Scandinavian Europe

DATE DUE

APR 4 - 2003		
AUG 1 5 2003		
JUN 1 5 2004		

DEMCO 38-296

LONELY PLANET PUBLICATIONS
Melbourne • Oakland • London • Paris

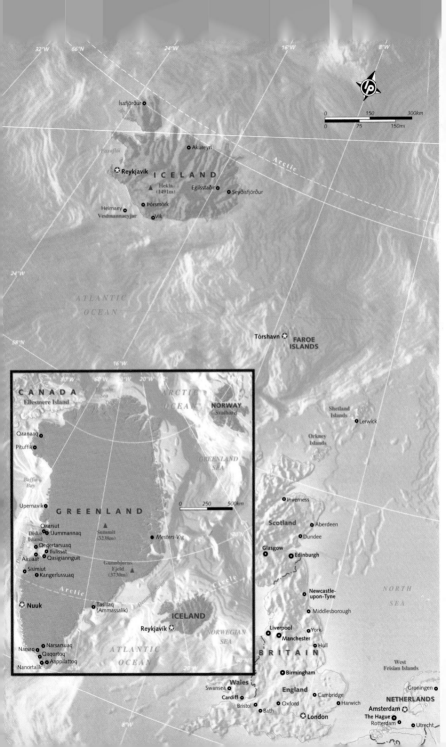

Scandinavian Europe
6th edition – February 2003
First published – January 1993

Published by
Lonely Planet Publications Pty Ltd ABN 36 005 607 983
90 Maribyrnong St, Footscray, Victoria 3011, Australia

Lonely Planet Offices
Australia Locked Bag 1, Footscray, Victoria 3011
USA 150 Linden St, Oakland, CA 94607
UK 10a Spring Place, London NW5 3BH
France 1 rue du Dahomey, 75011 Paris

Photographs
Many of the images in this guide are available for licensing from
Lonely Planet Images.
[w] www.lonelyplanetimages.com

Front cover photograph
Reindeer crossing a road in Arctic Norway in the winter (David Tipling)

ISBN 1 74059 318 9

Printed by SNP SPrint (M) Sdn Bhd
Printed in Malaysia

Although the authors and Lonely Planet try to make the information as accurate as possible, we accept no responsibility for any loss, injury or inconvenience sustained by anyone using this book.

Contents – Text

1

Contents – Maps

SWEDEN

The Authors

Graeme Cornwallis

Graeme wrote and updated the Greenland chapter in this book (based on Lonely Planet's *Iceland, Greenland & the Faroe Islands*). He also updated the introductory chapters and the Faroe Islands, Iceland and Norway chapters. Born and raised in Edinburgh, Graeme later wandered around Scotland before coming to rest in Glasgow. While studying astronomy at Glasgow University, he developed a passion for peaks – particularly the Scottish Munros – and eventually bagged all 284 summits over 3000ft in Scotland at least once. Graeme has travelled extensively throughout Scandinavia, Asia, North & South America and the Pacific. Mountaineering successes include trips to the Bolivian Andes, Arctic Greenland and Norway. When he's not hiking, climbing or travelling, Graeme teaches mathematics and physics at home in Glasgow.

Carolyn Bain

Carolyn updated the Sweden chapter. Melbourne-born Carolyn was raised on a diet of Abba music and the Muppet Chef, and first travelled around Scandinavia as a teenager, while living and studying in Denmark. That experience left her with a love of all the best that Scandinavia has to offer – open, egalitarian societies populated by unfairly attractive people, long summer nights and cosy winters, wonderful art and design, pickled fish (or perhaps not…) – and she jumped at the chance to return to Sweden for this project. After having obtained a degree in languages Carolyn embarked upon the obligatory tour of duty, living, working and travelling in Europe, Africa and North America. Upon her return to Australia she joined Lonely Planet as an editor for their European titles, but in time she decided guidebook authors have more fun than editors and joined their illustrious ranks. She has covered other fabulous, far-flung destinations for Lonely Planet, including the Greek Islands, New Zealand and Texas.

Des Hannigan

Des updated the Denmark chapter. Many years ago, Des set out from his native Scotland to look for unbroken sunshine in some exotic locale. He got lost on the way and ended up at sea, spending 15 years as a fisherman on the often unsunny waters of Britain's Atlantic approaches. Then he took up news reporting in the mistaken hope that it might make for an easier life. From hack work he moved into guidebook work and has written guides to Andalucia, Rhodes, Corfu, southern Spain, north Pakistan and most of northern Europe, including Denmark, as well as several walking and rock-climbing guides. He lives in sunny Cornwall, England.

Paul Harding

Paul researched and updated the Finland chapter. Melbourne-born, Paul spent his formative years as a newspaper reporter in country Victoria before being sucked into the backpacker vortex. After travelling extensively in Europe and South-East Asia, he worked as an editor of a London travel magazine before landing at Lonely Planet's Melbourne home for wayward travellers. Realising he was on the wrong side of the desk, he eventually swapped his red pen for a blue one and now works as a full-time writer and researcher. Paul is the author of Lonely Planet's *Read This First: Europe* and *Istanbul to Kathmandu* guides, and has contributed to *Australia, New Zealand, New South Wales, India, South India, Middle East* and *South-East Asia*.

FROM THE AUTHORS

Graeme Cornwallis Firstly, I'd like to thank Ingibjørg Jacobsen, Bjørga Jacobsen and family in Tórshavn for a wonderful stay in the Faroe Islands, and Kristin Bennick (Norges Turistråd, Oslo) for tremendous help with many Norway-related issues. Thanks also to: Deanna Swaney (Alaska), Andrew Bender (Los Angeles), Jimmy Pringle (Bishopton, Scotland), Wenche Berger (NSB, Oslo), Lisbeth Bjone (Use It, Oslo), Joar Eie (Trondheim), Ellen Frisvold (Stavanger), Erna Mufti (HSD, Bergen), Ann Helen Blakset (Stryn), Siw Møller Kristensen (Grønlands Turistråd, Copenhagen), Jesper Egede and Stig Rømer Winther (Greenland Tourism, Nuuk), Robert Peroni (Tasiilaq), Arne Niemann (Uummannaq), Samal Arnoldsson and Garry Flaws at Smyril Line, the staff at tourist offices in the Faroe Islands (especially Unn á Lað and Ingigerð á Trøðni), Aðalheiður Borgþórsdóttir (Seyðisfjörður, Iceland), Jón Illugasson (Reykjahlíð), Guðrún Bergmann (Brekkubær, Snæfellsnes), Markús Einarsson, Gauti Guðmundsson and Guðrún Fridriksdóttir (Reykjavík), Árni Gunnarsson at Flugfélag Íslands, and the staff at tourist offices throughout Norway, Iceland (particularly Inga Jóna Þórisdóttir in Akureyri and Inga Hallbjörnsdóttir in Reykjavík) and Greenland (including Janus Kleist and Salik Hard in Narsaq, Esther Jensen in Nuuk, as well as Inunguak Olsen in Kangerlussuaq).

Carolyn Bain Firstly, a big thank you to Graeme Cornwallis for advice and assistance, and for sharing some excellent Swedish contacts with me. *Tack så mycket* to Ann-Charlotte Carlsson and Emelie Klein at the Swedish Travel & Tourism Council in London for providing helpful big-picture information, and to Sylvie Kjellin of the Stockholm Information Service for her useful tips on the capital. The wonderful Magnus Welin provided a friendly welcome to Sweden and invaluable assistance for the duration of my research and beyond, for which I'm hugely grateful. I'm also indebted to the helpful staff at tourist offices throughout Sweden who answered all my questions and pointed me in the right direction; other tourist-industry folk also helped greatly – Monica Sansaricq, of the brilliant Ice Hotel, deserves a special thanks for her cheery assistance. I was fortunate to meet a number of fellow travellers and expats who offered further insight into the country; I'm especially grateful to Kieron Hayter for his company and ace driving skills in and around Stockholm, to Kenyan Kim in Helsingborg for fascinating conversation, and to Amy Archer for her fabulous company in and around Uppsala. *Kiitos* also goes to co-author Paul Harding for a very entertaining few days on the Sweden-Finland border; thanks to Paul for enduring Groundhog Day with me and for showing me the humppa! Jules Bain and John Foley once again gave me free run of their place in London before and after my trip – a mere thank you is not enough. Big cheers also to the fine folk at Lonely Planet's London office for giving me a place to write up my notes. Finally, my heartfelt appreciation, as ever, goes to family and friends for their unfailing encouragement and support, and for once again farewelling me and warmly welcoming me home.

Des Hannigan Many thanks to the always helpful and friendly staff of numerous tourist offices throughout Denmark. Thanks also to Mikael Boe Larsen of LBL in Copenhagen, Siv Jarto of Christiania, Rose Lundby of Aalborg, Craig Monk in Århus, Breda Ewé in Helsingør, Carsten Pedersen in Køge, and Michael Hjorth and friends for great company in Sandvig, Bornholm. A very special thanks to Marit Lehn Simonsen of Odense, and St Ives, Cornwall, and Charlotte Lehn Høeg of Hillerød for their insights, and for their help with the intricacies of the Danish language. To the many Danes I met along the way, my thanks for their unfailing kindness and courtesy, the hallmarks of the Danish people. My gratitude, above all, to Glenda Bendure and Ned Friary, who wrote the original *Denmark* guides, from which it was such a joy to work.

Paul Harding Thanks, as always, to the people at Lonely Planet who kindly enable me to keep travelling for a living. Thanks to Chris Wyness for the initial offer, Kieran Grogan, Csanád Csutoros and Mark Griffiths in Melbourne for early assistance, and Amanda Canning in London for patience and understanding. Everywhere I went in Finland I met many wonderful people from many walks of life. Thanks to James Luckhurst at the Finnish Tourist Board in London, Kaarina Pelkonen at the Finnish Tourist Board in Helsinki, staff at Helsinki Expert, and staff at many of the local tourist offices around Finland, particularly Turku, Tampere, Lappeenranta, Kuopio, Pori and Vaasa. Big thanks to Carolyn; to Markku, Jussi and everyone at Huvila in Savonlinna; and to Kaisa.

This Book

Many people helped create this 6th edition of *Scandinavian Europe* (previously *Scandinavian & Baltic Europe*). The major contributors to previous editions were Glenda Bendure, Jennifer Brewer, Graeme Cornwallis, Ned Friary, Steve Fallon, Steve Kokker, Clem Lindenmayer, Marcus Lehtipuu, Clay Lucas, Nick Selby and Nicola Williams. This edition was updated by Graeme Cornwallis, Carolyn Bain, Des Hannigan and Paul Harding.

Scandinavian Europe is part of Lonely Planet's Europe series, which includes *Central Europe, Eastern Europe, Mediterranean Europe* and *Western Europe*. In addition to these titles Lonely Planet also produces *Europe on a shoestring,* which features 40 countries, and phrasebooks to these regions.

FROM THE PUBLISHER

This 6th edition of *Scandinavian Europe* was commissioned by Chris Wyness in our Melbourne office. Amanda Canning was the commissioning editor for the book. Editing was coordinated by Marg Toohey and Darren O'Connell with the help of Kate James, Lara Morecombe, Cherry Prior, Diana Saad, Simon Sellars and Tom Smallman. Cartography and layout were coordinated by Birgit Jordan; she was assisted by Csanád Csutoros, Jimi Ellis, Karen Fry, Cris Gibcus, Joelene Kowalski, Sally Morgan, Adrian Persoglia, Corie Waddell and Wendy Wright. Project managers for this title were Bridget Blair and Kieran Grogan. The language chapter was produced and edited by Quentin Frayne and Emma Koch.

ACKNOWLEDGEMENTS

Thanks also to Mountain High Maps ® Copyright © 1993 Digital Wisdom, Inc.

THANKS
Many thanks to the travellers who used the last edition and wrote to us with helpful hints, advice and interesting anecdotes. Your names appear in the back of this book.

Foreword

ABOUT LONELY PLANET GUIDEBOOKS

The story begins with a classic travel adventure: Tony and Maureen Wheeler's 1972 journey across Europe and Asia to Australia. There was no useful information about the overland trail then, so Tony and Maureen published the first Lonely Planet guidebook to meet a growing need.

From a kitchen table, Lonely Planet has grown to become the largest independent travel publisher in the world, with offices in Melbourne (Australia), Oakland (USA), London (UK) and Paris (France).

Today Lonely Planet guidebooks cover the globe. There is an ever-growing list of books and information in a variety of media. Some things haven't changed. The main aim is still to make it possible for adventurous travellers to get out there – to explore and better understand the world.

At Lonely Planet we believe travellers can make a positive contribution to the countries they visit – if they respect their host communities and spend their money wisely.

Since 1986 a percentage of the income from each book has been donated to aid projects and human rights campaigns, and, more recently, to wildlife conservation.

> Although inclusion in a guidebook usually implies a recommendation we cannot list every good place. Exclusion does not necessarily imply criticism. In fact there are a number of reasons why we might exclude a place – sometimes it is simply inappropriate to encourage an influx of travellers.

UPDATES & READER FEEDBACK

Things change – prices go up, schedules change, good places go bad and bad places go bankrupt. Nothing stays the same. So, if you find things better or worse, recently opened or long-since closed, please tell us and help make the next edition even more accurate and useful.

Lonely Planet thoroughly updates each guidebook as often as possible – usually every two years, although for some destinations the gap can be longer. Between editions, up-to-date information is available in our free monthly email bulletin *Comet* (W www.lonelyplanet.com/newsletters). Lastly, the *Thorn Tree* bulletin board and *Postcards* section carry unverified, but fascinating, reports from travellers.

Tell us about it! We genuinely value your feedback. A well-travelled team at Lonely Planet reads and acknowledges every email and letter we receive and ensures that every morsel of information finds its way to the relevant authors, editors and cartographers.

Everyone who writes to us will find their name listed in the next edition of the appropriate guidebook. The very best contributions will be rewarded with a free guidebook.

We may edit, reproduce and incorporate your comments in Lonely Planet products such as guidebooks, websites and digital products, so let us know if you don't want your comments reproduced or your name acknowledged.

How to contact Lonely Planet:
Online: e talk2us@lonelyplanet.com.au, W www.lonelyplanet.com
Australia: Locked Bag 1, Footscray, Victoria 3011
UK: 10a Spring Place, London NW5 3BH
USA: 150 Linden St, Oakland, CA 94607

Introduction

Scandinavian Europe encompasses a huge area north of the Baltic Sea and right across the chilly North Atlantic Ocean, offering the visitor rugged wilderness, safe travel, spectacular scenery and wonderful natural sights such as gigantic icebergs, volcanoes, the aurora borealis and the midnight sun.

The countries covered in this book have everything from strikingly beautiful fjords, glaciers and mountains to treeless Arctic tundra. The region's cities range from cosmopolitan Copenhagen to the East-West blend of Helsinki, from trendy, modern Stockholm to quaint Tórshavn and the rough streets of Nuuk. Outdoor enthusiasts will get their fill of activities in Scandinavia, including ski-touring in Norway; exploring the glaciers, hot springs, geysers and volcanoes of Iceland; and bird-watching in the starkly beautiful Faroe Islands.

The range of attractions in the region is great. Norway has unspoiled fishing villages and rich historic sites, including Viking ships and medieval stave churches; Denmark has Viking ruins and pristine islands; Sweden has impressive museums and national parks with many walking trails. Visitors to Finland can cruise around giant lakes, experience the Russian influence in the south and see reindeer in the north. Most of Greenland is dominated by ice and its haunting landscapes are among the most magnificent on Earth.

Scandinavia is also a varied region offering vivid contrasts: there are popular swimming beaches along the coast of Denmark, whereas Greenland, Norway, Sweden and Finland all extend beyond the Arctic Circle. Sweden has, in the past, managed to combine socialist principles with some of the most successful capitalist enterprises on Earth. The tiny Faroe Islands intends to take steps towards full independence in the coming years, while enormous Greenland is still wedded to Denmark.

This book will take you through Scandinavian Europe, from predeparture preparations to packing your bag for the return home. There's information on how to get there and how to get around once you've arrived – whether it's by train through the Swedish forests, by bicycle along Danish cycling routes, by bus around Iceland, or by coastal ferry in Greenland.

Scandinavia is famed for its high costs, but prices are more affordable these days. Recent years of recession have brought real bargains to travellers and this book details the many ways of finding them, including staying in Denmark's *vandrerhjem* (hostels) and eating at Norway's *konditori* (bakeries).

There are extensive recommendations about where to stay, including camping in Greenland, traditional turf-roofed cabins in Norway, and farmhouse accommodation in Iceland. Dining possibilities are also covered thoroughly, from Denmark's famed *smørrebrød* (open sandwich) and Sweden's flashy restaurants to traditional Icelandic dishes you'd probably rather not know about like *hákarl* (putrefied shark meat).

Scandinavia offers travellers a real chance for adventure; a region where both natural and cultural frontiers can be explored. All you have to do is go.

Facts for the Visitor

THE BEST & WORST
The Top 10
There's so much to see in Scandinavian Europe that compiling a top 10 is almost impossible. However, we asked the authors of this book to list their personal highlights, and the results are as follows:

1. Geirangerfjord, Norway's western fjords
2. Frederiksborg Castle, Hillerød, Denmark
3. Mývatn, Iceland
4. Gamla Stan, Stockholm
5. Ice Hotel, Jukkasjärvi
6. Lofoten islands, northwest Norway
7. Ride on a working icebreaker ship, Finland
8. Tasermiut Fjord and Torssuqaatoq Sound, Greenland
9. The *Hurtigruten* coastal steamer trip from Bergen to Kirkenes, Norway
10. Ilulissat Kangerlua, Greenland

The Bottom 10
The writers were also asked to list the 10 worst sights and came up with the following:

1. Badly behaved children in public places, with indifferent parents, particularly in Sweden and Iceland
2. Foul-smelling timber pulp factories, Finland
3. Seal clubbing display at Polar Museum, Tromsø, Norway
4. Bloodthirsty swarms of mosquitoes in the forests of Sweden and Finland
5. Thick cigar smoke blighting cosy Danish cafés
6. Little Mermaid, Copenhagen
7. Legoland (Denmark) without kids
8. Blue Lagoon, Iceland
9. Pubs brawls in Greenland
10. Swedish tourists bingeing on duty-free booze on cross-Baltic ferries

PLANNING
There are those who would say that much of Scandinavia is so well developed you don't have to plan before your trip since anything can be arranged on the spot. As any experienced traveller knows, the problems you anticipated often turn out to be irrelevant or will sort themselves out once you're on the move.

That's fine if you've decided to blow a massive inheritance or lottery winnings. However, if your financial status is rather more modest, a bit of prior knowledge and careful planning can make your hard-earned budget stretch further than you thought it would, an important consideration in pricey Scandinavia. For more information you could consult Lonely Planet's *Read This First: Europe* when planning your trip.

When to Go
Make sure the things you plan to see and do are possible at the particular time of year when you'll be travelling. Any time can be the best time to visit Scandinavia, depending on what you want to do. Summer offers the most pleasant climate for outdoor pursuits in the northern half of the continent. In general, the short summers in Scandinavia last from June to August and temperatures can be relatively hot (even in Iceland!); this is the best time for comfortable travelling in the region.

Of course, everything will be crowded in summer at the popular tourist destinations, but there are also surprises. In many cities and towns, hotels cut their ordinary winter rates by as much as half, and the supply of beds grows enormously as youth hostels, school dormitories, camping grounds and holiday villages open up. And naturally, the so-called Right of Common Access (see Hiking under Activities later in this chapter) is really only useful in summer, when camping in the woods is an option. Also, when it comes to entertainment, summer is certainly the best time to go, with festivals and other events taking place all over Scandinavia.

Spring arrives in May or June, the precise time depending on latitude and altitude; this is a particularly good season to visit, with carpets of flowers and snow on the mountains. After August, most tourists disappear, many tourist-oriented activities wind down, and schools reopen. September is also a pleasant time to be in the region, but you most definitely get the impression it's already autumn.

In southern Scandinavia, if you want to enjoy the outdoor life, including concerts and beaches, the best time to visit is from late June to August. The shoulder seasons from May to June and from September to mid-October are less crowded, most sights are open and the weather is good.

Late June to mid-August is also the best time to visit northern parts of the Scandinavian mainland, unless you're into winter sports such as skiing or are in search of the aurora borealis (northern lights). This is when it's warmest, daylight hours are very long, hostels are open, the weather is normally at its best and there are fewer public holidays to disrupt travel plans.

If you're keen on winter sports, you can find good accommodation package deals in some Scandinavian cities before or after you visit your ski resort.

The Climate and When to Go sections in individual country chapters explain what to expect and when to expect it. As a rule, autumn and winter tend to be windier and wetter than spring and summer in most western parts (areas which have a maritime climate), but summer and early autumn are wetter further east, and in west Greenland (areas with continental climate).

The climate in the Faroe Islands and along the Norwegian coast is moderated by the warm Gulf Stream and is relatively wet all year. Be aware that climatic conditions in Greenland and Svalbard are unique in Scandinavian Europe.

Maps

Good maps are easy to come by once you're in Europe, but you might want to buy a few beforehand, especially if you're driving or cycling. The maps in this book are a useful first reference when you arrive in a city.

Otherwise, you can't go wrong with Michelin maps and, with their soft covers; they fold easily so you can stick them in your pocket. Some people prefer the meticulous Freytag & Berndt, Kümmerly + Frey or Hallwag maps, which have been recommended for Scandinavian countries. Falk Plan city maps are very usable and detailed, and the Falk map of Scandinavia is particularly good.

In Scandinavia (notably Denmark), tourist offices are an excellent source for free and up-to-date maps. Local automobile associations also provide detailed, free maps to their members or members of automobile associations with reciprocal rights (see information under Car & Motorcycle in the Getting Around chapter for more information).

The following shops sell Scandinavian maps, including motoring maps and topographic maps for hikers, by mail order:

World Heritage List

Unesco's list of 'cultural and natural treasures of the world's heritage' includes the following places in Scandinavian Europe:

Denmark
Jelling church, burial mounds and runic stones
Kronborg Castle
Roskilde Cathedral

Finland
Bronze-Age burial site of Sammallahdenmäki
Fortress of Suomenlinna
Petäjävesi church
Vanha Rauma (Old Rauma)
Verla Groundwood and Board Mill

Norway
Bryggen
Mining town of Røros
Rock drawings of Alta
Urnes stave church

Sweden
Agricultural landscape of southern Öland
Birka and Hovgården
Church village of Gammelstad, Luleå
Engelsberg ironworks
Falun mining area
Hanseatic town of Visby
Höga Kusten (High Coast)
Laponian area
Naval port of Karlskrona
Rock carvings at Vitlycke (Tanumshede)
Royal Domain of Drottningholm
Skogskyrkogården (southern Stockholm)

The Map Shop (☎ 01684-593146, fax 594559, Ⓦ www.themapshop.co.uk) 15 High St, Upton-upon-Severn, Worcestershire, WR8 0HJ, England
Map Land (☎ 03-9670 4383, fax 03-9670 7779, Ⓦ www.mapland.com.au) 372 Little Bourke St, Melbourne, VIC 3000, Australia
Omni Resources (☎ 336-227 8300, fax 227 3748, Ⓦ www.omnimap.com) 1004 S Mebane St, PO Box 2096, Burlington, NC 27216-2096, USA

What to Bring

Taking along as little as possible is the best policy. But while it's very easy to find almost anything you need along the way, most people tend not to buy as they travel in Scandinavia because of the high price of goods and value-added tax (VAT). Just be very selective as you pack and if you only think you *may* need an item or article of clothing, leave it out.

A backpack is still the most popular method of carrying gear as it is convenient, especially for walking. On the down side, a backpack doesn't offer too much protection for your valuables, the straps tend to get caught on things and some airlines may refuse to accept responsibility if the pack is damaged or tampered with.

Travelpacks, a combination backpack and shoulder bag, are popular. The backpack straps zip away inside the pack when they are not needed, so you almost have the best of both worlds. Some packs have quite sophisticated shoulder-strap adjustment systems and can be used comfortably, even on long hikes.

Versatile hybrid packs, which combine features of both backpacks and travelpacks, are an increasingly popular option.

Packs are much easier to carry than a bag or any kind of suitcase. A small padlock locking your pack will help deter would-be thieves.

As for clothing, the climate will influence on what you bring along. Remember that insulation works on the principle of trapped air, so several layers of thin clothing are warmer than a single thick one (and will be easier to dry, too).

You'll also be more comfortable if the weather suddenly warms up – though always be prepared for rain at any time of year. Jeans aren't advisable in wet climates; they're difficult to dry. A minimum packing list could include:

- swimming gear
- a pair of poly-cotton trousers and a pair of shorts, or trousers with zip-off legs that convert into shorts
- a few T-shirts and shirts
- a warm sweater
- a sturdy pair of walking shoes or hiking boots
- sandals or thongs (to wear in the shower)
- a coat or jacket
- a raincoat or waterproof jacket (with hood) or umbrella
- a medical kit
- a sewing kit
- a padlock
- a Swiss Army knife
- soap and towel
- toothpaste, toothbrush and other toiletries
- extra packs of tissues and toilet paper

A padlock is useful to lock your bag to a luggage rack in a bus or train; it may also be needed to secure your hostel locker. A Swiss Army knife comes in handy for all sorts of things. (Any brand of pocketknife is fine but make sure it includes such essentials as a bottle opener and strong corkscrew.) Soap, toothpaste and toilet paper are readily obtainable almost anywhere, as is paper in public toilets and those at camping grounds in Scandinavia. In Scandinavia, using toilets in public areas can cost a sizable chunk of change; plan visits carefully and use restaurant toilets discreetly. Tampons are available at pharmacies and supermarkets everywhere, including Greenland. Condoms are also widely available.

A tent and sleeping bag are vital if you want to save money by camping. Even if you're not camping, a sleeping bag is still very useful. It can double as a cushion on hard train seats, a seat for long waits at bus or train stations, and a blanket in cold guesthouses (buy one that unzips all the way and it can be used as a quilt). You will also need a sleeping bag to take advantage of the free accommodation along trekking routes in Finland. A cheap form of accommodation in Iceland is 'sleeping-bag accommodation' – a bed or mattress on which to roll out your sleeping bag.

A sleeping sheet with pillow cover (case) is necessary if you plan to stay in hostels. You may have to hire or purchase one if you don't bring your own. In any case, a sheet that fits into your sleeping bag is easier to wash than the bag itself. Make one out of old sheets (include a built-in pillow cover), or buy one from your hostel association. Silk liners are much smaller and lighter, but they cost more than the cotton variety.

Other optional items include a compass (buy one that's adjusted for use in the region you plan to visit), a torch (flashlight), an alarm clock, an adapter plug for any electrical appliances (such as a cup or coil immersion heater to save on tea and coffee), a universal bath/sink plug (the lid of a film canister sometimes works), sunglasses, a few clothes pegs, and premoistened towelettes or a large cotton handkerchief which you can wet and use to cool off while touring cities in the warm summer months. During city sightseeing, a small daypack is harder for would-be thieves to snatch. Consider using plastic carry bags or garbage-bin liners inside your backpack to keep things separate, but also dry, if the pack gets soaked.

Airlines lose luggage from time to time, but you have a much better chance of it not being yours if it is tagged with your name and address *inside* the bag as well as outside; outside tags can always fall off or be removed.

Appearances & Conduct

Dress standards are fairly informal in northern Europe and Greenland. By all means dress casually, but do ensure sufficient body cover (trousers or a knee-length dress) if your sightseeing includes churches, monasteries or synagogues. Wearing shorts away from the beach, camp site or back garden isn't very common among men in northern Europe. Some nightclubs and fancy restaurants may refuse entry to people wearing jeans, trainers (sneakers) or a tracksuit; men only need to pack a tie if they plan on dining out at very upmarket restaurants.

Nude bathing is usually limited to restricted beach areas, although topless bathing is common in many parts of Scandinavia, particularly on the beaches of Denmark. However, women should be wary, especially in Finland where topless bathing is uncommon and in Greenland where it's unheard of; if nobody else seems to be doing it, the rule is you don't either.

RESPONSIBLE TOURISM

Facilities for tourists are well developed throughout most of Scandinavia. However, a few problems have arisen due to some travellers abusing the Right of Common Access (see Hiking under Activities later in this chapter). Don't leave rubbish in huts and keep camping places clean. Using roadside laybys as public toilets is antisocial and presents a serious threat to public health, particularly in Norway. Using huts without paying and using emergency huts illegally (in Iceland) aggravates local people. Be sensible – don't exploit the land or the people, or other travellers following you will pay the price.

VISAS & DOCUMENTS
Passport

Your most important travel document is your passport. If it's about to expire, renew it before you go; renewal while travelling can be inconvenient and time-consuming. Some countries insist that your passport is valid for a specified minimum period (usually three months but sometimes up to six months) after your visit. Even if they don't insist on this, expect questions from immigration officials if your passport is due to expire.

If you don't have a passport, you'll have to apply for one, which can be an involved process. A renewal or application can take anything from an hour to several months, depending on many factors, so don't leave it until the last minute (it can sometimes be sped up with a good excuse, and payment of a higher fee). The wheels of bureaucracy usually turn faster if you can do everything in person at the actual passport-issuing office rather than relying on the mail or agents. Check first what you need to bring with you: photos of a certain size, birth certificate, population register extract, signed statements and exact payment in cash are just some of the possible requirements.

Australian citizens can apply at a post office or the passport office in state capitals; Britons can pick up application forms from major post offices, and the passport is issued by the regional passport office; Canadians can apply at regional passport offices; New Zealanders can apply at any district office of the Department of Internal Affairs; US citizens must apply in person (but may usually renew by mail) at a US Passport Agency office or some courthouses and post offices.

Citizens of many European countries may not need a passport to travel within the region; a national identity card may be sufficient. European Union (EU) citizens have the right of unrestricted travel throughout the EU (Scandinavian member countries of the EU are Denmark, Sweden and Finland). But if you want to take advantage of these options, check with your travel agent or the embassies of the countries you plan to visit.

Carry your passport at all times and guard it carefully (security procedures are outlined in the Copies section later in this chapter). Some countries require residents and aliens alike to carry personal identification.

Visas

A visa is a stamp in your passport or a separate piece of paper permitting you to enter the country in question and stay for a specified period of time. There's a wide variety, including tourist, transit and business visas.

Transit visas are usually cheaper than tourist or business visas, but they only allow a very short stay (one or two days) and can be difficult to extend. Often you can get the visa at the border or at the airport on arrival; check first with the embassies or consulates of the countries you plan to visit. If you need a visa to enter Denmark, note that you'll need a separate visa for entry to Greenland.

It's important to remember that visas have a 'use-by date', and you'll be refused entry after that period has elapsed. Visa requirements do change, and you should always check with the individual embassies or consulates or a reputable travel agent before leaving home. If you plan to get your visas as you go along rather than arranging them all beforehand, carry spare passport photos.

Citizens of the UK, the USA, Canada, Ireland, Australia and New Zealand, don't require visas to visit any Scandinavian country; South Africans, on the other hand, need a visa to enter all Scandinavian countries. With a valid passport most travellers will be able to visit Scandinavian countries for up to three (sometimes even six) months, provided they have some sort of onward or return ticket and/or 'sufficient means of support' (money). Except at international airports, it's unlikely that immigration officials will give you and your passport more than a cursory glance – if that.

Many EU countries have abolished passport controls between their borders and an identity card should be sufficient, but it's always safest to carry your passport.

Travel Insurance

A travel insurance policy to cover theft, personal liability, loss and medical problems is strongly recommended. There's a wide variety of policies available and travel agents will have recommendations. The International travel policies handled by STA Travel or other student travel organisations are usually good value. Always check the small print; some policies specifically exclude 'dangerous activities' such as skiing, motorcycling, mountaineering, scuba diving or even hiking.

Travel insurance also covers cancellation or delays in travel arrangements. (You could fall seriously ill two days before departure, for example.) Cover depends on your insurance so ask both your insurer to explain where you stand. Ticket loss is also covered by travel insurance.

Buy travel insurance as early as possible. If you buy it the week before you are due to fly, you may find that you're not covered for delays to your flight caused by strikes or other industrial actions that may have been in force before you took out the insurance.

Paying for your airline ticket with a credit card often provides limited travel accident insurance, and you may be able to reclaim the payment if the operator doesn't deliver. In the UK, for instance, institutions issuing credit cards are required by law to reimburse consumers if a company goes into liquidation and the amount involved is more than £100. Ask your credit card company what it's prepared to cover.

A policy that pays doctors or hospitals directly may be preferable to one where you pay on the spot and claim later. If you have to claim later, make sure you keep all documentation. Some policies ask you to phone (reverse charges) a centre in your home country where an immediate assessment of your problem can be made.

Check if the policy covers ambulances and an emergency flight home. If you have to stretch out you will need two seats and somebody has to pay for them!

EU citizens are covered for emergency medical treatment in all EU countries (Denmark, Finland and Sweden are Scandinavian EU members) on presentation of an E111 form. Inquire about these at your national health service or travel agent well in advance; in some countries post offices may have them. UK citizens can find out more on the website W www.doh .gov.uk/traveladvice/treatment2.htm. Similar reciprocal arrangements exist between individual countries; see the individual chapters for details. Australian Medicare covers emergency treatment in seven European countries, including Finland and Sweden. You may still have to pay on the spot, but you'll be able to reclaim these expenses at home. However, travel insurance is still advisable because of the flexibility it offers as to where and how you're treated, as well as covering expenses for ambulance and repatriation.

Driving Licence & Permits

Your local driving licence will probably be acceptable for motoring in the region but play it safe by getting an International Driving Permit (IDP) from your local automobile association before you leave – you will need a passport photo and a current licence. They are usually inexpensive and valid for one year only. An IDP helps Europeans make sense of your unfamiliar local licence (make sure you take that with you, too) and can make life much simpler, especially when hiring cars and motorcycles.

Also ask your automobile association for a Letter of Introduction (*Lettre de Recommendation*). This entitles you to services offered by affiliated organisations in Europe, usually free of charge (touring maps and information, help with breakdowns, technical and legal advice etc). See the Getting Around chapter for more details on driving your own vehicle.

Camping Card International

Your local automobile association also issues the Camping Card International, which is basically a camping ground ID. These are also available from local camping federations, and sometimes on the spot at camping grounds. They incorporate third-party insurance for damage you may cause, and many camping grounds offer a small discount if you sign in with one. However, these cards are not commonly recognised in Iceland, the Faroes or Greenland.

Hostel Card

While not mandatory in Scandinavia, a Hostelling International (HI) card gives a sizable discount every time you check in to an affiliated hostel. Some hostels will issue one on the spot or after a few stays, although this might cost a bit more than getting it in your home country. See Hostels in the Accommodation section of this chapter for more details.

Student & Youth Cards

The most useful of these is the International Student Identity Card (ISIC), a plastic ID-style card with your photograph, which provides discounts on numerous forms of transport (including airlines, international ferries and local public transport), reduced or free admission to museums and sights, and cheap meals in some student restaurants – a worthwhile way of cutting costs in expensive Scandinavia.

There's a global industry in fake student cards, and a number of places now stipulate a maximum age for student discounts or, more simply, they've substituted a 'youth discount' for a 'student discount'. If you're aged under 26 but not a student, you can apply for the Euro<26 card (W www.eyca .org), which goes by various names in different countries, or an IYTC (International Youth Travel Card, previously called the GO25 card). All these cards are available through student unions, hostelling organisations or youth-oriented travel agencies. They don't automatically entitle you to discounts and some companies and institutions refuse to recognise them altogether – but you won't find out until you try.

Seniors Cards

Museums and other sights, public swimming pools and spas, and transport companies frequently offer discounts to retirees/OAPs/those over 60 (sometimes slightly younger for women; and over 65 in Sweden). Make sure you bring proof of age; the ever proper, always polite Scandinavian ticket-collector is not going to believe you're a day over 39.

For a small fee, European nationals aged over 60 can get a Rail Plus pass as an add-on to their national rail senior pass. It entitles the holder to reduced fares in some European countries; percentage savings vary according to the route. See Cheap Tickets in the Train section of the Getting Around chapter. See also Rail Passes in the same section for details on the ScanRail Senior pass.

Vaccination Certificates

You'll need the yellow booklet only if you're coming to the region from certain parts of Asia, Africa and South America, where outbreaks of such diseases as yellow fever have been reported. For more information on jabs see Predeparture Planning in the Health section of this chapter

Copies

The hassles brought on by losing your passport can be considerably reduced if you have a record of its number and issue date, or even better, photocopies of the relevant data pages. A photocopy of your birth certificate can also be useful. All important documents (passport data page and visa page, credit cards, travel insurance policy, air/bus/train tickets, driving licence, serial numbers of your travellers cheques etc) should be photo-copied before you leave home. Leave one copy with someone at home and keep another with you, separate from the originals. Add some emergency money, say US$100 in cash, to this separate stash. If you do lose your passport, notify the police immediately to get a statement, and contact your nearest embassy or consulate.

It's also a good idea to store details of your vital travel documents in Lonely Planet's free online Travel Vault. Your password-protected Travel Vault is accessible online anywhere in the world – you can create your own at W www.ekno.lonelyplanet.com.

CUSTOMS

Since 1 July 1999 duty-free goods can no longer be sold to those travelling from one EU country to another, but duty-free is still available for anyone travelling to/from non-EU countries. For goods purchased at airports or on ferries *outside* the EU, the usual allowances apply – tobacco (eg, 200 cigarettes), alcohol (2L of wine, 1L of spirits) and perfume (60mL). Do not confuse these with *duty-paid* items (including alcohol and tobacco) bought at normal shops and supermarkets in one EU country and carried into another EU country, where certain goods might be more expensive. In this case the allowances are much more generous. See the individual country chapters for more details regarding customs regulations.

Customs inspections among EU countries have all but ceased. However, they can be quite thorough between liberal Denmark and more conservative Sweden. At most border crossings and airports elsewhere they are pretty cursory, but not always.

Scandinavia & the EU

country	EU member	currency
Denmark	yes	Danish krone (Dkr)
Faroe Islands	no	Faroese króna (Fkr) & Danish krone (Dkr)
Finland	yes	euro (€)
Greenland	no	Danish krone (Dkr)
Iceland	no	Icelandic króna (Ikr)
Norway	no	Norwegian krone (Nkr)
Sweden	yes	Swedish krona (Skr)

EMBASSIES & CONSULATES

See the individual country chapters for the addresses of embassies & consulates.

Getting Help from Your Embassy

It's important to realise the things your own embassy – the embassy of the country of which you are a citizen – can and can't do to help you. Generally speaking, it won't be much help in emergencies if the trouble you're in is your own fault. Remember that you are bound by the laws of the country you are in. Your embassy will not be sympathetic if you end up in jail after committing a crime locally, even if such actions are legal in your own country.

In genuine emergencies you might get some assistance, but only if other channels have been exhausted. For example, if you need to get home urgently, a free ticket home is exceedingly unlikely – the embassy would expect you to have insurance. If you have all your money and documents stolen, it might assist with getting a new passport, but a loan for onward travel is out of the question.

MONEY
Exchanging Money

All Scandinavian currencies are fully convertible. Most foreign currencies can be easily exchanged but US dollars, pounds sterling and euros are the best to carry. You may well decide, however, that other currencies suit your purposes better. You lose out through commissions and customer exchange rates every time you change money, so if you only visit Sweden, for example, you may be better off buying some kronor before you leave home. See the Money section in the relevant country chapters for further details.

Unlike in the rest of Europe, travellers should avoid banks in Scandinavia (except in the Faroes and Iceland, where banks tend to be a better option) in favour of *bureaux de change* (eg, Forex) or post offices, which tend to offer better rates and charge lower fees or commissions than banks. They usually also keep longer hours than the banks, which are closed at weekends and on public holidays (see the individual country chapters for lists). However, most airports, central train stations, some fancy hotels and many border posts have banking facilities outside working hours. If you visit several countries, the constant conversions can drive you crazy. Buy a cheap pocket calculator, cut out the list of exchange rates from a newspaper, and stick it to the back of the calculator for easy reference.

Cash Nothing beats cash for convenience...or risk. If you lose it, it's gone forever and very few travel insurers will come to your rescue; those who do will limit the payout to about US$300.

It's still a good idea, though, to bring some local currency in cash, if only to tide you over until you get to an exchange facility or find an automated teller machine (ATM). The equivalent of around US$100 should usually be enough. Some extra cash in an easily exchanged currency (eg, US dollars or pounds sterling) is also a good idea. Remember that banks will always accept foreign-currency paper money but very rarely coins, so you might want to spend (or donate) your local coins before you cross a border.

Travellers Cheques The main advantage of travellers cheques over cash is the protection they offer against theft, though they are losing their popularity as more travellers access money from their bank at home, withdrawing it from ATMs as they go. American Express, Visa and Thomas Cook cheques are widely accepted and have efficient replacement policies for lost and stolen cheques.

Keeping a record of the cheque numbers and those you have used is vital when it comes to replacing lost travellers cheques. You should keep this separate from the cheques themselves. Cheques are available in various currencies, but those denominated in US dollars, euros and pounds sterling are easiest to cash. Still, you might not be comfortable using a currency you're not familiar with, and watching it being converted into yet another currency is confusing and risky.

When you change cheques, don't just look at the exchange rate; ask about fees and commissions as well. There may be a per-cheque service fee, a flat transaction fee, or a percentage of the total amount irrespective of the number of cheques. In most European countries the exchange rate for travellers cheques is slightly better than the exchange rate for cash.

Cards & ATMs A credit card can be an ideal travelling companion. If you're not familiar with credit, cash card, credit/debit, debit and charge cards, ask your bank to explain the workings and relative merits of each. Make sure you know what to do in case of theft (usually call telephone hotlines).

With a credit card you can charge big expenses like airline tickets and save carrying so much cash and so many travellers cheques. Another major advantage is that they allow you to withdraw cash at selected banks or ATMs.

ATMs linked up internationally will give you instant cash as soon as you punch in your personal identification number (PIN). Cards (eg, Cirrus, Plus, Eurocard) are accepted widely throughout Scandinavian Europe, including Greenland (though they may be of limited use in the Faroe Islands); always make sure you know which ATMs abroad will accept your particular card. Remember that ATMs aren't completely fail-safe. If one swallows your card it can be a major headache. Note that many ATMs in Europe will not accept PINs of more than four digits.

Cash cards, which you use at home to withdraw money directly from your bank account, are also widely linked internationally – ask your bank at home for advice. Withdrawals may incur a transaction fee – usually a flat rate of about $US2 to $US5 – so it's more economical if you make fewer but larger withdrawals. Check with your credit-card provider about charges.

Charge cards like American Express and Diners Club have offices in most countries, and they can generally replace a lost card within 24 hours. That's because they treat you as a customer of the company rather than of the bank that issued the card. In theory, the credit they offer is unlimited and they don't charge interest on outstanding accounts, but they do charge fees for joining and annual membership, and payment is due in full within a few weeks of the account statement date. Charge cards may also be hooked up to ATM networks.

Credit and debit cards are very popular in Scandinavia; Visa is the most common one followed by MasterCard. They are more widely accepted than charge cards because they charge merchants lower commissions. Their major drawback is that they have a credit limit based on your regular income, and this limit can stop you in your tracks if you are charging major expenses like long-term car rental or long-distance airline tickets and travelling extensively. You can avoid this by depositing money into your card account before you begin your travels. Other drawbacks are that interest is charged on outstanding accounts, either immediately or after a set period (always immediately on cash advances) and the card can be very difficult to replace if lost abroad in remote areas.

If you use a credit card to withdraw money from an ATM, you pay interest on the money from the moment you get it. You can get around that by leaving the card in credit when you depart or by having somebody at home pay money into the card account from time to time. On the plus side, you don't pay commission charges to exchange money and the exchange rate is usually at a better interbank rate than that offered for travellers cheques or cash exchanges. Bear in mind that if you use a credit card for purchases, exchange rates may have changed by the time your bill is processed, which can work out to your advantage or disadvantage.

If you choose to rely on plastic, go for two different cards – a Visa or MasterCard, for instance, with an American Express or Diners Club backup. Better still is a combination of credit card and travellers cheques so you have something to fall back on if an ATM swallows your card or the banks in the area won't accept it for some inexplicable reason.

A word of warning: although it's not common in this region, fraudulent shopkeepers have been known to make several charge-slip imprints with customers' credit cards when they're not looking; they then simply copy the signature from the signed slip. Try not to let the card out of your sight, and always check your statements carefully.

Another option is Visa TravelMoney, a prepaid travel card that gives 24-hour access to your funds via Visa ATMs. The card is PIN-protected and its value is stored on the system, not on the card. So if you lose the card, your money's safe. Visa TravelMoney can be purchased from both Citicorp and Thomas Cook/Interpayment. More details are available at W www.international.visa.com /ps/products/vtravelmoney.

International Transfers If you run out of money, need more and your card won't work in the ATM, you can instruct your bank back home to send you a draft. Make sure you specify the city, the bank and the branch to which you want your money directed, or ask your home bank to tell you where a suitable one is.

The whole procedure will be easier if you've authorised someone back home to access your account. Also, a transfer to a tiny bank in a remote village in Lapland is obviously going to be more difficult than to the head office in Helsinki. If you have the choice, find a large bank and ask for the international division.

Money sent by telegraphic transfer (there will be costs involved, typically from US$40) should reach you within a week; by mail, allow at least two weeks. When it arrives, it will most likely be converted into local currency – you can take it in cash or buy travellers cheques.

You can also transfer money much faster through the use of the MoneyGram (W www .moneygram.com) service; its international agents are listed on the website. Western Union Money Transfers can be collected from banks throughout Scandinavian Europe.

Costs

First, a general disclaimer about all those prices that we list so faithfully throughout this book: they're likely to change, probably upwards, but if last season was particularly slow they just might come down. Nevertheless, relative price levels should stay fairly constant – if hotel A costs twice as much as hotel B, it's likely to stay that way.

Scandinavia is expensive, even by European standards. Nevertheless, it is possible to travel in the region without spending a fortune.

One secret is cheap accommodation. There is a highly developed network of camping grounds, some are quite luxurious, and they're great places to meet people. The hostel network, too, is well developed, and used equally by all age groups. The exception is Greenland, where camping and hostels are not so well developed, and the hostels that do exist tend to be expensive.

Other money-saving strategies include using a student or youth card, which offers worthwhile discounts (see Visas & Documents earlier in this chapter); various rail and transport passes (see the Getting Around chapter); and applying for consumer tax rebates on purchases (see Taxes & Refunds later in this chapter and the Facts for the Visitor sections of the individual country chapters). Avoiding alcohol in most of the Scandinavian countries is probably the best cash-saving strategy of all!

Including transport, but not private motorised transport, daily expenses could be around US$45 a day if you're on a rock-bottom budget. This means camping or staying in hostels, eating economically and using transport passes. Travel and accommodation costs in Greenland are much higher than elsewhere – see the Greenland chapter for details.

Travelling on a moderate budget you should be able to manage on US$70 to US$90 per day. This would allow you to stay at budget hotels, guesthouses or B&Bs. You could afford meals in economical restaurants and maybe even one or two beers!

Tipping

For the most part in Scandinavia, it's common for a service charge to be added to restaurant bills, in which case no tipping is necessary. In other cases, simply rounding up the bill is sufficient. See the individual country chapters for more details.

Taxes & Refunds

A kind of sales tax called value-added tax (VAT) applies to most goods and services throughout most of Scandinavia. International visitors can usually claim back the VAT on purchases (above a set minimum amount) that are being taken out of the country. Remember, though, that those people actually residing in an EU country are not entitled to a refund on VAT paid on goods bought in another EU country (eg, a Briton returning home with goods from Finland, Sweden or Denmark). The procedure for making the claim is usually pretty straightforward. For guidance, see the relevant country chapter.

POST & COMMUNICATIONS
Post

Airmail typically takes about a week to reach North American or Australasian destinations. Postage costs vary from country to country. Postal services are very efficient in Scandinavian countries.

You can collect mail from post office poste restante sections. Ask people writing to you to print your name clearly and underline your surname, as well as using capital letters. When collecting mail you may need a passport for identification. If an expected letter is not waiting for you, ask to check under your given name as letters are sometimes misfiled. Unless the sender specifies otherwise, mail will always be sent to the main post office of any city.

You can also have mail (but not parcels) sent to you at American Express offices so long as you have an American Express card or travellers cheques. When you buy American Express travellers cheques you can ask for a booklet listing all their office addresses worldwide.

Telephone

You can ring abroad from almost any phone box in Scandinavia. Public telephones accepting stored-value phonecards, available from post offices, telephone centres, newsstands or retail outlets, are the norm and, in some places, coin-operated phones are almost impossible to find. The card solves the problem of having the correct coins for calls. (In Iceland and the Faroes, however, phonecard phones are hard to find outside of Reykjavík and Tórshavn. Phonecards aren't available in Greenland.)

Reverse-charge (collect) calls are usually possible, and communicating with the local operator in English should not be much of a problem in Scandinavia. From some countries you can avoid the local operator, and dial direct to your home operator.

To call abroad you simply dial the international access code (IAC) for the country you are calling from (most commonly 00 in Europe), the country code (CC) for the country you are calling, the local area code (usually dropping the leading zero if there is one) and then the number. If, for example, you are

Telephone Codes

country	☎ CC	☎ IAC	☎ IO
Denmark	45	00	141
Faroe Islands	298	00	808080
Finland	358	00, 990, 994, 999	020222
Greenland	299	00	none
Iceland	354	00	533 5010
Norway	47	00	181
Sweden	46	00	118119

CC – country code (to call into that country)
IAC – international access code (to call abroad from that country)
IO – international operator (to make inquiries)

Changing Phone Numbers

Over the next few years, as EU telecommunications rules come into effect, many local telephone numbers are going to change. Check with the relevant tourist offices for the latest developments.

in Norway (international access code 00) and want to make a call to Sweden (country code 46), Stockholm (area code 08), number ☎ 123 4567, then you dial ☎ 00-46-8-123 4567. Check out ⓦ www.ekno.com/ekit/Info/Countryphoneguide for a list of international country codes.

Lonely Planet's ekno global communication service provides low-cost international calls – for local calls you're usually better off with a local phonecard. ekno also offers free messaging services, email, travel information and an online travel vault, where you can securely store all your important documents. You can join online at ⓦ www.ekno.lonelyplanet.com, where you will find the local-access numbers for the 24-hour customer-service centre. Once you have joined, always check the ekno website for the latest access numbers and updates on new features. Apart from the Faroes and Greenland, the Scandinavian countries are covered by ekno.

Various types of mobile phone network are operating in Scandinavia and your home mobile may not work in extensive areas. Ask your home network for advice before taking your mobile phone abroad; local telephone companies and national tourist offices can advise on coverage.

Rental of mobile phones is always possible – purchase is always an option, but it's expensive and you'll be unable to use your existing number in either case. Another option is to buy a local SIM card with a rechargeable account (particularly good value in Sweden and Finland).

Fax
You can send faxes and telegrams from most larger post offices.

Email & Internet Access
Travelling with a portable computer is a great way to stay in touch with life back home but, unless you know what you're doing, it can be fraught with problems. A good investment is a universal AC adapter for your appliance, so you can plug it in anywhere without frying the innards of your computer, if the power supply voltage varies. You'll also need a plug adapter for each country you visit, often easiest bought before you leave home.

Secondly, your PC-card modem may or may not work once you leave your home country and you won't know for sure until you try. The safest option is to buy a reputable 'global' or 'world' modem before you leave home, or buy a local PC-card modem if you're spending an extended time in any one country. Keep in mind that the telephone socket in each country you visit will probably be different from that at home, so ensure that you have at least a US RJ-11 telephone adapter that works with your modem. You can almost always find an adapter that will convert from RJ-11 to the local variety, or buy a local modem cable with the appropriate telephone jack at the end. For more information on travelling with a portable computer, see the World Wide Phone Guide on the Internet at ⓦ www.kropla.com or TeleAdapt at ⓦ www.teleadapt.com.

Internet service providers (ISPs) such as **AmericaOnline** (ⓦ www.aol.com), **Compu Serve** (ⓦ www.compuserve.com) and **AT&T** (ⓦ www.att.com) each have dial-in nodes throughout Europe, except for Greenland and the Faroe Islands; it's best to download a list of the dial-in numbers before you leave home. You can also get an Internet account with **MaGlobe** (ⓦ www.maglobe.com), which offers local access numbers throughout Scandinavia (except the Faroes and Greenland) and charges around US$5 per hour. If

Mobile Phones

Most populated parts of Scandinavia use GSM 900/1800, which is compatible with the rest of Europe and Australasia, but not with the North American GSM 1900 or the totally different system in Japan (although some North American GSM 1900/900 may work here). If you have a GSM phone, check with your service provider about using it in Scandinavia, and beware of calls being routed internationally (very expensive for a 'local' call). See also the individual country chapters for more specific details.

you access your Internet email account at home through a smaller ISP or your office or school network, your best option is either to open an account with a global ISP, like those previously mentioned, or rely on Internet cafés and other public access points to collect your mail.

If you do intend to rely on Internet cafés, check whether your ISP has a Web-based email collection point on their website. If not, you will need to have three pieces of information so you can access your Internet mail account: your incoming (POP or IMAP) mail server name, your account name and your password. Your ISP or network supervisor will give you these. Armed with this information, you should be able to access your Internet mail account from any net-connected machine in the world, provided it runs some kind of email software. It pays to become familiar with the process for doing this before you leave home.

Another popular option for collecting mail through Internet cafés is to open a free Web-based email account like **Hotmail** (W *www .hotmail.com*) or **Yahoo! Mail** (W *mail .yahoo.com*). You can then access your mail from anywhere in the world from any net-connected machine running a standard Web browser.

You'll find Internet cafés throughout Scandinavia and some are listed in the country chapters in this book; for an up-to-date list see W www.netcafeguide.com. You may also find public Internet access in post offices, libraries, hostels, hotels, universities and so on.

DIGITAL RESOURCES

The World Wide Web is a rich resource for travellers. You can research your trip, hunt down bargain air fares, book hotels, check on weather conditions or chat with locals and other travellers about the best places to visit (or avoid!).

There's no better place to start your Web explorations than the Lonely Planet website (W www.lonelyplanet.com). Here you'll find succinct summaries on travelling to most places on earth, postcards from other travellers and the Thorn Tree bulletin board, where you can ask questions before you go or dispense advice when you get back. You can also find travel news and updates to many of our most popular guidebooks, and the sub-WWWay section links you to the most useful travel resources elsewhere on the Web.

The following websites offer useful general information about European cities, transport systems, currencies etc:

Airline Information What airlines fly where, when and for how much
  W www.travelocity.com
Currency Converter Exchange rates of hundreds of worldwide currencies
  W www.xe.net/currency
Rail Information Train fares and schedules on the most popular routes in Europe, including information on rail and youth passes
  W www.raileurope.com
Tourist Offices Lists tourist offices at home and around the world for most countries
  W www.towd.com

NEWSPAPERS & MAGAZINES

If you want to keep up with the news in English, you can get the excellent *International Herald Tribune*, the European edition of the *Wall Street Journal* or the colourful but very superficial *USA Today* in large Scandinavian towns. The UK *Guardian* and *Financial Times* are also widely available. Other UK papers are often on sale, but are expensive and likely to be a day or so behind. *Time*, *Newsweek* and the *Economist* are widely available (exceptions include most of the Faroes, Greenland and rural Iceland).

RADIO & TV

In Scandinavia, the **BBC World Service** (W *www.bbc.co.uk)* can be found on long wave at 198kHz (1510m), medium wave at 648kHz, and on short wave at 6195, 9410 and 15485kHz, the appropriate frequency depends on your location and the time of day. **Voice of America** *(VOA;* W *www.voa.gov)* can usually be found on short wave at 15205kHz. You'll also find English-language programmes (including BBC World Service and VOA) on local AM radio stations.

Cable and satellite TV have spread across Europe with much more gusto than radio but networks like Sky TV, BBC World and CNN are usually only found in expensive hotels.

VIDEO SYSTEMS

If you want to record or buy videos to play back home, it won't work if the image registration systems are different. Most of Europe and Australia uses PAL (France and Poland use SECAM), which is incompatible with NTSC in North America and Japan.

PHOTOGRAPHY & VIDEO

Scandinavia is extremely photogenic, but where you'll be travelling and the climate will dictate what film to take or buy locally. In autumn, when the sky can often be overcast, photographers should bring film rated 200 or 400 ISO. In sunny weather (or under a blanket of snow) slower film (with a lower ASA) is the answer. It is worth noting that if you are taking pictures of icebergs (or in any brightly reflective conditions) you need to overexpose your shots. Otherwise automatic cameras think it's brighter than it really is and take on faster shutter speeds, resulting in dark photos. Batteries tend to run out quickly in cold conditions, carry a spare set. For more pointers, check out Lonely Planet's *Travel Photography*, by internationally renowned travel photographer Richard I'Anson. It's full colour and designed to be taken on the road.

Still and video film and camera equipment are available throughout Scandinavia, but it would be advisable to bring as much as possible with you, as prices can be exorbitant. Apart from Greenland, print processing is generally available in towns and cities around Scandinavia.

TIME

Scandinavian Europe sprawls across six time zones. See the country chapters for details.

ELECTRICITY

Voltages & Cycles

Most of the region runs on 220V, 50Hz AC. Check the voltage and cycle (usually 50Hz) used in your home country. Most appliances that are set up for 220V will handle 240V quite happily without modifications (and vice versa; the same goes for 110V and 125V combinations.

It's always preferable to adjust your appliance to the exact voltage if you can (some modern battery chargers and radios will do this automatically). Just don't combine 110/125V and 220/240V without a transformer (which will be built into an adjustable appliance).

Several countries outside Europe (eg, the USA and Canada) have 60Hz AC, which will affect the speed of electric motors even after the voltage has been adjusted to European values, so CD and tape players (where motor speed is all-important) will be useless. However, appliances like electric razors, hair dryers, irons and radios will be fine.

Plugs & Sockets

The standard here is the so-called europlug with two round pins, though some plugs in the Faroes have three pins and some in Iceland have two slanted prongs. Adaptors are available from most supermarkets. Many europlugs and some sockets don't have provision for earth since most local home appliances are double insulated; when provided, earth usually consists of two contact points along the edge.

WEIGHTS & MEASURES

The metric system is used exclusively in Scandinavia. Decimals are indicated by commas and thousands are indicated by points.

HEALTH

Scandinavia is a very healthy place in which to travel. Your main risks are likely to be viral infections in winter and sunburn and insect bites in summer. Foot blisters, and an upset stomach from overeating or drinking, can hit you any time.

Travel health depends on your predeparture preparations, daily health care while travelling and how you handle any medical problems that develop. If you are reasonably fit, the only thing you need to organise before departure is travel insurance that includes good medical cover. See Travel Insurance under Visas & Documents earlier in this chapter.

There are a number of excellent travel health sites on the Internet. From Lonely Planet's home page there are links at **w** www .lonelyplanet.com/weblinks/wlheal.htm.

Predeparture Planning

Jabs are not necessary for travel in the region, unless you have been travelling through a part of the world where yellow fever may be prevalent. Ensure that your normal childhood vaccinations (against measles, mumps, rubella, diphtheria, tetanus and polio) are up to date and/or you are still showing immunity.

Make sure you're healthy before you start travelling. If you are going on a long trip have a dental checkup. If you wear glasses take a spare pair and your prescription. You will have no problem getting new glasses made up quickly and competently in Scandinavia but you'll pay for the privilege.

Wearers of contact lenses should bring generous supplies of cleaning fluids and wetting solutions when travelling in rural areas

(Greenland in particular) as they aren't easy to find in small towns and may be more expensive than they are at home.

If you require a particular medication take an adequate supply, as it may not be available locally. Take part of the packaging showing the generic name rather than the brand, which will make buying further supplies easier. To avoid any problems, it's a good idea to have a legible prescription or letter from your doctor to show that you legally use the medication.

Health Insurance Make sure that you have adequate health insurance. See Travel Insurance under Visas & Documents earlier in this chapter for details.

Basic Rules

Food Although most stomach upsets in Scandinavia will be relatively minor, beware of breakfast buffets where food (including cold meats and fish) may have been out of the fridge for several hours on each of several consecutive days.

Salads and fruit should be safe. Ice cream is usually OK, but be wary of ice cream that has melted and been refrozen. Avoid undercooked meat and take great care with fish or shellfish (for instance, cooked mussels that haven't opened properly can be dangerous).

If a restaurant, café or shop looks clean and well run, and if the vendor also looks clean and healthy, then the food is probably safe. It is also a good sign if a place is packed with locals or travellers. Be careful with any food that has been cooked and left to go cold.

Mushroom picking is traditionally a favourite pastime in this part of the world as autumn approaches, but make sure you don't eat any mushrooms that haven't been positively identified as safe.

Water Tap water is always safe to drink in Scandinavia. However, always be wary of drinking natural water. The burbling stream may look crystal clear and very inviting but, before drinking from it, you want to be absolutely sure there are no people or animals upstream; take particular care in Iceland, the Faroe Islands, and southern Greenland. In Norway, Sweden, Iceland and Greenland, meltwater streams from glaciers should be avoided – the suspended silt in the water can cause kidney problems. Run-off from fertilised fields is also a concern.

Water Purification If you are planning extended hikes where you have to rely on natural water, the simplest way of purifying water is to boil it thoroughly. Vigorous boiling should be satisfactory; however, at high altitude water boils at a lower temperature, so germs are less likely to be killed. Boil it for longer in these environments.

If you cannot boil water it should be treated chemically. Chlorine tablets (Puritabs, Steritabs or other brands) will kill many pathogens, but not some parasites like giardia and amoebic cysts. Iodine is more effective in purifying water and is available in tablet form (such as Potable Aqua). Follow the directions carefully and remember that too much iodine can be harmful.

Medical Problems & Treatment

In Scandinavia, including Greenland, medical and dental facilities are generally good, even in small towns. If you fall ill, seek help initially at your hotel or hostel. Local pharmacies or neighbourhood medical centres are good places to visit if you have a minor medical problem and can explain what it is. Hospital casualty wards will help if it's more serious, and will tell you if it's not. Throughout this book, major hospitals are indicated on the maps and emergency numbers are mentioned in the text. Tourist offices and hotels can put you on to a doctor or dentist; your embassy will probably know one who speaks your language.

Environmental Hazards

Hypothermia Hypothermia occurs when the body loses heat faster than it can produce it and the core temperature of the body falls. It's surprisingly easy to progress from very cold to dangerously cold due to a combination of wind, wet clothing, fatigue and hunger, even when the air temperature is above freezing. It's best to dress in layers; silk, wool and artificial fibres like Capilene polyester are all good insulating materials. A hat is important, because a lot of heat is lost through the head.

A strong, waterproof outer layer is essential. A 'space' blanket should be carried for emergencies if you will be exposed to the elements, such as while hiking. Carry basic supplies, including food containing simple sugars (such as chocolate) to generate heat quickly, and fluid to drink.

Symptoms of hypothermia are exhaustion, numb skin (particularly toes and fingers), shivering, slurred speech, irrational or violent behaviour, lethargy, stumbling, dizzy spells, muscle cramps and violent bursts of energy. Irrationality may take the form of sufferers claiming they are warm and trying to take off their clothes.

To treat mild hypothermia, first get the person out of the wind and/or rain, remove their clothing if it's wet and replace it with dry, warm clothing. Give them hot liquids – not alcohol – and some simple, sugary food. Do not rub victims, but allow them to slowly warm themselves. This procedure should be enough to treat the early stages of hypothermia. The early recognition and treatment of mild hypothermia is the only way to prevent severe hypothermia, which is a critical condition.

Jet Lag A person experiences jet lag when they travel by air across more than three time zones (each time zone usually represents a one-hour time difference). It occurs because many of the functions of the human body (such as temperature and emptying of the bladder and bowels) are regulated by internal 24-hour cycles. When we travel long distances rapidly, our bodies take time to adjust to the 'new time' of our destination, and we may experience fatigue, disorientation, insomnia, anxiety, impaired concentration and loss of appetite. These effects will usually be gone within three days, but to minimise the impact of jet lag:

- Rest for a couple of days prior to departure
- Try to select flight schedules that minimise sleep deprivation; arriving late in the day means you can go to sleep soon after you arrive. For very long flights, try to organise a stopover.
- Avoid excessive eating (which bloats the stomach) and alcohol (which causes dehydration) during the flight. Instead, drink plenty of non-carbonated, non-alcoholic drinks such as fruit juice or water.
- Avoid smoking
- Make yourself comfortable by wearing loose-fitting clothes and perhaps bringing an eye mask and ear plugs to help you sleep
- Try to sleep at the appropriate time for the time zone you are travelling to

Sunburn You can get sunburnt surprisingly quickly, even through cloud. Use sunscreen, a hat, and a barrier cream for your nose and lips. Calamine lotion or Stingose are good for mild sunburn. Protect your eyes with good-quality sunglasses, particularly if you will be near water, sand, glacier ice or snow.

Infectious Diseases

Diarrhoea Simple things like a change of water, food or climate can all cause a mild bout of diarrhoea, but a few rushed toilet trips with no other symptoms is not indicative of a major problem.

Dehydration is the main danger with any diarrhoea, particularly in children or the elderly as it can occur quite quickly. Under all circumstances fluid replacement (at least equal to the volume being lost) is the most important thing to remember. Weak black tea with a little sugar, soda water, or soft drinks allowed to go flat and diluted 50% with water are all good. Stick to a bland diet as you recover.

If you're going trekking or wild camping, you'll want to know about *Giardia lamblia*, an intestinal parasite that causes giardiasis, commonly known as giardia or 'beaver fever'. Symptoms include stomach cramps, nausea, bloated stomach, watery, foul-smelling diarrhoea and frequent sulphurous gas. Giardiasis can appear several weeks after you've been exposed to the parasite. The symptoms may disappear for a few days and then return; this can go on for several weeks and will cause irreparable internal damage unless you seek medical advice. If this isn't possible, the recommended drugs are Tinidazole (Fasigyn) or metronidazole (Flagyl). Treatment is a 2g single dose of Fasigyn or 250mg of Flagyl three times daily for five to 10 days.

Fortunately, giardiasis is still rare in Scandinavia, but cases have been reported in Iceland. To minimise the risk, avoid drinking water from streams which may have been contaminated by people, sheep or cattle. And to minimise the risk to others, make sure you cause no contamination in streams or rivers – this includes waste food from washing dishes.

Hepatitis A general term for inflammation of the liver is hepatitis. There are a number of different viruses that cause hepatitis, and they differ in the way that they are transmitted. The symptoms are similar in all forms of the illness, and include fever, chills, headache, fatigue, feelings of weakness and aches and pains, followed by loss of appetite, nausea, vomiting, abdominal pain, dark urine, light-coloured faeces, jaundiced (yellow) skin and yellowing of the whites of the eyes. People who have had hepatitis A should avoid alcohol for some time after the illness, as the liver needs time to recover.

Hepatitis A is transmitted by contaminated food and drinking water. You should seek medical advice, but there is not much you can do apart from resting, drinking lots of fluids, eating lightly and avoiding fatty foods.

Hepatitis B is spread through contact with infected blood, blood products or body fluids, for example, through sexual contact, unsterilised needles and blood transfusions, as well as contact with blood via small breaks in the skin. Other risk situations include having a shave, tattoo or body piercing with contaminated equipment. The symptoms of hepatitis B may be more severe than type A and the disease can lead to lasting problems such as chronic liver damage, liver cancer or a long-term carrier state.

There are vaccines against hepatitis A and B, but following basic rules about food and water (hepatitis A) and avoiding risk situations (hepatitis B) are important preventative measures.

HIV & AIDS Infection with human immuno-deficiency virus (HIV) may lead to acquired immune deficiency syndrome (AIDS), which is a fatal disease. Any exposure to blood, blood products or body fluids may put the individual at risk. The disease is often transmitted through sexual contact or dirty needles – vaccinations, acupuncture, tattooing and body piercing can be potentially as dangerous as intravenous drug use.

Sexually Transmitted Diseases (STDs)

Gonorrhoea, herpes and syphilis are among these diseases; sores, blisters or rashes around the genitals and discharges or pain when urinating are common symptoms. In some STDs, such as wart virus or chlamydia, symptoms may be less marked or not observed at all, especially in women. Syphilis symptoms may even disappear completely but the disease continues and can cause severe problems in later years. While abstinence from sexual contact is the only 100% effective prevention, using condoms is also effective.

STDs are fairly common in Greenland due to a relatively high rate of promiscuous sexual activity. STD clinics are widespread in Scandinavia and can be found at hospitals in Greenland. Don't be shy about visiting them if you may have contracted something. Treatment of gonorrhoea and syphilis is with antibiotics. Different sexually transmitted diseases each require specific antibiotics.

Cuts, Bites & Stings

Insect Bites & Stings Bee and wasp stings are usually painful rather than dangerous. However, in people who are allergic to them severe breathing difficulties may occur and require urgent medical care. Calamine lotion or Stingose spray will give relief and ice packs will reduce the pain and swelling. Midges, small blood-sucking flies related to mosquitoes, are common in Arctic regions from June to August.

Mosquitoes and blackflies, as well as being a nuisance, can almost drive you insane during the summer months in northern Europe – Finland, with its many lakes, is particularly notorious, but Greenland can be worse. Midsummer is the worst period, and hikers will have to cover exposed skin and may even need special mosquito hats with netting to screen their faces. Seek local advice, as regular mosquito repellents and coils are hardly effective against the ravenous hordes that home in on you 24 hours a day. A mosquito-proof tent is essential. Fortunately, mosquito-borne diseases such as malaria are unknown in this part of the world, and the main risks are psychological (people have been literally driven mad by the incessant buzzing and itching).

Most people get used to mosquito bites after a few days as their bodies adjust and the itching and swelling become less severe. Antihistamine cream or tablets should help alleviate the worst symptoms.

Rabies Caused by a bite or scratch from an infected mammal, rabies is found throughout Europe (though Iceland and the Faroes are rabies-free), and the risk has increased since the physical and political barriers were removed between the East and West in 1989. Dogs are a noted carrier, but cats, foxes and bats can also be infected.

Any bite, scratch or even lick from a warm-blooded, furry animal should be cleaned immediately and thoroughly. Scrub with soap and running water, and then apply alcohol or iodine solution. Medical help should be sought promptly to receive a course of injections to prevent the onset of symptoms and death.

Ticks Disease-carrying ticks are a concern for hikers, particularly in Åland, Finland. You should always check all over your body if you have been walking through a potentially tick-infested area as ticks can cause skin infections and other more serious diseases. If a tick is found attached, press down around the tick's head with tweezers, grab the head and gently pull upwards. Avoid pulling the rear of the body as this may squeeze the tick's gut contents through the attached mouth parts into the skin, increasing the risk of infection and disease. Smearing chemicals on the tick will not make it let go and is not recommended.

Snakes They tend to keep a very low profile in Scandinavia (there are none in Iceland, Greenland or the Faroes) but to minimise your chances of being bitten always wear boots, socks and long trousers when walking through undergrowth where snakes may be present. Don't put your hands into holes and crevices, and be careful when collecting firewood.

Snakebite doesn't cause instantaneous death and antivenins are usually available. Immediately wrap the bitten limb tightly, as you would for a sprained ankle, and attach a splint to immobilise it. Keep the victim still and seek medical help. Don't attempt to catch or kill the snake – there's always the possibility of being bitten again and snakes are no longer needed for identification. Tourniquets and sucking out the poison are now comprehensively discredited.

Women's Health

Gynaecological Problems Use of antibiotics, synthetic underwear, sweating and contraceptive pills can lead to fungal vaginal infections, especially when travelling in hot climates. Fungal infections are characterised by a rash, itch and discharge and can be treated with a vinegar or lemon-juice douche, or with yoghurt. Nystatin, miconazole or clotrimazole pessaries or vaginal cream are the usual treatment.

WOMEN TRAVELLERS

Scandinavia, apart from Greenland, is one of the safest places to travel in all of Europe. Women often travel alone or in pairs around the region, which should pose no problems, but women do tend to attract more unwanted attention than men (especially in Greenland),

and common sense is the best guide to dealing with potentially dangerous situations like hitching, walking alone at night etc.

Recommended reading is the *Handbook for Women Travellers* by M & G Moss.

GAY & LESBIAN TRAVELLERS

Gays and lesbians should get in touch with their national organisation for more detailed information about Scandinavia. This book lists contact addresses and gay and lesbian venues in some of the individual country chapters, but your organisation should be able to give you more information. The *Spartacus International Gay Guide*, published by Bruno Gmünder Verlag (Berlin), is an excellent international directory of gay entertainment venues, but it's best used in conjunction with more up-to-date listings in local papers; as elsewhere, gay venues in the region can change with great speed.

Denmark, Iceland, Norway and Sweden allow gay and lesbian couples to form 'registered partnerships', which grant every right of matrimony except access to church weddings, adoption and artificial insemination.

DISABLED TRAVELLERS

Scandinavia, apart from Greenland, leads the world in terms of facilities for disabled people. For instance, by law every new restaurant in Finland must have a special toilet for people with a disability. There are wheelchair ramps to practically all public buildings and most department shops, shopping centres and many private shops and some train carriages are fitted with special lifts for wheelchairs.

If you have a physical disability, get in touch with your national support organisation (preferably the 'travel officer' if there is one) and ask about the countries you plan to visit. They often have complete libraries devoted to travel, and they can put you in touch with travel agents who specialise in tours for the disabled.

The **Royal Association for Disability & Rehabilitation** (RADAR; ☎ 020-7250 3222; W www.radar.org.uk; 12 City Forum, 250 City Rd, London, EC1V 8AF) can supply general advice for disabled travellers in Europe.

SENIOR TRAVELLERS

Senior travellers are entitled to many discounts in Scandinavia on public transport, museum admission fees etc, provided they show proof of their age. In some cases they might need a special pass. The minimum qualifying age is generally 60 or 65. See also Seniors Cards under Visas & Documents earlier in this chapter.

In your home country, a lower age may already entitle you to all sorts of interesting travel packages and discounts (on car hire, for instance) through organisations and travel agents that cater for senior travellers. Start hunting at your local senior citizens' advice bureau.

TRAVEL WITH CHILDREN

Successful travel with young children does require planning and effort. Don't try to overdo things; even for adults, packing too much into the time available can cause problems. Make sure the activities include the kids as well – balance a day at Copenhagen's Nationalmuseet with a day at Legoland. Include your children in the trip planning; if they've helped to work out where you will be going, they will be much more interested when they get there. Lonely Planet's *Travel with Children*, by Cathy Lanigan, is a good source of information.

Most of Scandinavia is very child-friendly (Iceland and Greenland are exceptions). There are many public parks for kids, and commercial facilities are numerous. Domestic tourism is largely dictated by children's needs – theme parks, water parks and so on. Many museums, such as the national ones in Stockholm, have a children's section with toys and activities. The Musikmuseet in that city, for instance, includes various 'hands on' musical instruments as part of its permanent collection.

Car-rental firms hire out children's safety seats at a nominal cost, but it's essential that you book them in advance. The same goes for highchairs and cots (cribs); they're standard in many restaurants and hotels, but numbers may be limited. The choice of baby food, infant formulas, soy and cow's milk, disposable nappies (diapers) etc is wide in the supermarkets of most Scandinavian countries. Remember, though, that opening hours may be quite different; but if you do happen to get caught out, there's always a 24-hour convenience store.

DANGERS & ANNOYANCES

Theft, usually pickpocketing, is becoming a serious problem in major Scandinavian cities. More threatening situations may also arise in Greenland. The police are notorious for inaction and incompetence, so it's best not to expect any assistance from them (although they must, by law, provide a statement detailing the crime). Take care of your belongings and remember that the greatest threat in places like Oslo, Copenhagen and Stockholm can actually be from fellow tourists, who thieve from others to fund their trips.

In remote rural areas, hypothermia, injury and getting lost are serious hazards. Because there are so few people around in such places, you'll have to accept those you do come across as they are – which is often suspicious of outsiders. The gloom that winter brings may lead to unpredictable behaviour and alcohol abuse.

Whatever you do, don't leave friends and relatives back home worrying about how to get in touch with you in case of emergency.

Mosquitoes and blackflies can be a real annoyance in some parts of the region. See Cuts, Bites & Stings in the earlier Health section.

Theft

As a traveller, you're often fairly vulnerable and when you do lose things it can be a real hassle. Theft is more of a problem in Greenland than elsewhere in Scandinavia – and here, it's not just other travellers you have to be wary of. The most important things to guard are your passport, other documents, tickets and money – in that order. It's always best to carry these next to your skin or in a sturdy leather pouch on your belt.

Train-station lockers or luggage storage counters are useful places to store luggage (but not your valuables) while you get your bearings in a new town. Be very suspicious about people who offer to help you operate your locker. Carry your own padlock for hostel lockers and watch out for thieves who strike at night in hostel dorms: keep your money and passport well out of reach.

Be careful, even in hotels; don't leave valuables lying around in your room. Parked cars are prime targets for petty criminals in most cities, and cars with foreign number plates and/or rental agency stickers are particularly targeted.

If possible, remove the stickers (or cover them with local football club stickers or something similar), leave a local newspaper on the seat and try to make it look like a local car. Don't ever leave valuables in the car, and remove all luggage overnight.

In case of theft or loss, always report the incident to the police and ask for a statement, or your travel insurance won't pay up.

Drugs

Always treat drugs with a great deal of caution. There's a fair bit of dope available in the region, sometimes quite openly, but that doesn't mean it's legal. Even a little hashish can cause a great deal of trouble.

Don't bother bringing drugs home with you. With 'suspect' stamps in your passport (including Copenhagen airport) energetic customs officials could well decide to take a closer look at your luggage.

ACTIVITIES

Scandinavia offers countless opportunities to indulge in more active pursuits than sightseeing. The varied geography and climate supports the full range of outdoor activities, including windsurfing, skiing, fishing, hiking, mountaineering, boating and cycling. For more local information, see the individual country chapters.

Hiking

Keen hikers can spend a lifetime exploring the region's many exciting trails. There are national parks, nature reserves and other interesting areas that may qualify as a trekker's paradise, depending on your preferences. You can hike on well-marked trails, and accommodation is available along the way. Be sure to bring food, and appropriate clothing and equipment with you.

The Right of Common Access law in Sweden, Norway, Finland and Iceland allows anyone to walk virtually anywhere, while respecting homeowners' and commercial premises' privacy. Greenland has a similar arrangement, but this doesn't cover the icecap. Naturally, there are certain rules of conduct. Huge national routes like Kungsleden in Sweden and the UKK route in Finland are popular, as are provincial or regional routes, spanning hundreds of kilometres, and extensive tracks through national parks. Local and regional tourist offices distribute free maps for shorter routes and sell excellent trekking maps for the national parks.

Skiing

Scandinavia is famous for winter sports and snow skiing is a popular activity. Skiing in Scandinavia is most often cross-country (nordic), on some of the world's best trails. Alpine or downhill skiing is quite expensive due to the costs of ski lifts, accommodation and the apres-ski drinking sessions.

Sweden and Norway have the longest downhill slopes but cross-country skiing is also very popular. Finnish and a few Icelandic ski areas are also fairly well equipped but, surprisingly, facilities are undeveloped in Greenland. Åre in Sweden is probably the single best area for alpine skiing and the top resorts in Norway are Geilo and Lillehammer, where telemark skiing is also popular.

Downhill skiing is always easier to arrange in Scandinavia as rentals can be organised easily. For cross-country skiing, travellers will normally have to either rely on friendly locals to lend their equipment, or plan on buying the skis, poles and boots. (Flea markets are the cheapest places to look.)

Skiing – especially cross-country – should only be attempted after studying the trails/routes (wilderness trails are identified by colour codes on maps and signposts). Wear appropriate clothing and carry food, extra clothing and emergency supplies, such as matches and something to burn. Skiers should be extra careful about darkness. In Scandinavia, days are very short in winter and, during the winter months of December and January, there's no daylight at all in the extreme north.

The skiing season generally lasts from early December to April. Snow conditions can vary greatly from one year to another and from region to region, but January and February, as well as the Easter holiday period, tend to be the best (and busiest) months. Snow cannons for producing artificial snow are common. Practically all towns and villages illuminate some skiing tracks.

Cycling

Along with hiking, cycling is the best way to really get close to the scenery and the people, keeping yourself fit in the process. It's also a good way to get around the cities.

Popular cycling areas include much of Denmark, greater Oslo, the islands of Gotland in Sweden and Åland in Finland. Be wary of western Norway, as beautiful as it is – there are tunnels galore which prohibit cyclists (some are over 5km long), the serpentine roads to/from mountain passes are killers and, unless you want to pedal an extra 50km around a fjord, you'll have to add on the expense of a ferry. Greenland is no place for cyclists, since there are virtually no roads or tracks outside the towns.

If you come from outside Europe, you can often bring your bicycle along on the plane for a surprisingly reasonable fee. Alternatively, this book lists places where you can rent one (make sure it has plenty of gears if you plan anything serious). The minimum rental period in Scandinavia is usually one day.

See the Getting Around chapter and the individual country chapters for more information on bicycle touring and tips on places to visit.

Boating
The many lakes, rivers and diverse coastlines in Scandinavia offer a variety of boating options unmatched anywhere in the world. You can ride the rapids in a canoe in Finland or, during winter, take a trip on an Arctic icebreaker; hire a rowing boat or cruise fjords or peaceful Lake Mjøsa in Norway; cruise from Helsinki to Stockholm; or kayak around the coast in Greenland – the possibilities are endless. The country chapters have more details.

Windsurfing
While this sport is not as popular as it was in the late 1980s, the beaches of Denmark continue to attract crowds of windsurfers in summer. Wetsuits enable the keener windsurfers to continue their sport throughout the colder months. Sailboards can be rented in some tourist centres, and courses are sometimes on offer for beginners.

COURSES
Apart from learning new physical skills by undertaking something like a downhill skiing course in Norway or learning to windsurf in Denmark, you can enrich your mind in a variety of structured courses on anything from a local language to alternative medicine. Language courses are often available to foreigners through universities, folk high schools or private institutions, and are justifiably popular since the best way to learn a language is in the country where it's spoken. You can also take courses in art, literature, architecture, drama, music, cooking, alternative energy, photography and organic farming, among other things. In general, the best sources of information are the cultural institutes,

tourist offices and embassies of Scandinavian countries abroad. The student-exchange organisations, student travel agencies, and organisations like the YMCA/YWCA and HI can also put you on the right track. Ask about special holiday packages that include a course.

WORK
Officially, a citizen of the EU is allowed to work in other EU countries. However, the paperwork isn't always straightforward for longer-term employment. Other country/nationality combinations require special work permits that are almost impossible to arrange, especially for temporary work.

That doesn't prevent enterprising travellers from topping up their funds occasionally, and not always illegally. Your national student-exchange organisation may be able to arrange temporary work permits to several countries through special programmes. For more details on working in Scandinavia, see Work in the Facts for the Visitor sections of the individual country chapters.

If you have a parent or grandparent who was born in an EU country, you may have certain rights you never knew about. Get in touch with that country's embassy and ask about dual citizenship and work permits – if you are eligible for citizenship, also ask about any obligations, such as military service, taxation and having to relinquish your first passport. Not all countries allow dual citizenship, so a work permit may be all you can get. Ireland is particularly easy-going about granting citizenship to people with Irish ancestry and, with an Irish passport, the EU is your oyster.

If you do find a temporary job, the pay may be less than that offered to locals, though this is not always the case in Scandinavia. Teaching English can pay well, but such work is hard to come by. Other typical tourist jobs (such as working in a restaurant, hotel or fish-processing plant) may come with board and lodging and the pay is little more than pocket money, but you'll have a good time partying with other travellers.

Work Your Way Around the World, by Susan Griffith, gives good, practical advice on a wide range of issues. Another useful title is *The Au Pair and Nanny's Guide to Working Abroad* by Susan Griffith & Sharon Legg.

If you play an instrument or have other artistic talents, you could try busking (street entertainment). It's fairly common in many major cities, but would be unwise anywhere in Greenland. In Sweden you'll need to get a busking permit, which is available from the police, although not everybody actually has the permit. In Copenhagen, acoustic music is allowed without a permit in pedestrian streets and squares between 4pm and 8pm on weekdays and noon to 5am at the weekend. Most other Scandinavian countries require municipal permits that can be hard to obtain. Talk to other buskers first.

Selling goods on the street is generally frowned upon and can be tantamount to vagrancy, apart from at flea markets. It's also a hard way to make money.

ACCOMMODATION

The cheapest places to stay in the region are camping grounds, followed by hostels and student accommodation. Cheap hotels are virtually unknown in most of the northern half of Europe, but guesthouses, pensions, private rooms and B&Bs can sometimes present good value. Self-catering flats and cottages are worth considering if you're travelling with a group, especially if you plan to stay in one place for a while.

See the Facts for the Visitor sections in the country chapters for an overview of the local accommodation options. During peak holiday periods, accommodation can be hard to find and, unless you're camping, it's advisable to book ahead. Even camping grounds, especially popular big-city ones, can fill up.

If you arrive in a country by train, there's often a hotel-booking desk at the railway station. Tourist offices in cities and towns tend to have extensive accommodation lists and the more helpful ones will go out of their way to find you something suitable. In most countries there's a small fee for this service, but if accommodation is tight, it can save you a lot of running around. This is also an easy way to get around any language problems. Agencies offering private rooms can be good value. Staying with a local family doesn't always mean that you'll lack privacy, but you'll probably have less freedom than in a hotel.

Camping

Camping is immensely popular in most of the region and is the cheapest accommodation. There's usually a charge per tent or site, per vehicle and per person. National tourist offices should have booklets or brochures listing camping grounds all over their country. See Documents earlier in this chapter for information on Camping Card International.

Although some camping grounds are commendably close to city centres, in most cases they will be some distance from the centre, especially in larger cities. For this reason camping is most popular among people with their own vehicles. If you're on foot the money you save by camping can quickly be outweighed by the money spent commuting to and from a town centre.

Unless the camping ground rents small cabins or chalets on site (common in Scandinavian countries except Greenland, Iceland and the Faroes), you'll also need a tent, sleeping bag and cooking equipment – easier to cart around if you have a vehicle.

Camping other than in designated camping grounds is not always straightforward. In Denmark and the Faroes, it's illegal without permission from the local authorities (the police or local council office) or from landowners (though don't be shy about asking, since you may be pleasantly surprised by their response). Take care to keep toilet activities away from all surface water and use bio-degradable soaps for washing up.

The Right of Common Access (see Hiking under Activities earlier in this chapter) applies to all forests and wilderness areas in Sweden, Norway, Finland and Iceland. Greenland has similar access rights, but these don't include access to the icecap. Camping for the night is always legal within the framework of these regulations but there are restrictions, and tourist offices usually stock official publications explaining these in English. See the Facts for the Visitor sections of the relevant country chapters for additional information.

Hostels

Hostels offer the cheapest roof over your head in Scandinavia, and you don't have to be a youngster to use them. Most hostels are part of the national YHA (Youth Hostel Association), which is affiliated with Hostelling International (HI). In Sweden and Greenland, many hostels aren't affiliated with HI – see Accommodation in the relevant country chapters for details.

Technically you're supposed to be a YHA or HI member to use affiliated hostels, but in practice most are open to anyone. You may have to pay a bit extra without a card but this may be offset against future membership. Stay enough nights as a nonmember and you automatically become a member.

In Scandinavian countries, the hostels are geared for budget travellers of all ages, including families with kids, and most have both dorms and private rooms. Many hostels (exceptions including most hostels in Iceland, Greenland and the Faroes) serve breakfast and almost all hostels have a communal kitchen. Note that there's only a handful of hostels in Greenland.

To join HI, ask at any hostel or contact your local or national hostelling office; check out the Internet at Ⓦ www.iyhf.org.

At a hostel, you get a bed for the night and use of communal facilities, usually including a kitchen where you can prepare your own meals. You're normally required to have a sleeping sheet and pillowcase or linen – simply using your sleeping bag is not permitted. If you don't have your own, you can usually hire or buy them.

Hostels vary widely in character but, increasingly, hostels are open longer hours, curfews are disappearing and 'wardens' with a sergeant-major mentality are an endangered species. Also the trend has been towards smaller dormitories with just four to six beds.

Many hostel guides are available, including HI's annually updated *Europe* guide. Some hostels accept reservations by phone or fax but usually not during peak periods; they'll often book the next one you're headed to for a small fee.

Bookings up to six months in advance can also be made through the International Booking Network (however not all hostels are in the network). You can also book hostels through national hostel offices. Popular hostels in capital cities can be heavily booked in summer and limits may be placed on how many nights you can stay.

For further information see the Facts for the Visitor sections in the country chapters.

University Accommodation

Some universities and colleges rent student digs from June to mid-August; in Finland this kind of accommodation is usually affiliated with HI. These will often be single or double rooms and cooking facilities may be available. Inquire directly at the college or university, at the student information service or at local tourist offices.

B&Bs, Guesthouses & Hotels

There's a huge range of accommodation above the hostel level. B&Bs, where you get a room and breakfast in a private home, can often be the real bargains in this field in some countries, except in Greenland, where B&Bs are about double the normal Scandinavian price.

Private accommodation may go under the name of pensions, guesthouses and so on. In Norway, for example, there are plenty of private guesthouses along main roads, and they're significantly cheaper than hotels.

Above this level are hotels, which are always much more expensive than B&Bs and guesthouses; in cities, luxury five-star hotels have five-star prices. Categorisation varies from country to country.

Check your hotel room and the bathroom before you agree to take it, and make sure you know what it's going to cost – discounts are often available at certain times and for longer stays. Also ask about breakfast; it's usually included but sometimes you may be required to have it and pay extra (which can be a real rip-off).

If you think a hotel is too expensive, ask if they have a cheaper room. If you're with a group or plan to stay for any length of time, it's always worth trying to negotiate a special rate.

FOOD

The Facts for the Visitor sections in the individual country chapters contain details of local cuisine, and there are many suggestions on places to eat in the chapters themselves. As a rule, Scandinavian food is rather bland, and some travellers might want to carry along a small collection of spices and condiments (pepper, chilli etc) to liven up some dishes.

Restaurant prices vary enormously. In Scandinavia, the cheapest places for a decent meal are often the self-service restaurants in department stores – though these don't exist in Iceland or the Faroes.

Official student cafeterias are also cheap and, though the food tends to be unexciting, it is of a better quality than at student cafeterias elsewhere in Europe.

Without a university card, you probably won't get the student discount, but you'll be allowed to eat there and prices are still low. Kiosks also sell cheap snacks that can be as much a part of the national cuisine as more complex dishes.

Self-catering can be a cheap and wholesome way of eating. Most campers and hostellers will end up preparing at least some of their meals (camping stove fuel is readily available), and hostels and student accommodation usually have cooking facilities. Even if you don't cook, a lunch in a park with some crispbread, local cheese and slivers of smoked fish or salami can be one of the recurring highlights of your trip. It also makes a really nice change from budget-restaurant food.

Vegetarians are fairly well catered for in Scandinavian cities, less so in towns and in Greenland and the Faroes. Many tourist offices can supply lists of vegetarian restaurants, and some are recommended in this book. Many standard restaurants have one or two vegetarian dishes, or at least a few items on the menu that don't contain meat. Restaurants open at lunchtime often have a salad bar, and pizzerias are good bets for the green stuff. Some restaurants can handle special

diets if approached in advance, and you can always ask the waiter to talk with the chef on your behalf. If all else fails, you'll have to put together your own meals from ingredients bought in shops and markets.

DRINKS

Coffee is the most widely consumed drink in Scandinavia. International and local brands of soft drinks are available throughout the region.

Unfortunately, alcohol prices are high throughout Scandinavia, so we can't recommend the region for a drinking holiday.

Local beers aren't always the favourite for visitors, with the exception of the famous Carlsberg in Denmark and some rather good brews in Iceland and Sweden.

Scandinavia is also known for its powerful spirit *aquavit*, but some of the flavourings are absolutely dreadful and beware of the home-distilled variety, which can knock your socks off.

Getting There & Away

Step one is to get to Europe and, in these days of severe competition among airlines, there are plenty of opportunities to find a cheap ticket. The range of 'gateway' cities to Europe includes London, Athens, Frankfurt, Berlin, Copenhagen, Oslo and Stockholm.

You can often find air fares from London that either match or beat surface alternatives in terms of cost. Travelling between airports and city centres isn't a problem in Scandinavia thanks to good transport networks.

Forget ships, unless by 'ships' you mean the many ferry services operating in the Baltic and North Seas and in the Atlantic Ocean between Iceland, the Faroe Islands, the UK, Norway and Denmark. There is just a handful of ships that still carry passengers across the Atlantic; they don't sail often and are very expensive, even compared with full-fare air tickets. See the Sea section later in this chapter for details.

Some travellers arrive in Scandinavia overland through Central Asia and Russia, which has borders with Norway and Finland. The trans-Siberian and Mongolian express trains now carry more people than ever to and from Europe. See Land later in this chapter for more information.

AIR
Tickets

For long-term travel there are plenty of discount tickets that are valid for 12 months and allow multiple stopovers with open dates. For short-term travel cheaper fares are available by travelling midweek, staying away at least one Saturday night or as part of short-lived promotional offers.

When you're looking for bargain air fares, your best bet is go to a travel agent rather than directly to an airline. Sometimes airlines do have promotional fares and special offers, but generally they only sell at the officially listed price. An exception to this rule is the expanding number of 'no-frills' carriers that operate in the USA and northwestern Europe, which mostly sell direct to travellers. Unlike 'full-service' airlines, no-frills carriers often have point-to-point one-way tickets which are exactly half the return fare, so it is easy to put together a return ticket that allows you to fly into one place but leave from another.

The other exception is by booking on the Internet. Many airlines, full-service and no-frills, offer some excellent fares to Web surfers. They may sell seats by auction or simply cut prices to reflect the reduced cost of electronic selling. Many travel agents have websites, which can make the Internet a quick and easy way to compare prices – a good start for when you're ready to negotiate with your favourite travel agency.

The days when some travel agents would routinely fleece travellers by running off with their money are, happily, almost over. Paying by credit card generally offers protection, as most card issuers provide refunds if you can prove you didn't get what you paid for. Similar protection can be obtained by buying a ticket from a bonded agent, such as one covered by the Air Transport Operators Licence (ATOL) scheme in the UK. Agents who only accept cash should hand over the tickets straight away and not tell you to 'come back tomorrow'. After you've made a booking or paid your deposit, call the airline and confirm that the booking was made. It's generally not advisable to send money (even cheques) through the post unless the agent is very well established – some travellers have reported being ripped off by fly-by-night, mail-order ticket agents.

You may decide to pay more than the rock-bottom fare by opting for the safety of a better known travel agent. Firms such as STA Travel, which has offices worldwide, are not going to disappear overnight and they do offer good prices to most destinations.

If you purchase a ticket and later want to make changes to your route or get a refund, you need to contact the original travel agent. Airlines only issue refunds to the purchaser of a ticket – usually the travel agent who bought the ticket on your behalf. Many travellers change their routes halfway through their trips, so think carefully before you buy a ticket which is not easily refunded.

Student & Youth Fares

Full-time students and people under 26 have access to better deals than other travellers. These may not always be cheaper fares, but can include more flexibility to change flights and/or routes. You'll need a document proving your date of birth or a valid International Student Identity Card (ISIC) when buying your ticket and boarding the plane. There are plenty of places where nonstudents can get fake student cards, but if are get caught using one your ticket could be confiscated.

Travellers with Specific Needs

Airlines can often make special arrangements for travellers if they're warned early enough, such as wheelchair assistance at airports or vegetarian meals on the flight. Children under two years travel for 10% of the standard fare (or free on some airlines) as long as they don't occupy a seat. They don't get a baggage allowance. 'Skycots', baby food and nappies should be provided by the airline if requested in advance. Children aged between two and 12 can usually occupy a seat for half to two-thirds of the full fare, and do get a baggage allowance.

The USA

The North Atlantic is the world's busiest long-haul air corridor and flight options are bewildering. Larger newspapers produce weekly travel sections where you'll find travel agents' ads for air fares to Europe.

You should be able to fly return from New York or Boston to Copenhagen, Oslo or Stockholm for around US$500 in the low season and US$1000 in the high season. Open-jaw tickets allow you to land in one city (Copenhagen, for example) and return from another (such as Oslo) at no extra cost.

Icelandair (☎ 1 800 223 5500; W www.icelandair.net) flies from New York, Boston, Baltimore–Washington DC, Minneapolis and Orlando (autumn and winter only) via Reykjavík (Keflavík) to many European destinations including Glasgow, London, Oslo, Stockholm and Copenhagen. It often offers some of the best deals and also allows a free three-day stopover in Reykjavík on all its transatlantic flights (not applicable to tickets purchased on the Internet), making it a great way to spend a few days in Iceland.

On the other hand, if you're planning to fly within Scandinavian Europe, **Scandinavian Airlines** (SAS; ☎ 1 800 221 2350, W www.scandinavian.net) offer various air passes, depending on the passenger's country of origin (see Air in the Getting Around chapter).

Airhitch (W www.airhitch.org) specialises in Internet purchases of stand-by tickets to Europe for US$210/278 one way from the east coast/west coast, but the destinations are by region (not a specific city or country), so you'll need to be flexible.

Discount Travel Agencies

Discount travel agents in the USA are known as consolidators. San Francisco is the American capital for ticket consolidators, although some good deals can also be found in Los Angeles, New York and other big cities. Consolidators can be found through the *Yellow Pages* or the major daily newspapers.

STA Travel (☎ 1 800 781 4040; W www.statravel.com) has offices in Boston, Chicago, Miami, New York, Philadelphia and San Francisco and other major cities. Call the toll-free number for office locations or visit its website.

Other travel agencies include:

Air-Tech (☎ 212-219 7000, W www.airtech.com) 588 Broadway, Suite 204, New York, NY 10012-5405
Airtreks (☎ 1 877 247 8735, W www.airtreks.com) 442 Post St, Suite 400, 4th floor, San Francisco, CA 94102
Cheap Tickets (☎ 1 888 922 8849, W www.cheaptickets.com)
Educational Travel Center (☎ 1 800 747 5551, W www.edtrav.com) 438 N Frances St, Madison, WI 53703-1084
Interworld Travel (☎ 305-443 4929, W www.interworldtravel.com) 1701 Ponce De Leon Boulevard, Coral Gables, FL 33134

Canada

Canadian discount air-ticket sellers are also known as consolidators but their ticket prices tend to be about 10% higher than those sold in the USA.

Travel CUTS (☎ 1 866 246 9762; W www.travelcuts.com), Canada's national student travel agency, has offices in major cities.

To Stockhom from Vancouver fares start from C$1390/2110 in low/high season. From Toronto you're looking at C$1200/1850 in low/high season. Airlines include British Airways, Northwest and Air Canada.

Australia

Quite a few travel offices specialise in selling discount air tickets. Some travel agents, particularly smaller ones, advertise cheap air fares in the travel sections of weekend newspapers

Two well-known agents are **STA Travel** (☎ 1300 733 035; W www.statravel.com.au) and **Flight Centre** (☎ 133 133; W www.flightcentre.com.au). STA Travel has offices in major cities and on many university campuses and Flight Centre has dozens of offices throughout Australia. Ring the Australiawide numbers or check the websites for the location of your nearest branch.

From Australia, flights to Scandinavian capitals require a couple of stopovers on the way, usually Singapore or Bangkok and another European city. Return fares range from A$1650 in low season to A$2350 in high season. Air France, Qantas, Cathay Pacific and KLM all offer some good deals.

New Zealand

Flight Centre (☎ 0800 243544; W www.flightcentre.co.nz) has a large **central office** (Shop 3B, 205-225 Queen St) in Auckland at the National Bank Towers, and there are many other branches throughout the country. **STA Travel** (☎ 0508 782 872; W www.statravel.co.nz) has a **main office** (☎ 09-309 0458; Shop 2B, 187 Queen St, Auckland); there are other offices in Auckland and other towns and cities in New Zealand.

From New Zealand, Lufthansa offers some of the best deals for travel to Scandinavia. Return fares to Oslo or Stockholm start from NZ$2299/2659 in low/high season.

The UK & Ireland

Currently, two no-frills airlines offer cheap flights to major entry points in Scandinavia.

Ryanair (☎ 08701 569569; W www.ryanair.com) flies from London to Århus and Esbjerg (Denmark), Oslo Torp (Norway), and Stockholm Skavsta, Gothenburg and Malmö (Sweden). They also fly between Glasgow Prestwick and Oslo Torp. Return fares start at under £100 but, if you're lucky, you may get a promotional return fare for under £40. Flying from London Stansted to Copenhagen is **easy-Jet** (☎ 0870 600 0000; W www.easyjet.com), with fares starting at around £70 return.

Other commercial airlines, including **SAS** (☎ 0845 607 2722; W www.scandinavian.net), offer return flights from London to Stockholm starting at around £120 return. **City Airline** (☎ 0870 330 8800; W www.cityairline.com) flies from London Gatwick and Manchester to Gothenburg and Linköping once or twice daily; special offers from £69 (plus tax) return are detailed on the website.

Atlantic Airways (W www.atlantic.fo) has flights from Aberdeen and London Stansted to Vágar (Faroe Islands); see the Getting There & Away section in the Faroe Islands chapter for details.

Another option is **Icelandair** (☎ 020-7874 1000; W www.icelandair.co.uk), which flies to the USA from London and Glasgow via Reykjavík. From London or Glasgow to Reykjavík, a 21-day advance-purchase return costs from around £180 (allowing a stay of up to one month and an obligatory Saturday night stopover). The cheapest tickets are only available via the Internet and slightly lower fares are offered to customers who have signed up for Icelandair's free Netclub. Check the website for further details.

If you're looking for a cheap way into or out of Scandinavia, London is Europe's major centre for discounted fares. Advertisements for many travel agents appear in the travel pages of the weekend broadsheets, in *Time Out* and in free magazines, such as *TNT*.

For students or travellers under 26 years old, the most popular travel agency in the UK is **STA Travel** (☎ 08701 600599; W www.statravel.co.uk) which has branches across the country. STA Travel sells tickets to all travellers but caters especially to young people and students. Charter flights can be a cheaper alternative to scheduled flights, especially if you don't qualify for the under-26 and student discounts.

Other travel agencies are: **Trailfinders** (☎ 020-7938 3939; 194 Kensington High St,

London, W8 7RG); **Bridge the World** (☎ *020-7734 7447;* 🔲 *www.bridgetheworld .com; 4 Regent Place, London, W1B 5EA)*; and **Ebookers** *(☎ 0870 010 7000;* 🔲 *www .ebookers.com).*

Continental Europe

Although London is the discount capital of Europe, there are several other European cities where you'll find a wide range of good deals, particularly Amsterdam, Athens and Berlin.

Atlantic Airways (🔲 *www.atlantic.fo)* and Maersk (🔲 *www.maersk-air.com)* fly to the Faroes from Copenhagen and Billund in Denmark, while Air Greenland (🔲 *www .greenlandair.gl)* flies to Greenland from Copenhagen. Icelandair (🔲 *www.icelandair .net)* flies to the USA via Reykjavík from numerous European cities.

Across Europe many travel agencies have ties with STA Travel, where cheap tickets can be purchased and STA-issued tickets can be altered (usually for a US$25 fee). STA and other discount outlets in important transport hubs include:

France
Voyages Wasteels (☎ 0803 88 70 04,
  🇪 parisdupuytren@wasteels.fr) 11 rue
  Dupuytren, F-75006 Paris

Germany
Alternativ Tours (☎ 030-881 2089,
  🇪 info@alternativ-tours.de)
  Wilmersdorferstrasse 94, D-10629 Berlin
STA Travel (☎ 069-703035,
  🇪 frankfurt.uni@statravel.de) Bockenheimer
  Landstrasse 133, D-60325 Frankfurt

Greece
ISYTS (☎ 01-0322 1267, 🇪 isyts@travelling.gr)
  11 Nikis St, First Floor, Syntagma Square,
  10557 Athens

Netherlands
Kilroy Travels (☎ 020-524 5100,
  🔲 www.kilroytravels.com) Singel 413-415,
  NL-1012 WP Amsterdam
My Travel (☎ 0180-393333, 🔲 www.mytravel
  .nl) Kleinpolderlaan 4, Postbus 281, NL-2910
  AG Nieuwerkerk aan den Ijssel

Switzerland
STA Travel (☎ 01-297 1111, 🔲 www.statravel
  .ch) Ankerstrasse 112, 8026 Zürich

Asia

Singapore and Bangkok are the discount plane-ticket capitals of the region. However,

be careful: not all agents are reliable. Ask the advice of other travellers before buying tickets. **Lauda Air** (🔲 *www.aua.com* flies to Vienna from Bangkok. **STA Travel** (🔲 *www .statravel.com)* has offices in both cities as well as Tokyo, Singapore, Bangkok, Taipei and Kuala Lumpur.

SAS has flights from Singapore to Oslo or Stockholm for S$1788 (US$1005). Thai Airways flies to Stockholm from Bangkok for US$795.

Mumbai and Delhi are India's air-transport hubs but tickets are slightly cheaper in Delhi. Aeroflot offers inexpensive deals from India to Europe.

LAND
Bus

If you're already in Europe and you don't have a rail pass, it's generally cheaper to get to Scandinavia by bus than by train or plane. Long bus rides can be tedious, so bring along a good book. On the plus side, some of the coaches are quite luxurious with toilet, aircon, stewards and snack bar.

Small bus companies occasionally come along with discount rates, although most of them don't remain in business for more than a year or two. Ask around at student and discount travel agencies for the latest information.

Eurolines (🔲 *www.eurolines.co.uk)* is one of the biggest, and best-established, express-bus services connecting Scandinavia with the rest of Europe. Most buses operate daily in summer and between two and five days a week in winter. Eurolines' representatives in Europe include:

Bohemia Euroexpress International (☎ 02-248
  14450, 🇪 informace@bei.cz) Krizikova 4–6,
  18600 Prague 8, Czech Republic
Deutsche Touring (☎ 069-790350) Am Römerhof
  17, D-60486 Frankfurt am Main, Germany
Eurolines (☎ 020-560 8788) Amstel Station, Julian-
  plein 5, 1097 DN Amsterdam, Netherlands
Eurolines (☎ 0870-514 3219) 52 Grosvenor
  Gardens, London, SW1W 0AG, UK
Eurolines (☎ 01-712 0453, 🇪 info@eurolines.at)
  Busstation Wien-Mitte, 1030 Vienna, Austria
Eurolines (☎ 70 10 00 10) Reventlowsgade 8,
  DK-1651 Copenhagen V, Denmark
Eurolines France (☎ 08-36 69 52 52)
  Gare Routiére Internationale, Boite 313, 28
  ave du Général de Gaulle, F-93541 Bagnolet,
  Paris, France
Eurolines/Nor-Way Bussekspress (☎ 81 54 44
  44) Bussterminalen Galleriet, N-0154 Oslo,
  Norway

Eurolines Sweden (☎ 08-440 8570) Busstop, Cityterminalen, Klarabergsviadukten 72, SE-11164 Stockholm, Sweden

These offices may have information on other bus companies and deals. Advance reservations and ticket purchases may be necessary on international buses; either call the companies directly or inquire at your local travel agency.

Sample Eurolines fares are: London to Copenhagen (from £69 return) or Stockholm (£140 return); and Berlin to Copenhagen (€69 return). There's a 10% discount for those under 26 years or over 60 years.

The Eurolines Pass covers unlimited travel to 46 cities in 26 European countries; the Scandinavian cities included are Gothenburg, Copenhagen and Stockholm. Other cities included in the pass are Edinburgh, Paris, Madrid, Warsaw and Rome. A youth pass for those under 26 years costs £186/205 for 30/60 days from 1 June to 15 September, £136/167 the rest of the year. Senior passes are available to travellers aged over 60 for the same rates. Otherwise, the adult pass costs £229/267 in the high season, £167/211 in the low season.

Train

Information about rail passes is in the Getting Around chapter.

The UK Going by train from the UK to Scandinavia can be more expensive than flying. From London, a return 2nd-class train trip will cost around £300 to Copenhagen and around £400 to Stockholm or Oslo, but these prices include couchettes and a five-day ScanRail pass. For reservations and tickets on any of these trains contact **Deutsche Bahn UK** (☎ 0870 243 5363).

The Channel Tunnel makes land travel possible between Britain and continental Europe. **Eurostar** (☎ 020-7928 5163; W www .eurostar.co.uk) passenger services connect London with Calais, Paris, Lille and Brussels. From Brussels connect to Hamburg, which is the main gateway to Scandinavia. Vehicles can be taken on the Channel Tunnel car-carrying train, **Eurotunnel** (☎ 0870 840 0046; W www.eurotunnel.com).

You can get a train ticket that includes the Channel crossing by ferry or SeaCat via Calais. Then you can travel via Lille to Brussels and on to Hamburg and Copenhagen. For more information on international rail travel (including Eurostar services) call the **Rail Europe Travel Centre** (☎ 0870 584 8848; W www .raileurope.co.uk; 178 Piccadilly, London W1).

Central Europe Hamburg is the main European gateway for Scandinavia but direct trains also run from Berlin. There are several direct trains daily to Copenhagen from Hamburg; the hour-long ferry trip is included in the ticket price. Direct trains from Berlin run daily to Malmö, via the Sassnitz to Trelleborg ferry (the ferry takes 3¾ hours), including an overnight sleeper.

In Poland, you can take a train to Świnoujście, Gdynia or Gdansk for a ferry to Sweden.

A good train deal you could use to get as close as possible to Scandinavia is the Sparpreis fare which allows a 2nd-class, round trip anywhere in Germany within one month for €99 (an accompanying person pays just €50). This ticket can be purchased at any German train station and unlimited stopovers along the direct route are allowed, but you must reach your outward destination by the first Monday after your journey starts. From northern Germany, you can easily make your way to Denmark and the rest of Scandinavia.

Asia Travelling across central and eastern Asia, a train can work out at about the same price as flying, depending on how much time and money you spend on the way – but it can be a lot more fun. Three routes cross Siberia to/from Moscow: the trans-Siberian to/from Vladivostok, and the trans-Mongolian and trans-Manchurian, both to/from Beijing. Prices can vary enormously, depending on where you buy the ticket and what is included – the prices quoted here are only a rough indication. Trains also run daily between Moscow and Helsinki, usually requiring changing at St Petersburg. Sleepers may be available on trains to/from Moscow and St Petersburg. In Russian, a sleeper is a *spalnyy vagon (SV)*, also known as *myngkih* (soft class).

The Trans-Siberian Railway takes just under seven days from Vladivostok to Moscow via Khabarovsk, but most travellers take the trans-Mongolian train, which passes through Mongolia en route from Beijing to Moscow and takes about 5½ days. A 2nd-class sleeper in a four-berth compartment on a trans-Mongolian package costs around US$350 (excluding visas) if purchased in Beijing, but cheaper tickets are available if you organise the trip yourself.

The trans-Manchurian option runs from Beijing, through Manchuria, and takes 6½ days, costing about US$400 when bought as a package in Beijing.

Monkey Business (*in Hong Kong* ☎ 2723 1376, *in Beijing* ☎ 6591 6519; ⓦ *www .monkeyshrine.com*) organises all-inclusive packages and visas for trips starting in Beijing. Its website includes information about visas.

Packages can also be bought in Europe, but they're more expensive; one well-known UK operator is **Regent Holidays** (☎ 0117-921 1711; ⓦ *www.regent-holidays.co.uk; 15 John St, Bristol, BS1 2HR*).

Lonely Planet's *Trans-Siberian Railway* is a comprehensive guide to the route.

Car & Motorcycle
Driving to Scandinavia usually requires taking a car ferry (see the following Sea section). The only land borders in the region are between Finland or Norway and Russia (and taking your own vehicle through Russia is no easy matter), or between Denmark and Germany. You can now drive through Denmark and onwards to Sweden using bridges and tunnels.

Bicycle
Cycling is a cheap, convenient, healthy, environmentally sound and, above all, enjoyable way of travelling. One note of caution: before you leave home, go over your bike with a fine-toothed comb and fill your repair kit with every imaginable spare, since replacements will probably be expensive and may be hard to find in rural areas. Check ahead with the airline about transporting your bicycle. See also the introductory Getting Around chapter and the Getting Around sections of the country chapters.

Hitching & Ride Services
Several European organisations can help you find a ride to/from Scandinavian countries. Besides hitchhiking, the cheapest way to get to northern Europe from elsewhere in Europe is as a paying passenger in a private car.

If you're leaving from or travelling within Germany, such rides are arranged by Mitfahrzentrale agencies in many German cities.

You pay a reservation fee to the agency and your share of petrol to the driver. Local tourist information offices will be able to direct you to several such agencies, or dial the city area code and ☎ 19444.

There are several organisations offering car-ride services in other European countries, including in France **Allostop Provoya** (☎ 01-53 20 42 42; 8 Rue Rochambeau, F-75009 Paris) and **Autopass** (☎ 03-20 14 31 9; 21 rue Patou, F-59800 Lille); and in Hungary **Kenguru** (☎ 1-266 5837; Köfaragó útca 15, Budapest).

Also check the Internet at ⓦ www.allostop .com and look for the long list of agencies available under the section 'Carpooling in Europe'.

For details of local conditions and laws, see the individual country chapters.

SEA
See the Getting There & Away sections of the country chapters for information about boat-trains or rail/ferry links within Scandinavian Europe. See also the Getting Around chapter for details of rail passes and their validity on ferries.

Boat Companies
The following details cover the larger ferry companies operating to Scandinavia.

DFDS Seaways A useful operator is DFDS Seaways (ⓦ *www.dfdsseaways.com*). It operates ferries from Oslo to Copenhagen via Helsingborg, Sweden; from Harwich, UK to Esbjerg, Denmark; and from Newcastle, UK, to Gothenburg, Sweden, via Kristiansand, Norway. Booking agents include:

Denmark (in Copengagen ☎ 33 42 30 00, in Esbjerg ☎ 79 17 79 17) Sankt Annæ Plads 30, DK-1295 Copenhagen K
Germany (☎ 040-389 0371) Van-der-Smissen-Strasse 4, D-22767 Hamburg
Norway (☎ 22 41 90 90, ⓔ booking@ dfdsseaways.no) Utstikker 2, Vippetangen, Oslo
Sweden (☎ 031-650600, ⓔ info@ dfdsseaways.se) Frihamnen, Box 8895, SE-40272 Gothenburg
UK (☎ 08705 333 000) Scandinavia House, Parkeston Quay, Harwich, Essex, CO12 4QG
USA (☎ 1 800 533 3755 ext 114, ⓔ Adminfo@dfdsusa.com), Cypress Creek Business Park, 6555 NW 9th Ave, Suite 207, Fort Lauderdale, FL 33309-2049

Stena Line Covering a variety of routes Stena Line (W *www.stenaline.co.uk*) runs ferries from Frederikshavn, Denmark, to Oslo in Norway and Gothenburg in Sweden; from Grenå, Denmark, to Varberg in Sweden; from Kiel (Germany) to Gothenburg (Sweden); and from Gdynia, Poland, to Karlskrona (Lyckeby), Sweden. Booking agents include:

Denmark (☎ 96 20 02 00, e info.dk@stenaline
  .com) Trafikhavnen, DK-9900 Frederikshavn
  (☎ 87 58 75 00) Stenaterminalen, DK-8500
  Grenå
Germany (☎ 0431-9099, e info.de@stenaline
  .com) Schwedenkai 1, D-24103 Kiel
Norway (☎ 23 17 90 00, e info.no@stenaline
  .com) Jernbanetorget 2, N-0154 Oslo
Sweden (☎ 031-858000, e info.se@stenaline
  .com) SE-40519 Gothenburg
  (☎ 0340-690 900) Stena Line, Box 94,
  SE-43222 Varberg (☎ 0455-366 300) Box
  6047, SE-37106 Lyckeby
UK (☎ 08705 707070, 01233-647022,
  e info.uk@stenaline.com) Charter House,
  Park St, Ashford, Kent, TN24 8EX

Color Line Ferries run by Color Line (W *www.colorline.com*) go from Hirtshals, Denmark, to Oslo and Kristiansand, Norway; from Kiel, Germany, to Oslo; and from Larvik, Norway, to Frederikshavn, Denmark. Booking agents include:

Denmark (☎ 99 56 19 77) Postboks 30,
  DK-9850 Hirtshals
  (☎ 99 56 19 77) Postboks 30, DK-9900
  Frederikshavn
France (☎ 01-42 85 64 50) c/o Scanditours,
  36 rue de St Pétersbourg, F-75008 Paris
Germany (☎ 0431-7300 300) Postfach 2646,
  D-24025 Kiel
Norway (in Oslo ☎ 22 94 44 00, 81 00 08 11,
  in Kristiansand ☎ 38 07 88 00) Postboks
  1422 Vika, N-0115 Oslo

Fjord Line Sailing between Hanstholm in Denmark and Egersund and Bergen in Norway; and between Newcastle (UK), Stavanger (Norway) and Bergen is Fjord Line (W *www .fjordline.com*). Booking agents include:

Denmark (☎ 97 96 30 00, e fjordline.dk@
  fjordline.com) Coastergade 10,
  DK-7730 Hanstholm
Norway (☎ 81 53 35 00, e booking@fjordline
  .com) Skoltegrunnskaien, Postboks 7250,
  N-5020 Bergen

UK (☎ 0191-296 1313) International Ferry
  Terminal, Royal Quay, North Shields, Tyne &
  Wear, NE29 6EG

Smyril Line Providing yet another option for ferry travel is Smyril Line (W *www .smyril-line.com*). It operates ferry services mid-May to mid-September from Lerwick in the Shetland Islands to Bergen, Norway, and to Tórshavn in the Faroe Islands; and also Hanstholm (Denmark)-Lerwick-Tórshavn-Lerwick-Hanstholm year-round; and Seyðisfjörður, Iceland. Booking agents include:

Denmark (☎ 96 55 03 60, e office@smyril-line
  .dk) Danmark, Trafikhavnsgade 7,
  DK-7730 Hanstholm
Faroe Islands (☎ 345900, e office@smyril-line
  .fo) Jónas Broncksgøta 37, PO Box 370,
  FO-110 Tórshavn
Iceland (☎ 587 1919, e smyril-iceland@isholf
  .is) Stangarhyl 3a, IS-110 Reykjavík
Norway (☎ 55 32 09 70, e office@smyril-line
  .no) Slottsgaten 1, Postboks 4135, Dreggen,
  N-5835 Bergen
UK (☎ 01595-690845, e office@smyril-line
  .com) Holmsgarth Terminal, Lerwick,
  Shetland, ZE1 0PR

Silja Line Silja Line (☎ 09-180 4510; W *www.silja.com; Bulevardi 1A, POB 659, FIN-00101 Helsinki*) runs ferries between Helsinki and Rostock (Germany), Tallinn (Estonia), and Stockholm; and from Turku, Finland, to Stockholm.

The Baltic Countries

There are regular sailings across the Baltic Sea from the three Baltic countries to Sweden and Finland; for schedules and fares, phone the relevant companies or check their websites.

Silja Line sails from Tallinn (Estonia) to Helsinki. **Tallink** (*in Stockholm* ☎ 08-666 6001, *in Tallinn* ☎ 640 9808; W *www.tallink .ee; Pärnu mnt 12, Tallinn*) sails from Tallinn to Stockholm and from Paldiski (Estonia) to Kapellskär (north of Stockholm). **VV Line** (*in Västervik* ☎ 0490-258080, *in Nynäshamn* ☎ 08-524 00850, *in Ventspils* ☎ 036-07358; W *www.vvline.com; 7 Plostu iela, LV-3600 Ventspils*) connects Paldiski (Latvia) with Västervik (Sweden) and Ventspils (Latvia) with Nynäshamn (Sweden).

There's also **Lisco Line** (*in Sweden* ☎ 0454-33680, *in Lithuania* ☎ 06-395111; W *www.shipping.lt; Lietuvininku sq 5, LT-5800 Klaipėda*), which shuttles between the

Lithuanian town of Klaipėda and Karlshamn, in Sweden.

For more details, see the Finland and Sweden chapters in this book.

Poland

Four regular ferries cross the Baltic Sea between Poland and Sweden. Stena Line (see the Boat Companies section earlier in this chapter) sails from Gdynia to Karlskrona and **Unity Line** *(in Sweden ☎ 0411-160110, in Szczecin ☎ 091-359 5692; W www.unityline.pl; Pl Rodla 8, 70-419 Szczecin)* connects Świnoujście (Poland) with Ystad (Sweden). **Polferries** *(in Sweden ☎ 08-520 18101, in Poland ☎ 091-321 6140; W www.polferries.com.pl; Ferry Terminal, ul Dworcowa 1, 76-206 Świnoujście)* links Gdansk with Nynäshamn (Sweden) and Świnoujście with Ystad. See the Sweden chapter for further details.

Germany

The **Scandlines** (W www.scandlines.se) train, car and passenger ferry from Puttgarden to Rødbyhavn (the quickest way to Copenhagen) runs every half-hour around the clock and takes 45 minutes. Frequent Scandlines ferries also run from Warnemünde to Gedser (Denmark).

From Kiel, there are Stena Line ferries to Gothenburg (Sweden) and Color Line ferries to Oslo (Norway); see Boat Companies earlier in this chapter. Five large Scandlines ferries run in each direction daily between Sassnitz, eastern Germany, and Trelleborg (south of Malmö in Sweden). Scandlines and **TT Line** *(in Sweden ☎ 0410-56200)* ferries run daily from Trelleborg to Rostock and Travemünde, Germany.

See also the relevant Getting There & Away sections in the individual country chapters.

The UK

DFDS Seaways ferry services run between Harwich and Newcastle (UK) and Esbjerg (Denmark). One of the most interesting Scandinavian travel possibilities is the weekly Smyril Line ferry service from the Shetland Islands to Tórshavn in the Faroe Islands. Other Smyril Line sailings link the Shetland and Faroe Islands with Norway, Iceland and Denmark (mid-May to mid-September only). From Newcastle, Fjord Line runs ferries all year to Stavanger and Bergen in Norway. DFDS Seaways has ferries from Harwich to

Esbjerg in Denmark and from Newcastle to Kristiansand and Gothenburg. See Boat Companies earlier in this chapter for details of agents and operators.

P&O North Sea Ferries *(☎ 0870 129 6002; W www.ponorthseaferries.co.uk)* runs a daily overnight service from Hull to Zeebrugge in Belgium from where you can travel by bus or train to Scandinavia. The shortest cross-Channel route (from Dover to Calais) is the busiest, although the Eurostar passenger train and Eurotunnel car and lorry train connecting the UK and France are now taking much of its business. Stena Line runs two ferries a day from Harwich to Hook of Holland in the Netherlands, from where you can head north by land.

See the relevant Getting There & Away sections in the individual country chapters for more details.

Transatlantic Passenger Ships & Freighters

Regular, long-distance passenger ships disappeared with the advent of cheap air travel and were replaced by a small number of luxury cruise ships. Cunard Line's **QE II** *(in the USA ☎ 1 800 728 6273, in the UK ☎ 0800 052 3840)* sails between New York and Southampton (UK) around nine times a year, taking five nights/six days per trip. The cost of a one-way crossing starts at around US$1800, but they also offer return and 'fly one-way' deals (including return on Concorde). In July, it does a circuit around the Arctic region, including Nordkapp (North Cape) in Norway. Most travel agents can provide the details.

A more adventurous (but not necessarily cheaper) alternative is as a paying passenger on a freighter. Freighters are far more numerous than cruise ships, and there are many more routes to chose from. With just a little bit of homework, you'll be able to sail to Europe from just about anywhere else in the world, with stopovers at exotic little-known ports. *Travel by Cargo Ship*, by Hugo Verlomme, covers this subject.

Passenger freighters typically carry six to 12 passengers (more than 12 would require a doctor on board) and, although they're less luxurious than dedicated cruise ships, they do provide a real taste of life at sea. Schedules tend to be flexible and costs vary, but normally hover around US$100 a day; vehicles can often be included for an additional charge.

ORGANISED TOURS

A package tour of Scandinavian Europe is worth considering if your time is very limited or you have a special interest such as canoeing, bird-watching, bicycling, mountaineering etc. Most national tourist offices can provide details of reputable tour operators.

Australia

Bentours (☎ 02-9241 1353, **W** www.bentours .com.au) Level 7, 189 Kent St, Sydney 2000. Bentours offers a range of tours covering most of the highlights in Scandinavia.

Denmark

Arctic Adventure (☎ 33 25 32 21, **W** www .arctic-adventure.dk) Reventlowsgade 30 st tv, DK-1651 Copenhagen V. Arctic Adventure offers well-organised all-year hotel-based tours and cruises around most of Greenland. There's also a variety of Iceland tours, and some combined Iceland-Greenland packages.

Grønlands Rejsebureau (☎ 33 13 10 11, **W** www .greenland-travel.dk) PO Box 130, Gammel Mønt 12, DK-1004 Copenhagen K. Grønlands Rejsebureau offers a slate of refreshingly original tour options in Greenland.

France

Grand Nord Grand Large (☎ 01-40 46 05 14, **W** www.gngl.com) 15 Rue du Cardinal Lemoine, 75005 Paris. This innovative company's list of destinations includes Finland, Greenland, Norway (including Svalbard) and Iceland.

Germany

Norden Tours (☎ 040-3770 2270, **W** www .norden-tours.de) Kleine Johannisstrasse 10, D-20457 Hamburg. Norden Tours organises a wide range of tours throughout Scandinavia, including cruises around Greenland and Svalbard (Norway).

Nordwind Reisen (☎ 08331-87073, **e** info@ nordwindreisen.com) Maximilianstrasse 17, D-87700 Memmingen. Nordwind Reisen's comprehensive list of tours covers Iceland, Greenland, the Faroes, Norway (including Svalbard), Sweden and Finland.

North America

Scantours (☎ 1 800 223 7226, **W** www.scantours .com). Scantours offers comfortable hotel-based excursions throughout Scandinavia.

Travcoa (in the USA ☎ 1 800 992 2003, in Canada ☎ 800 563 0005; **W** www.travcoa .com) 2350 SE Bristol, Newport Beach, CA 92660. Travcoa provides hotel-based highlights tours in most Scandinavian countries.

Norway

Brand Cruises (☎ 52 85 31 03, **W** www.brand .no) Postboks 33, N-4291 Kopervik. Brand Cruises offers high standards of catering and accommodation on its tours around Norway (including Svalbard) and Greenland.

UK

Arctic Experience Discover the World (☎ 01737-218800, **W** www.arctic-discover.co.uk) 29 Nork Way, Banstead, Surrey, SM7 1PB. This company offers wilderness and wildlife holidays in the Faroes, Iceland, Greenland and arctic Norway (including Svalbard).

Dick Phillips (☎ 01434-381440, **e** icelandick@ nent.enta.net) Whitehall House, Nenthead, Alston, Cumbria, CA9 3PS. Dick Phillips probably knows Iceland better than anyone else in Britain, with decades of experience leading cycling, hiking and trekking trips through remote areas. Rates are very reasonable but the trips are rigorous and not for anyone who requires pampering.

Tangent Expeditions International (☎ 01539-737757, **W** www.tangent-expeditions.co.uk) 3 Millbeck, New Hutton, Kendal, Cumbria, LA8 0BD. This excellent, experienced ski-mountaineering company concentrates on East Greenland, including unclimbed and unnamed peaks; there are also expeditions to Svalbard, and Greenland icecap crossings.

Getting Around the Region

Getting around Scandinavia is a hassle-free experience, with efficient public transport and great connections. Travelling around Greenland might not be quite so straightforward.

In Greenland, flight timetables exist mainly for convenience, but to rely on them may well amount to inconvenience; allow plenty of leeway (two days is usually enough) when booking connecting flights. See the Greenland chapter for details.

AIR

Since 1997 air travel within the EU has been deregulated. This affects Denmark, Sweden and Finland, the only EU members in Scandinavian Europe. The 'open skies' policy allows greater flexibility in routing (national airlines no longer have to include a domestic airport in routes and they can fly between EU cities) and also potentially greater competition and lower prices. Air travel is still dominated by the large state-run and private carriers, but these have been joined by a new breed of small no-frills airlines, such as the UK-based company easy-Jet and Ryanair, which sell budget tickets directly to customers. The cheapest fares may require 21-day advance purchase and a stay of at least one Saturday night.

London is a good centre for picking up inexpensive, restricted-validity tickets through discount operators. Amsterdam and Athens are other good places for tickets in Europe. Various classes of cheap air tickets are also available on routes within Scandinavian countries.

For longer journeys, you may find air fares are cheaper than land-based alternatives. Travelling between airports and city centres is rarely a problem in Scandinavian countries, thanks to good bus services.

Air travel is normally best viewed as a way of reaching the starting point of your itinerary rather than as your main means of travel, as it lacks the flexibility of ground transport. Also, if you fly relatively short hops it can be expensive, particularly as special deals are rarely available on internal flights. In Greenland, however, covering large areas of the country may require flying, which costs about three times as much as the cheapest boat ticket.

Open-jaw returns, where you can travel into one city and out of another, are worth considering (see the Getting There & Away chapter), though they usually work out more expensive than straightforward returns, but can be cheaper when bought through a good travel agent.

Air Passes

Visitors flying **SAS** *(in North America* ☎ *1 800 221 2350, in the UK* ☎ *0845 607 2727;* Ⓦ *www.scandinavian.net)* return to Norway, Sweden or Finland, either from within Europe (excluding Scandinavia), or from outside Europe, can buy tickets on a Visit Scandinavia or Visit Scandinavia/Europe air pass. The passes are also available to passengers of **Icelandair** *(*Ⓦ *www.icelandair.com)* flying from Iceland or from the USA (as these flights go via Iceland). The passes allow one-way travel on direct flights between any two Scandinavian cities serviced by SAS, Maersk, Widerøe, Skyways and other operators. You can buy up to eight tickets (for around US$65 each) which are valid for three months; tickets can be purchased after arriving in Scandinavia if you have a return SAS international ticket.

Flugfélag Íslands *(Air Iceland;* Ⓦ *www .airiceland.is)* sells a variety of passes for flights within Iceland. For details, see the Iceland chapter.

BUS
International Buses

Bus travel tends to take second place to train travel in most of Europe. In mainland Scandinavia (Denmark, Finland, Norway and Sweden), buses have the edge in terms of cost but they're generally slower and less comfortable than trains. Eurolines offers a variety of city 'loops' and the Eurolines Pass; see the Getting There & Away chapter for more details. On ordinary return trips, Eurolines youth fares cost 10% less than the ordinary adult fare. See the individual country chapters for details.

National Buses

Buses provide a viable alternative to the rail network in Scandinavian countries. Again, compared to trains, they're usually cheaper (though not in Finland) and slightly slower. Bus travel tends to be best for shorter hops such as getting around cities and reaching remote rural villages. There are no bus services between any of the towns in Greenland.

Buses are often the only option in regions where rail tracks fear to tread; these buses often connect with train services. Advance reservations are rarely necessary. However, you do need to pre-purchase your ticket before you board many city buses, and you cancel your own ticket on the bus. See the individual country chapters for details.

TRAIN

Trains are a popular way of getting around; they're good meeting places and in Scandinavia are comfortable, frequent and generally on time. Also in the Scandinavian countries, European train passes make travel affordable. Supplement and reservation costs are not covered by passes and pass-holders must always carry their passport on the train for identification purposes. There are no trains in Iceland, Greenland or the Faroes, or in most of far-northern Norway.

If you plan to travel extensively by train, it might be worth getting hold of the *Thomas Cook European Timetable*, which gives a complete listing of train schedules and indicates where supplements apply or where reservations are necessary. It's updated monthly and is available from Thomas Cook outlets in the UK, and in the USA and Canada from **Rail Pass Express** (☎ *1 800 722 7151, 614-793 7651*). If you're planning to do a lot of train travel in any country it might be worthwhile getting hold of the national rail timetable published by the state rail body.

Oslo, Stockholm, Helsinki and Copenhagen are important hubs for international rail connections. See individual city sections for details and budget ticket agents.

Express Trains

Fast trains in Europe, or ones that make few stops, are usually identified by the symbols EC (Eurocity) or IC (Intercity), although there are national variations; in Norway, some expresses are called Signatur trains, while in Finland they're also called Pendolino express trains and they're known as X2000 in Sweden. Supplements usually apply on fast trains and it's a good idea (sometimes obligatory) to make reservations at peak times and on certain lines.

Overnight Trains

Overnight trains will usually offer a choice of couchette or sleeper if you don't fancy sleeping in your seat with somebody else's head resting on your shoulder. Again, reservations are advisable and in Scandinavia they're often necessary as sleeping options are allocated on a first-come, first-served basis.

Couchettes are bunks numbering four (1st class) or six (2nd class) per compartment and are comfortable enough, if lacking a bit in privacy. In Scandinavia, a bunk costs around US$25 for most international trains, irrespective of the length of the journey.

Sleepers are the most comfortable option, offering beds for one or two passengers in 1st class and two or three passengers in 2nd class. All sleepers in Norway, for example, are either for one person (1st class only) or two to three people (2nd class); there are no couchettes as previously described, but the three-person, 2nd-class compartments function in the same way. When individual travellers book a bed in one (Nkr160), they'll be booked into a compartment with two other people of the same sex. Denmark has six-person compartments, as well as single and double cabins, with charges varying depending upon the journey, but tending to be significantly more expensive than couchettes.

Most long-distance trains have a dining car or drink-and-snack-laden trolley, wheeled through the carriages by an attendant, but prices tend to be steep so you're better off bringing your own snacks aboard.

Train Passes

ScanRail ScanRail (Ⓦ *www.scanrail.com*) is a flexible rail pass covering travel in the Scandinavian countries of Denmark, Norway, Sweden and Finland.

There are three versions. For travel on any five days within a two-month period, the pass costs £189/139 for 1st/2nd-class travel (£142/105 for travellers under 26). For travel on any 10 days within a two-month period, the pass costs £252/187 for 1st/2nd class (£189/140 for under 26s). For unlimited travel during 21 consecutive days, the cost of the pass is £291/216 for 1st/2nd class (£219/162 for those under 26). If you're aged 60 or over, then you're eligible for the ScanRail Senior pass, which will allow 1st/2nd-class travel over five days in a two-month period for £169/123, 10 days in a two-month period for £225/166 and 21 consecutive days for £259/192.

It's best to buy your ScanRail pass outside Scandinavia – otherwise, you'll face restrictions in availability: five travel days can only

RAILWAYS & FERRIES

be chosen from 15 days, the 10 days out of two months is unavailable and you're only allowed three days of travel in the country of purchase.

ScanRail passes are valid on trains run by Linx (Copenhagen–Oslo and Oslo–Stockholm), Connex (Gothenburg–Stockholm–Narvik), state railways in Denmark (DSB), Finland (VR), Norway (NSB) and Sweden (SJ), and Swedish Länstrafik trains, but not SL (Stockholm Local) trains. The pass also includes free travel on NSB-bus (from Trondheim to Storlien), buses between Luleå/Boden and Haparanda, as well as Helsingør to Helsingborg (Scandlines), Rødbyhavn to Puttgarden (Scandlines) and Trelleborg to Sassnitz (SJ/DFO) boat services.

There's a 50% discount if you're travelling on the following services:

destination	line
Copenhagen–Rønne	Bornholmstrafikken
Rønne–Ystad	Bornholmstrafikken
Hjørring–Hirtshals	train
Frederikshavn–Skagen	train
Frederikshavn–Oslo	Stena Line
Frederikshavn–Gothenburg	Stena Line
Grenå–Varberg	Stena Line
Hirtshals–Kristiansand	Color Line, daytime only
Hirtshals–Larvik	Color Line, daytime only
Hirtshals–Oslo	Color Line, daytime only
Frederikshavn–Larvik	Color Line, daytime only
Stockholm–Helsinki	Viking or Silja Line
Stockholm–Turku	Viking or Silja Line
Travemünde–Trelleborg	TT Line
Rostock–Trelleborg	TT Line
Nynäshamn–Visby	Destination Gotland
Oskarshamn–Visby	Destination Gotland
Stavanger–Bergen	Flaggruten
Sandefjord–Strömstad	Color Scandi Line

There's a 50% discount on most of Norway's northern express buses (including Bodø–Fauske–Narvik–Tromsø–Alta–Kirkenes); on the Lofotbus (Narvik–Harstad–Andenes–Svolvær–Leknes–Å); as well as on many other Norwegian buses. A few other boats offer discounts, including Hardanger Fjord and southern Hordaland ferries (HSD Snoggbåtene; 25% discount) and Rostock to Helsinki sailings with

Silja Line (variable discount). The Mora–Gällivare Inlandsbanan gives a 25% discount on a two-week unlimited travel ticket and the Myrdal–Flåm Flåmsbanen offers 30% discount. There's also a 20% discount offered on the Oslo Card (see the Oslo section in the Norway chapter).

Eurail In Scandinavia, the ScanRail pass (more information later in this section) is generally a better deal than the Eurail pass, so this information will only be of interest to travellers visiting other parts of Europe too.

Passes issued by **Eurail** (W *www.eurail .com*) can only be bought by residents of non-European countries (these include CIS countries in continental Europe, Turkey, Morocco, Algeria and Tunisia), and are supposed to be purchased before arriving in Europe. However, Eurail passes are available within Europe as long as your passport proves you've been there for less than six months. Outlets where you can purchase them are limited, and the passes are 10% more expensive than buying them outside Europe. For example, Copenhagen is the only city in Denmark and Oslo is the only place in Norway where you can buy Eurail passes (at the international ticket counters in the main train stations).

If you've lived in Europe for more than six months, you're eligible for an Inter Rail pass (see Inter Rail later in this section), which is a better buy.

Eurail passes are valid for unlimited travel on national railways and some private lines in Austria, Belgium, Denmark, Finland, France (which includes Monaco), Germany, Greece, Hungary, Ireland, Italy, Luxembourg, the Netherlands, Norway, Portugal, Spain, Sweden and Switzerland (including Liechtenstein). The passes do *not* cover the UK.

Eurail is also valid on ferries running between Italy and Greece, and from Sweden to Finland with Silja Line.

Eurailpass Youth offer reasonable value for people aged under 26. They're valid for unlimited 2nd-class travel for various time limits, including 15 days (US$401), one month (US$644) or two months (US$910). The Eurailpass Youth Flexi, also for 2nd class, is valid for a certain number of days within a two-month period: 10 days for US$473 or 15 days for US$622. Overnight journeys commencing after 7pm count as the following day's travel. The traveller must fill out in ink the relevant box in the calendar before starting a day's travel; not validating the pass or tampering with it (eg, using an erasable pen and later rubbing out days) will lead to a fine.

For those aged over 26, a Eurailpass Flexi (available in 1st class only) costs US$674/888 for 10/15 days within two months. The standard Eurail pass, also available in 1st class only, has five versions, costing from US$572 for 15 days unlimited travel up to US$1606 for three months. Two or more people travelling together can get good discounts on a Saverpass, which works like the standard Eurail pass. A 15/21-day Saverpass will cost US$486/630 per person. Eurail passes for children are also available – half price for those aged four to 11 years, and free for children under four.

Inter Rail Passes issued by **Inter Rail** (W *www.interrailnet.com)* are valid in 29 countries and are available to European residents (including CIS countries in continental Europe, Algeria and Tunisia) of at least six-months standing – passport identification is required. Terms and conditions vary slightly from country to country, but in the country of origin there's only a discount of around 50% on normal fares, rather than free travel.

The Inter Rail pass is split into eight zones. Zone A is the UK and Ireland; B is Sweden, Norway and Finland; C is Denmark, Germany, Switzerland and Austria; D is the Czech Republic, Slovakia, Poland, Hungary and Croatia; E is France, Belgium, Netherlands and Luxembourg; F is Spain, Portugal and Morocco; G is Italy, Greece, Turkey and Slovenia; H is Bulgaria, Romania, Yugoslavia and Macedonia. The price for any one zone is £169/119 (if aged over/under 26) for 12 days and £209/139 for 22 days. Multizone passes are better value and are valid for one month: two zones is £265/189, three zones is £299/209, and all zones is £355/249.

The pass also gives free travel on shipping routes from the Italian port of Brindisi to Patras in Greece, as well as 30% to 50% discounts on various other ferry routes (more routes than covered by Eurail) and certain river and lake services. Be sure to check for the latest information if considering buying a pass.

Euro Domino There is a Euro Domino pass (called a Freedom pass in Britain) for each of

the countries covered in the zonal Inter Rail pass. Check W www.europerailpass.co.uk for more details. Adults (travelling 1st or 2nd class) and youths under 26 can travel within one country on any three to eight days during one month. Examples of adult/youth prices for eight days in 2nd class are £174/130 for Sweden, £101/78 for Denmark, and £204/157 for Norway.

Cheap Tickets

European rail passes are only worth buying if you plan to do a reasonable amount of inter-country travelling within a short space of time. Some people overdo it, spending every night on the train and ending up too tired to enjoy the sightseeing.

When weighing up options, consider the cost of other cheap ticket deals. Travellers who are under 26 years of age can pick up BIJ (Billet International de Jeunesse) tickets, which may cut international fares by between 20% and 40%. Unfortunately, you can't always bank on a substantial reduction and these tickets are being phased out. The Rail Plus Pass (€15) is valid one year and allows 25% savings on youth (under 26) and senior (over 60) tickets on international routes, but they're not valid in Norway or Sweden.

Various agents issue youth tickets in Europe, including **STA Travel** (W *www.statravel .com)* and **Wasteels Rejser** (☎ *33 14 46 33;* W *www.wasteels.dk; Skoubogade 6, DK-1158 Copenhagen K, Denmark).*

CAR & MOTORCYCLE

Travelling with your own vehicle is the best way to get to remote places and it gives you the most flexibility. Unfortunately, the independence you enjoy tends to insulate you from the local people. Also, cars are usually inconvenient in city centres where it's generally worth ditching your vehicle and relying on public transport.

A useful general reference on motoring in Europe is Eric Bredesen's *Moto Europa* (Seren Publishing). It contains information on rental, purchase, documents, tax and road rules. Unfortunately, it's out of print, but you can try to get a second-hand copy.

Paperwork & Preparations

Proof of ownership of a private vehicle should always be carried (Vehicle Registration Document for British-registered cars) when touring Europe. An EU driving licence is acceptable for driving throughout Scandinavia, as generally are North American and Australian licences. However, to be on the safe side – or if you have any other type of licence – you should obtain an International Driving Permit (IDP) from your motoring organisation (see Visas & Documents in the Facts for the Visitor chapter).

Third-party motor insurance is a minimum requirement in most of Europe. Most UK motor-insurance policies automatically provide third-party cover for EU and some other countries. Ask your insurer for a Green Card (there may be a charge), an internationally recognised proof of insurance, and check that it lists all the countries you intend to visit. You'll need this in the event of an accident outside the country in which the vehicle is insured. Also ask your insurer for a European Accident Statement form, which can simplify things if worse comes to worst. Never sign statements you can't read or understand – insist on a written translation and only sign it if it's acceptable.

If you want to insure a vehicle you've just purchased (see the Purchase section later in this chapter) and have a good insurance record, you might be eligible for a considerable discount if you can show a letter to this effect from your insurance company back home.

A European breakdown-assistance policy, such as the AA Five Star Europe service or the RAC European Motoring Assistance, is a good investment. Expect to pay about £60 for 14 days' cover with a 10% discount for association members. It's also worth asking your motoring organisation for details about free and reciprocal services offered by affiliated organisations around Europe.

Every vehicle crossing an international border should display a sticker showing its country of registration. Almost everywhere it is compulsory to carry a warning triangle, to be used in the event of breakdown. Recommended accessories are a first-aid kit, a spare bulb kit and a fire extinguisher – in Iceland, carrying spare parts (including a fan belt and clutch cable) is also a good idea. Contact your automobile association or, in the UK, contact the **RAC** (☎ 0800 550 550; Ⓦ www .rac.co.uk) for more information.

Road Rules

You drive on the right in all northern European countries. Vehicles from the UK or Ireland should have their headlights adjusted to avoid blinding the oncoming traffic at night (a simple solution on older headlight lenses is to cover up the triangular section of the lens with a headlight deflector, available from motoring accessory shops). Priority is usually given to traffic approaching from the right. Some national motoring organisations publish booklets with summaries of motoring regulations in each country, including parking rules; check with your local organisation.

Take care with speed limits as they vary from country to country. Many driving infringements are subject to an on-the-spot fine in Scandinavian countries. If you receive a fine for any driving offence, make sure to get a receipt.

Scandinavian countries are particularly strict with their drink-driving regulations and the maximum blood-alcohol concentration (BAC) varies from 0.02% in Sweden to 0.08% in Denmark (see the Getting Around sections in the individual country chapters for details).

Roads

Conditions and types of roads vary widely across Europe, but it's possible to make some generalisations. The fastest routes are four- or six-lane dual carriageways. These tend to skirt cities and plough through the countryside in straight lines, often avoiding the most scenic areas. Motorways and other primary routes, with the exception of some roads in Iceland, are universally in good condition.

Road surfaces on minor routes are not so reliable in some countries although normally they will be more than adequate. These roads are narrower and progress is generally much slower. To compensate you can expect to pass through much better scenery and plenty of interesting villages along the way.

Motorways are being built in Sweden, while in Finland and Norway they're not as common, although the rate at which country roads are being surfaced is accelerating. Norway has some particularly hair-raising roads; some serpentine examples climb from sea level to 1000m in what seems no distance at all on a map. These roads will use plenty of petrol and strain your car's engine. Coming down, the strain will be on the brakes (and your nerves!).

In Norway, you must pay tolls for some tunnels, bridges and roads and practically all ferries crossing fjords. Tolls must also be paid to enter some of the larger towns and cities. Roads, tunnels, bridges and car ferries in Finland and Sweden are always free, though there's a hefty toll on the Øresund bridge between Denmark and Sweden.

In Scandinavia in winter, snow tyres are compulsory – the tyre chains common in the Alps are allowed in Norway.

There are virtually no roads outside the towns in Greenland.

Rental

Renting a car is very expensive in most Scandinavian countries (see the individual country chapters for details). The variety of special deals and terms and conditions attached to renting a car can be mind-boggling. However, there are a few pointers that can help you through the morass. The big international firms – Hertz, Avis, Eurodollar, Budget, and Europe's largest rental agency, Europcar – will give you reliable service and a good standard of vehicle. Usually you will have the (sometimes chargeable) option of returning the car to a different outlet at the end of the rental period.

Unfortunately, if you walk into an office and ask for a car on the spot, you will pay over the odds, even allowing for special weekend deals. If you want to rent a car and haven't prebooked, look for national or local firms, which can often undercut the big companies substantially.

Prebooked and prepaid rates are always cheaper, and there are fly/drive combinations and other programs that are worth looking into (eg, SAS often offers cheaper car rentals to its international passengers). The Scanrail 'n' Drive programme gives you a five-day rail pass and a car for two days to be used within two months. Prices start at US$309 for an adult on 2nd-class trains and an economy car (US$510 for two adults) with an option of retaining the car for US$55 per day.

Holiday Autos International (☎ 0870 400 0099; ⓦ www.holidayautos.com; *Holiday Autos House, Pembroke Broadway, Camberley, Surrey, GU15 3XD*) usually has good rates for rental, but you need to prebook; it has offices around Europe, including Denmark, Norway and Sweden. Ask in advance if you can drive a rented car across borders.

No matter where you rent, be sure that you understand what's included in the price (unlimited or paid kilometres, injury insurance, tax, collision damage waiver etc) and what your liabilities are. Always take the collision damage waiver, though you can probably skip the injury insurance if you and your passengers have decent travel insurance.

The minimum rental age is usually 21, sometimes even 23, and you'll probably need a credit card (or a mountain of cash for the deposit). Note that prices at airport rental offices are usually higher than at city-centre branches.

Motorcycle and moped rental isn't particularly common in Scandinavian countries, but it's possible in major cities. Inexperienced riders tend to leap on bikes and very quickly fall off them again. Take care!

Purchase

The purchase of vehicles in some European countries is illegal for nonresidents of that country. Britain is a good place to buy secondhand cars; prices are good and English speakers will find the absence of language difficulties helpful. Amsterdam is also not a bad place to buy second-hand cars.

Bear in mind that you'll be getting a car with the steering wheel on the right in Britain. If you want left-hand drive and can afford to buy new, prices are reasonable in Belgium, France, Germany, Luxembourg and the Netherlands. Cars are very expensive in Iceland, Norway and Finland, but somewhat cheaper in Sweden. Paperwork can be tricky wherever you buy; insurance is expensive and many countries have compulsory roadworthiness checks on older vehicles.

Leasing

A form of long-term rental, leasing a vehicle has none of the hassles of purchasing and can work out considerably cheaper than hiring over longer periods. Peugeot's European Self-Drive programme provides new cars for non-EU residents for periods of over 17 days; prices include unlimited kilometres, insurance and 24-hour roadside assistance. For a typical quote check out ⓦ www.autoeurope .com/lease_home.cfm. Unfortunately, the closest pick-up point to Scandinavia is Amsterdam airport.

Camper Van

A popular way to tour Europe is for three or four people to band together to buy or rent a camper van. London is the usual embarkation point. Look at the advertisements in London's free magazine *TNT* if you wish to form or join a group. *TNT* is also a good resource for purchasing a van, as is the *Loot* newspaper and the **Van Market** *(Market Rd, London N7)*, near the Caledonian Rd tube station, where private vendors congregate. Some second-hand dealers offer a 'buy-back' scheme for when you return from Europe, but buying and re-selling privately would be more advantageous.

Camper vans usually feature a fixed high-top or elevating roof and two to five bunk beds. Apart from the essential camping gas cooker, professional conversions may include a sink, fridge and built-in cupboards. You'll need to spend from at least £1700 (US$2400) for something reliable enough to get you around Europe. An eternal favourite for budget travellers is the VW Kombi; they aren't made any more but the old ones seem to go on forever, and getting spare parts isn't a problem. Once on the road you should be able to keep budgets lower than if you were backpacking using trains, but don't forget to set some money aside for emergency repairs.

The main advantage of travelling by camper van is flexibility; with transport, eating and sleeping requirements all taken care of in one unit, you're tied to nobody's timetable but your own.

A disadvantage of camper vans is that you're in a confined space for much of the time. Four adults in a confined space can be a volatile mix, particularly if the group has been formed at short notice. Tensions can be minimised if you agree on daily routines and itineraries before setting off.

Other disadvantages are that camper vans are not very manoeuvrable within towns and you'll often have to leave your gear unattended inside (many people bolt extra locks onto the van). Driving a camper van on mountain roads in Norway and Iceland isn't recommended. They're also expensive to buy in spring and hard to sell in autumn. As an alternative, consider a car and tent. Remember, too, that by travelling, sleeping and even eating in the self-contained little 'world' of a van, you'll be missing a lot of the outside world you came to see.

Motorcycle Touring

Europe is excellent for motorcycle touring, with good-quality winding roads, stunning scenery and an active motorcycling scene. Just make sure your wet-weather gear is up to scratch. The best time for motorcycle touring is from May to September.

The wearing of helmets by both rider and passenger is compulsory in Europe. Using headlights during the day is recommended and is compulsory in some parts of Scandinavia.

On ferries, motorcyclists rarely have to book ahead as they can generally be squeezed in. Take note of local custom about parking motorcycles on pavements (sidewalks). Although this is illegal in some countries, the police usually turn a blind eye so long as the vehicle doesn't obstruct pedestrians.

Anyone considering a motorcycle tour should read *Adventure Motorbiking Handbook,* by Chris Scott – it gives good advice on motorcycle touring worldwide.

Fuel

Fuel is very expensive in Scandinavia (except Greenland), due to heavy taxation. Most types of petrol, including unleaded 95 and 98 octane, are widely available, but leaded petrol may be unavailable. Always check carefully what type of fuel is being supplied – pumps with green markings and the word *Blyfri* deliver unleaded. Diesel is significantly cheaper than petrol in some countries.

BICYCLE

If you want to bring your own bicycle to Scandinavia, you should be able to take it along on the plane relatively easily. Check with your airline.

A tour of Europe by bike may seem a daunting, as well as exciting, prospect. It's particularly exciting to consider that you'll get around vast areas of wilderness on your own steam. One organisation that can help in the UK is the **Cyclists' Touring Club** *(CTC;* ☎ *0870 873 0060;* Ⓦ *www.ctc.org.uk; Cotterell House, 69 Meadrow, Godalming, Surrey, GU7 3HS)*. It can supply information to members on cycling conditions in Europe, including Scandinavia, as well as detailed routes, itineraries, maps and cheap specialised insurance. Tours around Denmark, Norway and Sweden are also organised for members.

Europe by Bike, by Karen & Terry Whitehill, is a bit out of date but has good descriptions of 18 cycling tours of up to 19 days' duration.

A primary consideration on a cycling tour is to travel light, but you should take a few tools and spare parts, including a puncture-repair kit and an extra inner tube as replacements may be pricey and hard to find in remote or rural areas. Panniers are essential to balance your possessions on either side of the bike frame. A bike helmet is also a very good idea. Take a good lock and always use it when you leave your bike unattended; theft is not uncommon in places like Helsinki and Copenhagen.

Seasoned cyclists can average 80km a day, but there's no point in overdoing it. The slower you travel, the more local people you're likely to meet. For more information on cycling, see Activities in the Facts for the Visitor chapter and in the individual country chapters.

Rental

It's easy to hire bikes throughout Scandinavia on a half-day, daily or weekly basis, and sometimes it's possible to return them to another outlet so you don't have to double back. Some train stations have bike-rental counters; see the country chapters for details.

Purchase

For major cycling tours, it's best to have a bike you are familiar with, so consider bringing your own rather than buying on arrival. There are plenty of places to buy a bike in Scandinavia, but you'll need lots of cash and a specialist bicycle shop for something capable of withstanding European touring. CTC can provide advice on purchasing.

Transporting a Bicycle

If you grow weary of pedalling or simply want to skip a boring section, you can put your feet up and take the train. On slower trains, bikes can usually be transported as luggage, subject to a small fee. Fast trains can rarely take bikes, which need to be sent as registered luggage and may end up on a different train from the one you take.

HITCHING

Hitching is never entirely safe in any country in the world, and we don't recommend it. Travellers who decide to hitch should understand that they're taking a small but potentially serious risk. People who do choose to hitch will be safer if they travel in pairs and let someone know where they're planning to go.

Also, be aware that hitching is neither popular nor particularly rewarding in most of Scandinavia. Finns are quite rightly wary of Russian criminals and Swedes worry about strangers dirtying their Volvos.

That said, with a bit of luck, hitchers can end up making good time in some areas, but obviously your plans need to be flexible in case a trick of the light makes you appear invisible to passing motorists. A man and woman travelling together is probably the best combination. Two or more men must expect some delays; two women together will make good time and should be relatively safe. A woman hitching on her own is always taking a risk – even in 'safe' Scandinavia.

Don't try to hitch from city centres; take public transport to suburban exit routes. Hitching is usually illegal on motorways – stand on the entrance ramps. Look presentable and cheerful, face the approaching traffic, and make a cardboard sign indicating your intended destination in the local language. Never hitch where drivers can't stop in good time or without causing an obstruction.

It's sometimes possible to arrange a lift in advance: scan student notice boards in colleges or contact car-sharing agencies (see Hitching & Ride Services under Land in the Getting There & Away chapter).

BOAT
Ferry

You can't really get around Scandinavia without extensive use of ferries although Denmark, which consists mostly of islands and is separated from Sweden by a narrow strait, is now well connected to mainland Europe and Sweden by bridges or tunnels. From mainland Denmark (Jutland), you'll need to catch a ferry for the shortest Denmark-Norway connection. The same applies to Sweden-Finland connections – unless you want to travel to the extreme north to see the area en route.

Ferries are usually good value. Tickets are very cheap on routes where there is competition and there are often duty-free prices on food and alcohol to consider. Transporting cars can be expensive but bicycles are usually carried free.

Avoid weekend ferries (especially on Friday nights) due to excessive noise, drinking and higher prices. Teenage travellers are banned on some Friday-night departures.

Several different ferry companies compete on the main ferry routes. The resulting service is comprehensive but complicated. Train pass-holders are entitled to a discount or free travel on some of the routes.

Food is often expensive on ferries so it's worth bringing your own when possible. It's also worth knowing that if you take your vehicle on board you can't access to it during the voyage, and car alarms must always be switched off.

For further information about the many ferry options available between the destinations in this book, see the Getting There & Away sections of the individual country chapters.

Steamers

Scandinavia's main lakes and rivers are served by steamers and diesel-powered boats during the summer. In general, consider extended boat trips as relaxing and scenic excursions; if you view them merely as a functional means of transport, they can be very expensive.

Sweden has probably the largest fleet of such boats in Scandinavia, and sailing on at least one is a must. Most leave from Stockholm and sail east to the Stockholm archipelago, a maze of 24,000 islands and islets, and west to historic Lake Mälaren, home base of the Swedish Vikings a millennium ago. You can also cruise the Göta Canal, which is the longest water route in Sweden.

In Finland, steamships ply Lakes Saimaa, Päijänne and Näsijärvi. There are also diesel-engine boats that are a bit faster and noisier but equally attractive.

ORGANISED TOURS

See Organised Tours in the Getting There & Away chapter for details of tours arranged from outside the individual countries. The individual country chapters have details of local organised tours.

Denmark

Denmark (Danmark) may be the smallest of the Scandinavian countries, but it packs within its boundaries a compelling mix of lively modern cities, historic provincial towns, sleepy villages, pastoral farmland, peaceful woods, and idyllic islands. The country is full of medieval churches, Renaissance castles, historic ports and harbours. Copenhagen, Scandinavia's largest and most cosmopolitan capital is a world-class destination with superb museums and a vibrant cultural life, while regional capitals, such as Århus and Odense, are sophisticated, and friendly university cities, brimming with art and music and with lively social scenes.

Denmark's historic treasures include the haunting remains of Neolithic burial chambers and of atmospheric Viking ruins that reflect the country's dramatic history and sea-centred character. The sea defines Denmark in every way. This most southerly of Scandinavian countries boasts kilometres of white sand beaches to match those of the Caribbean, and, though water temperatures may be a touch more bracing, these are the warmest seas in the Baltic. A wealth of archipelagoes and islands adds to the country's marvellous diversity.

Denmark's physical complexity makes for fascinating exploration, but the country is surprisingly easy to get around. Public transport is generally excellent and the Danish road system straightforward and efficient. The country is mainly flat, with only occasional areas of gentle hills, which, combined with an extensive network of cycle routes, makes Denmark a good place to explore by bike.

Facts about Denmark

HISTORY

Denmark was the ancient heart of Scandinavia. It was to the low-lying flatlands of what are now Jutland and Funen that prehistoric hunters and gatherers from central and southern Europe moved north as the ice sheets retreated. Neolithic people settled on this new landscape in 4000 BC and by 500 BC Iron Age farms and trading centres were well established.

At a Glance

Capital	Copenhagen
Population	5.3 million
Area	43,075 sq km
Official Language	Danish
GDP	US$162,817 billion
Time	GMT/UTC +0100
Country Phone Code	☎ 45

Highlights

- Exploring Copenhagen's pedestrianised Strøget and the intriguing tangle of squares and narrow streets to either side (p69)
- Enjoying the dazzling interiors and the lakeside location of Frederiksborg Slot at Hillerød (p85)
- Spending a few days on the idyllic island of Bornholm (p95)
- Taking a leisurely bike trip around the green lanes of Ærø (p107)
- Sampling the best of Jutland in fashionable Århus and in the nearby Lake District (p109)

Only the haunting remnants of burial chambers and vestigial fortifications survive from prehistory and it is to the arrival of the Danes, a tribe thought to have migrated south from Sweden around AD 500 that present-day Denmark traces its linguistic and cultural roots. In the late 9th century, warriors led by the Viking chieftain, Hardegon, conquered the Jutland Peninsula. The Danish monarchy, which is Europe's oldest, dates back to Hardegon's son, Gorm the Old, who established his reign in the early 10th century. Gorm's son, Harald Blue-tooth, completed the conquest of Denmark and spearheaded the conversion of the Danes to Christianity. Successive Danish kings went on to invade England and conquer most of the Baltic region.

In 1397 Margrethe I of Denmark established a union between Denmark, Norway and Sweden to counter the influence of the powerful Hanseatic League that had come to dominate the region's trade. Sweden withdrew from the union in 1523, and over the next few hundred years Denmark and Sweden had numerous border skirmishes and a few fully fledged wars, largely over control of the Baltic Sea. Norway remained under Danish rule until 1814.

In the 16th century the Reformation swept through the country, accompanied by church burnings and civil warfare. The fighting ended in 1536 with the ousting of the Catholic Church and the establishment of a Danish Lutheran Church headed by the monarchy.

Denmark's golden age was under Christian IV (1588–1648), with Renaissance cities, castles and fortresses flourishing throughout his kingdom. A wealthy upper class prospered and many of the most lavish mansions and palaces were built during this period. In 1625 Christian IV, hoping to neutralise Swedish expansion, entered an ill-advised and protracted struggle known as the Thirty Years' War. The Swedes triumphed and in 1658 Denmark lost Skåne and its other territories on the Swedish mainland.

Literature, the arts, philosophy and populist ideas flourished in the 1830s, and Europe's 'Year of Revolutions' in 1848 helped inspire a democratic movement in Denmark that led to the adoption of a constitution on 5 June 1849. As a result, King Frederik VII was forced to relinquish most of his power to an elected parliament and so became Denmark's first constitutional monarch. Denmark's involvement in a series of failed military campaigns resulted in a steady contraction of its borders, culminating in the ceding of the Schleswig and Holstein regions to Germany in 1864.

By the beginning of the 20th century, the political influence of large landowners had lost ground to farmers' cooperatives, and the country's government shifted from conservative to liberal with a socialist bent.

Denmark remained neutral throughout WWI and also declared its neutrality at the outbreak of WWII. Nevertheless, on 9 April 1940 an unfortified Denmark faced either a quick surrender or a full-scale invasion by German troops massed along its border. The Danish government settled for the former, in return for an assurance that the Nazis would allow the Danes a degree of autonomy. For three years the Danes managed to walk a thin line, basically running their own internal affairs under Nazi supervision, until in August 1943 the Germans took outright control. The Danish Resistance movement mushroomed and 7000 Jewish Danes were quickly smuggled into neutral Sweden.

Although Soviet forces heavily bombarded the island of Bornholm, the rest of Denmark emerged from WWII relatively unscathed. Denmark joined NATO in 1949 and the European Community – now the European Union (EU) – in 1973.

The Danes have been hesitant to support expansion of the EU. When the Maastricht Treaty, which established the terms of a European economic and political union, came up for ratification in 1992, it was rejected by Danish voters by a margin of 51% to 49%. After Denmark was granted exemptions from Maastricht's common-defence and single-currency provisions, Danes voted to accept the treaty, by a narrow majority, in a second referendum held in 1993.

The issue of the common currency remains a controversial topic. In April 2000, the ruling Social Democrats overwhelmingly endorsed adopting the common currency. However, that decision was rejected by a margin of 8% in a national referendum held at the end of September 2000. General support for the EU is tepid as many Danes fear the loss of local control to a European bureaucracy dominated by stronger nations.

Under the leadership of the Social Democrats, a comprehensive social welfare state was established in the postwar period, and Denmark provides its citizens with extensive cradle-to-grave social security.

In May of 2002 Denmark introduced tougher immigration laws in response to a Europe-wide anxiety about an increase in illegal immigration.

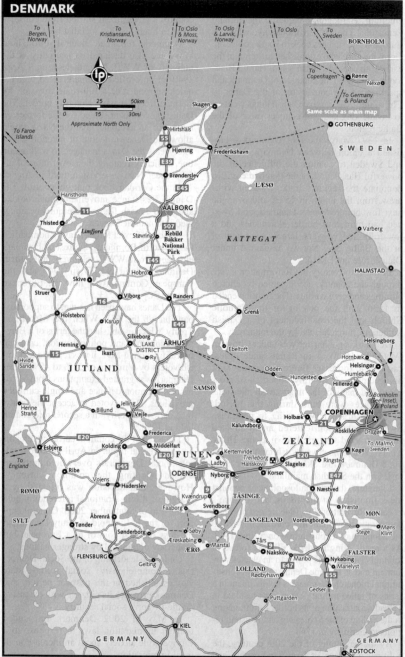

DENMARK

To Bergen, Norway
To Kristiansand, Norway
To Oslo & Moss, Norway
To Oslo & Larvik, Norway
To Oslo
To Sweden
BORNHOLM

To Copenhagen
Rønne
Nexø
To Germany & Poland

Same scale as main map

GOTHENBURG

0   25   50km
0   15   30mi
Approximate North Only

To Faroe Islands

SWEDEN

Skagen
Hirtshals
Hjørring
Frederikshavn
Løkken
Brønderslev
LÆSØ
Varberg

Hanstholm

AALBORG
Thisted
Limfjord
Støvring
Rebild Bakker National Park
HALMSTAD

KATTEGAT

Hobro
Skive
Struer
Viborg
Randers
Grenå
Holstebro
Karup
Helsingborg
Silkeborg
ÅRHUS
Hornbæk
Helsingør
Herning
LAKE DISTRICT
Ikast
Ry
Ebeltoft
Humlebæk
Hvide Sande
JUTLAND
Odden
Hillerød
Hundested
To Bornholm (see Inset) & Poland
Horsens
SAMSØ
Henne Strand
Jelling
Holbæk
COPENHAGEN
Billund
Vejle
Kalundborg
Roskilde
Drager
Esbjerg
Frederica
ZEALAND
To Malmö, Sweden
To England
Kolding
Middelfart
FUNEN
Kerteminde
Trelleborg
Køge
Ribe
Ladby
Halsskov
Slagelse
Ringsted
Vojens
ODENSE
Nyborg
Korsør
RØMØ
Haderslev
Kvændrup
TÅSINGE
Næstved
Præstø
MØN
Åbrenrå
Faaborg
Svendborg
LANGELAND
Vordingborg
SYLT
Tønder
Søby
Stege
Møns Klint
Sønderborg
Ærøskøbing
Marstal
Tårs
FLENSBURG
ÆRØ
Nakskov
Maribo
Nykøbing
FALSTER
Gelting
LOLLAND
Rødbyhavn
Marielyst
Gedser
Puttgarden

GERMANY
KIEL
GERMANY
ROSTOCK

55
E39
E45
507
E45
16
15
11
E20
E45
11
21
E20
E47
9
E47
E55

GEOGRAPHY

Denmark is a small country with a land area of 43,075 sq km, mostly on the peninsula of Jutland. There are 406 islands, 90 of which are inhabited. Copenhagen is on Zealand, the largest island.

Most of Denmark is lowland of fertile farms, marshland, rolling hills, beech woods and heather-covered moors. The highest point is a mere 173m. Except for its land border with Germany, Denmark is surrounded by the North and Baltic Seas.

CLIMATE

Denmark lies at approximately the same latitude as central Scotland and southern Alaska. Despite its northerly position, it has a relatively mild climate, moderated by the effects of the warm Gulf Stream Drift, which sweeps northward along the western coast.

In midwinter, the nation's average daytime maximum temperature hovers around freezing point. Winter, however, has the highest relative humidity (90%) and the cloudiest weather, both of which can make it feel much colder than the actual reading might indicate.

Expect to see rain and grey skies in Denmark at any time of the year. Rain falls on an average of 11 days in June and 18 days in November.

The average temperature is 2.1°C in March, 10.8°C in May, 15.6°C in July and August and 1.6°C in December. With its low-lying terrain and proximity to the sea, variations in climate throughout Denmark are minimal.

ECOLOGY & ENVIRONMENT

The Danish landmass has been heavily exploited by agriculture and 70% of its land is farmed mainly for barley and root crops, which are used to feed livestock. With almost 20% of farmland near sea level, many environmentally sensitive wetlands were made arable by draining. EU quotas now make farming such land less viable, and the Danish government has initiated an ambitious plan to restore these wetlands and reestablish marshes and streams throught the country. In doing so it's hoped that endangered species such as the freshwater otter will also make a comeback.

Still commonly seen in Denmark are wild hare, deer and many species of birds, including magpies, coots, swans and ducks.

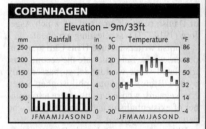

COPENHAGEN
Elevation – 9m/33ft

GOVERNMENT & POLITICS

Denmark is a constitutional monarchy. Queen Margrethe II has been on the throne since 1972 but legislative powers rest with the Folketing, Denmark's elected parliament. Social Democrats, Conservatives, Liberals and Socialists form the four main political parties, though in recent times there have been close to a dozen parties represented in the 179-seat parliament. The current prime minister, Anders Fogh Rasmussen, is a member of the ruling Centre-Right/Conservative coalition.

ECONOMY

Denmark has one of the world's highest per capita GDPs and a high standard of living. It's the world's leading exporter of canned meat and boasts the EU's largest fish catches. Other important exports include butter, cheese, beer, furniture, electronics, silverware and porcelain.

POPULATION & PEOPLE

Denmark's population is about 5.3 million, with 70% living in urban areas. The four largest cities are Copenhagen (1.5 million), Århus (285,000), Odense (184,000) and Aalborg (155,000). Foreign nationals account for 7.8% of Denmark's population, and 11.8% of Copenhagen's population.

ARTS

Before the 19th century Danish art was mainly formal portraiture, exemplified by the works of Jens Juel (1745–1802). A 'Golden Age' ushered in the 19th century with such fine painters as Wilhelm Eckersberg (1783–1853) and major sculptors such as Bertel Thorvaldsen (1770–1844). Later in the century the 'Skagen School' evolved from the movement towards outdoor painting of scenes from working life, especially of fishing communities on the northern coasts of Jutland and Zealand. Leading exponents were PS Krøyer and Michael Ancher and Anna Ancher. In the mid-20th century, a vigorous modernist school of Danish painting emerged, of which Asger Jorn (1914–73) was a leading exponent.

Danish writers include Hans Christian Andersen, whose fairy tales are the second most translated work worldwide, surpassed only by the Bible; religious philosopher Søren Kierkegaard, whose writings were a forerunner of existentialism; and Karen Blixen, who penned *Out of Africa*.

Blixen also wrote *Babette's Feast;* a movie adaptation by Danish film director Gabriel Axel won the Academy Award for Best Foreign Film in 1988. The following year, director Bille August won an Academy Award as well as the Cannes Film Festival's Palme d'Or for *Pelle the Conqueror,* adapted from the novel by Danish author Martin Andersen Nexø. In 1996 Bille August produced a film adaptation of *Smilla's Sense of Snow*, a suspense mystery by Denmark's foremost contemporary author, Peter Høeg. In 2000, Danish director Lars von Trier won the Cannes Film Festival's Palme d'Or for his film *Dancer in the Dark.*

The Royal Danish Ballet, which performs in Copenhagen's Royal Theatre from autumn to spring, is regarded as northern Europe's finest. The Royal Theatre is also the venue for the Royal Orchestra, Royal Opera and various theatrical performances.

On a different front, Denmark is a leader in industrial design, with a style marked by cool, clean lines applied to everything from architecture to furniture and silverware. Denmark has produced a number of leading 20th-century architects, including Jørn Utzon who designed Australia's Sydney Opera House.

SOCIETY & CONDUCT

Danes pride themselves on being thoroughly modern, and the wearing of folk costumes, the celebration of traditional festivals and the clinging to old-fashioned customs is less prevalent in Denmark than elsewhere in Scandinavia. There are, of course, traditional aspects of the Danish lifestyle that are not immediately apparent at first glance.

Perhaps nothing captures the Danish perspective more than the concept of *hygge,* which, roughly translated, means 'cosy and snug'. It implies shutting out the turmoil and troubles of the outside world and striving instead for a warm intimate mood. *Hygge* affects how Danes approach many aspects of

their personal lives and there's no greater compliment that a Dane can give their hosts than to thank them for a cosy evening.

Denmark's often difficult history at the heart of a volatile part of Europe has taught the modern Dane to avoid too much conflict or rivalry. Danes are refreshingly self-effacing and reserved about themselves and their achievements, but in a very subtle way. It springs from a long-standing belief among Danes that no-one should think of themselves as being better than the average and that you should always keep your feet firmly on the ground at all times. Travellers will find Danes to be relaxed, casual and not given to extremes or to ostentation. They are tolerant of different lifestyles; in 1989 Denmark became the first European nation to legalise same-sex marriages.

The national sport is soccer, there is a huge active involvement in athletics, especially running, while cycling, rowing, sailing and windsurfing are popular pastimes. Although Danes, especially in larger cities, tend to be eminently stylish in dress, travellers will get by with just casual clothing so long as upmarket dining isn't on the agenda.

RELIGION

About 90% of Danes belong to the state-supported National Church of Denmark, which is an Evangelical Lutheran denomination. Less than 5% are regular churchgoers.

Facts for the Visitor

SUGGESTED ITINERARIES

Depending on the length of your stay you might like to see and do the following:

Two days
Copenhagen – get a Copenhagen Card and explore the city
One week
Copenhagen, North Zealand's castles and beaches, Roskilde and Køge
Two weeks
Sights listed above plus Odense, Ærø, Århus, Ribe, Skagen and other Jutland sights of interest (or Bornholm)
One month
As above plus Bornholm, south Funen (including the islands of Tåsinge and Langeland), Møn and Falster
Two months
As above, but at a slower pace and including island hopping by bicycle

PLANNING
When to Go
Considering its northern latitude, Denmark has a fairly mild climate. May and June can be a delightful time to visit; the countryside is a rich green, accented with fields of yellow rapeseed flowers, the weather is generally warm and comfortable, and you'll beat the rush of summer tourists. While autumn can also be pleasant, it's not nearly as scenic, as fields and hedgerows have by then largely turned to brown.

July to August is the peak tourist season and the time of the year for open-air concerts, lots of street activity and basking on the beach. Other bonuses for travellers during midsummer are longer opening hours at museums and other sightseeing attractions and potential savings on accommodation, as some hotels drop their rates.

Maps
Most tourist offices have fairly good city and regional maps which they distribute free. If you're renting a car, you can usually pick up a suitable road map free from the rental agency. The most detailed road map of Denmark is published by Kort-og Matrikelstyrelsen in a handy atlas format (1:200,000) and can be bought in Danish bookshops for Dkr128.

What to Bring
If you visit Denmark during the warm season you can travel light. A jumper (sweater) will be the heaviest item you'll need. Consider a lightweight waterproof also. Summer rain in Denmark can be torrential and prolonged. If you're using hostels, bringing your own sleeping sheet will save a lot of money.

TOURIST OFFICES
Local Tourist Offices
Virtually every good-sized town in Denmark has a local tourist office, usually found in the *rådhus* (town hall) or elsewhere on *torvet* (the central square). Most can load you up with both regional and national brochures.

Tourist Offices Abroad
Danish tourist offices abroad include:

France (☎ 0033-15343 2626, e paris@dt.dk) Conseil du Tourisme de Danemark, 18 blvd Malesherbes, 75008 Paris

Germany (☎ 40 32 0210, e daninfo@.dt.dk) Dänisches Fremdenverkehrsamt, Glockengiesserwall 2, 20095 Hamburg
Norway (☎ 22 00 76 46, e danmark@dt.dk) Danmarks Turistkontor, Tollbugaten 27, Postboks 406 Sentrum, 0103 Oslo
Sweden (☎ 08 611 72 22, e info@dtab.se) Danmarks Turistråd, Box 5524, 114 85 Stockholm
UK (☎ 020-7259 5959, e dtb.london@dt.dk) Danish Tourist Board, 55 Sloane St, London SW1X 9SY
USA (☎ 212-885 8700, e info@goscandinavia .com) Danish Tourist Board, PO Box 4649, Grand Central Station, New York, NY 10163

VISAS & DOCUMENTS
Citizens of the EU, USA, Canada, Australia and New Zealand need a valid passport to enter Denmark, but don't need a visa for stays of less than three months. If you wish to apply for a visa make sure to do so at least three months in advance of your planned arrival.

EMBASSIES & CONSULATES
Danish Embassies
Danish embassies abroad include:

Australia (☎ 02-6273 2195) 15 Hunter St, Yarralumla, Canberra, ACT 2600
Canada (☎ 613-562 1811, W www .danish-embassy-canada.com) 47 Clarence St, Suite 450, Ottawa, Ontario K1N 9K1
Finland (☎ 9-684 1050, W www.kolumbus.fi /danmark) Centralgatan 1A, 00101 Helsinki
France (☎ 1-44 31 21 21, W www .amb-danemark.org) 77 ave Marceau, 75116 Paris
Germany (☎ 5050 2000, W www.daenemark .org) Rauchstrasse 1, 10787 Berlin
Iceland (☎ 56 21 230, W www4.mmedia.is /rekamb/) Hverfisgata 29, 121 Reykjavík
Ireland (☎ 1-475 6404, W www.denmark.ie) 121 St Stephen's Green, Dublin 2
Netherlands (☎ 70 302 59 50, W www.danishembassy.nl) Koninginnegracht 30, 2514 Den Haag
New Zealand Contact the embassy in Australia
Norway (☎ 22 54 08 00, W www .denmark-embassy.no) Olav Kyrres Gate 7, 0244 Oslo
Sweden (☎ 8-406 75 00, W www.danemb.se) Jakobs Torg 1, 11186 Stockholm
UK (☎ 020-7333 0200, W denmark.org.uk) 55 Sloane St, London SW1X 9SR
USA (☎ 202-234 4300, W www.denmarkemb .org) 3200 Whitehaven St NW, Washington DC 20008

Embassies & Consulates in Denmark

Foreign representation in Denmark includes:

Australia (☎ 70 26 36 76, W www.denmark
.embassy.gov.au) Dampfægevej 26,
Copenhagen
Canada (☎ 33 48 32 00, W www.canada.dk)
Kristen Bernikows Gade1, Copenhagen
Finland (☎ 33 13 42 14, W www.finamb.dk)
Sankt Annæ Plads 24, Copenhagen
France (☎ 33 67 01 00, W www.amba-france
.dk) Kongens Nytorv 4, Copenhagen
Germany (☎ 35 45 99 00, W www
.tyske-ambassade.dk) Stockholmsgade 57,
Copenhagen
Iceland (☎ 33 18 10 50) Dantes Plads 3,
Copenhagen
Ireland (☎ 35 42 32 33) Østbanegade 21,
Copenhagen
New Zealand Contact the British embassy
Netherlands (☎ 33 70 72 00, W www
.nlembassy.dk) Toldbodgade 33, Copenhagen
Norway (☎ 33 14 01 24, W www.norsk.dk)
Amaliegade 39, Copenhagen
Poland (☎ 39 46 77 00, W www.ambpol.dk)
Richelius Allé 12, Hellerup
Russia (☎ 35 42 55 85) Kristianiagade 5,
Copenhagen
Sweden (☎ 33 36 03 70, W www
.sverigesambassad.dk) Sankt Annæ Plads
15A, Copenhagen
UK (☎ 35 44 52 00, W www.britishembassy.dk)
Kastelsvej 36-40, Copenhagen
USA (☎ 35 55 31 44, W www.usembassy.dk)
Dag Hammarskjölds Allé 24, Copenhagen

CUSTOMS

One litre of spirits and 200 cigarettes can be brought into Denmark duty free if you're coming from outside the EU. Those coming from an EU country are allowed to bring in 300 cigarettes and 1.5L of spirits.

MONEY
Currency

The Danish *krone* is most often written as DKK in international money markets, Dkr in northern Europe and kr within Denmark.

The krone is divided into 100 øre; there are 25 and 50-øre, one, two, five, 10 and 20-kroner coins. Notes come in 50, 100, 200, 500 and 1000-kroner denominations.

Exchange Rates

The following currencies convert at these approximate rates:

country	unit		kroner
Australia	A$1	=	Dkr4.07
Canada	C$1	=	Dkr4.81
euro	€1	=	Dkr7.42
Iceland	Ikr10	=	Dkr0.88
Japan	¥100	=	Dkr6.23
Norway	Nkr1	=	Dkr0.99
New Zealand	$NZ1	=	Dkr3.58
Sweden	Skr	=	Dkr0.80
UK	UK£1	=	Dkr11.62
USA	US$1	=	Dkr7.58

Exchanging Money

All common travellers cheques are accepted in Denmark. Buy your travellers cheques in higher denominations as bank fees for changing money are a hefty Dkr25 to Dkr30 per cheque, with a Dkr40 minimum. If you're exchanging cash, there's a Dkr25 fee for a transaction. Travellers cheques command a better exchange rate than cash by about 1%.

Post offices will also exchange foreign currency at comparable rates to those at banks – the main benefit for travellers is that they're open Saturday morning. Major banks have ATMs, many of them accessible outside normal banking hours, which accept Visa, MasterCard and the Cirrus and Plus bank cards.

Visa, Eurocard, MasterCard, American Express (AmEx) and Diners Club credit cards are widely accepted throughout Denmark.

The Euro

Although Denmark remains outside the euro zone, acceptance of euros is commonplace at every level of non-governmental commercial life in Denmark. The ever-pragmatic Danes have always traded in other currencies, especially in those parts of Denmark close to neighbouring countries. Most hotels and restaurants will accept euros, as do many bars, cafés and shops, although you may find reluctance to do so in more remote areas or from very small businesses. Government institutions do not accept euros.

Costs

Costs in Denmark are not exorbitant if judged by Scandinavian standards generally, but nothing's particularly cheap either – partly due to the 25% value-added tax (VAT), *moms* in Danish, that's included in every price. The hidden bonus is a high standard of public services that, often invisibly, smooth your way.

Your costs will depend on how you travel. In terms of basic expenses, if you camp or stay in hostels and prepare your own meals you might get by on Dkr250 a day. If you stay in even modest hotels and eat at inexpensive restaurants, expect to spend about Dkr500 a day if you're doubling up, Dkr700 if you're travelling alone. Staying in private rooms arranged through tourist offices can knock Dkr150 to Dkr200 off this estimate.

To this you will need to add local transport, museum admission fees, entertainment and incidentals. Always check for admission-free days at museums. Long-distance transport is reasonably priced and it helps that Denmark is small – the most expensive train ticket possible between two points costs just Dkr300. If you're a student, bring your identity card with you, as it will warrant a few discounts, particularly at museums.

Tipping & Bargaining

Restaurant bills and taxi fares include service charges in the quoted prices, and further tipping is unnecessary. Bargaining is not a common practice in Denmark.

Taxes & Refunds

Foreign visitors who are not EU citizens can get a refund on the 25% VAT, less a handling fee, for goods costing more than Dkr300 purchased at stores participating in the Tax Free Shopping Global Refund plan. Present the tax-refund 'cheque' to the refund window at your departure point.

POST & COMMUNICATIONS
Post

Denmark has an efficient postal system. Most post offices are open 9am or 10am to 5pm or 5.30pm Monday to Friday and 9am to noon on Saturday. You can receive mail c/o poste restante at any post office in Denmark.

It costs Dkr4.75 to mail a postcard or letter weighing up to 20g to Western Europe, Dkr5.75 to other countries.

Telephone & Fax

There are no telephone area codes within Denmark; you must dial all eight numbers. It costs Dkr2 minimum to make a local call at coin phones. You get about twice as much calling time for your money on domestic calls made between 7.30pm and 8am daily and all day on Sunday.

If you're going to be making many calls, consider buying a phonecard, which is used in card phones that are typically found beside coin phones. The cards (Dkr30 to Dkr100) can be bought at post offices and newspaper kiosks.

The country code for calling Denmark from abroad is ☎ 45. To make international calls from Denmark dial ☎ 00 and then the country code for the country you're calling.

Faxes can be sent from hotels and some post offices.

Email & Internet Access

The largest cities have Internet cafés that charge about Dkr20 to Dkr30 an hour. Public libraries also have Internet-capable computers and visitors generally have access to them, but as computer time often requires advance sign-up, you may have to wait for a free slot.

DIGITAL RESOURCES

The Danish foreign ministry website ⓦ www .denmark.org has a wealth of information, including updated weather reports and exchange rates, as well as links to many sites, such as the Danish Tourist Board's website at ⓦ www.visitdenmark.com.

BOOKS

For travellers, Lonely Planet's *Denmark* is the most comprehensive all-round guidebook available. *Camping Danmark*, published each year by the Danish Camping Board (Campingrådet), has detailed information on all camping grounds in Denmark.

For a good overview of the Viking era, there's *A Short History of the Vikings* by Karsten Gabrielsen. *Denmark: A Modern History*, by W Glyn Jones, gives a comprehensive account of contemporary Danish society.

NEWSPAPERS & MAGAZINES

The *Copenhagen Post* (ⓦ www.cphpost.dk), a quality weekly newspaper, publishes Danish news and events in English; it can be picked up at hotels in Copenhagen or browsed online. The *International Herald Tribune* and many other foreign newspapers and magazines are readily available at train-station kiosks in larger towns.

RADIO & TV

You can listen to the news in English at 8.40am, 9.10am, 5.05pm and 10pm on Radio

Denmark (1062MHz in Copenhagen, 91.7 FM in Århus). British and US programmes are common on Danish TV. Foreign programmes broadcast domestically are typically in English with Danish subtitles, while those broadcast from neighbouring countries are usually dubbed.

TIME

Time in Denmark is normally one hour ahead of GMT/UTC, the same as in neighbouring European countries. When it's noon in Denmark, it's 11am in London, 6am in New York and Toronto, 3am in San Francisco, 9pm in Sydney and 11pm in Auckland.

Clocks are moved forward one hour for daylight-saving time from the last Sunday in March to the last Sunday in October. Denmark uses the 24-hour clock and all timetables and business hours are posted accordingly.

LAUNDRY

Møntvaskeri (laundrettes) are much easier to find in Denmark than in other Scandinavian countries, although there are signs that there is a decrease in their number.

You can usually find them in larger cities and towns, and hostels and camping grounds usually have some coin-operated machines. The cost to wash and dry a load of clothes is generally around Dkr50.

TOILETS

Toilets in Denmark are Western style. Public ones are generally free and easy to find at such places as train stations, town squares and ferry harbours.

HEALTH

There are no exceptional health precautions necessary for visiting Denmark. The Danish national health insurance program covers visitors from countries with reciprocal health arrangements with Denmark. Citizens of EU countries need to present EU form E111. All visitors, from wherever they originate receive free hospital treatment in the event of accident or sudden illness.

Emergency

In Denmark, dial the free number ☎ 112 when you need police, fire and ambulance services.

Controlled medicines are available only from a pharmacy.

There is an **AIDS advice line** (☎ *33 91 11 19; open 9am-11pm daily*).

WOMEN TRAVELLERS

The **Danish Centre for Information on Women & Gender** (KVINFO; ☎ *33 13 50 88;* Ⓦ *www.kvinfo.dk; Christians Brygge 3, Copenhagen*) has information on feminist issues, while **Kvindehuset** (☎ *33 14 28 04; Gothersgade 37, Copenhagen*) is a help centre and meeting place for women. Dial ☎ 112 for rape crisis or other emergencies.

GAY & LESBIAN TRAVELLERS

Denmark is a popular destination for gay and lesbian travellers. Copenhagen in particular has an active, open gay community and lots of nightlife options.

Landsforeningen for Bøsser og Lesbiske (LBL; ☎ *33 13 19 48;* ⓔ *kbh@lbl.dk; Teglgård-stræde 13, Copenhagen*) is the national organisation for gay men and lesbians. Branch offices in main towns are mentioned in relevant sections. A good English-language website with links to LBL and other gay organisations is Ⓦ www.copenhagen-gay-life.dk.

DISABLED TRAVELLERS

Overall, Denmark is a user-friendly destination for the disabled traveller. The Danish Tourist Board publishes *Access in Denmark – a Travel Guide for the Disabled,* which is an English-language booklet with information on accommodation, transportation and sightseeing options for disabled travellers. In addition, the main hostel and hotel guides use a symbol to indicate properties that are wheelchair accessible.

SENIOR TRAVELLERS

Senior citizens between the ages of 60 and 65 may be given discounts at most museums. Transportation is often discounted for seniors. The DSB railway system, for example, gives a 25% to 50% discount to those aged 65 and older.

TRAVEL WITH CHILDREN

It should come as no surprise that Denmark, home of the Lego block, has lots of attractions to entice kids. Legoland itself is the most visited children's site in Scandinavia, and the rest of Denmark abounds with amusement

DENMARK

parks filled with Ferris wheels, carousels and water slides. The biggest of these parks, Tivoli and Bakken, are in Copenhagen. An increasing number of local and regional tourist departments publish brochures that focus on children-orientated activities and attractions. Ask for details at tourist offices.

DANGERS & ANNOYANCES

Denmark is by and large a safe country and travelling presents no unusual dangers for the visitor. Nevertheless, be careful with your belongings, particularly in busy places such as Copenhagen's Central Station. In cities, you'll need to become accustomed quickly to the busy cycle lanes between vehicle roads and the pedestrian pavement, as these lanes are easy to step into accidentally.

LEGAL MATTERS

Although marijuana and hashish are available in Denmark, sometimes quite openly, all forms of cannabis, and harder drugs, are illegal.

If you are arrested for any offence in Denmark, you can be held up to 24 hours before appearing in court. You have a right to know the charges against you and a right to a lawyer. You are not obliged to answer police questions before speaking to the lawyer.

You can get free legal advice on your rights from the EU legal aid organisation **EURO-JUS** (☎ 33 14 41 40). Free legal advice clinics can be found in over 90 places across Denmark. You do not need to identify yourself and there is no means test. Advice is given on all legal matters, but it is initial advice only. For further legal help you will be referred to another lawyer, at which point fees may be required. The service is organised by the Danish bar, **Det Danske Advokatsamfund** (☎ 38 38 36 38). The registry of any court will provide the address of the nearest legal advice clinic, or you can get the same information from a local library.

BUSINESS HOURS

Office hours are generally 9am to 4pm Monday to Friday. Most banks are open 9.30am to 4pm Monday to Friday (to 6pm Thursday). Stores are usually open to 5.30pm Monday to Friday and 2pm on Saturday.

Throughout this chapter, we use the term 'summer' generally to refer to the months of May to September, while 'winter' refers to the remaining months.

PUBLIC HOLIDAYS & SPECIAL EVENTS

Summer holidays for schoolchildren begin around 20 June and end around 10 August. Many Danes go on holiday during the first three weeks of July. Public holidays observed in Denmark are:

New Year's Day 1 January
Maundy Thursday Thursday before Easter
Good Friday to Easter Monday March/April
Common Prayer Day Fourth Friday after Easter
Ascension Day Fifth Thursday after Easter
Whit Sunday Fifth Sunday after Easter
Whit Monday Fifth Monday after Easter
Constitution Day 5 June
Christmas Eve 24 December (from noon)
Christmas Day 25 December
Boxing Day 26 December

Beginning with **Midsummer's Eve** bonfires in late June, Denmark buzzes with outdoor activity throughout the summer. Main attractions are the 180 music festivals that run almost nonstop throughout the country, covering a broad spectrum of music that includes not only jazz, rock and blues but also gospel, folk, classical, country, Cajun and much more.

The acclaimed 10-day **Copenhagen Jazz Festival** is held in early July, with outdoor concerts and numerous performances in clubs around the city.

Roskilde hosts an internationally acclaimed **rock festival**, with big international names, on the last weekend of June; a single admission fee includes tent space and entry to all concerts.

There are **folk festivals** in Skagen near the end of June and in Tønder in late August. The 10-day **Århus Festival** in early September features an array of music and multicultural events.

For details on music festivals nationwide, contact **Dansk Musik Informations Center** (☎ 33 11 20 66; W www.mic.dk; Gråbrødre Torv 16, 1154 Copenhagen K).

ACTIVITIES

Cycling is a leading holiday activity in Denmark and there are thousands of kilometres of established cycling routes. Those around Bornholm, Funen and Møn, as well as the 440km Old Military Rd (Hærvejen) through central Jutland, are among the most popular.

Dansk Cyklist Forbund (DCF; ☎ 33 32 31 21; W www.dcf.dk; Rømersgade 7, 1362

Copenhagen K) publishes *Cykelferiekort,* a cycling map of the entire country, as well as more detailed regional cycling maps.

DCF also publishes *Overnatning i det fri,* which lists hundreds of farmers who provide cyclists with a place to pitch a tent for Dkr15 a night. Cycling maps can be purchased in advance from DCF or from tourist offices and bookshops upon arrival. Tourist offices also have information on packaged cycling holidays.

Even though Denmark does not have substantial forests, there are numerous small tracts of woodland that are crisscrossed by pleasant **walking** trails. **Skov og Naturstyrelsen** (Forest & Nature Bureau) produces brochures with sketch maps that show trails in nearly 100 such areas. The brochures can be picked up free at public libraries and some tourist offices. The coast in Denmark is public domain and in many areas there are scenic walking tracks along the shoreline.

Canoeing possibilities on Denmark's inland lakes are superb. Such areas as Jutland's Lake District are ideal for canoe touring between lakeside camp sites. You can hire canoes and equipment at many such camping grounds or at hiring companies in main centres such as Silkeborg. The lakes are generally undemanding as far as water conditions go although some experience is an advantage.

Denmark's remarkable coastline offers terrific **windsurfing** possibilities. There is not much swell for conventional surfing, but the configuration of headlands and bays and the often windy nature of Danish coastal weather creates ideal conditions for windsurfers. Good areas are along the northern coast of Zealand at places such as Smidstrup Strand, and in northwest Jutland. The Limfjord area of northwest Jutland is particularly suited to windsurfing and you can pick up an excellent leaflet, *Windsurfing in the Limfjord Area,* from most tourist offices in the area. There's an English version and it pinpoints 28 windsurfing areas by use of small maps.

COURSES

Scandinavia's unique *folkehøjskole,* literally 'folk high school' ('high' denotes an institute of higher learning), provides a liberal education within a communal living environment. Folk high schools got their start in Denmark, inspired by philosopher Nikolai Grundtvig's

concept of 'enlightenment for life'. The curriculum includes such things as drama, peace studies and organic farming. People aged 19 and older can enrol; there are no entrance exams and no degrees.

There are a number of schools offering **Danish-language** courses to foreigners, but most, understandably focus on those who are long-term residents. A useful place to try is **Hovedstadens Oplysnings Forbund** (HOF; ☎ 33 11 88 33; Købmagergde 26, Copenhagen), a privately run school that offers courses of two to three sessions a week over two months. The cost is about Dkr1600. **Arbejdernes Opysnings Forbund** (AOF; ☎ 39 16 82 00; Lersø Parkallé, Copenhagen) runs free courses for non-Danes, but you need to have a Danish social security number to enrol.

WORK

Overall, the job situation is generally bleak for those who are not Danes, doubly so for those who don't speak Danish.

Citizens of EU countries are allowed to stay in Denmark for a period of up to three months searching for a job, and it's fairly straightforward to get a residency permit if work is found. The main stipulation is that the job provide enough income to adequately cover living expenses.

Citizens of other countries are required to get a work permit before entering Denmark. This requires first securing a job offer and then applying for a work and residency permit while you're still in your home country. You can enter Denmark only after the permit has been granted. These permits are usually limited to people with specialised skills that are in high demand.

ACCOMMODATION
Camping & Cabins

Denmark's 516 camping grounds typically charge from Dkr50 to Dkr60 per person to pitch a tent. Many places add about Dkr20 for the tent space. Places with the simplest facilities have the cheapest rates. A camping pass is required (Dkr80) and covers a family group with offspring under 18 for the season. It can be picked up at any camping ground. If you do not have a seasonal pass you pay an extra Dkr20 a night for a temporary pass.

Many camping grounds rent simple cabins that sleep two to six people and cost from

Dkr225 to Dkr500 a day. Though cabins often have cooking facilities, bedding is rarely provided so you'll need your own sleeping bag.

Camping is restricted to camping grounds, or on private land with the owner's permission. While it may seem tempting, camping in a car along the beach or in a parking lot is definitely prohibited and can result in an immediate fine. Tourist offices usually have brochures listing camping grounds throughout Denmark.

Hostels

Most of Denmark's 100 *vandrerhjem* (hostels) in its Danhostel association, have private rooms in addition to dormitory rooms, making hostels an affordable alternative to hotels. Depending on the category of the hostel, dorm beds cost from about Dkr90 to Dkr100, while private rooms range from Dkr180 to Dkr300 for singles, Dkr250 to Dkr400 for doubles, depending on the season and the standard of facilities. The price paid is per room and the highest rates are usually for four-bedded rooms with private bath. The prices shown under individual hostels reflect the highest price for rooms. Some places charge the same per room for a single as they do for a double, but the price per room can rise by about 50% for more than two people. Blankets and pillows are provided at all hostels, but if you don't bring your own sheets you'll have to hire them for around Dkr40. Sleeping bags are not allowed.

Travellers without an international hostel card can buy one in Denmark for Dkr160 or pay Dkr30 extra a night. From May to September hostels can book out in advance; it's always a good idea to call ahead for reservations. Outside Copenhagen, check-in is generally between 4pm and 8pm or 9pm (but a few places close as early as 6pm); the reception office is usually closed and the phone not answered between noon and 4pm.

In spring and autumn, hostels can get crowded with children on school outings and many hostels require advance reservations from 1 September to 1 June. Most Danish hostels close in winter for any time from a few weeks to several months.

You can pick up a free 200-page hostel guide from tourist offices giving information on each hostel, including such matters as which have laundry facilities and wheelchair-accessible rooms.

All Danish hostels have an all-you-can-eat breakfast for Dkr45 or less and many also provide dinner (Dkr65 maximum). Nearly all hostels also have guest kitchens with pots and pans where you can cook your own food.

The national HI office is **Danhostel** (☎ 33 31 36 12; W *www.danhostel.dk; Vesterbrogade 39, 1620 Copenhagen V*).

Hotels

Hotels are in the centre of all major towns, with the lower end of the range starting at around Dkr450/600 for singles/doubles. While the cheapest places tend to be spartan, they're rarely seedy or unsafe. *Kro*, a name that implies country inn but is more often the Danish version of a motel, is a type of accommodation common along motorways near the outskirts of towns; they are generally cheaper than hotels by about a third. Both hotels and *kros* usually include an all-you-can-eat breakfast that varies from a simple meal of bread, cheese and coffee to a generous buffet.

In recent years many Danish hotels have either fully upgraded, or are in the process of doing so, to include private toilet and shower in each room. Where there are shared toilets and showers, these are generally kept spotlessly clean. Rates listed in this chapter include all taxes and are for rooms with toilet and shower. Where there is a mix of rooms, with and without toilet and shower, the terms 'with bath' and 'without bath' are used. Some hotels offer discount schemes from May to September, when business travel is light, and at weekends year-round.

The Danish Tourist Board's free *Hotels in Denmark* booklet, published annually, lists hotels and *kros* around the country and explains the discounts available.

Other Accommodation

Many tourist offices book rooms in private homes for a small fee, or provide a free list of the rooms so travellers can phone on their own. Rates vary, averaging about Dkr250/300 for singles/doubles. Standards of accommodation may vary widely and some rooms may be very basic. **Dansk Bed & Breakfast** (☎ 39 61 04 05; W *www.bbdk.dk; PO Box 53, 2900 Hellerup*) handles 300 homes throughout Denmark offering private rooms at similar rates. It'll make the bookings for you or you can order its brochure (Dkr20) listing the homes and book them directly yourself.

If you prefer accommodation in the countryside, **Landsforeningen for Landboturisme** (☎ 86 37 39 00, fax 86 37 35 50; **w** www
.bondegaardsferie.dk; Lerbakken 7, Følle, 8410 Rønde) books stays on farms throughout Denmark, some in rooms in family homes, others in separate flats. Prices vary, but average around Dkr200 a person a day. You can peruse sites and book online in advance. Alternatively, once in Denmark, stop by a tourist office to pick up its free illustrated booklet, which has mailing addresses for each farm so you can book them directly yourself.

Also, if you're cycling or driving around Denmark on your own, you'll come across farmhouses displaying 'værelse' (room) signs.

FOOD

Nothing epitomises Danish food more than smørrebrød (literally 'buttered bread'), an open-faced sandwich that ranges from very basic fare to some elaborate sculpture-like creations. Typically, it's a slice of rye bread topped with either roast beef, tiny shrimps, roast pork or fish fillet and finished off with a variety of garnishes. Though it's served in many restaurants at lunchtime, it is cheapest at bakeries and butcher shops.

The rich pastry known worldwide as a 'Danish' is called wienerbrød in Denmark, and nearly every second street corner has a bakery with mouth-watering varieties. For a cheap munch, stop at one of the ubiquitous pølsemandens, the wheeled carts that sell a variety of frankfurters for around Dkr15.

The cheapest restaurant food is generally pizza and pasta; you can eat your fill for about Dkr50 at lunch, Dkr70 at dinner. Danish food, which relies heavily on fish, meat and potatoes, generally costs double that. Dagens ret, which means daily special, is usually the best deal on the menu, while the børn menu is for children.

Typical Danish dishes include frikadeller (minced pork meatballs), kogt torsk (poached cod in mustard sauce), flæskesteg (roast pork with crackling), hvid labskovs (beef and potato stew) and hakkebøf (beef burger with fried onions). Then there's the koldt bord, a buffet-style spread of cold foods, including herring dishes, salads, cold cuts, smoked fish and cheeses.

Cafés commonly serve a variety of salads, and increasingly, mainstream restaurants are catering for vegetarians.

DRINKS

Denmark's Carlsberg and Tuborg breweries both produce excellent beers. The most popular spirit in Denmark is caraway-spiced Aalborg aquavit; it's drunk straight down as a shot, followed by a chaser of beer. Øl (beer), vin (wine) and spirits can be purchased at grocery stores during normal shopping hours and prices are reasonable compared to those in other Scandinavian countries. The minimum legal age for all alcoholic beverages is 18 years.

ENTERTAINMENT

Denmark's cities have some of the most active nightlife in Europe, with live music wafting through side-street cafés, especially in the university cities of Copenhagen, Århus and Odense. Little begins before 10pm or ends before 3am. Most towns have cinemas showing first-run, English-language films subtitled in Danish.

SHOPPING

Silverware, ceramics and handblown glass – all in the sleek style that is typical of Danish design – are popular though not inexpensive purchases. Amber, which washes up on the west-coast beaches of Jutland, makes lovely jewellery and prices are reasonable.

Getting There & Away

AIR

Scandinavian Airlines is the largest carrier serving Denmark. Other airlines flying into Copenhagen include Air France, Alitalia, Austrian Airlines, British Airways, British Midland, El Al, Finnair, Iberia, Icelandair, KLM, Lithuanian Airlines, LOT, Lufthansa, Maersk, Cimber Air, Olympic Airways, and Virgin Express. The budget carrier Ryanair has two flights a day from Stansted Airport, England to Århus airport. At the time of writing, booking well in advance with Ryanair can often secure remarkably cheap flights.

LAND
Germany

The E45 is the main motorway between Germany and Denmark's Jutland Peninsula. Three railway lines link the two countries; 2nd-class fares from Copenhagen to Frankfurt are Dkr1000. Eurolines operates buses from Copenhagen to Berlin (Dkr295) and Frankfurt (Dkr680) several times a week.

Norway

Trains operate daily between Copenhagen and Oslo; the 2nd-class fare (via Sweden) is Dkr430. Eurolines offers a daily bus service between Oslo and Copenhagen (Dkr220) via Gothenburg.

Sweden

Trains run many times a day between Denmark and Sweden via the Øresund Fixed Link, the longest bridge-tunnel of its type in the world. The bridge links Copenhagen with Malmö, Sweden. The 2nd-class train fare from Copenhagen is Dkr62 to Malmö, Dkr200 to Gothenburg and Dkr370 to Stockholm. If you're travelling by train, the bridge crossing is included in the fare, but for those travelling by car, there's a Dkr220 per-vehicle toll.

There are numerous buses between Copenhagen and Sweden, including Eurolines buses to Gothenburg (Dkr160) and Stockholm (Dkr346).

SEA
Germany

The frequent Rødbyhavn-Puttgarden ferry takes 45 minutes and is included in train tickets for those travelling by rail; otherwise, the cost per adult/child is Dkr45/25 and for a car with up to five passengers is Dkr345.

Other ferries run from Rømø to Sylt (Dkr35, one hour), Rønne on Borhholm to Sassnitz (Dkr130, 3½ hours) and Gedser to Rostock (Dkr60, two hours). See also the respective Getting There & Away sections for more information.

Iceland & the Faroe Islands

Smyril Line's (☎ 33 16 40 04; W www .smyril-line.fo) Norröna runs every week from Hanstholm to Tórshavn (Faroe Islands) and Seyðisfjörður (Iceland) from mid-May to early September. The boat leaves Hanstholm at 8pm Saturday, arriving in Tórshavn at 5am Monday. Visitors then have a two-day stop-over in the Faroe Islands (while the boat makes a run to Lerwick, Shetland, and Bergen, Norway), departing from Tórshavn at 6pm Wednesday and arriving in Seyðis-fjörður at 8am Thursday. The return boat departs from Seyðisfjörður at noon Thursday,

arriving in Tórshavn at 5am Friday and in Hanstholm at 3pm Saturday.

Midsummer fares to Tórshavn for a couchette (sleeping berth with mattress, but no bedding) are Dkr1638, and for a bunk in a four-berth cabin, Dkr1766. Fares to Seyðis-fjörður are, couchette Dkr2114, bunk in four-berth cabin Dkr2707: these fares are about 25% less for travel in low season (September to April). There's a 25% discount for students under 26, on presentation of a valid student card. You can take a bicycle to all destinations for about Dkr75 a motorcycle for about Dkr510 (Faroe Islands) and Dkr850 (Iceland); and a car for Dkr1290 (Faroe Islands) and Dkr2150 (Iceland).

Norway

A daily overnight ferry operates between Copenhagen and Oslo. Ferries also run from Hirtshals to Oslo, Kristiansand and Moss; from Hanstholm to Bergen; and from Frederikshavn to Oslo and Larvik. More details are provided in the relevant Getting There & Away sections of the cities.

Poland

Polferries (☎ 33 11 46 45) operates ferries to Świnoujście from both Copenhagen (Dkr380, 10 hours) and Rønne (Dkr180, 5½ hours).

Sweden

The cheapest and most frequent ferry to Sweden is the shuttle between Helsingør and Helsingborg (Dkr18, 20 minutes); ferries leave opposite the Helsingør train station every 20 minutes during the day and once an hour through the night. Passage for a car with up to five people costs Dkr230.

Other ferries go from Frederikshavn to Gothenburg (Dkr100 to Dkr160, two to 3¼ hours), Rønne to Ystad (Dkr150, 1½ hours) and Grenå to Varberg (Dkr100 to Dkr140, four hours). See also the relevant Getting There & Away sections in this chapter.

UK

DFDS Seaways (☎ 08705 333 000; W www .dfdsseaways.co.uk) sails from Esbjerg to Harwich at least three times a week at 6pm year-round. It takes 19 hours. The cost for passage in a chair ranges from Dkr600 in winter to Dkr1140 in midsummer, while the cheapest bed in a two-person cabin is between Dkr948 and Dkr1798. Add Dkr116 to Dkr232 for a motorcycle, and Dkr406 to Dkr640 for a car; bikes are carried free.

LEAVING DENMARK
There are no departure taxes to be paid when leaving Denmark.

Getting Around

AIR
Denmark's domestic air routes are operated by **Maersk Air** (☎ 70 10 74 74; ⓦ www .maersk-air.com), which connects Copenhagen with Billund, Esbjerg, Odense, Rønne and Vojens. The regular one-way fare from Copenhagen is Dkr869 to Bornholm and Dkr815 to Billund, but if you buy your ticket a week in advance and stay over the weekend, you can get cheaper deals.

SAS (☎ 70 10 30 00; ⓦ www.scandinavian .net) links Copenhagen with Aalborg and Århus, both about a dozen times a day. The one-way fare is Dkr740, and there are return fares in the same price range.

BUS
All large cities and towns have a local bus system and most places are also served by regional buses, many of which connect with trains. There are also a few long-distance bus routes, including from Copenhagen to Aalborg or Århus. The cost of travelling by bus on long-distance routes is about 20% less than travel by train.

TRAIN
With the exception of a few short private lines, the Danish State Railways (DSB) runs all train services in Denmark.

There are two types of long-distance trains. Sleek InterCity (IC) trains have ultramodern comforts and generally require reservations (Dkr20). Inter-regional (IR) trains are older and a bit slower, make more stops and don't require reservations. Both trains charge the same fares, as long as you avoid the InterCity-Lyn, a cushy express train that is aimed at businesspeople, has free drinks, fewer stops and a 50% surcharge. Rail passes don't cover reservation fees or surcharges.

Overall, train travel in Denmark is not expensive, in large part because the distances are short. Standard fares work out to about Dkr1 per kilometre, while the highest possible

fare between two stations in Denmark is Dkr300. People aged 65 and older are entitled to a 20% discount on Friday and Saturday and a 50% discount on other days. There are also generous discounts for children.

Scanrail, Eurail and other rail passes are valid on DSB ferries and trains, but not on the private lines. For rail pass information, see the Getting Around the Region chapter.

CAR & MOTORCYCLE
Denmark is a pleasant country for touring by car. Roads are in good condition and well signposted. Traffic is surprisingly manageable, even in major cities including Copenhagen (rush hours excepted).

Access to and from motorways is made easy since roads leading out of city and town centres are sensibly named after the main city to which they're routed. For instance, the road leading out of Odense to Faaborg is Faaborgvej, the road leading to Nyborg is Nyborgvej, and so on.

Denmark's extensive network of ferries carries motor vehicles for reasonable rates. Though fares vary, as a rule of thumb domestic fares for cars average three times the passenger rate. It's always a good idea for drivers to call ahead and make reservations.

You'll find the best prices for petrol at stations along motorways and at the unstaffed OK Benzin chain, which has self-serve pumps that accept Dkr100 notes as well as major credit cards.

Denmark's main motoring organisation is **Forenede Danske Motorejere** (FDM; ☎ 32 66 01 00; ⓦ www.mst.dk; Firskovvej 32, 2800 Lyngby).

Road Rules
In Denmark you drive on the right-hand side of the road, seat-belt use is mandatory and all drivers are required to carry a warning triangle in case of breakdowns. Speed limits are 50km/h in towns, 80km/h outside built-up areas and 110km/h on motorways. Cars and motorcycles must use dipped headlights at all times. It's a good idea for visitors to carry a Green Card (see the Paperwork & Preparations section in the Getting Around the Region chapter).

The authorities are very strict about drink driving. It's illegal to drive with a blood-alcohol concentration of 0.05% or greater, and driving under the influence is subject to stiff penalties and a possible prison sentence.

Car Rental

You'll generally get the best deal by booking through an international rental agency before you arrive in Denmark. Otherwise rates for the cheapest cars, including VAT, insurance and unlimited kilometres, begin at about Dkr680 a day, or Dkr520 a day on rentals of two days or more. Most companies offer a special weekend rate that allows you to keep the car from Friday afternoon to Monday morning and includes VAT and insurance for around Dkr1200. Request a plan that includes unlimited kilometres, as some begin tacking on an extra fee after the first 250km. Europcar offers unlimited kilometres and generally offers the cheapest, most flexible weekend deals, but it's wise to call around and compare.

The largest companies – Europcar, Avis and Hertz – have offices throughout Denmark.

Parking

To park in the street in city centres you usually have to buy a ticket from a *billetautomat* machine on the pavement. The billetautomat has an LCD read-out showing the current time, and the time advances as you insert coins. Put in enough money to advance the read-out to the time you plan to leave and then push the button to eject the ticket from the machine. Place the ticket, which shows the exact time you've paid for, face up inside the windscreen. The cost is generally Dkr10 to Dkr20 an hour. Unless otherwise posted, street parking is usually free from 6pm to 8am, after 2pm on Saturday and all day on Sunday.

In smaller towns, which are usually free of coin-hungry billetautomats, street parking is free within the time limits posted. You will, however, need a windscreen parking disc (available from tourist offices and petrol stations) which you set at the time you park. *Parkering forbudt* means 'No parking'.

BICYCLE

Cycling is a practical way to get around Denmark. There are extensive bike paths linking towns throughout the country and bike lanes through most city centres.

You can rent bikes in most towns for around Dkr60 a day, plus a deposit of about Dkr250. Bikes can be taken on ferries and most trains for a modest cost; make sure you pick up the DSB pamphlet *Cykler i tog*. See also Activities in Facts for the Visitor earlier in this chapter.

HITCHING

Hitching in Denmark is quite rare, generally not very good and illegal on motorways.

BOAT

A network of ferries links virtually all of Denmark's populated islands. Where there's not a bridge, there's usually a ferry. Specific ferry information is given under the individual destination sections.

LOCAL TRANSPORT

All cities and towns of any size in Denmark are served by local buses. As a rule, the main local bus station is adjacent to the train station or ferry depot. For more details, see the individual destination sections.

Taxi stands can be found at train stations and major shopping areas in Denmark. The fare is typically Dkr21 to Dkr30 flag fall and between Dkr10 and Dkr13 per kilometre, with the higher rates prevailing at night and at weekends.

Copenhagen

pop 1.5 million

Copenhagen (København) is Scandinavia's largest and liveliest city and is one of Europe's most seductive destinations. It began life as a fishing village and developed within the shelter of Slotsholm, the island that is now dominated by the monumental Christiansborg Palace. Slotsholm was fortified during the 12th century, and the settlement that developed around it was named Kømanshavn, later amended to København, meaning the 'port of the merchants'. The much-expanded settlement became the capital of Denmark during the early 15th century. Today, Copenhagen sprawls across a flat cityscape. No surrounding hills give it overall context, yet buildings are generally low rise and several splendid steeples and towers break the skyline.

Central Copenhagen has an active nightlife that rolls on well into the early hours of the morning, and there's a treasure trove of museums, castles and old churches to explore. The most outstanding museums are Ny Carlsberg Glyptotek, the Nationalmuseet and the Statens Museum for Kunst. The city's famous Tivoli amusement park and garden always draws local and visitor alike, but much of Copenhagen's allure lies in the irresistible

COPENHAGEN (KØBENHAVN)

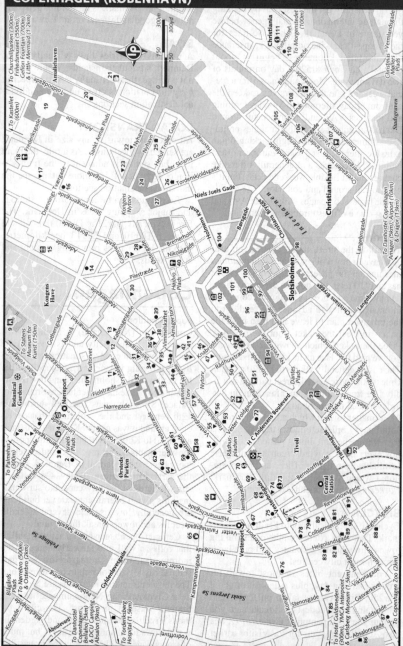

COPENHAGEN (KØBENHAVN)

PLACES TO STAY
1 Cab-Inn Scandinavia
3 Hotel Jørgensen
20 Copenhagen Admiral Hotel
25 Sømandshjemmet Bethel
26 Hotel Opera
53 Hotel Rainbow
80 Missionshotellet Nebo
81 Ibis Hotel
82 Selandia Hotel
83 Hebron Hotel
86 City Public Hostel
88 Tiffany Hotel
89 Absalon Hotel
90 Saga Hotel
91 Turisthotellet

PLACES TO EAT
7 Supermarket
8 Govindas
10 Klaptræet
11 Ankara
13 Studenterhusets
17 Ida Davidsen
22 Cap Horn
23 Nyhavns Færgekro
28 Reinh van Hauen Bakery
29 Netto Supermarket
30 Café Sommersko
31 Det Lille Apotek
35 Samos
36 Restaurant Gråbrødre Torv 21
37 Peder Oxe; Jensen's Bøfhus
38 Pasta Basta
41 Sebastian
42 Café de Paris;
   Restaurant Eastern
45 Café Sorgenfri
46 Heaven
47 Riz Raz
50 Restaurant Puk
55 Shawarma Grill House

56 Reinh van Hauen Bakery
57 7-Eleven
64 Reef n' Beef
69 Matahari; Italian Corner
74 Hard Rock Cafe
77 Astor Pizza
84 Ankara
85 Merhaba
105 Café Wilders
106 Christianshavns Bådudlejning
108 Oven Vanden Café

OTHER
2 Dansk Cyklist Forbund
   (Cycling Federation)
4 Petrol Station
5 Outpost Entertainment
6 Fjeld & Fritid
9 Rosenborg Slot
12 Rundetårn
14 Kvindehuset
15 Davids Samling
16 Ostehjørnet
18 Frederik's Kirke
   (Marmorkirken)
19 Amalienborg Palace
21 Boats to Oslo & Bornholm
24 Charlottenborg
   (Royal Academy of Arts)
27 Royal Theatre
32 University Library
33 Vor Frue Kirke
34 Kilroy Travels
39 Copenhagen Jazz House
40 St Nicolaj Kirke
43 GAD Bookshop
44 Wasteels
48 Huset
49 Use It
51 Mojo
52 Oscar
54 Politiken Boghallen Bookshop

58 Masken
59 Nordisk Korthandel Bookshop
60 Cosy Bar
61 Guf
62 LBL (National Gay &
   Lesbian Organisation)
63 Never Mind
65 Petrol Station
66 Pumphuset
67 Hertz Car Rental
68 Nordea
70 Forex
71 Rådhusarkaden Shopping
   Centre
72 Rådhus (City Hall)
73 Wonderful Copenhagen
   (Tourist Office)
75 Steno Apotek
76 Europcar Car Rental
78 Danwheel
79 Eurolines Office
87 Istedgades Møntvask
   Laundrette
92 Main Post Office
93 Ny Carlsberg Glyptotek
94 Nationalmuseet
95 Museum of Royal Coaches
96 Christiansborg Palace
97 Tøjhusmuseet (Royal Arsenal)
98 Royal Library
99 Teatermuseet
100 Folketing (Parliament)
101 Royal Reception Chambers
102 Thorvaldsens Museum
103 Ruins of Absalon's Fortress
104 Netto-Bådene Boats
107 Sofie Kælderen
109 Vor Frelsers Kirke
110 Loppe Building; Spiseloppen;
   Loppen Dance Club; Gallopperiet
111 Christiania Information Office

buzz of its central streets and squares and in the liveliness of its bars, cafés, restaurants and music venues – more than enough to satisfy any urban explorer.

Although it is a large and complex city, the best of Copenhagen is easy to navigate. As always there are main throughways that are torrents of traffic, but much of the central area is pedestrianised and the main roads have cycle lanes for those who prefer to move at a faster, yet still human, pace.

Orientation

The always bustling train station, Central Station (Hovedbanegården or København H), is flanked on its west by the main hotel zone, a dense grid of mildly down-at-heel streets and

grey-faced buildings, where modernised hotels rub shoulders, unfazed, with the occasional explicit sex shop or strip club. To the east of the station's main entrance, across the broad and busy Bernstorffsgade, is the Tivoli amusement park, barely visible behind lines of offices, shops and restaurants. The equally broad and traffic-bound HC Andersens Boulevarde flanks Tivoli on its northeastern corner. Beyond here lies the spacious Rådhuspladsen: the central city square, main bus transit point and gateway to the heart of Copenhagen.

From Rådhuspladsen, the narrow opening of Frederiksberggade is the unassuming introduction to Strøget, 'the world's longest pedestrian mall'. The mall is a linked sequence of lively, crowded streets that runs through the heart of the city linking Rådhuspladsen and the other great square of Kongens Nytorv, at the head of the Nyhavn canal. Strøget is made up of Frederiksberggade, Nygade, Vimmelskaftet, Amagertorv and Østergade. Other streets run north from Strøget into the university district and the so-called Latin Quarter, north of which lie Copenhagen's main parks and gardens. South of Strøget, is another scramble of quieter streets, but with their full share of lively cafés, bars and restaurants, that lead to the canal-bound Slotsholm and its monumental buildings and museums. Southeast of Slotsholm, across the inner harbour, is the relaxed canal district of Christianshavn and the ultimate alternative of the 'Freetown' of Christiania. Copenhagen is nothing if not wonderful in its variety.

Information

Tourist Offices The city tourist office, **Wonderful Copenhagen** (☎ 70 22 24 42, fax 70 22 24 52; W www.visitcopenhagen.dk; Bernstorffsgade 1; open 9am-8pm Mon-Sat, 10am-8pm Sun May-Aug; 9am-4.30pm Mon-Fri, 9am-1.30pm Sat Sept-Apr), north of Central Station, distributes the informative Tourist in Copenhagen and Copenhagen This Week, a free city map, and brochures for all regions of Denmark. It can get very crowded by mid-morning and there are separate ticket queuing systems for inquiries and for hotel bookings. In summer especially, the queues can be long and fretful.

Use It (☎ 33 73 06 20, fax 33 73 06 49; W www.useit.dk; Rådhusstræde 13; open 9am-7pm daily mid-June–mid-Sept; 11am-4pm Mon-Wed, 11am-6pm Thur, 11am-2pm Fri mid-Sept–mid-June) is a first class information centre aimed at young budget travellers, but open to all. It books rooms, stores luggage (by day only), holds mail, offers free Internet use and provides information on everything, from working in Denmark to cheap sleeps and affordable nightlife. Playtime is Use It's free annual guide to the city and around and is a bright, upbeat publication packed with information.

Copenhagen Card The Copenhagen Card secures unlimited travel on buses and trains around Copenhagen and North Zealand, and on the city's waterbuses. It also gives free or discounted admission to most of the region's museums and attractions. An adult card (aged 16 upward), costs Dkr215/375/495 for one/two/three days. The adult card covers two children under 10. A young people's card (aged 10 to 15) costs Dkr95/165/225 for one/two/three days. Cards are sold at the Wonderful Copenhagen tourist office, Copenhagen Airport's Terminal 3 Service Information centre, Central Station and other major DSB stations, and at many hotels, camping grounds and hostels. If you want to tick off a lot of sights in a few days this card can be a real bargain, but for a more selective and leisurely exploration of venues it may work out better to pay individual admissions and use one of the transport passes (see the Getting Around section later in this section).

Money Banks, all of which charge transaction fees, are found throughout the city centre. At Central Station the **Forex exchange booth** (open 8am-9pm daily) has the lowest fees. You'll find 24-hour, cash-exchange ATMs that exchange major foreign currencies for Danish kroner, minus a hefty Dkr25 to Kkr30 fee, at the **Den Danske Bank** (Central Station) and at **Nordea** (Axeltorv).

Banks in the airport arrival and transit halls are open 6am to 10pm daily.

Post Pick up poste-restante mail at the **main post office** (Tietgensgade 35-39; open 11am-6pm Mon-Fri, 10am-1pm Sat). There is a **post office** (open 8am-9pm Mon-Fri, 9am-4pm Sat, 10am-5pm Sun) in Central Station.

Email & Internet Access Internet access is available at **Outpost Entertainment** (☎ 33 93 22 63; Frederiksborggade 15) for Dkr30 an hour. If you just want to check your email, **Use It** (Rådhusstræde 13), offers free Internet access, within reasonable time restraints, or you can drop by the **Royal Library** at the southern side of Slotsholmen, where more than 100 on-line computers fill the hallways.

Travel Agencies Two agencies specialising in student and budget travel are **Kilroy Travels** (☎ 33 11 00 44; Skindergade 28) and **Wasteels** (☎ 33 14 46 33; Skoubogade 6).

Bookshops & Newsagents A superb collection of travel guides and maps can be found at **Nordisk Korthandel** (Studie-stræde 26-30). General bookstores in Copenhagen with English-language sections include **GAD**

(Vimmelskaftet 32) and **Politiken Boghallen** *(Rådhuspladsen 37)*. Pick up foreign newspapers at Central Station or newsstands.

Laundry There's a *møntvaskeri* at **Istedgades Møntvask** *(Istedgade 45; open 7am-9pm)* in the hotel district. Washing and drying a 10kg load costs about Dkr28.

Left Luggage At Central Station there are lockers (per 24 hours small/large Dkr25/35, maximum of 72 hours) in the lower level near the Reventlowsgade exit

Medical & Emergency Services Dial ☎ 112 for police emergencies or ambulance. **Frederiksberg Hospital** *(☎ 38 16 38 16; Nordre Fasanvej 57)*, west of the city centre, has a 24-hour emergency ward. Private doctor visits (☎ 33 93 63 00 for referrals) usually cost around Dkr350. **Steno Apotek** *(Vesterbrogade 6c)*, opposite Central Station, is a 24-hour pharmacy.

Walking Tour

Taking a half-day's walk from Rådhus (City Hall) to the Little Mermaid is a pleasant way of becoming familiar with the city as well as taking in some of the central sights.

The **Rådhus** *(☎ 33 66 25 82; open 9.30am-3pm daily)* building itself is worth a glance. The building dates from the late 19th century and reflects a dazzling mix of influences in the decor of its sumptuous rooms. You can take a look at the rooms for free or join a guided tour, Dkr30, with commentary in English, at 3pm Monday to Friday, 10am Saturday.

For Dkr20 you can walk 300 steps to the top of the Rådhus tower, at 10am, noon and 2pm Monday to Friday and noon Saturday. Take a look at **Jens Olsens World Clock** *(adult/child Dkr10/5)* in a side chamber of the entrance hall. The clock contains 15,448 individual parts and is a staggering expression of Danish ingenuity and precision.

From Rådhus stroll down Strøget, which, after a couple of blocks, cuts between the cobbled squares of **Gammel Torv**, the 'Old Square' on the left and **Nytorv**, the 'New Square' on the right. Gammel Torv has been a market square for hundreds of years and today jewellery, flowers and fruit are still sold from stalls. At the centre of Gammel Torv is the elegant *Caritas*, the 'Charity' Fountain.

Strøget now enters Nygade and then becomes Vimmelskafte before widening again into the lively square of **Amagertorv**. Ahead is the famous *Storkespringvandet* the 'Stork Fountain', a popular meeting place and venue for street entertainers, who can be exceptional, or eccentric. The busy shopping street of Købmagergade leads off left. To the right is Højbro Plads with, at its far end, the great statue of the city founder, Bishop Absalon on horseback and the handsome steeple of St Nikolaj Kirke rising above the red rooftops on the left. Beyond the Bishop Absalon statue is the exhilarating panorama of Christianborg Palace on the island of Slotsholmen and the spire of entwined dragons' tails that crowns the Børsen, the beautiful Renaissance stock exchange building.

From the lively heart of Amagertov, Strøget continues along the narrow Østergade. A few steps to the right will take you to **St Nikolaj Kirke** *(10 Nikolaj Plads; admission Dkr20; open noon-5pm daily)*, now a community art gallery, where some fine exhibitions are held. Strøget soon ends at Kongens Nytorv, a huge square circled by some gracious old buildings including the **Royal Theatre**, home to the Royal Danish Ballet, and **Charlottenborg**, a 17th-century Dutch baroque palace that houses the **Royal Academy of Arts** *(admission Dkr20; open 10am-5pm Mon-Sun, 10am-7pm Wed)*. The academy's rear building has changing exhibits of contemporary art.

On the eastern side of Kongens Nytorv is picturesque **Nyhavn** canal, dug 300 years ago to allow traders to bring their wares into the heart of the city. Nyhavn was once the haunt of sailors, local characters, and writers, such as Hans Christian Andersen, who lived for many years at No 67. Today it is given over entirely to busy pavement cafés on its sunny northern side, but is still lined with an attractive jumble of sailing craft and houseboats.

From the northern side of Nyhavn, head north on Toldbodgade, turn right into Sankt Annæ Plads and then turn left along the airy waterfront, where you're just as likely to see a Cayman Island's gin palace cruiser, or Greenpeace's Rainbow Warrior, moored temporarily alongside. When you reach a fountain, turn inland to the great cobbled square of Amalienborg Plads and to **Amalienborg Palace** *(adult/child Dkr40/5; open 10am-4pm daily May-Oct, 11am-4pm daily Nov-Apr)*, which has been the home of the royal family since 1794. The palace's four, nearly identical, rococo mansions surround the central square and are guarded by sentries. There is a rather lifeless element to the entire venue, but things are enlivened at noon by a ceremonial changing of the guard, a distinctly Hans Christian Andersen scenario, although these are serious soldiers beneath the greatcoats. You can view the interior of the northwestern mansion, with its royal memorabilia and the study rooms of three kings.

Head inland along Frederiksgade to the splendid **Frederikskirken** (admission free, guided tour adult/child Dkr20/10; open 10am-5pm Mon-Thur, noon-5pm Fri-Sun, tower tour 1pm & 3pm daily mid-June–Aug). It's known universally as Marmorkirken (Marble Church) because of its magnificent marble dome, a striking contrast to the rest of Copenhagen's exotic steeples and towers. The church was modelled on St Peter's in Rome. The panelled and gilded frescoes on the inside of the dome have breathtaking colours.

Back on Amalienborg Plads, head north along Amaliegade for 500m to reach Churchillparken, where you'll find **Frihedsmuseet** (admission Dkr30, Wed free; open 10am-4pm Tues-Sat, 10am-5pm Sun May–mid-Sept; 11am-3pm Tues-Sat, 11am-4pm Sun mid-Sept–Apr), which depicts the history of Danish Resistance against Nazi occupation.

Keep heading straight on from the Frihedsmuseet and in 150m you pass the spectacular **Gefion Fountain** that features the mythical goddess Gefion, ploughing the island of Zealand with her four sons yoked as oxen. Continue north along the waterfront for another 400 metres to the statue of the famed **Little Mermaid** (Den Lille Havfrue), a rather forlorn little bronze statue with an industrial harbour backdrop that tends to disappoint all but the most steadfast Hans Christian Andersen fans.

From the Little Mermaid continue on the road inland (west). In just a few minutes you'll reach steps leading down to a wooden bridge that crosses a moat into an interesting, 17th-century citadel called the **Kastellet**. It's a short walk south through the Kastellet, where a second bridge spans the moat and leads back into Churchillparken. From the park, turn right onto Esplanaden to Store Kongensgade, where it's just over half a kilometre's walk back to Kongens Nytorv; or you can catch bus No 6 back to Rådhus.

Latin Quarter
The university district north of Strøget, all narrow streets lined with cafés, bars and an eclectic mix of shops, has a lively atmosphere.

Climb the stairs of the **University Library** (enter from Fiolstræde) to see one quirky remnant of the 1807 British bombardment of Copenhagen – a cannonball in five fragments and the object it hit, a book titled *Defensor Pacis* (Defender of Peace).

Opposite the university is **Vor Frue Kirke** (admission free; open 8am-5pm daily, closed to viewing during services and concerts), Copenhagen's neoclassical cathedral. The building dates from 1829, but stands on the site of earlier churches. It has a strong classical design and with its high, vaulted ceiling and rather stark interior seems well suited for the museum-like display of the powerful statues of Christ and the 12 apostles, the most acclaimed works of the Golden Age sculptor, Bertel Thorvaldsen. A couple of blocks east of the cathedral is the pretty square of **Gråbrdre Torv** and its flanking restaurants. On the northern side of the Latin Quarter is **Kultorvet**, a lively square where on sunny days you'll almost certainly find impromptu street entertainment, as well as beer gardens, flower stalls and produce stands.

Rundetårn
The Round Tower (☎ 33 73 03 73, Købmagergade 52; adult/child Dkr20/5; open 10am-8pm Mon-Sat, noon-8pm Sun June-Aug; 10am-5pm Mon-Sat, noon-5pm Sun Sept-May) provides a fine vantage point for viewing the old city's red-tiled rooftops and abundant church spires. It was built by Christian IV in 1642 as an astronomical observatory. Halfway up the 209m spiral walkway is a hall with changing exhibits. Peter The Great of Russia is said to have ridden his horse up the ramp followed by the Czarina in a horse-drawn carriage; everyone else walks. The observatory offers winter **astronomy programmes** (open 7pm-10pm Tues & Wed Oct-May).

Rosenborg Slot
This 17th-century castle (☎ 33 15 32 86; adult/child Dkr60/10; open 10am-4pm daily May & Sept, 10am-5pm daily June-Aug, 11am-3pm daily Oct, 11am-2pm daily Nov-Apr) built by Christian IV in Dutch Renaissance style, stands at the edge of the peaceful Kongens Have, the King's Gardens. There are glorious marbled and painted ceilings,

gilded mirrors, Dutch tapestries, silver lions and gold and enamel ware. The Royal Treasury is in the castle basement and here the Danish crown jewels, including Christian IV's crown, the sword of Christian III and Queen Margrethe II's pearls, glow in the subdued lighting of soundless rooms.

Gardens

The green stretch of gardens along Øster Voldgade offers a refuge from the city traffic. **Kongens Have**, the large public park behind Rosenborg Slot, is a popular picnic spot. If timing allows, include a visit to the adjacent **Davids Samling** (admission free; open 1pm-4pm Tues-Sun), which houses Scandinavia's largest collection of Islamic art.

The extensive **Botanical Gardens** (admission free; open 8.30am-6pm daily May-Sept, 8.30am-4pm Tues-Sun Oct-Apr) on the western side of Rosenborg Slot has fragrant trails. The **Palmehus** (open 10am-3pm Mon, Tues, Thur & Fri; 1pm-3pm Wed, Sat, Sun & public hols) is a large, walk-through glasshouse with tropical plants. One entrance to the gardens is at the intersection of Gothersgade and Voldgade and the other is off Øster Farimagsgade.

Statens Museum for Kunst

Denmark's national gallery, (☎ 33 74 84 94; 𝕎 www.smk.dk; Sølvgade 48-50; adult/child Dkr50/free, Wed free; open 10am-5pm Tues & Thur-Sun, 10am-8pm Wed) contains an enormous collection of superb paintings. Taking everything in at one go can be exhausting. The main collection is on the 2nd floor and includes works by 19th-century Danish masters such as Jens Juel, CW Eckersberg, Constantin Hansen, PS Krøyer and Kristian Zahrtmann, as well as the 17th-century Dutch and Flemish masters, Rembrandt and Rubens. Leading European artists including Matisse, Picasso, Braque, Utrillo and Munch are well represented. There are contemporary, and often engagingly provocative, installations by Danish artists. The ground floor stages temporary exhibitions of major international paintings for which there is a separate admission fee. The museum's café offers engagingly artistic food, with equally artistic prices.

Slotsholmen

On an island separated from the city centre by a moat-like canal, Slotsholmen is the site of **Christiansborg Palace** (☎ 33 92 64 92) and the seat of Denmark's national government. Of the many sites the grandest is the **Royal Reception Chambers** (adult/child Dkr40/10, guided tours 11am, 1pm & 3pm daily May-Sept; 11am & 3pm Tues, Thur, Sat & Sun Oct-Apr) the ornate Renaissance hall where the queen entertains heads of state. The tours have commentary in English.

The **Ruins of Absalon's Fortress** (adult/child Dkr20/5; open 9.30am-3.30pm daily May-Sept; 9.30am-3.30pm Tues, Thur, Sat & Sun Oct-Apr) are the excavated foundations of Bishop Absalon's original castle of 1167, those of the original Slotsholmen castle of 1167 and of its successor, Copenhagen Slot. They can be visited in the atmospheric basement of the present palace tower.

Tøjhusmuseet (☎ 33 11 60 37; adult/child Dkr40/free, Wed free; open noon-4pm Tues-Sun), the royal arsenal built in 1600, has an impressive collection of hand weapons and old armour and a huge hall filled with historic cannons.

At the **Museum of Royal Coaches** (☎ 33 40 10 10; adult/child Dkr20/10; open 2pm-4pm Fri, Sat & Sun May-Sept; 2pm-4pm Sat & Sun Oct-Apr), the horses and carriages used for regal events can be viewed.

Teatermuseet (adult/child Dkr30/5; open 2pm-4pm Wed, noon-4pm Sat & Sun), which houses the royal stage, dates from 1766 and has many exhibits on Danish theatre history.

Thorvaldsens Museum (☎ 33 32 15 32; Bertel Thorvaldsens Plads; adult/child Dkr20/free; Wed free; open 10am-5pm Tues-Sun) features grand statues by the famed Danish sculptor Bertel Thorvaldsen, who was heavily influenced by Greek and Roman mythology. Enter from Vindebrogade.

The **Royal Library** (☎ 33 47 47 47; Søren Kierkegaards Plads; open 10am-7pm Mon-Sat) dates from the 17th century, but the focal point these days is its new ultramodern extension dubbed the 'Black Diamond' for its shiny black granite facade. The sleek, seven-storey building houses 21 million books and other literary items such as Hans Christian Andersen's original manuscripts. The building itself is open for **visits and guided tours** (adult/child Dkr25/10; open 10am-11pm daily) and for changing **exhibitions** (adult/child Dkr30/10; open 10am-9pm daily).

Nationalmuseet

The National Museum (Ny Vestergade 10; W www.natmus.dk; adult/child Dkr40/free, Wed free; open 10am-5pm Tues-Sun) holds the world's most extensive collection of Danish artefacts from the Palaeolithic period to the 19th century. Highlights include Bronze-Age burial remains in oak coffins and *lurs* (musical horns) that were used for ceremony and communication, ancient rune stones, a golden sun chariot, the silver Gundestrip cauldron and Viking weaponry. Other major collections cover the Middle Ages and Renaissance period, Egyptian and classical antiquities and there's even a **Children's Museum**.

Christianshavn

Christianshavn was established by King Christian IV in the early 1600s as a commercial centre and military buffer for the expanding city of Copenhagen. Still surrounded by ramparts and cut by canals, Christianshavn today is a mix of residential development and cultural enclave with a number of excellent cafés and bars. There's a distinctly relaxed lifestyle along the canalsides, and the area is attracting an increasing number of artists and craftspeople.

To get to Christianshavn, walk over the bridge from the northeastern side of Slotsholmen or take bus No 8 from Rådhuspladsen.

'Freetown' of Christiania Christianshavn is also the site of the remarkable 'Freetown' of Christiania, an alternative city community of about 1000 residents. It has its own commercial life, political structure, education system, radio station and weekly newspaper as well as a thriving music, theatre and social scene. It also has a relentless hash culture and hash, grass and skunk are openly, though illegally, sold on Pusherstreet from a variety of stalls. Passive smoking can be an occupational hazard for deep breathers.

Christiania has an **information office** (☎/fax 32 95 65 07; W www.christiania.org; Nyt Forum, Pusherstreet; open noon-6pm Mon-Thur, noon-4pm Fri) on the 1st floor of the music centre of Operæn.

In the early 1970s an abandoned military barracks on the eastern side of Christianshavn saw a huge and dynamic influx of squatters, hippies, artists, musicians, political activists and other urban escapees, all fired with the dream of an alternative 'New Society' run by

and for the community. During the next 10 years, the citizens of Christiania dug in amid sporadic, and often violent, confrontations with the state, especially when elections brought in less sympathetic governance.

By the start of the 1980s an acknowledged hard drugs problem resulted in police raids, a moral backlash from some quarters, and much soul-searching within Christiania itself. The result is, that while hash remains an almost Eucharistic feature of life in Christiania, there are tough community rules against the use of hard drugs.

The government eventually agreed to the continuation of Christiania as a 'social experiment' in communal living. Until recently progress was still punctuated by police actions and by bureaucratic conflicts, but Christiania has emerged as a viable community that pays duties from a common fund, supports a range of social organisations and businesses and is, inevitably, a tourist attraction.

It is a fascinating place to visit, although some ultra 'free spirits' may be repelled by a certain sense of claustrophobia and by the relentless hash culture that underlies much of Christiania life. Visitors are welcome to stroll through car-free Christiania. Taking photographs should be with consent at all times, and is forbidden on Pusherstreet. There are numerous cafés and other eating places as well as a range of often wonderfully eccentric shops. Music and theatre remain a vigorous part of community life. If you want to learn more about Christiania, there are guided tours most days in summer. Check with the information offices for details. There are plans to establish a new entrance to Christiania at the junction of Prinsessegade with Baadsmandsstrade.

Vor Frelsers Kirke Close to Christiania is the 17th-century Vor Frelsers Kirke (☎ 31 57 27 98; Sankt Annæ Gade 29; admission free, tower adult/child Dkr20/10; open 11am-4.30pm daily Apr-Aug, 11am-3.30pm Sept-Mar, no admission during services; tower closed Nov-Mar), which has an elaborately carved pipe organ and a baroque altar. If you really want to get literally high above Christiania's fog and gain a panoramic city view, climb the dizzying 400 steps of the church's 95m spiral tower. The last 160 steps run along the outside rim, narrowing to the point where they disappear at the top.

Tivoli

Right in the heart of the city, is Copenhagen's century-old amusement park, Tivoli (☎ 33 15 10 01; ⓦ www.tivoli.dk; adult/child Dkr50/25; open 11am-11pm Sat-Thur, 11am-1am Fri mid-Apr–mid-June & mid-Aug–mid-Sept; 11am-midnight Sun-Thur, 11am-1am Fri & Sat mid-June–mid-Aug). It's a mishmash of gardens, food pavilions, amusement rides, carnival games and various stage shows. Fireworks light up the skies at 11.45pm on Wednesday and Saturday.

Ny Carlsberg Glyptotek

This splendid museum (☎ 33 41 81 41; Dantes Plad 7, HC Andersens Blvd; adult/child Dkr30/free, Wed & Sun free; open 10am-4pm Tues-Sun) is housed in a grand period building near Tivoli. It has an exceptional collection of Greek, Egyptian, Etruscan and Roman sculpture, a wing of paintings by Gauguin, Monet and Van Gogh and a complete set of Degas bronzes.

Other Museums

It could take weeks to explore all of Copenhagen's museums. They cover almost every special interest, including Danish design, architecture, decorative art, erotica, medical sciences, geology, working-class cultural history, tobacco and pipes, Copenhagen city history, post and telegraph, shipbuilding, Danish naval history, European musical instruments, drawings of humorist Storm P, and the silver designs of Georg Jensen. Copenhagen This Week has a list of the full range of options with addresses, admission fees and hours.

Carlsberg Brewery

At the Carlsberg Brewery visitor centre (☎ 33 27 13 14; Gamle Carlsberg Vej 11; open 10am-4pm Tues-Sun) free self-guided tours provide the lowdown on the history of Danish beer, capped off with a sampling of the present-day product. Take bus No 6 westbound.

Copenhagen Zoo

The zoo (☎ 72 20 02 80; Roskildevej 32; adult/child Dkr80/40; open 9am-5pm daily June-Oct, 9am-4pm daily Nov-Mar), in the Frederiksberg area, has the standard collection of caged creatures, including elephants, lions, gorillas and polar bears. To get to the zoo take bus No 18.

Dragør

If Copenhagen begins to feel crowded, consider an afternoon excursion to Dragør, a quiet maritime town on the island of Amager a few kilometres south of the airport.

During the early 1550s King Christian II allowed Dutch farmers to settle in Amager to provide his court with flowers and produce, and Dragør still retains a hint of Dutch flavour.

Along the waterfront are fishing boats, smokehouses and the Dragør Museum (☎ 32 53 41 06 Havnepladsen; adult/child Dkr20/10; open noon-4pm Tues-Sun May-Sept), a half-timbered house holding ship paraphernalia, period furnishings and locally produced needlework. The winding cobblestone streets leading up from the harbour are lined with the thatch-roofed, mustard-coloured houses that comprise the old town.

It is a 35-minute ride on bus No 30 or 33 (Dkr21) from Rådhuspladsen.

Klampenborg

Klampenborg is a favourite spot for people taking family outings from Copenhagen. It is only 20 minutes from Central Station on the S-train's line C (Dkr28). Bellevue beach, 400m east of Klampenborg Station, is a sandy strand that gets packed with sunbathers in summer. A large grassy area behind the beach absorbs some of the overflow. A 10-minute walk west from the station is Bakken (☎ 39 63 73 00; Dyrehavevej 62; admission free; open noon-midnight daily Apr-late Aug), the world's oldest amusement park. A blue-collar version of Tivoli, it's a honky-tonk carnival of bumper cars, slot machines and beer halls.

Bakken is on the southern edge of Dyrehaven, an expansive woodland of beech trees and meadows crossed with peaceful walking and cycling trails. Dyrehaven was established in 1669 as a royal hunting ground and has evolved into the capital's most popular picnic area. At its centre, 2km north of Bakken, is the old manor house Eremitagen, a good vantage point for spotting herds of deer.

Frilandsmuseet

This sprawling open-air museum (☎ 33 13 44 11; Kongevejen 100; adult/child Dkr40/free; open 10am-5pm Tues-Sun mid-Apr–Sept, 10am-4pm Tues-Sun Oct) of old countryside homes, workshops and barns is in the town of Lyngby. It's a 10-minute walk from Sorgenfri

Station, which is 25 minutes from Central Station on the S-train's line B (Dkr28).

Louisiana Museum of Modern Art

Louisiana (☎ 49 19 07 91; Gl Strandvej 13; adult/child Dkr68/20; open 10am-5pm Thur-Tues, 10am-10pm Wed), Denmark's foremost modern art museum, is on a seaside knoll in a striking modernistic complex. It is surrounded by delightful grounds full of sculptures by the likes of Henry Moore and Alexander Calder. The permanent collection features works by Giacometti, Picasso, Warhol, Rauschenberg and many more and there are outstanding changing exhibitions. It's a fascinating place even if you're not passionate about modern art. There's a diverting **Children's Wing** and a lakeside **garden**.

The museum is a 10-minute walk north on Strandvej from Humlebæk Station, which is 35 minutes on the S-train's line C from Copenhagen (Dkr49).

Organised Tours

Bus Tours Copenhagen is so easy to get around that there's little need to consider a sightseeing bus tour. However, **Copenhagen Excursions and Vikingbus** (☎ 32 54 06 06) does offer various tours of the city in double-decker buses from Dkr100, children under 11 free, or half price on more expensive tour.

Quickshaw Tours Copenhagen's 'quick-shaws' are two-seater, open carriages powered from behind by remarkably fit young pedal-pushers. They operate daily and can be found at most main squares. Tours start at Dkr180 for an hour. They can also be used as taxis with payment by zone system. Rådhuspladsen to Nyhavn costs Dkr60.

Canal Tours For a different angle on the city, hop onto one of the hour-long boat tours that wind through Copenhagen's canals April to mid-October. Multilingual guides give a lively commentary in English as well as Danish.

The largest company, **DFDS Canal Tours** (adult/child Dkr50/20), leaves from the head of Nyhavn. However, the best deal is with **Netto-Bådene** (adult/child Dkr20/10). Its boats also leave from Nyhavn, as well as from Holmens Kirke, which is opposite the stock exchange. Both companies' tours pass by the Little Mermaid, Christianshavn and

Christiansborg Slot, and leave a few times an hour between 10am and 5pm.

Canal boats also make an excellent, traffic-free alternative for getting to some of Copenhagen's waterfront sites. DFDS Canal Tours charges Dkr40 for a one-day 'waterbus' pass from mid-May to mid-September. The boats leave Nyhavn every 30 minutes between 10.15am and 4.45pm (to 5.45pm mid-June to mid-August) and make a dozen stops, including at the Little Mermaid, Nationalmuseet and Vor Frelsers Kirke, allowing you to get on and off as you like. In addition, the **HT public transport system** has a new boat service (adult/child Dkr26/13) linking the Royal Library, Nyhavn and Nordre Toldbod, near the Little Mermaid, every 20 minutes until 7pm.

Special Events

The **Copenhagen Jazz Festival** (☎ 33 93 20 13; **W** www.cjf.dk) is the biggest event of the year, with 10 days of music in early July. The festival presents a wide range of Danish and international jazz, blues and fusion music. It's a cornucopia of some 500 indoor and outdoor concerts, with music wafting out of practically every public square, park, pub and café from Strøget to Tivoli.

Places to Stay

Rooms & Booking Services The **tourist office** (Bernstorffsgade 1) can book **rooms** in private homes from Dkr300/500 for singles/doubles. It also books unfilled hotel rooms, often at discounted rates. Expect even a double room with shared bath to cost around Dkr500 at many of the hotels listed in this section. However, hotel discounts are based on supply and demand and are not always available during busy periods. There's a Dkr60 fee charged per booking. The airport information booth outside customs offers a similar service.

Use It (Rådhusstræde 13) books private rooms (singles/doubles from Dkr175/250) free of booking fees, keeps tabs on which hostel beds are available, and is a good source of information for subletting student housing and other long-term accommodation.

Camping About 9km west of the city centre near Brøndbyøster Station on the S-train's line B is **DCU Camping Absalon** (☎ 36 41 06 00 fax 36 41 02 93; **e** absalon@dcu.dk; Korsdalsvej 132; adult/child/tent Dkr62/31/20).

Hostels Copenhagen has two HI hostels, each about 5km from the city centre. Both have laundry facilities and guest kitchens. They often fill early from May to September so it's best to call ahead for reservations. Most hostels charge Dkr20 to Dkr40 for hire of sheets.

Danhostel Copenhagen Bellahøj *(☎ 38 28 97 15, fax 38 89 02 10; e bellahoej@ danhostel.dk; Herbergvejen 8; dorm beds/ doubles Dkr95/250; 24hr reception, open 1 Mar-15 Jan)* is in a quiet suburban neighbourhood and has 250 dorm beds and a limited number of family rooms (doubles). You can take bus No 2-Brønshøj from Rådhuspladsen and get off at Fuglsangs Allé. The night bus is 82N.

Danhostel Copenhagen Amager *(☎ 32 52 29 08, fax 32 52 27 08; Vejlands Allé 200, Amager; dorm beds/doubles Dkr95/275; open 15 Jan-30 Nov)*, in an isolated part of Amager just off the E20, is one of the largest hostels in Europe with 528 beds in two-bed and five-bed rooms. Take the S-train to Sjælør Station, then change to bus No 100S, which stops in front of the hostel. Until 5pm Monday to Friday, bus No 46 runs from Central Station directly to the hostel.

Even when the HI hostels are full you can nearly always find a bed at one of the city-sponsored hostels. Though the larger ones tend to be a crash-pad scene, they're more central than the HI hostels and sleeping bags are allowed.

City Public Hostel *(☎ 33 31 20 70, fax 33 55 00 85; e info@city-public-hostel.dk; Absalonsgade 8; dorm beds Dkr130; 24hr reception, open early May–mid-Aug)* sleeps 200 people. There's one 72-bed dorm but the other rooms average six to 23 beds each. Breakfast is available for Dkr25, or Dkr20 if included with the bed price. There's a pleasant garden in front of the hostel. From Central Station, walk west for 10 minutes along Vesterbrogade then bear off left at Vesterbro Torv.

The city-run, 286-bed **Sleep-In** *(☎ 35 26 50 59, fax 35 43 50 58; e copenhagen@ sleep-in.dk; Blegdamsvej 132; dorm beds Dkr90; 24hr reception, open late June-31 Aug)*, in the pleasant Østerbro area, is a few kilometres north of the city centre. It occupies a sports hall that's partitioned off into 'rooms' with four to six beds. There's a group kitchen, a café and free lockers. This is a busy and popular place. Take bus No 1 or 6 from Rådhuspladsen to Trianglen and walk

300m south on Blegdamsvej. Night buses are 85N and 95N.

Sleep-In Green *(☎ 35 37 77 77; w www .sleep-in-green.dk; Ravnsborggade 18; dorm beds Dkr85; open mid-May–mid-Oct)* is in the Nørrebro area, close to cafés and bars. It has 68 dorm beds. Take bus No 5 or 16, or the S-train to Nørreport Station then walk northwest on Frederiksborggade over the canal.

The smallest operation is **YMCA Interpoint** *(☎ 33 31 15 74; Valdemarsgade 15; dorm beds Dkr85; reception 8.30am-11.30am, 3.30pm-5.30pm, 8pm-12.30am, open end June-early Aug)* in the heart of the Vesterbro area. There are only 28 dorm beds in all, so it fills early and calling ahead for reservations is advised. Bed sheets (Dkr15) and breakfast (Dkr25) are available; there's no kitchen. It's a 15-minute walk from Central Station (take Vesterbrogade west to Valdemarsgade), or you can take bus No 3, 6 or 16.

The privately run **Sleep-In Heaven** *(☎ 35 35 46 48; e morefun@sleepinheaven.com; Struenseegade 7; dorm beds Dkr120)*, in the Nørrebro area, has beds in a basement dorm. There is an age limit of 35 years. Breakfast is available for Dkr35, sheets for Dkr20. Take bus No 8 to the Kapelvej stop; the night bus is 92N.

An enjoyable alternative southwest of the city limits is **Belægningen Avedørelejren** *(☎ 36 77 90 84, fax 36 77 95 87; w www .beaegningen.dk; Avedøre Tværvej 10, Hvidovre; dorm beds Dkr100, singles/doubles from Dkr250/350)* in the renovated barracks of a former military camp. Sleeping bags are not allowed, but bed linen and towels are included in the price. Breakfast (Dkr40) is available and there's free Internet access, cheap bicycle rental and a group kitchen. The site also houses Denmark's main movie studios. Take bus No 650S from Central Station to Avedøre School.

Also see **Hotel Jørgensen** in the following Hotels section.

Hotels – Around Central Station Copenhagen's main hotel area lies in Vesterbro on the western side of Central Station, where rows of six-storey, century-old buildings house one hotel after the other. This is also Copenhagen's red-light district, though the only visible sign is a scattering of porn shops and strip clubs. Sad signs of drug use are occasionally evident, but there is no overt sense of unease and Vesterbro has an unthreatening, fairly cheerful atmosphere overall. Most hotels have upgraded their facilities in recent years to include toilet and shower in all rooms. Many are members of chains and reflect a rather bland business and conference ambience. Rates given in this section are for singles/doubles with bath, and with shared bath, where relevant. All rates include breakfast.

Turisthotellet (☎ 33 22 98 39; Reverdilsgade 5; double with bath Dkr450, singles/doubles with shared bath around Dkr250/350) is the area's cheapest hotel and is close to the station. It has small, depressing rooms and a generally shabby decor, but is convenient if you're on a budget and arrive late in the city. Otherwise, consider a hostel.

Hotel Guldsmeden (☎ 33 22 15 00; fax 33 22 15 55; e reception@hotelguldsmeden.dk; Vesterbrogade 66; singles/doubles Dkr795/995) opened in 2002 and is a sister hotel to Hotel Guldsmeden in Århus. It's over 1km from the city centre, but is an exceptionally stylish and welcoming place.

Saga Hotel (☎ 33 24 49 44, fax 33 24 60 33; e booking@sagahotel.dk; Colbjørnsensgade 18-20; singles/doubles Dkr650/800, with shared bath Dkr450/580) has pleasant, modernised room, all with phone and TV.

Tiffany Hotel (☎ 33 21 80 50; fax 33 21 87 50; e tiffany@hoteltiffany.dk; Colbjørnsensgade 28; singles/doubles Dkr895/1095) in a quiet location is an upmarket hotel that has spacious rooms with fridge, microwave cooker, and water-heating facilities. A rather mundane continental-style breakfast is delivered to your room.

Absalon Hotel (☎ 33 24 22 11, fax 33 24 34 11; e info@absalon-hotel.dk; Helgolandsgade 15; singles/doubles Dkr875/1095) has smartly turned out rooms in its main hotel and an annexe of fairly dull rooms where singles/doubles with shared bath are Dkr495/650.

Hebron Hotel (☎ 33 31 69 06; fax 33 31 90 67; e tophotel@hebron.dk; Helgolandsgade 4; singles/doubles Dkr725/950) has comfortable rooms, good facilities and a quiet ambience.

Centrum Hotel (☎ 33 31 31 11, fax 33 23 32 51; e centrum.hotel@adr.dk; Helgolandsgade 14; singles/doubles Dkr680/890) is clean and comfortable, but still shows signs of being in need of further upgrading.

Ibis Hotel (☎ 33 22 11 00, fax 33 21 21 86; e star@accorhotel.dk; Colbjørnsensgade 13; singles/doubles Dkr745) is a modernised hotel that has bright, straightforward rooms.

Missionshotellet Nebo (☎ 33 21 12 17, fax 33 23 47 74; e nebo@email.dk; Istedgade 6; singles/doubles Dkr820/930, with shared bath Dkr510/730) is only a few metres from Central Station. The rooms are small, and cramped in some cases, but are comfy and the shared showers are large and clean.

Selandia Hotel (☎ 33 31 46 10, fax 33 31 46 09; e hotel-selandia@city.dk; Helgolandsgade 12; singles/doubles Dkr775/950, with shared bath Dkr525/650) has reasonably sized, comfortable rooms although the fittings and decor are not enthralling.

Hotels – Elsewhere in Copenhagen A small, friendly and exclusively gay hotel in an excellent location, **Hotel Rainbow** (☎ 33 14 10 20; w www.copenhagen-rainbow.dk; Frederiksbergadde 25; rooms with shared bath Dkr720-835, room with bath Dkr890) is right near the Rådhus end of Strøget. The hotel is on the top floor and has just a few bright and airy rooms. Use the street-level intercom. It's advisable to book ahead.

Sømandshjemmet Bethel (☎ 33 13 03 70, fax 33 15 85 70; Nyhavn 22; singles/doubles Dkr595/745) is in a great location on Nyhavn. It has bright, pleasant rooms and views of Nyhavn's quays from some rooms, although you pay more for a harbour view.

Hotel Jørgensen (☎ 33 13 81 86, fax 33 15 51 05; e hotel@post12.tele.dk; Rømersgade11; dorm beds Dkr120, singles/doubles Dkr575/700, with shared bath dkr475/575), near Nørreport Station, is popular with gay travellers but open to all. Simple rooms have shared bath. The hotel also has 13 dorm rooms and 150 beds.

Cab-Inn Scandinavia (☎ 35 36 11 11, fax 35 36 11 14; e cabinn@cabinn.dk; Vodroffsvej 57; singles/doubles Dkr510/630) has 201 compact rooms that resemble cruise-ship cabins. Though small, the rooms are comfortable and have TV and private bath. If it's full, its sister hotel **Cab-Inn Copenhagen** (☎ 33 21 04 00, fax 33 21 74 09; e cabinn@cabinn.dk; Danasvej 32-34) costs the same and is a few blocks away.

Hotel Opera (☎ 33 47 83 00, fax 33 47 83 01; e hotelopera@arp-hansen.dk; Tordenskjoldsgade 15; singles/doubles Mon-Fri Dkr1160/1490, Sat & Sun Dkr795/995) has a pleasant old-world, if expensive, character.

Copenhagen Admiral Hotel (☎ 33 74 14 14, fax 33 74 14 16; e admiral@admiralhotel

.dk; Toldbodgade 24-28; singles/doubles Dkr1195/1435) is on the waterfront near Nyhavn. Occupying a renovated, 18th-century granary, its 366 rooms blend period charm and modern conveniences. Rates listed are for a harbour-view room, but there are cheaper options. Breakfast is an extra Dkr98.

Places to Eat

Around Central Station The extensive Middle Eastern buffet at **Ankara** *(☎ 33 31 14 99; Vesterbrogade 35; buffet noon-4pm Dkr39, 4pm-midnight Dkr69)* includes dishes such as calamari, chicken, lamb and salads. There's also a fast-food bar with a Dkr20 pitta bread sandwich and soda deal.

For a fancier setting there's **Merhaba** *(☎ 33 25 10 10; Vesterbrogade 39; 3-course dinners Dkr88)*, which has an array of three-course Mediterranean dinners.

For an all-you-can-eat deal there's the **Astor Pizza** *(Vesterbrogade 7; buffet 11am-5pm Dkr49, after 5pm Dkr59)*, just north of Central Station, which has a reasonable pizza-and-salad buffet.

Hard Rock Café *(Vesterbrogade 3)*, near the tourist office, has the expected burgers, brew and rock memorabilia decor.

Scala *(Vesterbrogade)*, opposite Tivoli, is a multistorey building full of fast-food eateries. Good outlets include **Matahari**, with wok-cooked dishes for around Dkr50, and **Italian Corner**, with various pizzas starting at Dkr22 and pasta plates for Dkr42

Central Station has a **DSB café** *(open 5.30am-12.45am Sun-Thur, 5.30am-1.45am Fri-Sat)*, a **supermarket** *(open 8am-midnight daily)*, the **Kringlen** bakery with good breads and pastries, a **fruit shop** and **fast-food** outlets. It also has **Gourmet Marked**, a complex of six deli-style eateries where Dkr36 buys a slice of pizza and a beer, or a quarter-chicken with fries. Most eateries open 6am to 11pm.

Rådhusarkaden, a shopping centre on Vesterbrogade near Rådhus, has the **Irma** grocery store and **Conditori Hans Christian Andersen**, offering sandwiches, pastries and coffee.

Around Strøget A pleasant place to dine is **Peder Oxe** *(☎ 33 11 00 77; Gråbrødre Torv; mains Dkr79-179)*, in a historic building in the cobbled square just north of Strøget. Tasty fish and organic meat dishes are served with a good salad buffet. Lunch is Dkr118.

Next door at **Jensen's Bøfhus** *(☎ 33 32 78 00; Gråbrødre Torv15)*, a branch of the chain steak restaurant, prices are much the same, but the food is less interesting.

On the southwest corner of the square is **Restaurant Gråbrødre Torv 21** *(☎ 33 11 47 07, mains around Dkr150, 3-course meal Dkr298)*, a top venue with good atmosphere both inside and on its outside terrace. Imaginatively prepared lamb and fish dishes are a good choice.

The stylish and friendly **Pasta Basta** *(☎ 33 11 21 31; Valkendorfsgade 22; mains Dkr79-159; open 11.30am-3am Sun-Thur, 11am-5am Fri & Sat)* has a superb selection of hot pasta dishes served with fish and meat mains. There's also an eat-as-much-as-you-like smorgasbord of cold pasta dishes and salads for Dkr30 to Dkr69, with or without other courses. It's worth booking ahead. Downstairs is the Coconut Beach Bar, open the same late hours and with good drink deals.

Samos *(☎ 33 33 00 25; Skindergade 29; buffet noon-5pm Dkr39, after 5pm Dkr79)* has an excellent buffet of Greek specialities and salads, with grilled meat dishes for under Dkr40.

At **Riz Raz** *(☎ 33 15 05 75; Kompagnistræde 20; buffet 11.30am-5pm Mon-Fri, 11.30am-4pm Sat & Sun Dkr49; evening buffet 5pm-11pm Mon-Fri, 4pm-11pm Sat & Sun Dkr59)*, just south of Strøget, you can feast on a Mediterranean-style vegetarian buffet including salads, pasta and felafels.

On the corner opposite Riz Raz is the popular **Heaven** *(☎ 33 15 19 00; Kompagnistræde 18; mains Dkr89-159)* a mostly gay place but welcoming to all. There are cheap drinks between 5pm and 9pm and a great selection of food, from pasta to burritos.

The corner pub **Café Sorgenfri** *(☎ 33 11 58 80; Brolæggerstræde 8)* features some reasonably priced Danish food. Items such as smørrebrød and pickled herring average Dkr38 to Dkr68, while a generous variety plate of traditional hot and cold dishes costs Dkr125.

Just across from Use It is **Restaurant Puk** *(☎ 33 11 14 17; Vandkunsten 8; lunch platter Dkr79-119)*, with a pleasant outside terrace that catches the sun. Next to Use It is a **bakery** that does delicious sandwiches for Dkr28 to Dkr35, including a vegetarian option.

Strøget has an abundance of cheap eateries including hot-dog, hamburger and ice-cream stands and numerous hole-in-the-wall kebab joints selling felafels and kebabs for under Dkr30. The best is **Shawarma Grill House** (16 Frederiksbeggade; open 11am-10pm daily, sandwiches Dkr23, kebabs Dkr44), a bustling spot a two-minute walk from Rådhuspladsen at the western end of Strøget. There's a 24-hour **7-Eleven** mini-market on the corner of Gameltorv.

Café de Paris (Vimmelskaftet 39; buffet Dkr39), in an arcade, has a simple pizza buffet. At **Restaurant Eastern** (buffet 11am-5pm Dkr49, after 5pm Dkr79), in the same arcade, a buffet of Indian and Pakistani dishes is offered.

There are several bakeries in the Strøget area. Recommended is **Reinh van Hauen**, which has a branch at the east end of Strøget and uses organic ingredients. **Netto** supermarket, near the eastern end of Strøget, has relatively cheap prices.

The Latin Quarter A good Turkish buffet of salads, rice and numerous hot and cold dishes and a three-course menu for Dkr99 can be foundin the Latin Quarter at **Ankara** (☎ 33 15 19 15; Krystalgade 8; noon-4pm Dkr39, 4pm-11pm Dkr69).

Studenterhusets (☎ 35 32 38 61; Købmagergade 52; open noon-midnight Mon-Fri) is a relaxed student hang-out with drinks and light eats, including vegetarian or meat sandwiches for Dkr20.

Another place popular with students is **Klaptræet** (Kultorvet 13; dishes under Dkr60), a café overlooking Kultorvet square, which serves burgers, chilli con carne and salads. Continental breakfast costs Dkr28. Kultorvet itself becomes a popular beer garden in summer.

Det Lille Apotek (☎ 33 12 56 06; Store Kannikestræde 15; lunch plates Dkr79-145, 3-course dinner Dkr185) offers Danish lunch plates that include fish fillet, pickled herring and roast pork.

Café Sommersko (Kronprinsensgade 6; dishes Dkr90-110; open 10am-midnight Mon-Fri, 10am-2am Sat) has a big selection of beers and a menu that includes salads at Dkr75, lasagna at Dkr85.

Reef n' Beef (☎ 33 33 00 30; Jarmers Plads 3; mains Dkr91-170), emphatically a meat eaters' paradise, offers traditional Australian dishes such as emu, kangaroo and crocodile. There's also seafood and steaks and good Aussie wines.

Elsewhere in Central Copenhagen For a thoroughly Danish experience, try the herring buffet at **Nyhavns Færgekro** (☎ 33 15 15 88; Nyhavn 5; herring buffet Dkr89), one of the more atmospheric restaurants on the canalside. There are 10 different kinds of prepared herring including baked, marinated and rollmops, with condiments to sprinkle on top and boiled potatoes to round out the meal.

The canalside **Cap Horn** (☎ 33 12 85 04; Nyhavn 21) has good Danish food, including a three-item smørrebrød plate for Dkr69 or a herring, steak and potato plate for Dkr105.

The gay and lesbian café **Sebastian** (Hyskenstræde 10; open noon-2am daily) does tasty sandwiches and light meals and turns into a disco, Le Mirage, on Saturday nights.

You can get good vegetarian food at **Govindas** (☎ 33 33 74 44; Nørre Farimagsgade 82; buffet noon-8.30pm Mon-Sat Dkr59), south of the Botanical Gardens, where the Hare Krishna members offer an all-you-can-eat buffet and vegan meals. Students and senior citizens pay Dkr45 for the standard buffet.

Ida Davidsen (☎ 33 91 36 55; Store Kongensgade 70; smørrebrød Dkr55-165), considered the top smørrebrød restaurant in Denmark, offers an extensive menu of smørrebrød options with some exotic fillings, often topped with raw egg.

The main city **produce market** (Israels Plads; open 9am-5pm Mon-Fri, 9am-2pm Sat), is a few minutes' walk west of Nørreport Station. On Saturday it doubles as a flea market.

Christianhavn & Christiania Both Christianhavn and the Freetown of Christiania have a mix of cheap eateries and pricier places.

Christianshavns Bådudlejning (☎ 32 96 53 53; Overgaden neden Vandet 29; fish & meat mains Dkr110-120) is a deservedly popular place on a canalside deck. It does a tasty lunch menu, including sandwiches for Dkr45 and salads Dkr60 to Dkr70. You can hire rowing boats as well – and just drift away.

Oven Vande Café (☎ 32 95 96 02; Overgaden oven Vandet 44; mains Dkr150-190) is a sunny, corner place with cheerful staff. As well as an evening menu it offers lunch dishes, including sandwiches and salads, for Dkr60 to Dkr70.

Café Wilders (☎ 32 54 71 83; Wildersgade 56; fish & meat mains Dkr135) is an unassuming eatery that does French-inspired food as well as tasty lunchtime salads and a buffet for Dkr58.

In the heart of Christiania, **Morgenstedet** *(Langgaden; mains Dkr35)* is a long-established vegetarian and vegan place where a main dish and salad costs Dkr50. It has a pretty garden and a nonsmoking interior. Typical of Christiania, Morgenstedet, which means 'the morning place', is actually open from noon to 9pm.

Spiseloppen *(☎ 32 57 95 58; Loppebygningen; fish & meat mains Dkr165-185)* is another Christiania institution and a general favourite in Copenhagen. Prices are not entirely budget, but it has excellent food, including a vegetarian main dish for Dkr130. Spiseloppen is in the big Loppe building that also houses the Loppen dance club (see Entertainment following) and the art gallery, **Gallopperiet.**

Entertainment

Copenhagen is a 24-hour party city. For free entertainment simply stroll along Strøget, especially between Nytorv and Højbro Plads, which is a bit like an impromptu three-ring circus of musicians, magicians, jugglers and other street performers. In addition, numerous free concerts are held throughout the summer in city parks and squares.

Copenhagen has scores of backstreet cafés with live music. Entry is often free on weeknights, while there's usually a cover charge averaging Dkr60 at weekends.

Available from Wonderful Copenhagen, the free publications *Nat & Dag, Musik Kalenderen, Film Kalenderen* and *Teater Kalenderen* list concerts and entertainment schedules in detail.

The westside Nørrebro area has a number of good entertainment spots, including **Rust** *(☎ 35 24 52 00; Guldbergsgade 8; admission Dkr30-50)* a multilevel dance venue attracting a college-age crowd; it can get busy and there are queues at weekends. **Stengade 30** *(☎ 35 36 09 38; Stengade 18; admission varies according to what's on)* has a spirited alternative live music and dance scene. **Vega** *(Enghavevej 40)*, in the Vesterbro area, stages hugely popular Friday and Saturday night sessions. Big-name rock bands and underground acts play the 'Big Vega' 1500 capacity venue.

Closer to the centre is **Pumphuset** *(☎ 70 15 65 65; Studiestræde 52)*, featuring rock and blues groups. Admission can be anything from

Dkr50 to Dkr285 for big names. **Copenhagen Jazz House** *(☎ 33 15 26 00; Niels Hemmingsens gade 10)* is the city's leading jazz spot and has a terrific ambience. Danish musicians and occasional international names feature, and after concerts on Thursday, Friday and Saturday nights, the place becomes a lively **disco** *(admission Dkr60; open 1am-5am)*. **Mojo** *(☎ 33 11 64 53; Løngangstræde 21)* is a prime spot for blues, with entertainment nightly. **Huset** *(☎ 33 15 20 02; Rådhusstræde 13)* is in the same courtyard as the Use It information centre. It houses a cinema, theatre, café and restaurant and offers music that includes good jazz. Many music events are free, but it costs about Dkr50 for special events.

In Christianhavn an engaging local bar is **Sofie Kælderen** *(☎ 32 57 27 87; Sofiegade 1)*. It opens noon and does lunches until 4pm and there's often live jazz and rock until late. **Loppen** *(☎ 32 57 84 22; Loppebygningen, Christiania; admission Dkr50-70; disco open 2am-5am Fri-Sat)* is a celebrated venue that has live music from soul to punk rock on various nights and a late disco.

There are numerous **cinemas** showing first-release movies along Vesterbrogade between Central Station and Rådhuspladsen.

Gay & Lesbian Venues Copenhagen has a good number of gay and lesbian bars and clubs and there's a great ease and confidence about gay life in this most civilised of cities. A popular meeting place for gay men is the central **Oscar** *(☎ 33 12 09 99; Rådhuspladsen 77; open noon-2am, kitchen noon-10pm)* near the Rådhus. The long-established **Never Mind** *(Nørre Voldgade 2; open 10pm-6am daily)* is a dance bar for mainly gay men, but with a dash of transgendered and lesbians enjoying its kitsch decor. **Kvindehuset** *(The Women's House; Gothersgade 37)* stages various dance nights for lesbians and has a café and bar. **Masken** *(Studiestræde 33)* is popular with students at weekends, not least because of its special drinks prices. There's a lesbians-only night in the basement section on Thursdays. Near Masken is **Cosy Bar** *(Studiestræde 24)*, a recently brightened up, late-night place for gay men, with a cruisy ambience. There are a fair number of erotic gay clubs in Copenhagen. Check the annual *Gay and Lesbian Guide to Copenhagen*, available in gay cafés and clubs, or check Ⓦ www.panbladet.dk.

Shopping

Copenhagen's main shopping street is Strøget where you can find speciality shops selling top-quality amber and Danish silver, china and glass. The upmarket department stores, **Magasin** and **Illum**, and the stylish **Illums Bolighus**, noted for its designer furniture, are also in the Strøget area. Good speciality shops include the delicatessen **Ostehjørnet** (☎ *33 15 50 11; Store Kongensgade 56)*, just along from Ida Davidsen restaurant, with terrific cheese, meat and wine selections. In the Latin Quarter, **Guf** *(Larsbjornsstræde 21)* is an excellent music shop with a big selection of discs and tapes. There are several outdoor suppliers along the north side of Frederiksborggade. **Fjeld & Fritid** is one of the best. The shops and craft galleries of Christiania are worth a look.

Getting There & Away

Air Copenhagen's modern international airport is in Kastrup, 10km southeast of the city centre. Most airline offices are north of Central Station near the intersection of Vester Farimagsgade and Vesterbrogade.

Bus International buses leave from Central Station; advance reservations on most routes can be made at **Eurolines** (☎ *33 88 70 00; Reventlowsgade 8)*.

Train Long-distance trains arrive and depart from Central Station, a huge complex with eateries and numerous services. There are public showers (Dkr15) at the underground toilets opposite the police office.

There are three ways of buying a ticket, and the choice can be important depending on how much time you have before your train leaves. *Billetautomats* are coin-operated machines and are the quickest, if you've mastered the zone-system prices. They are best for S-train tickets. If you're not rushed, then **DSB Billetsalg** *(open 8am-7pm Mon-Fri, 9.30am-4pm Sat)* is best for reservations. There's a numbered-ticket queuing system. **DSB Kviksalg** *(open 5.45am-11.30pm daily)* is for quick ticket buying, although queues can build at busy times.

Car & Motorcycle The main highways into Copenhagen are the E20, which goes west to Funen and east to Malmö, Sweden; and the E47, which connects to Helsingør. If you're coming into Copenhagen from the north on the E47, exit onto Lyngbyvej (route 19) and continue south to get into the heart of the city.

Car Rental As well as airport booths, the following agencies have city branches at:

Avis (☎ 33 15 22 99) Kampmannsgade 1
Europcar (☎ 33 55 99 00) Gammel Kongevej 13
Hertz (☎ 33 17 90 20) Ved Vesterport 3

Hitching Hitching is seldom rewarding, but if you want to try your luck it's best to start outside the city centre. For rides north, take bus No 1 to Vibenhus Runddel. If you're heading towards Funen, take the S-train's line A to Ellebjerg. **Use It** has a free message board that attempts to link up drivers and riders.

Boat The ferry to Oslo, operated by **DFDS Seaways** (☎ *33 42 30 00; Sankt Annæ Plads)*, departs daily at 5pm. **Bornholmstrafikken's** (☎ *33 13 18 66)* service to Bornholm departs nightly at 11.30pm. Both leave from Kvæsthusbroen, north of Nyhavn.

Getting Around

To/From the Airport A train links the airport with Central Station three times an hour (Dkr19.50, 12 minutes). If your baggage is light, you could also take local bus No 250S (Dkr19.50), which runs between Rådhuspladsen and the airport terminal – but it's much slower.

The airport is 15 minutes and about Dkr160 from the city centre by taxi.

Bus & Train Copenhagen has an extensive public-transit system consisting of a metro rail network called S-train, whose 10 lines pass through Central Station (København H), and a vast bus system, whose main terminus is nearby at Rådhuspladsen.

At the time of writing, a new underground Metro system is being constructed in Copenhagen. It was scheduled to open in 2003, but it is estimated that only part of the system will be open by then. The Metro will mainly be of use to suburban commuters; for travellers there will be a useful link from Copenhagen airport to stations at Kongens Nytorv and Nørreport.

Buses and trains use a common fare system based on the number of zones you pass through. The basic fare of Dkr14 for up to two zones covers most city runs and allows transfers between buses and trains on a single ticket as long as they're made within an hour. Third and subsequent zones cost Dkr7 more with a maximum fare of Dkr49 for travel throughout North Zealand. In place of a single destination ticket, you can buy a *klippekort* (clip card) good for 10 rides in two zones for adult/child Dkr90/45 (three zones for Dkr120/60) or get a 24-hour pass allowing unlimited travel in all zones for adult/child Dk85/42. Children under 12 travel free when accompanied by an adult.

On buses, fares are paid to the driver when you board, while on S-trains tickets are purchased at the station and then punched in the yellow timeclock on the platform.

Trains and buses run from about 5am to 12.30am, though buses continue to run through the night (charging double fare) on a few main routes. For schedule information about buses call ☎ 36 13 14 15; for trains call ☎ 33 14 17 01.

Taxi Taxis with signs saying *'fri'* can be flagged down or you can phone ☎ 35 35 35 35. The cost is Dkr22 flag fall plus about Dkr10 per kilometre from 6am to 3pm, Dkr11 from 3pm to 6am (Dkr13, 11pm to 6am Friday and Saturday). Most taxis accept credit cards.

Car & Motorcycle With the exception of the weekday-morning rush hour, when traffic can bottleneck coming into the city (and going out around 5pm), traffic is usually manageable. Getting around by car is not problematic other than for the usual challenges of finding a parking space in popular places. It's best to explore sights within the city centre on foot or by using public transport, but a car is convenient for reaching suburban sights.

For kerbside parking, buy a ticket from a streetside 'parkomat' and place it inside the windscreen. Search out a blue or green zone where parking costs Dkr7 to Dkr12 an hour; in red zones it's a steep Dkr20. Parking fees must be paid 8am to 6pm in blue and green zones and 8am to 8pm in red zones Monday to Friday, and 8am to 2pm in red and green zones on Saturday. Overnight kerbside parking is generally free and finding a space is not usually too much of a problem.

Bicycle At Central Station, **Københavns Cykler** rents bicycles for Dkr75 a day. For cheaper prices (Dkr40 a day) walk a few blocks northwest to **Danwheel** (*Colbjørnsensgade 3*).

If you just want to ride in the city centre, look for a free-use City Bike – they've got solid spokeless wheels painted with sponsors' logos. There are about 125 City Bike racks scattered throughout central Copenhagen, although available bikes are often few and far between. If you're lucky enough to find one with a bike, deposit a Dkr20 coin in the stand to release the bike. You can return the bicycle into any rack to get your money back.

Except during weekday rush hours, you can carry bikes on S-trains for Dkr12. If you're travelling with your own bike be careful, as expensive bikes are targets for theft on Copenhagen streets.

Zealand

Copenhagen does not entirely outshine the rest of Zealand (Sjælland) and there are numerous places on the island that offer a refreshing break from the capital's relentless charm. Northern Zealand has exhilarating beaches, likeable coastal towns and villages and some breathtaking castles, while a trip to the southern islands of Møn and Falster reveals rural Denmark at its most serene and absorbing.

NORTH ZEALAND
The northern part of Zealand is a compact region of wheat fields and beech woodlands interspersed with small towns and tiny hamlets and with a surprisingly remote northern coastline.

One of the most popular day trips from Copenhagen is a loop tour taking in Frederiksborg Slot in Hillerød and Kronborg Slot in Helsingør. With an early start you might even have time to reach one of the northshore beaches before making your way back to the city, although it is more rewarding to allow an extra day for wandering between shoreline towns.

If you're driving between Helsingør and Copenhagen ignore the motorway and take the coastal road, Strandvej (Route 152), which is far more scenic.

Frederiksborg Slot
Hillerød, 30km northwest of Copenhagen, is the site of Frederiksborg Slot (*adult/child Dkr50/10; open 10am-5pm daily Apr-Oct, 11am-3pm daily Nov-Mar*), an impressive

NORTH ZEALAND

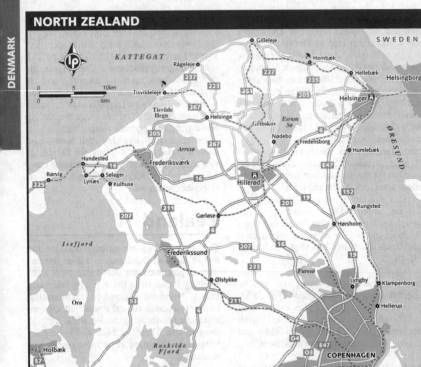

Dutch Renaissance castle that's spread across three islands. The oldest part of the castle dates from Frederik II's time, though most of the present structure was built by his son Christian IV in the early 1600s. After parts of the castle were ravaged by fire in 1859, Carlsberg beer baron JC Jacobsen spearheaded a drive to restore the castle and make it a national museum.

The sprawling castle has a magnificent interior with gilded ceilings, full wall-sized tapestries, royal paintings and antiques. The richly embellished **Riddershalen** (Knights' Hall) and the **coronation chapel**, where Danish monarchs were crowned between 1671 and 1840, are well worth the admission fee.

The S-train (A and E lines) runs every 10 minutes between Copenhagen and Hillerød

(Dkr49), a 40-minute ride. From Hillerød Station follow the signs to Torvet, then continue along Slotsgade to the castle, a 15-minute walk in all. Alternatively, take bus No 701 which can drop you at the gate.

Helsingør (Elsinore)

Helsingør is a busy, attractive port town, with ferries continuously shuttling across the Øresund Strait to and from Sweden. The **tourist office** (☎ 49 21 13 33; Havnepladsen 3; open 9am-5pm Mon-Thur, 9am-6pm Fri, 10am-3pm Sat, mid-June–July; 9am-4pm Mon-Fri, 10am-1pm Sat, Aug–mid-June) is opposite the train station.

PC Billig (☎ 49 21 52 93; Stengade 28D) is an Internet centre that charges Dkr20 an hour.

Things to See Helsingør's top sight is **Kronborg Slot** *(tour Dkr40; open 10.30am-5pm daily July-Sept, 11am-3pm Tues-Sun Nov-Mar)*, made famous as the Elsinore Castle of Shakespeare's *Hamlet*. Kronborg's primary function was not as a royal residence, but rather as a grandiose tollhouse, wresting taxes, the infamous and lucrative 'Sound Dues', for more than 400 years from ships passing through the narrow Øresund. You can cross the moat and walk around the courtyard for free. A guided tour of the chapel, dungeons and royal quarters costs Dkr40/15 per adult/child; or get a combined ticket that includes the **Danish Maritime Museum** for Dkr60/25 per adult/child. The castle is on the northern side of the harbour.

The town itself has been taken in hand over the years and careful preservation work, that has not impinged on Helsingør's commercial life, has created a busy, attractive centre. Øresund trade continues to thrive as crowds of Swedes pour off the ferries to buy bulk alcohol from Helsingør's countless drinks' outlets.

From the tourist office head up Brostræde and along Sankt Anna Gade. This will take you through the **medieval quarter** and past the old cathedral, **Sankt Olai Kirke** *(open 10am-4pm Mon-Sat Apr-Oct, 10am-2pm Mon-Sat Nov-Mar)*; the **City History Museum** *(adult/child Dkr10/free; open noon-4pm daily)*; and **Karmeliterklostret** *(admission Dkr10; open 10am-3pm Mon-Fri mid-May–mid-Sept, 10am-2pm mid-Sept–mid-May)* one of Scandinavia's best-preserved medieval monasteries. From here Sudergade leads to the tree-lined, cobbled central square of **Axeltorv**, which, on sunny days can have an almost Southern European ambience.

Places to Stay & Eat Beachside **Helsingør Camping Grønnehave** *(☎ 49 28 12 12; e campingpladsen@helsingor.dk; Strandalléen 2; adult/child/tent Dkr55/25/35)* is east of **Danhostel Helsingør** *(☎ 49 21 16 40, fax 49 21 13 99; e helsingor@danhostel.dk; Nordre Strandvej 24; dorm beds Dkr100, rooms Dkr250; open Feb-Nov)*. The hostel is 2km northwest of the centre and right on the Øresund.

The tourist office books **rooms** in private homes from Dkr200 to Dkr300/400 for singles/doubles, plus a Dkr25 booking fee. **Hotel Hamlet** *(☎ 49 21 05 91, fax 49 26 01 30; Bramstræde5; singles/doubles Dkr685/895)*

has pleasant rooms. **Hotel Skandia** *(☎ 49 21 09 02, fax 49 21 09 45; Bramstraede 1; singles/doubles with bath Dkr550/650, with shared bath Dkr395/495)*, just down the road, has been updated in recent years and has bright, airy rooms.

Kammercaféen *(sandwiches Dkr35, salads & meat dishes Dkr45-70)*, in the old customs house behind the tourist office, has healthy, well-priced light eats.

Or head for Axeltorv square, four blocks northwest of the train station, which has the moderately priced **Thai Cuisine** *(☎ 4925 15 11; Torvegade 5; mains Dkr85-94)* and **Kødbørsen** *(Sudergade 18B)*, a butcher's shop with cheap takeaway smørrebrød.

Another excellent smørrebrød outlet is **Slagter Baagø** *(☎ 49 21 11 84; Bjergegade 3)* where you can get a mixed lunch plate of fish and meat for Dkr95. Just across the way is the **Helsingør Flutebar** *(☎ 49 20 25 52; Bjergegade 6B; sandwiches around Dkr30)*, which does tasty sandwiches.

The **China Box** *(Stengade 28)* offers food box takeaways for Dkr27 to Dkr35. The nearby **Pakhus Pizzeria** *(☎ 49 21 10 50; Stengade 26C; pizzas & pastas Dkr44-57)* does omelettes for Dkr48 and a youngsters' menu for Dkr30 as well as pizzas and pastas.

Snack Baren *(☎ 49 21 10 18; Hovedvagtsstræde 7a; mains Dkr42)* is a worthwhile budget place that does a different lunch dish every day in the solid Danish meat and vegetables mode. A good breakfast costs Dkr41.

Madam Sprunck *(☎ 49 26 48 49; Stengade 48; mains Dkr145-205)* is a Helsingør institution. It is in a charming courtyard and as well as evening meals in its restaurant, it does a lavish brunch for Dkr88 to Dkr115, salads for Dkr65 and sandwiches for Dkr40 to Dkr85.

Restaurant Sundkroen *(☎ 49 21 37 36; Stationspladsen 3; 3-course menu Dkr198)* is in the old train station and has a good lunch menu.

Entertainment There are several pleasant **bars** in Helsingør, and for 'week-ending' there's **Main Street Dance Bar** *(Stengade 51; open 11pm-7am Fri & Sat)*.

Getting There & Away Trains from Hillerød (Dkr42, 30 minutes) run at least once hourly. Trains from Copenhagen run a few times hourly (Dkr49, 55 minutes). For information on ferries to Helsingborg (Dkr18, 20

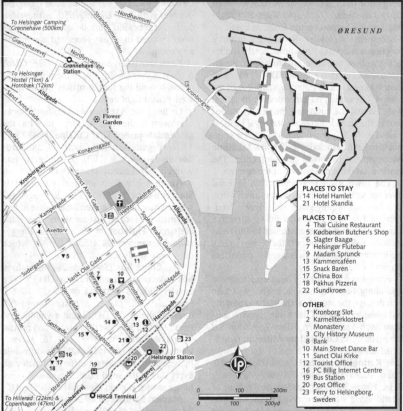

HELSINGØR

ØRESUND

To Helsingør Camping
Grønnehave (500km)
To Helsingør Hostel (1km) &
Hornbæk (12km)

Grønnehave Station

Flower Garden

PLACES TO STAY
14 Hotel Hamlet
21 Hotel Skandia

PLACES TO EAT
4 Thai Cuisine Restaurant
5 Kødbørsen Butcher's Shop
6 Slagter Baagø
7 Helsingør Flutebar
9 Madam Sprunck
13 Kammercaféen
15 Snack Baren
17 China Box
18 Pakhus Pizzeria
22 ISundkroen

OTHER
1 Kronborg Slot
2 Karmeliterklostret Monastery
3 City History Museum
8 Bank
10 Main Street Dance Bar
11 Sanct Olai Kirke
12 Tourist Office
16 PC Billig Internet Centre
19 Bus Station
20 Post Office
23 Ferry to Helsingborg, Sweden

Axeltorv

Helsingør Station

To Hillerød (22km) &
Copenhagen (47km)

HHGB Terminal

0   100   200m
0   100   200yd

---

minutes) see the Getting There & Away section in this chapter.

Zealand's North Coast

The north coast of Zealand has a scattering of small towns whose origins as fishing centres date from the 1500s. Along their backstreets you'll find half-timbered, thatch-roofed houses and flower-filled gardens. The small winter populations are swollen from May to September by throngs of visitors and the beaches are crowded with swimmers, sunbathers and windsurfers; but there's still a refreshing sense of escape from the city lights.

Hornbæk has the best beach on the north coast, a vast expanse of silky white sand that runs the entire length of the town. From the train station, it's a five-minute walk directly

down Havnevej to the harbour and yacht marina. Climb the dunes to the left and you're on the beach. The **library** (☎ 49 70 47 47; W www.hornbaek.dk; Vester Stejlebakke 2A; open 2pm-5pm Mon, Tues & Thur, 10am-5pm Wed & Fri, 10am-2pm Sat) doubles as the **tourist office**; when closed it's window displays a useful map showing local accommodation.

Zealand's northernmost town, **Gilleleje**, has the island's largest fishing port. Around the harbour and yacht marina there's always something interesting to watch, while the thatched houses of the town add to its character. The **tourist office** (☎ 48 30 01 74; W www .gilleleje.dk; Hovedgade 6; open 10am-6pm Mon-Sat mid-June–Aug; 9am-4pm Mon-Fri, 10am-1pm Sat, Aug–mid-June) is in the centre. There are **beaches** to either side of the town and others along the coast to the west, especially at Rågeleje and at Smidrup Strand, where conditions are often good for **windsurfing**.

Tisvildeleje is a pleasant seaside village with a long, straggling main street that leads to an even longer beach. The **tourist office** (☎ 48 70 74 51; ⓦ www.helsinge.com; Banevej 8; open noon-5pm Mon-Fri, 10am-3pm Sat) is in the train station, alongside the **post office**. Behind the beach is **Tisvilde Hegn**, a windswept forest of twisted trees and heather-covered hills laced with good paths.

Places to Stay & Eat Hornbæk has a camping ground, **CampingHornbæk** (☎ 49 70 02 23; ⓔ hornbaek@dcu.dk; Planetvej 4; adult/child/tent Dkr58/29/20). **Hotel Villa Strand** (☎/fax 49 70 00 88; Kystvej 2; singles/ doubles Dkr850/1350) is a pleasant, quiet place to the west of Hornbæk centre and close to the beach. There are cheaper doubles in garden bungalows.

You can get cheap food at the bars and fast-food places at the harbourside and at the western end of Øresundsvej, the road that runs parallel to the beach. On the main road, Nordre Strandvej, **Bella Italia** offers pizzas at Dkr30 and stays open late. **Café Paradis** (Havne Vej 1; meat & fish mains Dkr89-118) does salads for Dkr54.

At Rågeleje, about 10km southwest of Gilleleje, is **Camping Rågeleje** (☎ 48 71 56 40; ⓔ raageleje@dcu.dk; Heatherhill, Hostrupvej 2; adult/child/tent Dkr58/29/ 20). The tourist office in Gilleleje books **rooms** in private homes at around Dkr250/ 350 for singles/doubles, plus a Dkr25 booking fee. Gilleleje's **Hotel Strand** (☎ 48 30 05 12; ⓔ hotelstr@post7.tele.dk; Vesterbrogade 4; singles/doubles Dkr510/760) is a small hotel with reasonable rooms, although some singles are rather small. It's just west of the harbour. It's worth looking for 'room to let signs' especially in the low season when there are some good deals possible.

Gilleleje has several dockside smokehouses where you can buy cheap takeaway fish, but for a real treat there's the charming **Hos Karen & Marie** (☎ 48 30 21 30; Nordre Havnevej 3; fish & meat mains Dkr178) where you can get deliciously prepared hake and trout dishes among others. A terrific lunch platter of fish and meat costs Dkr149.

In Tisvildeleje, the modern 272-bed **Danhostel Tisvildeleje** (☎ 48 70 98 50; ⓔ info@ helene.dk; Bygmarken 30; dorm beds Dkr100, singles/doubles Dkr375/400), is a 10-minute walk from the beach.

The **Tisvildeleje Strandhotel** (☎ 48 70 71 19; ⓔ strand-hotel@strand-hotel.dk; singles/ doubles Dkr495/700, with shared bath Dkr395/590) is right on the main street and has pleasant accommodation that is being steadily updated. The hotel has a popular restaurant that does lunch for Dkr40 to Dkr100 and a five-course evening menu for Dkr350.

Getting There & Away Trains from Hillerød run to Gilleleje and to Tisvildeleje (Dkr32.50), but there's no rail link between the two. Trains from Helsingør go to Hornbæk (Dkr21, 25 minutes) and on to Gilleleje (Dkr42, 40 minutes) twice an hour Monday to Friday and once hourly at weekends. There are also buses, which cost the same, but take a little longer; from Helsingør Station bus No 340 runs to Hornbæk and Gilleleje. Bus No 363 runs every two hours, between Gilleleje and Tisvildeleje (Dkr21, one hour).

ROSKILDE
pop 43,000

Roskilde is ponderous with history. Yet, apart from its magnificent cathedral, there is little visible excitement left in the town centre's modern buildings to recall a remarkable medieval heritage. Roskilde was Denmark's original capital and was a thriving trading port throughout the Middle Ages. It was also the site of Zealand's first Christian church, built by Viking king Harald Bluetooth in AD 980. As Roskilde was the centre of Danish Catholicism, it suffered some decline after the Reformation, and its population shrank. Today it's a pleasantly low-profile place, serene and well ordered – even the public toilet in the main square has carpets. Its quietude is disturbed only during the annual Roskilde Festival.

Orientation & Information

You can walk between the main sights. Roskilde Domkirke is on Torvet, 10 minutes northwest of the train station; cut diagonally across the old churchyard and go left along Algade. The harbourside Viking Ship Museum is north of the cathedral, a pleasant 15-minute stroll through city parks.

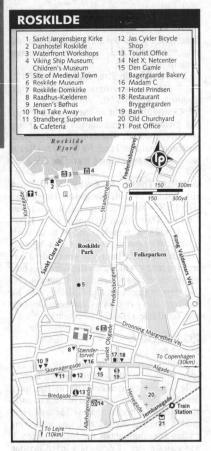

ROSKILDE

1 Sankt Jørgensbjerg Kirke
2 Danhostel Roskilde
3 Waterfront Workshops
4 Viking Ship Museum;
   Children's Museum
5 Site of Medieval Town
6 Roskilde Museum
7 Roskilde Domkirke
8 Raadhus-Kælderen
9 Jensen's Bøfhus
10 Thai Take Away
11 Strandberg Supermarket
   & Cafeteria
12 Jas Cykler Bicycle
   Shop
13 Tourist Office
14 Net X; Netcenter
15 Den Gamle
   Bagergaarde Bakery
16 Madam C
17 Hotel Prindsen
18 Restaurant
   Bryggergarden
19 Bank
20 Old Churchyard
21 Post Office

Roskilde has a helpful **tourist office** (☎ 46 35 27 00; W www.destination-roskilde.com; Gullandsstræde 15; open 9am-5pm Mon-Fri, 10am-1pm Sat June-Aug; 9am-5pm Mon-Thur, 9am-4pm Fri, 10am-1pm Sat Sept-June).

There are Internet cafés side by side at **Net-X** (Allehelgensgade 15) and **Netcenter** (Grønnegade 2), both charging about Dkr7 for 15 minutes.

Roskilde Domkirke

Though most of Roskilde's medieval buildings have vanished in fires over the centuries, the imposing cathedral (☎ 46 35 27 00; Domkirkepladsen; adult/child Dkr15/10; open 9am-4.45pm Mon-Sat, 12.30pm-4.45pm Sun Apr-Sept; 9am-4pm Mon-Fri, 10am-1pm Sat Aug–mid-June) still dominates the city centre. Started by Bishop Absalon in 1170, Roskilde Domkirke has been rebuilt and added to so many times that it represents a millennium of Danish church architectural styles. It's protected under Unesco's World Heritage List.

The cathedral has tall spiky **spires**, eye-catching in their disproportionate slenderness compared with the solidity of the rest of the building. The cathedral interior is splendid; its **crypts** contain the *sarcophagi* of 39 Danish kings and queens. Some are lavishly embellished and guarded by marble statues of knights and women in mourning. Others are simple and unadorned. There's something awesome about being able to stand so close to the remains of so many of Scandinavia's powerful historical figures, though again, the weight of all this history – the overwhelming solidity of the monuments themselves – bears down heavily on the spirit. For light relief, take a look at the 16th-century **clock** above the entrance, where a tiny St George on horseback marks the hour by slaying a yelping dragon.

The cathedral sometimes closes for weddings and funerals; check in advance by calling the tourist office.

Other Attractions

From the northern side of the cathedral, you can walk across a field where wildflowers blanket the unexcavated remains of Roskilde's original medieval town, continuing through a green belt all the way to the **Viking Ship Museum** (☎ 46 30 02 00; Vindeboder 12; adult/child Dkr60/35, low season Dkr45/28; open 9am-5pm daily 1 May-30 Sept, 10am-4pm daily 1 Oct-30 Apr).

This well-presented museum contains five reconstructed Viking ships (circa 1000), excavated from the bottom of Roskilde Fjord in 1962 and brought to shore in thousands of fragments.

A short walk west along the harbour will bring you first to the **waterfront workshops** where Viking ship replicas are being built using Viking-era techniques. Then continue west to the **Sankt Jørgensbjerg quarter**, where the cobbled Kirkegade walkway leads through a neighbourhood of old straw-roofed houses into the courtyard of the 11th-century **Sankt Jørgensbjerg Kirke**.

Roskilde Museum (☎ 46 36 60 44; Sankt Olsgade 15; adult/child Dkr25/free) has displays on Roskilde's rich history.

Special Events
The **Roskilde Festival** (W *www.roskilde-fes
tival.dk*), Northern Europe's largest music
festival, rocks Roskilde each summer on a
weekend in late June/early July. This is a
major European event that draws vast numbers of festivalgoers.

A special reception stall is set up in Copenhagen's main station a week before the event
and Roskilde's genteel centre is filled with alternative fashion – and alternative attitudes –
for days. The festival site is on the outskirts
of the town. There are half a dozen main
stages featuring about 150 bands and performers. Past stars include Bob Dylan, the Pet
Shop Boys, Robbie Williams and the Chem-
ical Brothers. The festival is also a showcase
for up-and-coming talent and new trends.
Camping is free, but tightly packed, and there
are subsidiary happenings and events.

There is a shuttle train service to the festival site from Roskilde Station and a shuttle
bus from the bus station. Roskilde Festival
2003 is scheduled for 26–29 June and 2004 is
set for 1–4 July.

Places to Stay & Eat
The tourist office books **rooms** in private
homes at Dkr175/350 for singles/doubles,
plus a Dkr25 booking fee. The harbourside
Danhostel Roskilde (☎ *46 35 21 84, fax 46
32 66 90;* e *danhostel.roskilde@post.tele
.dk; Vindeboder 7; dorm beds Dkr100,
rooms Dkr400*), is adjacent to the Viking
Ship Museum.

Hotel Prindsen (☎ *46 30 91 00;* e *info@
hotelprindsen.dk; Algade 13; singles/doubles
Dkr995/1295*) is a plush central hotel boasting past guests such as HC Andersen. Its
restaurant offers mains, starting at Dkr155
and a brunch buffet for Dkr115.

Budget eateries include **Madam C**, a food
kiosk in the main square open from April to
October and offering sandwiches for Dkr30.
Thai Take Away (*Skomagergade 42; mains
Dkr55-99*) does a Thai box for Dkr35. Also
on Skomagergade, **Strandberg Supermarket**
has a rooftop cafeteria with a daily lunch dish
for Dkr45 and sandwiches, including with
vegetarian fillings, for Dkr35; **Jensen's
Bøfhus** serves inexpensive steak lunches.
Den Gamle Bagergaarde (*Algade 6*) is a
bakery with good pastries and sandwiches.
Restaurant Bryggergården (☎ *46 35 01
03; Algade 15; menu Dkr188-208*) offers a
good selection of smørrebrød for Dkr38 to
Dkr68. For a treat, the atmospheric **Raadhus-
Kælderen** (☎ *46 36 01 00; Staændertorvet;
2-/3-course dinner Dkr218/238*) in the old
town hall (circa 1430) offers a fish lunch for
Dkr36 to Dkr68. On Friday and Saturday,
from 11.30pm to 5am, the restaurant is transformed into a disco for the 20 to 30 crowd.

Getting There & Away
Trains from Copenhagen to Roskilde are frequent (Dkr49, 25 minutes). From Copenhagen by car, route 21 leads to Roskilde;
upon approaching the city, exit onto route
156, which leads into the centre.

Getting Around
Parking discs are required in Roskilde. There
are car parks off Læderstræde, just south of
Aldgade, Roskilde Museum and near the
Viking Ship Museum.

A bicycle rental shop **Jas Cykler** (☎ *46 35
04 20; Gullandsstræde 3*), just off Skoma-
gagergade, rents distinctive yellow bikes for
Dkr50 per day.

KØGE
pop 33,500
The one-time medieval trading centre of
Køge, 42km south of Copenhagen, retains an
engaging core of historic buildings that line
the narrow streets leading off the broad and
busy main square, Torvet. The **tourist office**
(☎ *56 67 60 01;* W *www.visitkoege.com;
Vestergade 1; open 9am-5pm Mon-Fri, 9am-
2pm Sat*) is just off the square. There's an Internet centre, **Pc-Junglen** (*Nørregade 22E*)
in an arcade opposite Sankt Nicolai Kirke
that charges Dkr25 an hour.

You can park in Torvet, but for one hour
only during the day, and there are longer-
term car parks near the train station. Time
discs are required.

A stroll around central Køge is rewarding.
The tourist office's free magazine describes a
route that takes in 30 of the town's finest
buildings. You'll find Denmark's oldest **half-
timbered building** (circa 1527) at Kirke-
stræde 20, a marvellous survivor with a fine
raked roof. Køge's **historical museum** (☎ *56
63 42 42; Nørregade 4; admission Dkr20*) is
in a splendid building dating from 1619. Another gem is **Brogade 23**, decorated with
cherubs carved by the famed 17th-century
artist Abel Schrøder.

Places to Stay & Eat

Danhostel Køge (☎ 56 65 14 74, fax 56 66 08 69; e koegedanhostel@koegkom.dk; Vamdrupvej 1; dorm beds Dkr90, rooms Dkr400) is 2km northwest of the centre. The tourist office can book double **rooms** in private homes from Dkr450 plus a Dkr25 booking fee.

The busy **Centralhotellet** (56 65 06 96, fax 56 66 02 07; Vestergade 3; doubles with bath Dkr590, singles/doubles with shared bath Dkr270/490) is right on the edge of Torvet and has passable rooms. It's advised to book ahead.

Hotel Niels Juel (☎ 56 63 18 00; e eniel sjuel@post.tele.dk; Toldbodvej 20; singles/doubles Dkr930/1150), a Best Western hotel on a dockside road, has discounts from May to September for its typical business-bland, but comfy, rooms.

Guld Bageren, on the northern side of Torvet, does hearty baguette sandwiches for Dkr31, delicious cakes and pastries, and large coffees. An outstanding restaurant is **StigAnn** (☎ 56 63 03 30; Sankt Gertruds Stræd 2; 3-course menu Dkr288) where lunches of salmon, lobster or duck cost about Dkr70 and fish mains, including halibut, cost Dkr195.

Entertainment

Køge has a number of pleasant bars, one of the best being the atmospheric **Hugos Vinkjælder** (Brogade 19), tucked away off Brogade in the little courtyard of Hugos Gård. It has an eclectic selection of over 70 beers including brews from Eastern Europe to Scotland. There's summer jazz in the courtyard. For late night-early morning action, until 7am, **Ritz** (Torvet 22) caters for all tastes in three different dance venues.

Getting There & Away

Køge's train and bus stations are at Jernbanegade 12 on the east side of town. The train station is at the southernmost point of greater Copenhagen's S-train network, at the end of the E line. Trains to Copenhagen run three times an hour (Dkr49, 38 minutes). The bus to Copenhagen (Dkr49, one hour) leaves from outside the train station.

TRELLEBORG

Trelleborg (Trelleborg Allé; adult/child Dkr35/20; open 10am-5pm daily Easter-Oct, 1pm-3pm daily Nov-Easter), in the countryside of southern Zealand, is the best preserved of Denmark's four Viking ring fortresses.

The earthen-walled fortress, which dates from 980, has two compounds, the inner of which is cut with gates at the four points of the compass. The gates are linked by paths, one east-west, the other north-south, which divide the inner ward into four symmetrical quadrants. In Viking times, each quadrant contained four long elliptical buildings of wood that surrounded a courtyard. Each of the 16 buildings, which served as barracks, was exactly 100 Roman feet long (29.5m).

You can walk up onto the grassy circular rampart and readily grasp the geometric design of the fortress. Cement blocks have been placed to show the outlines of the house foundations. Plaques point out burial mounds and other features. It is a fascinating place, but the understandable absence of even vestigial wooden ruins creates a sense of anti-climax overall. Nearby is a replica longhouse built in stave style. It is now known to be an inaccurate design, but it does add a romantic sheen. There is a museum, and a separate area is given over to more reconstructions of typical Viking-period buildings. A few costumed interpreters demonstrate old trades and, for a small fee, you can try your hand at bread baking or archery. Spear throwing is free – as it no doubt always was. The museum and office building closes at 5pm, but you can still wander about the grounds in the evening.

Trelleborg is 7km west of Slagelse. To get there, take the train to Slagelse (Dkr52, 33 minutes from Roskilde) and then either catch the hourly bus No 312 to Trelleborg (Dkr12, 12 minutes), take a taxi, or rent a bicycle from a shop near the Slagelse tourist office.

MØN, FALSTER & LOLLAND

The three main islands south of Zealand – Møn, Falster and Lolland – are all reached from the mainland, and from each other, by various bridges. Møn is celebrated for its spectacular, and totally un-Danish, sea cliffs of bone-white chalk; Falster has fine sandy beaches, and Lolland, the largest and least interesting island, has a handful of scattered sights including a drive-through safari park.

Møn

It's worth spending some time on Møn, provided you're not looking for too much nightlife. Pleasant beaches lie at the end of narrow seaward lanes; the island's medieval churches have remarkable frescoes, and there are numerous prehistoric remains, including a couple of impressive passage graves. The main attractions on Møn are the white cliffs and the woods of Møns Klint on the east coast.

One downside is that the island's bus service is sketchy, and to get the best out of Møn, having your own transport is a help.

Stege, the main settlement on Møn, is an everyday place, but it is enlivened by its role as the island's gateway town and main commercial centre. Møn **tourist office** (☎ 55 86 04 00; W www.moen-touristbureau.dk; Storegade 2; open 10am-5pm Mon-Fri, 9am-6pm Sat, 11am-1pm Sun mid-June–Aug; closed Sun Sept–mid-June) is at the entrance to Stege and has good information on the entire island.

Stege Kirke (Provstesstræde; admission free; open 9am-5pm Tues-Sun) has unique medieval frescoes and a carved pulpit whose images reflect entertaining interpretations of the bible.

Møns Klint The chalk cliffs at Møns Klint were created during the final Ice Ages when the calcareous deposits from aeons of compressed seashells were uplifted from the ocean floor. The gleaming white cliffs rise sharply for 128m above an azure sea, presenting one of the most striking landscapes in Denmark. The cliffs are being constantly eroded and are friable. Black seams of flintstone and chert ripple across the face of the chalk like blackened teeth, and their broken fragments remain, after landfalls, as sea-washed pebbles on the narrow beach at the base of the cliffs. The chalk subsoil of the land above the cliffs supports a terrific variety of wild flowers including vivid orchids. There is a strict embargo on picking wild flowers.

Møns Klint is a very popular tourist destination and the wooded arrival point above the cliffs has a busy cafeteria, souvenir shops and picnic grounds; but none of this detracts from the natural appeal of the cliffs themselves. Parking costs Dkr25. Take care of your ticket; you need to expose it to a scanner at the exit barrier.

The woods of Klinteskoven, behind the cliffs, have a network of paths and tracks. From near the cafeteria you can descend the cliffs by a series of wooden stairways. It's quite a long descent and, consequently, a strenuous return. From the base of the steps turning south along the narrow beach leads in about 1km to another stairway at Gråryg Fald. These take you

steeply to the cliff top, from where a path leads back to the car park. Turning north at the base of the descent stairway leads, in just over 1km, to another stairway at Sandskredsfald that again takes you back to the cliff top. In winter, and after heavy rain, unstable lumps of chalk may break off and fall to the beach and you should keep this in mind. Warning notices and barriers should be heeded.

Passage Graves Møn has a wealth of prehistoric remains, although many are vestigial burial mounds. The best preserved sites are the Late-Stone-Age passage graves of **Kong Asgers Høj** and **Klekkende Høj**. Both are on the west side of the island within a 2km radius of the village of Røddinge, from where they are signposted. Kong Asgers Høj is close to the narrow road and parking space is minimal. The site is extremely well preserved and comprises a grassy mound pierced by a low passageway that leads to a splendid stone-lined chamber. Take a torch and mind your head. Klekkende Høj is on a hilltop amid fields. From a car park, follow a signposted track and path to reach the grave. The grave has a double chamber and again you need a torch and some agility to creep inside. One of the routes described in the cycle tour printout (see Cycling later) takes in these sites and others.

Churches of Møn Taking a leap forward from the passage graves of the Late Stone Age leads to the churches of Møn. These are tall, gaunt buildings that punctuate the landscape, with their striking, yet somehow inelegant crow-stepped towers. Most of the buildings are medieval and many are graced with the best-preserved primitive frescoes in Denmark. The frescoes depict biblical scenes, often interpreted through lighthearted rustic imagery. These frescoes were obliterated with whitewash by post-Reformation Lutherans fearful of what they saw as too much Roman exuberance. Ironically, the whitewash dealt a blow to bigotry by preserving the frescoes, and 20th-century restoration has revealed them in all their glory. The style of Møn fresco painting owes much to the Emelunde-mestteren (the Elmelunde Master), an accomplished stylist of unknown name. Some of his finest work can be see at **Elmelunde Kirke** (Kirkebakken 41; admission free; open 7am-5pm daily Apr-Sept, 8am-4pm daily Oct-May) on the road to Møns Klint.

Cycling Although robust at times, cycling on Møn is rewarding given the island's uncharacteristic hilliness. The tourist office has a route map and an excellent printout guide, in English, to seven bike tours on the island. All have special themes, including bird life and prehistory. One of the tours even takes in the nearby island of Bogø.

Places to Stay & Eat About 3km from the cliffs, **Camping Møns Klint** (✆ 55 81 20 25; e camping@klintholm.dk; open 1 Apr-1 Nov; adult/child/tent Dkr60/35/10) is in a pleasant woodland setting. **Danhostel Møns Klint** (✆ 55 81 20 30, fax 55 81 28 18; open 1 May-1 Oct; dorm beds Dkr100 rooms Dkr280) is in a former lakeside hotel opposite the camping ground.

Pension Elmehøj (✆ 55 81 35 35; e pension-moen@vip.cybercity.dk; Kirkebakken 39; singles/doubles with shared bath Dkr265/430), right next to Elmelunde Kirke, has pleasant, simple rooms and is an ideal base for exploring Møn. There is a summer café here where you can buy packed lunches for Dkr45 and an evening meal for Dkr100. There are also bikes for rent at Dkr42 per day.

At Møns Klint car park the **cafeteria** does a range of meals including fish and chips for Dkr59. In Stege, there are bakeries and supermarkets and a handful of cafés. For terrific smørrebrød, try the cheerful **Stig's Slagterforretning** (✆ 55 81 42 67; Storegade 59; fish & meat portions Dkr15-32) where a new restaurant should be open by the time you read this.

Getting There & Away From Copenhagen take the train to Vordingborg (Dkr92, 1½ hours) from where it's a 45-minute (Dkr32) bus ride to Stege. From late June to mid-August, buses make the 45-minute run (Dkr13) from Stege to Møns Klint a few times a day. The bus stops at the hostel and camping ground en route.

Falster

The east coast of Falster is lined with white sandy beaches that attract huge numbers of German and Danish holiday-makers, many of whom own tree-shrouded cabins along the wooded coastline.

The most glorious stretch of beach is at **Marielyst**, which is 12km from the island's main settlement of Nykøbing Falster. Marielyst has the building style of a Mediterranean resort, although from its main drag you can't see the beach for the trees. The beach draws crowds in summer, but it's so long that you can always achieve some sense of tenuous escape. You reach the sea down various lanes that slice through the tree line. Parking is not obvious and many of these lanes are the jealously guarded preserves of residents and holiday-cabin occupants. The most convenient access and parking is straight on from the junction of the resort's main street, Marielyst Strandvej with the north-south road, Bøtøvej. There is parking down seaward access lanes at roughly every kilometre as you go south along Bøtøvej from the crossroads.

The **tourist office** (✆ 54 13 62 98; w www.marielyst.org; Marielyst Strandpark 3; open 9am-5pm Mon-Sat mid-June–Aug; 9am-4pm Mon-Fri, 10am-2pm Sat Sept–mid-June) is in a modern complex on the western entrance to the resort as you come in from the E55. Go left at the big roundabout.

Places to Stay & Eat The central **Marielyst Camping** (✆ 54 13 53 07; Marielyst Strandvej 36; adult/child/tent Dkr60/15/15) has a long season and is popular with young families. The nearest hostel to Marielyst is **Danhostel Nykøbing F** (✆ 54 85 66 99; e nyk.f@danhostel.dk; OAllé 110; dorm beds Dkr100, rooms Dkr400), just 1km east of Nykøbing Falster's train station, and opposite the zoo.

The tourist office can arrange bed & breakfast on the island for about Dkr250 per person.

In Marielyst itself, **Hotel Marielyst Strand** (✆ 54 13 68 88; e info@hotel-marielyst.dk; Torvet; singles/doubles Dkr545/695) is a pleasant, central place with smart rooms.

Marielyst has plenty of cafés, hot-dog stands and ice-cream shops. A good alternative to fast food is **Schous Kødcenter** (✆ 54 13 62 71; Bøtøvej 8), which sells inexpensive cod cakes, grilled chicken and deli takeaways; there's a fruit and vegetable stand next door and there's a good bakery near the camping ground.

Getting There & Around Trains leave Copenhagen hourly for Nykøbing F (Dkr118, two hours), from where it's a Dkr22 bus ride to Marielyst (25 minutes) or Gedser (35 minutes) further south. From Gedser there are daily ferries every two hours from May to September, to Rostock, Germany. The trip takes two hours and costs Dkr35 per person. It's Dkr450 for a car with up to five people, but transforms into a rather monopolistic Dkr610 at weekends.

You can rent bikes – useful in Marielyst – for Dkr40 per day, next door to the tourist office at **Sydsol** (☎ 54 16 16 16).

Lolland

Lolland sounds thoroughly laid back by name alone and the island's landscape is flat and repetitive – the highest point is only 30m. But this is very Danish Denmark, there is a pleasant sense of escape from the mainstream and there are a handful of diverting sights.

The main town of **Maribo** has an engaging charm, not least because of its lakeside setting. Maribo's **tourist office** (☎ 54 78 04 96; W www.lolland-falster.dk; Torvet; open 10am-5pm Mon-Fri, 10am-1pm Sat) is on the attractive main square and has masses of information on the island. The town stands amid a scattering of lakes, and its handsome, 15th-century, red-brick **Domkirken** overlooks the gleaming waters of the Søndersø. There are pleasant lakeside **walks** and Maribo has a number of interesting **museums**.

About 7km north of Maribo is **Knuthenborg Safari Park** (☎ 54 78 80 88; Bandholm; adult/child Dkr88/46; open 9am-5pm May-Sept) a drive-through estate with rhinos, giraffes, zebras, tigers and other exotic animals roaming freely.

Maribo Sø Camping (☎ 54 78 00 71; e camping@maribo-camping.dk; Bangshavevej 25; adult/child/tent Dkr58/30/5) is in a pretty lakeside setting. **Danhostel Maribo** (☎ 54 78 33 14; W www.danhostel.dk/maribo; Søndre Boulevarde 82; dorm beds Dkr85, rooms Dkr255) is about 2km southeast of Torvet. The tourist office can book **rooms** at Dkr200/350 (singles/doubles). The pleasant **Ebsens Hotel** (☎ 54 78 10 44; Vestergade 32; singles/doubles Dkr500/625, with shared bath Dkr350/525) has some strikingly decorated larger rooms.

Vestergade, the main street running west from Torvet, has several cafés, a good bet being **Café Maribo** (Vestergade 6; mains Dkr59-98) with smørrebørd for Dkr15 to Dkr24 and sandwiches for Dkr38.

Trains run between Nykobing F on Falster to Maribo (Dkr30, 25 minutes) and on to Nakskov (Dkr48, 47 minutes) every hour Monday to Friday, less at weekends.

Bornholm

pop 44,000
You should take your time over Bornholm. This is no day-trip island, but a remarkable self-contained little world, 200 escapist kilometres east of Copenhagen and nearer to Sweden, Germany and Poland than to the mother country. Life is satisfyingly slow-paced, but never dull.

Bornholm's history reflects its position at the heart of the Baltic and in its time Sweden, Germany and Soviet Russia have occupied it. Always Danish, the island fell into Swedish hands in the 17th century, but was won back for Denmark by a fierce local rebellion. The island suffered cruelly in the chaos at the end of WWII.

It was occupied by the Nazis, but when Germany surrendered to the Allies in May 1945 the German commander on Bornholm resisted and Rønne and Nexø suffered heavy damage from Soviet air raids.

On 9 May the island was handed over to the Soviets who remained in situ until the following year, when Bornholm regained its essential Danishness.

The centre of the island is a lush swathe of wheat fields and forests. The coast is beaded with small fishing villages and stretches of powdery white sand. It is low-lying and accessible for most of its length, except in the northwest, where granite cliffs and reef-lined shores create a striking contrast.

Unique among Bornholm's attractions are its four 12th-century **round churches**, splendid buildings whose whitewashed walls, 2m-thick, are framed by solid buttresses and crowned with black, conical roofs. Each was designed not only as a place of worship, but also as a fortress against enemy attacks, with an upper storey pierced by gun slots. All four churches are still used for Sunday services, but are otherwise open to visitors from Monday to Saturday.

Getting There & Away

Bornholmstrafikken (☎ 33 13 18 66; W www.bornholmstrafikken.dk) operates ferries between Copenhagen and Rønne that leave at 11.30pm daily (in both directions), take seven hours and cost Dk224/112 (adult/child). Add Dkr74 for a dorm bunk, Dkr176 per person for a double cabin, or spread out your sleeping bag

DENMARK

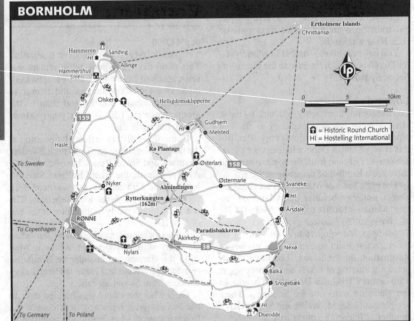

BORNHOLM

Ertholmene Islands
Christiansø

Hammeren · Sandvig
HI
Allinge
Hammershus Slot

Olsker · Helligdomsklipperne

159

Gudhjem
HI · Melsted

Hasle

Rø Plantage

Østerlars
HI
158

Nyker

Østermarie

Svaneke
HI

Almindingen

Rytterknægten (162m)

Årsdale

RØNNE
HI

To Copenhagen

Paradisbakkerne

Åkirkeby

To Sweden

Nylars

38

Nexø

Balka

Snogebæk

To Germany · To Poland

HI
Dueodde

🏛 = Historic Round Church
HI = Hostelling International

0 — 5 — 10km
0 — 3 — 6mi

in the lounge for free. This is the slowest route, but it also provides a cheap night's sleep. It costs Dkr62 to take a bicycle, Dkr172 for a motorcycle and Dkr460 for a car. From mid-June to mid-August there's also a day ferry, except on Wednesday, that leaves Copenhagen at 8.30am and returns from Rønne at 3.30pm.

Bornholmstrafikken also operates the ferry service that runs several times daily between Rønne and Ystad, Sweden (Dkr180 one way or same-day return, 1½ hours) and on a near-daily basis from May to September from Sassnitz-Mukran in Germany (Dkr130, 3½ hours). The Ystad and Sassnitz–Mukran prices are high season and can be about 20% less in the low season.

A quicker option is the train-ferry combination from Copenhagen to Rønne via Ystad, Sweden. This trip goes a few times a day, takes three hours and costs Dkr205. The same route by bus costs Dkr195 and takes 3½ hours.

The quickest option of all is to fly with **Cimber Air** (☎ 74 42 22 77; ⓦ www.cimber .dk), which operates several flights a day between Copenhagen and Bornholm. The trip takes just 35 minutes and costs Dkr869 one

way, although you can get cheaper prices by booking ahead.

Getting Around

To/From the Airport The island's airport, Bornholms Lufthavn, is 5km southeast of Rønne, on the road to Dueodde. Bus No 7 stops on the main road in front of the airport.

Bus A good, inexpensive bus service around the island is operated by **Bornholms Amts Trafikselskab (BAT)**. Fares are based on a zone system and cost Dkr8.50 per zone, with the maximum fare set at 10 zones. Ask the bus driver about a 'RaBATkort', which is good for 10 rides, can be used by more than one person and saves about 20%. There are also day/week passes for Dkr110/370. Buses operate all year, but schedules are less frequent from October to April. From May to September, bus No 7 leaves from the Rønne ferry terminal every two hours between 8am and 4pm and goes anti-clockwise around the island, stopping at Dueodde beach and all major coastal villages before terminating at Hammershus. Other buses make direct runs from Rønne to Nexø, Svaneke, Gudhjem and Sandvig.

DENMARK

Car & Scooter Motor scooters/cars can be rented from Dkr225/620 a day at **Europcar** (☎ 56 95 43 00; *Nordre Kystvej 1, Rønne*). The office is in the petrol station just along the road from the ferry terminal.

Bicycle Cycling is a great way to get around. Bornholm is crisscrossed by more than 200km of bike trails, many built over former rail routes. You can start right in Rønne, from where bike routes fan out to Allinge, Gudhjem, Nexø, Dueodde and the central forest. Rønne tourist office sells a 60-page English-language *Bicycle Routes on Bornholm* (Dkr40), which maps out routes and describes sights along the way.

In Rønne, **Bornholms Cykeludlejning** (☎ 56 95 13 59; e *bornholms.cykeludlejning@ teliamail.dk; Nordre Kystvej 5*), next to the tourist office, has a large fleet of bikes renting at Dkr60 a day. Bicycles can usually be rented from hostels and camping grounds around the island for about Dkr55 a day.

RØNNE

pop 15,000

Rønne is a charming little town with a number of engaging museums and an old quarter of cobbled streets flanked by pretty single-storeyed dwellings. It is the island's largest settlement and is a popular shopping destination for Swedes on day trips.

The **tourist office** (*Bornholms Velkomstcenter;* ☎ 56 95 95 00; *Nordre Kystvej 3; open 9.30am-5.30pm Mon-Fri, 10am-4pm Sat late June-Aug; 9am-4pm Mon-Fri, 10am-1pm Sat Mar, May, Sept & Oct; 9am-4pm Mon-Fri Nov-Feb)* is a few minutes' walk from the harbour and has masses of information on all of Bornholm.

Two very pleasant streets with period buildings are the cobblestoned **Laksegade** and **Storegade**.

Bornholms Museum (☎ 56 95 07 35; *Sankt Mortensgade 29; adult/child Dkr30/ 10; open 10am-5pm Mon-Sat)* has an entertaining collection of local history exhibits. **Hjorths Fabrik** (☎ 56 95 01 60; *Krystalgade 5; adult/child Dkr30/10; open 10am-5pm Mon-Sat)* is a ceramics museum complete with working features.

The handsome round church, **Nylars Rundkirke**, built in 1150 and decorated with 13th-century frescoes, is only a 15-minute ride from Rønne on bus No 6.

Galløkken Camping (☎ 56 95 23 20, fax 56 95 37 66; w *www.gallokken.dk; Strandvejen 4; open mid-May–Aug; adult/child Dkr56/28)* is just over 1km south of the town centre. It rents bikes for Dkr55 to Dkr65 per day. The 140-bed **Danhostel Rønne** (☎ 56 95 13 40, fax 56 95 01 32; e *rvh@post4.tele.dk; Arsenalvej 12; dorm beds Dkr100, singles/ doubles Dkr220/350)* is nearby. The tourist office books **rooms** in private homes at Dkr195/ 280 for singles/doubles; there's no booking fee.

Pleasant, central accommodation near the ferry terminal is **Sverre's Small Hotel** (☎ 56 95 03 03, fax 56 95 03 92; *Snellemark 2; singles/doubles from Dkr290/460)*. **Hotel Hoffmann** (☎ 56 95 03 86, fax 56 95 25 15, w *www.hotelteam-bornholm.dk; Nordre Kystvej 32; singles/doubles Dkr695/795)* is a modern hotel with a quiet atmosphere, just across the way from the tourist office.

The **Kvickly** supermarket, opposite the tourist office, has a good bakery that opens at 6.30am, and a handy bistro that offers sandwiches for Dkr39 to Dkr45 and steak and chips for Dkr62. You'll find numerous **fast-food eateries** on Store Torv, the central square.

Strøgets Spisehus (☎ 56 95 81 69; *Store Torvegade 39; mains Dkr122-160)* specialises in excellent Danish meat and vegetable dishes. **Zaren** (☎ 56 91 10 09; *Store Torvegade 14)* is a cheerful bar that draws a young crowd. You can get tasty sandwiches from Dkr46 to Dkr68 and it has live music at weekends when it's open to about 2am. **O'Malley's** (☎ 56 95 00 16; *Store Torvegade 2)* caters for an older crowd with an over-21 age limit for its Friday and Saturday late-night discos.

DUEODDE

Dueodde has a vast stretch of white-sand beach backed by woodlands and dunes. There's no village, just a bus stop with a single hotel, a restaurant, a cluster of kiosks selling ice cream and hot dogs, and necessary public toilets to cope with the rush from tour coaches in summer. It can be a crowded trek for a couple of hundred metres along boardwalks to reach the superb beach. Once there, head left, or right, for wide-open spaces.

The beachside **Dueodde Vandrerhjem & Campground** (☎ 56 48 81 19; e *info@ dueodde.dk; open Apr-Oct; adult/child/tent Dkr50/30/25)* is a 10-minute walk east of the bus stop, or it can be reached by car from the main road. It also has cabins for rent at

Dkr170/300 for one/two persons, rising to Dkr800 for eight. **Granpavillonen** (☎ 56 48 81 75; Fyrvej 5; meat & fish mains Dkr115-128) is a busy restaurant at Dueodde's main junction. It does pizzas for Dkr57 to Dkr69, a buffet for Dkr99 to Dkr142, and vegetarian dishes for Dkr98.

BORNHOLM'S EAST COAST

Bornholm's east coast tends to be fairly built up, but is punctuated by several settlements, all with some interest as stopping-off places.

Snogebæk a small shoreside fishing village that hangs on to its authenticity because of its small fleet of working boats and its scattering of fishing huts and cabins.

Just north of Snogebæk is the fine beach of **Balka Strand**.

Nexø is Bornholm's second-largest town. It took a hammering from Soviet bombers in WWII and today much of what you see from the harbour outwards is a fairly functional reconstruction. Yet, there are enough picturesque buildings to add colour to what is essentially a working port. **Nexø-Dueodde Turistinformation** (☎ 56 49 70 79; Postboks 65) is in the centre of town, two blocks inland from the harbour. **Nexø Museum** (☎ 56 49 25 56, Havnen 2; adult/child Dkr15/5; open 10am-4pm Mon-Fri, 10am-2pm Sat mid-May–mid-Oct) is at the harbour and features exhibits on Nexø's history and its fishing and seagoing.

The harbour town of **Svaneke** has award-winning historic buildings, especially those near the village church, a few minutes' walk south of the centre. The **tourist office** (☎ 56 49 70 79; Storegade 24) is in the post office building, two blocks north of the central square.

Places to Stay & Eat

A good base in the Snogebæk-Nexø area is the **Hotel Balka Strand** (☎ 56 49 49 49, fax 56 49 49 48, e mail@hotelbalkastrand.dk; Boulevarden 9; singles/doubles Dkr690/910), a friendly and smart place about 200m from Balka Strand beach. Rates are less outside peak summer weeks.

Møllebakken Familie Camping(☎/fax 56 49 64 62, e molcamp@post10.tele.dk, Møllebakken 8; open mid-May–mid-Sept; adult/child/tent Dkr49/24/15) is a two-star camping ground about 1km north of Svaneke. **Danhostel Svaneke** (☎ 56 49 62 42, fax 56 49 73 83, e info@danhostel-svaneke.dk;

Reberbanevej 9; dorm beds Dkr100, singles/doubles Dkr350/400; open Apr-Oct) is 1km south of the centre of Svaneke.

Down by Snogebæk's seafront, the smokehouse **SnogebækRøgeri** offers good herring and mackerel portions at Dkr39, smoked eel at Dkr42, 1kg of prawns at Dkr50, or an all-you-can-eat fish buffet for Dkr78. It rubs shoulders with souvenir shops and hand-blown glass galleries.

GUDHJEM
pop 1000

Gudhjem is a compact, attractive seaside village with half-timbered houses and sloping streets that rattle down to the pleasant harbour front. It's a popular eating-out place. The harbour was one of the settings for Bornholm novelist Martin Andersen Nexø's Oscar-winning film *Pelle the Conqueror*. The **tourist office** (☎ 56 48 52 10; Åbogade7; open 10am-4pm Mon-Sat mid-June–mid-Aug, 1pm-4pm Mon-Fri mid-Aug–Sept & Mar–mid-June) is a block inland from the harbour alongside the library. Gudhjem has narrow streets and parking is difficult. There's a public car park northwest of the harbour.

Stroll the **footpath** running southeast from the harbour for a pleasant coastal view. Gudhjem's shoreline is rocky, though sunbathers will find a small sandy **beach** at Melsted, 1km east. A bike path leads inland 4km south from Gudhjem to **Østerlars Rundkirke** the most impressive of the island's round churches; bus No 3 goes by the church.

Places to Stay & Eat

Danhostel Gudhjem (☎ 56 48 50 35, fax 56 48 56 35; e dgh@mail.tele.dk; dorm beds Dkr100, singles/doubles Dkr250/325) is just up from the harbourside bus stop. The management can book **rooms** in private homes for Dkr250/350 and also handles the pleasant **Therns Hotel** (Brøddegade 31; singles/doubles Dkr500/700).

The central **Jantzens Hotel**(☎ 56 48 50 17; e jantzenshotel@mail.dk; Brøddegade 33; singles/doubles Dkr525/925) is a fine, old building that has been refurbished and has stylish rooms and a restaurant. Next door is **Restaurant Venezia** (☎ 56 48 53 53; Brøddegade 33) that does pizzas for Dkr53 to Dkr75. Down on the harbour front, **Klint's Kokken** (☎ 56 48 56 26; Ejnar Mikkelsensvej 20; fish & meat mains Dkr128-158) has a pleasant terrace and serves light lunches for Dkr54 to Dkr80. Further along is the waterfront smokehouse **Gudhjem Rogeri** (☎ 56 48 57 08) with an all-you-can-eat buffet for Dkr78 and some challenging seating, including on the upper floor, which is reached by rope ladder. It has live folk, country and rock music most nights in summer.

You'll find a **bakery** and a few reasonably priced **cafés** along Brøddegade, a little inland from the harbour.

SANDVIG

Sandvig is tucked away under Bornholm's rocky northwestern tip of Hammeren and boasts an excellent sandy beach to add to its distinctive appeal. Bornholm's best-known sight, **Hammershus Slot**, is 3km south on the road to Rønne. The impressive, substantial ruins of this 13th-century castle are the largest of their kind in Scandinavia. They are perched dramatically on a height of land that is flanked by sea cliffs and a deep valley. One of the best ways of reaching the castle is by following footpaths from Sandvig through the heather-covered hills of Hammeren – a wonderful hour-long hike. The trail begins down by the camping ground. Sandvig has a mix of attractive old houses and several good eating places.

Places to Stay & Eat

Sandvig Familie Camping (☎ 56 48 04 47; Sandlinien 5; adult/child/tent Dkr50/25/15) is near the beach and handy for tracks onto Hammeren. **Danhostel Sandvig** (☎ 56 48 03 62, fax 56 48 18 62; e sandvig@danhostel .dk; Hammershusvej 94; dorm beds Dkr100, singles/doubles Dkr250/375; open 1 June– 1 Oct) is midway between Hammershus Slot and Sandvig. There are several pensions in the village, a good bet being **Hotel-Pension Langebjerg** (☎ 56 48 02 98; Langebjergvej 7; singles/doubles Dkr365/680).

Sandvig has a number of fairly touristy restaurants, but for real character head for the friendly **Café Bølgen** (☎ 56 48 00 09; Strandpromenaden 26), in a great position right on the beach and alongside Sandvig's indoor swimming pool. It offers good beers and wines to go with tasty Spanish-Mexican inspired dishes at Dkr38 to Dkr105 as well as bocadillos for Dkr42.

An unmissable place for good company and delicious Christiansø herring dishes (Dkr35) and meat mains (Dkr60 to Dkr95) is

Café Værftet (☎ 56 48 04 34; Jernbanegade 3). It's in an old boathouse whose entire front wall, complete with windows and coverings, can be raised open at the touch of a button from behind the bar – an entertaining event, especially if you've had a few *snaps* (akvavit) too many.

CHRISTIANSØ
pop 100

Tiny Christiansø is a charmingly preserved, 17th-century fortress-island an hour's sail northeast of Bornholm. A seasonal fishing hamlet since the Middle Ages, Christiansø fell briefly into Swedish hands in 1658, after which Christian V decided to turn the island into an invincible naval fortress. Bastions and barracks were built; a church, school and prison followed.

By the 1850s the island was no longer needed as a forward base against Sweden and the navy withdrew. Soldiers who wanted to stay on as fishermen were allowed to live as free tenants in the old cottages. Their offspring, and a few latter-day fisherfolk and artists, currently comprise Christiansø's 100 residents. The entire island is an unspoiled reserve – there are no cats or dogs, no cars and no modern buildings or additions intrude.

Christiansø is connected to a smaller island, Frederiksø, by a footbridge.

There's a small **local history museum** in Frederiksø's tower and a great 360-degree view from Christiansø **lighthouse**. Otherwise the main activity is **walking** the footpaths along the fortified walls and batteries that skirt the island. There are skerries with nesting **sea birds** and a secluded **swimming cove** on Christiansø's eastern side.

In summer, **camping** (☎ 30 34 96 05) is allowed in a small field at the Duchess Battery. **Christiansø Gæstgiveriet** (☎ 56 46 20 15; rooms Dkr460), the island's only inn, has a few rooms with shared bath (breakfast included) and a restaurant. Booking ahead for a room is advised. There's a small **food store** and a **snack shop**.

Boats sail to Christiansø daily from Gudhjem and Monday to Saturday from Allinge between mid-May and mid-September. The mailboat from Svaneke makes the trip Monday to Friday year-round. All boats charge Dkr150/75 per adult/child return on a day trip. There is a strict ban on taking cats, dogs or other pets onto Christiansø.

Funen

pop 472,000

Funen (Fyn) is Denmark's garden island. It is largely rural with rolling woodlands, and with pastures and cornfields peppered with old farmhouses and sleepy villages. The unspoilt islands of the South Funen archipelago, especially Langeland and Ærø, are delightful places to visit as are the main island towns of Svendborg and Faaborg, the jumping-off points to the smaller islands.

The railway line from Copenhagen runs straight through Odense, Funen's main city, and westward onto Jutland. Store Bælt (Great Belt), the channel that separates Zealand and Funen, is spanned by Europe's longest combined road and rail bridge. Opened in 1998, the Storebælts-forbindelsen (Great Belt Fixed Link) consists of a four-lane highway on two sleek suspension bridges that are connected via the uninhabited island of Sprogø, and an 8km train tunnel, which is second in length only to the UK-France Channel Tunnel. In all, the impressive span, which runs between the industrial towns of Korsør and Nyborg, covers 18km. If you're taking a train, the crossing is included in your train fare; if you're driving, there's a bridge toll of Dkr240 for vehicles under 6m, Dkr360 over 6m, Dkr120 for a motorbike.

ODENSE

pop 184,00

Denmark's third largest city takes great pride in being the birthplace of Hans Christian Andersen, though it seems that after a fairly unhappy childhood Andersen left Odense, with little regret. Odense is a friendly university city with busy, central pedestrianised areas, a good network of bike lanes, an interesting, cathedral and a number of worthwhile museums.

Orientation & Information

The cathedral is on Klosterbakken, just two minutes from the tourist office, and most other city sights are within walking distance.

The **tourist office** (☎ 66 12 75 20; w www.odenseturist.dk; open 9am-7pm Mon-Sat, 10am-5pm Sun mid-June–Aug; 9am-4.30pm Mon-Fri, 10am-1pm Sat Sept–mid-June), at Rådhus, is a 15-minute walk from the train station.

Odense has a handy 'adventure pass' that allows free entry into museums and free bus transport. You can buy it at the train station or tourist office for a reasonable Dkr100/140 for 24/48 hours.

Badstuen (☎ 66 13 48 66; Østre Stationsvej) is a youth and community centre that has a café and information point and also stages music events.

Boomtown Netcafé (Pantheonsgade 4) is an Internet place charging Dkr25 for an hour. There's free use of the Internet at **Odense Central Library** (Odense Banegård Center; open 10am-7pm Mon-Thur, 10am-4pm Fri & Sat).

At the train station **left-luggage** lockers cost Dkr10 for 24 hours.

HC Andersen Museums

The **HC Andersens Hus** (☎ 66 14 88 14; Hans Jensens Stræde 37-45; adult/child Dkr35/15; open 9am-7pm daily mid-June–Aug, 10am-4pm Tues-Sun Sept–mid-June) lies amid the picturesque little houses of the old poor quarter of Odense. It depicts Andersen's life story through his memorabilia and books. Near the museum is the charming **Fyrtøjet – Et Kulturhus For Børn** (Tinderbox – A Cultural Centre For Children; ☎ 66 14 44 11; Hans Jensens Stræde 21; admission Dkr45), where youngsters can explore the magical world of Hans Christian Andersen through play, storytelling and music. **HC Andersens Barndomshjem** (Munkemøllestræde 3; adult/child Dkr10/5; open 10am-4pm daily mid-June–Aug, 11am-3pm Tues-Sun Sept–mid-June) has a couple of rooms of exhibits in the small house where Hans grew up.

Sankt Knuds Kirke

Odense's 13th-century, Gothic cathedral (☎ 66 12 03 92; Flakhaven; admission free; open 9am-5pm Mon-Sat, noon-3pm Sun) reflects Odense's medieval wealth and stature. It has a handsome rococo **pulpit** and a dazzling, 16th-century **altarpiece** and a gilded wooden **triptych** crowded with over 300 carved figures and said to be one of the finest pieces of religious art in Northern Europe. In the cathedral's chilly crypt are **reliquaries** containing two skeletons claimed to be those of King Knud II and his brother Benedikt, who in 1806 fled into St Alban's and were killed at the altar by Jutland farmers during a revolt against taxes. Though less than saintly, in 1101 Knud was canonised Knud the Holy by the pope in a move to secure the Catholic church in Denmark.

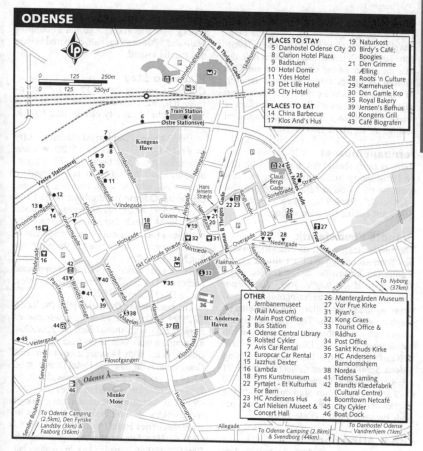

ODENSE

PLACES TO STAY
5 Danhostel Odense City
8 Clarion Hotel Plaza
9 Badstuen
10 Hotel Domir
11 Ydes Hotel
13 Det Lille Hotel
25 City Hotel

19 Naturkost
20 Birdy's Café;
   Boogies
21 Den Grimme
   Ælling
28 Roots 'n Culture
29 Kærnehuset
30 Den Gamle Kro
35 Royal Bakery
39 Jensen's Bøfhus
40 Kongens Grill
43 Café Biografen

PLACES TO EAT
14 China Barbecue
17 Klos And's Hus

OTHER
1 Jernbanemuseet
   (Rail Museum)
2 Main Post Office
3 Bus Station
4 Odense Central Library
6 Rolsted Cykler
7 Avis Car Rental
12 Europcar Car Rental
15 Jazzhus Dexter
16 Lambda
18 Fyns Kunstmuseum
22 Fyrtøjet - Et Kulturhus
   For Børn
23 HC Andersens Hus
24 Carl Nielsen Museet &
   Concert Hall

26 Møntergården Museum
27 Vor Frue Kirke
31 Ryan's
32 Kong Graes
33 Tourist Office &
   Rådhus
34 Post Office
36 Sankt Knuds Kirke
37 HC Andersens
   Barndomshjem
38 Nordea
41 Tidens Samling
42 Brandts Klædefabrik
   (Cultural Centre)
44 Boomtown Netcafé
45 City Cykler
46 Boat Dock

A few metres west of the coffin, stairs lead down to the remains of the original **St Alban's church**.

Den Fynske Landsby

This is a delightful open-air museum (☎ 66 14 88 14; adult/child Dkr55/15; open 10am-5pm daily Apr–mid-June & mid-Aug–Oct; 10am-7pm daily mid-Jun–mid-Aug; 11am-3pm daily Nov-Mar), furnished with period buildings authentically laid out like a small country village, complete with barnyard animals, a duck pond, apple trees and flower gardens.

The museum is in a green zone 4km south of the city centre via bus No 42. From May to September you can take a boat (adult/child Dkr32/22) from Munke Mose down the river to Erik Bøghs Sti, from where it's a 15-minute woodland walk along the river to Den Fynske Landsby.

Fyns Kunstmuseum

In a stately, neoclassical building, this museum (☎ 66 14 88 14; Jernbanegade 13; adult/ child Dkr30/5; open 10am-4pm Tues-Sun) has a serene atmosphere and contains a quality collection of Danish art. Highlights include PS Krøyer's *Italieneske Markarbejdere*, 'Italian Field Workers', Gustava Emilie Grüner's cheerful *Portraegruppe Familien Leunbach* and HA Brendekild's harrowing, but powerful *Udslidt*, 'Finished', depicting a prostrate worker and distressed woman in a vast, despairingly flat field. There are small collections of fine sculptures and of contemporary art; changing exhibitions are also staged.

Carl Nielsen Museet

This museum (☎ 66 14 88 14; Claus Bergs Gade 11; adult/child Dkr25/5; open 10am-4pm Tues-Sun), in Odense's concert hall, details the career of the city's native son Carl Nielsen, Denmark's best known composer. At various points you can don earphones and enjoy Nielsen's music. There are displays of works by Nielsen's wife, the accomplished sculptor Anne Marie Brodersen.

Jernbanemuseet

Railway buffs should not miss the collection of 19th-century locomotives at the rail museum (☎ 66 13 66 30; Dannebrogsgade 24; adult/child Dkr40/16; open 10am-4pm daily) just behind the train station.

Brandts Klædefabrik

The former textile mill on Brandts Passage has been converted into a cultural centre (combined admission ticket Dkr50; open 10am-5pm daily July & Aug, 10am-5pm Tues-Sun Sept-June) with a photography museum, a modern art gallery and a museum of graphics and printing. The combined ticket allows entry to all three museums or you can buy separate tickets for Dkr25 to Dkr30 each.

Nearby, in a large loft, is the charming Tidens Samling (Times Collection; ☎ 65 91 19 42; Brandt's Passage 29; adult/child Dkr25/15; open 10am-5pm daily), featuring a series of domestic interiors from various periods between 1900 and the 1980s.

Other Attractions

Strolling is a pleasure along the busy pedestrianised main street Vestergade and down side streets such as Lille Gråbrødstræd. The central square Flakhavn, framed by Odense Rådhus and Sankt Knuds Kirke, features Svend Wiig Hansen's giant bronze, the reclining Oceania, a joyful playground for children. The east side of the city centre has some of Odense's oldest buildings. You can trace a rewarding walking route from the centre by crossing the busy Torvegade and strolling down Nedergade, a cobblestoned street with leaning, half-timbered houses and antique shops, and then returning via Overgade. En route you'll pass the 13th-century Vor Frue Kirke (open 10am-noon Mon-Sat).

Around the corner, Møntergården (☎ 66 14 88 14; Overgade 48-50; admission Dkr25; open 10am-4pm Tues-Sun), a city museum, has various displays of Odense's history from the Viking Age and a couple of 16th- and 17th-century, half-timbered houses that can be visited.

Places to Stay

Odense Camping (☎ 66 11 47 02; Odensevej 102; adult/child/tent Dkr58/29/20) is 3.5km south of the city centre (take bus No 21 or 22).

The 143-bed Danhostel Odense City (☎ 63 11 04 25, fax 63 11 35 20; w www.cityhostel.dk; dorm beds Dkr100, singles/doubles Dkr310/360) is a bright, modern place alongside the train and bus stations. Danhostel Odense Vandrerhjem (☎ 66 13 04 25, fax 65 91 28 63; Kragsbjergvej 121; dorm beds Dkr94, rooms Dkr376), with 168 beds, occupies a former manor house round a grassy central square, 2km southeast of the centre via bus No 61 or 62.

The tourist office books rooms in private homes at Dkr200/350 for singles/doubles, plus a Dkr35 booking fee.

The pension-like Det Lille Hotel (☎/fax 66 12 28 21; Dronningensgade 5; singles/doubles Dkr350/500, with shared bath Dkr250/390), a 10-minute walk west of the train station, is a friendly place with 14 straightforward rooms. Good value is the 35-room Hotel Domir (☎ 66 12 14 27, fax 66 12 14 31; w www.domir.dk; Tausensgade 19; singles/doubles Dkr420/495-585), which has pleasant rooms, though some singles are a bit cramped. Nearby is its sister hotel Ydes Hotel (☎ 66 12 11 31, fax 66 12 17 82; Hans Tausensgade 11; singles/doubles Dkr360/450-550), which has 26 smaller, but similarly appointed, rooms.

Clarion Hotel Plaza (☎ 66 11 77 45, fax 66 14 41 45; @ info.plaza@clarion.choicehotels.dk; Østre Stationsvej 24; singles/doubles Dkr1045/1245) overlooks the green spaces of Kongens Have, and has 68 luxury rooms. City Hotel (☎ 66 12 12 58, fax 66 12 93 64; w www.city-hotel-odense.dk; Hans Mulesgade 5; singles/doubles Dkr675/895) is a comfortable modern hotel near the Hans Christian Andersen House Museum.

Places to Eat

There are numerous eateries along Kongensgade. China Barbecue (Kongensgade 66; lunch buffet noon-3pm, Dkr49) does takeaway boxes for Dkr22 to Dkr33, while Jensen's Bøfhus (Kongensgade 10) serves inexpensive steak and chicken lunches for Dkr39 to Dkr69. For tasty pastas, starting at Dkr30, there's **Kongens Grill** *(Kongensgade 19)*.

Café Biografen *(☎ 66 13 16 16; Brandts Klædefabrik; open 11am-midnight daily; brunch Dkr60)* is a cheerful place where ducks waddle happily around the terrace tables. It does a good selection of baguettes at Dkr38 and salads at about Dkr60, as well as cakes, pastries, coffees, light meals and beer at reasonable prices.

Klos And's Hus *(☎ 66 13 56 00; Vindegade 76; 2/3 course menu Dkr175/195)* is an atmospheric restaurant with a hint of the baronial about its decor; it does excellent meat dishes. Upstairs, a remarkable **whisky bar** opens at 10pm and has one of the biggest and best collections of whisky you're likely to find outside Scotland.

Another popular spot is **Birdy's Café** *(☎ 66 14 00 39; Nørregade 21-23; dishes around Dkr78; open 5pm-midnight Mon-Sat)*, which serves Mexican food.

Den Grimme Ælling *(☎ 65 91 70 30; Hans Jensens Straede 1; lunch buffet Dkr75-120)* is a charming little restaurant in a cobbled lane. It has a varied and delicious buffet selection, with lunch starting at Dkr75 for herring and salad. Evening buffet with wine is Dkr239.

Odense's showpiece restaurant is **Den Gamle Kro** *(☎ 66 12 14 33; Overgade 23; fish & meat mains Dkr158-258)*, which is spread throughout several rooms of a 17th-century house, its style intact. Fillet of sole stuffed with salmon and spinach costs Dkr189, peppered steak Dkr258.

The unique **Kærnehuset** *(Nedergade6)*, a vegetarian collective, in a 1st-floor room serves a Dkr40 meal at 6pm Tuesday to Friday and welcomes visitors. A few doors away is **Roots 'n Culture** *(Nedergade 12; brunch Dkr40)*, a small friendly café that does vegetarian meals.

Naturkost *(☎ 66 13 70 13; Gravene 8)* is a well-stocked health-food store. You'll find bakeries and fast-food outlets all around the city. **Royal Bakery** *(Vestergadev28)* opposite Jernbanegade, has good pastries and organic ice cream.

Odense Banegård Center, which incorporates the train and bus stations, has low-priced options including a **DSB Café** *(open 5am-10pm Mon-Fri, 8am-10pm Sat & Sun)*, a **supermarket** and a **pub**.

Entertainment

Ryan's *(Nørregade)* is a friendly Irish style pub set back from the busy Thomas B Thriges Gade. **Boogies** *(Nørregade 21)*, a dance place downstairs from Birdy's Café, is popular with students and opens at midnight. Admission is about Dkr35 on Friday and Saturday when there are bands. **Brandts Klædefabrik** has an outdoor amphitheatre that's a venue for free summer weekend concerts and the **Café Biografen** *(admission Dkr45-55)* shows first-run movies on three screens. **Biocity** is a cinema in the Odense Banegård Center.

Kong Graes *(☎ 66 11 18 16; Asylgade 7-9)* is a late-night dance club and **Jazzhus Dexter** *(66 13 68 88; Vindegade 65)* has good live groups. Odense's gay and lesbian centre **Lambda** *(☎ 66 17 76 92; Vindegade 100)* has a late-night café on Fridays and most Saturdays and a disco on the first and third Saturdays of each month. It's in an unsigned, red-brick building, about 30m beyond the roundabout just past Jazzhus Dexter, and on the other side of the road.

Getting There & Away

Odense is on the main railway line between Copenhagen (Dkr192, 1½ hours), Århus (Dkr168, 1¾ hours), Aalborg (Dkr257, three hours) and Esbjerg (Dkr151, two hours). The ticket office is open from about 6am to 8.15pm most days, but closes 5.15pm on Saturdays. Buses leave from the rear of the train station.

Odense is just north of the E20; access from the highway is clearly marked. Route 43 connects Odense with Faaborg; route 9 connects Odense with Svendborg. For car rental there are local offices of **Avis** *(☎ 66 14 39 99; Østre Stationsvej 37)* and **Europcar** *(☎ 66 14 15 44; Kongensgade 69)*.

Getting Around

In Odense you board city buses at the front and pay the driver (Dkr12) when you get off. You're strongly advised to have the correct change.

Driving in Odense is not difficult, outside rush hour, though many of the central sights are on pedestrian streets, so it's best to park your car and explore on foot. You can find substantial parking lots around Brandts Klædefabrik and the Carl Nielsen Museet Parking costs a minimum Dkr1 for about seven minutes, Dkr8 for one hour.

Bicycles can be rented at **Rolsted Cykler** (☎ 66 17 77 36; Østre Stationsvej 33; open 10am-5pm Mon-Tues, 10am-7pm Fri, 10am-2pm Sun) for Dkr85 a day, Dkr500 a week. Another hire place is **City Cykler** (☎ 66 13 97 83; e email@citycykler.dk; Vesterbro 27; open 9am-5.30pm Mon-Fri, 10am-2pm Sat) west of the city centre. Bikes are Dkr99 per day.

KERTEMINDE
pop 5500

Kerteminde is a fresh-faced seaside town with a relaxed pace and a couple of sea-centred attractions. A few fishing boats lend character to its waterfront, but leisure sailing is now the town's main seagoing trade. Kerteminde is fronted by a harbour and long marina, but there are sandy beaches on both sides of the town.

Kerteminde **tourist office** (☎ 65 32 11 21, fax 65 32 18 17; e ktb@kerteminde-turist .dk; open 9am-5pm Mon-Sat mid-June–Aug; 9am-4pm Mon-Fri, 9.30am-12.30pm Sat Sept–mid-June) has helpful staff with lots of information and even distributes a data-packed CD.

Farvergården

The local-history museum (☎ 65 32 37 27, Langegade 8; adult/child Dkr15/free; open 10am-4pm Tues-Sun Mar-Oct), in the town centre, is in the original section of a 17th-century merchant's house. Many of the rooms remain as they would have been in centuries past, with period furnishings, pottery and paintings.

Fjord & Bælt

Fjord & Bælt (☎ 65 32 42 00; Margrethes Plads 1; adult/child Dkr70/40; open 10am-6pm daily July–mid-Aug; 10am-4pm Mon-Fri, 10am-5pm Sat & Sun mid-Feb–June & mid-Aug–Nov) is a hugely popular sea centre. It's a great place for children, with porpoises and seals in harbour pools, a walk-through underwater tunnel and hands-on exhibits, all dealing with life in the fjord. The centre also runs one-hour boat trips for Dkr60 and two-hour snorkelling trips for Dkr140.

Places to Stay

Kerteminde Camping (☎ 65 32 19 71, fax 65 32 18 71, e kertemindecamp@dk-camp .dk, Hindsholmvej 80; adult/child/tent Dkr57/ 30/30; open Apr-Sept) is a three-star camping ground opposite the beach and just 1.5km north of the town centre.

Danhostel Kerteminde (☎ 65 32 39 29, fax 65 32 39 24, e info@dkhostel.dk, Skovvej 46; dorm beds Dkr100, rooms Dkr400) is at the edge of a pleasant wooded area just a five-minute walk from a sandy beach and 15 minutes south of the town centre.

The tourist office provides a list of **rooms** in private homes; singles/doubles cost around Dkr250/350.

Tornøes Hotel (☎ 65 32 16 05, fax 65 32 48 40, e tornoes@tornoeshotel.dk, Strandgade 2; singles/doubles Dkr650/845), a smart, well-appointed place, has a good central waterfront location and comfy rooms.

Places to Eat

There are a few places in central Kerteminde where you can get inexpensive food.

Burger Caféen (☎ 65 32 18 78, Langegade 19; burgers & sandwiches Dkr20-50) does burgers and a variety of sandwiches.

Café Wenzel (☎ 65 32 39 84; Strandgade 2; mains Dkr119-148) is part of the Tornøes Hotel and has a wide range of options from baguettes and salads at Dkr39 to fish and meat dishes and a children's menu for Dkr20 to Dkr39. The hotel restaurant does two-/three-course menus for Dkr135/178.

Getting There & Around

Kerteminde is on route 165, 19km northwest of Nyborg and 21km northeast of Odense.

There are hourly bus services connecting Kerteminde with Odense (Dkr27, 39 minutes) and Nyborg (Dkr27, 31 minutes).

You can hire bikes at **Cykelgården** (☎ 65 32 36 18; Strandgade 31) and the **Harbour Marina** (☎ 65 32 37 33) for about Dkr60 to Dkr75 a day.

LADBYSKIBET

Ladbyskibet (Ladby ship; ☎ 65 32 16 67, Vikingevej 123; adult/child Dkr25/free; open 10am-5pm daily June-Aug; 10am-4pm Tues-Sun Sept-Oct & Mar-Ma;, 11am-3pm Wed-Sun Nov-Feb) comprises the remains of a 22m-long Viking ship that has been skilfully preserved at the site where it was originally excavated in 1935. The ship, which once formed the tomb of a Viking chieftain, was buried in the 10th century and covered with an earthen mound. It is the only Viking Age ship burial site uncovered in Denmark to date.

All the wooden planks from the Ladby ship, which was buried in turf, decayed long ago. What is preserved is the imprint of the hull moulded into the earth, along with iron nails, an anchor and the partial remains of the dogs and horses that were buried with their master. This may sound unpromising, and at first glance, the grassy hillock covering the site seems more like a bomb shelter from the outside, but as soon as the automatic entrance doors hiss open most people are captivated by this compelling relic.

There's a separate visitor centre at the arrival car park with a 1:10-scale model of the ship and background information about the site.

Getting There & Away

In the little village of Ladby, 4km southwest of Kerteminde via Odensevej, turn north onto Vikingevej, a one-lane road through fields that ends after 1.2km at the Ladbyskibet car park. You enter through the little museum from where it's a few minutes' walk along a field path to the mound.

Local bus No 482 makes the six-minute trip from Kerteminde to the village of Ladby (Dkr13) eight times a day from Monday to Friday only. Check the schedule with the bus driver, as the last return bus is typically around 4pm. Also, you'll have to walk the Vikingevej section.

EGESKOV CASTLE

Egeskov (☎ 62 27 10 16; W www.egeskov .com; castle grounds adult/child Dkr75/37, plus castle interior Dkr55/28; open 10am-5pm daily May, June, Aug & Sept, 10am-7pm daily July) is a magnificent Renaissance castle, complete with moat and drawbridge. The castle exteriors are the best features. The interior is heavily Victorian in its furnishings and hunting trophies of now rare beasts. The grounds include century-old privet hedges, free-roaming peacocks, topiary and English gardens and there's an entertaining bamboo grass labyrinth, dreamed up by the contemporary Danish poet/artist Piet Hein.

The castle grounds usually stay open an hour longer than the castle. Admission to the grounds includes entry to an antique **car museum**.

Egeskov Slot is 2km west of Kvændrup on route 8. From Odense take the Svendborg-bound train to Kvændrup Station (Dkr45) and continue on foot or by taxi. Alternatively, for Dkr36 take bus No 801 to Kvændrup Bibliotek, where you can switch to bus No 920, which stops at the castle on its regular run between Faaborg and Nyborg.

FAABORG & AROUND
pop 7000

Faaborg is a south-facing sun trap and has a relaxing air. In the 17th century it was a bustling harbour town sustained by one of Denmark's largest commercial fleets. Today, Faaborg retains many vestiges of that earlier era in its picturesque, cobblestone streets and leaning, half-timbered houses. Faaborg's **tourist office** (☎ 62 61 07 07; Banegårdspladsen 2A; open 9am-5pm Mon-Sat June-Sept, 10am-5pm Mon-Sat Oct-May) is adjacent to the bus station and car park on the harbour front. You can hire bikes here for Dkr50 a day.

Things to See & Do

The main square, **Torvet**, is a pleasant spot to linger. It features the Svendborg sculptor Kai Nielsen's striking bronze fountain group *Ymerbrønd* that depicts a Norse fertility myth.

Running east from Torvet is the tree-lined main shopping street Østergade. Torvegade runs west from Torvet to join the cobbled Holkegade at a cluster of attractive buildings of contrasting style. They include a neoclassical, one-time chemist's shop with Tuscan pilasters, and the handsome, 18th-century merchant's house that is now the town museum, **Den Gamle Gaard** (Holkegade 1; adult/child Dkr30/free; open 10.30am-4.30pm daily mid-May–mid-Sept; 11am-3pm Sat & Sun Apr–mid-May & mid-Sept–Oct) complete with period furnishings.

Faaborg Museum for Fynsk Malerkunst (Grønnegade 75; adult/child Dkr35/free; open 10am-4pm daily Apr-Oct) is a former winery which, though small, contains a fine collection of Funen art, including works by leading Funenite artists such as Peter Hansen, Jens Birkholm, and Anna Syberg. Kai Nielsen's original granite sculpture of the *Ymerbrønd* is also here.

There are numerous daily ferries to the nearby islands of **Avernakø** and **Lyø** (Dkr70 return, bicycle Dkr20) and a passenger boat to **Bjørnø** (Dkr40 return).

Places to Stay & Eat
Holms Camping (☎ 62 61 03 99; e post@ holms-camp.dk; Odensevej 54; adult/child

Dkr54/25) is on route 43, 1km north of the town centre. The 69-bed **Danhostel Faaborg** (☎ 62 61 12 03, fax 62 61 35 08; Grønnegade 71-72; dorm beds Dkr100, rooms Dkr300) is in a half-timbered building next door to the Faaborg Museum for Fynsk Malerkunst.

The tourist office books **rooms** in private homes at singles/doubles for Dkr250/400 plus a Dkr25 booking fee. **Hotel Faaborg** (☎ 62 61 02 45; e post@hotelfaaborg.dk; Torvet; singles/doubles Dkr575/650) is very central and has good comfy rooms. Its restaurant does tasty herring dishes for Dkr80 and smørrebrød for Dkr38 to Dkr58. **Harlem Pizza** (Torvet) has long hours and does pizza, sandwiches and lasagne for about Dkr30 to Dkr40.

Getting There & Away
Faaborg has no train service. Bus Nos 961 and 962 from Odense (Dkr50, 1¼ hours) run at least hourly to 11pm. Getting to Faaborg by car is straightforward; from the north, simply follow route 43, which is called Odensevej as it enters town.

For information on ferries to Ærø, see the Ærø section.

SVENDBORG
pop 40,000
Down-to-earth Svendborg is South Funen's largest municipality and a transit point for travel between Odense and Ærø. The train and bus stations are two blocks northwest of the dock. The **tourist office** (☎ 62 2 1 09 08; Centrumpladsen 4; open 9.30am-6pm Mon-Fri, 9.30am-3pm Sat mid-June–Aug; 9.30am-5pm Mon-Fri, 9.30am-12.30pm Sat Jan– mid-June & Sept-Dec) has lots of information on South Funen as a whole.

A splendid natural harbour made Svendborg a major port and shipbuilding centre from medieval times onwards and today there is still enough marine heritage to counterbalance the fairly soulless modern docks that dominate the waterfront. The town has a number of maritime training schools to add to its salty ambience.

Things to See
At the southern end of Havnepladsen's cobbled quayside, opposite where the Ærø ferry docks, is **Sejlskibsbroen**, a jetty lined with splendidly preserved sailing ships and smaller vessels and with an adjoining marina that caters for the great number of yachts that

sail local waters. Ask at the tourist centre about the various trips that can be arranged on the old sailing ships.

Just over the bridge from Svendborg is the island of Tåsinge, with its pretty harbourside village of Troense and the nearby 17th-century castle **Valdemars Slot** (☎ 62 22 61 06; Slotsalléen 100; adult/child Dkr55/30; open 10am-5pm daily May-Sept). The castle's lavish interior is crammed with paintings and eccentric objects. In the grounds are **Denmark's Toy Museum** and the **Danish Yachting Museum**. The grounds of the castle and the nearby white-sand beach have free access. You can get to Valdemars Slot by bus but a better way is by the MS Helge, an old-style ferry that carries passengers from Svendborg to Troense and Valdemars Slot every few hours from May to September.

Places to Stay & Eat
The nearest **camping grounds** are on Tåsinge. **Danhostel Svendborg** (☎ 62 21 66 99, fax 62 20 29 39; e dk@danhostel-svendborg.dk; Vestergade 45; dorm beds Dkr100, rooms Dkr330) is in a renovated, 19th-century iron foundry in the town centre.

Hotel Ærø (☎ 62 21 07 60; Brogade 1 singles/doubles with shared bath Dkr250/400), opposite the Ærø ferry dock, has 13 straightforward but clean rooms.

At Tåsinge, the charming and friendly **Det Lille Hotel** (☎ 62 22 53 41; e eriksen@detlillehotel.dk; Badstuen 15; singles/doubles with shared bath Dkr400/520) has a few rooms in a typically picturesque cottage.

In Svendborg, there's a **bakery, ice-cream shop** and other inexpensive eateries along the pedestrian street, Brogade-Gerritsgade, in the town centre. **Jette's Diner** (☎ 62 22 16 97; Kullinggade 1) is a popular local place that does sandwiches and salads for Dkr40 to Dkr68. **Bella Italia** (☎ 62 22 24 55; Brogade 2; mains Dkr134-180) does tasty pizzas and pastas for Dkr56 to Dkr94.

At Valdemars Slot the popular **Restaurant Valdemars Slot** (☎ 62 22 59 00; Slotsalléen 100; mains Dkr85-95) offers a three-course meal for Dkr175. The nearby **Aeblehavn Café**, beside the car park, does pizza and sandwiches for Dkr20 to Dkr30.

Getting There & Away
Trains leave Odense for Svendborg about once an hour, cost Dkr53 and take one hour.

Ferries to Ærøskøbing depart five times a day, the last at 10.30pm in summer.

LANGELAND

The long, narrow island of Langeland, connected by bridge to Funen via Tåsinge, has a satisfying sense of isolation. It has some good beaches, enjoyable cycling and rewarding bird-watching. You can pick up information about the entire island from Langeland's **tourist office** (☎ 62 51 35 05; Torvet 5, Rudkøbing; open 9am-5pm Mon-Sat mid-June–Aug; 9.30am-4.30pm Mon-Fri, 9.30am-12.30pm Sat Sept–mid-June).

Things to See & Do

Langeland's main town of **Rudkøbing** has a fairly desolate harbour area, but the town centre is attractive and there are some fine old buildings around Rudekøbing Kirke, to the north of Brogade, the street leading inland from the harbour to the main square of Torvet. For beaches head for **Ristinge** about 15km south of Rudkøbing; for **bird-watching** you'll find a sighting tower at **Tryggelev Nor**, 5km south of Ristinge, and a sanctuary at **Gulstav Bog** at the island's southern tip.

Cycling is a good way to explore Langeland. The tourist office has an excellent English-language edition of a brochure and map (Dkr15) that describes six bike routes on the island. Bikes can be hired at **Cykelsmeden** (Bystrædt 3, Dkr60 per day), in the centre of town.

Langeland's top sight is the salmon-coloured **Tranekær Slot** a handsome medieval castle that has been in the hands of the one family since 1672. The castle is not open to the public, but its grounds are home to the fascinating **TICKON** (Tranekær International Centre for Art and Nature; admission to grounds Dkr25) a collection of art installations created by international artists and sited throughout the woodland and round a scenic lake. Children love searching out each feature. **Tranekær Slot Museum** and the **Souvenir Museum** are in the castle's old water mill and old theatre respectively. About 1km north of the castle is the **Castle Mill** (☎ 63 51 10 10; Lejbølleveje; adult/child Dkr20/free; open 10am-5pm Mon-Fri, 1pm-5pm Sat & Sun June–mid-Sept; 10am-4pm Mon-Fri, 1pm-4pm Sat & Sun mid-Sept–May), a 19th-century windmill, its remarkable wooden mechanics still intact.

Places to Stay & Eat

There are nine **camping grounds** scattered around the island of Langeland, including one at **Danhostel Rudkøbing** (☎/fax 62 51 18 30; e rudkobing@danhostel.dk; Engdraget 11; dorm beds Dkr100, rooms Dkr325) Langeland's only hostel, located in Rudkøbing centre. The tourist office maintains a list of **rooms** for rent in private homes with doubles costing about Dkr350 to Dkr400.

Det Gamle Hotel Rudkøbing (☎ 62 51 36 18; Havnegade 2; singles doubles Dkr380/595) on the edge of the harbour area has reasonable, if plain rooms. **Pension Skrøbelevgaard** (☎ 62 51 45 31; Skrøbelev Hedevej 4; singles/doubles with shared bath Dkr350/500) has simple rooms in part of an old manor farm outside Rudkøbing.

There are a number of cafés and restaurants in Rudkøbing. **Efes Restaurant** (☎ 62 51 22 23; Østergade 5; mains Dkr76-149) does tasty pasta dishes for Dkr52 to Dkr69 as well as grills and mainly meat mains.

Getting There & Away

Buses make the 25-minute run from Svendborg to Rudkøbing (Dkr30) at least hourly; most connect onwards to Tranekær. There are daily ferries from Rudkøbing to Marstal in Ærø and from Spodsbjerg to Tårs in Lolland.

ÆRØ

pop 7500

Ærø is an idyllic, captivating island with a gentle coastline and an interior of rolling green hills, patchworked with fields and farmsteads. Its mainly coastal towns are small and friendly. The country roads are winding and are enhanced by thatched houses and old windmills. As well, the island has ancient passage graves and dolmens to explore. There are some good small beaches, one of the best being **Risemark Strand** on the southern tip of the island. Ærø is a great place to tour by bicycle

Ærø has three main towns: Ærøskobing, Marstal and Søby. **Ærøskøbing tourist office** (☎ 62 52 13 00; Vestergade 1; open 9am-5pm Mon-Fri, 9am-2pm Sat, 9.30am-12.30pm Sun mid-June–Aug; 9am-4pm Mon-Fri, 9.30am-5.30pm Sat Jan–mid-June & Sept-Dec) is near the waterfront. **Marstal tourist office** (☎ 62 53 19 60; Havnegade 5; open 9am-5pm Mon-Fri, 9am-2pm Sat, 9.30am-12.30pm Sun mid-June–Aug; 9am-4pm Mon-Fri, 9.30am-5.30pm Sat Jan–mid-June

& *Sept-Dec*) is a few minutes' walk south of the harbour. The island's tourist website is (W www.aeroe-turistbureau.dk).

Ærøskøbing

Ærøskøbing was a prosperous merchants' town in the late 1600s; its older buildings are extremely well preserved. The narrow, cobblestone streets are tightly lined with 17th- and 18th-century houses, many of them gently crooked, half-timbered affairs with traditional handblown glass windows and decorative doorways beautified by streetside hollyhocks. The tourist office has an illustrated leaflet, with a separate insert in English, describing the finest buildings.

Apart from Ærøskøbing's overall charm a main tourist attraction is **Flaske Peters Samling** (☎ 62 52 29 51; *Smedegade 22; adult/child Dkr25/10; open 10am-5pm daily*). This museum is in the former poorhouse and, as well as displays of local folk art, there are examples of the work of ship's cook, Peter Jacobsen, 'Bottle Peter', who crafted 1700 ships-in-a-bottle during his long life. There are also two **local history museums** stuffed with antiques and period furnishings.

Søby

This fairly quiet little port has a shipyard, which is the island's biggest employer, a sizable fishing fleet and a busy yacht marina. Five kilometres beyond Søby, at Ærø's northern tip, there's a pebble beach with clear water and a stone **lighthouse** with a view.

Marstal

On the southeastern end of the island, Marstal is Ærø's most modern-looking town and has a web of busy shopping streets at its centre. Marstal has an emphatically maritime history – even its street names echo the names of ships and famous sailors. Its **Søfartsmuseum** (☎ 62 53 23 31; *Prinsensgade 1; adult/child Dkr35/10; open 9am-8pm daily July, 9am-5pm daily June & Aug, 10am-4pm daily Mar & Sept*) has an absorbing collection of nautical artefacts including ships' models and full-size boats. There is a reasonably good **beach** on the southern side of town.

Ancient Ærø

Ærø once had over 100 prehistoric sites and, although many have been lost, the island still has some atmospheric Neolithic remains,

especially in its southeast district, to the west of Marstal. At the small village of Store Rise is the site of **Tingstedet**, the remains of a passage grave in a field behind an attractive **12th-century church**. At **Lindsbjerg** is the superb hilltop site of a long barrow and two passage graves, one of which has a nicely poised capstone. Just over 1km south of here, following signs, and right on the coast, is the fascinating medieval relic of **Sankte Albert's Kirke** within a Viking defensive wall of about the 8th century. Another striking site is at **Kragnæs**, about 4km west of Marstal. Head through the village of Græsvænge and follow signs for 'Jættestue' along narrow lanes to reach a small car park, from where it's about 600m along field tracks to the restored grave site.

Places to Stay

There are **camping grounds** at Søby, Ærøskøbing and Marstal. **Danhostel Ærøskøbing** (☎ 62 52 10 44; e stormaeroe@mail.tele.dk; *open 1 Apr-31 Oct; dorm beds Dkr100, rooms Dkr240*) is 1km from town on the road to Marstal. **Danhostel Marstal** (☎ 63 52 63 58; e mav@adr.dk; *Færgestræde 29; open 1 May-1 Sept; dorm beds Dkr100, singles/doubles Dkr210/250*) is south of the harbour.

The tourist offices have a list of countryside **B&Bs** around the island; prices average Dkr215/340 for singles/doubles.

In Ærøskøbing, **Hotel Ærohus** (☎ 62 52 10 03; e mail@aeroehus.dk; *Vestergade 38; singles/doubles Dkr535/740, with shared bath Dkr265/420*) has comfortable modernised rooms and a garden annexe. Next door is the delightful **Pension Vestergade 44** (☎ 62 52 22 98; e pensionvestergade44@post.tele.dk; *Vestergade 44; singles/doubles with shared bath Dkr450/580*), an 18th-century house with stylish interiors. In Marstal, **Hotel Marstal** (☎ 62 53 13 52; *Dronningestræde 1A; singles/doubles with shared bath Dkr325/450*) is near the harbour and has adequate rooms.

Places to Eat

All three towns have bakeries, restaurants and food stores. In Ærøskøbing on Vestergade, just west of the ferry dock, there's a small grocery store, a **rogeri** with inexpensive smoked fish and moderately priced restaurants.

At Marstal's harbour, there's a small food store and **Restaurant Kabyssen** with sandwiches and grills for Dkr49 to Dkr59 and a children's menu for Dkr39. For something more substantial, **Hotel Marstal** has a two-course daily special for Dkr105.

As well as fish and meat dishes, **Den Gamle Vingaard** (☎ 62 53 13 25; Skolegade 15; fish & meat mains Dkr78-142), in the town centre, offers smørrebørd for Dkr48 to Dkr98, pastas and pizzas for Dkr50 to Dkr65. Just along the road is **Scruffy Murphy's** (☎ 62 53 13 23; Strandstræde 39B), brimming with Irish beers and with a strong, live, folk-music programme.

Getting There & Away

There are year-round **car ferries** (☎ 62 52 40 00; e info@aeroe-ferry.dk) to Søby from Faaborg, to Ærøskøbing from Svendborg and to Marstal from Rudkøbing. All run about five times a day, take about an hour and charge Dkr77/41 per adult/child, Dkr21 for a bike and Dkr169 for a car. If you have a car it's a good idea to make reservations, particularly at weekends and in midsummer.

There's also a **ferry** (☎ 62 58 17 17; e aero .als@get2net.dk) between Søby and Mammary that runs a few times daily from spring to autumn at comparable fares.

Getting Around

Bus No 990 runs from Søby to Marstal via Ærøskøbing hourly Monday to Friday, half as frequently at weekends. A pass for unlimited, one-day travel costs Dkr52.

You can **rent bikes** for Dkr45 a day at the **hostel** and **camping ground** in Ærøskøbing and at **Pilebækkens Cykel og Servicestation** (☎ 62 52 11 10; Pilebækken 11) opposite the car park on the outskirts of the town. In Marstal, **Nørremarks Cykelforretning** (☎ 62 53 14 77; Møllevejen 77) rents out bikes from a stance at the harbour car park between 10am and 11am each morning. **Søby Cykelforret- ning** (☎ 62 58 18 42; Langebro 4) rents out bikes in Søby. The tourist office in Marstal sells a Dkr20 cycling map of a round-island route.

Jutland

The Jutland (Jylland) Peninsula is where mainland Europe meets Scandinavia. The region was settled originally by the Jutes, a Germanic tribe whose forays included invading England in the 5th century. Not surprisingly Jutland's southern boundary has been a fluid one, last drawn in 1920 when Germany relinquished its holdings in Sønderjylland.

Jutland's west coast has endless stretches of windswept sandy beaches. Most of the main cities, including Århus and Aalborg, are along the more sheltered east coast.

The natural landscape of northern Jutland is largely coastal sand dunes and heathland, while southern Jutland is dominated by moors and marshes. Drainage and reclamation has turned most of Jutland into level farmland and modern agriculture has produced a landscape of tilled fields that are a brilliant green in spring and a monotonous brown in autumn. Parts of the interior, especially around the marginally hillier central areas, are forested,

ÅRHUS & AROUND
pop 285,000

Århus is the second largest city in Denmark and is one of Scandinavian Europe's most modern and sophisticated regional capitals. Yet the city retains all the friendliness and ease of a small country town. It lies midway along Jutland's eastern coastline and has been an important trading centre and seaport since Viking times.

The city is the cultural and commercial heart of Jutland. It has a thriving university with more than 20,000 students, whose numbers are refreshed annually by a new intake of several thousand. The city has one of Denmark's best music and entertainment scenes, a well-preserved historic quarter and plenty to see and do, ranging from good museums and period churches in the centre, to woodland trails and beaches along the city's outskirts.

Arhus began in about 900 as Aros, the 'place at the river's mouth' and during the medieval period it seesawed between prosperity and devastation as rival Vikings and warring kings entangled the city in their campaigns. In more peaceful times, the city stabilised and soon became the commercial focus of Jutland. Århus' progress towards becoming a university city was something of a battle against competing bids from other Jutland cities such as Viborg, but by 1934 Århus University was established.

Orientation

Århus is fairly compact and easy to get around. The train station is on the southern side of the city centre. The pedestrian shopping streets of Ryesgade, Søndergade and Sankt Clements Torv lead, in 1km, from the station to the cathedral at the heart of the old city.

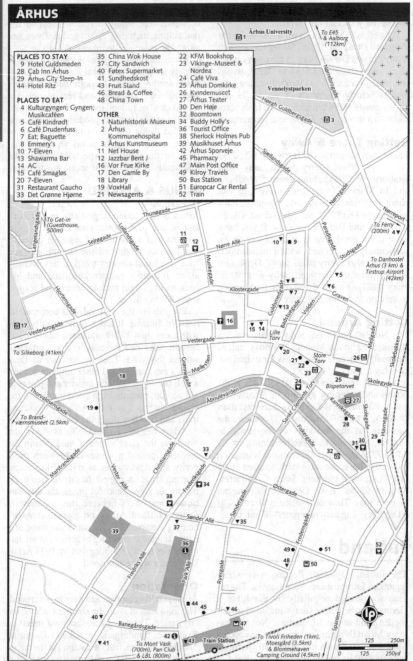

ÅRHUS

PLACES TO STAY
9   Hotel Guldsmeden
28 Cab Inn Århus
29 Århus City Sleep-In
44 Hotel Ritz

PLACES TO EAT
4   Kulturgyngen; Gyngen; Musikcaféen
5   Café Kindrødt
6   Café Drudenfuss
7   Eat; Baguette
8   Emmery's
10 7-Eleven
13 Shawarma Bar
14 AC
15 Café Smagløs
20 7-Eleven
31 Restaurant Gaucho
33 Det Grønne Hjørne
35 China Wok House
37 City Sandwich
40 Føtex Supermarket
41 Sundhedskost
43 Fruit Stand
46 Bread & Coffee
48 China Town

OTHER
1   Naturhistorisk Museum
2   Århus Kommunehospital
3   Århus Kunstmuseum
11 Net House
12 Jazzbar Bent J
16 Vor Frue Kirke
17 Den Gamle By
18 Library
19 VoxHall
21 Newsagents
22 KFM Bookshop
23 Vikinge-Museet & Nordea
24 Café Viva
25 Århus Domkirke
26 Kvindemuseet
27 Århus Teater
30 Den Høje
32 Boomtown
34 Buddy Holly's
36 Tourist Office
38 Sherlock Holmes Pub
39 Musikhuset Århus
42 Århus Sporveje
45 Pharmacy
47 Main Post Office
49 Kilroy Travels
50 Bus Station
51 Europcar Car Rental
52 Train

Information

The **tourist office** (☎ 89 40 67 00, fax 86 12 95 90; w www.visitaarhus.com; Park Allé; open 9.30am-6pm Mon-Fri, 9.30am-5pm Sat, 9.30am-1pm Sun mid-June–mid-Sept; 9.30am-5pm Mon-Fri, 10am-1pm Sat May–mid-June; 9.30am-4.30pm Mon-Fri, 10am-1pm Sat Jan-Apr & mid-Sept–Dec) is in Rådhuset, the city hall. It has a very friendly and helpful staff and offers numerous brochures and leaflets on the city and its surroundings, and on the rest of Jutland and Denmark. The city has introduced an **'info-bike' service** (open daily mid-June–mid-Sept, Sat & Sun mid-Sept–mid-June) with front-box bikes travelling round the city with leaflets, brochures and information.

There's a **bank** with an ATM at the front of the train station and many more along Søndergade.

The **main post office** (Banegardspladsen; open 9.30am-6pm Mon-Fri, 10am-1pm Sat), is beside the train station.

Århus has a couple of Internet places, heavily patronised by gamers, but with a few online stations. **Boomtown** (Åboulevarden 21; open 10am-2am Mon-Thur, 10am-8am Fri-Sat, 11am-midnight Sun) is part of a city chain.

Net House (Nørre Allé 66A; open noon-midnight daily) tucked away well off the street and up a flight of stairs. Both charge Dkr20 for one hour.

Kilroy Travels (☎ 86 20 11 44; Fredensgade 40) specialises in discount and student travel and has friendly, helpful staff.

Landsforeningen for Bøsser og Lesbiske (LBL; ☎ 86 13 19 48; w www.aarhus.lbl.dk; Jægergårdsgade 42), the Århus branch of the Danish national organisation for gays and lesbians is located next door to the Pan Club.

Mønt Vask (St. Paul's Gade 64) is a coin launderette. An average wash and dry costs Dkr45.

International newspapers are sold at the train station and there is an excellent **newspaper shop** at Store Torv 7. **KFM** (Store Torv 5) is a bookshop with a good range of books including travel guides.

Left-luggage lockers are available at the bus and train stations. Both charge Dkr10 for 24 hours.

Dial ☎ 112 if you need police or ambulance. **Århus Kommunehospital** (Nørrebrogade) has a 24-hour emergency ward.

Den Gamle By

Den Gamle By (The Old Town; ☎ 86 12 31 88; w www.dengamleby.dk; Viborgvej 2; adult/child Dkr70/25; open 9am-6pm daily June-Aug; 10am-5pm daily Apr-May & Sept-Oct; 10am-4pm daily Feb-Mar & Nov-Dec; 11am-3pm daily Jan) is an engaging open-air museum of 75 half-timbered houses brought here from around Denmark and reconstructed as a provincial town, complete with a functioning bakery, silversmith, bookbinder etc. It's on Viborgvej, a 20-minute walk from the city centre. After hours you can walk through the old streets for free – an interesting time to visit as the crowds are gone and the light is ideal for photography, though you won't be able to enter individual buildings. Bus Nos 3, 14, 25 and 55 will take you there.

The **Botanical Garden** with its thousands of plants and recreated Jutland environments occupies the high ground above Den Gamle By and can be reached through an exit from the Old Town or directly from Vesterbrogade.

Århus Domkirke

This impressive cathedral (☎ 86 12 38 45; Bispetorv; admission free; open 9.30am-4pm Mon-Fri May-Sept, 10am-3pm Mon-Fri Oct-Apr), is Denmark's longest, with a lofty nave that spans nearly 100m. The original Romanesque chapel at the eastern end dates from the 12th century, while most of the rest of the church is 15th-century Gothic.

Like other Danish churches, the cathedral was once richly decorated with **frescoes** that served to convey biblical parables to unschooled peasants. After the Reformation, church authorities who felt the frescoes smacked too much of Roman Catholicism, had them all whitewashed, but many have now been uncovered and restored. They range from fairy-tale paintings of St George slaying a dragon, to scenes of hellfire.

The cathedral's splendid, five-panel, gilt **altarpiece** is a highlight. It was made in Lubeck by the renowned woodcarver Bernt Notke in the 15th century. In its centre panel, to the left of the Madonna and child, is a gaunt-faced St Clement, to whom Århus Domkirke was dedicated. The ill-starred Clement drowned at sea with an anchor round his neck and became the patron saint of sailors for his pains.

The cathedral's other items worth note are the bronze baptismal **font** dating from 1481, the finely carved Renaissance **pulpit** created in 1588, the magnificent baroque **pipe organ** made in 1730, the large 18th-century **votive ship** and the baroque **sepulchre** in the Marselis family chapel.

Vor Frue Kirke

This church (☎ 86 12 12 43; Frue Kirkeplads; admission free; open 10am-2pm Mon-Fri, 10am-noon Sat), off Vestergade, has a carved wooden **altarpiece** dating from the 1530s. But far more interesting is what's in its basement – the **crypt** of the city's original cathedral, dating from about 1060. Enter via the stairway beneath the altar. To enter a third chapel, this one with 16th-century frescoes, go through the courtyard and take the left door.

Vikinge-Museet

There's more than the expected vaults in the bank basement of **Nordea** (☎ 89 42 11 00; Sankt Clements Torv 6; admission free; open 10am-4pm Mon-Wed &, Fri, 10am-6pm Thur) where there is an exhibition of artefacts from the Viking Age town that were excavated at this site in 1964 during the bank's construction.

The artefacts have been dated from the period 900 to 1400, suggesting that the heart of modern Århus housed one of the earliest settlements in the area. The display includes, a skeleton, a reconstructed house, 1000-year-old carpentry tools and pottery and photos of the excavation.

Århus Kunstmuseum

This museum (☎ 86 13 52 55; W www.aarhuskunstmuseum.dk; Høegh Guldbergs Gade 2; adult/child Dkr40/free; open 10am-5pm Thur-Sun & Tues, 10am-8pm Wed) is south of the university at Vennelystparken. It has a comprehensive collection of 19th- and 20th-century Danish art. Take bus No 1, 2, 3 or 6 to Nørreport. A new art museum is currently under construction.

Other Museums

At **Kvindemuseet** (☎ 86 13 61 44; W www.kvindemuseet.dk; Domkirkeplads 5; adult/child Dkr25/20; open 10am-5pm daily June-Aug; 10am-4pm Tues-Sun Sept-May), in the old city hall, is an absorbing exhibition that focuses on the life of women throughout history. Special exhibitions on particular themes are also staged.

Brandværnsmuseet (Danish Firefighting Museum; ☎ 86 25 41 44; Tomsagervej 25; adult/child Dkr45/15; open 10am-5pm daily Apr-Oct, 10am-4pm Tues-Sun Nov, Feb & Mar) is 4km southwest of the city centre and has one of Europe's largest collection of fire engines.

The **Naturhistorisk Museum** (☎ 86 12 97 77; Universitetsparken; adult/child Dkr40/15), on the campus of Århus University, has displays on Denmark's natural history.

Moesgård

The Moesgård Woods, 5km south of the city centre, make for an absorbing half-day outing. The focal point is **Moesgård Museum of Prehistory** (adult/child Dkr35/free; open 10am-5pm daily Apr-Sept, 10am-4pm Tues-Sun Oct-May), with quality displays from the Stone Age to the Viking Age, including a roomful of rune stones. The unique and most dramatic exhibit is the 2000-year-old Graubelle Man, or Grauballemanden, whose preserved body was found in 1952 at the village of Graubelle, 35km west of Århus.

A wound mark across the throat suggests that the Graubelle Man was either murdered, executed or the victim of ritual sacrifice. The date of his death has been pinpointed to the last century BC and one assumption is that he may have been a sacrificial victim to a fertility god of the Iron Age. Investigations show that the body is that of a man of about 30 years of age while analysis of stomach contents revealed that his final meal was a mix of rye and barley gruel. The tannic acids and iron oxide inherent in peat bogs preserved the body naturally by an effective tanning of the skin to a dark brown leathery consistency. The dehydrated, leathery body is remarkably intact, right down to red hair and fingernails.

A new exhibition, with the Graubelle Man as its focus, should be open by the time you read this.

The museum also stages a variety of changing exhibitions throughout the year.

An enjoyable **trail** dubbed the 'prehistoric trackway' or Oldtidsstien leads from behind the museum across fields of wildflowers, past grazing sheep and through beech woods down to **Moesgård Strand**, Århus' best sandy beach. The trail, marked by red-dotted stones, passes reconstructed historic sights including a dolmen, burial cists and an Iron-Age house. The museum has a brochure with details. You can walk one way and catch a bus from the beach back to the city centre or follow the trail both ways as a 5km round trip.

Bus No 6 from Århus train station terminates at the museum year-round, while bus No 19 terminates at Moesgård Strand from May to September; both buses run about twice an hour.

Tivoli Friheden

A good break for youngsters is this amusement park (☎ 86 14 73 00, Skovbrynet 1; adult/child Dkr35/15; open noon-10pm daily May-Aug, noon-9pm mid-Apr–May), 2km south of the city centre. It's at the northern edge of the Marselisborg woods, and is reached via Spanien and then Strandvejen; you can get there by bus No 1, 4, 6, 18 or 19. There are fairground rides, clown shows, flower gardens, fast-food eateries and cafés.

Swimming

There are sandy beaches to be found on the outskirts of Århus. The most popular one to the north is **Bellevue**, about 4km from the city centre (bus No 6 or 16), while the favourite to the south is Moesgård Strand (see Moesgård above).

Organised Tours

A guided 2½-hour bus tour leaves from the **tourist office** (☎ 89 40 67 00 for bookings) at 10am daily from mid-June to early September, giving a glimpse of the main city sights. The Dkr50 tour is a good deal as it includes entry into Den Gamle By and also leaves you with a 24-hour public bus pass.

Special Events

The 10-day **Århus Festival** (W www.aarhusf estuge.dk) in early September turns the city into a stage for nonstop revelry with jazz, rock, classical music, theatre and dance. The festival is of international significance and in its long history has hosted such varied bill toppers as the Rolling Stones, Anne-Sophie Mutter, Ravi Shankar, City of Birmingham Symphony Orchestra, New York City Ballet, Günter Grass and many more. Each year the festival has a special theme, such as dance, or even a big political issue of the day. Events take place all over the city and there is a fringe element also.

Places to Stay

Camping The nearest camping ground, **Blommehaven** (☎ 86 27 02 07; adult/child/ tent Dkr62/31/20; open mid-Mar–mid-Sept), right by beaches in the Marselisborg Woods, is 6km south of Århus and reached by bus No 19 or 6.

Hostels & Rooms The **Danhostel Århus** (☎ 86 16 72 98, fax 86 10 55 60; e danhostel .aarhus@get2net.dk; Marienlundsvej 10; dorm beds Dkr95 rooms Dkr400; open late Jan–mid-Dec), is in a renovated 1850s dance hall at the edge of the Risskov Woods, 4km north of the city centre, reached by bus No 6 or 9.

Århus City Sleep-In (☎ 86 19 20 55, fax 86 19 18 11; e sleep-in@citysleep-in.dk; Havnegade 20; dorm beds Dkr105, double room with bath Dkr360, without bath Dkr300; 24hr reception), run by a youth organisation, is in a central former mariners' hotel. It's casual, the rooms are a bit run down and it can be a noisy, but cheerful, place. Sheets can be hired for Dkr30. Safety boxes are Dkr10, with Dkr100 deposit. Key deposit is Dkr50. There's a TV and pool table, guest kitchen and laundry facilities. Bikes can be hired for Dkr50 a day.

The tourist office books **rooms** in private homes for Dkr200/300 singles/doubles, plus a Dkr25 booking fee.

Hotels The 62-room **Get-in** (☎ 86 10 86 14, fax 86 10 86 24; e get-in@get-in.dk; Jens Baggesensvej 43; singles/doubles with bath Dkr300/400, without bath Dkr250/350) is a guesthouse near Århus University, about 1.5km from the city centre. It has clean, adequate rooms and there's a TV room and guest kitchen. Breakfast is Dkr35. Take bus No 7 from the train station.

Cab-Inn Århus (☎/fax 86 75 70 00; e aarhus@cab-inn.dk; Kannikegade 14; singles/doubles Dkr510/630) is in an ideal central location opposite the Domkirke. The style is standard Cab-Inn with small, but comfy and spotless rooms.

Hotel Guldsmeden (☎ 86 13 45 50, fax 86 13 76 76; Guldsmedgade 40; singles/doubles from Dkr695/945), on the northern side of the city centre, is a friendly place with a relaxed and stylish ambience.

Hotel Ritz (☎ 86 13 44 44, fax 86 13 45 87; W www.hotelritz.dk; Banegårdsplads 12;

DENMARK

singles/doubles Dkr655/995), a member of the Best Western chain, gets a lot of business and conference trade and has plush rooms, although some singles are small.

Places to Eat

The narrow streets of the old quarter north of the cathedral are thick with cafés serving Danish and ethnic foods.

The café-restaurant of **Kulturgyngen** (Mejlgade 53; lunch/dinner Dkr38/75; open 11am-9pm Mon-Sat), an alternative cultural and youth complex, has a great atmosphere, and good food including sandwiches for Dkr25 and a choice of vegetarian or meat dinner nightly.

Café Drudenfuss (☎ 86 12 82 72; Graven 30; brunch Dkr55), is a pleasant relaxing bar/café with art work on the walls, photography exhibitions and a good range of sandwiches, starting at Dkr35, and salads for Dkr47.

A touch more sophisticated is **Café Kindrødt** (☎ 86 18 56 88; Studsgade 8; pastas Dkr55-65). It does salads for Dkr65 and tasty sandwiches starting at Dkr47, and has a good wine list.

Emmery's (☎ 86 13 04 00; Guldsmedgade 24-26; open 7.30am-6pm Mon-Fri 8am-4pm Sat & Sun; brunch Dkr95) is a stylish and friendly café-cum-delicatessen. It serves its own delicious bread, tapas at Dkr95 and sandwiches, including with vegetarian fillings. Breakfast is Dkr20. There's a terrific selection of cheeses, olive oil and coffee, from worldwide ethical sources.

Just along from Emmery's is **Eat** (Klostergade 17) with takeaway sandwiches for Dkr27 to Dkr32, salads Dkr35. Next door, **Baguette** (Klostergade 17) does well-filled small baguettes for Dkr18.50, large ones for Dkr31.

AC (☎ 86 12 95 67; Klostertorv 5; mains Dkr180-298) has modernist decor and modern prices to go with it. Brunch is Dkr78, lunch starts at Dkr65 for tasty fish cakes and there's a good choice of sushi from Dkr25 to Dkr98.

Café Smagløs (☎ 86 19 03 77; Klostertorv 7; brunch Dkr65), right next to AC, is a cosy, down-to-earth place with salads, sandwiches and vegetarian dishes for about Dkr35 to Dkr58. Another nearby option is the **Shawarma Bar**, (pitta-bread sandwiches Dkr25).

Det Grønne Hjørne (☎ 86 13 52 47; Frederiksgade 60; mains Dkr99-149, lunch buffet Dkr59, buffet after 4pm Dkr99), on the corner with Østergade, has a superb buffet spread with good vegetarian options.

China Town (Fredensgade 46; lunch specials under Dkr50), opposite the bus station, offers 10 daily lunch specials. Alternatively, for just Dkr20 you can get a box lunch from the unpretentious **China Wok House** (Søndergade). **City Sandwich** (Sønder Allé 5) does excellent baguettes for Dkr20 to Dkr35.

There is a string of fairly pricey riverside restaurants and bars with outside seating along the north of Aboulevarden to the west of Sankt Clemens Torv bridge. A small lager costs about Dkr25, lunch dishes Dkr60, sandwiches Dkr50. They all have entrances on Sankte Clemens Strade, the street one block north.

Restaurant Gaucho (Aboulevarden 200; mains Dkr109-159), on the east side of the bridge, specialises in Argentinean beef dishes. You get half-price meals between 4pm and 6pm. The train station has a **DSB café**, a **minifood bar** and a small **supermarket** (open until midnight). There's a **fruit stand** (Frugt og Blomster) out front, and a popular bakery/café, **Bread & Coffee**, across the street. Two blocks west on Frederiks Allé, is **Føtex supermarket**, with a cheap bakery and deli, and **Sundhedskost**, the city's largest health-food store. There's a useful **7-Eleven** 24-hour mini-market on the corner of Lille Torv and Immervad, and another branch at Guldsmedgade 33.

Entertainment

The monthly free publication What's On in Århus lists current happenings in detail and is available at the tourist office and other venues around town.

Århus has a vibrant music scene with something for all ages and tastes. **Train** (☎ 86 13 47 22; Toldbodgade 6; open until 5am Thur-Sat) is one of the biggest venues in Denmark. It stages concerts by international rock, pop and country stars and there's a late night disco.

Musikcaféen and the adjacent **Gyngen** (☎ 86 76 03 44; Mejlgade 53; open 8.30pm-2am Mon-Sat) are alternative and often vibrant venues with rock, jazz and world music. They are a showcase for hopefuls and up-and-coming acts.

VoxHall (☎ 87 30 97 97; Vester Allé 15; open 8pm-2am Mon-Sat) offers a very wide range of music and will sometimes features UK bands.

Jazzbar Bent J (☎ 86 12 04 92; Nørre Allé 66) is a jazz only, very long-established bar that has an impressive guest list. Entry is Dkr80 on guest nights.

Sherlock Holmes Pub (☎ 86 12 40 50; Frederiksgade 76d) has live music, a big screen for football matches and lots more. Drinks are half-price until 7pm. Just down the road is the three-floor dance and disco **Buddy Holly's** (☎ 86 18 08 55; Frederiksgade 29; open 10am-5am Mon-Thur, from 5pm Fri & 10pm Sat).

Café Viva (Aboulevarden/Sankte Clemens Strøde 22), a classy riverside restaurant, transforms into a late night disco upstairs.

There are a number of busy bars in Skolegade, where **Den Høje** (Skolegade 28) is popular with an easygoing young crowd, not least for its cheap beer. It's open most nights from 7pm to 5am, closed Sundays.

The main gay and lesbian social scene is at **Pan Club** (☎ 86 13 43 80; Jægergårdsgade 42). To find it head south down MP Bruuns Gade on the west side of the train station and then go right down Jægergårdsgade for 300m and it's on the left-hand side of the road. There's a late-night café on Tuesday, Thursday, Friday and Saturday and a disco on Thursday, Friday and Saturday. The Århus office of Landsforeningen for Bøsser og Lesbiske, the Danish national organisation for gays and lesbians is across the courtyard from Pan Club. Ask there about special events and private club contacts. The city concert hall, **Musikhuset Århus**, presents dance, opera and concerts by international performers.

Getting There & Away
Air The airport, in Tirstrup 43km northeast of Århus, has direct flights from Copenhagen and London.

Bus The bus station (Fredensgade) has a DSB café, a small supermarket and a photocopier. **Express buses** (☎ 70 21 08 88) run a few times daily between Århus and Copenhagen's Valby Station (adult/child Dkr210/105, students Dkr110, three hours). Buses run regularly to Silkeborg (Dkr46, 48 minutes) and Aalborg (Dkr110, two hours).

Train Trains to Århus, via Odense, leave Copenhagen on the hour from early morning to 10pm (Dkr267, 3¼ hours) and there's a night train at 2am. There are regular trains to Aalborg (Dkr135, one hour, 25 minutes) and Esbjerg (Dkr184, 2¾ hours). There's a ticket-queuing system at the station, red for internal, green for international. For local journeys,

unless you have mastered use of the quicker ticket machines, be prepared for quite long waits at busy times. Friday trains are always very busy and it's advised to reserve a seat for long journeys.

Car & Motorcycle The main highways to Århus are the E45 from the north and south and route 15 from the west. The E45 curves around the western edge of the city as a ring road. There are a number of turn-offs from the ring road into the city, including Åhavevej from the south and Randersvej from the north.

Cars can be rented from **Europcar** (☎ 89 33 11 11; Sønder Allé 35).

Boat The ferry operator is **Mols-Linien** (☎ 70 10 14 18). It runs car ferries from Århus to Odden (adult/child Dkr135-195/half price, car and five passengers Dkr435, 65 minutes) and Kalundborg (2½ hours).

Getting Around
To/From the Airport The airport bus to Århus train station costs Dkr55 and takes approx 45 minutes. Check times to the airport at the stands outside the train station; some services start only in August. The taxi fare to the airport is about Dkr470.

Bus Most in-town buses stop in front of the train station or around the corner on Park Allé. City bus tickets are bought from a machine in the back of the bus for Dkr13 and are good for unlimited rides within the time period stamped on the ticket, which is about two hours.

You can also buy a 24-hour pass for bus travel in Århus county (adult/child Dkr88/44) or in Århus municipality alone (Dkr50/25). Or get a two-/seven-day 'Århus Pass' (Dkr110/155) that includes both bus travel and entry into Århus museums. You can buy tickets and passes at **Århus Sporveje** (☎ 89 40 10 10; Banegårdspladsen 20; open 8am-6pm Mon-Fri, 10am-1pm Sat), the city transport service shop across from the train station.

Car & Motorcycle A car is convenient for getting to sights such as Moesgård on the city outskirts, though the city centre is best explored on foot. There's paid parking along many streets and in municipal car parks, including one on the southern side of Musikhuset Århus. Fees start at Dkr1 for six minutes and Dkr10 for one hour. Overnight (7pm to 8am) is free.

Taxi Taxis wait outside the station and at Store Torv. Expect to pay up to Dkr60 for destinations within the city.

JELLING

Jelling, in spite of its low-key, rural character is the location of one of Denmark's most important historic sites – the **Jelling church**. Inside the small whitewashed church are **frescoes** dating from the 12th century, and outside the door are two impressive **runic stones**.

The smaller stone was erected in the early 900s by King Gorm the Old, Denmark's first king, in honour of his wife, Queen Thyra. The larger one, raised by Harald Bluetooth and dubbed 'Denmark's baptismal certificate', is adorned with the oldest representation of Christ found in Scandinavia and reads:

Harald king bade this be ordained for Gorm his father and Thyra his mother, the Harald who won for himself all Denmark and Norway and made the Danes Christians.

Two huge **burial mounds** flank the church; the one on the north side is said to be that of King Gorm and the other of Queen Thyra, although excavators in the 19th century found no human remains and few artefacts. This could suggest much earlier grave robbing, but during the 1970s archaeologists excavated below Jelling Kirke and found the remains of three wooden churches. The oldest of these was thought to have been erected by Harald Bluetooth.

A burial chamber within this site was also uncovered and revealed human bones and gold jewellery that shared characteristics with artefacts previously discovered within the large northern burial mound. One suggestion is that the bones found beneath the church ruins are those of King Gorm and that they were moved there from the old pagan burial mound by Harald Bluetooth out of respect for his recently acquired Christian faith. Queen Thyra remains ephemeral. The Jelling mounds, church and rune stones are designated as a Unesco World Heritage Site.

Kongernes Jelling (☎ 75 87 23 50; Gormsgade 23; adult/child Dkr30/15; open 10am-5pm daily June-Aug; 10am-5pm Tues-Sun Mar-May & Sept; 1pm-4pm Tues-Sun Jan-Mar & Nov-Dec) is an information and exhibition centre just across the road from the church. It traces the history of the Jelling monuments. It has a **café** where you can get a pleasant smorgosbord lunch for Dkr45.

Jelling makes a good two-hour side trip off the Odense–Århus run. Change trains at Vejle for the ride to Jelling (Dkr21, 15 minutes). The church is 100m straight up Stationsvej from the Jelling train station.

THE LAKE DISTRICT

The Danish Lake District, the closest thing to hill country in Denmark, is a popular outdoor-activity area for Danes, and there is certainly excellent canoeing, biking and hiking to be had amid the woods and on the water. The scenery is placid and pastoral rather than stunning, but the area is delightful all the same and has a distinctive character. The Lake District contains the Gudenå, Denmark's longest river; Mossø, Jutland's largest lake; and Yding Skovhøj, Denmark's highest point. None of these are terribly long, large or high in terms of low altitude Denmark.

Silkeborg
pop 52,000

Silkeborg overcomes its rather bland modern character with a friendly openness. It is the Lake District's biggest town and is an ideal base for exploring the surrounding forests and waterways. The town has some excellent restaurants and lively bars and cafés. The helpful **tourist office** (☎ 86 82 19 11; ⓦ www.silkeborg.com; Åhavevej 2A; open 9am-5pm Mon-Fri, 9am-3pm Sat, 9.30am-12.30pm Sun mid-June–Aug; 9am-4pm Mon-Fri, 9am-noon Sat Sept–mid-June) is near the harbour and has lots of leaflets and brochures including detailed route descriptions of walks and cycle routes.

Internettet (Ngade 37) is an Internet café charging Dkr25 per hour.

Silkeborg Museum The main attraction at the Silkeborg Museum (☎ 86 82 14 99; Hovedgården; adult/child Dkr30/10; open 10am-5pm daily mid-May–Oct; noon-4pm Wed, Sat & Sun Nov–mid-May) is the Tollund Man. He is believed to have been executed in 200 BC and his leathery body, complete with the rope still around its neck, was discovered in a bog in 1950. The well-preserved face of the Tollund Man is hypnotic in its detail. Other attractions include displays on local trades and of fine Danish glasswork.

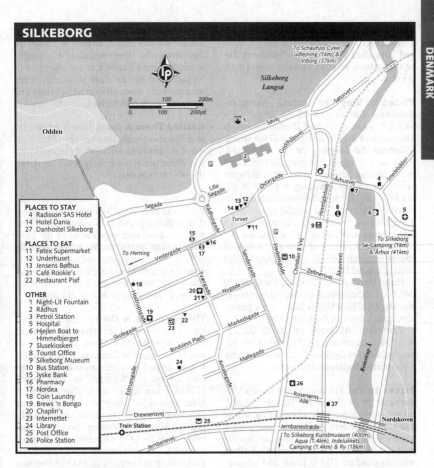

SILKEBORG

PLACES TO STAY
4 Radisson SAS Hotel
14 Hotel Dania
27 Danhostel Silkeborg

PLACES TO EAT
11 Føtex Supermarket
12 Underhuset
13 Jensens Bøfhus
21 Café Rookie's
22 Restaurant Piaf

OTHER
1 Night-Lit Fountain
2 Rådhus
3 Petrol Station
5 Hospital
6 Hjejlen Boat to
   Himmelbjerget
7 Slusekiosken
8 Tourist Office
9 Silkeborg Museum
10 Bus Station
15 Jyske Bank
16 Pharmacy
17 Nordea
18 Coin Laundry
19 Brews 'n Bongo
20 Chaplin's
23 Internettet
24 Library
25 Post Office
26 Police Station

Silkeborg Kuntsmuseum The museum
(☎ 86 82 53 88; Gudenåvej 7-9; adult/child
Dkr40/free; open 10am-5pm Tues-Sun Apr-
Oct, noon-4pm Tues-Fri Nov-Mar) is 1km
south of the town centre and features the
works of native son Asger Jorn and other
modern artists.

Aqua Situated 2km south of central Silkeborg, Aqua (☎ 89 21 21 89; Vejsøvej 55;
adult/child Dkr70/40; open 10am-6pm daily
June-Aug; 10am-4pm Mon-Fri, 10am-5pm
Sat & Sun Sept-Mar) is an entertaining aquarium and exhibition centre with lots of fishy
creatures and imaginative displays.

Activities Outdoor activities are at the heart
of the Lake District's appeal. The track of the

old railway from Silkeborg to Horsens is now
an excellent **walking** and **cycling** trail of
about 50km or so. It passes through the beech
forest of **Nordskoven**, itself crisscrossed with
hiking and bike trails. To reach Nordskoven
simply head south down Åhavevej from the
tourist office then go left over the old railway
bridge down by the hostel. The tourist office
has useful leaflets on Nordskoven and on the
Silkeborg-Horsens trail.

Canoeing is a marvellous way to explore
the Lake District and you can plan trips for several days staying at lakeside camp sites along
the way. The canoe-hire places can help plan
an itinerary. You can rent canoes for Dkr60/
300 an hour/day at **Slusekiosken** (☎ 86 80 08
93) at the harbour. Bike hire costs Dkr69 per
day at **Schaufuss Cykeludlejning** (☎ 86 81 39

38; *Nørreskov Bakke 93)*, which is about 1½km from Torvet across Silkeborg Langsø and is reached by Bus No 5. **Silkeborg Sø-camping** rents bikes and canoes from Dkr60 per day.

Places to Stay The camping ground, **In-delukkets Camping** *(☎ 86 82 22 01; Vejl-søvej 7; adult/child/tent Dkr60/30/25)*, is 1km south of the art museum amid woodland. **Silkeborg Sø-camping** *(☎ 86 82 28 24; Arhusvej 51; adult/child/tent Dkr60/30/25)* is in a lakeside setting 1.5km east of the town centre. **Danhostel Silkeborg** *(☎ 86 82 36 42, fax 86 81 27 77; e silkeborg@danhostel.dk; Åhavevej 55; dorm beds Dkr100; open 1 Mar–1 Dec)* has a scenic riverbank location and is a few minutes walk east of the train station.

The tourist office distributes a list of **rooms** in private homes, with singles/doubles costing around Dkr150/350.

Hotel Dania *(☎ 86 82 01 11, fax 86 80 20 04; e info@hoteldania.dk; Torvet 5; singles/doubles Dkr995/1195)* is Silkeborg's prime-site, luxury hotel in the heart of town.

Radisson SAS Hotel *(☎ 88 82 22 22; e info@radissonsas.com; Papirfabrikken 12; singles/doubles Dkr950/1180)* is a smoothly comfortable, business-class hotel.

Places to Eat For tasty meals there's **Un-derhuset** *(☎ 86 82 37 36; Torvet 7; fish & meat mains Dkr55-100)*. It's right on Torvet and does excellent Danish cuisine with a touch of French. A lunch platter of herring cost Dkr48. Next door is a **Jensen's Bøfhus** with its standard Dkr39 lunch and all-you-can-eat spare ribs for Dkr99.

There are a number of cheap food outlets on Søndergade, the pedestrianised main street. The **Føtex supermarket** *(Torvet)* has a bakery and an inexpensive café.

Nygade is Silkeborg's equivalent to Aal-borg's 'street of bars' Jomfru Ane Gade, but with more everyday shops. There are a number of grill bars and pizza places with quick bites for Dkr20 to Dkr35. **Restaurant Piaf** *(☎ 86 81 12 55; Nygade 31; mains Dkr180)* has French-inspired cuisine in cosy sur-roundings. The nearby **Café Rookie's** *(☎ 86 81 33 44; Nygade 18; sandwiches Dkr25-48)* is a relaxed place that does good sandwiches and has a vegetarian menu for Dkr25 to Dkr42. It stays open until the early hours on Thursday, Friday and Saturday.

Entertainment Nygade has several good music bars and discos. **Brews 'n Bongo** on the corner with Hostrupsgade is a late-night music bar and **Chaplin's** at the other end of Nygade, and behind Café Rookie's, opens until the early hours on Thursday, Friday and Saturday. Both bars admit over-18s only.

Getting There & Away Hourly trains con-nect Silkeborg with Skanderborg (Dkr39, 30 minutes) and Århus (Dkr60, 49 minutes) via Ry. There are regular daily buses to Århus (Dkr46, 48 minutes).

Ry

Ry is a smaller town in a more rural setting than Silkeborg and is a good place from which to base your exploration of the Lake District. The helpful **tourist office** *(☎ 86 89 34 22; w www.visitry.com; Klostervej 3; open 9am-5pm Mon-Fri, 9am-2pm Sat mid-June–Aug; 9am-4pm Mon-Fri, 9pm-noon Sat Sept–mid-June)* is in the train station.

Things to See & Do The Lake District's most visited spot is the whimsically named **Himmelbjerget** (Sky Mountain), which, at just 147m, is one of Denmark's highest hills. It was formed by water erosion during the final Ice Age as a 'false hill' or *kol*, the sides of which are quite steep. Himmelbjerget holds great significance for Danes. There are a number of interesting memorials surround-ing the hilltop's crowning glory, the 25m tower built in 1875 to commemorate King Frederick VII, who introduced constitutional government to Denmark in 1849. Admission to the tower, and to its superlative views, is Dkr5. Open-air meetings, both political and cultural have been held on the summit of Himmelbjerget. The summit can be reached via a marked 6km footpath from Ry, or by bus or boat.

Another good, half-day outing is to cycle from Ry to **Boes**, a tiny hamlet with pictur-esque, thatch-roofed houses and vivid flower gardens. From Boes continue cross country to **Øm Kloster** *(☎ 86 89 81 94; adult/child Dkr35/10; open 10am-6pm Tues-Sun July-Aug, 10am-5pm Mar-June & Sept, 10am-4pm Apr & Oct)*, the ruins of a medieval monastery, where glass-topped tombs reveal the 750-year-old bones of Bishop Elafsen of Århus and many of his abbots. The whole trip from Ry and back is 18km.

If you want to explore the lakes in the district, **Ry Kanofart** (☎ 86 89 11 67; Kyhnsvej 20) rents canoes for Dkr60 an hour. For walking and cycling routes ask at the tourist centre for the cycling and walking leaflets (Dkr20). **Cykeludlejning** (☎ 86 89 14 91; Skanderborgvej 19) rents bikes for Dkr50 a day.

Places to Stay & Eat The lakeside **Sønder Ege Camping** (☎ 86 89 13 75; e info@ sdregecamping.dk; Søkildevej 65; adult/child Dkr65/35) is 1km north of town. **Danhostel Ry** (☎ 86 89 14 07; e mail@danhostel-ry.dk; Randersvej 88; dorm beds Dkr100, rooms Dkr400) is on the same bathing lake. To get there from the train station cross the tracks, turn left and go 2.5km; or take the infrequent bus No 311. The tourist office books **rooms** in private homes from Dkr200/275 for singles/doubles.

Ry Park Hotel (☎ 86 89 19 11; e ryparkh otel@mail.dk; Kyhnsvej 2; singles/doubles Dkr690/890) is a modern complex with swimming pool, sauna and restaurant. It has sizable coach trade.

The **butcher's shop**, opposite the train station, has fried fish and a few other takeaway selections. There's a **bakery** next door and the nearby **Peking Grill** (☎ 86 89 24 84; Klostervej 26; mains Dkr45-65) is a good bet. In Skanderborgvej are cheap eateries **Gormand Sandwich** and **Pizza Express** while **Pizzeria Italia** (☎ 86 89 31 33; Skanderbrgvej 3; fish & meat mains Dkr109-147) offers tasty pastas at Dkr69 and a three-course menu for Dkr179.

Getting There & Away Hourly trains connect Ry with Silkeborg (Dkr25, 20 minutes) and Århus (Dkr35, 30 minutes).

VIBORG
pop 12,700
Viborg's rich history and religious associations rest happily with what has become a charming and very modern Danish town. Nearby lakes and surrounding woodland enhance its appeal. In 1060, Viborg became one of Denmark's eight bishoprics and grew into a major religious centre. Prior to the Reformation the town had 25 churches and abbeys though ecclesiastical remnants from that period are few.

Orientation & Information
The old part of town consists of the street around Viborg Domkirke. The train station is about 1km southwest of the tourist office.

Viborg **tourist office** (☎ 86 61 16 66; w www.viborg.dk; Nytorv 9; open 9am-5pm Mon-Fri, 9am-3pm Sat mid-June–Aug; 9am-5pm Mon-Fri, 9.30am-12.30pm Sat mid-May–mid-June; 9am-4pm Mon-Fri, 9.30am-12.30pm Sat Sept-Apr) is in the centre of town.

There is ample, and convenient, free parking behind the Sankt Mathias Gade Shopping Centre on the south side of town, but you must use a time disc.

Things to See & Do
The tourist office has excellent printouts, including English-language versions, that describe walks round the town with historical and cultural themes.

The multitowered **Viborg Domkirke** (☎ 87 25 52 50; Sankt Mogens Gade 4; admission free; open 10am-5pm Mon-Sat, noon-5pm Sun June-Aug; 11am-4pm Mon-Sat, noon-4pm Sun Apr-May & Sept; 11am-3pm Mon-Sat, noon-3pm Sun Jan-Mar) is one of Denmark's largest granite churches. The first church on the site dated from the Viking period. The cathedral's interior is awash with frescoes painted over five years (1901–06) by artist Joakim Skovgaard and feature scenes from the Old Testament and the life of Christ.

Skovgaard Museet (☎ 86 62 39 75; Domkirkestræde 2-4; adult/child Dkr10/free; open 10am-12.30pm & 1.30pm-5pm daily May-Sept; 1.30pm-5pm daily Oct-Apr) lies to the south of Viborg Domkirke. It also features work by Joakim Skovgaard, but here the scenes are more down to earth and include portraits, landscapes and nudes.

There's a local history museum **Viborg Stiftsmuseum** (☎ 87 25 26 20; Hjultorvet 9; adult/child Dkr20/free; open 11am-5pm daily mid-June–Aug; 2pm-5pm Tues-Fri, 11am-5pm Sat & Sun Sept–mid-June) that tells the story of Viborg's rich past.

Sankt Mogens Gade, between the cathedral and the tourist office, has some handsome old houses, including Hauchs Gård at No 7 and the Willesens House at No 9, both dating back to around 1520.

Places to Stay & Eat
Viborg So Camping (☎ 86 67 13 11, fax 86 67 35 29; e viborg@dcu.dk; Vinkelvej 36b; open late Mar-late Sept; adult/child/tent Dkr58/29/20) is a three-star camping ground on the east side of Lake Søndersø. **Danhostel**

Viborg (☎ 86 67 17 81; ⓔ viborg@danhostel
.dk), adjacent to Viborg So Camping, is just a
1km walk from town. It has bikes for hire.

Staff at the tourist office can book **rooms**
in private homes with singles/doubles starting at Dkr200/275 plus a Dkr25 booking fee.

Palads Hotel (☎ 86 62 37 00; ⓔ infor@
hotelplads.dk; Sankt Mathias Gade; singles/
doubles Dkr895/1195; Sat & Sun year-round,
daily May-Sept Dkr795 per room) is a long-
established hotel, now part of the Best Western chain. It has bright, pleasant rooms and is
just a short walk north of the train station.

The huge **Sankt Mathias Gade Centre** has
cafés, a supermarket, fruit shop, a butcher
and a baker.

Ristorante Pizzeria Italia (☎ 86 62 42 43;
Sankt Mathias Gade 74; buffet lunch Dkr49)
does tasty pastas for Dkr45, pizzas for Dkr45
to Dkr50 and a children's pizza for Dkr29.
Bone's (☎ 86 60 36 66; Prieisler's Plads 3;
meals from Dkr100), 300m west of the tourist
office, offers large helpings of steak and
spare ribs.

Kafé Arthur (☎ 86 62 21 26; Vestergade
4; 2-course dinner Dkr210) is a stylish venue
for an evening out; it also does a good lunch
menu for about Dkr70.

Café Vogue (☎ 86 62 63 32; Sankt Mathias Gade 28; brunch Dkr53-71) has pasta salads and sandwiches for Dkr40 to Dkr53 and
Mexican dishes for Dkr59 to Dkr65. It's a
popular place with bright, cheerful decor.

Getting There & Around
Viborg is 66km northwest of Århus on route 26
and 41km west of Randers on route 16. Trains
from Århus (Dk94, 70 minutes) run hourly
Monday to Friday, less frequently at weekends.

The **tourist office** has a few bikes for hire
at Dkr50 a day. **Byens Cykler** (☎ 86 62 36
53, fax 86 61 10 89; Vesterbrogade 19A) is
west of Sankt Mathias Gade and rents bikes
for Dkr60 a day.

AALBORG
pop 155,000
People soon warm to Aalborg's unassuming
style. This is Jutland's second largest city, an
industrial and trading centre without many
great buildings or much medieval quaintness
to enliven its commercialism. Yet Aalborg is
a friendly, down-to-earth place with plenty of
good shops and a lively nightlife. It has some
worthwhile sites, not least the remarkable

Lindholm Høje, Denmark's largest Viking
burial ground. Linked by bridge and tunnel,
the city spreads across both sides of the Limfjord, the long body of water that cuts Jutland
in two.

Orientation & Information
The town centre is a 10-minute walk from the
train and bus stations, north on Boulevarden.
There is a very helpful **tourist office** (☎ 98
12 60 22; ⓦ www.visitaalborg.com; Østerågade 8; open 9am-5.30pm Mon-Fri, 10am-
1pm Sat mid-June; 10am-4pm Sat July;
9am-4.30pm Mon-Fri, 10am-1pm Sat Jan–
mid-June & Sept-Dec). The tourist office has
masses of information, including a diary of
events, What's On In Aalborg.

The **Danish Emigration Archives** (☎ 99
31 42 20; Arkivstræde 1), behind Vor Frue
Kirke, helps foreigners of Danish descent
trace their roots.

The office of **Landsforeningen for Bøsser
og Lesbiske** (LBL; ☎ 98 16 45 07; Toldbodgade 27, PO Box 1244) is the local branch
of the Danish national organisation for gays
and lesbians.

There's an Internet centre at **Net-City** (Nytorv 13A) that charges Dkr20 for one hour.
Free Internet access can be had at the city library **Hovedbiblioteket** (Rendsburggade 2;
open 10am-8pm Mon-Fri, 10am-3pm Sat).

Old Town
The whitewashed **Buldolfi Domkirke** marks
the centre of the old town, and has colourful
frescoes in the foyer. About 75m east of the
cathedral is the **Aalborg Historiske Museum**
(Algade 48; adult/child Dkr20/10; open
10am-5pm Tues-Sun) with interesting artefacts and the Renaissance furnishings.

The alley between the museum and church
leads to the rambling **Monastery of the Holy
Ghost**, which dates from 1431; the tourist office arranges guided tours (Dkr40). Northeast of the cathedral on Østerågade are three
noteworthy historic buildings: the **old town
hall** (circa 1762), five-storey **Jens Bangs
Stenhus** (circa 1624) and **Jørgen Olufsens
House** (circa 1616).

In addition, the half-timbered neighbourhoods around **Vor Frue Kirke** are worth a
stroll, particularly the cobbled Hjelmerstald.
Aalborghus Slot, near the waterfront, is more
administrative office than castle, but there's
a small dungeon you can enter for free.

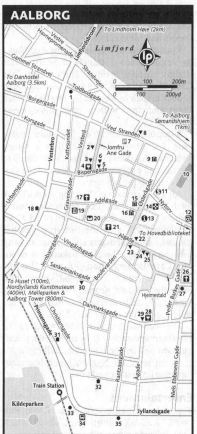

AALBORG

PLACES TO STAY
18   Helnan Phønix Hotel
31   Prinsens Hotel
32   Park Hotel

PLACES TO EAT
2   Frytøjet
3   Rendez Vous
5   7-Eleven
6   Benzons
8   Café Casa Blanca
22   Bakery
23   Schak Nielsen
24   Café Underground
25   Kronen
29   Ali-Baba
30   Akropolis

OTHER
1   Landsforeningen for Bøsser og Lesbiske (LBL)
4   Royal Pub
7   Parking Garage
9   Jørgen Olufsens House
10   Aalborghus Slot
11   Bank
12   Net-City
13   Tourist Office
14   Salling Department Store
15   Jens Bangs Stenhus
16   Old Town Hall
17   Monastery of the Holy Ghost
19   Aalborg Historiske Museum
20   Post Office
21   Budolfi Domkirke
26   Vor Frue Kirke
27   Danish Emigration Archives
28   Pan Aalborg Club
33   Avis Car Rental
34   Bus Station
35   Europcar Car Rental

Nordjyllands Kunstmuseum

This regional art museum (☎ 98 13 80 88; Kong Christian Allé 50; adult/child Dkr30/free; open 10am-5pm daily July-Aug, 10am-5pm Tues-Sun Sept-June) in a marble building designed by Finnish architect Alvar Aalto, has a fine collection of Danish modern art, including work by Asger Jorn and JF Willumsen.

To get to the museum, take the tunnel beneath the train station; it leads to Kildeparken, a green space with statues and water fountains.

Go directly through the park, cross Vesterbro and then continue through a wooded area to the museum, a 10-minute walk in all; or take bus No 5, 8, 10 or 11 from the centre of town.

Aalborg Tower

The hill behind the art museum has an ungainly tower (☎ 98 77 05 11; Søndre Skovvej; Dkr20; open 11am-5pm daily Apr-Sept, 10am-7pm daily July) with a panoramic view of the city's steeples and smokestacks. The tower sits on the edge of an expansive wooded area, **Mølleparken**, which has walking trails, views and a zoo.

Lindholm Høje

On a hill-top pasture overlooking the city, Lindholm Høje (admission free; open dawn-dusk daily) is the site of nearly 700 graves from the Iron Age and Viking Age. Many of the **Viking graves** are marked by stones placed in the outline of a Viking ship, with two larger end stones as stem and stern. There is a compelling

DENMARK

atmosphere at the site. A **museum** (☎ 96 31 04 29; adult/child Dkr30/15; open 10am-5pm daily Apr-Oct) depicts, in an imaginative way, the site's history; it is adjacent to the field. Lindholm Høje is 15 minutes from Aalborg centre on bus No 6.

Places to Stay
Danhostel Aalborg (☎ 98 11 60 44, fax 98 12 47 11; e aalborg@danhostel.dk; Skydebanevej 50; dorm beds Dkr100, rooms Dkr460) is at the marina 4km west of the centre and has an adjacent camping ground with cabins. Take bus No 8.

The tourist office books **rooms** in private homes for Dkr200/300 for singles/doubles plus a Dkr25 booking fee.

Prinsens Hotel (☎ 98 13 37 33, fax 98 16 52 82; Prinsensgade 14; w www.prinsen-hotel .dk; singles/doubles from Dkr695/895) has modern rooms, although some are rather small.

Aalborg Sømandshjem (☎ 98 12 19 00, fax 98 11 76 97; e hansen@hotel-aalborg .com; Østerbro 27; singles/doubles Dkr500/ 680), about 1km east of the centre, has comfortable, quiet rooms.

Park Hotel (☎ 98 12 31 33, fax 98 13 31 66; e parkhotel@email.dk; Boulevarden 41; singles/doubles from Dkr725/859) has comfortable rooms and traditional decor and is just 100m from the train and bus stations.

Helnan Phønix Hotel (☎ 98 12 00 11, fax 98 10 10 20; e hotel@helnan-phoniz-hotel .dk; singles/doubles Dkr755/955), a smart modern hotel with plush rooms, has its own fitness and sauna suite.

Places to Eat
A good place for food, drink and diversion is Aalborg's famous Jomfru Ane Gade, a lively, pedestrian street lined with restaurants and bars, most with pavement tables and competitive prices. It could do with a few non-food and -drink outlets to break the pace, but it is the heart of Aalborg's nightlife and most places are open to the early hours.

If you want just food rather than fun, there's a 24-hour **7-Eleven** mini-market on the corner with Bispensgade. At the popular **Rendez Vous** (☎ 98 16 88 80; Jomfru Ane Gade 5; fish & meat mains Dkr69-90) you can get a tasty brunch for Dkr69, including a 'fitness' healthy eating version. Just opposite is **Benzons** (☎ 98 16 34 44; Jomfru Ane Gade 8), with good Danish dishes and a lunch buffet for

Dkr69, and **Frytøjet** (☎ 98 13 73 77; Jomfru Ane Gade 17; dishes around Dkr60) with Danish and Mexican fare.

Round the corner from Jomfru Ane Gade, on Ved Stranden a straggle of eateries offer slightly cheaper options. The popular **Café Casa Blanca** (☎ 98 16 44 45; Ved Stranden 4) does brunch or a buffet for Dkr59 between 11am and 4pm with a youngsters' menu for Dkr39.

Akropolis (☎ 98 11 42 55; Sankelmarksgade 1A; menu Dkr209-279) is a Greek restaurant that does grilled dishes for Dkr79 to Dkr128 and might make you think of the sun, if it's raining Danish rain.

Algade, a pedestrian shopping street a block south of the tourist office, offers inexpensive options, including **Schak Nielsen** (☎ 98 12 35 92; Algade 23) a terrific fish shop that has takeaway salmonburgers and a range of tasty fish specialities. There's a **bakery** just opposite. **Café Underground** (Algade 21) offers natural ice cream, crêpes and sandwiches, while the splendid **Kronen** (☎ 98 12 04 10; Algade 17) sells specialist coffee and other delicacies on the corner with Mollegade.

The well-stocked **Ali-Baba** (☎ 98 12 73 11; Danmarksgade 27) is an excellent delicatessen just by the Pan Club. **Salling**, a department store on Nytorv, has a basement supermarket with a good deli.

Entertainment
A popular drinking spot is the **Royal Pub** (☎ 98 13 20 80; Jomfru Ane Gade 3), which has a fulsome range of beers and spirits.

Jomfru Ane Gade has a number of early hours dance bars and discos. Away from the street of bars, **Huset** (☎ 98 16 76 66; Hasserisgade 10) is a cultural centre that stages jazz, folk and world music events. **Pan Aalborg Club** (☎ 98 12 22 45; Danmarksgade 27A; open 11pm-2am Thur, 10pm-5am Fri & Sat) is Aalborg's main gay venue and has a bar and disco.

Getting There & Away
Train Trains run at least hourly to Århus (Dkr135, one hour 25 minutes) and every two hours to Frederikshavn (Dkr68, one hour). **Express buses** (☎ 70 10 00 30) run daily to Copenhagen (Dkr220, five hours).

Car & Motorcycle The E45 bypasses the city centre, tunnelling under the Limfjord,

DENMARK

whereas the connecting route 180 leads into the centre. To get to Lindholm Høje or points north from Aalborg centre, take route 180 (Vesterbro), which crosses the Limfjord by bridge.

Avis (☎ 98 13 30 99) is at the train station. **Europcar** (☎ 98 13 23 55; Jyllandsgade 4) is a short distance to the west.

Getting Around

City buses leave from the intersection of Østerågade and Nytorv. The bus fare is Dkr13 to any place in greater Aalborg.

Other than for a few one-way streets and the often-confusing outer roads that may have you driving in circles, central Aalborg is fairly easy to get around by car. There's metered parking in the city centre (Dkr8/64, one/24 hours) and time-limited, free parking along many side streets, but you need to use a parking disc. If you're unable to find a parking space, there's a large parking garage, Palads Parking, at Ved Stranden 11.

REBILD BAKKER NATIONAL PARK

Rebild Bakker National Park is a great place to unwind from too much urban experience. It was founded in 1912 by Danish-Americans and is best known for its US-style Fourth of July celebration, the largest held outside of the USA.

There's a Lincoln log cabin and a few souvenir shops near the centre, but the rest of the park is an unspoiled area of rolling hills and heathland. A 4km trail begins in a sheep meadow opposite the Lincoln cabin, and numerous other trails crisscross the park and the adjacent Rold Skov, Denmark's largest forest.

The Ministry of the Environment publishes a useful leaflet *Rebild Bakker Himmerland* that gives basic directions for a number of rewarding walks. One of the best is the 3km Ravnkilde-Nordre Dybdal trail, which takes in some good views and passes interesting old buildings and ruins.

The **Rebild Festival** is an annual event on 4 July celebrating Danish-American connections. It celebrates and commemorates over 300,000 Danish immigrants to the USA during the late 19th and early 20th centuries and the strong familial bonds that survive between the USA and Denmark. The festival has a strong American flavour. There are concerts by military and civilian orchestras and bands, receptions, picnics, dancing and

rock and country music shows. Aalborg itself takes on a distinctly American hue with most festivalgoers staying in the city.

Safari Camping (☎ 98 39 11 10; Rebildvej 17; adult/child Dkr60/35) is nearby. You can get meals at the park cafeterias. The thatch-roofed **Danhostel Rebild** (☎ 98 39 13 40; e rebild@danhostel.dk; dorm beds Dkr100, rooms Dkr350) is next to the park entrance.

From Aalborg, Århus-bound trains stop in Skørping (Dkr39, 16 minutes), from where it's 3km to Rebild. Bus No 104 runs between Aalborg and Rebild (Dkr36, 45 minutes), via Skørping, 10 times daily Monday to Friday, six times daily at weekends.

FREDERIKSHAVN
pop 26,000

Frederikshavn is a major ferry town and industrial port with a fairly featureless dockside area; but the town has a pleasant pedestrianised centre with plenty of shops and several attractive bars and restaurants.

An overhead walkway leads from the ferry terminal to the **tourist office** (☎ 98 42 32 66; w www.frederikshavn-tourist.dk; Skandiatorv 1; open 8.30am-7pm Mon-Sat, 8.30am-5pm Sun July–mid-Aug (until 5pm daily last 2 weeks June & Aug), 9am-4pm Mon-Fri, 11am-2pm Sat Sept–mid-June). The train station and adjacent bus terminal are a 10-minute walk to the north.

Bangsbo Museum

Bangsbomuseet (☎ 98 42 31 11; Margrethesvej 6; adult/child Dkr30/5; open 10am-5pm daily June-Aug, 10.30-5pm Sept-May, closed Mon Nov-May), 3km south of Frederikshavn centre, is an old country estate with an interesting mix of exhibits. In the manor house, there are displays of antique furnishings and collectibles, while the old farm buildings hold ship figureheads, military paraphernalia and exhibits on Danish resistance to the German occupation. The most intriguing exhibit is the *Ellingå* ship, reconstructed remains of a 12th-century Viking-style merchant ship that was dug up from a nearby stream bed. Bus No 3 from central Frederikshavn stops near the entrance to the estate, from where it's an enjoyable 500m walk through the woods to the museum. The adjoining **Bangsbo Botanical Gardens** with its deer park makes a pleasant additional visit.

Krudttårnet

If you're waiting for a train, you might want to climb the nearby whitewashed Krudttårnet (☎ 98 42 31 11; Kragholmen 1; adult/child Dkr15/5; open 10.30am-5pm daily June-Sept). It's an old gun tower and a remnant of the 17th-century citadel that once protected the port.

Places to Stay & Eat

Danhostel Frederikshavn (☎ 98 42 14 75, fax 98 42 65 22; ℮ frederikshavn@danhostel .dk; Buhlsvej 6; dorm beds Dkr90, singles/ doubles Dkr200/270; open Feb–mid-Dec) is 2km north of the ferry terminal.

The tourist office books **rooms** in private homes from Dkr150/175 for singles/doubles, plus a Dkr25 booking fee.

Hotel Herman Bang (☎ 98 42 21 66, fax 98 42 21 07; ﹗ www.hermanbang.dk; Tordenskjoldsgade 3; singles/doubles with bath Dkr595/795, without bath Dkr395/595) is central and has bright, comfortable rooms.

Scandic Stena Line Hotel Frederikshavn (☎ 98 43 32 33; fax 98 43 33 11; ℮ frederi kshavn@scandic-hotels.com; Tordenskjoldsgade 14; singles/doubles Dkr915/1115) is a pricey option, but comes with a full scale swimming pool, bubble bath, wave machine and bar.

Damsgaard Supermarked (Havnegade) beside the tourist office, has a cheap cafeteria with a harbour view, and there are pizzerias on nearby Danmarksgade and Søndergade. A busy little place just off the south end of Søndergade, **Ar Buchetto** (☎ 98 43 34 36; Rimmensgade 4b; pizzas & pastas Dkr40-60) does salads and baguettes (Dkr45) as well as pizzas and pastas.

If you're catching a ferry, **Havne Super**, a supermarket at the harbour, has a cafeteria and long hours. Consider picking up provisions if you're going on to expensive Norway.

Getting There & Away

Bus & Train Frederikshavn is the northern terminus of the DSB train line. Trains run about hourly south to Aalborg (Dkr71.50) and on to Copenhagen (Dkr310). **Nordjyllands Trafikselskab** (NT) has both a train (40 minutes) and bus service (one hour) north to Skagen (Dkr39).

Boat From Frederikshavn to Gothenburg, Sweden, **Stena Line** (☎ 96 20 02 00) runs ferries six to 10 times daily (adult/child Dkr80/40 to Dkr160/80, two to 3¼ hours). It also runs to Larvik, Norway, daily from May to September, fewer days in winter (Dkr125 to Dkr300, 6¼ hours), prices depending on time of year and day of week.

Color Line (☎ 99 56 20 00) has daily ferries to Larvik, Norway (adult/child Dkr170/ 85 to Dkr360/180, 6¼ hours). Both Stena and Color Line also carry vehicles, with prices varying by the day and season.

SKAGEN
pop 10,500

Artists discovered Skagen's luminous light and its colourful, heath-and-dune landscape in the mid-19th century and fixed eagerly on the romantic imagery of the area's fishing life that had earned the people of Skagen a hard living for centuries. Painters such as Michael and Anna Ancher and Oscar Björck followed the contemporary fashion of painting *en plein air*, out of doors, often regardless of the weather. Their work established a vivid figurative style of painting that became known as the 'Skagen School'.

Today, Skagen is a major tourist resort, packed to its figurative gunwales in high summer. But the sense of a more picturesque Skagen survives and the town's older neighbourhoods are filled with distinctive, yellow-washed houses, each with red-tile roofs that are painted with distinctive bands of white-wash at their edges. The custom dates from a time when the edges of thatched roofs were treated with protective lime, and the mortar of slate roofs with whitewash. Skagen is now a mix of arts, crafts and conspicuous tourism, with plenty of art galleries, souvenir shops and ice-cream parlours. The peninsula is lined with fine beaches, including a sandy stretch on the eastern end of Østre Strandvej, a 15-minute walk from the town centre.

Orientation & Information

Sankt Laurentii Vej, Skagen's main street, runs almost the entire length of this long thin town, and is never more than five minutes from the waterfront. The **tourist office** (☎ 98 44 13 77; ﹗ www.skagen-tourist.dk; Sankt Laurentii Vej 22; open 9am-7pm Mon-Sat, 9am-4pm Sun late June-early Aug; closes rest of June & Aug at 5pm; 9am-4pm Mon-Sat, 10am-4pm Sat & Sun May & Sept, otherwise earlier closing) is in the train/bus station.

Skagen is very busy with traffic in high season. There is convenient metered parking (Dkr10 for one hour) just by the train station.

Grenen

Denmark's most northerly point is the culmination of a long, curving sweep of sand at Grenen, about 3km northeast of Skagen along route 40. Where the road ends there's a car park, café and souvenir shops, plus, in high summer, what seems like everyone else in Denmark. Crowds head along the last stretch of beach for the 30-minute walk to the narrow tip where the waters of the Kattegat and Skagerrak clash and you can put one foot in each sea; but not too far. Bathing is strictly forbidden here because of the ferocious tidal currents and often-angry seas. A special tractor-drawn bus, the *Sandormen*, leaves from the car park every half hour, waits for 15 minutes at the beach end, then returns (adult/child return for Dkr15/10). From May to September, buses run from Skagen Station to Grenen hourly (Dkr13) until 5pm. Taxis, available at the train station, charge about Dkr60 to Grenen.

Skagens Museum

This fine museum (☎ 98 44 64 44; Brøndumsvej 4; Dkr50; open 10am-5pm or 6pm daily May-Aug; 11am-4pm Tue-Sun Apr; 1pm-5pm Wed-Fri, 11am-4pm Sat, 11am-3pm Sun Nov-Mar) displays the paintings of Michael and Anna Ancher and PS Krøyer, and of other artists who flocked to Skagen between 1830 and 1930.

Michael & Anna Ancher's Hus

This poignant domestic museum (☎ 98 44 30 09; Markvej 2-4; adult/child Dkr40/10; open 10am-6pm daily mid-June–mid-Aug; 10am-5pm daily May–mid-June; 11am-3pm daily Apr & Oct; 11am-3am, Sat & Sun Nov-Mar) is in the house that the Ancher's bought in 1884 and in which their daughter Helga lived until 1960.

Skagen By-og Egnsmuseum

This well-presented, open-air museum (☎ 98 44 47 60; Pk Nielsonvej 8-10; adult/child Dkr30/5; open 10am-5pm daily May-Sept; 10am-6pm daily July; 10am-4pm Mon-Fri Mar-Apr & Oct-Nov) depicts Skagen's maritime history and includes a picturesque old windmill as well as the period homes of

fisherfolk. It's a 15-minute walk from the train station, west down Sankt Laurentii Vej, then south on Vesterled.

Tilsandede Kirke

This whitewashed medieval church tower (☎ 98 44 43 71; adult/child Dkr8/4; open 11am-5pm daily 1 June-1 Sept) still rises above the sand dunes that buried the church and surrounding farms in the late 1700s. The tower, in a nature reserve, is 5km south of Skagen and well signposted from route 40. By bike, take Gammel Landevej from Skagen.

Råbjerg Mile

These undulating 40m-high hills comprise Denmark's largest expanse of shifting dunes and are great fun to explore. Råbjerg Mile is 16km south of Skagen, off route 40 on the road to Kandestederne. From May to September, bus No 99 runs six times a day from Skagen Station (Dkr19.50, 25 minutes).

Places to Stay

Grenen Camping (☎ 98 44 25 46; adult/child Dkr65/37), 1.5km northeast of Skagen centre, has a fine seaside location, semi-private tent sites and pleasant four-bunk huts. The 112-bed **Danhostel Skagen** (☎ 98 44 22 00, fax 98 44 22 55; e danhostel.skagen@adr.dk; Rolighedsvej 2; dorm beds Dkr100, singles/doubles from Dkr250/300) is 1km west of the centre.

The tourist office books **rooms** in private homes for around Dkr200/350 for singles/doubles, plus a Dkr50 booking fee.

Marienlund Badepension (☎ 98 44 13 20, e badepension@marienlund.dk; Fabriciusvej 8; singles/doubles with bath Dkr450/740, without bath Dkr330/590) is on the quieter west side of town near the open-air museum.

Clausens Hotel (☎ 98 45 01 66; e bestilling@clausenhotel.dk; singles/doubles with bath Dkr550/795, without bath Dkr495/525) is just across from the train station and has comfortable rooms.

Brøndums Hotel (☎ 98 44 15 55; e info@broendums-hotel.dk; singles/doubles with bath Dkr680/990, without bath Dkr550/810) is a pleasantly old-fashioned hotel with comfy rooms. It's in the heart of the old town right across from the Skagens Museum. It had close associations with Skagen's artists in its day.

DENMARK

The harbourside **Skagen Sømandshjem** (☎ 98 44 25 88; Østre Strandvej 2; singles/ doubles with bath Dkr550/740, without bath Dkr410/630) has bright, pleasant rooms.

Places to Eat

You'll find a couple of **pizzerias**, a **kebab shop**, a **burger joint** and an **ice-cream shop** clustered near each other on Havnevej. **Super Brugsen** (Sankt Laurentii Vej 28), a grocery store just west of the tourist office, has a bakery.

Restaurant Pakhuset (☎ 98 44 20 00; Rødspættevej 6; mains Dkr150-200) on the harbour, has long hours and good Danish fish dishes. Its downstairs café offers cheaper dishes at Dkr60 to Dkr110.

Jakobs (☎ 98 44 16 90; Havnevej 4; mains Dkr138-188) is a popular restauraunt on Skagen's busy main street. It does brunch for Dkr70, children's brunch for Dkr35 and sandwiches, salads and pastas for Dkr45 to Dkr75.

Entertainment

Skagen has a branch of **Buddy Holly's** (Havnevej 16) with its usual brand of late night-early morning pubbing and clubbing.

Getting There & Away

Either a bus or a train leaves Skagen Station for Frederikshavn (Dkr39) about once an hour. The seasonal Skagerakkeren bus (No 99) runs half a dozen times daily between Hirtshals and Skagen (Dkr32.5, 1½ hours) from mid-June to mid-August. The same bus continues on to Hjørring and Løkken.

Getting Around

Cycling is an excellent way of exploring Skagen and the surrounding area. **Skagen Cykeludlejning** (☎ 98 44 10 70; Banegårds-spladsen) rents bicycles for Dkr75 a day and has a stand on the western side of the train station and at the harbour.

HIRTSHALS
pop 7000

Hirtshals takes its breezy and friendly character from its commercial fishing harbour and ferry terminal. The essentially modern main street, pedestrianised Nørregade, is lined with a mix of cafés and shops and with supermarkets that cater to Norwegian shoppers who pile off the ferries to load up with relatively cheap Danish meats and groceries.

The seaward end of Nørregade opens out into a wide, airy space, Den Grønne Plads, the 'Green Square', that overlooks the fishing harbour and its tiers of blue-hulled boats. There is a **tourist office** (☎ 98 94 22 20; e pj@ hirtshals-tourist.dk; Nørregade 40; open 9am-5pm Mon-Sat, 10am-noon Sun mid-July–Aug, 9am-4pm Mon-Fri, 9am-noon Sat Aug-June).

Hirtshals' main sight for nonshoppers is the **Nordsømuseet** (☎ 98 94 44 44; Willemoesvej 2; adult/child Dkr90/45; open 10am-8pm daily mid-June–mid-Aug, 10am-5pm daily mid-Aug–mid-June), an impressive aquarium that re-creates a slice of the North Sea in a four-storey tank that's Europe's largest. There are coastal cliffs and a **lighthouse** on the town's western side. If you want beaches and dunes, there's a lovely unspoiled stretch at **Tornby Strand**, 5km to the south.

Places to Stay & Eat

Hirtshals Camping (☎ 98 94 25 35; Kyst-vejen 6) is about 1km west of the train station. **Hirtshals Hostel** (☎ 98 94 12 48; e danhostel.hirtshals@adr.dk; Kystvejen 53; dorm beds Dkr95, singles/doubles Dkr300/ 400; open Mar-Nov) is nearby.

Staff at the tourist office can book **rooms** in private homes starting at Dkr150 plus a Dkr25 booking fee.

Hotel Hirtshals (☎ 98 94 20 77; fax 98 94 21 07; e info@hotelhirtshals.dk; Havnegade 2; singles/doubles Dkr645/785), right on the main square above the fishing harbour, has bright, comfortable rooms, with good views at the front.

There are **cafés** and a good **bakery** at the northern end of Hjørringgade, and a couple of **pizza and kebab places** on Nørregade.

Restaurant Rosa (☎ 98 94 19 44; pizzas Dkr48-58) specialises in tasty pizzas, but also does Mexican food and pasta and has a children's menu for Dkr35.

Hirtshals Kro (☎ 98 94 26 77; Havnegade; mains Dkr139-169) is a delightful restaurant in a very old kro that has retained its character. Not surprisingly there are tasty fish and seafood dishes including a mixed fish plate for Dkr179.

Getting There & Away

Bus From May to September there's a bus from Hirtshals Station to Hjørring (Dkr19.50) that stops en route at Tornby Strand six times a day.

Train Hirtshals' main train station is 500m south of the ferry harbour, but there's also a stop near the Color Line terminal. The railway, which is operated by a private company, connects Hirtshals with Hjørring (Dkr19.50), 20 minutes to the south. Trains run at least hourly, with the last departure from Hjørring to Hirtshals at 10.25pm. From Hjørring you can take a DSB train to Aalborg (Dkr54) or Frederikshavn (Dkr39).

Boat The ferry company **Color Line** (☎ 99 56 20 00) runs year-round ferries to the Norwegian ports of Oslo (8½ hours, 10 times daily From May to September) and Kristiansand (2½ to five hours, four times daily from May to September). Fares on both routes are from Dkr170 midweek in the low season to Dkr400 on summer weekends for passengers, from Dkr150 to Dkr290 for a motorcycle and from Dkr200 to Dkr680 for a car.

HJØRRING
pop 24,800
Hjørring's well-kept streets are enlivened by some 150 statues and bronze sculptures, and the town is a lively place behind its sometimes staid exterior.

The oldest part of Hjørring is built around the central squares, the broad focal point of Springvandspladsen and the nearby Sankt Olai Plads. The latter is bordered by three medieval churches. Springvandspladsen is a short five-minute walk north from the train station along Jernbanegade; continue 200m farther north on the pedestrian walkway Strømgade to reach Sankt Olai Plads.

The **tourist office** (☎ 98 92 02 32, fax 98 92 04 52; W www.visithjoerring.dk; open 9am-5pm Mon-Fri, 9am-2pm Sat mid-June–Aug, 9am-4pm Mon-Fri, 9am-noon Sat Sept–mid-June)) is a bit out of the centre on Markedsgade 9, 750m east of the train station.

Things to See & Do
Hjørring is unique in that three of its medieval churches survived the Reformation intact. All three churches, **Sankt Olai Kirke**, **Sankt Catharinæ Kirke** and **Sankt Hans Kirke** are within 200m of each other, on the northern side of Sankt Olai Plads.

The town museum, **Vendsyssel Historiske Museum** (☎ 96 24 10 50; Museumsgade 3; adult/child Dkr30/free; open 10am-5pm daily Apr-Oct, 11am-4pm Mon-Fri Nov-Mar)

is about 250m south of Sankt Catharinæ Kirke. It features exhibits from prehistoric times, as well as an ecclesiastical art collection, period furnishings and displays on farming.

There's also an art museum, **Vendsyssel Kunstmuseum** (☎ 98 92 41 33, Brinck Seidelinsgade 10; adult/child Dkr25/free; open 10am-4pm Tues-Sun), a five-minute walk northeast of the train station, that's devoted to regional art and crafts.

Places to Stay & Eat
Both the camping ground and hostel are about 2.5km northeast of the train station and can be reached by local bus.

Hjørring Campingplads (☎ 98 92 22 82, fax 98 91 06 99; Idræts Allé 45; adult/child Dkr55/25; open May–mid-Sept) is a small, three-star camping ground with an outdoor swimming pool. **Danhostel Hjørring** (☎ 98 92 67 00, fax 98 90 15 50, e danhostel .hjoerring@adr.dk, Thomas Morildsvej 11; open Mar-Sept; dorm beds Dkr100, singles/ doubles Dkr350/380) is a large modern hostel about 2.5km east of Springvandspladsen.

Hotel Phønix (☎ 98 92 54 55, fax 98 90 10 37, e hotel@phoenix-hjoerring.dk, Jernbanegade 6; singles/doubles Dkr650/850) is a central hotel with comfy rooms. It has a sizable tour-coach trade.

There are a number of cheap eateries in Jernbanegade. **Pizza King**, opposite the station, has pizzas starting at Dkr29. The station has a **DSB café**. For a terrific selection of takeaway smørrebrød and other dishes try **Hartmann Petersen** (☎ 98 92 01 97; Jernbanegade 1), a butcher's shop near Hotel Phønix, that has tasty items at Dkr16 to Dkr48 and a herring platter for Dkr85 to Dkr125. **Bøf og Van** (☎ 98 92 21 88; Jernbanegade 10; 3-course menu Dkr158-208) has good Danish cuisine and does main dishes for Dkr70 to Dkr98.

Getting There & Away
Hjørring is 35km west of Frederikshavn on route 35 and 17km south of Hirtshals on route 55 or the E39.

Trains run to Hirtshals (Dkr19.50), Frederikshavn (Dkr39), Aalborg (Dkr58.50) and Århus (Dkr160).

LØKKEN
pop 1300
Løkken has an intriguing history as a long-established sea trading and fishing centre on

the unforgiving North Sea coast of Jutland. Its history is not submerged entirely by the hordes of summer visitors who pack the many camping grounds of the area and throng the bars, cafés and souvenir shops of the town itself. Down on the vast beach, the long line of white beach huts fronting the dunes in summer, are matched by Løkken's sturdy fishing vessels. These boats seem to be trapped deep in the sand when they are drawn up on the beach, but they are launched through a clever combination of winching and tractor power.

The **tourist office** (☎ 98 99 10 09, fax 98 99 11 59; W www.loekken.dk; Harald Fischers Vej 8; open 9am-5pm Mon-Sat June-Aug; 10am-2pm Sun mid-July–Aug; 9am-4pm Mon-Fri, 10am-1pm Sat Sept-May), is a few blocks east of Torvet, the central square.

Things to See & Do

Løkken's **beach** is broad and long and has excellent sand. The town itself has an older neighbourhood to the north of the centre.

The charming little **Løkken Museum** (Nørregade 12; adult/child Dkr10/free; open 10am-4pm Mon-Fri, 2pm-5pm Sun June-Aug) and the **Coastal Fishing Museum** (☎ 20 66 13 07; Ndr Strandvej; adult/child Dkr10/free; open 10am-4pm Mon-Fri, 2pm-5pm Sun June-Aug), perched above the beach, tell the story of Løkken seagoing.

Places to Stay & Eat

There is a string of **camping grounds** along Søndergade, the street that runs south from Torvet. Most of them charge in the region of Dk60/30 per adult/child in high season.

Most of the **hotels** and **apartment complexes** in Løkken are geared to holidaymakers planning longer stays and offer their best prices for weekly bookings although you might catch an overnight stay for about Dkr600 in the low season. The tourist office can provide a booklet with a brief description of each place and a detailed price list. In the low season it's worth checking out any 'room to let' signs for good deals.

There are several places offering cheap **fast food** on Torvet and along Nørregade and Strandgade, which radiate out from Torvet.

Løkken Fiske-Restaurant; (☎ 98 99 02 00; Nørregade 9; mains Dkr119-200) has good fish dishes, including a tasty fish soup. It also does fish lunches for Dkr55 to Dkr69 and some meat dishes.

Getting There & Away

Løkken is on route 55, 18km southwest of Hjørring. Buses run every couple of hours between Løkken and Hjørring (Dkr26, 30 minutes) and between Løkken and Aalborg (Dkr52, one hour).

ESBJERG
pop 83,000

Esbjerg is a newcomer to Denmark, having been established as a port in 1868 following the loss of the Schleswig and Holstein regions to Germany. It is now Denmark's fifth largest city, the centre of Denmark's North Sea oil activities and the country's largest fishing harbour. Although Esbjerg has its fair share of early-20th-century buildings, it lacks the intrigue found in the older quarters of other Danish cities. For most travellers it's a transit point, but the town has a lot to offer and is worth a stopover.

Orientation & Information

Torvet, the city square where Skolegade and Torvegade intersect, is bordered by cafés, a **bank**, the **post office** and the **tourist office** (☎ 75 12 55 99; W www.visitesbjerg.com; Skolegade 33; open 9am-5pm Mon-Fri; 9am-2.30pm Sat mid-June–Aug; 10am-1pm Mon-Fri & 10am-1pm Sat Sept–mid-June). The train and bus stations are about 300m east of Torvet, the ferry terminal 1km south.

Kilroy Travels (☎ 70 15 40 15; Kongensgade 8) specialises in discount and student travel and has friendly staff.

Pentagon net Café (Kongensgade 28) is an Internet centre open until the early hours most nights and charges Dkr5 for 15 minutes.

Things to See & Do

The **Fiskeri og Søfartsmuseet** (☎ 76 12 20 00; Tarphagevej 2; adult/child Dkr70/35, low season Dkr60/30; open 10am-6pm daily July & Aug, 10am-5pm daily Jan-June & Sept-Dec), at Tarphagevej 4km northwest of the centre, has an aquarium, outdoor seal pool and a number of fisheries exhibits. Take bus No 1 or 6.

There are also a few local museums in the centre. **Esbjerg Kunstmuseum** (☎ 75 13 02 11; Havnegade 20, adult/child Dkr30/free; open 10am-4pm daily) has a fine collection of Danish modern art. **Esbjerg Museum** (☎ 75 12 78 11; Torvegade 45; adult/child Dkr30/10, open 10am-4pm daily) contains historical collections and an amber display.

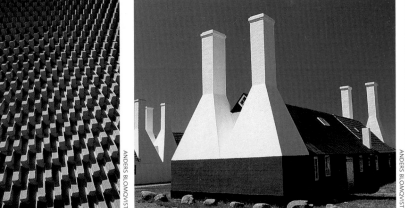

Copenhagen scenes (from top left): Tivoli park has amused the city since 1843; Ny Carlsberg Glyptotek houses an outstanding art collection; the city's many parks and gardens are perfect for a picnic; striking wall feature at the Louisiana Museum of Modern Art. **Bottom right:** smokehouses at a Bornholm fishery

Jazzing it up at Copenhagen's famous festival

Refuel at Copenhagen's Café Sommersko

A cyclist's wonderland, idyllic Bornholm offers more than 200km of scenic bike trails

Stroll Copenhagen's Strøget for stylish shops...

...or kick ice at the Royal Theatre skating rink

Places to Stay

The nearest camping ground, **Ådalens Camping** (☎ 75 15 88 22; ⓔ info@adal.dk; Gudenåvej 20; adult/child Dkr59/29), is 5km north of the city via bus No 1 or 7.

Danhostel Esbjerg (☎ 75 12 42 58, fax 75 13 68 33; ⓔ esbjerg@danhostel.dk; Gammel Vardevej 80; bus Nos 4 & 12; dorm beds Dkr100, singles/doubles Dkr275/380; open 1 Feb-1 Dec) is in a former folk high school 3km northwest of the city centre. The tourist office books **rooms** in private homes at Dkr175/300 for singles/doubles.

Cab-Inn Esbjerg (☎ 75 18 16 00, fax 75 18 16 24; ⓔ cab-inn@cab-inn.dk; Skolegade14; singles/doubles Dkr475/585) has 82 pleasantly renovated rooms with TV and private bath.

Hotel Britannia (☎ 75 13 01 11, fax 75 45 20 85; singles/doubles Dkr930/1030, doubles May-Sept Dkr725), a Best Western hotel at Torvet, has smoothly comfortable rooms.

Hotel Ansgar (☎ 75 12 82 44; fax 75 13 95 40; Skolegade 36; singles/doubles Dkr560/815) is a friendly place with modernised, comfortable rooms.

Places to Eat

There are a number of restaurants in and around Torvet.

As well as main dishes **Dronning Louise** (☎ 75 13 13 44; Torvet 19; mains Dkr110-168) does sandwiches, burgers and lunch fish plates for Dkr38 to Dkr58.

Papa's Cantina (☎ 75 13 08 00; Torvet 17; mains Dkr119-149) has a big range of Mexican and Latin American food including a buffet lunch.

Restaurants and grocery stores are east of Torvet on Kongensgade. **Midt-I** shopping centre, on Kongensgade near Torvet, has a bakery and cafeteria. The popular **Sunset Boulevard** has small/large submarine sandwiches for Dkr30/50, as well as ice cream. **Hong Kong Restaurant** (Kongensgade 34; 3-course meals Dkr108-188) does box takeaways for Dkr33 to Dkr43.

Jensen's Bøfhus (☎ 75 18 18 70; Kongensgade 9; mains Dkr109-169), just off the street, offers its standard feast of barbecue ribs for Dkr99. Next door is **Downtown Pizza** where you can get pizza slices for Dkr20 to Dkr30.

As well as spare ribs **Bones** (☎ 75 13 61 19; Skolegade 17; spare ribs Dkr104-125) has

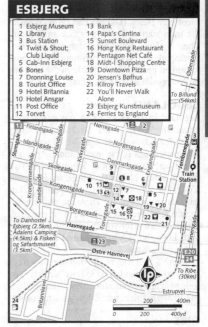

ESBJERG

1 Esbjerg Museum
2 Library
3 Bus Station
4 Twist & Shout;
   Club Liquid
5 Cab-Inn Esbjerg
6 Bones
7 Dronning Louise
8 Tourist Office
9 Hotel Britannia
10 Hotel Ansgar
11 Post Office
12 Torvet
13 Bank
14 Papa's Cantina
15 Sunset Boulevard
16 Hong Kong Restaurant
17 Pentagon Net Café
18 Midt-I Shopping Centre
19 Downtown Pizza
20 Jensen's Bøfhus
21 Kilroy Travels
22 You'll Never Walk Alone
23 Esbjerg Kunstmuseum
24 Ferries to England

chicken dishes for Dkr84 to Dkr94. There's 25% off between 4.30pm and 7pm.

Entertainment

For an English-style pub there's **You'll Never Walk Alone** (Kongensgade 10), which has UK brews and big-screen broadcasts of British football. **Club Liquid** and **Twist & Shout** (☎ 76 12 10 22; Skolegade 9) are late-night dance clubs, opening on Friday and Saturday overnight until 5 am. Entry is free until midnight and Dkr30 after; you can get drinks for Dkr10 up until midnight.

Getting There & Away

Trains connecting the towns of Esbjerg and Copenhagen (Dkr260, 3¼ hours) run about hourly until 10pm.

If you're driving into Esbjerg from the east, the E20 leads into the city centre. If you're coming from the south, route 24 merges with the E20 on the city outskirts. From the north, route 12 makes a beeline into the city, ending at the harbour.

For details of ferry services to the UK see the Getting There & Away section at the start of this chapter.

Getting Around

Most city buses (Dkr14) can be boarded at the train station. Parking is free in Esbjerg. There's also a convenient car park on Danmarksgade, but it has a two-hour limit; some unlimited parking is available in the car park on Nørregade east of the library.

LEGOLAND

Legoland (☎ 75 33 13 33; ⓦ www.lego.com; adult/child 3-13 years Dkr160/140; open 10am-8pm daily 1 Apr-late Oct, to 9pm early July-early Aug) is the internationally popular theme park in the town of **Billund**. Forty-five million plastic blocks have been arranged into a world of miniature cities, Lego pirates, safari animals and lots more. There are also amusement rides, which are included in the entry fee. This is Paradise for youngsters who have lived with Lego, but adults may need to grit their teeth after a while.

There's a frequent, 25-minute bus from Vejle to Legoland (Dkr35), as well as bustour packages from numerous cities, including Esbjerg. Inquire at Esbjerg tourist office.

RIBE
pop 8000

Ribe sells its quaintness with great efficiency. Dating from 869, it is said to be the oldest town in Scandinavia and was an important medieval trading centre. The crooked, cobblestoned streets and half-timbered, 16th-century houses, certainly impart a sense of history and the entire old town is a preservation zone, with more than 100 buildings under the care of the Danish National Trust.

The town is compact and is easy to explore, although for most of the summer be prepared to share the experience with huge crowds of fellow sightseers. Almost everything, including the hostel and train station, is within 10 minutes' walk of Torvet, the town square, which is dominated by a huge Romanesque cathedral.

At the **tourist office** (☎ 75 42 15 00; Torvet; ⓦ www.ribetourist.dk; open 9.30am-5.30pm Mon-Fri, 10am-5pm Sat, 10am-2pm Sun July & Aug, 9am-5pm Mon-Fri, Apr-June & Sept-Oct, 10am-1pm Sat Apr-Jun & Sept-Dec) you can obtain the publication *Sommer I Ribe*, a good events magazine.

Gamer's Gateway (Saltgade 20; open noon-midnight) is an Internet café charging Dkr5 for 12 minutes, Dkr25 for one hour.

Things to See & Do

For a pleasant stroll, head along any of the picturesque streets that radiate out from Torvet, especially Puggårdsgade or Grønnegade from where narrow alleys lead down and across Fiskegarde to Skibbroen and the old harbour. Boats still tie up alongside the quay, and there is a replica of the 19th-century cargo vessel the *Johannes Dan*.

Ribe Domkirke (☎ 75 42 06 19; Torvet; adult/child Dkr12/5) dominates the heart of the town and boasts a variety of styles from Romanesque to Gothic. Its monumental presence is literally sunk into the heart of Ribe. The cathedral floor is over a metre below the level of the surrounding streets. You can climb the **cathedral steeple** for a breathtaking view of the surrounding countryside and for a realisation of just how small and compact Ribe is.

Ribes Vikinger (☎ 76 88 11 22; Odins Plads 1; adult/child Dkr50/20; open 10am-6pm daily July & Aug; 10am-4pm daily Apr-June, Sept & Oct; 10am-4pm Tues-Sun Nov-Mar), a substantial museum opposite the train station, has archaeological displays of Ribe's Viking history, including a reconstructed marketplace and Viking ship, with lots of hands-on features.

Ribe Vikingecenter (☎ 75 41 16 11; Lustrupvej 4; adult/child Dkr50/20; open 11am-4.30pm daily July & Aug; 11am-4pm Mon-Sun May-June & Sept), 3km south of the centre, is a re-created Viking village complete with working artisans and interpreters decked out in period costumes. Bus No 51 (Dkr15) will take you there from Ribe.

Ribe Kunstmuseum (☎ 75 42 03 62; Sankt Nicolajgade 10; adult/child Dkr30/free) has a fine collection of 19th-century 'Golden Age' and 'Silver Age' Danish art, including Ludvig Abelin Schou's magnificently romantic *Death of Chione*. There are a couple of local-history museums, including one at the **Old Town Hall** (adult/child Dkr15/5) that displays the formidable axe of the fortunately long-gone formidable executioner.

A costumed **night watchman** makes the rounds from Torvet at 8pm and 10pm from May to September and you can follow him for free as he sings his way through the old streets.

Places to Stay & Eat

The modern, 140-bed **Danhostel Ribe** (☎ 75 42 06 20, fax 75 42 42 88; ⓔ ribe@danhhostel .dk; Sankt Pedersgade 16; dorm beds Dkr100,

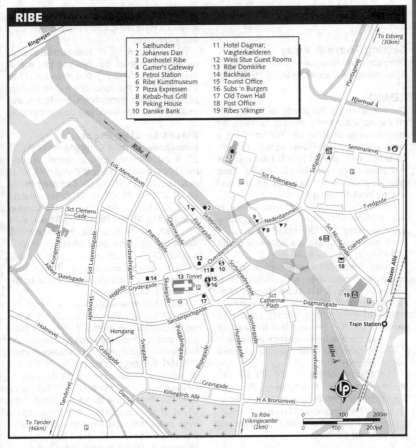

RIBE

1 Sælhunden	11 Hotel Dagmar;
2 Johannes Dan	Vægterkælderen
3 Danhostel Ribe	12 Weis Stue Guest Rooms
4 Gamer's Gateway	13 Ribe Domkirke
5 Petrol Station	14 Backhaus
6 Ribe Kunstmuseum	15 Tourist Office
7 Pizza Expressen	16 Subs 'n Burgers
8 Kebab-hus Grill	17 Old Town Hall
9 Peking House	18 Post Office
10 Danske Bank	19 Ribes Vikinger

singles/doubles Dkr250/295) has friendly staff and a good, uncrowded location.

The tourist office maintains a list of **rooms** in private homes from Dkr250/350 for singles/doubles.

The central **Hotel Dagmar** (☎ 75 42 00 33; fax 75 42 36 52; e dagmar@hoteldagmar.dk; *Torvet; singles/doubles Dkr795/995)* claims to be the oldest hotel in Denmark and has pleasant rooms and a comfy atmosphere.

The friendly **Backhaus** (☎ 75 42 11 01, fax 75 42 52 87; *Grydergade 12; singles/doubles without bath Dkr250/500, double with bath Dkr750)* does an evening meal for Dkr105 to Dkr180.

Weis Stue (☎ 75 42 07 00; *Torvet; singles/doubles Dkr400/500)* has guest rooms in a handsome, old building. For breakfast you are ushered across the road to the restaurant at Hotel Dagmar.

There are several fast-food outlets along Nederdammen, including **Kebabhus & Grill** with burgers and kebabs round about Dkr30 to Dkr48, **Pizza Expressen**, with pizza at Dkr45, and **Peking House** offering Chinese lunch specials from Dkr30. **Subs 'n Burgers** *(Torvet)* does tasty half/full baguettes for Dkr27/47.

Vægterkælderen *(Torvet; lunch menu Dkr105-135)*, a basement restaurant in the Hotel Dagmar, shares a kitchen with the hotel's upstairs restaurant, but has cheaper dishes, including a generous spare ribs plate for Dkr169.

Saelhunden (☎ 75 42 09 46; *Skibbroen 13; fish & meat mains Dkr46-186)* is a handsome, old restaurant right on the quayside. A tasty lunch of smoked herring or smoked ham costs Dkr75.

Getting There & Away

There are trains from Esbjerg to Ribe (Dkr50, 40 minutes) and from Århus to Ribe (Dkr192).

RØMØ

The unrelentingly flat island of Rømø, lies off the mainland coast, midway between the historic towns of Ribe and Tønder and is a mere 30-minute drive from either. It's connected to the mainland by a 10km causeway that passes over marshlands, where sheep graze happily on the nontidal pasture and wading birds forage for food.

During the 18th century, many islanders were captains of German and Dutch whaling ships working off Greenland, their lives lived, home and away, in a flat world of unbroken horizons.

Today, Rømø is a hugely popular holiday destination, especially with visitors from nearby Germany. It has its fair share of caravan parks, but red-walled, thatch-roofed houses of great charm shelter amid pine woods, vast sand beaches line the western shore and the North Sea air is exhilarating.

The northern end of the island is an out of bounds military zone.

The **tourist office** (☎ 74 75 51 30; w www.romo.dk; Havnebyvej 30; open 9am-6pm daily mid-June–mid-Sept, 9am-5pm daily mid-Sept–mid-May) is on the eastern side of Rømø, 1km south of the causeway exit on to the island.

Things to See & Do

Rømø's **beaches** are most easily reached at Lakolk on the central west coast and if you have **windsurfing** gear, conditions are often perfect although the sea can be more than a kilometre away from the shoreline at low water. The inland section of the island has **trails** through heather moors and wooded areas that offer quiet hiking. There's an **old church** with unique Greenlandic gravestones on the main road in Kirkeby.

An unmissable place is **Kommandørgården** (☎ 74 75 52 76; Juvrevej 60, Toftum; adult/child Dkr15/free; open 10am-6pm Tues-Sun May-Sept, 10am-3pm Tues-Sun Oct), the preserved home of one of Rømø's 18th-century whaling captains, on the northeastern side of the island. Dutch tiles line

many of the walls, the woodwork is painted in rococo style and the furnishings come from many countries.

About 1km north of Kommandørgården, on the east side of the road and just past a blue sign for Vestervej, is a remarkable but thought-provoking sight. It's a short section of fencing made from whales' jaw bones, and looking for all the world like concrete pillars.

Places to Stay & Eat

Kommandørgårdens Camping (☎ 74 75 51 22; e info@kommandergaarden.dk; Havnebyvej 201; adult/child/tent Dkr55/ 30/20) is near the hostel and **Lakolk Camping** (☎ 74 75 52 28; fax 74 75 53 52; Lakolk; adult/ child Dkr61/31) is on the west-coast beach at Lakolk. The 91-bed **Danhostel Rømø** (☎ 74 75 51 88, fax 74 75 51 87; e sonderborg@ danhostel.dk dorm beds Dkr100, singles/ doubles Dkr300/325; open 15 Mar-1 Nov), on the southeastern side of Rømø near Havneby, is in a delightful traditional building with a thatched roof.

Hotel Kommandørgården (74 75 51 22; e info@kommanddoergaarden.dk; Havnevej 201; singles/doubles 595/795) is a busy place that also rents huts and apartments and has its own swimming pool and mini-market.

Hotel Færgegaarden (☎ 74 75 54 32; e info@faegegaarden.com; Vestergade 1, Havneby; singles/doubles750/990) is a thatch-roofed place at the southern end of the island. It has pleasantly comfy rooms and a huge restaurant capacity. Two-/three-course menus are Dkr135/165 and a herring lunch platter costs Dkr85, a steak dish Dkr89.

Otto & Ani's Fisk (☎ 74 75 53 06; Havnepladsen), right on the harbourside at Havneby, offers a big range of fish dishes from Dkr45 for basic fish and chips to Dkr175 for a two-person platter of mixed fish. There's a children's menu for Dkr35 to Dkr55.

There are **grocery stores** and a **bakery** within walking distance of the hostel, and there are numerous **cafés** and other eateries near the beach-road end at Lakolk.

Getting There & Around

Rømø is 14km west of the town of Skærbæk and route 11. Buses run from Skærbæk to Havneby (Dkr12, 35 minutes) numerous times a day. From Skærbæk there's a train service to Ribe, Tønder and Esbjerg about once an hour. Car ferries connect Havneby with Germany's island of Sylt (adult/child Dkr34/24, one hour) many times a day.

From May to September, a limited public bus service connects villages on the island. Rømø is a good place for cycling; bicycles can be rented in several places, including the camping grounds.

TØNDER & AROUND

Tønder is historic southern town that was in and out of border history for centuries and retains a few pleasingly curved and cobble-stoned streets with half-timbered houses, such as Uldgade, Nørregade and Spikergade. There is a **tourist office** (☎ 74 72 12 20; w www.visittonder.dk; Torvet 1; open 9.30am-5.30pm Mon-Fri, 9.30am-3pm Sat mid-June–Aug; 9am-4pm Mon-Fri, 9am-noon Sat Sept–mid-June) with information on the town and its surrounding area.

Things to See

The **Tønder Museum** (☎ 74 72 26 57; Kongevej 51; adult/child Dkr30/free; open 10am-5pm daily June-Aug, Tues-Sun Sept-May) has a wing with regional-history exhibits including a collection of Tønder lace, once considered among the world's finest. Another wing features Danish surrealist and modern art. The museum is a 10-minute walk east of the train station.

The 16th-century **Tønder church** (Torvet) has a fine interior of ornate woodwork and paintings.

Special Events

Tønder's high point is the last weekend of August when the **Tønder Festival** (☎ 74 72 46 10; w www.tf.dk), one of Denmark's largest, attracts a multitude of international and Danish folk musicians.

Places to Stay

Tønder Camping (☎/fax 74 72 18 49; Holmevej 2; adult/child/tent Dkr55/25/20) is just beyond the hostel. **Danhostel Tønder** (☎ 74 72 35 00, fax 74 72 27 97; e danhostel@tonder-net.dk; Sønderport4; dorm beds Dkr100, singles/doubles Dkr225/ 300), on the eastern side of the centre and a 15-minute walk

from the train station, has comfortable rooms with dorm beds and singles/doubles with private bath.

The tourist office maintains a list of **rooms** in private homes at about Dkr200/300 for singles/doubles.

Hotel Tønderhus (☎ 74 72 22 22; e info@hoteltoenderhus.dk; Jomfrustien 1; singles/doubles Dkr775/900) is a recently restored place in the Classics Hotel chain. It has bright, comfortable rooms.

Places to Eat

A short walk east of the central square of Torvet is **Spisehuset Asian** (Østergade 37; mains Dkr45), which has inexpensive Chinese and grilled items, **Pizzeria Italiano** (Østergade 40; pizza & pasta dishes Dkr50-65) and an adjacent **bakery**. You can buy fresh fruit and cheese at the **market** (Torvet), which is open on Tuesday and Friday mornings.

Getting There & Away

Tønder is on route 11, about 4km north of the German border. Trains run hourly Monday to Friday, somewhat less frequently at the weekend from Ribe (Dkr53, 50 minutes) and Esbjerg (Dkr76, 1½ hours).

Møgeltønder

Slotsgade, the main street of the fetching village of Møgeltønder, is cobblestoned and lined with thatch-roofed, period houses that have colourful, wooden doors. At one end of Slotsgade is the private **castle** of Prince Joachim and a small **public park**. At the other end is the 12th-century **Møgeltønder Kirke** (☎ 74 73 85 96; Slotsgade 1; admission free; open 8am-4pm daily May-Sept, 9am-4pm daily Sept-Apr) with one of the most lavish interiors in Denmark (a splendid mix of the Romanesque, Classical and Gothic) and filled with frescoes, wall paintings and beautiful artefacts.

Mogeltønder is just 4km west of Tønder. Buses run from Tønder about hourly Monday to Friday, less frequently at weekends. Another option is to rent a bicycle for about Dkr55 a day from **Top Cykler** (☎ 74 72 18 81; Jernbanegade 1C)

Faroe Islands

The 18 Faroe Islands (Føroyar) make up an independent nation within the Kingdom of Denmark. The Faroes is one of those mysteriously remote sorts of places, like the Aleutians or the Falklands, which most people would be hard-pressed to find on a map. Here the forces of nature, the old Norse culture and today's technology all combine to create a slice of modern Europe superimposed on a stunning natural and traditional background.

The islands, which measure only 110km from north to south, are home to a rather reserved, stoic and self-reliant sea-faring people, known for their hospitality, independent spirit and remarkable prowess at international football.

Visitors aren't usually prepared for the beauty of the landscape and, apart from news about the traditional *grindadráp* (pilot-whale slaughters), these North Atlantic islands receive very little press.

Facts about the Faroe Islands

HISTORY

The first Norse settlers, primarily farmers and pastoralists, arrived in the uninhabited Faroes in the early 9th century from southern Norway and Orkney. The *Færinga Saga*, written in Iceland in the 13th century, tells of Norse life and times, including the violent conversion to Christianity around 1000.

From early on, the administration of these islands lay in the hands of a parliamentary body known as the Alting. In 1380 parliamentary procedures ceased and the Alting simply became a royal court. The legislative body was renamed the Løgting. With the Kalmar Union of 1397, in which Norway, Sweden and Denmark merged politically, the Faroes became a Danish province. In 1535 Denmark imposed both the religious influences of the Protestant Lutheran Church and a trade monopoly, which lasted until 1856.

During the 19th century, Denmark increasingly dominated the Faroes and, in 1849, the Danish Rigsdag (parliament) incorporated the islands into Denmark. However, this stirred up notions of independence,

At a Glance

Capital	Tórshavn
Population	47,120
Area	1399 sq km
Official Language	Faroese
GDP	US$1.2 billion (2001 estimate)
Time	GMT/UTC
Country Phone Code	☎ 298

Klaksvík p150

Tórshavn p144
Central Tórshavn p146

GREENLAND

ICELAND   NORWAY   SWEDEN   FINLAND

FAROE
ISLANDS

DENMARK

Highlights

- Exploring the quaint Tinganes peninsula in Tórshavn (p143)
- Taking the fantastic tour of the Vestmanna bird cliffs (p148)
- Enjoying an afternoon in the rustic village of Gjógv on Eysturoy (p149)
- Walking to the lighthouse at Kallur on Kalsoy (p151)
- Visiting Mykines, the paradise of birds (p151)

which are only now beginning to bear fruit. During WWII the British occupied the Faroes to secure the strategic North Atlantic shipping lanes and prevent German occupation.

On 23 March 1948 the Act on Faroese Home Rule was passed and the Faroes' official status changed from 'county of Denmark' to 'self-governing community within the Kingdom of Denmark'. When Denmark joined the

EEC (now EU), the Faroes refused to follow because of the hot issue of fishing rights. Despite the Faroese claim to a 200mi (320km) fisheries exclusion limit, stocks dwindled as a result of overfishing. In the early 1990s, after years of big spending by government, there was a serious recession; unemployment peaked at 26% and many people left for Denmark. Ten years later, the economy has perked up with the cod fisheries becoming more profitable again, unemployment has dropped, the resident population has risen again – and moves towards independence received a kick-start after a referendum in 2001.

GEOGRAPHY

The mountainous Faroe Islands, covering 1399 sq km, lie 400km southeast of Iceland and 280km north of Scotland. Most western flanks of the islands (those facing the Atlantic Ocean) consist of sheer cliffs up to 620m high. There are four distinct areas: the two large, central and most populated islands, Streymoy and Eusturoy; Vágar and Mykines, to the west of Streymoy; the rugged finger-like islands in the northeast; and the southern islands, including Sandoy and Suðuroy.

CLIMATE

The Faroes have a temperate maritime climate, characterised by extensive cloud cover and frequent storms; average temperatures vary from 3°C in January to 11°C in July and rain in one form or another can probably be expected 280 days of the year. Fortunately, the weather is somewhat localised. Tune to Útvarp Føroya radio (89.9MHz FM, 531kHz MW; 94.2MHz FM in Klaksvík) at 8.50am on weekdays, June to August, for weather information in English.

ECOLOGY & ENVIRONMENT

Although water and air pollution is minimal and the marine environment is the cleanest in the North Atlantic, fish farming has caused localised pollution problems. Despite fairly large numbers of sheep, giardia has not been reported. The low tourist volume barely affects the environment but wild camping is illegal since many streams and rivers are used for domestic drinking water supplies.

FLORA & FAUNA

Trees are virtually nonexistent on the Faroes, partly due to large numbers of sheep, but also

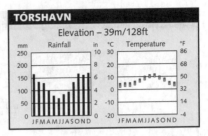

because of salt spray. Classic images of the islands feature bare, grassy hillsides soaring out of the sea.

Coastal cliffs provide nesting sites for large numbers of sea birds such as puffins, fulmars and kittiwakes, while inland you'll find great skuas, ducks and many species of wading birds. The national bird is the *tjaldur* (oystercatcher). Saltwater fish and shellfish have declined due to overfishing, but pilot whales aren't unusual in Faroese waters. There are also five species of freshwater fish. Land mammals are mainly cattle and sheep: there are twice as many sheep as people!

GOVERNMENT & POLITICS

The Faroes had a long tradition of left- or right-wing coalitions, but in recent years a stronger divide has appeared, with home-rule parties opposed by unionists. After four years of coalition government supporting full independence from Denmark, the general election in April 2002 revealed an increase in anti-independence feeling. Now the parties are evenly split and, at the time of writing, Anfinn Kallsberg was prime minister, leading a coalition consisting of the Conservatives, the Republicans, the Christian Folk Party and Conservative Republicans. Full-independence negotiations with Denmark continue.

ECONOMY

The economy, based almost entirely on fishing and fish processing, is currently fairly buoyant. The cod fisheries are doing well enough due to healthy stocks, but prices have fallen recently.

Preliminary drilling for oil began in 2001, but results have not been favourable. In 1999 the Faroes recorded a trade surplus of Dkr293 million (excluding ships). In March 2002 the unemployment rate was 3% and in 2001 inflation was 2.7%.

FAROE ISLANDS

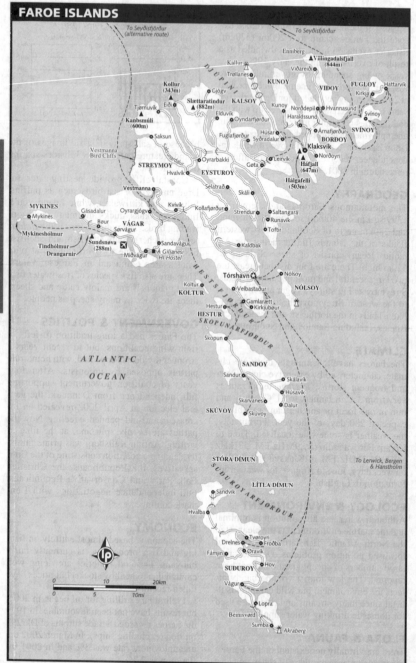

FAROE ISLANDS

To Seyðisfjörður
(alternative route)

To Seyðisfjörður

Enniberg

Villingadalsfjall
(844m)

Kallur

Trøllanes

Viðareiði

FUGLOY

KUNOY

Hattarvík

Kollur
(343m)

Gjógv

VIDOY

Kirkja

Tjørnuvík

Eiði

Slættaratindur
(882m)

KALSOY

Kunoy

Norðdepil

Hvannasund

SVÍNOY

Svínoy

Kanbsmúli
(600m)

Elduvík

Haraldssund

Árnafjørður

Saksun

Oyndarfjørður

Húsar

BORDOY

Fuglafjørður

Syðradalur

Klaksvík

Norðoyri

Vestmanna
Bird Cliffs

Saksunardalur

Oyrarbakki

Leirvík

Gøta

Háfjall
(647m)

STREYMOY

Hvalvík

EYSTUROY

Selatrað

Skáli

Hálgafelli
(503m)

Vestmanna

Kvívík

Kollafjørður

Strendur

Saltangará

Oyrargjógv

Runavík

MYKINES

Gásadalur

Mykines

Bøur

Sørvágur

VÁGAR

Sandavágur

Á Giljanesi
HI Hostel

Toftir

Mykineshólmur

Tindhólmur
Drangarnir

Sundsnøva
(288m)

Miðvágur

Kaldbak

ATLANTIC

OCEAN

Tórshavn

Nólsoy

Koltur

Velbastaður

NÓLSOY

KOLTUR

Gamlarætt
Kirkjubøur

Hestur

HESTUR

SKOPUNARFJØRÐUR

Skopun

SANDOY

Sandur

Skálavík

SKÚVOY

Skarvanes

Húsavík

Dálur

Skúvoy

STÓRA DÍMUN

LÍTLA DÍMUN

To Lerwick, Bergen
& Hanstholm

SUÐUROYARFJØRÐUR

Sandvík

Hvalba

SUDUROY

Drelnes

Tvøroyri
Froðba

Fámjin

Øravík

Hov

Vágur

Lopra

Beinisvørð

Sumba

Akraberg

0   10   20km
0   5   10mi

POPULATION & PEOPLE

At last count, 47,120 people lived in the Faroes; 16,842 of them in the capital, Tórshavn, and 4773 in Klaksvík. There are around 100 other communities of varying size. The natural annual increase in population (0.6%), is due largely to a birth rate of 1.4%.

The majority of Faroese are of Nordic origin, descended from early Norwegian settlers who arrived during the Viking era. While on first appearances the Faroese may seem somewhat reserved, on getting to know them you'll discover the friendliest and most hospitable people in the North Atlantic region.

ARTS

Individual artistic expression really only emerged during the 20th century, mainly due to a general lack of time in subsistence households. Although Faroese was long regarded as a 'peasant' dialect that inhibited poetry and literature, modern writers, including Heðin Brú, are popular both at home and abroad. Awareness of sculpture and painting has also arisen in modern times – one of the most renowned painters is Sámal Joensen Mikines.

Unlike elsewhere in Scandinavia, chain dancing has survived intact from medieval times and visitors can take part during special tourist shows.

RELIGION

Religion is important to the Faroese and 85% of the population is 'registered' with the official Evangelical-Lutheran Church. There are also several sects and a small number of Roman Catholics.

Facts for the Visitor

SUGGESTED ITINERARIES

Depending on the length of your stay you might like to include these highlights:

Two days
Tórshavn and a tour of the Vestmanna bird cliffs or a visit to a village such as Saksun, Gjógv or Kirkjubøur

One week
As earlier plus Klaksvík, and the islands of Viðoy (for the tough walk to the Enniberg cliff, the highest sheer cliff face in Europe), Kalsoy and Nólsoy

Two weeks
As earlier plus the islands of Vágar, Mykines and Suðuroy

PLANNING

When to Go

The best season to visit is between May and August, when most tourism-related facilities are open. For information on what to bring, see the Iceland chapter.

Maps

A handy booklet of topographic maps covering the Faroe Islands at 1:100,000 scale is available at tourist offices and bookshops throughout the islands for Dkr115, or directly from the publishers **Kort og Matrikelstyrelsen** (☎ 45-35 87 50 50, fax 45-35 87 50 51; Rentemestervej 8, DK-2400 Copenhagen, Denmark).

The islands are also mapped at 1:20,000-scale (Dkr70). The tourist board distributes the 1:200,000 scale Faroe Islands Map (free), which includes street plans of larger settlements plus accommodation, services, bus and ferry information.

TOURIST OFFICES

For local tourist offices, see Organised Tours in the Getting Around section of this chapter and Information under Tórshavn; ask for the free Tourist Guide – Faroe Islands. Representatives abroad include:

Denmark (☎ 33 14 83 83, ☒ annette@tourist.fo)
Færøernes Repræsentationskontor, Hovedvagtsgade 8, 2 sal, DK-1103 Copenhagen K
UK (☎ 020-7333 0200, ☒ jor@tinganes.fo)
Faroese Representative to the UK, Royal Danish Embassy, 55 Sloane St, London, SW1X 9SR
USA (☎ 212-885 9700, ☒ info@goscandinavia .com) 655 Third Avenue, 18th floor, New York, NY 10017

VISAS & DOCUMENTS

Citizens of Western European countries, the USA, Canada, Australia and New Zealand need only a valid passport to visit the Faroes for up to three months.

Bring your HI membership card to get a Dkr20 discount at hostels. Student identity cards also yield discounts.

EMBASSIES

The Faroes are represented abroad by Danish embassies (☒ www.ambassade-info.dk). See also under Embassies & Consulates in the Facts for the Visitor section of the Denmark chapter.

CUSTOMS

Visitors over 15 years of age may import 200 cigarettes, 50 cigars or 250g of tobacco; those over 18 can also bring 1L of wine (up to 22%) or 2L of table wine (up to 12%), 1L of spirits (from 22% to 60% proof) and 2L of beer (less than 5.8% alcohol, and in long-necked bottles only). Perfume and confectionery are limited to 50g and 3kg per person, respectively. Nonrecyclable containers are forbidden and animals may not be brought in.

MONEY

Although the Faroes issues its own currency, the Faroese króna (Fkr) is tied to the Danish krone (Dkr) and both are used interchangeably throughout the Kingdom of Denmark.

Foreign currency may be exchanged at any Faroese bank; most are open 9.30am to 4pm Monday to Friday (until 6pm Thursday). The exchange bank at Vágar airport opens 10am to 1pm for most arriving or departing international flights (otherwise, use the ATM opposite the cafeteria). In the Faroes, ATMs only dispense cash from 6am to midnight daily.

Often a small commission is charged for exchange services. Outside banking hours, hotels, tourist information offices and travel agencies usually exchange money. All brands of travellers cheques and major currencies are accepted. Postal cheques may be exchanged at post offices in larger towns.

Currency

One króna is equal to 100 oyru (Danish: krone, øre). Notes come in denominations of 50, 100, 200, 500 and 1000 krónur; the Danish coins in use include 25 and 50 øre, one krone and two, five, 10 and 20 kroner.

Exchange Rates

See the Denmark chapter for the Danish krone's rates.

Costs

The minimum price of a single hotel room is Dkr475, but there are also guesthouses, youth hostels and camping grounds offering more economical options. Eating out, supermarket food and bus travel are expensive compared to most other Western European countries. Tipping isn't required. Holders of student identity cards get discounts on bus and ferry fares and at camping grounds.

There's a 25% value-added tax (VAT) included in all quoted prices. If you spend over Dkr300 in tax-free shops, you'll get a VAT receipt, which you should give to the customs officer when you leave the Faroes. You'll be given an on-the-spot VAT refund in cash.

POST & COMMUNICATIONS

Post

The postal service, Postverk Føroya, has offices in many towns (most have a one- to three-hour lunch break). The **central post office** (open 10am-4pm Mon-Wed & Fri, 10am-6pm Thur) in Tórshavn offers reliable poste restante; have your mail sent to Poste Restante, Central Post Office (miðbynum), FR-100 Tórshavn, Faroe Islands. The cost of sending a letter or postcard up to 20g economy/priority air mail is Dkr4.50/5 locally, Dkr6 (priority only) to Iceland, Dkr6/6.50 to Europe and Dkr7.50/8 to the rest of the world.

Telephone

Make international telephone calls and send faxes from the **telephone office** (☎ 303030; e tele@ft.fo; Tinghúsvegur 64, Tórshavn; open 8am-9pm daily). The public fax number here is 315546. Telephone cards with denominations of Dkr30, Dkr50 and Dkr100 are available.

From public phones, there's a Dkr0.40 connection charge; local calls then cost Dkr0.32 per minute (8am to 6pm, Monday to Saturday), otherwise Dkr0.22 per minute. A three-minute call to the USA costs Dkr13.50 at all times.

For telephone information and directory assistance ring ☎ 118.

The Faroes' international country code is ☎ 298. To dial out of the Faroes, you must dial ☎ 00 then the destination country code, area or city code and phone number.

The GSM mobile-phone network covers almost the entire country (but it's incompatible with North American GSM). Contact the telephone office for further details regarding mobile telephone use in the Faroes.

Email & Internet Access

Internet cafés have opened around the Faroes in recent years; tourist offices keep current listings.

DIGITAL RESOURCES

There's lots of tourist and general information on the website ⓦ www.faroeislands.com, but

you can also try W www.framtak.com, W www
.puffin.fo/travel, and Postverk Føroya's phi-
lately service home page (W www.stamps.fo).
Whaling and the *grindadráp* have Internet
pages at W www.whaling.fo. You can find
out more about the Faroese parliament and
government at W www.logting.fo.

BOOKS
For more detailed background and practical
information, consult the Lonely Planet guide
Iceland, Greenland & the Faroe Islands. Another background text is *The Faroe Islands*
by Liv Kjørsvik Schei and Gunnie Moberg.

The English translation of the *Færinga
Saga, The Faroese Saga,* by GVC Young and
Cynthia Clewer, describes the adventures of
the early Norse settlers. *The Far Islands and
Other Cold Places,* by Elizabeth Taylor, originally written in a witty and down-to-earth style
covering the years between 1895 and 1919,
gives another good historical perspective.

NEWSPAPERS & MAGAZINES
There are six local, Faroese-language newspapers. London and New York papers and international news magazines are flown in and
are sold at the airport kiosk and the newsagent
in the SMS shopping centre in Tórshavn.

RADIO & TV
Útvarp Føroya (89.8MHz FM, 531kHz MW;
94.2 MHz in Klaksvík), broadcasts from 7am
to between 10pm and 1am; the English-
language weather report is at 8.50am on
weekdays.

Sjónvarp Føroya, the Faroes' television station, screens films in the original language
with Danish or Faroese subtitles. Foreign television programming, including BBC World,
BBC Prime and MTV, is available by satellite.

PHOTOGRAPHY & VIDEO
Film and print processing is available in Tórshavn, but supplies elsewhere may be limited; a 36-exposure roll of Kodak or Fuji print
film costs Dkr30 and 24-hour developing
costs Dkr102. Fujichrome Sensia slide film
costs Dkr65 for 36 exposures (excluding
processing).

TIME
Between the last Saturdays in October and
March, local time in the Faroes is GMT/UTC,
the same time as London, five hours ahead of

New York, eight hours ahead of Los Angeles
and 10 hours behind Sydney. The rest of the
year, it's on GMT plus one hour.

WOMEN TRAVELLERS
Women travellers rarely face problems in the
Faroe Islands. The local women's crisis centre
is **Kvinnuhúsið** (☎ 317200; e *kvinhusi@
post.olivant.fo; Hoydalsvegur 6, Tórshavn).*

GAY & LESBIAN TRAVELLERS
Gay couples are advised to be discreet to
avoid upsetting the more traditional and religious locals. There are no specifically gay
bars or clubs on the islands.

DISABLED TRAVELLERS
Most public transport in the Faroes can take
at least one passenger in a wheelchair. Some
hotels and hostels are accessible to people in
wheelchairs and the telephone office has a
computer-phone for people who are deaf. For
further details, contact the **Faroese Association for the Handicapped** (☎ 317373; *Ís-
landsvegur 10c, FO-100 Tórshavn).*

SENIOR TRAVELLERS
Senior travellers with proof they are aged over
65 receive 20% to 50% discount on bus and
passenger ferry fares and some travel passes.

TRAVEL WITH CHILDREN
Unpleasant weather conditions may make
camping with children an ordeal. Children
aged seven to 13 get 20% to 50% discount off
bus and passenger ferry fares (including
travel passes), and discounts are usually
available on tours; inquire when booking.
Museum entrance fees are either reduced or
free for children.

Lonely Planet's *Travel with Children,* by
Cathy Lanigan, gives all sorts of useful general advice.

BUSINESS HOURS
Shops are generally open 9am to 5.30pm or
6.30pm Monday to Friday (some close as late
as 7pm on Friday) and 9am to noon or 2pm

FAROE ISLANDS

on Saturday. For bank and post office opening hours, see under Money and Post & Communications earlier in this section.

PUBLIC HOLIDAYS & SPECIAL EVENTS

The Faroese observe the following holidays:

New Year's Day 1 January
Maundy Thursday Thursday before Easter
Good Friday to Easter Monday March/April
Flag Day 25 April (afternoon only)
Labour Day 1 May (some workers only)
Common Prayers Day April/May
Ascension Day May/June
Whit Sunday, Whit Monday May/June
Constitution Day 5 June
Ólavsøka (Faroese National Day and Festival) 28 (afternoon only) & 29 July
Christmas Eve 24 December (some shops open until noon)
Christmas Day 25 December
Boxing Day 26 December
New Year's Eve 31 December (afternoon only)

Every summer there are local festivals where you'll see the traditional Faroese chain dance.

The largest festival takes place in Tórshavn on Ólavsøka (Faroese National Day); highlights include the village rowing competition and other sporting events.

Throughout the islands during the first two weeks in August there's the excellent annual Faroese arts festival Listastevna (W www.listastevna.com).

ACTIVITIES

Activities in the Faroe Islands include **birdwatching** (particularly on Nólsoy and the Mykines and Vestmanna cliffs), **fishing** and **hiking**.

Most of the hiking trails on the main islands are marked on the 1:100,000 map (see under Planning earlier in this section for more information); more adventurous hikers may wish to climb the highest peak, Slættaratindur (882m), from Eiði or Gjógv.

It's perfectly possible to hike where there are no trails, but watch out for crumbly cliffs, which may not be obvious from above.

One of the best fishing spots in the Faroes is the tidal pool below Saksun village, where no licence is required.

Ask tourist offices for licence details in other locations.

WORK

Due to unemployment in the Faroes and the fact that job applicants with fluency in Faroese will always take precedence, foreigners have little chance of finding paid work. If you find a prospective employer – eg, a cannery, fishing boat or construction company – you'll need to apply to the police in Tórshavn for a work permit.

ACCOMMODATION

Those with webbed feet can try camping! The main camping ground is in Tórshavn on Streymoy. Most hostels allow camping on their land and you can also camp by the guesthouse on Mykines, and by the hotel at Eiði on Eysturoy. Camping isn't permitted outside designated areas.

There are a number of gistiheimilið (guesthouses) and ferðamannaheim (youth hostels) belonging to the **Danish Youth Hostels Association** (HI; W www.farhostel.fo), scouts and other associations. Hostels have kitchen facilities and dormitory rates are typically set at Dkr100/120 for members/nonmembers. Singles/doubles are usually available for around Dkr250/400.

Try bed and breakfasting in someone's home for an excellent introduction to the Faroese lifestyle. Prices start at Dkr250/360 for singles/doubles, including breakfast. You must book in advance through local tourist offices or the more expensive agency **Tora Tourist Traffic** (☎ 315505; W www.tora.fo; PO Box 3012, Niels Finsensgøta 21, FO-100 Tórshavn). You can also book self-catering houses and apartments throughout the Faroes (from Dkr440 per day).

Most hotels in the Faroes are fairly characterless but facilities are usually good enough; en suite hotel rooms average Dkr600/800 (singles/doubles). Around the same price, in Tórshavn and Klaksvík there are Sjómansheimið (seamen's homes), established by the Danish Lutheran Church as safe lodging for sailors and fishermen, but now open to all travellers. Christianity is enforced – no carousing – with formal prayers every morning. They have cafeterias that serve breakfast, lunch, pizzas and smørrebrød (open sandwiches) all day, as well as meals for several hours in the evening.

FOOD & DRINKS

Supermarkets are found in all towns and all but the smallest villages. Smaller kiosks stay open until 11pm Monday to Friday and varying hours Saturday and Sunday. Snacks such as burgers and chips are available at grill-bars and cafeterias in most towns and villages, and at some petrol stations. Apart from in Tórshavn, there are relatively few restaurants or cafeterias that serve full meals. Meals usually consist of stodgy meat-and-two-veg, but finer restaurants have fish and Faroese specialities such as lamb and puffin. Service standards are often poor – we recommend you only tip for good service.

Traditional foods include boiled, baked or roasted puffin, *skerpikjøt* (wind-dried mutton), horse and offal sausage, birds' eggs, sheep heads and whale meat. You'll even see sheep heads peering at you from inside plastic bags in supermarket freezers. Strangely, fresh fish isn't easily obtained – ask at a harbour if anyone has any spare fish for sale. Vegetarians are as rare as hens' teeth in the Faroes and any vegetarian traveller will need to resort to buying their own from a supermarket.

Alcohol is available from state alcohol stores, local brewery outlets and also some licensed bars, clubs and restaurants.

ENTERTAINMENT

In Tórshavn, there's a cinema, several pubs/cafés and nightclubs/discos, a swimming pool and a sports complex. Klaksvík and the smaller communities are distinctly quieter. 'Faroese evenings' feature traditional food, singing and chain dancing; contact tourist offices for the latest programme.

Getting There & Away

AIR

Through buses to the Faroes' international airport on Vágar run twice daily, leaving Tórshavn around three hours before flight departures. For information, contact any tourist office or call ☎ 343030.

Atlantic Airways (W *www.atlantic.fo*) flies to the Faroe Islands from Aberdeen in Scotland (two or three weekly, year-round), London Stansted (twice weekly, mid-June to mid-August only), Reykjavík in Iceland (twice weekly, April to October) and Oslo in Norway (twice weekly, mid-June to mid-August). Once weekly, the Oslo flight goes via Stavanger (Norway).

Maersk Air (W *www.maersk-air.com*) and Atlantic Airways fly between Copenhagen and Vágar daily all year. From mid-June to August, they also fly to/from Billund (Denmark) up to four times weekly each.

Atlantic Airways return Apex fares from Aberdeen/London to Vágar start at £230/277 (plus tax). Copenhagen to Vágar return is Dkr3095 with both Maersk Air and Atlantic Airways, and Oslo to Vágar return is Nkr2652. For these tickets, you must stay one Saturday night and the maximum stay is one month. Nondiscounted return fares vary, but can be nearly double the discounted deals. Weekend fares are usually available (Dkr2460 return from Copenhagen with Atlantic Airways) and there are special fares for those under 26, those over 65, and groups.

SEA

Smyril Line's new *Norröna* operates year-round from Hanstholm (Denmark) to Tórshavn. From mid-May to mid-September, the *Norröna* also connects with Iceland, the Shetland islands and Norway; it departs Hanstholm on Saturday evening and arrives in Tórshavn on Monday morning. Iceland-bound passengers must disembark while the ship continues to Lerwick (Shetland) and Bergen (Norway). After returning to Tórshavn on Wednesday, it collects the Iceland passengers and sails overnight to Seyðisfjörður. It returns to Tórshavn on Friday morning, and continues to Hanstholm for another circuit. See the Iceland chapter for further details.

For more time in the Faroes, Iceland-bound passengers have to break the journey and pay for two sectors. From Hanstholm to Tórshavn, the one-way, high-season, couchette fare is Dkr1640, with 25% discount for student cardholders (under 26 years old). Transporting vehicles up to 5m long costs Dkr1240. Above couchette, there are four classes of en suite cabins and a luxury suite. The ship also has a bar/nightclub, a cafeteria, two restaurants, duty-free shops and a swimming pool.

Those coming from mainland Scotland can travel with **NorthLink Ferries** (W *www .northlinkferries.co.uk*) from either Aberdeen or Kirkwall (Orkney) to Lerwick, then connect with the *Norröna* from there. The one-way, high-season, couchette fare between Lerwick and Tórshavn is £80, with a 25% discount for student card-holders. Transporting vehicles up to 5m in length costs £60.

FAROE ISLANDS

For further information, contact **Smyril Line Shetland** (☎ 01595-690845; **w** www .smyril-line.com; Holmsgarth Terminal, Lerwick, Shetland, ZE1 0PR).

Getting Around

Remember that the weather has the final say on whether transport services will actually run.

AIR

There's only one airport in the Faroe Islands, the international terminal on Vágar, so all interisland air travel is by helicopter (tyrlan, pronounced **toor**-lan). Several times a week, helicopters connect Vágar airport with Tórshavn, Klaksvík, Skúvoy, Froðba and Stóra Dímun. There are also routes from Vágar airport to Mykines and Gásadalur and from Klaksvík to Svínoy and Fugloy. The flights to Mykines are popular, so book early.

Helicopter services are operated by **Atlantic Airways** (☎ 241000; **w** www.atlantic .fo; Vágar Airport, FO-380 Sørvágur). The Tórshavn heliport is 500m north of the camping ground. Helicopter flights from Tórshavn to Klaksvík, Froðba (Suðuroy) or Vágar all cost Dkr215; and from Vágar to Mykines costs Dkr145. Prices and schedules are posted on the website.

BUS

The **Strandfaraskip Landsins** (**w** www.ssl .fo) Bygdaleiðir long-distance bus service is excellent. It follows a strict and convenient schedule and, when combined with the ferry services, links virtually every corner of the country, including some fairly remote outposts. The bus timetable and map Ferðaætlan is issued annually (free). Bus fares are steep but visitors can buy the SL Visitor Travelcard for Dkr500/800 for four/seven days of unlimited travel on all buses and interisland ferries (50% child discount, seven to 13 years). Passes are available from the tourist information desk at the airport or the Farstøðin (harbour) transport terminal in Tórshavn.

CAR & MOTORCYCLE

In the Faroes, vehicles drive on the right. There are only a few unsurfaced roads and outlying islands are connected to Tórshavn by car ferries, bridges or tunnels. The greatest hazards are fog, sheep and precipitous drops. Some of the numerous tunnels, especially those in the northeastern islands, are wide enough for only one vehicle to pass through but there are bays every few hundred metres. If they're marked 'V', pull in and allow the other car to pass. If marked 'M', the other car has to give way.

The drink-driving laws are strict, maximum 0.05% blood alcohol content or you lose your licence.

Be extremely alert in thick fog; motorists must take financial responsibility for anything they hit. If you hit a sheep, phone the **police** (☎ 311448) in Tórshavn. Speed limits are 80km/h on the open highway and 50km/h through villages. Front and rear seatbelt use is compulsory.

In Tórshavn, you must place a parking disc (set at the time you parked your car) in the front window. These discs are available free from tourist offices and banks. Legal parking spaces are marked with a 'P' followed by a number and the word tíma, which indicates the maximum permitted parking time. Blýfrítt (unleaded petrol) is always available at petrol stations. Unleaded petrol costs around Dkr7.50 per litre.

Rental agencies tack on a Collision Damage Waiver (CDW), but with your own vehicle; you'll need some proof of third-party insurance (eg, a Green Card) or be prepared to purchase it (at great expense) from the customs department upon entering the country. See also under Car & Motorcycle in the Getting Around the Region chapter.

Rental

You must be at least 18 years old to rent a car. It's expensive and there may be a per kilometre charge, but the daily rate decreases the longer you keep the car. Car hire typically costs around Dkr700 per day, including VAT and insurance; a deposit may be required. Car-rental outlets include:

Avis Føroyar (☎ 332765, fax 333155, **e** avis@ post.olivant.fo) Vágar Airport, FO-380 Sørvágur

Avis Føroyar (☎ 313535, fax 317735) v/Johs Berg, Staravegur 1, FO-110 Tórshavn

Eyðbjørn Hansen (☎ 313375, fax 311495) Varðagøta 75, FO-100 Tórshavn

Hertz (☎ 312107, fax 315716, **e** hertz@ff.fo) Hoydalsvegur 17, PO Box 3225, FO-110 Tórshavn

BICYCLE

Although there are lots of steep hills, tunnels, wind and rain, the Faroes aren't too bad for cycling because all highways are surfaced. Don't take Faroese cycling too lightly; warm, windproof and waterproof clothing is essential. If the weather gets too wretched, remember that buses accept bicycles as luggage for Dkr30 per ride.

The biggest obstacles for cyclists are long road tunnels, which are best avoided (especially Kollafjørður–Kaldbaksfjørður and Oyrarbakki–Vesturdalur); toxic gases can be trapped in the more congested tunnels. You'll need a good bicycle lamp, both front and back, visible for several kilometres. Hills are steep, highways are wet and drop-offs severe so check your brakes carefully. Note that off-road biking is prohibited in the Faroes.

Currently, bike rental is only available in Klaksvík.

BOAT

All islands except Koltur and the Dímuns are connected by ferry and/or the bus system. Some ferries take vehicles and others only carry passengers. Children (seven to 13 years), students and people over 65 receive 14% to 50% discounts. Some ferry trips, especially those to Mykines, Svínoy and Fugloy, are through open seas in small boats and are frequently cancelled because of the weather. Keep plans as flexible as possible.

ORGANISED TOURS

Tours and bookings are available from the following organisations:

Eysturoyar Kunningarstova (☎ 449449, e infoey-r@post.olivant.fo) FO-600 Saltangará. Hiking tours to Slættaratindur

Gunnar Skúvadal (☎ 424305, e skuvadal@puffin .fo) FO-350 Vestmanna. Exceptionally friendly boat tours to the Vestmanna bird cliffs

Kunningarstovan (☎ 315788, w www.visittorsh avn.fo) Niels Finsensgøta 13, PO Box 379, FO-110 Tórshavn. Trips to the storm petrel colony on Nólsoy; hiking trips on Streymoy and surrounding islands; sea angling; bus tours; and town walks

Kunningarstovan Suðuroy (☎ 372480, e sout-inf@ post.olivant.fo) FO-800 Tvøroyri. Guided hikes on Suðuroy, bus tours and fishing

MB Tours (☎ 322121, e mb-tours@mb-tours .com) Bryggjubakki 2, PO Box 3021, FO-110 Tórshavn. Day tours by bus; destinations include Saksun, Gjógv and Kirkjubøur

Norðoya Kunningarstova (☎ 456939, e info@ klaksvik.fo) Nólsoyar Pálsgøta 32, FO-700 Klaksvík. Hiking on the northern islands (including the Enniberg cliffs), sightseeing around Kalsoy by boat, and bus tours

Palli Lamhauge (☎ 424155, e sight@sightseeing .fo) FO-350 Vestmanna. Boat tours to the Vestmanna bird cliffs and (for groups) Eiði, Saksun and Mykines

Smyril Line Tours (☎ 345900, e incoming@ smyril-line.fo) Jónas Bronckgøta 37, PO Box 370, FO-110 Tórshavn. Sailing trips to Hestur or Nólsoy, bus tours, hiking, (including the highest peak Slættaratindur) and trips to Sandoy

Tora Tourist Traffic (☎ 315505, w www.tora.fo) Niels Finsensgøta 21, PO Box 3012, FO-100 Tórshavn. Day tours by bus

Vágar Tourist Association (☎ 333455, e vagar@ post.olivant.fo) FO-370 Miðvágur. Pony trekking, hiking and boat trips

Tórshavn

pop 16,842

The capital and largest community of the Faroes, Tórshavn has a relaxed atmosphere and enjoys picturesque charm. A stroll around Tinganes, the small headland where the town began nearly a thousand years ago, will endear this quiet and rainy little place to most visitors. The rest of Tórshavn, a mixture of pleasant harbour areas, colourful homes and even a city park proudly boasting that forests are growing in the Faroes, all hold quaint appeal.

Orientation

Tórshavn is easy to walk around. The older, central section surrounds the two harbours, which are separated by the historical Tinganes peninsula. The Eastern Harbour is the ferry terminal and the Western Harbour is for commerce. Uphill from the harbours, there's a modern centre with most shops, restaurants and services, including the SMS indoor shopping centre on RC Effersøesgøta.

Information

Tourist Offices The **Faroe Islands Tourist Board** (☎ 316055, fax 310858; e tourist@ tourist.fo; Undir Bryggjubakka 17; open 7am-5pm Mon & Fri, 8am-5pm Tues-Thur, 2pm-5pm Sun June-Aug; shorter hrs Sept-May) is by the Western Harbour. There's also the **Kunningarstovan city tourist office** (☎ 315788, fax 316831; e torsinfo@post.olivant.fo; Niels Finsensgøta 13; open 7am-5.30pm Mon & Fri, 8am-5.30pm Tues-Thur, 9am-2pm Sat

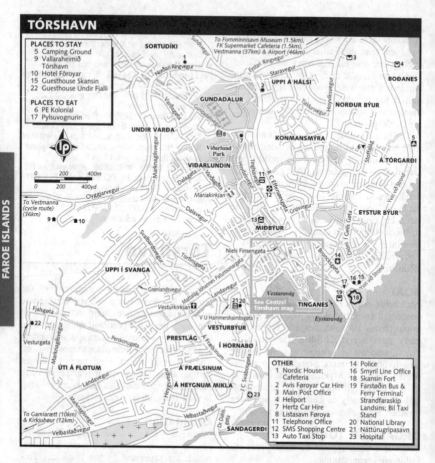

TÓRSHAVN

PLACES TO STAY
5 Camping Ground
9 Vallaraheimið Tórshavn
10 Hotel Føroyar
15 Guesthouse Skansin
22 Guesthouse Undir Fjalli

PLACES TO EAT
6 PE Kolonial
17 Pylsuvognurin

OTHER
1 Nordic House; Cafeteria
2 Avis Føroyar Car Hire
3 Main Post Office
4 Heliport
7 Hertz Car Hire
8 Listasavn Føroya
11 Telephone Office
12 SMS Shopping Centre
13 Auto Taxi Stop
14 Police
16 Smyril Line Office
18 Skansin Fort
19 Farstøðin Bus & Ferry Terminal; Strandfaraskip Landsins; Bil Taxi Stand
20 National Library
21 Náttúrugripasavn
23 Hospital

mid-May–Aug; slightly shorter hrs Sept–mid-May). Both offices distribute the free booklet *Tourist Guide – Faroe Islands*, which details sights and tourist facilities around the country.

Money Tórshavn's banks are open 9.30am to 4pm on weekdays (late closing at 6pm on Thursday); all handle foreign exchange. Outside normal banking hours, the Kunningarstovan city tourist office will exchange money (except Icelandic króna), as does Hotel Hafnia, which charges a higher commission but is open evenings and Sunday. Visa, Plus, Eurocard, MasterCard and Cirrus are accepted by the **Føroya Banki ATM** *(Niels Finsensgøta 15)*.

Post & Communications The **central post office** *(Posthúsbrekka; open 10am-4pm*

Mon-Wed & Fri, 10am-6pm Thur) on Vaglið (the town square) provides philatelic services. There's also the **main post office** *(Óðinshædd 2; open 9am-5pm Mon-Fri)*.

Purchase telephone cards, send or receive faxes and make international calls at the **telephone office** *(Tinghúsvegur 64; open 8am-9pm daily)*.

Teledepelin *(Niels Finsensgøta 10; open 9am-5.30pm Mon-Wed, 9am-6pm Thur & Fri, 10am-2pm Sat)* has two free Internet terminals available for browsing.

There's also free Internet access (with bookable one-hour slots) at the **National Library** *(☎ 311626; JC Svabosgøta; open 10am-8pm Mon-Wed, 10am-5pm Thur & Fri mid-Aug–mid-June; 1pm-5pm Mon-Fri mid-June–mid-Aug)*.

Historic buildings on the Tinganes peninsula, Faroe Islands

The one that didn't get away!

The towering Vestmanna bird cliffs are home to fulmars, kittiwakes, guillemots, razorbills and puffins

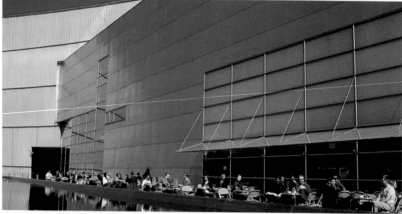

JONATHAN SMITH

Helsinki's Kiasma offers daring contemporary art and a chance to kick back and relax with the Finns

JOHN BORTHWICK

Lap up the wilderness in Lapland: hike or take a peaceful boat cruise in Lemmenjoki National Park

JEROEN VAN MARLE

Just push off! Winter recreation in Kaivopuisto Park, Helsinki

Bookshops The best place to find foreign-language publications is **HN Jacobsens Bókahandil** (☎ *311036; Vaglið*). **Bókasølan**, upstairs at the SMS shopping centre, carries some English and German titles.

Medical Services There's a casualty service at the **hospital** (☎ *313540; JC Svabosgøta*).

Things to See

Until the late 1800s, Tórshavn didn't extend beyond the Tinganes peninsula. Narrow Gongin lane, still lined with some lovely 19th-century wooden houses, was the main street. Today, plenty of interesting buildings remain on the peninsula.

Probably dating from the 15th century, **Munkastovan** had a religious role as a lodging house for monks. The **Leigubúðin**, built in the 16th century, was the king's storehouse. When most of the old buildings on Tinganes burnt down in 1673, both this and Munkastovan were spared. **Reynargarður**, once a vicarage, was constructed in 1630 and is an excellent example of Faroese architecture from the 17th century. **Skansapakkhúsið**, at the southern end of Tinganes, was built in 1750 for storage of artillery. The stone **Myrkastovan** (Dark House), dating from 1693, was a guardhouse.

Skansin (*admission free; always open*), the fort whose ruins are on the edge of the Eastern Harbour, was ostensibly constructed to keep pirates and smugglers from upsetting the local monopoly trade. It affords a great view of the harbour.

Listgalleríið Friðriksvágur (☎ *314382; 1st floor, Vágsbotnur 12; admission free; open 4pm-5.30pm Mon-Fri, 11am-noon Sat*) is a decent gallery of Faroese and modern art. Items on display are usually for sale.

The modern **Løgting** (Parliament) is across the pedestrian street from Vaglið. The distinctive, turf-roofed Løgting building was originally constructed in 1856 and has since been expanded.

The **Niels R Finsen Memorial** (*Laða Brekka*) commemorates the Faroese physician who won the Nobel Prize for medicine in the early 20th century and who is now considered the father of radiology. As a child, he carved his initials into a rock in what is now a tiny city park.

The architecturally interesting, turf-roofed **Nordic House** (☎ *317900;* 🔲 *www.nlh.fo; Norðari Ringvegur 10; admission free; open*

10am-6pm Mon-Sat, 2pm-6pm Sun) dates from 1983. The spacious interior is used as a theatre and a conference, concert and exhibition hall; there's also a library and a cafeteria. For information on any visiting exhibitions by Scandinavian artists, check the website.

The bright and airy Faroese Museum of Art, **Listasavn Føroya** (☎ *313579; Gundadalsvegur 9; adult/child Dkr20/free; open 11am-5pm Mon-Fri, 2pm-6pm Sat & Sun June-Aug; 2pm-5pm Tues-Fri, 2pm-6pm Sat & Sun Sept–mid-Dec & mid-Jan–May*), has a fine collection of works by Faroese artists.

The excellent historical museum **Fornminnissavn** (☎ *310700; Brekkutún 6, Hoyvík; adult/child Dkr30/free; open 10am-5pm Mon-Fri, 2pm-5pm Sat & Sun mid-May–mid-Sept, 3pm-5pm Sun mid-Sept–mid-May*), 2km north of the city centre, contains religious and maritime artefacts, boats, early art, and various practical household and farming implements from the Viking Age and the medieval period to modern times. It's well worth a visit. Red bus Nos 2 and 3 pass near the museum, on Hvítanesvegur.

The natural history museum **Náttúrugripasavn** (☎ *312306; VU Hammershaimbsgøta 13; adult/child Dkr20/free; open 11am-4pm Mon-Fri, 3pm-5pm Sat & Sun June-Aug, 3pm-5pm Sun Sept-May*) features marine mammal skeletons, stuffed birds and a wacky stuffed giant squid, which is nearly 6m long.

Places to Stay

Camping The **camping ground** (☎ *315788, 320739; Yviri við Strond;* 🄴 *torsinfo@post .olivant.fo; tent sites per person Dkr50; open mid-May–mid-Sept*), 1500m north along the coast from the centre, has acceptable kitchen and bathroom facilities, but the ground is rather hard and prone to flooding.

Hostels On the hillside 2km west of central Tórshavn is the clean and tidy **Vallaraheimið Tórshavn** (☎ *345900;* 🄴 *booking@smyril-line .fo; Oyggjarvegur; beds HI non-members/ members Dkr145/130; open 2 Jan-23 Dec*). Accommodation is in two- to six-bed dormitories. Advance booking is only accepted from Smyril Line passengers – otherwise, just turn up. Breakfast costs Dkr70 extra but cooking facilities are available.

Bládýpi (☎ *311951, fax 319451; Dokta Jakobsensgøta 14-16; beds HI members/ nonmembers Dkr100/120, singles/doubles*

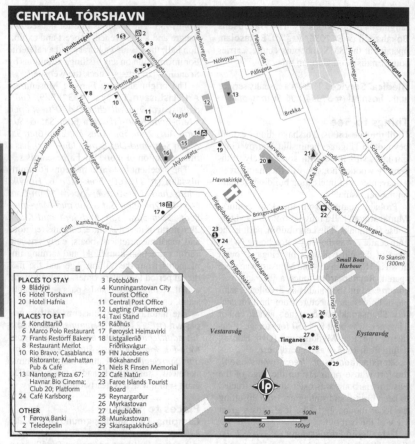

CENTRAL TÓRSHAVN

PLACES TO STAY
9   Bládýpi
16 Hotel Tórshavn
20 Hotel Hafnia

PLACES TO EAT
5   Konditaríið
6   Marco Polo Restaurant
7   Frants Restorff Bakery
8   Restaurant Merlot
10 Rio Bravo; Casablanca
    Ristorante; Manhattan
    Pub & Café
13 Nantong; Pizza 67;
    Havnar Bio Cinema;
    Club 20; Platform
24 Café Karlsborg

OTHER
1   Føroya Banki
2   Teledepilen

3   Fotobúðin
4   Kunningarstovan City
    Tourist Office
11 Central Post Office
12 Løgting (Parliament)
14 Taxi Stand
15 Ráðhús
17 Føroyskt Heimavirki
18 Listgalleriið
    Friðriksvágur
19 HN Jacobsens
    Bókahandil
21 Niels R Finsen Memorial
22 Café Natúr
23 Faroe Islands Tourist
    Board
25 Reynargarður
26 Myrkastovan
27 Leigubúðin
28 Munkastovan
29 Skansapakkhúsið

Dkr240/380) is in a nice part of town and offers hostel-style rooms with shared bathroom facilities. Book in advance or you may find the place deserted.

B&Bs & Guesthouses The Kunningarstovan city tourist office keeps lists of families who offer B&B (singles/doubles from Dkr250/360).

Guesthouse Undir Fjalli (☎ 317177, 320527; ℮ nuf@hsh.fo; Vesturgøta 15; singles/doubles Dkr360/490; open mid-June–mid-Aug) has modernised rooms that include shower and breakfast; kitchen facilities are available. **Guesthouse Skansin** (☎ 312242, fax 310657; Jekaragøta 8; singles/doubles Dkr390/540; open 2 Jan-23 Dec), near the harbour, also offers a guest

kitchen and clean rooms, with breakfast included.

Hotels In the centre of town, near Vaglið square, **Hotel Tórshavn** (☎ 350000, fax 350001; Tórsgøta 4; singles/doubles from Dkr590/750; open 2 Jan-23 Dec) has pleasant rooms with bath and great harbour views; rates include breakfast. The professionally run **Hotel Hafnia** (☎ 313233; ℮ hafnia@hafnia.fo; Áarvegur 4-10; singles/doubles Dkr800/995; open 3 Jan-23 Dec) offers well-appointed en suite accommodation, including breakfast.

Up on the hill, **Hotel Föroyar** (☎ 317500; ℮ hotel-fo@post.olivant.fo; Oyggjarvegur; singles/doubles from Dkr790/950) has the finest views and flash facilities, including en suite rooms, TV, phone and minibar.

Places to Eat

Restaurants At Hotel Hafnia (☎ 313233; Áarvegur 4-10; buffet breakfast/lunch/ dinner Dkr65/78/175) you'll find huge buffet meals – lunch is particularly recommended. Two-course lunches cost Dkr110 and Faroese specialities (including fried puffin) cost from Dkr85 to Dkr205. The lunch buffet isn't available on weekends.

The stylish **Restaurant Merlot** (☎ 311121; Magnus Heinasonargøta 20; mains Dkr178-218) serves a range of fine beef, lamb and fish dishes.

Rio Bravo (☎ 319767; Tórsgøta 11; steaks Dkr155-185; open 6pm-midnight Mon-Thur, 5pm-midnight Fri-Sun) has an emphasis on steaks, but there's also a solitary salmon on the menu (Dkr165). Downstairs, the Italian-style **Casablanca Ristorante** (☎ 319696; dishes Dkr85-175; open noon-10.30pm daily) serves a variety of pasta, meat and fish dishes, and a lunch buffet (Dkr 59) Monday to Friday.

The **Marco Polo Restaurant** (☎ 313430; Sverrisgøta 12; dishes Dkr155-210) serves venison, lamb and beef, but the lunch buffet (Dkr59) is basically stodge. The Chinese restaurant **Nantong** (☎ 318698; Tinghúsvegur 8; Tues-Fri lunch buffet Dkr59) is a better lunch choice. In the same building, **Pizza 67** (dishes Dkr54-130) rustles up pizzas, Mexican fare (burritos, nachos, quesadillas etc) and the best burgers and chips in town.

Cafeterias Hotel Tórshavn's **Pizzacafé** (Tórsgøta 4; dishes Dkr55-90) serves pizza, pasta and kebabs. The food's consistently good although the service can be a bit odd.

You'll find a good cafeteria in the **Fk supermarket** (Brekkutún 9; daily specials Dkr38) near the Fornminnissavn museum in Hoyvik and there's also a pleasant **cafeteria** (most dishes Dkr20-30) in the Nordic House, which serves decent soup (Dkr20), sandwiches and cakes.

Fast Food Try **Kondittaríið** (Niels Finsensgøta 11; snacks Dkr10-30) for various inexpensive dishes. The wonderful **Café Karlsborg** (Undir Bryggjubakka 18; snacks Dkr10-55) is better, but it's not always open. For hot dogs, burgers and chips, try the basic **Pylsuvognurin** (snacks from Dkr17) opposite the Farstøðin transport terminal, or **City Burger** (Tórsgøta 17; burgers Dkr30-46; open 11am-11pm Mon-Sat, 2pm-11pm Sun).

Self-Catering The best-stocked supermarket is **Miklagarður** (RC Effersøesgøta 31; open Mon-Sat), in the SMS shopping centre. Around town, you'll also find a number of small grocery kiosks, including **PE Kolonial** (Stoffalág 33), near the camping ground. In the centre, you can buy groceries and excellent baked goods at **Frants Restorff Bakery** (Tórsgøta; open 7am-11pm daily).

Entertainment

For theatre and other events, including 'Faroese evenings', contact the tourist office.

Bars & Clubs Most weeks, **Café Natúr** (Áarvegur 7) has live music from Thursday to Saturday. Black Sheep lager costs Dkr50 per half litre.

The nightclub/disco **Club 20** (Tinghúsvegur 8), in the same building as the cinema, attracts locals in the 18 to 25 age group. The adjacent nightclub **Platform** appeals to the 20 to 30 age group and sometimes features live bands. The **Manhattan Pub & Café** (Sverrisgøta 15) regularly has live music along with a younger clientele after 1am on weekends.

Cinema The two-screen cinema, **Havnar Bio** (☎ 311956; Tinghúsvegur 8; tickets Dkr60), shows between three and six films every night. Films are shown in their original language with Danish subtitles.

Shopping

Stock up on film at **Fotobúðin** (Niels Finsensgøta 8); one-hour print processing is also available here. Handknitted woollen garments are for sale at **Føroyskt Heimavirki** (Vágsbotnur 14).

Getting There & Away

Long-distance buses and international and inter-island ferries depart from the Farstøðin transport terminal, by the Eastern Harbour. For a concise schedule of buses and ferries, pick up a copy of Ferðaætlan (free, from tourist offices or Strandfaraskip Landsins at the terminal). See also the Getting There & Away section earlier in this chapter.

For information on helicopter flights, see the introductory Getting Around section in this chapter.

Smyril Line (☎ 345900; e office@smyri l-line.fo; Jónas Broncksgøta 37) operates ferry services to Europe, the UK and Iceland from the Farstøðin transport terminal.

Getting Around

To/From the Airport The airport bus (No 100; Dkr100) leaves from the Farstøðin transport terminal approximately three hours before international flight departures and runs to the international airport on Vágar via the new Streymoy–Vágar undersea tunnel. Bookings aren't possible. For information, contact tourist offices or phone ☎ 343030.

Bus The red Bussleiðin city buses (Dkr10 per ride) cover most of the city, running half-hourly on weekdays and hourly in the evening.

Taxi You'll find **taxis** (☎ *311234, 311444*) at the Auto and Bil stands on Niels Finsens-gøta and at Farstøðin, respectively, and at the Ráðhús. Bil offers special rates (Dkr25 per person) for *Norröna* passengers wishing to stay at the Vallaraheimið Tórshavn HI hostel or Hotel Föroyar.

Around the Faroes

KIRKJUBØUR
pop 65

Kirkjubøur, on Streymoy, was the largest and wealthiest farm in the Faroes and the episcopal centre of the country during medieval times. Its most striking ruin is the '**unfinished cathedral**' *(admission free)*, a grand Gothic church intended to be dedicated to St Magnus, Earl of Orkney, but never completed. Consequently, the nearby **St Olav's church**, originally constructed in 1111, served as the Faroes' ecumenical heart right through to the Reformation. **Roykstovan** (☎ *328089; adult/child Dkr30/free; open 10am-5.30pm Mon-Sat, 2pm-5pm Sun June-Aug)*, a 900-year-old, turf-roofed farmhouse at Kirkjubøur, is a large two-storey, split-log building. The interior of the building is laid out to reflect the Faroese lifestyle during medieval times.

From Tórshavn, Kirkjubøur is reached on foot over the mountain (8km) or by taking bus No 101 (Dkr20, 30 minutes) from the Farstøðin transport terminal to Gamlarætt and walking 2km from there (with advance booking, some buses continue to Kirkjubøur).

VESTMANNA BIRD CLIFFS

The magnificent boat tours to the wild Vestmanna bird cliffs of northwestern Streymoy are probably the finest highlight of the Faroe Islands. When the weather's fine, you sail from Vestmanna along the west coast of Streymoy to towering cliffs and sea stacks that teem with fulmars, kittiwakes, guillemots, razorbills and, occasionally, puffins. If the sea is calm, the boats pass through some beautiful sea caves that lie beneath the cliffs.

The recommended tour (adult/child Dkr175/85) is with **Gunnar Skúvadal** in his 8m-long Faroese wooden launch *Urðardrangur* or his more modern fibreglass speedboat *Barbara*. If his tours are full, there's also **Palli Lamhauge** in his boats *Frígerð* or *Silja*. For contact details, see Organised Tours in the introductory Getting Around section earlier in this chapter.

Vestmanna (pop 1241) itself is of little interest, but there are several pleasant walks in the area. If you want to stay, the **La Carreta** (☎ *424610;* e *carreta@post.olivant.fo; á Bakka; dorm beds HI members/nonmembers Dkr100/120, singles/doubles Dkr275/390; hostel open June-Aug)* hostel, guesthouse and restaurant will be happy to accommodate you. **Kaffistovan**, at the ferry dock, serves quick grills and microwave snacks.

Buses to Vestmanna run fairly frequently from the Farstøðin bus and ferry terminal in Tórshavn (Dkr40, 50 minutes).

SAKSUN
pop 32

Saksun, on Streymoy, has a magnificent and unusual setting, making it a wonderful tourist destination. Downstream from the village is the beautiful and almost perfectly round tidal lake **Pollur**. The turf-roofed **Saksun church**, which overlooks Pollur, was moved to its present position from Tjørnuvík in 1858.

At the end of the northern road in Saksun is the 19th-century turf farmhouse **Dúvugarður** (☎ *310700; admission Dkr20; open 2pm-5pm Fri-Wed mid-June–mid-Aug)*, now a fascinating folk museum conveying the rigours of Faroese life from the medieval era to the 19th century.

There are several good day **hikes** around Saksun, including the Saksunardalur valley, the mountain pass to Tjørnuvík (the path isn't easy to find), and the route northwest to the fantastic Kambsmúli viewpoint, which passes several small lakes with profuse bird life.

Daily except Sunday, from 25 June to 15 August, there are two buses (No 204) to/from Oyrarbakki (on Eysturoy) 'connecting' with buses (No 400) to/from Tórshavn; sometimes you'll have a long wait. The fare from Tórshavn is Dkr50. Otherwise, MB-Tours run a Tuesday tour from Tórshavn to Saksun.

EIÐI

pop 720

Eiði (**oy**-yeh) sits on a pass between the Eysturoy mainland and the Kollur peninsula (which makes for a great hike, with excellent views of the Risin og Kellingin sea stacks). The **village church**, built in 1881, has several votive ships and is one of the nicest in the Faroes. The folk museum, **Látrið** (☎ *423597; admission Dkr20; open 2pm-4pm Wed & Sun June-Aug, or by arrangement*), has an interesting collection of several traditional turf-roofed houses complete with box beds, furniture, tools and other equipment.

Hotel Eiði (☎ *423456; e hotel-ei@post .olivant.fo; camping Dkr50, singles/doubles Dkr600/650; open May-Aug*) looks rather impersonal, but it's quite nice inside and the staff are friendly. However, the meals can be rather variable. There's a basic camping area by the hotel, but it may move in the future.

The village **supermarket** sells a full range of groceries.

From Tórshavn, take bus No 400 to Oyrarbakki then bus No 200 to Eiði (Dkr50, one hour, two to nine daily).

GJÓGV

pop 59

The quiet village of Gjógv in northern Eysturoy is one of the most picturesque in the Faroes. It's named after its harbour, which is an unusual sea-filled gorge. Gjógv is a good base for hiking to **Slættaratindur** (882m), the Faroes' highest peak; set off from the highest point on the Eiði–Funningur road. There's also a great walk west from Gjógv to Ambadalur, with impressive views of the Búgvin cliffs and sea stack (at 188m, the highest in the Faroes).

The excellent **Gjáargarður Youth Hostel** (☎ *423171; e mail@gjaarhostel.dk; camping per person Dkr50, dorm beds HI members/ nonmembers Dkr100/120, singles/doubles Dkr275/385; open mid-June–mid-Aug*) is a pleasant, grass-roofed building with balconies, originally intended to resemble a traditional Faroese farmhouse.

To reach Gjógv from Tórshavn, take bus No 400 to Oyrarbakki then connect with bus No 205, which runs twice on weekdays, once or twice on Saturday (Dkr50, 1¾ hours).

KLAKSVÍK

pop 4773

Klaksvík, on the island of Borðoy, is the Faroes' second largest town and it's ideal for exploring the northeastern Faroes. Like most Faroese towns, its economy is based on fishing and fish processing, but the country's only brewery, Föroya Bjór, is also located here.

Information

The tourist office is **Norðoya Kunningarstova** (☎ *456939; e info@klaksvik.fo; Nólsoyar Pálsgøta 32; open 9am-5pm Mon-Fri, 10am-1pm Sat mid-June–mid-Aug; 10am-noon & 1pm-4pm Mon-Fri mid-Aug–mid-June*). The **post office** (*Klaksvíksvegur 2*) is at the head of the harbour and the **telephone office** (*Biskupsstøðgøta 3*) is just to the east. For Internet and email, the **library** (*Biskupsstøðgøta 9; open 1pm-6pm Mon-Fri, 10am-1pm Sat*) has bookable one-hour slots. All three banks in town exchange foreign currency and travellers cheques. The **hospital** (☎ *455463; Vikavegur 40-44*) has a casualty ward.

Things to See & Do

Klaksvík's most interesting site is **Christianskirkja** (*Kirkjubrekka 6; admission free; open 10am-11am & 1pm-4pm Mon-Sat mid-May–Aug*), a church with a 4000-year-old sacrificial bowl from a pagan temple as a baptismal font. The gables are reminiscent of early Viking halls, the stone walls call to mind those of St Magnus' Cathedral at Kirkjubøur and the design of the gable windows was inspired by those of Faroese boathouses.

There are good local exhibits in **Norðoya Fornminnasavn** (*North Islands Museum;* ☎ *456287; Klaksvíksvegur 84; admission Dkr20; open 1pm-4pm daily mid-May–mid-Sept*), housed upstairs in an old store from the Danish monopoly days. Look out for the float made from a dead cat.

A popular half-day trip from town is the steep climb up the 647m peak **Háfjall** (meaning high mountain) and/or the 503m **Hálgafelli**. Follow the road towards the heliport, slanting uphill and heading south from the southern end of the harbour. Turn right for 500m, leave the track and ascend directly

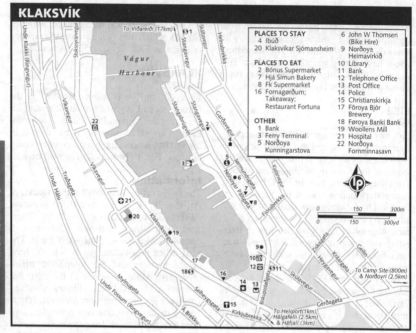

KLAKSVÍK

PLACES TO STAY
4 Ibúð
20 Klaksvíkar Sjómansheim

PLACES TO EAT
2 Bónus Supermarket
7 Hjá Símun Bakery
8 Fk Supermarket
16 Fornagørðum;
   Takeaway;
   Restaurant Fortuna

OTHER
1 Bank
3 Ferry Terminal
5 Norðoya
   Kunningarstova
6 John W Thomsen
   (Bike Hire)
9 Norðoya
   Heimavirkið
10 Library
11 Bank
12 Telephone Office
13 Post Office
14 Police
15 Christianskirkja
17 Føroya Bjór
   Brewery
18 Føroya Banki Bank
19 Woollens Mill
21 Hospital
22 Norðoya
   Fornminnasavn

---

towards the pass between the two peaks, then follow the ridges (easier on the western sides) to either peak.

If you'd like to visit the **Föroya Bjór brewery** (*Klaksvíksvegur 24*) or see the spinning and washing processes at the **woollens mill** (*Klaksvíksvegur 54*), ask at the tourist office.

Places to Stay & Eat

Free **camping** (☎ 456939; open mid-June–mid-Aug), with kitchen and toilet facilities, is allowed 1.5km from town in the direction of Norðoyri; turn left up the hill just before the graveyard.

The very nice (if a bit quirky) hostel, **Ibúð** (☎/fax 457555; e ibudkl@post.olivant.fo; Garðavegur 31; dorm beds HI members/nonmembers Dkr100/120, singles/doubles Dkr220/350; open mid-May–Aug), is best reached by a circuitous signposted route.

The **tourist office** (☎ 456939; B&B singles/doubles Dkr250/450) can arrange B&B and self-catering options.

The Seamen's Home, **Klaksvíkar Sjómansheim** (☎ 455333, fax 457233; Víkavegur 38; singles Dkr345-595, doubles Dkr495-795; open year-round), has some good en

suite rooms. The recommended and filling meals here cost Dkr40/80/80 for breakfast/lunch/dinner.

Popular **Fornagørðum** (*Klaksvíksvegur 22; dishes from Dkr45*) serves pizzas and grilled fare all day. The **takeaway** next door offers fish and chips for Dkr42. Upstairs, **Restaurant Fortuna** (*Klaksvíksvegur 22; specials around Dkr55-75*) serves fish and beef dishes, including traditional options.

You'll find excellent gooey concoctions at the **Hjá Símun bakery** (*Nólsoyar Pálsgøta 16*). The two main supermarkets are **Fk** (*Nólsoyar Pálsgøta 12*) and **Bónus** (*Stangavegur 10*).

Shopping

Norðoya Heimavirkið (*Biskupsstøðgøta 11*) sells high-quality, handmade pullovers and other woollen goods.

Getting There & Away

Buses from Tórshavn connect with ferries to Klaksvík 10 times on weekdays, seven times on Saturday and five times on Sunday (Dkr80, two hours). There is a **heliport** (☎ 241000) in town with services to/from Tórshavn (Dkr215), Svínoy (Dkr110) and

Fugloy (Dkr110) which operate three days each week. The **ferry terminal** (☎ 343030) is located on Varpabrúgvin.

Getting Around
For taxi service, ring **Bil** (☎ 212900). Bicycles may be rented from **John W Thomsen** (☎ 455858; Nólsoyar Pálsgøta 26; at most Dkr40/day, plus at least Dkr200 deposit).

KALSOY
pop 141
Ferry-bound travellers pass enigmatic Kalsoy on their way to Klaksvík. Its four tiny villages are connected by a partly unsurfaced road that spends half its length in dark and wet tunnels. A bus takes you to Trøllanes, from where you should take the two-hour return walk to the Kallur **lighthouse** – it's well worth the effort. It's also possible to **hike** along parts of the ridge at the southern end of the island.

You should contact the Klaksvík **tourist office** (☎ 456939; e info@klaksvik.fo) for details of self-catering accommodation on Kalsoy. The bus (Dkr20) connects at Syðradalur with the ferry (Dkr30) from Klaksvík, which runs two to four times daily.

VIÐAREIÐI
pop 337
The most northern village in the Faroe Islands is Viðareiði, occupying a windy pass near the northern end of Viðoy. Looking west from the village, the view to the headlands of northern Borðoy, Kunoy and Kalsoy is absolutely spectacular.

The main attraction on Viðoy is the stiff walk up to **Enniberg** (750m), the highest sheer cliff face in Europe. The route goes via the 844m summit of Villingadalsfjall; take the 1:100,000-scale map (available from tourist offices) and allow six or seven hours.

The village **church** is noteworthy for its silver altar and silver crucifix. Ask Klaksvík tourist office for the key. The rectory is reputedly haunted.

Hotel Norð (☎ 451244, fax 451245; singles/doubles Dkr475/675) is an ideal remote retreat for anyone seeking solitude. Accommodation and meals must be booked in advance.

Bus No 500 makes seven runs each weekday between Klaksvík and Viðareiði (Dkr30, 45 minutes). There are three runs on Saturday, and four on Sunday.

VÁGAR
pop 2737
Vágar's main attractions are its lakes, its precipitous western and southern coasts, and its mountain country. There are **tourist offices** at the airport and in Miðvágur.

The finest hike is from Sørvágur to Lambadalur, following a path along the southern shore of the fjord. From Lambadalur, easy grassy slopes lead up to the back of the 288m sheer precipice of **Sundsnøva**, with magnificent views of the Drangarnir and Tindhólmur islets. Allow three to four hours return.

Gásadalur makes a great destination for a day hike. A well-marked path begins in Bøur, 4km west of Sørvágur, and follows a beautiful but steep and marginally treacherous route as high as 425m before descending to Gásadalur village.

The rather quirky, prefabricated HI hostel **Á Giljanesi** (☎ 333465; e giljanes@post .olivant.fo; camping Dkr50, beds HI members/nonmembers Dkr100/120, singles/doubles Dkr300/400) lies about halfway between Sandavágur and Miðvágur. Meals can be ordered in advance. There are **supermarkets** in Sørvágur, Sandavágur and Miðvágur.

The airport bus runs to/from Tórshavn twice daily via the new undersea tunnel between Streymoy and Vágar; bus No 300 shuttles between the villages on Vágar. Helicopters fly to/from various destinations around the Faroes from the international airport.

Vágar is home to the Faroes' only airport, serviced by two airlines: **Atlantic Airways** (☎ 341010) and **Maersk** (☎ 340000). See under Air in the Getting Around section earlier in this chapter for more information.

MYKINES
pop 22
Most visitors agree that Mykines, the westernmost of the islands, is the jewel of the Faroes. Climb the 135 steps from the ferry landing to Mykines' single village, a magical place, with earthen streets and bright, turf-roofed houses.

Make a point of visiting **Lundaland** (land of puffins) on the islet of Mykineshólmur, which is connected to Mykines by a footbridge over a 35m gorge.

The **lighthouse** on the islet's westernmost cape has a magnificent location and it's surrounded by some of the world's most densely populated bird colonies. In three or four

FAROE ISLANDS

hours, you can hike to the highest peak on Mykines, **Knúkur** (560m).

For longer stays, there's a small guesthouse/snack bar, **Kristianshús** (☎/fax 310985; e mykines@post.olivant.fo; camping per person Dkr50, B&B per person Dkr195; open May-Aug), with tiny rooms and space for tents outside.

Access to Mykines is by a weather-dependent ferry service (Dkr60 one way, twice daily mid-May to August) from Sørvágur (Vágar), or by helicopter three days per week from the international airport on Vágar.

NÓLSOY
pop 264

Just east of Tórshavn, the island of Nólsoy is well worth a day visit. A cairned trail leads 7km from the village to the lighthouse at the southeastern cape.

The island boasts the Faroes' largest collection of stuffed birds and you are able to watch the extraordinary procedure in the workshop.

Ask the tourist office in Tórshavn for details regarding viewing and the location of the house where it takes place (it's at the northwestern end of Nólsoy village)

The fairly average **Kaffistovan Guesthouse** (☎ 327175, fax 327176; sleeping-bag accommodation Dkr100, singles/doubles Dkr200/350) is the only accommodation option; it also has a 'restaurant'.

From Tórshavn, the ferry sails two to five times daily (Dkr30).

SUÐUROY
pop 5064

Beautiful Suðuroy, the southernmost of the Faroes and relatively rarely visited by tourists, is marginally drier and warmer than the other islands.

Things to See & Do

The overgrown village of Tvøroyri is of little interest, but there's a good hike across the island to **Fámjin**, arguably the most charming village on Suðuroy. From Tvøroyri, at the head of Trongisvágsfjørður, climb the slope up the 330m pass Oyrnaskarð, then traverse the Dalsá valley. North of Tvøroyri, on the western coast near **Hvalba**, there are impressive cliffs, caves and a blowhole. The road south from Tvøroyri leads to the more rustic village **Vágur**, which also has an impressive western coast. Just south of Vágur, a tunnel (or the magnificent mountain road via the cliffs of **Beinisvørð**) will take you from Lopra to the charming village of **Sumba**, the southernmost place in the Faroes.

Places to Stay & Eat

In Øravík, **Hotel Øravík** (☎ 371302; e uni@ post.olivant.fo; camping per person Dkr50; dorm beds HI members/nonmembers Dkr100/ 120; singles Dkr350-550; doubles Dkr500-825; open year-round) is the best choice for accommodation on Suðuroy – only 2.5km south of the Drelnes ferry terminal. Meals can be ordered in the restaurant (breakfast/ lunch Dkr50/118, dinner mains Dkr140 to Dkr175).

Getting There & Away

Helicopters fly between Tórshavn and Froðba (2km east of Tvøroyri) twice weekly (Dkr215). Ferries sail between Tórshavn and Drelnes (Dkr70, 2¼ hours) at least twice daily, with a once weekly sailing via Vágur (Dkr70, 2½ hours).

Getting Around

From Tvøroyri, buses head south to Øravík (Dkr20), Vágur (Dkr30) and Sumba (Dkr30), and north to Hvalba (Dkr20); frequencies range from three to seven services daily.

Finland

For much of the 20th century, Finland was the least visible of the Scandinavian countries; Sweden had ABBA, Norway had all those lovely fjords, but Finland stirred few notions in the average traveller's mind.

With the rise of mobile communications and the Internet, though, Finland has hit the world stage; companies such as Nokia are exploring areas of communications that were once imagined only in science fiction. As the techno wave breaks into the 21st century, Finland appears set to play an important role in the way the future is mapped out. But what's in it for the traveller? In contrast to this hi-tech revolution, Finland is for the most part a land of quietness, where a ramshackle cottage by a lake and a properly stoked sauna is all that's required for happiness. Finland is a vast expanse of forests and lakes and more forests, punctuated by towns full of people genuinely surprised to find tourists visiting them. It's a country waiting to be 'discovered', which is an attraction in itself. Sophisticated Helsinki is deservedly becoming a popular travel destination (but is still far from being overrun with tourists), and the historic towns of Turku and Savonlinna have plenty to draw travellers. Then there's Lapland, with its Sami reindeer herders, Santa Claus connections, northern lights and sheer, unadulterated wilderness. If you visit Finland in summer, there's always a feeling that something big is happening. Festivals explode everywhere and you could easily plan your trip around them.

Finns and Finland have a reputation for being quiet and mysterious, but if you have the time to look under the surface, you'll find some of the warmest people you'll ever meet.

Facts about Finland

HISTORY

Human settlement in Finland dates back almost 10,000 years. Before arriving on the north of the Baltic coast, the Finns' ancestors appear to have dominated half of northern Russia. They established themselves in the forests, driving the nomadic Sami people to the north, where a small number still live in Lapland.

At a Glance

Capital	Helsinki
Population	5.2 million
Area	338,000 sq km
Official Language	Finnish, Swedish
GDP	€114 million
Time	GMT/UTC +0200
Country Phone Code	☎ 358

Highlights

- Enjoying Finland's wealth of summer festivals, from the jazz festival in Pori (p196) to the month-long opera festival in Savonlinna (p200)
- Picnicking, exploring the fortress ruins and watching the ferries roll in on Helsinki's Suomenlinna Island (p176)
- Exploring the historic port town of Turku, with its spectacular castle, folk museum and riverside bars (p182)
- Sweating it out in the world's largest smoke sauna in Kuopio (p203)
- Experiencing the endless midnight-sun days in Lapland and visiting Santa's post office at the Arctic Circle near Rovaniemi (p214)

By the end of the Viking era, Swedish traders had extended their interests to Ladoga and throughout the Baltic region. The growth of power at this time in Sweden and Russia

FINLAND

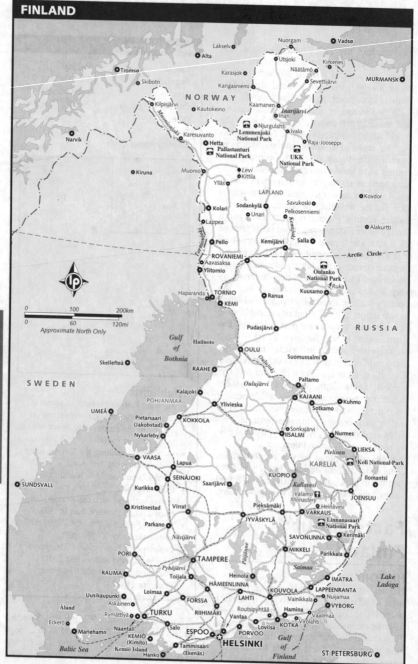

FINLAND

Finland

anticipated Finland's fate in the political sandwich between the two countries.

In 1155 the Swedes made Finland a province, and Swedish culture was swiftly imposed, beginning with the establishment of the first university in the capital Turku. But the heavy-handedness of Sweden's Protestant monarch, Gustav II Adolf, soon split the country along religious lines, and most Orthodox believers fled to Russia; famine then killed a third of the remaining Finnish population.

In 1809, after a bloody war, Sweden ceded Finland to Russia under Tsar Alexander. As a result, Finland gained greater autonomy as a Grand Duchy, keeping its Swedish laws, Lutheran Church and Finnish senate. The capital moved to Helsinki in 1812. Nationalism surged, which suited the tsars until the 1880s, when there was a firm policy to dismantle the Finnish state and incorporate it into Russia.

The Communist revolution of October 1917 brought the downfall of the Russian tsar and enabled the Finnish senate to declare independence on 6 December 1917.

Divisions between socialists and conservatives in the new government led to a bloody civil war in which 30,000 Finns died. The conservatives, led by CGE Mannerheim, were victorious, and were gradually replaced by moderate social democrats.

During the Depression of the 1930s Finland gained fame internationally as a brave new nation, as the only country to pay its debts to the USA and as a sporting nation (long-distance runner Paavo Nurmi won seven gold medals in three Olympics).

Anticommunist violence broke out during the 1930s and relations with the Soviet Union remained uneasy. Finland sought neutrality, but Soviet deals with Nazi Germany and supposed security concerns led to demands for Finland's eastern Lakeland. In November 1939 the Winter War between the two countries began. It was a harsh winter, with temperatures falling to -40°C; soldiers from both sides died in their thousands. After 100 days, the massively outnumbered Finns were defeated, and Finland was forced to cede part of eastern Lakeland (Karelia). When no Western allies would help it against the Soviet threat, Finland accepted assistance from Germany, and in return allowed the transit of German troops across Finnish soil. With aid from Germany, Finland resumed hostilities with the Soviets in 1941 and won back large swathes of Karelia in

what became known as the Continuation War. This, the last of more than 40 wars with Russia, cost Finland almost 100,000 lives.

By September 1944, growing Soviet strength forced another armistice, under the terms of which Finns turned and fought German forces entrenched in Lapland.

Under President Paasikivi, Finland took a new line in its Soviet relations and signed a new treaty. It recognised Soviet security concerns and agreed to Soviet aid in defending the frontier. This developed further during the 25 years of Urho Kekkonen's presidency, and Finland crafted an independent stance in East-West relations during the Cold War.

With this new security came the opportunity for Finland to develop its economy and welfare system, and its Scandinavian links through the Nordic Council. The various Helsinki conferences and accords were significant in the gradual end to the Cold War and the dismantling of the Soviet Union. Finland solved its worst postwar recession despite an endless number of bankruptcies and economic reforms, and by the end of the 20th century had gone from strength to strength economically.

Finland joined the EU in 1995, giving this oft-forgotten country new opportunities.

GEOGRAPHY

Finland is Europe's seventh-biggest country, with one-third beyond the Arctic Circle. Helsinki is the second most northerly European capital, and the world's fourth coldest. Glacial lakes are the country's dominant feature; altogether, there are 187,888 lakes in Finland (with 98,050 islands) fed by a network of rivers and 5100 rapids. Compared to Sweden and Norway, Finland is a flat country with a scattering of fells (forested hills) in the northern Lakeland and Lapland area, some of which are cleared and used for downhill skiing. The highest peak is Halti Fell (1328m) near Kilpisjärvi.

CLIMATE

The four seasons differ enormously in Finland, ranging from continuing darkness in the Arctic winter to a two-month 'day' in northern Lapland's summer. In most parts of the country snow first falls in October and vanishes by the end of March, but in Lapland it lingers from September to late May. Temperatures can be surprisingly warm in summer (June to August), especially in the south of the country.

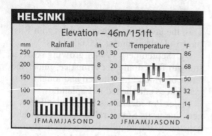

However, you should pack some warm clothes at any time of year. Temperatures can drop unexpectedly at any time of year, especially in Lapland, but even on the southern coast.

FLORA & FAUNA

Forests cover two-thirds of Finland; the main types of forest are pine, spruce and birch. Much of this forest is managed and timber harvesting is an important industry.

Elk, brown bears and wolves are native to Finland's forests, although sightings are rare. In Lapland, the Sami keep commercial herds of some 230,000 reindeer. Hundreds of species of migratory birds arrive in the Arctic each spring, making Finland a bird-watcher's paradise.

National Parks

Finland boasts over 120,000 sq km of publicly owned lands and waters in 32 national parks, some of the last great wilderness areas in Europe. The best for hiking include Oulanka National Park in southeast Lapland, Urho Kekkonen National Park in Lapland's Saariselkä Wilderness, Linnansaari National Park in eastern Finland and Lemmenjoki National Park in Lapland. For more information, contact **Metsähallitus** (☎ 09-270 5221; Ⓦ www.metsa.fi) in Helsinki.

GOVERNMENT & POLITICS

Finland is a presidential republic, and a prime minister is elected every four years by the 200-member parliament; the prime minister until 2003 is Paavo Lipponen.

Members of parliament are elected from 14 national districts. There are 12 *lääni* (provincial administrations) and 450 *kunta* (municipalities).

The president, chosen by the people, has a six-year term and, in council with the prime minister and cabinet, forms the executive government. Tarja Halonen was elected in 2000 and is Finland's first woman president.

Åland has a small local parliament and a high degree of autonomy. It also sends one member of parliament to Helsinki.

ECONOMY

Government spending constitutes a majority of GDP, although most businesses are privately owned. Finland borrows heavily in order to finance an excellent welfare system; as a result, tax rates in Finland are high. The unemployment rate in 2002 was 7.8%.

Industry only developed fully after WWII, but has delivered strong annual growth of around 4% to 5% ever since – with the exception of a major recession that lasted from 1991 to 1995. The metals and technology sectors dominate foreign exchange earnings, with the best known examples being cruise ships and telecommunications (Nokia is possibly what many know best about Finland).

POPULATION & PEOPLE

Finland has a population of 5.2 million, more than half of whom live in the south. Finland is one of Europe's most sparsely populated countries, with 17 people per square kilometre. There are around 300,000 Swedish-speaking Finns in the west, as well as in fishing communities along the coast and on the Åland islands; and a smaller number of Roma (Gypsies) in the south.

The Sami population of 6500 in the deep north consists of three distinct groups, each speaking its own dialect. The Scandinavian Sami region has its own flag, and many Samis look across the border at the more developed Sami community in Norway for a deeper cultural identity.

Samis (Lapps) have traditionally been nomads, herding their reindeer in the large area of Lapland which spans the region from the Kola peninsula in Russia to the southern Norwegian mountains. Their traditional dwelling, the *kota*, resembles the tepee or wigwam of native North Americans, and is easily set up as a temporary shelter. Old traditions are vanishing, though: most Samis now live in permanent villages and use motor vehicles, snowmobiles and mobile phones while still herding their reindeer.

Samis inhabited all of Finland 6000 years ago but have been pushed farther north ever since. They were forcibly converted to (Protestant) Christianity in the 17th century, and their religious traditions were made illegal.

There are three Sami (Lapp) languages used in Finland today, the most common being Fell Sami. Inari Sami and Skolt Sami are spoken by only a few hundred people. Sami is taught in local schools, and legislation grants Samis the right of Sami usage in offices in northern Lapland.

ARTS

Tove Jansson, who died in 2001, is internationally famous for her Moominland children's stories; another high-profile Finn is the late architect Alvar Aalto, whose design work features in public buildings and furniture.

Jean Sibelius, one of the most famous late-Romantics, was a Finn at the forefront of the nationalist movement. His stirring tone-poem *Finlandia* has been raised to the status of a national hymn. Sibelius and the nationalistic painter Akseli Gallen-Kallela fell under the spell of 'Karelianism', a movement stemming from the folk songs collected in the 1830s by Elias Lönnrot to form the national epic the *Kalevala*. Perhaps the greatest Finnish writer, Aleksis Kivi was not regarded as a romantic during his lifetime. Quite the contrary; his so-called crudities met with fierce opposition. But it did not take long before he gained the immense popularity which he has retained to this day.

The Finnish film industry is small, but some of the greatest achievements are in documentary work. The best-known Finnish film maker is probably Aki Kaurismäki, director of the 1989 *Leningrad Cowboys Go America* (many say his film *Ariel* is a better work).

SOCIETY & CONDUCT

A capacity for silence and reflection are the traits that best sum up the Finnish character (however, get a Finn near a stack of duty-free liquor and see if this remains the case). The image of a log cabin with a sauna by a lake tells much about Finnish culture: independence, endurance (*sisu* or 'guts') and a love of open space and nature.

The stark simplicity of modern Finnish design also speaks volumes about the Finnish psyche, but perhaps the great Finnish distance runners sum up the society best by their very resilience.

The Finns are a naturally reserved people, and at first meeting can be very polite and more formal than you may be used to. The seemingly icy front that many present never lasts, though, and almost every visitor to Finland leaves with a story of unusual and unexpected kindness from a Finn.

RELIGION

Eighty-six per cent of Finns are Evangelical Lutherans, 1.1% Orthodox and the remainder unaffiliated. Minority denominations, including Roman Catholic, make up only a few per cent.

LANGUAGE

Finnish is a Uralic language spoken by just six million people, all but a few of whom live in Scandinavia and Russian Karelia. The most widely spoken of the Finno-Ugric family is Hungarian, but its similarities with Finnish are few.

Finnish is not a Scandinavian language, nor is it related to Indo-European languages. However, many words have been borrowed from Baltic, Slavic and Germanic languages, and many words derive from English. In Finnish Finland is known as Suomi, and the language as Suomi.

Staff at hotels, hostels and tourist offices generally speak fluent English, however, bus drivers and restaurant and shop staff outside the cities may not – but they'll always fetch a colleague or bystander who does. You can certainly get by with English in Finland, but don't assume everyone speaks it.

Swedish is spoken on Åland, as well as on the west ('Swedish') coast and around Helsinki and Turku, and all Finns learn Swedish at school.

See Language at the back of the book for a guide to pronunciation, and useful words and phrases.

Facts for the Visitor

SUGGESTED ITINERARIES

Depending on the length of your stay you might like to see and do the following things:

Two days

On your first day in Helsinki visit Kiasma or Mannerheim Museum, then stroll over to Pohjoisesplanadi for lunch. Afterwards, wander down to the market square, visit the impressive Senaatintori, have a drink at the famous Kapelli beer terrace, then join the locals for a night of bar-hopping. The next day either hop on a ferry to Suomenlinna or visit Porvoo.

One week

After a day or two in Helsinki (with a possible day trip to Tallin), either explore the eastern cities of Savonlinna, Lappeenranta and Kuopio, or take an overnight train to Lapland (Rovaniemi) or to Oulu for a couple of days. The Helsinki–Savonlinna–Kuopio–Rovaniemi–Helsinki route is a good option.

Two weeks

Spend a few days in Helsinki, then visit Turku and Tampere, then on to Savonlinna and the beautiful eastern Lakeland. After this go up to Rovaniemi in Lapland, and perhaps as far as Inari. You could also incorporate a summer festival, a trip into North Karelia (Ilomantsi or Lake Pielinen) or a quick visit to Åland.

One month

You can cover practically all major regions, and include a bicycle tour in Åland, or a trek in Lapland or Karelia

PLANNING
When to Go

May to September are the best months to visit Finland. The tourist season in southern and central Finland is in full swing from early June to the end of August, when all attractions, hostels and camping grounds are open and festivals abound. During the rest of the year, tourist infrastructure hibernates.

Lapland's tourist season is different from the rest of the country; the mosquitoes are annoying in July but September is delightful with its *ruska* (autumn) colours. October and February/March are good times to visit Lapland to view the aurora borealis (northern lights) and enjoy winter activities. The Christmas holiday period is also delightful.

Maps

Tourist offices give out perfectly good city and regional maps. Trekking, canoeing and road maps are available from **Karttakeskus** (☎ *0204-45 5911; Unioninkatu 32, 00100 Helsinki*).

What to Bring

Bring what you can from home to avoid the relatively high prices of Finnish shops. Even in summer you should have warm clothes and a waterproof and windproof jacket. An inner sheet and pillowcase are essential if you're staying in hostels (to save on hire costs). If you're travelling on a tight budget in summer, take camping gear and make use of Finland's relatively well-equipped, inexpensive campsites.

TOURIST OFFICES

Every Finnish town has a tourist office with piles of English-language brochures, free maps and helpful staff (in summer they're often staffed by students studying tourism). The **Finnish Tourist Board** (☎ *09-4176 9300;* ⓦ *www.mek.fi; Eteläesplanadi 4, Helsinki)* also has a mailing address, PO Box 249, 00131 Helsinki.

Tourist Offices Abroad

These offices can assist you with tourist promotional material and inquiries but are generally not offices where you can walk in for information. A better source is the **Finnish Tourist Board** (ⓦ *www.mek.fi).*

Denmark (☎ 3313 1362, ⓔ findland.dk@mek.fi)
Finlands Turistbureau, Nyhavn 43A, 1051
Copenhagen K
Estonia (☎ 06-997 010, ⓔ mek.tal@mek.fi)
Soome Turismiar-endamise, Uus 32, 10111
Tallinn
Norway (☎ 2316 2430, ⓔ finland.no@mek.fi)
Finlands Turistkontor, Lille Grensen 7, 0159
Oslo 1
Sweden (☎ 08-587 69121, ⓔ finland.se@mek.fi)
Finska Turistbyrån Snickarbacken 2, 111 39
Stockholm
UK (☎ 7365 2512, ⓔ finlandinfo.lon@mek.fi)
Finnish Tourist Board, PO Box 33213, London
W68JX
USA (☎ 212-885 9700) Finnish Tourist Board,
655 Third Ave, New York, NY 10017

VISAS & DOCUMENTS

A valid passport is required to enter Finland. Citizens of EU countries (except Greece), Norway and Iceland can, however, come and go with only an identity card. Most Western nationals don't need a tourist visa for stays under three months; South Africans require a Schengen visa. The **Directorate of Immigration** (☎ *09-476 5500;* ⓔ *ulkomaalaisvirasto@uvi .fi; Panimokatu 2A, 00580 Helsinki)* handles visas and work permits.

EMBASSIES
Finnish Embassies

Finland maintains embassies in the following countries:

Australia (☎ 02-6273 3800, ⓔ sanoman.can@
formin.fi) 10 Darwin Ave, Yarralumla, ACT
2600
Canada (☎ 613-236 2389, ⓔ sanoman.ott@
formin.fi) 55 Metcalfe St, Suite 850, Ottawa
K1P 6L5

Denmark (☎ 3313 4214, e sanomat.kob@
  formin.fi) Sankt Annae Plads 24, 1250
  Copenhagen K
Estonia (☎ 610 3200, e sanomat.tal@formin.fi)
  Kohtu 4, EE-0100 Tallinn
France (☎ 01-44 18 19 20, e sanomat.par@
  formin.fi) 1 Place de Finlande, 57007 Paris
Germany (☎ 030-505030, e sanomat.ber@
  formin.fi) Rauchstrasse 1, 10787 Berlin
Ireland (☎ 01-478 1344, e sanomat.dub@
  formin.fi) Russell House, Stokes Pl, St
  Stephen's Green, Dublin 2
Latvia (☎ 371-707 8300, e sanomat.rii@
  formin.fi) Kalpaka bulvāris 1, LV-1605 Rīga
Netherlands (☎ 070-346 9754, e sanomat
  .haa@formin.fi) Groot Hertoginnelaan 16,
  251r EG Den Haag
New Zealand Honorary Consulate General
  (☎ 499 4599) 44–52 the Terrace, Wellington.
  Or contact the Australian embassy.
Norway (☎ 2212 4900, e sanomat.osl@
  formin.fi) Thomas Heftyes gate 1, 0244 Oslo
Russia (☎ 095-787 4174, e sanomat.mos@
  formin.fi) Kropotkinskij Pereulok 15/17,
  119034 Moskva G-34
Sweden (☎ 08-676 6700, e info@finland.se)
  Gärdesgatan 11, 11527 Stockholm
UK (☎ 020-7838 6200, e sanomat.lon@formin
  .fi) 38 Chesham Place, London SW1X 8HW
USA (☎ 202-298 5800, e sanomat.was@
  formin.fi) 3301 Massachusetts Ave NW,
  Washington DC 20008

Embassies in Finland
The following embassies are in Helsinki:

Australia (consulate: ☎ 447233) Museokatu
  25B, Vantaa; nearest embassy is in Stockholm
Canada (☎ 171 141) Pohjoisesplanadi 25B
Denmark ☎ 684 1050) Keskuskatu 1A
Estonia (☎ 622 0288) Itäinen Puistotie 10
France (☎ 618 780) Itäinen Puistotie 13
Germany (☎ 458 580) Krogiuksentie 4
Ireland (☎ 646 006) Erottajankatu 7
Latvia (☎ 4764 7244) Armfeltintie 10
Lithuania (☎ 608 210) Rauhankatu 13A
Netherlands (☎ 228 920) Eteläsplanadi 24A
New Zealand Contact the Australian consulate
Norway (☎ 686 0180) Rehbinderintie 17
Russia (☎ 661 876) Tehtaankatu 1B
Sweden (☎ 687 7660) Pohjoisesplanadi 7B
UK (☎ 2286 5100) Itäinen Puistotie 17
USA (☎ 171 931) Itäinen Puistotie 14A

CUSTOMS
Travellers should encounter few problems
with Finnish customs. Those from outside the
EU can bring currency and gifts up to the
value of €200 into Finland without declaration, as well as 15L beer, 2L wine and 1L
spirits.

MONEY
Currency
The Finnish markka was officially replaced
by the euro in 2001. Euro notes come in five,
10, 20, 100 and 500 denominations and coins
in five, 10, 20, 50 cents and €1 and €2.

Swedish krona (including coins) are accepted on Åland and in western Lapland, and
Norwegian krona can be used in areas near
the Norwegian border in northern Lapland.

Exchange Rates
At the time of printing the following exchange rates prevailed:

country	unit		euro
Australia	A$1	=	€0.55
Canada	C$1	=	€0.64
Denmark	Dkr1	=	€0.64
Iceland	Ikr10	=	€0.11
Japan	¥100	=	€0.86
New Zealand	NZ$1	=	€0.47
Norway	Nkr1	=	€0.13
Sweden	Skr1	=	€0.10
UK	UK£1	=	€1.57
USA	US$1	=	€1

Exchanging Money
Finland has three national banks (Osuus-
pankki, Nordea and Sampo) with similar
rates and charges. In cities, independent ex-
changers such as Forex are a better alternative for exchanging cash and travellers
cheques; they charge a flat €2 per cheque.
Finnish ATMs ('Otto') are linked to the international networks Cirrus, EC, Eurocard,
Visa, MasterCard and Plus. Credit cards are
widely accepted and Finns are dedicated
users of the plastic – purchasing a beer in a
bar with a credit card is not unusual and it's
commonplace to pay for accommodation and
restaurant meals in this way. Banks open 9am
to 4.15pm weekdays.

There is no American Express office that
changes travellers cheques in Finland, but
Thomas Cook is represented (through Trav-
elex) in Helsinki and Turku.

Costs
For the traveller, overall costs are lower than
they have been for decades and five-star comforts are almost cheap compared to Sweden
and Norway. Finland is still expensive but it's
comparable to much of Western Europe. Your

costs will depend on how you travel, and where; if you stick to the big cities like Helsinki and Tampere, costs will be higher than in smaller towns. If you camp or stay in hostels, prepare your own meals and don't move around too much, it's possible to get by on €25 a day. This wouldn't allow room for nightlife or tours. If you stay in guesthouses (or private rooms in hostels) and eat at inexpensive restaurants, expect to pay about €60 a day if travelling alone or €50 each with a partner.

To this you need to factor in museum admission fees, entertainment, transportation and incidentals. Trains are cheaper than buses, unlike in Sweden. Petrol is expensive, but there are no extra charges (such as road tolls or ferry charges) for car travel. A single night on the town can wreck your budget, thanks to the huge 'sin tax' on alcohol, but buying alcohol from supermarkets or Alko stores is reasonable.

Students with valid ID and seniors receive substantial discounts on museum admission prices quoted in this chapter, as well as on transport (including ferries) – if you fit the bill, always ask.

Tipping & Bargaining
Tipping is not necessary and Finns generally don't do it; however, in cities such as Helsinki the hospitality industry expects it so it's polite to tip for good service at a restaurant. Bargaining is not common, except at flea markets.

Taxes & Refunds
The value-added tax (VAT) of 22% can be deducted if you post goods from the point of sale. Alternatively, at stores showing the 'Tax Free for Tourists' sign, non-EU citizens can get a 12% to 16% refund on items priced over €45. Present the tax-refund 'cheque' to the refund window at your departure point from the EU.

POST & COMMUNICATIONS
Post
Posti (post offices) are generally open 9am to 5pm Monday to Friday, but stamps can be bought at bus or train stations and R-kiosks (newsagents). Postcards and letters weighing up to 20g cost €0.60 to anywhere in the world (including within Finland) by *lento-posti* (airmail). International parcel post is expensive in Finland (almost twice the price of sending from Sweden). Poste restante is at the main post offices in cities.

Telephone
Some public phones accept coins, but most accept only plastic Telecards. In a few cities such as Turku there are public telephones that accept only a local telephone card which is completely useless elsewhere.

With the proliferation of mobile phones in Finland, public phones don't get much of a work-out.

International calls are expensive but are much cheaper if you buy one of the prepaid calling cards from any R-kiosk. The cheapest are those placed between 10pm and 8am on weekdays and all day Saturday and Sunday. A three-minute call to the USA during peak time will cost about €4. For national directory assistance dial ☎ 020 202; for international help, ☎ 020 208.

Finland has 13 area codes, each starting with a zero. Include the zero when dialling within Finland, but omit it if you are calling from abroad. The country code for calling Finland from abroad is ☎ 358. To make an international call from Finland, first dial an international prefix (☎ 00, 990, 994 or 999) and then the country code for the country you're calling.

Mobile Phones Finland has one of the world's highest rates of mobile-phone usage, which is hardly surprising since Nokia is Finnish. Don't be surprised to see more Finns, of all ages, playing with their phones here than anywhere else.

So advanced is their technology that Finns can even send a text message from their phone to many vending machines, which will then deliver, say, a soft drink and the charge will be on their next phone bill.

Getting hooked up to the mobile-phone network is easy with the prepaid system using either Sonera or Telia (the two companies merged in 2002).

You can bring your own phone and simply buy a starter kit from a phone shop or any R-kiosk. It costs €50 which includes €40 worth of call time and a SIM card, then you can buy recharge cards from the same outlets.

The main company offering connection to the GSM network in Finland is Radiolinja, but unless you're planning on staying long-term, it's cheaper and easier to use the prepaid system.

For more information see the Telephone section in the Facts for the Visitor chapter.

Fax
Faxes can be sent from public telephone offices (usually adjacent to the post office in big cities). Hotels and some hostels will receive faxes free and send them for a fee.

Email & Internet Access
All public libraries offer free Internet access, though in many cases you need to book hours or even days in advance. An increasing number of businesses and tourist offices have at least one terminal that you can use free for 15 minutes. Because of this free access, Internet cafés are not as common in Finland as elsewhere.

DIGITAL RESOURCES
Finland probably has more websites per capita than any other country – all tourist offices have a site, and so, it seems, does every other person, place and institution in the country. A few good websites are those of the **Finnish Tourist Board** (MEK; W www.mek.fi), the **Finnish Youth Hostel Association** (SRM; W www.srmnet.org), the **Forest & Park Service** (Metsähallitus; W www.metsa.fi) and the **Helsinki city tourist office** (W www.hel.fi). Most Finnish sites offer an English-language version.

BOOKS
Lonely Planet's *Finland* is the most comprehensive guidebook available.

Guides to the architecture of Helsinki are available in that city's bookstores.

For a readable history, check out the paperback *A Short History of Finland* by Fred Singleton. *The Kalevala – Poems of the Kaleva District*, compiled by Elias Lönnrot, is the national folk epic and provides an insight into the country and its people.

Some great Finnish authors, including Mika Waltari and Väinö Linna, have been translated by American as well as Finnish publishers. Edited by Herbert Lomas, *Contemporary Finnish Poetry* highlights the best poets, and *A Way to Measure Time* (from the Finnish Literature Society) contains contemporary Finnish literature from over 50 authors.

NEWSPAPERS & MAGAZINES
There is no local daily English-language newspaper, but the *International Herald Tribune*, several British newspapers and various English-language magazines are available at train stations and R-kiosks in larger towns (don't be surprised to pay up to €5 for an international newspaper

The weekly *Keltainen pörssi* and *Palsta* are the best sources of ads for used cars and bicycles.

RADIO & TV
A summary of world news is broadcast in English at 10.55pm on the national radio stations YLE 3 and YLE 4. Capital FM (FM 103.7Mhz), in Helsinki, broadcasts English-language programmes such as BBC World News, Voice of America as well as Radio Australia.

The two national TV networks broadcast British and US programmes in English with Finnish and Swedish subtitles.

PHOTOGRAPHY & VIDEO
Print and slide film as well as video tapes are readily available in Finnish cities, and film processing is quick and of high quality. A standard roll of 36 prints costs €6 and a 36-exposure slide film costs €9.

TIME
Finland is two hours ahead of GMT/UTC and daylight-saving time applies from early April to late October, when clocks go forward one hour. When it's noon in Finland it's 10am in London, 5am in New York, 2am in San Francisco, 5am in Toronto, 7pm in Sydney, 10pm in Auckland, 11am in Stockholm, Copenhagen and Oslo and 1pm in Moscow and St Petersburg.

LAUNDRY
Laundrettes are listed in the telephone book as *pesuloita* but are thin on the ground. The traveller's best options are hostels and camping grounds with washing machines (€2), but some hotels will arrange for your laundry to be done (allow 24 hours) for around €5 to €8.

TOILETS
The world's most expensive pee is to be had in Finnish bus stations – over one US dollar! Other public toilets also charge. However, by law all restaurants and cafés must have a wheelchair-accessible public toilet. Libraries, department stores and hotels also have free toilets.

HEALTH

Visitors whose home countries have reciprocal medical-care agreements with Finland are charged the same as Finns: €8 to visit a doctor, €21 per day for hospitalisation. Those from other countries are charged the full cost of treatment. *Apteekki* (pharmacies) are plentiful and provide medicine and advice.

For more health information see the Regional Facts for the Visitor chapter earlier in this book.

WOMEN TRAVELLERS

The only annoyance you're likely to find is harassment by drunken men. Ignore them, and avoid neighbourhood pubs in the evening. **Unioni Naisasialiitto Suomessa** *(Union for Women's Affairs;* ☎ *643 158; Bulevardi 11A, Helsinki)* is the national feminist organisation.

GAY & LESBIAN TRAVELLERS

Though you won't find the equivalent of Copenhagen's or Stockholm's active gay community in Finland, it is as tolerant as the other Nordic countries and there's a growing scene in Helsinki. Current information is available from the Finnish organisation for gay and lesbian equality, **Seksuaalinen tasavertaisus** *(SETA;* ☎ *681 2580;* Ⓦ *www.seta.fi; Hietalahdenkatu 2B 16, Helsinki).*

DISABLED TRAVELLERS

By law, most public and private institutions must provide ramps, lifts and special toilets for disabled people, making Finland one of the easiest countries to negotiate. Some national parks offer accessible trails.

TRAVEL WITH CHILDREN

Families with children will love Finland; most hostels have family rooms, the supermarkets stock everything your children need and many trains and ferries have special play areas. Plus there are some fantastic theme parks for kids, such as Moomin World in Naantali, Wasalandia in Vaasa and Särkänniemi in Tampere.

DANGERS & ANNOYANCES

Violence mostly occurs in association with drunk males, but even in this regard Finland is remarkably safe compared with many countries. Foreign males of dark complexion run the highest risk of being harassed on the street, though reports of race-related violence are becoming less common. In Helsinki, it's best to avoid the main train station late at night.

Weather extremes in Lapland can be an unexpected danger at any time of the year. Exposure kills lone trekkers almost every winter, and cold rain can be a problem in summer. Also, if hiking in the wilderness there's the remote possibility of encountering wild animals. Wolves are out there but are not common, and bears generally avoid people, though if they feel threatened females with cubs may attack. A bigger problem in summer are insects such as mosquitoes, which grow as big as your hand and swarm relentlessly.

LEGAL MATTERS

Traffic laws are strict, as are drug laws. However, police usually treat bona fide tourists politely in less serious situations. Fines (such as traffic fines) are calculated according to your income and assets. You *must* obtain a permit if you plan to fish in Finland.

BUSINESS HOURS

Shops are generally open 9am to 5pm weekdays, and to 1pm on Saturday. Banks are open 9.15am until 4.15pm weekdays. Many supermarkets and Helsinki department stores stay open until 9pm or 10pm on weeknights and open all day on Saturday and Sunday. Town markets begin about 7am on weekdays and Saturday and continue until about 2pm. Public holidays are taken seriously in Finland – absolutely everything shuts at 6pm on holiday evenings and reopens the morning after the holiday ends.

PUBLIC HOLIDAYS & SPECIAL EVENTS

Finland grinds to a halt twice a year – around Christmas (sometimes including the New Year) and during the Midsummer weekend. Plan ahead and avoid travelling during those times. The public holidays are:

Emergency

In Finland, dial ☎ 112 for an ambulance; ☎ 10023 in case of emergency or in need of medical advice. Car accidents should be promptly reported to the Motor Insurers' Bureau (☎ 09-680 401; Bulevardi 28, 00120 Helsinki).

New Year's Day 1 January
Epiphany 6 January (usually)
Good Friday to Easter Monday March/April
May Day Eve & May Day (Vappu) 30 April &
  1 May
Ascension Day 40 days after Easter
Whit Sunday Late May or early June
**Juhannus (Midsummer's Eve & Midsummer's
  Day)** Third weekend in June
All Saints Day 1 November
Independence Day 6 December
Christmas Eve 24 December
Christmas Day 25 December
Boxing Day 26 December

Just about every town and city in Finland puts on a barrage of festivals between mid-June and mid-August. The foremost events are the **Opera Festival** in Savonlinna and the **Jazz Festival** in Pori, but there's also **Provinssrock** at Seinäjoki, a festival of international rock music held in mid-June, and the **Folk Festival** at Kaustinen, which is held over a week in mid-July and attracts thousands of people to see Finnish and international folk concerts and dance performances. Midsummer is a big deal in any part of Finland, though for most Finns it's a family time when they disappear to their summer cottages. The Lapp town of Sodankylä holds the annual Midnight Sun International Film Festival. A few smaller communities arrange some of the weirdest events imaginable (the Wife Carrying World Championships in Sonkajärvi and the Air Guitar World Championships in Oulu, for instance). Pick up the *Finland Festivals* booklet in any tourist office or contact or check out ⓦ www.festivals.fi.

Anyone who has been in Finland on *vappu* (May Day) will know it's a big day for Finns, and that more alcohol is consumed in the 48 hours surrounding 1 May than over a similar period at any other time of year.

ACTIVITIES
Swimming & Sauna
What would Finland be without the physically and mentally cleansing sauna? The traditional sauna is a wooden room with benches and a properly stoked wooden stove, although most Finnish saunas now have modern electrical heating. Temperatures from 80°C to 100°C are proper, and bathing is done in the nude.

A cold swim afterwards completes the refreshment (fanatics roll in snow or jump in icy lakes during winter). Most hotels – and many hostels and camping grounds – have men's and women's saunas that are free with a night's stay or may be used for a small fee, even by nonguests.

*Uimahalli (*indoor swimming centres) can be found in most towns and they usually have spa and sauna facilities in addition to a pool. *Kylpylä (*spa hotels) are another option for getting hot and wet and some have spectacular facilities as well as massage and hydrotherapy. Nonguests can use them for a fee (usually around €8).

Hiking
Hiking or trekking (often called fell walking in Finland) is best from June to September, although in July mosquitoes and other biting insects can be a big problem in Lapland. In summer, given the continuous daylight in northern Finland, you can comfortably walk all night if you feel like it! Wilderness huts line the northern trails (they are free and must be shared). According to the law, a principle of common access to nature applies, so you are generally allowed to hike in any forested or wilderness area, and camp for a night anywhere outside any inhabited, privately owned areas. See the National Parks section for some good trekking areas.

Canoeing & Rafting
Canoes and kayaks can be hired in most towns near a lake, often from camping grounds – prices start at around €10 a day. Transport to the start/finishing points of popular river trips can usually be arranged at an extra cost.

Good places for organised white-water rafting include the area around Kuhmo, the Kitkajoki river north of Kuusamo, the rapids of the Tornionjoki and Munionjoki rivers on the Finland-Sweden border, and the Ruunaa Recreation in North Karelia.

Fishing
To fish you need a one-week (€5) or one-year (€15) fishing licence (except if you are under 18 years of age), available at banks, post offices and the **Forest and Park Service information office** (ⓦ *www.metsa.fi; Etelä-esplanadi 20, Helsinki*). Fishing in Northern Lapland requires a separate regional licence. In winter, ice-fishing is popular. Most fishing spots are owned privately or by the local or national authorities, so as well as a licence you also need a local permit for the day or

week (available from municipal or forestry authorities or from whoever owns the waters – ask at the tourist offices). Check local rules before you cast out.

Skiing

Nordic skiing is popular and there are cross-country trails of varying difficulty (some lit). Downhill skiers head for the northern resorts such as Ylläs or Levi in north-west Lapland, Ruka in Kuusamo or Koli in North Karelia. Expect to pay €20 to €26 a day for lift passes and €20 to hire a complete cross-country or downhill kit (skis or snowboard, boots and poles). The season runs from October to April and, although daylight is limited before Christmas, you can ski in nocturnal twilight in Lapland from late October.

Finnish winter resorts offer a range of activities including dog sledding, snowmobile safaris, reindeer sleigh tours and ice-fishing, but these are all expensive pastimes.

WORK

There's very little permanent work open to foreigners due to high local unemployment, but students can apply for limited summer employment. Au pair arrangements are allowed for up to 18 months, busking is a possible money-earner, and many foreigners find bar work, particularly in Irish pubs in cities such as Helsinki, Tampere and Turku.

A work permit is required of all non-EU foreigners, and employment must be secured before applying for the permit.

ACCOMMODATION

Camping is the cheapest way to travel around Finland, but it's far from convenient in cities such as Helsinki, Tampere and Turku. Camping grounds are most often located next to lakes, in forests or on the coast. Most are closed in winter and popular spots are crowded during July. As well as tent sites (from €8 to €15), there are cabins ranging from basic two-bed huts (from €30) to self-contained cottages with private sauna.

The **Finnish Youth Hostel Association** (SRM; ☎ 09-64 0377; e info@srm.inet.fi; Yrjönkatu 38B, 00100 Helsinki) operates 133 hostels, with about half open all year. They're a little disappointing compared with hostels elsewhere in Scandinavia. Summer hostels are invariably student accommodation, which means the facilities are good (many of the rooms are apartment-style with private kitchen and bathroom). Most offer singles and doubles as well as dormitory accommodation. Hostel prices quoted in this chapter are those given to holders of a valid HI card; nonmembers should add €2.50.

The invaluable free publication *Camping & Hostels*, published by the **Finnish Tourist Board** (W www.mek.fi), gives a full listing of hostels and camping grounds.

In contrast to much of the rest of the world, hotels in Finland offer lower rates on weekends (usually Friday and Saturday nights) and in summer. Finnish hotels offer few surprises – they're invariably spotlessly clean, efficiently run and always have a sauna. Common chain hotels include Sokos, Scandic and Cumulus.

If you're staying in hotels, Finncheques are vouchers that give discounted accommodation in 140 designated hotels; €34 per person in a double room. They're valid from May to September and can be purchased at participating hotels and travel agencies. However, if you're travelling during July and August, when hotels offer discounted rates anyway, you may find Finncheques unnecessary and perhaps even overpriced!

Holiday cottages can be booked through the regional tourist offices. They vary from very basic lakeside cottages with few facilities to luxurious houses. Rental starts at about €200 per week for four people. For listings on the mainland and booking information, contact **Lomarengas** (☎ 09-3516 1321; e sales@lomarengas.fi; Malminkaari 23, 00700 Helsinki).

FOOD

Typically Finnish food is similar to what you get elsewhere in Scandinavia – lots of fish such as Baltic herring, salmon (the salmon soup is delicious) and whitefish – along with heavy food such as potatoes, dark rye bread and the like. Reindeer is commonly served in Finnish and Lappish restaurants, but it's not cheap.

Restaurant meals are generally expensive, particularly dinner. Fortunately, most restaurants offer special lunch menus for around €7, and these include salad, bread, milk, coffee and dessert, plus big helpings of hearty fare – sausage and potatoes or fish and potatoes are common.

Most hotels include a breathtaking breakfast buffet with the price of your room, something to consider when factoring in daily costs – a mammoth, healthy, all-you-can-eat breakfast can cut down food costs for the rest of the day.

Most towns have a *kauppahalli* (covered market) where you can get sandwiches and snacks cheaply.

The *grilli* is the venue for a takeaway meal of hamburgers or hot dogs for less than €3. Turkish kebab joints offer good value, and inexpensive pizzerias are everywhere. The Finns are very attached to chain restaurants (familiarity is important here!). Hesburger is the local equivalent of McDonald's, Golden Rax Pizza is a low quality but cheap all-you-can-eat place, and chains such as Rosso and Amarillo can be found in most towns.

DRINKS
Strong beers, wines and spirits are sold by the state network, beautifully named Alko (much more appealing than Sweden's Systembolaget!). There are stores in every town and they're generally open from 10am to 6pm Monday to Thursday, till 8pm on Friday and until 2pm Saturday. Drinks containing more than 20% alcohol are not sold to those aged under 20; for beer and wine purchases the age limit is 18. Beer and cider with less than 4.7% alcohol content are readily available in supermarkets and surprisingly cheap at around €7 for a six-pack. Even imported wine is reasonably priced at Alko – you can get a drinkable bottle from €6 to €10.

Drinking in bars and restaurants, however, is costly. A pint of beer or cider (the latter is made from apple or pear) costs from €3.50 to €5.50. Alcohol is taxed by content, so the stronger it is, the more expensive. Uniquely Finnish drinks to look out for include: *salmiekkikoska*, a handmade spirit combining dissolved liquorice/peppermint flavoured sweets with the abrasive koskenkova vodka (an acquired taste!); *sahti*, a sweet, high-alcohol beer traditionally made at home by farmers' wives – you can find it in a couple of pubs in Lahti and Savonlinna; cloudberry or cranberry liqueurs, and vodka mixed with cranberry.

If Finns are lovers of alcohol, it's nothing compared to their passion for coffee. Every restaurant, café, petrol station and market stall has a self-serve pot of coffee on the warmer.

ENTERTAINMENT
For many Finns, talking and socialising over a few drinks is entertainment enough, though you'll find live music venues for rock, jazz and maybe folk in most major towns. For older Finns, taking to the dance floor and dancing the tango or *humppa* to a live band is the epitome of a great night out. In summer, temporary stages are often set up for live music.

Nightclubs typically charge €5 after 11pm (the minimum age for entry is 18 or 20 years, sometimes 24). Note that in nightclubs and some bars, even when there's no cover charge, you'll have to pay a 'coat charge' of around €2, which usually goes to the doorman.

Cinema tickets cost around €8; foreign films are in their original language and have subtitles in Finnish and Swedish.

Theatre performances are always in Finnish, and operas tend to have Finnish and Swedish subtitles. Classical concerts and festivals – many held outdoors – are very popular during summer.

SPECTATOR SPORTS
Ice hockey is Finland's number one national passion, but you'll have to visit in winter to see a game. The season is between late September and March. The best place to see a quality match in the national league is Tampere (home of the ice hockey museum), but Helsinki, Turku, Oulu and Rovaniemi also have major stadiums. Another popular winter spectator sport is ski-jumping – Lahti, with its vast sports centre, is the best place to see it, but Kuopio also has a jump on Puijo Hill.

In summer, football (soccer) is the national team sport although it's not as popular here as elsewhere in Europe. *Pesäpallo* is the Finnish version of baseball, and is a popular spectator sport.

SHOPPING
Beautifully designed home wares and crockery are Finnish specialities, though slick Nordic design doesn't come cheap; a tea cup and saucer by Finlandia (one of the best brands) can cost up to US$20.

Check the labels on the attractive wool sweaters you see in Finnish markets – they probably were made in Norway. *Duodji* are authentic handicrafts produced according to Sami traditions. A genuine item, which can be expensive, should carry a round, coloured 'Duodji' token. The range of items in bone, hide, wood and metals includes jewellery, clothing and the knives characteristic of the Sami communities.

FINLAND

Good places to shop for handicrafts include the *kauppatori* (market square) in Helsinki, Rovaniemi, Napapiiri and Inari in Lapland, Savonlinna in the lake district, and Kuusamo.

Trekkers may want to purchase a *kuksa* (cup) made in traditional Sami fashion from the burl of a birch tree.

Getting There & Away

AIR

All major European carriers have flights to/from Helsinki, though the majority of services are with **Finnair** (W *www.finnair.com*) or **SAS** (W *www.scandinavian.net*). You may also find a cheap flight to Helsinki from the USA or Asia – bucket shops include Helsinki as a standard European destination. From London, it's worth considering a cheap flight to Stockholm with Ryanair and the ferry from there to Turku or Helsinki.

Holders of the International Youth Travel Card (IYTC) or International Student Identity Card (ISIC) from student travel agents should also be able to pick up discount flights; in Finland, contact **Kilroy Travels** (☎ 680 7811; *Kaivokatu 10C*) in Helsinki. They also have offices in Turku, Tampere, Jyväskylä, Vaasa and Oulu.

LAND
Sweden

There are six crossings from northern Sweden to northern Finland over the Tornionjoki (Torneälv) and Muonionjoki Rivers. There are no passport or customs formalities and if you're driving up along the border you can easily alternate between countries. From Norway or southern Sweden, there are trains to Boden and buses (train passes are valid) to the Swedish town of Haparanda, from where you can easily walk across (or take another bus) to the Finnish town of Tornio.

Norway

There are six border crossings by road plus several legal crossings on wilderness trails. Buses run between Rovaniemi and the Norwegian border, and most buses continue on to the first Norwegian town.

The main Nordkapp route will take you from Rovaniemi via Inari and Kaamanen to Karigasniemi and across the border to Karasjok and Lakselv. Many bus services run from Ivalo to Karasjok. Two alternative routes, which are not as well served by bus, go through western Lapland, via Hetta and on to Karasjok; or along highway 21 to Kilpisjärvi and along the coast to Alta. The latter route is also the quickest way to Tromsø and anywhere south in Norway.

The road from the northernmost point of Finland, at Nuorgam, will take you to Tana Bru, with connections to various parts of Finnmark in Norway. Buses take you to the border, 4km from Nuorgam.

To get to Kirkenes from Finland, cross the border at Näätämö to reach Neiden, 10km away, which has bus connections to Kirkenes and to other centres in Finnmark. You may have to hitchhike from Näätämö to Neiden.

Russia

There is a badly overworked single rail line and two road crossings along the heavily travelled Helsinki–Vyborg–St Petersburg corridor. The rail crossing is at Vainikkala (Luzhayka). Highways cross the Finnish border posts of Nuijamaa (Russian side: Brusnichnoe) and Vaalimaa (Russian side: Torfyanovka), just north of Vainikkala.

You may be able to drive from Joensuu to the Finnish post of Niirala (Russian side: Vyartsilya) and 500km on to Petrozavodsk.

From Ivalo a road goes to Murmansk via the Finnish border post of Raja-Jooseppi.

If you drive, you'll need an International Driving Permit (IDP) and certificate of registration, passport, visa and insurance. **Ingosstrakh** (☎ 09-694 0511; *Salomonkatu 5C, 00100 Helsinki*) is the only Russian insurer in Helsinki; it will cover you in Russia only, and no other republics.

Bus Daily express buses run from Turku and Helsinki to St Petersburg and Vyborg, and a visa is required. These buses stop at other Finnish cities, notably Porvoo and Hamina. Check timetables and book tickets at the bus station or a travel agency. Of course, the train is a far more romantic way to reach Russia. There are also Gold Line buses from Rovaniemi and Ivalo to Murmansk.

Train There are three daily trains from Helsinki to Russia, travelling via the Finnish stations of Lahti, Kouvola and Vainikkala.

You must have a valid Russian visa but border formalities have been fast-tracked so that passport checks are now carried out on board the moving train.

The *Tolstoi* sleeper departs from Helsinki daily at 5.42pm, arrives in Moscow at 8.30am the next day and costs €83/124 in 2nd/1st class one way. It departs Moscow daily at 10.20pm. The fare includes a sleeper berth in both classes. The *Sibelius* and *Repin* have daily services between Helsinki and St Petersburg (5½ hours) via Vyborg (3¾ hours). The *Sibelius* (a Finnish train) departs Helsinki at 7.42am (€44.10/77.90 2nd/1st class, seats only). The Russian *Repin* departs at 3.42pm and has 2nd-class seats (€49.10) or 1st-class sleeping berths (€86.10). Return fares are roughly double. Fares to Vyborg are €38.40/ 61.80 on *Sibelius* and €35.40/70.50 on *Repin*. From St Petersburg departures are at 4.48pm *(Sibelius)* and 7.48am *(Repin)*.

Buy Russian rail tickets in Helsinki at the special ticket counter in the central station. There are discounts for seniors and children under 15, but no student discounts. If you can rustle up a group of six people under 15, the group can get a whopping 60% discount. Check timetables at w www.vr.fi.

SEA

The Baltic ferries are some of the world's most impressive seagoing craft and are justifiably described as floating hotels and shopping plazas. They certainly qualify as mini-cruise ships, with bars, karaoke, cabaret, gaming rooms and nightclubs, and many Scandinavians use them simply for overnight boozy cruises. The ferry is an excellent way to arrive or depart Finland – in Helsinki they sail virtually into the centre of the city! Service between major cities is year-round; you should book when travelling in July, especially if you have a car.

Many ferries offer 50% discounts for holders of Eurail, Scanrail and Inter Rail passes. Some services offer discounts for seniors and for those with ISIC and IYTC cards. Fares are slightly complicated and depend on the season, day (Friday to Sunday is more expensive), whether it's day or overnight and, of course, the class of travel.

Sweden

The Stockholm to Helsinki, Stockholm to Turku, and Kapellskär (Sweden) to Mariehamn

(Åland) runs are operated by Silja Line and Viking Line, with daily departures. Birka Cruises travels between Mariehamn and Stockholm.

Cabins are compulsory on Silja Line. On Viking they're optional – instead you can just buy a passenger ticket and sleep in the salons or any spare patch of inside deck (or just not sleep at all, as many partying passengers do). There are luggage lockers on board. Friday night departures on Viking in the low season are considerably more expensive than departures on other nights of the week. In summer, overnight crossings (passenger ticket only) from Stockholm start at €33 to Turku (11 to 12 hours) and €40 to Helsinki (16 hours).

Eckerö Line sails from Grisslehamn north of Stockholm to Eckerö in Åland – at three hours and €5.50 (€8.90 in summer) it's the quickest and cheapest crossing from Sweden to Finland.

RG Lines (w www.rgline.com) sails from Vaasa in Finland, to Umeå, Sweden (€41 or Skr360, three hours, one or two times daily in summer, less often in winter).

Estonia

Several ferry companies ply the Gulf of Finland between Helsinki and Tallinn in Estonia. Since most nationalities (except Canadians) don't require a visa and the trip is so quick and cheap, it's a very popular day trip from Helsinki. See the boxed text 'Tripping to Tallinn' in the Helsinki section of this chapter.

Competition between the companies keeps the price low and if you're heading to Estonia for onward travel it can be cheaper to get a same-day return ticket than a one-way ticket. Car ferries cross in 3½ hours, catamarans and hydrofoils in about 1½ hours. Service is heavy year-round, although in winter there are fewer departures, and the traffic is also slower due to the ice.

Eckero Line has only one departure daily but is the cheapest with a return fare of just €12 from Tuesday to Thursday, except in July and August when it's €22. Tallink and Silja Line have several daily departures. Catamarans and hydrofoils cost from €25 to €65 return depending on the company, time of year and the day of the week. Linda Line is the cheapest fast boat, but it also has the smallest boats. Nordic Jet Line is the priciest.

Germany

Finnlines *(Helsinki:* ☎ *09-251 0200;* W *www .finnlines.fi)* has service from Helsinki to Travemünde (32 to 36 hours) with bus service to Hamburg. Rates for Helsinki–Travemünde are from €272 one way.

Superfast ferries *(Helsinki:* ☎ *09-2535 0640, fax 09-2535 0601;* W *www.superfast .com),* at Melkonkatu 28 in Helsinki, runs a ferry between Rostock and Hanko on the south coast of Finland (22 hours), daily except Sunday. The ferries all depart in the evening and the minimum one-way fare is €138/69 adult/child.

Russia

At the time of writing there was no ferry service between Finland and Russia, although **Kristina Cruises** *(*☎ *05-218 1011)* does operate visa-free cruises between Helsinki and St Petersburg, and **Karelia Line** *(*☎ *05-453 0380)* offers visa-free cruises to Vyborg from Lappeenranta. On both trips you must return with the same cruise.

LEAVING FINLAND

There are no departure taxes when leaving Finland.

Getting Around

AIR

Finnair (W *www.finnair.com)* and **SAS** (W *www.scandinavian.net)* run fairly comprehensive domestic services between the big centres and to Lapland.

Full fares are not cheap (eg, Helsinki–Rovaniemi €223, Helsinki–Kuopio €167) but if you plan ahead you can get reasonable discounts.

Advance-purchase return tickets give up to 50% discount, and summer and weekend deals are cheaper still.

Seniors and children aged under 12 years receive a 70% discount. If you're aged between 17 and 24 the discount is 50%, but better still you can fly stand-by to anywhere in Finland for €50 or €64 one-way depending on the flight – a huge saving on a flight from, say, Helsinki to Rovaniemi (cheaper, in fact, than the train).

To qualify you need to arrive at the airport one hour before the flight of your choice and wait to see if there are any seats available.

BUS

Buses are the principal carriers outside the railway network – they travel on 90% of Finland's roads. You may buy your ticket on board or book at a bus station or travel agency (Monday to Friday only). Restricted services operate on weekends and public holidays. Long-distance and express bus travel is handled by **Oy Matkahuolto Ab** *(*☎ *09-682 701)* in Helsinki. Private lines operate local services, but all share the same ticketing system. National timetables are available from bus stations and at tourist offices. In Lapland the main bus service is **Gold Line** (W *www.goldline.fi).*

Ticket prices depend on the length of journey – a 100km trip costs €12.40/14.60 regular/ express. From Helsinki to Rovaniemi by express bus (13½ hours) costs €82.60 one way. Return tickets are about 10% cheaper than two one-way fares. Discounts are available for students and seniors, though usually only if the ticket is booked and the trip is more than 80km. Children aged from four to 11 pay half fare, and from 12 to 16 get 30% off.

On some routes, buses accept train passes.

TRAIN

Finnish trains are efficient, fast and much cheaper than in Sweden and Norway. On longer routes there are two- and three-bed sleepers. Rovaniemi is the main northern rail terminus. Eurocity expresses are known as EP trains in Finland (EC in other EU countries), and other classes include the faster (and slightly more expensive) InterCity (IC) trains, the most expensive Pendolino trains, and the cheaper regional trains (2nd class only). Tickets bought in advance include a seat reservation on all services except regional trains.

VR Ltd Finnish Railways *(*☎ *09-707 3519;* W *www.vr.fi)* in Helsinki has its own travel bureau at main stations and can advise on all tickets. An open return ticket is valid for 15 days and costs the same as two one-way tickets. Students, seniors and children under 17 pay half fare, and children under six travel free (without a seat).

International rail passes accepted in Finland include the Eurail pass, Eurail Flexipass, ScanRail Pass, Euro Domino and Inter Rail Ticket. Note that if you buy a ScanRail Pass within Finland, you can only use it for up to three days in Finland (this restriction doesn't apply if you purchase it outside Finland).

The Finnrail Pass is a one-month pass good for unlimited rail travel for three/five/10 days; 2nd class travel costs €114/154/208. 1st class is about 50% more. The Euro Domino pass is similar. These passes may be purchased before arrival in Finland (consult your local travel agent) and are only available to non-residents of Finland. Check at the train station on arrival for summer and regional special fares. So-called Green Departures offer a 15% discount on off-peak trains on certain routes. Sleeping berths cost a flat rate of €42 for a single berth, and €20.20/10 per person for double/triple berths, although these prices are about 30% higher at peak travel times.

CAR & MOTORCYCLE

Finland's road network is good between centres, although there are only a handful of motorways emanating from major cities. In the forests you'll find many unsurfaced roads and dirt tracks. There are no road tolls. Petrol is expensive in southern Finland – between €0.98 and €1.15 a litre for 95e unleaded – and even more so in Lapland.

Your headlights must be turned on at all times outside built-up areas. Foreign cars must display their nationality and visitors must be fully insured. Accidents should be reported promptly to the **Motor Insurers' Bureau** (☎ 09-680 401; Bulevardi 28, 00120 Helsinki).

Wearing seat belts is mandatory for all passengers. The blood alcohol limit is 0.05%. The speed limit is 50km/h in built-up areas, from 80km/h to 100km/h on highways, and 120km/h on a few motorways. Traffic keeps to the right.

Beware of elk and reindeer, which do not respond to motor horns. By law, police must be notified about accidents involving these animals. Several thousand accidents involving elk are reported in Finland each year – it's ironic that the only time you may get to see an elk in the wild is when it's careering through your windscreen. Reindeer, on the other hand, are very common in Lapland and often wander along the road in semi-domesticated herds.

Buying a car in Finland is not really practical unless you plan to stay for quite a while. Small 10-year-old saloons and old vans can cost less than €1500, but those costing less than €800 should have been recently *katsastettu* (inspected).

Finland's national motoring organisation is **Autoliitto** (*Automobile & Touring Club of Finland;* ☎ 09-774 761; Ⓦ *www.autoliitto.fi; Hämeentie 105A, 00550 Helsinki*).

Winter Driving

Snow and ice on Finland's roads from September to March or April (and as late as June in Lapland) make driving a hazardous activity without snow tyres (chains are illegal); cars hired in Finland will be properly equipped.

Car Rental

Car hire in Finland is not cheap, but with a group of three or four it can work reasonably economically, especially if your time is short and you want to get off the beaten track. Rental companies such as **Budget** (☎ *686 6500*), **Hertz** (☎ *0800-112 233*) and **Europcar** (☎ *09-7515 5300*) have offices in most cities. Avoid renting from airports where rates are highest. In Helsinki there are cheaper local car-hire companies. The smallest car costs from €40 per day plus €0.30 per kilometre. Weekly rentals with unlimited mileage cost from €350 a week.

BICYCLE

Finland is flat and as bicycle friendly as any country you'll find, with miles of bike paths – which cyclists share with inline skaters in summer. The only drawback to an extensive tour is distance, but bikes can be carried on most trains and buses. Daily/weekly hire at about €10/50 is possible in most cities, although hiring decent bikes in smaller towns is becoming difficult, as bike shops find it unprofitable – check with the local tourist office. Helmets are advisable but not compulsory. The **Finnish Youth Hostel Association** (*SRM;* Ⓦ *www.srmnet.org*) offers a cycling and hostel package that takes in the flat south and lakes and costs €249/431 for 7/14 days, including bike rental and accommodation.

New bikes are expensive in Finland, starting from €250 for a hybrid, but good second-hand models may cost less than €100.

HITCHING

Hitching in Finland is fairly easy, especially if you try outside the biggest cities and look clean. However, compared with elsewhere in Europe it's uncommon to see hitchhikers in Finland and you can expect long waits on minor roads.

FINLAND

BOAT

Lake and river ferries operate over the summer period (most lakes are frozen over in winter!). They're more than mere transport, which is just as well, because they're more expensive than the bus – a lake cruise taking you from one town to another via southern Finland's sublime system of waterways is a bona fide Finnish experience. The most popular routes are Tampere–Hämeenlinna, Savonlinna–Kuopio, Lahti–Jyväskylä and also Joensuu–Koli–Lieksa. The popular sea routes are Turku–Naantali, Helsinki–Porvoo, Uusikaupunki–Hanko via Turku, and the archipelago ferries to the Åland islands. Many of the ferries that run between the islands along the coast are free, especially in Åland.

LOCAL TRANSPORT

The only tram and metro networks are in Helsinki. There is a bus service in all Finnish cities and towns. As a rule, train and bus stations are reasonably close together, and train and bus timetables are designed so that incoming trains meet outgoing buses, or vice versa. These timetables are executed with clinical precision right around the country, so be on time. Tickets can be bought at the bus station but on weekends, when bus station ticket offices are closed, you must buy the ticket on board, unless you have a bus pass or have bought it in advance.

Hail taxis at bus and train stations or call one by telephone (they are listed in the phone book under *Taksi*). Taxis are expensive – typically the fare is €3 plus a per-kilometre charge.

ORGANISED TOURS

Many Finnish towns offer a great variety of tours – but there are not always enough takers. Helsinki, Turku and Rovaniemi offer weekly tour programmes during the summer and winter high seasons. In places like Lieksa, Kuusamo and Lapland, tours can be the cheapest, or indeed the only way to visit isolated attractions.

Helsinki

☎ 09 • pop 540,000

For many travellers, Helsinki is Finland. And while the nation still struggles a little to gain the attention of tourists, Helsinki is fast becoming one of Europe's hottest destinations.

Although this is by far Finland's largest and most vibrant city, Helsinki is small and intimate compared to other Scandinavian capitals. Walking or cycling is the best way to appreciate its cafés, parks, markets and nearby islands, which are an absolute delight in summer.

Nor does Helsinki bear much resemblance to other Scandinavian or Baltic cities. Rather than the ornate and grandiose buildings of Stockholm, it's a low-rise city of understated, functional architecture. But in summer, the appeal is as much in the atmosphere and upbeat nature of the people as in any particular sight. Strolling around the harbour area, picnicking on Suomenlinna island or joining the throngs sunning themselves in the many cafés and beer terraces is every bit as good as ticking off the museums.

The area has only been settled since 1550. When the Swedes (whose name for the city is Helsingfors) were here in the 18th century they erected a mammoth fortress on the nearby island of Suomenlinna. After falling to the tsar in 1808, Helsinki became the seat of the Russian Grand Duchy – although in the process much of the town was wrecked. The monumental buildings of Senaatintori (Senate Square) were designed by 19th-century German architect Carl Ludwig Engel to give the new city an appropriate measure of oomph.

Orientation

Helsinki occupies a peninsula and is linked by bridge and boat to nearby islands. The city centre surrounds the main harbour, Eteläsatama, and the kauppatori, which lies between the huge international ferry terminals. The main street axes are the twin shopping avenues of Pohjoisesplanadi and Eteläesplanadi, and Mannerheimintie.

Information

Tourist Offices The busy but helpful **Helsinki City Tourist Office** (☎ 169 3757; W www.hel.fi; Pohjoisesplanadi 19; open 9am-7pm Mon-Fri, 9am-3pm Sat & Sun May-Sept & 9am-5pm Mon-Fri, 9am-3pm Sat Oct-Apr) is near the market square. In summer you'll probably see uniformed 'Helsinki Helpers' wandering around – collar these volunteers for any sort of tourist information.

The **Finnish Tourist Board** (☎ 4176 9300; W www.mek.fi; Eteläesplanadi 4; open 9am-5pm Mon-Fri year-round, 10am-4pm Sat May-Sept) has an office opposite the city tourist office, with brochures, maps and information for destinations around the country.

Tikankontti (☎ 270 5221 or 0203-44 122; w www.metsa.fi; Eteläesplanadi 20; open 10am-6pm Mon-Fri, 10am-3pm Sat) is the Helsinki office of Metsähallitus, the Finnish Forest and Park Service. It has information and maps for national parks and hiking areas, cabin rentals and sports fishing.

Kompassi (☎ 3108 0080; w www.lasipalatsi.fi/kompassi; Mannerheimintie 22-24; open 11am-6pm Tues-Thur, 11am-4pm Fri & 11am-6pm Sun) is a youth information centre offering youth cards and general advice and support.

Pick up free copies of the useful *Helsinki This Week* (published monthly) and the newspaper-style *City in English* from tourist offices and hotels.

Helsinki Card This pass gives free urban travel, plus free entry to more than 50 attractions in and around Helsinki and discounts on day tours to Porvoo and Tallinn. A card valid for 24/48/72 hours costs €24/33/39 (€9.50/12.50/15 for children). It's well worth the price if you plan to visit several museums, use the island ferries and organise your day wisely; take the free 1½-hour sightseeing bus tour first up. Buy the card at the city tourist office, or at hotels, R-kiosks and transport terminals.

Money With branches at the train station, **Forex** (open 8am-9pm daily), on the Pohjoisesplanadi and on Mannerheimintie, offers good rates and is the best place to change cash or travellers cheques (€2 flat fee). They also offer commission-free cash advances on credit cards. There are currency exchange counters at the airport and the Katajanokka ferry terminal. **Western Union** (open 9am-9pm Mon-Fri, 9am-6pm Sat) is on the 7th floor of the Stockman department store on Mannerheimintie.

Post & Communications The **main post office** (Mannerheiminaukio 1; open 10am-7pm Mon-Fri, 11am-4pm Sat & Sun) is opposite the train station. The **poste restante office** (open 8am-9pm Mon-Fri, 9am-6pm Sat & 11am-9pm Sun) is in the same building (00100 Helsinki).

Email & Internet Access Internet access at Helsinki's public libraries is free. The best place is the **Kirjakaapeli library** (Cable Book Library; ☎ 3108 5000; Mannerheimintie 22-24), upstairs in the Lasipalatsi Multimedia Centre. There are some terminals available on a first-come-first-served basis, or you can book a half-hour slot in advance. There are several terminals at the central **Rikhardinkadun Library** (Rikhardinkatu 3).

Although email is discouraged, the best place to surf the Net is the impressive **Helsinki University Library** (Unioninkatu 36), which has 20 terminals at the rear of the 2nd floor that can be used free without booking.

Roberts Coffee, on the ground floor of Stockman department store, has two free terminals for customers, as does **Wayne's Coffee** (Kaisaniemenkatu 3).

Travel Agencies Specialising in student and budget travel is **Kilroy Travels** (☎ 680 7811; Kaivokatu 10C). **Helsinki Tour Expert** (☎ 2288 1599), in the city tourist office, is an agency handling travel around Finland and to Tallinn and St Petersburg.

Bookshops The biggest bookshop in Finland, **Akateeminen Kirjakauppa** (Pohjoisesplanadi 39), stocks a huge range of books, newspapers and periodicals in 40 languages. It has a big travel section, including maps.

Laundry A load of washing at **Easywash** (☎ 406 982; Runeberginkatu 47; open 10am-8pm Mon-Thurs, 10am-6pm Fri & Sat) costs €3 to €4; drying is €2. Tram No 3 stops right outside.

Left Luggage Luggage can be left at the main train station, bus station and ferry terminals. Lockers cost €2/3 for small/large, and the train station and Viking Line ferry terminal have left-luggage counters charging €2 per piece per day.

Medical & Emergency Services Dial ☎ 112 for ambulance service, ☎ 10022 for police, and ☎ 10023 for 24-hour medical advice. The police have stations at Helsinki's main train and bus stations, and there's a police **lost-property office** (☎ 189 3180; Päijänteentie 12A).

English speakers should use the 24-hour clinic at **Töölö Hospital** (☎ 4711; Töölönkatu 40). There's a 24-hour **pharmacy** at Mannerheimintie 96.

FINLAND

FINLAND

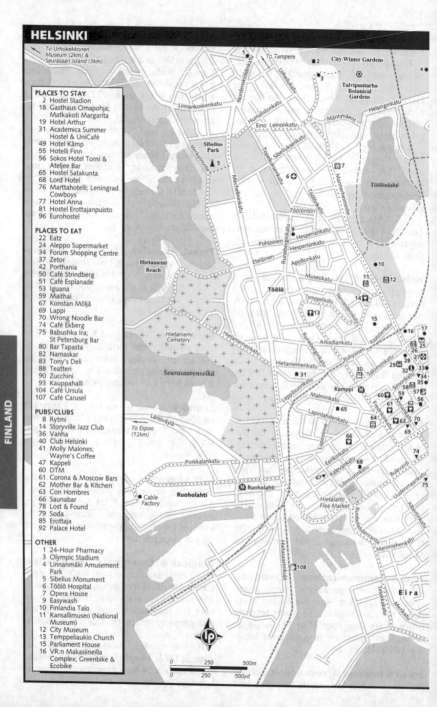

HELSINKI

To Urhokekkonen
Museum (2km) &
Seurasaari Island (3km)

To Tampere

City Winter Gardens

Talvipuutarha
Botanical
Gardens

PLACES TO STAY
2 Hostel Stadion
18 Gasthaus Omapohja;
 Matkakoti Margarita
19 Hotel Arthur
31 Academica Summer
 Hostel & UniCafé
49 Hotel Kämp
55 Hotelli Finn
56 Sokos Hotel Torni &
 Ateljee Bar
65 Hostel Satakunta
68 Lord Hotel
76 Marttahotelli; Leningrad
 Cowboys
77 Hotel Anna
81 Hostel Erottajanpuisto
96 Eurohostel

PLACES TO EAT
22 Eatz
24 Aleppo Supermarket
34 Forum Shopping Centre
37 Zetor
42 Porthania
50 Café Strindberg
51 Café Esplanade
53 Iguana
59 Maithai
67 Konstan Möljä
69 Lappi
70 Wrong Noodle Bar
74 Café Ekberg
75 Babushka Ira;
 St Petersburg Bar
80 Bar Tapasta
82 Namaskar
83 Tony's Deli
88 Teatteri
90 Zucchini
93 Kauppahalli
104 Café Ursula
107 Café Carusel

PUBS/CLUBS
8 Rytmi
14 Storyville Jazz Club
36 Vanha
40 Club Helsinki
41 Molly Malones;
 Wayne's Coffee
47 Kappeli
60 DTM
61 Corona & Moscow Bars
62 Mother Bar & Kitchen
63 Con Hombres
66 Saunabar
78 Lost & Found
79 Soda
85 Erottaja
92 Palace Hotel

OTHER
1 24-Hour Pharmacy
3 Olympic Stadium
4 Linnanmäki Amusement
 Park
5 Sibelius Monument
6 Töölö Hospital
7 Opera House
9 Easywash
10 Finlandia Talo
11 Kansallismuseo (National
 Museum)
12 City Museum
13 Temppeliaukio Church
15 Parliament House
16 VR:n Makasiineilla
 Complex; Greenbike &
 Ecobike

Sibelius
Park

Hietaniemi
Beach

Töölö

Hietaniemi
Cemetery

Seurasaarenselkä

To Espoo
(12km)

Länsiväylä

Porkkalankatu

Cable
Factory

Ruoholahti

Töölönlahti

Kamppi

Malminkatu

Lapinlahdenkatu

Ruoholahti

Hietalahti
Flea Market

Eira

0 250 500m
0 250 500yd

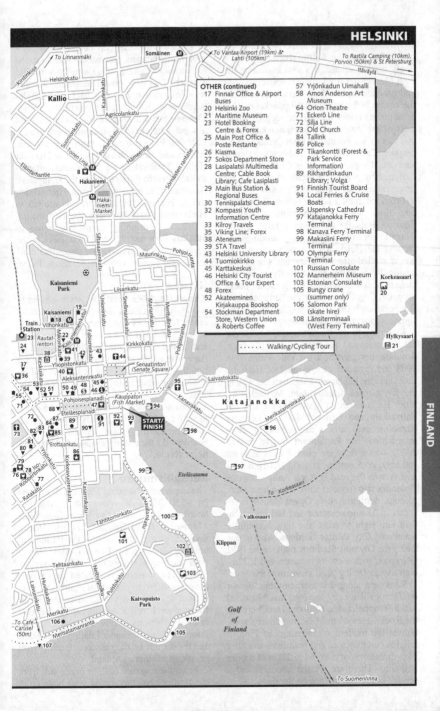

HELSINKI

To Linnanmäki
Somäinen
To Vantaa Airport (19km) & Lahti (105km)
To Rastila Camping (10km), Porvoo (50km) & St Petersburg
Itäväylä

Kirstinkuja
Helsinkikatu

Kallio

Kaarenkatu

Agricolankatu

Suomenkatu
V-tonen Linja
Porthaninkatu
Hämeentie
Eläintarhantie

Hakaniemi
Haka-niemi Market

Siltasaarenkatu
Sörnaisten rantatie

Maurinkatu
Pohjoisranta

Kaisaniemi Park
Liisankatu
Snellmaninkatu
Mariankatu
Meritullinkatu

Kaisaniemi
Uonkatu

Train Station
Vilhonkatu
Kaisaniemenkatu
Fabianinkatu
Kirkkokatu

Rautatientori
Mikonkatu

Keskuskatu
Yliopistonkatu

Senaatintori (Senate Square)

Pohjoisranta

Aleksanterinkatu

Kauppatori (Fish Market)

Pohjoisesplanadi
Eteläesplanadi

START/FINISH

Erottajankatu

Yrjönkatu
Korkeavuorenkatu
Kasarmikatu

Iso-Roobertinkatu

Ratakatu

Laivastokatu
Katajanokka
Merikasarminkatu

Kanavakatu

Tähtitorninkatu

Eteläsatama

Tehtaankatu
Neitsytpolku
Puistokatu

Laivanvarustajankatu

Huvilakatu
Laivurinkatu

Kaivopuisto Park

To Cafe Carúsel (50m)

Merisatamanranta
Merikatu

Gulf of Finland

Valkosaari
Klippan

To Korkeasaari

To Suomenlinna

Korkeasaari
20

Hylkysaari
21

FINLAND

OTHER (continued)
17 Finnair Office & Airport Buses
20 Helsinki Zoo
21 Maritime Museum
23 Hotel Booking Centre & Forex
25 Main Post Office & Poste Restante
26 Kiasma
27 Sokos Department Store
28 Lasipalatsi Multimedia Centre; Cable Book Library; Cafe Lasiplasti
29 Main Bus Station & Regional Buses
30 Tennispalatsi Cinema
32 Kompassi Youth Information Centre
33 Kilroy Travels
35 Viking Line; Forex
38 Ateneum
39 STA Travel
43 Helsinki University Library
44 Tuomiokirkko
45 Karttakeskus
46 Helsinki City Tourist Office & Tour Expert
48 Forex
52 Akateeminen Kirjakauppa Bookshop
54 Stockman Department Store, Western Union & Roberts Coffee

57 Yrjönkadun Uimahalli
58 Amos Anderson Art Museum
64 Orion Theatre
71 Eckerö Line
72 Silja Line
73 Old Church
84 Tallink
86 Police
87 Tikankontti (Forest & Park Service Information)
89 Rikhardinkadun Library; Volga
91 Finnish Tourist Board
94 Local Ferries & Cruise Boats
95 Uspensky Cathedral
97 Katajanokka Ferry Terminal
98 Kanava Ferry Terminal
99 Makasiini Ferry Terminal
100 Olympia Ferry Terminal
101 Russian Consulate
102 Mannerheim Museum
103 Estonian Consulate
105 Bungy crane (summer only)
106 Salomon Park (skate hire)
108 Länsiterminaali (West Ferry Terminal)

· · · · · Walking/Cycling Tour

Walking Tour

Helsinki is easy to get around on foot or by bicycle. Start at the **kauppatori**, Helsinki's lively market square. It's also known as the Fish Market but it's largely a souvenir, craft and produce market these days. Just south of the square is the **kauppahalli** (market hall), a great place to stock up on gourmet provisions. East of the market, on Katajanokka island, you can't miss the magnificent Orthodox **Uspensky Cathedral**. The red-brick exterior supports 13 gilded cupolas ('onion domes' designed by a Russian architect of the tsar) representing Christ and his disciples.

From the market square follow Sofiankatu one block north to **Senaatintori** (Senate Square), Helsinki's majestic central square. Ringed with early 19th-century buildings, including the Helsinki University, the square was modelled after St Petersburg's and is occasionally used by B-list Hollywood film makers who want a dramatic 'Russian' backdrop. CL Engel's stately white **Tuomiokirkko** (Lutheran cathedral), finished in 1852, is the square's most prominent feature.

Returning to the market square, check out the fountain and mermaid statue of **Havis Amanda**, designed by artist Ville Vallgren in 1908 and regarded as a symbol of Helsinki. From here the Esplanade Park stretches west to the city's main thoroughfare, Mannerheimintie. Head north to visit **Kiasma** and the **Kansallismuseo** (National Museum; see under Kansallismuseo later in this section for more information) and **Parliament House** (☎ 432 2027), where there are guided tours at 11am and noon on Saturday, at noon and 1pm Sunday. Across the road is Alvar Aalto's angular **Finlandia talo** (concert hall). If you have time, continue north to Aalto's **Opera House** on the corner of Mannerheimintie and Helsinginkatu, then turn right to reach the tiny, beautifully manicured **City Winter Gardens**. Also in this area is the **Olympic Stadium**, built for the 1952 Olympics, with a sports museum and a 72m-high tower offering good views over the city.

Returning along Mannerheimintie, detour on Temppelikatu (by the National Museum) to the **Temppeliaukio Church** (The Church in the Rock). Hewn into rock, the church symbolises the modern meanderings of Finnish religious architecture and features a stunning 24m-diameter roof covered in 22km of copper stripping. There are regular concerts and a service in English at 2pm on Sundays.

Walk down Fredrikinkatu then east on Lönnrotinkatu to the small park (and old cemetery – look for the ancient gravestones littered round the square) where there's a lovely **Old Church**. This is a popular lunchtime meeting spot in summer. Heading back down Bulevardi (away from the city), you come to **Hietalahden tori** where there's a market hall and a popular **flea market** on summer evenings.

If you have a bicycle, from here you can ride around the southern shoreline of Helsinki (follow Telakkakatu then Merisatamanranta) to **Kaivopuisto Park** and on to the kauppatori. Alternatively, head north from Hietalahden tori to Hietaniemenkatu and ride around to **Hietaniemi Beach**, the closest beach to central Helsinki. Continuing north you come to **Sibelius Park** and the steel monument to the great Finnish composer. The organ-like cluster of steel pipes is said to represent the forest.

Kiasma

Kiasma (*☎ 1733 6501;* **w** *www.kiasma.fi, Mannerheiminaukio 2; adult/student/child under 18 €5.50/4/free; open 9am-5pm Tues, 10am-8.30pm Wed-Sun*) is in the curvaceous and quirky chalk-white building designed by American architect Steven Holl. It exhibits a rapidly growing collection of Finnish and international modern art from the 1960s to the 1990s.

Kiasma is a local meeting point in summer – its café and terrace are hugely popular, locals sunbathe on the grassy fringes and skateboarders do their thing around the **Mannerheim statue**.

Kansallismuseo

The impressive National Museum of Finland (*☎ 4050 9544;* **w** *www.nba.fi; Mannerheimintie 34; open 11am-8pm Tues-Wed, 11am-6pm Thurs-Sun; adult/student/child €4/ 3.50/free*), just north of the Parliament building, looks a bit like a Gothic church with its heavy stonework and tall square tower. The museum is divided into rooms covering different periods of Finnish history, including prehistory and archaeological finds, church relics, ethnography and cultural exhibitions. Look for the imperial throne of Tsar Alexander I dating from 1809, and the display on the reindeer-herding Sami people of northern Lapland.

From the entrance hall, or better still from the 1st-floor balcony, crane your head up to

Tripping to Tallinn

Although Finland can seem very remote from the rest of Europe at times, Helsinki is remarkably close to the Continental mainland and a day or overnight trip to the Estonian capital of Tallinn is a must. The chalk-and-cheese contrast between modern Helsinki and the turrets and spires of Tallinn's compact medieval Old Town is fascinating.

It's 80km across the Gulf of Finland to Tallinn; catamarans and hydrofoils do the 1½-hour trip several times daily. The trip costs as little as €25 return – see the Getting There & Away sections at the beginning of this chapter and under Helsinki for more information. Most nationalities (except Canadians) don't need a visa.

The trip itself is something of a 'booze cruise' for many Finns, but unlike the overnight trips to Sweden, it's not the cruise itself they are interested in, but the destination. Alcohol in Estonia is substantially cheaper than anywhere in Scandinavia – less than half the price in liquor shops – so it's not unusual to see tipsy Finns tottering aboard with trolleys loaded up with beer and vodka (within customs limits of course). The ferries have the usual bars and cafeteria-style restaurants – check-in early if you want a seat in one of the lounges.

The highlight of Tallinn is undoubtedly the walled **Old Town** – a Unesco World Heritage Site – and the lofty **Toompea Castle**. It's only about a 15-minute walk (follow Mere puiestee) from the ferry terminals to **Viru Gate**, the main entrance to Old Tallinn. A short walk along the cobbled, restaurant-lined Viru brings you to the central square **Raekoja plats**, which has been a marketplace since the 11th century. Dominating the south side of the square is the Gothic **town hall**, dating from 1371, and opposite is the **tourist office** (☎ 645 7777), considerably younger but a great source of information and the place to buy your Tallinn Card if you intend to visit lots of attractions.

The Old Town will seem pretty touristy after Helsinki, but with its tangle of narrow, cobbled streets and impossibly quaint medieval houses (many now studios, galleries, cafés, museums and craft shops), it demands to be explored on foot. Climb the hill to **Toompea**, dominated by the Alexandr Nevsky Cathedral, the Parliament building and Toompea Castle. Back in the Lower Town, take a stroll along Pikk tänav, lined with old merchants' houses and guilds, and a couple of interesting museums and galleries.

Take the time to splurge at one of Tallinn's traditional restaurants or terrace cafes – although dining is generally a bit pricier in the Old Town, it's still much cheaper than Finland and the atmosphere is unbeatable. There are plenty of eateries along Viru and around Raekoja plats. If you plan to stay overnight try **Vana Tom** (☎ 631 3252; Väike-Karja tänav 1; dorm beds HI members/nonmembers 210/225EEK, rooms from 590EEK), just 30 seconds walk from Raekoja plats.

If you've got a lazy €120 and want to get to Tallin in style, Copter Line (☎ 0200 18181) has hourly helicopter flights (about 14 a day) from Helsinki to Tallin. It takes just 18 minutes and you can get the ferry back. There's a small discount for return flights.

see the superb frescoes on the ceiling arches, depicting scenes from the epic *Kalevala*, painted by Akseli Gallen-Kallela.

Ateneum

The list of painters at the National Gallery (☎ 173 36275; Ⓦ www.fng.fi/ateneum; Kaivokatu 2; adult/student €5.50/4; open 9am-6pm Tues & Fri, 9am-8pm Wed & Thur, 11am-5pm Sat & Sun) reads like a 'Who's Who' of Finnish art. It houses Finnish paintings and sculptures from the 18th century to the 1950s including works by Albert Edelfelt,

Akseli Gallen-Kallela, the Von Wright brothers and Pekka Halonen, along with Rodin's famous sculpture *The Thinker*.

Mannerheim Museum

This fascinating museum (☎ 635 443; Kalliolinnantie 14; adult/student €7/540; open 11am-4pm Fri-Sun) in Kaivopuisto Park was the home of CGE Mannerheim, former president, commander-in-chief of the Finnish army and Civil War victor. Such was the national regard for Mannerheim that the house was converted into a museum less than a year after his death in 1951. Entry includes a mandatory but enthusiastic guided tour (around one hour) in one of six languages, and free plastic booties to keep the hallowed floor clean.

Cable Factory
This massive factory (☎ 4763 8303; Tallberginkatu 1C), off Porkkalankatu and on the way to Espoo, was once used for manufacturing sea cable and later became Nokia's main factory until the 1980s. When Nokia moved out, artists moved in, renting every spare space on offer. Theatre, art exhibitions and dance performances take place here now, and there's a café and restaurant.

Amos Anderson Art Museum
This museum (☎ 684 4460; Yrjönkatu 27; adult/child €7/1.50; open 10am-6pm Mon-Fri, 11am-5pm Sat & Sun) houses the collection of publishing magnate Amos Anderson, one of the wealthiest Finns of his time, and includes Finnish and European paintings and sculptures. Unless you have a Helsinki Card, admission is a bit steep.

Seurasaari Open-Air Museum
North-west of the centre, Seurasaari island is home to this open-air museum (☎ 4050 9660; adult/child €4/free; open 11am-5pm daily, 11am-7pm Wed June-Sept) with 18th- and 19th-century houses from around Finland. Guides dressed in traditional costume demonstrate folk dancing and crafts such as spinning, embroidery and troll-making.

Seurasaari is a venue for Helsinki's Midsummer bonfires. Take bus No 24 from the central train station.

Urho Kekkonen Museum Tamminiemi
The large house (☎ 4050 9652; Seurasaarentie 15, Tamminiemi; adult/child €3.50/free; open 11am-5pm daily, to 7pm Wednesday mid-May–mid-Aug) was a presidential residence for 30 years, right up until Urho Kekkonen's death, when it was turned into a museum. From central Helsinki, take bus No 24, or tram No 4 and walk.

Helsinki Zoo & Maritime Museum
One of the world's northernmost zoos, the spacious Helsinki Zoo (☎ 169 5969; adult/child €5/3, with ferry ride €8/4; open 10am-8pm daily May-Oct) is on Korkeasaari

island and is best reached by ferry from the kauppatori. Established in 1889, it has animals and birds from Finland and around the world housed in large natural enclosures, as well as a tropical house, small farm and a good cafe and terrace. On the adjoining Hylkysaari island is the Maritime Museum (☎ 4050 9051; adult/child €1.50/free; open 11am-5pm daily May-Oct) with exhibitions on Finnish shipbuilding and seafaring.

Suomenlinna
An essential day or half-day trip from Helsinki is by boat to the island fortress of Suomenlinna (Swedish: Sveaborg). Set on a tight cluster of islands, the World Heritage-listed fortress was founded by the Swedes in 1748 to protect the eastern part of the empire against the Russians. It worked for a while, but following a prolonged attack, Sveaborg was surrendered to the Russians after the war of 1808.

At the bridge connecting the two main islands – Iso Mustasaari and Susisaari – is the Inventory Chamber Visitor Centre (☎ 668 800) with tourist information, maps and guided walking tours in summer. In the same building is the Suomenlinna Museum (adult/student/child €5/4/2.50), covering the island's history. There's a scale model of Suomenlinna as it looked in 1808, and an illuminating half-hour audio-visual.

You can ramble around the old bunkers, crumbling fortress walls and cannons at the southern end of Susisaari island, and there are several museums scattered around, including the Ehrensvärd Museum (adult/child €3/1; open 10am-5pm daily May-Aug) which preserves an 18th-century officer's home. Three museums relating to Suomenlinna's military history can be visited with a combination ticket (adult/student €5.50/2). Maneesi commemorates the battles of WWII and displays heavy artillery. The Coastal Defence Museum displays still more heavy artillery in a bunker-style exhibition. U-boat Vesikko is one of the few WWII submarines remaining in Finland.

There are some good cafés on Suomenlinna, but most locals bring picnicking supplies (including lots of booze) and find a grassy spot among the fortress ruins. There's also a HI hostel here (see Places to Stay).

HKL ferries depart every 40 minutes from the passenger quay at the kauppatori. Buy tickets (€2) for the 15-minute trip at the pier.

The Helsinki Card is valid for all ferries and attractions at Suomenlinna.

There's nowhere to hire bikes, but they can be brought across on the ferries.

Activities

No visit to Helsinki is complete without a sauna and swim at the **Yrjönkadun Uimahalli** (☎ 3108 7400; Yrjönkatu 21; admission €5-10). This sleek Art Deco complex was first opened in 1928, and its powerful Nordic elegance has been beautifully restored. There are separate hours for men and women, and bathing suits are not allowed in the pool or saunas.

Inline skates can be hired at **Salomon Park** (☎ 040-525 7787), a kiosk on Merisataman-ranta, west of Kaivopuisto park. For bicycle hire, see Getting Around at the end of this section. In summer (late July to August) you can bungy-jump from a 130m crane set up over the water at Kaivopuisto park. A jump costs €70.

Organised Tours

Helsinki Expert (☎ 2288 1600; adult/child €19/10, €6 with Helsinki Card) runs excellent 1½-hour sightseeing bus tours daily in summer on the hour from 10am to 2pm. They depart from the Esplanade Park, near the tourist office, and taped commentary (in 11 languages) is via a headset. In winter the tour departs only at 10am from the Olympia ferry terminal.

Royal Line (☎ 612 2950) and **Sun Line** (☎ 727 7010) operate 1½-hour sea cruises (adult/child €14/5) with daily departures in summer from the kauppatori.

Places to Stay

It's wise to make bookings at least a week in advance for hostels and hotels from June to August. The **Hotel Booking Centre** (☎ 2288 1400; e hotel@helsinkiexpert.fi; open 9am-7pm Mon-Fri, 9am-6pm Sat, 10am-6pm Sun June-Aug; 9am-5pm Mon-Sat Sept-May), in the central hall of the train station, can help in a pinch. There's also a branch at the city tourist office.

Camping In Vuosaari, 10km east of the centre, **Rastila Camping** (☎ 321 6551; fax 344 1578; e rastilacamping@hel.fi; camping per person/group €9/14, cabins for 2/4 people €40/62, log cottages €95) is easily reached by metro – the Rastila metro stop is only about 50m from the camp (turn right as you exit).

There's also a summer **youth hostel** here, with dorm beds from €13.50 and singles/doubles €22.50/42.50.

Hostels Helsinki has two year-round hostels and three that are open in summer only plus there's a hostel on Suomenlinna island.

Eurohostel (☎ 622 0470; fax 655 044; W www.eurohostel.fi; Linnankatu 9; dorm beds €18.50, singles/doubles/triples €32/37/55.50; 24hr reception), a high-rise place on Katajanokka island less than 500m from the Viking Line terminal, is an efficiently run, friendly and very busy HI hostel. Rates include morning sauna. Take tram No 4 or 2 from the centre or walk – it's not that far. Check-in starts at 2pm.

Hostel Erottajanpuisto (☎ 642 169, fax 680 2757; Uudenmaankatu 9; dorm beds €19.50-22.50, singles/doubles €43.50/55) is definitely the most laid-back hostel in Helsinki, and has the best location on a lively street close to the heart of the city.

Hostel Stadion (☎ 477 8480, fax 477 84811; W www.stadionhostel.com; Pohjoinen Stadiontie 3B; dorm beds from €12, 4–5-bed rooms €15, singles/doubles with linen €24/34) is a 162-bed HI hostel in the Olympic Stadium. It's in a relatively dead part of town and a bit of a relic.

Academica Summer Hostel (☎ 1311 4334, fax 441 201; W www.hostelacademica.fi; Hietaniemenkatu 14; dorm beds €13.50-18.50, singles/doubles/triples from €38.50/31/63.50; open June-Aug) has no large dorms as such but each room, with ensuite and kitchenette, can be used as a dorm (without linen) or as a private room (with linen and breakfast included). It's in a quiet part of town.

Hostel Satakunta (☎ 6958 5231, fax 685 4245; e ravintola.satakunta@sodexho.fi; Lapinrinne 1A; dorm beds €12, singles/doubles/triples/quads €36.50/51/58.50/66; open June-Aug) is a student apartment building. The dorms are not flash but they are the cheapest in Helsinki. The private rooms are clean and include a fridge. Buffet breakfast is included in the price.

Suomenlinna Hostel (☎ 794 481, W www.leirikoulut.com; dorms €20.50, singles/doubles €37.50/55), in an old red-brick building near the ferry quay on Suomenlinna island, is a peaceful and interesting alternative to staying in central Helsinki.

Guesthouses Just around the corner from the train station, **Gasthaus Omapohja** (☎ 666 211; Itäinen Teatterikuja 3; singles/doubles from €40/60, with bathroom €58/75) is a fine old guesthouse without any of the sleazy characteristics of some Helsinki guesthouses. Rooms are spotless and management is friendly.

Matkakoti Margarita (☎ 622 4261; Itäinen Teatterikuja 3; singles/doubles with shared bath €37/50), next door, is not quite as charming but again it's clean and reasonably good value.

Hotels The spotless and friendly **Martta-hotelli** (☎ 618 7400, fax 618 7411; ⓦ www .martahotelli.fi; Uudenmaankatu 24; singles/ doubles/triples €94/112/135, discounted to €70/80/100) is a central but most rooms face a quiet inner courtyard with free parking. Rates include a superb buffet breakfast and there's a small sauna.

Hotel Arthur (☎ 173 441, fax 626 880; ⓦ www.hotelarthur.fi, Vuorikatu 19; singles/ doubles/triples from €89/106/126, discounted to €71/88/108), near the train station, is another welcoming place.

Hotelli Finn (☎ 684 4360, fax 6844 3610; ⓦ www.hotellifinn.fi; Kalevankatu 3B; singles/doubles €65/80, Fri & Sat €55/70) is a small hotel occupying the top floors of a central city building.

Hotel Anna (☎ 616 621, fax 602 664, ⓦ www.hotelanna.com; Annankatu 1; singles/doubles from €100/135) is a popular mid-range hotel that fills up fast. Rates include buffet breakfast but sauna is extra.

Hotel Kämp (☎ 576 111, fax 576 1122; ⓦ www.hotelkamp.fi; Pohjoisesplanadi 29; doubles from €330) is Helsinki's finest, and most exclusive, hotel. The original building dates from 1887 and it was restored and reopened in 1998. The rooms vary from standard to spectacular – but even the luxurious Mannerheim Suite is way over the top at €2624 per night! You can take in a little of the opulence in the front bar.

Places to Eat

Unsurprisingly, Helsinki has far and away the best range of cafés and Finnish and international restaurants in the country – take advantage of it. If you're self-catering, stock up at **Aleppo**, a supermarket in the pedestrian tunnel by the train station. The **kauppahalli**

(Eteläranta 1) is a brilliant place for cheap filled sandwiches, snacks and fresh produce. The **kauppatori** is the place to fill up on fish soup and other Finnish snacks.

For cheap fast food, it's hard to go past the basement of the sprawling **Forum shopping centre** (Mannerheimintie 20) which has an atrium-covered food court with everything from Asian noodles to burgers and kebabs.

Cafés Helsinki University has numerous student **cafeterias** around the city, where meals cost less than €5. These include **UniCafé** (Hietaniemenkatu 14) below Hostel Academica, **Porthania** (Hallituskatu 11-13) and the huge **Ylioppilasaukio** (Mannerheimintie 3B), next to Zetor in the city centre.

There are a number of good cafés around Esplanadi Park. On any budget, **Café Esplanade** (Pohjoisesplanadi 37; sandwiches €3-5) is perfect, with oversized Danish pastries and Finnish *pulla* (wheat bun) for €2, as well as spectacular salads. **Café Strindberg** (Pohjoisesplanadi 33) is twice the price, but twice as classy; tables at the front (waiter service) are at a premium, and the upstairs lounge is all class.

Café Ekberg (Bulevardi 9; buffet breakfast & lunch €7.20) is Helsinki's oldest café and one of the best places for breakfast in the city. The lunch buffet is also great value.

Café Lasipalasti, on the ground floor of the multimedia centre, specialises in Finnish food and has a €7 soup and salad buffet.

Wayne's Coffee (Kaisaniemenkatu 3) is unbeatable for its muffins and the salads, sandwiches and coffee aren't bad either.

Down by Kaivopuisto Park, with great views down to Harakka Island is **Café Ursula** (☎ 652 817; Ehrenströmintie 3). A little further west around the peninsula, **Café Carusel** is cheaper, less pretentious and a good waterfront café with excellent foccacias.

Restaurants Serving up genuine Lappish specialities is **Lappi** (☎ 645 550; Annankatu 22; mains €15-30). It's a delightfully rustic restaurant with costumed staff. Dishes include breast of snowgrouse and sirloin of elk, as well as various reindeer preparations.

Konstan Möljä (☎ 694 750; Hietalahdenkatu 14; lunch/dinner buffet €7.50/11.50) is the place to go for hearty home-style Finnish fare in a pleasant atmosphere. The buffet always includes reindeer.

Russia's best restaurants are said to be in Helsinki – try a blini or borscht at the tiny and romantic **Babushka Ira** (☎ 680 1405; *Uudenmaankatu 28)* to judge for yourself.

Bar Tapasta *(☎ 640 724; Uudenmaankatu 13)* is an intimate place with a welcoming atmosphere and wonderful tapas and salads from €2 to €7. Wash it all down with a jug of sangria (€16.80).

The ultra-modern and trendy **Wrong Noodle Bar** *(Annankatu 21; meals €6.50-7; open 11am-10pm Mon-Fri, 3pm-10pm Sun)* is hard to beat for a filling bowl of ramen noodles, laksa, satay or curry, including vegetarian.

Iguana *(mains €4.50-10.50)* is a good-value American-style Tex Mex chain with three branches in central Helsinki, including one on Keskuskatu and another on Mannerheimintie.

Maithai *(☎ 685 6850; Annankatu 31-33; mains €10-16; open 11am-11pm Mon-Fri, noon-11pm Sat & Sun)* is an intimate, authentic little place and a local favourite for Thai food.

Tony's Deli *(☎ 641 100; Bulevardi 2; mains €8.50-11.50)* is a stylish, low-key Italian place, with pasta from €10 and Helsinki's best antipasto. The antipasto buffet on Monday evenings is not cheap at €16, but is something special and includes tiramisu for dessert.

Zetor *(☎ 666 966; Mannerheimintie 3-5; mains €8-12)* is a spoofy Finnish restaurant with deeply ironic tractor decor. It's owned by film maker Aki Kaurismäki and designed by those crazy guys from the Leningrad Cowboys.

Eatz *(☎ 687 7240; Mikonkatu 15; mains €10-20)* manages to serve up everything from Thai and Indian to Italian and even has a sushi bar. It's also the cornerstone of Helsinki's biggest summer beer terrace.

Entertainment

Helsinki has a lively and sophisticated nightlife scene that's fast becoming the envy of northern Europe. In summer, drinking starts early at the many **beer terraces** that have sprouted up all over town. Helsinki's biggest summer terrace is along Mikonkatu where hundreds of chairs and tables crowd the sidewalk in front of Eatz, On the Rocks and Barfly. After about 4pm on a sunny day it's difficult to score a seat here, but the atmosphere is fantastic.

Bars, Pubs & Clubs In summer the bright red pub tram, **Spårakoff** *(€7, beer €5)* shuttles around the city. The terminus is on Mikonkatu, opposite Eatz restaurant and departing on the hour between 2pm and 7pm from Tuesday to Saturday.

Vanha *(Mannerheimintie 3)*, a music bar in a beautiful 19th-century students' house, is popular with students, though it's more interesting from the outside than within.

Kappeli, in the middle of Esplanade Park near the kauppatori, has one of the city's most popular summer terraces, facing a stage where various bands and musicians regularly play in summer. Inside, there's a vault-like brewery pub in the cellar.

Ateljee Bar *(Yrjönkatu 26)* is a tiny perch on the roof of the Sokos Hotel Torni, and is worth ascending just for the views of the city. Another bar-with-a-view is on the roof of the **Palace Hotel.**

Molly Malone's *(Kaisaniemenkatu 1C)* is a typically exuberant Irish pub and one of the best places in Helsinki to meet travellers, expats and Finns. There's live music on most nights upstairs, where it's shoulder-to-shoulder Guinness consumption.

If you're young and/or beautiful, or just trying, **Soda** *(Ⓦ www.barsoda.fi; Uudenmaankatu 16-20)* is for you; its house and techno music draw shiny happy people most nights. The ultra chic club above is **Teatter** *(Pohjoisespa 2)*, which has space for 300 people and a beautifully designed bar on the middle level.

More down-to-earth is the stylish **Mother Bar & Kitchen** *(☎ 612 3990; Eerikinkatu 2)*, with DJs playing drum & bass and acid jazz music four nights a week, giving off a wonderful vibe.

Corona *(Eerikinkatu 15)* and **Moscow** next door are run by film makers Aki and Mika Kaurismäki; both attract a savvy, grungy crowd. Corona has about 20 pool tables. Farther down the street, the **Saunabar** *(☎ 685 5550; Eerikinkatu 27)*, downstairs at the rear of the building, is popular with students and does indeed have saunas.

Away from the centre, in the suburb of Kallio, **Rytmi** *(Toinen Linja 2)* is a funky little bar with DJs playing on weekends.

If you're partying late, **Club Helsinki** *(Yliopistonkatu 8)* is a mainstream dance club open till 4am and popular with a youthful Helsinkian crowd.

Gay & Lesbian Venues By Scandinavian standards, Helsinki has a low-key gay scene but **Lost & Found** (☎ 680 1010; Annankatu 6; open until 4am) and the associated **Hideaway Bar** is a sophisticated place that gets busy around midnight. More vibrant are **DTM** (Annankatu 32), and the industrial 'eurobar' **Con Hombres** (☎ 608 826; Eerinkinkatu 14).

Jazz One of Helsinki's best jazz clubs is **Storyville** (☎ 408 007; Museokatu 8). An older crowd with deeper wallets boogie-woogie to traditional, Dixieland and New Orleans jazz most nights. Bands start at 8pm and usually play till 4am.

Cinemas One of Europe's largest multiplex cinemas, screening mostly recent American movies is **Tennispalatsi** (☎ 0600-007 007; Salomonkatu 15); there are several other big cinemas in the centre. The **Orion Theatre** (☎ 6154 0201; Eerikinkatu 15) is a cinema with a fondness for Woody Allen.

Opera, Theatre & Ballet For concerts and performances, see Helsinki This Week or inquire at the tourist office. Opera, ballet and classical concerts are held at the **Opera House** (Helsinginkatu 58; tickets from €10), but not during summer.

Spectator Sports

Sporting events in Helsinki are numerous; the best is ice hockey in the city's indoor arena at the Olympic Stadium off Mannerheimintie, with matches played between September and March. Ask at the tourist office – or any bar – for match times.

Getting There & Away

Air There are flights to Helsinki from all major European cities. Vantaa airport, one of Europe's most user-friendly terminals, is 19km north of Helsinki.

Finnair (☎ 0203-140160 for reservations; Asema-aukio 3; open Mon-Sat) flies to 20 Finnish cities, generally at least once a day but several times daily on routes such as Turku, Tampere, Rovaniemi and Oulu. Its office is near the train station.

Bus Purchase long-distance and express bus tickets at the **main bus station** (open 7am-7pm Mon-Fri, 7am-5pm Sat & 9am-6pm

Sun), which is off Mannerheimintie, or on the bus itself.

Train A pedestrian tunnel links the train station to Helsinki's metro system. There is a separate counter for buying tickets for the international trains.

Express trains run daily to Turku, Tampere and Lappeenranta, and there's a choice of day and overnight trains to Oulu, Rovaniemi and Joensuu. There are also daily trains to the Russian cities of Vyborg, St Petersburg and Moscow.

Boat International ferries depart from four terminals and travel to Stockholm, Tallinn, and Travemünde in Germany. See this chapter's introductory Getting There & Away section for details.

Ferry tickets can be bought at the terminals, from the ferry companies' offices in the centre or (in some cases) from the city tourist office. Book tickets in advance from June to August.

Silja Line (☎ 0203-74552) offices are at Mannerheimintie 2 and in the Olympia ferry terminal. The **Viking Line** (☎ 123 577) office is at Mannerheimintie 14 and in the Katajanokka terminal.

Nordic Jet Line (☎ 681 770) is in the Kanava terminal. **Eckerö Line** (☎ 228 8544) is at Mannerheimintie 10 and the Länsiterminaali (West Terminal).

Tallink (☎ 2282 1222) is at Erottajankatu 19. A catamaran service to Tallinn departs from Kanava Terminal.

Kanava and Katajanokka terminals are served by bus No 13 and tram Nos 2, 2V and 4; Olympia and Makasiini terminals by tram Nos 3B and 3T; and Länsiterminaali by bus No 15.

Getting Around

To/From the Airport Bus No 615 (€3; 30 minutes, Helsinki Card not valid) shuttles between Vantaa airport (all international and domestic flights) and platform No 10 at Rautatientori (Railway Square) next to the main train station.

Finnair buses (€4.90) depart from the Finnair office at Asema-aukio, also next to the main train station, every 20 minutes from 5am to midnight. There are also door-to-door **airport taxis** (☎ 10 64 64; W www.airporttaxi .fi) at €16.80 per person.

FINLAND

Public Transport Central Helsinki is easy enough to get around on foot or by bicycle, but there's also a metro line and a reasonably comprehensive tram, bus and train network. A one-hour flat-fare ticket for the bus, tram, metro, Suomenlinna ferry and local trains within Helsinki's HKL network (W www .hel.fi/HKL) costs €2 when purchased on board, €1.40 when purchased in advance. The ticket allows unlimited transfers but should be validated in the stamping machine on board when you first use it. A single tram ticket (no transfers) is €1.50/1.

Tourist tickets are available at €4.20/8.40/ 12.60 for one/three/five days; 10-trip tickets cost €12.80. Alternatively, the Helsinki Card gives you free travel anywhere within Helsinki (see the Information section earlier for details).

There are also regional tickets for travel by bus or train to neighbouring cities such as Vantaa and Espoo which cost €3 for a single one-hour ticket, €7.50 for one day and €22 for the 10-trip ticket. Children's tickets are usually half-price. The penalty for travelling without a valid ticket is €42.

HKL offices at the Rautatientori and Hakaniemi metro stations (open weekdays) sell tickets and passes, as do many of the city's R-kiosks.

The *Helsinki Route Map*, available at HKL offices and the city tourist office, is good for making sense of local transport.

Bicycle Helsinki is ideal for cycling: the small inner city is flat, and there are well-marked and high-quality bicycle paths. Pick up a copy of the Helsinki cycling map from the tourist office.

The city of Helsinki provides 300 distinctive green 'City Bikes' at stands within a radius of 2km from the kauppatori – although in summer you'll wonder where they're all hiding.

These bikes are free: you deposit a €2 coin into the stand which locks them, then reclaim it when you return the bike to any stand.

For something a bit more sophisticated, **Greenbike** (☎ 8502 2850), in the old railway goods sheds, rents quality bikes for €10 per day, or €15 for 24 hours.

Ecobike is a smaller operation in the small yellow hut across the road from Parliament House.

AROUND HELSINKI
Espoo
☎ 09 • pop 217,000
Espoo is an independent municipality just west of Helsinki and while it ranks as the second-largest city in Finland, it's virtually a suburb of the capital.

The most important sight in Espoo is the **Gallen-Kallela Museum** (☎ 541 3388; W www.gallen-kallela.fi; Gallen-Kallelantie 27; adult/child €8/4; open 10am-6pm daily, closed Mon in Sept), the pastiche studio-castle of Akseli Gallen-Kallela, one of the most notable of Finnish painters. The Art Nouveau building was designed by the artist and is now a museum of his work. Take tram No 4 from central Helsinki to Munkkiniemi, then walk 2km or take bus No 33 (Saturday and Sunday only).

The **Espoo Car Museum** (☎ 855 7178; Pakankylän Kartano Manor; adult/child €5/ 2; open 11am-5.30pm Tues-Sun June-Aug) has more than 100 vintage motor vehicles dating from the early 20th century.

Architecture buffs should check out the **Otaniemi University** campus – the main building and library were designed by Alvar Aalto.

Espoo's annual **Jazz Festival** (☎ 8165 7234), held in late April, is top-notch.

Porvoo
☎ 019 • pop 43,000
Porvoo (Swedish: Borgå), a picturesque medieval town and Finland's second-oldest (founded in 1346), makes a perfect day or overnight trip from Helsinki, 50km away. Porvoo has a distinctly Swedish feel around the cobbled **Old Town.** Its charming wooden houses, meandering streets and active riverfront make it great for exploring.

The historic **Porvoo church** and several good **museums** – including the preserved 19th-century home of Finland's national poet JL Runeberg – are the main sights; there are guided walks in the Old Town and river cruises in summer. The **tourist office** (☎ 520 231; W www .porvoo.fi; Rihkamakatu 4) has details.

The HI **Porvoo Hostel** (☎/fax 523 0012; W www.porvoohostel.cjb.net; Linnankos-kenkatu 1-3; dorm beds €.10.50, singles/ doubles €24.50/27, linen hire €4) is in a lovely old building with spotless rooms and a well-equipped kitchen. You can pitch a tent at **Camping Kokonniemi** (☎ 581 967; e myyntipalvelu@lomaliitto.fi; tent sites

€15, 4-person cabins €62; open June–mid-Aug), 2km south of Porvoo town.

Porvoo has some good cafés and bars in the Old Town and along the waterfront. Try **Café Blanka** on the old town square, and the inexpensive **Café Old Town**, where 'young' Porvoo sits outside and watches 'old' Porvoo drift by. Good bars include **Poorvoon Paahtimo** (*Mennerheiminkatu 2*), right at the bridge and with a great little terrace hanging over the water; and the eccentric **Café Beach**, with Porvoo's biggest summer terrace and weirdest crowd.

The boat restaurant **Glückauf** (☎ 54761; mains €10-20) is a 19th-century sailing ship specialising in seafood, and there's a cheaper terrace menu (ie, you eat on the river bank rather than the boat) for €6 to €8.

There are buses every 30 minutes between Porvoo and Helsinki (€7.90, one hour), but the best way to reach Porvoo in summer is by ferry.

The steamship **JL Runeberg** (☎ 019-524 3331) sails daily except Thursday from Helsinki in summer (one way/return €20/29). Since the trip takes almost four hours, you can opt to return by bus or, on Saturdays in summer, on the vintage diesel train (combined ferry/boat ticket €27).

Järvenpåå & Tuusulan Rantatie

The Tuusulan Rantatie (Tuusula Lake Road; W www.jarvenpaa.fi) is a narrow road along Tuusula Lake (Tuusulanjärvi) about 40km north of Helsinki. A major stop along the 'museum road' is **Halosenniemi** (*adult/child €5/2; open 11am-4pm Tues-Sun*), the Karelian-inspired, log-built National Romantic studio of artist Pekka Halonen.

Closer to the town of Järvenpää is the family home of composer Jean Sibelius, now a museum. **Ainola** (☎ 287 322; Ainolantie; W www.ainola.fi; adult/student/child €5/2/1; open 10am-5pm Tues-Sun May-Sept), built on this beautiful forested site in 1904, contains original furniture, paintings, books and a piano owned by the Sibelius family.

Järvenpää Camping & Hostel (☎ 7425 5200; W www.matkailukeskus.com; Stålhanentie 5; tent sites €12, 2-5–person cabins €20-50, hostel rooms €17.50-60.50) is a camping resort on the western shore of Tuusulanjärvi about 2.5km from Järvenpää town centre.

Turku & the Southern Coast

Nowhere in Finland are there so many historical monuments as along the southern coast between Turku and Hamina. This region is dotted with medieval churches, old manors and castles, and is strongly influenced by early Swedish settlers.

The historic 'King's Road', which runs from Turku to St Petersburg, passes through here.

TURKU
☎ 02 • pop 171,000

Though you might not know it due to its predominantly modern buildings, Turku (Åbo) is the oldest city in Finland, founded in the 13th century, and also the former Swedish capital. For many travellers it's their first taste of Finland since there are regular ferry connections from Sweden via the Åland islands. Turku has an impressive castle, a wonderfully active riverside (in summer at least) and, if you have time, is the ideal base for exploring the convoluted southwestern archipelago.

Information

The busy city **tourist office** (☎ 262 7444; W www.turkutouring.fi; Aurakatu 4; open 8.30am-6pm Mon-Fri, 9am-4pm Sat & Sun) hires out bikes and sells the **Turku Card** (€21/28 for one/two days) which gives free admission to most museums and attractions in the region, free public transport and various other discounts.

Forex (Eerikinkatu 12; open 8am-7pm Mon-Fri, 8am-5pm Sat) is the best place to exchange cash and travellers cheques. The **main post office** is at Humalistonkatu 1.

There are several Internet terminals at the **public library** (Linnankatu 2; open Mon-Sat), and there's one free terminal (15 minutes) at the tourist office. **Surf City** (Aninkaistenkatu 3) is an Internet café charging €2 for 30 minutes, with discounts for students.

Things to See & Do

Vocal locals are quick to claim that Turku has more museums than Helsinki, though only a handful stand out. The city's 50 museums are generally open daily in summer, closed Monday in winter and charge €3.40 admission.

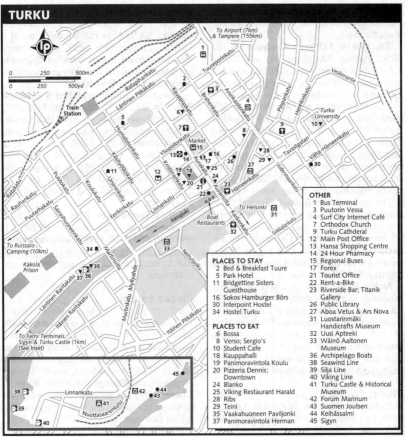

TURKU

To Airport (7km) & Tampere (155km)

Train Station

Market

To Helsinki

Boat Restaurants

To Ruissalo Camping (10km)

Kakola Prison

To Ferry Terminals, Sigyn & Turku Castle (1km) (See Inset)

Linnankatu

Nuottasaarenkatu

Turku University

OTHER
1 Bus Terminal
3 Puutorin Vessa
4 Surf City Internet Café
7 Orthodox Church
9 Turku Cathdral
12 Main Post Office
13 Hansa Shopping Centre
14 24 Hour Pharmacy
15 Regional Buses
17 Forex
21 Tourist Office
22 Rent-a-Bike
23 Riverside Bar; Titanik Gallery
26 Public Library
27 Aboa Vetus & Ars Nova
31 Luostarinmäki Handicrafts Museum
32 Uusi Apteeki
33 Wäinö Aaltonen Museum
36 Archipelago Boats
38 Seawind Line
39 Silja Line
40 Viking Line
41 Turku Castle & Historical Museum
42 Forum Marinum
43 Suomen Joutsen
44 Keihässalmi
45 Sigyn

PLACES TO STAY
2 Bed & Breakfast Tuure
5 Park Hotel
11 Bridgettine Sisters Guesthouse
16 Sokos Hamburger Börs
30 Interpoint Hostel
34 Hostel Turku

PLACES TO EAT
6 Bossa
8 Verso; Sergio's
10 Student Cafe
18 Kauppahalli
19 Panimoravintola Koulu
20 Pizzeria Dennis; Downtown
24 Blanko
25 Viking Restaurant Harald
28 Ribs
29 Teini
35 Vaakahuoneen Paviljonki
37 Panimoravintola Herman

A visit to the mammoth **Turku Castle** (☎ 262 0300; adult/child €6.50/4.50, guided tours €1.50; open 10am-6pm daily mid-May–mid-Sept, shorter hrs winter), near the harbour, is a must. Founded in 1280 at the mouth of the Aurajoki, the castle has been growing ever since. Notable occupants have included Count Per Brahe, founder of many towns in Finland, and Sweden's King Eric XIV, who was imprisoned in the castle's Round Tower in the late 16th century, having been declared insane. Guided tours of the stronghold area are given in English at 11am, 12.10pm, 1.10pm, 2.10pm, 3.10pm and 4.10pm, but do not include the Renaissance rooms on the upper floor, or the extensive museums in the bailey section of the castle, so allow time to explore those yourself.

The open-air **Luostarinmäki Handicrafts Museum** (☎ 262 0350, Luostarinmäki; adult/child €3.40/2.60, guided tours €1.60/1.40; open 10am-6pm daily mid-Apr–mid-Sept, 10am-3pm Tues-Sun mid-Sept–mid-Apr), in the only surviving 18th-century area of this medieval town (Turku has been razed 30 times by fire), is the best of its kind in Finland. In summer artisans work inside its 40 old wooden houses and musicians stroll its paths.

Forum Marinum (☎ 282 9511; Linnankatu 72; adult/child €10/5) is an impressive new maritime museum near the castle. As well as a better-than-average exhibition space devoted to Turku's shipping background, it incorporates three **museum ships**: the mine layer *Keihässalmi*, the three-masted barque *Sigyn*; and the impressive 1902 sailing ship

Suomen Joutsen (Swan of Finland). The ships can be visited independently of the museum for €4/2.

The **Wäinö Aaltonen Museum** (☎ 262 0850; Itäinen Rantakatu 38; adult/child €3.40/2.60) on the south side of the river has permanent exhibitions of this important Finnish artist's sculptures and paintings.

The **Aboa Vetus** and **Ars Nova** (☎ 250 0552; Itäinen Rantakatu 4-6; adult/child to each €7/5, combined ticket €9.50/7; open 11am-7pm daily May–mid-Sept, Thurs-Sun Sept-Dec), two museums under the one roof, are respectively an archaeological exhibition and a modern art collection. The **Titanik** gallery nearby often has great contemporary work.

The commanding **Turku Cathedral** (*Tuomiokirkkokatu*), dating from the 13th century, is the national shrine and 'mother church' of the Evangelical-Lutheran Church of Finland. Services are still held here regularly and there's a **museum** (€2; open daily) containing church relics and artworks.

Archipelago cruises are a popular activity in summer, with daily departures from Martinsilta bridge. The best option is a cruise out to Naantali aboard the steamship **SS Ukkopekka** (☎ 515 3300; w www.ukkopekka.fi; one way/return €13/18) daily at 10am and 2pm from June to August. The trip takes 1½ hours and you can have lunch on board (€10 to €13).

Places to Stay

Ruissalo Camping (☎ 262 5100, fax 262 5101; tent sites €9, double rooms €23, villa €59; open June-late Aug) is on Ruissalo island, 10km west of the city centre. There are no cabins, but there is a villa with two- to four-bed rooms, and nice beaches. Take Bus No 8 from the market square

HI-affiliated **Hostel Turku** (☎ 231 6578, fax 231 1708; Linnankatu 39; dorm beds €11, singles & doubles €34.50; reception open 6am-10am & 3pm-midnight daily) is well located on the river close to the town centre and is one of the busiest hostels in Finland. Facilities include a well-equipped kitchen, laundry (€1 per hour), lockers and bike hire.

Interpoint Hostel (☎ 231 4011, fax 231 2584; Vähä-Hämeenkatu 12a; beds €8.50-10.50) is a friendly, central YMCA place open only for a month between 15 July and 15 August. It's the cheapest place in Turku but for good reason – 30 mattresses on the floor and one shower!

The **Bridgettine Sisters Guesthouse** (☎ 250 1910; Ursininkatu 15A; singles/doubles €42/61) is run by the nuns of a Catholic convent. The clean, simple rooms are a bargain and include breakfast. Silence is expected around the corridors and reception areas after 10pm. Book ahead.

Close to the bus terminal, **Bed & Breakfast Tuure** (☎ 233 0230; Tuureporinkatu 17C; singles/doubles €34/47) is another secure, friendly option. Clean rooms have shared bath.

Park Hotel (☎ 251 9666, fax 251 9696; Rauhankatu 1; singles/doubles €105/130, discounted to €80/105), in a lovely Art Nouveau building dating from 1904, is Turku's most romantic and ambient hotel by a long shot.

Sokos Hamburger Börs (☎ 337 381; Kauppiaskatu 6; singles/doubles €120/140, discounted to €70), overlooking the market square, is the town's swishest business hotel with an assortment of popular nightclubs and restaurants.

Places to Eat

There are plenty of cheap eateries around Turku's market square, and in the **kauppahalli** (open Mon-Sat). It's always possible to get a cheap meal at the Turku University **cafeteria**.

Next to the bridge is the ultra-chic **Blanko** (☎ 233 3966; Aurakatu 1), where Turku's gorgeous young things shake their booty to DJs on Friday and Saturday night. When not striking a sullen pose the staff whip up an excellent tapas menu.

Pizzeria Dennis (☎ 469 1191; Linnankatu 17; meals €8-11) doesn't look much from the outside, but within is a warren of cosy rooms adorned with chianti bottles and strings of garlic. The traditional Italian menu includes an innovative range of pizzas and pasta.

Verso (Linnankatu 3; lunch from €6) is a fine vegetarian restaurant offering lunch specials. A few doors down the street is **Sergio's** (Linnanlatu 1; mains €8-9.50), an Italian restaurant serving great pasta, Italian wines and the best coffee in town.

Across the river, **Ribs** (mains €12-20) is a trendy steakhouse with a great summer terrace; the speciality is ribs and wings. For something more Finnish, **Teini** (Uudenmaankatu 1; mains €7-12) across the square has traditional local cuisine, including vegetarian dishes; at the rear of the restaurant is a fantastic underground bar.

The riverfront **Vaakahuoneen Paviljonki** (☎ 515 3324; Linnankatu 38; mains €7-15, fish buffet €8) is *the* place to go for great value food and entertainment. As well as an à la carte menu of snacks, pasta, pizzas and steak, there's a daily 'archipelago fish buffet' (11am-10pm), plus a changing ethnic buffet (Thai, Vietnamese, Indian etc). On top of this there's live music, usually traditional jazz, most days in summer.

Panimoravintola Koulu (☎ 274 575;, Eerikinkatu 18) is in an enormous former schoolhouse built in 1889. Upstairs is an upmarket restaurant (mains €11.60 to €15), downstairs a brewery pub, beer garden and wine bar serving decent €7 lunches. **Panimoravintola Herman** (Läntinen Rantakatu 37) is another decent brewery pub/restaurant near Hostel Turku.

Viking Restaurant Harald (☎ 276 5050; Aurakatu 3; mains €11-21) is a theme restaurant where you get to mix with Norse warriors and eat with your hands. There are three-course set meals from €24.

Turku has some good ethnic restaurants. **Bossa** (☎ 251 5880; Kauppiaskatu 12; mains €11-16) is probably the only Brazilian restaurant in Finland. It's an intimate place with live Latin music most nights.

Entertainment

In summer the heart of Turku's nightlife scene is along the river. The evening usually begins on any of half a dozen **boats** lining the south bank of the river. Although some of these also serve food, they are primarily floating beer terraces with music and lots of shipboard socialising.

Hard-up locals gather on the grassy riverbank drinking takeaway alcohol. Nearby, the **Riverside Bar** is a good spot with street dancing on Tuesday night.

South of the river, **Uusi Apteeki** (Kaskenkatu 1) is a wonderful bar in a converted old pharmacy; the antique shelving and desks have been retained, but they are filled with hundreds of old beer bottles. For pure novelty value, **Puutorin Vessa**, in the middle of a small square near the bus terminal, is worth popping into. It was once a public toilet!

There's live jazz most days at **Vaakahuoneen Paviljonki** (see Places to Eat). For live rock music, the slightly down-at-heel **Downtown**, on the corner near Pizzeria Dennis, is worth a look.

Getting There & Away

Finnair flies regularly from Stockholm and Helsinki to the Turku airport, 8km north of the city.

From the main bus terminal at Aninkaistentulli here are hourly express buses to Helsinki (€20.90, 2½ hours), and frequent services to Tampere (€16.80, two hours), Rauma (€11.40, 1½ hours) and other points in southern Finland. Regional buses depart from the market square.

Express trains run frequently to and from Helsinki (€19.80, two hours), Tampere (€16.60, 1¾ hours), Oulu (€60.20, seven hours), Rovaniemi (€67.40, 10 hours). For Oulu and Rovaniemi you'll need to change in Tampere. There are direct train connections from Turku harbour to Helsinki. Bus No 30 shuttles between the centre and the train station.

Silja Line and Viking Line ferries sail from Stockholm (9½ hours) and Mariehamn (six hours). Seawind Line sails to Stockholm via Långnäs (Åland). All three have offices at the harbour, and Silja Line and Viking Line also have offices in the Hansa shopping centre opposite the market square.

Getting Around

Bus No 1 runs to and from the airport and between the centre (€1.80, 25 minutes). This same bus also goes from the market square to the harbour.

The city and regional bus services (both gold and blue buses) are frequent and cost €1.80 for a single journey or €4.20 for a 24-hour ticket.

Bikes can be hired from **Rent-A-Bike** (☎ 041-5123430), on the river just around the corner from the tourist office, for €9/45 a day/week, or from the tourist office itself.

AROUND TURKU
Naantali

☎ 02 • pop 12,500

Naantali, 13km west of Turku, is one of Finland's loveliest seaside towns, but that can sometimes be lost on the hordes of Finnish families descending on their star attraction, the extraordinarily popular **Moomin World** theme park (day pass €13; open June-Aug). It's a sort of Disneyland based on the popular children's books written by Tove Janssen and set on an island linked to the mainland by a footbridge.

FINLAND

The village was developed after the founding of a convent in the 1440s and today the harbour, lined with cafés and restaurants, the delightful cobbled **Old Town** and the huge **Convent Church** are enough incentive for a day trip here from Turku. Tourist information is available at **Naantali Tourist Service** (☎ 435 9800, fax 435 0852; Kaivotori 2; open 9am-6pm Mon-Fri, 10am-3pm Sat & Sun June–mid-Aug, 9am-4.30pm Mon-Fri mid-Aug–May) near the harbour.

Kulturanta, the summer residence of the president of Finland, is a fanciful stone castle on nearby Luonnonmaa island, surrounded by a 56ha estate with beautiful, extensive rose gardens. It can only be visited by guided tour; book through the tourist office.

Places to Stay & Eat Although an easy day trip from Turku, spending a night here is a good way to beat the crowds. **Naantali Camping** (☎ 435 0855, 435 0850; Kuparivuori; tent sites €13-17, 2–6-person cabins €30-100; open April-Oct), 400m south of the town centre, is an exceptional camping ground.

Naantali Summer Hotel (☎ 445 5660; Opintie 3; rooms per person €31; open June–mid-Aug) is a modern hostel-type place near to, and run by, the spa hotel.

Hemtellet Kotelli (☎ 435 1419; Luostarinkatu 13; singles/doubles €55/60, breakfast €5) is a fine early-19th-century villa, beautifully kept and furnished. The dining room has heaps of style.

Naantali has some great restaurants curving around the harbour, plus a couple of good cafés in the Old Town. **Merisali** (Nunnakatu 1; buffet lunch/dinner €9/10.50, Sun lunch €12), just below the Convent Church, has a shaded terrace and a mind-blowing smorgasbord for lunch and dinner – pack an appetite!

Café Antonius (Mannerheiminkatu 9) is an unbeatable café in Villa Antonius, with homemade gingerbread and other mouthwatering sweets.

Getting There & Away There are buses every 15 minutes from Turku (€3.40, 20 minutes), and in summer the steamship *Ukkopekka* cruises between Turku and Naantali several times daily (see the Turku section for details).

Louhisaari Manor

The village of Askainen, 30km north-west of Turku, is the setting for stunning Louhisaari

Manor (☎ 431 2555; adult/child €3.50/1; open 11am-5pm daily mid-May–Aug) and its lavishly decorated rooms, including a 'ghost room', and its extensive museum and gardens. The five-storey Dutch Renaissance-style manor was purchased by the Mannerheim family in 1795, and Finland's greatest military leader and president, CGE Mannerheim, was born here in 1867. There are three to four buses daily from Turku to Askainen.

KEMIÖ ISLAND
☎ 02

Kemiö Island offers excellent possibilities for bicycle tours. The access point is the village of Kemiö, which has a **tourist office** (☎ 423 572; Arkadiantie 13). The many 18th-century churches and the museums of **Sagalund** and **Dalsbruk** are worth a visit.

The Kasnäs harbour, on a small island south of Kemiö Island, is the main jumping-off point for regional archipelago ferries. Visit **Sinisimpukka** (Naturum; ☎ 466 6290; open 10am-6pm daily June-Aug) for information on the South-West Archipelago National Park.

Pensionat och Vandrarhotell (☎ 424 553; Kulla; dorm beds €15.50, singles/doubles €17.50/26, with attached bath & breakfast €39/64; open Mar-Dec) in the village of Dragsfjärd is one of the homeliest hostels in Finland. It's beautifully furnished, has several common areas, a kitchen, a big garden, a sauna and bicycles and boats for rent.

All buses and trains between Helsinki and Turku stop at Salo, which has half a dozen daily bus connections to Kemiö Island.

TAMMISAARI
☎ 019 • pop 14,700

The seaside town of Tammisaari (Ekenäs), 96km south-west of Helsinki, is one of Finland's oldest. In 1546 King Gustav Vasa intended it to be a trading port to rival Tallinn in Estonia; the idea failed, but the attractive Gamla Stan (Old Town) still stands. Free walking tours are offered by the **tourist office** (☎ 263 2212) in summer. Although a popular family resort, Tammisaari is not as quaint as Hanko, a little further down the coast.

Nearby is the region's most impressive sight, the 14th-century **Raseborg castle ruins** (☎ 234015; adult/child €1/0.50; open 10am-8pm), 15km east of Tammisaari, and about 2km from the village of Snappertuna.

Ormnäs Camping *(☎ 241 4434; sites per person/tent €6.50/10, 2/4-person cottages €31/42; open April-Sept)* is at the seaside 1km from the town centre, next to Ramsholmen Natural Park. There's a café and bikes and boats can be rented here.

Ekenäs Vandrarhem *(☎ 241 6393, fax 241 3917; Höijerintie 10; dorm beds from €10, singles/doubles €19.50/24; open mid-May–mid-Aug)*, is an HI-affiliated summer hostel with tidy, modern apartment-style rooms (four rooms share a kitchen and bathroom). Reception is open from 3pm to 9pm and there's a sauna and a laundry.

There are frequent daily bus and train services from Turku and Helsinki to Tammisaari, continuing on to Hanko.

HANKO
☎ 019 • pop 10,600

Hanko (Hangö) blossomed as a resort town in the late 19th and early 20th centuries, when it was a glamorous summer retreat for Russian nobles, artists and tsars. These visitors built grand wooden **villas** on the sandy shore east of the harbour. Some of these villas are now guesthouses – providing uniquely Finnish accommodation.

Hanko Camping Silversand *(☎ 248 5500;* W *www.lomaliitto.fi; Hopeahietikko; tent sites €13.50, cabins from €48; open June–mid-Aug)* is 4km from town on a stretch of beach. There's also a **motel** here with singles/doubles for €51/73.

Villa Doris *(☎ 248 1228; Appelgrenintie 23; singles/doubles from €53/65)* and **Villa Maija** *(☎ 248 2900; Appelgrenintie7; singles/doubles from €50/70)* are among the stylish B&B villas in the area known as the spa park. Rooms, with shared bathroom, are beautifully decorated.

Across from the East Harbour is a string of excellent restaurants in converted wooden storehouses, most specialising in seafood. Try **Origo** for fine dining, or the inexpensive **Mad Dog** for cheap *grilli* food. **Park Café**, in the spa park, is an excellent Belgian café-bar with free Internet access.

EAST OF HELSINKI
Ruotsinpyhtää
☎ 019 • pop 3200

This lovely village is a good place to while away a day or two. At its heart are the quaint brick ruins of the 18th-century **Strömfors**

Iron Works, which is now a museum. The area is famous for its **fishing**.

Finnhostel Krouvinmäki *(☎ 618 474, 0400-492 161, fax 618 475; singles/doubles €23/45.50; open June–mid-Aug or by prior arrangement)* is a wonderful HI-affiliated hostel in a renovated former tavern house. All rooms are twins and there's a good kitchen and laundry.

Myllyravintola is in a 17th-century former mill on a lovely quiet pond. In summer the restaurant has a terrace with live music and dancing. The menu includes light meals, wood-fired pizzas and some Finnish specialities – the salmon soup is something special.

HAMINA
☎ 05 • pop 10,000

Just 40km west of the Russian border, the small town of Hamina is surrounded by crumbling **fortifications**, begun by panicky Swedes in 1722 after they lost Vyborg to Russia (the wall wasn't paranoia: shortly after it was built, in marched the Russians). There's not a lot left of the fortress, but Hamina's unusual octagonal town plan, several museums and a lively harbour scene provide enough interest if you're taking the coastal route towards Karelia.

The main **tourist office** *(☎ 749 5251;* W *www.hamina.fi; Raatihuoneentori 1; open 9am-4pm Mon-Fri)* is in the town hall building in Old Hamina, but there's a **summer office** *(open 9am-6pm Mon-Fri, 10am-3pm Sat & Sun June–mid-Aug)* in the Lipputorni (Flagtower) at the kauppatori.

The most interesting place to stay in Hamina during summer is aboard the historic steamship **SS Hyöky** *(☎ 040-763 3757; singles/doubles €30/40)*, moored in Tervasaari harbour. There are nine tiny cabins, each with a set of bunks, plus the 'captain's cabin' above deck. The ship also has a bar, a cluttered museum and even a tiny sauna (free for guests).

Hotel Gasthaus *(☎ 354 1434; Kaivokatu 4; singles/doubles €37/55)* is a rustic, central pub with 10 rooms upstairs.

There are several places to eat around the kauppatori and down at the harbour. **Ravintola Patiisa** *(☎ 353 2444; Satamakatu 11; mains €8-15, pizzas €9)* has a popular 1st-floor terrace overlooking the market square.

Express buses go west to Helsinki and east to Vyborg and St Petersburg. There is also a regular local service from Kotka.

FINLAND

Åland

☎ 018 • pop 25,400

The Åland islands are unique and autonomous, with their own flag and culture. A number of Swedish dialects are spoken, and few Ålanders speak Finnish. This situation goes back to a League of Nations' decision in 1921 after a Swedish-Finnish dispute over sovereignty. Åland took its own flag in 1954 and has issued stamps (prized by collectors) since 1984.

Although Åland joined the EU along with Finland in 1995, it was granted a number of exemptions, including duty-free tax laws which allowed the essential ferry services between the islands and mainland Finland and Sweden to continue operating profitably.

The islands are popular for cycling and camping holidays, and Midsummer celebrations here are among the best in Finland. There are medieval parish churches, ruins and fishing villages.

The capital and main (only) town of Åland is Mariehamn, in the south of the main island group. You can take your wheels almost anywhere around the islands using the bridges or the network of car and bicycle ferries.

History

The first settlers set foot on Åland 6000 years ago. More than a hundred Bronze and Iron Age cemeteries have been discovered, and they are clearly signposted as *fornminne*. There are also ruins of Viking Age fortresses in Saltvik. Medieval churches date from the 12th to 15th centuries, and the ones in Finström, Kumlinge, Lemland, Saltvik and Sund are not to be missed, although Hammarland, Eckerö and Jomala's churches are older. Kastelholm Castle, established in the 14th century, is Åland's most striking attraction.

Information

The main tourist office is **Elands Turistinformation** (☎ 24000; 🖳 *www.goaland.net; Storagatan 8*) in Mariehamn, and there are smaller offices in the ferry terminal in Eckerö and at Godby. For accommodation bookings, **Ålandsresor** (☎ 28040; 🖳 *www.alandsresor.fi; Torggatan 2*) in Mariehamn handles hotel, guesthouse and cottage bookings for the entire island and is often the *only* way to secure accommodation. Viking Line and Eckerö Line also make bookings.

Both the euro and Swedish krona are legal tender on Åland. There are ATMs accepting international cards in Mariehamn, and credit cards are as easily used here as on mainland Finland. Finnish telephone cards can be used on Åland, but there are also local cards. Åland uses the Finnish mobile phone network – Sonera and Radiolinja work here but Telia (even if purchased in Finland) does not.

In emergencies call ☎ 112, for police ☎ 10022 and for medical service ☎ 10023.

Getting There & Away

Air Finnair has an office at Skarpansvägen 24 in Mariehamn. There is a weekday direct service to/from Stockholm and daily service to/from Helsinki (€154) via Turku. The airport is 4km north of Mariehamn and there's a connecting bus service.

Boat The main companies operating between Finland and Åland (and on to Sweden) are **Viking Line** and **Silja Line**, while **Eckerö Line** and **Birka Cruises** operate only between Åland and Sweden.

Viking and Silja lines have daily ferries to Mariehamn from Turku as part of their links with Stockholm: you can stop off 'between' countries, which is what many Swedes and Finns do to take advantage of the duty-free shopping on board the ferries. Viking Line also sails from Kapellskär in Sweden.

Birka Cruises sails only between Stockholm and Mariehamn. Eckerö Line sails from Grisslehamn to Eckerö – the latter is the cheapest and quickest route from Sweden to Åland.

Another alternative if you have the time is the smaller local ferries that sail from minor Finnish ports to the remote northern and southern archipelago islands of Åland. Free travel for pedestrians and cyclists is possible from mainland Finland via Korppoo (southern route, from Galtby passenger harbour) or Kustavi (northern route, from Osnäs passenger harbour), but only if you break your journey to stay on one or more islands.

Getting Around

Bus Five main bus lines depart from Mariehamn's regional bus terminal on Torggatan in front of the library. No 1 goes to Hammarland and Eckerö; No 2 to Godby and Geta; No 3 to Godby and Saltvik; No 4 to Godby, Sund and Vårdö (Hummelvik); and No 5 to Lemland and Lumparland (Långnäs).

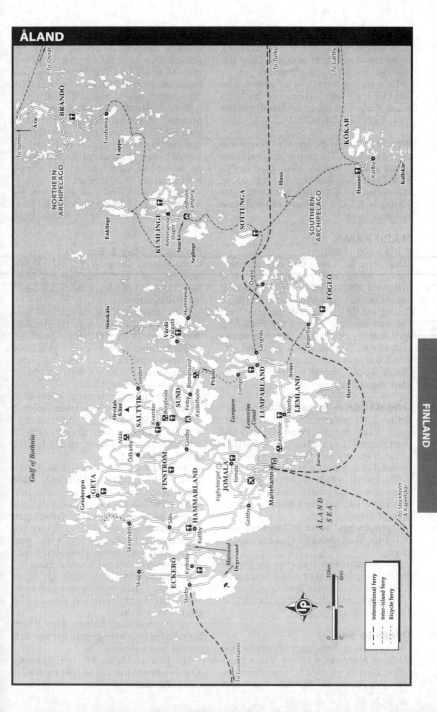

ÅLAND

Boat Ferries are constantly plying the shorter straits, and are free. For longer routes, ferries run according to schedule. These ferries take cars, bikes and pedestrians.

There are also three bicycle ferries in summer (€6 to €9 with bicycle). For timetables ask at the tourist office or **Ålandstrafiken** (*Strandgatan 25, Mariehamn*).

Bicycle Bicycle is the best way to see these flat, rural islands. The most scenic roads have clearly marked separate bike lanes. **Ro-No Rent** (☎ 12 820) has bicycles available at Mariehamn and Eckerö harbours with rates starting at €7/35 a day/week (€13/65 for a mountain bike).

MARIEHAMN
☎ 018 • pop 11,000

Mariehamn, the 'town of a thousand linden trees', is Åland's main port and largest town. In summer it becomes the town of a thousand tourists but still manages to retain its village flavour, and the marinas at the East and West Harbours are quite pretty when loaded up with gleaming sailing boats. The main pedestrian street, Torggatan, is a colourful and crowded hive of activity, and there are some fine museums – enough to allow a leisurely day's exploration.

Orientation & Information
The town lies on a peninsula and has two harbours, Västra Hamnen (West Harbour) and Östra Hamnen (East Harbour). The main ferry terminals are at Västra Hamnen but the more colourful local marina is at Östra Hamnen.

The **tourist office** (☎ 24000; W www .goaland.net; *Storagatan 8*), on the main east-west Esplanade, has free Internet access, as does the **library**.

The **main post office** in Torggatan sells collectible Åland postage stamps and changes money.

The **police** station is next to the library, and the main **hospital** (☎ 5355; *Norragatan 17*) is one block north of the tourist office.

There is luggage storage in lockers (€2) at the ferry terminal.

Things to See
The stalwarts of Åland are mariners and the **Maritime Museum** (☎ 19930; *Västra Hamnen; adult/child €4.50/2.50; open 9am-5pm daily May-August, till 7pm July, 10am-4pm*

other times), a kitsch museum of fishing and maritime commerce, is devoted to all things nautical. Outside is the museum ship *Pommern* (*€4.50/2.50*), a beautifully preserved four-masted barque built in Glasgow in 1903. A combined ticket to both is €7/3.50.

The fine **Ålands Museum** and **Åland Art Museum** (☎ 25426; *Stadhusparken; adult/ child €2.50/1.70; open 10am-4pm daily, till 8pm Tuesday, closed Monday Sept-April*) are housed jointly. The museum gives an absorbing account of Åland's history and culture, from prehistory to the present.

There are trade and craft displays at the **Köpmannagar** (*Merchant's House; Parkgatan; admission free; open 1pm-3pm Mon-Fri June-Aug*).

Places to Stay & Eat
Gröna Uddens Camping (☎ 21121; *Osternäsvägen; tent sites €17.50; open mid-May-Aug*), 1km south of town, is the closest camping to Mariehamn.

In the absence of any hostels, the next cheapest accommodation is the shabby **Gästhem Kronan** (☎ 12617; *Neptunigatan 52; singles/doubles June-Aug €37/55*). Basic but cleanish rooms have shared bathroom, and the owners also have another guesthouse up the road if Kronan is full.

There are plenty of hotels in Mariehamn. The cheapest and best value is **Hotel Esplanad** (☎ 16444; *Storogatan 5; singles/doubles €53/66; open June-Aug*). Rooms (with TV and attached bath) are not special but it's friendly and central.

Mariehamn has some good cafés and the most active nightlife on the islands. **Café Julius** (*Torggatan 10*) on the pedestrian strip opens early and has plenty of cheap sandwiches, pastries and snacks. **Kaffestugan Svarta Katten** (*Norragatan 15*) is a lovely spot to sample the local speciality, Åland pancakes, made with semolina and served with prunes or strawberry and whipped cream.

Buffalo Saloon (*Strandgatan 12; mains €8-15*) is a popular meeting spot with enormous hamburgers, pasta and pizza, and a great outdoor decking.

On Esplanadgatan, **Buffalo After Beach bar** is a chic little open-fronted bar and club popular with a young crowd.

The boat restaurant **FP von Knorring** (*Östra Hamnen*) has a great beer terrace for sunny afternoons.

SUND
☎ 018 • pop 950

Åland's most striking attraction is the medieval **Kastelholm** *(adult/child €5/3.50; open daily June-Aug)*, in Sund 20km northeast of Mariehamn. You can only visit the castle on a guided tour, run frequently (in English) from June to August. Next to the castle, **Jan Karlsgarden Museum** *(admission free; open 10am-5pm daily June-Aug)* is a typical open-air museum consisting of about 20 wooden buildings, including three windmills, transported here from around the archipelago.

Farther east, the ruins of the Russian fortress at **Bomarsund** are accessible all year, as are the cemeteries on **Prästö Island**. The impressive Russian fortifications date from the 1830s and were destroyed during the Crimean War (1853–56). Near Bomarsund is **Puttes Camping** *(☎ 44016; camping per person €2.50; open May-Aug)*, which also rents cabins.

Café Uffe på Berget is popular for its splendid view over the islands from its 30m observation tower is superb. It's on the main Mariehamn–Sund road near the town of Godby, just before the bridge to Sund.

ECKERÖ
☎ 018 • pop 800

Finland's westernmost municipality, Eckerö is linked by ferry to Sweden, and is thus an extremely popular holiday spot for Swedish families. The ferry terminal is at Storby village, and its historic **Post & Customs building** now houses a café, post office and bank. Bus No 1 runs to Mariehamn.

East from Storby on the road to Mariehamn, the medieval **Eckerö Church** has some beautiful interior paintings. There are other medieval churches worth visiting along the road between Storby and Mariehamn – watch for the signs.

If you're camping head for **Käringsund Camping** *(☎ 38309; Storby; tent sites €8, cabins for 3/4 persons €33/44)*. **Ängstorp Gästhem** *(☎ 38665; Storby; singles/doubles June-Aug €51/59)* is one of the nicest places to stay in Åland. **Storby Logi** *(☎ 39462; singles/doubles €27/52)* is a simple but cheap option right in the village.

NORTHERN ARCHIPELAGO ROUTE

You can visit Jurmo, Brändö, Kumlinge, Lappo and Enklinge islands on the northern archipelago route. The ferries are free for bicycles and pedestrians if you stop en route.

On Kumlinge island, **Ledholm Camping** *(☎ 55647)*, near Seglinge ferry pier, has cheap camping and cabins. On Brändö Island, the top-end **Hotell Gullivan** *(☎ 28040; singles/doubles June-Aug €63/80)*, in Björnholam village, has a restaurant.

Take bus No 4 from Mariehamn to Hummelvik harbour on Vårdö Island. From Turku, take a bus to Kustavi, and on to Vartsala Island to reach the harbour of Osnäs (Vuosnainen).

SOUTHERN ARCHIPELAGO ROUTE

You can visit Kökar, Husö, Sottunga and Föglö islands along the southern route between Finland and Åland, or take the ferry across from Långnäs. Kökar Island is the most quaint, with hiking trails, a 14th-century abbey and an 18th-century church. There are boat trips from Kökar to the tiny island of Källskär in summer on board the **MS Kristina** *(☎ 55737; adult/child return €20/15)*.

Accommodation on Kökar includes **Sanvik Camping** *(☎ 55911)* near the pier, with tent sites and cabins; **Antons Guesthouse** *(☎ 55729; singles/doubles June-Aug €64/68)*; and **Hotell Brudhäll** *(☎ 28040; singles/doubles June-Aug €91/108)* in Karlby, which also has a nice restaurant.

From Mariehamn, take bus No 5 to Långnäs harbour. On the mainland ferries depart from Galtby harbour on Korppoo Island, 75km from Turku (take the Saaristotie bus from Turku).

South-Central Finland

TAMPERE
☎ 03 • pop 189,500

Tampere, Finland's third-largest city, is set between the Näsijärvi and Pyhäjärvi lakes. Once known for its powerful textile industry, dozens of red-brick chimneys from former factories point skyward in this 19th-century manufacturing centre; most have now been transformed into cultural centres, bars or restaurants. Long known as the 'Manchester of Finland', on a grey day, Tampere takes on a sort of Dickensian (or maybe Orwellian) quality. But if this paints a bad picture, don't

FINLAND

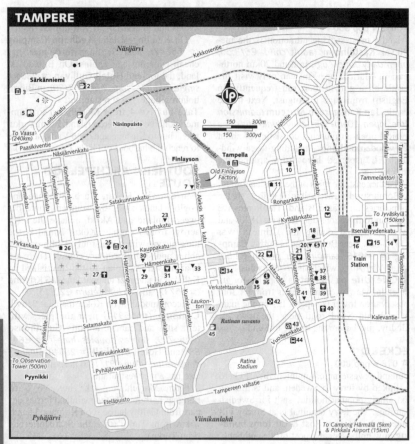

be put off: Tampere works beautifully, some-how combining working-class energy with Finnish sophistication.

Information

The efficient city **tourist office** (☎ 3146 6800, fax 3146 6463; ⓦ www.tampere.fi; Verkatehtaankatu 2; open 8.30am-8pm Mon-Fri, 10am-5pm Sat & Sun June-late Aug; 10am-5pm Mon-Fri other times) is right in the city centre, just north of the big Koskikeskus shopping centre. It has two free Internet terminals and can help out with accommodation.

There are also free Internet terminals available at the **public library** (☎ 314 614; Pirkankatu 2), and the **Vuoltsu Internet Café** (Vuolteenkatu 13).

There's a **Forex** (Hämeenkatu 1; open daily June-Aug, Mon-Sat Sept-May).

For English-language books and news-papers check out **Akateeminen Kirjakauppa** (Itämeenkatu 6).

Things to See & Do

Vapriiki Museum Centre (☎ 3146 6966; Veturiaukio 4; adult/child €4/1; open 10am-6pm Tues-Sun) is Tampere's premier exhibition space, in a renovated Tampella mill factory building. Also here is the **Ice Hockey Museum**, a small display dedicated to Finland's winter passion with photos, jerseys, sticks and pucks galore.

The tiny **Lenin Museum** (☎ 276 8100; Hämeenpuisto 28; adult/child €4/2; open 9am-6pm Mon-Fri, 11am-4pm Sat & Sun)

TAMPERE

PLACES TO STAY	41	Donatello		21	Café Europa
10 Hostel Tampere YWCA	46	Laukontori Market		22	Vahna Posti & Henry's Pub
11 Sokos Hotel Tammer				24	Moominvalley & Mineral
13 Hotelli Victoria	**OTHER**				Museum
26 Hostel Uimahallin Maja	1	Särkänniemi Amusement		25	Public Library
38 Hotel Iltatähti		Park		27	Aleksanteri Church
	2	Särkänniemi Quay		28	Lenin Museum
PLACES TO EAT	3	Sara Hildén Taidemuseo		31	Teerenpeli
7 Panimoravintola Plevna	4	Näsinneula Observation		34	City Transport Office &
14 Attila House		Tower			Local Buses
19 Pikkupapu	5	Zoo & Dolphinarium		35	Verkaranta Arts &
20 Coffee House;	6	Mustalahti Quay			Crafts Centre
Memphis East	8	Vapriiki Museum Centre		36	Tourist Office
23 Anttila Supermarket	9	Tampere Cathedral		39	O'Connell's Irish Bar
29 Thai Non Khon	12	Main Post Office		40	Orthodox Church
30 Tây-Do	15	Telakka		42	Koskikeskus Shopping Centre
32 Viking Restaurant Harald	16	Tullikamari Klubi		43	Vuoltsu Internet Café
33 Kauppahalli	17	Forex		44	Main Bus Station
37 Salud	18	Akateeminen Kirjakauppa		45	Laukontori Quay

gives an interesting insight into the work of the Russian revolutionary leader. The **Sara Hildén Taidemuseo** (☎ 214 3134; Särkänniemi; adult/child €4/1; open 11am-6pm daily) concentrates on modern and Finnish art and sculpture. Beautiful textiles and handicrafts are sold at the **Verkaranta Arts & Crafts Centre** (Verkatehtaankatu 2; adult/child €2.50/2), where there's also a café in a stunning spot by the river if you're here when the sun's out.

In the basement of the public library is **Moominvalley** (☎ 3146 6578; Hämeenpuisto 20; adult/child €4/2), an exhibition based on the children's books of Tove Jansson. It features original drawings and tableaux models from this Finnish cultural phenomenon. In the same building the small **Mineral Museum** is devoted to rocks and gemstones and has the same hours and admission as Moominvalley.

Särkänniemi amusement park (☎ 248 8111; ⓦ www.sarkanniemi.fi; adult/child pass €27/16) boasts carnival rides, an aquarium, a children's zoo, a planetarium and the Dolphinarium. A pass gives unlimited rides, or you can pay as you go (€3.50 per attraction). The park's **Näsinneula Observation Tower** (€3.50) is, at 168m, the tallest in Finland and has a rotating restaurant at the top.

Tampere's **cathedral** (Tuomiokirkonkatu, open 9am-6pm daily), which is built in the National Romantic style, features the weird frescoes of Hugo Simberg. There is a small but ornate **Orthodox church** (open 9.30am-3pm Mon-Fri May-Aug) south of the train station area.

Pyynikki Ridge, rising between the two lakes, is a forested area of walking trails with fine views on both sides. There's an **observation tower** (adult/child €1/0.50; open 9am-8pm daily) on the ridge, which also has a great café serving Tampere's best doughnuts.

Lake cruises are popular in summer; **Tammerlines** (☎ 254 2500) has cruises from Laukontori quay (adult/child from €8/2). SS Tarjanne, a steam ship, departs from Mustalahti quay for longer trips on the 'Poet's Way' to Virrat.

Special Events
Tammerfest in mid-July is a big weekend of rock music with the main concert venue at the Ratina Stadium, but plenty of smaller gigs around town.

Places to Stay
Camping Härmälä (☎ 265 1355 or in winter ☎ 6138 3210; Leirintäkatu 8; tent sites €13.50, 3–5-person cabins €27-60) is 5km south of the centre (take bus No 1). There are lakeside saunas and rowing boats, and an adjacent **summer hostel** (singles/doubles €30.50/47.50) with self-contained rooms.

There are two HI-affiliated hostels at opposite ends of town. **Hostel Tampere YWCA** (☎ 254 4020, fax 254 4022; Tuomiokirkonkatu 12A; dorm beds €11-12.50, singles/doubles €28.50/39; open June-Aug) is simple and clean, with kitchen and laundry facilities.

Hostel Uimahallin Maja (☎ 222 9460, fax 222 9940; Pirkankatu 10-12; dorm beds €16.50) has a slightly higher room standard.

Hotel Iltatähti *(☎ 315 161, fax 3151 6262; Tuomiokirkonkatu 19; singles/doubles €37/45.50, with bathroom €55.50/63; reception 9am-7pm Mon-Fri, noon-6pm Sat & Sun)* is a guesthouse in a reasonably quiet but central street near the train station.

Hotelli Victoria *(☎ 242 5111, fax 242 5100; ⓦ www.hotellivictoria.fi; Itsenäisyydenkatu 1; singles/doubles €90/110, discounted to €70/75)* has good rooms. The best hotel in town, **Sokos Hotel Tammer** *(☎ 262 6265, fax 262 6266; Satakunnankatu 13; singles/doubles €129/147, discounted to €85/103)* overlooks the river.

Places to Eat

The frightening Tampere speciality, *mustamakkara*, a black sausage made with cow's blood, can be found lurking in the **kauppahalli** *(Hameenkatu)*.

There are dozens of cafés lining Hämeenkatu, but one of the best in town, certainly for coffee, is **Pikkupapu** (Little Bean), tucked away down Tuomiokirkonkatu. It's a tiny European-style café with espresso, cappuccino, great smoothies and crepes and sandwiches. **Coffee House**, back on Hämeenkatu, is another good place specialising in various styles of coffee.

The central **Koskikeskus shopping centre** *(Hatanpään Valtatie)* has lots of fast-food outlets and a few chain restaurants; and the **Old Finlayson Factory** is another place to head for American-style fast food. Tampere University's student cafeteria in **Attila House** *(Yliopistonkatu 38; open 8.30am-5pm Mon-Fri, lunch Sat)* has cheap meals.

Both **Thai Non Khon** *(Hämeenkatu 29; lunch from €6)* and **Tây-Do** *(Hämeenkatu 22)*, a tiny Vietnamese restaurant across the street, offer some good vegetarian dishes.

Panimoravintola Plevna *(☎ 260 1200; Itäinenkatu 8; mains €7-17; open daily)*, a brewery pub and restaurant in the old Finlayson textile mill, is one of the most enjoyable places to dine in Tampere. As well as Finnish-style fish and steak dishes, the speciality here is German sausages such as bratwurst and bockwurst (€6.70 to €9.80), washed down with a pint of Plevna's award-winning strong stout (€5.60).

Donatello *(Aleksanterinkatu 37; buffet €6)* sets out a lavish all-you-can-eat pizza and pasta buffet for lunch and dinner – cheaper and tastier than Golden Rax. **Salud**

(☎ 223 5996; Tuomiokirkonkatu 19; dishes €6-17) is a favourite for Spanish-style gourmet food.

Entertainment

Tampere is arguably the friendliest place in Finland to hit the town. **Café Europa** *(☎ 223 5526; Aleksanterinkatu 29)* is easily the coolest bar in Tampere, but gets very crowded on weekend evenings. Furnished with 1930s-style couches, it's a romantic old-world European-style place with Belgian and German beers and a good summer terrace. Upstairs is a small dance club called **Attic** which opens at 10pm.

O'Connell's *(Rautatienkatu 24)* is an unpretentious Irish pub with a strong local following. It's a good place to meet travellers, expats and Tampere locals.

Teerenpeli *(Hämeenkatu 25)* is another good pub with home-brewed beer and cider and a cavernous club downstairs. Of the many bars on Hämeenkatu, **Vanha Posti** *(Hämeenkatu 13A)* is a perennial favourite with a good terrace. **Henry's Pub**, in the basement of the same building, has live music (country and rock bands) – you'll probably have to queue to get into either place late on a Friday or Saturday.

Telakka *(☎ 225 0700; Tullikamarinaukio 3)* is a bohemian bar-theatre-restaurant in another of Tampere's restored red-brick factories. There's live music here regularly, theatre performances and a brilliant summer terrace.

The enormous **Tullikamari klubi** near the train station is Tampere's main indoor venue for rock concerts. Big-name Finnish bands sometimes perform here and the cover charge varies from free to €15. This is also the venue for the film festival and jazz events.

Getting There & Away

There are daily Finnair services from Pirkkala airport (15km south-west of the centre) to Helsinki, as well as direct flights from Scandinavia's capital cities.

The **main bus station** *(Hatanpäänvaltatie 7)* is a block south from the Koskikeskus shopping centre. Regular express buses run from Helsinki (€23.10, 2½ hours) and Turku (€16.80, two hours).

Express trains run hourly to/from Helsinki (€21.40; two hours). Intercity trains continue to Oulu (€50, five hours) and there are direct trains to Turku, Pori, Jyväskylä, Vaasa and Joensuu.

You can cruise down to Hämeenlinna by lake ferry in summer. **Suomen Hopealinja** *(Finnish Silverline;* ☎ *212 4804;* W *www .finnishsilverline.com)* operates cruises from Tampere's Laukontori quay daily (€37 one-way, eight hours); they also have cruises north to Virrat (€42, eight hours).

Getting Around

The bus service is extensive and a one-hour ticket costs €2. A 24-hour Traveller's Ticket is €4. Bus No 61 goes to the airport (€2).

HÄMEENLINNA

☎ 03 • pop 47,500

Historical Hämeenlinna is at the southern tip of a lake network, 100km northwest of Helsinki, and linked by lake ferry to Tampere. The **Häme Tourist Service** *(☎ 621 2388; Linnankatu 6; open 9am–5pm Mon–Fri, plus 9am–2pm Sat mid-June–mid-Aug)* has plenty of information and a free Internet terminal.

The main attraction here is the medieval **Häme Castle** *(☎ 675 6820; adult/child €4/ 2.50; open 10am–6pm daily May–mid-Aug, 10am–4pm daily other times)* which was built by the Swedes in the 1260s and converted into a jail in 1837. There are free guided tours and an extensive museum inside. Around the castle are three more **museums** which can be visited on a combined ticket with the castle (€12).

Finland's most famous composer, Jean Sibelius, was born in Hämeenlinna and his childhood home is now an unassuming **museum** *(☎ 621 2755; Hallituskatu 11; adult/ child €3/1; open 10am–4pm daily June-Aug, noon–4pm other times)*.

Trains and express buses from Tampere and Helsinki are frequent. Many visitors catch a ferry from Tampere (see Tampere's Getting There & Away section).

LAHTI

☎ 03 • pop 95,000

About 100km north of Helsinki by motorway, Lahti is in some ways a satellite of the capital and thus has a modern, business city feel compared to other Lakeland towns. Its claim to fame is as a winter sports centre: the sports complex close to the centre has three sky-high jumps which are used in winter and summer (for training), and world championship events have been staged here. There's a **Skiing Museum** at the centre, and you can take a chairlift to the **Ski Jump Observation Terrace**.

The **tourist office** *(☎ 877 677;* W *www .lahtitravel.fi; Aleksanterinkatu 13)* has information on other museums and attractions in town.

Laden Kansanopisto *(☎ 878 1181, fax 878 1234; Harjukatu 46; dorm beds from €15.50, singles/doubles €29.50/41, with bath €35.50/51; open June–mid-Aug)*, the local folk college, is a HI summer hotel with a variety of rooms and an equipped kitchen.

JYVÄSKYLÄ

☎ 014 • pop 75,300

Jyväskylä (**yuh**-vahskuhllah), the bustling capital of south-central Finland, is known among architecture lovers for its Alvar Aalto buildings, in particular the university campus, and for the interesting **Alvar Aalto Museum** *(☎ 624 809; Alvar Allonkatu 7; adult/student €6/2)*, which shows as much about his interior design as exterior. You can pick up an Aalto walking tour booklet at the **tourist office** *(☎ 624 903;* W *www.jyvaskyla.fi; Asemakatu 6)*.

There are several **museums** (all are closed on Monday), a **winter sports centre** with some frightening ski jumps, and plenty of **lake traffic** (cruises and ferries to Lahti) to keep you occupied, but nothing in the 'must-see' category.

Although a provincial capital, Jyväskylä's centre is incredibly compact, with a lively pedestrian strip that has some of the best student-inspired nightlife outside Helsinki or Tampere.

Laajari *(☎ 624 885; Laajavuorentie 15; dorm beds from €14.50)* is a HI hostel in the Laajavuori ski-centre complex. More central is the 3rd-floor **Pension Kampus** *(☎ 338 1400;* e *pensionkampus@kolumbus.fi; Kauppakatu 11; singles/doubles €52/70, discounted to €43/60)*.

There are lots of good places to eat and bar-hop on Kauppakatu, especially the pedestrian section at the northern end. The **Old Bricks Inn** *(☎ 616 233; Kauppakatu 57; meals €5-13.50)* ranks as one of the best spots in town with filling meals and a big range of international beers. **Katrina** *(mains €7-8.50)* is a cute little vegetarian café next to Pension Kampus, with veg pasta, curries and ratatouille.

There are regular trains from Helsinki (€36.30, 5½ hours) via Tampere, and some quicker direct trains.

AROUND JYVÄSKYLÄ

In the tiny village of Petäjävesi, 35km west of Jyväskylä, is a bizarre cross-shaped wooden church, probably the most notable example of 18th-century peasant architecture in Finland. The **Petäjävesi church** (€2; open 10am-6pm June–mid-Aug), an odd combination of Renaissance and Byzantine, is on the Unesco World Heritage List and now functions only as a museum.

There are hourly buses between Jyväskylä and Petäjävesi.

West Coast

The flat coastal area called Pohjanmaa, facing the Gulf of Bothnia, is also known as the 'Swedish coast' due to the number of Swedish-speakers, or the 'tomato belt' for the dozens of glass hothouses that dot its fields.

RAUMA

☎ 02 • pop 38,000

Some 600 wooden houses from the 18th and 19th centuries make up Vanha Rauma (Old Rauma), Finland's first Unesco World Heritage Site and the main attraction of this seaside town. Rauma itself is not particularly appealing, but the old town, with its narrow cobbled streets, cafés, **house museums** (€4 for a combined ticket) and 15th-century **Church of the Holy Cross**, makes it worthy of a stop along the west coast.

The **tourist office** (☎ 834 4551, 834 4552; W www.rauma.fi; Valtakatu 2; open 8am-6pm Mon-Fri, 10am-3pm Sat, 11am-2pm Sun June-late Aug; 8am-4pm Mon-Fri other times), publishes a free map and a self-guided walking tour.

Places to Stay & Eat

Poroholma Camping & Hostel (☎ 8388 2500, fax 8388 2502; Poroholmantie; camping per person/site €8/13.50, cottages €42-51, hostel beds from €7, singles/doubles €17.50/25; open mid-May–late Aug) is on Otanlahti bay about 2km northwest of the town centre.

Kesähotelli Rauma (☎ 824 0130; Satamakatu 20; shared beds €9.50, singles/doubles €30.50/48; open June-Aug) is a summer hostel with typical twin-share student rooms with private kitchen and bathroom shared between two rooms.

The **kauppatori**, in the Old Town, is where you'll find cheap food stalls and a market in summer. Charming cafés are plentiful in Vanha Rauma – **Kontion Leipomo** (Kuninkaankatu 9) is a perennial favourite – a great place for coffee, cakes or pastries, and there's a large garden at the back.

Wanhan Rauman Kellari (☎ 866 6700; Anundilankatu 8; lunch €9.50, mains €10-21), on the edge of Vanha Rauma, is a very popular cellar restaurant with a terrific rooftop beer terrace open in summer.

PORI

☎ 02 • pop 76,500

Despite being one of Finland's oldest towns, the industrial city of Pori would be of minor interest to travellers if it wasn't host to the internationally renowned **Pori Jazz Festival**. The festival is held over two weeks in July and is known worldwide among jazz and blues performers. Many scheduled and impromptu performances are free, while the big names play on an open-air stage on Kirjurinluoto. For tickets and information contact **Pori Jazz** (☎ 550 5550; W www.porijazz.fi; Pohjoisranta 11, 28100 Pori).

Local sights include **Pori Taidemuseo** (Eteläranta 1; open Tues-Sun), one of Finland's better modern galleries; and the **Juselius Mausoleum**, a poignant memorial built by a local businessman for his 11-year-old daughter who died of tuberculosis. The original frescoes inside were painted by Akseli Gallen-Kallela.

Regular accommodation during the festival is very hard to find, but the **tourist office** (☎ 621 1273; W www.pori.fi; Hallituskatu 9) can help organise a cheap bed (around €30 to €45) on a first-come, first-served basis, either in a private home or on the floor of a school classroom.

Matkakoti Keskus (☎ 633 8447; Itäpuisto 13; singles/doubles €29/39) is a very basic guesthouse with simple rooms and shared bath, but it's nice and central. There's no breakfast.

During festival time, the waterfront Eteläranta becomes 'Jazz Street', a pulsating and infectious strip of makeshift bars and food stalls. Otherwise, **Café Juselia** (buffet lunch €7) is a good lunch spot and coffee shop. **Beerhunters**, across from the market square, is a brilliant pub-brewery that also serves food.

Express buses go to Pori from Turku, Tampere and Helsinki, and there are frequent trains to/from Tampere.

VAASA
☎ 06 • pop 55,000

The bilingual city of Vaasa (Wasa) was founded in 1606 by Charles IX of Sweden. Some travellers use this as an entry or exit point to or from Sweden (see Getting There & Away later). As the largest town along the west coast between Turku and Oulu, Vaasa has a lively, bustling air but lacks the character of smaller places.

The busy **tourist office** (☎ 325 1145; W www.vaasa.fi; Kaupungintalo; open 8am-8pm Mon-Fri, 10am-6pm Sat & Sun, shorter hrs Sept-May), in the town hall building just off Raastuvankatu, books accommodation and rents bikes.

The most interesting of the numerous museums and art collections is the **Museum of Ostrobothnia** (☎ 325 3800; Museokatu 3; adult/child €4/2, Wed free; open 10am-5pm daily, 10am-8pm Wed) with one of the best collections of art from Finland's Golden Era, and artefacts from all over Pohjanmaa. In the basement level is the **Bothnia Straits Nature Centre**, with displays on the region's geology, flora and fauna.

On Vaskiluoto island, linked by a bridge to the town centre, is Finland's mini-Disneyland amusement park, **Wasalandia**, and a 'tropical spa', **Tropiclandia**, both very popular with Finnish families.

Vaasa is a good base for bicycle tours to the **Stundars Handicraft Village** (☎ 344 2200; W www.stundars.fi; adult/child €4/2; open noon-6pm daily mid-May–mid-Aug, noon-6pm Sat & Sun mid-late Aug), in Solf 16km away. In summer, costumed artisans demonstrate crafts and folk-dancing.

Places to Stay & Eat
Vaasa Camping (211 1255; Niemeläntie; tent sites €7 plus per person €4; cabins €9 plus per person €4), on Vaskiluoto 2km from the centre, is generally full of families visiting the nearby amusement parks. **Kenraali Wasa Hostel** (☎ 0400-668 521, fax 3121 394; Korsholmanpuistikko 6-8; singles/doubles/triples €37/46/50) is the best of the few budget places in Vaasa. It's a friendly place with a well-equipped kitchen and cosy rooms (shared bathrooms).

The 2nd-floor **Bertel's Panorama** (Vaasanpuistikko 16; lunch special €7.40) serves a generous lunch buffet which you can eat overlooking the market square. For a drink with a

bird's eye view, head to the **Sky Terrace** on the rooftop of the Sokos Hotel Vakuna. The best place for a meal or drink in summer is **Strampen**, a restaurant and terrace bar in the waterfront Hovioikeuden park.

Getting There & Away
There are frequent buses up and down the coast from the terminal on Vöyrinkatu, and daily trains from Helsinki (€35.60, five hours) via Tampere or Seinäjoki.

In summer there are daily ferries between Vaasa and the Swedish town of Umeå (Uumaja) with **RG Lines** (☎ 320 0300; W www.rgline.com; €41; 3hrs).

PIETARSAARI
☎ 06 • pop 20,000

Although the international ferries have ceased, the quaint town of Pietarsaari (Jakobstad) is distinctively Swedish and the most interesting place to sample the curious world of *Parallelsverige* (Parallel Sweden).

The **tourist office** (☎ 723 1796; W www.jakobstad.fi; Kauppiaankatu 12; open 8am-6pm Mon-Fri, 9am-3pm Sat Jun-Aug; shorter hrs Sept-May), is next to the town square, and there's free Internet access at **After Eight**, a café and youth drop-in centre on Isokatu.

Skata, the town's historic area filled with 18th-century wooden houses, is worth a stroll. Among Pietarsaari's quirky museums is the fascinating Arctic museum **Nanoq** (☎ 729 3679; Pörkenäsintie 60; adult/child €6/3.50), about 7km from town on the way to Faboda.

In the old harbour area at Gamla Hamn is the pride of Pietarsaari, the **Jacobstad Wapen** (adult/child €4/2), modelled after a 17th-century sailing vessel.

Svanen-Joustsen (☎ 723 0660; Luodontie 50; tent sites €14, 2-/4-person cabins €22-28/38-65; open mid-May–late Aug) is a HI youth hostel and camping ground 6km north of town. **Hostel Lilja** (☎ 786 6500; Isokatu 6; shared room €20, singles/doubles €37.50/40) is a stylish new HI hostel attached to **Musikcafé After Eight** in the town centre.

Westerlund Resandehem (☎ 723 0440; Norrmalmsgatan 8; singles/doubles €27/43) is a lovely B&B in the old part of town.

There are plenty of cheap places to eat and drink along the partly pedestrian Kävelykatu, one block north of the market square. **Café Trend** lives up to its name – Pietarsaari's beautiful people crowd the terrace or read magazines over coffee inside. **Ella's** (*Raatiuoneenkatu 3; buffet lunch €6*) is open for lunch only with a typical all-you-can-eat spread.

There are regular buses to/from Vaasa (€12.40) and north to Oulu (€26.70) via Kokkola (the closest convenient train station).

Eastern Finland

Eastern Finland is a romantic region of lakes, rivers, locks and canals. It encompasses Karelia, part of which was taken by Russia in the bitter Winter War, and the Savo region of which Savonlinna is the centre. This Lakeland area is a highlight of any trip to Finland, so if you've only got the time or money to visit one destination outside Helsinki, make this the place.

Finns come here en masse in spring, summer and early autumn, and rent holiday cottages so they can enjoy trekking, boating, fishing and, of course, long saunas at night.

LAPPEENRANTA
☎ 05 • pop 57,000

The capital of South Karelia, Lappeenranta was a frontier garrison town until the construction of the Saimaa Canal in 1856 made it an important trading centre. Despite the surrounding pulp factories, it's one of the most attractive stops on Lake Saimaa, Finland's largest lake.

The day cruise along the Saimaa Canal to Vyborg, which was Finland's second-largest city until it was lost to Russia in WWII, is one of Lappeenranta's main attractions.

Information

The **main tourist office** (☎ 667 788; e *matkailuoy@lappeenranta.fi; open 9am-6pm Mon-Fri June-late Aug, 9.30am-4.30pm Mon-Fri other times*) is on the south side of the market square. A **summer tourist office** at the harbour is open daily from 9am to 9pm June to late August.

The **public library** (*Valtakatu 47*), has free Internet terminals (book ahead). **I@Café** (*Kauppakatu 63; €5 per hour*) is a better bet for Internet access.

Things to See

The fortifications in **Linnoitus** (Fortress) were started by the Swedes and finished by the Russians in the 18th century. Some of the

fortress buildings have been turned into mildly interesting **museums** (*combined ticket adult/student/child €5/4.20/3.40; all open 10am-6pm Mon-Fri, 11am-5pm Sat & Sun June-late Aug; 11am-5pm Tues, Thur, Sat & Sun Sept-late May*). They include the **South Karelia Museum**, with folk costumes and a scale model of Vyborg as it looked before it fell to the Russians in 1939; the **South Karelia Art Museum**, with a permanent collection of paintings by Finnish and Karelian artists; and the small **Cavalry Museum** which exhibits portraits of commanders, uniforms, saddles and guns.

In the city centre, the **Wolkoff Talomuseo** (☎ 616 2258; Kauppakatu 26; adult/student/child 3.40/2.50/1.20; open 10am-6pm Mon-Fri, 11am-5pm Sat & Sun June-late Aug; 11am-5pm Fri & Sat Sept-May) is the preserved home of a Russian emigrant family. Obligatory guided tours are held on the hour.

Organised Tours

Short cruises (adult/child on *Camilla* €11/6, on *El Faro* €10/5) on Lake Saimaa are popular and there are daily departures in summer. Better still are the day cruises to Vyborg in Russia (adult/child €40/20; on Saturday and from 24 June to 10 August €50/25) aboard the MS *Carelia*. A Russian visa is not required, but you'll need to provide passport details a week in advance, and book well ahead. Boats leave at around 7.30am and return as late as 10pm. The **Karelia Line** office (☎ 453 0380, fax 411 9096) at the harbour sells tickets.

Places to Stay

Huhtiniemi (☎ 451 5555; ⊞ www.huhtiniemi.com; Kuusimäenkatu 18; open mid-May–Sept; tent & van sites €17.50, cottages for 2/4 people €30/41, apartments €34-74) is a well-kept, slightly officious camping ground on the shores of Lake Saimaa, about 2km west of the centre (bus No 6 runs past). Also here is the **Huhtiniemi Hostel** (*dorm beds €7.50; open June–mid-Aug*), with six-bed dorms and the cheapest accommodation in town, and the upmarket **Finnhostel Lappeenranta** (*singles/doubles €42.50/52*) with linen, breakfast and a morning swim and sauna included.

Karelia Park (☎ 675 211, fax 452 8454; Korpraalinkuja 1; dorm beds €14, singles/doubles €40.50/45; open June-late Aug), 300m west of Huhtiniemi, is good-value budget

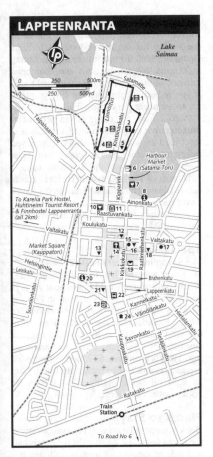

LAPPEENRANTA

PLACES TO STAY
9   Scandic Hotel Patria
24   Gasthaus Turistilappee

PLACES TO EAT
5   Kahvila Majurska
12   Old Park; Matkahuolto Office
13   Gram Marie
16   Tassos
18   Tiglio's
21   Drive-In Elvis

OTHER
1   South Karelia Museum
2   Orthodox Church
3   South Karelia Art Museum
4   Cavalry Museum
6   Passenger Quay & Karelia Line
7   Princessa Armaada & SS Suvi-Saamai
8   Summer Tourist Office
10   Kolme Lyhtyä; Birra
11   Wolkoff Talomuseo; Cafe Wolkoff
14   Lappee Church
15   Pharmacy
17   Public Library
19   Post Office
20   Main Tourist Office
22   Bus Station
23   I@Café

accommodation. Spotless two-bed rooms each have kitchen facilities and attached bath.

Gasthaus Turistilappee (☎ 415 0800; *Kauppakatu 52; singles/doubles/triples €33.70/50.50/57.20*) is not far from the train station, and offers tidy rooms with attached bath, and breakfast and a sauna included.

Scandic Hotel Patria (☎ 677 511; *Kauppakatu 21; singles/doubles €102/125, discounted to doubles €75*), close to the harbour, is Lappeenranta's top hotel, with good views, sauna, restaurant and bar.

Places to Eat

At stalls at the **kauppatori** and at the harbour you can try *vety* (meat pie or sandwich with ham, eggs and butter), a local Karelian favourite.

Drive-In Elvis (*Kauppakatu 45*) is a classic *grilli* with pizzas, burgers and kebabs from €2.

Kahvila Majurska (*Kristiinankatu 7*), in an 18th-century wooden building at the fortress complex, is one of the most charming cafés in Finland and serves delicious homemade cakes and quiches.

Gram Marie (☎ 451 2625; *Kauppakatu 41; lunch buffet €7.20*) is a lunch restaurant specialising in Finnish food with an all-you-can-eat buffet. It's on the 5th floor.

Lappeenranta has a surprisingly decent range of international restaurants. **Tiglio's** (☎ 411 8311; *Raatamiehenkatu 18; pasta & pizza €9-11, other mains €12-22*) is a pleasant find – an authentic Italian restaurant with reasonably priced meals.

Tassos (☎ 678 6565; *Valtakatu 41; mains €12-22*) is a fine Greek place which is a bit pricier for dinner but has a good-value lunch special.

Café Wolkoff (*Kauppakatu 26; mains €16-25*) adjacent to the Wolkoff Museum, is a stylish restaurant specialising in Finnish cuisine such as whitefish, reindeer, elk and cloudberry soup.

Entertainment

In summer, the SS *Suvi-Saamai* and the *Prinsessa Armaada*, at the harbour, serve as busy beer terraces.

Kolme Lyhtyä *(Kauppakatu 21)*, across from Café Wolkoff, is a typical eastern Finland bar, and next door is **Birra** *(Kauppakatu 19)*, an ugly, modern bar where Lappeenranta's student population congregates to drink cheap beer.

The **Old Park** *(Valtakatu 36)* is an Irish pub that gets very crowded most nights.

Getting There & Away

Finnair has daily flights between Helsinki and Lappeenranta; take bus No 4 to the airport.

All bus and train tickets can be booked at the central office of **Matkahuolto**, next to Café Galleria. Regular bus services include: Helsinki (€26.70, four hours), Savonlinna (€18.50, three hours via Parikkala), Mikkeli (€14.60, 2½ hours) and Imatra (€5.70, 45 minutes). For Kuopio (€30.90) change at Mikkeli.

There are frequent direct trains to/from Helsinki (€33, 2¾ hours), and to Savonlinna (€18.40, 2½ hours; change at Parikkala).

SAVONLINNA
☎ 015 • pop 28,700

Savonlinna grew up between lakes near the stronghold of Olavinlinna Castle in some of the prettiest of Finland's waterscapes. As a summer destination or opera venue it's unbeatable, and if you're in Finland for more than a few days try to make it here.

The **tourist office** *(☎ 517 510; e savonl inna@touristservice-svl.fi; Puistokatu 1; open 8am-6pm daily June, 8am-8pm daily July, 8am-6pm Mon-Fri Aug, 9am-5pm Mon-Fri Sept-May)* is a good place for opera festival information.

The **public library** *(☎ 571 5100; Tottinkatu; open 11am-7pm Mon-Fri, 10am-2pm Sat)* has Internet terminals which you can book in advance. **Café Knut Posse** *(Olavinkatu 44)*, adjacent to the bookshop of the same name, has one free terminal, as does the café at **Hotel Seurahone**.

Things to See & Do

The best-preserved medieval castle in the northern countries is **Olavinlinna** *(☎ 531 164; adult/student & child €5/3.50; open 10am-5pm daily June-Aug, 10am-3pm daily*

Sept-May). It was used by both Swedish and Russian overlords, but is today best known as the setting for the month-long Savonlinna Opera Festival. To tour the castle, including its original towers, bastions and chambers, join one of the excellent hourly guided tours. If you're here in late June and July you may get to see opera stars rehearsing.

Across from the castle is the **provincial museum** with exhibits related to local history, and two **museum ships** *(combined ticket adult/child €3/2; open 11am-5pm Tues-Sun Aug-Jun, 11am-5pm daily July)*.

Dozens of 1½-hour **scenic cruises** *(adults €7-10)* leave from the harbour at the kauppatori daily in summer, and there are ferries to Rauhalinna Manor, Linnansaari National Park and Punkaharju.

Special Events

The **Savonlinna Opera Festival** *(☎ 476 750; w www.operafestival.fi; Olavinkatu 27, 57130 Savonlinna)*, held throughout July, is perhaps the most famous festival in Finland with an international cadre of performers which includes touring productions from Covent Garden. The setting, in the covered courtyard of Ovanlinna Castle, is breathtaking. Tickets cost from €37 to €95 (more for premieres), but can be picked up for as little as €20 on some nights. Tickets can be booked over the Internet.

Places to Stay

Book accommodation well in advance during the opera festival – six months for hotels and a couple of months for hostels, although it's always worth a phone call to see if you can get in on any given day. Prices at hotels rise by as much as 100% during this time.

Vuohimäki Camping *(☎ 537 353; e myyntipalvelu@lomaliitto.fi; tent sites €15.50, cabins €70-80, bunk rooms from per person €17)*, 7km west of town, has good facilities but fills up quickly in July.

During summer the **SS Heinävesi** *(☎ 533 120; cabins upper/lower deck per person €19/17)* offers two-person cabin accommodation after the last cruise every evening.

Vuorilinna *(☎ 739 5495, fax 272 524; e casino.myynti@svlkylpylaitos.fi; Kylpylaitoksentie; dorm beds €18.50, singles/doubles €51.50/66; open June-late Aug)* is an HI-affiliated hostel near to (and run by) the spa hotel on Kasinosaari (Casino Island).

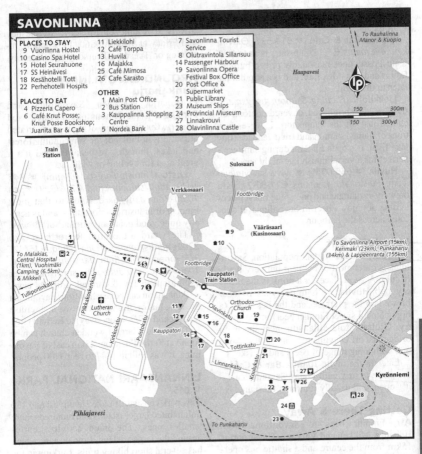

SAVONLINNA

PLACES TO STAY
9 Vuorilinna Hostel
10 Casino Spa Hotel
15 Hotel Seurahuone
17 SS Heinävesi
18 Kesähotelli Tott
22 Perhehotelli Hospits

PLACES TO EAT
4 Pizzeria Capero
6 Café Knut Posse;
Knut Posse Bookshop;
Juanita Bar & Café

11 Liekkilohi
12 Café Torppa
13 Huvila
16 Majakka
25 Café Mimosa
26 Cafe Sarasto

OTHER
1 Main Post Office
2 Bus Station
3 Kauppalinna Shopping
Centre
5 Nordea Bank

7 Savonlinna Tourist
Service
8 Olutravintola Sillansuu
14 Passenger Harbour
19 Savonlinna Opera
Festival Box Office
20 Post Office &
Supermarket
21 Public Library
23 Museum Ships
24 Provincial Museum
27 Linnakrouvi
28 Olavinlinna Castle

FINLAND

Malakias (☎ 739 5430, fax 272 524; Pihlajavedenkuja 6; shared room €18.50, singles/doubles €39.50/52; open June-early Aug), 2km north-west of town, is another summer hotel with two-room apartments sharing a kitchen and bath.

Kesähotelli Tott (☎ 575 6390, fax 514 504; Satamakatu 1; singles/doubles from €70/85; open early June-late Aug) is a comfortable summer hotel close to the harbour and market square. Some rooms are apartment-style, with kitchen.

Of Savonlinna's many hotels, the best is the cosy and fashionable **Perhehotelli Hospits** (☎ 515 661; Linnankatu 20; singles/doubles €70/80) near the castle. Top-notch rooms with a romantic view of the lake at the **Casino Spa Hotel** (☎ 739 5430, fax 272 524; Kasinosaari; singles/doubles €78/115, Fri & Sat €64/88) are a steal at this price, though you're unlikely to get a room in July.

Places to Eat

The lively market at the **kauppatori** is the place to find local pastries such as *omenalörtsy*, a tasty apple turnover (€1.50). Also on the kauppatori, **Café Torppa** is a popular student-run kiosk for coffee and late night snacks.

Pizzeria Capero (Olavinkatu 51; pizza & pasta €6-8) is the best place in town for a quick pizza and it's open till 10pm every night.

Majakka (☎ 531 456; Satamakatu 11; lunch specials from €7) opposite the harbour is a good restaurant with a nautical theme.

Café Mimosa (☎ 532 257; Linnankatu; light meals €6-10), near the castle, has a fine terrace and bar, and serves salads, cakes and light meals.

Juanita Bar & Café (☎ 514 531; Olavinkatu 44; mains €7-12), upstairs next to Café Knut Posse, does reasonably priced burgers, fajitas and Tex-Mex fare, and is a popular bar later in the night.

Liekkilohi (Flaming Salmon; fishy mains €7-8.50) is a bright-red, covered pontoon anchored just off the kauppatori. It serves portions of flamed salmon and fried vendace (tiny lake fish). It's open till 2am during summer – perfect for a very Finnish late-night snack.

Huvila (☎ 555 0555; ⓦ www.savonniemi .com; Puistokatu 4; mains €11.50-21) is a brewery-restaurant and one of the finest places to dine or enjoy a beer in Savonlinna. It's located across the harbour.

Entertainment

With only a small student population, Savonlinna is quiet most of the year but very lively in July. A good place for a drink is the brewery pub **Huvila**, with three types of beer brewed on the premises and the best *sahti* (a high alcohol sweet Finnish beer) in the country. **Olutravintola Sillansuu**, near the main bridge just off Olavinkatu, is an English-style pub with a big range of beers and whiskeys.

Later in the night, **Juanita Bar & Café** is the place to mix with young Savonlinnans – it's open, and usually jumping, till 4am.

Getting There & Away

Air Finnair flies to Savonlinna from Helsinki, Mikkeli and Varkaus. The airport is 15km from the centre and a shuttle bus operates during the opera festival (€6).

Bus From the bus station on the western side of town there are regular buses to Helsinki (€35.40, 4½ hours), Joensuu (€18.50, two hours), Mikkeli (€17, 1½ hours), Kuopio (€23.10, two hours) and Kerimäki (€4.20, 30 minutes).

Train There are trains from Helsinki (€42.20, five hours) via Parikkala – note that you must change to a regional train or connecting bus service at Parikkala, otherwise you'll wind up in Joensuu (€21.40, 2½ hours). For Kuopio, you need to take a bus to Pieksämäki and a train from there. The main train station is a long walk from Savonlinna's centre; get off at the kauppatori platform instead.

Boat In summer the lake ferry MS *Puijo* travels to Kuopio on Monday, Wednesday and Friday at 9.30am (€60, 11½ hours), returning on Tuesday, Thursday and Saturday.

AROUND SAVONLINNA
Punkaharju

Punkaharju, between Savonlinna and Parikkala, is the famous pine-covered sand ridge (*esker*) that is one of the most overrated attractions in Finland; the surrounding forest and lakes, though, are beautiful and it's a great area for cycling or walking.

Lusto (Finnish Forest Museum; ☎ 345 1030; adult/student/child €7/6/3.50; open 10am-7pm daily) is devoted to that most Finnish of industries – forestry – and is actually quite good in an educational sort of way.

The weird art centre, **Retretti** (☎ 775 2200; adults/senior/student/child €15/12/ 9/5; open 10am-5pm daily June & Aug, 10am-6pm daily July), has superb summer exhibitions in a walk-through artificial cave.

Punkaharju can be reached from Savonlinna by train, bus or, in summer, a two-hour cruise (adult/child €7/3.50 one-way) to Retretti jetty.

The world's largest wooden church can be found at **Kerimäki**, about 23km east of Savonlinna. It was built in 1847 to seat 3300 people!

LINNANSAARI NATIONAL PARK
☎ 015

This park consists of Lake Haukivesi and 130 uninhabited larger islands and hundreds more smaller ones. The main activity centres around the largest island, Linnansaari, which has several short hiking trails. Lurking in the park's waters is a tiny population of the near-extinct Saimaa ringed seal; in 1999 there were 50 known seals in the park, although there are around 200 in Lake Saimaa.

In summer, there's a regular daily boat service to Linnansaari from Mustalahti quay, 3km from Rantasalmi village. However, the best way to see the park is to pack camping gear and food, rent a rowing boat in Rantasalmi or Oravi (on the eastern shore of the lake) and spend a few days exploring. Boats, kayak and canoes can be hired from Saimaan Eräpalvelu Oravi Oy (☎ 050-563 3257) or Saimaan Eräelämys (☎ 015-64303). Contact the **Lakeland Centre** (☎ 0205-645916) in Rantasalmi for more information.

On the island you can stay at the established **campsites** for free, or there's a private camping ground (☎ 0500-275 458) with huts, tent sites and sauna.

There are regular buses to both Oravi and Rantasalmi from Savonlinna.

UUSI-VALAMO
☎ 017

The Valamo monastery (☎ 570 111, fax 570 1510; W www.valamo.fi; Valamontie 42, 79850 Uusi-Valamo) – Finland's only Orthodox monastery – is one of Savo's most popular attractions. The original Valamo monastery was annexed by the Red Army during WWII; the latest church was consecrated in 1977. The monastery is 4km north of road No 23 to Joensuu from Varkaus. Like all good monks, the clergy at Valamo produce their own wine (around €9 a bottle) using berries such as crowberries, raspberries, strawberries and blackcurrants.

You can stay in the simple Valamo Guesthouse (singles €22, 2–5-bed rooms per person €20) or the more comfortable Valamo Hotel (singles/doubles €32/47). Breakfast is included and there's also a restaurant here.

If you are looking for something even more peaceful, visit the nearby Lintula Orthodox Convent (☎ 563 225; singles/doubles €18/28) which also has accommodation. In summer there are regular cruises through lakes and canals from Valamo to Lintula (€13/15 one-way/return).

It's also possible to visit Valamo and Lintula from Kuopio on a monastery cruise (adult/child 51/25). The return journey is by bus.

MIKKELI
☎ 015 • pop 46,700

Mikkeli is a major provincial Lakeland town, but is not one of the most attractive – most travellers merely pass through on the way to Savonlinna or Kuopio. The town does have some historical interest: this was the headquarters of the Finnish army during WWII, and it was from here that the great military leader CGE Mannerheim directed the Winter War campaign against the Soviets. The Päämaja-museo (Headquarters Museum; ☎ 194 2427; Päämajamkuja 1-3; adult/child €4/free) was the command centre, and Jalkaväkimuseo (Infantry Museum; ☎ 369 666; Jäärkärinkatu 6-8; adult/child €3.50/1.50) is one of the largest military museums in Finland.

For information on local attractions contact the Mikkeli tourist office (☎ 194 3900; Porrassalmenkatu 15).

The Mikkeli Music Festival (W www .mikkelimusic.net), held here in late June/early July, is a week-long classical music event featuring top Finnish and Russian conductors.

KUOPIO
☎ 017 • pop 86,000

Kuopio is the most enjoyable of the northern Lakeland cities. It's a vibrant place with lots to see and do and enjoys a beautiful location, surrounded by forest and lakes. Time your visit for a Tuesday or Friday so you can steam it up in the world's biggest smoke sauna.

The helpful tourist office, Kuopio Travel Shop (☎ 182 585, fax 261 3538; W www .kuopioinfo.fi; Haapaniemenkatu 17; open 9.30am-5pm Mon-Fri, 10am-3pm Sat July; 9.30am-4.30pm Mon-Fri Aug-June) is right behind the impressive town hall on the north side of the market square.

Things to See & Do

In a land as flat as Finland, Puijo Hill is highly regarded. Take the lift to the top of the 75m-high Puijo Tower (€3) for spectacular views of Lake Kellavasi and the surrounding forests. The hill is a popular spot for mountain-biking, walking and cross-country skiing. There's also an all-season ski jump here and you can often see jumpers in training.

Don't miss the chance to sweat in the world's largest smoke sauna (Jätkänkämpällä; adult/child €10/5; open 5pm-10pm Tues & Fri) near the Hotel-Spa Rauhalahti. This 60-person log sauna is mixed and guests are given wraps to wear. Bring a swimsuit for a dip in the lake – devoted sauna-goers do so even when the lake is covered with ice! You can get there by boat from Kuopio harbour.

A museum card (€11), available from the tourist office, gets you into six city museums, including the following: Kuopio Art Museum (☎ 182 633; Kauppakatu 35; adult/child €2.50/free) has excellent contemporary exhibitions. Old photos and special exhibitions are featured at the top-class VB Photographic Centre (☎ 261 5599; Kuninkaankatu 14-16; adult/child €2.50/free; open Tues-Sun). History museums include the Kuopio Museum (☎ 182 603; Kauppakatu 23; adult/student & child €4/2; open 9am-4pm Mon-Sat, 11am-8pm Sun), housed in a medieval castle-like

FINLAND

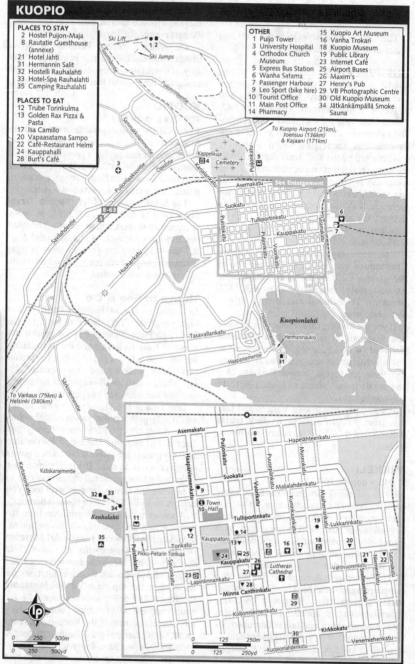

KUOPIO

PLACES TO STAY
2 Hostel Puijon-Maja
8 Rautatie Guesthouse (annexe)
21 Hotel Jahti
31 Hermannin Salit
32 Hostelli Rauhalahti
33 Hotel-Spa Rauhalahti
35 Camping Rauhalahti

PLACES TO EAT
12 Trube Torinkulma
13 Golden Rax Pizza & Pasta
17 Isa Camillo
20 Vapaasatama Sampo
22 Café-Restaurant Helmi
24 Kauppahalli
28 Burt's Café

OTHER
1 Puijo Tower
3 University Hospital
4 Orthodox Church Museum
5 Express Bus Station
6 Wanha Satama
7 Passenger Harbour
9 Leo Sport (bike hire)
10 Tourist Office
11 Main Post Office
14 Pharmacy
15 Kuopio Art Museum
16 Vanha Trokari
18 Kuopio Museum
19 Public Library
23 Internet Café
25 Airport Buses
26 Maxim's
27 Henry's Pub
29 VB Photographic Centre
30 Old Kuopio Museum
34 Jätkänkämpällä Smoke Sauna

Ski Lift
Ski Jumps

Kappelikuja
Cemetery

To Kuopio Airport (21km),
Joensuu (136km)
& Kajaani (171km)

Asemakatu
Suokatu
Tulliportinkatu
Kauppakatu

See Enlargement

Kuopionlahti

Hermaninaukio

Tasavallankatu
Haapaniementie

To Varkaus (75km) &
Helsinki (380km)

Katiskaniementie

Rauhalahti

Asemakatu
Hapelähteenkatu
Puijonkatu
Haapaniementie
Suokatu
Puuseppänkatu
Musekatu
Maljalahdenkatu
Maaherrankatu
Vuorikatu
Kuninkaankatu
Lukkarinkatu

Town Hall

Tulliportinkatu

Kauppatori
Torikatu
Kauppakatu
Pikku-Pietarin Torikuja
Savonkatu
Puistokatu
Lapinlinnankatu
Minna Canthinkatu
Kolionniemenkatu
Vahtivuorenkatu
Niemenkatu
Hellmäninkatu
Satamakatu

Lutheran Cathedral

Kirkkokatu
Venemiehenkatu
Kuopionlahdenkatu

0   250   500m
0   250   500yd

0   125   250m
0   125   250yd

building, and the **Old Kuopio Museum**
(☎ 182 625; Kirkkokatu 22; adult/child
€2.50/free).

The **Orthodox Church Museum** (☎ 287
2244; Karjalankatu 1; adult/child €5/3; open
10am-4pm Tues-Sun May-late Aug; noon-
3pm Mon-Fri, noon-5pm Sat & Sun late Aug-
Apr) is a fascinating museum with collections
brought here from monasteries, churches and
tsasouni (chapels) in USSR-occupied Karelia.

Special Events
Kuopio's main event is the **Dance Festival**
(☎ 282 1541; Ⓦ www.kuopiodancefestival
.fi) in mid-June. There are open-air classical
and modern dance performances and the
town is buzzing at this time.

Places to Stay
Camping Rauhalahti (☎ 361 2244; Kivin-
iementie; tent sites per person/family €10/
16, 2-4-person cabins €30-54; open mid-
May–Sept), adjacent to the Rauhalahti spa
complex, has a lovely lakeside location.

Hostelli Rauhalahti (☎ 473 111, fax 473
470; Katiskaniementie 8; share bed €30.50,
singles/doubles €54.50/61) is a hostel next
to the spa hotel in the Rauhalahti tourist
centre complex, 5km southwest of the centre.
It's handy for the smoke sauna if you're there
on the right days, but pricey for backpacker
accommodation. You get to use the hotel facilities, which include a gym, spa and pool.
Take bus No 7 from the kauppatori.

Hostel Puijon Maja (☎ 255 5250, 255
5266; Puilontornintie; dorm beds €14.50,
with linen & breakfast €25.50, singles/
doubles €47.50/51) is a lovely hostel perched
on top of Puijo Hill. It's popular with groups,
including practicing ski jumpers, so book
ahead. Unfortunately, there's no public transport from the town centre.

Hermannin Salit (☎ 364 4961, fax 364
4911; Hermanninaukio 3A; dorm beds €13,
singles/doubles €25.50/35) is Kuopio's
cheapest and most central hostel, about 1.5km
south of the market square. It's a small,
friendly place.

Rautatie (☎ 580 0569, fax 580 0654;
Asemakatu 1; singles/doubles €46/75) is in
the railway station building but is a surprisingly comfortable and peaceful guesthouse.
Nearby, at Vuorikatu 35 (same phone), is another small guesthouse with slightly cheaper
rooms (€36/56).

Hotel Jahti (☎ 264 4400; Snellmaninkatu
23; singles/doubles €50/65), down towards
the harbour, is the best mid-range hotel.

Places to Eat
There are indoor (kauppahalli) and outdoor
markets in the main square where you can try
kalakukko, a local fish baked inside a rye loaf
(eaten hot or cold). The 2nd-floor **Golden
Rax Pizza & Pasta** (Puijonkatu 45; buffet
lunch & dinner €7) serves the usual all-you-
can-eat cardboard.

Burts Café (☎ 262 3995; Puijonkatu 15) is
the best place in town for coffee and home-
made cakes and pastries. **Café-Restaurant
Helmi** (Kauppakatu 2; pizzas €7-10), in an
old stone building near the harbour, is an atmospheric bar and restaurant specialising in
great pizzas. There's often live music in the
courtyard at the side.

Vapaasatama Sampo (☎ 261 4677; Kauppakatu 13; meals €8.50-13) is the town's oldest restaurant and is famous all over Finland for
its muikku (whitefish), served in various forms.
Sampo is also very much a typical Finnish pub
and a good place to meet locals.

Isa Camillo (☎ 581 0450; Kauppakatu 25;
mains €9-21), in a beautifully renovated
bank, is one of Kuopio's finest restaurants,
but is reasonably informal and affordable.
The menu is international with plenty of
Finnish specialities and there's a good enclosed terrace at the side.

Entertainment
Most of Kuopio's nightlife is along Kauppakatu, running east from the market square
to the harbour. **Wanha Satama** (☎ 197 304),
down at the harbour, is a lively pub with a
sprawling terrace during the summer, and
occasional live music. **Vanha Trokari** (Kauppakatu 29) is another popular pub and brewery with a busy summer terrace and a jazz
bar attached.

Henry's Pub (Käsityökatu 17) is one of the
best in town with live rock Friday and Saturday nights. Around the corner, **Maxim's**
(Kauppakatu), draws a younger late-night
crowd, combining a happening music bar on
two levels, with a nightclub playing house
and drum & bass.

Getting There & Away
Finnair flies to the airport, 20km north of
town, several times daily from Helsinki.

Kuopio is easily reached by train or bus from Helsinki or Kajaani. The express bus station is north of the train station.

In summer, the lake ferry **MS Puijo** departs for Savonlinna on Tuesday, Thursday and Saturday at 9.30am (€60, 8½ hours), going via Heinävesi and Oravi. It returns from Savonlinna on Monday, Wednesday and Friday.

IISALMI
☎ 017 • pop 23,500

This pretty little riverside northern Savo town, 85km north of Kuopio, is home to the large Olvi brewery, which provides ample excuse for the numerous beer terraces and an annual **beer festival** in early July.

Iisalmi has a **tourist office** (☎ 830 3391; Kauppakatu 22; open 9am-6pm Mon-Fri) opposite the bus station. Trains and buses connect the town with Kajaani and Kuopio.

Kuappi, at the harbour's edge, bills itself as the world's smallest restaurant – it has one table, two seats, a bar and a toilet! You can't actually eat in here, but in summer they may open up the bar (it's listed in the Guinness Book of Records as the world's smallest pub). The building dates back to 1907 when it was a hut for railway workers.

Just north of the centre, the HI-affiliated **YMCA Hostel** (☎/fax 823 940; Sarvikatu 4C; beds from per person €17.50; open June & July) is an austere block with clean rooms with kitchen and sauna. Reception is open from 5pm to 11pm.

Olutmestari (☎ 8381 430; mains €8-18), at the harbour, is an atmospheric bar and restaurant with a good summer terrace. The food is not cheap but it's very good.

AROUND IISALMI
The tiny village of Sonkajärvi, 18km east of Iisalmi, hosts the annual **Wife Carrying World Championships** in early July. The event attracts competitors from around the world. Entrants carry any (consenting) woman over the age of 17 over a 253m obstacle course that includes a water hazard and two hurdles; dropping the woman incurs a 15-second time penalty. The winner takes home, among other prizes, his passenger's weight in beer. The preceding day you can warm up with the **Finnish Barrel Rolling Championships**. It's an entertaining and boozy weekend – accommodation is tight but the Iisalmi or Kuopio tourist offices may be able to help.

JOENSUU
☎ 013 • 54,000

Joensuu is a university town and the provincial capital of North Karelia. Although a pleasant enough riverside town, it's really just a jumping-off point for hikes into surrounding wilderness areas. The gentle Pielisjoki rapids divide the town into two parts: most of the town centre is west of the river, but the bus and train station are to the east.

The **tourist office** (☎ 267 5300; Koskikatu 5) is in the Carelicum Centre, which also has a café, free Internet and the town's best museum. Another good place for Internet access is Kansalaistalo coffee shop, where you can also hire bikes for €6 a day.

Carelicum Museum (North Karelian Museum; ☎ 267 5222; adult/student/child €4.20/2.50/1.70; open 10am-5pm Mon-Fri, 11am-4pm Sat & Sun) is one of the finest museums in the eastern Lakeland area. It charts the history, traditions and culture of Karelia, part of which is now in Russia.

Places to Stay
Linnunlahti Camping (☎ 126 272; Linnunlahdentie 1; camping per person/site €7/12, 4–6-person cabins €35-42), just south of the centre, has a pleasant lakeside location.

There are three HI-affiliated hostels in Joensuu. **Partiotalon Retkeilymaja** (☎ 123 381; Vanamokatu 25; dorm beds €7.50-11.50; open June-late Aug) has basic accommodation in the slightly run-down old scout hall, but it's certainly the cheapest in town. Reception is open from 9am to 11am and 4pm to 10pm.

Finnhostel Joensuu (☎ 267 5076; e finnhostel@islo.jns.fi; Kalevankatu 8; shared rooms per person €22.50, singles/doubles €38.50/48.50) is at the high end of hostel accommodation. Very comfortable twin rooms include linen and TV, and have their own bath and fully equipped kitchen.

Summer Hotel Elli (☎ 225 927, fax 225 763; e hotel.elli@kolumbus.fi; singles/doubles €33.50/47) has good-value apartment-style rooms with kitchenette and breakfast is included.

Places to Eat & Drink
As usual the **kauppatori** is packed with stalls selling cheap snacks, including Karelian pies. **Matilda** (Torikatu 23; lunch from €4.50), just north of the market square, is a good bakery, restaurant and café.

FINLAND

Mama's Bar & Kitchen *(Kirkkokatu 25; mains €5-13)* is an inexpensive lunch restaurant open on weekdays in summer.

The oldest and best known pub is the rustic **Wanha Jokela** *(☎ 122 891; Torikatu 26)*. In summer there's plenty of drinking at the harbour café **Tuulaki** where the passenger ferries dock.

Getting There & Away
Finnair flies daily to/from Helsinki. The airport is 11km from town; bus service is €4 one-way and departs from Kirkkokatu 25.

Buses arrive and depart from the bus station near the railway. Services include buses to Kuopio (€18.50), Savonlinna (€18.50), Jyväskylä (€29.10), Helsinki (€40.42), Kuhmo (€24.70), Ilomantsi (€10.40) and Nurmes (€16.80).

Direct trains run to/from Helsinki (€49; 5¼ hours).

In summer the MS *Vinkeri II* operates twice-weekly from Joensuu to Nurmes via Koli (€30/40 one-way/return; 6½ hours), from where you can connect with another ferry to Lieksa, across Lake Pielinen. The ferry departs at 9.30am on Thursday and Saturday, returning from Koli at 12.30pm on Wednesday and Friday. Book through **Saimaa Ferries** *(☎ 481 244)*.

ILOMANTSI
☎ 013 • 8500
Ilomantsi, 72km east of Joensuu, is Finland's most Karelian, Orthodox and eastern municipality and the centre of a charming region.

The excellent **tourist office** *(☎ 881 707; W www.travel.fi/fin/ilomantsi; Mantsintie 8; open 8.30am-5pm Mon-Fri)* can help with just about everything from cottage reservations to information on trekking routes and hire of camping equipment, snowshoes and cross-country ski gear. This should be your first stop if you're planning trips into the Karelian countryside.

The village centre itself is modern and quite ugly, having been trampled by the Russians, but it's the surrounding region that demands exploration. The **wine tower** is worth ascending, for the views and to sample the locally made berry wine. There's also a café at the top. **Parppeinvaara** *(€3.50/1; open 10am-6pm daily mid-June–mid-Aug)* is the oldest and most interesting of Finland's Karelian theme villages.

Places to Stay
Lomakeskus Ruhkaranta *(☎ 843 161; Ruhkarannantie 21; tent sites €10, cottages from €25; open May-Sept)* is 9km east of Ilomantsi. Located in a thick pine forest, it has spectacular views of several lakes. There's a traditional smoke sauna here but it takes six hours to heat up and costs €200 a session!

Anssilan Monola *(☎ 881 181; Anssilantie; singles/doubles €25/46, cottage €86)* is a former dairy farm on a hill 3km south of the village centre and about 500m off the main road. The friendly family rents rooms in their converted farmhouse building.

TREKS AROUND KARELIA
Some of the best trekking routes in North Karelia have been linked up to create **Karjalan Kierros**, an 800km loop of marked trails between Ilomantsi and Lake Pielinen. For more information on these and other routes contact the Lieksa or Ilomantsi tourist offices, or **Metsähallitus** *(☎ 0205-64 5500; Urheilukatu 3A, Lieksa)*, the information office for the Forest & Park Service's eastern region.

Karhunpolku
The Bear's Trail (not to be confused with the Bear's Ring in Lapland) is a 133km marked hiking trail of medium difficulty leading north from Patvinsuo National Park near Lieksa, through a string of national parks and nature reserves along the Russian border. The trail ends at Teljo, about 50km south of Kuhmo. You'll need to arrange transport from either end.

Sustaival
The 100km Wolf's Trail is a marked trail running south from the marshlands of Patvinsuo National Park to the forests of Petkeljärvi National Park, 21km east of Ilomantsi. This links with the Bear's Trail.

LAKE PIELINEN REGION
The sixth-largest lake in Finland, Lake Pielinen is surrounded by some of the most attractive and action-packed countryside in North Karelia.

Lieksa
☎ 013 • pop 16,000
The small centre of Lieksa, about 100km north of Joensuu, is primarily a base and service town if you're planning any outdoor activities in the region.

FINLAND

The local **tourist office** (Lieksan Matkailu Oy; ☎ 689 4050; Ⓦ www.lieksa.fi/travel; Pielisentie 7; open 8am-6pm Mon-Sat June-Aug; 11am-3pm Sun July; 8am-4pm Mon-Fri Sept-May) has information on accommodation, fishing, canoeing, smoke saunas and national parks, as well as local hiking maps.

One of Finland's largest open-air museums, the **Pielinen Museum** (☎ 689 4151; Pappilantie 2; adult/child €4/1.50; open 10am-6pm daily mid-May–mid-Sept) is a complex of almost 100 Karelian buildings and exhibits – along with an indoor museum of local war and folk history. The indoor hall is also open in winter.

In winter, **husky tours** and **snow-mobile safaris** along the Russian border are popular; Lieksan Matkailu Oy can provide a list of tour operators.

Places to Stay & Eat Timitraniemi Camping (☎ 521 780; Timitra; tent sites €11, cabins €30-80; open June-Aug) is at the river mouth on Lake Pielinen, and has plenty of facilities including log cabins, lakeside saunas and bikes and boats for hire.

The small Vuonislahti train station 28km south of Lieksa is the jumping-off point for the brilliant lakeside hostel **Kestikievari Herranniemi** (☎ 542 110; ⓔ reception@herranniemi.com; Vuonislahdentie 185; dorm beds €10, cabins €22.50-65.50, B&B singles/doubles €38.50/55.50). The farm building has a restaurant, a range of comfortable accommodation, two lakeside saunas and rowing boats.

Most places to eat and drink are on Lieksa's main street, Pielisentie. **Café Sanna** (Pielisentie 2-6; meals €6-8) offers reasonably priced home-cooked lunches. **Tinatähti** (☎ 521 914; Pielisentie 28) is a lively pub that also serves meals.

Getting There & Away Trains and buses run regularly to/from Joensuu and Nurmes, but the most pleasant way to arrive here is by ferry from Joensuu (via Koli, see the Joensuu section). The huge 250-person car ferry runs twice a day between Lieksa and Koli from June to mid-August, departing at 9.30am and 3.30pm (adult/child €14/7 one-way, car/bicycle €7/2; 1¾ hours).

Ruunaa Recreation Area

The Ruunaa Recreation Area, 30km east of Lieksa, is great for **fishing**, **white-water rafting** and easy **hiking**. The **Ruunaa Nature Centre** (☎ 0205-645 757; open 9am-7pm daily summer) near the bridge over the Naarajoki River is where most boat trips end.

There are six rapids, and several daily launches of wooden and inflatable boats during summer. A two- to four-hour trip costs €34/17 per adult/child and the nature centre or Lieksa tourist office can line you up with an operator. Walking trails cover the entire area, and there are bridges, campsites and free lean-to laavu (shelters).

In addition to accommodation and services at Naarajoki, the **Neitikoski Hiking Centre** (☎ 533 170; tent sites €10, cabins from €75) has a large café, camping sites, kitchen, sauna and luxurious four- to six-bed cabins. A boardwalk goes a short distance from here to the Neitikoski rapids, a popular fishing and kayaking spot.

Koli National Park

Finns regard the views from the heights of Koli, overlooking Lake Pielinen, as the best in the country – the same views inspired several Finnish artists from the National Romantic era. In summer, the national park offers scenic hiking routes, and there's a ferry service between Koli and Lieksa (less than two hours; see the Lieksa section) or Joensuu (seven hours). In winter, Koli attracts skiers with two slalom centres (Loma-Koli and Ukko-Koli) and more than 60km of cross-country trails, including 24km of lit track.

There's a regular bus service from Koli village up to the top of the hill. At the top, the **Ukko-Koli Heritage Centre** (☎ 688 8400) has displays and information on the national park.

Kolin Lomaranta (☎ 040-729 5030; Merilänrannantie 15; tent sites €10, cabins €20-34; open June-Aug) has camping sites and 'outbuildings' for 2-5 people.

The family-run **Koli Hostel** (☎ 673 131; dorm beds from €9.50), on a gravel road 5km from the bus stop, has a kitchen, smoke sauna and beds. It's a great getaway – if you call ahead you may be able to arrange a pick-up.

Nurmes

☎ 013 • pop 10,000

Much like Lieksa, Nurmes is a base for wallet-draining activities such as dog sledding, snow-mobiling, ice-fishing and cross-country skiing tours in winter, and canoeing and farmhouse tours in summer. It's a more pleasant town in its own right though, with an 'old town' area (Puu-Nurmes) of historical wooden buildings along Kirkkokatu. A highlight is **Bomba House**, part of a delightful re-creation of a Karelian village 3km southeast of the centre. The village features a summer market, craft shops and cafés.

For local information and to book activities, the **Loma-Nurmes tourist office** (☎ *481 770;* ✉ *matkailu@nurmes.fi; open 8am-10pm daily June-Aug, 8am-5pm Mon-Fri Sept-May)* is at the Hyvärilä holiday complex, which is also the obvious place to stay. **Hyvärilä** (☎ *481 770; tent sites €7-12, dorm beds €11.50, singles/doubles from €35/50)* is a sprawling lakeside complex with a camping ground, two youth hostels, an upmarket hotel, restaurant and even a golf course.

Nearby, **Bomba Spa Hotel** (☎ *687 200; Suojärvenkatu1; singles/doubles from €78/95)* is a stylish set-up where you can pamper yourself with the spa and sauna facilities.

There are regular buses from Nurmes to Joensuu, Lieksa, Kajaani and Kuopio; and regional trains from Joensuu (€15.20, two hours) via Lieksa.

In summer there are cruises on Lake Pielinen and ferries to Koli and Joensuu on Wednesday and Friday (€35, 10 hours).

North-Central Finland

KAJAANI
☎ 08 • pop 40,000

Kajaani is the centre of the Kainuu region, and although a pleasant enough riverside city (once noted as Finland's largest tar-producer), for travellers it's mainly a transport hub and stopover on the haul between the south and Lapland. The **tourist office** (☎ *615 5555; Kauppakatu 21)* is just off the town square.

The town's greatest historical claim to fame is that writer Elias Lönnrot, author of the epic *Kalevala*, used Kajaani as a base for his travels. The **regional museum** near the train station has a good section on Lönnrot.

At the Ämmäkoski waterfall, near the remnants of Kajaani castle, is a **tar-boat canal**, a type of lock built in 1846 to enable the boats laden with tar barrels to pass. There's a small **museum** *(admission free; open 11am-5pm*

Tues-Sun) in the old lock-keeper's cottage, and tar boat shows at 11am on Saturdays in July.

Places to Stay & Eat
Retkeilymaja Huone ja Aamiainen (☎ */fax 622 254; Pohjolankatu 4; singles/doubles/ triples €24.50/35.50/47.50)* is a pretty basic HI-affiliated place but the rooms are clean and it's the cheapest in town, with breakfast and linen included. Reception opens at 4pm.

Kartanohotelli Karolineburg (☎ *613 1291;* ⓦ *www.karolineburg.com; Karoliinantie 4; singles/doubles from €70/80, double with sauna €117, suites €100-250)* is easily the most romantic place to stay in Kajaani. It's an elegant 19th-century wooden manor house across the river from the centre.

The partly pedestrianised Kauppakatu – leading from the market square to the town square – is the main street and has many restaurants. **Pikantti** *(cnr Kauppakatu & Urho Kekkonenkatu)* has excellent lunch buffets until 5pm weekdays.

When it's warm, the outside chairs at the **Brahe Public house** *(cnr Kauppakatu & Linnankatu),* in the cute cobbled town square, is Kajaani's best spot to sit with a beer or coffee and watch the passing parade.

Also in the town square is a rustic **stall** where Finnish pancakes are whipped up while you wait.

Getting There & Away
Finnair flies to/from Helsinki, and trains connect with Kuopio, Nurmes and Oulu.

KUHMO
☎ 08 • pop 13,000

Kuhmo, like Kajaani, was once a major tar producer, but is now a modern service town in the heart of accessible wilderness territory – it makes an excellent jumping-off point for the UKK trekking route, Finland's longest marked trek.

The town is also famous for the annual **Kuhmo Chamber Music Festival** (☎ *652 0936, fax 652 1961;* ✉ *kuhmo.festival@ kuhmofestival.fi; Torikatu 39),* held mid-July to August, which attracts musicians from around the world.

The **tourist office** (☎ *655 6382; Kainuuntie 82; open 8am-6pm Mon-Fri, 10am-4pm Sat June-late Aug, 8am-5pm Mon-Fri rest of the year)* is good for national park and festival information.

The **Kalevala Village theme park** (*☎ 652 0114; adult/child €10/5; open 9.30am-6pm daily June-late Aug*), 3km from the centre, is the main sight in Kuhmo. It consists of a series of Karelian buildings along a walking track.

Places to Stay & Eat
Kalevala Camping (*☎ 655 6388, fax 655 6384; tent sites €11, 2-/4-person cabins from €26/34; open June-late Aug*), on the lake near the Kalevala Village theme park, has good facilities including a smoke sauna and boats.

Kuhmo Youth Hostel (*☎ 655 6245; Kainuuntie 113; dorm beds €8.50, singles/ doubles €22.50/26.50; open July*) is a HI place in the Piilolan school building, but it's open only in July when the town is crowded with music lovers.

Kuhmon Matkakoti (*☎/fax 655 0271; Vienantie 3; singles/doubles/triples €25/ 44/56*) is a friendly, good-value guesthouse near the town centre.

Despite the naff name, **Ristorante Pizz Burger** (*☎ 652 0144; Kainuuntie 84; mains €6.50-12*) is a reasonably good pizza, pasta and salad restaurant with a filling lunchtime buffet (€7.20), booth seating and a small terrace.

Getting There & Away
There are numerous daily buses to/from Kajaani (€14.60, 1½ hours), where you can get connections to elsewhere west and south, and direct buses to Nurmes (€10.40, 1½ hours) and Joensuu (€27.10, four hours).

UKK Trekking Route
The 240km Urho K Kekkonen (UKK) route is Finland's longest marked trail, passing through pockets of the now-rare Finnish wilderness on the way from Koli Hill in North Karelia to Iso-Syöte Hill far to the north of Kuhmo. Two of the finest sections of the UKK route are the Kuhmo to Hiidenportti leg and the Kuhmo to Lentiira leg.

The trail is well maintained in the Kuhmo area, with clear markings and *laavu* (simple shelters) spaced every 10km to 20km. In summer, carry a sleeping bag and *plenty* of mosquito repellent.

You can pick up route maps and information at the Kuhmo tourist office or the **Kainuu Nature Centre** (*☎ 877 6380; ⓔ kaapalinna@ metsa.fi*), also in Kuhmo.

OULU
☎ 08 • pop 117,500
Oulu is the largest city north of Tampere and is a lively, fast-growing university town. Technology companies have set up shop here in recent years, giving Oulu an affluent, progressive air.

The city was founded by King Karl IX of Sweden in 1605 and rebuilt after a fire in 1822; few old buildings remain. While Oulu lacks any 'must see' sights and suffers a dearth of budget accommodation, its summertime energy (in June and July it never gets dark), cosmopolitan air and frenetic nightlife make it well worth a stop on the road north.

Information
The city **tourist office** (*☎ 5584 1330; Ⓦ www.oulutourism.fi; Torikatu 10; open 9am-6pm Mon-Fri, 10am-3pm Sat mid-June–mid-Aug; 9am-4pm Mon-Fri mid-Aug–mid-June*) publishes the useful guide *Look at Oulu*.

On the waterfront, the large **public library** (*open daily*) has eight Internet terminals and a reading room. There are also two Internet terminals (€1 for 10 minutes; free to customers) at **Pint Netti Baari**, a pub on the pedestrian Rotuaari strip.

Things to See & Do
Visiting **Tietomaa** (*☎ 5584 1340; Ⓦ www .tietomaa.fi; adult/child €10/8.50; open 10am-6pm daily, till 8pm July*) Scandinavia's largest science museum, can occupy a full day, but it's essentially for kids. **Oulu City Art Museum** (*adult/child €3/1, admission Fri free; open Tues-Sun*), nearby, has some intriguing temporary international and Finnish exhibitions.

The imposing, 19th-century **cathedral** (*Kirkkokatu*) was designed by Carl Engel and has Finland's oldest portrait (dating from 1611) hanging in its vestry. The **kauppatori**, near the quay, is one of the most colourful in Finland with its red wooden storehouses (now housing restaurants, bars and craft shops), market stalls and bursting summer terraces.

In summer you can take a boat out to the folksy **Turkansaari Open-Air Museum** (*☎ 5586 7191; €2.50; open 11am-8pm daily June-late Aug, to 5pm daily early–mid-Sept*) on Turkansaari island, 13km south-east of the city. There are various old buildings and displays of tar-burning, log-rolling and folk

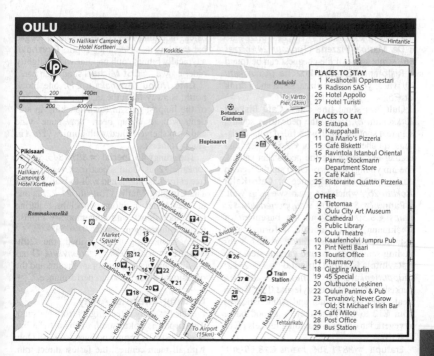

OULU

PLACES TO STAY
1 Kesähotelli Oppimestari
5 Radisson SAS
26 Hotel Appollo
27 Hotel Turisti

PLACES TO EAT
8 Eratupa
9 Kauppahalli
11 Da Mario's Pizzeria
15 Café Bisketti
16 Ravintola Istanbul Oriental
17 Pannu; Stockmann
   Department Store
21 Café Kaldi
25 Ristorante Quattro Pizzeria

OTHER
2 Tietomaa
3 Oulu City Art Museum
4 Cathedral
6 Public Library
7 Oulu Theatre
10 Kaarlenholvi Jumpru Pub
12 Pint Netti Baari
13 Tourist Office
14 Pharmacy
18 Giggling Marlin
19 45 Special
20 Oluthuone Leskinen
22 Oulun Panimo & Pub
23 Tervahovi; Never Grow
   Old; St Michael's Irish Bar
24 Café Milou
28 Post Office
29 Bus Station

music and dancing. The MS *Sympaatti* departs from Värtto Pier daily except Monday at noon (€17 return) from June to August. Otherwise take bus No 3 or 4.

One of Oulu's best features is the extensive network of wonderful **bicycle paths** and nowhere is the Finns' love of two-wheeled transport more obvious than here in summer. Bikes can be hired from the train station, or from shop 24 at the kauppatori, and a route map is available from the tourist office.

Places to Stay

Nallikari Camping (☎ 5586 1350; e *nallikari .camping@ouka.fi; Hietasaari; tent sites per person/family €10/15.50, 2-4-bed camping cabins €29, cottages from €58*) is Oulu's saviour for budget travellers, not only because you can pitch a tent or rent a cheap cabin, but because it's mercifully close to the city centre. It's on Hietasaari island, 5km northwest of the city centre – but only 2.5km by foot or bicycle via the pedestrian bridges. Nearby is the good Nallikari beach.

Kesähotelli Oppimestari (☎ 884 8527, fax 884 8772; Nahkatehtaankatu 3; singles/ doubles €35/50; open June-early Aug), across

from the Tietomaa Science Centre, is a summer hotel and has the cheapest rooms in Oulu.

Hotel Kortteeri (☎ 550 9700, fax 550 9843, e *oluotsi@pohto.fi, Vellamontie 12; doubles €57; open mid-June–mid-Aug*) is a summer hotel in the Pohto college campus on Hietasaari island. Rooms are hotel-style (ie, no kitchen) with TV.

Hotel Turisti (☎ 5636 100, fax 3110 755; Rautatienkatu 9; singles/doubles/triples €70/ 85/95) is directly opposite the train station in a slightly seedy area but it's a surprisingly bright and tidy place with decent-sized rooms.

Hotel Apollo (☎/fax 52211, fax 372060; e *hotel@apollo.inet.fi; Asemakatu 31-33; singles/doubles from €78/100, discounted to €64/78*) is a small but reasonably stylish hotel with attractive summer rates.

Places to Eat

The best and cheapest snacks and local specialities can be found in the lively **kauppatori** and the classic indoor **kauppahalli** on the southern side of the square. In summer there are stalls selling fresh salmon, cheese bread, paella and more. Oulu's hungry student population means there are plenty of cheap kebab

FINLAND

and pizza places (including no fewer than 11 branches of Koti Pizza!). The best pizzas are at **Da Mario's Pizzeria** (*Torikatu 24; pizzas €6*), while some of the cheapest can be found at **Ristorante Quattro Pizzeria** (*Asemakatu 20*) where you can get pizza, salad and a drink for €5.

Oulu has some fine cafés. **Café Bisketti** (*Kirkkokatu 8*), facing the pedestrian square, is a great spot for lunch with filled rolls, croissants, quiche and cakes for €2.50 to €5, and a small terrace facing the pedestrian square. The hip young crowds of Oulu sip their green tea in the Nordish elegance of **Café Kaldi** (*Isokatu 25*), which has great sweets as well.

Pannu (*☎ 815 1600, Kauppurienkatu 12; mains €6.50-19.50*), in the basement of Stockmann, is a fantastic, informal grill restaurant with a huge range of dishes including snails, ostrich, and various steaks.

Ravintola Istanbul Oriental (*☎ 311 2922; Kauppurienkatu 11; dishes €12-24*) is a Turkish restaurant with style and flair. Kebab meals, such as Iskender and Anatolian, cost from €12 to €15, and there's a good range of vegetarian options, including felafels (€11 to €13).

Eratupa (*☎ 8811 300; mains €18.50-30*), in one of the red storehouses on the waterfront, is a pricey restaurant but the food is high quality and includes everything from whitefish to wild boar.

Entertainment

There's plenty going on in Oulu at night – the number of bikes lined up outside pubs and bars on summer weekends has to be seen to be believed.

Kaarlenholvi Jumpru Pub (*Kauppurienkatu 6*) is an Oulu institution and a great place for meeting locals. It has an enclosed terrace, which is a perennial favourite, and a warren of cosy rooms inside.

Oluthuone Leskinen (*Saaristonkatu 15*) is a friendly bar with an extraordinary range of Finnish and international beers. This is where expats working for Nokia start (and often end) their night, so it's a good place to find out where to head next.

The main pedestrian strip between the kauppatori and Isokatu is called Rotuaari and along here you'll find plenty of bars and cafés, including **Oulon Panimo & Pub** (*Kauppurienkatu 13*), a brewery pub with three home-grown tap beers and a good atmosphere.

On Hallituskatu is a small strip of bars and cafés, including **Never Grow Old**, a reggae bar that hits its stride after 10pm; **Tervahovi**, a typically Finnish pub popular with a slightly older crowd; and **St Michael's**, an Irish bar.

Café Milou (*Asemakatu 21*), one block north, is away from the main strip but is one of the hippest bars in town, packing in students with its cheap beer, 'way gone' vibe and bookshelves filled with comics (Tin Tin among others).

The grungy **45 Special** (*☎ 881 1845; Saaristonkatu 12*) is Oulu's best rock venue, with free entry most nights and wall-to-wall patrons. The **Giggling Marlin** (*Torikatu 21-22*) is one of a new brand of 'Suomi pop' clubs, featuring two dance floors with contemporary Finnish pop and international music.

For something more refined, the **Oulu Theatre** (*☎ 5584 7600; Kaarlenväylä 2*) has classical music, contemporary theatre and the occasional Shakespearian performance.

Getting There & Away

Finnair has daily direct flights from Helsinki. The airport is 15km south of town (take bus No 19; €4.40). Trains and buses connect Oulu with all main centres; the fastest direct train from Helsinki takes only six hours (€53.40). Bus services include Rovaniemi (€26.70), Tornio (€19.20) and Kajaani (€20.90).

KUUSAMO
☎ 08 • pop 19,000

Kuusamo is a frontier town 200km northeast of Oulu, and similar in feel to the towns of Lapland. It's the base for trekking or canoeing trips in Oulanko National Park, and is close to one of Finland's most popular ski resorts (Ruka).

There are many possibilities for cross-country skiing, hiking and fishing and fast, rugged rapids on the **Kitkajoki River**. Inquire about organised tours at the **tourist office** (*☎ 850 2910; Torangintaival 2*).

Kuusamon Kansanopisto (*☎ 852 2132, fax 8521 1134; Kitkantie 35; dorm beds from €7.50, singles/doubles €14.50/26.50; open Midsummer-Aug*), is a rambling summer HI hostel close to the town centre.

Finnair flies daily to Helsinki. Buses run daily from Kajaani, Oulu and Kemijärvi.

Oulanko National Park

This is one of the most visited national parks in Finland, thanks mainly to the 80km

Karhunkierros Trail (Bear's Ring), a spectacular three- or four-day trek through rugged cliffs, gorges and suspension bridges starting from either the Hautajärvi Visitor Centre or the Ristikallio parking area, to Ruka, 25km north of Kuusamo.

There are shelters and free overnight huts on the trail. Get the *Rukatunturi-Oulanka* map (1:40,000) for trail and hut information.

Juuma is another gateway to the region, with accommodation and accessibility to some of the main sights, such as the **Myllykoski** and **Jyrävä** waterfalls. If you don't have the time or resources for the longer walk, you can do the 12km **Little Bear's Ring** from Juuma in around four hours. The trail starts at **Lomakylä Retkietappi** (*☎ 863 218*), where there's camping and cabins.

Lapland

Lapland is Finland's true wilderness and a place of extremes: continuous daylight in summer and continuous night in winter; and average daytime temperatures that range from -15°C in December to 15°C in June. If you care to brave the Arctic winter, October, February and March are ideal times to see the stunning aurora borealis (northern lights).

From September, the period known locally as *ruska* produces exceptional autumn colours and in the far north *kaamos*, the season of eerie bluish light, begins late in October.

Finnish Lapland is home to some 6500 Sami people and their living culture is best seen in the villages of Hetta, Inari or remote Utsjoki. The Sami take pride in their heritage and still wear traditional dress on festival days and keep close contact with their Norwegian counterparts across the border. However, increasing numbers of Sami define themselves not as Sami but as Finns.

Reindeer farming, fishing and forestry are the largest industries in Lapland, although there's a tourist industry in handicrafts. Lake Inarijärvi, 300km north of Rovaniemi, is a popular destination, but most of Lapland remains wilderness where the Sami pasture their reindeer herds of some 230,000 head.

TORNIO
☎ 016 • pop 23,200
The Swedish town of Haparanda across the Tornionjoki is Tornio's twin, and they're geographically – if not culturally – melded into one. This is the most southerly land crossing between the two countries.

The **Green Line Centre** (*☎ 432 733;* Ⓦ *www.tornio.fi; open 8am-8pm Mon-Fri, 10am-8pm Sat & Sun June–mid-Aug; 8am-11.30am & 12.30pm-4pm Mon-Fr mid-Aug–May*), near the bridge on the Tornio side of the border, acts as the tourist office for both towns, with information on Finland and Sweden. There's free Internet access, and there are a couple of terminals at the **public library**, next to the Aine Art Museum.

Things to See & Do
The **Green Zone golf course** (*☎ 431 711*) is justifiably famous (or should be). Not only can you play midnight golf (with the sun shining), but the course actually straddles the border. You can tee off in Finland and hit the ball into Sweden, which means if you start at, say, 12.30am, the ball will remain in the air for an hour and land in yesterday. The price for this novelty is €22 for green fees (18 holes) plus around €10 if you need to hire a shoddy set of clubs. To play after 10pm you need to book in advance.

Catch a salmon in the Tornio River, which runs through town; local guide **Risto Mämmioja** (*☎ 470 093 or 040-551 1283*) will give you tips. Rafting trips are popular in summer on the 3.5km-long **Kukkola rapids**, 15km north of town.

Places to Stay & Eat
Camping Tornio (*☎ 445 945;* ⓔ *sirkka.hyry@ pp.inet.fi; Matkailijantie; tent sites €15, cabins €39-54*) is about 3km from town on the road to Kemi.

Hostel Tornio (*☎ 211 9244;* ⓔ *pptoim isto@ppopisto.fi, Kivirannantie 13-15; singles/ doubles €11/22, with attached bath €22.50/ 35; open June-Aug*) is a typical HI-affiliated summer hostel in a poor location east of the river about 3km from the centre. Facilities are good, including kitchen, lounge, laundry and a small gym.

A better choice for hostellers is the **STF Youth Hostel** (*☎ 0046 611 71, fax 0046 61784; Strandgatan 26*) in Haparanda. Reception is open from 5pm and there's a good café here.

Ristorante Dal Laziale (*☎ 481 009; Kauppakatu 12; pasta €10, pizza €4-8*) is a popular Italian place with reasonably priced meals.

FINLAND

It's open till 11pm. **Karkiaisen Leipomo** (*Länsiranta 9*) has the best fresh pastries, cakes and *donitsi* (doughnuts) in town.

For entertainment Finnish-style, head to **Umpitunneli**, near the bridge on Hallituskatu. It's an open-air dance pub where you can see the *humppa* in full swing from Wednesday to Saturday.

Getting There & Away

From Kemi (see next entry), take a bus from the train station (€4.50, free with Finnrail pass; 30 minutes). Road No 21 leads from Tornio to the north, and there are frequent direct buses to Rovaniemi (€16.80).

KEMI

☎ 016 • pop 25,000

Kemi is an industrial town with huge pulp factories creating a strong whiff of that distinctive sulphur smell. That may not sound terribly appealing, but Kemi is home to one of Lapland's blockbuster winter attractions – a four-hour cruise aboard the *Sampo*, an authentic Arctic icebreaker ship and the only one in the world that accepts passengers. The trip includes ice swimming in special drysuits, as well as a walk or snowmobile trip on the ice – a remarkable experience. The *Sampo* sails at noon on Thursday, Friday and Saturday from mid-December to late April and costs a whopping €162 per person. Contact **Sampo Tours** (☎ 256 548, fax 256 361; **W** *www.sampotours.com; Torikatu 2*).

Another reason to visit in winter is the **Snow Castle** (☎ 259 502; **W** *www.snowcastle.net; adult/child €5/2.50; open 10am-6pm Mon-Thurs, 10am-8pm Fri-Sun Feb–mid-Apr*). The castle, first built in 1996, features an ice restaurant with bar, ice tables covered with reindeer fur, and ice sculptures. It's also possible to stay overnight in the **snow hotel** where heavy-duty Arctic sleeping bags keep you warm in -5°C room temperature!

The **tourist office** (☎ 259 467; **W** *www .kemi.fi; Kauppakatu 19; open daily June-Aug, Mon-Fri Sept-May*), in the Gemstone Gallery, can direct you to a handful of other attractions in town.

Places to Stay & Eat

Kemi has no hostel, but in summer there is **Hotel Relletti** (*233 541; Miilukatu 1; singles/doubles €25/40*), 1.5km southeast of the train station.

Hotel Palomestari (☎ 257 117; *Valtakatu 12; singles/doubles from €67/71*) is more central – only a few hundred metres from the bus and train stations.

Café Sufe (*Kauppakatu 15*) is the best place for coffee and cakes in Kemi, and there's a €6 lunch buffet. **Hullu Pohjola** (☎ 458 0250; *Meripuistokatu 9*) is a pub offering Tex-Mex fare such as burritos and fajitas.

The **Sampo** (*mains €12-15*) serves as an atmospheric daytime restaurant in summer, but you'll need your own transport to get to Ajos Harbour, 9km away.

Getting There & Away

There are trains from Helsinki (€64.20; 8½ hours) and Rovaniemi (€15; 1½ hours). Buses to/from Tornio are free with a Finnrail pass.

ROVANIEMI

☎ 016 • pop 35,400

Rovaniemi is the capital of and gateway to Lapland. Many travellers make a beeline here from Helsinki, either to say they've visited Lapland or to 'cross' the Arctic Circle. Neither is a major event in its own right, but there's a lot to be said for this latitude in summer – when the midnight sun really does shine – and in winter this is a convenient base for expensive **dog or reindeer sledding, skiing** or **snowmobile safaris**.

The town itself is quite modern and relatively uninteresting, built from a plan by Alvar Aalto after its complete destruction in WWII (the main streets radiate out from Hallituskatu in the shape of reindeer antlers, in a twee salute to local business, but this would only be obvious from the air!). The official Arctic Circle marker and Santa Claus village is only 8km away, so the tour buses thunder through all year.

Information

The tourist office shamelessly goes by the name **Santa Claus Tourist Centre** (☎ 346 270; **W** *www.rovaniemi.fi; Koskikatu 1; open 8am-6pm Mon-Fri, 10am-4pm Sat & Sun June-late Aug; 8am-4pm Mon-Fri late Aug-May*) but is an excellent source of information for all of Lapland.

Etiäinen (☎ 647 820; *open 10am-5pm daily*) at Napapiiri is the information centre for the national parks and trekking regions, with information on hiking and fishing in Lapland.

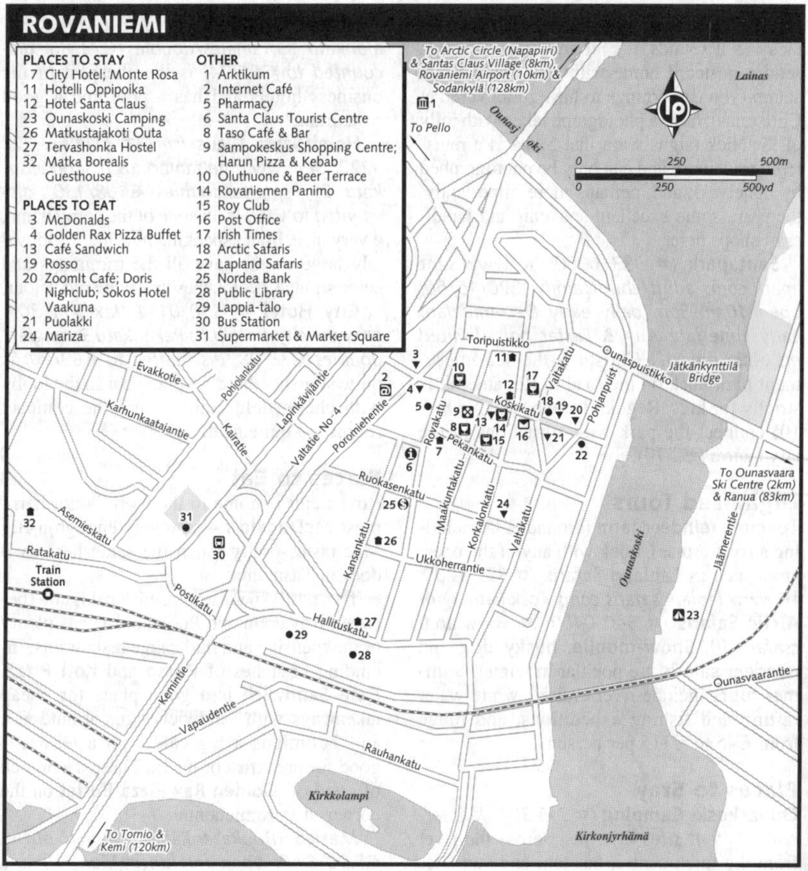
ROVANIEMI
PLACES TO STAY
7 City Hotel; Monte Rosa
11 Hotelli Oppipoika
12 Hotel Santa Claus
23 Ounaskoski Camping
26 Matkustajakoti Outa
27 Tervashonka Hostel
32 Matka Borealis Guesthouse
PLACES TO EAT
3 McDonalds
4 Golden Rax Pizza Buffet
13 Café Sandwich
19 Rosso
20 ZoomIt Café; Doris Nighclub; Sokos Hotel Vaakuna
21 Puolakki
24 Mariza
OTHER
1 Arktikum
2 Internet Café
5 Pharmacy
6 Santa Claus Tourist Centre
8 Taso Café & Bar
9 Sampokeskus Shopping Centre; Harun Pizza & Kebab
10 Oluthuone & Beer Terrace
14 Rovaniemen Panimo
15 Roy Club
16 Post Office
17 Irish Times
18 Arctic Safaris
22 Lapland Safaris
25 Nordea Bank
28 Public Library
29 Lappia-talo
30 Bus Station
31 Supermarket & Market Square
To Arctic Circle (Napapiiri) & Santas Claus Village (8km), Rovaniemi Airport (10km) & Sodankylä (128km)
To Pello
Ounasjoki
Lainas
0 250 500m
0 250 500yd
Jätkänkynttilä Bridge
Toripuistikko
Ounaspuistikko
Evakkotie
Pohjolankatu
Karhunkaatajantie
Lapinkävijäntie
Kairatie
Valtatie No 4
Poromiehentie
Rovakatu
Koskikatu
Valtakatu
Pohjanpuisto
Pekankatu
Ruokasenkatu
Maakuntakatu
Korkalonkatu
To Ounasvaara Ski Centre (2km) & Ranua (83km)
Asemieskatu
Ratakatu
Train Station
Kansankatu
Ukkoherrantie
Ounaskoski
Jäämerentie
Postikatu
Hallituskatu
Kemintie
Vapaudentie
Ounasvaarantie
Rauhankatu
Kirkkolampi
To Tornio & Kemi (120km)
Kirkonjyrhämä

The **post office** is at Koskikatu 9 but most visitors prefer to send their postcards from the busy Santa Claus post office at Napapiiri. The **public library** *(Hallituskatu 9; open Mon-Sat)*, has several Internet terminals, and there is an **Internet café** on Poromiehentie (€3 an hour).

Bicycles can be rented from Arctic Safaris (€18 for 24 hours) at Koskikatu 6.

Things to See & Do

Arktikum *(☎ 317 840; W www.arktikum.fi; Pohjoisranta 4; adult/student/child €10/8.50/5; open 9am-8pm daily mid-June–mid-Aug, 10am-6pm daily early June-Sept, 10am-4pm daily Oct-Apr)*, with its beautifully designed glass tunnel, is one of the best museums in Finland. Exhibition spaces include superb static and interactive displays focusing on Arctic flora and fauna as well as the Sami and other people of Arctic Europe, Asia and North America. There's also a multivision theatre. Give yourself at least a couple of hours to get around it.

Rovaniemi has several Alvar Aalto designed buildings, including the library, town hall and the **Lappia-talo** *(☎ 322 2745; Hallituskatu 11-13)*, an impressive concert hall.

Across the Ounasjoki river and 3km above the town, the **Ounasvaara Ski Centre** has six downhill ski slopes and three ski jumps, plus a summer tobogganing run.

The official **Arctic Circle marker** *(Napapiiri; bus No 8 or 11)* is 8km north of Rovaniemi, and built on top of it is the 'official' **Santa Claus Village**. The Santa Claus post office receives close to a million letters each year. As tacky as it sounds, it's all good fun. You can send a postcard home with an official Santa stamp (you can arrange to have it delivered at Christmas); have a photograph taken with jolly ol' St Nick (signs warn that Santa is a registered trademark and can only be photographed by his elves); and, perhaps more importantly, there are some excellent souvenir and handicraft shops here.

Santapark (☎ 333 0000; W www.sant apark.com; adult/child/family €20/15/50; open 10am-8pm daily early Dec–mid-Jan; early June-late Aug & Easter hols; limited hrs other times), a Christmas-themed amusement park back on the road to Rovaniemi, is strictly for kids. Regular local buses (No 8 or 10) connect the park with attractions in the city centre (€2.70).

Organised Tours
To tour a **reindeer farm** (around €45 including a river cruise), book with any of the operators such as **Lapland Safaris** (☎ 331 1200; W www.laplandsafaris.com; Koskikatu 1) or **Arctic Safaris** (☎ 340 0400; W www.arcti csafaris.fi). **Snow-mobile, husky dog** and **reindeer safaris** are popular in winter. **Summer tours** include river cruises, white-water rafting and fishing expeditions, and range from €45 to €115 per person.

Places to Stay
Ounaskoski Camping (☎ 345 304; Jäämerentie 1; tent sites €5), just across the river from the town centre, has tent and van sites only.

Tervashonka Hostel (☎ 344 644; Hallituskatu 16; dorm beds €11.50, singles/doubles €25.50/31) is an 'old school' hostel but is no worse for that – facilities are not flash but it has plenty of character. Reception is closed from 10am to 5pm, and closes again at 10pm (ring ahead if you're coming in on the night train).

Matka Borealis (☎/fax 342 0130; Asemieskatu 1; singles/doubles €40/52), opposite the train station, is a friendly guesthouse offering clean, simple rooms with breakfast included.

Matkustajakoti Outa (☎ 312 474; Ukkoherrantie 16; single/doubles €30/40) is another cheap no-frills guesthouse with shared bathrooms, but this one is right in the town centre.

Hotelli Oppipoika (☎ 338 8111; Korkalonkatu 33; singles/doubles €73/86, discounted to €61/74) is the cheapest of the business hotels and has a pool and a good restaurant.

Hotel Santa Claus (☎ 321 321, fax 321 3222; W www.hotelsantaclaus.fi; Korkalonkatu 29; singles/doubles €108/130, discounted to €83) is, in spite of the corny name, a very nice, brand spanking new hotel. Unusually large rooms have all the trimmings and some strange 70s touches involving red velour.

City Hotel (☎ 330 0111, fax 311 304; W www.city-hotelli.fi; Pekankatu 9; singles/doubles €78/98, discounted to €69/80) is quite stylish – there's a piano bar in the lobby with chesterfield couches and the compact rooms are quite neat.

Places to Eat
Rovaniemi is home to the world's northernmost **McDonald's** – strangely enough a Big Mac tastes pretty much the same here as it does in Tasmania.

The partly pedestrianised Koskikatu (between Rovakatu and Pohjanpuist) has plenty of inexpensive and mid-range restaurants, including branches of **Rosso** and **Koti Pizza**. **Café Sandwich** is a good place for cheap takeaways with sandwiches for around €3, and **ZoomIt** is a big café with a terrace – good for breakfast or lunch. There's a branch of good ol' **Golden Rax Pizza Buffet** on the corner of Poromiehentie.

Mariza (Ruokasenkatu 2; lunch buffet €5.90-6.50; open for lunch Mon-Fri) is a simple working-class place offering a fabulous lunch buffet of home-cooked Finnish food including hot dishes, soup and salad.

Monte Rosa (Pekankatu 9; mains €9-12), attached to the City Hotel, serves up a range of pasta, Tex-Mex (fajitas etc) and American-Finnish dishes, and has a great terrace at the side.

Puolakki (Valtakatu; mains €15-25) is arguably Rovaniemi's best restaurant when it comes to traditional Lappish cuisine. It's not cheap and the restaurant itself is unassuming, but the food is delicious and includes reindeer, whitefish and cloudberry desserts.

Entertainment
Discounting the winter ski resorts, Rovaniemi is the only place north of Oulu with a half-decent nightlife. In summer it's hard to

resist sitting out under the midnight sun in the open beer terrace of **Oluthuone**, set up on the pedestrian part of Koskikatu.

Rovaniemen Panimo (*Koskikatu 11*) is a popular English-style pub with cosy seating arrangements, a small terrace and international beers on tap. Despite the name, no beer is brewed on the premises.

Irish Times (*Valtakatu 35*) has a great heated terrace at the back, pool tables downstairs and is a cosy place to be in winter.

Taso Café & Bar (*Maakuntakatu*) is the trendiest place in Rovaniemi with loungy, lime-green retro furniture, magazines, a hip young crowd and quality DJs on weekend evenings.

Across the road, the basement **Roy Club** (*Maakuntakatu 24*) takes over some of the Taso crowd after 2am and is usually packed with students.

Doris Nightclub, in the Sokos Hotel Vakuna, is open till 4am and attracts a slightly older crowd (must be over 22 on Friday and Saturday).

Getting There & Away

Finnair has daily flights from Helsinki, Kemi and Oulu; there's an airport bus that meets all flights (€3.50).

Frequent buses travel to Kemi (€14.60) and Oulu (€26.70) to the south; Muonio, Enontekiö (Hetta) and Kilpisjärvi in the northwest, Kuusamo in the east; and to Sodankylä (€16.80), Ivalo and Inari in the north, continuing on to Norway.

The train is the best way to travel between Helsinki and Rovaniemi (€69.20, 10 to 12 hours) – it's considerably quicker and cheaper than the bus. There are eight daily trains (via Oulu), including four overnight services. There's one train connection daily to Kemijärvi, farther north (1½ hours).

RANUA WILDLIFE PARK

Ranua, 83km south of Rovaniemi on road No 78, is home to the excellent Ranua Wildlife Park (*☎ 355 1921; adult/child & student €10/8.50; open 9am-8pm daily June–mid-Aug, shorter hrs mid-Aug–May*). Its 30 mammal and 30 bird species, including brown and polar bears, lynx, Arctic fox and several species of owl, are housed in spacious natural enclosures, and are all native to Finland or Scandinavia. As with any zoo, seeing the animals active is a matter of chance but

you'll certainly get a look at the normally elusive *hirvi* – the Finnish elk.

There are daily buses to Ranua from Oulu and Kajaani, and several daily connections from Rovaniemi.

SODANKYLÄ
☎ 016

The busy market town of Sodankylä is a reasonable place to break the journey between Rovaniemi and northern Lapland. It's also a base for visiting the **Lampivaara Amethyst Mine** (*☎ 2709 0203;* [W] *www.amethystmine.fi; Lampivaara Fell; adult/child € 11/6; open 11am-5pm daily early June-Sept*), 38km south in Luosto.

The small **tourist office** (*☎ 618 168;* [W] *www.sodankyla.fi; Jäämerentie 7*) is at the back of a craft shop on the main shopping street.

Sodankylä is known for the **Midnight Sun International Film Festival** held every June. Tickets are available from the tourist office.

Camping Sodankylä Nilimella (*☎ 612 181, fax 611 503; tent sites €12.60, cabins €34-42; open June–mid-Aug*) is across the river from the village. It's a friendly place – if you're travelling alone the owners may let you have a cabin for €17.

Majatalo Kolme Veljestä (*☎ 611 216; Ivalontie 1; singles/doubles/triples €35/50/60*) is a simple guesthouse about 500m north of the bus station with tidy rooms and a guest lounge and kitchen.

There are six buses daily to/from Rovaniemi (€16.80, 1¾ hours).

IVALO
☎ 016 • pop 3500

Ivalo is the administrative and commercial centre of the Inari district, but it's a modern centre with no special attractions – Inari, 40km further north, is a better place to stop. Ivalo is somewhere to stock up on provisions, make bus connections, or meet some crusty old gold-panners who come to town to trade their gold chips for beer. There's no tourist office.

Ukonjärvi Lomakylä (*☎ 667 501, fax 667 516; tent/caravan sites €12/16, cottages €47-75; open May-late Sept*), north of Ivalo at the lake of the same name, has good facilities, including boats and a good restaurant and bar.

Express buses from Rovaniemi run twice daily, and continue north to Nordkapp (Norway) before returning. Gold Line buses run

FINLAND

from Ivalo to Saariselka, Inari, Roveniemi and Murmansk (Russia).

INARI
☎ 016 • pop 550

As unprepossessing as it seems at first, the tiny village of Inari (Sami: Anár) is the most interesting point of civilisation in far northern Lapland. This is the main Sami community in the region, and a centre for genuine Sami handicrafts – although the collection of galleries and boutique shops has a distinct air of commercialism, this is the best place in Finland to shop for genuine Lappish and Sami handmade textiles, jewellery, silverware and woodwork.

Inari is a good base for exploring northern Lapland but it has some fine attractions of its own. Spend at least a day here visiting the Siida museum, trekking to the Wilderness Church, and perhaps taking an afternoon cruise on lake Inarijärvi.

One of the finest conceptual and open-air museums in Finland, **Siida** (☎ 665 212; W www.samimuseum.fi; adult/student & pensioner/child €7/6/3; open 9am-8pm daily June-Sept, 10am-5pm Tues-Sun Oct-May) should not be missed. The exhibition successfully brings to life Sami origins, culture, lifestyle and present-day struggles. Outside is a fine open-air museum featuring Sami buildings, handicrafts and artefacts.

There's a marked 7.5km walking track (starting from the Siida parking area) to the 18th-century **Pielpajärvi wilderness church**, with a hut and a sauna nearby. If you have a vehicle, there's another parking area 3km closer.

In summer, boat trips leave for the prominent **Ukko Island**, an ancient cult site for the Inari Samis. The two-hour cruise on Lake Inarijärvi costs €12/6 (adult/child).

Places to Stay
About 3km from Inari on the road to Lemmenjoki is a small, free **camping ground** with firewood and a pit toilet. **Uruniemi Camping** (☎ 671 331, fax 671 200; tent sites €11, cottages from €17 a double, for four people €34-42; open Mar-late Sept), about 2km south of town, is a well-equipped lakeside camping ground with cottages, café, sauna and boats and bikes for hire.

The nearest youth hostel is the HI-affiliated **Hostel Jokitörmä** (☎ 672 725, fax 672 745; tent sites €12.60, dorms €13.20, single/double cabins €12.50/21.80), on the Arctic

Hwy about 23km north of Inari. It's a great place with cosy two- and four-person rooms, and a separate set of cottages, each with their own kitchen and bathroom facilities – it's a pity it's not closer to Inari, but all buses will stop here on request.

Hotel Inari (☎ 671 026; singles/doubles €33.50/38) is the hub of the village and has decent rooms with attached bath. It also has a good **restaurant** (mains €10-13, pizzas €4-8) with all the Lappish dishes – plenty of reindeer and salmon prepared in a variety of ways. Pizzas include 'sauteed reindeer, peach and onion', and there are inexpensive burgers.

Inarin Kultahovi (☎ 671 221; mains €11-24) has a classy à la carte menu of Lappish specialities and a set three-course lunch and dinner menu (€16). Appetisers include crepes filled with forest mushrooms (€5.10).

Getting There & Away
The Arctic Highway runs through Inari so buses from Rovaniemi ply the route right through to Nordkapp. Gold Line buses run daily to/from Ivalo (€5.70, 40 minutes) with connections south to Rovaniemi.

LEMMENJOKI NATIONAL PARK
At 2855 sq km, Lemmenjoki is Finland's largest national park, and one of its most diverse. Hiking trails extend for over 70km through the vast reserve and there are several free wilderness huts within the nature reserve.

The **Lemmenjoki nature centre** (☎ 0205-647 793; open 9am-9pm daily June-Sept) is just before the village of Njurgulahti, about 50km southwest of Inari. It has a small interpretive exhibition, a powerful set of binoculars, and you can purchase maps and fishing permits here.

Even if you're not keen on an extended trek, you can take a **boat cruise** (€14/27 one way/return) along the Lemmenjoki valley in summer, from Njurgulahti village to the Kultahamina wilderness hut at Gold Harbour. A 20km marked trail also follows the course of the river, so you can take the boat one-way, then hike back.

Accommodation at Njurgulahti includes two very cheap camping grounds. **Ahkun Tupa** (☎/fax 061-673 435; camping per person €2, 2-/4-person cabins from €21/39) is a switched-on place with a restaurant, canoe hire and boat trips.

In summer, Gold Line buses run at least once a day from Ivalo and Inari to Lemmenjoki (two hours).

NORTHWESTERN LAPLAND

As an alternative trans-Lapland route, the western road No 21 gives you the possibility of crossing the border into Sweden across the Tornionjoki and Muonionjoki rivers; there are six border crossings – Tornio, Aavasaksa, Pello, Kolari, Muonio and Karesuvanto – with no formalities or passport control. After the last border crossing at Karesuvanto, the scenery becomes progressively more barren until the snow-capped mountains mark the point where Finland ends and Norway begins. This route is far more dramatic (though longer) than the more popular eastern route to Nordkapp.

In winter, this part of Lapland is a centre for downhill skiing, with two major resorts and a couple of smaller ones. In summer there are good opportunities for hiking, mountainbiking, canoeing and white-white rafting.

Ylläs
☎ 016

Ylläs, 35km north-east of the border town of Kolari, is a popular **ski resort** and the highest fell in Finland with downhill skiing. There are 37 slopes and 20 lifts; passes are €26 per day. In summer Ylläs is a mecca for mountain bikers, and there are trekking opportunities around the fells. **Kellokas Nature Centre** (☎ 647 039) is a national park visitor centre at the foot of Ylläs fell.

You can rent bikes (from €11.80 a day) and canoes and organise summer and winter activities through **Ylläs Holiday Service** (☎ 569 666; W www.yllasholiday.com) in the village of Äkäslompolo. Also here is **Ylläs Matkailu Oy** (☎ 569 721), the regional booking and information service. Most of the accommodation is deserted in summer (and many places are closed), so it's easy enough to find a bed, but book well ahead in winter.

If you arrive by train in Kolari, there is a connecting bus that goes first to Ylläsjärvi then on to Äkäslompolo.

Muonio
☎ 016

Muonio is the last significant town on road No 21 before the road continues on towards Kilpisjärvi. It offers all services, and the **Kiela**

Naturium (☎ 532 280; e kiela@munio.fi; open 10am-6pm daily July–mid-Aug, 11am-5pm Mon-Fri April-May & Sept-Dec) combines tourist information with a nifty 3D-multimedia fells nature display, and planetarium with aurora borealis show (adult/child €10/6; every 20 minutes).

South of the centre, the **Harriniva Holiday Centre** (☎ 530 0300, fax 532 750; W www .harriniva.fi) rents equipment and has a vast programme of summer and winter activities, as well as accommodation. Harriniva has a husky farm with 160 huskies (guided tour €6/3.50 adult/child). In winter, there are dogsledding safaris from one hour (€52) to two days (€390), as well as snowmobile and reindeer safaris. In summer, the centre offers daily guided white-water rafting trips from €22 for a 1½ hour trip.

Lomamaja Pekonen (☎ 532 237, fax 532 236; Lahenrannantie 10; single/double rooms €26/40, cottages €27-59), near the town centre, has rooms and a range of cottages sleeping two to four people.

Levi & Sirkka
☎ 016

Levi is a major skiing centre built around the village of Sirkka. This is one of the most popular ski resorts in Lapland, particularly with the party crowd. The **tourist office** (☎ 639 3300, fax 643 469; W www.levi.fi; Myllyojantie 2) handles accommodation bookings as well as snowmobile safaris, dog-sled treks and reindeer rides.

The resort has 45 downhill slopes and 19 lifts. Ski passes cost €22/105 per day/week in the winter high season, and equipment can be rented for around €19 a day. Two lifts operate in summer, and mountain bikes can be hired from the ski rental shop (€20 per day).

Accommodation prices are through the roof in the peak season of February to May and in December. In summer (May to September), however, you can get a comfortable cabin sleeping up to five people for as little as €45 a night and hotel prices drop to rates comparable to anywhere else in Finland.

Hetta & Pallastunturi National Park

One of the easiest long-distance walks in Lapland is the excellent 60km trekking route between the northern village of **Hetta** (previously known and still signposted as

FINLAND

Enontekiö) and **Hotelli Pallas** (☎ *016-532 441)*. The marked trail passes through the Pallastunturi National Park and can easily be completed in four days. There are seven free wilderness huts, but they could be packed with people in summer so it's wise to carry a tent. At the Hetta end of the route, you will have to catch a boat taxi across the lake for a small fee.

There's plenty of accommodation in Hetta, and there's the **Fell Lapland Nature Centre** (☎ *533 056; Peuratie)* which is the combined local tourist office and a visitor centre for the Pallastunturi National Park.

There are daily buses from Muonio to Pallastunturi (to the hotel; €4.50, 45 minutes) and one bus a week direct from Rovaniemi to Pallas. Buses to Hetta run daily from Rovaniemi (€35.20, five hours) via Kittilä and Muonio.

Kilpisjärvi
☎ 016

Some of Finland's highest mountains (which aren't very high) can be seen in this small, remote trekking centre on the shores of Lake Kilpisjärvi. Most people climb the **Saana** (1029m), or walk (or take a boat taxi, €13) to the **Malla Nature Park**, which has access to the joint border post of Sweden, Norway and Finland (you can visit three countries in a matter of seconds). Serious trekkers can walk to the **Halti Fell**, the highest in Finland. There are wilderness huts en route but a map is essential. Information is available from the hiking centre at Kilpisjärven Retkeilykeskus.

Kilpisjärven Retkeilykeskus (☎ *537 771, fax 537 702; @ retkeilykeskus@sunpoint.net; tent sites €12, singles/doubles €37/50, 4-person cottage €49; open early Aug-late Sept)*, close to the Norwegian border, is convenient to the trekking routes and is a centre for information. There's a range of rooms and cottages all with attached bath.

Peera Hiking Centre (☎/fax *532 659; beds €16.50-20.50; open late Feb-late Oct)* is a HI-affiliated hostel that, although only 25km from Kilpisjärvi, is a real wilderness place. It's very cosy and welcoming – spend time here walking, fishing and relaxing. There's a kitchen, sauna, laundry, and a café.

There is a daily bus connection between Rovaniemi and Kilpisjärvi (€45.70, eight hours) via Kittilä and Muonio.

Greenland

It's said that once a traveller has seen the world, there's always Greenland, the world's largest island (excluding the island-continent of Australia). Beyond Ilulissat and Kulusuk (the world's most unusual day trips), travellers can still find a lot of space between rucksacks. However, as a growing number of visitors are discovering this vast wilderness, anyone who's saving Greenland for last may not beat the crowds.

Greenland, known as Kalaallit Nunaat in Greenlandic, has a beautiful, rugged and dramatic landscape that can be forbidding, and the country's diversity is expressed in subtle variations on arctic conditions: rocky, treeless mountains; dry or boggy tundra; long, sinuous fjords choked with huge icebergs; and expansive sheets and tortured rivers of ice. However, what Greenland lacks in range, it makes up for in quality.

Greenland also exemplifies what is perhaps the most successful meeting of European and indigenous cultures in the colonial world. Its intriguing people, their resourceful and practical traditions and the haunting beauty of their land will never be forgotten by anyone who experiences them first-hand.

Facts about Greenland

HISTORY
The Inuit
The Inuit (pronounced **Inn**-ooit) people, sometimes called Eskimos ('eaters of raw meat' in native American languages – this name is now out of favour), are the predominant population group in Greenland.

There's evidence that the Inuit sailed from Siberia to Alaska by *umiaq* (skin boat) around 7000 to 8000 years ago. It's thought that the first Stone Age Greenlanders, known as Independence I, migrated from Ellesmere Island in northern Canada to far northern Greenland around 5000 years ago. These hardy people survived by hunting polar bears, musk oxen, arctic hares and other animals. They were either supplanted by or developed into the culture known as Independence II, which inhabited northern Greenland from

At a Glance

Capital	Nuuk
Population	56,540
Area	2,415,100 sq km
Official Language	Greenlandic
GDP	US$1 billion
Time	GMT/UTC-0300
Country Phone Code	☎ 299

Hiking Around
Ilulissat p256
Ilulissat (Jakobshavn) p255
Kangerlussuaq to
Sisimiut Trek pp252-3
Sisimiut (Holsteinsborg)
p250
Tasiilaq
(Ammassalik)
p262
Nuuk (Godthåb)
p246
Narsarsuaq
p236
Around Narsarsuaq,
Narsaq & Qaqortoq p239
Narsaq p240
Qaqortoq
(Julianehåb) p242
Nanortalik p244
GREENLAND
NORWAY
ICELAND
FAROE
ISLANDS
DENMARK

Highlights
- Trekking from Qaqortoq to Igaliku via the Hvalsey church ruins, South Greenland (p243)
- Cruising past the soaring granite peaks in Tasermiut Fjord, near Nanortalik in South Greenland (p244)
- Sitting and contemplating the extraordinary Ilulissat Kangerlua (Ilulissat icefjord) (p254)
- Visiting Uummannaq, arguably the finest town in arctic Greenland (p258)
- Visiting Tasiilaq and hiking to the top of Qaqqartivagajik, East Greenland (p261)

about 3400 to 2600 years ago. Independence II people travelled in hunting groups of 20 to 40 and lived in tents.

Archaeological sites associated with the Saqqaq culture, which migrated from Canada to West Greenland around 3800 years ago, have been discovered in East Greenland and

221

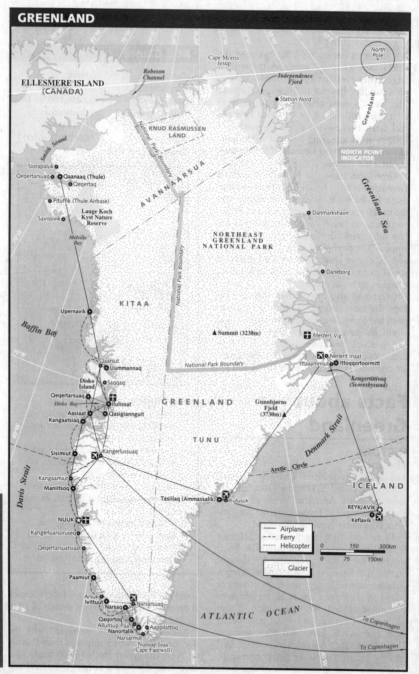

GREENLAND

North Pole

Greenland

NORTH POINT INDICATOR

Cape Morris Jesup

Independence Fjord

ELLESMERE ISLAND (CANADA)

Robeson Channel

Station Nord

KNUD RASMUSSEN LAND

National Park Boundary

AVANNAARSUA

Smith Sound

Siorapaluk

Qeqertarsuaq ○ Qaanaaq (Thule)
○ Qeqertaq

Pituffik (Thule Airbase)

Lauge Koch Kyst Nature Reserve

Savissivik

Melville Bay

Danmarkshavn

NORTHEAST GREENLAND NATIONAL PARK

Greenland Sea

Daneborg

KITAA

Baffin Bay

Upernavik

▲ Summit (3238m)

National Park Boundary

✠ Mesters Vig

National Park Boundary

Qaarsut
○ Uummannaq

Disko Island

Saqqaq

Disko Bay

Qeqertarsuaq ○ ✠ Ilulissat

Aasiaat ○ Qasigiannguit

Kangaatsiaq ○

GREENLAND

Gunnbjørns Fjeld (3730m) ▲

TUNU

✠ Nerlerit Inaat
Ittaajimmiut ○ Ittoqqortoormitt

Kangertittivaq (Scoresbysund)

Sisimiut ○ ✠

Kangerlussuaq

Kangaamiut ○

Maniitsoq ○

Arctic Circle

Tasiilaq (Ammassalik) ✈
○ Kulusuk

Denmark Strait

ICELAND

NUUK ✠

Kangerluarsoruseq ○

Qeqertarsuatsiaat ○

REYKJAVIK ✈
Keflavik ✠

Davis Strait

Paamiut ○

Arsuk ○
Ivittuut ○
Narsaq ○ ✈ Narsarsuaq
Alluitsup Paa ○ ○ Aappilattoq
Qaqortoq ○
Nanortalik ○
Narsarmiut ○ Nunaap Isua (Cape Farewell)

ATLANTIC OCEAN

To Copenhagen

To Copenhagen

	Airplane
- - -	Ferry
.....	Helicopter

Glacier

0   150   300km
0   75   150mi

GREENLAND

along the west coast as far north as Upernavik. The Saqqaq people lived in tents (small summer hunting groups) and more elaborate 'houses' (for the extended family group in winter). It is thought that there were large Saqqaq gatherings, probably during the hunting season. Around 2500 years ago, however, the climate turned colder and the Saqqaq culture mysteriously disappeared; they either combined with the Independence II people (who had migrated southwards), retreated westwards to Canada, or developed into the Dorset culture.

The Dorset culture thrived since it was more technologically advanced and lived in more communal societies than its predecessors. Its people carved weapons and artistic pieces from bone and ivory, used sleds to transport belongings and burned oil from whale and seal blubber for heat and light. However, archaeological research on the Saqqaq and Dorset periods is ongoing and the results may radically alter long-held theories.

The Thule culture apparently migrated from Canada during the warmer 10th century and spread all over Greenland in less than 150 years, absorbing or supplanting all other cultures. However, it's possible that Independence II didn't migrate south around 2500 years ago, but stayed in the far north and developed into the Thule culture, which eventually moved south across the entire island.

The Thule culture developed the *qajaq* (kayak), the harpoon and the dogsled, all of which are still used today. The modern-day Greenlandic Inuit – known as the Inussuk culture – have almost certainly descended from the Thule.

The Norse Colonies

The two main accounts of Norse history in Greenland are the *Grænlendinga Saga,* or *Tale of the Greenlanders,* and the *Saga of Eiríkur Rauðe*, both written well after the fact and not particularly reliable.

According to the sagas, the first European discovery of Greenland was in AD 900 when Gunnbjörn Ulfsson discovered the Gunnbjarnar Skerries, near present-day Tasiilaq on the east coast. In AD 978, to escape the long arm of the law, Snæbjörn Galti and some companions set sail from Iceland and landed at the icy fjord Bláserk, near Tasiilaq. However, cabin fever gripped the party and they fell out, so only a couple of them returned to Iceland alive.

In AD 982 Eiríkur Rauðe Þorvaldsson (Erik the Red) was outlawed for murder and he sailed for Greenland, calling at Bláserk. Eiríkur sailed around Cape Farewell, wintered on tiny Eiríksey (Eiríkur's Isle) and the following summer, continued up Eiríkur's Fjord and built his farm at Brattahlíð (Steep Hillside).

Eíríkur returned to Iceland in AD 986 to report that Grænaland was rich, fruitful and ripe for settlement. This was a bit of an overblown assessment, but the ploy worked and 14 ships successfully sailed for Eíríkur's Østerbygd (Eastern Settlement). Vesterbygd (Western Settlement) was later established near Nuuk, several hundred kilometres up the coast.

At their peak, the Greenland colonies included some 300 farms with around 5000 inhabitants who successfully ran sheep, cattle and hogs, and hunted seals, caribou, walrus and polar bears.

In 1261 Norway annexed Greenland and a trade monopoly was imposed, allowing two ships to visit annually with supplies and carry locally made goods back to Europe. Unfortunately, the late 13th century became much cooler, causing glaciers to advance. Animals died, the seas choked with ice, shipping became impossible and, in 1380, the largest of the merchant ships that carried goods from Greenland to Norway sank.

The last report from the Østerbygd is from 14 September 1408, when a wedding took place at the Hvalsey church and the couple returned to Iceland to provide a detailed account.

No-one really knows what happened to the colonies. Some people believe the Inuit wiped them out, but there's no supporting evidence. Other suggestions include devastating climatic change, epidemics, inbreeding, emigration to North America, absorption into the Inuit community and kidnapping by English pirates. Strangely, there is evidence of pirate attacks, ranging from papal epistles to Inuit legends. However, the disappearance of Greenland's Norse colonies remains one of the great mysteries of history.

Recolonisation

Greenland next came to the attention of Europeans in 1575, when Martin Frobisher sailed up the west coast while looking for the Northwest Passage, a possible route to the Far East. Over the next two centuries, up to 10,000 men arrived annually on Danish, Norwegian, British, Dutch, German and Basque whaling

GREENLAND

vessels to hunt in the Arctic waters. Many of them came ashore, leading to interbreeding with the Greenlandic people.

In 1605 the Danish king Christian IV claimed Greenland for Denmark. Colonisation began in 1721 when Hans Egede founded a trading post and Lutheran mission, which was relocated to Nuuk (formerly Godthåb: 'Good Hope') in 1728. Denmark imposed a trade monopoly in 1776 and this lasted until 1950.

During the late 19th and early 20th centuries, the more remote parts of Greenland were explored by Europeans. The Norwegian Fridtjof Nansen crossed the inland ice in just over five weeks in 1888 and Robert Peary explored the far north in the years before leading the first successful expedition to reach the North Pole, in 1909.

In 1924, Norway challenged the Danish claim to sovereignty over East Greenland, but the dispute was settled in Denmark's favour during the 1930s.

In 1940 Hitler occupied Denmark and, in early 1941, the US military opened bases at Kangerlussuaq (Søndre Strømfjord, or 'Bluie West Eight') and Narsarsuaq ('Bluie West One'), which later served as a refuelling stop for Allied aircraft crossing the Atlantic.

In 1953 Greenland became a county of Denmark and Greenlanders acquired full Danish citizenship. On 1 May 1979 the county council was replaced by the Landsting (parliament) and the Landstyre (Home Rule government), but Greenland retains two representatives in the Danish parliament.

GEOGRAPHY & GEOLOGY

With an area of 2,415,100 sq km and a 40,000km-long coastline, Greenland is the world's largest island – 52 times the size of mainland Denmark. About 83% of Greenland is covered in ice; the immense icecap, up to 3000m thick and measuring 2500km north–south and up to 1000km east–west, spills down to the coasts in thousands of valley glaciers. It contains over four million cubic kilometres of ice, which amounts to one billion litres of water for every person on Earth!

Greenland is the northernmost country in the world. Its southernmost point, Cape Farewell (Nunaap Isua), lies at 59°45'N, while the Oodaaq Island group, off the north coast, is the world's most northerly land at 83°40'N.

All but the southern quarter of Greenland lies north of the Arctic Circle. In the far north, the sun is visible for nearly three months during the summer, but nowhere on the island is there darkness between late May and mid-July (so Greenland really is the land of the midnight sun). During mid-winter, southern Greenland experiences several hours of real daylight.

Greenland is geographically part of North America – its nearest neighbour is Canada, whose Ellesmere Island lies only 20km away across Robeson Channel from the northwest coast. At its nearest point, Iceland is about 300km away across the Denmark Strait and Svalbard (Norway) lies about 500km east off the northeast coast.

Greenland's rocks are the oldest yet discovered. Gneiss from the Nuuk area is reckoned to be 3.87 billion years old, close to the Earth's age of 4.6 billion years.

CLIMATE

Almost all of Greenland has a relatively stable but rather extreme Arctic climate. In summer, maximum daytime temperatures average between 10°C and 18°C in the south and between 5°C and 10°C in the north. In July and August, south and southwest Greenland can get enduring bouts of wet and windy conditions. Even on calm summer days, coastal fog is common. In winter in the far south, temperatures of -20°C can be expected, but further north it can be -40°C or lower for weeks on end.

For local weather forecasts, check out W www.dmi.dk/vejr/gron/index.html.

ECOLOGY & ENVIRONMENT

Interest in the environment is clearly lacking in and around some Greenlandic towns, with rubbish dumped everywhere and, north of the Arctic Circle, lots of smelly sledge dogs on the outskirts of towns and villages. Recycling is limited to drinks bottles – everything else is burnt or dumped. Due to the Arctic climate,

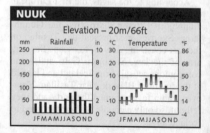

NUUK
Elevation – 20m/66ft

there are virtually no trees and this is unlikely to change. However, away from the sledge dogs, air and water pollution are insignificant and Greenland has one of the cleanest, purest environments in the world. Cores from the inland ice have been used as a test of atmospheric purity over the last few millennia.

Greenland allows whaling for subsistence purposes only. Strictly controlled, this doesn't affect the overall whale population, which is increasing regardless of hunting.

FLORA & FAUNA

Greenland's national flower is rosebay, also called the broad-leafed willow herb. Arctic vegetation is fairly limited and typically stunted but, in sheltered areas around Qaqortoq and Narsarsuaq, there are stands of dwarf birch, alder, juniper and willow. Typical tundra vegetation includes huckleberries, crowberries and lowbush cranberries, as well as miniature flowering plants (such as saxifrage), mosses, sedges, lichens and grasses.

Greenland's fabulous Arctic wildlife is relatively sparse, due to the harsh climate and limited food supply. You may see larger land mammals at Kangerlussuaq, where caribou and musk oxen are abundant. Other prominent mammal species include polar bears (the national animal, mainly seen in East Greenland), lemmings, arctic hares, arctic wolves and arctic foxes.

Marine mammals – including porpoises, pilot whales, fin whales, sei whales, minke whales, orcas (killer whales) and humpback whales – are regularly seen from coastal ferries. More rare is the beautiful and unusual beluga (white whale) and the narwhal, which has a long spiral tusk. Fin and minke whales, as well as the narwhal, may be hunted. Narwhal display the unusual characteristic of travelling in fairly large groups with their tusks above the surface – this may be seen in areas north of the Arctic Circle in October and November. Walruses, ringed seals, hooded seals, bearded seals, spotted seals and harp seals are common in some areas. Harp seals are particularly valuable to the Greenlandic fur industry.

National Parks

Greenland has only one national park, the remote Northeast Greenland National Park, but it's the world's largest! For more information, see the East Greenland section later in this chapter.

GOVERNMENT & POLITICS

In 1979, after a referendum, Greenland became a self-governing, overseas administrative division of the Danish kingdom. It opted out of the EU in 1985.

Legislative responsibility belongs to the 31-seat Landsting (parliament), which meets three times annually; general elections are held every four years. Foreign relations, defence, security, currency and most of the judicial system are handled directly by the Danish government; the Danish parliament includes two MPs from Greenland. The head of state is the Danish Queen Margrethe II, who is highly respected by most Greenlanders.

At the time of writing, Greenland was ruled by a centre-left coalition of the Siumut and Atassut parties; the premier is Siumut's Jonathan Motzfeldt.

The main political issues in Greenland are its relationship with Denmark, fishing rights and international relations. Fishing rights (including the offshore fishing distance, who is allowed to fish, how much can be caught, and what happens to the catch) are a particularly thorny issue between Greenland, Canada, Iceland and the EU.

ECONOMY

Since the 1960s, traditional hunting, weapons, navigational technology and communications have been largely replaced by Western technology. Danish government policy has ensured nearly all manufactured and consumer goods, machinery, food, animals and petroleum products have been imported from Denmark and subsidised to keep prices on par with those on the mainland. As a result Greenlandic people have become reliant on Denmark for their current standard of living.

While the public sector accounts for two thirds of employment, Greenland's real economy is predictably based on fishing and related industries, which employ around 15% of the workforce. The west-coast shrimp fishery is particularly lucrative. Fish products account for around 95% of Greenlandic exports. The fish 'catch' is worth approximately US$250 million per year.

In northern and eastern Greenland, 80% of employment is based on subsistence hunting and fishing, but it's only about 20% in far southern Greenland. Special dispensations are allowed by the International Whaling Commission (IWC) regarding 'aboriginal

GREENLAND

subsistence whaling', but catches are strictly regulated to 19 fin whales and 185 minke whales per year.

Greenland's living standards are comparable to those of mainland Europe but around half of the country's annual Gross Domestic Product is provided by Danish subsidies. In 2001 inflation was 4.1% and 'official' unemployment around 6%.

POPULATION & PEOPLE

88% of Greenland's population are Inuit or mixed Danish and Inuit; the remaining 12% are of European extraction, mainly Danish. Most Greenlanders live on the west coast, although there are isolated communities on the east coast and in the far north. The capital and largest city, Nuuk, has 13,889 people.

ARTS & CULTURE
Tupilak

Greenlandic *tupilak* (small carvings made from bone, skin or chunks of peat) were traditionally used around Tasiilaq to cast misfortune and even death on enemies.

Modern *tupilak* are no longer intended to project misfortune, but are produced and sold as art and souvenirs. They're carved from caribou antler, soapstone, driftwood, narwhal tusk, walrus ivory and bone. Some represent polar bears, birds or marine mammals but most are just hideous imaginary beings.

Literature

Written literature is a recent addition to Greenlandic culture. The only Greenlandic works available in English translation are in Michael Fortescue's *From the Writings of the Greenlanders/Kalaallit Atuakkiaanit*, which includes excellent folk tales and some interesting excerpts from novels.

Music

Greenland produces more music CDs per head of population than anywhere else in the world, most of it modern rock or pop; one of the more melodic bands is Qulleq, and traditional drum music can be found on some CDs. Ask tourist offices for advice on the latest compilations.

SOCIETY & CONDUCT

Greenlanders are known as peace-loving people who have never waged war with each other or anyone else. Typically, both Greenlandic men and women are passionate about

speedboats, fishing, hunting and football. Many of them are immensely proud of their country. Greenlanders are also very musical and their love of music (and, to a lesser extent, dance) is renowned.

Greenlanders still care for the elderly within the extended family, a practice which has almost disappeared in many Western cultures.

Traditionally, Greenlanders love the land and the sea and aren't sentimental about the death of animals or the relationship between animals and humans. Children aren't chastised or disciplined, which is very hard for Westerners to understand.

Always take off your shoes when entering a Greenlandic home. Greetings are carried out as in Western cultures, with a handshake. When eating avoid tucking in before the host has started.

Alcohol-related problems are more visible in Greenland than in most other cultures. While most inebriated Inuit are of the friendly variety, you're advised to steer clear of local drinking dens. If you are apprehended by someone who has been drinking, it's much better to respond to a friendly greeting than to ignore it.

RELIGION

Inuit people may have believed that Europeans were the product of a union between Inuit women and dogs, but that didn't prevent them accepting Christianity. South Greenland was converted by 1800 and most of the rest of Greenland had converted by the early 20th century. However, Greenlanders still adhere to certain aspects of their traditional shamanistic religion, especially in times of hardship.

Early Inuit religion was characterised by belief in an all-pervading soul that survived death, and in familiar spirits who helped or hindered individuals. The Inuit did not fear death but they did fear *toornat*, the spirits of the dead, *tupilat*, the hideous creatures that populate nightmares and *qivittut*, the outlandish zombie-like creatures who could possess any person who saw one.

Facts for the Visitor

SUGGESTED ITINERARIES

Depending on the length of your stay you might wish to see and do the following:

GREENLAND

Two to five days
Visit Kulusuk and Tasiilaq in East Greenland
One week
Visit Narsarsuaq and hike from Qassiarsuk to Narsaq, or take ferries from Narsarsuaq and visit Qaqortoq and Narsaq
Two weeks
As for one week, plus Nanortalik, Tasermiut Fjord and Aappilattoq; or spend two weeks in the Disko Bay area
One month
As for two weeks, plus cruising the west coast to include at least Nuuk, Ilulissat and Uummannaq
Two months
As for one month, but include more hiking and visits to destinations such as Kangerlussuaq and Disko Island

PLANNING
When to Go
Greenland's tourist season begins in early July and continues to the first week in September. In May the winter snows haven't yet melted and new snow is possible until early June. Depending on latitude, spring is anytime between May and July. Summer is in July and/or August and the wonderful autumn tundra colours arrive by late August. By mid-September, there's new snow and genuinely cold weather.

The mosquito season generally runs from late June to early August and anyone attached to their sanity should wear long clothing and invest in a head net.

The best time for 'winter' dogsledding and skiing tours is between late March and early May. Viewing the aurora borealis is best done in southern Greenland (as far north as Disko Bay) from late August to early April.

Maps
Greenland Tourism has produced an excellent series of hiking maps at scales of 1:75,000 or 1:100,000. All maps include hiking and other practical information on the back. They can be bought from Greenland Tourism in Nuuk (see under Tourist Offices later in this section) and local tourist offices for around Dkr80 each.

Saga Maps (W *www.sagamaps.com*) publishes 20 regional maps covering all populated areas of Greenland. It also publishes historic maps/guides to the Eastern and Western Settlements and Tasiilaq/Ammassalik. To place an order, contact **Atuagkat Boghandel** (☎ 321737; W *www.atuagkat.gl; Imaneq 9, DK-3900 Nuuk*).

TOURIST OFFICES
Local Tourist Offices
Tourist information offices in Greenland are officially overseen by **Greenland Tourism** (☎ 342820; W *www.greenland.com; PO Box 1615, Hans Egedes vej 29, DK-3900 Nuuk*). For details, see the individual destinations in this book. Most offices provide maps and brochures and some organise day tours and activities.

Some tourist offices are run by private tour companies or hotels, which may result in monopoly prices and a tendency to discourage budget or nonpackage travellers. The most objective offices – at Nuuk, Nanortalik, Narsaq, Tasiilaq and Sisimiut – welcome independent travellers.

Tourist Offices Abroad
Greenland Tourism (☎ 33 69 32 00; W *www .greenland.com; PO Box 1139, Pilestræde 52, DK-1010 Copenhagen K, Denmark*) is the official national tourist board of Greenland. Ask for the excellent *Explore Greenland Tour Guide* and the four regional *Experiences Of A World Apart* booklets, which are available free.

In addition to Greenland Tourism, Danish Tourist Boards dispense limited Greenland information: see the listing in the Tourist Offices Abroad section of the Denmark chapter of this book, or check out W www.visitdenmark.com.

VISAS & DOCUMENTS
Citizens of Nordic countries – Norway, Sweden, Finland (including Åland), Iceland, the Faroe Islands and Denmark – need only a valid identification card to enter the island of Greenland.

Citizens of countries not requiring visas, including Australia, New Zealand, Canada, Japan, Turkey, the US and EU countries, need only a valid passport for stays of up to three months.

Citizens of most other countries require visas – for details, contact your nearest Danish embassy. If you need a visa to enter Denmark, note that you'll need a separate visa for entry to Greenland.

EMBASSIES
Danish embassies and consulates (W *www .ambassade-info.dk*) represent Greenland abroad. See Embassies & Consulates in the Denmark chapter.

GREENLAND

CUSTOMS

Travellers over 18 may import duty-free 1L of spirits (over 22% alcohol by volume) or 2L of fortified wine (15% to 22% alcohol), 2.25L of wine (under 15% alcohol) and 2L of beer. Anyone over 17 can bring in 250g of tobacco and 200 cigarette papers, or 200 pre-rolled cigarettes. All travellers are allowed a maximum 2kg of confectionery, 1kg of coffee or tea, 2L of carbonated drinks and 5kg of meat or meat products. Importation of live animals of any kind is prohibited.

If you're taking animal products out of Greenland, you'll need a CITES (Convention on International Trade in Endangered Species) export permit, issued at the point of sale. Only East Greenlandic narwhal, polar bear and walrus, and West Greenlandic minke whale, beluga whale, narwhal, polar bear, wolf and walrus products may be exported (check with your home country regarding importation; the US and Australia prohibit imports of marine-mammal products). Without an approved form, your souvenirs may be confiscated by customs. These regulations also apply to Danish citizens.

MONEY
Currency

The Danish krone (Dkr) is legal tender in Greenland; one krone is equal to 100 øre. Notes come in denominations of 50, 100, 200, 500 and 1000 kroner, and coins in 25 and 50 øre and one, two, five, 10 and 20 kroner denominations.

Exchange Rates

See the Exchange Rates section in the Denmark chapter for the Danish krone's rates.

Exchanging Money

All brands of travellers cheques and all Scandinavian and other major currencies may be exchanged for kroner in any bank. It's extremely wise to carry plenty of cash if you'll arrive late or on a weekend.

Grønlandsbanken has branches in Nuuk, Qaqortoq, Maniitsoq, Sisimiut and Ilulissat and charges Dkr75 commission per travellers cheque. In towns and villages without banks, Post Greenland (the post office) may have an ATM, but don't count on it.

ATMs & Credit Cards ATMs are found at banks (and at post offices in most towns without banks), although it's *not* a 24-hour service. Cash can usually be withdrawn from ATMs using credit cards or Cirrus and Plus ATM cards.

Visa and MasterCard are accepted at tourist restaurants and hotels in larger towns (including Narsarsuaq and Kangerlussuaq), and cash advances are available (but not recommended) at Grønlandsbanken, some Pisiffik supermarkets and some tourist offices.

Costs

Thanks to Danish subsidies, food, restaurant bills and consumer goods costs are similar to those in Copenhagen. However, accommodation and transport costs remain high. Greenland has no highways and only expensive ferries, charter boats or air links to population centres. Some places in Greenland, including Tasiilaq and surrounding villages, can often only be reached by helicopter. Long helicopter journeys are prohibitively expensive: the 40-minute Narsarsuaq–Qaqortoq helicopter flight costs Dkr914 and the 15-minute Kulusuk–Tasiilaq flight is Dkr545. Children travel at 40% to 90% discount. Assuming you're in a fixed location, not taking organised tours and self-catering in hostels, you'll spend between Dkr200 and Dkr300 per day (sights such as museums are usually free in Greenland).

POST & COMMUNICATIONS
Post

All Greenlandic towns have a Post Greenland office, which also offers fax and telephone facilities – most are open from 9am to 3pm Monday to Friday. An airmail postcard/letter costs Dkr4.50 within Greenland, Dkr4.75 to Europe and Dkr5.75 to other countries.

Poste restante is available at post offices in all main towns.

Telephone & Fax

At **Tele Greenland** *(PO Box 1002, DK-3900 Nuuk)* telephone offices (associated with post offices) you can phone or fax by direct dialling to anywhere in the world. However, reverse-charge calls are not accepted and there's no international operator number.

Greenland's country code is ☎ 299 and there are no area codes. To access an international line (including Denmark), dial ☎ 00, then the desired country code, area code and phone number.

International directory assistance can be reached on ☎ 118 (Dkr3 per call). A one-minute call to the US costs Dkr2.95 from a private line. Mobiles and public telephones are only slightly dearer. There are no phone cards and coin-operated public phones accept Dkr1, Dkr5 and Dkr 10 coins only. For an international call, you'll need to insert at least Dkr10.

For visitors who bring their mobile phone from home, check with your service provider before using it in Greenland and ask Tele Greenland for the latest info on NMT and GSM coverage. Tele Greenland telephone offices (in towns and in Kangerlussuaq) charge Dkr2000 returnable deposit for mobile-phone rental, but you also have to pay Dkr100 per day plus the call charges.

Email & Internet Access

Only a few places currently offer public Internet access – see the Kangerlussuaq, Narsaq, Nuuk, Sisimiut and Tasiilaq sections for details. Accessing the Internet using a laptop is hopeless: no well-known, non-Greenlandic Internet service providers have nodes in Greenland.

DIGITAL RESOURCES

The **Greenland Guide** (Ⓦ *www.greenland-guide.gl*) is Greenland's most comprehensive tourism website. **Atagu** (Ⓦ *www.atagu.ki.gl*) is another tourist-oriented site with lots of useful links. **Greenland Homerule Government** (Ⓦ *www.nanoq.gl*) covers the government and economy, while also featuring general information about Greenland. **Greenland Iceberg Paradise** (Ⓦ *www.geocities.com/Yosemite/Rapids/4233*) has details on attractions and activities from icebergs to dogsledding, and you can find out about kayaks at Ⓦ *home.att.net/~jimcoburn*. Marine mammal and hunting issues are covered by Ⓦ *www.highnorth.no*, with Santa at his website Ⓦ *www .santa.gl*.

BOOKS

The best English-language book selection on Greenland and Arctic themes is at Atuagkat Boghandel in Nuuk (see under Maps in the Facts for the Visitor section earlier). Some books on Greenland are virtually unobtainable outside the country, but Atuagkat will always be happy to help.

Lonely Planet's *Iceland, Greenland & the Faroe Islands* is the most comprehensive

guide to the region, and the following books may also be of interest:

Arctic Dreams, by Barry Lopez, deals with Greenland and other parts of the Arctic

Arctic Wars, Animal Rights, Endangered Peoples, by Finn Lynge, passionately supports the rights of indigenous hunters and criticises conservationists

The Frozen Echo: Greenland and the Exploration of North America, ca AD 1000–1500, by Kirsten Seaver, is a detailed investigation of the Norse colonies in Greenland

The Greenlanders, by Jane Smiley, is a haunting fictional account of the Norse settlers

Ice!, by Tristan Jones, is an entertaining account of a sailing trip to parts of

Last Places – A Journey in the North, by Lawrence Millman, is an amusing account of travel and contact with local people.

Miss Smilla's Feeling for Snow (published in the USA as *Smilla's Sense of Snow*), by Peter Høeg, a compelling thriller set in Denmark and Greenland, was made into a film in 1997

My Wide, White World, by Ivars Silis, is one of the finest coffee-table photographic books available on Greenland

This Cold Heaven, by Gretel Ehrlich, is one of the very few novels about Greenland, and particularly recommended

Trekking in Greenland, by Torbjørn Ydegaard, is a must for anyone heading into the wilderness and contains detailed route descriptions

NEWSPAPERS & MAGAZINES

Large tourist hotels can provide out-of-date, foreign-language newspapers.

For a good range of Greenland-related topics in Danish, English and Greenlandic, check out *SULUK*, the Air Greenland in-flight magazine, distributed free on aircraft and in airline and tourist offices. For sub-scription details, contact **Atuagassiivik/ Eskimo Press** *(PO Box 939, DK-3900 Nuuk)*.

RADIO & TV

Radio programmes are broadcast around the country in Danish and Greenlandic. Most local TV is in Danish or has Danish subtitles – there isn't enough room on the screen for Greenlandic! British, US and Canadian satel-lite channels are available in some hotels.

PHOTOGRAPHY & VIDEO

Photographers worldwide sing the praises of the magical Arctic light; add spectacular scenery and colourful human aspects and you

GREENLAND

have a photographer's paradise. Film and print processing is available in the larger towns in Greenland and is fairly expensive. You're strongly advised to bring a large supply of film with you and wait until you get home for processing. In winter extreme cold may stop camera batteries from functioning.

TIME
Almost all of Greenland is three hours behind London, two hours ahead of New York, five hours ahead of Los Angeles and 14 hours behind Sydney (12 hours behind Sydney from late March to late October). Exceptions include the Northeast Greenland National Park, which is one hour ahead of the rest of the country. Greenland has daylight saving time from late March to late October, when clocks are turned forward one hour.

LAUNDRY
Reasonably priced services are limited to seamen's homes and youth hostels, but you're advised to bring your own soap and do your laundry by hand.

HEALTH
Although Greenland is a fairly healthy place, campers and hikers should be careful with drinking water, especially near settlements and sheep pastures (see Health in the Regional Facts for the Visitor chapter).

Rabies exists in Greenland and dogs and foxes can be stricken with this deadly disease (see Health in the Regional Facts for the Visitor chapter).

A few shops and hotels sell head nets to protect you from the diabolical summer onslaught of mosquitoes and blackflies, and exposed skin can be protected with 100% diethylmetatoluamide (DEET), although this may be dangerous if used too frequently.

WOMEN TRAVELLERS
In Greenland, local men are known to harass solo women travellers (wolf whistling, staring, passing comments), but serious incidents are very rare. However, be sensible and avoid anyone who has been drinking (see the Dangers & Annoyances section following and the Society & Conduct section earlier). The climate doesn't encourage skimpy clothing, but even when temperatures are warmer women are advised to stay reasonably well covered to avoid attracting unwelcome attention.

Emergency
Emergency telephone numbers vary across the country; those for major towns are listed here. In towns without an emergency number for fire, fire alarms are located on posts in the street.

town	police (☎)	fire (☎)	hospital (☎)
Ilulissat	943222	113	943211
Kangerlussuaq	841222	-	841037
Nanortalik	613222	-	613211
Narsaq	661222	-	661211
Nuuk	321448	113	344112
Qaqortoq	642222	-	642211
Qasigiannguit	911222	-	911211
Qeqertarsuaq	921222	113	921211
Sisimiut	864222	113	864211
Tasiilaq	981448	-	981211
Upernavik	961222	-	961211
Uummannaq	951222	-	951211

DANGERS & ANNOYANCES
On Friday and Saturday nights, some parts of Greenland can resemble the Wild West, especially on the east coast in Qaqortoq, Nuuk and Ilulissat. Although alcohol-related violence is a problem, crimes are rarely aimed at tourists. Ask locally which pubs, clubs and discos should be avoided.

BUSINESS HOURS
Weekday shopping hours are 9am to 5.30pm or 6pm, although some shops open at 8am and close at 4pm or later. On Saturday, shops usually open at 9am or 10am and close between noon and 4pm. Post offices, banks and Arctic Umiaq Line ferry offices are usually open 9am to 3pm weekdays only.

PUBLIC HOLIDAYS & SPECIAL EVENTS
Greenland observes the following public holidays:

New Year's Day 1 January
Epiphany 6 January (half-day)
Easter Maundy Thursday, Good Friday, Easter Sunday, Easter Monday March or April
Labour Day 1 May (half-day)
Common Prayer's Day May
Ascension Day May
Whitsunday, Whitmonday June
National Day, Ullortuneq (Longest Day) 21 June

Christmas Eve 24 December
Christmas Day 25 December
Boxing Day 26 December
New Year's Eve 31 December (afternoon only)

Several local festivals are staged around the country. In northern Greenland, a celebration – and a sigh of relief – marks the end of the polar night, when the sun returns after its sojourn below the horizon. In Ilulissat this occurs in mid-January, and early February in Upernavik. Around Easter, towns north of the Arctic Circle hold dogsled races accompanied by festivities.

In June, Narsaq or Qaqortoq hold a sort of 'sheep rodeo', which includes shearing, herding and other ovine-related competitions. The Nuuk marathon is held in July or August. In mid-August, don't miss the first day of primary school, when parents and children dress in national costume. In late August or early September, the Grønlandsmesterskab national football tournament is held in different venues throughout Greenland. It includes a week or two of play-offs and stirs up lots of excitement.

The Greenland Summer Festival, a one- or two-week cultural and political gathering, features presentations of traditional theatre, drum dances and folk and rock music. It starts around 15 July and is held in Narsarsuaq.

Details of all special events are available from Greenland Tourism (see under Tourist Offices earlier in this section).

ACTIVITIES
Hiking
Hiking in Greenland isn't much like hiking anywhere else. Apart from the odd sheep track in South Greenland and a few tracks around Narsarsuaq and Tasiilaq, trails are essentially nonexistent and hiking routes are unmarked. However, the most fantastic thing about Greenland is its stunning scenery: the soaring peaks, huge glaciers, roaring rivers and iceberg-choked fjords. Get yourself out of town on foot for a few days to experience the best the country can offer.

Hikers in Greenland will need to be experts with map and compass: for the applicable latitude, you'll need to know compass deviations (shown on all Greenland Tourism hiking maps), and be able to find your way through virtually empty, rugged landscapes. This isn't to put you off hiking – there is no better way to appreciate the wilderness – but

outdoor skills, good equipment, careful preparation and advance planning are of utmost importance. All hikers should carry a tent, stove, food, fuel and a sleeping bag.

Always tell someone about hiking plans and your estimated time of return. Rescue helicopters cost around Dkr40,000 per hour and it's the missing hiker who pays. If you advise someone of your itinerary and change it without notifying them, you could very quickly end up poor. Also, it's illegal to set off on an expedition to the inland ice without first obtaining a permit and purchasing compulsory search-and-rescue insurance.

More detailed descriptions of hiking routes are given in Lonely Planet's *Iceland, Greenland & the Faroe Islands*.

Mountaineering
Greenland offers plenty of scope for first ascents, but most unclimbed peaks are in extremely remote districts. Of the country's major climbing areas, Tasiilaq and Nanortalik are the most accessible. Greenland's highest peak, Gunnbjørns Fjeld (3730m), lies 500km northeast of Tasiilaq, but the finest climbing is on the immense granite walls that rise above Tasermiut Fjord near Nanortalik.

Fishing
Greenlandic lakes, particularly in the south, are rich in arctic char and salmon, while the fjords teem with cod that seem to snap at anything, so it makes sense for trekkers to carry a fishing rod and lures. These can be difficult to hire, so it may be better to purchase them or bring your own. You'll need to buy a nonresident licence from a post office or tourist office – a one-day/week/month noncommercial fishing licence costs Dkr75/200/500. Ask for a list of regulations when purchasing a licence.

Dogsledding
Organised trips with a dogsled and driver are increasingly popular in areas north of the Arctic Circle (including Kulusuk on the east coast), but they're fairly expensive. Trips can last from an hour or two up to several days. The best season is around March and April when daylight hours are fairly long, but the land and sea are still in the grip of winter. Arguably the finest location for dogsledding is Uummannaq in northwest Greenland (in mid-March to May). For further details, see the Organised Tours sections in the individual destination sections.

WORK

Since Greenland has opted out of the EU, non-Danish citizens may not work there and there's no shortage of unskilled labour, so few foreign jobseekers have luck finding work. Even fishing and fish-processing jobs almost invariably go to locals. Contracts with cushy fringe benefits are only available to persons relocating from Denmark.

However, if you have a marketable skill and are keen to work in Greenland, contact a Danish embassy and see what sort of advice it can offer. Those who speak Danish and/or an Inuit dialect have the best chances of success.

ACCOMMODATION
Camping

Narsarsuaq, Ilulissat and Tasiilaq have organised camping grounds; most other towns have camping areas, but without facilities or charges.

There are no restrictions on wilderness camping, but in the interests of the fragile Arctic ecosystems you should practise minimal-impact camping. In particular, avoid contaminating watercourses with human and food waste by burying all waste at least 200m from the nearest running water. Carry out all rubbish and any other waste.

For stoves that burn methylated spirits (denatured alcohol), use *Borup Husholdnings Sprit 93%*, available from supermarkets. Petrol-burning stoves can use *bensin*, available from petrol pumps for only Dkr3.25 per litre. The local name for Coleman fuel (white gas, Shellite) is *rense bensin*. It may be available from youth hostels, tourist offices, shops and petrol stations and costs Dkr100 per 5L container.

Paraffin (kerosene) burning stoves can use *lugtfri petroleum* or *A1 Jet Fuel*, available from most hardware stores (and possibly supermarkets) at Dkr15 for 500mL, but only Dkr2.50 per litre at petrol stations.

Mountain Huts

In South Greenland, sheep stations in the Narsaq, Qaqortoq and Nanortalik districts offer basic but comfortable dormitory-style accommodation in hostel-like huts for Dkr150 per person. They're locally called 'youth hostels' and cooking facilities are available.

These huts shouldn't be confused with the much more spartan shepherds' huts, which are scattered around sheep-grazing areas of South Greenland and can be used by walkers as emergency shelters.

Youth Hostels

Most budget and mid-range travellers wind up staying in at least one *vandrehjem* (youth hostel). They're maintained independently by villages, tourist offices, travel agencies or private individuals and most towns have one. The least expensive places charge around Dkr120, the average is Dkr150 and the most expensive is Dkr315! There's no discount for HI members. Some hostels are used as student accommodation from August to June but are open to travellers in July.

Most hostels have hot showers and cooking facilities, and some offer laundry facilities; they aren't overly concerned with rules, regulations and curfews, and meals aren't usually available. Although some hostels provide bedding for an additional cost, you're strongly advised to bring your own sleeping bag.

B&Bs

Bed and breakfast (B&B) in private homes isn't particularly cheap in Greenland. Beds can only be booked through tourist offices and typically cost Dkr300 to Dkr350 per person.

Seamen's Homes

At the rather expensive Christian-oriented seamen's homes, staff begin the day with formal prayers and hymn-singing, but the homes are actually quite good and a viable alternative to hotels. Some rooms have private bathrooms with showers; usually there's also a common room with a TV.

Double rooms with/without bath cost around Dkr860/695, including breakfast. All seamen's homes have cafeterias that serve snacks and great-value set menus at mealtimes. Alcohol is prohibited.

Hotels

Most Greenlandic towns have at least one hotel – as with most North Atlantic hotels, they're typically rather drab and priced for businesspeople with bottomless expense accounts. However, most are very comfortable and their restaurants and pubs may even serve as a town social centre.

The cheapest double rooms, including a buffet breakfast, start at around Dkr600, while tourist-class hotels may charge around Dkr1600.

FOOD
Traditional Foods

Although some visitors are put off traditional Greenlandic fare for sentimental or ideological reasons, remember that whales and seals have dominated the Inuit subsistence hunting culture for thousands of years with no adverse effects on populations. It was European commercial whaling that brought about the decline in cetacean numbers.

Traditional Inuit practise neither commercial nor recreational whaling or sealing; animals are only hunted on a small scale for subsistence purposes and every bit is used. Whale steaks, which cost from Dkr50 per kilogram, taste like fine beef and are rich and filling fare. *Mattak* (whale blubber), relatively tasteless and difficult to chew, is rich in vitamins and unsaturated fatty acids.

Frozen seal meat is sold in supermarkets, but you'll also find fresh seal at the *kalaaliaraq* or *brædtet* (harbour market). Seal is tougher than whale and tastes fishier. It can be cooked by cutting it into chunks and boiling it for an hour; it's popular to prepare the resulting stock as *suaassat* (seal broth with rice and onions).

In addition to marine mammals, harbour markets also sell a range of fish, including sea trout, salmon and capelin, as well as sea birds, caribou and, occasionally, musk ox. Meat and fish, particularly capelin, are dried for the winter and salmon is salted and smoked.

Wild foods such as berries, camomile and mushrooms appear during the short summers. A favourite is the celery-like angelica, which may be eaten raw with sugar or boiled cod liver; it's also used in jams and desserts or as a salad accompaniment to game dishes. The most delicious mushroom is large and chocolate-coloured with a spongy centre (called 'slippery jack' in English); it peaks in early August.

Restaurants

Apart from the tourist hotels, Greenland has relatively few restaurants. Hotel fare is predictably expensive but normally quite good – look out for the occasional Greenlandic buffet.

Seamen's homes do acceptable cafeteria meals, typically consisting of a fish, mutton or beef dish accompanied by the boiled potatoes and frozen vegetables that are ubiquitous in the North Atlantic. A growing number of smaller cafés serve up popular dishes – even Thai cuisine! For a quick snack, you can resort to the *grill-baren* (grill bars), which specialise in hot dogs, chips and burgers.

Self-Catering

Economy-conscious travellers will want to buy supermarket food and prepare it themselves on a camping stove or in hostels. Supermarkets usually have an amazing variety of groceries, but don't bank on it.

The Brugsen cooperative has shops in Sisimiut, Maniitsoq, Nuuk, Paamiut, Narsaq, Qaqortoq and Nanortalik, while Pisiffik and Pilersuisoq are represented in all major towns. In larger towns, both chains may also have smaller kiosks that stay open longer hours, possibly Sunday as well.

Every town has a bakery – sometimes associated with a supermarket – that supplies fresh bread, cakes, doughnuts and biscuits daily (except Sunday).

DRINKS
Nonalcoholic Drinks

The choice of fizzy soft drinks includes the Faxe Kondi brand, which is quite palatable and reminiscent of Sprite. Coffee is a national institution and may be served up at any time of day.

Alcohol

The most popular beers are Danish Carlsberg and Tuborg, sold in 330mL bottles for Dkr17 in shops and Dkr30 to Dkr42 in bars and restaurants.

In shops, the 2.2% beer costs around Dkr7 per 330mL bottle. Wines from around the world are available; a 750mL bottle of table wine costs from Dkr55.

Due to the prevalence of alcoholism, the government restricts times when alcohol can be sold. Full-strength beer, wine and spirits is sold in kiosks and supermarkets from 9am to 6pm Monday to Friday and from 9am to 1pm on Saturday, or in licensed pubs and bars in the afternoon and evening.

The recommended 'Greenlandic Coffee', an intriguing mix of whisky, Kahlúa, black coffee and whipped cream, is flambéed with Grand Marnier and typically costs Dkr140 in restaurants.

Viiniaaraq wine, bottled and sold in Greenland, isn't bad, but may be too sweet for some tastes. There's also the foul, homebrew beer *imiaq*, which is illegal.

GREENLAND

SHOPPING

Most Greenlandic towns have hotels or craft shops where visitors can buy soapstone, caribou antler, and walrus- and narwhal-ivory carved to make *tupilak*, which are more expensive in East Greenland; the best carvings are found in Tasiilaq, Nuuk and Sisimiut. A walrus ivory 'Thule necklace' will cost Dkr5000 to Dkr10,000 (see under Customs earlier for details of compulsory export permits for souvenirs). Beadwork and silver jewellery also make fine souvenirs. Note that animal souvenirs are only a by-product of the food industry and many Greenlanders rely on sales to tourists for their livelihood.

Shops in Narsaq and Ilulissat specialise in local stones, including garnets, amazonite, moonstone, several types of quartz and granite, and *tuttupit*, a pink stone unique to the Narsaq area. *Nuumit*, the so-called 'Opal of Greenland', comes from the Nuuk area.

Getting There & Away

AIR

International travel to Greenland is through one of four airports: Narsarsuaq in South Greenland; Kangerlussuaq (Søndre Strømfjord) in Southwest Greenland; Kulusuk in East Greenland; and Nerlerit Inaat (Constable Pynt) in Northeast Greenland. Charter flights may also use the airfield at Mesters Vig in Northeast Greenland.

Narsarsuaq, which gets a fair bit of foggy weather, lacks sophisticated radar – planes must make a visual approach, so don't be surprised if your Narsarsuaq flight is diverted to more hi-tech, climatically stable Kangerlussuaq. When this happens, **Air Greenland** *(☎ 343434; Ⓦ www.greenlandair.gl)* pays passengers' expenses at Kangerlussuaq. Air Greenland flies one to three times weekly from Copenhagen to Narsarsuaq (from Dkr4500 return). Flights from Reykjavík (Iceland) to Narsarsuaq ceased in 2000, but as they're scheduled to resume in 2003, check with Flugfélag Íslands (Air Iceland) or Air Greenland.

From 27 May to 21 September, **Flugfélag Íslands** *(in Reykjavík ☎ 570 3030; Ⓔ websales@airiceland.is; Ⓦ www.airiceland.is)* offers excursion flights once or twice daily (except Sunday), between Reykjavík and Kulusuk in East Greenland, for Ikr31,300/41,415 in low/high season (high season is 16 June to 20 August). You can also opt for a day tour, which amounts to four hours on Kulusuk Island, including a tour of Kulusuk village, 3km from the airport. Otherwise you can continue by helicopter (Dkr1090 return) to Tasiilaq for several days before returning to Iceland, or continue to the west coast of Greenland (for more information, see the Getting Around section following).

Air Greenland flies between Copenhagen and Kangerlussuaq several times weekly; check with the airline as frequency may increase. One-way tickets start at Dkr2800.

Getting Around

Getting around in Greenland will probably be your biggest expense and greatest source of uncertainty; consider getting to know one area well and minimise travelling around. Even in summer, bad weather can disrupt schedules, so allow plenty of time between connections – two days is usually enough! Travelling by coastal ferry is recommended and tends to be far more reliable than travel by air.

Outside the towns and villages, there are virtually no roads in Greenland: in fact, only two small communities in the whole country are actually connected by road! There are no bus or rail services between any of the Greenlandic towns or villages and car hire isn't a practical option unless you're a long-term resident worker.

AIR

From 2003, watch out for airport closures, switches from fixed-wing to helicopter flights, and changes of operator.

Currently, Air Greenland links most settlements with a fleet of helicopters and fixed-wing aircraft. Narsarsuaq, Kangerlussuaq, Nuuk, Maniitsoq, Sisimiut, Aasiaat, Ilulissat, Qaarsut, Upernavik, Qaanaaq and Kulusuk have fully fledged runways.

All airports have Air Greenland offices, but in small towns, tickets and bookings are normally handled by Arctic Umiaq Line (AUL) offices. In Denmark, contact **Grønlands Rejsebureau** *(Greenland Travel; ☎ 33 13 10 11; Ⓔ tour@greenland-travel.dk; Gammel Mønt 12, PO Box 130, DK-1004 Copenhagen K)*.

GREENLAND

The fares and flight frequencies described in this book apply only between mid-June and early September. In winter, flights are less frequent and disruptions are more common. You'll find the timetable and standard fares on the Internet; red tickets are available at 30% discount (purchase at least seven days in advance). Contact Air Greenland for details of any special fares (such as the 'cheap' Takuss return ticket) and make your bookings many months in advance. Children aged two to 12 and seniors over 60 get 50% discount.

Air Alpha (☎ 943004; W www.airalpha .com) operates a fleet of small helicopters, serving communities around Disko Bay and the Tasiilaq area in East Greenland.

The outrageously high airport taxes (typically Dkr346 for domestic flights) are always included in ticket prices.

BOAT
Ferry
Arctic Umiaq Line (AUL; ☎ 349900; W www .greenland-guide.gl/aul; Vandsøvej 10, Postboks 608, DK-3900 Nuuk) owns a fleet of coastal ferries used to transport passengers along the west coast between Aappilattoq (near Cape Farewell) in the south and Upernavik in the north. For soft sightseeing and meeting Greenlanders, you can't beat them. They're not cruise ships by any description, but they're safe and comfortable and will take you past soaring peaks and through seas choked with mountainous icebergs and ice floes. You'll even see the occasional whale.

Regular passenger routes are handled by three large boats, the *Sarpik Ittuk*, *Sarfaq Ittuk* and *Saqqit Ittuk*. These may be juggled around depending on the season and the year but, typically, each one handles one of three sections: Qaqortoq to Ilulissat, Nuuk to Uummannaq or Nuuk to Upernavik.

Note that the routes overlap and that sailings to Ilulissat and Uummannaq don't run from mid-December to late May and mid-November to mid-June, respectively. In summer, at least one weekly boat calls (both northbound and southbound) at Narsarsuaq and Kangerlussuaq.

Each ferry has couchettes, cabins (most are like dormitories with space for four people and no locks on the doors, but there are plusher two-person cabins), showers and cafeterias where you can eat, socialise or watch videos (the *Sarpik Ittuk* has a comfortable TV lounge). Breakfast, lunch and dinner (two courses) are reminiscent of bad school meals and cost Dkr50/80/80; a coffee is Dkr6. The ships are too large to dock at smaller villages, requiring a tender (usually the lifeboat!) to take people ashore.

There are also smaller, short-haul ferries that serve places around Disko Bay and between Narsarsuaq and Aappilattoq, but routes vary from year to year. Ask AUL for details of the cargo boats that carry supplies and passengers to remote settlements.

The larger ferries and some smaller boats usually get fully booked quite early so you're advised to buy tickets at least six months in advance, otherwise you'll end up on the waiting list, which isn't recommended. Grønlands Rejsebureau (see under Air earlier) can book summer itineraries as early as January, even before the timetable is available to the public.

In this book, summer deck class (couchette) fares are given; to work out cabin fares, add approximately 60%. Children aged two to 11 years pay half-fare, as do seniors (except from mid-June to mid-August, when seniors get only a 25% discount); children under two get 90% discount. Tickets bought on board are subject to a Dkr50 surcharge.

ORGANISED TOURS
In Greenland, transport difficulties often make organised tours the only way to get to many places; although rather expensive, they're usually well worth the money.

For independent travellers, a great option is to join a day tour, especially one run by a local operator. In many towns, tourist offices and private operators run day tours for Dkr400 to Dkr900 per person.

Great places for organised tours include Narsaq, Ilulissat, Uummannaq and Tasiilaq. See the relevant sections for details.

Greenland Outfitters
Specially trained guides and tour organisers known as 'Greenland Outfitters' provide customised itineraries, including hiking, mountaineering, kayaking, sailing, dogsledding, snowmobiling, fishing and hunting. Most speak at least some English and are licensed and insured to guide travellers. For a complete list of Greenland Outfitters, check out W www.greenland.com.

GREENLAND

South Greenland

In Greenlandic, South Greenland is some-times known affectionately as 'Sineriak Ba-naaneqarfik' (Banana Coast), but don't be fooled: it was also the source of the island's verdant-sounding name.

Many visitors to Greenland get their first taste of the country here in the south, and it's an overwhelming introduction. Nestled amid spectacular scenery are hundreds of Norse and Eskimo ruins, colourful towns, tiny vil-lages, sheep farms and even a hot spring where you can bathe while watching the ice-bergs drift past in the fjord.

NARSARSUAQ
pop 182
Narsarsuaq's magnificent setting makes a beautiful introduction to Greenland: while there's plenty to see and do, this odd village owes its existence to the international airport, so it's not a representative view of the country.

The original US airbase at Narsarsuaq, known as 'Bluie West One', was constructed practically overnight in July 1941. During WWII it was used as a refuelling stop for bombers crossing the Atlantic; by 1945 it had become Greenland's largest settlement, with a population of 12,000 and all the trappings of a small US town. Although the base was sched-uled for decommissioning at the end of the war, it didn't close until 1958. In 1959 Den-mark established the current civilian airfield on the site.

Information
The **tourist office** (☎ 665301; e south .tourist@greennet.gl), at the Blue Ice Café, dis-tributes leaflets, books tours and assists with hiking information. There's also a tourist in-formation desk by the southern entrance to the airport, open for Copenhagen arrivals. The youth hostel (a good source for hiking infor-mation) and Hotel Narsarsuaq also offer tourist advice. The Arctic Adventure office in the lobby of the hotel provides details of its tours.

Hotel Narsarsuaq and the Airport Admin-istration office exchange cash and travellers cheques, but rates aren't too good. The **post office** (open 2pm-3pm Mon & Tues, 11am-3pm Wed-Fri) is in the airport terminal building. Laundry service is available at the youth hostel for Dkr25 per load.

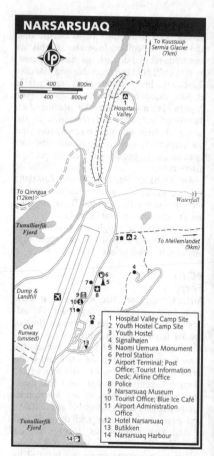

NARSARSUAQ

1 Hospital Valley Camp Site
2 Youth Hostel Camp Site
3 Youth Hostel
4 Signalhøjen
5 Naomi Uemura Monument
6 Petrol Station
7 Airport Terminal; Post Office; Tourist Information Desk; Airline Office
8 Police
9 Narsarsuaq Museum
10 Tourist Office; Blue Ice Café
11 Airport Administration Office
12 Hotel Narsarsuaq
13 Butikken
14 Narsarsuaq Harbour

Things to See & Do
The **Naomi Uemura Monument**, opposite the airport terminal, honours Naomi Uemura, the Japanese national hero who went solo to the North Pole and crossed Greenland's in-land ice from south to north.

The extensive and worthwhile **Narsarsuaq Museum** (☎ 665499; admission Dkr20; open 10am-6pm daily mid-May–mid-Oct) in-cludes a library of books on Greenland and a variety of (unfortunately) outdated historical exhibits on the Norse people, sheep farming and the US presence.

For the climb to the radio tower atop the 226m **Signalhøjen** (Signal Hill), start from behind the youth hostel or head up the gravel track which begins behind the Butikken supermarket.

About 3km north of Narsarsuaq is **Hospital Valley**, with lots of detritus left behind after the US pullout. Two species of orchid flower bloom here in August, and there are great views from the ridge between the valley and the river, or from the little pass at the extreme north end of the valley.

The **Blue Ice Café** (☎ 665499) rents out mountain bikes for Dkr75/100 per half-day/day and fishing equipment for Dkr100/350 per day/week. It also hires out single/double sea kayaks for Dkr400/500 per day or Dkr2000/2500 per week.

Organised Tours

The respected outfitter **Jacky Simoud** (☎ 497371; e blue.ice.outfitting@greennet.gl) runs transfers to Qassiarsuk for Dkr120/240 one way/return and offers various tours in the area, including boat trips to the Qooroq Icefjord (Dkr400) and glacier hiking on Kuussuup Sermia (Dkr450).

Arctic Adventure (☎ 665240), with an office in the lobby of Hotel Narsarsuaq, runs guided day trips to Narsaq (Dkr975), Itilleq and Igaliku (Dkr875), Qooroq Icefjord (Dkr450), Qassiarsuk (from Dkr400) and Qassiarsuk/Tassiusaq (Dkr675); walks to Kuussuup Sermia (Dkr350); and helicopter flights to the inland ice (Dkr1500). Tours are best booked several days in advance.

Places to Stay & Eat

For **wild camping**, head out to Hospital Valley, 4km northeast of the airport.

At the pleasant **Youth Hostel** (☎ 665221; e vandrehjemmet-uak@greennet.gl; camping per person Dkr95, beds Dkr195; open mid-June–Sept), campers will find the ground fairly hard. It's popular, however, so book a bed well in advance.

Despite looking like a block of council-owned flats, the well-appointed **Hotel Narsarsuaq** (☎ 665253; e reception.narsarsuaq@glv.gl; B&B dorm beds Dkr265, singles Dkr640-990, doubles Dkr775-1180) is very nice inside, but it's often packed with tour groups. The cheaper rooms have shared bathroom.

The hotel **dining room** (mains Dkr135-195) serves good à la carte meals, and a twice-weekly Greenlandic buffet for Dkr210. The less extravagant **cafeteria** (mains around Dkr50; open 6.30am-7.45pm daily) serves reasonable grub, including pasta bolognese and fish and chips.

The **Butikken supermarket** (open 10am-6pm Mon-Fri & 9am-1pm Sat) is in a block of flats south of the hotel.

Getting There & Away

Air With an office at the airport terminal, **Air Greenland** (☎ 665287; open 8am-3pm Mon-Fri) flies to/from Copenhagen one to three times weekly. In high season, these flights stop en route at Keflavík (Iceland). Check with the airline for the latest.

Air Greenland runs four or five weekly helicopter connections to Qaqortoq (Dkr914) and Narsaq (Dkr684), but only two to four times weekly to Nanortalik (Dkr1439). It also has flights to Nuuk (Dkr3344), up to six times weekly.

Boat AUL South Greenland boats call at Narsarsuaq harbour three times weekly from 20 May to 18 August, with service to Qassiarsuk (Dkr185), Itilleq (Dkr185), Narsaq (Dkr185) and Qaqortoq (Dkr265). Tickets are available from Air Greenland at the airport terminal (tickets bought on the boat are subject to a Dkr50 surcharge).

On Wednesdays, from 23 May to 25 September, one of the big coastal ferries visits Narsarsuaq then heads for Qaqortoq and Ilulissat.

Getting Around

A free bus shuttles passengers between the airport, the harbour and the hotel. Transfers in the youth hostel van run to/from the harbour, airport or Hospital Valley.

AROUND NARSARSUAQ
Narsarsuaq Valley Hike & The Inland Ice

The pleasant and easy walk through Hospital Valley and into Narsarsuaq Valley (also called Blomsterdalen, or Flower Valley) follows a proper walking track.

From the northern end of Hospital Valley, the track climbs over a rise, then continues in the relatively luxuriant Narsarsuaq Valley, with trees up to 3m high in some sheltered enclaves. Casual walkers usually turn back near the head of the valley, by a beautiful 125m-high cascade (the Kuussuup Sermia glacier snout may just be seen between crags to the north). However, it's worth the 200m ascent to a haunting lake flanked by tundra and glacier-scraped boulders. From the lake, the

GREENLAND

trail makes a 1.5km descent to the flank of Kuussuup Sermia, which is a spur of the inland ice. Allow at least six hours for the round-trip; Arctic Adventure offers this as a guided day hike for Dkr350, including lunch (for contact details see Organised Tours in the Nasarsuaq section).

QASSIARSUK (BRATTAHLID)
pop 56

Qassiarsuk, across Tunulliarfik (Eiríks Fjord) and 15 minutes by boat from Narsarsuaq, is reputedly the site of Brattahlid, Eiríkur Rauðe's 10th-century farm. It's a wonderfully scenic spot on a warm summer's day, with thick grass in the fields and a fjord dotted with icebergs in the background.

Two of the finest reconstructions in Greenland, a 10th-century **Viking longhouse** and **Þjóðhildur's church** *(admission Dkr40; open 9am-9pm daily July & Aug)* are open on request – ask the guide for details about Viking-themed activities. There's also a smaller reconstruction of an **Inuit turf hut**, which is always open and has sealskins and reindeer furs. The memorial to Eiríkur Rauðe, in red and white Igaliku sandstone, is now dwarfed by the impressive **Leifur Eiríksson statue** on the hill above. Look out for the small modern **rune stone** at the bottom of the hill.

There are several **Norse ruins**, including the first Christian church in the New World, foundations of a **manor house** and a **byre**. Also in the village, there's a modern **church** and a small **museum** with photos of life in Qassiarsuk; ask locally for admission.

Organised Tours

The three-hour Arctic Adventure tour from Narsarsuaq (Dkr400) offers a brief introduction to the Norse in Greenland. For an extra Dkr275, you can add lunch and a guided trip to Tasiusaq. Ask if it's possible to stay in Qassiarsuk or Tasiusaq and return to Narsarsuaq on a later tour.

Places to Stay & Eat

The yellow-painted **Youth Hostel** *(☎/fax 665010; beds Dkr165)* offers basic beds and cooking facilities. Next to the hostel, there's good grass for **camping** at Dkr65 per person, including use of hostel facilities. Wild campers should head north, at least 2km from the village.

The small **Pisiniarfik** shop stocks a surprising range of groceries.

Getting There & Away

AUL South Greenland boats sail between Narsarsuaq and Qassiarsuk three times weekly, from 20 May to 18 August (Dkr185), and from Qassiarsuk to Qaqortoq (Dkr245). The moderately priced **Jacky Simoud** *(☎ 497371)* transfers from the Narsarsuaq run several times daily for Dkr120/240 (one way/return). You can book directly or through the Narsarsuaq Youth Hostel (see Places to Stay under Narsarsuaq).

QASSIARSUK TO NARSAQ TREK

Thanks to the youth hostels on the trail, Qassiarsuk to Narsaq may well be the best-trodden trek in Greenland. The sheep farms on the northern half of the peninsula are mostly linked by tractor tracks, so walking is relatively easy, but the southern half of the walk is much more challenging. Although you can stay in youth hostels for two or three nights, you'll need a tent for the last one or two nights (unless you arrange boat transport to Narsaq from Ipiutaq).

The rugged scenery at the Narsaq end of the peninsula is some of the most impressive in the area.

To start, follow the track which heads west to Nunataaq from the modern church in Qassiarsuk (there are no signs). The first day crosses the peninsula by tractor track from Qassiarsuk to Nunataaq (9km), where there's an excellent **Youth Hostel** *(VHF radio 0084 'Nunataaq 43'; beds Dkr150, camping Dkr65)* in an old farmhouse – it's like a private home, with varnished floors and gas-cooking facilities.

Next day, return 3km inland, then follow the partly marked route southwards over the peninsula to Sillisit, where there's the slightly shabby **Sillisit Youth Hostel** *(VHF radio 0084 'Sillisit 29'; beds Dkr150)*, with old furniture and gas cooking.

On day three, the most direct route heads inland again; keep north of Peak 786 and look for a place to camp before climbing up to the pass north of Peak 936. The following day, continue over this pass and head southwest towards the 1050m-high Naakkalaaq Pass, where the ground is steep and route finding is difficult.

After Naakkalaaq, head south and camp well before you reach the lake Taseq (which supplies drinking water to Narsaq). A steep descent, keeping north of Peak 643, leads

AROUND NARSARSUAQ, NARSAQ & QAQORTOQ

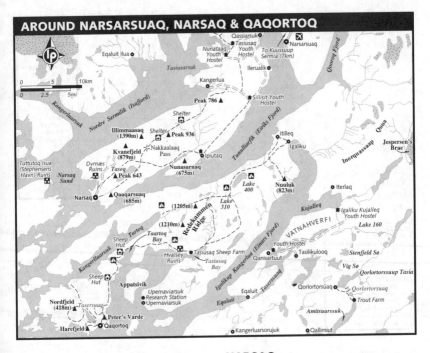

down to the Narsaq river, then it's fairly flat for the final 6km to Narsaq.

An alternative route from Sillisit heads southwest, keeping parallel with – but only 1km to 2km from – the coast. After about 15km, you'll return to the coast at Ipiutaq, where there's another **Youth Hostel** *(VHF radio 0084 'Ipiutaq 19'; beds Dkr125)*, similar to Sillisit.

After a night there, head inland and keep north of the mountain Nunasarnaq, where there's a difficult river crossing just upstream from the 2.5km-long lake. After that, follow the coast (with some moderate river crossings) and look for somewhere to camp before climbing up to Taseq, where you'll meet the direct route from Sillisit to Narsaq.

Most of the route is unmarked so you'll have to rely on your map and compass; the best map is Greenland Tourism's 1:100,000-scale *Narsaq* sheet.

There are two emergency shelters on the difficult and exposed high-level section from Sillisit through to Nakkaalaaq Pass.

For more details of this route, see Lonely Planet's *Iceland, Greenland & the Faroe Islands*.

NARSAQ
pop 1693
Rather pleasant Narsaq (The Plain) sprawls across level land at the end of the Narsaq Peninsula, with a great view of the iceberg-studded Narsaq Sund.

Narsaq is incredibly industrious, with several factories and factory shops. A local company also collects icebergs to make ice cubes and sells them in Denmark and Germany!

The excellent **tourist office** (☎ 661325; e info@2narsaq.gl; Søndervej B157) provides brochures and information, changes travellers cheques and offers cash advance on credit cards. The **post office** *(Erik Egedes Plads B989)* has ATMs and **Netsiden** *(Tobiasvej B262)* provides Internet access at Dkr25/45 for 30/60 minutes.

Things to See & Do
The excellent and recommended **Narsaq Harbour Museum** (☎ 661666; admission Dkr10; open 1pm-4pm daily June–mid-Sept) takes in the 1883 Nordprøven trading station buildings beside the picturesque old harbour: a cooperage/blubber storage house, stable, chapel, shop, Frederik Høegh's printworks

GREENLAND

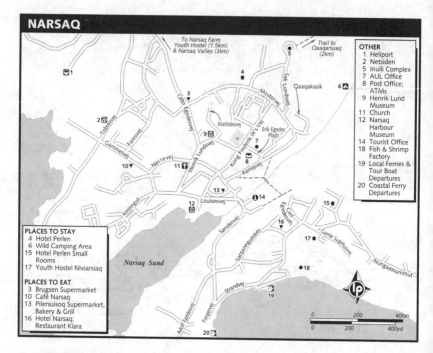

NARSAQ

To Narsaq Farm
Youth Hostel (1.5km)
& Narsaq Valley (3km)

Trail to
Qaaqarsuaq
(2km)

Qaaqakasik

OTHER
1 Heliport
2 Netsiden
5 Inuili Complex
7 AUL Office
8 Post Office;
    ATMs
9 Henrik Lund
    Museum
11 Church
12 Narsaq
    Harbour
    Museum
14 Tourist Office
18 Fish & Shrimp
    Factory
19 Local Ferries &
    Tour Boat
    Departures
20 Coastal Ferry
    Departures

Matildesvej
Erik Egedes
Plads

PLACES TO STAY
4 Hotel Perlen
6 Wild Camping Area
15 Hotel Perlen Small
    Rooms
17 Youth Hostel Niviarsiaq

PLACES TO EAT
3 Brugsen Supermarket
10 Café Narsaq
13 Pilersuisoq Supermarket,
    Bakery & Grill
16 Hotel Narsaq;
    Restaurant Klara

Narsaq Sund

Louisesvej

0   200   400m
0   200   400yd

(built in 1830), several stone houses and a recent replica of a traditional sod hut. The main exhibition building houses a large collection of fascinating cultural exhibits and artefacts, including a piece of a Norse harp and locally made replicas of Norse wool clothing.

The **Henrik Lund Museum** (☎ 661666; *Matildesvej; open 2pm-4pm daily June–mid-Sept*) was the home of the Greenlandic priest, poet and painter, Henrik Lund, who composed the Greenlandic national anthem. The interesting interior has been left intact and dates from the 1930s, '40s and '50s.

Qaaqarsuaq, the prominent 685m-high peak behind the town, makes a popular day hike (two hours up, one hour down), or you can climb up to the 350m-high saddle for great views of Narsaq and the icebergs in the fjord; start from behind the Inuili complex (Greenland's only catering school).

Organised Tours

The tourist office arranges a geological hike on Kvanefjeld (Dkr450); a walking tour of Narsaq (Dkr150); a hike to Dyrnæs Norse ruins (Dkr250); a twice-weekly Greenlandic national costumes show and buffet (Dkr230); a Green-

landic barbecue (Dkr250, minimum two people); a botanical walk learning about Arctic flora (Dkr150); sailing trips to the Bredefjord tidewater glacier (Dkr800); and other boat trips (Dkr500). In spring, six-hour ice-fishing trips cost Dkr450. Folk dances, choirs and kayak shows can be arranged for groups.

Places to Stay

There are lots of **campsites** out toward the Narsaq Valley, but the most convenient site is uphill from the town centre, in the valley behind the tourist office.

The **Narsaq Farm Youth Hostel** (☎ 572073; e *helgioutfitter@greennet.gl; beds Dkr165; open May-Sept*) is 2km north of town, toward Narsaq Valley. **Youth Hostel Niviarsiaq** (☎ 661290; e *hotelniv@greennet.gl; Gamle Sygehusvej B503; beds per person Dkr225*) offers clean, fresh rooms with shared facilities.

Hotel Perlen (☎ 661290; e *hotelniv@ greennet.gl; Mestervej B999; singles/doubles Dkr650/900*) offers fine rooms with shower and toilet; rates include breakfast. The hotel can arrange small **rooms** (*Savaasit Qaqqaat B247*) with shared facilities and kitchen for Dkr250 per person; one is reputedly haunted!

GREENLAND

Places to Eat

Despite its size and importance, Narsaq is short of places to eat. Posh and cosy **Restaurant Klara** (☎ 661740; Sarqannguaqvej B819; mains Dkr149-178), in Hotel Narsaq, serves a range of excellent gourmet dishes, including minke whale, musk ox and fantastic desserts.

Café Narsaq (Gammelvej) rustles up fried food, including chicken and burgers – the burger meal deal is around Dkr40.

The well-stocked **Pilersuisoq** (Niaqornarssangmut B842) and **Brugsen** (Mestervej B1230) supermarkets sell everything needed for self-catering.

Pilersuisoq also has a bakery and a grill selling burgers and hot dogs.

Getting There & Away

The **Air Greenland** (☎ 661488) chopper to/from Narsarsuaq (Dkr684) flies four or five times weekly, and to/from Qaqortoq (Dkr469) three or four times weekly.

For boat tickets, contact the **AUL office** (☎ 661444; Erik Egedes Plads). Coastal ferries call in once weekly all year in either direction, en route between Qaqortoq (Dkr185) and Nuuk (Dkr1400).

AUL South Greenland runs between Qaqortoq, Narsaq and Narsarsuaq (Dkr185) three days weekly, with two extra sailings between Qaqortoq and Narsaq.

QAQORTOQ (JULIANEHÅB)
pop 3086

Tidy and brightly coloured Qaqortoq (pronounced like **kra**-kror-tok) is South Greenland's big city and hub. It was founded as a trading station in 1775, and originally named Julianehåb after Queen Juliane Marie of Denmark.

The **tourist office & souvenir shop** (☎ 642444; W www.iserit.greennet.gl/tourist; Torvevej B68) organises excursions; ask here for details of local hiking routes and the Qaqortoq Greenland Tourism map. The **Grønlandsbanken bank** (Olesvej B1216; open 10am-3pm Mon-Fri) has an ATM.

Dangers & Annoyances

Drunken brawls, even among women, are notorious in the local bars – visitors are recommended to exercise extreme caution, especially on pay day (the last Friday of the month) and weekends.

Things to See

The busy and colourful **harbour** and the **historic district** by the town square are both popular with photographers. The Torvet (Town Square) **fountain** dates from 1928 and was the first one in Greenland.

The highly regarded **Qaqortoq Museum** (☎ 641080; Torvevej B29; admission free; open 10am-noon & 1pm-4pm Mon-Fri, 1pm-4pm Sat & Sun June-Sept) exhibits include drawings and photos of early indigenous sealskin qajaqs (kayaks) and other ingenious hunting and fishing implements, as well as artefacts from the Thule and Greenlandic cultures.

The brilliant Stone & Man project, the brainchild of Greenlandic artist Aka Høegh, attempts to turn amphitheatre-shaped Qaqortoq into a sculpture gallery by creating shapes and reliefs from natural stone formations all over town. Some of the best are just behind the tourist office – ask there for a free map.

The beautiful **Frelserens Kirke** (Skolevej) – also called the old church – was built in 1832 and contains a votive ship from 1837, made by the crew of a stranded ship with nothing else to do. Greenland's current prime minister was previously a priest in this church; the tourist office has the key and can take you on a quick, free guided tour.

The **Great Greenland tannery** (Havnevej B1274) turns seals into fur coats and is one of Qaqortoq's economic mainstays. The tourist office arranges one-hour tours for a minimum of four people (Dkr40).

Organised Tours

The **tourist office** (☎ 642444) runs various tours by arrangement, most requiring a minimum of eight people (prices are per person).

One of the best tours is the five-hour guided boat trip to the excellent Hvalsey Norse church ruins (Dkr450); the eight-hour boat trip to the Kangerluarsorujuk sheep farm costs Dkr800 (including lunch and guide).

The impressive Bredefjord tidewater glacier tour (Dkr800) takes 11 hours. An eight-hour sailing excursion (Dkr800, including lunch and guide) takes you to the extraordinary 34°C Uunartoq hot springs, set among fields of wildflowers. While bathing, you can watch huge icebergs drift by in the fjord.

Town tours (Dkr150, minimum four people) feature a three-hour stroll through old Qaqortoq, a visit to the old church and fountain, and

GREENLAND

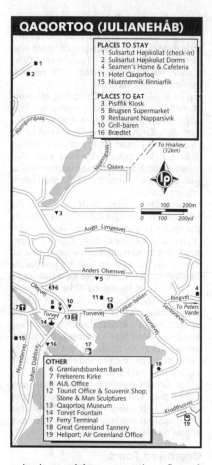

QAQORTOQ (JULIANEHÅB)

PLACES TO STAY
1 Sulisartut Højskoliat (check-in)
2 Sulisartut Højskoliat Dorms
4 Seamen's Home & Cafeteria
11 Hotel Qaqortoq
15 Niuernermik Ilinniarfik

PLACES TO EAT
3 Pisiffik Kiosk
5 Brugsen Supermarket
9 Restaurant Napparsivik
10 Grill-baren
16 Brædtet

To Hvalsey (32km)

OTHER
6 Grønlandsbanken Bank
7 Frelserens Kirke
8 AUL Office
12 Tourist Office & Souvenir Shop; Stone & Man Sculptures
13 Qaqortoq Museum
14 Torvet Fountain
17 Ferry Terminal
18 Great Greenland Tannery
19 Heliport; Air Greenland Office

a circuit around the most prominent *Stone & Man* sculptures.

If you're willing to help with fishing or hunting work, you may be able to arrange informal trips (price on agreement). Just head to the harbour and ask around for someone who'll take you along.

Places to Stay

Camping is difficult due to rocks, swarms of flies and wet ground. There's no official site and you're advised to get well out of town before putting up a tent.

Sulisartut Højskoliat (☎ 642466; e sulih oj@greennet.gl; Kamikorfik B1021; hostel beds Dkr165, rooms from Dkr500) has basic dorm beds, grubby cooking facilities and rather better guesthouse-style rooms with all

meals included (and some with en suite). The six luxury student houses at the business college, **Niuernermik Ilinniarfik** (☎ 642444; e qaqtourist@greennet.gl; Vestervej; beds per person Dkr175; open June & July), are considerably better. There's no permanent attendant, so make arrangements with the tourist office and ask them to meet your boat or helicopter.

The friendly and recommended **Seamen's Home** (☎ 642239; e shjqaq@greennet.gl; Ringvej B40; singles Dkr495-635, doubles Dkr695-835) is the red building midway up the hill from the harbour. Rooms are small but clean and the higher-priced ones have attached bathrooms. Guests can use the comfy sitting room with a library of books in several languages.

Hotel Qaqortoq (☎ 642282; e hotelsyd@ greennet.gl; Anders Olsensvej B1254; singles/doubles Dkr885/1095), perched on the hill overlooking the harbour, offers good en suite B&B.

Places to Eat

The fine **Restaurant Napparsivik** (☎ 643067; Torvet B67; mains Dkr168-188) serves fine meals (including lamb, reindeer and whale) in a historic half-timbered house built in 1783. The **Seamen's Home cafeteria** (Ringvej B40; small/large daily specials Mon-Sat Dkr40/46, Sun Dkr46/54; open 7am-8pm Mon-Sat, 8am-8pm Sun) serves fairly tasty hot meals.

Grill-baren (Olesvej B578; snacks & meals from Dkr18) rustles up hamburgers, chips, ice cream and the like; fish and chips costs Dkr45.

The large and well-stocked **Brugsen supermarket** (Anders Olsensvej B852) has a good-value liquor store. There's also the **Pisiffik Kiosk** (Nipinngaaq), open until 10pm nightly. Fresh fish, whale and seal are sold at **brædtet**, near the harbour.

Getting There & Away

Ferry and air tickets can be purchased from the helpful **AUL office** (☎ 642240; Torvevej B23) in the historical area.

Air Contact **Air Greenland** (☎ 642188; Krudthusvej B1193) for scheduled helicopter flights to/from Narsarsuaq (Dkr914, once daily except Monday, Friday and Sunday) and to/from Narsaq (Dkr469, three or four times weekly).

GREENLAND

Boat AUL South Greenland boats run five days per week between Qaqortoq and Nanortalik (Dkr350); some days there's a return trip, other days it's only one way. There are also three return sailings weekly between Qaqortoq and Narsarsuaq (Dkr265) via Narsaq (Dkr185) and Qassiarsuk (Dkr245), plus two extra weekly sailings between Qaqortoq and Narsaq.

Large AUL coastal ferries call in once or twice weekly in either direction, en route between Narsarsuaq (Dkr265, mid-May to September only), Narsaq (Dkr185) and Nuuk (Dkr1435).

QAQORTOQ TO IGALIKU TREK

The four- or five-day trek from Qaqortoq to Igaliku, one of Greenland's premier walks, offers a combination of Norse history and wonderful scenery. It's a fairly difficult route and overnight camping in your own tent is required. You'll need the Greenland Tourism 1:100,000 scale maps *Qaqortoq* and *Narsaq*.

The route, now marked most of the way and following some sheep tracks, begins at the end of Qaava street in Qaqortoq, crosses a low pass, then follows the rather rough shore of an arm of Qaqortoq Fjord for about 15km to a narrow isthmus with a lake in the middle. You'll find several good camping spots here. On day two, keep to the steep and rocky coast around Taartoq bay, cross a low pass (100m), then climb through mossy boulders and bushes over a 350m-high pass. This is followed by a long and tedious descent to the mouth of a river that's usually knee-deep. Another hour along the steep bouldery coast leads to the extraordinary **Hvalsey church ruins**, about 32km from Qaqortoq; camping is not allowed within 50m of the church.

The ruins are the most extensive and best-preserved of all the Norse ruins in Greenland. Alone and abandoned in the wilderness, they elicit a sense of timeless awe. The now roofless church, one of the last built during the Norse era, measures 16m by 8m at the base and was constructed of hewn granite and lime mortar; it was obviously well made, because the walls and gables are still intact.

The rest of the route to Igaliku requires at least one more night of camping – it's fairly straightforward, but still involves several climbs and some problematic boulder fields.

Follow the shore from Hvalsey, past the Tasiusaq sheep farm and into the valley at the head of Tasiusaq Bay. From there, it's a matter of picking your way through hills and valleys to Igaliku. There are two main hiking routes: one continues up the broad valley above Tasiusaq, while the other, better route bears east above the head of Tasiusaq (crossing the knee-deep river on its delta) and continues northeast past a series of lakes to Lake 400, before descending to Igaliku. The route to Igaliku and suggested campsites (there's good camping by Lake 310) are clearly shown on the Greenland Tourism maps.

In Igaliku there's a cosy **Youth Hostel** (☎ 666151; e *jlynge@greennet.gl; Augo Lyngesvej 579; beds Dkr175; open May-Aug)*, which serves meals. Groceries are sold at the small **Pilersuisoq** shop. From Igaliku, it's an easy 3km hike over the peninsula to Itilleq, where AUL South Greenland boats call three days weekly on the run between Qaqortoq (Dkr235) and Narsarsuaq (Dkr185).

For more details, see Lonely Planet's *Iceland, Greenland & the Faroe Islands*.

NANORTALIK & AROUND
pop 1544

Located on a small offshore island, Nanortalik, which is more traditional than most places in South Greenland, has some of the country's friendliest people and most spectacular surroundings. The area includes the imposing granite peaks and spires of the Nunaap Isua (Cape Farewell) and Tasermiut Fjord regions.

The useful **Nanortalik Tourism Service** (☎ 613633, 490298; w *www.nanortalik.gl; Lundip Avquta B128)* is particularly helpful to independent travellers. There's no bank, although the **post office** *(Lundip Avquta B128)* has two ATMs. The **Pilersuisoq supermarket** *(Qujanarteq B340)* and the tourist office offer cash advance on credit cards.

Things to See & Do

Nanortalik's wonderful **old harbour** area, south of the town centre, seems too picturesque to be real. Most of the historical buildings are constructed from stone and heavy timber and date from the 19th century. The excellent and worthwhile town **museum** (☎ 613606; *Kivfap Avquta B7; admission free; open 1pm-4pm Sun-Thur)* includes photos, *qajaqs, tupilaks*, copies of Norse costumes from Herjolfsnes and other relics from Greenland's past.

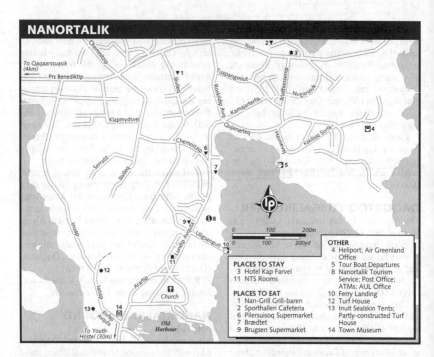

NANORTALIK

To Qaqaarssuasik (4km)
Prs Benediktip

To Youth Hostel (30m)

Old Harbour

PLACES TO STAY
3 Hotel Kap Farvel
11 NTS Rooms

PLACES TO EAT
1 Nan-Grill Grill-baren
2 Sporthallen Cafeteria
6 Pilersuisoq Supermarket
7 Braedtet
9 Brugsen Supermarket

OTHER
4 Heliport; Air Greenland Office
5 Tour Boat Departures
8 Nanortalik Tourism Service; Post Office; ATMs; AUL Office
10 Ferry Landing
12 Turf House
13 Inuit Sealskin Tents; Partly-constructed Turf House
14 Town Museum

Just west of the old harbour, a traditional Greenlandic **turf house** has been reconstructed to show visitors how Greenlanders used to live. Someone from the museum or the tourist office will unlock it and explain things for you. Across the road there's a group of **Inuit summer sealskin tents**.

The lovely, double-topped 559m-high **Qaqaarssuasik** (Storfjeldet), 4km out of town, is Nanortalik island's highest peak, and either summit presents quite a surprise. After you've slogged up the boulder fields to the northern summit, from the head of the bay west of Nanortalik you'll reach several cairns and a breathtaking drop-off into the sea. You can continue southwards to the slightly higher southern summit.

The wonderful 63km-long **Tasermiut Fjord** winds its way northeast from Nanortalik, past magnificent granite peaks including **Ulamertorsuaq** (1858m) and **Uiluit Qaaqa** (2003m), which dominates the monastery ruins in **Klosterdalen** with its sheer 1400m wall. The fjord ends at the spectacular face of the tidewater glacier Sermitsiaq, which spills steeply down from the inland ice. The tourist office organises boat tours.

Equally fantastic for a day trip is the once-weekly AUL ferry journey to rough Aappilattoq (Dkr450 return), via Torssuqaatoq Sound and Narsaq Kujalleq. The soaring peaks and ice-choked seas present some of the most startling views in Greenland.

Organised Tours

The tourist office can suggest affordable boat charters to places such as Klosterdalen, the Tasermiut glacier face, the Uunartoq hot springs, Herjolfsnes, Cape Farewell and Lindenows Fjord. Speedboats for up to five passengers cost Dkr1800 per day but a smaller motor boat for up to four persons is Dkr1200 per day. A new 12-passenger tourist motorboat started cruising the area in 2002.

The tourist office also runs two-hour town walks at Dkr150 per person, for a minimum of two people.

Places to Stay & Eat

Nanortalik's best accommodation is the cosy and historic little **Youth Hostel** (☎/fax 613633; ℮ nanortalik@greennet.gl; Nuuk; beds from Dkr175, camping Dkr80), in the old harbour area. Book well in advance.

NTS Rooms *(☎ 573386; e nicoh@greennet .gl; Lundip Avquta; singles/doubles Dkr550/ 700)* offers en suite accommodation in the former store, just south of the ferry quay. Four-bed apartments cost Dkr900. **Hotel Kap Farvel** *(☎ 613294; e kapfarvel@greennet.gl; Isua B304; singles/doubles Dkr625/900)* offers rooms with shared facilities; book in advance or you may find it locked. Eating in the bar-dining room (mains around Dkr150) is recommended – it's reckoned to be one of the best restaurants in Greenland.

The **Nan-Grill Grill-baren** *(Ilivileq B1344)* and the **Sporthallen Cafeteria**, off Isua, serve hot snacks and soft drinks. At the **brædtet harbour market**, you'll find whale and seal meat. Nanortalik has **Pilersuisoq** *(Qujanarteq B340)* and **Brugsen** *(Lundip Avquta B376)* supermarkets, with a **bakery** inside Brugsen.

Getting There & Away
Book and purchase ferry tickets at the **AUL office** *(☎ 613544; Lundip Avquta B128)* in the post office building. **Air Greenland** *(☎ 613288; Qujanarteq B1371)* has an office at the heliport.

Air Nanortalik often experiences fog, which disrupts helicopter schedules. Normally, Air Greenland flies two to four times weekly to/from Narsarsuaq (Dkr1439).

Boat AUL South Greenland sails once weekly on the beautiful run from Nanortalik to Aappilattoq (Dkr225), ice conditions permitting. The fabulous trip from Qaqortoq takes 6½ to 12 hours (Dkr350).

Southwest Greenland

The southwestern coast of Greenland stretches northwards from Narsaq to beyond the Arctic Circle. Unfortunately, southern parts of the region, especially the capital, Nuuk, are notorious for poor weather.

Historically, Ameralik Fjord (Lysefjord) in the Nuuk region is known as the site of the Norse Vesterbygd, the 'Western Settlement', which disappeared in the 15th century, before the Østerbygd in South Greenland (which disappeared in the early 16th century). The Nuuk area later served as headquarters for Greenland's first two Christian missions.

NUUK (GODTHÅB)
pop 13,889
Nuuk, which proudly claims to be the world's smallest capital city, was originally named Godthåb (Good Hope) in 1728 by its founder Hans Egede. Nuuk was founded as a Christian mission and trading post. In 1733, Moravian missionaries arrived and set up a rival mission nearby. In 1736, there was a smallpox epidemic – Hans Egede's wife, Gertrud Rask, died, along with many other Greenlanders and Europeans. Modern Nuuk houses 24% of Greenland's population, many in monumentally ugly housing projects, and the current sprawl spawned by urban drift has lent it an impersonal, non-Greenlandic air.

However, the wonderful Kolonihavnen historical district is a magnet for visitors: you can watch humpback whales swimming and diving just off shore. Hikers will also find lots of interest in the surrounding area.

Information
Tourist Offices The **tourist office** *(☎ 322700;* w *www.greenland-guide.gl/nuuktour; Hans Egedesvej 29; open 9am-5pm Mon-Fri, noon-4pm Sat mid-June–mid-Sept; 10am-5pm Mon-Fri mid-Sept–mid-June)* distributes maps and brochures, organises varied and interesting tours, and rents out tents and outdoor equipment.

Money The **Grønlandsbanken bank** *(Naapittarfik; open 10am-3pm Mon-Fri)* has ATMs, which are open 6am to 6pm daily and accept Visa, MasterCard, Plus and Cirrus. The bank charges Dkr75 to change travellers cheques.

Post & Communications The main **post office** *(Aqqusinersuaq 4; open 10am-3pm Mon-Wed & Fri, 10am-5pm Thur & 10am-1pm Sat)* contains the **telephone office**. Public phones can be found in supermarkets and restaurants.

The **Nuuk NetCafé** *(Industrivej 2B; open 4pm-midnight Sun-Thur, noon-1am Fri & Sat)* charges Dkr30/45 for 30/60 minutes of Internet access. The **Public & National Library** *(☎ 321156; Imaneq 26; open noon-6pm Mon, Tues & Thur, 10am-6pm Wed, noon-5pm Fri, 11am-2pm Sat)* offers free Internet access but book well in advance.

Travel Agencies Helpful **Greenland Travel** *(☎ 321205; e nuuk@greenland-travel.gl;*

GREENLAND

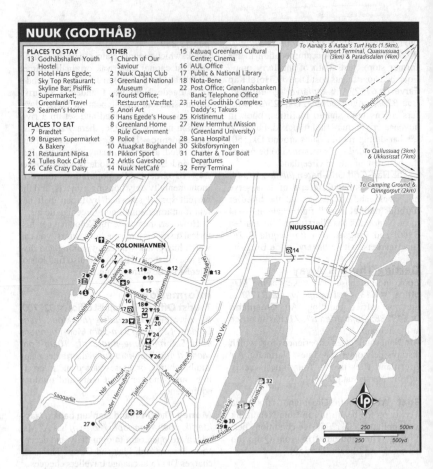

NUUK (GODTHÅB)

PLACES TO STAY
13 Godhåbshallen Youth
   Hostel
20 Hotel Hans Egede;
   Sky Top Restaurant;
   Skyline Bar; Pisiffik
   Supermarket;
   Greenland Travel
29 Seamen's Home

PLACES TO EAT
7 Brædtet
19 Brugsen Supermarket
   & Bakery
21 Restaurant Nipisa
24 Tulles Rock Café
26 Café Crazy Daisy

OTHER
1 Church of Our
   Saviour
2 Nuuk Qajaq Club
3 Greenland National
   Museum
4 Tourist Office;
   Restaurant Værftet
5 Anori Art
6 Hans Egede's House
8 Greenland Home
   Rule Government
9 Police
10 Atuagkat Boghandel
11 Pikkori Sport
12 Arktis Gaveshop
14 Nuuk NetCafé

15 Katuaq Greenland Cultural
   Centre; Cinema
16 AUL Office
17 Public & National Library
18 Nota-Bene
22 Post Office; Grønlandsbanken
   Bank; Telephone Office
23 Hotel Godthåb Complex:
   Daddy's; Takuss
25 Kristinemut
27 New Herrnhut Mission
   (Greenland University)
28 Sana Hospital
30 Skibsforsyningen
31 Charter & Tour Boat
   Departures
32 Ferry Terminal

Aqqusinersuaq 3A) can assist with all flight and boat arrangements.

Bookshops Greenland's largest bookshop is **Atuagkat Boghandel** (☎ 321737; **W** www .atuagkat.gl; *Imaneq 9*). It stocks a huge range of works, mainly in Danish or Greenlandic. Mail order can be arranged.

Emergency Emergency services in Nuuk include the **police** (☎ 321448), **Sana hospital** (☎ 344000; *Tjalfesvej 11*), **fire brigade** (☎ 000) and **ambulance** (☎ 344112).

Things to See
New Herrnhut Mission (*Soder Herrnhutvej*), built in 1747, was the early headquarters of the Greenland Moravian Mission, which was

dispatched by King Christian IV and instructed to assist Hans Egede. The building is now home to the University of Greenland, which has several faculties and around 100 full-time students.

About 4km from the city centre, just off the airport road, **Aanaa & Aataa's Turf Huts** (*admission Dkr40*), reconstructions of traditional Greenlandic homes, fly a flag to indicate someone's in. Both have wooden beds, tables, small stoves and benches. Admission includes coffee and cake.

Kolonihavnen
Most of the buildings in this quiet and picturesque colonial quarter date from the 18th and 19th centuries, and formed the heart of old Nuuk before the new industrial harbour

was constructed. On some summer weekends and evenings, you may catch a *qajaq* demonstration at the headquarters of the **Nuuk Qajaq Club**, beside the National Museum. At any time, keep a lookout for humpback whales diving just 500m from the shore.

Church of Our Saviour The lovely Church of Our Saviour *(Hans Egedesvej)* was consecrated on 6 April 1849, with several renovations since. If it's unlocked, take a look inside. The chalices date from 1722 and bear the initials of King Christian IV, and the altar has the mark of King Frederik VII. You'll also find artistic marble reliefs depicting Hans Egede and Gertrude Rask.

Hans Egede's House The yellow house *(Hans Egedesvej)* where Hans Egede lived while overseeing his Nuuk mission was built in 1728, making it the oldest 'useful' structure in Greenland. It's now used for VIP receptions by the Home Rule government.

Greenland National Museum The fine National Museum (☎ 322611; *Hans Egedesvej 8; admission free; open 10am-4pm Tues-Sun June-Sept, 1pm-4pm Tues-Sun Oct-May)* occupies three buildings in Kolonihavnen and depicts 4500 years of Greenlandic culture, including historical *qajaqs* and *umiaqs*. Other excellent exhibits include artefacts from the earliest Greenlandic cultures, the extraordinary 15th-century Qilakitsoq mummies, traditional hunting tools and methods, historical and modern Greenlandic dress, geology (with local ores and details of the formation of Greenland), Inuit handicrafts and Norse history.

Katuaq Greenland Cultural Centre Within the intriguing iceberg-like exterior of the **Katuaq Greenland Cultural Centre** (☎ 328528; *w* www.katuaq.gl; *Imaneq 21; main hall admission free, theatre tickets Dkr50-70; open 11am-7pm Tues-Sun)*, visitors can experience concerts, theatre and a variety of cultural arrangements, including art displays, drum dancing, choir singing and seal-skin shows. There's also a good café.

Hiking
The best hikes will take you up the peaks Quassussuaq (Lille Malene; 443m) and Ukkusissat (Store Malene; 772m), or 16km around Quassussuaq through Paradisdalen. The landscape

on much of the rest of the Nuuk peninsula consists of spectacular jagged peaks – the views are great on a clear day. Quassussuaq is an easy climb from the airport – follow the ski lift. For the Paradisdalen loop, start at the parking area for Aanaa and Aataa's Turf Huts and follow the well-trodden route clockwise around Quassussuaq, via the lovely lake Qallussuaq (Cirkusøen). The route to the twin summits of Ukkusissat heads off from the Paradisdalen loop at its highest point, above Qallussuaq. Use Greenland Tourism's 1:75,000 *Nuuk* map, sold at the tourist office and several shops in town.

On weekdays, bus No 3 runs hourly to Aanaa and Aataa's Turf Huts and to the airport from opposite Hotel Hans Egede.

Organised Tours
The tourist office organises numerous day tours and hikes, but it's best to book ahead.

Popular options include a hike to Quassussuaq (Dkr475, four hours), a city-sights tour (Dkr160, two hours), a cruise around the Cook Isles and Little Narsaq (Dkr495, four hours – with a good chance of seeing whales), a cruise to the abandoned settlement of Kangeq (Dkr550, five hours), and a cruise to Sermitsiaq Island and beyond to the Bjørneøen Eskimo ruins (Dkr785, seven hours).

The arts and handicrafts tour (Dkr150, 1½ hours) visits a *qajaq*-building workshop, the leather-tanning shop (Kittat) and local artists' workshops. The Home Rule tour (Dkr100, one hour) takes you through the Greenland Home Rule Government offices, where the corridors are lined with Greenlandic art and sculpture; government procedures are explained and you'll see the Landsting Hall debating chamber.

Special Events
Every March, there's a snow-sculpture festival – visit *w* www.snow.gl for details. The Nuuk Festival in early August features a week of live music, art exhibitions and food stalls.

Places to Stay
In Nuuk, budget accommodation is hard to find and B&B isn't a cheap option. There's no organised campsite, but **wild camping** is possible east of town, near the airport, or south of the airport around Qinngorput.

Godthåbshallen Youth Hostel (☎ 322700; *e* info@nuuk-tourism.gl; *Vandsøvej 2; beds Dkr95)* is attached to a sports hall; facilities

GREENLAND

have been recently improved, but it's still fairly basic.

The **tourist office** keeps a list of B&Bs, which offer rooms and breakfast in family homes, but they're expensive at Dkr300 per person.

The best mid-range place to stay is the clean and tidy **Seamen's Home** (☎ 321029; ⓔ nuuk@soemandshjem.gl; Marinevej 3; singles Dkr495-735, doubles Dkr695-960), near the coastal ferry terminal. Rooms vary from basic, with communal facilities, to excellent hotel-standard en suite accommodation.

The fairly luxurious **Hotel Hans Egede** (☎ 324222; ⓔ hhe@greennet.gl; Aqqusinersuaq 1-5; singles/doubles from Dkr1145/1445) offers excellent rooms with breakfast, private bathrooms, TV/video, radio, minibar and telephone. Look out for the stuffed polar bear opposite the reception desk.

Places to Eat
The best place to eat in town is undoubtedly **Restaurant Værftet** (☎ 311000; Hans Egedesvej 29; mains Dkr175-229; open dinner Thurs-Tues), near the tourist office, which serves international-style Greenlandic specialities from lamb to musk ox.

At Hotel Hans Egede, the elegant restaurant **Sky Top** (☎ 324222; Aqqusinersuaq 1-5; mains Dkr110-198) serves international cuisine and gourmet versions of Greenlandic cuisine, including reindeer steaks, salmon and whale.

Restaurant Nipisa (☎ 321210; Aqqusinersuaq 6; mains Dkr178-225, 2-course/3-course dinner Dkr265/285) serves excellent lamb, reindeer, musk ox, beef and fish dishes and is also open for traditional Danish and Greenlandic lunches (from Dkr55).

The pub-style **Tulles Rock Café** (Aqqusinersuaq 7; dishes Dkr30-198) emulates Hard Rock Café and serves up large portions of simple but good value specials (Dkr40) from noon to 8pm daily. More down to earth is the attached **Kristinemut** (☎ 348090; specials Dkr40), which has adopted an odd cowboy theme and rustles up the same menu (see Entertainment following).

The unassuming **Café Crazy Daisy** (Aqqusinersuaq 9; dishes Dkr16-87) has a menu ranging from hot dogs, burgers and chips to full meals (specials Dkr45), including fish, shrimps, steaks, pizza, chicken and Chinese and Thai cuisine. The **Seamen's Home** cafeteria (Marinevej 3; meals Dkr35-55) dishes up basic but tasty hot meals.

For self-catering, you can choose between the well-stocked **Brugsen supermarket** (Aqqusinersuaq 2; open daily), which has an attached bakery, or the extensive **Pisiffik supermarket** (Aqqusinersuaq 1), on the ground floor of Hotel Hans Egede. The **brædtet fish market** (John Møllersvej) is in Kolonihavnen.

Entertainment
The quiet and upmarket rotating **Skyline Bar** (Aqqusinersuaq 1-5), in Hotel Hans Egede, attracts businesspeople and has a view over the bright lights of Nuuk. It offers low-key dancing and less of the drunken mayhem (before midnight on pay day, at least!).

The **Hotel Godthåb complex** (Imaneq 30; cloakroom Dkr20) offers dancing on Friday and Saturday nights. There's also free live music on weekends in the **restaurant**, adjacent to **Daddy's** in the same complex. The rougher locals' bar **Takuss** also features free live music nightly.

Kristinemut (Aqqusinersuaq 7; cloakroom Dkr50) is a western-themed nightspot with live music and dancing 8pm to midnight, Sunday to Thursday, and 8pm to 3am on weekends. This place can be rough and it's inadvisable to enter alone.

The one-screen **cinema** (Imaneq 21) in the Katuaq Greenland cultural centre shows two or three films daily.

Shopping
Nuuk is good for buying high-quality art and craftwork, including carvings, books, artwork and furs. **Arktis Gaveshop** (HJ Rinksvej 23) offers a good selection while **Anori Art** (Tuapannguit) stocks some interesting and unusual designs. The airport and the good-value Seamen's Home keep limited supplies of souvenirs.

Film can be bought from **Nota-Bene** (Imaneq 23A) and various other places.

For outdoor equipment, try **Pikkori Sport** (Aantuukasiip Aqq). You can buy camping stove fuel at **Skibsforsyningen** (Trawlerkaj).

Getting There & Away
Air Contact **Air Greenland** (☎ 343434) for direct flights between Nuuk and Ilulissat (Dkr4234, seven weekly), Sisimiut (Dkr2314, daily except for Sunday), Kangerlussuaq (Dkr2354, one to six daily except Sunday)

and Narsarsuaq (Dkr3344, three to six per week). There are also twice weekly flights to/from Kulusuk (Dkr6584) via Kangerlussuaq, connecting with flights to/from Reykjavík.

Boat Make your bookings at the **AUL office** (☎ 349934; Ilivinnguaq; open 9am-3pm Mon-Fri).

At least once weekly, the big ferries connect the capital with Qaqortoq (Dkr1435) via Narsaq (Dkr1400), and with Ilulissat (Dkr1565), Kangerlussuaq (Dkr1380), Sisimiut (Dkr880), Qeqertarsuaq (Dkr1435) and Qasigiannguit (Dkr1505). Runs to Uummannaq (Dkr2145) are twice weekly and once weekly there's a boat to Upernavik (Dkr2715). To Qaqortoq takes about 29 hours and to Ilulissat, 42½ to 56 hours.

Getting Around

The Nuuk airport lies 7km northeast of town. Airport transport is fairly good, with an efficient taxi service (Dkr110 for up to three people) and hourly buses (weekdays only), which cost Dkr13.

Bus No 3 (Dkr13 per ride) connects the Seamen's Home, the city centre, Nuussuaq and the airport hourly from 6.30am to 9.30am and from 1.30pm to 5.30pm Monday to Friday.

For taxi services, ring ☎ 322222 or ☎ 321818.

Pikkori Sport (☎ 321888; Aantuukasiip Aqq 5) hires out a few mountain bikes for Dkr100 per day.

SISIMIUT (HOLSTEINSBORG)
pop 5222

Lovely Sisimiut, founded in 1764 and developed as a whaling centre, now depends on the shrimp industry. It lies 75km north of the Arctic Circle and is Greenland's northernmost, all-year, ice-free port. It's also the country's second-largest town and is known for the gruelling Arctic Circle ski race, held around the end of March. Oddly enough, Sisimiut has an outdoor heated swimming pool.

Information

Head to the **tourist office** (☎ 864848; [w] www .info-sisimiut.gl; Jukkorsuup Aqq 6) or **Arctic Circle Tours** (☎ 866652; Aqqusinersuaq 54) for local information.

You'll find an ATM at the **Grønlandsbanken bank** (Kaaleeqqap Aqq 4; open 10am-3pm Mon-Fri). The **post office** (Kaaleeqqap

Aqq 6) is by the police station and the **Ilimmarsa Netc@fé** (Aqqusinersuaq 64) charges Dkr25/45 per half-hour/hour online.

For souvenir books, try the **Sisimiut Atuagaarniarfik bookshop** (Aqqusinersuaq 33).

Things to See

Sisimiut's **old town**, near the tourist office, dates from the mid-18th to mid-19th centuries, and you enter it beneath a whalejawbone arch. **Gammelhuset** (Old House), which houses most of the town museum, was originally constructed around 1756. Other exhibits are housed in the **Gamla Materialhandel** (the old general shop), which was built in 1825. The blue **Bethel Church**, Greenland's oldest church, was consecrated in 1775.

The **museum** (☎ 865087; Jukkorsuup Aqq 7; adult/child Dkr25/10; open 2pm-5pm Tues-Sun June-Aug) displays the usual Greenlandic gamut of settlement history, hunting and fishing boats, tools and relics, and local art. Ask here for the Bethel Church key.

About 1km west of the harbour, **Teleøen** is reached from Sisimiut by a short bridge – features include ruins from the Saqqaq culture, graves, whale meat storage houses and an old telegraph station. Ask the tourist office for a free map.

Hiking

The climb to the top of spectacular 784m-high **Nasaasaaq** is quite steep and the return trip will take five to seven hours. On a clear day views are wonderful. Route finding on this mountain isn't particularly easy, although there are guided trips and you can follow the blue paint marks on cairns. Use Greenland Tourism's 1:100,000 scale map Sisimiut or the local tourist office hiking map (Dkr20).

Begin by heading east past the old heliport and the lake east of town, then head up the ravine north of the massif, bearing left at the top onto the level area beneath the summit. From there, turn east and follow the clear route directly up to the summit; at one very steep bit, there are ropes to assist you. The summit is marked with a large cairn.

Organised Tours

The tourist office recommends a mind-boggling list of tours, including cultural varieties, wildlife, boat trips, hiking, and winter dogsled, skiing and snowmobile trips; most have minimum participation numbers, so pre-booking is

GREENLAND

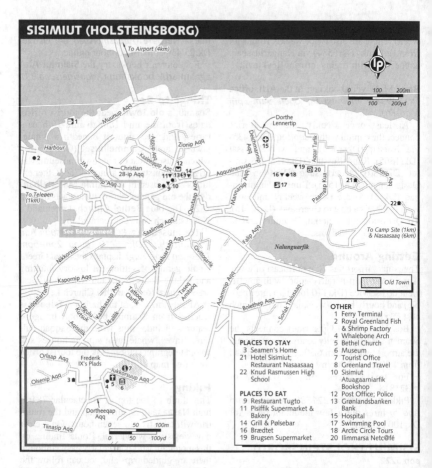

SISIMIUT (HOLSTEINSBORG)

OTHER
1 Ferry Terminal
2 Royal Greenland Fish
   & Shrimp Factory
4 Whalebone Arch
5 Bethel Church
6 Museum
7 Tourist Office
8 Greenland Travel
10 Sisimiut
   Atuagaarniarfik
   Bookshop
12 Post Office; Police
13 Grønlandsbanken
   Bank
15 Hospital
17 Swimming Pool
18 Arctic Circle Tours
20 Ilimmarsa Netc@fé

PLACES TO STAY
3 Seamen's Home
21 Hotel Sisimiut;
   Restaurant Nasaasaaq
22 Knud Rasmussen High
   School

PLACES TO EAT
9 Restaurant Tugto
11 Pisiffik Supermarket &
   Bakery
14 Grill & Pølsebar
16 Brædtet
19 Brugsen Supermarket

advisable. The biggest operator is **Arctic Circle Tours** (☎ 866652; **W** www.arcticcircletours.gl; Aqqusinersuaq 54).

You can tour the **Royal Greenland Fish & Shrimp Factory** (☎ 864088; Umiarsualivimmut 25) for free, if it's not too busy – try between 9am and 4pm on weekdays.

Places to Stay
The recommended **campsite**, 2.5km east of the ferry terminal, is free and has toilets; the river water is OK for drinking.

Arctic Circle Tours (see the Organised Tours section earlier) arranges **B&B** for Dkr295 per night; it can also book **houses** (two-bed/six-bed rooms Dkr475/1200) and organise accommodation at the modern, renovated **Knud Rasmussen High School** (Aqqusinersuaq 99; singles/doubles Dkr225/520; open July) student residence. Breakfast isn't included, but kitchen facilities are available.

The **Seamen's Home** (☎ 864150, fax 865791; Frederik IX's Plads 5; singles/doubles Dkr635/860) has nicely renovated rooms with private facilities. **Hotel Sisimiut** (☎ 864840; **e** hotsisi@greennet.gl; Aqqusinersuaq 86; singles/doubles Dkr895/1250) has stylish en suite accommodation and offers excellent walk-in rates (singles/doubles around Dkr375/650).

Places to Eat
Restaurant Nasaasaaq (Aqqusinersuaq 86; mains Dkr130-250, 3-course dinner Dkr248) at Hotel Sisimiut serves a good breakfast, lunch and dinner. The Greenlandic buffet on Friday is best booked in advance (Dkr195).

The Seamen's Home **cafeteria** (Frederik IX's Plads 5; meals Dkr45-55) serves continental breakfast, smørrebrød (small, open savoury sandwiches) and simple hot meals.

The basic **Restaurant Tugto** (Aqqusinersuaq 31; lunch/dinner Dkr45/128) serves full, good value Greenlandic meals; there's dancing and disco music every night except Monday. For inexpensive snacks, try the **Grill & Pølsebar** (Ane Sofiap Aqq 1).

Sisimiut also has a **brædtet market** (Aqqusinersuaq 54), and **Brugsen** (Aqqusinersuaq 52) and **Pisiffik** (Kaaleeqqap Aqq) supermarkets (the latter with a **bakery**).

Getting There & Away

There's no AUL or Air Greenland office in town – visit **Greenland Travel** (☎ 865747; Aqqusinersuaq 23) to buy tickets.

The airport is 4.5km west of town. Air Greenland flies from Sisimiut to Kangerlussuaq (Dkr1094, six weekly), Nuuk (Dkr2314, daily except Sunday) and Ilulissat via Kangerlussuaq (Dkr2154, twice weekly).

Two or three big ferries call in once weekly in either direction most of the year. Sample couchette fares include Qasigiannguit (Dkr765), Ilulissat (Dkr820) and Nuuk (Dkr880).

Getting Around

Regular town buses cost Dkr10 per ride.

KANGERLUSSUAQ (SØNDRE STRØMFJORD)

pop 487

Kangerlussuaq lies just north of the Arctic Circle in Greenland's widest ice-free zone (200km), at the head of its third-longest fjord. The area is officially a desert, with an extreme but stable polar climate, and it's also the best place in Greenland to observe native wildlife.

History

The Sondrestrom airbase (Bluie West Eight) was officially founded by the US on 7 October 1941, and overnight a military airfield and a host of personnel barracks were constructed. During WWII, it was the main way-station for bombers and cargo carriers flying between North America and Europe, and over 8000 military personnel were stationed there.

After the Soviet Union collapsed, the US military finally departed on 30 September 1992 and the base was taken over by the Home Rule government; Kangerlussuaq is now officially a village in Sisimiut district.

Information

Most items of interest to tourists are at the airport terminal, including the Tele-Post Center, Hotel Kangerlussuaq, the Air Greenland desk, the gift shop and the restaurant, bar and cafeteria.

The **tourist office** (☎ 841920; e kangerlussuaq@gt.gl) is in the airport terminal. Change money and travellers cheques at the reception desk in Hotel Kangerlussuaq, which also offers cash advance on credit cards.

The **Gate 3 Internetcafé** (Umimmak building), about 1km south of the airport terminal, offers Internet access for Dkr30/45 per 30/60 minutes.

Black Ridge

A road from Kangerlussuaq heads south and crosses the Watson River; turn left after the bridge and follow the road to Black Ridge (1½ hours), where there's a great view of the outwash plain south of the airport. You may also see musk oxen or reindeer on the ridge, especially near the curious salt-lake Store Saltsjø (three hours walk from the airport).

Activities

Kangerlussuaq is the Arctic equivalent of Club Med thanks to the US military, which left behind a host of recreational facilities, including a gymnasium, a bowling alley, an indoor swimming pool and an 18-hole golf course! Ask the tourist office for details.

Organised Tours

Kangerlussuaq Tourism (☎ 841098; e kangtour@greennet.gl) runs various tours, but some must be booked at least one day in advance. Winter tours, including dog sledding, ice fishing and northern lights viewing (with Greenlandic food), are also available. The 1½-hour 'Musk Ox Photo Safari' (Dkr175) runs daily. There's also a three-hour jeep tour up Sandflugtdalen to the Russell Glacier (Dkr475) and sightseeing around Kangerlussuaq by car or bus (Dkr250, two hours). **Rejsegruppen** (☎ 841433; e rejsegruppen@greennet.gl) offers similar tours and is usually cheaper.

Places to Stay

The free **camping ground**, west of the airport terminal, only has a cold-water tap, although showers are available at Hotel Kangerlussuaq and toilets are available at the airport terminal itself.

The no-frills and slightly shabby **Rejsegruppen Youth Hostel** *(☎ 841433; e rejsegruppen@greennet.gl; dorm beds from Dkr135, B&B singles/doubles Dkr500/600)* has renovated toilet facilities and is 1km south of the airport terminal.

Kangerlussuaq Tourism runs the flash and nicely renovated hostel, **Vandrehjemmet Old Camp** *(☎ 841648; e kangtour@greennet.gl; beds Dkr275, singles/doubles Dkr550/750)*, 2km west of the airport terminal. Breakfast is included in the price but lunch and dinner costs an extra Dkr105.

At the airport terminal, **Hotel Kangerlussuaq** *(☎ 841180; e kangbook@glv.gl; B&B singles Dkr500-980, doubles Dkr750-1225)* has spacious, modern rooms (most include an en suite) and corridors lined with Saga maps.

From mid-December to mid-April, a temporary **Ice Hotel** *(singles/doubles Dkr495/ 842)* across the road offers real igloos at -12°C. Beds are on ice blocks, with musk ox skins and good sleeping bags.

Places to Eat

The **Hotel Kangerlussuaq restaurant** *(mains Dkr165-178, 3-course meals Dkr248; open 6pm-9.30pm daily)* offers decent à la carte dining. The more basic but very reasonable **cafeteria** *(snacks & mains Dkr13-128, specials Dkr54; open 6.30am-8.30pm or 9.30pm daily)* serves breakfast, sandwiches and good-value hot lunches and dinners.

Buy your groceries at **Butikken**, opposite the airport terminal.

Getting There & Away

Air Greenland *(☎ 841142)* flies between Kangerlussuaq and Copenhagen. For more information, see the introductory Getting There & Away section earlier.

Air Greenland also has direct flights between Kangerlussuaq and Ilulissat (Dkr2119), Sisimiut (Dkr1094), Nuuk (Dkr2354), Qaarsut (Dkr3279) and Kulusuk (Dkr4469).

AUL coastal ferries call in once weekly (16 June to 11 August only) at Kangerlussuaq harbour; passengers and cargo must be ferried to/from the shore in the lifeboat. Ferries travel southbound to Nuuk (Dkr1380) and northbound to Sisimiut (Dkr995), Ilulissat

KANGERLUSSUAQ TO SISIMIUT TREK

(Dkr1855) and Uummannaq (Dkr2355). Free buses or vans connect the airport terminal with the harbour about two hours before ferry sailings. AUL tickets are handled by **Air Greenland** (☎ 841142) at the airport.

Getting Around
Blue town buses cover the road between the Vandrehjemmet Old Camp youth hostel and the museum, twice hourly from 5.15am to 7pm on weekdays (Dkr10).

Kangerlussuaq Tourism (☎ 841098) runs transfers to the harbour/Kellyville (Dkr500 for up to four people). **Rejsegruppen** (☎ 841433) hires out bikes for Dkr75/350 per day/week.

KANGERLUSSUAQ TO SISIMIUT TREK
This popular 150km-long trek between Kangerlussuaq and Sisimiut is relatively accessible, with an airport and coastal ferries at either end. There are six free huts about 16km to 30km apart – camp in the middle of the long sections.

The trek takes 10 to 14 days and requires careful planning, but anyone who is fit and good with route finding and river crossings should handle it. The trip begins easily in Kangerlussuaq, becoming more difficult further west. Notify the tourist office of your intentions and report your safe arrival.

The description in this book is intended as a rough guide only. You'll need the essential 1:100,000 Greenland Tourism maps – *Kangerlussuaq*, *Pingu* and *Sisimiut* – which show the route in detail.

Start at Kangerlussuaq harbour and follow the gravel track for 4km towards Mt Evans; from there, the trail heads west over an undulating plateau with a chain of lakes. At the eastern tip of the vast Amitsorsuaq lake is an eight-person hut, but it's 26km from Kangerlussuaq harbour so you'll probably camp en route. From the eastern tip, a hard, 18km, eight-hour day along the southern shore of Amitsorsuaq leads to its western end, where there's a big 30-person hut.

From Amitsorsuaq, the route follows the lake's outlet stream to an even larger lake, Tasersuaq. About 2km from the western end of Tasersuaq, there's a hiker's hut for your next night. From there, the route descends to the marshy valley Itinneq, then heads north and west to avoid Iluliumanersuup Portornga

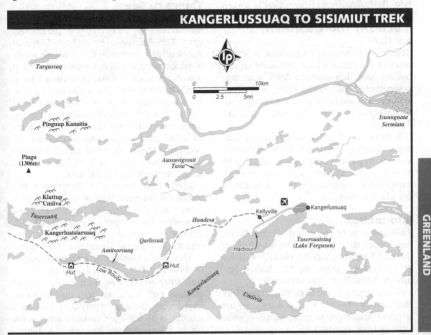

KANGERLUSSUAQ TO SISIMIUT TREK

GREENLAND

(there are two difficult river crossings in this section and you'll need to camp en route). Follow another chain of fairly large lakes northwards and westwards along their western or southern shores to Hut Lake, where there's an eight-person hut.

Continue west, keeping near the 500m contour, then descend the narrow valley towards the fjord Kangerluarsuk Tulleq; about 18km from Hut Lake there's another free mountain hut. The route down to the fjord is reasonable and there's another hut 2km west of the head of the fjord. Keep high on the hillside and cross the Qerrortusup Majoriaa pass. Follow the river westwards on the other side and pass through the gap between Nasaasaaq and Alanngorsuaq, which takes you to Sisimiut.

Disko Bay

Disko Island, the largest off the Greenland coast, shelters Disko Bay, an iceberg-studded expanse 300km north of the Arctic Circle. Visitors heading north up the coast feel their first real taste of the high Arctic here, which gets the midnight sun from late May to mid-July. The bay normally freezes over in winter.

ILULISSAT (JAKOBSHAVN)
pop 4200
Ilulissat, on Greenland's west coast, is 300km north of the Arctic Circle. However scruffy and unkempt, Ilulissat is the Arctic you came to see: there's cold, mirror-like seas crowded with icebergs and floes, and a disorderly spirit noticeably missing from the tidier towns farther south.

Ilulissat was founded as a religious mission and trading centre in 1741. In addition to tourism, its present economy is bolstered by its fishing fleet and several shrimp- and halibut-processing plants. It's now Greenland's third-largest town.

Information
Ilulissat has three competing tourist offices, which open daily from mid-June to August. **Ilulissat Tourist Service** (☎ 944322; W www .its.gl; Kussangajaannguaq 11), **Tourist Nature** (☎ 944420; e touna@greennet.gl; Kussangajaannguaq 5) and **Greenland Tours Elke Meissner** (☎ 944411; W www.iserit.greennet .gl/gtem; Kussangajaannguaq 18) all organise tours and sell souvenirs.

The **Grønlandsbanken bank** (Kussangajaannguaq 4; open 10am-3pm Mon-Fri) has an ATM. The **post and telephone office** (Alanngukasik 1) is in the Pisiffik complex. The Ilulissat Tourist Service charges Dkr40 per half-hour for Internet access.

Ilulissat Kangerlua
The main tourist attraction of Ilulissat is the astonishing Ilulissat Kangerlua (Ilulissat Icefjord), caused by the 5km-wide and 1100m-thick glacier Sermeq Kujalleq (Jakobshavns Isbræ), which breaks up 45km east of Ilulissat. The glacier flows an average of 25m daily and is the world's most prolific outside Antarctica, producing a tenth of the icebergs floating in Greenlandic waters, amounting to 20 cubic kilometres every year.

The icefjord is most easily reached from the old heliport 1km south of Ilulissat, where a well-trodden 15-minute track leads to the shore (for more information see Hiking later). From there, you can continue east along the shoreline to Seqinniarfik or all the way to Inussunnuaq (both great icefjord vantage points), or return via the partially marked coastal route.

Things to See
The **Knud Rasmussen Museum** (☎ 943643; Nuissarianguaq 9; adult/child Dkr25/free; open 9am-4pm Mon-Fri & 1pm-4pm Sun Apr-Sept; 1pm-4pm daily Oct-Mar) is a lovely house that once served as the town vicarage. It was also the home of Knud Rasmussen, Greenland's favourite son – the Arctic explorer, anthropologist and author was born here on 7 July 1879. It now houses the town museum and is dedicated to Kunuunnguaq (little Knud), his anthropological and linguistic studies, and expeditions. Other exhibits deal with Greenlandic traditions, early Danish life in Greenland and ancient Inuit artefacts and history.

Most of the works in the **Emanuel A Petersen Art Museum** (☎ 944443; Aaron Mathiesenip Aqq 7; adult/child Dkr25/free; open noon-4pm Sun-Fri) are by a prolific Danish artist whose intriguing pictures mostly concern ships, water and Greenlandic landscapes.

The town's **Hunting & Fishing Museum** (☎ 944484; off Noah Møgårdip Aqq; admission free) emphasises Inuit traditions and contains both traditional and modern tools, implements and conveyances, as well as a wooden boat. It's open variable hours – ask for the key at the Knud Rasmussen Museum.

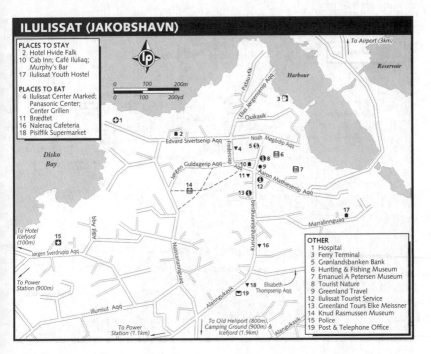

ILULISSAT (JAKOBSHAVN)

PLACES TO STAY
2 Hotel Hvide Falk
10 Cab Inn; Café Iluliaq;
   Murphy's Bar
17 Ilulissat Youth Hostel

PLACES TO EAT
4 Ilulissat Center Marked;
   Panasonic Center;
   Center Grillen
11 Brædtet
16 Naleraq Cafeteria
18 Pisiffik Supermarket

OTHER
1 Hospital
3 Ferry Terminal
5 Grønlandsbanken Bank
6 Hunting & Fishing Museum
7 Emanuel A Petersen Museum
8 Tourist Nature
9 Greenland Travel
12 Ilulissat Tourist Service
13 Greenland Tours Elke Meissner
14 Knud Rasmussen Museum
15 Police
19 Post & Telephone Office

GREENLAND

Hiking

Use Greenland Tourism's 1:100,000 *Ilulissat*
map or the two 1:20,000 new sheets, *Ilulissat
North* and *Ilulissat South*.

Sermermiut The easiest and most popular
walk from Ilulissat will take you to the ruins
of Sermermiut, Ilulissat Kangerlua and
113m-high **Seqinniarfik** (Holms Bakke), a
good viewpoint.

Walk southwest along the obvious track
from the old heliport, 1km south of town, past
a picturesque cemetery, then descend toward
the shore. In a prominent grassy patch lie the
remains of Sermermiut, an Eskimo winter settlement, first inhabited around 3500 years ago.

Check out the prominent peninsula that
juts into the icefjord – at its base is the intriguing **Kællingekløften** (Witch's Gorge),
also called Suicide Gorge after the cliff at its
southern end, where old people reputedly
jumped to their deaths.

If you follow the well-marked track up the
icefjord (on either the Ridge Trail, which goes
via Seqinniarfik, or the Icefjord Trail), you'll
reach a narrow lake; head inland above its
western shore and you'll strike the Qilakitsoq

trail back to Ilulissat via Qilakitsoq Pass. An alternative route back to town follows a marked
route northwards, which parallels the coast (at
25m to 50m altitude) until you reach the power
station immediately west of Ilulissat.

Vandsøen This five-hour circuit across the
Ilulissat plain, past the five Vandsøen lakes,
makes a pleasant and easy day hike, but the
ground gets soggy in places. The area is
noted for its rare flowers in July and August.

Cross the bridge above the harbour and
continue to the reservoir, where you leave the
airport road and follow the reservoir's southern shore. You'll pass three small ponds, then
the larger Vandsø No 4, before descending to
Vandsø No 5. From its south end, continue
south over the hill to a long, narrow lake.
Walk west, above its northern shore, and follow the obvious trail over Qilakitsoq pass to
Ilulissat, or continue to Sermermiut.

Organised Tours

The three tourist offices run a range of similar
tours through Ilulissat's dramatic surroundings.

The Ilulissat Tourist Service offers a two-
hour town walk (Dkr150); a two-hour hike to

HIKING AROUND ILULISSAT

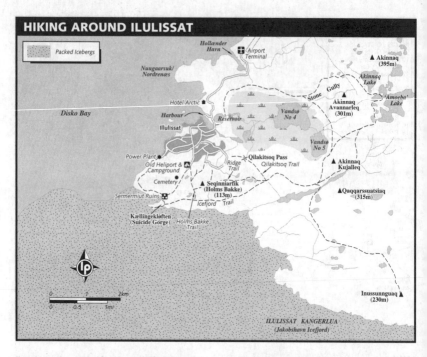

Sermermiut and the icefjord (Dkr150); a five-hour hike to Sermermiut, returning via Qilakitsoq Pass (Dkr275, including lunch); and a two-day hike to the cabin Himmelhytten (Dkr1775). It runs an impressive array of boat trips, including a 2½-hour sail around the icebergs (Dkr400), a midnight sail to the icefjord (Dkr450), a boat trip to Oqaatsut (Dkr850, including lunch), and the highly recommended 10-hour trip to the tidewater glacier Eqip Sermia and Port Victor (Dkr1195, including lunch). Several fantastic helicopter tours are also offered (from Dkr1395), including the excellent trip to the Sermeq Kujalleq glacier face. Dogsled tours run November to April and are extremely popular. Trips range from a quick spin around town (Dkr750, two hours) to longer expeditions on the sea ice (eg, Dkr4250 for three days), with overnight stays in hunting huts or igloos. The Ilulissat Tourist Service offers 12-day expeditions to Uummannaq for real tough-nuts; prices are by agreement.

Places to Stay

Ilulissat is packed with tourists from mid-June to late August; book accommodation well in advance or bring a tent.

Camping (☎ 944322; ℮ info@its.gl; camping per person Dkr35), with toilets and showers, is available at the old heliport, 1.5km south of the town centre. Don't leave food unattended in tents or encourage dogs: sledge dogs caught thieving face execution by firing squad.

The popular and rather smart **Ilulissat Youth Hostel** (☎/fax 943377; ℮ vhjav@greennet.gl; Marralinnguaq 47-49; beds Dkr195-250) has good facilities but can be taken over by large tour groups. Contact any of the tourist offices for other hostel options.

The **tourist offices** can arrange B&B in private homes (Dkr325 per person) and accommodation in self-catering houses (singles Dkr400 to Dkr450, doubles Dkr450 to Dkr700), all good options.

The pleasant, motel-style **Hotel Icefjord** (☎ 944480; ℮ hotel.icefjord@greennet.gl; Jørgen Sverdrupip Aqq 10; singles/doubles from Dkr 625/895) offers spacious en suite rooms with breakfast.

At the **Cab Inn** (☎ 942242; ℮ cab-inn@icecaphotels.gl; Fredericiap Aqq 5; singles/doubles Dkr500/800) the rooms have en suites but are rather small. The luxurious but unpretentious **Hotel Hvide Falk** (☎ 943343;

Admire the aurora borealis from Kuusamo

Pillars of faith: Helsinki's Tuomiokirkko

Colourful waterfront houses at Porvoo

See Finland's north by exhilarating snowmobile safari; Samis now use these beasts to herd reindeer

A trawler nudges through icebergs, Greenland

When I grow up I want to pull a sledge

The sun sets over Disko Island, marking the start of the long winter darkness

Football under the midnight sun, Tasiilaq

Skiing in Northeast Greenland National Park

e *hhf@greennet.gl; Edvard Sivertsenip Aqq 18; singles/doubles from Dkr945/1245)* includes breakfast and harbour/airport transfers in its rates – ask for a room in the excellent Norwegian-style annexe.

Places to Eat

Fine dining is available at **Hotel Hvide Falk** *(Edvard Sivertsenip Aqq 18; 2-course/3-course dinner Dkr189/248, Greenlandic buffets Mon & Thur Dkr198)*, with Danish, French, Chinese, Thai and Greenlandic options.

For good cafeteria meals and reasonably priced dinners, visit the **Naleraq Cafeteria** *(Kussangajaannguaq 23; specials Dkr60-80)*. **Café Iluliaq** *(Fredericiap Aqq 5; specials Dkr55, mains Dkr75-99)*, with outdoor seating, is a busy place with burgers, salads and fish, lamb and beef dishes. For hot dogs, snacks or coffee, try **Center Grillen** *(Fredericiap Aqq)*.

The best-stocked supermarkets are the **Ilulissat Center Market** *(Fredericiap Aqq; open daily)* and the **Pisiffik supermarket complex** *(Alanngukasik 1)*. The **brædtet market** *(Fredericiap Aqq)* is in the centre, oddly distant from the harbour area.

Entertainment

The **Naleraq Cafeteria** *(Kussangajaannguaq 23; cloakroom Dkr10-20)* engages Greenlandic bands – there's either disco or live music and dancing nightly. The pub at **Hotel Hvide Falk** *(Edvard Sivertsenip Aqq 18)* features live international music, and **Murphys bar** *(Fredericiap Aqq 5)*, at Cab Inn, has a disco with happy hour from 10pm to 11pm. Unless you're feeling particularly pugnacious, avoid other local bars and discos.

Shopping

All three tourist offices sell local art and carvings. Camera supplies are available from **Panasonic Center** *(Ilulissat Center Marked, Fredericiap Aqq 1A)*.

Getting There & Away

Air Alpha *(☎ 943004)* has direct helicopter flights to/from Qasigiannguit (Dkr945, six per week) and Qeqertarsuaq (Dkr945, 12 per week). **Air Greenland** *(☎ 943988)* flies to Kangerlussuaq (Dkr2119), Nuuk (Dkr4234), Sisimiut (Dkr2154), Qaarsut (Dkr1399) and Upernavik (Dkr3234).

Greenland Travel *(☎ 943246; Kussangajaannguaq 7; open 10am-4.30pm Mon-Thur,* *10am-4pm Fri)* handles all AUL and Air Greenland inquiries.

As a major ferry terminal, Ilulissat is served three times weekly from Nuuk (Dkr1565), once or twice weekly from Qeqertarsuaq (Dkr290), twice weekly from Uummannaq (Dkr740) and once weekly from Upernavik (Dkr1150). Two local AUL ferries chug around Disko Bay, connecting Ilulissat with Qeqertarsuaq (Dkr290) and other places.

Getting Around

There's currently no airport bus. A **taxi** *(☎ 944944)* costs Dkr70 to Dkr100 and the Ilulissat town bus operates on demand – flag it down for Dkr10.

DISKO ISLAND (QEQERTARSUAQ)

The main attraction on Disko Island is hiking through the weird, striated, mesa-like mountains. Geologically, Disko Island is some of the newest land in Greenland – only about 50 million years old – and includes some coal seams.

Qeqertarsuaq (Godhavn)
pop 1011

Qeqertarsuaq, the Greenlandic name for both Disko Island and its town, means 'big island' (it's not to be confused with the town of the same name near Qaanaaq). The only significant permanent inhabitation on the island, Qeqertarsuaq was a European whaling port long before it was actually founded in 1773. From this time it gradually grew into the trading centre of northern Greenland and remained the most important town north of Nuuk until 1950. Visitors will usually see a cluster of stranded icebergs just offshore.

For tourist, hiking and tour information, try the **tourist office** *(☎ 921628;* W *www .qeqertarsuaq.gl; Adam Mølgård-ip Aqq B82)*.

Things to See

The **Qeqertarsuaq Museum** *(☎ 921153; Juaanngup Aqq B5; adult/child Dkr10/free; open 10am-2pm Mon-Fri, 10am-4pm Sat)* features permanent local exhibits, including the history of the Arctic Research Station and paintings by Jakob Danielsen, local artist and hunter. You can also visit the unique and odd-looking 1915 octagonal **church** *(Oqaluffiup Aqq)*, and the **Arctic Research Station** 800m east of town – make arrangements through the tourist office.

GREENLAND

About 2km south of town lies the whalers' lookout tower **Qaqqaliaq** – it's like a box painted with the Danish flag, and the chances of seeing a whale are fairly remote.

Hiking

Disko Island, a vast wilderness, measures 120km across. For experienced hikers, trekking is limited to the most accessible areas on the southern peninsula near Qeqertarsuaq: west towards Itilleq (Laksebugt) and north towards Diskofjord. The new Greenland Tourism 1:100,000 sheet *Qeqertarsuaq* shows some suggested routes. For more details, see Lonely Planet's *Iceland, Greenland & the Faroe Islands*.

Organised Tours

Summer dogsledding is available on the glacier Lyngmarksbræen from Dkr700. Other tours include hiking trips to the rock formations at Kuannit or the Valley of Winds (Dkr150, three to five hours), and dogsledding (from Dkr600, two hours) and snowmobile safaris (from Dkr450) from 15 February to 30 April. For details and bookings contact the tourist office.

Places to Stay & Eat

Free **camping** is available beside the river Rødeelv, with dry toilet facilities and stream water also available.

The tourist office organises accommodation at several **Youth Hostels** and **B&Bs** (☎ 921628; e qeq.tourism@greennet.gl; beds per person Dkr195-475); standards vary from mundane to excellent. The eight-room **Hotel Disko** (☎ 921310; e qalut@greennet.gl; Aqqalualiip Aqq 3; singles/doubles Dkr800/ 1100) has modern en suite rooms and a cheaper annexe with shared facilities (B&B from Dkr400 per person).

Fish and meat courses are available at the **Nikifik Café & Bar** (Aqqalualiip Aqq 5; mains Dkr60-65; open Mon-Sat). For burgers and hot dogs, head for the **grill bar** (Oqaluffiup Aqq 4). There's also a **bakery** (Adam Mølgård-ip Aqq) for bread and pricey sandwiches, a **Pilersuisoq supermarket** (PH Rosendahlip Aqq 2) and the **brædtet harbour market**.

Getting There & Away

Air Alpha (☎ 943004) helicopters fly to/from Ilulissat (Dkr945) 12 times weekly.

At least once weekly, a big AUL ferry serves Qeqertarsuaq from Ilulissat (Dkr290). Local AUL Disko Bay boats sail to/from Ilulissat twice weekly.

Northwest Greenland

Northwest Greenland offers some of the most exciting travel opportunities in Scandinavian Europe. However, the traditional Arctic cultures described by Knud Rasmussen and other polar explorers are changing fast. Only 40 years ago, society in Northwest Greenland still lived and hunted as it had for thousands of years. However, although the traditional hunting culture has by no means disappeared, particularly in the Qaanaaq and Upernavik districts, it has now been extended to include junk food, alcohol, videos, snowmobiles, mobile phones, speedboats and warm, comfortable prefab housing.

UUMMANNAQ

pop 1464

Wonderful Uummannaq, with its 1170m-high red gneiss peak, is known as Greenland's sunniest spot and the dry climate does wonders keeping the summer mosquitoes at bay. Uummannaq has successfully transformed from a hunting-based to a halibut-fishing district.

The town rambles over steep rocky hills, anchored with pipes and cables – one wonders whether a big wind might not blow the lot away.

If you want to see the extraordinary narwhal (a 4m-long mottled whale with a tusk up to 2m long), you're advised to visit in late October or November. In March or April, a nine-hole golf course is constructed on the sea ice, with icebergs instead of bunkers!

Uummannaq Tourist Service (☎ 951518; e uummannaq@icecaphotels.gl; Trollep Aqq B1343) is at Hotel Uummannaq.

The **AUL ticket office** (☎ 951246) and the **post office** (at the Tele-Post Center, with ATMs) are 100m from the harbour.

Things to See

Ask the tourist office for the key to the unique 1935 stone-built **Uummannaq church** (Kussangajaannguaq), which is just inland from the harbour. Climb up to the bell tower for a nice harbour view. The three traditional 20th-century **turf huts** on the church lawn are preserved as national historical buildings. The yellow-washed **Blubber House**, opposite the turf huts, was built in 1860 and served as a whale-oil warehouse.

Uummannaq Museum (☎ 954461; Alfred Berthelsen-ip Aqq B9B; admission Dkr20; open 10am-noon & 1pm-3pm Tues-Fri), near the church, is one of Greenland's better town museums, with fine exhibits on local expeditions, archaeology, history, the Qilakitsoq mummies (the naturally mummified remains of eight 15th-century Eskimos, found in a cave near Uummannaq in 1972), the whaling era and the history of the museum itself (which dates from 1880).

Uummannaq sits on a small, precipitous island, with limited walking opportunities. However, you can get part of the way up the extraordinary 1170m-high **Uummannaq Mountain**, or hike to the **Blue Lake** on the mountain's western flank, via the turf hut known as **Santa Claus' Castle**.

Organised Tours

Uummannaq is among the best places in the world for traditional dogsled trips with local seal hunters, who guide tourists across the frozen sea from mid-March to May.

Friendly **Lucia Ludvigsen** (☎ 549529) can organise informal boat and dogsled trips and accommodation in district villages. A boat with three passengers will cost Dkr500 for a trip through impressive fjords to Maarmorilik (nine hours), Dkr400 for a visit to the Ikerasak hunting village and a calving glacier (six hours), or Dkr300 to the Qilakitsoq Eskimo ruins and mummy cave (four hours). **Hotel Uummannaq** (☎ 951518) offers excellent four- or seven-hour cruises for Dkr500 or Dkr1000 per person. The four-hour option includes Qilakitsoq and the weird Storøen desert; for the latter, add the Qingartarssuaq bird cliff and Sattut village.

Places to Stay & Eat

There are a few free, level, and grassy **camping spots** near the police station and around Santa Claus' Castle, 1.5km north of the ferry terminal. Arrange beds with the tourist office for the **Youth Hostel** (per person Dkr225) or **B&Bs** (per person Dkr350).

At the modern **Hotel Uummannaq** (☎ 951518; e uummannaq@icecaphotels.gl;

Trollep Aqq B1343; singles Dkr575-850, doubles Dkr725-1150), in its superb position overlooking the harbour, the more expensive rooms have en suites; for full board add Dkr250.

For a great meal, try **MH Mortensen-ip Restaurant** (Trollep Aqq B1343; lunch/dinner specials Dkr100/148), which frequently puts on Greenlandic buffets. Otherwise there's the **grill-baren** (Aqqusinersuaq B799A) at the harbour, or the **Sporthallen cafeteria** (Aqqusinertaaq B905).

The **brædtet market** is opposite the ferry landing, near the hotel. Just inland from the harbour area is the **Pilersuisoq supermarket** (Frederinnguup Aqq B14), which houses an exceptional **bakery**.

Getting There & Away

Air Greenland (☎ 951289; Frederiksenip Aqq B1515) helicopters (Dkr500) fly from the heliport six times weekly to connect with direct aeroplane flights from Qaarsut to Ilulissat (Dkr1399) and Kangerlussuaq (Dkr3279). Qaarsut airport may close, in which case flights to/from Ilulissat will be replaced by a helicopter service.

AUL coastal ferries serve Uummannaq twice weekly on runs from Nuuk (Dkr2145) via Ilulissat (Dkr740). There's also a weekly sailing to Upernavik (Dkr800).

UPERNAVIK
pop 1185

Fascinating and traditional Upernavik, the most northerly ferry terminal in Greenland, is nearly 800km north of the Arctic Circle at a latitude of 72°50'N. The average summer temperature is only 5°C.

The **tourist office** (☎ 961700; e turist@greennet.gl; Napparsimaviup Aqq B656) is in the **Tele-Post Center** (Napparsimaviup Aqq B656); here you'll find an ATM.

Things to See & Do

The entire historical district of the village is basically an outdoor museum. Upernavik's **Old Town Museum** (☎ 961085; Niuertup Ottup Aqq B12; admission Dkr25; open 1pm-3pm Tues-Fri & Sun), Greenland's oldest, is a real surprise. Most interesting is the original qajaq ensemble complete with harpoon, throwing stick, bird skewer, knife, seal-stomach float (to prevent seals diving after being hit or sinking after being killed) and a line made of leather thong.

The tourist office can advise on local hikes and boat charter, and local supply boat schedules for outlying places, including the **Apparsuit bird colonies** and the **Kullorsuaq rock pinnacle**.

Places to Stay & Eat

The hills and valleys north of town offer lots of free, scenic **camp sites**.

The **tourist office** can arrange accommodation in private homes or at the STI School from Dkr250 per person, but you must book in advance. **Restaurant Upernavik** (☎ 961595; ℮ restupv@greennet.gl; Mittarfiup Aqq B748; B&B per person from Dkr275), 1km northeast of town and near the airport, offers no-frills accommodation and serves decent meals. The **Pilersuisoq supermarket & bakery** (Umiarsualiviup Aqq B143) is near the harbour.

Getting There & Away

Air Greenland (☎ 961148), at the airport, flies three times weekly between Ilulissat (Dkr3234) and Upernavik.

AUL (☎ 961044; Napparsimaviup Aqq B676) has a once-weekly sailing to Uummmannaq (Dkr800), Ilulissat (Dkr1150) and Nuuk (Dkr2715).

East Greenland

Isolated East Greenland is radically different from the west coast, both culturally and linguistically, and many people remain dependent on subsistence hunting and fishing. Around half of East Greenland is protected by the immense Northeast Greenland National Park.

In the 15th and 16th centuries, Inuit people migrated from Northwest Greenland to several sites on the east coast, but by 1800, all but Tasiilaq (Ammassalik) had been abandoned. In the late 19th century, the Danish Umiaq expedition discovered a community of 416 Inuit near the site of present-day Tasiilaq.

KULUSUK (KAP DAN)

pop 310

Kulusuk island is a popular destination for day trippers from Reykjavík, only a two-hour flight away. The international airport was built in 1958 to service the US Distant Early Warning line radar station and was once home to 2000 US military personnel (more than the entire East Greenlandic population).

Visitors get a splendid impression of Greenland, as Kulusuk is a textbook village: a tiny isolated settlement, it clings to a rocky island planted beside an iceberg-choked bay and backed by dramatic peaks. Even now, few of the houses have running water, almost all have toilet buckets and there's a communal laundry.

Things to See & Do

The haunting 'new' **cemetery** (between the village and the airport) is festooned with colourful plastic flowers set against a bleak backdrop, while the overcrowded **old cemetery** in the village makes for excellent photos, with an ice-packed sea in the background.

Flugfélag Íslands (Air Iceland) organises an informal **qajaq demonstration** and **drum dance performance** for day-trippers.

The most popular **walk** is the 40-minute stroll along the track between the airport and Kulusuk village. Another great walk will take you straight up the hill, south of the airport, to an eerie mountain lake. It's easy to ascend the first peak on the ridge and you may see ptarmigan and arctic fox.

Organised Tours

Hotel Kulusuk (☎ 986993) offers a two-hour cruise to the tidewater glacier on Apusiaajik island (Dkr295), 1½-hour coastal hiking trips (Dkr75), and a 1½-hour mountain jeep tour to Isikajia (Dkr195). In winter, it also offers dogsledding (from Dkr495), snowmobile tours (Dkr300 per hour) and a superjeep snow tour (Dkr295).

Local outfitter **Frede Kilime** (☎ 986801; ℮ kilimeoutfitter@greennet.gl) arranges dogsledding, accommodation and skiing.

Places to Stay & Eat

Camping is possible about 1.5km southwest of the airport, but there are no facilities.

In the village, the adequate 30-bed **Kulusuk Youth Hostel** (☎ 986888; ℮ johannb@hi.is; beds Dkr200) has cooking facilities. **Kulusuk Turiststation** (☎ 986800; ℮ mogm@greennet.gl; per house Dkr300) offers reasonable accommodation in a five-person house in Kulusuk village. The excellent **Hotel Kulusuk** (☎ 986993; ℮ kushot@greennet.gl; singles/doubles Dkr795/985), midway between the village and the airport, has comfortable en suite rooms; the restaurant serves good traditional meals (Dkr165 for lunch or dinner).

The village **shop** sells a range of groceries and has a fast-food outlet.

Shopping

East Greenlandic carvings, beadwork and other gifts are of consistently high quality; the **souvenir shop** sells *tupilaks*, seal-skin bags, narwhal tusk, reindeer horn etc (from Dkr150). Items are also sold by relaxed street vendors.

Getting There & Away

Flugfélag Íslands *(Iceland* ☎ *570 3030;* W *www.airiceland.is)* has once- or twice-daily (except Sunday) flights between Reykjavík City Airport (Iceland) and Kulusuk (from Ikr31,300 return). Twice weekly, **Air Greenland** *(*☎ *986988)* flies to Kangerlussuaq (Dkr4469) and Nuuk (Dkr6584).

Air Alpha *(*☎ *981313;* e *air.alpha.agm@ greennet.gl)* helicopters meet incoming flights, shuttling passengers between Kulusuk and Tasiilaq (Dkr545 each way).

Ice conditions permitting, **Royal Arctic Line** *(*☎ *981133)* connects Tasiilaq to Kulusuk (Dkr205, two hours, once weekly).

TASIILAQ (AMMASSALIK)

pop 1816

Tasiilaq, on Ammassalik Island, is the largest community on Greenland's east coast; it enjoys stunning surroundings and many of its people still hunt and fish for personal food supplies. Tasiilaq has attracted some of the most interesting personalities in Greenland and, although parts of the town can become a bit wild (especially on payday, the last Friday in any month), it's a fascinating place to visit.

Information

The **tourist office** *(*☎ *981543;* e *gatetogl@ ammassalik.gl; Ujuaap Aqqulaa B48)* is in the Skæven souvenir shop.

The **post office** *(Umiartsualivimmut B817)* has an ATM inside. Travellers cheques can be cashed only at Hotel Angmagssalik.

The **Neriusaaq bookshop** *(Nappartsimavimmut B156)* has a pay phone, a public fax service and Internet access for Dkr1 per minute.

Things to See & Do

The modern, pentagonal, hill-top **church** *(Kaaralip Aqqulaa; open 10am-4pm Mon-Fri, 8am-noon Sun)* has an unusual steeple, appealing interior decor – blending traditional and modern Greenlandic art – and a model *umiaq* votive ship.

The **Tasiilaq Museum** *(*☎ *981311; Ruttelip Aqqulaa B41; admission free; open 10am-noon & 1pm-5pm Mon-Fri, 1pm-4pm Sun)*, housed in an old church, contains a wealth of exhibits and information on the history and culture of East Greenland. Just west of the museum, there are several buildings (not open to the public) dating from the late 19th or early 20th centuries, including the **Potato House** (still used to store vegetables), **The Citadel** (the oldest building in town, from 1894), the **Missionaries' House** and the **Trade Manager's House**. Down at the harbour, there's a former **warehouse** (circa 1920).

Follow the river easily upstream to **Narsuuliartarpiip** (Blomsterdalen, or Flower Valley), with a variety of Arctic flora – after around an hour you'll reach some wonderful lakes and waterfalls and may see snow buntings.

From Hotel Angmagssalik it's a stiff but straightforward climb up 679m-high **Qaqqartivagajik** (Sømandsfjeldet); allow four or five hours return. On clear days, the summit view encompasses Tasiilaq, Kong Oscars Havn, the inland ice and the wild iceberg- and floe-studded coastline. It may well be the most spectacular sight you've ever seen. Use Greenland Tourism's 1:100,000 *Tasiilaq/ Kulusuk* map.

Organised Tours

The tourist office can help arrange informal tours with local hiking and fishing guides.

Robert Christensen *(*☎ *981052)* rents out snowmobiles for Dkr1000 per day, or Dkr250 per hour with driver.

In summer (mid-June to mid-August), **Hotel Angmagssalik** *(*☎ *981293;* W *www .arcticwonder.com)* offers a walk in Narsuuliartarpiip (Dkr75), a recommended iceberg cruise (Dkr285), and a five-hour cruise (Dkr485) to a glacier. Helicopter tours to 900m-high Mittivakkat glacier (Dkr955) take 10 minutes each way, but allow 30 minutes on the ice. The hotel also organises winter/ spring activities, including dogsledding at Dkr495/985 per half/full day, and offers ski rental to guests.

Red House Tours *(*☎ *981650;* W *www .eastgreenland.de)* runs town sightseeing tours (Dkr100, one to two hours), tailor-made hunting and dogsled expeditions, guided hiking trips (Dkr100 to Dkr480), whale watching

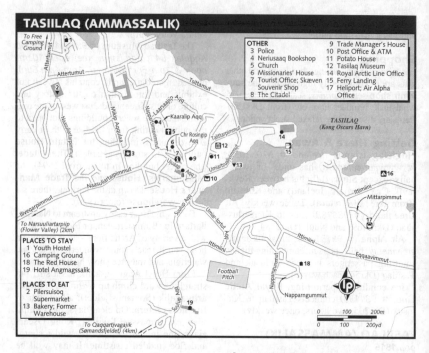

TASIILAQ (AMMASSALIK)

OTHER
3 Police
4 Neriusaaq Bookshop
5 Church
6 Missionaries' House
7 Tourist Office; Skæven
   Souvenir Shop
8 The Citadel
9 Trade Manager's House
10 Post Office & ATM
11 Potato House
12 Tasiilaq Museum
14 Royal Arctic Line Office
15 Ferry Landing
17 Heliport; Air Alpha
   Office

PLACES TO STAY
1 Youth Hostel
16 Camping Ground
18 The Red House
19 Hotel Angmagssalik

PLACES TO EAT
2 Pilersuisoq
   Supermarket
13 Bakery; Former
   Warehouse

(Dkr450, two to three hours), and support for mountaineering expeditions, including equipment hire.

Places to Stay

The best free **camping grounds** are 2km northwest of town, below Præstfjeld mountain. The Red House has an organised **camping ground** (☎ 981650; off Ittimiini; @ tuning@greennet .gl; camping per person Dkr50) near the heliport, with water, showers and toilets.

The **Youth Hostel** (☎/fax 981543; @ gatet ogl@ammassalik.gl; beds Dkr200; open late June-early Aug), at the northern edge of town in the secondary-school dormitory, has kitchen facilities; bring your own sleeping bag.

The **Red House** (☎ 981650; @ tuning@ greennet.gl; Napparngummut B1025; beds Dkr200-300) offers clean, straightforward rooms with shared facilities and is highly recommended.

Also recommended is **Hotel Angmagssalik** (☎ 981293; @ arcwon@greennet.gl; Suulup Aqqulaa B725; singles Dkr395-795, doubles Dkr595-985), with comfortable rooms and the best view of any hotel in Greenland.

Places to Eat

The **Hotel Angmagssalik** (Suulup Aqqulaa B725; meals Dkr 145-165) dining room offers nonguests lunch and dinner (advance reservations only).

The **Red House** (Napparngummut B1025) does breakfast, packed lunches and dinner (Dkr50/80/160). Nonguests are welcome at the Red House and the food and atmosphere here are great: here's your chance to eat tasty and filling traditional foods with local hunters.

Self-caterers can resort to the **bakery** by the harbour or the new **Pilersuisoq supermarket** (Attertumut B1600).

Getting There & Away

All air access to Tasiilaq is via Kulusuk; the 15-minute **Air Alpha** (☎ 981313) shuttle between Kulusuk and Tasiilaq costs Dkr545. For Air Greenland, Air Alpha and Air Iceland tickets, contact Hotel Angmagssalik.

The Royal Arctic Line supply boat runs once weekly (from early July, ice conditions permitting) between Tasiilaq and neighbouring villages, including Kulusuk (Dkr205) – the office is at the harbour.

NORTHEAST GREENLAND NATIONAL PARK

The world's largest national park, established in 1974 and expanded in 1988 to encompass a total of 972,000 sq km, takes in the entire northeastern quarter of Greenland and extends 1400km from southeast to northwest. The park's vast coastal tundra expanses provide a haven for musk oxen, polar bears, caribou, arctic wolves, foxes, hares and a variety of delicate plant life, while the fjords shelter seals, walruses and whales.

The park offers an overpowering sense of remoteness and the chance to explore unclimbed peaks and ground untouched by human feet (this is literally true: large parts of the park have never been visited by people before). There is wild mountainous scenery and the weather is usually good.

Most of the park, however, lies on the icecap. Access is extremely difficult and almost all visitors arrive as part of an organised tour (see the Getting Around section earlier). Tour operators outside Greenland who can help include:

Arcturus Expeditions (☎ 01389-830204; Ⓦ www.arcturusexpeditions.co.uk) PO Box 850, Gartocharn, Alexandria, Dunbartonshire, G83 8RL, Scotland. Organises adventurous hiking expeditions to the Mesters Vig area in the national park

Tangent Expeditions International (☎ 01539-737757; Ⓦ www.tangent-expeditions.co.uk) 3 Millbeck, New Hutton, Kendal, Cumbria, LA8 0BD, UK. Runs ski mountaineering expeditions to remote and spectacular areas of the national park, and offers first ascents of unclimbed peaks

Iceland

Nowhere are the powerful forces of nature more evident than in Iceland (Ísland), which offers glaciers, hot springs, geysers, active volcanoes, icecaps, tundra, snowcapped peaks, vast lava deserts, waterfalls, craters and even Snæfell, Jules Verne's gateway to the centre of the Earth. On the high cliffs that characterise much of the coastline are some of the most densely populated sea-bird colonies in the world, and the lakes and marshes teem with waterfowl. The island is also a backdrop for the sagas, considered by literary scholars to be the finest of all Western medieval works.

Facts about Iceland

HISTORY

Irish monks were the first to arrive on Iceland around AD 700. Although they regarded Iceland as a hermitage until the early 9th century, the Age of Settlement is traditionally defined as the period between 874 and 930 when political strife on the Scandinavian mainland caused many Nordic people to flee westward.

The human history of Iceland was chronicled from its beginning. The *Íslendingabók* was written by the 12th-century scholar Ari Torgilsson (Ari the Learned) about 250 years after the fact. He also compiled the more detailed *Landnámabók*, a comprehensive chronicle of that era. The *Íslendingabók* credits first permanent settlement to Norwegian Ingólfur Arnarson. He set up in 874 at a place he called Reykjavík (Smoky Bay) because of the steam from thermal springs.

The early Icelanders decided against a Scandinavian-style monarchy in favour of the world's first democratic parliamentary system. In 930, Þingvellir (Parliament Plains) near Reykjavík was declared the site of the national assembly or parliament, the Alþing. Iceland was converted to Christianity around the year 1000.

In the early 13th century, after 200 years of peace, violent feuds and raids by private armies ravaged the countryside, and the chaos eventually led to the cession of control to Norway in 1281. In 1397, the Kalmar Union (of Norway, Sweden and Denmark) brought Iceland under Danish rule. As a result of disputes between church and state during the Reformation of

At a Glance

Capital	Reykjavík
Population	286,575
Area	103,000 sq km
Official Language	Icelandic
GDP	US$7.7 billion (2001)
Time	GMT/UTC+000
Country Phone Code	☎ 354

Highlights

- Crawling through the pubs, cafés and discos of Reykjavík all night long (p284)
- Viewing Gullfoss and Geysir: two of nature's most amazing wonders in water (p294)
- Visiting Vestmannaeyjar for the finest views and friendliest people in Iceland (p295)
- Enjoying the spectacular volcanic scenery around Mývatn and Krafla (p303)
- Exploring the incredible Landmannalaugar geothermal area (p311)

1550, the Danes seized church property and imposed Lutheranism.

At the end of the 16th century, Iceland was devastated by natural disasters. Four consecutive severe winters led to crop failure; 9000 Icelanders starved to death and thousands were uprooted from their homes.

In 1602, the Danish king imposed a trade monopoly whereby Swedish and Danish firms were given exclusive trading rights in Iceland. This resulted in large-scale extortion, importation of inferior goods and more suffering.

Over the next 200 years, natural disasters continued. In 1783, Lakagígar (Laki) erupted for 10 months and devastated much of southeastern Iceland, spreading a poisonous haze that destroyed pastures and crops. Nearly 75% of Iceland's livestock and 20% of the human population perished in the resulting famine.

By the early 1800s, a growing sense of Icelandic nationalism was perceived in Copenhagen. Free trade was restored in 1855, thanks to lobbying by the Icelandic scholar Jón Sigurðsson and by 1874 Iceland had drafted a constitution. The Republic of Iceland was established on 17 June 1944.

After the German occupation of Denmark, and Iceland's declaration of sovereignty in 1940, the island's vulnerability became a matter of concern for the Allied powers. Without any military forces, Iceland couldn't defend its strategic position against German aggression, so British troops occupied the island. When the British withdrew in 1941, the government allowed US troops to take over Keflavík, now the site of Reykjavík's international airport. Despite protests up to the 1980s by the government and people, the USA continues to operate a NATO military base at Keflavík.

In the 1970s, Iceland extended its offshore fishing limit to 200mi (322km), precipitating the 'Cod War' with the British Royal Navy and fishing fleet. The British eventually accepted the fishing limit in 1976. However, in the 1980s and '90s there were clashes between Icelanders and conservation groups over Icelandic whaling policy. Although whaling from 1986 to 1989 was limited in scale, the conservation groups saw it as the 'thin end of the wedge'. In May 2002, after the International Whaling Commission rejected an Icelandic application for membership, Iceland announced its intention to restart commercial whale hunting.

GEOGRAPHY
Covering an area of 103,000 sq km, Iceland is the second-largest island in Europe. The southeastern coast is 798km from Scotland, the eastern end is 970km from Norway, and the Westfjords lie 287km east of Greenland.

Iceland, a juvenile among the world's land masses, is characterised by desert plateaus

(52%), lava fields (11%), *sandur* or sand deltas (4%) and icecaps (12%). Over 50% of the country lies above 400m and its highest point, Hvannadalshnúkur, rises 2119m above sea level. Only 21% of the land, all near the coast, is considered arable and habitable. The bulk of the population and agriculture is concentrated in the southwest, between Reykjavík and Vík.

GEOLOGY
Iceland is prone to earthquakes and volcanic eruptions because of its position on the mid-Atlantic ridge. The active zone runs through the middle of the country, from southwest to northeast; here, new land can appear at any time. Recent eruptions were at Krafla (1984), Hekla (1991 and 2000) and Gjálp (1996). Rocks in the northwest and east form the oldest parts of Iceland.

Active-zone geological features include lava flows, lava tubes, geysers, hot springs, fumaroles and volcanoes. You'll find rocks such as basalt, pumice, rhyolite and obsidian. Old lava flows, occasionally with wonderful columnar structures, are common.

CLIMATE
Warm Gulf Stream waters and prevailing southwesterly winds combine to give the southern and western coasts mild temperatures. However, rain is the result when this warm air meets cold polar seas and mountainous coastlines. In January, Reykjavík enjoys an average of three entirely sunny days and in July, only one. Fierce, wind-driven rains alternate with partial clearing, drizzle, gales and fog to create a miserable climate. Basically, it's a matter of 'if you don't like the weather now, wait five minutes – it will probably get worse'. May, June and July are the 'driest' months of the year.

Further north and east around Akureyri, Mývatn and Egilsstaðir, the situation improves. The interior deserts are also more prone to clear weather than coastal areas, but they may experience blizzards at any time of year, with icy winds whipping up grit and dust into opaque sandstorms.

Similar conditions occur on the sand deltas of the northern and southern coasts; it can be a nasty experience if you're caught outdoors.

The weather forecast, in English and updated daily, is available from the **Icelandic Meteorological Office** (☎ 902 0600 extension 44; W *www.vedur.is/english*).

ICELAND

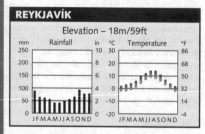

REYKJAVÍK

Elevation – 18m/59ft

Rainfall | Temperature

Rikisins (☎ 570 7400; ⓔ natturuvernd@
natturuvernd.is; ⓦ www.natturuvernd.is; Skú-
lagata 21, IS-101 Reykjavík).

GOVERNMENT & POLITICS

Since 1944, Iceland has been a democratic republic with a president elected to four-year
terms by majority vote. Presidential duties
are similar to those of the monarch in a constitutional monarchy, and legislative powers
rest with the Alþing (parliament). Executive
functions are performed by the prime minister and a cabinet of ministers. Every citizen
over 18 has voting rights.

Vigdís Finnbogadóttir, the first woman
elected to the presidency of a democratic
country, held office from 1980 until standing
down in 1996, when Ólafur Ragnar Grímsson
was elected.

After the 1999 parliamentary election there
was little change in the distribution of support
for the main political parties, and the tradition
of coalition government continues. However,
the new Left Green Movement snatched 9.1%
of the vote, indicating a growing awareness of
environmental issues. The largest party is the
conservative Independence Party (Sjálfstæð-
isflokkurinn) with 40.7% of the vote, led by
Prime Minister David Oddson.

ECONOMY

Iceland's economy depends on fishing. The
nationwide fleet of 896 vessels employs 3.8%
of Iceland's workforce and fish processing
occupies another 4.3%. The total catch was
1.987 million tonnes in 2001, and most was
exported. This was 11% of the 2001 gross domestic product (GDP), representing about
US$844 million and making it the 13th-
largest fishing industry in the world.

Icelanders are also employed in agriculture, aluminium smelting, construction,
tourism and transport, government services
and finance.

In 2002, inflation was 4.8% and, in April
2002, the unemployment rate was 3.2%.

POPULATION & PEOPLE

Most Icelanders are descended from the early
Scandinavian and Celtic settlers. Nowadays,
immigration is strictly controlled, so foreigners
living in the country are mainly temporary
workers or spouses of citizens. The population
of 286,575 is increasing by only 1.21% annually and 62% (178,030) of these people live in

ECOLOGY & ENVIRONMENT

While the small population in Iceland causes
little pollution, severe ecosystem degradation
has resulted from sheep farming and the extreme climate. However, the Icelandic government, Non Governmental Organisations
and ordinary people are successfully cooper-
ating to restore tree cover and other ecosystems across the country.

FLORA & FAUNA

Birch trees grow in sheltered parts of the
Þingvellir and Jökulsárgljúfur National Parks.
However, the native flora in most other places
consists only of grasses, mosses and lichens.

The only indigenous land mammal is the
Arctic fox. Introduced species include reindeer and mice. Polar bears occasionally turn
up on the north coast, but their life expectancy
in Iceland is very short. While Iceland lacks a
diversity of land animals and flora, it certainly
compensates for this with vast numbers of
birds and a rich marine fauna. Kittiwakes, fulmars, puffins and gannets form large coastal
colonies. Among other bird species, there are
the aggressive Arctic terns, golden plovers,
ducks, swans, divers and geese. Vast amounts
of plankton and great varieties of fish are attracted to the coastal waters. Seals aren't uncommon, and 17 species of whale (including
blue whales) have been observed.

National Parks & Nature Reserves

Found throughout the country are *þjóðgarður*
(national parks) and *friðland* (nature reserves),
the most significant being Mývatn Nature Reserve, and the Þingvellir, Snæfellsjökull,
Jökulsárgljúfur and Skaftafell National Parks.
Parks and reserves are open to visitors at all
times. Wild camping is restricted in national
parks and some nature reserves. For national
park or conservation information, contact the
nature conservation council, **Náttúruvernd**

Reykjavík and its environs. Iceland has a literacy rate of 100% and its inhabitants have one of the highest life expectancies in the world – 77.6 years for men and 81.4 years for women.

Icelanders' names are constructed from a combination of their Christian name and their father's (or mother's) Christian name. Girls add the suffix *dóttir*, meaning daughter, to the patronymic and boys add *son*. Therefore, Jón, the son of Einar, would be Jón Einarsson. Guðrun, the daughter of Halldór, would be Guðrun Halldórsdóttir. Telephone directories are alphabetised by Christian name rather than patronymic, so Guðrun Halldórsdóttir would be listed before Jón Einarsson.

ARTS
Literature
The traditions of Icelandic poetry mostly date from prior to the 14th century. Poetry divides neatly into two categories: Eddic poetry, actually more like free-metre prose; and Skaldic poetry, which employs a unique and well-defined syntax and vocabulary. Eddic poetry deals primarily with two themes: the heroic and the mythical. The heroic Eddas are based on Gothic legends and German folk tales, while the mythical Eddas are derived primarily from stories of Norse gods. It's believed that Skaldic poetry was composed by Norwegian court poets to celebrate the heroic deeds of Scandinavian kings.

The most popular early literary works were the sagas. They were written in Old Norse, which differed little from modern Icelandic. During the Saga Age (the late 12th and 13th centuries), epic tales of settlement, romance and dispute were recorded and sprinkled liberally with dramatic licence. For commoners, they provided entertainment and a sense of cultural heritage. One of the best known, *Egils Saga*, is a biography of the Skaldic poet Egill Skallagrímsson. Authorship is attributed to Snorri Sturluson, Iceland's greatest historian.

Some of the sagas are available in English. Since they're mainly anonymous works, they're found in catalogues and bookshops under the names of their translators, in most cases Magnús Magnússon, Hermann Pálsson or both. Available titles include *Hrafnkels Saga*; *Egils Saga*; *Laxdæla Saga*, the tragic account of a northwest Iceland family; *King Haralds Saga*; *Grettis Saga*, about a superhuman outlaw; and *Njáls Saga*, perhaps the most popular of all.

Icelanders have also contributed to modern literature. In the late 1800s, Jón Sveinsson (Nonni), a priest from Akureyri, wrote a body of juvenile literature that was translated into 40 different languages. Jóhann Sigurjónsson wrote *Eyvind of the Hills*, a biography of the 18th-century outlaw Fjalla-Eyvindar. The best-known modern Icelandic writer is Nobel Prize-winner Halldór Laxness, whose work deals with daily life in Iceland. His *Independent People* describes harsh living conditions in the Icelandic countryside. Einar Kárason's *Devil's Island*, concentrating on Reykjavík life in the early 1950s and '60s, was made into a film in 1996. These, and works of other authors, have been published in English.

Music
The pop music world was astounded in 1986 when the Icelandic band Sugarcubes arrived on the scene; its most successful compilation is *World Domination or Death*. The music scene continues to flourish as new bands appear; some of the more successful include Quarashi, Sigur Rós and Múm. Björk, former lead singer of the Sugarcubes and now a successful solo artist, is currently the most famous Icelander.

SOCIETY & CONDUCT
Icelanders are noted for being self-reliant, stoic and reserved, which gregarious visitors may find a little disconcerting. Objecting too vocally to whaling and bird hunting may upset locals, who are likely to be sensitive about these issues.

RELIGION
Before the year 1000, the Icelandic Norse followed the pagan church of the day, which submitted to a pantheon of Norse deities: Þór, the main god; Óðinn, the god of war and poetry; and Freyr, the god of fertility and sensuous pleasure. The Norse belief system was simple and unburdened with theology or dogma, with no salvation possible or necessary. Immortality came only to warriors who died in battle; they'd be gathered up by the Valkyries, the warrior-maids, and carried into Valhalla to indulge in mead, feasting and women until the gods themselves fell in battle.

Iceland officially converted to Christianity around 1000. With the Reformation of 1550 the Danes imposed Lutheranism, which still prevails today.

ICELAND

ATLANTIC OCEAN

Hornvík
Hornbjarg
Aðalvík
HORNSTRANDIR
Jökulfirðir
Furufjörður
Bolungarvík
Suðureyri
Ísafjörður
Unaðsdalur
Flateyri
Suðavík
Norðurfjörður
61
Drangajökull
Gljúfur
Þingeyri
Reykjanes
Djúpavík
Gláma
60

Skagafjörður
76

Skagaströnd
Bíldudalur
Westfjords Peninsula
Hólmavík
Húnaflói
Sauðárkrókur
Patreksfjörður
F66
Blönduós
Breiðavík
Brjánslækur
60
Hóp
1
Látrabjarg
61
Hvammstangi
Flatey
F35
Breiðafjörður
Stykkishólmur
Búðardalur
Brú
ARNARVATNSHEIÐI
Stórisandur Route
Blandá
Kjölur Route
57
F578
Hellissandur-Rif
Ólafsvík
57
Grundarfjörður
Hveravellir
Snæfellsjökull National Park
54
SNÆFELLSNES
Summer Ski School
Snæfellsjökull (1446m)
Búðir
Eiríksjökull
Hrútfell
Hellnar
Arnarstapi
Hraunfossar, Barnafoss
F550
Langjökull
Hvítárvatn
Kerlingarfjöll
54
Deildartunguhver
Faxaflói
Kleppjárnsreykir
Reykholt
Ok
Þórisjökull
F35
Borgarnes
52
Kaldidalur Route
Hvítá
Borgarfjörður
Þingvellir NATIONAL PARK
Akranes
New Tunnel
Geysir
Gullfoss
36
REYKJAVÍK
Þingvallavatn
Kópavogur
Keflavík
Hafnarfjörður
26
Njarðvík
Hveragerði
Fjallabak Reserve
Blue Lagoon
Krísuvík
Selfoss
Grindavík
Þorlákshöfn
1
Hella
Tindfjallajökull
F210
Hvolsvöllur
261
Fljótsdalur
Þórsmörk
ATLANTIC OCEAN
(1666m)
(1450m)
Eyjafjallajökull
Skógar
Heimaey
Vestmannaeyjar
ATLANTIC OCEAN

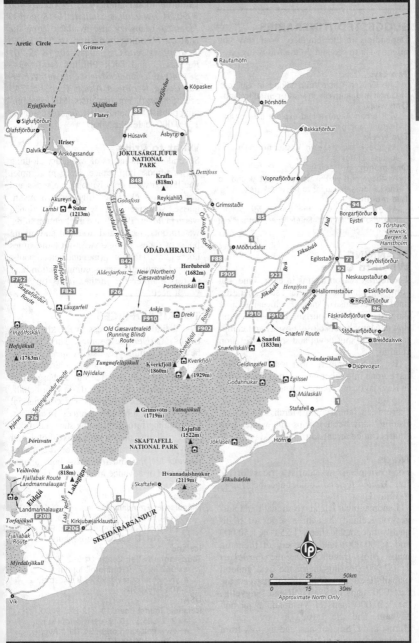

ICELAND

ICELAND

Facts for the Visitor

SUGGESTED ITINERARIES
Depending on the length of your stay you might wish to see and do the following:

Two days
The Golden Circle tour, taking in Gullfoss, Geysir and Þingvellir in south-central Iceland
One week
Visit urban Akureyri and explore the volcanic features and birdlife of Mývatn
Two weeks
As above plus take in Vestmannaeyjar and Jökulsárgljúfur
One month
As above plus visit Skaftafell, Fjallabak and do the Landmannalaugar to Þórsmörk trek
Two months
As above plus visit the Westfjords, Askja, Kverkfjöll, Lakagígar, Snæfellsnes, Vatnajökull and east Iceland

PLANNING
When to Go
The tourist season begins in early June, but some highland bus tours don't start operating until July because of snow. Each year after 31 August Icelandic tourism begins to wind down. Many hotels close, hostels and camping grounds shut down and some buses stop running.

By 30 September, most tourist facilities have gone into hibernation, apart from some in Reykjavík and Akureyri, and some bus and jeep tours.

Between January and March, skiing, ice-fishing, snow-scooter trips and winter jeep safaris can be arranged from Reykjavík.

Maps
For town plans, ask tourist offices for the free *Around Iceland* booklet and the *Map of Reykjavík*.

Landmælingar Íslands (National Land Survey of Iceland) has three series of high-quality topographic sheets (1:25,000, 1:50,000 and 1:100,000) and a variety of thematic maps. Most travellers use the *Ferðakort 1:500,000* (touring map), the best general map of the country. Other useful maps are the 1:25,000 maps of Skaftafell and Þingvellir, the 1:50,000 maps of Vestmannaeyjar and Mývatn, and the 1:100,000 coverage of Hornstrandir, Snæfellsnes, and the trek from Landmannalaugar to Þórsmörk.

For a catalogue or mail order form contact **Landmælingar Íslands** (☎ 430 9000, fax 430 9090; W www.lmi.is; Stillholt 16-18, IS-300 Akranes). Maps are also available from the **Mál og Menning bookshop** (☎ 515 2500; e shopping@edda.is; Laugavegur 18, IS-101 Reykjavík) and **Dick Phillips** (☎ 01434-381440; e icelandick@nent.enta.net; Whitehall House, Nenthead, Alston, Cumbria, CA9 3PS, England). For motorists, Mál og Menning publish the handy *Kortabók* road atlas at 1:300,000 scale (Ikr2900).

What to Bring
Several efficient layers of warm dry clothing are of utmost importance. Even in summer you'll need wool or polypropylene socks and underwear, thick gloves, high protection sunglasses, sunscreen, a hat with ear protection, a warm pullover, T-shirts and thick cotton shirts, waterproofs (jacket and trousers) and hiking boots or shoes. Bring a swimsuit (sometimes not required!) for hot springs and heated pools.

See Camping under Accommodation later in this chapter for further ideas on what you'll need.

TOURIST OFFICES
You'll find tourist offices in Reykjavík and towns all over the country. They're very helpful and employees usually speak Scandinavian languages, English, German and French. Services are free but a charge may apply to telephone calls made on your behalf.

National park brochures and commercial maps are sold at bookshop prices. In addition to providing information, the staff will book tours, sell bus passes and make hotel and transport reservations. Ask for the useful *Around Iceland* and *Iceland* – both annual and free. For advance information, contact:

Germany
Isländisches Fremdenverkehrsamt (☎ 06102-254484, fax 06102-254570, e info@icetourist.de) City Center, Frankfurter Strasse 181, D-63263 Neu-Isenburg
Iceland
Tourist Information Centre (☎ 562 3045, fax 562 3057, e tourinfo@tourinfo.is, W www.tourist.reykjavik.is) Bankastræti 2, IS-101 Reykjavík
USA
Icelandic Tourist Board (☎ 212-885 9700, fax 212-885 9710, e usa@icetourist.is, W www.goiceland.org) 655 Third Ave, New York, NY 10017

ICELAND

VISAS & DOCUMENTS

Scandinavians only need to provide proof of citizenship when entering Iceland from another Nordic country. Scandinavians entering from elsewhere, and citizens of EU countries need only their passport. Citizens of the USA and Commonwealth countries need valid passports to enter as tourists. Stays of up to three months during a nine-month period are usually granted with proof of sufficient funds for the declared length of stay. Officials are fairly liberal with this requirement but if they think you may run short of cash (eg, less than US$20 per day) they may ask to see an onward ticket. Lengths of stay may be extended at police stations.

HI hostel cards give discounts of Ikr350 at hostels. Student cards are of little use (see Costs later).

EMBASSIES & CONSULATES
Iceland Embassies & Consulates

A full list of Icelandic embassies and consulates is available on the website ⓦ www .mfa.is. Icelandic representation abroad includes the following:

Australia & New Zealand (☎ 02-9365 7345, ⓔ iceland@bigpond.net.au) 16 Birriga Road, Bellevue Hill, Sydney
Denmark (☎ 33 18 10 50, ⓔ icemb.coph@utn.stjr .is) Dantes Plads 3, DK-1556 Copenhagen V
Faroe Islands (☎ 311155, ⓔ solva@faroeyard.fo) JC Svabosgøta 31, Box 65, Tórshavn
France (☎ 01-44 17 32 85, ⓔ icemb.paris@utn .stjr.is) 8 ave Kléber, F-75116 Paris
Germany (☎ 030-5050 4000, ⓔ icemb.berlin@utn .stjr.is) Rauchstrasse 1, D-10787 Berlin
Greenland (☎ 981293, ⓔ arcwon@greennet.gl) c/o Hotel Angmagssalik, Sulup Aqq B725, Postbox 117, Tasiilaq
UK (☎ 020-7599 3999, ⓔ icemb.london@utn .stjr.is) 2a Hans St, London SW1X 0JE
USA & Canada (☎ 202-265 6653, ⓔ icemb.wash@utn.stjr.is) 1156 15th St NW, Suite 1200, Washington, DC 20005-1704
Permanent Mission of Iceland to the UN:
(☎ 212-593 2700, ⓔ icecon.ny@utn.stjr.is) 800 Third Ave, 36th floor, New York, NY 10022

Embassies in Iceland

The following countries have representation in Reykjavík:

Denmark (☎ 562 1230, ⓔ ambdan@mmedia.is) Hverfisgata 29
France (☎ 551 7621, ⓔ amb.fran@itn.is) Túngata 22
Germany (☎ 530 1100, ⓔ embager@li.is) Laufásvegur 31

Sweden (☎ 520 1230, ⓔ sveamb@itn.is) Lágmúli 7
UK (☎ 550 5100, ⓔ britemb@centrum.is) Laufásvegur 31
USA (☎ 562 9100, ⓔ amemb@itn.is) Laufásvegur 21

CUSTOMS

Icelandic customs regulations are posted on the Internet at ⓦ www.tollur.is. Visitors are permitted to import up to Ikr10,000 worth of food provided it doesn't weigh more than 3kg and doesn't include animal products. Those aged over 20 years may import duty-free 1L of spirits (22% to 79% alcohol) and 1L of wine (less than 22%); or 1L of spirits and 6L of foreign beer; or 1L of wine and 6L of beer; or 2L of wine. Those aged over 18 may bring in 200 cigarettes or 250g of other tobacco products.

To prevent contamination of Icelandic waters by foreign fish diseases, recreational fishing equipment – lines, rubber boots and waders – requires a veterinarian's certificate stating that it has been disinfected for at least 10 minutes by immersion in 2% formaldehyde solution. Alternatively, officials can disinfect the gear when you arrive (Ikr1200 to Ikr2200). Riding clothing and equipment are subject to similar regulations.

Vehicle import duty is waived for students and visitors staying less than one year, but vehicles cannot be sold without payment of duty.

MONEY
Currency

The Icelandic unit of currency is the *króna* (Ikr), which is equal to 100 *aurar*. Notes come in denominations of 500, 1000, 2000 and 5000 krónur. Coins come in denominations of one, five, 10, 50 and 100 krónur.

Exchange Rates

At the time of printing the following exchange rates prevailed:

country	unit		króna
Australia	A$1	=	Ikr47.99
Canada	C$1	=	Ikr54.74
Denmark	Dkr1	=	Ikr11.49
euro	€1	=	Ikr85.29
Japan	¥100	=	Ikr70.29
New Zealand	NZ$1	=	Ikr41.84
Norway	Nkr1	=	Ikr11.59
Sweden	Skr1	=	Ikr9.27
UK	UK£1	=	Ikr135.63
USA	US$1	=	Ikr86.86

Exchanging Money

Travellers cheques in foreign denominations, postal cheques and banknotes may be exchanged for Icelandic currency at banks for a small commission (there's no commission at Landsbanki Íslands). Beware of using other exchange offices; commissions can reach 8.75% and exchange rates are lower. Any leftover krónur may be exchanged for foreign currency before departure.

ATMs, Debit & Credit Cards Cash can be withdrawn from banks using a MasterCard, Visa or Cirrus ATM card; exchange rates for ATM cards are usually good. Maestro, EDC and Electron debit cards are widely accepted.

MasterCard and Visa can be used at many retail outlets; Diners Club and American Express (AmEx) are rarely accepted. Icelanders use cards for buying groceries and other small purchases.

Costs

The lowest price of a double hotel room in Reykjavík, with shared bathroom, is Ikr8100. If you stay in hostels, eat at snack bars and travel using bus passes, you can keep expenses to about Ikr4500 a day. Rock-bottom budget travel in Iceland is only possible with near-total exposure to the difficult weather conditions. If you must get by on less than Ikr1500 a day, you'll have to camp, self-cater and hitchhike, cycle or walk.

Student cards get you substantial discounts on flights, museum admissions and bus fares (in winter). Students and holders of Iceland bus passes receive 5% to 10% discount on most camping fees, sleeping-bag accommodation at Edda hotels and some restaurants. Discounts aren't advertised and many are available only if you purchase vouchers in conjunction with bus passes from Destination Iceland at the BSÍ bus station in Reykjavík.

Bringing a camper van or caravan allows comfortable travel on a fairly low budget. Minimise petrol costs by sharing expenses with travellers without vehicles.

Unfortunately, as tourism grows in Iceland, costs of many tourist services are spiralling into orbit – at up to four times the rate of inflation!

Tipping & Bargaining

Tipping isn't required in Iceland; restaurants automatically add service charges to the bill. If you want to tip for particularly good or friendly service, however, you won't be refused. Bargaining isn't standard practice in Iceland.

Taxes & Refunds

The 24.5% Icelandic *söluskattur* (VAT) applies to many goods and services and it's included in marked prices.

If you spend over Ikr4000 in a shop with the sign 'Iceland Tax-Free Shopping', you'll get a tax-refund coupon worth up to 15% of the cost price. If you spent more than Ikr40,000, present your coupons and goods (except woollens) to customs before check-in at Keflavík, Reykjavík city airport, Akureyri airport, or Seyðisfjörður; this isn't necessary for purchases between Ikr4000 and Ikr40,000. Collect your refund in cash from the duty-free stores at Reykjavík and Akureyri, the banks at Keflavík airport and a desk at the ferry terminal in Seyðisfjörður.

POST & COMMUNICATIONS
Post

The Icelandic postal system (W www.postur.is) is reliable and efficient. An airmail letter/postcard to Europe costs Ikr55; outside Europe it costs Ikr80. Poste restante is available in all cities and villages, but Reykjavík is best set up to handle it. Mail should be addressed with your name to Poste Restante, Central Post Office, Pósthússtræti 5, IS-101 Reykjavík, Iceland.

Telephone

Direct dialling is available via satellite to Europe, North America and elsewhere. After dialling the international access code (☎ 00 from Iceland), dial the country code, area or city code and the telephone number. Iceland's country code is ☎ 354 and there are no area codes; from outside Iceland, follow with the seven-digit number. Within Iceland, just dial the seven-digit number. For operator assistance, call ☎ 533 5310. Directory assistance is ☎ 118 (local) or ☎ 1811 (international). Reverse-charge (collect) calls may be made to many countries, and many charge cards are accepted. Beware of public telephones in bars and restaurants – most eat up your money at an incredible rate.

Using the Síminn Ikr500 phonecard, a three-minute phone call to the USA or the UK costs Ikr105 at all times.

Take a steamy dip in Reykjavík's Laugardalur pool

Basalt columns at Aldeyjarfoss waterfall, Iceland

Birch trees at Jökulsárgljúfur National Park

Dome-shaped Perlan restaurant, atop the Öskjuhlíð water tanks, is a Reykjavík landmark

Summer wildflowers near Skaftafell National Park

Vast and volcanic: Viti hot lake at Askja

Dettifoss is Europe's most powerful waterfall

Strokkur, at Geysir, spouts every eight minutes

Mud pies anyone? Boiling mudpots at Krísuvík

GRANT DIXON

GRANT DIXON

GRANT DIXON

GRAEME CORNWALLIS

GRAEME CORNWALLIS

Mobile Telephones Information for GSM users, including the latest details on coverage, can be obtained from **Síminn** *(Iceland Telecom;* ☎ *550 8200;* ⓦ *www.siminn.is; Laugavegur 15, Reykjavík).* Mobile calls to anywhere in the world are cheaper from 7pm to 8am weekdays and from 7pm Friday to 8am Monday.

Fax
Telefax services are available at the public telephone offices in Reykjavík and most post offices around the country. Send all incoming public faxes to **Síminn** *(fax 550 6609; Laugavegur 15, Reykjavík)* or the **Central Post Office** *(fax 580 1191; Posthússtræti 5, Reykjavík).*

Email & Internet Access
Internet access is available in public libraries around the country (usually closed at weekends); most are free, but you have to pay around Ikr200 per half-hour in Reykjavík, Húsavik and some other places. There are also rather expensive Internet cafés in Reykjavík, Akureyri, Ísafjörður and elsewhere. You can arrange Internet access for your laptop with AOL and CompuServe in Iceland; see Email & Internet Access in the Regional Facts for the Visitor chapter earlier.

DIGITAL RESOURCES
The **Icelandic Tourist Board** (ⓦ *www.icet ourist.is,* ⓦ *www.goiceland.org)* has detailed country information, as well as tips on organised tours, accommodation and festivals. Other tourist-oriented websites include ⓦ www.east.is, ⓦ www.nice.is, ⓦ www.west .is and ⓦ www.south.is.

For a huge list of links covering news, local information, tours, accommodation and culture, surf to ⓦ www.iceland.com. The websites ⓦ www.nat.is and ⓦ www.icelandreview.is also have comprehensive information (with links) for anyone interested in Iceland. Statistical details are on the Internet at ⓦ www .statice.is.

For information on Reykjavík, check ⓦ www.tourist.reykjavik.is, ⓦ www.whatson .is and ⓦ www.reykjavik.com.

BOOKS
There are several good bookshops in Reykjavík and Akureyri. Lonely Planet's *Iceland, Greenland & the Faroe Islands* is the most

comprehensive guide to the region, and the following books may also be of interest:

A Guide to the Flowering Plants & Ferns of Iceland by Hörður Kristinsson
Hiking Trails in Iceland – The Western Fjords by Einar Guðjohnsen
Iceland Saga by Magnús Magnússon
Iceland's 1100 Years by Gunnar Karlsson
Land of Lava – A Geological Saga by Guðmundur Páll Ólafsson
Last Places – A Journey in the North by Lawrence Millman
Letters from High Latitudes by Lord Dufferin & Vigds Finnbogadottir
Letters from Iceland by WH Auden & Louis Mac-Neice
The Visitor's Key to Iceland edited by Örlygur Hálfdanarson

See also Literature under Arts, earlier in this chapter.

NEWSPAPERS & MAGAZINES
The informative English-language magazine *Iceland Review* is available on subscription from **Edda** *(☎ 522 2000;* ⓦ *www.edda.is; Suðurlandsbraut 12, IS-108 Reykjavík).*

German, French and English-language periodicals, including *Der Spiegel, Time* and *Newsweek,* are available at Eymundsson's in Reykjavík and at Bókval in Akureyri.

RADIO & TV
The English-language BBC World Service is relayed at FM 90.9 in Reykjavík. A recorded newscast is available in English by phoning ☎ 515 3690; it's also on teletext (National TV Channel One), page 130. The state-run TV station and three private stations operate mainly during afternoon and evening hours; subtitled British and US programmes dominate prime time.

PHOTOGRAPHY & VIDEO
Crystal-clear air combined with long, red rays cast by a low sun create excellent effects on film. However, because of glare from water, ice and snow, photographers should use a UV or skylight filter and a lens shade. Although photographic supplies (including standard and camera-size videotapes) are available in Reykjavík and Akureyri, they're quite expensive, so it's wise to bring a good supply of film. Photographic equipment and camera repairs are also expensive. Specialised processing for Kodachrome isn't available locally.

ICELAND

TIME

From late October to late March, Iceland is on the same time as London (GMT/UTC), five hours ahead of New York, eight hours ahead of Los Angeles and 11 hours behind Sydney. Iceland doesn't have daylight-saving time so, in the northern hemisphere summer, it's one hour behind London, four hours ahead of New York, seven hours ahead of Los Angeles and 10 hours behind Sydney.

LAUNDRY

You'll find *þvottahús* (laundrettes) are thin on the ground. Some hostels and camping grounds (including those in Reykjavík and Akureyri) have washing machines for guests. Large hotels also offer laundry services.

HEALTH

Travellers face few health hazards. Tap water is safe and surface water is drinkable except in urban areas. Glacial river water may appear murky, but it should be drinkable in small quantities. Just to be safe, it's a good idea to purify drinking water because most unpopulated land in Iceland serves as sheep pasture. Giardiasis does exist, but it isn't a major problem.

Sunburn and windburn are concerns on snow and ice. The sun burns you, even if you feel cold, and wind causes dehydration and chafing of skin. Use a good sunscreen and a moisturising cream on exposed skin, even on cloudy days.

A hat is recommended, as is zinc oxide for your nose and lips. Reflection and glare from ice and snow can cause snow blindness, so high-protection sunglasses are essential for glacier and ski trips.

Health centres and doctors operate within the National Health system and can be found in all towns and some villages. By reciprocal agreement, citizens of Nordic countries and the UK are automatically covered for medical treatment and are charged the same as Icelanders; other visitors need travellers' health insurance coverage. Dental treatment is handled privately in Iceland.

Emergency

In Iceland, in case of emergency dial ☎ 112 for police, ambulance and fire services.

WOMEN TRAVELLERS

Women travelling in Iceland are unlikely to face any problems but it's still better to travel with a friend. As in any country avoid drunken men, who can be a nuisance. The **Womens' Crisis Centre** (☎ 561 1205) is available 24 hours a day.

GAY & LESBIAN TRAVELLERS

Icelanders generally hold a fairly open attitude towards gays and lesbians. Contact the gay and lesbian organisation **Samtökin '78** (☎ 552 7878, fax 552 7820; e office@samtokin78.is; *Reykjavík Gay Centre, Laugavegur 3, IS-101 Reykjavík*) or check out the website w www .gayiceland.com.

DISABLED TRAVELLERS

Many hotels, restaurants and large shops have facilities for people with disabilities. The airlines can take disabled passengers, as can two of the coastal ferries, the *Baldur* and the *Herjólfur*. Flugfélag Íslands (Air Iceland) offers discounts to disabled travellers. Facilities aren't available on scheduled bus services, but tours on specially equipped buses can be arranged. For details, contact the tourist information centre in Reykjavík, or the organisation for the disabled, **Sjálfsbjörg** (☎ 552 9133; w *www.sjalfsbjorg.is; Hátún 12, IS-105 Reykjavík*).

SENIOR TRAVELLERS

Senior travellers rarely get discounts or any form of special treatment in Iceland, but some museums offer discounts and Flugfélag Íslands (Air Iceland) offers discounted fares.

TRAVEL WITH CHILDREN

Camping and hiking aren't great options for children visiting Iceland due to frequent spells of bad weather.

Children aged two to 11 pay half fare on Flugfélag Íslands (Air Iceland) flights and tours, and are charged half price for farmhouse and some other accommodation. Destination Iceland buses and tours charge half fare for those aged four to 11. There's a 50% discount at swimming pools and admission to museums and cinemas varies from full price to free. Always check age limits.

DANGERS & ANNOYANCES

Iceland has a low crime rate, so there are few dangers or annoyances for travellers. Police don't carry guns, and prisoners go home on public holidays.

When visiting geothermal areas avoid thin crusts of lighter coloured soil around fumaroles (vents for hot gases) and mudpots, snowfields that may overlie hidden fissures, loose sharp lava chunks, and slippery slopes of scoria (volcanic slag).

Be careful when using taxis, especially to or from the Keflavík international airport or the Reykjavík city airport; there have been reports of rip-offs. Take care when dealing with car rental agencies. If you have a grievance, see Car Rental in the Getting Around section.

BUSINESS HOURS

Weekday shopping hours are 9am to 6pm, although some shops may open at 8am and close as early as 4pm. Shops usually open at 9am or 10am and close between 1pm and 4pm on Saturday. Petrol stations, kiosks and some supermarkets are open 9am to between 10pm and 11.30pm daily. Some shops in Reykjavík open on Sunday. Post offices have variable opening hours, but most open 8.30am or 9am to 4.30pm or 5pm Monday to Friday. Banking hours are 9.15am to 4pm Monday to Friday.

PUBLIC HOLIDAYS & SPECIAL EVENTS

The following public holidays are observed in Iceland:

New Year's Day 1 January
Maundy Thursday Thursday before Easter
Good Friday to Easter Monday March/April
First Day of Summer April
Labour Day 1 May
Ascension Day May
Whit Sunday & Whit Monday May
Independence Day 17 June
Shop & Office Workers' Holiday First Monday in August
Christmas Eve 24 December (afternoon)
Christmas Day 25 December
Boxing Day 26 December
New Year's Eve 31 December (afternoon)

The largest nationwide festival is **Independence Day** on 17 June, celebrating the day in 1944 on which Iceland gained independence from Denmark.

Tradition has it that the sun is not supposed to shine on this day, perhaps a psychological concession to what normally happens, anyway!

Reykjavík hosts a biennial **arts festival** (W www.listahatid.is) in May (even-numbered years), with a wide range of events, including painting exhibitions, song and dance.

The first day of summer, or **Sumardagurinn fyrsti**, is celebrated in carnival style on the third Thursday in April, with the biggest bash staged in Reykjavík. The first day of winter, **Fyrsti vetrardagur**, falls on the third Saturday of October but it is not, of course, an occasion that inspires much merriment.

Sjómannadagurinn, celebrated on the first Sunday in June, is dedicated to seafarers. The Seamen's Union sponsors a celebration in each coastal town, where it may be the greatest party of the year.

Midsummer is celebrated around 24 June in Iceland, but with less fervour than on the Scandinavian mainland.

Another earth-shaking festival, **Þjóðhátíð Vestmannaeyjar**, occurs in early August in Vestmannaeyjar, commemorating the day in 1874 when foul weather prevented the islands from celebrating the establishment of Iceland's constitution. Elsewhere in Iceland, **Verslunarmannahelgi** is held on the same weekend, with barbecues, horse competitions, camping and family reunions. It's not an ideal weekend to visit the national parks or Þórsmörk because excessive alcohol consumption may lead to things getting out of control.

On a Saturday in mid-August, there's the **Culture Night** in Reykjavík; it's great fun, with art, music, dance and a finale of fireworks.

During September in the highlands the *réttir* (autumn sheep roundup) is also an occasion for rural camaraderie and festivities.

Iceland also stages several arts and music festivals and sports tournaments as well as an international chess tournament, but dates vary from year to year.

ACTIVITIES
Hiking, Trekking & Mountaineering

Most visitors to Iceland agree that the best way to see the country is on foot, whether on an afternoon hike or a two-week wilderness trek. The weather is variable, and can be a nuisance: rain is common and snow may fall in any season at higher altitudes. The best months for walking in the highlands are July, August and September. At other times, some routes will be impassable without complete winter gear. At any time of year, unbridged rivers may be difficult to cross. Negotiating lava fields may be unpleasant, but strong boots will help.

Use caution when walking with children, especially in fissured areas such as Mývatn and Þingvellir where narrow cracks in the earth can be hundreds of metres deep.

You can hike or trek in many areas (including national parks and nature reserves), the most popular being **Hornstrandir**, **Mývatn**, **Skaftafell** and **Landmannalaugar to Þórsmörk**. With proper equipment and maps, you'll find many other trekking opportunities. If you're into mountaineering, there are some serious routes, including **Hvannadalshnúkur** (2119m), Iceland's highest peak.

For details on hiking and mountaineering, contact **Ferðafélag Íslands** (☎ 568 2533; e fi@fi.is; w www.fi.is; Mörkin 6, IS-108 Reykjavík), or **Íslenski Alpaklúbburinn** (☎ 581 1700; Mörkin 6, IS-108 Reykjavík).

Reykjavík has several outdoor equipment shops – see Shopping under Reykjavík for details.

Whale Watching

Boat trips to see whales and dolphins are popular with travellers. Regular sailings depart from Húsavík, Keflavík, Reykjavík/ Hafnarfjörður, Vestmannaeyjar, Stykkishólmur and Ólafsvík.

Swimming

Thanks to an abundance of geothermal heat, every city and village has at least one *sundlaug* or *sundhöll* (public swimming hall) with pools and Jacuzzis. Some places also have flumes. A session, including shower and sauna, costs around Ikr250/125 for adults/children. Alternatively, visit one of Iceland's many natural hot springs.

Skiing

Skiers who enjoy out-of-the-way slopes will find some pleasant no-frills skiing in Iceland. In winter, Nordic skiing is possible throughout the country, and in the highland areas it continues until early July. The greatest drawbacks are the lack of winter transport in rural areas and almost constant bitterly cold winds. Both **Reykjavík** and **Akureyri** have winter resorts for downhill skiing, and a summer ski school operates at **Kerlingarfjöll** near Hofsjökull in central Iceland.

Fishing

Salmon fishing seems like a great idea but a one-day licence may cost anything from Ikr20,000 to Ikr200,000, which is far too much for most people. However, you can fish for rainbow trout, sea trout and Arctic char on a more reasonably priced voucher system. Trout fishing is possible from April to mid-September but ice-fishing is possible in some areas in winter. Contact local tourist offices for further details.

Horse Riding

The Icelandic horse has been prominent in the development of the country. This small (about 133cm high) but sturdy animal weighs between 390kg and 400kg and is perfectly suited to the rough Icelandic terrain. They assist with farm work but are also used recreationally, and are known for their *tölt* (a smooth, distinctive gait).

You can hire horses and organise riding expeditions through farm stays, tour agencies and individual farmers throughout the country. Icelandic horses are gentle, and novice riders should have no problems. Horse tours are usually expensive, costing between Ikr6500 and Ikr11,000 per day; multi-day tours with tent or hut accommodation can sometimes be arranged. Short-term rental costs from Ikr1200 per hour. In September, you can also volunteer for the *réttir*, or sheep roundup; the job normally provides room and board as well as an interesting experience. Arrangements are made through tourist offices and some tour operators.

WORK

High-paying jobs on fishing boats are hard to come by and normally go to friends and relatives of boat owners. Most foreign workers in Iceland find themselves gutting fish eight hours a day for well below the national average wage. However, some companies include food and/or accommodation in the deal; your best chance of finding employment is in spring. If you intend to work in Iceland, you'll need to have a job offer before you actually arrive in the country, then apply for a work permit. Icelandic embassies abroad keep lists of businesses hiring seasonal employees.

ACCOMMODATION
Camping

Camping provides the most effective relief from high accommodation prices. Bring only an easily assembled, stable, seam-sealed and well-constructed tent (storm-force winds and deluges aren't uncommon in summer). A porch for storing wet gear, cooking implements and boots is vital. You'll also need a good sleeping bag.

Only a small amount of land in Iceland is privately owned. If you'd like to camp on a private farm, ask the owner's permission first. Otherwise, apart from national parks and nature reserves where camping is either forbidden or restricted to certain areas, you're free to camp anywhere. Take care to go to the toilet well away from all surface water and use biodegradable soaps for washing up.

Organised camping grounds are known as *tjaldsvæði*. Some places provide washing machines, cooking facilities, hot showers and common rooms; others have only a cold-water tap and a pit toilet. Charges vary, but usually you'll pay about Ikr400 to Ikr700 per person. Several remote communities attract visitors off the Ring Road by offering free camping, complete with excellent facilities!

Natural fuel shortages and Icelandic regulations preclude campfires, so carry a stove and enough fuel for the duration of your trek. Butane cartridges are found in shops and petrol stations. *Blýlaust* (unleaded petrol) and *hreinsað bensín* (white spirits) are found at most petrol stations. Coleman fuel may be purchased at the Reykjavík camping ground and at **Nanoq** (☎ 575 5100; *Kringlan shopping centre, Reykjavík*). *Steinólíu* (paraffin/kerosene) works in all stoves fitted with a paraffin/kerosene jet; it's available at some petrol stations and ironmongers (hardware stores). Methylated spirits is expensive and it's sold only in chemists and at ÁTVR State Monopoly stores. A similar but cheaper alternative is *rauðspritt*, available from the Reykjavík camping ground.

Emergency Huts

The Lifesaving Association and the Icelandic Automobile Association maintain orange-coloured emergency huts on high mountain passes, remote coastlines and other places subject to life-threatening conditions. They're stocked with food, fuel and blankets and must only be used in emergencies.

Mountain Huts

Ferðafélag Íslands (the Icelandic Touring Club) and smaller local clubs maintain a

system of *sæluhús* (mountain huts). Several of these, such as those at Landmannalaugar and Þórsmörk, are accessible by 4WD vehicle, but most are in wilderness areas. Huts along the popular Landmannalaugar to Þórsmörk route must be reserved and paid for in advance through the club office or through wardens at the Þórsmörk or Landmannalaugar huts. Some have cooking facilities but guests must carry food and sleeping bags.

The huts are open to anyone. In the more rudimentary ones, Icelandic Touring Club members pay Ikr750 while nonmembers pay Ikr1000. In posher places, members pay Ikr1000 and nonmembers Ikr1500. For more information, contact **Ferðafélag Íslands** (☎ 568 2533; e fi@fi.is; *Mörkin 6, IS-108 Reykjavík*).

Útivist (☎ 562 1000; e utivist@utivist.is; w www.utivist.is; *Laugavegur 178, IS-105 Reykjavík*) operates huts at Goðaland and Fimmvörðuháls along the Þórsmörk to Skógar route.

Hostels

Icelandic HI hostels are called *farfuglaheimili*, which translates into something like 'little home for migrating birds'. All hostels have hot water, duvets and pillows, cooking facilities, luggage storage and opportunities to meet other travellers. There are normally no curfews. Sleeping bags are welcome, so guests don't have to provide or rent sleeping sheets. For a dorm bed, HI members pay Ikr1200 to Ikr1600 and others pay Ikr1500 to Ikr2000 (children aged five to 12 pay half price). Single and double rooms may be available. Sheet hire costs Ikr500 per stay and breakfast (when available) costs Ikr600 to Ikr800 extra.

For more information on hostels, contact the **Icelandic Hostel Association** (*Bandalag Íslenskra Farfugla*; ☎ 553 8110, fax 588 9201; e info@hostel.is; w www.hostel.is; *Sundlaugavegur 34, IS-105 Reykjavík*).

Guesthouses

There are several types of *gistiheimilið* (guesthouses), from private homes that let out rooms to bring in extra cash, to others that are quite elaborate. Most are only open seasonally; between October and May, room rates are significantly cheaper than they are from June to September. Some guesthouses offer rooms reminiscent of prison cells and charge excessive prices; always ask to see the room before checking in, and beware of hidden extras, such as breakfast, which may not be included in the price. Breakfast is usually served buffet-style, with cold dishes only.

Hostel-style sleeping-bag accommodation may be available for Ikr1400 to Ikr3000 (usually excluding breakfast); double rooms range from Ikr3000 to Ikr9000; and self-contained units cost between Ikr5600 and Ikr18,500. Rooms are always cheaper if booked through a travel agency abroad.

Edda Hotels & Summer Hotels

Most summer hotels, including **Edda Hotels** (W *www.hoteledda.is)*, run by Icelandair Hotels, are schools that are used as tourist accommodation during summer holidays (early June to late August). Some offer sleeping-bag accommodation (a bed or mattress on which to roll out your sleeping bag) in rooms or classrooms (the latter become dormitory facilities), in addition to more conventional lodging. Singles start at Ikr4700 and doubles at Ikr5800. Sleeping-bag accommodation ranges from Ikr1000 (for a mattress on the floor in a classroom) to Ikr1900 per person.

Hotels

Major towns have at least one upmarket hotel, sometimes rather characterless, but with all amenities – restaurant, pub, private bathroom, telephone and TV. In Reykjavík, paying an average of Ikr14,000 for a double in a mid-range hotel gets you these creature comforts, as well as a buffet breakfast.

Farm Holidays

In Iceland some farms date from the Settlement Era and are mentioned in the sagas. Farm holidays allow you to become acquainted with everyday country life. Made-up beds are always available and many places also offer the sleeping-bag option. Some farms offer meals but others just have cooking facilities. Many also organise fishing, horse rental or guided horse tours. From September to May, accommodation must be booked in advance. For detailed listings, contact **Icelandic Farm Holidays Ltd** (☎ 570 2700, fax 570 2799; e ifh@farmholidays.is; Síðumúli 13, IS-108 Reykjavík). For current prices, ask local tourist offices, the farms themselves (English may not always be spoken), or Icelandic Farm Holidays.

FOOD

Traditionally, Icelanders showed very little culinary imagination due to the lack of ingredients. Nowadays, however, there are cafés and restaurants catering to most tastes. Amazingly, the outrageously expensive fish dishes can be disappointing – some chefs destroy delicate fishy flavours with inappropriate sauces and others fry the flavours out of the fish entirely! Lamb dishes are usually a better option.

Though traditional delicacies may remind foreigners of the nightmare feast in *Indiana Jones and the Temple of Doom*, they aren't always as bad as they sound. The glaring exception is *hákarl*, putrefied shark meat that has been buried in sand and gravel for three to six months to ensure sufficient decomposition. It reeks of a cross between ammonia and old roadkill. Few foreigners appreciate it and some people take ill due to the foul stench alone!

Other oddities include *súrsaðir hrútspungar*, rams' testicles pickled in whey and pressed into a cake, and *svið*, singed sheep's head (complete with eyes but minus the brain) sawn in two, boiled and eaten either fresh or pickled.

Moving towards the less bizarre, Icelanders make a staple of *harðfiskur*, haddock that's cleaned and dried in the open air until it has become dehydrated and brittle. It's torn into strips and eaten with butter as a snack. Icelanders also eat broiled *lundi*, or puffin, which looks and tastes like calf liver.

A unique Icelandic treat is the delicious yoghurt-like concoction *skyr*, made of pasteurised skimmed milk and bacteria culture. Surprisingly, this rich and decadent dessert is actually low in fat, but it's often mixed with sugar, fruit and cream to give it a creamy, pudding-like texture.

Snack Bars, Fast Food & Restaurants

Relatively inexpensive chips, hot dogs, sandwiches, doughnuts, ice cream and coffee are available at petrol stations and kiosks. For a light meal of chips, hot dog, mustard and excellent chopped onions, you'll pay about Ikr400. In larger towns, you'll find kiosks selling pizza, pastries and pre-packaged, pop-it-in-the-microwave items.

There are fast-food outlets in Reykjavík, and a fried chicken outlet in Akureyri. Pizza restaurants are quite popular and are found around Iceland.

In Reykjavík and Akureyri, several good-value restaurants offer soup and all the salad you can eat for between Ikr950 and Ikr1050. Reykjavík also has intimate pub-style cafés where you can drink beer, eat a meal or chat over coffee for hours without attracting comment. These places are great value, with light meals for about Ikr800.

The word 'restaurant' usually denotes an upmarket establishment, often associated with an expensive hotel. Standards of catering and service vary enormously. Breakfast is usually served buffet-style but lunch and dinner are normally à la carte. Generally, main courses range from about Ikr1600 to Ikr3000 per person – and some restaurants *do* provide gourmet-quality food for these prices.

Reykjavík has an increasing variety of ethnic restaurants, including Thai, Vietnamese, Chinese, Italian, Indian and Mexican. The Asian restaurants are usually good value.

Self-Catering

Self-catering minimises your food costs. Every town and village has at least one *kaupfélagið* (cooperative supermarket), the key to inexpensive dining in Iceland. The most economical supermarket chain is Bónus; good-value food includes *skyr*, canned fish and dried fruit. Bread typically costs an extortionate Ikr250 for a 550g loaf, but only Ikr99 for a 1kg loaf at Bónus. Otherwise, look for the previous day's bread at half price in bakeries. Some supermarkets also have good-value self-service salad bars. Petrol stations usually sell basic groceries and are open outside normal supermarket shopping hours.

Icelandic greenhouse produce is very good, but imported vegetables are often already past their best when they hit the shelves.

DRINKS
Nonalcoholic Drinks

Coffee is a national institution in Iceland and is available free for customers in some shops. A 500g bag of decent coffee costs about Ikr300 in Bónus supermarkets, and a cup of filter coffee will cost from Ikr220 (ask if a free refill is available).

The only nonalcoholic traditional drink (although it may be spiked with alcohol) is *jólaöl* or 'Christmas brew'. British travel writer Tony Moore disparagingly described the taste as 'de-alcoholised Guinness seasoned with Marmite'.

Alcoholic Drinks

Iceland is what is popularly referred to in European jargon as a 'nanny state', one in which high taxes are levied on alcohol in the hope that they will discourage excessive consumption. If you want to see how successful this has been, just look around Reykjavík on any Friday night! In fact, beer didn't become legal until 1989.

Beer, wine and spirits are available to people aged over 20 from licensed bars, restaurants and ÁTVR shops (State Monopoly stores; some are called *vínbúðin*). The inexpensive 2.2% beer sold in supermarkets and petrol stations costs from Ikr75 per 500mL can.

Drinking in restaurants and pubs is definitely for the wealthy. A glass of house wine costs about Ikr600, and beer costs up to Ikr800 for 500mL.

The traditional Icelandic alcoholic brew is *brennivín* (burnt wine), a sort of schnapps made from potatoes and caraway. Its nickname, *svarti dauði* (black death) may offer some clues about its character but it's actually quite good.

Note that drink-driving laws are strict and some people may reach the legal limit of 0.05% blood alcohol content after one drink.

ENTERTAINMENT

Apart from some cinemas, there's not much entertainment outside Reykjavík and Akureyri. See those sections for details.

SHOPPING

Many visitors to Iceland seem to end up with a *lopapeysa* (woolly pullover), although you can also buy hats and gloves. Pullovers come in many designs but the traditional ones, which are more expensive than the delicate pastel fashion sweaters, are thicker and have white and blue, violet or earth tones. Factory-made pullovers start at around Ikr7000. Hand-knitted garments are more expensive, with prices from around Ikr8000.

Handmade ceramics, glassware and silver jewellery can be bought from various outlets in central Reykjavík, especially around Austurstræti. Icelandic music, from folk to rock, is available from many shops around the country.

Iceland's beautiful stamps are a favourite with collectors. For details, contact the national philatelic service, **Postphil** (☎ 580 1050; @ stamps@postur.is; w www.stamps .is; Storhöfði 29, IS-110 Reykjavík).

ICELAND

Getting There & Away

AIR

Icelandair (W *www.icelandair.net*), Iceland's national carrier, offers shorter-stay 'cheap' tickets with very limited possibilities for rescheduling.

Icelandair operates services to Keflavík direct from a number of European airports, including Amsterdam, Copenhagen, Frankfurt, Glasgow, London, Oslo, Paris and Stockholm. In the high season, Copenhagen–Keflavík flights operate three or four times daily and the London flight operates twice daily.

A standard return ticket from Copenhagen to Reykjavík costs Dkr4200 (including taxes) and must be purchased at least seven days in advance; special offers start at around Dkr3200. Flights from the UK to Iceland are cheaper, starting at around £180 return from Glasgow or London (if you purchase at least 21 days in advance, and stay for one Saturday night and a maximum of one month). For details of special fares, check Icelandair's UK website.

During the high season (20 May to 29 September) there are daily Icelandair Keflavík–Boston and Keflavík–Baltimore/Washington DC flights. Flights to New York JFK go five times weekly and those to Minneapolis go six times weekly. In autumn and winter there are four weekly flights to Orlando. For the latest information, call ☎ 1 800 223 5500 toll-free within the USA.

Flugfélag Íslands (☎ 570 3030; W *www .airiceland.is*) and **Atlantic Airways** (W *www .atlantic.fo*) fly between Reykjavík and the Faroe Islands twice weekly from April to October, then from the Faroes to Aberdeen two or three times weekly (and to London Stansted twice weekly from mid-June to mid-August only). The discounted Apex return fare for Vágar (Faroes) to Reykjavík is Dkr2470, but you must stay one Saturday night and the maximum stay is one month.

Flugfélag Íslands also flies from Kulusuk (Greenland) to Reykjavík, with variable frequency (twice weekly to at least once daily). Fares from Greenland start at Ikr62,600 return; tickets must be bought at least 14 days in advance, and the maximum stay is one month. Flights from Nerlerit Inaat (Constable Pynt, Greenland) to Reykjavík are mainly used by Inuit people and mountaineering groups.

In summer, other airlines serving Iceland from France and Germany include **LTU** (*Germany* ☎ 0211-941 8466, *Reykjavík* ☎ 587 1919; W *www.ltu-airways.com*), which flies from Düsseldorf to Keflavík and Egilsstaðir in May to October and June to September, respectively.

Combined air and ferry tickets to Iceland are now available from the UK and Scandinavia. Contact your travel agency for full details.

SEA
Ferry
You can travel from the European mainland by ferry. Although this takes longer than flying and isn't much cheaper, it allows you to take a vehicle.

Smyril Line's new *Norröna* operates from mid-May to mid-September out of Hanstholm in Denmark. The *Norröna* sails from Hanstholm on Saturday, arriving in Tórshavn in the Faroe Islands on Monday morning. All passengers bound for Iceland must disembark while the ship continues to Lerwick (Shetland) and Bergen (Norway). It returns to Tórshavn on Wednesday, gathers up the Iceland passengers, and sails overnight to Seyðisfjörður. On the return journey, it sails back to Tórshavn on Thursday, arriving on Friday morning, then returns to Hanstholm to begin another circuit.

Note that Iceland passengers cannot remain aboard while the ship sails to Norway; they must spend two nights in the Faroes en route. To stay longer in the Faroes, you'll have to break your journey there and pay for two sectors. The high-season couchette fare between Hanstholm and Seyðisfjörður is Dkr2480 each way. Hanstholm to Tórshavn is Dkr1640 and Tórshavn to Seyðisfjörður is Dkr1420, adding up to Dkr3060 for the broken trip. Discounts of 25% are available to student-card holders aged under 26. Avoid changing money on the ship; exchange rates are poor and the commission is high.

To transport a vehicle up to 5m long between Hanstholm and Seyðisfjörður will cost Dkr2040. Motorcycles cost Dkr800 and bicycles are Dkr80. Above deck class (couchette) there are four classes of cabins and a luxury suite. For more information, contact **Smyril Line** (☎ 298-345900; e *office@smy ril-line.fo*; *Jónas Broncksgøta 37, PO Box 370, FO-110 Tórshavn, Faroe Islands*).

In Scotland, contact **Smyril Line Shetland** (☎ 01595-690845; e *office@smyril-line.com*;

www.smyril-line.com; Holmsgarth Terminal, Lerwick, Shetland, ZE1 0PR).

Coming from mainland Scotland, you can travel with **NorthLink Ferries** (w *www.northlinkferries.co.uk)* from either Aberdeen or Kirkwall (Orkney) to Lerwick (Shetland), then connect with the *Norröna* to Iceland from there.

Cargo Ship
The Icelandic cargo-shippers, **Eimskip** (w *www.eimskip.com),* can take up to four passengers each on its vessels *Dettifoss* and *Goðafoss.* The ships sail almost every alternate Thursday from Reykjavík to mainland Europe via the Faroe Islands, arriving in Rotterdam on Monday and Hamburg on Tuesday, and returning via Denmark, Sweden, Norway and the Faroes.

The trip from Rotterdam costs single/double €470/660 each way (full board). From Hamburg it takes four days and costs single/double €560/790. To transport a car less than 5.9m long costs €370.

For further information, see the Eimskip website or contact the sales agent in Iceland: **Úrval-Útsýn Travel** (☎ *585 4000, fax 585 4079;* e *aslaug@uu.is; Lágmúli 4, IS-108 Reykjavík).*

LEAVING ICELAND
Iceland levies a hefty airport departure tax, but it's always included in ticket prices. There's no departure tax when leaving Iceland by ferry or cargo ship.

Getting Around

AIR
Iceland's main domestic airline, **Flugfélag Íslands** *(Air Iceland;* ☎ *570 3030, fax 570 3001;* w *www.airiceland.is)* has daily flights (June to August) between Reykjavík and Akureyri, Egilsstaðir, Höfn and Ísafjörður. Other destinations from Akureyri, including Grímsey, are served up to six times weekly. Flexible travel plans are essential, since inclement weather can lead to postponed or cancelled flights.

Flight passes are available, but they must be bought outside Iceland; four/five/six sector passes cost from Ikr24,600/28,000/32,200. There's also a 12-day fly-as-you-please ticket for Ikr39,100 to Ikr43,400, but you'll have to

pay the domestic airport tax (Ikr415) separately for every departure.

Íslandsflug flies from Reykjavík to Vestmannaeyjar; for information and tickets, contact Flugfélag Íslands. Flight passes aren't valid on this route.

BUS
Although Iceland is small and has a well-established public transport system, there are no railways and the highway system is in Europe's least developed. Parts of National Highway 1, the 'Ring Road', which was completed in 1971, remain unsurfaced.

Destination Iceland (☎ *591 1000, fax 591 1050;* w *www.dice.is; BSÍ bus station, Vatnsmýrarvegur 10, IS-101 Reykjavík),* a travel agency serving Iceland's long-distance bus operators, covers the country with feasible connections. Many routes are straightforward, but on some minor routes connections may take up to two days. Many buses stop running in September and don't resume until June. Interior routes rarely open before mid-June and most close by early to mid-September.

Destination Iceland offers travellers two bus passes, the Hringmiði ('Ring Pass' or Full-Circle Pass) and the Tímamiði ('Time Pass' or Omnibuspass). The former allows a circuit of the Ring Road in either direction (without reversing your route), stopping wherever you like. It costs Ikr19,300 (Ikr28,600 with the Westfjords extension) – not much below the normal fare, but you're entitled to a 5% or 10% discount at camping grounds and other accommodation when vouchers are purchased from Destination Iceland. There's also a 5% discount on some organised tours bought from Destination Iceland.

The Tímamiði (Omnibuspass) is good for one to four weeks and allows unrestricted travel on all but interior bus routes and some other special routes. On interior routes, there are substantial discounts for Tímamiði holders; on some bus tours, 5% discount is offered. The pass also offers accommodation discounts when vouchers are purchased from Destination Iceland.

With the one- and two-week passes, you'd have to do a lot of travelling to get your money's worth, but three- and four-week passes are good value. One/two/three/four-week passes cost Ikr21,100/30,700/39,300/43,700; from October to April, only the one-week pass is available (Ikr12,400).

The free *Destination Iceland* booklet includes detailed bus timetables.

CAR & MOTORCYCLE
Private Vehicles

It's relatively easy to bring a vehicle on the ferry from mainland Europe. Drivers must carry the vehicle's registration documents, proof of valid insurance and a driving licence. After vehicle inspection, a free temporary import permit will be issued if the driver isn't employed in Iceland. Incredibly, diesel vehicles have to pay a tax on entry to the country (Ikr1813 per week for vehicles under 1000kg). In June 2002, unleaded 95 octane *(blýlaust)* cost Ikr96 per litre around the country – some of the most expensive petrol on earth! Leaded petrol and LRP (lead replacement petrol) aren't available.

Travellers in the interior must have a 4WD vehicle. Bear in mind that petrol and diesel may only be available at Hrauneyrar and Kerlingarfjöll and there are no repair services on the F-numbered (interior) highway system. A suggested spares and repair kit includes: extra oil, brake fluid, extra petrol, sealing compound for the radiator and petrol tank, a distributor cap, rotor arm, condenser, fuel filter, fan belt, at least two spare tyres and a puncture repair kit, spark plugs, insulated wire, headlights and fuses. You will also need to have the expertise to identify all this stuff and fix any mechanical problems.

Also required are large-scale maps, a compass, extra food rations, a shovel and some means of protecting your eyes and skin from wind-driven sand. Tool kits should include a tow rope, a crowbar, the relevant sockets and wrenches, a jack, a torch, batteries, flares and a fire extinguisher.

In the interior, it's best to travel with another vehicle. Unbridged rivers pose the greatest threats but drifting sand is also a hazard – even 4WD vehicles get bogged in sand drifts. Glacial rivers change course and fords change nature. Warm days may cause heavy glacial melting and placid rivers can become torrents without warning. Tyre marks leading into the water do not mean a river can be crossed.

If possible, try to check the depth and condition of the riverbed before driving in. Only cross where there are rocks or gravel, never on sand. The narrowest fords are usually the deepest. Before entering the water, remove the fan belt, cover the distributor and ignition system with a woollen rag and switch off headlights. Don't stop in midstream unless you cannot continue and you want to reverse out.

Details of the current conditions of mountain roads and tracks are available from **Vegagerðin** *(Public Roads Administration;* ☎ *1777).*

Most Icelandic highways aren't suitable for high-speed travel (try telling that to Icelanders). Headlight and radiator protection from dust and flying rocks is advisable. For further information, contact **Félag Íslenska Bifreiðaeigenda** *(Icelandic Automobile Association;* ☎ *562 9999, fax 552 9071;* **w** *www .fib.is; Borgartún 33, IS-105 Reykjavík).*

Road Rules

In Iceland, you drive on the right, but beware of dangerous drivers on gravel roads – some drive in the middle and force oncoming drivers onto the soft verge, where overturning is a real possibility. The use of seat belts (front and rear) is compulsory. The speed limit on unpaved roads is 80km/h; unfortunately, it's universally ignored. In urban areas, the speed limit is 50km/h or less.

Drink-driving laws are very strict in Iceland and the legal limit is set at 0.05% blood-alcohol content. The penalty for driving over the limit is loss of your licence plus a large fine.

Car Rental

A few years ago, the Sultan of Brunei would have thought twice before renting a car in Iceland. Prices started to drop considerably, but they've risen steeply again in the last couple of years. Even worse, readers have reported illegal dual pricing, with locals getting a lower price list and tourists being ripped off. If you've been cheated, complain to the **Consumers' Association of Iceland** *(☎ 545 1200;* **e** *ns@ns.is;* **w** *www.ns.is; Siðumúli 13, IS-108 Reykjavík).*

The cheapest vehicles, such as the Nissan Micra, normally cost from Ikr4000 per day, with 100km free per day and 24.5% VAT included. After your 100km, add Ikr25 to Ikr45 per km, compulsory insurance (around Ikr1000 per day) and expensive petrol to the price. Rental charges for 4WD vehicles are two to three times the above. Ask the tourist office in Reykjavík for details of special offers.

You must be at least 20 years old to rent a car from most of the following agencies:

Átak (☎ 554 6040, ⓔ atak@atak.is) Smiðjuvegur 1, IS-200 Kópavogur
Bílaleiga Íslands/Europcar (☎ 545 1300, ⓔ carrental@carrental.is) Barónstígur 2, IS-104 Reykjavík. This company offers the best deals.
Icelandair/Hertz (☎ 505 0600, ⓔ hertz@hertz.is) Reykjavík airport, IS-101 Reykjavík. Other offices are in Keflavík (☎ 425 0221), Akureyri (☎ 461 1005), Egilsstaðir (☎ 471 1210), Höfn (☎ 478 1250) and Vestmannaeyjar (☎ 481 3300).
RB Car Rental (☎ 557 4266)
Reykjavík HI Hostel (☎ 553 8110, ⓔ info@hostel .is) Sundlaugavegur 34, IS-105 Reykjavík
Avis (☎ 568 8888) Dugguvogur 10, IS-104 Reykjavík. Avis also has offices in Akureyri (☎ 461 2428) and Keflavík (☎ 421 1690).

BICYCLE

In Iceland the wind, rough roads, gravel, river crossings, intimidating vehicles, sandstorms and horrid weather conspire against cyclists. Hard-core cyclists will find Iceland a challenge, but you should come prepared to pack up your bike and travel by bus when things become intolerable. The Kjölur route through the interior has bridges over all major rivers, so it's accessible to cyclists.

In areas best suited to cycling, such as in Mývatn or urban Reykjavík and Akureyri, bicycles can be hired for around Ikr1500 per day, plus deposit. Domestic airlines usually accept bicycles as checked luggage and they may provide bike bags free. Bikes may be carried on long-distance buses for Ikr500 to Ikr1000 if there's space, but there are lots of cyclists in the summer, so don't count on it.

Cyclists are advised to avoid the main roads (dual carriageways) through Reykjavík. Many Icelandic motorists drive as if theirs is the only vehicle on the road and cyclists are extremely vulnerable.

HITCHING

Summer hitching is possible but can be inconsistent. If there's traffic you'll get a ride eventually, but long waits are common in most areas, especially in the Westfjords. It's best not to hitch in a group of more than two people. See Hitching in the Getting Around chapter.

BOAT

The main car ferries operating in Iceland are *Herjólfur*, between Þorlákshöfn and Vestmannaeyjar; *Baldur*, between Flatey, Stykkishólmur and Brjánslækur; and *Sæfari*, between Dalvík, Hrísey and Grímsey.

Most ferries connect well with buses, described in detail in the *Destination Iceland* timetable.

LOCAL TRANSPORT

Reykjavík, Hafnarfjörður and Akureyri have good local bus and taxi services; the bus service in Ísafjörður is more limited. Taxis with an English or German-speaking driver are available in most towns. Sightseeing trips for up to four passengers typically cost Ikr3500 for one hour or Ikr27,600 per day.

ORGANISED TOURS

Many of the best sights in Iceland are in remote locations where public transport isn't available. If you don't have a hardy vehicle and don't want to walk, endure difficult hitching conditions or attempt cycling, tours provide the only access.

The least expensive and most loosely organised tours are those offered by Destination Iceland, the consortium of long-distance bus companies, in association with small local operators. They run much like ordinary bus services, but stop at points of interest. Sometimes a guide is included. It's also possible to leave nonguided tours at any time and rejoin at a later specified date. Destination Iceland also offers glacier tours and various boat trips, including whale-watching trips. Watch out for the Tour of the Week, which is discounted by up to 30% and announced by Destination Iceland on Sundays in June and August. Some readers have complained about the quality of overnight accommodation booked by Destination Iceland in conjunction with multi-day tours.

Several companies and groups operate hiking, rafting, jeep, horse-riding, whale-watching or photography tours. There are also upmarket bus tours that provide accommodation in tents and mountain huts. Contact the following companies:

Destination Iceland (☎ 591 1000, Ⓦ www.dice.is) Umferðarmiðstöðin, Vatnsmýrarvegur 10, IS-101 Reykjavík
Ferðafélag Íslands (☎ 568 2533, Ⓦ www.fi.is) Mörkin 6, IS-108 Reykjavík
Guðmundur Jónasson (☎ 511 1515, Ⓦ www .gjtravel.is) Borgartún 34, IS-105 Reykjavík
Highlanders (☎ 568 3030, Ⓦ www.hl.is) Suðurlandsbraut 10, IS-108 Reykjavík
Reykjavík Excursions (☎ 562 4422, Ⓦ www.re.is) Bankastræti 2, Reykjavík

Nonni Travel (☎ 461 1841, Ⓦ www.nonnitravel
.is) Brekkugata 5, PO Box 336, IS-602 Akureyri
Útivist (☎ 562 1000, Ⓦ www.utivist.is)
Laugavegur 178, IS-105 Reykjavík

Reykjavík

pop 178,030

Reykjavík is the world's most northerly capital city and also one of its smallest. By European standards, Reykjavík is historically and architecturally unexciting, but politically, socially, culturally, economically and psychologically, it dominates Iceland. In essence, everything that happens in Iceland happens in Reykjavík.

Reykjavík was the first place in Iceland to be intentionally settled. The original settler,

Ingólfur Arnarson, tossed his high-seat pillars overboard in 874, and built his farm near where they washed ashore, between Tjörnin (the Pond) and the sea, where Aðalstræti now intersects with Suðurgata. He called the place Reykjavík (Smoky Bay) because of the steam rising from nearby geothermal features. Ingólfur claimed the entire southwestern corner of the island, then set about planting his hayfields at Austurvöllur, the present town square.

Now known as the 'smokeless city' thanks to its ample winds and reliance on geothermal heat, Reykjavík boasts a symphony orchestra and theatre, ballet and opera companies, plus all the usual trappings of a modern European city. Neat rows of painted concrete houses with bright roofs extend out to the relatively uninteresting suburbs.

REYKJAVÍK

Orientation

Reykjavík's heart is still between Tjörnin and the harbour, and many old buildings remain. Nearly everything in the city lies within walking distance of the old settlement, and most meeting and lounging activity takes place around Lækjartorg and the adjacent pedestrian shopping street, Austurstræti. This is also where you'll find the central post office and tourist information centre. The shopping district extends east along Laugavegur from Lækjargata to the Hlemmur bus station.

Information

Tourist Offices The main tourist information centre, **Upplýsingamiðstöð Ferðamála** (☎ 562 3045; e tourinfo@tourinfo.is; Banka-straeti 2; open 8.30am-6pm daily June-Aug, shorter hours Sept-May) is near Lækjargata. A second branch is at the **Raðhus** (City Hall; ☎ 563 2005; Tjarnargata 11; open 8.20am-4.30pm Mon-Fri, noon-6pm Sat & Sun mid-May–mid-Sept, Mon-Sat mid-Sept–mid-May). There's another helpful desk in the BSÍ bus station. Pick up your free copies of Reykjavík This Month and the Map of Reykjavík.

Reykjavík Tourist Card This pass, available at tourist offices, gives you free entry to museums, swimming pools, etc, and includes a bus pass. It costs Ikr1000/1500/2000 for one/two/three days.

Money Banks can all be found on Austurstræti and Bankastræti. **The Change Group**

REYKJAVÍK

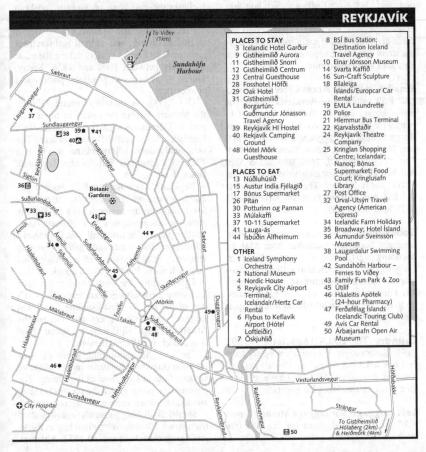

PLACES TO STAY
3 Icelandic Hotel Garður
9 Gistiheimilið Aurora
11 Gistiheimilið Snorri
12 Gistiheimilið Centrum
23 Central Guesthouse
28 Fosshotel Höfði
29 Oak Hotel
31 Gistiheimilið Borgartún; Guðmundur Jónasson Travel Agency
39 Reykjavík HI Hostel
40 Rekjavík Camping Ground
48 Hótel Mörk Guesthouse

PLACES TO EAT
13 Núðluhúsið
15 Austur Indía Fjélagið
17 Bónus Supermarket
26 Pítan
30 Potturinn og Pannan
33 Múlakaffi
37 10-11 Supermarket
41 Lauga-ás
44 Ísbúðin Álfheimum

OTHER
1 Iceland Symphony Orchestra
2 National Museum
4 Nordic House
5 Reykjavík City Airport Terminal; Icelandic/Hertz Car Rental
6 Flybus to Keflavík Airport (Hótel Loftleiðir)
7 Öskjuhlíð
8 BSÍ Bus Station; Destination Iceland Travel Agency
10 Einar Jónsson Museum
14 Svarta Kaffið
16 Sun-Craft Sculpture
18 Bilaleiga Íslands/Europcar Car Rental
19 EMLA Laundrette
20 Police
21 Hlemmur Bus Terminal
22 Kjarvalsstaðir
24 Reykjavík Theatre Company
25 Kringlan Shopping Centre; Icelandair; Nanoq; Bónus Supermarket; Food Court; Kringlusafn Library
27 Post Office
32 Úrval-Utsýn Travel Agency (American Express)
34 Icelandic Farm Holidays
35 Broadway; Hotel Ísland
36 Ásmundur Sveinsson Museum
38 Laugardalur Swimming Pool
42 Sundahöfn Harbour – Ferries to Viðey
43 Family Fun Park & Zoo
45 Útilíf
46 Háaleitis Apótek (24-hour Pharmacy)
47 Ferðafélag Íslands (Icelandic Touring Club)
49 Avis Car Rental
50 Árbæjarsafn Open Air Museum

(*Bankastræti 2; open 8.30am-6pm daily June-Aug, 9am-5pm Mon-Fri, 10am-2pm Sat Sept-May*), in the tourist office, charges commissions ranging from 2.75% to 8.75%. Head for **Landsbanki Íslands** (*Austurstræti*) for a better deal, if you can. After-hours banking is available at **The Change Group** (*Keflavík international airport*), open for flight arrivals and departures. During non-banking hours, you can exchange foreign currency at hotels, but they charge a high commission. ATMs accept MasterCard, Cirrus, Visa and Electron.

Post & Communications Reliable poste restante and fax services are available at the **Central Post Office** (*fax 580 1191; Posthússtræti 5; open 9am-4.30pm Mon-Fri*). Substations include the **post office** at Skipholt 50a.

Public phones are hard to find in mobile-crazy Reykjavík. Phones accepting coins and cards are found in the main tourist office, in the street opposite Laugavegur 38, and in the Kringlan shopping centre.

Email & Internet Access Free Internet access isn't available in Reykjavík unless you buy a library card for Ikr1000. The best libraries for Internet access (including email) are **Borgarbókasafn** (*Tryggvagata 15; Ikr200/300 per 30/60 minutes; open 10am-8pm Mon-Thur, 11am-7pm Fri, 1pm-5pm Sat & Sun*) and **Kringlusafn** (*Kringlan shopping centre; Ikr200 per half-hour*). There's also access at the **BSÍ bus station** (*Vatnsmýrarvegur 10; Ikr250 per half-hour*).

Bookshops The widest varieties of English-language books are available from **Mál og Menning** (☎ 515 2500; ✉ shopping@edda.is; *Laugavegur 18*), which also sells good topographic maps, and **Eymundsson** (*Austurstræti 18*). For used paperbacks at reasonable prices, go to the friendly **second-hand bookshop** at Vesturgata 17.

Laundry The EMLA Laundrette (☎ 552 7499; *Barónsstígur 3; open 8am-6pm Mon-Fri*) has a laundry service. The Reykjavík camping ground and HI hostel have self-service washing machines for guests.

Left Luggage For **luggage storage** (*open 7.30am-7pm daily*), head for the BSÍ bus station in Reykjavík .

Medical & Emergency Services The 24-hour emergency ward is at the **city hospital** (☎ 525 1000; *Fossvogur*), near Áland. Nonurgent cases should consult the **Health Centre** (☎ 585 2600; *Vesturgata 7*), but appointments are required. There's also a 24-hour pharmacy, **Háaleitis Apotek** (☎ 581 2101; *Háaleitisbraut 68*). Dentists are listed under *tannlæknar* in the phone book, or ring ☎ 575 0505 at any time.

Use the same number, ☎ 112, to call the police, ambulance or fire brigade.

Things to See
Old Reykjavík The **old town** of Reykjavík includes the area bordered by Tjörnin, Lækjargata, the harbour and the nearby suburb of Seltjarnarnes. The historical centre of the city includes the east bank of Tjörnin and both sides of Lækjargata. The Lækjartorg area is the socialising centre of town.

Houses on the south side of **Hafnarstræti** were used by Danish traders during the trade monopoly between 1602 and 1855. Today, tourist shops here sell woollens, pottery and souvenirs.

Old Reykjavík grew up around **Tjörnin**, the pleasant lake in the centre of town. The park at Tjörnin has jogging and bike trails, a fountain and colourful flower gardens. The octagonal gazebo, **Hljómskálinn**, was built in 1922 as a rehearsal hall for the Reykjavík Brass Band.

Reykjavík's new **Raðhus** (*City Hall; ☎ 563 2005; open 8am-7pm Mon-Fri, 10am-6pm Sat & Sun*), on the northern bank of Tjörnin, could be described as a sort of postmodern floating palace. The main hall contains a tourist information desk, a café and a gallery featuring temporary exhibitions, as well as a huge relief map of Iceland. It's well worth a look.

Stjórnarráðið, the white building opposite Lækjartorg, contains government offices. It's one of the city's oldest buildings, and was originally an 18th-century jail. On nearby **Árnarhóll** (Eagle Hill) there's a statue of the first settler, Ingólfur Arnarson.

The grey basalt building south of Austurvöllur (Ingólfur's hayfields and the old town square), built in 1881, houses the **Alþing**. The government has outgrown the present building and an extension is currently being constructed.

Sheriff Skúli Magnússon's weaving shed (*Aðalstræti 10*) is the oldest building in Reykjavík, originally built around 1752. Although the shed burnt down in 1764, it was immediately replaced on the same foundation and now houses a pub.

Þjóðmenningarhúsið *(Culture House; ☎ 545 1400; Hverfisgata 15; adult/child Ikr300/200; open 11am-5pm daily)* has impressive temporary exhibits about Vikings and other aspects of Icelandic cultural heritage, and a permanent exhibit of original saga manuscripts.

New Reykjavík Reykjavík's most imposing structure, the immense church **Hallgrímskirkja** *(☎ 510 1000; Skólavörðuholt; open 10am-5pm daily)*, was consecrated in 1986 and was unashamedly designed to resemble a mountain of basaltic lava. The stark, light-filled interior is enhanced by the great view from its 75m tower. The lift costs Ikr300/50 per adult/child. Outside the church, there's a **statue of Leifur Eiríksson**, presented by the USA in 1930 on the 1000th anniversary of the Alþing.

The extraordinary **Icelandic Phallological Museum** *(☎ 566 8668; Laugavegur 24; admission Ikr400; open 2pm-5pm Tues-Sat May-Aug, 2pm-5pm Tues & Sat Sept-Apr)* claims to be the only museum in the world with a collection of penises from all local mammals (except homo sapiens)!

The **National Gallery** *(☎ 515 9600; Fríkirkjuvegur 7; admission Ikr400, admission free Wed; open 11am-5pm Tues-Sun)* is worth visiting for its exhibitions by Icelandic artists. This bright and airy museum features everything from wonderful Icelandic landscapes to some extraordinarily pretentious modern art.

Iceland's **Nordic House** *(☎ 551 7030; Sæmundargata; exhibition admission Ikr300; open noon-5pm daily during exhibitions)*, south of Tjörn, serves as a Scandinavian cultural centre and offers a cafeteria, travelling exhibitions, concerts, lectures, films based on Nordic themes and a library of Scandinavian literature.

To appreciate Vestmannaeyjar or Mývatn, it's well worth paying a visit to the excellent **Volcano Show** *(☎ 551 3230; Hellusund 6a; admission 2/1-hour show Ikr950/750)*. Filmed by locals Vilhjálmur and Ósvaldur Knudsen, the show offers an insight into the volcanic spectre under which Icelanders live. The daily two-hour shows (in English) begin at 11am, 3pm and 8pm in July and August; shows are once or twice daily from September to June.

French programmes are shown at 6pm daily while German programmes are shown at 1pm (Saturday only, July and August).

The **National Museum** *(☎ 552 8888; Suðurgata 41; admission Ikr400; open 11am-5pm Tues-Sun mid-May–mid-Sept, shorter hours mid-Sept–mid-May)* is obligatory for anyone who is interested in Norse culture and Icelandic history. The most renowned artefact is the **Valþjófsstaður church door** (from East Iceland), which was carved around 1200 and depicts a Norse battle scene. Other fine exhibits include Settlement Era religious and folk relics and tools, nautical and agricultural artefacts, fishing boats and ingenious early farm implements.

The **Öskjuhlíð** tanks store geothermally heated water for use around the city (that's why your hot shower in Reykjavík smells sulphuric). Perched atop the tanks is the swish Perlan restaurant, which is now a city landmark; there's also a cafeteria, a new waxworks museum and a viewing area. To get there, take bus No 7 from Lækjartorg.

Jóhannes Kjarval, born in 1885, is one of Iceland's most popular artists. The surrealism that characterises his work was derived from the ethereal nature of the distinctive Icelandic landscape.

The impressive **Kjarvalsstaðir** *(☎ 552 6131; Flókagata; adult/child Ikr500/free, admission Mon free ; open 10am-5pm daily)* has an extensive Kjarval collection and it includes temporary exhibits by other Icelandic artists.

Near Hallgrímskirkja is the cube-shaped **Einar Jónsson Museum** *(☎ 551 3797; Njarðargata; adult/child Ikr400/free; open 2pm-5pm Tues-Sun June–mid-Sept; 2pm-5pm Sat & Sun mid-Sept–May)*, a worthwhile exhibit of work by Iceland's foremost 20th-century sculptor which includes his apartment and sculpture garden.

Jónsson's mystical work mostly deals with classical and religious themes, which he created while in a self-imposed state of seclusion.

The well-respected, igloo-shaped **Ásmundur Sveinsson Museum** *(☎ 553 2155; Sigtún; adult/child Ikr500/free, admission Mon free ; open 10am-4pm daily May-Sept, 1pm-4pm daily Oct-Apr)* features massive but graceful concrete sculptures on Icelandic saga and folklore themes, plus smaller works in wood and various metals, by Ásmundur

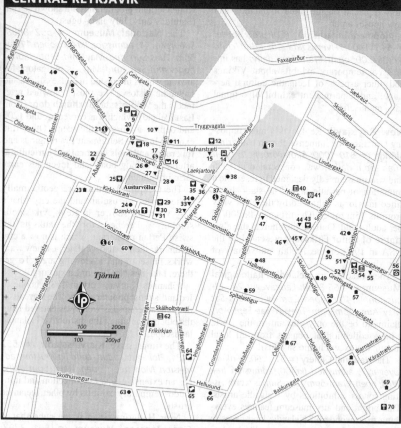

CENTRAL REYKJAVÍK

Sveinsson. Oddly enough, there's also an igloo-shaped bus stop shelter outside!

On the shore near the bay end of Klapparstígur stands the astonishing **Sun-Craft sculpture**, which resembles a distinctly porous Viking ship and certainly merits a photo.

The popular **family fun park & zoo** (☎ 585 7800; Laugardalur; adult/child Ikr450/350; open 10am-6pm daily mid-May–Aug, 10am-5pm daily Sept–mid-May) is in the vast park south of Reykjavik HI Hostel.

It contains a huge sandbox with kid-sized earth-moving equipment, a driving course which teaches the fundamentals in mini-cars, a replica Viking longship, farm animals, seals and reindeer.

Nearby, the wonderful **Botanic Gardens** (☎ 553 8870; Laugardalur; admission free;

open 10am-10pm daily Apr-Sept, 10am-5pm daily Oct-Mar), which contains 72% of native Icelandic plant species and a magnificent array of colourful seasonal flowers, are good for a pleasant evening stroll.

Árbæjarsafn (Open Air Museum; ☎ 577 1111; Árbær; bus No 10 from Hlemmur or No 110 from Lækjartorg; adult/child Ikr500/free; open 11am-4pm Mon, 9am-5pm Tues-Fri, 10am-6pm Sat & Sun June-Aug; shorter hours Sept-May) is a 12.5-hectare historic farm set up as a museum in 1957.

It includes an interesting collection of old homes with period furniture, workshops and other buildings moved from various places to illustrate life in early Iceland. Don't miss the excellent 25-minute audio-visual presentation on the history of Reykjavík.

ICELAND

CENTRAL REYKJAVÍK

PLACES TO STAY
1. Guesthouse Vikingur
2. Gistiheimilið Ísafold
3. Icelandic City Hotel
23. Salvation Army Guesthouse
30. Hótel Borg
49. Gistiheimilið Jörð
57. Tower Guesthouse
59. Gistiheimilið Luna
67. Gistiheimilið Óðinn
68. Gistiheimilið Svala
69. Hótel Leifur Eiríksson

PLACES TO EAT
6. Naust
10. Pizza 67
15. Nonnabiti
19. Einar Ben
27. Café Paris
31. Restaurant Salatbarinn
32. Kína Húsið
33. Amigo's
36. Kebabhúsið
39. Hús Málarans
44. Ítalía
45. Asía
46. Grænn Kostur
47. Prikið

51. Á næstu grösum
52. Pasta Basta
55. Sjanghæ
60. Restaurant Íðno

OTHER
4. Second-Hand Bookshop
5. Health Centre
7. Borgarbókasafn Library
8. Glaumbar
9. Gaukur á Stöng
11. Djúpið; Hornið Restaurant
12. Spotlight
13. Árnarhóll & Ingólfur Arnarson Statue
14. Lækjartorg Bus Terminal; Miðbæjarmyndir
16. Central Post Office
17. Landsbanki Íslands Bank
18. Dubliner
20. Vik Wool
21. Kaffileikhúsið í Hlaðvarpanum
22. Sheriff Skúli Magnússon's Weaving Shed
24. Alþing
25. NASA
26. ÁTVR (State Alcohol Store)

28. Eymundsson Bookshop
29. Kaffi Brennslan
34. 66j Norður
35. Astro
37. Tourist Information Centre; The Change Group; Reykjavík Excursions
38. Stjórnarráðið
40. Þjóðmenningarhúsið
41. National Theatre
42. Borgarhjól Bicycle Rental
43. Tres Locos
48. Útivist Travel Agency
50. Mál og Menning Bookshop
53. 22
54. Icelandic Phallological Museum
56. Public Telephone
58. Handknitting Association of Iceland
61. Ráðhús (City Hall) & Tourist Information
62. National Gallery
63. Hljómskálinn
64. US Embassy
65. UK Embassy
66. Volcano Show
70. Hallgrímskirkja

Activities

Hiking Spreading out southeast of Elliðavatn lake, immediately southeast of Reykjavík, is **Heiðmörk** (Heath Woods), a 2800-hectare city park. There are lots of hiking tracks, picnic sites and forested areas; ask the tourist office for a map. You can reach the western end of the park by taking bus No 140 from Hlemmur to Ásgarður, then change to No 57 to Vífilsstaðir. From there, it's just a short walk to Vífilsstaðavatn lake at the park entrance.

Viðey, 1km north of Reykjavík's Sundahöfn harbour (near Laugardalur), is served by daily ferries (see the Getting Around section later). From the ferry landing, walk uphill to the **church** and the **farmhouse**. The latter dates from 1755 and is the oldest original building in Iceland (it now contains a restaurant). The two ends of the island are about 1km north or 800m south of the church, respectively; there are several walking tracks.

Swimming The **Laugardalur swimming pool** (☎ 553 4039; Sundlaugavegur; bus No 5; adult/child Ikr200/100; open 7am-9.30pm Mon-Fri, 8am-8pm Sat & Sun) is conveniently situated near the Reykjavík HI Hostel and camping ground.

Places to Stay

In summer, finding a place to stay may be difficult. Bring a tent or book accommodation in advance if you'd rather not risk being left out in the cold.

Camping The immense **Reykjavík Camping Ground** (☎ 568 6944; Sundlaugavegur; tent sites per person Ikr700, 2-bed cabins Ikr3800 per night; open mid-May–mid-Sept) has cooking (Ikr50 for 20 minutes) and laundry (Ikr300) facilities. It's 15 minutes on bus No 5 from Lækjartorg or a Ikr1000 to Ikr1200 taxi ride from the BSÍ bus station. From 1 June to 31 August, a free shuttle bus runs from the camping ground to the BSÍ bus station at 7.15am.

Hostels Beside the camping ground is the clean, environmentally friendly, award-winning **Reykjavík HI Hostel** (☎ 553 8110, fax 588 9201; @ info@hostel.is; Sundlaugavegur 34; beds HI members/nonmembers Ikr1500/ 1850, en suite private rooms per person Ikr2000-3150). Breakfast is Ikr700. The excellent facilities include a wide-screen TV and two PCs with Internet access (Ikr400 per half-hour). Book well in advance.

Guesthouses The cheapest guesthouse is the no-frills **Salvation Army Guesthouse** (☎ 561 3203; e guesthouse@guesthouse.is; Kirkjustræti 2; sleeping-bag accommodation Ikr1700-2200, singles Ikr3700-4000, doubles Ikr5100-5500), which has shared bathrooms and cooking facilities; breakfast is Ikr800 extra. The bright and clean **Gistiheimilið Jörð** (☎ 562 1739, fax 562 1735; Skólavörðustígur 13a; singles Ikr3000-4000, doubles Ikr4000-6000) has shared bathrooms, and breakfast is Ikr600.

About 10 minutes' walk from the BSÍ bus station, the smart and friendly hostel-style **Central Guesthouse** (☎ 552 2822; e central guesthouse@visir.is; Bólstaðarhlíð 8; sleeping-bag accommodation Ikr1400-1800, singles Ikr2400-3600, doubles Ikr3600-4800) offers shared bathrooms. Internet access costs Ikr200 per half-hour and breakfast is Ikr700 (but cooking facilities are available).

The acceptable **Gistiheimilið Snorri** (☎ 552 0598; e gausar@li.is; Snorrabraut 61; sleeping-bag accommodation Ikr1500, singles/doubles from Ikr5500/7500) has kitchen facilities and some en suite rooms.

At the straightforward **Guesthouse Viking-ur** (☎ 562 1290; e ghviking@isholf.is; Ránargata 12; B&B singles/doubles Ikr5200/7900; open June-Aug) there are shared bathrooms.

The architecturally bizarre **Tower Guesthouse** (☎ 896 6694; e towerguesthouse@hot mail.com; Grettisgata 6; doubles Ikr7900-9300) has a spiral staircase and welcomes gay travellers. Readers have recommended another gay guesthouse, **Gistiheimilið Luna** (☎ 511 2800; e luna@islandia.is; Spítalastígur 1; apartments Ikr5900-11,900 per day), which offers seven bright and cheerful apartments.

There are plenty of other options. **Gistiheimilið Svala** (☎ 562 3544; e svala_guesth ouse@visir.is; Skólavörðustígur 30; singles Ikr3500-5000, doubles Ikr5000-7500) is an old house on a quiet, central street; confirm on booking that rates include breakfast. A little more upscale is the friendly **Gistiheimilið Centrum** (☎ 562 0100; e farfa@centrum.is; Njálsgata 74; B&B singles/doubles/triples Ikr5500/7500/9500; open June-Aug), with shared bathrooms.

Gistiheimilið Óðinn (☎ 552 2313; e odinn@vortex.is; Óðinsgata 9; B&B singles/doubles/triples Ikr5500/7500/9500) can accommodate 20 Viking warriors, mostly in pleasant rooms with wooden floors. Recom-

mended by readers, **Gistiheimilið Ísafold** (☎ 561 2294; e isafold@itn.is; Bárugata 11; singles/doubles Ikr6300/8500, en suite double apartment Ikr10,500) lies in the heart of old Reykjavík and offers fine Icelandic hospitality, breakfast included.

Another favourite is the even more comfortable **Gistiheimilið Borgartún** (☎ 511 1500; e gjtravel@gjtravel.is; Borgartún 34; en suite B&B singles/doubles Ikr7400/9800), run mainly for guests of Guðmundur Jónasson tours, but welcome to anyone.

You could also try the recommended **Gistiheimilið Aurora** (☎ 552 5515, fax 551 4894; Freyjugata 24; sleeping-bag accommodation Ikr1900, B&B singles/doubles without bath Ikr5500/7500).

Hótel Mörk Guesthouse (☎ 568 3600; e vidarhg@islandia.is; Mörkin 8; 2-person flats Ikr9000) has well-equipped flats.

Friendly **Gistiheimilið Hólaberg** (☎ 567 0980; e holaberg@centrum.is; Hólaberg 80; sleeping-bag accommodation Ikr1650, singles/doubles Ikr3900/5300) is quite a long way out, but there's free pick-up from the city airport or the BSÍ bus station if you're booked in.

Hotels On the university campus, **Icelandic Hotel Garður** (☎ 551 5656; e hotelgardur@ icelandichotels.is; Hringbraut; sleeping-bag accommodation Ikr2300, B&B singles/doubles Ikr6900/8100; open 25 May-26 Aug), is a straightforward 43-room student residence hall with shared bathrooms.

Fosshótel Höfði (☎ 552 6477; e bokun@ fosshotel.is; Skipholt 27; B&B basic singles/doubles Ikr6900/8900, en suite singles/doubles Ikr8900/11,900; open June-Aug) offers reasonable deals and has a variety of quite acceptable rooms.

Icelandic City Hotel (☎ 511 1155; e cit yhotel@icelandichotels.is; Ránargata 4a; singles Ikr6100-9100, doubles Ikr8100-13,000) has excellent B&B in en suite rooms with TV, minibar and phone.

A similar option is the en suite B&B at the nicely decorated and friendly **Hótel Leifur Eiríksson** (☎ 562 0800; e hotel-leifur@vortex .is; Skólavörðustígur 45; singles Ikr5400-9200, doubles Ikr7100-12,000).

The renovated and particularly recommended **Oak Hotel** (☎ 511 3777; e oakho tel@vortex.is; Brautarholt 22-24; B&B singles Ikr5400-9200, doubles Ikr7100-12,000) has bright, spacious and comfortable rooms.

The central **Hótel Borg** (☎ 551 1440; e reservations@hotelborg.is; Pósthússtræti 9-11; B&B singles Ikr10,200-16,800, doubles Ikr14,600-38,000) has impressive retro 1930s decor and individually decorated en suite rooms throughout.

Places to Eat

There's no shortage of places to eat with acceptable standards for any budget.

Restaurants Just up the street from the HI hostel, **Lauga-ás** (☎ 553 1620; Laugarásvegur 1; mains Ikr1490-2990 inc. soup) has a nice atmosphere and serves meat and fish dishes – the lamb is particularly good. Friendly and rather posh, **Potturinn og Pannan** (☎ 551 1690; Brautarholt 22; soup & salad buffet Ikr1050, mains with soup & salad buffet Ikr1590-3800) serves fish, lamb and beef dishes; burgers and meat dishes are especially recommended.

Ítalía (☎ 562 4630; Laugavegur 11; pasta dishes Ikr1350-1650, pizzas about Ikr1450) rustles up a good Icelandic variation on Italian food. The recommended **Pasta Basta** (☎ 561 3131; Klapparstígur 38; lunch buffet Ikr1190, mains Ikr1530-2980) has a generous buffet lunch, including soup, bread, home-made pasta, vegetables and salad.

Sjanghæ (☎ 551 6513; Laugavegur 28b; lunch buffet Ikr980, most mains Ikr1600-2700) serves Westernised Chinese dishes, including a six-course, Asian buffet lunch, but the service is a bit strange. For other Chinese and Japanese options, there's **Asía** (☎ 562 6210; Laugavegur 10; buffet lunch Ikr950). A more basic Chinese option is **Kína Húsið** (Lækjargata 8; specials from Ikr750). The recommended **Austur Indía Fjélagið** (☎ 552 1630; Hverfisgata 56; mains Ikr1795-3595) serves up genuine fare from India.

The excellent vegetarian restaurant **Á næstu grösum** (Laugavegur 20b; meals Ikr750; daily special lunch/dinner Ikr900/990; open lunch & dinner Mon-Sat, dinner Sun) serves macrobiotic and standard vegetarian meals. **Grænn Kostur** (Skolavörðustígur 8; veg special Ikr800) does two great vegetarian daily specials. **Restaurant Salatbarinn** (Pósthússtræti 13; veg & nonveg buffet Ikr980/1290 before/after 5pm; open 11am-9pm daily) offers a rather good, all-you-can-eat buffet including soups, two hot courses, 20 different salads, yoghurt, fruit and drinks.

On the 2nd and 3rd floors of the oldest theatre in Iceland (1897), **Restaurant Iðnó** (☎ 562 9700; Vonarstræti 3; 3-course dinner Ikr2400) offers excellent traditional Icelandic cuisine. The fine seafood restaurant **Naust** (☎ 552 3030; Vesturgata 6-8; fish buffet Ikr3300) is housed in a former salt cellar and has a heavy nautical theme. A vast range of seafood and some of Iceland's more bizarre traditional dishes are on offer (hákarl and brennivin cost from Ikr1000). The recommended **Einar Ben** (☎ 511 5090; Veltusund 1; 2-course special Ikr2450, mains Ikr2190-4450) serves great food, including whale steaks (Ikr3190).

For good Mexican food, try the popular **Amigo's** (☎ 511 1333; Lækjargata 6a; mains Ikr1190-2395; open lunch & dinner). Enchiladas cost Ikr1385 to Ikr1560.

Cafés & Cafeterias There are several pub-style cafés serving inexpensive food in central Reykjavík. At the popular but stuffy **Café Paris** (Austurstræti 14; light lunch Ikr450-870), you'll get a coffee for Ikr220 and light continental lunches. Iceland's only bohemian café (complete with art gallery) is the intriguing **Hús Málarans** (Bankastræti 7a). The more ordinary **Prikið** (Bankastræti 12) serves rather good coffee.

Highly recommended is the funky **Svarta Kaffið** (Laugavegur 54), which serves up great light meals, including home-made soup in bread roll bowls (Ikr1000, including 500mL beer).

The no-frills workers' cafeteria, **Múlakaffi** (Hallarmúli; meals Ikr890-1290) offers a decent soup and salad buffet, with filling fish, beef or lamb mains and coffee included. Inexpensive sandwiches are also available.

The particularly good-value **food court** (Kringlan, Miklabraut), upstairs at the Kringlan shopping centre, has several inexpensive cafeterias.

Fast Food & Pizza For a quick bite on the run, nothing beats the **snack kiosks** on Hafnarstræti and the Austurstræti mall. **Nonnabiti** (Hafnarstræti 18; dishes Ikr280-640) serves burgers and fried snacks and **Kebabhúsið** (Lækjargata 2; kebabs from Ikr640) dishes up kebabs and tasty fish and chips (Ikr770). Delicious and filling Thai meals are served at the cafeteria-style **Núðluhúsið** (Vitastígur 10; mains Ikr780-950).

For a change, try the great pitta sandwiches at **Pítan** (Skipholt 50c; sandwiches Ikr550-760).

Pizza 67 (Tryggvagata 26; pizzas Ikr650-2510) is a pleasant, hippie-theme pizza-pub, which also serves burgers, sandwiches and desserts.

The best ice cream in Reykjavík is at **Ísbúðin Álfheimum** (Álfheimar 2); delectable gigantic cones with dip cost from Ikr130.

Self-Catering For a large selection of groceries, visit the **Bónus supermarket** (Kringlan shopping centre; open daily). There's another **Bónus** (Laugavegur 59; open Mon-Sat) in town. You'll find a more basic and expensive **10-11 supermarket** (Laugalækur) near the HI hostel and camping ground.

Entertainment
Clubs For an unforgettable cultural experience, try a Friday or Saturday night crawl with the beautiful youth through Reykjavík's 'in' bars and clubs. Cover charges average Ikr1000 and there are huge queues on weekend evenings. The city rocks until 5am or later and streets are thronged with inebriated clubbers all night long. Things change fast here – for an up-to-date listing, see Reykjavík This Month. Avoid the strip joints: 'dancers' aren't locals and most work under dubious conditions.

NASA (Austurvöllur) is the latest hot spot, popular with people in their 20s; you'll get dance music and chart sounds here. Other popular places include **Astro** (Austurstræti 22), with techno and dance music; the enduring **Gaukur á Stöng** (Tryggvagata 22), which features live music most nights; the wild gay bar/club **Spotlight** (Hafnarstræti 17); and the more sedate **Broadway** (Ármúli 9) in Hótel Ísland.

Pubs Some of the best pubs include sporty **Glaumbar** (Tryggvagata 20), **22** (Laugavegur 22) and the Irish-style, wood-panelled **Dubliner** (Hafnarstræti 4). Also recommended is the salsa bar at **Tres Locos** (Laugavegur 11), and the quiet **Djúpið** (Hafnarstræti 15), in the cellar of the Hornið restaurant. Another option is **Kaffi Brennslan** (Pósthússtræti 9), which boasts up to 62 varieties of beer.

The pub/café **Svarta Kaffið** (Laugavegur 54) serves some of the cheapest beer in Reykjavík (Ikr400 for 500mL), between 6pm and 9pm daily.

Theatre Reykjavík has several theatre groups, an opera, a symphony orchestra and a dance company.

Important box offices are the **National Theatre** (☎ 551 1200; Hverfisgata 19), the **Iceland Symphony Orchestra** (☎ 545 2500; Hagatorg), the **Reykjavík Theatre Company** (☎ 568 8000; Listabraut 3, Kringlan) and **Kaffileikhúsið í Hlaðvarpanum** (☎ 551 9030; Vesturgata 3b). For other venues, check daily papers for information or contact the tourist information centre for details and tickets.

Cinemas Reykjavík has seven cinemas; listings, times and addresses can be found in daily newspapers. Films are shown in their original language with Icelandic subtitles; most features cost Ikr800.

Shopping
The **Handknitting Association of Iceland shop** (Skólavörðustígur 19) charges from Ikr7900 for a traditional handknitted sweater. Rock-bottom prices (from Ikr6000) and inconsistent quality are found in street stalls on Austurstræti.

Vik Wool (Hafnararstræti 3) is a recommended outlet with competitive prices for woollen goods and other souvenirs.

For outdoor equipment, go to **Nanoq** (☎ 575 5100; Kringlan shopping centre) or **66° Norður** (☎ 535 6606; Lækjargata 4). If you need to hire camping equipment, try **Útilíf** (☎ 545 1500; Álfheimar & Vatnsmýrarvegur 9).

At **Miðbæjarmyndir** (Lækjartorg), a 36-exposure roll of Fujichrome Sensia 100 or Fujichrome Velvia 50 costs Ikr1000 or Ikr1150, respectively.

For boozers, there's the state alcohol store, **ÁTVR** (Austurstræti 10a).

Getting There & Away
Air Reykjavík city airport serves all domestic destinations, the Faroe Islands and Greenland (Kulusuk and Constable Pynt). All other flights operate through Keflavík international airport, 50km west of Reykjavík. **Icelandair** (☎ 505 0300/0100; Kringlan shopping centre) has an office in Kringlan.

Bus Early June to mid-September, bus services ply between Reykjavík's **BSÍ bus station** (☎ 591 1000; Vatnsmýrarvegur 10) and

Akureyri (Ikr5300, daily), Mývatn (Ikr9500, daily), Skaftafell (Ikr4690, daily), Höfn (Ikr6620, daily), Reykholt (Ikr1800, twice weekly), Stykkishólmur (Ikr2600, daily) and Þorlákshöfn (Ikr850, daily). Other services include daily (except Thursday) runs to Ísafjörður (via Snæfellsnes and the Stykkishólmur-Brjánslækur ferry, or via Hólmavík). Travellers between Reykjavík and Egilsstaðir must stay overnight in Akureyri, Mývatn or Höfn. There are fewer services during the rest of the year.

Getting Around

To/From the Airport The Flybus to Keflavík international airport leaves Hótel Loftleiðir two hours prior to international departures (Ikr900, 50 minutes). The first bus leaves from the Reykjavík HI hostel daily at 5am then picks up at all main hotels. Buses from Keflavík airport into town leave about 35 minutes after the arrival of an international flight.

Bus Reykjavík's excellent **city bus system** (☎ 551 2700; W www.bus.is) runs from 7am to midnight, with night buses at weekends. Buses pick up and drop off passengers only at designated stops (marked with the letter S). The two central terminals are at Hlemmur near the corner of Laugavegur and Rauðarárstígur, and on Lækjargata near the square, Lækjartorg.

The fare is Ikr200 (no change given), but *skiptimiði* (transfer tickets) are available. The Reykjavík Tourist Card includes a bus pass.

Taxi There are four taxi companies in the Reykjavík area: **Hreyfill-Bæjarleiðir** (☎ 588 5522), **BSR** (☎ 561 0000), **Borgarbíll** (☎ 552 2440) and **BSH** (☎ 555 0888). Taxis are only moderately expensive, and there's no tipping. Make sure you are advised in advance of charges for any service offered.

Bicycle Bikes may be hired from **Borgarhjól** (☎ 551 5653; Hverfisgata 50), as well as from Reykjavík HI Hostel and the camping ground. All these places charge Ikr1750/10,500 per day/week.

Boat Ferries to Viðey depart three to five times daily from **Sundahöfn harbour** (☎ 892 0099; bus No 4 from Lækjartorg) for Ikr500 return.

AROUND REYKJAVÍK
Hafnarfjörður
pop 22,568
Although it's now a suburb of Reykjavík, Hafnarfjörður (W www.hafnarfjordur.is) maintains old architectural charm and is well worth a visit in its own right. The **tourist office** (☎ 565 0661; Vesturgata 8) is in a 19th-century timber building near the harbour.

Things to See The interesting **Icelandic Maritime Museum** (☎ 565 4242; Vesturgata 8; adult/child Ikr300/free; open 1pm-5pm daily June-Sept), in a warehouse built around 1865, contains nautical artefacts outlining Iceland's maritime history, including displays of old boats and items of equipment. The worthwhile **Hafnarfjörður Museum** (☎ 565 5420; Vesturgata 6; admission included in maritime museum ticket; open 1pm-5pm daily June-Sept) is in the town's oldest house (1805) and several other buildings; exhibits include 19th-century furnishings.

Places to Stay & Eat The picturesque **Viðistaðatún Campground** (Hjallabraut; tent sites per person Ikr700; open June-Sept) is associated with the **Hraunbyrgi HI Hostel** (☎ 565 0900; e hostel@hraunbuar.is; Hjallabraut 51; beds HI members/nonmembers Ikr1500/1850). At the recommended **Helguhús** (☎ 555 2842; e gax@islandia.is; Lækjarkinn 8; singles/doubles with shared bath Ikr4000/6200), breakfast is included.

The novel **Fjörukráin** (☎ 565 1213; Strandgata 55; lunch Ikr550-990, mains Ikr1450-3100, 3-course dinner Ikr4600) occupies an 1841 structure which features Viking-era architecture, pagan feasts and (occasionally) staff in Viking outfits. One section resembles an English pub but specialises in fresh seafood.

The steakhouse **Hrói Höttur** (☎ 565 2525; Hjallahraun 13; burgers & steaks Ikr400-1990) also does takeaway pizzas (from Ikr680). The cosy café **Súfistinn** (Strandgata 9; light meals Ikr400-1000) serves delectable fresh coffee and hot chocolate (from Ikr220). The **Samkaup supermarket** (Hjallabraut) has a good-value salad bar.

Getting There & Away The bus station is on Fjarðargata, by the harbour. From Reykjavík, take bus No 140 from Hlemmur or Lækjartorg (use bus No 150 in the evening

ICELAND

and on the weekend). The **Flybus** (☎ 562 1011) to/from Keflavík airport stops for reserved passengers.

Krísuvík

The geothermal area Krísuvík (or Krýsuvík) lies about 20km south of Hafnarfjörður. After earthquakes in the 1920s and a huge explosion in June 2000, this fantastic and colourful area of steaming vents, fumaroles, mud pots and solfataras increased in activity. It can be explored on a series of boardwalks, but there's lots of steam and, when the wind blows from the west, visitors get drenched.

From May through to September, Destination Iceland runs a daily guided tour (Ikr4900, six hours) on a circular route from Reykjavík (1.10pm) via Hafnarfjörður, Krísuvík, Grindavík and the Blue Lagoon. Otherwise, you'll need a vehicle or get lucky with hitching.

Blue Lagoon

The Blue Lagoon (Bláa Lónið) isn't a lagoon, but rather a pale-blue, 20°C pool of effluent from the Svartsengi power plant, about 50km southwest of Reykjavík. Its deposits of silica mud, combined with an organic soup of dead algae, have been known to relieve psoriasis and the pool is a popular day trip for people from Reykjavík. However, its over-zealous promotion attracts many more visitors than it deserves.

Even so, a swim can be an ethereal experience with clouds of vapour rising and parting at times to reveal the stacks of the power plant and moss-covered lava in the background. Bring enough shampoo for a number of rinses or your hair will become a brick-like mass afterwards.

You can use the **pool** (adult/child Ikr880/ 440; open 9am-9pm daily June-Aug, shorter hours Sept-May) for a maximum of three hours.

From the BSÍ bus station in Reykjavík, take one of four daily Grindavík buses (Ikr850 one way).

The South

THE GOLDEN TRIANGLE

The 'Golden Triangle' refers to Gullfoss, Geysir and Þingvellir, the 'big three' destinations for Icelandair's stopover visitors.

If Iceland has a star attraction, it's **Gullfoss**, where the Hvitá River drops 32m in two falls. On sunny afternoons, you may see a rainbow through the spray.

Ten kilometres down the road is **Geysir**, after which all the world's spouting hot springs are named. The **Great Geysir** died in the mid-20th century, plugged by debris tossed in by thoughtless tourists to encourage it to perform. However, it now irregularly erupts up to 15m as a result of ground movements during the powerful earthquakes in June 2000. There's also the faithful stand-in **Strokkur** (Butter Churn), which spouts up to 35m approximately every eight minutes. There's a good exhibition of volcanic, geysir, earthquake, folk and natural history exhibits at the **Geysisstofa Geocentre** (☎ 486 8915; adult/child Ikr400/200; open 10am-7pm daily June-Sept, noon-5pm daily Oct-May).

Þingvellir is Iceland's most significant historical site, since the Alþing was established here in AD 930. The site was selected because of its topography, acoustics and proximity to population. In 1928, its history and wealth of natural attractions led to the creation of Iceland's first national park.

Most of the historical buildings are concentrated in a small area of the park and the remainder is left to nature. A maze of hiking trails crisscrosses the plain, leading through scenic areas and woods to points of interest. Of particular interest are **Almannagjá**, a large tectonic rift with the waterfall **Öxaráfoss**; **Lögberg** (Law Rock), which served as the podium for the Alþing from 930 to 1271; **Þingvallavatn**, Iceland's largest lake; and the clear blue wishing spring, **Peningagjá**.

Places to Stay & Eat

Þingvellir has **Hótel Valhöll** (☎ 468 1777; e valholl@vortex.is; B&B singles/doubles Ikr12,100/14,600), near the church, with three dining rooms (dinner mains are Ikr1490 to Ikr3320) and fairly elegant en suite accommodation. Nearby, at Leirar, is the main **camping ground** (☎ 482 2660; tent sites per person including shower Ikr500), with a park information office and an outlet selling basic snacks.

Hótel Geysir (☎ 486 8915; e geysir@ geysircenter.is; sleeping-bag accommodation Ikr950, singles/doubles from Ikr3900/5600), at Geysir, offers acceptable rooms and has a fairly good restaurant with mains from Ikr1200 to Ikr2500. There's also a nearby camping ground (☎ 486 8915; tent sites per person including shower Ikr500). The **souvenir shop/café** sells hot dogs, sandwiches, burgers, pizzas and chips (Ikr180 to Ikr990).

Getting There & Away
The popular Reykjavík Excursions and Destination Iceland Golden Circle day tours to Gullfoss, Geysir and Þingvellir cost Ikr5900, without lunch. They depart from the BSÍ bus station in Reykjavík at 8.40am daily.

Destination Iceland buses run between Reykjavík, Gullfoss and Geysir, departing at 8.30am and 12.30pm daily (June to August) from BSÍ (Ikr3740 round-trip). Public buses between Reykjavík and Þingvellir depart from the BSÍ bus station at 1.30pm daily (Ikr1700 return).

VESTMANNAEYJAR
pop 4457
These 15 islands were formed by submarine volcanoes between 10,000 and 5000 years ago. In 1963, the world witnessed the birth of its newest island, Surtsey. Only Heimaey (Home Island) supports a permanent population. Characterised by brightly coloured roofs, the town spreads across about a third of the island.

Its spectacular setting is defined by the *klettur* (rock) escarpments that rise abruptly behind the well-sheltered harbour, the red peak of Eldfell (which erupted in 1973), and the conical hill Helgafell. The **tourist office** (☎ 481 3555) is at the ferry terminal and the **library** (off Skólavegur) offers free Internet access.

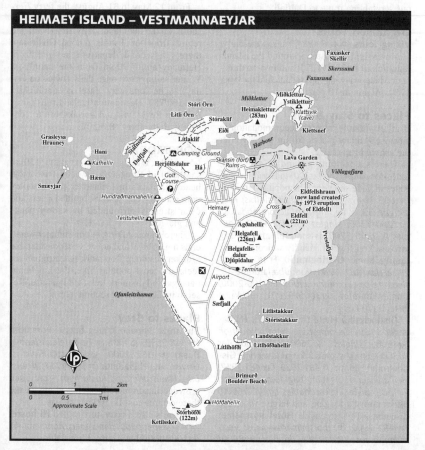

HEIMAEY ISLAND – VESTMANNAEYJAR

Things to See & Do

Vestmannaeyjar Natural History Museum
(☎ 481 1997; Heðarvegur 12; adult/child
Ikr450/150, includes admission to folk museum; open 11am-5pm daily May–mid-Sept)
has an aquarium of bizarre Icelandic fish, a
live video link to a puffin colony and a wonderful collection of polished agate and jasper
slices. The worthwhile **folk museum** (☎ 481
1194; Raðhúströð; adult/child Ikr450/150,
includes admission to natural history museum) is upstairs in the library. The excellent
Volcano Show (☎ 481 1045; Heiðarvegur;
admission Ikr600), in the cinema, features
local explosive action.

Opportunities for **hiking** abound on
Heimaey, including the walk to Stórhöfði and
climbs of Helgafell, Eldfell and the treacherous scrambling route to Dalfjall.

Organised Tours

Viking Tours (☎ 488 4884) runs twice-daily,
1½-hour sightseeing tours around the islands
(adult/child Ikr2500/1250) and two- to three-
hour whale-watching trips (adult/child Ikr3500/
1750, minimum 10 persons).

Places to Stay & Eat

If at all possible, reserve accommodation in
advance – many places fill up quickly after
the arrival of the ferry.

There's a **camping ground** (☎ 481 2075;
tent sites per person Ikr700) in Herjólfsdalur.
Rates include showers. The popular **Hreiðrið**
(☎ 699 8945; e eyjamyndir@isholf.is; Fax-
astígur 33; sleeping-bag accommodation
Ikr1200-1500, singles Ikr2000-3200, doubles Ikr3800-5200) is soon full after a ferry
arrives. You'll get a friendly welcome at the
family home **Gistiheimilið Erna** (☎ 481
2112, fax 481 1280; Kirkjubæjarbraut 15;
sleeping-bag accommodation Ikr1400-2000,
singles/doubles Ikr3600/5200); breakfast
costs Ikr700 extra.

Gistiheimilið Hvíld (☎ 481 1230; Höfða-
vegur 16; sleeping-bag accommodation
Ikr1500, singles Ikr2500-3500, doubles
Ikr3000-5400) is known for good service. **Gistiheimilið Heimir** (☎ 481 2929, fax 481 2912;
Heiðarvegur 1; sleeping-bag accommodation
Ikr1500, B&B singles/doubles Ikr4000/6500)
offers no-frills lodging and large low-season
discounts. The expensive **Hótel Þórshamar**
(☎ 481 2900; e thorshamar@eyjar.is; Vest-
mannabraut 28; singles/doubles Ikr8400/

11,900) has a moderately priced guesthouse,
Sunnuhöll (sleeping-bag accommodation
Ikr1800).

The dining room at **Hótel Þórshamar** (Vest-
mannabraut 28; mains from Ikr2000) is the upmarket choice. For Vestmannaeyjar delicacies,
try the excellent **Lanterna** (Bárustígur 11;
mains Ikr1000-2500). The place for a pizza is
Pizza 67 (Heiðarvegur 5) and **Café Maria**
(Skólavegur 1) serves snacks and coffee. The
takeaway grill **Toppurinn** (Heiðarvegur) serves
good burgers and sandwiches. For self-catering,
visit **11-11 supermarket** (Goðahraun 1).

Getting There & Away

Íslandsflug (☎ 481 3300) flies two or three
times daily to/from Reykjavík (from Ikr4490
one-way), but weather can interrupt schedules.

From 12 May to 31 August, the ferry Herjólfur sails from Vestmannaeyjar to Þorlákshöfn, on the mainland, daily at 8.15am, and
returns from Þorlákshöfn at noon. On Friday,
there's a second departure at 4pm from
Heimaey and 7.30pm from the mainland.
Winter sailings are once daily (twice on Friday). The one-way fare is adult/child
Ikr1500/750. Destination Iceland runs buses
between Reykjavík and Þorlákshöfn to connect with the ferry (Ikr850).

ÞÓRSMÖRK

Þórsmörk (Woods of Thor), about 130km
southeast of Reykjavík, is one of the most
beautiful places in Iceland, a glacial valley
with scrub birch, flowers, braided rivers and
clear streams surrounded by snowy peaks
and glaciers.

There's great **hiking** but on summer weekends it gets busy and noisy, with considerable
drunken disorder. Þórsmörk is a terminal for
Iceland's most popular hike, the Landmannalaugar to Þórsmörk trek (see Fjallabak Reserve in The Interior section later).

Places to Stay

The three Þórsmörk area huts – **Þórsmörk**
(☎ 568 2533; e fi@fi.is; Ferðafélag Íslands),
Básar (☎ 562 1000; e utivist@utivist.is;
Útivist) and **Húsadalur** (☎ 545 1717; e aust
urleid@austurleid.is; Austurleið) – are often
crowded in summer. Tent sites at any of the
three centres cost Ikr500 per person.

There's also a cosy, turf-roofed **HI hostel**
(☎ 487 8498; beds HI members/nonmembers
Ikr1000/1350) at nearby Fljótsdalur.

Getting There & Away

During summer (June to mid-September), buses run between Reykjavík and Húsadalur (over the hill from Þórsmörk) once or twice daily (Ikr3200 one way).

To reach Fljótsdalur, get off the Ring Road bus at Hvolsvöllur, then walk or hitch the 27km along route 261. From mid-July to mid-August, the Syðri Fjallabaksleið bus runs once daily from Reykjavík to Fljótsdalur via Hvolsvöllur.

The North

UPPER BORGARFJÖRÐUR

Upper Borgarfjörður, east of the Ring Road about 90km north of Reykjavík, has several places well worth visiting.

Things to See

Reykholt (population 50), 22km east of the Ring Road, is best known for **Snorri's Pool**. This haunting saga site consists of a circular bath 4m in diameter, which is lined with stones and fed by a stone aqueduct from a nearby hot spring. The passage behind the pool is believed to lead to the cellar where Iceland's greatest saga writer Snorri Sturluson was murdered in 1241; the adjacent farm site is currently being excavated.

Deildartunguhver, 4km west of Reykholt, is Iceland's most powerful and prolific hot spring. It pours out at a rate of 180L per second – a path allows impressive public viewing. About 18km northeast of Reykholt is the astonishing **Hraunfossar**, a series of 'magic waterfalls' where a substantial river mysteriously emerges from beneath a lava flow. From there, a walking track leads upstream to the waterfall **Barnafoss** where the constricted river Hvítá roars through a narrow gorge. The name was derived from a legend that two children fell into the river from a natural bridge.

Places to Stay & Eat

Camping (*Kleppjárnsreykir; tent sites per person Ikr400*) is available 1km from Deildartunguhver. **Hótel Reykholt** (☎ 435 1260; ℮ hotelreykholt@isholf.is; Reykholt; sleeping-bag accommodation Ikr1525, singles/doubles from Ikr3990/5150) has a restaurant and bar; the standard rooms have shared facilities and breakfast is Ikr800 extra. Two-course lunches/dinners start at Ikr950/1900.

Getting There & Away

Buses run from Reykjavík to Reykholt (via Deildartunguhver) on Friday and Sunday afternoons (Ikr1800). You'll need your own transport (or hitch) to reach Hraunfossar and Barnafoss.

SNÆFELLSNES

The 1446m-high volcano Snæfell, at the western end of the 100km-long Snæfellsnes peninsula, is capped by the Snæfellsjökull glacier. It served as the gateway to the underworld in Jules Verne's adventure, *A Journey to the Centre of the Earth*. Most of Snæfellsnes' population is strung along the north coast in the villages of Stykkishólmur, Grundarfjörður, Ólafsvík and Hellissandur-Rif. The area is very scenic, with steep mountains, old rambling lava flows, waterfalls and scattered Icelandic farmhouses between the villages.

Stykkishólmur

pop 1235

Stykkishólmur, Snæfellsnes' largest village, lies on the southern shore of Breiðafjörður. From there, ferries go to Brjánslækur in the Westfjords. Follow the causeway out to the islet **Súgandisey**, just north of and sheltering the harbour – it's made up of interesting basalt columns.

Snæfellsjökull

Visitors wanting to climb Snæfell have several options. The most interesting way is from the western end of the peninsula, along the Móðulækur stream (4WD vehicles can go 4km up the track). This route goes via the red scoria craters of Rauðhólar, the waterfall Klukkufoss and scenic Eysteinsdalur Valley. It will take you a couple of days, so make sure you're fully equipped. You may need crampons and ice axes to reach the summit.

Organised Tours

Sæferðir (☎ 438 1450; ℮ saeferdir@saeferdir.is; Stykkishólmur) runs excellent, three-hour whale-watching trips (daily, mid-May to August) from Ólafsvík for Ikr4200.

Places to Stay & Eat

Stykkishólmur has an excellent but exposed **camping ground** (☎ 438 1150; tent sites per person Ikr500) and a fine **HI hostel** (☎ 438 1095; Höfðagata 1; beds HI members/nonmembers Ikr1400/1700).

The small guesthouse, **Heimagisting María Bæringsdóttir** (☎ 438 1258; Höfðagata 11; B&B singles/doubles Ikr4800/6800) offers shared facilities. At the bland-looking **Hótel Stykkishólmur** (☎ 430 2100; e hotelstykki sholmur@simnet.is; Borgarbraut 6; en suite B&B singles/doubles from Ikr7500/9800) there's a posh dining room (mains Ikr1450 to Ikr3800) and a great view. **Skjöldur** (☎ 438 1535; tent sites per person Ikr500, sleeping-bag accommodation Ikr1000), at Helgafellsveit, 8km south of Stykkishólmur, has kitchen facilities.

About 1km east of Ólafsvík, just off the road to Stykkishólmur, lies the sheltered **camping ground** (☎ 436 1543; tent sites per person/tent Ikr200/200). In Ólafsvík itself, **Hótel Höfði** (☎ 436 1650; e info@hotelh ofdi.is; Ólafsbraut 20; sleeping-bag accommodation Ikr1800, B&B singles/doubles from Ikr6200/8400) offers comfortable rooms. Across the street is **Prinsinn** (Ólafsbraut; dishes from Ikr500), which serves burgers and pizzas.

Hellnar has a cosy, ecological guesthouse **Brekkubær** (☎ 435 6820; e gudrun@hellnar .is; camping per person/tent Ikr500/100, sleeping-bag accommodation Ikr1200, singles/ doubles from Ikr5200/7400). The restaurant serves fine organic dinners for Ikr2100.

Getting There & Away

The daily bus journeys between Reykjavík and Stykkishólmur take three hours and cost Ikr2600. Buses between Reykjavík, Ólafsvík and Stykkishólmur meet at a remote intersection called Vegamót (or Gröf), then passengers sort themselves out according to destination. See the following Westfjords section for details of the Stykkishólmur–Brjánslækur ferry and connecting buses.

THE WESTFJORDS

Extending claw-like towards Greenland, the Westfjords Peninsula, attached to the mainland by a narrow isthmus, is the most rugged and remote corner of Iceland.

Ísafjörður

pop 2741

Ísafjörður, the Westfjords' commercial centre, is the region's largest settlement and has a wonderful location on a narrow spit in the Skutulsfjörður fjord. There's a **tourist office** (☎ 456 5121; e info@vestfirdir.is; Aðalstræti 7) as well as a **bank** (Pólgata 1) and **post office** (Aðalstræti 18).

Things to See & Do The **Westfjords Maritime Museum** (☎ 456 3293; Neðstíkaupstaður; admission Ikr300; open 1pm-5pm daily June & Aug, 10am-5pm daily July), one of Iceland's finest, has both recent and historical displays and lovely old photographs of the early settlement.

Other items of interest include the huge **whale jawbone arch** in the town park, the odd-looking **church** nearby, and the new **art museum & library** (☎ 456 3296; Hafnararstræti; Internet Ikr100/hour), a former hospital built in 1925.

Hiking in the mountains around Ísafjörður isn't particularly easy, but the views are rewarding; for advice, contact the tourist office.

Organised Tours There's an extensive programme at **West Tours** (☎ 456 5111), which includes a four-hour trip to Hesteyri on Hornstrandir on Wednesday, Friday and Sunday (Ikr3900).

Places to Stay & Eat The two **camping grounds**, one 3km southwest of town in **Tungudalur** (☎ 456 5081; tent sites per person Ikr750) and the other behind **Mentaskólinn Torfnes** (☎ 456 4485; Skutulsfjarðarbraut; per tent/person Ikr550/330), both have good facilities. The nearest **HI hostel** (☎ 456 7808; e korpudalur@centrum.is; beds HI members/ nonmembers Ikr1500/1850; open June- Aug) is at the head of Önundarfjörður, 14km southwest of Ísafjörður.

The pleasant, old guesthouse, **Gamla Gistihúsið** (☎ 456 4146; e fmg@snerpa.is; Mánagata 5; sleeping-bag accommodation Ikr1600-1800, beds per person Ikr2500-2700), charges Ikr800 for breakfast.

Mentaskólinn Torfnes (☎ 456 4485; e info@hotelisafjordur.is; Skutulsfjarðarbraut; sleeping-bag accommodation Ikr1100-3300, B&B singles/doubles Ikr6100/8800; open June–mid-Aug) offers no-frills rooms with shared facilities.

The fine **Hótel Ísafjörður** (☎ 456 4111; e info@hotelisafjordur.is; Silfurtorg 2; B&B singles/doubles Ikr11,500/ 13,800) offers smart rooms with private bathrooms, a good breakfast (Ikr800 for nonresidents) and excellent restaurant dinners (two courses for Ikr2100).

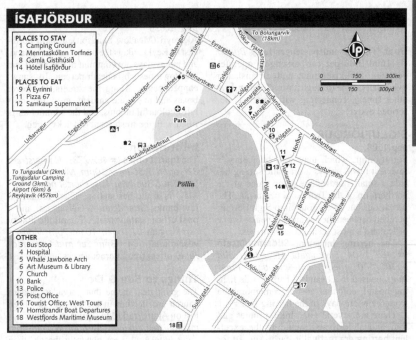

ÍSAFJÖRÐUR

PLACES TO STAY
1 Camping Ground
2 Menntaskólinn Torfnes
8 Gamla Gistihúsið
14 Hótel Ísafjörður

PLACES TO EAT
9 Á Eyrinni
11 Pizza 67
12 Samkaup Supermarket

OTHER
3 Bus Stop
4 Hospital
5 Whale Jawbone Arch
6 Art Museum & Library
7 Church
10 Bank
13 Police
15 Post Office
16 Tourist Office; West Tours
17 Hornstrandir Boat Departures
18 Westfjords Maritime Museum

Central **Pizza 67** *(Hafnarstræti 12; meals from Ikr550)* serves pizzas, burgers, meat and fish. **Á Eyrinni** *(☎ 456 5267; Mánagata 1; pizzas from Ikr630)* serves up pizza, burgers and pitta sandwiches in an 1884 house with a pleasant solarium. You'll find a **summer café** at the museum. For great value, visit the salad bar at the **Samkaup supermarket** *(Austurvegur 2)*.

Hornstrandir

The wildest corner of the Westfjords, the Hornstrandir peninsula was abandoned in the 1950s and now offers excellent hiking and camping. For details see Lonely Planet's *Iceland, Greenland & the Faroe Islands*. The peninsula is accessible by boat from Ísafjörður and one-way fares are about Ikr3000; contact the Ísafjörður tourist office for details. There's basic accommodation at **Hesteyri** *(☎ 456 3879)*, **Bolungarvík** *(☎ 852 8267)* and **Reykjarfjörður** *(☎ 853 1615)*.

Látrabjarg

The Látrabjarg cliffs have one of the greatest populations of **birds** in Iceland. Lying at the westernmost end of the Westfjords, the 12km-long cliffs range from 40m to 511m high. Puffins and the occasional seal are the main attractions.

There's a beautifully located but simple **guesthouse** *(☎ 456 1575; e breidavi@li.is; sleeping-bag accommodation Ikr1500, made-up beds Ikr2000-2400)* at Breiðavík, 12km from the cliffs.

Getting There & Away

Air There are flights between Reykjavík and Ísafjörður available two or three times daily (from Ikr5445) with **Flugfélag Íslands** *(☎ 456 3000)*

Bus Buses between Reykjavík and Ísafjörður require a change at Brú, leave Reykjavík on Tuesday, Friday and Sunday at 10am (June to August). On Monday and Wednesday at 8.30am, and Saturday at 1pm, you can go from Reykjavík to Ísafjörður via the Stykkishólmur (Snæfellsnes) to Brjánslækur (Westfjords) ferry (Ikr6400, nine to 13½ hours).

The Ísafjörður–Brjánslækur–Látrabjarg bus runs via Breiðavík Monday, Wednesday and Saturday (June to August) and allows 1¼ hours at Látrabjarg.

Travelling between Ísafjörður and Akureyri requires a connection in Brú.

Boat The car and passenger ferry *Baldur* (Ikr1600/1600 per car/passenger) operates between Stykkishólmur and Brjánslækur twice daily, June to August (less frequently at other times), connecting with buses as described above.

SIGLUFJÖRÐUR
pop 1508

Siglufjörður, which may well be Iceland's loveliest town, enjoys a dramatic setting beside a small fjord of the same name at the northern tip of the Tröllskagi peninsula. The precarious but lovely route into Siglufjörður, perched between the sea and the peaks, is one of Iceland's most scenic coastal drives.

The herring museum, **Síldarminjasafn** (☎ 467 1604; *Snorragata 15; adult/child Ikr300/100; open 10am-6pm daily June-Aug*), housed in a beautiful harbourside fishing hostel, contains nostalgic memorabilia from the boom days of the herring fishery.

There are several good hiking routes and four annual festivals, including the excellent **herring era festival** in early August; for details, check out the festival's website **W** www.siglo.is.

Places to Stay & Eat

The main **camping ground** (*per person Ikr400*) is near the harbour and town square. In an old hotel from the 1930s, the cosy **Gistiheimilið Hvanneyri** (☎/fax 467 1378; *Aðalgata 10; sleeping-bag accommodation Ikr1200, beds per person Ikr2000*) has rooms with shared facilities and kitchen access.

The cinema-inspired **Bíó Café Restaurant** (☎ 467 2233; *Aðalgata 30; dishes from Ikr400*) serves good-value burgers, pizzas and beef and fish dishes. Self-caterers should head for the **Strax supermarket** (*Suðurgata*). The **fishmonger** (*Aðalgata*) sells fresh fish (including excellent catfish) and *harðfiskur*.

Getting There & Away

Íslandsflug (☎ 570 8090) flies between Reykjavík and Sauðárkrókur up to six days per week (from Ikr5865), with Flybus connections to Siglufjörður (Ikr500, one hour).

Buses run between Reykjavík and Siglufjörður (Ikr4000) three times a week in either direction (June to September only).

AKUREYRI
pop 15,635

Akureyri (Meadow Sandspit), 250km northeast of Reykjavík, is the best of urban Iceland, and sunny days are common in this small and tidy town nestled beneath perpetually snowcapped peaks. Along the streets, in flower boxes and in private gardens, grow Iceland's most colourful blooms, and the summer air is filled with the fresh scent of sticky birch.

Information

The **tourist office** (☎ 462 7733; *Hafnarstræti 82; open 7.30am-7.30pm Mon-Fri, 8am-5pm Sat & Sun June-Aug, shorter hours Sept-May*) is at the bus station. There are also a few **banks** (*Strandgata & Geislagata*) and a **post office** (*Hafnarstræti*). The **public library** (*Brekkugata 17; open 10am-7pm Mon-Fri year-round, 10am-3pm Sat mid-Sept–mid-June*) offers free Internet access.

Things to See & Do

The geological theme that pervades modern church architecture in Iceland has not been lost on **Akureyrarkirkja** (*Eyrarlandsvegur; admission free; open 10am-noon & 2pm-4pm daily June-Aug*). Less blatantly 'basalt' than Reykjavík's Hallgrímskirkja, Akureyrarkirkja is basalt, nonetheless. Note the angel sculpture by renowned Danish sculptor Bertel Thorvaldsen.

Most of Akureyri's **museums** are former homes of 'local boys made good'. Icelanders proudly commemorate their artists, poets and authors, but, unless you have a particular admiration for their work, it may be of limited interest. The best of them is **Nonnahús** (☎ 462 3555; *Aðalstræti 54b; adult/child Ikr300/free; open 10am-5pm daily June–mid-Sept*), the childhood home of children's writer Reverend Jón Sveinsson (nicknamed 'Nonni') who lived from 1857 to 1944. This cosy old home, built in 1850, is a good example of an early village dwelling. **Minjasafn Akureyrar** (*Akureyri Folk Museum;* ☎ 462 4162; *Aðalstræti 58; adult/child Ikr400/free; open 11am-5pm daily June–mid-Sept*) houses artwork and historical household items. **Lystigarður Akureyrar** (*Akureyri Botanical Gardens; Eyrarlandsvegur; admission free; open 8am-10pm Mon-Fri, 9am-10pm Sat & Sun June-Oct*), opened in 1912, includes every native Icelandic species and high-latitude and high-altitude plants from around the world.

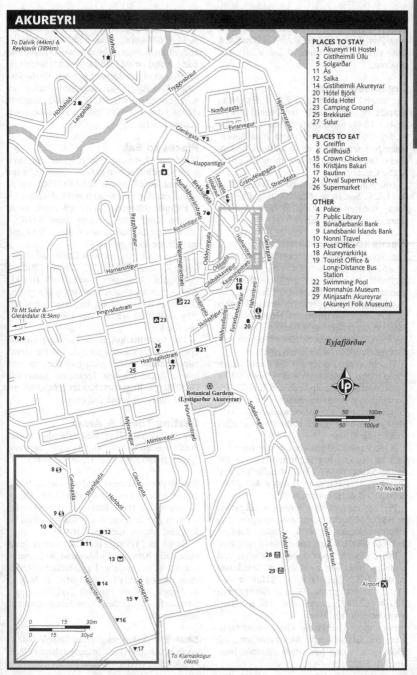

AKUREYRI

PLACES TO STAY
1 Akureyri HI Hostel
2 Gistiheimili Úllu
5 Solgarðar
11 Ás
12 Salka
14 Gistiheimili Akureyrar
20 Hótel Björk
21 Edda Hotel
23 Camping Ground
25 Brekkusel
27 Sulur

PLACES TO EAT
3 Greiffin
6 Grillhúsið
15 Crown Chicken
16 Kristjáns Bakari
17 Bautinn
24 Úrval Supermarket
26 Supermarket

OTHER
4 Police
7 Public Library
8 Búnaðarbanki Bank
9 Landsbanki Íslands Bank
10 Nonni Travel
13 Post Office
18 Akureyrarkirkja
19 Tourist Office & Long-Distance Bus Station
22 Swimming Pool
28 Nonnahús Museum
29 Minjasafn Akureyrar (Akureyri Folk Museum)

To Dalvík (44km) & Reykjavík (389km)

Eyjafjörður

To Mt Sulur & Glerárdalur (8.5km)

To Mývatn

Botanical Gardens (Lystigarður Akureyrar)

To Kjarnaskógur (4km)

Airport

There's also a recommended **swimming pool** (*Þingvallastræti 7; admission Ikr270; open 7am-9pm Mon-Fri, 8am-6.30pm Sat & Sun*) with flumes suitable for adults and children.

Organised Tours

The **tourist office** (☎ 462 7733), **Flugfélag Íslands** (☎ 460 7000) and **Nonni Travel** (☎ 461 1841; *Brekkugata 5*) run very popular day tours to **Grímsey island**. It has lots of seabirds, interesting rock formations, and includes the only part of Iceland north of the Arctic Circle.

Tour prices range from Ikr4000 to Ikr11,230. See Boat in the Getting There & Away section for details of how to reach Grímsey by bus and ferry.

Places to Stay

The spacious, central **camping ground** (☎ 462 3379; ☻ hamrar@scout.is; *Þorunnarstræti; tent sites per person Ikr500*) has laundry facilities (wash and dry Ikr400).

Advance booking for the central and highly recommended **Akureyri HI Hostel** (☎ 462 3657; ☻ storholt@nett.is; *Stórholt 1; beds HI members/nonmembers Ikr1500/1900, singles/doubles Ikr3600/5800*) is advised.

The maximum price for the cartel guesthouse rooms in Akureyri is Ikr4500/6000 for single/double made-up beds and Ikr3000 for sleeping-bag accommodation (the average for sleeping-bag accommodation is Ikr2200). Most places have shared bathrooms and offer cooking facilities.

A recommended guesthouse with rooms as well as sleeping-bag accommodation is the central **Salka** (☎ 461 2340; ☻ salka@nett.is; *Skipagata 1*). Even nicer is **Ás** (☎ 461 2248; *Skipagata 4 & Hafnarstræti 77*).

Perhaps the best deal in town is **Sólgarðar** (☎ 461 1133; *Brekkugata 6; sleeping-bag accommodation Ikr1800, singles/doubles Ikr3200/4700*), which has cooking facilities.

More sleeping-bag accommodation and made-up beds are available at **Brekkusel** (☎ 461 2660; *Byggðavegur*), **Súlur** (☎ 461 1160; *Þórunnarstræti 93*) and **Gistiheimili Úllu** (☎ 462 3472; *Langahlíð 6*), which doesn't have cooking facilities.

For a nicer guesthouse with en suite facilities, try **Gistiheimili Akureyrar** (☎ 462 5588; *Hafnarstræti 104; singles/doubles from Ikr4500/6900*).

Hótel Björk (☎ 461 3030; ☻ bjork@ hotelkea.is; *Hafnarstræti 67; singles/doubles Ikr11,300/14,400*) is an odd-looking black-and-white former printer's workshop. The **Edda Hotel** (☎ 461 1434; ☻ edda@edda.is; *Eyrarlandsvegur 28, entry from Hrafngilsstræti; sleeping-bag accommodation in schoolrooms/rooms Ikr1000/1400, singles/doubles from Ikr4700/5800*) is in the town grammar school.

Places to Eat

If you only have one splurge in Iceland, save it for **Greifinn** (*Glerárgata 20; soup & salad lunch bar Ikr950; mains Ikr1090-3990*), which serves excellent beef, lamb and fish dishes.

Bautinn (*Hafnarstræti 92; all-you-can-eat soup & salad Ikr990, mains about Ikr1600*) offers meat and fish courses; prices for these include the soup and salad.

For pizza, try the pleasant **Grillhúsið** (*Geislagata 7; pizzas from Ikr750*). **Crown Chicken** (*Skipagata 12; burgers & filled pitta Ikr400-750*) serves reasonable fast fare; half a grilled chicken is Ikr750. Along the pedestrian shopping mall there are two small **kiosks** selling fast food.

The **supermarket** at the camping ground opens evenings and weekends but the **Úrval supermarket** (*Hrísalundur*) is cheaper and has a home cooked Icelandic food bar (Ikr998/kg). **Kristjáns Bakarí** (*Hafnarstræti 100*) sells fresh bread and cakes.

Getting There & Away

Air In summer, **Flugfélag Íslands** (☎ 460 7000) has up to nine flights daily between Akureyri and Reykjavík (from Ikr5445).

Bus Between Akureyri and Reykjavík, buses depart at least once daily (Ikr5300). Buses travelling over the Kjölur route to Reykjavík, through the interior, leave daily at 9am in July and August and cost Ikr6400.

Buses to Mývatn (Ikr1800) run at least once daily between 13 May and 30 September; buses continue to Egilsstaðir (Ikr4500) three times weekly or daily. From 27 May to 31 August, buses to Húsavík (Ikr1500) depart three to five times daily (and less frequent at other times).

Boat The *Sæfari* sails from Dalvík (44km north of Akureyri) to Grímsey Island at 9am on Monday, Wednesday and Friday, returning from Grímsey at 4pm. The trip takes 3½ hours each way and costs Ikr3500 return (or Ikr4000 return, including the bus from Akureyri to Dalvík).

AROUND AKUREYRI

Just an hour's walk south of the town centre you'll find Iceland's most visited 'forest', **Kjarnaskógur**. A good day walk from Akureyri follows the **Glerárdalur** valley as far as Lambi mountain hut. You can hike up and down **Mt Sulur** (1213m) from Akureyri in about eight hours.

About 50km east of Akureyri, by the Ring Road, there's the fine waterfall **Goðafoss**. Legend has it that an Icelander threw his statues of the old Norse gods into the falls when he converted to Christianity in 1000. Buses from Akureyri to Mývatn pass the falls.

HÚSAVÍK

pop 2420

Húsavík, about 90km northeast of Akureyri (by road), is an important base for whale-watching trips. In town, there's the extensive and fascinating **whale centre/tourist office** *(☎ 464 2520; Hafnarstétt; adult/child Ikr400/ 150; open 9am-9pm daily mid-June–mid-Aug, shorter hours other times)*, featuring skeletons, models and the story of Icelandic whaling. There's also a fine **church** *(Heðins-braut; admission free; open 9am-noon & 1pm-6pm daily June-Aug)* and an interesting folk and natural history **museum** *(☎ 464 1860; Stórigarður 17; adult/child Ikr300/50; open 10am-6pm daily June-Aug)*, with local fisheries exhibits and a stuffed polar bear, which was shot on Grímsey in 1969.

Norðursigling *(☎ 464 2350)* does up to four daily three-hour **whale-watching trips** for Ikr3600/1800. You're most likely to see minke whales, dolphins and humpbacked whales.

Places to Stay & Eat

The friendly **camping ground** *(☎ 464 2220; tent sites per person Ikr500)* is on the northern edge of the village. For rooms, try the clean and friendly **Gistiheimilið Árból** *(☎ 464 2220; Ásgarðsvegur 2; singles/doubles Ikr5250/ 6770)*. Otherwise, ask the tourist office for details of **private homes** with sleeping-bag accommodation for around Ikr1500 and singles/doubles for Ikr3200/4600. The expensive **Fosshótel Húsavík** *(☎ 464 1220; e husavik@fosshotel.is; Ketilsbraut 22;*

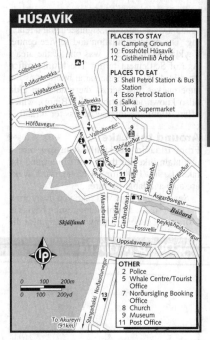

HÚSAVÍK

PLACES TO STAY
1 Camping Ground
10 Fosshótel Húsavík
12 Gistiheimilið Árból

PLACES TO EAT
3 Shell Petrol Station & Bus Station
4 Esso Petrol Station
6 Salka
13 Úrval Supermarket

OTHER
2 Police
5 Whale Centre/Tourist Office
7 Norðursigling Booking Office
8 Church
9 Museum
11 Post Office

0   100   200m
0   100   200yd

To Akureyri (91km)

singles/doubles from Ikr11,400/15,400) has en suite rooms and breakfast is included.

Cosy **Salka** *(Garðarsbraut 6; snacks & pizzas Ikr550-1500, mains Ikr1350-1750)* serves some traditional dishes. The **Shell petrol station** *(Heðinsbraut 6; snacks and mains Ikr170-1195)*, where the buses stop, has a good-value snack bar. **Esso petrol station** *(Heðinsbraut 2)* is similar. The **Úrval supermarket** *(Garðarsbraut 64)* has excellent meat and fish counters and sells locally grown vegetables.

Getting There & Away

There are three to five daily buses to Akureyri (Ikr1500) from 27 May to 31 August. Daily service go to Ásbyrgi (not on weekends from September to mid-June). Buses to Reykjahlíð (Mývatn) depart up to three times daily from 27 May to 31 August (Ikr1300, 45 minutes).

MÝVATN

The Mývatn basin sits on the spreading zone of the mid-Atlantic ridge and, although most of the interesting sights are volcanic or geo-thermal features, the centrepiece of the reserve is wonderful Lake Mývatn and its diverse waterfowl. Here, travellers can settle in and spend a week camping, sightseeing and relaxing. The main population and service centre, **Reykjahlíð** (pop 250), was one of the area's Age of Settlement farms. The **tourist office** (☎ 464 4390) is in the same building as the supermarket, just across the road from **Eldá** (also known as Gistiheimilið Bjarg), which offers 30-minute Internet access for Ikr250.

Around the Lake

From Eldá in Reykjahlíð you can hire a mountain bike for the 37km trip around the lake (Ikr900/1400 for six/12 hours). Kayaks are also available for hire.

Several side trips will take you away from the main roads. The most interesting begins at **Stóragjá**, a rather scummy hot spring near the

village. After a few minutes, the walk comes to a dead end at a pipeline. There you should turn left and walk several hundred metres until the track turns southward. It crosses an overgrown lava field before reaching **Grjótagjá**, a 44°C hot spring in a cave, then continues to the prominent tephra crater, **Hverfell**, and **Dimmuborgir**, a 2000-year-old maze of oddly shaped lava pillars and crags.

Other sites of interest around the lake include the forested lava headland of **Höfði**; the *klasar* pinnacle formations at **Kálfaströnd**; the pseudocraters at **Skútustaðir**, where ponds, bogs and marshlands create havens for nesting birds; the climb up **Vindbelgjarfjall** (529m); and the high-density waterfowl **nesting area** along the northwestern shore (off-road entry is restricted between 15 May and 20 July).

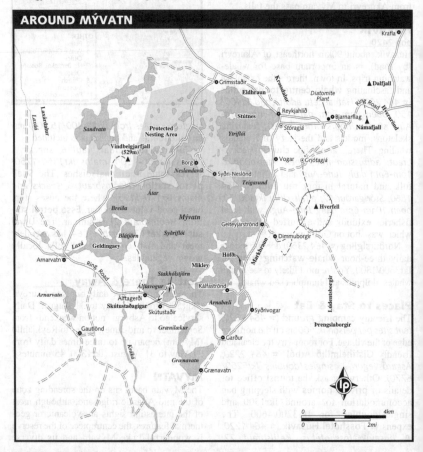

AROUND MÝVATN

Námafjall & Hverarönd

Produced by a fissure eruption, the pastel-pink Námafjall ridge lies south of the Ring Road, 6km east of Reykjahlíð. It sits squarely on the spreading zone of the mid-Atlantic rift and contains numerous steaming vents. At its foot is the Hverarönd geothermal field with fumaroles and solfataras (sulphurous vents).

Krafla

The incredible steaming fissure **Leirhnjúkur** is Krafla's prime attraction. From there you can look out across the **Krafla Caldera**, where lava flows created by the original Mývatnseldar eruptions and from those of 1975 are overlain in places by 1984 lava. Nearby **Viti**, meaning 'hell', is a 320m-wide explosion crater and lake (now apparently inactive). The 30-megawatt **Krafla Geothermal Power Station** (☎ 464 8200; admission free; open 9am-3.30pm daily June-Aug) gets steam from 17 boreholes around the volcano and is worth a visit to see the two 10-minute videos.

Organised Tours

Most tours operate only in summer (usually mid-June to August). A 2¾-hour tour of Mývatn and Krafla departs from Reykjahlíð at 1pm daily (pick-up from Skútustaðir may be arranged) and costs Ikr3100. The Volcanic Wonders tour (Ikr5400) leaves Eldá at 8.15am on Tuesday, Thursday and Sunday. The morning segment is a 3½-hour tour around local volcanic features; then, in the afternoon, it visits Krafla. A Mývatn–Krafla tour operates from Akureyri.

Eldá's highly recommended Dettifoss Super Tour (Ikr5500 to Ikr6000, 11 to 12 hours) runs three days weekly and includes the sights in the Jökulsárgljúfur National Park and a coastal puffin colony. There's also an excellent five-hour tour (Ikr5500) to Lofthellir, a lava cave with magnificent natural ice sculptures; departures are from Eldá at 8.15am on Tuesday, Thursday and Saturday in July and August.

Places to Stay & Eat

Reykjahlíð Reserve regulations prohibit camping away from designated areas, so most travellers head for Reykjahlíð. **Hlíð** (☎ 464 4103; e hlid@isholf.is; camping per person Ikr500, sleeping-bag accommodation Ikr1500), 300m inland from the church, offers good grassy tent sites and basic hostel-style rooms. The highly recommended **Gistiheimilið Bjarg**

(Eldá; ☎ 464 4220; lakeshore tent sites Ikr600, sleeping-bag accommodation Ikr1900, B&B singles/doubles Ikr5200/7300) is a more popular choice. About 2.5km south of the village is **Gistiheimilið Vogar** (☎ 464 4399; camping per person Ikr550, sleeping bag accommodation Ikr2100-3100, B&B singles/doubles Ikr5000/8000).

Hótel Reykjahlíð (☎ 464 4142; e reykjahlid@islandia.is; singles/doubles Ikr7400/10,100) is a friendly nine-room hotel on the lakeshore. The larger **Hótel Reynihlíð** (☎ 464 4170; e rhlid@mmedia.is; singles/doubles from Ikr11,800/13,800) offers en suite B&B and has a **dining room** (2-course specials around Ikr2100).

Pleasant **Gamli Bærinn** (mains Ikr890-1800), by the hotel, offers meat or fish soup for Ikr900. In cheaper **Hverinn** (snacks & mains Ikr550-1650), campers can dry out and munch reasonable burgers and chips.

Try to sample hverabrauð (hot spring bread), a gooey, cake-like concoction baked underground using geothermal heat. It's available at the **Strax supermarket** or the shop by Gamli Bærinn. For smoked salmon and Arctic char at good prices, try **Reykhúsið Geiteyjarströnd** near Dimmuborgir, 5km south of Reykjahlíð.

Skútustaðir Skútustaðir, at the southern end of the lake, has a general store, cafeteria and a restaurant at the petrol station. There's a **camping ground** (☎ 464 4212; tent sites Ikr500, beds per person Ikr3300) at Skútustaðir farm. You can sleep on a mattress on the floor at the community centre **Skjólbrekka** (☎ 464 4164; sleeping-bag accommodation Ikr1250). **Stöng Guesthouse** (☎ 464 4252; sleeping-bag accommodation Ikr2050, singles/doubles Ikr4000/5300), 8km west of Skútustaðir, then 5km south, is a friendly place that serves excellent home-made dinners.

Getting There & Away

The main long-distance bus station is at Hótel Reynihlíð in Reykjahlíð, but buses between Mývatn and Akureyri also stop at Skútustaðir. From 13 May to 30 September, there's at least one daily bus doing the 1½-hour trip between Akureyri and Mývatn (Ikr1800), and three per week or daily buses run from Mývatn to Egilsstaðir (Ikr2700). See the Húsavík section for details of Mývatn-Húsavík buses. Twice a week, there are buses to/from Reykjavík via

Sprengisandur (see Sprengisandur Route in The Interior section later for details). There are also three buses per week between Mývatn and Reykjavík via Kjölur (Ikr9500, July and August) and between Mývatn and Landmannalaugar via Sprengisandur (Ikr5900, mid-July to mid-August).

JÖKULSÁRGLJÚFUR NATIONAL PARK

The nearly unpronounceable name (**Yew**-kl-sour-**glyu**-fr) of this national park means 'glacial river canyon', but this belies the fact that it contains a myriad of other wonderful natural features. Sometimes called 'Iceland's Grand Canyon', Jökulsárgljúfur is also known for its sticky-birch forests, bizarre rock formations and **Ásbyrgi**, a canyon formed by a flood of biblical proportions, which came from a glacier 200km away. The swirls, spirals, rosettes, honeycombs and columns at **Hljóðaklettar** (Echo Rocks) are quite extraordinary, and near the park's southern boundary is the impressive 44m-high **Dettifoss**, Europe's most powerful waterfall.

Destination Iceland runs daily buses (18 June to 31 August) from Akureyri and Húsavík to major sites in the park (Ikr6200 return from Akureyri). Highly recommended is Eldá's Dettifoss Super Tour from Mývatn (Ikr5500 to Ikr6000), which offers a luggage transfer service for hikers.

The park offers excellent hiking and trekking opportunities but camping inside its boundaries is limited to sites at **Ásbyrgi** *(tent sites per person Ikr600)*, **Vesturdalur** *(tent sites per person Ikr600)* and **Dettifoss** *(free, hikers only)*. Meals are available only at the snack bar, supermarket and petrol station at the **Ásbyrgi farmstead** *(route 85)*.

The daily scheduled bus between Húsavík and Ásbyrgi costs Ikr1300 and takes 50 minutes. There's also a daily Mývatn-Dettifoss bus via Krafla from 18 June to 31 August.

The East

The main eastern attraction is sunshine. You can expect cool but clear summer weather with the odd rainy day thrown in to keep things interesting. Iceland's largest forest and longest lake are found here, along with a wealth of rugged and remote peaks and headlands, and some lovely waterfalls.

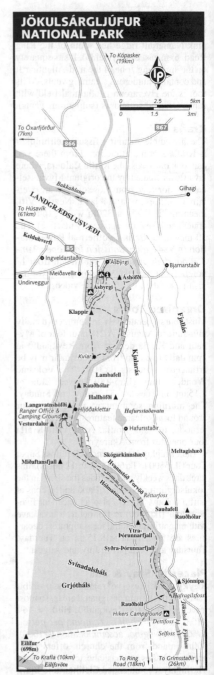

JÖKULSÁRGLJÚFUR NATIONAL PARK

EGILSSTAÐIR
pop 1608

Egilsstaðir, which began as a large farm in the late 19th century, is now the transport and commercial hub of eastern Iceland. The petrol station, cafeteria, bank, supermarkets, tourist office and associated camping ground are all clustered near the central crossroads.

Egilsstaðir sits beside the long, narrow **Lake Lögurinn**, which reputedly has a Nessie-like monster. The main attractions, accessible by car, bicycle or tour bus (three days per week in July and August, contact the tourist office for details), are the **Hallormsstaður woods** with a wooded camping ground; and the magnificent waterfall, **Hengifoss**, on the opposite shore. The interesting **cultural museum** (☎ 471 1412; Laufskógar 1; adult/child Ikr400/200; open 11am-5pm Tues-Sun June-Aug) includes a 10th-century Viking grave and a reconstructed farmhouse.

Places to Stay & Eat

The friendly, central **camping ground** (☎ 471 2320; Kaupvangur 10; tent sites per person Ikr500, sleeping-bag accommodation Ikr1300) offers cooking facilities. **Gistihúsið Egilsstaðir** (☎ 471 1114; e gilsstadir@isholf.is; sleeping-bag accommodation Ikr2500, singles/doubles from Ikr4500/7000) is 300m west of the central crossroads and all prices include breakfast.

Fosshótel Valaskjálf (☎ 471 1000; e valaskjalf@valaskjalf.is; Skógarlönd 3; singles/doubles from Ikr4750/7450) is large and bland, but it has a cinema.

For meals, there's the flash **Hótel Hérað dining room** (2-course lunch/dinner Ikr1450/2850), the **Shell petrol station** (Fagradalsbraut 13; snacks & meals Ikr390-1350), **Pizza 67** (Lyngás 1) for the best pizzas in town, and **Café Nielsen** (Tjarnarbraut 1; snacks & mains Ikr520-2900), a very pleasant coffee shop-cum-restaurant. The **supermarkets** are well stocked with travellers' supplies.

Getting There & Away

Air There are two or three **Flugfélag Íslands** (☎ 471 1210) flights daily between Reykjavík and Egilsstaðir (from Ikr6245).

Bus Late May to mid-September, it's possible to travel between Akureyri and Höfn via Egilsstaðir in one day. The main terminal is at the camping ground.

Between 1 June and 10 September the Seyðisfjörður bus runs at least twice daily, Monday to Friday (Ikr700, 30 minutes). On Wednesday and Thursday, it does additional runs in either direction to accommodate passengers travelling to Europe on the ferry *Norröna*. Buses also run once a day on Saturday and Sunday in July.

SEYÐSFJÖRÐR
pop 765

Seyðisfjörður, the terminal for ferries from the European mainland, is a pleasant introduction to Iceland for many travellers. It's an architecturally interesting town surrounded on three sides by mountains and on the other by a deep, 16km-long fjord.

The **tourist office** (☎ 472 1551; e ferdamenning@sfk.is; Austurvegur 42) has Internet access for Ikr150 per hour. The **bank** is 400m from the dock. The information desk in the **Smyril Line office** will book your onward accommodation.

A great introduction to walking in Iceland is the popular trip up the valley Vestdalur and around Mt Bjólfur to the Seyðisfjörður–Egilsstaðir road.

The **camping ground** (☎ 472 1551; Ránargata; tent sites Ikr400) is beside the Shell petrol station. Otherwise, there's the **Hafaldan HI Hostel** (☎ 472 1410; e thorag@simnet.is; Ránargata 9; beds HI members/nonmembers Ikr1450/1800). Contact the tourist office for details of hotel accommodation.

For meals, try the basic **cafeterias** at the Shell and Esso petrol stations, or the recommended bistro and Internet café **Skaftfell** (Austurvegur 42; mains Ikr600-1500).

For bus information, see the Egilsstaðir section earlier. Details of the ferry service from mainland Europe are described in the Getting There & Away section of this chapter.

STAFAFELL
pop 10

Stafafell, about 100km south of Egilsstaðir, is a great hiking area with an excellent location between the **Lón** lagoon and the colourful **Lónsöræfi** mountains.

Jeep tours to Kollumúli, in the Lónsöræfi mountains, are highly recommended. They cost Ikr4000 with **Stafafell Travel Service** (☎ 478 1717) – arrange these at the HI hostel. The hostel can also advise on about a dozen local walking routes.

For accommodation, there is an excellent **Stafafell HI Hostel & Guesthouse** (☎ 478 1717; ⓔ stafafell@eldhorn.is; beds for HI members/nonmembers Ikr1500/1850, B&B singles/doubles from Ikr4500/6000), and a **camping ground** (tent sites per person Ikr500), which also has cabins. Meals are available for hostel and guesthouse guests and campers using the camping ground (Ikr1200 to Ikr1800); they must be reserved in advance.

There's one daily bus to Egilsstaðir at 8.55am (Ikr4270, four hours), and another to Höfn at 5.15pm (Ikr520, 30 minutes).

VATNAJÖKULL

The 8400-sq-km icecap Vatnajökull, which reaches a thickness of 1km in places, is Iceland's greatest glacier. Scores of smaller valley glaciers flow down from Vatnajökull as crevasse-ridden rivers of sculptured ice.

To reach the icecap, take the 9am daily (June to early September) Austurleið bus from Höfn to Jöklasel (Ikr4220 return), near the edge of the ice, allowing time for a terrific one-hour skidoo tour (Ikr6900 extra). Return to Höfn via Jökulsárlón (with time for a cruise) or continue to Skaftafell (Ikr3930, July and August). The trip is also possible in a day from Skaftafell in July and August. Book through **Glacier Jeeps** (☎ 478 1000; ⓔ glacierjeeps@simnet.is).

The 17-sq-km and 600m-deep **Jökulsárlón lagoon**, near the Ring Road, is more or less an obligatory stop between Skaftafell and Höfn. It's getting bigger and it's full of icebergs calved from the glacier Breiðamerkurjökull, which descends from Vatnajökull.

In **Höfn** (pop 1753), there's a **tourist office** (☎ 478 1500; Hafnarbraut 52) with a **camping ground** (tent sites per person Ikr500), an **HI hostel** (☎ 478 1736; Hafnarbraut 8; beds HI members/nonmembers Ikr1500/1850), a **hotel** and several **guesthouses**. Accommodation is available at **Jöklasel Hut** (☎ 478 1000; sleeping-bag accommodation Ikr1800), near the edge of the ice.

Warning

Hiking around the Jöklasel Hut isn't advised due to the danger of falling into a crevasse.

SKAFTAFELL NATIONAL PARK

Skaftafell National Park, beneath a breathtaking backdrop of peaks and glaciers, is ideal for day walks and longer wilderness hiking

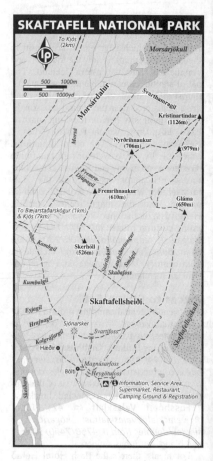

SKAFTAFELL NATIONAL PARK

trips, but don't approach or climb the glaciers without proper equipment and training.

One of the most popular walks is the easy one-hour return route to **Skaftafellsjökull** glacier. The track begins at the service centre and leads to the glacier face where you will experience evidence of glacial activity: bumps, groans and flowing water, as well as the brilliant blue hues of the ice itself.

Skaftafell's most photographed feature is **Svartifoss**, a waterfall flanked by unusual overhanging basalt columns. A well-worn trail leads uphill from the camping ground; allow 1½ hours return. If the weather's fine, follow the recommended loop walk around **Skaftafellsheiði**. The longer day walks from the camping ground to **Kristínartindar** (1126m), **Kjós** or the glacial lagoon in

Morsárdalur are tiring but enjoyable; plan on about seven hours for each return trip.

Places to Stay & Eat
The immense, grassy **camping ground** *(tent sites per person Ikr600)* is broken only by the odd windbreak hedge or barbecue spit. The service area has an information office, coffee shop, cafeteria, supermarket and shower and toilet block.

Another option is the farm **Bölti** *(☎ 478 1626; Skaftafellsheiði; dormitory sleeping-bag accommodation Ikr1900, singles/doubles Ikr5000/6400; open Mar-Oct)*; breakfast is Ikr850.

Getting There & Away
The daily buses (1 June to 15 September) between Reykjavík and Höfn stop at Skaftafell, passing at 2.35pm eastbound and 11.10am westbound. The ride to/from Höfn (1¾ to 2¾ hours) costs Ikr1930; to/from Reykjavík (5¼ to 5¾ hours) is Ikr4690. The more expensive Fjallabak Nyrðra bus (Ikr6660), which runs from 21 June to 7 September, follows the more scenic inland route via Landmannalaugar and Eldgjá rather than the coastal Ring Road.

KIRKJUBÆJARKLAUSTUR
pop 170
Kirkjubæjarklaustur has a very agreeable setting and several interesting sights, so it's worth spending a day there en route between Reykjavík and Skaftafell. During the late-18th-century Laki eruptions, lava averaging 12m thick covered an area of 565 sq km and destroyed many farms. It amounted to a volume of over 12 cubic km, making it the largest recorded lava flow from a single eruption.

Kirkjugólf, the smoothed upper surface of vertical basalt columns, lies in a field about 400m north of the central Skaftárskáli petrol station. **Systrafoss** is the prominent waterfall near the hotel. The lake **Systravatn**, a pleasant short walk above the falls, was reputedly a bathing place for nuns.

Organised Tours
The best access to the fantastic Lakagígar area, with its 25km-long crater row, is with the exceptionally good-value, 9½-hour Destination Iceland tour (Ikr4500) which departs at 9am daily (July and August), from **Hótel Kirkjubæjarklaustur** *(☎ 487 4900)*.

Places to Stay & Eat
The popular **Kirkjubæ II Campground** *(☎/fax 487 4612; per person Ikr450)* offers hot showers and both cooking and laundry facilities. **Summerhótel Kirkjubæjarklaustur** *(☎ 487 4838, fax 487 4815; open mid-June–mid-Aug; sleeping-bag accommodation classrooms/rooms Ikr1100/2000, singles/doubles Ikr4800/6100)* has a swimming pool *(adult/child Ikr300/150)* and charges Ikr840 for breakfast.

Hótel Kirkjubæjarklaustur *(☎ 487 4900)* has a good restaurant *(mains Ikr1680-3290)*. For grill snacks, try the **Skaftárskáli petrol station**. The **Kjarval supermarket** is just east of the chapel, and includes the **Systrakaffi** pizzeria.

Getting There & Away
The bus station is at Hótel Kirkjubæjarklaustur. Buses run daily between Reykjavík (Ikr3830), Kirkjubæjarklaustur, Skaftafell (Ikr860) and Höfn (Ikr2790). The Fjallabak Nyrðra bus between Reykjavík, Landmannalaugar, Kirkjubæjarklaustur and Skaftafell runs from 21 June to 7 September.

The Interior

The vast, barren interior of Iceland comprises one of Europe's greatest wilderness areas. Gazing across the expanses, you could imagine yourself in Tibet, Mongolia or, as some have noted, on the moon. In fact, the Apollo astronauts held training exercises here in preparation for lunar landings. This is seriously remote wilderness and there are practically no tourist facilities, no accommodation, no bridges and no guarantees should something go awry.

If you're planning to visit this area as an independent traveller, careful preparations are essential.

ROUTES OF CENTRAL ICELAND
Historically, the interior routes were used as summer short cuts between the northern and southern coasts. The harsh mountains, valleys and broad expanses were considered the haunt of *utilegumenn*, outlaws fleeing revenge. For commoners, the vast deserts were regarded as undesirable places of fear and tragedy.

The country map at the beginning of this chapter shows the following routes.

Kjölur Route

The Kjölur (Keel) Route (F35) was named in reference to its topographic shape. Though it was greener, more interesting and geographically more inviting than its counterpart, the Sprengisandur Route, it was historically less popular, probably due to legends of superhuman outlaws inhabiting its remote ranges.

Kjölur's main attraction for the modern visitor is **Hveravellir**, a geothermal area of fumaroles and multicoloured hot pools at the northern end of the pass. Ferðafélag Íslands has a **mountain hut** here.

The Kjölur Route is better suited to walking or cycling than other interior routes thanks to its smoother nature and lack of sand and lava flows.

Organised Tours Most travellers opt for the 9¼-hour Destination Iceland tour, which departs at 9am daily from Reykjavík or Akureyri. The standard fare is Ikr6400 but Omnibuspass holders get a large discount. If you have the Hringmiði (Full Circle Pass), you can opt to replace the Akureyri-Reykjavík section of the Ring Road with the Kjölur Route (Ikr1600 supplement).

Sprengisandur Route

The Sprengisandur Route (F26) may be the least interesting of the interior routes, but it has great views of the Vatnajökull, Tungnafellsjökull and Hofsjökull icecaps, as well as Askja and Herðubreið from the west. You may want to break the journey at Nýidalur, where there's a **camp site** and two Ferðafélag Íslands **huts** *(staffed July & Aug)*. From the huts, you can take leisurely hikes up the valley or a day hike to the pass, **Vonarskarð** (1000m), a colourful saddle between Tungnafellsjökull, the green Ógöngur hills and Vatnajökull.

Organised Tours Buses depart from Reykjavík for Mývatn via Sprengisandur and the magnificent waterfall Aldeyjarfoss (flanked with basalt columns) at 8am on Wednesday and Saturday. From north to south, they leave from Hótel Reynihlíð (Mývatn) at 8.30am on Thursday and Sunday. The journey costs Ikr9500 and takes 12 hours.

Öskjuleið Route

Herðubreið and Askja on the Öskjuleið Route (F88) are the most visited wonders of the Icelandic desert.

Herðubreið This oddly shaped 1682m-high mountain has been said to resemble a birthday cake, a cooking pot and a lampshade, but the tourist industry calls it 'Queen of the Icelandic Desert'. The track around it makes a nice day hike from **Herðubreiðarlindir**, a grassy oasis created by springs flowing from beneath the lava. There's a **tourist office**, a **camp site** and Ferðafélag Íslands' **Þorsteinsskáli Hut** *(open June-Aug)* with gas and coal stoves. It's an ideal overnight stop before continuing to Askja or returning to Mývatn.

Askja Askja is an immense 50-sq-km caldera (a volcano that has collapsed into its magma chamber) that sets one thinking about the power of nature. Part of this collapsed magma chamber contains the sapphire-blue (when it's liquid) **Öskjuvatn**, Iceland's deepest lake at 217m. At its northeastern corner is **Víti**, a hot lake in a tephra crater, which was formed in 1875 after a volcanic eruption. Nearby **Dreki Hut** at **Drekagil** (Dragon Ravine) accommodates 20 people but the cold is brutal, so go prepared and make sure you have warm and hefty sleeping bags.

Organised Tours Tours depart from Reykjahlíð (Mývatn) from 15 June to 14 July three times weekly (and daily between 15 July and 15 August) – *if* the road is passable. It's a gruelling 12 to 13-hour return trip and many participants opt to stay at Herðubreiðarlindir or Drekagil and rejoin the tour later. The fare is Ikr7000.

Kverkfjöll Route

The 108km-long Kverkfjöll Route (F905, F910 and F902) connects Möðrudalur on the Ring Road with the Ferðafélag Íslands **Sigurðarskáli hut and camping ground**, 3km from the impressive **lower Kverkfjöll ice caves**. A hot river from a vast geothermal area flows from beneath the cold glacier ice; clouds of steam swirl over the river and melt shimmering patterns on the ice walls, and there you have it – a tourist attraction. Perhaps this was the source of the overworked fire and ice cliche! There are other ice caves high up on the glacier (four hours return) and there's a **hot waterfall** (30°C) at Hveragil, five hours return from Sigurðarskáli (ask at the hut for directions).

Organised Tours Three-day tours to Kverkfjöll from Akureyri, Húsavík or Mývatn are run by **Ice & Fire Expeditions** (☎ 462 4442; e sba@sba.is). You must bring your own food, warm clothing and sleeping bag (and a tent if you're camping). Hiking boots are essential. Tours run twice weekly in July and August (Ikr16,400 from Húsavík or Mývatn, Ikr16,900 from Akureyri, not including hut or camping fees).

FJALLABAK RESERVE

The Fjallabak Reserve consists of rainbow-coloured rhyolite peaks, rambling lava flows, blue lakes and soothing hot springs – it can hold you captive for days.

The star attractions around **Landmannalaugar** are: the **Laugahraun** lava field; the **hot springs** 200m west of the Landmannalaugar hut; the hot vents at colourful **Brennisteinsalda** (Burning Stones Crest); the incredible red crater lake **Ljótipollur**; and the blue lake **Frostastaðavatn**, just over the rhyolite ridge north of Landmannalaugar. **Bláhnúkur** (Blue Peak), immediately south of Laugahraun, offers a scree scramble and fine views from the 943m peak.

Places to Stay

Ferðafélag Íslands' **hut** at Landmannalaugar accommodates 75 people on a first-come, first-served basis. In July and August, it's usually booked out by tour groups and club members. Others will probably have to use the **camping ground** (tent sites per person Ikr500), which has toilet and expensive shower facilities.

Getting There & Away

The only public transport over the Fjallabak Nyrðra Route is the Destination Iceland mountain bus, which operates daily between Reykjavík and Skaftafell from 21 June to 7 September, snow and river conditions permitting.

Leaving from either direction, it stops at Landmannalaugar between 1pm and 2.45pm. Buses to/from Skaftafell stop at Eldgjá (Fire Gorge) allowing an hour for a walk to the nearby waterfall, Ófærufoss. The return fare from Reykjavík to Landmannalaugar is Ikr7520; holders of bus passes pay Ikr2420/4840 single/return.

LANDMANNALAUGAR TO ÞÓRSMÖRK TREK

The wonderful three- to four-day trek from Landmannalaugar to Þórsmörk (or vice versa) is the premier walk in Iceland. It can be completed by anyone in reasonably good physical condition between mid-July and early September. There are also many possible side trips. Most people walk the track from north to south because of the net altitude loss. Some continue on to Skógar, making it a six-day trip (which can be difficult in bad weather). The best map of the route is Landmælingar Íslands' Þórsmörk/Landmannalaugar (1:100,000).

The public huts along the track now have wardens. Dates when wardens are present may vary from year to year, and the huts may be booked out by the ubiquitous tour groups, so check with Ferðafélag Íslands in Reykjavík before you set out. Wardens can answer questions and provide information on trail conditions. Due to at least two substantial river crossings, this route may not be suitable for children.

From Landmannalaugar hut, cross the **Laugahraun** lava field and ascend **Brennisteinsalda** (840m). Cross some rhyolite hills, then descend to the steaming vents at **Stórihver** and continue across the moors (covered in chunks of obsidian and extensive snowfields) and a mountain pass to the **Hrafntinnusker hut**. From Hrafntinnusker, the track bounces over parallel rhyolite ridges before ascending steeply to a ridge studded with hot springs and fumaroles. Cross more ridges of descending altitude then drop steeply from the **Jökultungur** ridge into the **Álftavatn** valley, where a 4WD track leads to two **huts**.

There are several stream crossings in the area south of Álftavatn; after 5km, you'll pass the privately owned **Hvanngil hut and camp site**. Cross the raging Kaldaklofskvísl on a footbridge, then follow the route posted 'Emstrur/Fljótshlíð' and ford the knee-deep Bláfjallakvísl. The track then enters a lonely and surreal 5km stretch of black sand and pumice desert, skirting the obtrusive pyramid-shaped peak, **Stórasúla**. The next barrier is the murky river **Innri-Emstruá**, which is bridged but may have a knee-deep side channel. After the bridge, continue up to the crest and watch on your left for the 'FÍ Skáli' signpost, which directs you through a desolate desert to the **Botnar (Emstrur) huts**.

Cross a small heath then drop steeply to cross the roiling **Fremri-Emstruá** on a small footbridge. From there, the trail is relatively flat to the Ljósá footbridge. Over the next hill is the more difficult unbridged river **Þrongá**.

ICELAND

LANDMANNALAUGAR TO ÞÓRSMÖRK TREK

Laugahraun

Brennisteinsalda (840m)

Grænagil

Bláhnúkur (943m)

To Þórsmörk

0   0.5   1km

0   0.25   0.5mi

Frostastaðavatn   F208   To Reykjavík (198km)

See Enlargement

To Eldgjá (12km) & Kirkjubæjar-klaustur (80km)

Brennisteinsalda (840m)   ▲ Bláhnúkur (943m)

Kirkjufell   F208

Stórihver

Hrafntinnusker Hut

Jökultungur

Háskerðingur (1278m)

Torfajökull

Kaldaklofsfjöll

Álftaskarð

Torfahlaup

Bratthálskvísl

Álftavatn

Hvanngil Hut & Camp Site

Ford

Footbridge

Stóra Grænafell (850m)   Stórasúla (880m)

Kaldaklofskvísl

Bláfjallakvísl

Mælifellssandur   F210

Blessárjökull

Tindfjallajökull

Innri-Emstrua

Ford & Bridge

Mosar

SLÉTTJÖKULL

Markarfljótsgljúfur

Fremri-Emstrua

Botnar (Emstrur) Hut

Slyppagil

Markarfljót

Entujökull

Ljósá

0   5   10km

0   2.5   5mi

F261

Footbridge

Prongá

Húsadalur Hut

Ford

Sottarhellir

Valahnúkur (Þórsmörk Hut)

Þórsmörk   Krossá

MÝRDALSJÖKULL

4WD Tracks   Básar Hut

1   Hot Springs
2   Landmannalaugar Hut & Camp Site
3   Lava Field
4   Landmannalaugar-Þórsmörk Track
5   Steaming Vents & Fumaroles

The onward route on the opposite bank isn't obvious; look for a V-shaped ravine just west of the marked crossing point. There, the track enters the **Þórsmörk** woodland, studded with grassy birch and mushrooms. When you reach

a junction, the right fork leads to Austurleið's **Húsadalur hut** and the left fork to the Ferðafélag Íslands' **Þórsmörk hut**. Camping is restricted to sites near the huts. For more on Þórsmörk, see The South section earlier.

Norway

Norway (Norge) is a ruggedly beautiful country of high mountains, deep fjords and icy blue glaciers. The mainland stretches 2000km from beach towns in the south to treeless Arctic tundra in the north; 1000km further north, there's Svalbard, Norway's breathtaking high Arctic archipelago. The country offers incredible wilderness hiking, year-round skiing and some of the most scenic ferry, bus and train rides imaginable. Summer days are delightfully long, and in the northernmost parts the sun doesn't set for weeks on end.

In addition to the lure of the spectacular western fjords, Norway has pleasantly low-key cities, unspoiled fishing villages and rich historical sites with Viking ships and medieval stave churches.

Norway retains something of a frontier character and its largest cities are virtually surrounded by forest. There are also several extensive, virtually untouched national parks and other wilderness areas.

Facts about Norway

HISTORY
The first settlers to Norway arrived around 11,000 years ago with the end of the Ice Age. As the glaciers melted, the earliest hunters and gatherers moved in from Siberia, pursuing migrating reindeer herds. Shortly afterwards, nomadic European hunters arrived in the south of the country. During the Bronze Age, people migrated into southern Norway from Sweden and created rock carvings showing ships and various symbols.

Norway's greatest impact on history was during the Viking Age, a period usually dated from the plundering of England's Lindisfarne monastery by Nordic pirates in AD 793. Over the next century, the Vikings conducted raids throughout Europe and established settlements in the Shetland, Orkney and Hebridean islands, the Dublin area (Ireland), and in Normandy (the latter named after the 'North men'). The Viking leader, Harald Hårfagre (Fairhair), unified Norway after the decisive naval battle at Hafrsfjord near Stavanger in AD 872; King Olav Haraldsson, adopting the

At a Glance

Capital	Oslo
Population	4.5 million
Area	385,155 sq km
Official Language	Norwegian
GDP	US$166 billion (2001)
Time	GMT/UTC+0100
Country Phone Code	☎ 47

Highlights

- Travelling on the scenic Oslo–Bergen railway (p359)
- Exploring the wonderful streets and passageways of historic Bergen (p360)
- Viewing the astonishing fjords, especially Geirangerfjorden (p373)
- Enjoying the midnight sun beneath towering peaks in a Lofoten fishing village (p386)
- Visiting the easily accessed Arctic wonderland of Svalbard (p398)

religion of the lands he had conquered, converted the Norwegians to Christianity and founded the Church of Norway in 1024.

With their sleek ships, the Vikings were the first to cross the Atlantic Ocean, beginning in earnest with Erik the Red's visit to Greenland in AD 982. Shortly after, in AD 1000 (according to the sagas), Leif Eriksson,

NORWAY

ARCTIC OCEAN

BARENTS SEA

NORWEGIAN SEA

SVALBARD

Svalbard
Jan Mayen
NORWAY

Nordaustlandet

Ny Ålesund

Spitsbergen

Barentsøya

Longyearbyen
Barentsburg

Sveagruva

Edgeøya

To Jan Mayen

To Norway mainland

Approximate North Only

Nordkapp
Honningsvåg
Hammerfest
Tana Bru
Vardø
Vadsø
Kirkenes
Storskog
Alta
Finnmark
Karasjok
Finnmarksvidda
Kautokeino

RUSSIA

Fjordgard
Husøy
Mefjordvær
Skaland
Gryllefjord
Andenes
Stø
Nyksund
Harstad
Stokmarknes
Melbu
Sortland
Svolvær
Stamsund
Storjord
Skutvik
Kjerringøy
BODØ
Fauske
Sattstraumen
Nordland
Svartisen IceCap

Tromsø
Finnsnes
Troms
Narvik

Vesterålen
Lofoten
Vestfjorden

FINLAND

Arctic Circle

ATLANTIC OCEAN

Mo i Rana

Mosjøen

Nord Trøndelag

Steinkjer

TRONDHEIM
Hell
Sør Trøndelag
Røros

SWEDEN

Bottenhavet

See Western Fjords & Central Norway Map

ÅLESUND
Åndalsnes
Måløy
Nordfjord
Geiranger
Stryn
Dombås
Rondane
Balestrand
Lærdal
Jotunheimen
Galdhøpiggen (2469m)
Sognefjorden
Voss
Flåm
Geilo
Finse
E16
BERGEN
Hardangervidda
Odda
Rjukan
Håukeligrend
Haugesund
Telemark
Tau
STAVANGER
SKIEN
Sørlandet
Kragerø
Risør
Lillesand
Arendal
Mandal
Grimstad
KRISTIANSAND

Lillehammer
Hamar

Notodden
OSLO
Kongsberg
Moss
FREDRIKSTAD
Halden
Larvik

Bø

Skagerrak

STOCKHOLM

HELSINKI

TALLINN

ESTONIA

BALTIC SEA

Erik the Red's son, explored the coast of North America, parts of which he called Markland and Vinland.

The Viking Age went into decline after 1066, with the defeat of the Norwegian king, Harald Hardråda, at the Battle of Stamford Bridge in England. Norwegian naval power was finished off for good when Alexander III, King of Scots, defeated a Viking naval force at the Battle of Largs (Scotland) in 1263.

In the early 14th century, Oslo emerged as a centre of power and a period of prosperity and growth followed until 1349, when the bubonic plague swept the country, wiping out nearly two-thirds of the population. In 1380, Norway was absorbed into a union with Denmark that lasted over 400 years.

Denmark's ill-fated alliance with France in the Napoleonic Wars resulted in its ceding of Norway to Sweden in January 1814 under the Treaty of Kiel. Tired of forced unions, on 17 May 1814 a defiant Norway adopted its own constitution, though its struggle for independence was quickly quelled by a Swedish invasion. The Norwegians were allowed to keep their new constitution but were forced to accept the Swedish king.

In 1884 a parliamentary government was introduced in Norway and a growing nationalist movement eventually led to a peaceful secession from Sweden in 1905. In a referendum, Norwegians voted in favour of a monarchy over a republic. Having no royal family of its own, Norway's parliament selected Prince Carl of Denmark to be king. Upon acceptance, he took the title Håkon VII and named his infant son Olav, both prominent names from Norway's Viking past.

Norway stayed neutral during WWI. Despite restating its neutrality at the start of WWII, it was attacked by the Nazis on 9 April 1940, falling to the Germans after a two-month struggle. King Håkon set up a government in exile in England, and placed most of Norway's merchant fleet under the command of the Allies. Although Norway remained occupied until the end of the war, it had an active Resistance movement.

As part of one of the most renowned sabotage efforts of WWII, Norwegian Resistance fighters parachuted into the German heavy-water plant at Rjukan in southern Norway, blowing the plant sky-high and shattering Germany's attempts to develop an atomic bomb. During their retreat at the end of the war, the Nazis torched and levelled nearly every town and village in northern Norway.

The royal family returned to Norway in June 1945. King Håkon died in 1957 and was succeeded by his son, Olav V, a popular king who reigned until his death in January 1991. The current monarch is Harald V, Olav's son, who was crowned in June 1991.

Norway joined the European Free Trade Association (EFTA) in 1960, but has been reluctant to forge closer bonds with other European nations, in part due to concerns about the impact on its fishing industry and small-scale farming industry. In 1972, Norwegians voted against joining the European Community (EC) amid a divisive national debate. It took two decades for membership to once again become a high-profile issue. During 1994 a second national referendum was held, this time on joining the EC's successor, the European Union (EU), and voters rejected that as well. Sentiments continue to favour staying outside the EU.

GEOGRAPHY

Norway, occupying the western part of the Scandinavian peninsula, has a land area of 385,155 sq km and shares borders with Sweden, Finland and Russia. The country is long and narrow, with a coastline deeply cut by fjords – long, narrow inlets of the sea bordered by high, steep cliffs. Mountains, some capped with Europe's largest glaciers, cover more than half of the land mass. Only 3% of the country is arable.

With a combination of mountains and a wet climate, it's hardly surprising that Norway has many spectacular waterfalls, including several of the top 10 highest in the world (although the number varies according to the list you're looking at).

'The Land of the Midnight Sun' is more than just a promotional slogan: nearly a third of Norway lies north of the Arctic Circle, the point at which there is at least one full day when the sun never sets and one day when it never rises.

CLIMATE

The typically rainy climate of mainland Norway is surprisingly mild for its latitude – thanks to the Gulf Stream (a relatively warm ocean current originating in the Gulf of Mexico), all its coastal ports remain ice-free throughout the year.

NORWAY

NORWAY

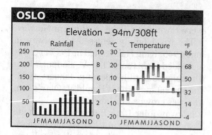

Average July temperatures are 16°C in the Oslo area and 11°C in the north. However, temperature extremes are also possible, even in the Arctic region. In winter, heavy snowfalls are common and make for superb skiing. In January, the average maximum temperature is 1°C in the south and -3°C in the north. However, it can get much colder, especially in areas away from the coast.

Climate details and weather forecasts can be found at **w** www.dnmi.no.

ECOLOGY & ENVIRONMENT

In Norway industrial waste is highly regulated, recycling is popular, there's little rubbish along the roadsides and general tidiness is a high priority in both urban and rural environments. Plastic bottles and cans may be exchanged for cash at supermarkets. On the other hand, loss of habitat has placed around 900 species of plants and animals on the endangered or threatened species lists; sport hunting and fishing are more popular here than in most of Europe; hydroelectric schemes have devastated some mountain landscapes and waterfalls; and the past sin of over-fishing has come back to haunt the economy.

In 1993 Norway resumed commercial hunting of minke whales in open defiance of an international whaling ban. Norway supports the protection of other threatened species, but the government contends that the estimated 70,000 to 186,000 North Atlantic minke whales can sustain a limited harvest. Despite strong resistance by Greenpeace, the international response has been quite limited. Norwegian whalers killed 487 minke whales in 2000, down from 625 in 1998.

FLORA & FAUNA

Flora varies with location, but pine, spruce and other conifers grow throughout the country, except in Svalbard, parts of Finnmark, and exposed offshore islands; deciduous trees,

including oak, maple and ash, grow in the relatively mild coastal regions in the south.

Norway has wild and semi-domesticated reindeer herds, thriving elk populations and a scattering of lynx, musk oxen, bears and wolverines. Lemmings occupy mountain areas through 30% of the country. Since the ban on hunting came into force in 1973, polar bear numbers have increased to over 5000, although they're only found in Svalbard; polar bears usually eat seals but have been known to kill and eat humans (Arctic travellers – take note). Walruses are rare and are confined to Svalbard, but several species of seal, dolphin and whale (especially minke whales) may be seen around most western and northern coasts.

Bird life is prolific in coastal areas and puffins, fulmars and kittiwakes are commonly seen. Rarer species include ospreys, golden eagles and magnificent white-tailed sea eagles.

Norway has 21 relatively low-key national parks, which are really designed to prevent development of wild areas rather than encourage large numbers of visitors.

GOVERNMENT & POLITICS

Norway is officially a constitutional monarchy under King Harald V and Queen Sonja, but it also enjoys a parliamentary democratic form of government. General elections are held every four years for the 165 seats in parliament (Storting); the Labour Party, with 43 seats, is the largest of the six major parties represented in parliament. However, in the 2001 election Labour was voted out of office and Kjell Magne Bondevik of the Christian Democrats took the helm as Prime Minister, leading a right-of-centre coalition of Christian Democrats, Conservatives and Liberals.

Until recently, Norway's politics had few extremes; the Conservative Party is quite moderate by European standards, but the far-right-wing Progress Party and the far-left Socialist Left Party gained considerable support in the 2001 election.

ECONOMY

North Sea oil fields, discovered on the Norwegian continental shelf in the 1960s, have brought prosperity to Norway, which has one of the world's highest per capita incomes. In 2001, the Norwegian GDP was US$166 billion or US$36,700 per capita.

Fishing, fish farming and shipping are traditional mainstays of the economy: Norway is the tenth-largest fishing nation in the world and fish products are the second-largest net export earner. Abundant hydroelectric power provides the basis for a number of industries, including aluminium, steel and paper production. Tourism is also significant.

Norway has a comprehensive cradle-to-grave social-welfare system, funded by high levels of taxation: all citizens are entitled to free university education and free hospital treatment, as well as a guaranteed pension.

In January 2002, the 'official' inflation rate was 1.3%. The unemployment rate was 3.3% in the last quarter of 2001.

POPULATION & PEOPLE

Norway has 4,524,000 people and one of the lowest population densities in Europe. The majority of modern Norwegians are middle class and life expectancies are high, being 76 years for men and 81.4 years for women. Immigration is strictly controlled and only bona fide refugees are admitted. The largest cities are Oslo with 508,726 residents, Bergen with 230,829, Trondheim with 135,879 and Stavanger with 106,000.

Most Norwegians are of Nordic origin, and are thought to have descended from central and northern European tribes who migrated northwards around 8000 years ago. In addition, there are about 40,000 Sami (formerly known as Lapps), who are the indigenous people of the far north of Norway and now make up the country's largest ethnic minority. Some Sami still live a traditional nomadic life, herding reindeer in Finnmark.

ARTS

Norway's best-known artists include the moody painter Edvard Munch (whose work *The Scream* is internationally renowned), the superb landscape painter JC Dahl, classical composer Edvard Grieg, sculptor Gustav Vigeland and famed playwright Henrik Ibsen, whose works include the classic *A Doll's House*.

Classical music and jazz are very popular in Norway and there are annual music festivals around the country, the most significant being in Bergen, Molde and Kongsberg. For details of music festivals, visit W www.norwayfestivals .com or contact the Norwegian Tourist Board.

Although not so well known today, the writer Bjørnstjerne Bjørnson was popular in the second half of the 19th century for his descriptions of contemporary Norwegian rural life and social problems. In 1903, he was the first Norwegian writer to be awarded the Nobel Prize in Literature.

Norwegians Sigrid Undset and Knud Hamsun won the Nobel Prize for Literature in 1928 and 1920, respectively. Undset is best known for *Kristin Lavransdottir*, a trilogy portraying the struggles and earthy lifestyle of a 14th-century Norwegian family, while Hamsun won the Nobel Prize for his 1917 novel *The Growth of the Soil*. However, many Norwegians remember Hamsun most for his collaboration with the Nazis during WWII and subsequent imprisonment as a traitor.

In the field of architecture, Norway's unique stave churches are some of the oldest wooden buildings on Earth, having one foot in the Viking Age and the other in the 11th-century early-Christian era. The stave churches, named for their vertical supporting posts, are distinguished by dragon-headed gables that resemble the ornately carved prows of Viking ships and by their undeniably beautiful, almost Oriental forms. However, of the 500 to 600 originally built, only about 20 of those remaining retain many original components.

Other significant architectural features in the country include the Norwegian 'dragon style', reflected in some historic wooden hotels, and the Art Nouveau style, best observed in Ålesund in western Norway.

SOCIETY & CONDUCT

Norwegians tend to be independent and outdoor-oriented: on summer weekends hiking, fishing and boating are popular, while in winter Norwegians head for the ski runs. 'No trespassing' signs are virtually unknown and public access to wilderness areas is guaranteed.

Norway holds on to many of its cultural traditions. The wearing of the *bunad*, an elaborate folk costume with regional variations, is still commonplace at weddings and other festive events. Interest in traditional folk music, dancing and singing has experienced a resurgence and visitors can enjoy these activities at festivals around the country.

Storytelling is another centuries-old tradition, with trolls figuring prominently in Norwegian folklore and forming the basis for the fireside storytelling custom that helped pass the dark winter months. Trolls are especially associated with mountainous areas, and while

NORWAY

NORWAY

some could be befriended, others were pesky creatures who lived in the ground under houses and barns, serving as a convenient source of blame for all of life's woes. Trolls live on in Norway's place names, as mascots and carved figurines, and as the subjects of scores of folk tales.

Although most Norwegians are straightforward and easy-going, as a guest in a Norwegian home, remove your shoes at the front door and don't touch your drink before your host makes the toast 'skål' (which you should return).

RELIGION

Around 86% of Norwegians belong to the Church of Norway, a Protestant Evangelical Lutheran denomination, but most Norwegians only attend church twice a year. The Humanist & Ethical Union has around 68,000 members and there are a number of smaller Christian denominations, as well as around 50,000 Muslims and 1000 Jews.

Facts for the Visitor

SUGGESTED ITINERARIES

Depending on the length of your stay you might wish to see and do the following:

Two days
Visit Bergen, then travel by rail to Flåm and take a combination boat/bus trip back to Bergen allowing you to see some fjords
One week
Spend two days in Oslo, two days in Bergen and go on a three-day jaunt through the western fjords, including Fjærland and Geiranger
Two weeks
As for one week, then continue north through Åndalsnes, Trondheim and Lofoten
One month
As for two weeks, plus a coastal steamer cruise from Lofoten to Kirkenes, breaking the trip at Tromsø and Nordkapp; or fly from Tromsø to Longyearbyen in Svalbard and take a cruise up the west coast of Spitsbergen
Two months
Explore the country thoroughly and spend some time skiing or hiking in Jotunheimen, Hardangervidda or the far north

PLANNING
When to Go

Due to the warming effects of the Gulf Stream flowing north along the Norwegian coast, the coastal areas have a surprisingly temperate climate. The average winter monthly temperature in Bergen never drops below 0°C, and in Vardø in the far north, the average temperature in December is only -4°C. Mountainous inland areas have a more extreme climate, and temperatures over 30°C in summer and lower than -30°C in winter aren't uncommon. Svalbard has an Arctic climate, with an average July maximum of 6°C in Longyearbyen and January minimums often below -30°C.

Norway is at its best and brightest from May to September. Late spring is a particularly pleasant time: fruit trees are in bloom, daylight hours are long and most hostels and sights are open but uncrowded.

Midnight-sun days, when the sun never drops below the horizon, extend from 20 April to 21 August at Longyearbyen (Svalbard), 13 May to 29 July at Nordkapp and from 28 May to 14 July in Lofoten. Even southern Norway has full daylight from 4am to 11pm in midsummer.

Unless you're heavily into winter skiing or searching for the aurora borealis of the polar nights, Norway's cold dark winters are not the prime time to visit.

Maps

The best road maps are the Cappelens series, sold in Norwegian bookshops for Nkr95. The *Veiatlas Norge* (Norwegian Road Atlas), published by Statens Kartverk (the national mapping agency), is revised every two years (Nkr220). Most local tourist offices distribute free town plans, and topographical hiking maps can be purchased from local bookshops and DNT, which has offices throughout Norway. For more information see Hiking under Activities later, and the Maps section in the Facts for the Visitor chapter.

What to Bring

Norwegians are quite casual and most travellers are unlikely to need dressy clothes. As the weather can change quickly it's best to bring layers that can be added and taken off as needed.

Even in summer you won't regret having a jacket for windy fjord cruises and the high country. Good walking shoes are important and you should bring hiking boots if you plan to hike. Budget travellers shouldn't be without a tent, a sleeping sheet (for hostels) and a warm sleeping bag (when camping). Consider bringing snacks such as trail mix, peanut butter and instant coffee to save money. Hostellers will save money by bringing their own sheets, as linen hire adds Nkr40 to Nkr50 to the bill.

TOURIST OFFICES
Local Tourist Offices
There are tourist offices in nearly every town in Norway, usually near the train station, dock or town centre. In smaller towns they may be open only during peak summer months, while in cities they're open year-round.

For general brochures and books on travel in Norway, contact **Norges Turistråd** (*Norwegian Tourist Board, formerly NORTRA; ☎ 24 14 46 00, fax 24 14 46 01; W www.visitnorway .com; PO Box 722 Sentrum, N-0105 Oslo*).

Tourist Offices Abroad
Australia (☎ 6273 3444, e emb.canberra@mfa .no) Royal Norwegian Embassy, 17 Hunter St, Yarralumla, ACT 2600

Denmark (☎ 33 19 36 09, e denmark@ntr.no) Norges Turistråd, Amaliegade 39, DK-1256 Copenhagen K

France (☎ 53 23 00 50, e france@ntr.no) Office National du Tourisme de Norvége, PB 47, F-75366 Paris

Germany (☎ 0180-500 1548, e germany@ntr .no) Norwegisches Fremdenverkehrsamt, Postfach 113317, D-20433 Hamburg

Sweden (☎ 791 8300, e sweden@ntr.no) Norges Turistråd, PO Box 3363, SE-10367 Stockholm

UK (☎ 0906 302 2003, e greatbritain@ntr.no) Norwegian Tourist Board, 5th Floor, Charles House, 5 Lower Regent St, London, SW1Y 4LR (no personal callers)

USA & Canada (☎ 885 9700, e usa@ntr.no) Norwegian Tourist Board, 655 Third Ave, Suite 1810, New York, NY 10017

VISAS & DOCUMENTS
Citizens of the USA, Canada, the UK, Ireland, Australia and New Zealand need a valid passport to visit Norway, but do not need a visa for stays of less than three months. The same is true for EU and European Economic Area (EEA – essentially EU and Scandinavia) countries, most of Latin America and most Commonwealth countries (except South Africa and several other African and Pacific countries).

Motorists should bring their driving licence and vehicle registration documents. The HI (Hostelling International) card saves Nkr25 per night in hostels; students with an International Student Identity Card (ISIC) or International Youth Travel Card (IYTC) can

get discounts on transport, museum admission and meals in some student restaurants. Seniors (usually those 67 years and older) and children (under 16 years) with proof of age can get similar discounts.

EMBASSIES & CONSULATES
Norwegian Embassies
There's an up-to-date listing of Norwegian embassies and consulates at W www.embassies .mfa.no.

Australia (☎6273 3444, e emb.canberra@mfa .no) 17 Hunter St, Yarralumla, ACT 2600

Canada (☎ 238 6571, e emb.ottawa@mfa.no) Royal Bank Centre, 90 Sparks St, Suite 532, Ottawa, Ontario K1P 5B4

Denmark (☎ 33 14 01 24, e emb.copenhagen@ mfa.no) Amaliegade 39, DK-1256 Copenhagen K

Finland (☎ 171234, e emb.helsinki@mfa.no) Rehbinderintie 17, FIN-00150 Helsinki

France (☎ 53 67 04 00, e emb.paris@mfa.no) 28 Rue Bayard, F-75008 Paris

Germany (☎ 505050, e emb.berlin@mfa.no) Rauchstrasse 1, D-10787 Berlin

Ireland (☎ 662 1800, e emb.dublin@mfa.no) 34 Molesworth St, Dublin 2

Sweden (☎ 665 6340, e emb.stockholm@mfa .no) Skarpögatan 4, SE-11593 Stockholm

UK (☎ 7591 5500, e emb.london@mfa.no) 25 Belgrave Square, London, SW1X 8QD

USA (☎ 333 6000, e emb.washington@mfa.no) 2720 34th St NW, Washington DC 20008

Embassies & Consulates in Norway
Australia (☎ 22 47 91 70) Jernbanetorget 2, N-0106 Oslo

Canada (☎ 22 99 53 00) Wergelandsveien 7, N-0167 Oslo

Denmark (☎ 22 54 08 00) Olav Kyrres gate 7, N-0273 Oslo

Finland (☎ 22 43 04 00) Thomas Heftyes gate 1, N-0264 Oslo

France (☎ 23 28 46 00) Drammensveien 69, N-0271 Oslo

Germany (☎ 22 27 54 00) Oscars gate 45, N-0258 Oslo

Ireland (☎ 22 01 72 00) Haakon VIIs gate 1, N-0244 Oslo

New Zealand (☎ 66 77 53 30) Billingstadsletta 19B, Postboks 113, N-1376 Billingstad

Russia (☎ 22 55 32 78) Drammensveien 74, N-0271 Oslo

Sweden (☎ 24 11 42 00) Nobelsgata 16A, N-0244 Oslo

UK (☎ 23 13 27 00, e britemb@online.no) Thomas Heftyes gate 8, N-0264 Oslo

USA (☎ 22 44 85 50), Drammensveien 18, N-0255 Oslo

CUSTOMS

Alcohol is expensive in Norway, so you might want to seize your duty-free opportunity: 1L of spirits and 1L of wine (or 2L of wine), plus 2L of beer. European (EEA)/non-European residents may also import 200/400 cigarettes duty-free.

Importation of fresh food and controlled drugs is prohibited.

MONEY
Currency

The Norwegian krone is most often written NOK in international money markets, Nkr in northern Europe and kr within Norway.

One Norwegian krone equals 100 øre. Coins come in denominations of 50 øre and one, five, 10 and 20 kroner, and bills in denominations of 50, 100, 200, 500 and 1000 kroner.

Exchange Rates

The following exchange rates prevailed at the time of printing:

country	unit		kroner
Australia	A$1	=	4Nkr
Canada	C$1	=	5Nkr
Denmark	Dkr10	=	11Nkr
euro	€1	=	7Nkr
Iceland	Ikr10	=	1Nkr
Japan	¥100	=	6Nkr
New Zealand	NZ$1	=	4Nkr
Sweden	Skr10	=	8Nkr
UK	UK£1	=	12Nkr
USA	US$1	=	8Nkr

Exchanging Money

Some post offices and all banks will exchange major foreign currencies and accept all travellers cheques, which command a better exchange rate than cash (by about 2%).

Post offices charge a service fee of Nkr10 per travellers cheque (minimum Nkr20, maximum Nkr100), and Nkr30 for cash transactions of any size. Some banks, including Nordea and Den Norske Bank, have slightly higher fees but similar exchange rates. Other banks tend to charge steeper travellers cheque commissions, which means you're better off with higher denomination cheques.

ATMs & Credit Cards Those with plastic can get cash any time at ATMs (adjacent to many banks and at busy public places such as shopping centres); most accept major credit cards, and Cirrus and Plus bank cards.

Visa, Eurocard, MasterCard, American Express and Diners Club cards are widely accepted throughout Norway – generally you'll be better off using a credit card as you avoid the hefty fees involved in exchanging money. Credit cards can be used to buy train tickets but are not accepted on domestic ferries, apart from the *Hurtigruten* coastal steamer.

Costs

Norway can be very expensive, but if you tighten your belt there are ways to take out some of the sting.

If you only stay in camping grounds and prepare your own meals, you might squeak by on Nkr180 a day. If you plan to stay at hostels, breakfast at a bakery, lunch at an inexpensive restaurant and shop at a grocery store for dinner, you should be able to get by for Nkr300 a day. If you stay at 'cheap' hotels that include a buffet breakfast and have one meal at a moderately priced restaurant, eating a snack for the other meal, expect to spend Nkr500 a day if doubling up and Nkr700 if travelling alone. This is still barebones budgeting, and doesn't include day trips, entertainment, alcohol and soft drinks.

Once your daily needs are met, you'll need to add transport costs – if you have a rail pass these will be low. Trying to cover the whole country by bus and ferry can be quite expensive because the distances are so great.

Admission to museums is rarely free, but seldom more than Nkr70 – students who flash their ID usually get a discount.

Tipping & Bargaining

Service charges and tips are included in restaurant bills and taxi fares, with no additional tip expected. As for bargaining, it's as rare in Norway as bargains themselves.

Taxes & Refunds

The 24% MVA (the equivalent of Value-Added Tax in many countries; sales tax in the USA), locally known as MOMS, is normally included in marked prices for goods and services, including meals and accommodation. One exception is car rental, where quoted rates may or may not include MVA.

At shops marked 'Tax Free for Tourists', goods exceeding Nkr308 in value are eligible for an MVA refund, less a service charge (10% to 17% of the purchase price). Ask the shop for a 'Tax-Free Shopping Cheque', which should be presented along with your purchases at your departure point from the country (ferry passengers normally collect their refund from the purser during limited hours once the boat has sailed).

POST & COMMUNICATIONS
Post
In most towns, post offices are open from 9am to 4pm (or 5pm) Monday to Friday and 10am to 2pm Saturday. Postal rates are high and continue to soar: cards and letters weighing up to 20g cost Nkr5.50 within Norway, Nkr7 to other Nordic countries, Nkr9 to elsewhere in Europe and Nkr10 to the rest of the world. Mail can be received c/o poste restante at almost all post offices in Norway.

Telephone & Fax
Norway has no telephone area codes; when making any domestic call all eight digits must be dialled.

Most pay phones accept Nkr1, Nkr5, Nkr10 and Nkr20 coins and will return unused coins but won't give change. The minimum charge for domestic and international calls is Nkr5. Domestic calls get 33% discount between 5pm and 8am weekdays, and on weekends (from 5pm Friday to 8am Monday). Directory assistance (☎ 180) costs Nkr8 per minute. So-called 'free' calls with ☎ 800 prefixes are charged for at cardphones and in hotels.

Telekort (phonecards) are sold in Nkr40, Nkr90, Nkr140 and Nkr210 denominations and work out cheaper than using coins. Cards can be purchased at post offices and the ubiquitous Narvesen and MIX kiosks. Credit cards can also be used in many card phones.

The country code for calling Norway from abroad is ☎ 47. To make an international call from Norway, dial ☎ 00, then the appropriate country code, area code and number you're calling. A three-minute call to the USA costs Nkr12 using the Nkr140 phonecard.

GSM mobile telephone networks cover 80% of populated areas in Norway. There are two service providers, **Telenor Mobil** (☎ 22 78 50 00) and **NetCom** (☎ 22 88 82 00). However, ask your home network for advice before taking your mobile phone abroad. Mobile phone rental isn't possible in Norway but you could buy one from any Telehuset shop (from around Nkr300, including charge card) and sell it before departure.

Faxes can be sent or received from most post offices or hotels.

Email & Internet Access
Many public libraries have online computers, but access for travellers may be restricted. Internet access at public libraries is generally free, but there are usually long queues of locals waiting to get online. Librarians may insist that the computers are available only to local residents and many places require advance booking.

Internet cafés are found in the larger cities and some large hotels have expensive credit-card-accessible Internet computers in their lobbies.

For laptop users, **AOL** (W *www.aol.com*) and **Compuserve** (W *www.compuserve.com*) share two ISDN modem access numbers in Norway: ☎ 73 50 38 00, with a baud rate of 57.6 bits per second and a US$6 surcharge per connection, and ☎ 23 35 83 00, which transfers at 9.6 bits per second but only carries a US$2.50 surcharge per connection.

DIGITAL RESOURCES
General and tourism-related information about Norway can be accessed at W www.visitnorway.com. The most useful tourist-oriented website for western Norway is W www.fjordnorway.com. For tour suggestions, attractions and accommodation throughout the country, check out W www.touristguide.no. Travel, shopping, genealogy and more can be found at W www.norway.com.

The Norwegian government website, W www.odin.dep.no, covers general information and governmental issues, as well as daily news updates.

The helpful Norwegian *Yellow Pages* list almost every business in Norway at W www.gulesider.no.

BOOKS
For extensive travel in the country, the best all-round guide is Lonely Planet's *Norway*. To help with communication, pick up Lonely Planet's *Scandinavian phrasebook*, which includes a section on Norwegian.

Erling Welle-Strand's concise *Motoring in Norway* and the flashier *Adventure Roads in Norway* both describe many of Norway's most scenic driving routes. In *Mountain Hiking in Norway*, Welle-Strand details wilderness trail information, including hiking itineraries, sketch maps and details on huts. *Norwegian Mountains on Foot*, by the Norwegian Mountain Touring Association (DNT), is similar and easier to obtain.

Highlights of Norway, by Gro Stangeland et al, is a superb coffee-table publication that describes some of Norway's finest attractions. An amusing cultural direction is offered in *Culture Shock! Norway: A Guide to Customs & Etiquette* by Elizabeth Su-Dale.

James Graham-Campbell's *The Viking World* traces the history of the Vikings by detailing excavated Viking sites and artefacts. If you're interested in Norse mythology and folk tales, look for *Gods & Myths of Northern Europe* by HR Ellis Davidson, and the colourful *Norwegian Folk Tales – from the collection of Peter Christen Asbjørnsen and Jørgen Moe.*

NEWSPAPERS & MAGAZINES

Domestic newspapers, such as Oslo's *Aftenposten* and Bergen's *Bergens Tidende*, are available nationwide, but they're published only in Norwegian. Foreign newspapers, like The *Guardian, International Herald Tribune* and *USA Today*, can be found, along with English-language magazines, at major transport terminals and large city newsstands.

RADIO & TV

Although most TV broadcasts are in Norwegian, a fair amount of US and British programs are presented in English with Norwegian subtitles. Hotels with cable TV often have CNN and English-language movie and sports channels. The BBC World Service broadcasts to Norway on 9410kHz.

PHOTOGRAPHY & VIDEO

Although print and slide film is readily available in major cities, prices are high. A 24/36-exposure roll of Fuji Superia costs around Nkr45/55, plus Nkr99/119 to process. A 36-exposure Fujichrome Sensia/Velvia slide film costs Nkr49/75.

TIME

Time in Norway is one hour ahead of GMT/UTC, the same as Sweden, Denmark and most of Western Europe. When it's noon in Norway, it's 11am in London, 1pm in Finland, 6am in New York and Toronto, 3am in San Francisco, 9pm in Sydney and 11pm in Auckland.

Norway observes daylight-saving time, with clocks set ahead one hour on the last Sunday in March and back an hour on the last Sunday in October. Timetables and business hours are posted according to the 24-hour clock.

When telling the time, Norwegians use 'half' to mean half before rather than half past: if a Norwegian tells you it's 'half two', the time will be 1.30.

LAUNDRY

Myntvaskeri (coin laundries) are expensive and extremely rare, although washers and dryers can often be found at hostels and camping grounds. It's a good idea to bring a little soap and plan on doing some washing by hand.

TOILETS

Toilets are Western style and not hard to find. Some places, such as train stations, charge Nkr5.

HEALTH

Norway is a very healthy place and no special precautions are necessary when visiting. The biggest risks are likely to be viral infections in winter, sunburn and insect bites in summer, and foot blisters from too much hiking.

For a medical emergency dial ☎ 113, or visit a local pharmacy or medical centre if you have a minor medical problem and can explain what it is. Hospital casualty wards will help if the problem is more serious. Nearly all health professionals in Norway speak English; tourist offices and hotels can make recommendations.

WOMEN TRAVELLERS

Norway is a relatively safe country for women travellers. The main Norwegian women's organisation is **Kvinnefronten** (☎ 22 37 60 54; e *kvinnefronten@online.no; Holsts gate 1, N-0473 Oslo*). Women who have been attacked or abused can call the **Krisesenter** (*in Oslo* ☎ 22 37 47 00, *nationwide* ☎ 112).

GAY & LESBIAN TRAVELLERS

Norwegians are generally tolerant of different lifestyles, but public displays of same-sex affection are not common practice. Gay and lesbian travellers can find gay entertainment spots in the larger cities. For gay issues and activities, contact **Landsforeningen for Lesbisk og Homofil frigjøring** (*LLH*; ☎ 22 36 19 48; e *llh@c2i.net; St Olavs plass 2, N-0165 Oslo*).

DISABLED TRAVELLERS

Norway can be a challenging destination for disabled travellers, and those with special needs should plan ahead. The Norwegian Tourist Board's main accommodation brochure and the hostel association's handbook both list nationwide accommodation that is wheelchair accessible. Most, but not all, trains have coaches designed for wheelchair users. **Norges Handikapforbund** (☎ 22 17 02 55; W www.nhf.no; Schweigaards gate 12, Postboks 9217 Grønland, N-0134 Oslo) publishes a brochure in English with information for disabled travellers – copies may be available at tourist offices.

SENIOR TRAVELLERS

Seniors (qualifying age varies from 60 to 67 years) are often entitled to discounts on museum admissions, air tickets and other transport. A few hotels offer discounts for seniors – inquire whenever you make a reservation. See Train in the Getting Around the Region chapter for information on the ScanRail Senior pass.

TRAVEL WITH CHILDREN

Many towns have attractions and sections of museums specifically aimed at the youngsters – one of the finest is the Dyrepark in Kristiansand, which offers an open-air zoo, pirate-ship battles, and family accommodation in the fantasy town of Kardamomme By.

Most attractions admit children up to about six years of age for free and admission for those up to 16 or so is half-price (or substantially discounted).

Family tickets are occasionally available. Hotels, HI hostels, camping sites and other accommodation options often have 'family rooms' or cabins for up to two adults and two children.

In hotels, this may cost little more than the price of a regular double.

DANGERS & ANNOYANCES

Sadly, Norway is no longer as safe as it was and robbery is becoming more common; watch your wallet at all times, especially at night. Svalbard presents some particular dangers: in the land of the hungry polar bear you must *never* venture from the immediate vicinity of Longyearbyen without a loaded rifle. Otherwise, you run a very real risk of being eaten.

BUSINESS HOURS

Business hours are generally 9am or 10am to 4pm or 5pm Monday to Friday and 10am to 2pm Saturday, although some shops stay open to around 7pm or 8pm on Thursday.

Be aware that many museums have short hours (11am to 3pm is quite common), which can make things tight for sightseeing.

On Sunday most stores – including bakeries and supermarkets, and some restaurants – are closed. Throughout this chapter, 'summer' generally refers to the months of May to September, while 'winter' refers to the remaining months.

PUBLIC HOLIDAYS & SPECIAL EVENTS

The following public holidays are observed in Norway:

New Year's Day 1 January
Maundy Thursday Thursday before Easter
Good Friday March/April
Easter Monday March/April
Labour Day 1 May
Constitution Day 17 May
Ascension Day The 40th day after Easter
Whit Monday The eighth Monday after Easter
Christmas Day 25 December
Boxing Day 26 December

Constitution Day, 17 May, is Norway's biggest holiday, with events throughout the country and many Norwegians taking to the street in traditional folk costumes. The biggest celebration is in Oslo, where marching bands and thousands of schoolchildren parade down Karl Johans gate to Det Kongelige Slott (the Royal Palace) to be greeted by the royal family.

Midsummer's Eve, celebrated by bonfires on the beach, is generally observed on 23 June, St Hans day. The Sami (Lapps) hold their most colourful celebrations at Easter in Karasjok and Kautokeino, with reindeer races, *joik* (traditional chanting) concerts and other festivities.

NORWAY

On 13 December, Christian children celebrate the feast of Santa Lucia by dressing in white and holding a candlelit procession.

ACTIVITIES
Hiking
Norway has some of northern Europe's best hiking, ranging from easy trails in the forests around the cities to long treks through the mountains. Due to deep winter snows, hiking in many areas is seasonal; in the highlands, it's often limited to the period of late June to September. The most popular wilderness hiking areas are Jotunheimen, Rondane and Hardangervidda, but many other areas are just as attractive (or even more so). There are also organised glacier hikes in Briksdal and on Nigardsbreen; Åndalsnes and Lofoten are the main centres for mountain climbing. For more information on hiking and climbing, contact the Norwegian Mountain Touring Association, **Den Norske Turistforening** (DNT; ☎ 22 82 28 22; W www.turistforeningen.no; Postboks 7 Sentrum, N-0101 Oslo).

Skiing
'Ski' is a Norwegian word and Norway makes a credible claim to having invented the sport. It's no exaggeration to say that it's the national winter pastime and you're seldom far from a ski run: Norway has thousands of kilometres of maintained cross-country (nordic) ski trails and scores of resorts with excellent downhill runs. The Holmenkollen area near Oslo, Geilo, on the Oslo–Bergen railway line, and Lillehammer and the surrounding Gudbrandsdalen region are just a few of the more popular spots. If you're a summer skier, head for the glaciers near Finse, Stryn or Jotunheimen. DNT is a good source for information about skiing throughout Norway.

Rafting
Norway's wild and scenic rivers are ideal for rafting, with trips ranging from short Class II doddles to Class III and IV adventures and rollicking Class V punishment. **Norges Padleforbund** (☎ 21 02 98 35; W www.padling.no; Service boks 1, Ullevål stadion, N-0840 Oslo) provides a comprehensive list of rafting operators.

Fishing
Norway's salmon runs are legendary – in June and July, you can't beat the rivers of Finnmark. No licence is required for saltwater fishing. In fresh water, a national licence (available from post offices for Nkr90 to Nkr180) is mandatory and often a local licence (available from tourist offices, sports shops, hotels and camping grounds for Nkr50 to Nkr300 per day) will also be required.

WORK
Norway has a relatively low unemployment rate, so foreigners can sometimes land a job, particularly in the poorly paid areas of hospitality and cleaning – you generally need to speak Norwegian and preference is typically given to Scandinavians.

As a member of the EEA, Norway grants citizens of other EEA countries the right to look for work for three months without obtaining a permit. Those who find work have the right to remain in Norway for the duration of their employment.

Other foreigners must apply for a work permit through the Norwegian embassy or consulate in their home country before entering Norway. Such work permits are rare and mainly granted in cases where highly skilled workers are in demand in a specialised occupation.

ACCOMMODATION
Camping & Cabins
Norway has around 1000 camping grounds. Tent space costs from Nkr50 at the most basic sites to Nkr180 in Oslo and Bergen, and many camping grounds also rent simple cabins from about Nkr250 a day. The cabins often have basic cooking facilities, though linen and blankets are rarely provided, so you'll need your own sleeping bag. **Reiselivsbedriftenes Landsforening** (☎ 23 08 86 20; e britt.larsen@rbl.no; Postboks 5465 Majorstua, N-0305 Oslo) publishes a free annual camping guide that lists many camping grounds.

Norway has an *allemannsretten* (Right of Common Access) dating back around 1000 years. This allows you to pitch a tent anywhere in the wilderness for two nights, as long as you camp at least 150m from the nearest house or cottage and leave no trace of your stay. From 15 April to 15 September lighting a fire in the proximity of woodlands is strictly forbidden.

DNT maintains an extensive network of mountain huts, a day's hike apart, in much of

Norway's mountain country, ranging from unstaffed huts with just a few beds to large, staffed lodges with more than 100 beds and generally superb service. At unstaffed huts, keys must be picked up in advance at DNT offices in nearby towns; at staffed huts hikers simply show up – no-one is turned away, even if there's only floor space left. For DNT members/nonmembers, nightly fees n a room with one to three beds is Nkr170/220, but cheaper options may be available. Basic membership for one calendar year will set you back Nkr365/175 for adult/concession.

Novasol (in Oslo ☎ 815 44 270, in Denmark ☎ 45-73 75 66 11; Ⓦ www.novasol .com; Postboks 309 Sentrum, N-0103 Oslo) publishes an English-language photo catalogue describing nearly 2000 self-catering cabins and chalets throughout Norway. Prices for a week's rental start from around Nkr1000 for a simple place in the low season to about Nkr13,000 for the most elaborate in midsummer. Most cabins sleep at least four people, some as many as 12.

Hostels

Norway has 72 *vandrerhjem* (hostels) affiliated with Hostelling International (HI). Some are quite comfortable lodge-style facilities, open year-round, while others operate out of school dorms in summer only. Most have two to six beds per room. The cost for a dorm bed varies from Nkr90 to Nkr250 per person, with breakfast generally included at the higher-priced hostels. Most hostels also have single, double and family rooms at higher prices. Guests must bring their own sleeping sheet and pillowcase, although most hostels hire sleeping sheets for Nkr40 to Nkr60 for as long as your stay. From May to September it's best to call ahead and make reservations, particularly for popular destinations.

Prices given throughout this chapter are for hostel members with an HI card; non-members pay Nkr25 extra per night.

Hostels that don't provide breakfast in their rate usually offer a buffet-style breakfast for an additional Nkr40 to Nkr70. Some also offer dinner for around Nkr70 to Nkr130 and nearly all hostels have kitchens where guests can cook their own meals.

You can pick up a brochure in English listing all hostels from tourist offices, or get the detailed *Opplev Norge med Norske Vandrerhjem* (free at hostels).

The Norwegian Hostelling Association is **Norske Vandrerhjem** (☎ 23 13 93 00, fax 23 13 93 50; Ⓦ www.vandrerhjem.no; Torggata 1, N-0181 Oslo). You can book hostels via the website.

Private Rooms & Pensions

Private rooms, usually bookable through tourist offices, average Nkr225/350 for singles/doubles and breakfast isn't normally included. Many towns also have pensions and guesthouses with singles in the Nkr270 to Nkr400 range, but linen and/or breakfast will only be included at the higher-priced places. A couple of useful listings can be found at Ⓦ www.bbnorway.com and Ⓦ www.bedandbr eakfast.no.

Along highways, you may see *Rom* signs, indicating informal accommodation for around Nkr100 to Nkr250 (without breakfast).

Hotels

Although normal hotel prices are high, most hotels substantially reduce their rates on Saturday and Sunday and in the summer season, slow periods for business travel. Nationwide chains like Rainbow Hotels and Rica offer particularly good summer and weekend deals. With Rainbow, you'll get the lowest rates by buying a Scan+ Hotel Pass (sold at hotels for Nkr90) – it usually pays for itself on the first night. Doubles start at Nkr295 per person.

One important consideration in this land of sky-high food prices is that hotels usually include an all-you-can-eat buffet breakfast, while most pensions do not.

The Norwegian Tourist Board's annually updated accommodation brochure lists most of the country's hotels and is available free on request.

FOOD

Food prices can be a real shock. To keep within a budget, expect to frequent supermarkets and bakeries. Some supermarkets have a reasonably priced deli where you can pick up salads sold by weight, or a roast chicken for as little as Nkr30.

Common throughout all of Norway is the *konditori*, a bakery with a few tables where you can sit and enjoy pastries and a relatively inexpensive sandwich. Other moderately cheap eats are found at *gatekjøkken* (food wagons and streetside kiosks), which generally have hot dogs for about Nkr20 and

NORWAY

hamburgers for Nkr40. Only marginally more expensive, but with more nutritionally balanced food, are *kafeterias*, with simple meals from about Nkr50. Main courses at moderately priced restaurants typically cost from Nkr80 to Nkr120, and many places feature a *dagens rett* (daily special) for about Nkr80. By international standards, Norwegian restaurant food is fairly bland, often heavy and difficult to digest. However, there are some magnificent restaurants that serve excellent food, but main course prices may be well in excess of Nkr200.

Norwegian specialities include grilled or smoked *laks* (salmon), *gravat laks* (marinated salmon), *reker* (boiled shrimp), *torsk* (cod) and other seafood. Expect to see sweet brown goat cheese called *geitost* (Gudbrandsdalsost is a popular brand) and *sild* (pickled herring) alongside the breads and cereals included in breakfast buffets at hostels and hotels. One of the finest Norwegian desserts is warm *moltebær syltetøy* (cloudberry jam) with ice cream – it's fantastic! *Lutefisk*, dried cod made almost gelatinous by soaking in lye, is popular at Christmas but it's definitely an acquired taste.

DRINKS
If Norway has a national drink, it's coffee and most Norwegians drink it black and strong. In bakeries and cafeterias a small cup normally costs around Nkr14, and refills from Nkr6 to Nkr10.

The legal drinking age is 18 years for beer and wine, 20 years for spirits. Beer can be purchased in supermarkets or at a *ølutsalg* (beer outlet), but wine and spirits are only available at Vinmonopolet (government liquor stores). Unfortunately, liquor stores are only found in the largest towns and cities. Wine is the most reasonably priced alcoholic beverage, costing from Nkr69 a bottle. In Svalbard, alcohol is available duty-free.

ENTERTAINMENT
Although Norway isn't known for having a riveting entertainment scene, you can find reasonable nightlife in the bigger cities. Expect to dig deep into your pockets – admissions to cinemas vary from Nkr40 to Nkr75 and cover charges for nightclubs average Nkr70. Beer typically costs Nkr50 for a 400mL glass, and a glass of house wine around Nkr50; spirits start at Nkr40 for 4cL.

SPECTATOR SPORTS
For thousands of years, skis were the only practical means of winter transport in much of Norway – as a result, Norwegians excel in winter sports. Major ski-jumping events normally take place at Holmenkollen near Oslo, and other winter events occur at the former Olympic venues in Hamar and Lillehammer.

SHOPPING
While Norway has high-quality products at high prices, there's no shortage of cheaper kitsch. The finest specialities include attractive wool sweaters and other hand-knitted clothing, pewter ware, silver jewellery, Sami sheath knives, reindeer-leather products, wooden toys and woodwork decorated with rosemaling (painted or carved floral motifs).

Getting There & Away

AIR
SAS, British Airways, KLM, Air France, Lufthansa, Swiss Airlines, Alitalia, Finnair and Icelandair link Oslo's Gardermoen airport with major European and North American cities. The budget airline Ryanair flies from both London Stansted and Glasgow Prestwick to Oslo Torp. Bergen, Stavanger and Trondheim also have direct flight connections with international destinations. For more details, see the introductory Getting There & Away chapter.

LAND
Denmark
The E6 Ekspressen bus from Copenhagen to Oslo (Dkr245/345, 9¼ hours, twice daily) runs via Malmö in Sweden; the lower fare is valid Monday to Thursday.

Trains from Copenhagen to Oslo (from Dkr330, from 8¾ hours, twice daily) requires changing in Gothenburg, Sweden; lowest fares require booking at least seven days in advance.

Finland
The E8 highway runs from Tornio, Finland, to Tromsø in Norway and there are secondary highways connecting Finland with Kautokeino, Karasjok and Tana Bru. Finnish company **Eskelisen Lapin Linjat** (in Finland ☎ 016-342 2160; W www.eskelisen-lapinlinjat .com) runs buses from Rovaniemi (Finland)

to Tanu Bru (year-round), Karasjok (year-round), Nordkapp (via Karasjok; from 1 June to 24 August), Kautokeino (from 1 June to 10 August) and Tromsø (from 1 June to 14 September).

Russia
Russia has a short border with northern Norway and buses run three times weekly between Kirkenes and Murmansk (for details see the Kirkenes section later).

Sweden
Bus For express buses, **Nor-Way Busseks-press** (☎ 815 44 444; [w] www.nor-way.no) runs between Oslo, Gothenburg (Skr175/255, 4¼ hours, six daily) and Malmö (Skr280/400, 8½ hours, five daily). Three or four daily buses run between Stockholm and Oslo (Skr300/425, eight hours); the lower fares are valid Monday to Thursday.

There are also buses between Skellefteå and Bodø (Skr480, 8¾ hours, once daily Sunday to Friday), and between Umeå and Mo i Rana (Skr244, 7½ to 8¾ hours, once daily).

Train Daily trains run from Stockholm (from Skr340, seven hours), Gothenburg (from Skr190, four hours) and Malmö (from Skr450, 8¼ hours) to Oslo; the cheapest tickets must be booked at least seven days in advance. Journeys from Östersund to Trondheim via Storlien require changing trains at the border. **Connex** (in Sweden ☎ 08-629 5050; [e] info@connex.se) trains run between Stockholm and Narvik (Skr1307, 18¾ hours, once daily).

Car & Motorcycle The main highways between Sweden and Norway are the E6 from Gothenburg to Oslo, the E18 from Stockholm to Oslo, the E14 from Sundsvall to Trondheim and the E12 from Umeå to Mo i Rana. Many secondary roads also cross the border.

SEA
Denmark
DFDS Seaways (in Denmark ☎ 33 42 30 00, in Norway ☎ 22 41 90 90; [w] www.dfdsseaways.com) runs daily overnight ferries between Copenhagen and Oslo, with the cheapest fares ranging from Dkr525 (Sunday to Thursday from 4 November to 31 January) to Dkr885 (from 20 June to 11 August). With a student card, cabin fares are discounted by 25%. Cars cost Dkr305. All cabin categories

are quite comfortable and you can take advantage of an excellent dinner buffet en route. The departure time in either direction is 5pm, with arrival at 9am the following day.

Color Line (in Denmark ☎ 99 56 19 77, in Norway ☎ 22 94 44 00; [w] www.colorline.com) runs ferries between Hirtshals and Kristiansand, the route with the shortest connection (from 4½ hours) and the most frequent service (two to five sailings daily) between Norway and Denmark. Color Line also operates once or twice daily between Frederikshavn and Larvik (from 6¼ hours) and once daily between Hirtshals and Oslo (eight hours). Fares are the same for all routes – depending on the day of the week and the time of year, they range from Dkr170 to Dkr360 for passengers and from Dkr200 to Dkr430 for cars. At certain times, there are special discount car packages on these routes.

Fjord Line (in Denmark ☎ 97 96 30 00, in Norway ☎ 55 54 88 00, 815 33 500; [w] www.fjordline.com) sails from Hanstholm to Egersund (from 6¾ hours), once or twice daily for most of the year; some sailings continue to Bergen. Hanstholm–Egersund fares range from Dkr260 (on some days from October to April) to Dkr550 (all weekends in July). Cabins start at Dkr100 per person (reclining chairs are Dkr50); cars cost from Dkr250 to Dkr630.

Stena Line (in Denmark ☎ 96 20 02 00, in Norway ☎ 23 17 91 00, 02010; [w] www.stenaline.com) operates daily ferries between Frederikshavn and Oslo (from Dkr90, 12 hours), except Monday from 2 September to 10 June. A car with driver costs from Dkr470 to Dkr675.

Germany
Color Line (in Germany ☎ 0431-7300 300, in Norway ☎ 22 94 44 00; [w] www.colorline.com) operates a ferry between Kiel and Oslo (from 19½ hours, once daily) – departures are at 2pm from Kiel and 1.30pm from Oslo; from 14 June to 18 August (high season), reclining chairs start at €88. The cheapest two-person cabin ranges from €84 at midweek in the low season (19 August to 13 June), to €116 on Saturday and Sunday in the high season (14 June to 18 August).

Iceland & the Faroe Islands
Smyril Line (in Iceland ☎ 587 1919, in the Faroes ☎ 345900, in Norway ☎ 55 32 09 70; [w] www.smyril-line.com) runs once weekly

from 18 May to 7 September between Bergen and Seyðisfjörður (Iceland), via Lerwick (Shetland; see the UK section later) and the Faroe Islands. One-way low/high season fares to Bergen begin at Dkr630/870 from Tórshavn in the Faroes and Ikr15,990/22,790 from Seyðisfjörður. High season is mid-June to 31 July, with some sailings in August. The boat arrives/departs Bergen at noon/3pm on Tuesday; it takes 23 to 26½ hours to Tórshavn, and 43 hours/five days to/from Seyðisfjörður.

Sweden

DFDS Seaways (in Sweden ☎ 042-266000, in Norway ☎ 22 41 90 90; ⓦ www.dfdsseaways .com) runs daily overnight ferries between Helsingborg and Oslo (from Skr575 to Skr975, 14 hours). The boat leaves the port at Helsingborg at 7pm northbound and Oslo at 5pm southbound.

DFDS Seaways also sails between Gothenburg and Kristiansand (passenger/car fares start at Skr150/240, from seven hours, three days weekly).

Two to six times daily, **Color Line** (in Sweden ☎ 0526-62000; ⓦ www.colorline.com) does the 2½-hour run between Strömstad (Sweden) and Sandefjord (Norway). From 28 June to 11 August, passengers/cars pay Skr188/206, and at other times Skr153/159.

UK

Fjord Line (in the UK ☎ 0191-296 1313, in Norway ☎ 815 33 500; ⓦ www.fjordline.com) sails from Newcastle to Bergen, via Haugesund and Stavanger, thrice weekly from mid-May to mid-September, and twice weekly at other times. Summer sailings are on Wednesday, Friday and Sunday from Newcastle and Tuesday, Thursday and Saturday from Bergen. The trip from Newcastle to Bergen takes from 20½ hours. Passenger fares range from £50 in winter to £110 on summer weekends. Pleasant cabins are available with extra charges starting at £10; reclining seats (available 21 March to 20 September only) are included in the fare. Car/motorcycle fares start at £60/30.

Smyril Line (in the UK ☎ 01595-690845; ⓦ www.smyril-line.com) sails between Lerwick (Shetland) and Bergen, from 20 May to 2 September, taking from 11½ hours. Couchette fares in low/high season are £42/59 and cars up to 5m long cost £34/50 (see the Iceland & the Faroe Islands section earlier).

DFDS Seaways (in the UK ☎ 08705 333000, in Norway ☎ 38 17 17 60; ⓦ www .dfdsseaways.com) sails between Newcastle and Kristiansand and takes from 16½ hours. Return fares start at £104 for foot passengers and £359 for four people in a car.

LEAVING NORWAY

Norwegian airport departure tax (Nkr213) is always included in the price of your airline ticket. There's no departure tax when leaving Norway overland or by ferry.

Getting Around

Public transport in Norway is quite efficient, with trains, buses and ferries often timed to link effectively. The handy *NSB Togruter*, available free at train stations, has rail schedules and information on connecting buses. Boat and bus departures vary with the season and the day, so pick up the latest *ruteplan* (timetables) from regional tourist offices. The Norwegian Tourist Board also publishes a free, annual national transport timetable.

When planning your route, particularly if heading into more remote areas, keep in mind that Saturday and Sunday bus services are often greatly reduced, and some are nonexistent on Saturday.

AIR

Norway has nearly 50 airports, with scheduled commercial flights, from Ny Ålesund (Svalbard) in the north to Kristiansand in the south. Air travel is worth considering, even by budget travellers, due to the great distances involved in overland travel.

Norway's main domestic airlines are **SAS** (ⓦ www.scandinavian.net), **Braathens** (ⓦ www.braathens.no) and **Widerøe** (ⓦ www .wideroe.no). Typical economy return fares from Oslo are Nkr1414 to Trondheim and Nkr2074 to Tromsø. Discounts are available for children aged two to 15, youths aged 16 to 25, and family groups. It's worth checking for stand-by tickets and other discount schemes.

In addition, there are some good-value passes. Widerøe offers foreign travellers US$63 Summerpass tickets (valid from 1 June to 31 August) for flights within any one of four sectors, divided at Trondheim, Bodø and Tromsø (although some short flights cost US$51). For example, flights from Oslo to

Stavanger or Trondheim cost US$63, while multisector flights from Oslo cost US$126 to Bodø, US$189 to Svolvær (Lofoten) and US$252 to Nordkapp.

Widerøe's Minipris ticket, valid for one month, costs 40% less than the normal return fare, but you'll have to stay at least one Saturday night or complete your return journey on Saturday or Sunday.

Braathens Northern Light Pass divides Norway into northern and southern sectors at Trondheim. Flights between any two points in one sector cost US$84, including taxes (except flights between Tromsø and Longyearbyen, which cost US$159), and US$159 when your travel involves two sectors. Tickets can be purchased from Braathens after arrival in Norway, but budget seats are limited so reserving well in advance is advised.

Norwegian domestic airport departure taxes (Nkr87 per flight) are included in ticket prices.

In addition to these domestic discount fares, there are regional air passes that include Norway (see the Getting Around the Region chapter).

BUS

Norway has an extensive bus network and long-distance buses are quite comfortable with reclining seats and onboard toilets. Fares are based on distance, averaging Nkr140 for the first 100km. Many bus companies offer child, student, senior, group (two or more people travelling together) and family discounts of 25% to 50% – always ask.

Nor-Way Bussekspress operates a far-reaching network of modern express buses, with routes connecting every main city from Mandal in the south to Alta in the north, and offers a bus pass covering travel on all its routes for 21 consecutive days (Nkr2300). Some independent long-distance companies provide similar prices and levels of service.

In Nordland, several Togbuss (train-bus) routes offer half-price fares to Eurail, Inter-Rail and ScanRail pass holders. They run between Fauske and Bodø, Narvik, Tromsø, Svolvær and Harstad. InterRail and ScanRail passes get half-price bus tickets to/from the western fjords, between Oslo and Åndalsnes, Ålesund, Molde, Måløy, as well as various other routes in southern Norway.

If you're planning to use buses extensively, pick up the free Nor-Way Bussekspress *Rutehefte Inn og Utland* timetable.

TRAIN

Norway has an excellent, though somewhat limited, national rail system. Almost all railway lines are operated by **NSB** *(Norges Statsbaner or Norwegian State Railways;* ☎ *815 00 888;* W *www.nsb.no)*. The main lines connect Oslo with Stavanger, Bergen, Bodø and Åndalsnes; there are also lines between Sweden and Oslo, Trondheim and Narvik.

Second-class travel, particularly on long-distance trains, is comfortable, with reclining seats and footrests. First-class travel, which typically costs 30% to 50% more, isn't worth it for budget travellers, but standards of service in Signatur Pluss are high and the food is superb.

The Norway Rail Pass, which allows unlimited train travel within the country, can be purchased either before or after you arrive in Norway. Prices for 2nd-class travel are US$146/146/202 for three/four/five days travel within one month. Children get 50% discount and seniors pay US$117/146/162; 1st-class tickets cost 30% more. The short, private Flåm line isn't covered (there's a 30% discount) but otherwise the pass takes you any place in Norway with a rail line and there's also 50% discount on Bergen-Stavanger ferries. For details on ScanRail, Eurail and other international passes valid in Norway, see the Getting Around the Region chapter.

If you're not travelling with a rail pass, there's a Minipris ticket available for travel on all long-distance trains, but tickets must be bought at least five days in advance.

Regular/Minipris fares from Oslo are Nkr633/360 to Bergen, Nkr609/290 to Åndalsnes, Nkr740/360 to Stavanger and Nkr707/360 Trondheim (all prices include the Nkr40 seat reservation).

There's a 50% discount on train travel for people aged 67 and older and children under 16. Children under four travel free. Students at Norwegian colleges and universities get 60/40% discount on departures marked green/white in timetables.

To be assured of a seat you can always make reservations for an additional Nkr40 – on many long-distance trains, including all between Oslo and Bergen, reservations are mandatory.

Second-class sleepers offer a good cheap sleep: a bed in a three-berth cabin costs Nkr160, while two-berth cabins cost Nkr245 per person in old carriages and Nkr300 in new carriages. Breakfast is included in the

NORWAY

price for two-berth cabins; in Oslo and Bergen, a huge buffet breakfast is served at a hotel near the station. 'Sleeperettes' (halfway between a chair and a bed) are available on the Trondheim–Bodø line for Nkr70.

Most train stations have luggage lockers for Nkr10 to Nkr40 and many also have a baggage-storage room.

Self-guided combination tours by boat and train are also available (see the Organised Tours section later).

CAR & MOTORCYCLE

If you plan to drive through mountainous areas in winter or spring, check first to make sure the passes are open, as some are closed until May or June. The **Road User Information Centre** (☎ 175) can tell you about the latest road conditions. Main highways, such as the E16 from Oslo to Bergen and the E6 from Oslo to Kirkenes, are kept open year-round. Cars in snow-covered areas should have studded tyres or carry chains.

If you plan to travel along Norway's west coast, keep in mind that it isn't only mountainous, but deeply cut by fjords. While it's a spectacular route, travelling along the coast requires numerous ferry crossings, which can be time-consuming and costly. For a full list of ferry schedules, fares and reservation phone numbers, consider investing in the latest copy of *Rutebok for Norge*, the comprehensive transport guide (Nkr210) available in larger bookshops and Narvesen kiosks. Some counties publish free booklets detailing bus and ferry timetables – tourist offices usually stock copies.

Leaded and unleaded petrol is available at most petrol stations. Regular unleaded averages Nkr9 per litre in the south, and can be well over Nkr10 per litre in the north. Diesel costs around Nkr1 per litre less. In towns, there are some 24-hour petrol stations, but most close by 10pm or midnight. In rural areas, many stations close in the early evening and don't open at all on weekends.

For more motoring information, contact the national automobile club, **Norges Automobil-Forbund** (NAF; ☎ 22 34 14 00; Storgata 2, N-0105 Oslo). For 24-hour breakdown assistance call the NAF on ☎ 81 00 05 05.

Road Rules

In Norway, you drive on the right side of the road. All vehicles, including motorcycles, must have their headlights on at all times. The use of seat belts is mandatory, and children under the age of four must have their own seat or safety restraint.

On motorways and other main roads, the maximum speed is generally 80km/h (a few roads have segments allowing 90 or 100km/h), while speed limits on through roads in built-up areas are generally 50km/h, unless otherwise posted. Speed cameras and mobile police units lurk at road sides to enforce these absurdly low speed limits (which don't seem to affect Norway's appalling driving standards and high death-rate for motorists).

Tolls are now common on highways, bridges and tunnels. Cities are effectively sealed-off by toll booths at places where no onward public transport is available, and parking, even in small towns, is subject to exorbitant fees. Make sure you have plenty of cash (and loose change) to pay for tickets; if you pass an automatic toll station without paying, call in at the next petrol station or tourist office and ask for assistance on how to pay in retrospect and avoid a whopping fine. Rental-car agencies will automatically add fines (including speed-camera tickets) to your credit-card bill.

Drink-driving laws are strict in Norway: the maximum permissible blood alcohol concentration is 0.02% and violators are subject to severe fines and/or imprisonment.

You're required to carry a red warning triangle in your car for use in the event of breakdown. Third-party car insurance is compulsory and carrying a Green Card (see the Getting Around the Region chapter) is recommended.

UK-registered vehicles must carry a vehicle registration document (Form V5), or a Certificate of Registration (Form V379, available from the DVLA in the UK). For vehicles not registered in the driver's name, you'll require written permission from the registered owner.

Motorcycle helmets are mandatory; motorcycles cannot park on the pavement and must follow the same parking regulations as cars.

The speed limit for caravans (and cars pulling trailers) is usually 10km/h less than for cars. There are a few mountain roads where caravans are forbidden and numerous other roads that are only advisable for experienced drivers, as backing up may be necessary to allow approaching traffic to pass. For a map outlining these roads, and caravan rules, contact **Vegdirektoratet** (☎ *22 07 35 00; Gaustadalleen 25, N-0371 Oslo*).

Car Rental

Major car-rental companies, such as Hertz, Avis and Europcar, have offices at airports and in city centres. Car rentals are expensive: the walk-in rate for a compact car with 200km free is about Nkr1050 a day, including VAT and insurance. Although you'll get much better deals by booking with an international agency before you arrive in Norway, **Rent-a-Wreck** (☎ *23 37 59 49;* 🖳 *www.rent-a-wreck .no; Østre Akersvei 21, N-0581 Oslo*) offers reasonable rates.

One relatively good deal readily available is the weekend rate offered by major car-rental companies, which allows you to pick up a car after noon on Friday and keep it until 10am on Monday for about Nkr1200 – make sure it includes unlimited kilometres.

BICYCLE

Given its great distances, hilly terrain and narrow roads, Norway is not ideally suited for extensive touring by bicycle. A number of regions, however, are good for cycling. The *Sykkelguide* series of booklets, with maps and English text, is available from larger tourist offices for Nkr120 each – routes include Lofoten, Rallarvegen, and the North Sea Cycle Route (from the Swedish border at Svinesund to Bergen). Bikes can be rented at some tourist offices, hostels and camping grounds.

Rural buses, express ferries and non-express trains carry bikes for various additional fees (around Nkr100), but express trains don't allow them at all and international trains treat them as excess baggage (Nkr250). Nor-Way Bussekspress charges half the adult fare to transport a bicycle!

HITCHING

Hitching isn't terribly common in Norway and traffic to many places is very light. Still, with a bit of luck and a lot of patience, some people do manage to get rides; expect long waits in bad weather, and uneven results. A good approach is to ask for rides from truck drivers at ferry terminals and petrol stations. When leaving a city or large town, take public transport to the outskirts of the area before starting to hitch.

BOAT

An extensive network of ferries and express boats links Norway's offshore islands, coastal towns and fjord districts. See specific destinations for details.

Hurtigruten Coastal Steamer

For more than a century Norway's legendary coastal steamer, **Hurtigruten** (☎ *810 30 000;* 🖂 *booking@ovds.no*), has been the lifeline linking the fishing villages and towns scattered along the western and northern coasts.

One ship heads north from Bergen every night of the year, pulling into 35 ports on its six-day journey to Kirkenes, where it then turns around and heads back south. If the weather's agreeable, the fjord and mountain scenery along the way is nothing short of spectacular.

The ships are accommodating to deck-class travellers, offering free sleeping lounges, baggage rooms, a shower room, a 24-hour cafeteria and a coin laundry. Deck passengers can also rent cabins ranging from Nkr300 to Nkr2950 per night (June to September rates).

Sample deck-class fares for trips from Bergen are Nkr1446 to Trondheim, Nkr2464 to Stamsund, Nkr2965 to Tromsø, Nkr3738 to Honningsvåg and Nkr4600 to Kirkenes. One stopover is allowed with these fares, and cars can also be carried for an extra fee. Accompanying spouses, children, students, and seniors over 67 all receive 50% discount.

There are some great low-season deals: from 1 September to 30 April, passengers get 40% discount off basic fares for sailings on any day except Tuesday, with return journeys at a further 50% reduction on the return portion of the ticket (en-route stopovers aren't allowed with these tickets).

The coastal steamer can also be booked as an all-inclusive cruise (see Organised Tours later).

LOCAL TRANSPORT

Cities and towns in Norway are served by public buses and local ferries. As a general rule, the local bus station is adjacent to the train station or ferry quay. For more details, see the relevant destinations.

Taxi

Taxis are readily available at train stations; daytime fares are Nkr26.80 flag fall and Nkr12 per kilometre. Rates are 21% to 45% higher at night, on weekends, and on public holidays.

ORGANISED TOURS

Norway's most popular tour is the cruise on the *Hurtigruten* coastal steamer from Bergen to Kirkenes. The one-way six-day journey, including flights to/from the UK, internal flights, meals and cabin, starts at about £675 October to May and £1235 June to September (per person, based on double occupancy). For reservations, contact **Norwegian Coastal Voyage** (☎ 212-319 1300; e *info@coastalvoyage .com)* in the USA and Canada, **Norwegian Coastal Voyage** (☎ 020-8846 2666; w *www .norwegiancoastalvoyage.com)* in the UK, and **Bentours International** (☎ 02-9241 1353; e *scandinavia@bentours.com.au)* in Australia.

Self-guided combination tours by boat and train are offered at w www.fjord-tours.com. The popular Oslo–Bergen–Stavanger–Oslo 'Triangle Tour' costs Nkr1295/685 (adult/child) and tickets are valid for two months. Contact the Norwegian Tourist Board for details of tour operators who can book accommodation along with these tours.

Oslo

pop 508,730

Founded by Harald Hardråda in 1048, Oslo is the oldest of Scandinavia's capitals. In 1299, King Håkon V constructed the Akershus Festning (Fortress) here, to counter the Swedish threat from the east. Levelled by fire in 1624, the city was rebuilt in brick and stone by King Christian IV who renamed it Christiania, after his humble self. In 1925 the city reverted to its original name, Oslo, and has since flourished as the capital of modern Norway.

Despite being Norway's largest city, for a European capital Oslo is remarkably low-key, casual and manageable. The city centre is a pleasant jumble of old and new architecture.

Oslo sits at the head of Oslofjorden, an inlet of the Skagerrak. Its northern border is Nordmarka, an extensive forest crossed by hiking and skiing trails. The city has good museums, plenty of parks and an abundance of statues. The Nobel Peace Prize is awarded in Oslo each December.

Oslo's highlights include the Bygdøy peninsula with its Viking ships and folk museum, Vigeland Park in Frognerparken featuring the sculptures of Gustav Vigeland, and Akershus Festning (Akershus Fortress) with its castle and harbour views.

Orientation

Oslo's central train station (Oslo Sentralstasjon or Oslo S) is at the eastern end of the city centre. From there the main street, Karl Johans gate, leads through the heart of the city to the Royal Palace. The brick-built Rådhus (City Hall) is between Karl Johans gate and the harbour.

Oslo is easy to get around. Most central city sights, including the harbourfront and Akershus Fortress, are within a 15-minute walk of Karl Johans gate, as are the majority of Oslo's hotels and pensions. Many sights outside Oslo centre, including Vigeland Park and Munchmuseet (the Munch Museum), are a short bus ride away, and even Bygdøy peninsula is a mere 10-minute ferry ride across the harbour. The trails and lakes of the Nordmarka wilderness are easily reached by T-bane.

Information

Tourist Offices Near the harbour and west of Rådhus, **Oslo Promotion** (☎ 23 11 78 80, fax 22 83 81 50; w *www.visitoslo.com; Brynjulf Bulls plass 1; open 9am-7pm daily June-Aug, 9am-5pm Mon-Sat Apr-May & Sept, 9am-4pm Mon-Fri Oct-Mar)* has tourist information for Oslo, as well as brochures to a few destinations elsewhere in Norway. It also maintains a **tourist information window** (*Oslo S; open 8am-11pm daily May-Sept, 8am-5pm Mon-Sat Oct-Apr)* at the central train station. Be sure to pick up the useful *Oslo Guide*, available at these offices and many hotels.

The staff at **Use It** (☎ 22 41 51 32; w *www .unginfo.oslo.no; Møllergata 3; open 9am-6pm Mon-Fri July & Aug, 11am-5pm or 6pm Mon-Fri Sept-June)*, the youth information office, can give you the lowdown on what's happening in and around Oslo, and provide advice on everything from cheap accommodation to hitching; pick up a copy of its free, informative *Streetwise* guide.

Oslo Card & Oslo Package If you plan on a lot of sightseeing, consider buying an Oslo Card, which provides free entry to most museums and attractions and free travel on Oslo public transport. It costs Nkr180/270/360 for one/two/three days (Nkr60/80/110 for children) and is sold at tourist offices, hotels and some Narvesen kiosks. Students and seniors, who get half-price entry at many sights, may do better buying a public-transport pass and paying separate museum admissions.

The Oslo Package must be booked from abroad and costs from Nkr395 to Nkr1560 per person per day – it includes a hotel room, breakfast and the Oslo Card, and up to two children included free. Contact your local travel agent for details and bookings.

Money You can change money at the **airport bank** (*Gardermoen airport departure hall; open 5.30am-8pm Mon-Fri, 5.30am-6pm Sat, 6.30am-8pm Sun*), the **post office** (*street level, Oslo S; open 7am-6pm Mon-Fri, 9am-3pm Sat*), **Forex** (*Oslo S; open 9am-6pm Mon-Fri*) and at **Nordea bank** (*Oslo S; open 7am-7pm Mon-Fri, 8am-5pm Sat & Sun*), near the airport train platform. There's also a 24-hour ATM across the concourse from the bank at Oslo S. Banks, many with ATMs that accept international bank and credit cards, can be found along Karl Johans gate and in neighbouring streets.

If you're changing a small amount you'll usually get the best deal from **American Express** (*Fridtjof Nansens plass 6; open 9am-4.30pm Mon-Fri, 10am-3pm Sat, 11am-3pm Sun July & early Aug*), north of the Rådhus. It exchanges cash and all types of travellers cheques without transaction fees, though its rates may be somewhat lower.

Post & Communications The **main post office** (*Dronningens gate 15; open 9am-5pm Mon-Fri*) handles all postal requirements. To receive mail, have it sent to Poste Restante, Oslo Sentrum Postkontor, Dronningens gate 15, N-0107 Oslo. There are branch post offices at Oslo S and at Karl Johans gate 23B, opposite Stortinget.

Check your email at **Coffee & Juice Netcafe** (*Nedre Slottsgate 12; open 10am-1am Mon-Sat, noon-midnight Sun*) or **Studenten Nett-Café** (*Karl Johans gate 45; open noon-8pm Tues-Sat, noon-10pm Sun & Mon*); both charge Nkr30/55 per 30/60 minutes.

Travel Agencies Although it specialises in student and youth travel, **Kilroy Travels** (☎ 02633; *Nedre Slottsgate 23*) caters for all. Otherwise, you'll find a handful of travel agencies near the Rådhus, including the American Express office.

Bookshops For comprehensive selections of maps, English-language books and travel guides, try **Tanum Libris** (*Karl Johans gate*

43) and nearby **Norli** (*Universitetsgata*). The travel bookshop **Bokkilden** (*Akersgata 34*) has an excellent Scandinavian map selection.

Libraries You can read foreign newspapers at the public library, **Deichmanske Bibliotek** (*Henrik Ibsens gate 1; open 10am-8pm Mon-Fri & 9am-3pm Sat Sept-May, 10am-6pm Mon-Fri & 9am-2pm Sat June-Aug*). It also has Internet and email access, with free half-hour bookable slots.

Laundry A coin laundry 400m north of the intersection of Akersgata and St Olavs gate, **Selva As** (*Ullevålsveien 15; open 8am-9pm daily*) charges Nkr30/30 to wash/dry, including soap powder.

Medical & Emergency Services The emergency phone numbers are **police** (☎ 112) and **ambulance** (☎ 113). **Jernbanetorget Apotek** (*opposite Oslo S*), is a 24-hour pharmacy. The medical clinic **Oslo Kommunale Legevakten** (☎ 22 11 80 80; *Storgata 40*) provides 24-hour emergency services.

Walking Tour

Many of Oslo's finest sights can be combined in a half-day walking tour. From Oslo S, head west along Karl Johans gate, the main pedestrian street; it's lined with shops and pavement cafés and is a haunt for street musicians.

After walking a couple of blocks you'll reach **Oslo Domkirke** (*open 10am-4pm daily*), the city cathedral, which dates from 1697 and has elaborate painted glass and ceiling, and an exceptional altarpiece dating from 1748 depicting the Last Supper.

Midway along Karl Johans gate is **Stortinget** (*Karl Johans gate 22; admission free; guided tours 10am & 1pm daily 1 July-15 Aug, otherwise Sat only*), the oddly shaped yellow-brick parliament building. Also architecturally notable is the stately **Grand Hotel** across the street, built in the 1870s, a decade after Stortinget.

Eidsvolls plass, a city square filled with fountains and statues, stretches between Stortinget and **Nationaltheatret**, the national theatre. The theatre, with its lavish rococo hall, was built a century ago to stage Ibsen's plays.

Opposite the theatre is the University of Oslo's law and medical campus, and one block north lies the university's **Historisk Museet** (Historical Museum) and **Nasjonalgalleriet**

NORWAY

NORWAY

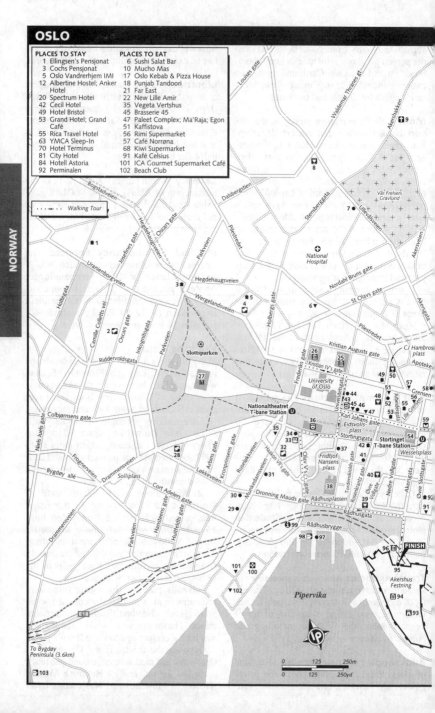

OSLO

PLACES TO STAY
1 Ellingsen's Pensjonat
3 Cochs Pensjonat
5 Oslo Vandrerhjem IMI
12 Albertine Hostel; Anker Hotel
20 Spectrum Hotel
42 Cecil Hotel
49 Hotel Bristol
53 Grand Hotel; Grand Café
55 Rica Travel Hotel
63 YMCA Sleep-In
70 Hotel Terminus
81 City Hotel
84 Hotell Astoria
92 Perminalen

PLACES TO EAT
6 Sushi Salat Bar
10 Mucho Mas
17 Oslo Kebab & Pizza House
18 Punjab Tandoori
21 Far East
22 New Lille Amir
35 Vegeta Vertshus
45 Brasserie 45
47 Paleet Complex; Ma'Raja; Egon
51 Kaffistova
56 Rimi Supermarket
57 Café Norrøna
68 Kiwi Supermarket
91 Kafé Celsius
101 ICA Gourmet Supermarket Café
102 Beach Club

····· Walking Tour

OSLO

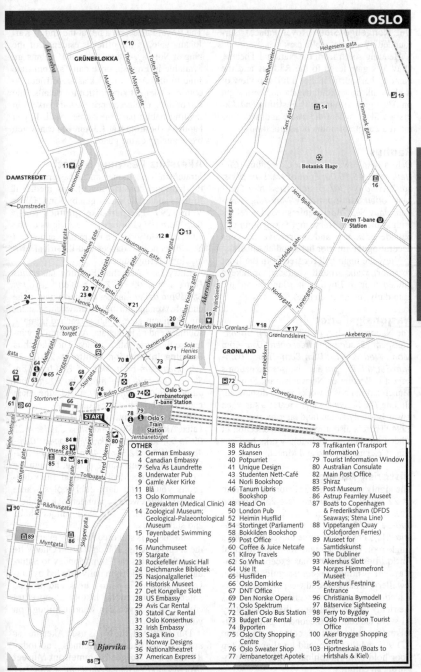

OTHER
2 German Embassy
4 Canadian Embassy
7 Selva As Laundrette
8 Underwater Pub
9 Gamle Aker Kirke
11 Blå
13 Oslo Kommunale Legevakten (Medical Clinic)
14 Zoological Museum; Geological-Palaeontological Museum
15 Tøyenbadet Swimming Pool
16 Munchmuseet
19 Stargate
23 Rockefeller Music Hall
24 Deichmanske Bibliotek
25 Nasjonalgalleriet
26 Historisk Museet
27 Det Kongelige Slott
28 US Embassy
29 Avis Car Rental
30 Statoil Car Rental
31 Oslo Konserthus
32 Irish Embassy
33 Saga Kino
34 Norway Designs
36 Nationaltheatret
37 American Express

38 Rådhus
39 Skansen
40 Potpurriet
41 Unique Design
43 Studenten Nett-Café
44 Norli Bookshop
46 Tanum Libris Bookshop
48 Head On
50 London Pub
52 Heimin Husflid
54 Stortinget (Parliament)
58 Bokkilden Bookshop
59 Post Office
60 Coffee & Juice Netcafe
61 Kilroy Travels
62 So What
64 Use It
66 Husfliden
66 Oslo Domkirke
67 DNT Office
69 Den Norske Opera
71 Oslo Spektrum
72 Galleri Oslo Bus Station
73 Budget Car Rental
74 Byporten
75 Oslo City Shopping Centre
76 Oslo Sweater Shop
77 Jernbanetorget Apotek

78 Trafikanten (Transport Information)
79 Tourist Information Window
80 Australian Consulate
82 Main Post Office
83 Shiraz
85 Post Museum
86 Astrup Fearnley Museet
87 Boats to Copenhagen & Frederikshavn (DFDS Seaways; Stena Line)
88 Vippetangen Quay (Oslofjorden Ferries)
89 Museet for Samtidskunst
90 The Dubliner
93 Akershus Slott
94 Norges Hjemmefront Museet
95 Akershus Festning Entrance
96 Christiania Bymodell
97 Båtservice Sightseeing
98 Ferry to Bygdøy
99 Oslo Promotion Tourist Office
100 Aker Brygge Shopping Centre
103 Hjortneskaia (Boats to Hirtshals & Kiel)

(National Gallery). Karl Johans gate ends at **Det Kongelige Slott** (Royal Palace), surrounded by a large public park.

Heading south from the National Theatre, Olav V's gate leads to the **Rådhus** and the bustling harbourfront. For a hill-top view of it all, walk down Rådhusgata and turn right on Akersgata to **Akershus Festning** and **Akershus Slott**, where the castle and museums merit a couple of hours of exploration.

Rådhus

Oslo's twin-towered red-brick Rådhus *(City Hall; ☎ 22 46 16 00; Fridtjof Nansens plass; adult/child Nkr30/15, admission free Sept-May; open 9am-5pm daily May-Aug, 9am-4pm daily Sept-Apr)* features wooden reliefs with scenes from Norse mythology lining its outside entrance, and impressive frescoes decorating the interior halls and chambers.

View the main hall for free from the front corridor, walk around yourself, or take a guided tour in English at 10am, noon and 2pm daily (no extra charge).

Nasjonalgalleriet

The National Gallery *(☎ 22 20 04 04; Universitetsgata 13; admission free; open 10am-6pm Mon, Wed & Fri; 10am-8pm Thur; 10am-4pm Sat; 11am-4pm Sun)* houses the nation's largest collection of Norwegian art. Some of Munch's best known works are on display, including *The Scream*, which created a stir when it was brazenly stolen (and later recovered) in 1994. There's also a respectable collection of other European art, including works by Gauguin, Cézanne, Picasso and Monet.

Historisk Museet

The highly recommended Historical Museum *(☎ 22 85 99 12; Frederiks gate 2; admission free; open 10am-4pm Tues-Sun mid-May–mid-Sept, 11am-4pm Tues-Sun mid-Sept–mid-May)* consists of three museums under a single roof. On the ground floor, the **National Antiquities Collection** has exceptional displays of Viking-era coins, gold treasure, jewellery, ornaments and weapons, as well as a medieval church art section that includes the richly painted ceiling of the 13th-century Ål stave church. The second level has a **numismatic collection of coins** dating from AD 995, while the second level and the top floor hold **ethnographical displays** on non-European cultures.

Det Kongelige Slott

The Royal Palace, on a hill at the end of Karl Johans gate, is the official residence of the king of Norway. Guided tours of 15 rooms are available in English, once daily at 2pm (late June to mid-August). Tickets are difficult to obtain – ask the tourist office for details. The rest of the grounds comprises Slottsparken, an inviting public park open free to all. If you happen to be around at 1.30pm you can watch the changing of the guard.

Akershus Festning & Slott

Strategically positioned on the eastern side of the harbour, construction of this medieval fortress and castle was begun by King Håkon V in 1299. The park-like **grounds** *(open 6am-9pm daily)* offer excellent views of the city and Oslofjorden, and are the venue for a host of concerts, dances and theatrical productions during summer.

Entry into Akershus Festning *(Akershus Fortress; ☎ 23 09 39 17; admission free; open 6am-9pm daily)* is either through a gate at the end of Akersgata or over a drawbridge spanning Kongens gate, which is reached from the southern end of Kirkegata. After 6pm in winter use the Kirkegata entrance. The **Akershus Festning Information Centre** *(☎ 23 09 39 17; open 9am-5pm Mon-Fri & 11am-5pm Sat & Sun mid-June–mid-Aug, 11am-4pm daily mid-Aug–mid-June)*, inside the main gate, has a brief historical display.

In the 17th century, Christian IV renovated Akershus Slott *(Akershus Castle; ☎ 23 09 35 53; adult/child Nkr30/10; open 10am-4pm Mon-Sat, 12.30pm-4pm Sun May–mid-Sept)* into a Renaissance palace, though the front remains decidedly medieval. In its dungeons you'll find dark cubbyholes where outcast nobles were kept under lock and key, while the upper floors have banquet halls and staterooms.

The chapel is still used for army events and the crypts of Kings Håkon VII and Olav V lie beneath it. Tours (at 11am Monday to Saturday, and 1pm and 3pm daily) are led by university students in period dress, and provide entertaining anecdotal history at no extra cost; otherwise you can wander through on your own.

During WWII, the Nazis used Akershus as a prison and execution grounds, and today it's the site of **Norges Hjemmefront Museet** *(Norwegian Resistance Museum; ☎ 23 09 31*

38; adult/child Nkr25/10; open 10am-3pm Mon-Fri, 11am-4pm Sat & Sun, longer hrs mid-Apr–Sept), providing a vivid and moving account of the tyrannical German occupation and the Norwegian struggle against it.

Of interest mainly to history buffs, **Christiania Bymodell** (☎ 22 33 31 47; admission free; open noon-5pm Tues-Sun May-Sept), just outside the northern wall of the fortress, features a model of the old city and a multimedia display of its history.

Modern Art Museums

Museet for Samtidskunst (Museum of Contemporary Art; ☎ 22 86 22 10; Bankplassen 4; adult/child Nkr40/free; open 10am-5pm Tues, Wed & Fri; 10am-8pm Thur; 11am-4pm Sat; 11am-5pm Sun), in a classic Art Nouveau building that once housed the Central Bank of Norway, features post-WWII Scandinavian and international art.

A block to the east is the **Astrup Fearnley Museet** (☎ 22 93 60 60; Dronningens gate 4; adult/child Nkr50/25; open 11am-5pm Tues, Wed & Fri; 11am-7pm Thur; noon-5pm Sat & Sun), with worthwhile modern Norwegian and international art exhibitions.

Post Museum

The well-presented Post Museum (☎ 23 14 80 59; Kirkegata 20; admission free; open 10am-5pm Mon-Fri, 10am-2pm Sat, noon-4pm Sun) has exhibits on Norway's 350 years of postal history, including a reindeer sledge once used for mail delivery and Norway's largest stamp collection. It's well worth a visit if you're a postal buff and want to buy commemorative stamps. There is a free museum booklet in English.

Munchmuseet & Around

Dedicated to the life work of Norway's most renowned artist, Edvard Munch (1863–1944), Munchmuseet (Munch Museum; ☎ 23 24 14 00; Tøyengata 53; T-bane Tøyen; adult/child Nkr60/30; open 10am-6pm daily June–mid-Sept, shorter winter hrs) is a repository for some 5000 drawings and paintings that Munch bequeathed to the city of Oslo. Despite the artist's tendency towards tormented visions, all is not grey: you'll see works like The Sick Child and The Maiden & Death, but lighter themes, such as The Sun and Spring Ploughing, are also represented.

Next to Munchmuseet is the university's **Zoological Museum** (☎ 22 85 17 00; Sars gate 1; open 11am-4pm Tues & Thur-Sun, 11am-8pm Wed) with well-presented displays of stuffed Norwegian wildlife; admission prices are variable. The adjacent **Geological-Palaeontological Museum** (☎ 22 85 17 00; Sars gate 1; open 11am-4pm Tues & Thur-Sun, 11am-8pm Wed) features displays on the history of the solar system, Norwegian geology, and examples of myriad minerals, meteorites and moon rocks; again, admission prices are variable. These museums are inside a fragrant **Botanisk Hage** (botanical garden; ☎ 22 85 17 00; Sars gate 1; admission free; open 7am-8pm Mon-Fri, 10am-8pm Sat & Sun Apr-Sept, shorter hrs Oct-Mar), with over 1000 alpine plants as well as tropical and temperate specimens.

Frognerparken & Vigeland Park

Frognerparken is a wonderful city park with expansive green spaces, duck ponds and rows of shady trees – a fine place for leisurely strolls and picnics. Its central walkway, Vigeland Park, is lined with life-sized statues by Gustav Vigeland (1869–1943). In nearly 200 highly charged works of granite and bronze, Vigeland presents the human form in a range of emotions, from screaming pot-bellied babies to entwined lovers and tranquil elderly couples.

The most impressive piece is the monolith of writhing bodies, said to be the world's largest granite sculpture. The circle of steps beneath the monolith is lined with voluptuous stone figures and is a popular spot for sitting and contemplation. The park is free and always open, making this a good place to come in the evening when other sights have closed. To get there, take tram No 12 or 15 from Jernbanetorget or Nationaltheatret.

Vigeland Museum

For a more in-depth look at the development of Gustav Vigeland's work, visit the Vigeland Museum (☎ 22 54 25 30; Nobels gate 32; adult/child Nkr40/20; open 10am-6pm Tues-Sat, noon-6pm Sun May-Sept, noon-4pm Tues-Sun Oct-Apr), opposite the southern entrance to Frognerparken. The museum was built by the city as a home and workshop for Vigeland in exchange for the bulk of his life's work and contains his early statuary, plaster moulds, woodblock prints and sketches.

NORWAY

Holmenkollen

The **Holmenkollen Ski Jump** (☎ 22 92 32 00; Kongeveien 5; T-bane Holmenkollen, adult/child Nkr70/35; open 9am-8pm daily June-Aug, 10am-5pm daily May & Sept, 10am-4pm daily Oct-Apr), perched on a hillside above Oslo, draws the world's top jumpers in a ski festival each March and doubles as a concert venue in summer. To get there follow the signs up the hill from Holmenkollen T-bane station. From the top of the ski jump tower, there's a bird's-eye view of the steep ramp, as well as a panoramic view of Oslo city and fjord; a lift goes partway up and then you climb 114 steps. The admission fee includes entry to a **ski museum**, leading you through the 4000-year history of skiing in Norway. Highly worthwhile are the exhibits on the Antarctic expeditions of Amundsen and Scott, and Fridtjof Nansen's slog across the Greenland icecap.

Tryvannstårnet

North of the ski jump, this observation tower (☎ 22 14 67 11; Voksenkollen; adult/child Nkr40/20; open 10am-8pm daily July & Aug, 10am-6pm daily June, 10am-5pm daily May & Sept, 10am-4pm daily Oct-Apr) offers superb views of the Nordmarka forest, as well as snow-capped Mt Gausta to the west, Oslofjorden to the south and the boundless Swedish forests to the east. The admission fee includes a lift which zips you up to the top.

To get to Tryvannstårnet from Holmenkollen, get back on the T-bane for the scenic ride to Frognerseteren, where the line ends in the woods. A 20-minute walk along a signposted trail leads to the tower.

Bygdøy

The Bygdøy (roughly pronounced 'big day') peninsula holds some of Oslo's finest attractions, including excavated Viking ships, an open-air folk museum, Thor Heyerdahl's raft the *Kon-Tiki*, and the *Fram* polar exploration ship. You could rush around all the sights in half a day, but allotting a few extra hours will make the whole experience more enjoyable.

Although only minutes from central Oslo, Bygdøy has a rural character and good **beaches**. The royal family maintains a summer home on the peninsula, as do quite a number of Oslo's other well-to-do residents.

From 12 April to 6 October, ferries make the run to Bygdøy (Nkr22, 15 minutes, every 20 to 40 minutes), starting at 7.45am (9.05am on Saturday and Sunday). The last boat back is at 9.25pm from 25 May to 18 August (otherwise 5.25pm).

The ferries leave from Rådhusbrygge 3 (opposite Rådhus) and stop first at Dronningen, from where it's a 10-minute walk up to the folk museum (avoid the overpriced tourist train). The ferry continues to Bygdøynes, where the *Kon-Tiki*, *Fram* and maritime museums are clustered. You can also take bus No 30 to the folk museum from Jernbanetorget. From the folk museum it's a five-minute walk to the Viking ships and 20 minutes more to Bygdøynes. The route is signposted and makes a pleasant walk.

There's a fruit stand opposite the entrance to the folk museum and cafés at the folk and maritime museums.

Norsk Folkemuseum More than 140 buildings, mostly from the 17th and 18th centuries and gathered from around the country, are clustered according to region in Norway's largest open-air museum, the Norsk Folkemuseum (Norwegian Folk Museum; ☎ 22 12 37 00; Museumsveien 10; adult/child Nkr70/40 mid-May–mid-Sept, Nkr50/30 mid-Sept–mid-May; open 10am-6pm daily mid-June–mid-Sept, 11am-3pm Mon-Fri, 11am-4pm Sat & Sun mid-Sept–mid-June). The folk museum is great for an overview of architectural styles around the country. Dirt paths wind past sturdy old barns, *stabbur* (storehouses on stilts) and rough-timbered farmhouses with sod roofs sprouting wildflowers. There's also a reproduction of an early-20th-century Norwegian town, including a village shop and an old petrol station.

One of the highlights is a restored **stave church**, built around 1200 in Gol and brought to Bygdøy in 1885. Also not to be missed is the **exhibition hall** just inside the main entrance, with extensive displays of folk art, festive costumes and Sami culture.

Sunday is a good day to visit, as there's usually folk music and dancing at 2pm (summer only).

Vikingskipshuset The magnificent Viking Ship Museum (☎ 22 13 52 80; Huk Aveny 35; adult/child Nkr40/20; open 9am-6pm daily May-Sept, 11am-4pm daily Oct-Apr) houses three Viking ships excavated from Oslofjorden region. The ships had been brought ashore and used as tombs for nobility, who were buried with all they were expected to need in the hereafter, including jewels, furniture, food and servants. Built of oak in the 9th century, these Viking ships were buried in blue clay, which preserved two of them amazingly well.

The impressive **Oseberg ship**, buried in AD 834 and festooned with elaborate dragon and serpent carvings, is 22m long and took 30 people to row. The burial chamber beneath it held the largest collection of Viking-age artefacts ever uncovered in Scandinavia, but had been looted of all jewellery. A second ship, the 24m-long **Gokstad**, is the world's finest example of a longship. Of the third ship, the **Tune**, only a few boards remain.

Kon-Tiki Museum This curious museum (☎ 23 08 67 67; Bygdøynesveien 36; adult/child Nkr35/20; open 9.30am-5.45pm daily June-Aug, 10.30am-4pm or 5pm daily Sept-May) is dedicated to the Kon-Tiki balsa raft, on which Norwegian explorer Thor Heyerdahl sailed from Peru to Polynesia in 1947 to demonstrate that Polynesia's first settlers could have come from South America.

There's also the papyrus reed boat Ra II, which Heyerdahl used to cross the Atlantic in 1970, and fascinating displays on Easter Island and the Galapagos Islands.

Polarskip Fram Opposite the Kon-Tiki Museum, Fridtjof Nansen's excellent 39m rigged schooner Fram is held in a **museum** (☎ 23 28 29 50; Bygdøynes; adult/child Nkr30/10; open 9am-6.45pm daily mid-June–Aug, shorter hrs Sept-May). The Fram, launched in 1892, was used for polar expeditions, including Roald Amundsen's successful first expedition to the South Pole in 1911. You can clamber around inside the boat, go down to the hold where the sledge dogs were kept, and view fascinating photographic displays of the Fram trapped in polar ice. The museum also includes an interesting rundown on the history of polar exploration.

Norsk Sjøfartsmuseum The Norwegian Maritime Museum (☎ 24 11 41 50; Bygdøynesveien 37; adult/child Nkr30/20; open 10am-6pm daily mid-May–Sept, shorter hrs Oct–mid-May) describes Norway's relationship with the sea, including the fishing and whaling industry, the seismic fleet (which searches for oil and gas) and shipbuilding. Check out the amazing model ships, the film of the Norwegian coastline and the top-floor balcony of the larger wing, which provides fine views over the islands of Oslofjorden. Outside the museum there's Roald Amundsen's Gjøa, the first ship to completely transit the Northwest Passage (from 1903 to 1906).

Islands & Beaches

Ferries to half a dozen islands in Oslofjorden leave from Vippetangen quay, southeast of Akershus Festning. **Hovedøya**, the closest island, has a rocky coastline, but its southwestern side is a popular sunbathing area. There are walking paths all around the perimeter, some old cannons and the ruins of a 12th-century monastery. Boats to Hovedøya leave from Vippetangen once or twice hourly, between 6.17am and midnight daily from late May to mid-August, with fewer runs the rest of the year.

Farther south, the undeveloped island of **Langøyene** offers far better swimming. It has both sandy and rocky beaches, including one designated for nude bathing. Boats to Langøyene depart 9.35am to 8.25pm daily, 26 May to 19 August.

The Bygdøy peninsula also has two popular beaches, **Huk** and **Paradisbukta**, which can be reached by taking bus No 30 from Jernbanetorget to its last stop. While there are some sandy patches, most of Huk comprises grassy lawns and large, smooth rocks ideal for sunbathing. It's actually separated into two beaches by a small cove; the beach on the northwestern side is open to nude bathing. If Huk seems too crowded, a 10-minute walk through the woods north of the bus stop leads to the more secluded Paradisbukta.

For freshwater swimming, try the eastern side of lake **Sognsvann**, at the end of T-bane line 5, about 6km north of central Oslo.

Other Sights

Oslo's oldest building is **Gamle Aker Kirke** (Akersbakken 26; admission free; open noon-2pm Mon-Sat), a medieval stone church built in 1080 and still used for services. Take bus No 37 from Jernbanetorget, get off at Akersbakken and walk up past the cemetery.

The skewed wooden homes of the quirky-looking **Damstredet** district, some dating from the early 19th century, add a splash of character to the area just north of the city centre.

NORWAY

Oslo also has a number of more esoteric museums, including ones dedicated to ice skating, technology, architecture, children's art, customs and tolls, the armed forces, theatre, and playwright Henrik Ibsen. For more details see the *Oslo Guide*.

Hiking

A network of trails leads into Nordmarka from Frognerseteren, at the end of T-bane line 1. One good, fairly strenuous walk is from Frognerseteren over to Lake Sognsvann, where you can take T-bane line 5 back to the city. If you're interested in wilderness hiking, contact the **DNT office** (☎ *22 82 28 22; Storgata 3*).

Cycling

Contact the tourist office for the latest information on bicycle hire.

One popular outing is to take the *sykkeltoget* (weekend bike train) to Stryken, 40km north of Oslo, and cycle back through Nordmarka. The train leaves Oslo S at 9.15am on Saturday and Sunday from May to October. For a shorter ride, take the T-bane to Frognerseteren and cycle back.

For cycling information contact the local club, **Syklistenes Landsforening** (☎ *22 47 30 30*).

Skiing

Oslo's ski season is roughly from December to March. There are over 1000km of ski trails in the Nordmarka area north of Oslo, many of them floodlit; easy-access tracks begin right at the T-bane stations Frognerseteren and Sognsvann. **Tomm Murstad Skiservice** (☎ *22 13 95 00;* W *www.skiservice.no; Tryvannsveien 2*), at Voksenkollen T-bane station, hires out snowboards and nordic skis.

A set of skis, boots and poles costs Nkr140/180 for one/two days. **Skiforeningen** (*Ski Society;* ☎ *22 92 32 00; Kongeveien 5, N-0787 Oslo*) can provide more information on skiing, or check out the society's website W www.holmenkollen.com.

Swimming

Oslo has two outdoor swimming pools, **Frognerbadet** (☎ *22 44 74 29; Middelthuns gate 28; adult/child Nkr75/35; open variable hrs mid-May–mid-Aug*) and **Tøyenbadet** (☎ *23 30 44 70; Helgesens gata 90; adult/child Nkr75/35; open variable hrs*).

Organised Tours

Oslo is so easy to get around that there's little need for organised tours. However, if time is tight, **Båtservice Sightseeing** (☎ *23 35 68 90; Pier 3, Rådhusbrygge*) does a tidy 7½ hour tour of the Bygdøy sites, Vigeland Park and the Holmenkollen ski jump, plus a cruise of Oslofjorden, for a reasonable Nkr425 (24 May to 8 September); a three-hour version minus the cruise costs Nkr280. Båtservice's frequent 50-minute 'minicruise' of Oslofjorden is a great orientation of the city from 24 May to 31 August; it costs Nkr90, or is free with the Oslo Card.

The popular 'Norway in a Nutshell' day tours cost Nkr1440 – they can be booked through any tourist office or travel agency, or directly through NSB (the national rail operator) at train stations. From Oslo, the typical 'Norway in a Nutshell' route includes a rail trip from Oslo across Hardangervidda to Myrdal, a rail descent to Flåm along the dramatic Flåmbanen, a cruise along Nærøyfjorden to Gudvangen, a bus to Voss, a connecting train to Bergen for a short visit, then an overnight return rail trip to Oslo (including a 2nd-class sleeper compartment).

Special Events

Oslo's most festive annual event is the 17 May Constitution Day celebration, when city residents descend on the Royal Palace in traditional garb.

In March, the Holmenkollen Ski Festival attracts nordic skiers and ski jumpers from around the world. During the last weekend in July there's the Summer Parade, an indoor and outdoor music and dance festival dominated by techno music. August sees the Oslo International Jazz Festival, and October the Scandinavia-oriented Ultima Contemporary Music Festival.

For details of these and other events, contact the tourist office.

Places to Stay

Camping The two main camping grounds in Oslo have full facilities, including kitchens (without cooking implements), but they're overpriced, charging around Nkr120 to Nkr180 for one or two people with tent. **Ekeberg Camping** (☎ *22 19 85 68;* e *ekeberg@ bogstadcamping.no; Ekebergveien 65; bus No 34 from Oslo S; open 24 May-2 Sept*), on a hill 10 minutes by bus southeast of (and overlooking) the city, is often seriously over-crowded in peak season and the facilities wilt under the pressure. **Bogstad Camping** (☎ 22 51 08 00; e mail@bogstadcamping.no; Ankerveien 117; bus No 32 from Oslo S) offers forested sites but currently has a reputation for overnight noise and other unpleasantries.

Oslo Fjordcamping (☎ 22 75 20 55; e fjordcamp@online.no; Ljansbrukveien 1; bus Nos 76, 79, 83; tent sites Nkr110-140, on-site caravan Nkr300-400), a family-friendly camping ground by Oslofjorden about 8km south of the city, is a very good alternative. There are showers, a kiosk selling simple snacks, and a nearby restaurant.

Hostels The Oslo area has four HI-affiliated hostels.

The newly extended **Oslo Vandrerhjem Haraldsheim** (☎ 22 22 29 65, fax 22 22 10 25; e oslo.haraldsheim.hostel@vandrerhjem.no; Haraldsheimveien 4; tram Nos 12, 13 or 17 from city centre; dorm beds with/without bath Nkr190/170, singles Nkr360/290, doubles Nkr480/400) is a busy place, 4km from the city centre. The hostel has kitchen and laundry facilities, 270 beds (mostly in four-bed rooms) and prices include breakfast.

Oslo Vandrerhjem IMI (☎ 22 98 62 00; Staffelsgata 4, enter from Linstowsgata; dorm beds Nkr170-190, singles/doubles from Nkr275/430; open 4 June-19 Aug) is a 46-bed summer hostel in a boarding school conveniently just north of Det Kongelige Slott. There's a kitchen, but prices include breakfast. Tram Nos 10, 11 and 17 stop nearby.

Oslo Vandrerhjem Holtekilen (☎ 67 51 80 40, fax 67 59 12 30; e oslo.holtekilen.hostel@vandrerhjem.no; Michelets vei 55, Stabekk; bus Nos 151, 153, 161, 162, 251, 252, 261; dorm beds Nkr180, singles/doubles Nkr280/460), 8km southwest of Oslo, has 195 beds and rates include breakfast.

Oslo Vandrerhjem Ekeberg (☎ 22 74 18 90, fax 22 74 75 05; Kongsveien 82; dorm beds Nkr175, singles/doubles Nkr280/440; open 1 June-27 Aug), 4km southeast of Oslo, offers 68 beds in an atmospheric old house. Rates include breakfast. Take tram No 18 or 19 towards Ljabru and get off at Holtet; from there, it's about 100m along Kongsveien.

The bright and airy **Albertine Hostel** (☎ 22 99 72 10, fax 22 99 72 20; e albertine@anker.oslo.no; Storgata 55; beds in 4-bed/6-bed rooms with bath Nkr155/135, rooms for

1 or 2 people Nkr400; open 6 June-24 Aug), used as a student residence except over summer, is a convenient non-HI option at the rear of the Anker Hotel. Breakfast costs Nkr55 extra; linen and towels also cost Nkr55.

YMCA Sleep-In (☎ 22 20 83 97; Grubbegata 4; dorm mattresses Nkr130; open 3 July-12 Aug) has a great position, only 10 minutes' walk from Oslo S, and fills up quickly. There's no bedding so you'll need a sleeping bag; basic shower and kitchen facilities are available.

Private Rooms & Pensions When all other options seem unlikely, **Use It** (☎ 22 41 51 32; Møllergata 3) can usually find a place, helping travellers book double rooms in private homes for Nkr300 to Nkr350 (excluding breakfast). There's no minimum stay and no booking fee. If you arrive on a Saturday or Sunday, when the office is closed, call ahead and they'll give you phone numbers and/or email addresses of possible rooms.

The Oslo S tourist office window also books rooms in private homes; these cost Nkr225/350 (singles/doubles, excluding breakfast), plus a Nkr35 booking fee; there's a supplement for one-night stays. Also worth checking out is w www.bbnorway.com, which lists around a dozen B&Bs in the city.

Ellingsen's Pensjonat (☎ 22 60 03 59, fax 22 60 99 21; Holtegata 25; singles Nkr300-420, doubles Nkr490-560), in a neighbourhood of older homes five blocks north of the Royal Palace, is a good-value pension with 20 small but adequate rooms.

Cochs Pensjonat (☎ 23 33 24 00, fax 23 33 24 10; Parkveien 25; singles/doubles from Nkr350/500), a bit pricier but closer to the centre, is just north of the Royal Palace. Most of the 65 rooms are rather spartan, but some are en suite with kitchenette.

Perminalen (☎ 23 09 30 81; e perminalen@statenskantiner.no; Øvre Slottsgate 2; bunks in 4-bed rooms Nkr275, singles/doubles Nkr495/650) is a central 55-room pension that caters to military personnel, but it's open to everyone. All rooms have TV and private bath, and prices include breakfast.

Hotels The tourist offices book unfilled hotel rooms at discounted rates, which can be worth pursuing during the week but are generally close to the rates that you can book directly from hotels on Saturday or Sunday.

There's a Nkr35 booking fee. Discounts are also offered to holders of hotel passes, such as the Scan+ Hotel Pass (which can be purchased at hotels for Nkr90), at weekends and during the summer period, usually mid-June to mid-August. Room rates quoted here include breakfast.

The relatively inexpensive **City Hotel** (☎ 22 41 36 10; e booking@cityhotel.no; Skippergata 19; singles Nkr475-635, doubles Nkr595-835) has a historical ambience but the rooms are mostly fairly basic, with shared bath. Anyone who's sensitive to traffic noise should request a courtyard room. A modern no-frills alternative with very clean en suite rooms is the **Anker Hotel** (☎ 22 99 75 10, fax 22 99 75 20; e booking@anker.oslo.no; Storgata 55; singles Nkr450-750, doubles Nkr600-900).

The **Tulip Inn/Rainbow Hotels chain** (central reservations ☎ 23 08 00 00, fax 23 08 00 72; w www.rainbow-hotels.com) offers reasonably good weekend and summer rates, available to holders of the Scan+ Hotel Pass; the following four in the chain have modern rooms with full amenities from private baths and cable TV to trouser presses (should you need a knife-edge crease). **Spectrum Hotel** (☎ 23 36 27 00; Brugata 7; singles Nkr610-995, doubles Nkr790-1245), near the diverse ethnic Grønland neighbourhood, is probably the best deal, with comfortable rooms. Two similarly priced Rainbows closer to Oslo S are **Hotel Terminus** (☎ 22 05 60 00; Stenersgata 10), noted for its fine breakfasts and is quite comfortable, and the recommended **Hotell Astoria** (☎ 24 14 55 50; Dronningens gate 21), with smaller rooms but a more central location. Rainbow's **Cecil Hotel** (☎ 23 31 48 00; Stortingsgata 8; singles/doubles Nkr650/850 Sat & Sun & daily mid-June–mid-Aug, otherwise from Nkr1120/1370) is in the heart of the city, just a stone's throw from the parliament. The well-appointed rooms circle a quiet interior courtyard.

Rica Travel Hotel (☎ 22 00 33 00, fax 22 33 51 22; Arbeidergata 4; singles Nkr695-905, doubles Nkr895-1060) is a good-value business hotel. Rooms are compact, pleasant and modern, and all have private bath, TV and minibar.

The best value of the city's classic hotels is **Hotel Bristol** (☎ 22 82 60 00; e booking@bristol.no; Kristian IV's gate 7; singles Nkr880-1350, doubles Nkr1150-1860). The large rooms have full amenities, while the

halls and lobby are filled with antiques, chandeliers and old-world charm.

The regal **Grand Hotel** (☎ 23 21 20 00; e grand@rica.no; Karl Johans gate 31; singles Nkr995-2740, doubles Nkr1190-2990) is another top-end place brimming with period character.

Places to Eat

Eating can be an expensive proposition in Oslo. One way to save money is to frequent bakeries, many of which sell reasonably priced sandwiches as well as pastries and hearty wholegrain breads. The **Baker Hansen** chain has numerous shops around Oslo. Among grocery stores, you'll find some of the best prices at **Kiwi**, a prolific chain with branches throughout the city.

Oslo S & Around The main section of Oslo S and the Byporten complex at the northern end of the station includes a small **Kiwi** food mart, the **Bit** Italian-style food stand, a **bakery**, a **Peppe's Pizza** and various fast-food chains. The south wing, Østbanehallen, has more fast food, along with **Rooster Coffee**, a good espresso bar, **Baker Nordby**, with pastries and sandwiches, and a **Rimi supermarket**.

Oslo City, a shopping complex opposite Oslo S, has bakeries, a baguette outlet, a grill joint, and Chinese and Mexican restaurants.

The **Galleri Oslo bus station** has a couple of small stores with fruit and snacks, and a **Baker Nordby** bakery (open 7am-4.30pm Mon-Fri).

Grønland This neighbourhood of Asian and Middle Eastern immigrants, a few minutes' walk northeast of the bus station, has good, affordable ethnic eating places. It's also opening up as the in-place for eating, drinking and dancing among the 20- to 30-year-old crowd.

Recommended is the **Punjab Tandoori** (Grønland 24; mains around Nkr55; open 11am-11pm daily), which serves chicken tandoori, rice and naan bread; a basic chicken curry is a bargain at Nkr35. At the **Oslo Kebab & Pizza House** (Grønlandsleiret 2; dishes from Nkr30), you'll get a kebab for Nkr30, fish and chips for Nkr69, and large pizzas from Nkr99.

Aker Brygge This former shipyard turned shopping complex, along the western side of the harbour, has a food court with various eating options, including fast-food chains, sushi, tapas, pizza and pasta places, the **Noodle Bar** *(Chinese dishes Nkr70-95)* and a baked-potato stall.

Behind Aker Brygge, the **ICA Gourmet supermarket café** sells filled baguettes (Nkr45), wok dishes (Nkr59) as well as salads (Nkr59). The popular American-themed **Beach Club** *(☎ 22 83 83 82; Bryggetorget 14; dishes Nkr85-190)*, serving burgers and the like, has outdoor seating and is great for a sunny afternoon. It's one of the very few places to serve a full American breakfast (Nkr95).

Lining the **harbour** are ice cream and hot-dog vendors, as well as docked boats that have been converted into pricey beer halls and restaurants.

Elsewhere in Oslo North of the city centre, Grünerløkka is an inner suburb with several trendy bars and restaurants, including the recommended **Mucho Mas** *(Thorvald Meyers gate 36; mains Nkr61-126)*, which serves quesadillas, burritos and tacos.

Back in town, **Brasserie 45** *(Karl Johans gate 45; mains from Nkr63)* features good food at honest prices, including salmon, lasagne, grilled catfish and fried chicken.

The friendly **Kaffistova** *(Rosenkrantz gate 8; mains Nkr82-92)* cafeteria serves traditional Norwegian food, including reindeer or elk carbonades (locally defined as meat cakes), meatballs, pork chops and fish cakes; salad is always included. **Café Norrøna** *(Grensen 19; mains Nkr55-188)* serves a lunch buffet daily except Sunday (from Nkr80).

Popular with businesspeople is the all-you-can-eat salad-and-sandwich lunch buffet at the **Cecil Hotel** *(Stortingsgata 8; lunch buffet Nkr50; buffet 11.30am-1pm Mon-Fri)*, which comes with coffee.

Vegeta Vertshus *(Munkedamsveien 3B; small/large plate Nkr85/95, all-you-can-eat Nkr135; open 11am-11pm daily)*, near the National Theatre, has a vegetarian buffet that includes wholegrain pizza, casseroles and salads.

A better vegetarian option is **Krishna's Cuisine**, *(Kirkeveien 59B; all-you-can-eat Nkr90; food available noon-8pm Mon-Fri)*, near the Majorstuen T-bane station, which serves up soup, salad, vegies and a hot dish.

For straightforward Indian fare, try the recommended **Curry & Ketchup** *(Kirkeveien 51; mains Nkr69-99)* for its excellent naan bread, and balti and korma dishes.

Also tasty is the modern **Far East** *(Bernt Ankers gate 7; most mains Nkr68-88; open 2pm-midnight daily)*, with a full menu of good-value Thai and Vietnamese meals. The Libyan-style **New Lille Amir** *(Torggata 18; open 11am-2am Sun-Thur, 11am-5am Fri & Sat)* has good felafels (Nkr30) and large shwarmas (Nkr50). You can get a good take-away sushi at **Sushi Salat Bar** *(Pilestredet 31; 10-piece lunch Nkr89, sushi Nkr59-159)*.

Local art students hang out at **Kafé Celsius** *(Rådhusgata 19; mains Nkr94-198; open 11am-midnight Mon-Sat, 1pm-10pm Sun)*, a low-key café with a pleasant courtyard beer garden serving salads and pastas.

The **Grand Café** *(Karl Johans gate 31; daily special Nkr145; daily special available 11am-6pm Mon-Sat)*, at the Grand Hotel, has been serving Oslo's cognoscenti for more than a century; as a reminder, a wall mural depicts the restaurant in the 1890s bustling with the likes of Munch and Ibsen. The best deal is the traditional daily special.

The shopping complex **Paleet** *(Karl Johans gate 37)* has some of the best food deals in the city centre, including **Ma'Raja** *(lunch buffet Nkr59-79)* with its Indian lunch buffets, and **Egon** *(pizza & salad buffet Nkr97; buffet available 10am-6pm Tues-Sat, 10am-11pm Sun & Mon)*.

Good central supermarkets include **Kiwi** *(Storgata 11)* and **Rimi** *(Lille Grensen 1)*.

Entertainment

The tourist office's monthly *What's On in Oslo* brochure lists concerts, theatre and special events, but the best publication for night owls and clubbers is the free *Streetwise*, published annually in English by Use It (see Information in the Oslo section earlier). Dress to impress or risk being refused entry to nightspots.

The Dubliner *(☎ 22 33 70 05, Rådhusgata 28; cover charge Nkr60)* is a friendly Irish pub with an authentic feel, featuring live Irish folk bands several times weekly. If you prefer a down-to-earth drinking-den atmosphere, try **Stargate** *(Grønlandsleiret 2)*, which offers the best-value beer in town: 500mL of draught is only Nkr24 to Nkr29. The weirdly named (and appropriately, if oddly, decorated) **Underwater Pub** *(Dalsbergstien 4)* is worth a visit on Tuesday and Thursday, when students of the State School of Opera lubricate their vocal chords and treat patrons to their favourite arias.

NORWAY

Head On *(Rosenkrantz gate 11B)* features funk and house with international DJs; it's currently the hottest place for clubbers.

Skansen *(Rådhusgata 25)*, inside a former public toilet, is one of the city's hottest dance clubs, resounding to the beats of house, funk, jazz and techno. For a laudable attempt at salsa, visit Shiraz *(Dronningens gate 17)*. So What *(Grensen 9)* is a café and club with alternative music and a young crowd. At Blå *(Brenneriveien 9C)*, reputedly the best modern jazz spot in Oslo, you can catch new artists and bands before they hit the big time.

The main disco hang-out for gay men is the London Pub *(CJ Hambros plass 5)*, with a good mix of chart sounds. Lesbians favour Potpurriet *(Øvre Vollgate 13)* with its emphasis on techno, latin and salsa music.

Of the city's largest concert halls, Oslo Spektrum *(Sonja Henies plass 2)* features contemporary music, Oslo Konserthus *(Munkedamsveien 14)* has an emphasis on jazz and classical, and the Rockefeller Music Hall *(Torggata 16)* attracts big-name international contemporary musicians. Every month except July, Oslo's opera company stages opera, ballet and classical concerts at Den Norske Opera *(☎ 815 44 488; Storgata 23; tickets from Nkr300, 50% student discount)*. The six-screen cinema, Saga Kino *(Stortingsgata 28)*, shows first-run movies in their original languages; the entrance is on Olav V's gate.

Take advantage of summer's long daylight hours and spend evenings outdoors: go down to the harbour and enjoy live jazz wafting from the floating restaurants, have a beer at one of the outdoor cafés at Vigeland Park, or take a ferry out to the islands in Oslofjorden.

Shopping

Traditional Norwegian sweaters are popular purchases; for good prices and selections, check out the Oslo Sweater Shop *(Biskop Gunnerus gate 3)* near Oslo S, or Unique Design *(Rosenkrantz gate 13)*. Husfliden *(Møllergata 4)* and Heimen Husflid *(Rosenkrantz gate 8)* are larger shops selling Norwegian clothing and crafts, with items ranging from carved wooden trolls to elaborate folk costumes. An excellent modern design outlet is Norway Designs *(Olav V's gate)*, but it's pricey. If you want to buy wine or spirits, there's a Vinmonopolet in the Oslo City shopping complex.

Getting There & Away

Air Most flights land at Oslo's main international airport in Gardermoen, 50km north of the city.

SAS *(☎ 815 20 400)* and Braathens *(☎ 815 20 000)* have ticket offices in the basement at Oslo S. Ryanair *(☎ 820 61 100)* flies from London Stansted and Glasgow Prestwick to Oslo Torp, 112km south of the city.

Bus Long-distance buses arrive and depart from the Galleri Oslo bus station, about a 10-minute walk east from Oslo S.

Train All trains arrive and depart from Oslo S in the city centre. The reservation desks are open 6.30am to 11pm daily. There's also an information desk *(☎ 815 00 888)* where you can get details on travel schedules throughout Norway. Oslo S has various sizes of lockers for Nkr20 to Nkr45 per 24 hours.

Car & Motorcycle The main highways into the city are the E6, from the north and south, and the E18, from the east and west. Unless you're on a motorcycle you'll have to pay a Nkr15 toll each time you enter Oslo.

Car Rental All major car-rental companies have booths at Gardermoen airport. The following also have offices in the city centre:

Avis *(☎ 23 23 92 00)*, Munkedamsveien 27
Budget *(☎ 23 16 32 40)*, Oslo Spektrum, near Oslo S
Statoil *(☎ 22 83 35 35)* Dronning Mauds gate 10B

Boat Boats to and from Copenhagen, operated by DFDS Seaways *(☎ 22 41 90 90)*, and from Frederikshavn (Denmark), operated by Stena Line *(☎ 23 17 91 00)*, use the docks off Skippergata, near Vippetangen. Bus No 60 brings you to within a couple of minutes' walk of the terminal.

Boats from Hirtshals (Denmark) and Kiel (Germany), run by Color Line *(☎ 22 94 44 00)*, dock at Hjortneskaia, west of the central harbour. Connecting buses run to Oslo S, or take tram Nos 10 or 13.

Getting Around

Oslo has an efficient public-transport system with an extensive network of buses, trams, T-bane trains (metro/underground) and ferries. A one-way ticket on any of these services costs

Nkr22 and includes one transfer within an hour of purchase; buy tickets from staff on ferries, from bus or tram drivers, and from service desks or automatic machines in T-bane stations. A *dagskort* (unlimited day ticket) costs Nkr50, but can't be used between 1am and 4am. Weekly/monthly cards cost Nkr160/620 (Nkr80/310 for people under 20 and seniors over 67). You can buy these with cash only at Trafikanten, Narvesen kiosks, staffed T-bane and train stations, and some 7-Eleven stores.

Bicycles can be taken on Oslo's trams and trains for an additional Nkr11. Note that while it may seem easy to board the subway and trams without a ticket, if confronted by an inspector you'll receive an automatic Nkr750 fine.

Trafikanten *(☎ 815 00 176; open 7am-8pm Mon-Fri, 8am-6pm Sat & Sun)*, below the Oslo S tower on Jernbanetorget, provides free schedules and a handy public-transport map, *Sporveiskart Oslo*. Dial ☎ 177 from 7am to 11pm daily (from 8am at weekends) for schedule information.

To/From the Airport High-speed trains run between Oslo S and Oslo International airport in Gardermoen (Nkr130, 24 minutes, every 10 minutes). Alternatively, you can take a local train (Nkr70, from 26 minutes, hourly but fewer on Saturday) or an express airport bus (Nkr90, 40 minutes, three or four hourly).

Bus & Tram Bus and tram lines crisscross the city and extend into the suburbs. There's no central station but most buses and trams converge at Jernbanetorget in front of Oslo S. Most westbound buses, including those to Bygdøy and Vigeland Park, also stop on the southern side of Nationaltheatret.

The service frequency drops dramatically at night, but on Saturday and Sunday only, *Nattlinjer* night buses No 200 to 218 follow the tram routes until 4am or later (tickets Nkr50; passes not valid).

T-bane The five-line T-bane metro train network, which goes underground in the city centre, is faster and goes farther outside the city centre than most bus lines. All lines pass through Nationaltheatret, Stortinget and Jernbanetorget stations.

Car & Motorcycle Oslo has its fair share of one-way streets, which can complicate city driving, but otherwise traffic is not too challenging. Still, the best way to explore central sights is to walk or take local transport, though a car can be quite convenient for outlying areas such as Holmenkollen.

Metered street parking, identified by a solid blue sign with a white 'P', can be found throughout the city centre. Hours written under the sign indicate when the meters need to be fed, typically from 8am to 5pm Monday to Friday, with Saturday hours in parentheses. Unless otherwise posted, parking is free outside that time and on Sunday. Parking at most meters costs from Nkr20 to Nkr35 per hour. There are many multistorey car parks in the city centre, including those at major shopping centres such as Oslo City and Aker Brygge. The Oslo Card gives free parking in municipal car parks.

Taxi Taxis charge up to Nkr91.50 at flagfall and from Nkr10 to Nkr16 per kilometre. There are taxi stands at Oslo S, shopping centres and city squares. Any taxi with a lit sign is available for hire. Otherwise, phone **Taxi2** *(☎ 02202)*, **Norgestaxi** *(☎ 08000)* or **Oslo Taxi** *(☎ 02323)*. Meters start running at the point of dispatch, adding to what will become a gigantic bill! Oslo taxis accept major credit cards.

Boat Ferries to Bygdøy leave from Rådhusbrygge every 20 to 40 minutes, while ferries to the islands in Oslofjorden leave from Vippetangen.

AROUND OSLO
The Østfold region, on the eastern side of Oslofjorden, is a mixture of farmland and small industrial towns dependent on the timber trade. The most interesting places to visit are Frederikstad and Halden, with their ancient fortresses.

Fredrikstad
pop 67,420
Fredrikstad, founded by King Fredrik II, has an enclosed fortress town (Gamlebyen) complete with moats, gates and a drawbridge, built in 1663 as protection against a belligerent Sweden. Gamlebyen's central square has an ATM, a café and an unflattering statue of King Frederik II.

Things to See & Do You can walk around the perimeter of the **fortress walls**, once ringed by 200 cannons, and through the narrow,

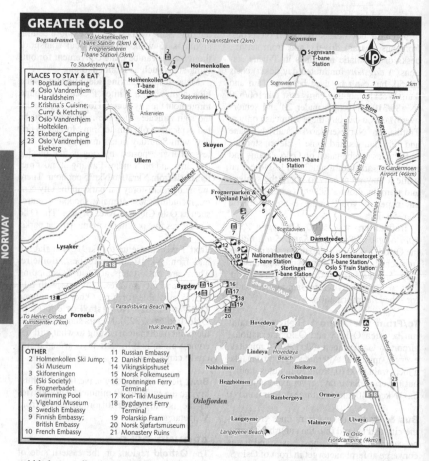

GREATER OSLO

PLACES TO STAY & EAT
1 Bogstad Camping
4 Oslo Vandrerhjem Haraldsheim
5 Krishna's Cuisine; Curry & Ketchup
13 Oslo Vandrerhjem Holtekilen
22 Ekeberg Camping
23 Oslo Vandrerhjem Ekeberg

OTHER
2 Holmenkollen Ski Jump; Ski Museum
3 Skiforeningen (Ski Society)
6 Frognerbadet Swimming Pool
7 Vigeland Museum
8 Swedish Embassy
9 Finnish Embassy; British Embassy
10 French Embassy
11 Russian Embassy
12 Danish Embassy
14 Vikingskipshuset
15 Norsk Folkemuseum
16 Dronningen Ferry Terminal
17 Kon-Tiki Museum
18 Bygdøynes Ferry Terminal
19 Polarskip Fram
20 Norsk Sjøfartsmuseum
21 Monastery Ruins

cobbled streets lined with still-lived-in historic buildings, most dating from the 17th century. The fort's infantry barracks have been converted into tourist accommodation.

Across the moat, 15 minutes' walk down Kongens gate, is the intact **Kongsten Festning** (Kongsten Fort; admission free), which sits on a bluff above a city park and dates from 1685. It makes for pleasant strolling and it's fun to scramble around the turrets, embankments, walls and stockade.

Places to Stay & Eat In the grounds of Kongsten Fort, the fairly average **Fredrikstad Motell & Camping** (☎ 69 32 05 32; Torsnesveien 16; camping with/without car Nkr140/90, motel singles/doubles Nkr390/490, 2/4-person cabins Nkr260/360) is the only choice

for budget accommodation; call in advance or you may find it closed. At the renovated **Artillery Barracks** (☎ 69 32 30 40; Gamlebyen; 4-person room Nkr500), room rates exclude breakfast and there aren't any kitchen facilities.

In Gamlebyen, the recommended **Major-Stuen** (☎ 69 32 15 55; Voldportgata 73; mains Nkr125-199) has an international menu but specialises in traditional Norwegian dishes. Just off the central square in Gamlebyen, **Lille Frederik** (Torvgaten; burgers with salad Nkr49-84) is the place for burgers, snacks and coffee.

Getting There & Away Trains to Fredrikstad leave roughly hourly from Oslo S (Nkr146, 1¼ hours). All continue to Halden (Nkr50, 35 minutes).

Getting Around From Fredrikstad station it's a five-minute walk to the riverfront, where a frequent ferry (Nkr6, one minute) shuttles across the Glomma River to the fortress' main gate. Alternatively, take bus No 362 from the city centre towards Torsnes and get off at Torsnesveien.

Halden
pop 21,120
Halden is quiet enough now, but it has the imposing 17th-century fortified hill-top **Fredriksten Festning** (☎ 69 18 54 11; adult/child Nkr40/10, tours Nkr45/20; open 10am-5pm daily 18 May-20 Aug), the site of many fierce battles between Norway and Sweden. Its crowning event came on 11 December 1718, when the warmongering Swedish King Karl XII was shot dead on the site (a monument now marks the spot). There are several museums in the fortress, all covered by the general admission fee.

The convenient **Fredriksten Camping** (☎ 69 18 40 32; tent sites Nkr110, 4-person cabins Nkr275-300), in the fortress grounds, offers a quiet green spot to pitch a tent. **Halden HI Hostel** (☎ 69 21 69 68; e halden .hostel@vandrerhjem.no; Brødløs; dorm beds Nkr100, singles/doubles Nkr135/255; open 25 June-8 Aug), at the suburban Tosterød school, offers standard rooms in ordinary modern buildings. Take bus Nos 102 to 104 (marked Gimle) from Busterud Park.

Near the waterfront, the **Pub Royal** (Olav V's gate 1) is a local favourite, with steaks, pizza (from Nkr65) and à la carte pasta and chicken dishes. **Dragon House** (☎ 69 18 44 67; Borgergata 3; mains from Nkr70) serves a wide range of acceptable Chinese dishes. By the main square, **Lunsjbaren** serves decent sandwiches, ice cream, burgers, lasagne and chips (from Nkr25).

Trains run roughly hourly from Oslo to Halden (Nkr180, 1¾ hours) via Fredrikstad (Nkr50, 35 minutes), while two trains a day continue on to Gothenburg in Sweden.

Southern Norway

Sørlandet, the curving south coast, is magnetic for Norwegians when the weather turns warm. The coast is largely rocky with a heavy scattering of low stone islands, and Sørlandet's numerous coves and bays are ideal for Norwegian holiday-makers with their own boats. The attraction is generally not as great for foreign travellers, the majority of whom have just arrived from places with warmer water and better beaches.

The Sørland train line, which runs 586km from Stavanger to Oslo via Kristiansand, stays inland most of the way, but buses meet the trains and link the rail line with most south-coast towns. The main highway follows a winding route from Stavanger to Kristiansand (E39) then on to Oslo (E18).

STAVANGER & AROUND
pop 106,000
Stavanger, Norway's fourth largest city, was once a bustling fishing centre and, in its heyday, had more than 70 sardine canneries. By the 1960s, the depletion of fish stocks had brought an end to the industry, but the discovery of North Sea oil spared Stavanger from hard times. The city now holds the title 'Oil Capital of Norway'; that's perhaps no greater tourist draw than pickled herring, but it has brought prosperity and a cosmopolitan community with nearly 3000 British and US oil people.

Most visitors to Stavanger arriving on the ferry from England make a beeline for Bergen or Oslo. However, it's well worth spending at least a day in Stavanger – it has a historic harbour area, a medieval cathedral and several excellent local museums.

Orientation & Information
The adjacent bus and train stations are a 10-minute walk from the harbour. Most of Stavanger's sights are within easy walking distance of the harbour. The Kulturhus holds the public library, a cinema, an art gallery and the new children's museum. On sunny days the pedestrian streets by the Kulturhus are alive with students, street musicians and pavement vendors.

Ask the **tourist office** (☎ 51 85 92 00; e info@visitstavanger.com; Rosenkildetorget 1; open 9am-8pm daily June-Aug, shorter weekly hrs & closed Sun Sept-May) for details of the 12 annual festivals in Stavanger.

Preikestolen & Lysefjord
The area's most popular outing is the two-hour hike to the top of the incredible Preikestolen (Pulpit Rock), 25km east of Stavanger. You can inch up to the edge of its flat top and peer

NORWAY

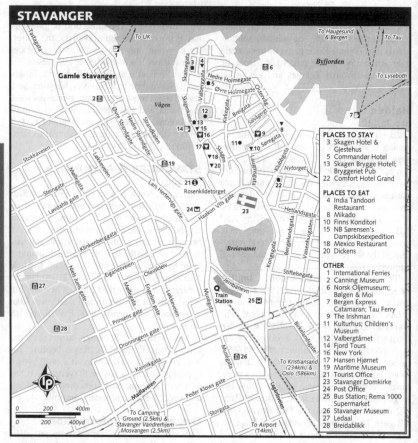

STAVANGER

PLACES TO STAY
3 Skagen Hotel &
    Gjestehus
5 Commandør Hotel
13 Skagen Brygge Hotell;
    Bryggeriet Pub
22 Comfort Hotel Grand

PLACES TO EAT
4 India Tandoori
    Restaurant
8 Mikado
10 Finns Konditori
15 NB Sørensen's
    Dampskibsexpedition
18 Mexico Restaurant
20 Dickens

OTHER
1 International Ferries
2 Canning Museum
6 Norsk Oljemuseum;
    Bølgen & Moi
7 Bergen Express
    Catamaran; Tau Ferry
9 The Irishman
11 Kulturhus; Children's
    Museum
12 Valbergtårnet
14 Fjord Tours
16 New York
17 Hansen Hjørnet
19 Maritime Museum
21 Tourist Office
23 Stavanger Domkirke
24 Post Office
25 Bus Station; Rema 1000
    Supermarket
26 Stavanger Museum
27 Ledaal
28 Breidablikk

600m straight down to the Lysefjord. From Stavanger take the 8.20am ferry to Tau (Nkr30, 40 minutes), from where a connecting bus (Nkr45) takes you to the trailhead (mid-June to August only), then returns at 4.15pm.

If you'd rather look up at Pulpit Rock from the bottom, the **Fjord Tours** (☎ 51 53 73 40) sightseeing boat leaves Stavanger daily from 18 May to 31 August to cruise the steep-walled Lysefjord. Tickets (adult/child Nkr250/125) can be purchased at the tourist office.

A good outing, if you have a vehicle, is to take the **car ferry** (reservations ☎ 51 86 87 80) from Stavanger all the way to Lysebotn, at the head of the Lysefjord. From there, drive up the mountain pass to Sirdal, along a narrow road that climbs 1000m with 27 hairpin turns, for a scenic ride back to Stavanger. Starting at the Øygardsstølen Café car park, near the top of the bends, a strenuous 10km-return hike leads to the second wonder of Lysefjord, the **Kjeragbolten** boulder, or chockstone, lodged between two rock faces about 2m apart but with 1000m of empty space underneath! The ferry takes four hours, leaving 8.30am daily from mid-June to mid-August; it costs Nkr266 for a car with driver plus Nkr117 for each additional passenger (or pedestrians). Advance reservations are advised.

Other Attractions

A fun quarter for strolling about is **Gamle Stavanger**, on the west side of the harbour, where cobblestone walkways lead through rows of well-preserved early-18th-century whitewashed wooden houses.

Stavanger Domkirke *(Haakon VIIs gate; open 11am-6pm Mon & Tues, 10am-6pm Wed-Sat, 1pm-6pm Sun mid-May–mid-Sept, shorter hrs mid-Sept–mid-May)* is an impressive medieval stone cathedral dating from around 1125. An atmospheric time to visit is during the organ recital at 11.15am on Thursday.

The unusual and interesting **Norsk Olje-museum** *(Norwegian Petroleum Museum;* ☎ *51 93 93 00; Kjeringholmen; adult/child Nkr75/35; open 10am-7pm daily June-Aug, 10am-4pm Mon-Sat & 10am-6pm Sun Sept-May)* traces the history of oil formation and exploration in the North Sea.

You can get a good view of the city and the harbour from **Valbergtårnet**, a 150-year-old tower at the end of Valberggata.

The entertaining **Children's Museum** *(*☎ *51 91 23 93; Kulturhus; adult/child Nkr65/35; open 10am-4pm Tues-Sat, 12.30-5pm Sun)* includes a tree hut and a wide variety of exhibits made by kids themselves.

The following **museums** *(*☎ *51 84 27 00)* are all open 11am to 4pm daily from mid-June to mid-August (shorter hours early June and late August) and have combined same-day admission costs of adult/family Nkr40/90. **Stavanger Museum** *(Muségata 16)* has the standard collection of stuffed animals in one wing and local history exhibits in another. More interesting are the **Maritime Museum** *(Nedre Strandgate 17)*, in two restored warehouses, which gives a good glimpse of Stavanger's maritime history, and the fascinating **Canning Museum** *(Øvre Strandgate 88A)* in an old sardine cannery. There are also two 19th-century manor houses built by wealthy ship owners: the recently restored **Ledaal** *(Eiganesveien 45)* serves as the residence for visiting members of the royal family, and the excellent **Breidablikk** *(Eiganesveien 40A)* is just across the road.

Places to Stay

There's a **camping ground** *(*☎ *51 53 29 71; Tjensvoll 1B; tent camping from Nkr80, huts for 2/4 people Nkr260/350)* near the lakeside HI hostel **Stavanger Vandrerhjem Mosvangen** *(*☎ *51 87 29 00;* e *stavanger.mosvangen .hostel@vandrerhjem.no; Henrik Ibsens gate 21; dorm beds Nkr145, doubles Nkr290; open June-Aug, Sept-May with advance booking)*, 3km from the city centre (bus No 78 or 79).

The turf-roofed HI hostel **Preikestolen** *(*☎ *97 16 55 51;* e *preikestolen.hostel@vandrerhjem .no; dorm beds from Nkr140, doubles from Nkr375; open June-Aug)* is within walking distance of Pulpit Rock (for directions see the Preikestolen & Lysefjord section earlier).

Contact the tourist office to book **B&Bs**, with singles/doubles around Nkr250/420 (plus Nkr25 booking fee). **Skagen Hotel & Gjestehus** *(*☎ *51 93 85 00;* e *lbjorgum@ world-online.no; Skansegata 7; singles/ doubles from Nkr525/625)* has renovated en suite rooms.

The friendly **Commandør Hotel** *(*☎ *51 89 53 00;* e *comhot@online.no; Valberggata 9; singles/doubles from Nkr500/650)* offers pleasant accommodation with private bathrooms.

An evening buffet, and breakfast, is included at the aptly named **Comfort Hotel Grand** *(*☎ *51 20 14 00;* e *booking.stavanger@comfort.cho icehotels.no; Klubbgata 3; singles/doubles from Nkr495/596)*. The large and opulent **Skagen Brygge Hotell** *(*☎ *51 85 00 00;* e *booking@skagenbryggehotell.no; Skagenkaien 30; singles/doubles from Nkr700/ 850)* offers particularly good weekend value.

Places to Eat

The imaginative menus at the stylish **Bølgen & Moi** *(*☎ *51 93 93 51; Norsk Oljemuseum, Kjeringholmen; mains Nkr110-295)* include monkfish, lamb and veal; desserts are highly recommended. **NB Sørensen's Dampskibsexpedition** *(*☎ *51 84 38 20; Skagen 26; specials Nkr80-120, mains Nkr119-255)* offers fine Norwegian food with a daily special in the pub and a pricier gourmet seafood restaurant upstairs.

Rustic **Dickens** *(Skagenkaien 6; mains Nkr59-176)* has a varied menu and a decent pizza buffet for Nkr76. **India Tandoori Restaurant** *(Valberggata 14; dishes Nkr89-209)* offers authentic northern Indian dishes, and at the **Mexico Restaurant** *(Skagenkaien 12; mains Nkr135-249)* there's high-quality Mexican fare. The Chinese/Japanese-oriented **Mikado** *(Østervåg 9; lunch Nkr48-79, most dinner mains Nkr83-150)* serves a good range of far-eastern dishes.

There's a moderately priced **Caroline Café** at the train station and a **fast-food eatery** and **Rema 1000** supermarket at the bus station. In the centre, opposite the Kulturhus, **Finns Konditori** has good pastries and bread.

NORWAY

Entertainment

There's good jazz at the **Bryggeriet Pub** (Skagen 28) on weekends. **The Irishman** (Høleberggata 9) features live folk music five nights weekly. There's also live music several times weekly at **Hansen Hjørnet** (Skagenkaien 18; no cover charge). On weekends, **New York** (Skagenkaien 24) provides fun and dancing for the young and funky.

Getting There & Away

Buses (Nkr50) leave frequently for the airport (14km south of town) in connection with international flights (serving Aberdeen, Copenhagen, London Heathrow, Newcastle and Stockholm) and internal flights.

The Nor-Way Bussekspress bus to Oslo (Nkr620, 10¼ hours) leaves Stavanger at 8.30am daily. Buses from Bergen to Stavanger (Nkr370, 5¾ hours) run roughly every two hours. Stavanger's only railway line runs to Oslo (Nkr700, 7¾ hours, one to three daily) via Kristiansand (Nkr336, three hours, four to seven daily). Daily (except Saturday) there's an overnight train, which leaves Stavanger at 10.45pm.

The **HSD Flaggruten** (☎ 51 86 87 80), express passenger catamaran to Bergen (Nkr620, 4¼ hours) and Haugesund, leaves two or three times daily; Eurail, Norway Rail and ScanRail pass-holders get 50% discounts.

For information on the boat from the UK, see the introductory Getting There & Away section of this chapter.

Getting Around

The city centre is a combination of narrow streets and cobbled pedestrian walkways that are best explored on foot. You'll find car parks next to the post office and on the southern side of the bus station.

MANDAL

pop 12,800

Mandal, Norway's southernmost town, is best known for having the country's finest bathing beach. For information, contact **Mandal Tourist Information** (☎ 38 27 83 00; Bryggegaten 10).

Things to See & Do

The 800m-long **Sjøsanden** beach, about 1km from the centre, is Norway's Copacabana and the forest backdrop is as lovely as the sand and sea itself. **Mandal Museum** (☎ 38 27 30 00;

Store Elvegata 5/6; adult/child Nkr10/free; open 11am-5pm Mon-Fri, 11am-2pm Sat & 2pm-5pm Sun 24 June-18 Aug) displays a host of historical maritime and fishing artefacts and works by local artists, including Mandal's favourite son, Gustav Vigeland.

At the southernmost point in Norway, 36km west of Mandal, you'll find wild coastal scenery and historical exhibitions at the classic lighthouse, **Lindesnes Fyr** (☎ 38 26 19 02; Lindesnes; adult/child Nkr30/free; open 10am-6pm daily May, 10am-8pm daily June & Sept, 10am-9pm daily July & Aug). Buses from Mandal (Nkr49, one hour) travel to the lighthouse on Monday, Wednesday and Friday.

Places to Stay & Eat

The **Sandnes Naturcamp** (☎ 38 26 51 51; Sandnes; tent sites Nkr100, rooms from Nkr250) lies pleasantly by the river Mandalselva, 2km north of town. The basic rooms in the atmospheric **Kjøbmandsgaarden Hotel** (☎ 38 26 12 76; e kjobmand@online.no; Store Elvegaten 57; singles/doubles Nkr450/670, with bathroom Nkr680/970), formerly a hardware shop dating from 1863, seem overpriced but they are clean.

If you just want a reasonable mid-range meal, try **Vertshuset Smak & Behag** (Store Elvegate 47B; pizzas from Nkr99, mains Nkr179-239). **Dr Nielsen's** (Store Elvegate 47A; mains around Nkr70-80) serves Greek food, including pasta, chicken and some fish dishes.

Getting There & Away

Express buses run two to four times daily between Stavanger (Nkr305, 3¾ hours) and Kristiansand (Nkr70, 45 minutes) via Mandal.

KRISTIANSAND

pop 57,040

Busy Kristiansand, the capital of Sørlandet and the fifth largest city in Norway, is Norway's closest port to Denmark and offers the first glimpse of the country for many ferry travellers from the south. Kristiansand has a grid pattern, or kvadraturen, of wide streets laid out by King Christian IV, who founded the city in 1641. It's a busy seaside holiday resort for Norwegians, but foreign visitors generally pile off the ferries and onto the first train, missing most of what the area has to offer.

KRISTIANSAND

Baneheia

0   125   250m
0   125   250yd

To Oddernes Kirke (1km),
Kristiansand Dyrepark (9km)
& Oslo (330km)

E18

Kongsgård-allé

Olavs vei

Parkveien

Tordalsveien

Marvikveien

Otra

To Rolighedan
Camping (2km)

Østerveien

Elvegata

Kuholmsveien

POSEBYEN

To Mandal
(42km) &
Stavanger
(250km)

Oddemesveien

Tordenskiolds gate

Festningsgata

Kristian IV gate

Skippergaten

Gyldenløves gate

Radhus gate

Holbergs gate

Kronprinsens gate

Town
Square

Tollbodgata

Dronningens gate

Kongens gate

Skansen

16

17

Markens gate

Train
Station

Vestre Strandgate

Kirkegata

Østre Strandgate

Strandpromenaden

4
3
1
2
10
14
7
9
8
11
12
13
15
5
6

To Hirtshals (Denmark),
Gothenburg (Sweden)
& Newcastle (UK)

Yacht
Harbour

NORWAY

PLACES TO STAY
8 Clarion Hotel Ernst
12 Hotel Norge
14 Sjøgløtt Hotel
17 Kristiansand
   Vandrerhjem Tangen

PLACES TO EAT
1 Peppe's Pizza
4 Mega Cafeteria
7 Bakery
10 Produce Vendors

11 McDonald's
13 Sjøhuset
16 Snadderskiosken

OTHER
2 Domkirke (Cathedral)
3 Tourist Office
5 Bus Station
6 Ferry Terminal
9 Post Office
15 Christiansholm
   Festning

Orientation & Information

The train, bus and ferry terminals are together on the west side of the city centre. Markens gate, a pedestrian street a block inland, is the central shopping and restaurant area.

Ask the **tourist office** (☎ 38 12 13 14; e destinasjon@sorlandet.com; Vestre Strandgate 32) for details about tours, including boat trips and elk safaris. Banks are numerous, but the **post office** (Markens gate 19) has longer hours and lower exchange fees.

Things to See & Do

The most prominent feature along Strandpromenaden is **Christiansholm Festning** (admission free; open 9am-9pm daily mid-May–mid-Sept), built between 1662 and 1672; there's a fine coastal view from the cannon-ringed wall. From there, walk inland along the tree-lined Festningsgata and turn left onto Gyldenløves gate, passing the **town square** and **domkirke** (cathedral; Kirkegata; open 9am-2pm or 4pm Mon-Fri June-Aug, 10am-2pm Sat late June-early Aug), which is Norway's largest church. You can climb the tower for adult/child Nkr20/10.

It's also worth taking a slow stroll around the enchanting **Posebyen**, or Old Town, which takes in most of 14 blocks at the northern end of Kristiansand's characteristic kvadraturen.

Baneheia, a park with lakes and trails, is just north of the city centre. The 11th-century Romanesque **Oddernes kirke**, about 1.5km further northeast, contains a rune stone, and a baroque pulpit from 1704; it's open variable hours.

Kristiansand Dyrepark (☎ 38 04 98 00; adult/child Nkr80/65 to Nkr215/180; open 10am-7pm daily late June-early Aug, variable daily hrs early Aug-late June) has gradually expanded into one of Norway's most popular and fun-filled domestic attractions. Mainly catering to families with children, the park includes a funfair, an excellent zoo, a 'nordic wilderness' (where you can spot wolves, lynx and elk) and the fantasy village of Kardamomme By. It's off the E18, 9km east of town; Dyreparkbussen and bus No 1 run to the park more or less hourly from June to August.

Places to Stay
Roligheden Camping (☎ 38 09 67 22; bus No 15; camping per tent site/person Nkr100/Nkr25, 4-person apartments Nkr650-1100) is at a popular beach 3km east of town. The HI hostel, **Kristiansand Vandrerhjem Tangen** (☎ 38 02 83 10; e kristiansand.hostel@vandrerhjem.no; Skansen 8; dorm beds Nkr190, singles/doubles Nkr380/420; open mid-Jan–mid-Dec), is a modern place, about 10 minutes' walk east of the fortress; prices include breakfast.

The cosy **Sjøglott Hotel** (☎/fax 38 02 21 20; e sjoglott@sjoglott.no; Østre Strandgate 25; singles/doubles with shared bathroom Nkr350/630, en suite Nkr590/780) has 10 rooms. The best upmarket options are the traditional **Hotel Norge** (☎ 38 17 40 00; e firmapost@hotel-norge.no; Dronningens gate 5; singles/doubles from Nkr630/890) and the more modern **Clarion Hotel Ernst** (☎ 38 12 86 00; e booking.ernst@clarion.choicehotels.no; Rådhus gate 2; singles Nkr645-1145, doubles Nkr850-1250), which serves excellent breakfasts in a glass-roofed courtyard.

Places to Eat
For a splurge, the harbourside **Sjøhuset** (☎ 38 02 62 60; Østre Strandgate 12A; mains Nkr135-249) offers good seafood and a scenic setting.

Peppe's Pizza (Gyldenløves gate 7) serves pizzas (Nkr134) that will feed two people. The **Mega Cafeteria**, in the supermarket opposite the train station, has cheap eats. For a great meal deal, follow the locals to **Snadderkiosken** (Østre Strand gate 78A; dishes Nkr13-79), which offers a relatively vast and great-value menu, including things like meatballs or cod with mashed potato, and grilled chicken. There

are good **bakeries** on Rådhus gate near the post office and diagonally opposite the extraordinary **McDonald's** (Markens gate 11), housed in a former bank. **Produce vendors** sell fresh fruit and vegetables on the southeastern side of the cathedral.

Getting There & Away
Express buses head north once or twice daily to Haukeligrend, with connections to Bergen (from Kristiansand: Nkr580, 12 hours). Trains run to Stavanger (Nkr336, three hours, four to seven daily) and Oslo (Nkr462, 4¾ hours, three to six daily), as well as express buses.

Regional buses depart hourly for towns along the south coast, including Arendal (Nkr93, 1½ hours) and Mandal (Nkr52, 45 minutes). For Risør (Nkr160, 2¾ hours), Nor-Way Bussekspress allows you to get off the Oslo express, departing Kristiansand at 2pm daily.

The E18 runs along the northern side of the city centre and is reached via Vestre Strandgate. For information on ferries to Denmark, Sweden and the UK see this chapter's introductory Getting There & Away section.

LILLESAND
pop 3000
Between Kristiansand and Grimstad you'll pass Lillesand, which has a wonderful unspoiled village centre of old whitewashed houses befitting the 'white town' image that so many south-coast towns claim. It's well worth wandering around for an hour or two. For tourist information, contact **Lillesand Turistkontor** (☎ 37 26 16 80; Tollboden; open 10am-6pm Mon-Fri, 10am-4pm Sat & noon-4pm Sun, mid-June–mid-Aug).

Accommodation options are rather expensive, but it's worth checking out the excellent dining room at the atmospheric **Lillesand Hotel Norge** (☎ 37 27 01 44; Strandgata 3; snacks & mains Nkr75-260), a historic relic which dates from 1837.

Nettbuss runs hourly to Kristiansand (Nkr46, 40 minutes), Grimstad (Nkr37, 25 minutes) and Arendal (Nkr59, one hour).

GRIMSTAD
pop 8180
Grimstad, renowned as the sunniest spot in Norway, is one of the loveliest of the 'white towns' on the Skagerrak coast and has a charming pedestrianised centre with narrow

streets. The current low-key atmosphere belies Grimstad's past as a major shipbuilding centre – at one point in the 19th century the town had 40 shipyards, and 90 ships were under construction simultaneously.

The helpful **Grimstad Turistkontor** (☎ 37 04 40 41; Smith Petersensgata 3; open 8.30am-4pm Mon-Fri, longer hrs June-Aug), near the waterfront, can suggest various boat trips to the outlying skerries (rocky islets).

Ibsenhuset & Grimstad By Museum

In 1847, Henrik Ibsen started work at the Lars Nielsen pharmacy, where he lived in a small room and cultivated his interest in writing. By the time he left Grimstad for university studies in Christiania (Oslo), Ibsen had qualified as a pharmacist's assistant and was on his way to future renown as a writer. Some of his finest works are set in Grimstad's offshore skerries.

The excellent Grimstad By Museum (☎ 37 04 46 53; Henrik Ibsens gate 14; adult/child Nkr40/15; open 11am-5pm Mon-Sat, 1pm-5pm Sun May–mid-Sept) includes the virtually untouched Lars Nielsen pharmacy and Ibsenhuset (the Ibsen house), which contains many of the writer's belongings.

Places to Stay & Eat

For camping, the nearest option is **Bie Appartement & Feriesenter** (☎ 37 04 03 96; off Arendalsveien; tent sites Nkr185, cabins Nkr450-1200), 800m northeast of the centre along Arendalsveien. The modern **Norlandia Sørlandet Hotel** (☎ 37 09 05 00; e service@sorlandet.norlandia.no; Televeien 21; singles/doubles from Nkr610/790) offers fine rooms in a quiet woodland setting on the western edge of town.

The highly recommended **Apotekergården** (☎ 37 04 50 25; Skolegaten 3; mains from Nkr198) is an excellent gourmet restaurant with outdoor seating. For tasty fish dinners, you can't beat **Dr Berg** (☎ 37 04 44 99; Storgata 2; dishes around Nkr140), right at the harbour.

Also down at the harbour, you can get good hotdogs for only Nkr10 from the **Dampen kiosk**.

Getting There & Away

The bus station is on Storgata, at the harbour. Nor-Way Bussekspress runs between Oslo

(Nkr360, five hours) and Kristiansand (Nkr74, one hour) via Grimstad three to five times daily. Nettbuss buses to/from Arendal run once or twice hourly (Nkr36, 30 minutes).

ARENDAL

pop 25,440

Picturesque Arendal, the administrative centre of Aust-Agder county, is centred on the Pollen harbour. **Arendal Turistkontor** (☎ 37 00 55 44, Langbrygga 5; open 9am-7pm Mon-Sat & noon-7pm Sun mid-June–mid-Aug, 9am-4pm Mon-Fri mid-Aug–mid-June), on the eastern side of Pollen, dispenses tourist information.

Things to See & Do

Just a few minutes' walk south of the bus station brings you into the old harbourside area of **Tyholmen**, with its attractively restored 19th-century wooden buildings. Check out the unusual **Rådhus** (☎ 37 01 30 00; Rådhusgata 10; admission free; open 9am-3pm Mon-Fri), originally a shipowner's home dating from 1815, later becoming the town hall in 1844. It features an elegant original staircase and portraits of Norwegian royalty.

The **Aust-Agder Museum** (☎ 37 07 35 00; Parkveien 16; adult/child Nkr20/10; open 9am-5pm Mon-Fri, noon-5pm Sun 24 June-19 Aug, closing 3pm 20 Aug-23 June) displays objects brought home by the town's sailors (from 1832), as well as relics of Arendal's shipbuilding, timber and import-export trades, and decent collections of folk art, furniture, farming implements and sailing paraphernalia.

Ask the tourist office for details of the offshore islands.

Places to Stay & Eat

For anything inexpensive, you'll have to head out of town. **Nidelv Brygge og Camping** (☎ 37 01 14 25; Vesterveien 251, Hisøy; tent sites Nkr60-80, cabins Nkr250-600) lies on the Nidelv river at Hisøy, 6km west of Arendal. From town, take any half-hourly bus for Kristiansand or Grimstad (Nkr22). The curious **Ting Hai Hotel** (☎ 37 02 22 01; e ting@online.no; Østregate 5; singles/doubles from Nkr580/800) is associated with a recommended Chinese restaurant (mains from Nkr100).

Madam Reiersen ((☎ 37 02 19 00; Nedre Tyholmsvei 3; mains Nkr125-238) offers reasonably sophisticated fare, with an emphasis on pasta dishes. American-run **Café Det Lindvedske hus** *(Nedre Tyholmsvei 7B; dishes Nkr48-88)*, with atmospheric 200-year-old decor, offers a good choice of sandwiches, salads and pasta.

For a tasty snack, stop at the waterfront **fish market**, which sells inexpensive fish cakes.

Getting There & Away
Nor-Way Busekspress buses between Kristiansand (Nkr97, 1¾ hours) and Oslo (Nkr340, four hours) call in several times daily at the Arendal bus station, in a large square a block west of Pollen harbour. Regional buses connect Arendal with Grimstad (Nkr36, 30 minutes, once or twice hourly) and Kristiansand (Nkr93, 1½ hours, hourly).

Arendal is connected with the main rail system by a trunk line from Nelaug.

RISØR
pop 4000
Risør, with its cluster of historic, white houses built up around a busy little fishing harbour, is one of the most picturesque villages on the south coast. It's a haunt for artists, and many well-to-do yachties make it their summer base.

Things to See & Do
The small but interesting quayside **Risør Aquarium** *(☎ 37 15 32 82; Dampskips-brygga; adult/child Nkr40/20; open 11am-7pm daily 25 June-5 Aug, otherwise shorter hrs)* houses saltwater fish, crustaceans and shellfish common to Norway's south coast. For the lowdown on the geology, fishing economy and 275-year history of Risør, visit the **Risør Museum** *(☎ 37 15 17 77; Prestegata 9; adult/family Nkr30/50; open 11am-5pm daily mid-June–mid-Aug)*.

Next to wandering around the harbour and the narrow streets in the old town, one of the most popular activities is to visit the offshore islands, which can be reached by inexpensive water taxis. The most frequented island, **Stangholmen**, has an old lighthouse with a restaurant.

Places to Stay & Eat
Most visitors to Risør stay on their boats. The closest camping ground, **Moen Camping** *(☎ 92 23 74 75; Moen; tent sites from Nkr80, cabins Nkr400-500)*, is 11km west of town

and 2km from the E18, but there are regular buses. **Risør Kunstforum** *(☎ 37 15 63 83; Tjenngata 76; singles/doubles Nkr400/500)*, 1km west of the harbour, offers do-it-yourself breakfast as well as art and sculpture classes. Rooms at the only in-town hotel, the **Risør Hotel** *(☎ 37 15 07 00; singles Nkr695-995, doubles Nkr995-1495)*, are pricey.

The recommended **Brasserie Krag** *(Kragsgata 12; mains Nkr98-186)* has a fairly diverse menu. You will find a couple of moderately priced pavement **cafés** at the harbour. Ice-cream shops abound and there's fresh produce at the harbourside **market**; a **bakery** *(Kragsgata)* is one block west.

Getting There & Away
Buses to/from Risør (Nkr51, 45 minutes) connect with the train at Gjerstad several times daily. Nor-Way Busekspress buses between Kristiansand (Nkr140, three hours) and Oslo (Nkr320, 3¾ hours) connect at Vinterkjær with local buses to/from Risør (Nkr26, 20 minutes).

TELEMARK
Most of the Telemark region is sparsely populated and rural, with steep mountains, deep valleys, high plateaus and countless lakes.

Apart from routes to Kongsberg, public transport in this region isn't particularly convenient; most buses run infrequently and the rail lines cover only the southeastern part of Telemark, so sightseeing is best done by car. Telemark's westernmost train station is at Bø; from there, connecting buses lead west to Dalen, Åmot and on to Odda in Hardanger. For tourist information, contact **Telemark-reiser** *(☎ 35 90 00 20; Postboks 3133, Handelstorget, N-3707 Skien)*.

Telemark Canal
The Telemark canal system, 105km of lakes and canals with 18 locks, runs from the industrialised city of **Skien** to the small town of **Dalen**.

Daily from 17 June to 10 August, a couple of century-old **sightseeing boats** *(☎ 35 90 00 30)* make the unhurried, if not sluggish, 11-hour journey (adult/child Nkr310/155 one way). At other times between mid-May and early September, they run three times weekly.

Trains run every hour or two between Skien and Oslo (Nkr231, 2¾ hours).

Places to Stay One kilometre from the Dalen dock, **Buøy Camping Dalen** (☎ 35 07 75 87; tent sites Nkr80-140, singles/triples Nkr200/350, cabins Nkr450-890) has a reasonable camping ground with hostel-style rooms and cabins. Skien's **HI hostel** (☎ 35 50 48 70; Moflatveien 65; dorm beds Nkr130, singles/doubles Nkr280/400) has rooms and tent space for campers; breakfast is included. Nearby **Hotell Herkules** (☎ 35 59 63 11; Moflatveien 59; singles/doubles Nkr525/720) is a reasonably good mid-range choice.

Notodden
pop 8000

Notodden is an industrial town of little note, but the nearby **Heddal stave church** (☎ 35 02 04 00; Heddal; adult/child Nkr30/free, Sun services free; open 10am-5pm daily 20 May-19 June & 21 Aug-10 Sept, 9am-7pm daily 20 June-20 Aug) is Telemark's most visited attraction. It's a mighty impressive structure and possibly dates from 1242, but parts of the chancel date from as early as 1147. Of great interest are the 'rose' paintings, the runic inscription, the bishop's chair and the altarpiece. On Sundays from Easter to November, services are held at 11am (visitors are welcome, but to avoid disruption, you must remain for the entire one-hour service); after 1pm, the church is again open to the public.

From Notodden, buses heading for Seljord and Bondal stop at Heddal. Between Kongsberg and Notodden (Nkr70, 35 minutes), TIMEkspressen buses run once or twice an hour.

Rjukan
pop 3730

The long, narrow industrial town of Rjukan is squeezed into the deep Vestfjord Valley at the base of the 1883m **Mt Gausta**, Telemark's highest peak. The route to the top starts at lake Heddersvann (1173m), 16km southeast from town (by road Fv651).

Ask the **tourist office** (☎ 35 09 12 90; www.rjukan-turistkontor.no; Torget 2) about local activities, including fun **rail bicycle rides**.

The **Industrial Workers Museum** (☎ 35 09 90 00; adult/child Nkr55/30; open 10am-6pm daily May-Sept), 7km west of Rjukan, has an exhibit about the Norwegian Resistance's daring sabotage of the heavy-water plant that was used here by the Nazis during WWII. Take the Bybuss westbound (Nkr23, five minutes, three daily Monday to Friday).

From the top station of the Krossobanen cable car (Nkr35), above Rjukan, it's an eight-hour walk north to the Kalhovd mountain hut and a network of trails that stretches north and west across the expansive moors of **Hardangervidda**, a popular wilderness hiking area that boasts Norway's largest wild reindeer herd.

Acceptable camping is available at **Rjukan Hytte og Caravan Park** (☎ 35 09 63 53; rjukanhycar@c2i.net; tent sites Nkr30-40, camping per person Nkr12-14, cabins Nkr235-450), about 7km east of the town centre – take the Bybuss (Nkr23, five minutes). The rather plush centrally located **Park Hotell** (☎ 35 08 21 88; Sam Eydes gate 67; singles/doubles from Nkr495/645) has a fine restaurant. On the main square, the straightforward and popular **Torgkroa** (Sam Eydes gate 93; mains Nkr85-169) serves burgers (Nkr39 to Nkr70) and a variety of dinners, including pizzas from Nkr140.

An express bus connects Rjukan to Oslo (Nkr260, 3½ hours) via Kongsberg (Nkr160, 1¾ hours), two or three times daily.

Kragerø
pop 5460

A popular seaside resort with narrow streets and whitewashed houses, Kragerø has long served as a retreat for Norwegian artists, including Edvard Munch. The forested island **Jomfruland**, the most popular local destination, measures about 10km long and up to 600m wide and has mostly sandy beaches. Ferries between Kragerø and Jomfruland (Nkr29, 50 minutes) are run by **Kragerø Fjordbåtselskap** (☎ 35 98 58 58) two or three times daily.

At the fine **HI hostel** (☎ 35 98 57 00; Lovisenbergveien 20; dorm beds Nkr220, singles/doubles 405/440; open 24 June-18 Aug), about 2km from town, rates include breakfast. **Stim** (☎ 35 98 30 00, Storgata 1; 2-course meal Nkr350) is a highly recommended fish and fowl restaurant, with a contemporary international menu and fresh local produce. Alternatively, you'll find simple Norwegian fare at **Kafe Edvard** (Edvard Munchsvei 2; lunch specials from Nkr70).

The simplest approach is by rail from Oslo or Kristiansand to Neslandsvatn, where most of the trains meet a connecting bus to Kragerø.

NORWAY

BUSKERUD

The mainly forested county of Buskerud stretches northwest from Oslofjorden to the central highlands of Norway. Mineral resources, particularly silver, have been thoroughly exploited in Buskerud's hills and mountains.

Kongsberg
pop 15,730

Kongsberg was founded in 1624 following the discovery of one of the world's purest silver deposits in the nearby Numedal Valley. During the resulting silver rush, it briefly became the second-largest town in Norway. The Royal Mint is still in town, but the last mine, no longer able to turn a profit, closed in 1957.

Today, Kongsberg attracts people with its historic sites and winter skiing. The town's **tourist office** (☎ 32 73 50 00; W www.visitk ongsberg.no; Storgata 35) is opposite the train station.

Things to See The **Norwegian Mining Museum** (☎ 32 72 32 00; Hyttegata 3; adult/ child Nkr50/10; open 10am-5pm daily July– mid-Aug, shorter hrs mid-Aug–July) is in the town centre, just over the bridge on the west side of the Numedalslågen River. Set in an 1844 smelter, it has exhibits of mining, minerals, the Royal Mint, the local armaments industry, and skiing.

The **Lågdal folk museum** (☎ 32 73 34 68; Tillischbakken 8-10; adult/child Nkr40/10; open 11am-5pm daily mid-June–mid-Aug, shorter hrs mid-Aug–mid-June) has a collection of period farmhouses, WWII exhibits and an indoor museum with re-created 19th-century workshops and a fine optics section. It's 10 minutes' walk south of the train station: turn left on Bekkedokk, take the walkway parallel to the tracks and follow the signs.

Up on the hillside at Håvet, about 1km west of town and well signposted, you'll find curious **royal monograms** carved into a cliff.

In July and August, there are daily tours of the old **silver mines** (adult/child Nkr75/30) at Saggrenda, 8km from Kongsberg, which include a 2.3km train ride through cool subterranean shafts – bring a sweater! Tour times should be checked with the tourist office. The Oslo-Notodden TIMEkspressen bus runs from Kongsberg to Saggrenda (Nkr40, 10 minutes, hourly), then it's a 15-minute walk.

Places to Stay & Eat The Kongsberg **HI Hostel** (☎ 32 73 20 24; Vinjesgata 1; dorm beds Nkr195, singles/doubles from Nkr395/ 500) is about 1km from the train station: walk south on Storgata, cross the bridge, turn right and take the pedestrian walkway over the main road to Saggrenda. Rates include breakfast.

The comfortable **Gyldenløve Hotel** (☎ 32 86 58 00; Hermann Fossgata 1; singles/ doubles from Nkr675/835) is highly recommended and has good rates.

At the fine **Skrågata Mat & Vinhus** (☎ 32 72 28 22; Nymoens Skrågate; dinner mains Nkr86-240) the menu includes sandwiches, salads, pasta and beef and fish dishes. In the Old Town, west of the river, **Jeppe's Pizza** (Kirkegata 6; mains Nkr86-219) also offers steaks, fish and chips, Mexican-style dishes, spare ribs and salads. Pizzas start at Nkr85. With an authentic blast of Middle Eastern music, **Delfin's Kebab** (Schwabesgate 3; kebabs Nkr52-85) offers a range of kebabs and burgers. There's a bakery at the **Rimi supermarket**, 250m northwest of the station.

Getting There & Away Kongsberg is a 1½-hour train ride from Oslo (Nkr134, hourly). TIMEkspressen buses connect Kongsberg with Oslo (Nkr130, 1½ hours) and Notodden (Nkr70, 35 minutes) at least hourly throughout the day and overnight. An express bus connects Kongsberg and Rjukan (Nkr160, 1¾ hours) two or three times daily.

Central Norway

The central region of Norway, stretching west from Oslo towards the western fjords, includes vast swathes of forested fells, the country's highest mountains and some of the best-known national parks. The scenic Oslo–Bergen railway climbs through forests and alpine villages to Norway's cross-country skiing paradise, the stark Hardangervidda plateau.

HAMAR
pop 22,220

The commercial town of Hamar, sitting beside lake **Mjøsa**, Norway's largest lake, is the capital of Hedmark county and boasts proudly of hosting several Olympic events in 1994. The impressive **Northern Lights amphitheatre**, the world's largest wooden hall, was built for figure skating and short track-skating events. The town's landmark, however, is the **Vikingskipshuset sports arena**, an amazingly graceful structure with the lines of an upturned Viking ship; there's a **tourist office** (☎ 62 51 75 03) inside.

The extensive open-air **county museum** (☎ 62 54 27 00; Strandveien 100; adult/child Nkr65/30; open 10am-6pm mid-June–mid-Aug), 1.5km west of the town centre, includes 18th- and 19th-century buildings, a local folk history exhibit featuring the creepy Devil's Finger, and the extraordinary 'glass cathedral'. Take bus No 6 from the town library (Nkr20, once hourly).

From 25 June to 11 August, **Skibladner** (☎ 61 14 40 80; ⓦ www.skibladner.no), the world's oldest operating paddle steamer, cruises around lake Mjøsa. On Tuesday, Thursday and Saturday the boat sails at 11.15am from Hamar to Lillehammer (Nkr200/300 one way/return), leaving Lillehammer at 3.15pm for the return trip to Hamar.

The HI hostel, **Vikingskipet Motell og Vandrerhjem** (☎ 62 52 60 60; ⓔ hamar.hostel@vandrerhjem.no; Åkersvikavegen 24; dorm beds Nkr135, singles/doubles Nkr260/360) offers good-value accommodation within 100m of the sports arena. Breakfast is Nkr60 extra. Centrally located **Seiersted Pensjonat** (☎ 62 52 12 44, fax 62 55 22 48; Holsetgata 64; singles/doubles Nkr350/695) offers a homely atmosphere, with dinner available from Nkr55.

Reasonable **Pizzaninni** (Torggata 24) charges from Nkr80 for pizza; pasta dishes are all Nkr95. There's also **Seaside** (☎ 62 52 62 10; Brygga; mains Nkr179-235, 5-course dinner Nkr395), by the lake, which offers meat, fish and vegetarian dishes.

Nor-Way Bussekspress buses run to/from the western fjords several times daily. Frequent trains run between Oslo and Hamar (Nkr185, 1½ hours, once or twice hourly); some services continue to Trondheim (Nkr542, five hours, four or five daily) via Lillehammer. Trains also run to Røros (Nkr390, 3¼ hours, three to five daily), some with connections for Trondheim.

LILLEHAMMER & AROUND
pop 18,560
Lillehammer, at the northern end of lake Mjøsa, has long been a popular ski resort for Norwegians and, since hosting the 1994 Winter Olympics, it has attracted foreign visitors as well.

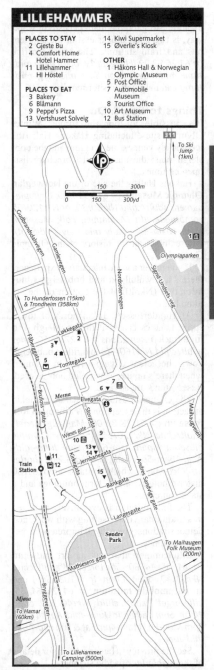

LILLEHAMMER

PLACES TO STAY
2 Gjeste Bu
4 Comfort Home Hotel Hammer
11 Lillehammer HI Hostel

PLACES TO EAT
3 Bakery
6 Blåmann
9 Peppe's Pizza
13 Vertshuset Solveig

14 Kiwi Supermarket
15 Øverlie's Kiosk

OTHER
1 Håkons Hall & Norwegian Olympic Museum
5 Post Office
7 Automobile Museum
8 Tourist Office
10 Art Museum
12 Bus Station

NORWAY

Lillehammer's centre is small and easy to explore. Storgata, the main pedestrian walkway, is two short blocks east of the adjacent bus and train stations. The **tourist office** (☎ 61 25 92 99; Elvegata 19; open daily mid-June–mid-Aug, Mon-Sat mid-Aug–mid-June) can help with visitor inquiries.

Things to See & Do

It's possible to tour the former Winter Olympic sites, including Håkons Hall (the ice-hockey venue), the ski jump and the bobsleigh runs; the main tourist brochure lists opening times.

Håkons Hall is the site of the **Norwegian Olympic Museum** (☎ 61 25 21 00; Olympiaparken; adult/child Nkr60/30, or Nkr120/55 combined with Maihaugen Folk Museum; open 10am-6pm daily mid-May–mid-Sept), with exhibits on the history of the Olympic Games.

If you prefer a more interactive experience, there's a downhill **ski and bobsleigh simulator ride** (Nkr40) at the bottom of the ski jump hill.

At Hunderfossen, 15km north of town, speed fanatics can visit the **bobsleigh and luge track** (reservations ☎ 61 27 75 50; rides adult/child Nkr160/80) and ride a bobsleigh down the actual Olympic run; in summer, when there's no ice, a 'wheeled bob' is used. Reservations are advised.

The Olympics aside, Lillehammer's main attraction is the exceptional **Maihaugen folk museum** (☎ 61 28 89 00; Maihaugveien 1; adult/child Nkr120/55, including Olympic museum; open 9am-6pm daily June–mid-Aug, 10am-5pm daily mid-Aug–Sept, shorter hrs Oct-May), which contains around 180 historic houses, shops, farm buildings and a stave church.

The folk museum is evocatively arranged in a traditional village setting with workshop demonstrations given by interpreters in period costumes.

Lillehammer also has an **art museum** (☎ 61 05 44 60; Stortorget 2; adult/child Nkr50/40; open 11am-4pm Tues-Sun) and an **automobile museum** (☎ 61 25 61 65; Lilletorget; adult/child Nkr40/20; open 10am-6pm daily mid-June–mid-Aug, 11am-3pm Mon-Fri, 11am-4pm Sat & Sun mid-Aug–mid-June).

See the previous Hamar section for details of the Skibladner paddle steamer.

Places to Stay & Eat

Lillehammer Camping (☎ 61 25 33 33; Dampsagveien 47; tent sites from Nkr80, cabins Nkr300-550), on lake Mjøsa 700m south of the Skibladner dock, offers good camping facilities and modern cabins. **Lillehammer HI Hostel** (☎ 61 24 87 00; e lillehammer.hostel@vandrerhjem.no; dorm beds Nkr175, singles/doubles Nkr350/460), upstairs at the bus station, has 27 two- or four-bed rooms, each with shower and toilet. Breakfast is included.

A good budget option is **Gjeste Bu** (☎ 61 25 43 21; e ss-bu@online.no; Gamlevegen 110; dorm beds from Nkr100, singles/doubles from Nkr200/300; reception open 9am-11pm), a guesthouse with simple rooms and shared bathrooms. There's a group kitchen, free coffee and a TV room. Breakfast is available at a nearby **bakery**.

The charming **Comfort Home Hotel Hammer** (☎ 61 26 35 00; e hammer@comfort.choicehotels.no; Storgata 108; singles/doubles from Nkr650/850) includes dinner in its rates and offers high-standard rooms.

Storgata is lined with shops, bakeries and restaurants; you can get a reasonably priced meal at several places, including **Peppe's Pizza** (Storgata 69; buffet Nkr79-93 11am-3pm Mon-Fri), the unassuming **Vertshuset Solveig** (Storgata 68B; dishes Nkr59-163) and **Blåmann** (Lilletorget 1; mains Nkr58-285), which has good sandwiches, Mexican food and pastas. Friendly **Øverlie's Kiosk** (Storgata 50; dishes Nkr41-85) is the best place for filling, inexpensive meals, including traditional dishes, kebabs, burgers and pizzas. There's also a **Kiwi supermarket** on Storgata.

Getting There & Away

Nor-Way Bussekspress runs services to/from Oslo (Nkr240, three hours, three or four times daily). Rail services run between Lillehammer and Oslo (Nkr257, 2¼ hours, 12 to 17 times daily), and between Lillehammer and Trondheim (Nkr486, 4¼ hours, four or five times daily).

DOMBÅS
pop 1500

Dombås, a popular adventure and winter sports centre, makes a convenient break for travellers between the highland national parks and the western fjords. The **tourist office** (☎ 61 24 14 44) is by the central car park and commercial complex.

The **Dovrefjell-Rondane Nasjonalpark-senter** (☎ 61 24 14 44; admission free; open 9am-8pm daily mid-June–mid-Aug, shorter hrs mid-Aug–mid-June), at the tourist office, has interesting displays on all Norwegian national parks. **Dovrefjell National Park**, 30km north of town, protects the 2286m-high Snøhetta massif and provides a habitat for arctic foxes, reindeer, wolverines and musk oxen. **Dovrefjell Activitetssenter** (☎ 61 24 15 55), by the tourist office in Dombås, organises wildlife tours (musk ox safaris are Nkr180), climbing trips with instruction (Nkr550) and rafting adventures (Nkr320 to Nkr600).

Bjørkhol Camping (☎ 61 24 13 31; tent sites Nkr50-60, cabins Nkr160-600), Norway's best value (and probably friendliest) camping, is 7km south of Dombås by the E6. The excellent **Dombås Vandrerhjem Trolltun** (☎ 61 24 09 60, e dombaas.hostel@vandrerhjem.no; dorm beds Nkr180, singles/doubles from Nkr350/500) is about 1.5km north of the centre and off the E6; breakfast is included. The more central **Dombås Hotell** (☎ 61 24 10 01; e dombas.hotel@online.no; singles/doubles from Nkr705/ 845) offers atmospheric rooms, a restaurant and a nightclub.

The main central commercial complex includes **Frich's Kafeteria** (dishes Nkr56-159) and **Senter-Grillen** (dishes Nkr49-119), which serves pizza, burgers and kebabs.

Dombås lies on the railway line between Oslo (Nkr454, four hours, four or five daily) and Trondheim (Nkr303, 2½ hours). The spectacular Raumabanen line runs down Romsdalen valley from Dombås to Åndalsnes (Nkr169, 1¼ hours, two or three times daily).

JOTUNHEIMEN NATIONAL PARK

The Sognefjellet road between Lom and Sogndal passes the northwestern perimeter of Jotunheimen National Park, Norway's most popular wilderness destination. Hiking trails lead to some of the park's 60 glaciers, up to the top of Norway's loftiest peaks (the 2469m Galdhøpiggen and 2452m Glittertind) and along ravines and valleys with deep lakes and plunging waterfalls. There are DNT huts and private lodges along many of the routes. For park information, as well as the maps and information you need to hike, contact **Lom tourist office** (☎ 61 21 29 90).

Dramatic **Galdhøpiggen**, with its cirques, arêtes and glaciers, is a fairly tough eight-hour day hike from Spiterstulen, with 1470m of ascent, accessible by a toll road (Nkr60 per car). **Krossbu** is in the midst of a network of trails, including a short one to the **Smørstabbreen glacier**; **Krossbu Turiststasjon** (☎ 61 21 29 22) offers four- to six-hour guided glacier hikes and courses for Nkr250. From **Turtagrø**, a rock-climbing and hiking centre midway between Sogndal and Lom, there's a three-hour hike to Fannaråkhytta, Jotunheimen's highest DNT hut (2069m), which offers great panoramic views.

The private **Spiterstulen lodge** (☎ 61 21 14 80; singles/doubles with shared bathroom Nkr300/400, camping per person Nkr50), at an old sæter (summer dairy), is the jumping-off point for Galdhøpiggen.

Beautiful Bøverdalen, 18km south of Lom, has a great riverside **HI hostel** (☎ 61 21 20 64; dorm beds Nkr95, singles/doubles Nkr190/ 240; open June-Sept). Near the head of Bøverdalen, the no-frills **Krossbu Turiststasjon** (☎ 61 21 29 22; Krossbu; doubles from Nkr360) has 85 rooms, most with shared bath.

The fantastically located **Turtagrø Hotel** (☎ 57 68 61 16; Turtagrø; e post@turtagro .no; singles/doubles Nkr830/1100 inc. breakfast, bunks Nkr200-240) offers great food and service. Breakfast is Nkr95 and a three-course dinner is Nkr350.

From mid-June to late August, two daily buses run between Otta (on the Oslo–Trondheim railway line) and Sogndal via Bøverdalen, Sognefjellet and Turtagrø (Nkr255, 4½ hours).

OSLO TO BERGEN

The Oslo–Bergen railway line is Norway's most scenic, a seven-hour journey past forests and alpine villages, and across the starkly beautiful **Hardangervidda** plateau.

Midway between Oslo and Bergen is **Geilo**, a ski centre where you can practically walk off the train and onto a lift. From 1 July to mid-September, **Geilo Aktiv** (☎ 32 09 59 30) runs rafting tours (Nkr650 to Nkr750). There's also good summer **hiking** in the mountains around Geilo and the town has an **HI Hostel** (☎ 32 08 70 60; Lienvegen 137; dorm beds/doubles from Nkr120/360), near the train station.

From Geilo the train climbs 600m through a tundra-like landscape of high lakes and snow-capped mountains to the tiny village of **Finse**, near the **Hardangerjøkulen** icecap.

NORWAY

Finse has year-round **skiing** and is in the midst of a network of summer **hiking trails**. One of Norway's most frequently trodden trails winds from the Finse train station down to the fjord town of **Aurland**, a four-day trek. There's breathtaking mountain scenery along the way as well as a series of DNT and private mountain huts a day's walk apart – the nearest is Finsehytta, 200m from Finse station. There's also a bicycle route from Finse to Flåm on the century-old **Rallarvegen** railway construction road. **Geilo Aktiv** (☎ 32 09 59 30) offers glacier trekking on Hardangerjøkulen (Nkr520), Monday, Wednesday and Friday from 1 July to 15 September.

Myrdal, further west along the railway line, is the connecting point for the spectacularly steep Flåm railway, which twists and turns its way down 20 splendid kilometres to **Flåm** village on Aurlandsfjorden, an arm of Sognefjorden.

Many people go down to Flåm, have lunch and take the train back up to Myrdal where they catch the next Oslo–Bergen train. A better option is to take the ferry from Flåm to Gudvangen (via spectacular Nærøyfjorden, with its thundering waterfalls and lofty peaks), where there's a connecting bus that climbs a steep valley on the dramatically scenic ride to Voss. From Voss, trains to Bergen run roughly hourly. To include a cruise of the Nærøyfjorden in a day trip from Oslo to Bergen, you'll need to take the 8.11am train from Oslo, which connects with the afternoon ferry from Flåm. For details on Flåm, see the Sognefjorden section later in this chapter.

Bergen & The Western Fjords

The formidable, sea-drowned glacial valleys of the western fjords, flanked by almost impossibly rugged terrain, haven't deterred Norwegians from settling and farming their slopes and heights for thousands of years. The region presents some of the most breathtaking scenery in Europe and, not surprisingly, is the top destination for travellers to Norway.

Information on the entire region is available from **Fjord Norge** (☎ 55 30 26 40; W www.fjordnorway.com; Postboks 4108 Dreggen, N-5835 Bergen).

BERGEN
pop 230,830
Bergen was the capital of Norway during the 12th and 13th centuries and in the early 17th century had the distinction of being Scandinavia's largest city, with a population of around 15,000.

Set on a peninsula surrounded by seven mountains, Bergen's history is closely tied to the sea. It became one of the central ports of the Hanseatic League of merchants, which dominated trade in northern Europe during the late Middle Ages. The Hanseatic influence is still visible in the sharply gabled row of buildings that lines Bergen's picturesque harbourfront.

Even though it's Norway's second-largest city, Bergen has a pleasant, slow pace. A university town and cultural centre of western Norway, it has theatres, good museums and a noted philharmonic orchestra.

Although you can reliably expect rain or showers on at least 275 days of the year, all this precipitation keeps the place clean, green and flowery, lending it a sense of cheeriness on even the dullest of days.

Bergen is the main jumping-off point for journeys to the western fjords, with numerous buses, trains, passenger ferries and express boats setting off daily.

Orientation
The central area of hilly Bergen remains pleasantly compact and easily manageable on foot. The bus and train stations lie only a block apart on Strømgaten, just a 10-minute walk from the ferry terminals. Most of the restaurants, hotels, museums, tourist sites and picturesque streets and passages cluster around Vågen, the inner harbour.

Information
Tourist Offices The helpful **tourist office** (☎ 55 55 20 00; W www.visitbergen.com; Vågsallmenningen 1; open 8.30am-10pm daily June-Aug, 9am-8pm daily May & Sept, 9am-4pm Mon-Sat Oct-Apr), opposite the inner harbour, has brochures on destinations throughout Norway. Be sure to pick up the free *Bergen Guide* booklet.

Bergen Card The Bergen Card allows free transport on local buses, free parking, funicular-railway rides and admission to most museums and historic sights. The Schøtstuene and

BERGEN

PLACES TO STAY
15 Skansen Pensjonat
21 Kjellersmauet Gjestehus
27 Bergen Vandrerhjem YMCA
38 Radisson SAS Hotel Norge
41 Crowded House
48 Marken Gjestehus
49 Olsnes Guesthouse
53 Grand Hotel Terminus
55 Intermission
58 Nygård Apartment
64 Steens Hotell
65 Hotel Park Pension

PLACES TO EAT
5 Sparmarket
10 Café Colomba
11 Bryggeloftet & Stuene
17 Sol Brød
18 Torget Fish Market
19 Zachariasbryggen Complex
23 Café Opera
25 Lido
28 Godt Brød
35 Wesselstuen
36 Pars
37 Dickens
42 Kinsarvik Frukt
46 Stenersens Café
51 Ma-Ma Thai
67 Pasta Sentral

OTHER
1 Bergen Aquarium
2 International Ferries
3 Håkonshallen
4 Rosenkrantztårnet
6 Mariakirken
7 Bryggens Museum
8 Schøtstuene (Hanseatic Assembly Hall)
9 Theta Museum
12 Hanseatic Museum
13 Cyberhouse
14 Funicular Station
16 Jarlens Vaskoteque Laundrette
20 Express Boats (Strandkaiterminalen); Ferry Terminals
22 Bergen Kino (Cinema)
26 Rick's
26 Tourist Office; Budget Car Rental
29 Domkirke (Cathedral)
30 Sykkelbutikken (Bike Hire)
31 Nordea Bank
32 Husfliden (Crafts Shop)
33 Main Post Office
34 Galleriet (Shopping Centre); Augustus
39 Kilroy Travel
40 Fotballpuben
43 Kafé Fincken
44 Garage
45 Bergen Art Museum
47 Bergen Turlag DNT Office
50 Leprosy Museum
52 Library
54 Old Town Gate
56 Bus Station; Storsenter; Pharmacy
57 Grieghallen Concert Hall
59 Natural History Museum
60 Cultural History Museum
61 Maritime Museum
62 Coastal Steamer Quay
66 Hulen
66 Avis Car Rental
68 Medical Clinic

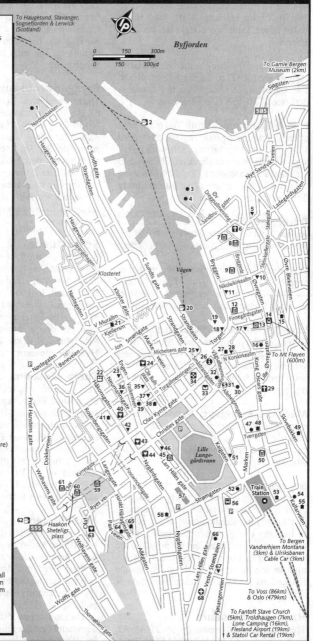

NORWAY

Hanseatic Museum are not covered. A 24/48-hour Bergen Card costs Nkr165/245 (Nkr70/105 for children) – it's sold at the tourist office, some hotels and most camping grounds.

Money Change money at the **Nordea bank** (Allehelgensgate 2) or the nearby post office. The tourist office changes money commission-free at 3% less than bank rates.

Post & Communications The **main post office** (Småstrandgaten; open 8am-6pm Mon-Fri, 9am-3pm Sat) can help with postal requirements. You can check email for Nkr40 per hour at **Cyberhouse** (Vetrlidsalmenning 13; open 24 hrs), or free at the **public library** (Strømgaten 6).

Travel Agencies Although specialising in student tickets, **Kilroy Travels** (☎ 02633; Vaskerelven 16) also handles regular bookings.

Libraries The **public library** (Strømgaten 6; open 10am-8pm Mon-Thur, 10am-4.30pm Fri, 10am-2pm Sat, shorter hrs mid-May–Sept) has a good selection of foreign newspapers.

Laundry At **Jarlens Vaskoteque** (Lille Øvregate 17; open 10am-6pm Mon, Tues & Fri; 10am-8pm Wed & Thur; 10am-3pm Sat) you can use the self-service (from Nkr50 for wash and dry) or pay a bit extra and have the manager do your wash.

Medical & Emergency Services There's a **medical clinic** (☎ 55 32 11 20; Vestre Stromkaien 19; open emergencies 24 hrs daily), and a **pharmacy** (open to midnight daily) at the bus station.

Bryggen

World Heritage–protected Bryggen, the site of the old medieval quarter, is a compact area that's easily explored on foot. The streetside of Bryggen's long timber buildings is home to museums, restaurants and shops, while the alleys that run along their less-restored sides offer an intriguing look at the stacked-stone foundations and rough-plank construction of centuries past.

Hanseatic Museum

This fascinating museum (☎ 55 31 41 89; Finnegårdsgaten 1A; adult/child Nkr40/free;

open 9am-5pm daily June-Aug, 11am-2pm daily Sept-May), in a timber building dating from 1704, retains its period character and furnishings and gives a glimpse of the austere working and living conditions of Hanseatic merchants. The entry ticket is also valid for Schøtstuene.

Bryggens Museum

The archaeological Bryggens Museum (☎ 55 58 80 10; Dregsalmenning 3; adult/child Nkr30/free; open 10am-5pm daily May-Aug, 11am-3pm Mon-Fri, noon-3pm Sat, noon-4pm Sun Sept-Apr) was built at the site of Bergen's earliest settlement. The 800-year-old foundations unearthed during the construction have been incorporated into the museum's exhibits along with excavated medieval tools, pottery, human skulls and rune stones.

Schøtstuene

Schøtstuene (☎ 55 31 60 20; Øvregaten 50; adult/child Nkr40/free; open 10am-5pm daily June-Aug, 11am-2pm daily May & Sept, 11am-2pm Sun Oct-Apr) houses one of the original assembly halls where the fraternity of Hanseatic merchants once met for their business meetings and beer guzzling. Schøtstuene's ticket is also valid for the Hanseatic Museum.

Theta Museum

This excellent one-room reconstruction of a clandestine Resistance headquarters, uncovered by the Nazis in 1942, is now Norway's tiniest museum (Enhjørningsgården; adult/child Nkr20/5; open 2pm-4pm Tues, Sat & Sun mid-May–mid-Sept). Appropriately enough, finding it is still a challenge – it's at the back of the Bryggen building with the unicorn figurehead; pass through the alley and up the stairs to the 3rd floor.

Mariakirken

This stone church (Dreggen; adult/child Nkr10/free, mid-May–Aug only; open 11am-4pm Mon-Fri mid-May–Aug, noon-1.30pm Tues-Fri Sept–mid-May), with its Romanesque entrance and twin towers, dates from the 12th century and is Bergen's oldest building.

The interior has 15th-century frescoes and a splendid baroque pulpit which was donated by Hanseatic merchants in 1676.

Rosenkrantztårnet

Opposite the harbour, the intriguing Rosenkrantz Tower (☎ 55 31 43 80; Bergenhus; adult/child Nkr20/10; open 10am-4pm daily mid-May–Aug, noon-3pm Sun Sept–mid-May) was built in the 1560s by Bergen's governor as a residence and defence post. The tower incorporates parts of an earlier building from 1273. You can climb up spiral staircases past halls and sentry posts to the lookout on top.

Håkonshallen

This large ceremonial hall (☎ 55 31 60 67; adult/child Nkr20/10; open 10am-4pm daily mid-May–Aug, noon-3pm Fri-Wed, 3pm-6pm Thur Sept–mid-May), adjacent to Rosenkrantztårnet, was completed by King Håkon Håkonsson in 1261 for his son's wedding. The roof was blown off in 1944 when a Dutch munitions boat exploded in the harbour; the building has since been extensively restored.

Other Attractions

City Sights The waterfront **fish market** at Torget is a good starting point for an exploration of the city's historic district. Bergen has lots of quaint cobblestone streets lined with older homes; one particularly picturesque area good for strolls is near the funicular station on Øvregaten.

The university has a **Natural History Museum** (☎ 55 58 29 20; Muséplass 3) full of stuffed creatures and mineral displays, and a **Cultural History Museum** (☎ 55 58 31 40; Haakon Sheteligs plass 10) with Viking weaponry, medieval altars, folk art and period furnishings. The Nkr30/free (adult/child) admission covers both museums, which are open 10am to 3pm Tuesday to Saturday and 11am to 4pm Sunday from mid-May to August (otherwise, shorter hours). The nearby **Maritime Museum** (☎ 55 54 96 00; Haakon Sheteligs plass 15; adult/child Nkr30/free; open 11am-3pm daily June-Aug, 11am-2pm Sun-Fri Sept-May) has exhibits on Norway's maritime history, including models of Viking ships.

The **Bergen Art Museum** (☎ 55 56 80 00; Rasmus Meyers Allé 3 & 7, Lars Hilles gate 10; adult/child Nkr50/free; open 11am-5pm daily mid-May–mid-Sept, shorter hrs mid-May–mid-Sept), housed in three buildings opposite the lake fountain, has a superb collection of Norwegian art from the 18th and 19th centuries, including many works by Munch and JC Dahl, as well as contemporary works by Picasso, Klee and others.

Bergen Aquarium (☎ 55 55 71 71; Nordnesbakken 4; adult/child Nkr80/50; open 9am-8pm daily May-Sept, 10am-6pm daily Oct-Apr), near the northern tip of the Nordnes peninsula, has an outdoor tank with seals and penguins, plus indoor fish tanks. Take bus No 11 or walk from the city centre (20 minutes). The public **park** just beyond the aquarium has shaded lawns, sunbathing areas and an outdoor heated swimming pool.

There's also a **Leprosy Museum** (☎ 55 32 57 80; Kong Oscars gate 59; adult/child Nkr30/15; open 11am-3pm daily mid-May–Aug), which details Norway's contributions to leprosy research.

Bergen Environs The interesting open-air museum, **Gamle Bergen** (☎ 55 39 43 04; Sandviken), with around 40 buildings from the 18th and 19th centuries, is 4km north of the city centre and can be reached by bus Nos 20 to 23. Tours cost Nkr50/25 (adult/child) and leave hourly from 10am to 5pm daily, mid-May to August. Entrance to the grounds is free and available year-round.

The **Fantoft stave church** (☎ 55 28 07 10; Paradis; adult/child Nkr30/5; open 10.30am-6pm daily mid-May–mid-Sept) was built in Sognefjorden around 1150 and moved to the southern outskirts of Bergen in 1883. An arsonist burned it down in 1992, but it has been painstakingly reconstructed. From Bergen take any bus from platforms 19 to 21, get off at Fantoft and walk uphill for 10 minutes.

If you want to continue on to the former lakeside home and workshop of composer Edvard Grieg, get back on the bus until the Hopsbroen stop and follow the signs to **Troldhaugen** (☎ 55 92 29 92; Hop; adult/child Nkr50/free; open 9am-6pm daily May-Sept, shorter hrs Oct-Apr), a 20-minute walk. Although Grieg fans will best appreciate this well-conceived presentation, the main house has excellent period furnishings and is generally interesting.

Cable Cars & Hiking

For an unbeatable city view, take the **funicular** from Øvregaten to the top of Mt Fløyen (320m). If you also want to do some hiking, well-marked trails lead into the forest from the hill-top station. Trails 1 and 3 are the longest, each making 5km loops through hilly woodlands. For a delightful 40-minute walk back to the city, take trail 4 and connect with trail 6. The funicular runs at least twice hourly from 7.30am to 11pm (until midnight from May to August) and costs Nkr50/25 (adult/child) return.

The **Ulriksbanen cable car** to the top of Mt Ulriken (642m) offers a panoramic view of the city, the fjords and mountains. The tourist office sells a ticket for Nkr120/60 (adult/child) that includes the cable car and a return bus from Bergen. It's also possible to take the cable car one way and walk (about three hours) across a well-beaten trail to the funicular station at Mt Fløyen.

For information on wilderness hiking and huts, contact the **Bergen Turlag DNT office** (☎ 55 32 22 30; *Tverrgaten 4*).

Organised Tours
The railway sells the 'Norway in a Nutshell' ticket combining morning trains from Bergen to Flåm, a ferry along the spectacular Aurlandsfjorden and Nærøyfjorden to Gudvangen, a bus to Voss and a train back to Bergen in time for a late dinner. It makes for a very scenic day trip at Nkr630.

HSD (☎ 55 23 87 80), whose boats leave from Strandkaiterminalen, organises various boat trips around local fjords and islands, including an 11-hour 'veteran boat cruise' (Nkr390), in an older boat.

Special Events
The Bergen International Festival, held for 12 days at the end of May, is the big cultural event of the year with quality dance, music and folklore events taking place throughout the city.

Places to Stay
Camping A good camping option is the lakeside **Lone Camping** (☎ 55 39 29 60; e *booking@lonecamping.no; Hardangerveien 697, Haukeland; camping per tent/person Nkr95/Nkr15, cabins & rooms Nkr340-715*), 30 minutes east of Bergen by bus No 900.

Hostels Bergen's 200-bed HI-affiliated **Bergen Vandrerhjem YMCA** (☎ 55 31 35 52; e *bergen.ymca.hostel@vandrerhjem.no; Nedre Korskirkealmenning 4; dorm beds/ rooms Nkr100/600; open 20 June-20 Aug*) is a central place to crash but it can be noisy.

Breakfast is extra (Nkr40) but there's a supermarket and a good bakery just metres away.

Of a higher standard is the 37-bed **Intermission** (☎ 55 30 04 00; *Kalfarveien 8; dorm beds Nkr100; open mid-June–mid-Aug*), in a period home, where the hospitable Christian Student Fellowship serves free waffles to guests on Monday and Thursday nights. A kitchen, laundry facilities and breakfast is available for Nkr30 .

The 332-bed, HI-affiliated **Bergen Vandrerhjem Montana** (☎ 55 20 80 70; e *bergen .montana.hostel@vandrerhjem.no; Johan Blyttsvei 30; dorm beds Nkr120-185, singles/ doubles from Nkr300/500; open 3 Jan-20 Dec*) is 5km from the city centre by bus No 31. Breakfast is included.

Right in the city centre, the recommended **Marken Gjestehus** (☎ 55 31 44 04; e *mark engjestehus@smisi.no; Kong Oscars gate 45; beds Nkr190/165 in 4/6-bed dorms; doubles per person Nkr220*) offers breakfast from Nkr55. Amenities include a kitchen, coin laundry, TV room and lockers.

Private Rooms & Pensions The tourist office books single/double **rooms** in private homes from Nkr230/340 (plus Nkr30 to Nkr50 booking fee); it can also find you last-minute hotel discounts.

Olsnes Guesthouse (☎ 55 31 20 44; *Skivebakken 24; singles/doubles from Nkr230/340; open mid-May–Sept*), in a quiet neighbourhood of older homes only a five-minute walk from the train station, has nine adequate rooms, a shared kitchen and a nice mix of Norwegian and foreign travellers. The centrally located and friendly **Skansen Pensjonat** (☎ 55 31 90 80; e *mail@skansen-pensjonat.no; Vetrlidsalmenningen 29; singles/doubles from Nkr300/550*) has 14 clean but simple rooms, most with shared bathroom.

Crowded House (☎ 55 23 13 10; e *info@ crowded-house.com; Håkonsgaten 27; singles/ doubles Nkr390/590*) is a former local hotel that has been spruced up to attract travellers with its 34 simple but clean rooms, each with a wash basin (toilets are in the hall). There are free laundry and kitchen facilities.

Kjellersmauet Gjestehus (☎/fax 55 96 26 08; e *kj-gj@online.no; Kjellersmauet 22; apartments Nkr300-1200*) offers a number of well-equipped apartments with bathroom and kitchen. The 60-bed **Nygård Apartment** (☎ 55 32 72 53; e *markengjestehus@smisi.no;*

Nygårdsgaten 31; singles/doubles from Nkr355/500; open June–mid-Aug) offers small student rooms, some with private bathroom. All rooms have access to cooking facilities.

Hotels At Steens Hotell *(☎ 55 31 40 50, fax 55 32 61 22; Parkveien 22; singles/doubles from Nkr510/750)*, a relatively inexpensive 19th-century-style choice, the en suite rooms all have phone and TV. For a decent family-owned hotel with 19th-century atmosphere and lots of antiques, try **Hotel Park Pension** *(☎ 55 54 44 00; e booking@parkhotel.no; Harald Hårfagresgate 35; singles/doubles from Nkr580/830)*.

Opposite the train station, the historic **Grand Hotel Terminus** *(☎ 55 21 25 00; e booking@ grand-hotel-terminus.no; Zander Kaaesgate 6; en suite singles/doubles Nkr690/990 to Nkr1260/1460)* has small rooms, but the wonderful decor more than compensates.

The classy and comfortable **Radisson SAS Hotel Norge** *(☎ 55 57 30 00; e reservations .bergen@radissonsas.com; Ole Bulls plass 4; singles Nkr995-1745, doubles Nkr1195-1945)* is spacious with full amenities, a fitness centre and an indoor pool.

Places to Eat

Top End The richly decorated **Wesselstuen** *(☎ 55 55 49 49, Ole Bulls plass 6; light meals Nkr109-139, dinner mains Nkr149-199)* offers excellent mid-range value and is especially popular with Bergen intellectuals.

The popular **Dickens** *(☎ 55 36 31 30; Kong Olav Vs plass 4; light meals Nkr85-139, dinner mains Nkr179-220)* has a sunny dining room overlooking the pedestrian square. Light dishes include salads, soup, burgers and nachos.

In the middle of the historic district, the two-storey **Bryggeloftet & Stuene** *(☎ 55 31 06 30; Bryggen 11; specials Nkr89, mains Nkr95-275)* serves traditional Norwegian fare (including reindeer, venison, *bacalao* – a cod dish – catfish and whale) in a pleasant atmosphere.

Mid-Range A cosy Asian restaurant, **Ma-Ma Thai** *(Kaigaten 20; lunch Nkr65-76, dinner mains Nkr98-168)* attracts university students with a discounted student menu (Nkr54 to Nkr67).

The recommended **Augustus** *(Galleriet, Torgallmenningen 8; specials Nkr99, mains Nkr79-135)* serves modern international dishes. **Café Colomba** *(Øvregaten 17; dishes around Nkr150)* is a trendy, international place with a menu of good Greek, Italian and Turkish dishes.

The kitschy atmosphere at the **Pars** *(Sigurdsgate 5; mains Nkr79-179)* Persian restaurant belies the excellent cuisine, including inexpensive vegetarian choices (Nkr79 to Nkr89).

Budget Trendy **Café Opera** *(Engen 18; dishes Nkr56-128)*, popular with artists and students, serves good, reasonably priced food, including ciabatta sandwiches, salads and smoked salmon.

Lido *(Torgallmenningen 1; mains Nkr99-135)* is an inexpensive cafeteria with good traditional Norwegian grub, but the toilets cost Nkr5!

The unassuming **Pasta Sentral** *(Vestre Strømkaien 6; dishes Nkr59-87)*, which isn't all that central, has great pizza, pasta and desserts, with a good range of vegetarian choices.

For a cultural treat there's **Stenersens Café**, on the ground floor of the **Bergen Art Museum** *(Rasmus Meyers Allé)*, with good pastries, baguette sandwiches and light meals at reasonable prices.

The **Sparmarket** *(Nye Sandviksveien)* sells groceries and has an astonishing takeaway deli with whole grilled chickens for only Nkr30.

A great place for a snack is the bustling **Godt Brød** *(Nedre Korskirkealmenningen 12; open 7.15am-6pm Mon-Fri, 7.15am-3.30pm Sat)*, with delicious organic breads and pastries and café tables. Many other bakeries in the centre offer reasonably priced sandwiches; **Sol Brød** *(cnr Vetrlidsalmenning & Kong Oscars gate)* also has recommended bread and pastries.

The waterfront **Zachariasbryggen complex**, at the inner harbour, houses several pubs and eateries, including the **Baker Brun** *konditori* with good pastries and sandwiches, a **Peppe's Pizza**, various other restaurants and an **ice-cream shop**.

Storsenter, at the bus station, has outlets serving inexpensive sandwiches, a **bakery**, a burger outlet, Vinmonopolet, and **Rimi** and **Spar** supermarkets. In the **fish market** at Torget you'll find a choice of fresh fruit and seafood snacks, including tasty open-faced salmon rolls for Nkr15; or pick up 500g of

NORWAY

boiled crab legs or shrimp for Nkr35 to Nkr75 and munch away at the harbour.

Kinsarvik Frukt *(Olav Kyrres gate 38)* is a small grocery store with a health-food section.

Entertainment

For details and schedules of entertainment events, including classical concerts, contact the tourist office (or see **w** www.visitbergen.com). Atop Mt Fløyen, classical concerts are held nightly at 8pm from mid-June to mid-August (Nkr160).

Bergen brews its own beer under the Hansa label. Among Norway's best-value beer venues is the sports bar **Fotballpuben** *(Vestre Torggate 9)*, where 500mL of lager will set you back only Nkr31.

Rick's *(Veiten 3)*, just off Ole Bulls plass, is one of the city's most popular entertainment venues with live music, a disco, a bar and pub. Bergen's top rock music venue, **Garage** *(Christies gate 14)*, attracts students, as does the cave-like **Hulen** *(Olaf Ryes vei 47)* behind the student centre. **Kafé Fincken** *(Nygårdsgaten 2A)* is the main gay and lesbian venue in town.

Bergen Kino *(Neumannsgate 3)*, a 13-screen cinema, shows first-run movies.

Shopping

The broadest selection of handicrafts, wooden toys and traditional clothing can be found at **Husfliden** *(Vågsallmenningen 3)*. The **Galleriet shopping centre**, northwest of the post office, has boutiques, camera shops, a grocery store and a good bookshop, **Norli**. The bus station contains another large shopping centre.

Getting There & Away

Air The airport is in Flesland, 19km southwest of central Bergen. Direct flights connect Bergen with major cities in Norway, plus a handful of international destinations. **Braathens** *(☎ 815 20 000)* and **SAS** *(☎ 815 20 400)*, both at the airport, fly frequently between Oslo and Bergen.

Bus Daily express buses run to Odda in Hardanger (Nkr233, 3½ hours) and to the western fjord region. From Bergen it costs Nkr395 (6½ hours) to Stryn, Nkr588 (9½ to 10 hours) to Ålesund and Nkr755 (14½ hours) to Trondheim. There's a bus from Bergen to Stavanger (Nkr370, 5¾ hours) roughly every two hours.

Train Trains to Oslo (Nkr593, 6½ to 7¾ hours) depart four or five times daily; seat reservations are required. In addition, local trains run between Bergen and Voss (Nkr134, 1¼ hours) every hour or two. Lockers at the train station cost Nkr15 to Nkr40.

Car There's a Nkr10 toll for vehicles entering the city from 6am to 10pm Monday to Friday.

Car Rental The following companies have offices in Bergen:

Avis (☎ 55 55 39 55) Lars Hilles gate 20A
Budget (☎ 55 27 39 90) Bergen tourist office, Vågsallmenningen 1
Statoil (☎ 55 99 14 90) Flyplassvegen 425, near Flesland airport

Boat Daily Sognefjorden express boats to Balestrand and Flåm, northbound express boats to Måløy and southbound express boats to Stavanger, leave from Strandkaiterminalen on the western side of Vågen.

The coastal steamer, *Hurtigruten*, leaves from the quay south of the university at 8pm daily from April to September, and 10.30pm otherwise. Details are in the introductory Getting Around section of this chapter.

International ferries to Newcastle, Lerwick (Shetland) and Denmark dock north of Rosenkrantztårnet (for details see the introductory Getting There & Away section earlier).

Getting Around

To/From the Airport Flybussen runs between the airport and Bergen bus station (Nkr60, 45 minutes, at least twice hourly), stopping on Olav Kyrres gate near Radisson SAS Hotel Norge and at the SAS Hotel beside the Bryggens Museum.

Bus City buses cost Nkr17, while fares beyond the centre are based on the distance travelled. Route information is available on ☎ 177. Free bus No 100 runs between the main post office and the bus station.

Car & Motorcycle If you have a car, it's best to park it and explore the city centre on foot. Except in spots where there are parking meters, street parking is reserved for residents with zone-parking stickers; if you see a 'P' for parking but the sign has '*sone*' on it, it's a reserved area. Metered parking has a 30-minute limit in the busiest spots and two hours elsewhere, including lots on the southwestern side of the Grieghallen concert hall and the northern side of Lille Lungegårdsvann. Less restricted are the parking areas at Sydnes, near Nostegaten, which allow up to nine hours (free at night), and the indoor car parks – the largest one is **Bygarasjen** *(open 24 hrs)*, at the bus station.

Taxi Taxis (☎ 07000) line up on Ole Bulls plass.

Bicycle You can hire cycles from **Sykkelbutikken** *(☎ 55 32 06 20; Østre Skostredet 5)*.

VOSS
pop 6000
Voss is a year-round sports centre with an attractive lakeside location. The busy **tourist office** *(☎ 56 52 08 00; W www.visitvoss.no; Uttrågata)* is a 10-minute walk east from the train and bus stations.

Things to See & Do
The tourist office can advise on **activities**, including skiing (December to April), whitewater rafting (Nkr590), canyoning (from Nkr620), waterfall abseiling (Nkr490) and riverboarding (Nkr650).

The 13th-century stone **church** *(Uttrågata; adult/child Nkr15/free; open 10am-4pm daily June-Aug)* is worth a look, but it has been significantly altered over the centuries. The **Mølstertunet Museum** *(☎ 56 51 15 11; Mølstervegen 143; adult/child Nkr35/free; open 10am-5pm daily May-Sept, shorter hrs Oct-Apr)*, on the hillside north of town, features historic farm buildings, which date from the mid-17th to mid-19th centuries and display various facets of life in earlier times. A **cable car** *(Nkr50; 11am-5pm daily mid-May–Aug)* whisks you up to the spectacular view from Mt Hangur every 15 minutes.

Places to Stay & Eat
The lakeside **Voss Camping** *(☎ 56 51 15 97; Prestegardsalléen 40; tent sites Nkr80, cabins Nkr300-350)* is 300m south of the tourist office. The modern **Voss Vandrerhjem** *(☎ 56 51 20 17; e voss.hostel@vandrerhjem.no; Evangervegen 68; dorm beds Nkr195, singles/ doubles Nkr420/540)* has en suite rooms throughout and a fine lakeside position, 600m west of the train station; breakfast/dinner costs Nkr45/90. The hostel has bicycles,

canoes, kayaks and rowing boats for hire and there's a free sauna.

For historic character, the wealthy can check out the enormous but beautiful **Fleischer's Hotel** *(☎ 56 52 05 00; e hotel@fleischers.no; Evangervegen; beds per person from Nkr350)*, opened in 1888. The dining room serves a fine lunch/dinner buffet (Nkr195/325).

For cakes and snacks (Nkr19 to Nkr28) and mains (Nkr84 to Nkr92), try the **Vangen Café** *(Vangsgata 42)*. Traditional Norwegian food is served at **Indremisjonskaféen** *(Vangsgata 46; mains Nkr72-95)*. The **Coop Mega supermarket** *(Strandavegen)* is on the eastern side of the town centre.

Getting There & Away
Buses stop at the train station. NSB rail services on the renowned Bergensbanen to/from Bergen (Nkr134, 1¼ hours, roughly hourly) and Oslo (Nkr510, 5½ to six hours, four or five daily) connect at Myrdal (Nkr78, 50 minutes) with the scenic line down to Flåm.

HARDANGERFJORDEN
Hardangerfjorden, the second longest fjord in Norway, stretches inland from a cluster of rocky coastal islands to the frozen heights of the **Folgefonn** and **Hardangerjøkulen** icecaps. The area is known for its orchards, including apples and plums.

The villages along the east coast of the central part of the fjord (also called Kvinnheradsfjorden) are now connected to the national road network by an 11km-long tunnel under the Folgefonn; **Rosendal** and **Sunndal** are the top destinations, with great mountain and glacier scenery. Rosendal has the interesting 1665 **Baroniet Rosendal** *(☎ 53 48 29 99; adult/child Nkr75/10)*, Norway's only baronial mansion, with period interiors – there's hourly guided tours at variable hours, daily from May to August. From Sunndal, an easy walk leads 3km to lake Bondhusvatnet and the impressive glacier **Bondhusbreen**.

On the other side of Folgefonn, **Odda** is an industrial town with a dramatic location. For information on hikes and glacier tours, contact the **tourist office** *(☎ 53 64 12 97)* near the Sørfjorden shore. **Tyssedal**, 6km north of Odda, has a **hydro-electric power plant museum** *(☎ 53 65 00 50; adult/child Nkr50/free; open 10am-5pm daily mid-May–August, otherwise shorter hrs)* and a mighty impressive **funicular railway**.

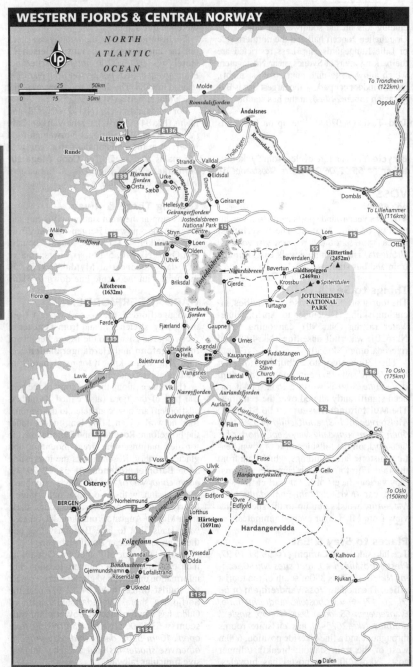

WESTERN FJORDS & CENTRAL NORWAY

NORTH
ATLANTIC
OCEAN

NORWAY

At picturesque **Utne**, 55km north of Odda, you'll find an interesting collection of old buildings at the **Hardanger Folk Museum** (☎ *53 66 69 00; adult/child Nkr40/free; open 10am-4pm daily May & June, 10am-6pm daily July & Aug)*, and the **Utne Hotel** (see Places to Stay & Eat).

At the innermost reaches of Hardangerfjorden you'll find the **Eidfjord** area, with sheer mountains, huge waterfalls and spiral road tunnels. Extraordinary **Kjeåsen**, a deserted farm perched on a mountain ledge about 6km northeast of Eidfjord, is reached by a road tunnel. The excellent **Hardangervidda Natursenter** (☎ *53 66 59 00, Øvre Eidfjord; adult/child Nkr70/35; open 10am-6pm daily Apr, May, Sept & Oct, 9am-8pm daily June-Aug)* has a must-see 19-minute movie, interactive displays and interesting natural history and geology exhibits. For tourist information, contact **Eidfjord tourist office** (☎ *53 67 34 00)*.

Places to Stay & Eat
In Rosendal, the ornate **Rosendal Gjestgiveri** *(☎/fax 53 47 36 66; Skålagato 17; singles/ doubles Nkr500/700)* dates from 1887 and offers atmospheric B&B in rooms with shared bath. The restaurant serves beef and chicken dishes, pizzas and salads for Nkr75 to Nkr155.

The historic wooden **Utne Hotel** (☎ *53 66 10 88;* e *kildehot@online.no; Utne; singles/ doubles from Nkr300/500)*, known for its fabulous decor, was built in 1722 and has been in business ever since. Meals are available in the dining room.

Lofthus has the new **Lofthus HI Hostel** (☎ *53 67 14 00;* e *lofthus.hostel@vandrerh jem.no; dorm beds Nkr180, singles/doubles Nkr260/460; open 20 May-10 Aug)*. Prices include breakfast.

In Eidfjord, the **Eidfjord Hotel** (☎ *53 66 52 64;* e *post@eidfordhotel.no; singles/doubles Nkr650/850)* has comfortable en suite rooms and the restaurant serves good, filling dinners. The nicely located **Sæbø Camping** (☎ *53 66 59 27; Øvre Eidfjord; tent sites Nkr60, cabins Nkr200-500)* has good facilities.

Getting There & Away
Buses run between Rosendal and Odda via Sunndal (about one hour, three to seven times daily). There are also bus and ferry connections between Rosendal and Bergen (Nkr125, 3½ hours, twice daily).

One to three daily Nor-Way Bussekspress buses run between Bergen (Nkr233, 3¾ hours) and Oslo (Nkr440, 7¼ hours) via Odda and Utne, with connections at Haukeligrend for Kristiansand.

Buses run between Geilo and Odda via Øvre Eidfjord, Eidfjord and Lofthus once or twice daily in summer (July to September), with extra runs between Øvre Eidfjord and Odda year-round. Ferries between Eidfjord and Norheimsund/Utne (Nkr160/97, three/1¼ hours) sail two or three times daily; buses to/from Bergen connect at Norheimsund.

SOGNEFJORDEN
Sognefjorden, Norway's longest (204km) and deepest (1308m) fjord, cuts a deep slash across the map of western Norway. In some places sheer lofty walls rise more than 1000m above the water, while in others there is a far gentler shoreline with farms, orchards and small towns.

The broad main waterway is impressive, but by cruising into the fjord's narrower arms, such as the deep and lovely Nærøyfjorden to Gudvangen, you'll have idyllic views of sheer cliff faces and cascading waterfalls.

Tourist information is dispensed by **Sognefjorden** (☎ *57 67 30 83;* w *www.sognefjorden .no; Postboks 222, N-6852 Sogndal)*.

Getting There & Away
Fylkesbaatane (☎ *55 90 70 70;* w *www .fylkesbaatane.no)* operates a daily year-round express boat between Bergen and Sogndal, stopping at 10 small towns along the way. Students and InterRail pass holders get a 50% discount.

From mid-May to mid-September, Fylkesbaatane runs a second express boat along the same route, except that it terminates in Flåm instead of Sogndal.

This summer boat leaves Bergen at 8am daily and arrives in Flåm at 1.25pm. The return boat leaves Flåm at 3.30pm, arriving in Bergen at 8.40pm. From Bergen it costs Nkr370 to Balestrand, Nkr510 to Flåm.

There are numerous local ferries linking the fjord towns and an extensive (though not always frequent) network of buses, all are detailed in *Sogn og Fjordane Rutehefte* (w www .ruteinfo.net/en/index.html), the 208-page timetable available free at tourist offices and some transport terminals.

NORWAY

Flåm

pop 400

A tiny village scenically set at the head of Aurlandsfjorden, Flåm is a jumping-off spot for travellers taking the Gudvangen ferry or the Sognefjorden express boat. It's also the only place on Sognefjorden with rail connections, and is the turnaround point for those doing the 'Norway in a Nutshell' tour. The **tourist office** (☎ 57 63 21 06), at the train station, rents bikes. The docks are just beyond the train station.

Places to Stay & Eat The pleasant **Flåm Camping & Hostel** (☎ 57 63 21 21; e flaam .hostel@vandrerhjem.no; dorm beds Nkr115, singles/doubles Nkr185/320; open May-Sept) has just 31 beds – book early. It's a few minutes' walk from the station: go up the riverside track and over the bridge. **Heimly Pensjonat** (☎ 57 63 23 00; e post@heimly.no; singles/ doubles from Nkr350/690) has rooms with great fjord views; breakfast is included.

Near the station, the novel **Togrestauranten** (mains Nkr85-115), housed in several wooden rail cars, serves some traditional Norwegian dishes and vegetarian choices. The **Furukroa Cafeteria** (mains Nkr78-100), at the ferry dock, offers fast food as well as Norwegian meals. Self-caterers will find a **Coop** supermarket behind Togrestauranten.

Getting There & Away The Flåm railway runs between Myrdal and Flåm (Nkr125) numerous times daily, in sync with the Oslo–Bergen service. At Flåm, buses and boats head out to towns around Sognefjorden.

The most scenic boat ride from Flåm is the ferry up Nærøyfjorden to Gudvangen (Nkr160/ 200 one-way/return), leaving at 3pm daily year-round and also at 9am, 11am and 1.15pm mid-June to mid-August. All ferry tickets and the ferry-bus combination from Flåm to Voss (Nkr230) are sold at the tourist office.

In addition to the Sognefjorden express boat between Flåm and Bergen, the Flåmekspressen boat runs once daily (except Saturday and Sunday) from Flåm to Aurland, and Sogndal.

Lærdal & Around

pop 2200

The 24.5km-long Lærdalstunnelen, the world's longest road tunnel, on the main E16 highway from Oslo to Bergen, now brings more visitors than ever to the wonderful **Borgund stave church** (☎ 57 67 88 40; adult/child Nkr50/25; open 8am-8pm daily June–mid-Aug, 10am-5pm daily May & mid-Aug–Sept), about 30km up the valley from Lærdal. **Lærdalsøyri**, at the fjord end of Lærdal, makes for pleasant strolling through the collection of intact 18th- and 19th-century timber homes. The **Norsk Villakssenter** (Norwegian Wild Salmon Centre; ☎ 57 66 67 71; Lærdal; adult/child Nkr70/ 35; open 10am-7pm daily June-Aug, shorter hrs May & Sept) reveals all you'd ever want to know about the Atlantic salmon and its peculiar habits.

Borlaug Vandrerhjem (☎ 57 66 87 80; e borlaug.hostel@vandrerhjem.no; dorm beds Nkr110, singles/doubles Nkr180/270) is a friendly roadside HI hostel, 10km east of Borgund. Breakfast is Nkr50, and a two-course dinner costs Nkr85. The rustic **Potter's Kafé & Konditori** (Øyragata 15; Lærdal; mains Nkr50-100) serves good chicken dishes, pies, pizzas, omelettes and burgers.

Buses to/from Bergen run via Borgund once daily and Lærdal (Nkr260, 3¾ hours) three to seven times daily. Buses between Lærdal and Sogndal (Nkr72, 50 minutes) run two to seven times daily.

Vangsnes & Vik

pop 1500

Vangsnes, across the fjord from Balestrand, is a little farming community crowned with a huge hill-top statue of Fridtjof, a hero of the Norwegian sagas. Although it has both ferry and express boat connections, there's not much to the village. There's a **snack bar** (pizzas from Nkr69) at the dock, and **Solvang Camping** (☎ 57 69 66 20; tent sites from Nkr40, cabins & rooms Nkr300-600), a few minutes inland, has cabins and motel rooms.

Frequent local buses run between Vangsnes and the industrial town Vik (Nkr23, 15 minutes), which has an excellent 12th-century **stave church** (☎ 56 67 88 40; Hopperstad; adult/child Nkr40/free; open 10am-5pm daily mid-May–mid-June & mid-Aug–mid-Sept, 9am-7pm daily mid-June–mid-Aug), about 1km south from its centre. Buses run from Vik (via Vangsnes) to Sogndal (Nkr67, 1½ hours, daily) and Vangsnes (via Vik) to Bergen (Nkr225, 3½ hours, daily except Saturday). The Sognefjorden express boat also stops in Vik.

Balestrand

pop 1000

Balestrand, the main Sognefjorden resort destination, enjoys a mountain backdrop and a genteel but low-key atmosphere. The **tourist office** (☎ 57 69 12 55), at the dock, rents bikes for Nkr75 per half day.

Things to See & Do The road that runs south along the fjord has little traffic and is a pleasant place to stroll. It's lined with apple orchards, ornate older homes and gardens, a **19th-century English church** and **Viking burial mounds**. One mound is topped by a statue of the legendary King Bele, erected by Germany's Kaiser Wilhelm II who spent his holidays here regularly until WWI.

For a longer **hike**, take the small ferry (Nkr15) across the Esefjord to the Dragsvik side, where there is an abandoned country road which forms the first leg of an 8km walk back to Balestrand.

Places to Stay & Eat At **Sjøtun Camping** (☎ 57 69 12 23; tent sites from Nkr30, cabins Nkr200), a 15-minute walk south along the fjord, you can pitch a tent amid apple trees or rent a rustic four-bunk cabin.

Balestrand HI Hostel (☎ 57 69 13 03; e balestrand.hostel@vandrerhjem.no; dorm beds/doubles Nkr180/520; open late June–mid-Aug) is a pleasant lodge-style place; breakfast is included.

Midtnes Pensjonat (☎ 57 69 11 33; e booking@midtnes.no; singles/doubles from Nkr500/660), next to the English church, is popular with returning British holidaymakers; breakfast is included. Also near the church, **Balestrand Pensjonat** (☎ 57 69 11 38; e epalmer@online.no; singles/ doubles from Nkr520/690) is a comfortable, modern place.

There's a **supermarket** and a fast-food **café** opposite the dock, the **hostel** restaurant serves dinner for Nkr110 and for a splurge there's an upmarket restaurant at the fjordside **Kvikne's Hotel** (mains Nkr215-595).

Getting There & Away In addition to the Sognefjorden express boat, local boats run daily to Hella (from Dragsvik, 10km by road north from Balestrand) and Fjærland.

Buses go to Sogndal (Nkr83, 1¼ hours) and Bergen (Nkr220, 3½ hours). The latter departs from Vik, reached by boat (Nkr48, 15 minutes), departing Balestrand 7.55am Monday to Friday. This service is cheaper than the express boat, and more scenic.

Fjærland

pop 300

The location of this farming village at the head of the beautiful Fjærlandsfjorden, near two arms of the **Jostedalsbreen** icecap, makes it one of the most inviting destinations in Norway.

Balestrand tourist office sells a packaged ticket (Nkr345) that includes the morning ferry to Fjærland, a connecting sightseeing bus and the afternoon return ferry. The tour includes the **Norwegian Glacier Museum**, which has extensive displays on Jostedalsbreen, and visits two arms of the glacier: the **Supphellebreen**, where you can walk up to the glacier's edge and touch the ice, and the creaking, blue-iced **Bøyabreen**, where it's not uncommon to witness ice breaks plunging into the lake beneath the glacier tongue. Alternatively, a taxi from the Fjærland dock to the glacier, with waiting time, costs about Nkr350 return.

Overnight visitors can stay at **Bøyum Camping** (☎ 57 69 32 52; dorm mattresses Nkr100, tent sites Nkr95, doubles Nkr250-300, 6-bed cabins Nkr530-630), near the glacier museum, or the excellent olde-worlde **Hotel Mundal** (☎ 57 69 31 01; e hotelmundal@fjordinfo.no; Mundal), which also has a fine dining room and is only five minutes walk from the quay.

Ferries run twice daily from 25 May to 9 September between Fjærland and Balestrand (Nkr130, 1¼ hours). Buses connect Fjærland and Sogndal (Nkr78, 45 minutes, three to seven daily) and Stryn (Nkr150, two hours).

Sogndal & Around

pop 3000

Sogndal, a modern regional centre, is a starting point for day trips in the area. Of most interest is the **Nigardsbreen glacier** 70km to the north, followed by Norway's oldest **stave church** (circa 1150 and on the Unesco World Heritage List) in Urnes across the Lustrafjord, and the **Sogn Folkemuseum** near Kaupanger, 11km east of Sogndal. Also in Kaupanger, there's a superb **stave church** dating from 1184. Sogndal's **tourist office** (☎ 57 67 30 83; Kulturhus, Gravensteinsgaten) is about 500m east of Sogndal bus station.

NORWAY

The tourist office books **rooms** in private homes from Nkr150 per person. There's an **HI Hostel** (*☎ 57 67 20 33; dorm beds Nkr100, singles/doubles Nkr165/230; open mid-June–mid-Aug)*, only 15 minutes east of the bus station.

The hotel restaurant **Compagniet** (*☎ 57 62 77 00; Hotel Sogndal, Gravensteinsgaten 5; buffet Nkr220)* has great evening buffets, but there's also a cheaper section with some meals under Nkr100. For an inexpensive meal, try the cafeteria in the **Domus** supermarket on Gravensteinsgata.

Buses run from Sogndal to Kaupanger (Nkr23, 10 minutes, hourly) and Balestrand (Nkr83, 1¼ hours, six to nine daily). Twice daily buses (17 June to 26 August) go northeast past Jotunheimen National Park to Lom (Nkr185, 3½ hours) and on to Otta (Nkr255, 4½ hours), on the Oslo–Trondheim railway line.

Nigardsbreen

The most attractive arm of the Jostedalsbreen glacier, Nigardsbreen is a popular summer destination, with guided **hikes** from late May to mid-September across the glacier's rippled blue ice. These outings include easy 1½-hour family walks (Nkr100) and challenging four-hour, blue-ice treks (Nkr300), crossing deep crevasses and requiring hiking boots and warm clothing (instruction and technical equipment included); there's also a full-day option. More information on glacier walks is available from **Jostedal Breheimsenteret** (*☎ 57 68 32 50; W www.jostedal.com)* or at nearby tourist offices.

A bus leaves Sogndal at 8.25am (Monday to Friday) for the glacier, and a return bus leaves Nigardsbreen at 5pm. The fare is Nkr90 each way. Although this will give you time to do a short hike, if you're doing a longer hike you might want to stay at the nearby **Nigardsbreen Camping** (*☎ 57 68 31 35; tent sites Nkr75, cabins Nkr275)*.

NORDFJORD

Sognefjorden and Geirangerfjorden are linked by a road that winds around the head of the 100km-long Nordfjord, past the villages of Utvik, Innvik, Olden and Loen to the larger town of Stryn.

The chief Nordfjord attraction is the **Briksdal glacier**, one of Jostedal's icy arms. Although a barrage of package-tour buses drive up Olden Valley to Briksdal, there's only one public bus. It leaves Stryn (Nkr58, 10am) and Olden (Nkr39, 10.15am) daily from mid-June to mid-August, arriving at Briksdal at 11am. The return bus leaves Briksdal at 2pm.

The **Jostedalsbreen National Park Centre** (*☎ 57 87 72 00; adult/child Nkr60/30; open 10am-4pm or 6pm daily May-Sept)*, which is 15km east of Stryn, contains glacier-oriented exhibits, a decent audiovisual presentation, and displays on avalanches, local minerals and meteorites.

From Briksdal, it's a 3km hike to the glacier – allow yourself about two hours return. Briksdal has a lodge, **Briksdalsbre Fjellstove**, and there's also a **camping ground**, a **cafeteria** and a souvenir shop. **Pony-cart rides** (*☎ 57 87 68 05; adult/child Nkr250/125)* run to the glacier for those who don't want to walk (but you'll still have to hike the final 15 minutes on a rough path). **Glacier hiking tours** (Nkr250-550) are operated by **Briksdal Breføring** (*☎ 57 87 68 00)* and **Olden Activ** (*☎ 57 87 38 88)* five times daily in summer.

Places to Stay & Eat

There are lots of camping and cabin options in the area. Budget travellers should head for the no-frills **Alda Camping** (*☎/fax 57 87 31 38; tent sites from Nkr40, 4-bed huts Nkr190-290; open June-Aug)*, by the river in the heart of Olden, or the **HI hostel** (*☎ 57 87 11 06; Geilevegen 14; dorm beds Nkr170, singles/doubles Nkr250/400; open June-Aug)* in Stryn.

The roadside inn, **Olden Krotell** (*☎ 57 87 34 55; Olden; singles/doubles Nkr400/600; open June-Aug)*, offers en suite rooms with breakfast.

In Briksdal, **Briksdalsbre Fjellstove** (*☎ 57 87 68 00; e post@briksdalsbre.no; singles/doubles from Nkr300/400; open Apr-Oct)* offers comfortable rooms near the glacier; traditional meals are available in the restaurant (Nkr99 to Nkr164). The wonderful 19th-century Swiss-style **Visnes Hotel** (*☎ 57 87 10 87; e vibeke@visnes.no; Prestestegen 1; singles/doubles from Nkr550/850)* in Stryn has a good traditional restaurant that serves three-course dinners for Nkr325.

Getting There & Away

There are buses between Fjærland and Stryn (Nkr150, two hours), including a southbound one at 8.45am (Monday to Friday only, continuing to Sogndal, Lærdal and Bergen).

Buses that run between Stryn, Hellesylt (Nkr74, 50 minutes, two to four daily) and Ålesund (Nkr203, 3½ hours, one to four daily) connect with the Geiranger ferry at Hellesylt.

HELLESYLT
pop 500

Although quieter and less breathtaking than Geiranger, Hellesylt is still spectacular, lulled by a roaring waterfall that cascades through the centre. The **tourist office** (☎ 70 26 50 52) is near the ferry dock.

The convenient but rather exposed **Helle-sylt Camping** (☎ 70 26 51 88; camping per tent site/person from Nkr40/Nkr12) is right in the centre. A fine **HI hostel** (☎ 70 26 51 28; dorm beds Nkr120, singles/doubles Nkr220/300; open June-Aug) is perched just above the village and has great fjord views. The rustic old 1875 **Grand Hotel** (☎ 70 26 51 00; @ grandhotel.hellesylt@c2i.net; singles/doubles from Nkr560/760) has fjord-view rooms and its dining room serves fish, chicken and beef dishes (Nkr109 to Nkr185).

Buses heading south to Stryn (Nkr74, 50 minutes) leave from the pier where the ferry pulls in.

NORANGSDALEN & SUNNMØRESALPANE

One of the most inspiring parts of the western fjords is Norangsdalen, a hidden valley west of Hellesylt. The partially unsealed Rv665 road to the villages of Øye and Urke, and the Leknes–Sæbø ferry on beautiful Hjørundfjorden is served by bus from Hellesylt once daily, Monday to Friday mid-June to mid-August.

Hikers and climbers will find plenty of scope in the dramatic peaks of the adjacent Sunnmørsalpane, including the incredibly steep scrambling ascent of Slogen (1564m) from Øye and the superb Råna (1586m), a long and tough scramble from Urke.

Superb en suite accommodation is available at **Saksa Feriehytter** (☎/fax 70 06 20 82; @ saksehyt@online.no; Urke; 6-person chalets from Nkr360).

GEIRANGERFJORDEN

The towering walls of the narrow and twisting 20km-long Geirangerfjorden have a scattering of abandoned farms clinging to the cliffs and breathtakingly high waterfalls with names such as The Seven Sisters, The Suitor and The Bridal Veil.

The cruise by public ferry along Geiranger-fjorden, between Geiranger and Hellesylt, is Norway's most stunning and shouldn't be missed.

Geiranger
pop 270

Geiranger, at the head of Geirangerfjorden, is surrounded by high mountains with cascading waterfalls. Although the village is tiny, it's one of Norway's most visited spots. Nevertheless, it's reasonably serene in the evening when the cruise ships and tour buses have gone. The **tourist office** (☎ 70 26 30 99), near the pier, opens daily from mid-May to early September and has an album detailing trails. Ask for details of the new **exhibition centre**, which describes local culture and history.

There's great hiking all around Geiranger to abandoned farmsteads, waterfalls and some beautiful view points. One special walk is to **Storseter waterfall**, a 45-minute hike that actually takes you between the rock face and the cascading falls. You'll get the most spectacular fjord views from **Flydalsjuvet**, about 5km uphill from Geiranger on the Stryn road, and from **Ørnevegen**, about 4km from Geiranger towards Valldal and Åndalsnes.

The highest and most splendid view of the Geiranger valley and fjord is from the **Dal-snibba** lookout (1500m); there's a bus (Nkr100 return) from Geiranger at 9.40am from 15 June to 20 August.

Places to Stay & Eat Hotels in Geiranger can be quickly booked out by package tours, but cabins and camping spots are plentiful. A dozen camping grounds skirt the fjord and hillsides, including **Geiranger Camping** (☎ 70 26 31 20; tent sites from Nkr70; open 20 May-10 Sept), right in the centre of Geiranger.

Vinjebakken (☎ 70 26 32 05; dorm beds Nkr130, plus sheets Nkr50; open July–mid-Aug), a hostel-style chalet about 15 minutes' uphill walk from the dock, has a beautiful fjord view and friendly management. If you arrive by bus get off at the octagonal church, 100m from the hostel.

You'll see *Rom* signs around the village advertising **rooms** at around Nkr200/300 (singles/doubles) – the tourist office maintains a list and can help book one for you.

The **Grande Fjord Hotell** (☎ 70 26 30 90; @ kirstamu@online.no; singles/doubles from Nkr700/800), at a scenic spot on the fjord

NORWAY

2km northwest of the village, also has cabins and tent space nearby. The buffet breakfasts (included) and dinners (Nkr172 to Nkr250) are particularly good here.

Naustkroa *(mains Nkr85-178)*, near the pier in the town's centre, has affordable fish, beef and chicken dishes, and the nearby **Olebuda** *(mains Nkr55-154)* offers sandwiches, burgers, sausages, salmon, steaks and Mexican dishes. You can pick up groceries at the central **Joker supermarket**, even on Sunday, and it serves takeaway waffles with jam, cream and a coffee for only Nkr25.

Getting There & Away From mid-June to late August, buses to Åndalsnes (Nkr137, three hours) leave Geiranger at 1pm and 6.10pm; change at Linge for buses to Ålesund (Nkr160). The Geiranger–Hellesylt ferry (passengers/cars Nkr34/107, one hour) cruises the fjord four to 10 times daily from 1 May to 24 September.

ÅNDALSNES
pop 3500

By Romsdalsfjorden, Åndalsnes is the northern gateway to the western fjords. Most travellers arrive on the train from Dombås, a scenic route that descends through a deeply cut valley with dramatic waterfalls. Just before reaching Åndalsnes, the train passes **Trollveggen**, a sheer 1500m-high rock face whose jagged and often cloud-shrouded summit is considered the ultimate challenge among Norwegian mountain climbers. Highway E136 between Dombås and Åndalsnes runs parallel to the railway line and is equally spectacular.

The town itself is rather nondescript, but the scenery is top notch, camping grounds are plentiful and it has one of the finest hostels in Norway. The **tourist office** (☎ 71 22 16 22) is at the train station.

Things to See & Do

The **Norsk Tindemuseum** *(☎ 71 22 12 74; adult/child Nkr30/15; open 1pm-5pm daily 20 June-20 Aug, or by appointment)*, 2.5km from the centre, on the road to Åndalsnes Camping, has exhibits on the climbing expeditions of renowned mountaineer Arne Randers Heen.

The mountains and valleys surrounding Åndalsnes offer excellent **hiking** – contact the tourist office for details of guided trips.

One good trail, which goes to the top of **Nesaksla** (715m), starts right in town 50m north of the roundabout and makes a fine half-day outing. While the path is quite steep, at the top you'll be rewarded with a terrific view of the surrounding fjords and mountains. In summer the ascent can be hot in the midday sun, so get an early start and be sure to take water.

Places to Stay & Eat

Åndalsnes Camping *(☎ 71 22 16 29; tent sites from Nkr70, basic cabins Nkr160, cabins with kitchen & shower Nkr650)*, 2km from the centre on the southeastern side of the Rauma River, has a good range of cabins and rents bicycles/canoes for Nkr100/200 per day.

The best place to stay is the turf-roofed **Åndalsnes Vandrerhjem Setnes** *(☎ 71 22 13 82;* e *aandalsnes.hostel@vandrerhjem.no; dorm beds Nkr180, singles/doubles Nkr280/450; open 20 May-10 Sept, advance bookings other times)*, 2km from the train station on highway E136 towards Ålesund. This wonderfully rustic HI hostel has pleasant rooms with wonderful views and rates include a splendid breakfast. If you don't want to walk, catch the Ålesund bus, which meets the train and passes the hostel.

The pleasant and modernised **Alpe Hotel** *(☎ 71 22 21 00;* e *alpehotel@sensewave .com; dorm beds Nkr200; singles/doubles Nkr395/495)* is just 50m from the train station. Near the hostel, **Romsdal Hytteutleie** *(☎ 71 22 13 83; Veblungsnes; 2-bedroom en suite cabins with kitchen Nkr600-700)* is highly recommended.

The **shop** at the train station sells basic snacks; just 50m away is **Måndalen Bakeri** *(Havnegate 5)*, with good pastries and bread. The nearest cafeteria to the hostel is **Vertshuset Rauma** *(Øran Vest; mains around Nkr85-140)*, on the E136 on the north bank of the river. There are also a couple of **grocery stores** and three cafeteria-style **restaurants** in the centre.

Getting There & Away

The train from Dombås runs to Åndalsnes three or four times daily (Nkr171, 1¼ hours), in sync with Oslo-Trondheim trains. Buses to Ålesund (Nkr162, 2¼ hours) meet the trains. Buses to Geiranger (Nkr137, three hours), via the spectacular Trollstigen road, operate from mid-June to late August, leaving Åndalsnes at 8.30am and 5.30pm. If you have your own car, the mountain pass is cleared of snow and opens by at least 1 June every year – early in the season it's an awesome drive between immense vertical walls of snow.

ÅNDALSNES TO GEIRANGER

The **Trollstigen** (Troll's Path) winding south from Åndalsnes is a thriller of a road with hairpin bends, a 1:12 gradient and, to add a daredevil element, it's practically one lane all the way. On request, the bus makes photo stops at the thundering, 180m-high **Stigfossen waterfall** on its way up to the mountain pass. At the top, the bus usually stops long enough for you to walk to a lookout with a dizzying view back down the valley.

There are waterfalls galore smoking down the mountains as you descend to **Valldal**. You could break your journey here – there are camping grounds, cabins and a hotel – though most travellers continue on, taking the short ferry ride from Linge across to **Eidsdal**. From there, a waiting bus continues along the **Ørnevegen** (Eagle's Highway), with magnificent bird's-eye views of Geirangerfjorden during the descent into Geiranger village.

ÅLESUND
pop 24,320

The lovely coastal town of Ålesund, crowded onto a narrow fishhook-shaped peninsula in the sea, is considered by many to be even more beautiful than Bergen, and is far less touristy. The central streets are lined with handsome Art Nouveau buildings, erected after a sweeping fire in 1904. The **tourist office** (☎ 70 15 76 00; ⓦ www.visitalesund.com), in the town hall, runs guided walks daily from 10 June to 17 August. The **post office** is on Korsegata. For free Internet, visit the **public library** (Kremmergaarden, Korsegata).

Things to See & Do

The most popular thing to do is to walk the 418 steps up **Aksla** for a splendid view of Ålesund and the surrounding islands. Take Lihauggata from Kongensgata, pass the **Rollon statue**, and begin the 20-minute puff to the top of the hill.

The town **museum** (☎ 70 12 31 70; Rasmus Rønnebergs gate 16; adult/child Nkr30/10; open 11am-4pm Mon-Fri, noon-3pm Sat & Sun mid-June–mid-Aug, shorter hrs mid-Aug–mid-June) concentrates on local history, including sealing, fishing, shipping, the fire of

NORWAY

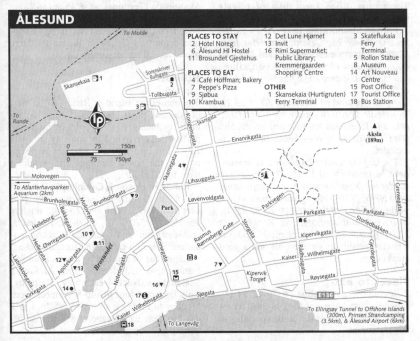

ÅLESUND

PLACES TO STAY
2 Hotel Noreg
6 Ålesund HI Hostel
11 Brosundet Gjestehus

PLACES TO EAT
4 Café Hoffman; Bakery
7 Peppe's Pizza
9 Sjøbua
10 Krambua

12 Det Lune Hjørnet
13 Invit
16 Rimi Supermarket;
   Public Library;
   Kremmergaarden
   Shopping Centre

OTHER
1 Skansekaia (Hurtigruten)
  Ferry Terminal

3 Skateflukaia
  Ferry
  Terminal
5 Rollon Statue
8 Museum
14 Art Nouveau
   Centre
15 Post Office
17 Tourist Office
18 Bus Station

1904, the German occupation during WWII and the town's distinctive architecture.

By the time you read this a new **Art Nouveau centre** should be open in Ålesund; ask the tourist office for details.

The recommended aquarium **Atlanterhavsparken** (☎ 70 10 70 60; *Tueneset; adult/child Nkr85/55; open 10am-7pm Sun-Fri & 10am-4pm Sat mid-June–mid-Aug, shorter hrs mid-Aug–mid-June*), 3km from the centre at the western extreme of the fishhook peninsula, introduces visitors to the astonishing marine life around the Norwegian coast.

Ålesund is a good base for touring the surrounding islands, including Runde (see the Runde section later). Ferries depart Skateflukaia Ferry Terminal.

Monday to Friday from 1 May to 25 September there's a scenic bus-ferry day trip (Nkr395) that includes a cruise down Geirangerfjorden, 2¾ hours in Geiranger and a return to Ålesund via Ørnevegen. There's also a day tour via Geiranger and Trollstigen (Nkr540, 12½ hours).

Places to Stay
The tourist office keeps lists of **private rooms** that start at around Nkr200 per person.

Prinsen Strandcamping (☎ 70 15 52 04, fax 70 15 49 96; *Gåseid; tent sites from Nkr50, cabins Nkr250-900, rooms Nkr200-400*), 5km east of town, has good facilities and luxurious cabins; take bus No 13, 14, 18 or 24.

At the **Ålesund HI Hostel** (☎ 70 11 58 30; e *aalesund.hostel@vandrerhjem.no; Parkgata 14; dorm beds Nkr180, singles/doubles Nkr370/470; open May-Sept*), breakfast is included.

The large hotel-standard rooms at **Brosundet Gjestehus** (☎ 70 12 10 00; e *post@brosundet.no; Apotekergata 5; singles/doubles from Nkr590/790*) have great harbour views, while the fine **Hotel Noreg** (☎ 70 12 29 38; e *noreg@rainbow-hotels.no; Kongensgata 27; singles/doubles from Nkr650/ 850*) offers comfortable en suite rooms and a good breakfast.

Places to Eat
Rustic and stylish **Sjøbua** (☎ 70 12 71 00; *Brunholmgata 1A; mains Nkr248-346*) serves gourmet meals; fish is the house speciality at this restaurant.

The menu at the atmospheric **Krambua** (*Apotekergata 2; dishes Nkr56-189*) pub-restaurant includes traditional Norwegian food and a daily special for Nkr94; there's live music some evenings.

Café Hoffmann (*Kongensgata 11; mains Nkr78-125*) offers a fine harbour view and soup for Nkr40; there's a **bakery** in the same shopping centre. Bright and cheery **Det Lune Hjørnet** (*Apotekergata 10; snacks Nkr12-40*) is a combined bookshop and coffeeshop. The modern-design espresso bar **Invit** (*Apotekergata 9; snacks Nkr15-48*) serves the best coffee in town.

You'll find a **Rimi supermarket** downstairs in Kremmergaarden, behind the tourist office, and **Peppe's Pizza** (*Kaiser Wilhelmsgata 25; lunch buffet Nkr79-93*) one block east of the supermarket.

Getting There & Away
Ålesund has daily flights to Oslo and other Norwegian cities. There are buses to Stryn (Nkr203, 3½ hours, one to four daily) via Hellesylt and to other major coastal and fjord towns.

Hurtigruten coastal steamers arrive/depart Skansekaia Terminal at 8.45am/ 6.45pm northbound and at 11.45pm/12.45am southbound; on the northbound run, there's a popular detour via Geiranger (hence the large gap in arrival and departure times).

RUNDE
pop 160
The impressive island of Runde, 27km west of Ålesund, plays host to half a million sea birds, including 100,000 pairs of migrating puffins that arrive in May and stay until late July. Most bird-watching sites are best seen by sea; the hostel arranges bird-watching tours for Nkr100.

Runde HI Hostel & Camping (☎ 70 08 59 16; e *runde.hostel@vandrerhjem.no; tent sites from Nkr75, dorm beds Nkr110, singles/ doubles Nkr220/270*), on the harbourside, provides clean and comfortable accommodation. There's a **café** 300m from the hostel.

Runde can be reached by a catamaran-bus combination that departs from Ålesund's Skateflukaia (Nkr144 each way, 2½ hours) daily from mid-June to mid-September; from Monday to Friday it's possible to do it as a day trip, leaving Ålesund at 8.30am and returning at 7.30pm.

Northern Norway

The counties of Sør Trøndelag, Nord Trøndelag, Nordland, Troms and Finnmark comprise a vast and varied area stretching over 1500km, mostly north of the Arctic Circle. The terrain ranges from majestic coastal mountains that rise above tiny fishing villages and scattered farms to the barren, treeless, Arctic plateau in the far north.

Trains run as far north as Bodø; for destinations further north, there are buses and boats. Since distances are long, bus travel costs can add up, though Inter-Rail and ScanRail pass-holders get a 50% discount on most long-distance bus routes. An interesting alternative to land travel is the *Hurtigruten* coastal steamer, which pulls into every sizable port between Bergen and Kirkenes, passing some of the best coastal scenery in Scandinavia.

RØROS
pop 2590

Røros is a wonderful old copper-mining town with a well-preserved historic district, protected under Unesco's World Heritage List.

The first mine opened in 1644 but in 1977, after 333 years of operation, the company went bankrupt. The town makes for delightful strolling and everything's within easy walking distance. The **tourist office** (☎ 72 41 11 65; *Peder Hiortsgata 2*) can advise on cycling trips, canoeing, fishing and hiking.

Things to See & Do

Røros' main attractions are turf-roofed **miners' cottages** and other centuries-old timber buildings, a prominent 1784 **church** (*Kjerkgata; tours adult/child Nkr25/free; open 10am-5pm Mon-Sat, 2pm-4pm Sun, 21 June-15 Aug; tours 2pm daily*) with an excellent baroque interior, **slag heaps**, and the old smelting works, now a **mining museum** (☎ 72 40 61 70; *Malmplassen; adult/child Nkr60/30; open 10am-7pm daily mid-June–mid-Aug, shorter hrs mid-Aug–mid-June*). The museum features brilliant intricate scale models of life in the mines.

You can also visit the now defunct **Olavsguva mine** (☎ 72 41 11 65; *Kojedalen; tours adult/child Nkr60/30*), 13km northeast of town. From 21 June to 15 August, subterranean tours into the old copper mine (5°C – bring a

NORWAY

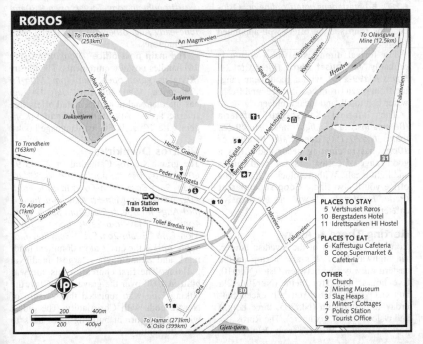

RØROS

To Trondheim (253km)
An Magritveien
To Olavsguva Mine (12.5km)
Svenhusveien
Speil Olaveien
Kvernhusveien
Johan Falkbergets vei
Hyttelva
Åstjørn
Falunveien
Doktortjørn
1
2 🏛
Henrik Grønns vei
5 🏠
Kjerkgata
Bergmannsgata
Mørkstugata
●4
3
31
8
6
7
Peder Hiortsgata
9 ⓘ
To Trondheim (163km)
Train Station & Bus Station
▪ 10
Dalsveien
To Airport (1km)
Stormoveien
Tollef Bredals vei
Falunveien
11 ▪
Øra
30
11 ▪
To Hamar (273km) & Oslo (399km)
Gjett-tjørn

0   200   400m
0   200   400yd

PLACES TO STAY
5 Vertshuset Røros
10 Bergstadens Hotel
11 Idrettsparken HI Hostel

PLACES TO EAT
6 Kaffestugu Cafeteria
8 Coop Supermarket & Cafeteria

OTHER
1 Church
2 Mining Museum
3 Slag Heaps
4 Miners' Cottages
7 Police Station
9 Tourist Office

sweater!) are given every 90 minutes, with the first at 11am and the last at 5pm. To get there, use your own wheels or take a taxi (Nkr400 return).

Organised Tours

In winter, the tourist office organises ski tours and excursions by dogsled (Nkr600 to Nkr800 for two to five hours) or horse-drawn sleigh (Nkr600 per hour for four people). Bizarre **UFO safaris** (☎ 72 41 55 55; W *www .hessdalen.org*) are also available.

Places to Stay & Eat

Idrettsparken HI Hostel (☎ 72 41 10 89; Øra 25; tent sites Nkr60, dorm beds Nkr190, cabins Nkr380-600, singles/doubles from Nkr340/400), at the edge of a sports stadium, offers a wide range of options with good standards. Prices include breakfast.

Perhaps the best-value choice is **Vertshuset Røros** (☎ 72 41 24 11; Kjerkgata 34; singles/doubles from Nkr685/850, 2-person apartments per person from Nkr395), which has 24 inviting rooms (breakfast included) and self-catering apartments. The cosy and down-to-earth **Bergstadens Hotel** (☎ 72 40 60 80; e bergstadens.hotel@online.no; Oslo-veien 2; singles/doubles from Nkr780/980), near the train station, offers well-appointed rooms.

For formal dining, the finest option is probably **Vertshuset Røros** (Kjerkgata 34; mains Nkr99-215), with a good menu ranging from pizza (from Nkr85), beef and freshwater fish to elk and local reindeer.

The informal **Kafestuggu cafeteria** (Bergmannsgata 18; light meals Nkr49-55, mains Nkr70-150; open daily to 8pm or 10pm) has fascinating decor and offers a good range of coffee, pastries, cold snacks and light meals. Within a block of the tourist office you'll also find a **Coop supermarket** (Peder Hiortsgata 7), with an inexpensive cafeteria.

Getting There & Away

Røros is 46km west of the Swedish border, via highway Rv31. It's also a stop on the eastern railway line between Oslo (Nkr510, five hours) and Trondheim (Nkr204, 2½ hours). Overnight buses run daily except Saturday to Trondheim (Nkr205, three hours) and Oslo (Nkr450, six hours). The Røros airport is served by Widerøe from Oslo.

TRONDHEIM
pop 135,880

Trondheim, Norway's third-largest city and original capital, is a lively university town with a rich medieval history. It was founded at the estuary of the winding Nidelva River in AD 997 by the Viking king Olav Tryggvason. After a fire razed most of the city in 1681, Trondheim was redesigned, with wide streets and a Renaissance flair, by General Caspar de Cicignon. Today, the steeple of the medieval Nidaros Domkirke (Nidaros Cathedral) is still the highest point in the city centre.

Orientation & Information

The central part of town is on a triangular peninsula that's easy to explore on foot. The train station, bus station and coastal-steamer quay are across the canal, a few minutes north of the centre.

On and around **Torvet**, the central square, are the tourist office, a produce market, a **statue of King Olav** and the 13th-century stone church **Vår Frue Kirke**. From Torvet there's a head-on view of the cathedral, Nidaros Domkirke, to the south.

The **tourist office** (☎ 73 80 76 60; W *www .visit-trondheim.com*; Torvet; open 8.30am-10pm Mon-Fri, 10am-8pm Sat & Sun, late June-early Aug, otherwise shorter hrs) helps with inquiries.

The **main post office** (Dronningens gate 10) handles postal requirements. The **library** (Kongens gate; open 9am-4pm Mon-Fri year-round, 10am-3pm Sat 1 July-12 Aug) has international newspapers and offers free Internet access. **Ark Bruns Bokhandel** (Kongens gate 10) sells English-language books.

Nidaros Domkirke

The grand Nidaros Cathedral (☎ 73 53 91 60; Kongsgårdsgata; adult/child Nkr35/20; open 9am-6pm Mon-Fri mid-June–mid-Aug, 9am- 3pm Mon-Fri May–mid-June & mid-Aug– mid-Sept; 9am-2pm Sat & 1pm-4pm Sun May–mid-Sept; noon-2.30pm Mon-Fri, 11.30am-2pm Sat, 1-3pm Sun mid-Sept– Apr) is the city's most dominant landmark and Scandinavia's largest medieval building. The first church on this site was built in 1070 over the grave of St Olav, the Viking king who replaced the worship of Nordic gods with Christianity. The oldest wing of the current building dates back to the 12th century.

TRONDHEIM

PLACES TO STAY
10 Chesterfield Hotel
11 Gildevangen Hotell
18 Britannia Hotel
21 Lilletorget Hotell
31 Trondheim Hotell
37 Gammeldagshuset
44 Trondheim InterRail Centre & Studentersamfundet

PLACES TO EAT
2 Solsiden Shopping Centre & Restaurants
6 Café Dali
7 Scapa
8 Det Lille Franske
9 Akropolis
13 Credo
16 Helios Trondheim (Health Foods)
20 Egon
23 Dickens
25 Peppe's Pizza
32 Rema 1000 Grocery Shop
35 Zia Teresa

OTHER
1 Bus Station
3 Maritime Museum
4 Airport Bus Stop; Budget Car Rental
5 Olavshallen & Olavskvartalet Cultural Centre
12 Rio
14 Ferries to Munkholmen
15 Ravnkloa Fish Market
17 Stiftsgården (Royal Residence)
19 Post Office
22 Avis Car Rental
24 Old Waterfront Warehouses
26 Library; Church Ruins; Kafé Gjest Baardsen
27 SpareBank1 Midt-Norge & Church Ruins
28 King's Cross
29 Ark Bruns Bokhandel (Bookshop)
30 Torvet
33 Tourist Office
34 Vår Frue Kirke
36 Museum of Decorative Arts
38 University Museum of Natural History & Archaeology
39 Trondheim Kino (Cinema)
40 Trondheim Kunstmuseum
41 Nidaros Domkirke
42 Archbishop's Palace
43 Rustkammeret Military Museum

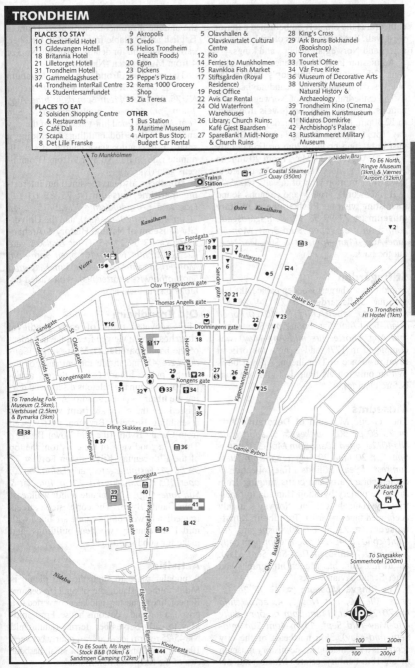

NORWAY

One of the most spectacular features of the cathedral is the ornately embellished exterior west wall, lined with statues of biblical characters and Norwegian bishops and kings.

Admission includes entrance to the adjacent 12th-century **Archbishop's Palace**, the oldest secular building in Scandinavia.

The cathedral, the site of Norwegian coronations, displays the **crown jewels** from 9am to 12.30pm, Monday to Thursday, and Saturday, 1pm to 4pm on Sunday (1 June to 20 August only), and noon to 2pm on Friday only from 20 August to 31 May. From 20 June to 20 August, visitors can climb the cathedral tower for a rooftop view of the city (Nkr5).

If old swords, armour and cannons sound interesting, visit the **Rustkammeret military museum** (☎ 73 99 58 31; Kongsgårdsgata; admission free; open 9am-3pm Mon-Fri June-Aug, 11am-4pm Sat & Sun Mar-Nov) out the back.

Stiftsgården

Scandinavia's largest wooden palace, the late baroque **Stiftsgården** (☎ 73 84 28 80; Munkegata; adult/child Nkr40/20; open 10am-5pm Mon-Sat, noon-5pm Sun, June–mid-Aug, shorter hrs mid-Aug–May) was completed in 1778 and is now the official royal residence in Trondheim. Admission is by tour only (on the hour; last tour one hour before closing).

Museums

The eclectic **Museum of Decorative Arts** (☎ 73 80 89 50; Munkegata 5; adult/child Nkr40/20; open 10am-5pm Mon-Sat, noon-5pm Sun 20 June-20 Aug, 11am-5pm Tues-Sun rest of year) exhibits a fine collection of contemporary arts and crafts ranging from Japanese pottery by Shoji Hamada to tapestries by Hannah Ryggen, Norway's highly acclaimed tapestry artist. **Trondheim Kunstmuseum** (☎ 73 53 81 80; Bispegata 7B; adult/child Nkr40/20; open 10am-5pm daily June-Aug, 11am-5pm Tues-Sun Sept-May), an art museum, has Munch lithographs and other Scandinavian works.

The **Ringve Museum** (☎ 73 92 24 11; Lade Allé 60; bus Nos 3, 4; adult/child Nkr70/25; open 11am-3pm or 5pm daily mid-May–mid Sept, 11am-4pm Sun mid-Sept–mid-May), 3km northeast of the city centre, is a fascinating music-history museum in an 18th-century estate. Music students

from the university give tours, demonstrating the antique instruments on display. Tours in English are available from April to October; call the museum for details. Take bus No 3 or 4 from Munkegaten (Nkr22).

The excellent **Trøndelag Folk Museum** (☎ 73 89 01 00; Sverresborg Allé; adult/child Nkr75/25; open 11am-6pm daily June-Aug, 11am-3pm Mon-Fri, noon-4pm Sat & Sun Sept-May) has good hill-top views of the city and over 60 period buildings, including a small, 12th-century stave church. It's a 10-minute ride on bus No 8 or 9 from Dronningens gate (Nkr22).

Trondheim also has the small but interesting **maritime museum** (☎ 73 89 01 00; Fjordgata 6A; adult/child Nkr25/15; open 10am-4pm daily June-Aug), and the **University Museum of Natural History & Archaeology** (☎ 73 59 21 45; Erling Skakkes gate 47; adult/child Nkr25/10; open 9am-4pm Mon-Fri, 11am-4pm Sat & Sun May–mid Sept, otherwise shorter hrs), with varied exhibits on the local area.

Old Trondheim

The excavated **ruins of early medieval churches** can be viewed free in the basement of the bank **SpareBank1 Midt-Norge** (Søndre gate 4), and inside the entrance of the nearby public library (where there's a display of two human skeletons discovered during the library's construction). Also not to be missed are the old **waterfront warehouses** resembling Bergen's Bryggen, best viewed from Gamle Bybro (the Old Town Bridge). There's a good view of the city from the top of the 17th-century **Kristiansten Fort** (☎ 73 99 58 31; Festningsgaten; admission Nkr10; open 10am-3pm Mon-Fri, 11am-4pm Sat & Sun June-Aug), a 10-minute uphill walk east from Gamle Bybro. The cobblestone streets immediately west of the centre are lined with mid-19th century wooden buildings and make for good strolling.

Activities

A popular place to sunbathe and picnic is **Munkholmen** island, site of an 11th-century Benedictine monastery and later converted to a prison, a fort and a customs house. From mid-May to early September, ferries (adult/child Nkr45/25 return) leave at least hourly between 10am or noon, and 6pm from the small harbour east of the **Ravnkloa fish market**.

The western side of Trondheim is bordered by the **Bymarka**, a woodland area crossed with good skiing and wilderness trails. To get there, take the tram (Nkr22) from St Olavs gate to **Lian**, which has good city views, a bathing lake and hiking paths.

Places to Stay

The nearest camping ground is **Sandmoen Camping** (☎ 72 88 61 35; ☻ tras@online.no; bus No 46; tent sites from Nkr100, cabins Nkr450-900), 12km south of the city on the E6.

From late June to mid-August, university students operate an informal crash pad called **Trondheim InterRail Centre** (☎ 73 89 95 38; ☻ tirc@stud.ntnu.no; Elgesetergate 1; dorm beds Nkr115), a five-minute walk south of the cathedral. Breakfast is included. This friendly operation is free of curfews and has a café with Nkr45 dinners, inexpensive beer and free Internet access.

The rather good **Trondheim HI Hostel** (☎ 73 87 44 50; ☻ trondheim.hostel@vandre rhjem.no; Weidemannsvei 41; bus No 63; dorm beds Nkr198, singles/doubles Nkr400/530; open 3 Jan-18 Dec), 2km east of the train station, includes breakfast in its rates.

At the **Singsaker Sommerhotel** (☎ 73 89 31 00, fax 73 89 32 00; Rogertsgata 1; dorm beds Nkr125-155, singles/doubles Nkr345/550; open early June–mid-Aug), 200m south of Kristiansten Fort, has breakfast included in the price.

The tourist office books **rooms** in private homes, mostly on the city outskirts, averaging Nkr250/400 for singles/doubles plus a Nkr20 booking fee.

For B&B with kitchen facilities and a quiet woodland location about 10km south of the centre, try **Ms Inger Stock** (☎/fax 72 88 83 19; Porsmyra 18, Tiller; bus No 46 to Tonstadgrenda; singles/doubles Nkr300/380). In a centrally located rustic house from 1837, the recommended **Gammeldagshuset** (☎/fax 73 51 55 68; Hvedingsveita 8; per person Nkr490; open summer) serves a traditional Norwegian breakfast.

Two Rainbow hotels – the **Trondheim Hotell** (☎ 73 50 50 50; ☻ trondheim@rainb ow-hotels.no; Kongens gate 15) and the historic **Gildevangen Hotell** (☎ 73 87 01 30; ☻ gildevangen@rainbow-hotels.no; Søndre gate 22) – offer full amenities and rates from Nkr650/850.

At the **Lilletorget Hotell** (☎ 73 80 63 00; ☻ lilletorget@lilletorget.no; Cicignons plass; singles/doubles from Nkr545/740) there are comfortable beds and particularly good breakfasts.

The quirky and personal **Chesterfield Hotel** (☎ 73 50 37 50; ☻ hotel@online.no; Søndre gate 26; singles/doubles from Nkr600/775) has commodious en suite rooms and free Internet facilities for guests. Rooms on the seventh floor have huge skylights and broad city views. Discounts are offered for Scan Rail pass holders.

The historic **Britannia Hotel** (☎ 73 80 08 00; ☻ britannia@britannia.no; Dronningens gate 5; singles/doubles from Nkr690/850) has a wonderful ambience and professional staff.

Places to Eat

The gourmet restaurant **Credo** (☎ 73 53 03 88; Ørjaveita 4; 3/5-course dinner Nkr380/470) has an excellent reputation and different wines served with each course; reserve several days in advance. Trondheim's most popular restaurant is **Egon** (☎ 73 51 79 75; Thomas Angells gate 8; mains Nkr84-209, pizza buffet Nkr93), which has something for everyone.

Zia Teresa (Vår Frue strete 4; mains Nkr75-185) is a cosy bistro with authentic Italian food, including pasta dishes averaging Nkr90. **Akropolis** (Fjordgata 19; mains Nkr108-245) offers full Greek meals. **Dickens** (Kjøpmannsgata 57; mains Nkr77-195), inside a restored canalside warehouse from 1740, has moderately priced meat and fish dishes, pizzas and salads.

The stylish bar and café **Scapa** (Brattørgata 12B; light meals Nkr55-99, dinner mains Nkr145-188) serves great food at reasonable prices.

For a more traditional experience, visit **Vertshuset** (☎ 73 87 80 70; Sverresborg Allé 11; mains Nkr99-235), a historic (1739) spot with rotating specials of traditional Norwegian fare, or just coffee and waffles.

The **Solsiden shopping centre**, on the east bank of the river, has several restaurants with outdoor tables and is great on a sunny day.

Right on the water, **Peppe's Pizza** (Kjøpmannsgata 25; pizzas Nkr134-182) features the standard Peppe's menu.

Kafé Gjest Baardsen (Kongens gate; light meals Nkr42-89), in the library, is a gathering place for international students and has

NORWAY

inexpensive cakes, salads and sandwiches. On the north side of the city, you'll find **Café Dali** *(Brattørgata; snacks & mains Nkr55-145)*, with simple meals and alternative music; it's popular with students.

From Monday to Friday, travellers stumbling off the night train can head to **Det Lille Franske** *(Søndre gate 25, enter from Brattørgata)*, which opens early and has coffee, good pastries and a pavement table.

Helios Trondheim *(Prinsens gate 53)* is a health-food store. For more standard fare, **Rema 1000** *(Torvet)* has good prices on groceries and bakery items – or munch out on inexpensive fish cakes from the **Ravnkloa fish market**.

Entertainment

Ask the tourist office for the lowdown on pubs and clubs – things change fast in Trondheim.

The new English pub, **King's Cross** *(Nordre gate)*, features live music some weekends, imported beer on tap, live wide-screen UK football and bar meals for around Nkr90.

Studentersamfundet *(Elgesetergate 1)*, the university student centre, has a pub, a cinema and some good alternative music, though most of the activities wind down in the summer. **Rio** *(Nordre gate 23)* is currently the hottest dance club for twentysomethings; it's almost too crowded on weekends.

Olavshallen *(Kjøpmannsgata 44)*, at the Olavskvartalet cultural centre, is the city's main concert hall, hosting performers ranging from the Trondheim Symphony Orchestra to international rock and jazz musicians.

For cinema, try **Trondheim Kino** *(☎ 73 80 88 00; Prinsens gate 2B)*.

Getting There & Away

Air From the airport in Værnes, 32km east of Trondheim, SAS and Braathens fly to major Norwegian cities. SAS also flies daily to Copenhagen.

Bus Nor-Way Bussekspress services run to/from Ålesund (Nkr477, 7¼ hours), Bergen (Nkr755, 14½ hours) and Oslo Sunday to Friday (Nkr590 to Nkr620, 9½ hours), the latter via Røros or Lillehammer.

Train There are four or five trains to Oslo daily (Nkr667, 6½ hours) and two or three to Bodø (Nkr773, 10 hours). If you're in a hurry

to get north, consider taking the overnight train from Oslo, tossing your gear into a locker at the station and spending the day exploring Trondheim before continuing on an overnight train to Bodø (which, incidentally, goes through Hell just after 10.50pm).

There are also trains or buses from Trondheim to Storlien in Sweden (Nkr153, 1¾ hours) at 11.57am and 3.10pm (Monday to Friday) or 4.20pm (Saturday and Sunday), with onward connections to Stockholm.

Car & Motorcycle The E6, the main north–south motorway, passes west of the city centre and tolls total Nkr35, both northbound and southbound (on the Trondheim–Stjørdal section). There's also a Nkr15 toll on vehicles entering the city 6am to 6pm from Monday to Friday.

For car rentals, there's **Avis** *(☎ 73 84 17 90; Kjøpmannsgata 34)* and **Budget** *(☎ 73 52 69 20; Kjøpmannsgata 73)*.

Boat On its northbound journey, the *Hurtigruten* coastal steamer arrives in Trondheim at 8.15am (6am from October to May) and departs at noon; southbound, it arrives at 6.30am and departs at 10am.

Getting Around

To/From the Airport Airport buses (Nkr54) leave from the train station, the Britannia Hotel and the Radisson SAS Royal Garden Hotel (Kjøpmannsgata 73) in conjunction with SAS and Braathens flights.

Bus The central transit point for all city buses is the intersection of Munkegata and Dronningens gate. The bus fare is Nkr22, or you can buy a 24-hour ticket for Nkr55 to Nkr70 (both paid to the driver, exact change needed).

Car & Motorcycle If you have a car, it's easy to drive between sights on the outskirts of town, but best to explore the centre on foot. There's metered parking along many streets at zones marked *P Mot avgift*, though car parks (there's one near the train station) are generally cheaper.

Bicycle About 30 stands spread around the city centre have free **bicycles** that can be borrowed by inserting a Nkr20 coin in the lock – return the bike to reclaim your coin.

MO I RANA & AROUND
pop 19,750

Friendly Mo i Rana, the third-largest city in the north, is the gateway to the spruce forests, caves and glaciers of the Arctic Circle region, one of Europe's largest wilderness areas. The **tourist office** (☎ 75 13 92 00) can assist with queries.

Things to See & Do

The **natural history museum** (☎ 75 14 61 80; Moholmen 15; admission Nkr10; open 9am-3pm Mon-Fri year-round & 7pm-10pm mid-June–mid-Aug) concentrates on the geology, ecology, flora and wildlife of the Arctic Circle region.

There are two **caves** open for tourist visits; the straightforward 30-minute tour through **Grønligrotta** (☎ 75 16 23 05; Grønli; adult/child Nkr70/35; tours hourly 10am-7pm mid-June–mid-Aug), 22km northeast of Mo i Rana, is illuminated by electric light and is particularly good fun.

The eastern part of the **Svartisen icecap** is readily accessible by car or bicycle from Mo i Rana. From Svartisdal, 33km north of Mo i Rana, boats chug along the lake Svartisvatnet at least four times daily from 20 June to 31 August.

Then it's an easy 6km return hike to the impressive Austerdalsisen glacier tongue, which calves whopping icebergs into a large glacial lake.

Places to Stay & Eat

About 12km out of town, toward Svartisen and by the E6 highway, the riverside **Anna's Camping** (☎ 75 14 80 74; Røssvoll; caravans/cabins from Nkr60/105) offers basic accommodation with shared kitchen and bathroom facilities. In a quiet location on a hill in town, there's the pleasant **Mo Hotell og Gjestgård** (☎ 75 15 22 11, fax 75 15 23 38; Hans Wølners gate 10; singles/doubles Nkr400/500).

The Holmen Hotel's **Karjolen Mat og Vinhus** (☎ 75 15 14 44; TV Westens gate 2; mains Nkr80-225) is recommended for its traditional Norwegian cuisine and extensive wine list.

Eivinds Gatekjøkken (☎ 75 15 04 33; Fridtjof Nansensgata 1) stays open late on weekends with burgers, chips and the like from Nkr57 to Nkr100. The **Bunnpris super-market** is opposite the tourist office.

Getting There & Away

Mo i Rana's unique octagonal train station gets two to four daily trains from Trondheim (Nkr612, six to seven hours) or Bodø (Nkr332, three hours). For bus journeys to/from Umeå, Sweden, see the introductory Getting There & Away section in this chapter.

BODØ
pop 33,020

In addition to being the terminus for the northern railway line, Bodø is Nordland's largest town and a jumping-off point for Lofoten. Since the town was flattened during WWII air raids and completely rebuilt in the 1950s, Bodø itself is really quite ordinary in appearance – but it does have a lovely mountain backdrop.

The **tourist office** (☎ 75 54 80 00; W www .bodoe.com; Sjøgata 3) is near the waterfront. There are several banks with ATMs in the central area, and a **post office** (Havnegata 9).

Things to See & Do

Nordlandsmuseet (☎ 75 52 16 40; Prinsens gate 116; adult/child Nkr30/15; open 9am-3pm Mon-Fri, noon-3pm Sun year-round, noon-3pm Sat Sept-Apr, 10am-3pm Sat May-Aug) covers Nordland history. There's also a modern **cathedral** (Kongens gate; open 9am-2.30pm Mon-Fri mid-June–Aug). The excellent **aviation museum** (☎ 75 50 78 50; Olav V gate; adult/child Nkr70/40; open 10am-7pm Sun-Fri, 10am-5pm Sat mid-June–mid-Aug, 10am-4pm Mon-Fri, 11am-5pm Sat & Sun mid-Aug–mid-June), 2km southeast of town, includes some scary simulations of jet-fighter flying. About 1km southeast but quite intriguing **Bodin Kirke** (Gamle riksvei 68; open 10am-3pm Mon-Fri late June–mid-Aug), a little onion-domed stone church dating from around 1240.

Places to Stay

The nearest camping ground is **Bodøsjøen Camping** (☎ 75 56 36 80; Kvernhusveien; tent sites from Nkr130), 3km from town via bus No 12. The 60-bed **Bodø HI Hostel** (☎ 75 52 11 22; e bodo.hostel@vandrerhjem.no; Sjøgata 55; dorm beds Nkr150, singles/doubles Nkr250/330; open May-Sept) is conveniently located upstairs at the train station.

The tourist office books **private rooms** from Nkr150 per person. The charmingly

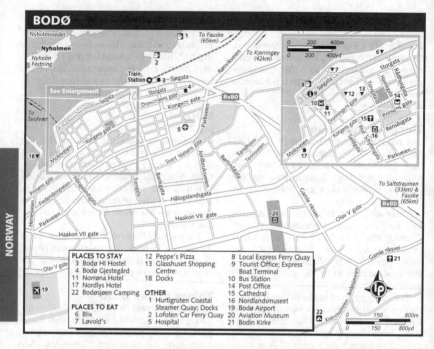

BODØ

PLACES TO STAY
3 Bodø HI Hostel
4 Bodø Gjestegård
11 Norrøna Hotel
17 Nordlys Hotel
22 Bodøsjøen Camping

PLACES TO EAT
6 Blix
7 Løvold's

12 Peppe's Pizza
13 Glasshuset Shopping
  Centre
18 Docks

OTHER
1 Hurtigruten Coastal
  Steamer Quay; Docks
2 Lofoten Car Ferry Quay
5 Hospital

8 Local Express Ferry Quay
9 Tourist Office; Express
  Boat Terminal
10 Bus Station
14 Post Office
15 Cathedral
16 Nordlandsmuseet
19 Bodø Airport
20 Aviation Museum
21 Bodin Kirke

renovated guesthouse **Bodø Gjestegård** (☎ 75 52 04 02; e johansst@online.no; Storgata 90; singles/doubles Nkr350/550) is at the edge of the centre.

The **Norrøna Hotel** (☎ 75 52 55 50; e norrona.hotell@radissonsas.com; Storgata 4B; singles/doubles from Nkr400/500), opposite the bus station, has comfortable rooms with private bath and affordable July and August prices. Bodø's newest and most stylish hotel, the **Nordlys Hotel** (☎ 75 53 19 00; e nordlys@rainbow-hotels.no; Moloveien 14; singles/doubles from Nkr490/690), has Scandinavian design touches throughout.

Places to Eat

Perhaps Bodø's most dignified restaurant, **Blix** (☎ 75 54 70 99; Sjøgata 23; mains Nkr172-206) serves beef and fish and has a nice wine list. The dockside **Molostua** (☎ 75 52 05 30; Moloveien 9; mains Nkr84-209) specialises in fish and regional cooking, and has unbeatable views.

At **Peppe's Pizza** (Storgata 3; pizzas Nkr134-182), you'll find the trademark pizza and salad lunch buffet (Nkr79 to Nkr93). The historic quayside cafeteria

Løvold's (Tollbugata 9; dishes Nkr23-115) offers sandwiches, grills and hearty Norwegian fare.

For inexpensive food, head to the **docks** for fresh shrimp, or **Glasshuset** (Storgata 12), with a supermarket and several fast-food choices.

Getting There & Around

The airport is served by SAS, Braathens and Widerøe.

Trondheim trains arrive in Bodø at 9.10am, 6.30pm and 0.25am (Nkr773, 10 hours). If you're continuing north by bus, be sure to get off 40 minutes before Bodø at Fauske, where the two daily express buses to Narvik (Nkr313, five hours) connect with the train. Southbound trains leave Bodø at 11.35am and 9pm daily.

The northbound *Hurtigruten* coastal steamer arrives in Bodø at 12.30pm and departs at 3pm; southbound, it's in port from 1.30am to 4am. The coastal steamer and Lofoten car-ferry quays are a five-minute walk north of the train station, while express catamaran boats dock near the tourist office. Information on Lofoten boats is in the Lofoten section, later in this chapter.

The tourist office rents **bikes** for Nkr60 per day, plus a deposit.

AROUND BODØ

The timber-built 19th-century trading station at sleepy **Kjerringøy**, by luminescent turquoise seas and soaring granite peaks 42km north of Bodø, has been preserved as an **open-air museum** (☎ 75 51 12 57; adult/child Nkr40/20; open 11am-5pm daily 25 May-18 Aug). Daily buses run from Bodø to Kjerringøy (Nkr73, 1½ hours), but schedules may not be convenient for daytrippers. You can stay 1km away at the old rectory, now **Kjerringøy Prestegård guesthouse** (☎ 75 50 77 10; hostel beds Nkr150, doubles from Nkr500), which offers simple rooms.

There are also buses (No 900) that go 33km south from Bodø (Nkr46, 45 minutes) to **Saltstraumen**, claimed to be the world's largest maelstrom – at high tide an immense volume of water swirls and churns its way through a 3km-long strait that links two fjords; unfortunately, although it may pack a lot of power, there isn't all that much to see, unless you're there at the right time. The Bodø tourist office can advise on the best times (which vary daily).

NARVIK

pop 14,140

Narvik was established a century ago as an ice-free port for the rich Kiruna iron-ore mines in Swedish Lapland. The town is bisected by a monstrous transshipment facility, where the ore is off-loaded from rail cars onto ships bound for distant smelters. In April and May 1940, during WWII, fierce land and naval battles took place around the town as the Germans and the Allies fought to control the iron-ore trade.

Ask the helpful Narvik **tourist office** (☎ 76 94 33 09; e post@narvikinfo.no; Kongens gate 26) for details of local hiking routes. The **post office** is 300m south on Kongens gate, the train station is at the north end of town, and the Lofoten express boat dock is on Havnegata, just over 1km south of the centre, down Kongens gate.

Things to See & Do

The impressive **Red Cross War Museum** (☎ 76 94 44 26; Kongens gate; adult/child Nkr45/10; open 10am-10pm Mon-Sat, 11am-5pm Sun 10 June-20 Sept, 11am-3pm

daily 1 Mar-9 June & 20-30 Sept) admirably illustrates WWII military campaigns.

The town's unique **Ofoten Museum** (☎ 76 96 00 50; Administrasjonsveien 2; adult/child Nkr25/5; open 11am-3.30pm Mon-Fri, noon-3pm Sat & Sun July, 10.30am-3.30pm Mon-Fri Aug-June) occupies a wonderful building dating from 1902, and tells of Narvik's farming, railway building and ore transshipment heritage.

Weather permitting, the Fjellheisen **cable car** (☎ 76 94 16 05; Mårveien; return fare adult/child Nkr80/45; 10am-1am daily mid-June–July, 1pm-9pm daily early June & Aug) soars up 656m for breathtaking views of the midnight sun and the surrounding peaks and fjords.

Organised Tours

Arrange sightseeing, fishing and whale-watching on the boat **Delphin Senior** (☎/fax 76 95 71 51); during the herring runs between October and December you may see orcas (killer whales). In October and November, **Tysfjord Turistsenter** (☎ 75 77 53 70; Storjord; w www .orca-tysfjord.nu) runs extraordinary orca-watching cruises from Storjord, about 85km south of Narvik on the E6. The Nor-Way Bussekspress bus to/from Fauske passes less than 1km from Storjord.

Places to Stay & Eat

The nearest camping ground is **Narvik Camping** (☎ 76 94 58 10; Rombaksveien 75; tent sites Nkr70, cabins Nkr450-650), 2km northeast of town on the E6.

Narvik HI Hostel (☎ 76 96 22 00; e narvik .hostel@vandrerhjem.no; Tiurveien 22; dorm beds Nkr160, singles/doubles Nkr215/320; open 24 June-17 Aug) is about a 20-minute walk west of the centre; breakfast is Nkr50 extra. More central is **Breidablikk Gjesthus** (☎ 76 94 14 18; e post@breidablikk.no; Tore Hunds gate 41; dorm beds Nkr185, singles/ doubles Nkr475/650), a pleasant pension with a hillside fjord view.

Made for backpackers and in former rail cabins by the tracks, the new **Spor 1 Gjestegård** (☎ 76 94 60 20; e post@spor1.no; Brugata 2; dorm beds/doubles Nkr160/500) has well-kept dorm rooms, charming hosts, a sauna and a well-equipped and spotlessly clean kitchen.

Around the corner from the tourist office, the **Nordstjernen Hotell** (☎ 76 94 41 20;

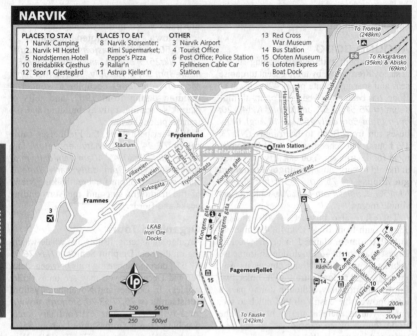

NARVIK

PLACES TO STAY	PLACES TO EAT	OTHER	13 Red Cross
1 Narvik Camping	8 Narvik Storsenter;	3 Narvik Airport	War Museum
2 Narvik HI Hostel	Rimi Supermarket;	4 Tourist Office	14 Bus Station
5 Nordstjernen Hotell	Peppe's Pizza	6 Post Office; Police Station	15 Ofoten Museum
10 Breidablikk Gjesthus	9 Rallar'n	7 Fjellheisen Cable Car	16 Lofoten Express
12 Spor 1 Gjestegård	11 Astrup Kjeller'n	Station	Boat Dock

e *nhnarvik@online.no; Kongens gate 26; singles/doubles from Nkr595/695)* has tidy, basic rooms and a breakfast buffet recommended by readers.

There are several places to eat within easy walking distance of the tourist office, including **Astrup Kjeller'n** *(Kinobakken 1; mains Nkr83-239)*, with its old-time feel and huge servings of pastas, steaks and local specialties. For good pasta and Italian fare there's **Rallar'n** *(Kongens gate 64)* in the Grand Royal Hotel. The **Narvik Storsenter shopping centre** *(Kongens gata 66)* 300m west of the train station has a **Peppe's Pizza** and a **Rimi supermarket**.

Getting There & Away

Narvik's airport is served by Widerøe from Bodø and Tromsø.

Some express bus connections between Fauske and Tromsø require an overnight break in Narvik. Nor-Way Bussekspress buses run to/from Fauske (Nkr313, five hours, twice daily) and to/from Tromsø (Nkr305, four to five hours, two or three daily). The Narvik–Lofoten Ekspressen runs daily between Narvik and Svolvær (Nkr388, eight to 9¼ hours).

Two trains run daily to Kiruna in Sweden, with overnight connections to Stockholm. Information on the express boat to Svolvær is in the following Lofoten section.

LOFOTEN

The spectacular glacier-carved mountains of Lofoten, separated from the mainland by Vestfjorden, soar straight out of the sea –from a distance they appear as an unbroken line, known as the Lofoten Wall.

Lofoten is Norway's prime winter fishing ground. The warming effects of the Gulf Stream draw spawning arctic cod from the Barents Sea south to the Lofoten waters each winter, followed by migrating north-coast farmer-fishermen, who for centuries have drawn most of their income from seasonal fishing. Although fish stocks have dwindled greatly in recent years, fishing continues to be Lofoten's largest industry and cod is still hung outside to dry on ubiquitous wooden racks through early summer.

Many of the fishing community's *rorbu* (winter shanties) and *sjøhus* (former fishermen's bunkhouses) have been converted into luxurious tourist accommodation, and are priced accordingly. They provide some of Norway's most atmospheric accommodation.

The main islands of Austvågøy, Vestvågøy, Flakstadøy and Moskenesøy are all ruggedly beautiful. Artists are attracted by Austvågøy's light and there are art galleries in Svolvær, Kabelvåg and the busy fishing village of Henningsvær. Vestvågøy has Lofoten's richest farmland. Flakstadøy and Moskenesøy have sheltered bays and fjords, sheep pastures and sheer coastal mountains looming above strikingly picturesque fishing villages.

The four main islands are all linked by bridge or tunnel, with buses running the entire length of the Lofoten road (E10) from Fiskebøl in the north to Å at road's end in the southwest. Ask **Nordtraffik Buss Lofoten** (☎ 76 06 40 40), the regional transport company, if there are currently any discount offers on group travel (two or more people) and return tickets. Bus fares between Bodø and Svolvær are half-price for holders of rail passes.

Tourist information is available at ⓦ www .lofoten-tourist.no and ⓦ www.lofoten-info.no.

Svolvær
pop 4140
By Lofoten standards the main port town of Svolvær on the island of Austvågøy is busy and modern. On the square facing the harbour, you'll find a couple of banks, a taxi stand and the helpful regional tourist office, **Destination Lofoten** (☎ 76 07 30 00; ⓔ tourist@ lofoten-tourist.no).

Daredevils, or just plain crazy mountaineers, like to scale **Svolværgeita** (The Svolvær Goat), a distinctive, two-pronged peak visible from the harbour, and then jump the 1.5m from one horn to the other – a graveyard at the bottom awaits those who miss! For phenomenal views, hikers can ascend the steep path to the base of the Goat and up the slopes behind it. There's also a rough route from the Goat over to the extraordinary **Devil's Gate**; ask the tourist office for details.

A fun excursion from Svolvær is a boat trip into the **Trollfjord**, a spectacularly steep and narrow fjord. Tours run five to 10 times daily between about 10 June and 20 August and cost Nkr300 per person; the tourist office has details.

Places to Stay & Eat A rustic beach house, **Svolvær Sjøhuscamping** (☎ 76 07 03 36; ⓔ noetnes@online.no; Parkgata 12; singles &

doubles per person Nkr350) has a dockside location: turn right on the first road past the library, and it's a five-minute walk east of the harbour. The down-to-earth **Havna Hotel** (☎ 76 07 10 55; OJ Kaarbøesgata 5; singles/ doubles from Nkr595/795), near the tourist office, has comfortable rooms with private bath.

There are a couple of atmospheric (and expensive) restaurants, including **Kjøkkenet** (☎ 76 06 84 80; Lamholmen; mains Nkr200-280), which looks like an old-time kitchen and has a bar made from a WWII Polish troop ship lifeboat. There's a **bakery** on the square and a **Rimi supermarket** (Torggata) a block inland.

Getting There & Away Svolvær has a small airport where you can catch Widerøe flights to Bodø.

Buses to/from Vesterålen travel between Svolvær and Sortland (Nkr124, 3¼ hours), crossing the dramatically scenic waters of the Fiskebøl-Melbu ferry (Nkr68 for car and driver). Buses to Leknes (Nkr88, two hours), with connections to Å (Nkr163, 3½ hours), leave Svolvær at least four times daily. The Narvik–Lofoten Ekspressen runs daily between Svolvær and Narvik (Nkr388, eight to 9¼ hours).

Express boats ply the waters between Svolvær and Bodø (Nkr246, 3½ hours) and Narvik (Nkr286, 3½ hours), daily except Saturday (but there's no Monday sailing from Svolvær to Narvik).

Svolvær is also a stop on the Hurtigruten coastal steamer; it departs at 10pm northbound and 7.30pm southbound.

Kabelvåg
The road into the quiet village of Kabelvåg passes Norway's second-largest **wooden church**; built a century ago to minister to the influx of seasonal fisherfolk, its 1200 seats far surpasses the village's current population.

Kabelvåg's small harbourfront square has a post office and outdoor market.

Behind the old prison, a trail leads uphill to the **statue of King Øystein**, who in 1120 ordered the first rorbu to be built to house fishermen who had been sleeping under their overturned rowing boats – not just a touch of kindness, as the tax on the exported dried fish was the main source of the king's revenue.

Some of these original rorbuer have been excavated as part of the **Lofoten Museum**

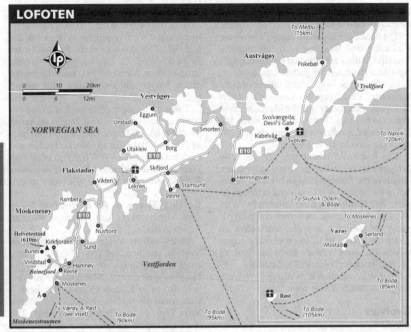

(see inset)

(☎ 76 07 82 23; Storvågan; adult/child Nkr40/15; open 9am-6pm daily mid-June–mid-Aug, 9am-3pm daily mid-Aug–mid-June), a regional history museum on the site of the first town in the polar regions.

Nearby, the sea-front **Lofoten Aquarium** (☎ 76 07 86 65; Storvågan; adult/child Nkr70/25; open 10am-9pm daily mid-June–mid-Aug, 11am-3pm daily mid-Aug–Nov & Feb–mid-June) shows you some of the faces which made Lofoten great, including the heroic cod and some harbour seals in an outdoor tank.

Ørsvågvær Camping (☎ 76 07 81 80; e booking@orsvag.no; Ørsvågvær; tent sites Nkr70, cabins Nkr290-890), located 3km and two inlets west of Kabelvåg, has basic cabins. The **Kabelvåg HI Hostel** (☎ 76 06 98 98, fax 76 06 98 81; e kabelvaag.hostel@ vandrerhjem.no; dorm beds Nkr210, singles/ doubles Nkr370/540; open June–mid-Aug) is at a school 10 minutes north of the village centre; breakfast is included. The hostel has a **cafeteria** with sporadic hours, and the charming fish, sandwich and pizza pub **Præstenbrygga** (Torget; mains Nkr33-149) is in the village centre.

From Svolvær you can walk the 5km to Kabelvåg or catch one of the roughly hourly buses (Nkr18, 10 minutes).

Henningsvær

Henningsvær's nickname, 'The Venice of Lofoten', is a tad overblown, but few people would disagree that this bohemian enclave and active fishing village is the brightest and trendiest place in the archipelago. Especially on weekends, the outdoor seating at the waterside bars and restaurants is ideal for observing the lively scene. There are also a couple of **art galleries** and a **climbing school**.

Henningsvær lacks an HI hostel, but the climbing school's **Den Siste Viking** (☎ 76 07 49 11, fax 76 07 46 46; Misværveien 10; dorm beds Nkr150) crosses a Lofoten rorbu with an English pub and a Himalayan trekkers' lodge. Its **Klatrekafeen** serves up a small selection of homemade light meals (Nkr75 to Nkr130) and snacks, as well as coffee and desserts.

Buses shuttle between Svolvær (Nkr39, 35 minutes), Kabelvåg (Nkr36, 25 minutes) and Henningsvær two to eight times daily.

Lofotr Vikingmuseum

This 83m-long chieftain's house, Norway's largest Viking building, has been excavated at Borg, near the centre of Vestvågøy. The site's Lofotr Vikingmuseum (☎ 76 08 49 00; adult/child Nkr80/40; open 10am-7pm daily mid-May–Aug) offers an insight into life in Viking times, complete with a scale-model reconstruction of the building, guides in Viking costume and a replica Viking ship, which you can row daily at 2pm (Nkr20). The museum is a stop on the Svolvær–Leknes bus route.

Stamsund

The traditional fishing village of Stamsund makes a fine destination largely because of its dockside hostel, a magnet for travellers who sometimes stay for weeks on end.

A **Joker supermarket**, post office and bus stop are a couple of minutes uphill from the hostel, and there's a **Hansen** bakery by the main road at the south end of the village.

At the wonderful old beach house **Justad HI Hostel/Rorbuer** (☎ 76 08 93 34, fax 76 08 97 39; bunks Nkr90, doubles from Nkr200, cabins from Nkr400; open mid-Dec–mid-Oct), rowing boat rental is free – catch and cook your own dinner! Bicycle rental and laundry facilities are available.

The *Hurtigruten* coastal steamer stops en route (7.30pm northbound, 9.30pm southbound) between Bodø (Nkr306) and Svolvær (Nkr109). From 20 August to 24 June, buses from Leknes to Stamsund (Nkr29, 25 minutes) run up to eight times daily, less often on Saturday and Sunday, with the last bus departing from Leknes at 8.50pm.

Reine & Hamnøy

The delightful village of Reine, on the island of Moskenesøy, is on a calm bay backed by ranks of mountain cliffs and pinnacles. With its almost fairy-tale setting, it easy to see why the village has been voted the most scenic place in all of Norway. All buses from Leknes to Å stop in Reine.

Ferries run from Reine to **Vindstad** (Nkr21, 40 minutes) through the scenic Reinefjord. From Vindstad, it's a one-hour hike over a ridge to the abandoned settlement of **Bunes** on the other side of the island, with a magnificent beach, vast quantities of driftwood and the 610m-high cliff of **Helvetestind**. On weekdays except Tuesday, you can take a morning ferry from Reine and then catch an afternoon ferry back – call ☎ 76 09 12 78 or ☎ 94 89 43 05 for the current schedule.

The quiet and pretty little fishing islet of Hamnøy, 4.5km north of central Reine, has **Eliassan Rorbuer** (☎ 76 09 23 05; e rorbuer@online.no; Hamnøy; 2/4 person rorbuer Nkr550/700) right on the water. Linen costs Nkr80 extra. The new **Hamnøy Mat og Vinbu** (☎ 76 09 21 45; Hamnøy; mains Nkr130-165) restaurant is already well regarded for local specialities, including *bacalao* and cod tongues.

There's a **Coop supermarket** in Reine.

Å

Å is a very special place – a preserved fishing village, the shoreline lined with red-painted *rorbu*, cod drying on racks everywhere and picture-postcard scenes at almost every turn.

Many of Å's 19th-century buildings are set aside as the **Norwegian Fishing Village Museum** (☎ 76 09 14 88; open 10am-5pm daily late June-late Aug, 11am-3pm Mon-Fri late Aug-late June), complete with old boats and boat-houses, a bakery from 1844, Europe's oldest cod liver oil factory, storehouses and so on. A second period museum, the **Norwegian Stockfish Museum** (☎ 76 09 12 11; open 11am-5pm daily mid-June–mid-Aug, 11am-4pm Mon-Fri rest of June, otherwise by appointment), details the history of cod fishing, taking in every step from catching to cooking. A ticket to tour both museums costs adult/child Nkr65/45.

The camping ground at the end of the village has a good hillside view of Værøy island, which lies on the other side of **Moskenesstraumen**, the swirling maelstrom that inspired the fictional tales of, amongst others, Jules Verne and Edgar Allen Poe.

Places to Stay & Eat Just south of Å, you'll find the basic **Moskenesstraumen Camping** (☎ 76 09 13 44; tent sites from Nkr60, cabins Nkr290-490). **Å HI Hostel** (☎ 76 09 11 21; e aa.hostel@vandrerhjem .no; dorm beds Nkr125, doubles Nkr250) offers accommodation in some of the museum's historic seaside buildings. The inviting **Å-Hamna Rorbuer** (☎ 76 09 12 11; e aa-hamna@lofoten-info.no; dorm beds Nkr100, rorbuer Nkr600-950), also at the museum, has pleasant rooms in a restored 1860s home and cosy *rorbu* with four to eight beds each.

NORWAY

Food choices are limited – the only restaurant is the high-end over-water **Brygga restaurant** (☎ 76 09 11 21; mains Nkr155-215), so your best bet is to use the kitchen where you're staying. You can buy fresh **fish** from local fishers and pick up other supplies at the small **food shop** behind the hostel office.

Getting There & Away Daily buses run from Leknes to Å (Nkr84, 1¾ hours).

Ofotens og Vesteraalens Dampskibsselskab (OVDS; ☎ 76 96 76 00; W www.ovds .no) runs car ferries from Bodø to Moskenes, 5km north of Å. The trip takes four hours, costs Nkr122 for a passenger, Nkr441 for a car, and operates up to five times daily from 28 June to 11 August (otherwise, once or twice daily except Saturday). Some of these ferries operate via Værøy and Røst.

Værøy & Røst
pop 1445

Lofoten's southern islands of Værøy and Røst have some of the finest **bird-watching** in Norway, with large colonies of fulmars, guillemots, kittiwakes and terns. There are puffins as well, but the population has dropped by more than 50% in the past decade as a result of dwindling stocks of herring, the main food source for puffin chicks.

Craggy Værøy has only 775 people, but 100,000 nesting sea birds. **Hiking trails** take in some of the more spectacular sea-bird rookeries. The main trail goes along the west coast, beginning about 300m past the island airstrip, and continues south all the way to the virtually deserted fishing village of Mostad. This 10km hike makes for a full day's outing and is not too strenuous, but it's exposed to the elements, so it's best done in fair weather. Other bird-watching outings, including boat tours, can be arranged through the hostel.

Røst, south of Værøy, enjoys one of the mildest climates in northern Norway, thanks to its location in the middle of the Gulf Stream. Access to the best bird-watching requires a boat, as the largest rookeries are on offshore islands. **Kårøy Sjøhus** (☎ 76 09 62 38) can arrange all-day boat trips (Nkr125) that cruise past major sea-bird colonies and stop at an 1887 **lighthouse** and a vista point. En route it's common to see **seals** and there are occasional sightings of **orcas** (killer whales). Røst itself is flat and, other than the boat trip, there's not much to do.

Places to Stay & Eat Værøy **HI Hostel** (☎ 76 09 53 75; dorm beds Nkr100, singles/ doubles Nkr190/250; open 1 May-15 Sept) provides atmospheric and authentic rorbu accommodation, but it's about an hour's walk north of the ferry landing. Værøy's only nightlife option, the **Kornelius Kro** (☎ 76 09 52 99; @ korn-kro@online.no; Sørland; rooms Nkr300-500), also has a restaurant (mains Nkr55 to Nkr150), a pub and a few simple but clean cottages out the back.

On Røst, budget accommodation and a guest kitchen are available at **Kårøy Sjøhus** (☎ 76 09 62 38; dorm beds Nkr100). For meals, try the **Querini Pub og Restaurant**.

Getting There & Away From 29 June to 12 August there's at least one ferry daily between Bodø and Værøy (Nkr112, four to six hours) and six days a week between Moskenes and Værøy (Nkr49, 1½ hours). There's a boat service from Værøy to Røst (Nkr60, two hours, five days a week) and from Røst to Bodø (Nkr134, 4¼ hours, once or twice daily). Sailing durations given are for direct ferries, but not every boat is direct. If your trip begins and ends in Bodø, ask about discounted return fares. Detailed schedules are available at boat terminals and tourist offices.

VESTERÅLEN

The islands of Vesterålen aren't quite as dramatic as Lofoten, but they're still very attractive to visitors. For tourist information, consult **Vesterålen Reiseliv** (☎ 76 11 14 80; Kjøpmannsgata 2, Sortland).

Vesterålen is connected by ferry from **Melbu** on Hadseløya to Fiskebøl on Austvågøy (Lofoten). Melbu has a couple of **museums** and a famous **music festival**, featuring classical, jazz and blues, every July. The other main town, **Stokmarknes**, is a quiet market community best known as the birthplace of the Hurtigruten coastal steamer.

Nyksund on Langøya is a former abandoned fishing village that's now re-emerging as an artists' colony. There's a great **walk** over the headland from Nyksund to Stø (three hours return), at the northernmost tip of Langøya. Ask the tourist office for details of **whale-watching tours** from Stø.

Andenes on Andøy seems a long way from anywhere, but there's whale-watching, a whale centre, a natural history centre, a lighthouse and a couple of museums. **Whale Safari**

(☎ 76 11 56 00; e booking@whalesafari.no; w www.whalesafari.no) runs popular three-to five-hour whale-watching cruises from the whale centre between late May and mid-September. Trips depart at least once daily (at 10.30am) and cost Nkr650. Sightings of sperm whales are guaranteed, or your next trip is free.

Places to Stay & Eat
In Nyksund, the cosy and historic **Holmvik Brygge** (☎ 76 13 47 96; e nickel@online.no; singles/doubles Nkr175/320) offers rooms with shared facilities; sheets are Nkr45 extra.

Stø Bobilcamp (☎ 76 13 25 30, fax 76 13 45 91; Stø; tent sites Nkr100) offers camping and a small restaurant serving fish, whale and land-roving animals.

At **Andenes Camping** (☎ 76 14 12 22; Andenes; tent sites Nkr80) you can camp on a seaside meadow. The timber-built **Andenes HI Hostel** (☎ 76 14 28 50; Havnegata 31, Andenes; dorm beds Nkr125, singles/doubles Nkr190/250; open June-Aug), which includes the Lankanholmen Sjøhus, is a wonderful old building and a nice base for a couple of days; breakfast is Nkr60 extra.

The rooms in the charming lighthouse keepers' cottage **Den Gamle Fyrmesterbolig** (☎ 76 14 10 27; Richard Withs gate 11, Andenes; singles/doubles from Nkr250/300) are another great option.

The sparkling **Aurora Borealis** (☎ 76 14 83 00; Sjøgata 19; mains Nkr53-184), whose menu will excite even the most jaded palate, is almost too sleek for tiny Andenes. There's also an informal **café** at the Andenes whale centre.

Getting There & Away
Sortland is the main transport hub in Vesterålen. Both Sortland and Stokmarknes are stops for the *Hurtigruten* coastal steamer.

The express bus between Tromsø (Nkr463, 7¼ hours), and Å (Nkr284, 6¼ hours) runs from Monday to Friday, via Sortland and Melbu. The Narvik–Lofoten Ekspressen between Narvik (Nkr247, 3¾ hours) and Svolvær (Nkr124, 2½ hours) operates daily except Saturday and the Fauske–Lofoten Ekspressen between Fauske (Nkr301, 5¼ hours) and Svolvær runs daily. Times and fares are from Sortland.

From 25 June to 19 August, one to four daily buses connect Sortland with Andenes (Nkr124, two hours) via Risøyhamn. Services are reduced at other times.

SENJA
Senja, Norway's second largest island, rivals Lofoten with its landscapes yet attracts very few visitors. Finnsnes, the town at the mainland side of the bridge to Senja, has no redeeming features.

Senja's Innersida, facing the mainland, features a broad agricultural plain and extensive forest. The western and northern coasts, Yttersida, include a convoluted series of peninsulas and jagged peaks that rise directly from the Arctic Ocean. Colourful, isolated **fishing villages** including Gryllefjord, Skaland, Mefjordvær, Fjordgard and Husøy are accessible via tiny back roads, making for remote getaways. The road to Mefjordvær is particularly dramatic, but the most outrageous-looking mountains are nearest to Fjordgard.

For tourist information, contact the **tourist office** (☎ 77 85 07 30; Finnsnes).

The suitably remote **Hamn i Senja** (☎ 77 85 98 80; e post@hamnisenja.no; Skaland; singles/doubles from Nkr340/540) features a combination of old and new buildings hugging the seashore.

From April to October (with a different timetable at other times of year) buses connect Finnsnes and Senja villages (but not necessarily daily), including Skaland (Nkr36, 30 minutes), Gryllefjord (Nkr93, 1½ hours), Fjordgard (Nkr82, 1½ hours) and Mefjordvær (Nkr100, 1¾ hours). Express ferries connect Finnsnes with Tromsø (Nkr190, 1¼ hours). Buses also run from Finnsnes to Tromsø (Nkr179, 2¼ hours, two to four daily).

TROMSØ
pop 47,100
Tromsø, at latitude 69°40'N, is the world's northernmost university town. In contrast to some of the more sober communities dotting the north coast of Norway, Tromsø is a spirited place with street music, cultural happenings and more pubs per capita than any other Norwegian town – it even has its own brewery.

A backdrop of snowcapped peaks provides spectacular scenery, excellent hiking in summer and great skiing and dogsledding from September to April. Many polar expeditions have departed from Tromsø, earning the city the nickname 'Gateway to the Arctic'. A statue of explorer Roald Amundsen, who headed some of the expeditions, stands in a little square down by the harbour.

NORWAY

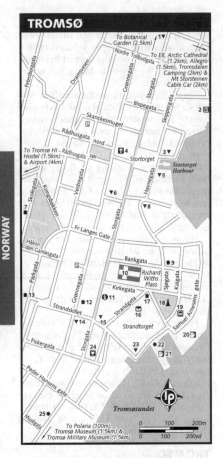

TROMSØ

PLACES TO STAY
7   Ami Hotel
9   Radisson SAS Hotel Tromsø
12 Rainbow Polar Hotel
13 Hotell Nord
17 Comfort Hotel Saga

PLACES TO EAT
1   Hong Kong Village
3   Coop Mega Supermarket Cafeteria
5   Peppe's Pizza
6   Amtmandens Datter
8   Aunegården
14 Meieriet
15 Paletten
23 Arctandria; Skarven

OTHER
2   Polar Museum
4   Catholic Church
10 Tromsø Domkirke
11 Tourist Office
16 Post Office
18 Roald Amundsen Statue
19 Bus Station
20 Coastal Steamer Quay
21 Express Boats
22 Food Kiosk
24 Blå Rock Cafe
25 Mack Brewery; Ølhallen

(Storgata 94), both built in 1861. However, Tromsø's most striking church is the **Arctic Cathedral** (☎ 77 64 76 11; Hans Nilsensvei 41; adult/child Nkr20/free; open 10am-8pm June-Aug), which is on the mainland just over the bridge. It's a modernist building that bears an interesting resemblance to the Sydney Opera House.

Tromsø Museum (☎ 77 64 50 00; Lars Thøringsvei 10; adult/child Nkr30/15; open 9am-8pm daily June-Aug, shorter hrs Sept-May), at the southern end of Tromsøya, is northern Norway's largest museum and has some well-presented displays on Arctic wildlife, Sami culture and regional history. Take bus No 28 from Stortorget. Nearby, the restored WWII fort at the **Tromsø Military Museum** (☎ 77 62 85 40; Solstrandveien; adult/child Nkr20/10; open noon-5pm Wed-Sun June-Aug; noon-5pm Sun May & Sept) includes a former ammunition store with an exhibition on the 52,600-tonne German battleship *Tirpitz*, which was sunk by British air forces at Tromsø on 12 November 1944.

The harbourside **Polar Museum** (☎ 77 68 43 73; Søndre Tollbugata 11; adult/child

Orientation & Information

Tromsø's city centre and airport are on the island of Tromsøya, which is linked by bridges to overspill suburbs on both the mainland and the much larger outer island Kvaløya.

The town's **tourist office** (☎ 77 61 00 00; 🖲 www.destinasjontromso.no; Storgata 61; open 8.30am-6pm Mon-Fri, 10am-5pm Sat, 10.30am-5pm Sun June–mid-Aug; 8.30am-4pm Mon-Fri mid-Aug–June) can help with information. Send or collect your mail from the main **post office** (Strandgata 41).

Things to See & Do

The city centre has many period buildings, including the old cathedral, **Tromsø Domkirke** (Storgata 25) – one of Norway's largest wooden churches – and a **Catholic church**

Nkr40/10; open 10am-7pm daily mid-June–mid-Aug, shorter hrs daily mid-Aug–mid-June) has exhibits on the Arctic frontier, some interesting and others – such as those on hunting furry Arctic creatures – of less universal appeal.

The modern and well-executed **Polaria** *(☎ 77 75 01 00; Hjalmar Johansens gate 12; adult/child Nkr75/40; open 10am-7pm daily mid-May–mid-Aug, noon-5pm daily mid-Aug–mid-June)*, on the city's southern waterfront, has extensive displays on polar topics ranging from exploration to natural history, a 180-degree cinema showing an interesting film about Svalbard, and an aquarium with Arctic fish and four bearded seals.

Take a stroll through the two-hectare **botanical garden** *(☎ 77 64 50 00; Breivika; bus Nos 20, 32; admission free; open daily Jan-Dec)*, which blooms brightly despite its northern locale.

Established in 1877, the **Mack Brewery** *(☎ 77 62 45 00; Storgata 5; tours Nkr70; open for tours 1pm Tues & Thur)* produces Macks Pilsner, Isbjørn, Haakon and several dark beers; the tour fee includes a beer stein, beer and souvenir.

You can get a fine city view by taking the **cable car** 420m up Mt Storsteinen. It runs from 10am to 5pm daily April to September, and until 1am on clear nights from 20 May to 20 August when the midnight sun is in view (adult/child return Nkr70/30). Take bus No 26 from Stortorget harbour.

Places to Stay
Tromsdalen Camping *(☎ 77 63 80 37; bus No 26 from Stortorget; tent sites Nkr100, cabins Nkr300-900)* is on the mainland, 2km east of the Arctic Cathedral.

The clean and tidy **Tromsø HI Hostel** *(☎ 77 65 76 28;* e *tromso.hostel@vandrerhjem.no; Åsgårdveien 9; dorm beds Nkr125, singles/doubles Nkr225/300; open 20 June-18 Aug)*, 1.5km west of the city centre, is a good place to crash; phone for directions.

The tourist office books **rooms** in private homes for around Nkr250/450 for a single/double.

Up on the hillside just west of the centre, **Hotell Nord** *(☎ 77 68 31 59;* e *info@hotell nord.no; Parkgata 4; singles/doubles from Nkr450/590)* feels like an informal guesthouse; staff are knowledgeable and friendly, and rates include breakfast. Rooms are available with or without en suite bathroom. At the similar **Ami Hotel** *(☎ 77 68 22 08;* e *email@amihotel.no; Skolegata 24; singles/doubles from Nkr450/580)*, request a room at the front for great views of the city.

Rainbow Polar Hotel *(☎ 77 68 64 80, fax 77 68 91 36; Grønnegata 45; singles/doubles from Nkr615/770)* has modern guestrooms and a cheery breakfast room with city views.

The **Comfort Hotel Saga** *(☎ 77 68 11 80;* e *post@sagahotel.com; Richard Withs plass 2; singles/doubles from Nkr695/895)* lives up to its name with up-to-date rooms, a fine breakfast buffet *and* a dinner buffet.

At the plush **Radisson SAS Hotel Tromsø** *(☎ 77 60 00 00;* e *sales@toszh.rdsas.com; Sjøgata 7; singles/doubles from Nkr695/895)*, you'll find highly professional service.

Places to Eat
The upscale **Arctandria** *(☎ 77 60 07 25; Strandtorget 1; mains Nkr125-245)* serves filling ocean catches including seal and whale.

Popular **Peppe's Pizza** *(Stortorget 2)* serves its usual menu. An excellent pizza option is **Allegro** *(☎ 77 68 80 71; Turistveien 19; dishes Nkr60-240)*, between the Arctic Cathedral and the cable car, which also bakes Italian-style pies in a birch-fired oven.

The multi-level sports-bar **Paletten** *(Storgata 51; mains Nkr45-96)* serves everything from inviting sandwiches to lasagne and cakes, occasionally enhanced by live music. The pub-like **Amtmandens Datter** *(Grønnegata 81)* has reasonable prices, and patrons may use its newspapers, books, board games and free Internet access.

The inviting, more café-like **Meieriet** *(Grønnegata 37; mains Nkr56-136)* serves cakes, snacks and meals, including Mexican and Chinese dishes. For coffee, pastries or a meal, visit traditional **Aunegården** *(Sjøgata 29)*.

Tromsø's fast-food scene is led by various **kebab carts**; other choices include **Hong Kong Village** *(Storgata 132)* for Chinese takeaway food and a **food kiosk** at the express boat dock.

You can buy fresh boiled shrimp from **fishing boats**, at Stortorget harbour. The harbourside **Coop Mega supermarket** *(Stortorget 1)* has a cheap 2nd-floor cafeteria and a nice view over the water.

NORWAY

Entertainment

Tromsø enjoys a thriving nightlife and, on Friday and Saturday, most nightspots stay open until 4am. Many also serve light meals. The bustling, youthful **Blå Rock Café** (Strandgata 14) features theme evenings, 75 types of beer, live concerts and dance music on weekends. The waterfront **Skarven** (Strandtorget 1) offers fine bar meals and is mainly a hangout for over-25s.

You can try Tromsø's own Mack beer at pubs, cafés or at **Ølhallen** (Storgata 4), near the brewery.

Getting There & Away

Tromsø is the main airport hub for northern Norway, with direct flights to Oslo, Bergen, Bodø, Trondheim, Alta, Hammerfest, Honningsvåg, Kirkenes and Longyearbyen. Airport buses depart from the Radisson SAS Hotel Tromsø.

There two or three daily express buses between Tromsø and Narvik (Nkr305, four to five hours). Buses to/from Alta (Nkr345, 6¾ hours) run once daily.

The *Hurtigruten* coastal steamer arrives at 2.30pm and departs at 6.30pm northbound and arrives at 11.45pm and departs at 1.30am southbound. Fares are Nkr946 to Bodø and Nkr650 to Hammerfest.

Getting Around

The airport bus (Nkr35) can be picked up at the Radisson SAS Hotel; a taxi to the airport costs about Nkr80. Thoroughly exploring Tromsø can take time, as the city is spread out and many of the sights are outside the centre. Rides on city buses cost Nkr20, but a better deal is to buy a 24-hour tourist bus pass for Nkr55.

If you have your own car, you'll find it convenient for getting around. Tromsø has numerous parking areas spread around the city, including a huge underground car park off Grønnegata. Express boats connect Tromsø with Finnsnes (Nkr190, 1¼ hours, two to four daily), the ferry terminal for Senja.

FINNMARK

Finnmark's curving north coast is cut by dramatic fjords and dotted with fishing villages. The interior is populated by Sami people who for centuries have herded their reindeer across the vast upland plateau, **Finnmarksvidda**, a stark wilderness with only two major settlements, Karasjok and Kautokeino.

Virtually every town in Finnmark was razed to the ground at the end of WWII by retreating Nazis whose scorched-earth policy was intended to delay the advancing Soviet troops. Unfortunately, the rebuilt towns all look rather similar, with most buildings constructed in a plain box-like style.

You can get information about the entire region from **Finnmark Tourist Board** (☎ 78 44 00 20; ⓦ www.visitnorthcape.com; Sorekskriverveien 13, N-9511 Alta).

Alta
pop 17,000

Alta is a sprawling town with fishing and quarrying industries. The town's two main centres, Sentrum and Bossekop, are 3km apart. Alta **tourist office** (☎ 78 45 77 77; Sorenskriverveien 13) is near the bus stop in Bossekop, as is a post office.

Things to See & Do Alta's main sight is the impressive, World Heritage-protected, **prehistoric rock art** (☎ 78 45 63 30; Altaveien 19; adult/child Nkr70/free; open 8am-11pm daily mid-June–mid-Aug; 8am-8pm daily early June & late Aug; 9am-6pm daily May & Sept) at Hjemmeluft, on the E6, 4km southwest of Bossekop. A 3km-long network of boardwalks leads past many of the 3000 rock carvings of hunting scenes, boats, fertility symbols, bears and reindeer that date back as far as 4000 BC. The admission charge includes guiding and the adjacent **Alta Museum**, with regional exhibits.

The Altaelva river rushes through the scenic 400m-deep **Sautso**, northern Europe's grandest canyon, best seen on the four-hour tour, which leaves the tourist office at 4pm daily in July (Nkr350, minimum five people). The tour includes the Alta Power Station dam and a snack in a traditional Sami *lavvo* (tent).

Alta is also renowned for its **salmon run**; several local companies provide fishing tours.

Places to Stay & Eat The award-winning **Wisløff Camping** (☎/fax 78 43 43 03; ⓔ lilly@wisloeff.no; Øvre Alta; tent sites from Nkr70, cabins Nkr275-350) has happy little beige and red cabins, 4km south of Bossekop, by highway Rv93. The FFR Alta–Kautokeino bus passes nearby two or three times daily (except Tuesday, Thursday and Saturday, when there's no service). **Alta HI Hostel** (☎ 78 43 44 09; ⓔ alta.hostel@vandrerhjem.no; Midtbakkveien 52; dorm beds Nkr125, singles/

doubles Nkr240/270; open 20 June-20 Aug) is a short walk from the Sentrum bus stop.

The cosy, art-filled and secluded **Hotel Aurora Borealis** (☎ 78 45 78 00; *Saga; singles/doubles Nkr700/860*), about 6km east of Bossekop by the E6, has a fine restaurant. The Hammerfest and Nordkapp buses pass here, running four days a week from 20 August to 24 June. In a timber-built former farmhouse, the friendly **Vica Hotell** (☎ 78 43 47 11; @ *post@vica.no; Fogdebakken 6; singles/doubles from Nkr745/ 995*) in Bossekop offers free sauna and Internet access.

Alta's finest dining establishment, **Altastua** (☎ 78 44 55 54; *Løkkeveien 2; mains Nkr219-262*) in Sentrum serves huge portions from a menu that includes reindeer, elk, salmon and cloudberries. **Alta Bistro** (*Svaneveien 7; mains Nkr39-165*) in Bossekop is a simple choice that serves grills, burgers and pizzas. Self-caterers should head for the **Coop Prix supermarket** (*Trudvang 2, Bossekop*).

Getting There & Away One daily Nor-Way Bussekspress service runs between Tromsø and Alta (Nkr345, 6¾ hours). FFR buses run to/from Kautokeino (Nkr181, 2½ hours), Hammerfest (Nkr170, 2¾ hours), and Nordkapp (Nkr271, 5¾ hours).

The **Express 2000 bus** (☎ 78 44 40 90) leaves Alta at noon on Monday and travels to Oslo (Nkr1850, 26½ hours), via Finland and Sweden. From Oslo, it leaves at 9am on Wednesday.

Hammerfest
pop 7030

Most visitors to this fishing town arrive on the *Hurtigruten* coastal steamer and have an hour or two to look around. The **tourist office** (☎ 78 41 21 85; *Kirkegata 21*) is a few minutes' walk from the dock. At the same site is the **Reconstruction Museum** (☎ 78 42 26 30; *Kirkegata 21; adult/child Nkr40/15; open 10am-6pm daily mid-June–Aug, 11am-2pm daily Sept–mid-June*), which details the rebuilding of Hammerfest after WWII. Nearby, in the town hall, the rather bizarre **Royal & Ancient Polar Bear Society** (☎ 78 41 31 00; *Rådhuset; admission Nkr20; open 6am-5.30pm daily 24 June-10 Aug, otherwise shorter hrs*) has Arctic hunting and local history displays.

Just west of the tourist office on Kirkegata is Hammerfest's contemporary **church**, where you can often find reindeer grazing in the graveyard. For lovely views of the town, coast and mountains, climb the 86m-high **Salen Hill**; the 10-minute trail begins behind the small park directly up from the town hall.

Places to Stay & Eat NAF Camping Storvannet (☎ 78 41 10 10; *Storvannsveien; cabins Nkr320-340; open late May–late Sept*), 2km east of the town centre, offers cooking facilities. Rooms at the **Quality Hotel Hammerfest** (☎ 78 42 96 00; @ *hammerfest@ quality.choice.no; Strandgata 2; singles/ doubles from Nkr645/795*) have loads of character – some resemble cabins on ocean liners.

Hammerfest's gourmet option for meat and seafood is **Odd's Mat & Vinhus** (☎ 78 41 37 66; *Strandgata 24; mains Nkr190-325*). The popular grill, **Hårek Grillkjøkken** (*Strandgata 43; mains Nkr36-120*) serves up various fast foods, but there's also an inexpensive cafeteria in the **Domus supermarket** (*Strandgata 14-18*), just east of the town hall. However, the nicest place to pick up snacks is the **Sandberg bakery** (*Strandgate 19*).

Getting There & Away The *Hurtigruten* coastal steamer stops daily at 4.45am northbound and 11.45am southbound.

Once or twice daily (four days weekly from mid-August to late June), buses run between Hammerfest and Alta (Nkr170, 2¾ hours). There's also a bus between Hammerfest and Kirkenes (Nkr682, 10¼ hours), via Karasjok (Nkr283, 4¾ hours).

Honningsvåg
pop 2900

Honningsvåg is the only sizable settlement on the island of Magerøya, now reached by undersea tunnel from the mainland. It claims proudly to be the world's most northerly town – other settlements further north are apparently too small to qualify as actual towns. The **tourist office** (☎ 78 47 25 99), by the bus station, covers the Nordkapp area and from October to April can arrange snowscooter expeditions to Nordkapp. The town has a recommended little **museum** and a 19th-century **church**, but the centre of attention is Nordkapp, 34km away.

Places to Stay & Eat Nordkapp Camping (☎ 78 47 33 77; *Skipsfjord; dorm beds Nkr135, doubles Nkr500, cabins Nkr480-800;*

NORWAY

open 10 May-20 Sept) is 8km north of Honningsvåg on the road to Nordkapp (Nkr20 by bus); the doubles have private bath.

Honningsvåg's extremely expensive hotels are just a money-spinning racket – well worth a body swerve. Alternatively, the recommended **Havstua** (☎ *78 47 51 50;* [e] *havstua@havstua.no; Kamøyvær; singles/doubles Nkr430/650),* in a former fishermen's cottage 11km north of Honningsvåg, features five small rooms on the pier; the waves beneath lull you to sleep. If full, they'll rent out other rooms in town, and there's also a well-regarded Arctic restaurant.

There's a **Rimi supermarket** *(Storgata 16),* uphill from the coastal steamer quay. **Corner** *(Fiskerveien 2A; mains Nkr99-160)* serves seafood and pizza.

Getting There & Away From early June to mid-August, once or twice daily (except Saturday) express buses connect Honningsvåg with Alta (Nkr241, 4½ to 5½ hours) and Nordkapp (Nkr66, one hour). There's also service between Hammerfest and Honningsvåg townships (Nkr230, 3¾ hours) several times a week.

The *Hurtigruten* coastal steamer stops at Honningsvåg at 11.45am, with a 3¾-hour northbound stop and an optional tour to Nordkapp (Nkr490).

Nordkapp

Nordkapp (North Cape), a high rugged coastal plateau at 71°10'21''N latitude, claims to be the northernmost point in Europe and it's the main destination for most visitors to the far north (Knivskjelodden is actually the northernmost point – see later in this section for details). The sun never drops below the horizon from mid-May to the end of July. To many visitors, Nordkapp, with its steep cliffs and stark scenery, emanates a certain spiritual aura – indeed, long before other Europeans took an interest in the area, Nordkapp was considered a power centre by the Sami people.

It was Richard Chancellor, the English explorer who drifted this way in 1553 on a search for the Northeast Passage, who named North Cape. Following a much-publicised visit by King Oscar II in 1873, Nordkapp became a pilgrimage spot of sorts for tourists.

Nowadays, there's a rip-off Nkr175 entrance fee and a touristy complex with exhibits, eateries, souvenir shops and a post office. The 180-degree theatre runs a rather repetitious short film but, if you want to really appreciate Nordkapp, take a walk out along the cliffs. If the weather is fair you can perch yourself on the edge of the continent and watch the polar mist roll in.

The continent's real northernmost point, **Knivskjelodden** (latitude 71°11'08'') is inaccessible to vehicles, but you can hike 18km return (five hours) to this lovely promontory from a marked car park about 9km south of Nordkapp.

An asphalt road winds across a rocky plateau and past herds of grazing reindeer up to Nordkapp. Depending on snow conditions, it's usually open from May to mid-October; **Road User Information Centre** (☎ *175)* gives opening dates.

From mid-May to the end of August, local buses run daily at 12.15pm and 9pm between Honningsvåg and Nordkapp (Nkr66, one hour), with an additional service at 8.20pm between 2 June and 16 August and another at 10.55pm between 2 June and 9 August. Between 2 June and 9 August, the last bus departs Nordkapp at 1.10am, allowing views of the midnight sun. Avoid so-called 'tours', which may charge considerably more for similar services.

Vardø
pop 2800

Vardø, Norway's easternmost town, is on an island linked to the mainland by a 2.9km-long tunnel under the Barents Sea.

The main sight of interest is the small star-shaped **fort** (☎ *78 18 85 02; Festningsgate 20; admission Nkr20; open 8am-9pm daily mid-Apr–mid-Sept, 10am-6pm daily mid-Sept–mid-Apr)* dating from 1737, with cannons and sod-roof buildings. It's a five-minute walk directly up from the coastal steamer quay. The **Pomor Museum** (☎ *78 98 80 75; Per Larssens gate 32; admission Nkr20; open 9am-6.30pm daily mid-June–mid-Aug, 9am-3pm Mon-Fri mid-Aug–mid-June)* covers local natural history, polar expeditions and trade with Russia prior to 1917.

The **tourist office** (☎ *78 98 84 04; Kaigata 12)* organises short cruises, from April to mid-October, to the teeming bird cliffs on Hornøya, Norway's easternmost point. At 31°10'4''E, it's almost on the same longitude as Cairo!

Accommodation options aren't great; the **student rooms** (singles/doubles Nkr275/450) rented by the tourist office are the best bet. The historic, wood-panelled pub **Nordpol Kro** (☎ 78 98 75 01; Kaigata 21; pizzas Nkr49-162) is recommended for its pizza.

Vardø is a stop on the *Hurtigruten* coastal steamer route but, otherwise, it's well off the beaten track for all but the most die-hard travellers. Buses run from Vardø to Vadsø and Tana Bru on the E6, from where buses run to Kirkenes and Hammerfest.

Kirkenes
pop 4500
The former mining town of Kirkenes was Norway's most bombed place during WWII, with over 1000 air raid alarms. The town is not a major tourist destination, but it does get some visitors since it's the end of the line for the *Hurtigruten* coastal steamer and a jumping-off point into Russia. The **tourist office** (☎ 78 99 25 44; Kongens gate 1-3) is at the Rica Arctic Hotel.

A cold **cave** (cnr Presteveien & Tellef Dahls gate; tours adult/child Nkr100/50; mid-June–mid-Aug) was used as a WWII air-raid shelter. Tours are held at noon, 3pm, 6.15pm & 9pm daily during the opening period. Up on a nearby hill, there's a **statue** dedicated to the Soviet soldiers who liberated the town. The rather good **Sør-Varanger Grenselandmuseet** (☎ 78 99 48 80; Førstevannslia; adult/child Nkr30/free; open 10am-6pm daily mid-June–Aug, 10am-3.30pm daily Sept–mid-June) has displays on WWII history, local geography, culture, religion and Sami crafts.

Visiting Russia Day and weekend bus tours from Kirkenes to Murmansk in summer are arranged by **Sovjetrejser** (☎ 78 99 25 01; e polarscout@grenseland.no, Kongensgate 1-3). The guided bus tour, including lunch and sightseeing, costs Nkr1090/1290 day/weekend but you'll have to add on the cost of a Russian visa, typically Nkr550 to Nkr1000, depending upon your nationality. Travellers interested in visiting Russia on their own can take the bus one way to Murmansk (4½ hours, Nkr350/700 one way/ return), plus the visa fee, but you'll need an 'official invitation'. Contact the **Russian Consulate** (☎ 78 99 37 37; Kirkegata) for a visa. Buses leave Kirkenes Monday to Friday at 2pm (and

Sunday at 4pm) from the Rica Arctic Hotel and return from the Hotel Polyarny Zory in Murmansk at 2pm and noon respectively. Visa processing takes 12 days, so make sure you contact Sovjetreiser or the consulate well in advance.

Places to Stay & Eat Six kilometres west of town off the E6 in Hesseng is **Kirkenes Camping** (☎ 78 99 80 28; tent sites Nkr90, cabins Nkr320-600; open June-Aug).

Around the back of a house near the *Hurtigruten* pier is **Milly's B&B** (☎ 78 99 12 48; Prestøyveien 28A; singles/doubles Nkr250/400), with three rooms and a small garden. Self-catering facilities are available. **Barbaras B&B** (☎ 78 99 32 07; e barbara@trollnet.no; Henrik Lunds gate 13; singles/doubles Nkr300/500) has two rooms and free Internet access.

The **Rica Arctic Hotel** (☎ 78 99 29 29; Kongensgate 1-3; singles/doubles mid-June–mid-Aug Nkr760/1275) offers the finest rooms in town and has a good restaurant.

Casablanca (Dr Wessels gate 6; mains Nkr89-175) actually features dishes from India, Mexico and Thailand. **Ritz** (Dr Wessels gate 17; mains Nkr59-203) is the main place for pizzas. The **Must Bakery** (Kirkegata 2) serves breakfasts and light lunches, and for self-catering, try the **Rimi supermarket** on the main square.

Getting There & Around SAS, Braathens and Widerøe fly into Kirkenes' airport, a 20-minute drive from town; flying in/out of Ivolo, Finland, some 250km away, may be cheaper. The airport bus costs Nkr50 and a taxi is about Nkr200.

By land, buses serve Karasjok (Nkr414, 5½ hours), Hammerfest (Nkr682, 10¼ hours) and Alta (Nkr719, 12¾ hours), and many points in between.

Kirkenes is the terminus of the *Hurtigruten* coastal steamer.

Karasjok
pop 2900
Karasjok is the most accessible Sami town and the site of the **Sami parliament**. It has Finnmark's oldest **church** (1807), the only building left standing in Karasjok after WWII. The **tourist office** (☎ 78 46 88 10; Porsangerveien 1), in Sami Park at the junction of E6 and route Rv92, can book winter

dogsled rides, and arranges salmon fishing, riverboat trips and other summer activities.

The **Sami Park** (☎ 78 46 88 10; *Porsangerveien 1; adult/child Nkr90/60; open 9am-7pm daily mid-June–late Aug, otherwise shorter hrs)* theme park and reindeer farm is flashy and high-tech, but the more interesting **Sami museum** (☎ 78 46 99 50; *Museumsgata 17; adult/child Nkr25/5; open 9am-6pm Mon-Sat, 10am-6pm Sun 9 June-19 Aug, otherwise shorter hrs)*, just 500m northeast of the town centre, covers Sami history and culture in more depth.

Karasjok Camping (☎ 78 46 61 35; *Kautokeinoveien; cabins Nkr230-850)*, 500m south of the Samiland Centre, has a variety of cabins. The wonderful **Karasjok HI Hostel** (☎ 78 46 71 66; e *karasjok.hostel@vandrerhjem.no; dorm beds Nkr150, singles/doubles Nkr275/350)* is 6km west of town; breakfast costs Nkr60, dinner is available and a variety of summer and winter tours is on offer. The Sami-run **Anne's Overnatting** (☎ 78 46 64 32; *Tanaveien 40; cabins Nkr320-400, singles/doubles Nkr390/490)* is another option; breakfast isn't included but kitchen facilities are available.

Rustic **Storgammen** (☎ 78 46 74 00; *Porsangerveien 1; mains Nkr189-254; open mid-May–mid-Aug)*, at Sami Park, offers traditional Sami dishes. In the central shopping centre, **Márkan Kafe** (*Markangeaidnu 1; dishes Nkr25-75)* sells sandwiches and omelettes at bargain prices, and there's a nearby **supermarket**. **Sillju Café & Gatekjøkken** (*Finlandsveien 2; dishes Nkr50-119)* specialises in burgers and chicken.

Buses connect Karasjok with Hammerfest (Nkr283, 4¾hours, daily except Saturday) and Kirkenes (Nkr414, 5½ hours). The Finnish Lapin Linjat buses to Ivalo (Nkr121, 3¾ hours) and Rovaniemi (Nkr310, 5½ hours) also pass through Karasjok.

Kautokeino
pop 3075

In Kautokeino, around 85% of the townspeople have Sami as their first language; the town is unlike anywhere else in Norway and it's not uncommon to see locals dressed in traditional garb. The **tourist office** (☎ 78 48 65 00) is in a kiosk by the main road through town.

The fascinating **Kautokeino Museum** (☎ 78 48 71 00; *Boavonjarga 23; adult/child Nkr20/free; open 9am-7pm Mon-Fri, noon-*

7pm Sat & Sun mid-June–mid-Aug, 9am-3pm Mon-Fri mid-Aug–mid-June)* presents a traditional Sami settlement, complete with an early home, temporary dwellings, a trapping exhibit and several agricultural and pastoral outbuildings.

Kautokeino Camping (☎ 78 48 54 00; *Suomalvodda 16; tent sites Nkr100, cabins Nkr280-300, motel rooms Nkr480-850)*, south of the river, is a good option and has a Sami *lavvo* with an open fire. **Svein's Grill** (☎ 78 48 50 65; *Cuonjalvodda; dishes Nkr45-125)* does very simple grills, while **Alfred's Kro** (*Hannoluohkka 4; mains Nkr48-125)*, north of the river, gets slightly more upscale with reindeer on the menu.

Buses connect Kautokeino with Alta (Nkr181, 2½ hours). You can also travel on the Lapin Linjat bus between Kautokeino and Rovaniemi, Finland (Nkr235, 7¼ hours).

Svalbard

Svalbard is *the* destination for an unforgettable holiday. This wondrous archipelago is an assault on the senses; it's the world's most readily accessible piece of the polar north and one of the most spectacular places imaginable. Vast icebergs and floes choke the seas, and icefields and glaciers frost the lonely heights, but Svalbard also hosts a surprising variety of flora and fauna, including seals, walrus, arctic foxes and polar bears.

History

Although known to the Icelanders as early as 1194, the official discovery of Svalbard (then uninhabited) is credited to Dutch voyager Willem Barents in 1596. During the 17th century Dutch, English, French, Norwegian and Danish whalers slaughtered the whale population. They were followed in the 18th century by Russians hunting walrus and seals. The 19th century saw the arrival of Norwegians, who hunted polar bears and arctic fox. During the late 19th and early 20th centuries, several (mostly unsuccessful) expeditions to the North Pole were mounted from Svalbard. In 1906, commercial coal mining began and is continued today by the Russians (at Barentsburg) and the Norwegians (at Longyearbyen and Sveagruva). The 1920 Svalbard Treaty granted Norwegian sovereignty over the islands.

Orientation & Information

Longyearbyen, the largest settlement on Svalbard, has an airport with flights to/from Tromsø. You'll find all the usual facilities, including a post office, a bank (with an ATM), and a library. Barentsburg, the Russian settlement, is about 40km west, while Ny Ålesund, a Norwegian research station with an airstrip, is about 100km northwest. Apart from the immediate vicinity of the settlements, there are no roads and most tourists will travel around with organised tours – on foot, by sea or, in winter, by snowmobile.

The friendly and helpful **tourist office** (☎ 79 02 55 50; **W** www.svalbard.net), in central Longyearbyen, distributes the handy *Svalbard* brochure.

Organised Tours

Dozens of exciting options are listed on the tourist office website. Accommodation, transport and meals are usually included in longer tours, but day tours are also available (see under Longyearbyen). The most popular tour operators are:

Spitsbergen Tours (☎ 79 02 10 68, **e** info@terrapolaris.com) Postboks 6, N-9171 Longyearbyen. Adventurous options include week-long trips combining cruises, hikes, dogsledding and snowmobile trips, depending on the season (from Nkr8000)

Spitsbergen Travel (☎ 79 02 61 00, **W** www.spitsbergentravel.no) Postboks 548, N-9171 Longyearbyen. This company offers week-long cruises, dogsledding trips, four-day snowmobile safaris, six- and 12-day trekking tours and 13-day ski treks

Svalbard Wildlife Service (☎ 79 02 10 35, **W** www.wildlife.no) offers varied tours including camping, kayaking and glacier exploration

Getting There & Away

SAS and Braathens fly regularly from Tromsø to Longyearbyen. Schedules and fares are subject to variation, but a typical return fare is around Nkr3200.

Warning

The danger of being killed by a polar bear cannot be overstated. Never venture from the settlements in Svalbard unless you are armed with a loaded rifle and know how to use it.

Longyearbyen
pop 1500

This frontier-like community, strewn with abandoned coal mining detritus, enjoys a superb backdrop including two glacier tongues, Longyearbreen and Lars Hjertabreen.

At the **Svalbard Museum** (☎ 79 02 13 84; *Skjæringa; admission Nkr30; open 11am-7pm Mon-Fri, noon-4pm Sat, 1pm-7pm Sun July & Aug, otherwise shorter hrs*), west of the centre, exhibits cover mining, and the history, climate, geology, wildlife and exploration of the archipelago.

Organised Tours Many short trips and day tours that vary with the season are on offer, including fossil hunting (Nkr300); mine tours (Nkr580); boat trips to Barentsburg and Pyramidien (Nkr900); dogsledding (Nkr750); dogsledding on *wheels* (Nkr400); diving trips (Nkr1200); glacier hiking (Nkr480); ice-caving (from Nkr520); kayaking (from Nkr510); mountain biking (Nkr400); horseback riding (Nkr400); and snowmobiling (from Nkr1250). Contact the tourist office for more details.

Places to Stay & Eat Many visitors head straight for **Longyearbyen Camping** (☎ 79 02 10 68; *per person Nkr70; open late June-early Sept*), next to the airport and about an hour's walk from town.

Mary-Ann's Polar Rigg (☎ 79 02 37 02; *singles/doubles Nkr375/500*) is a simple guesthouse with a kitchenette. Linen is Nkr100 extra and breakfast is Nkr75. **Spitsbergen Nybyen Gjestehus** (☎ 79 02 63 00; **e** nybyen@spitra.no; *Nybyen; dorm beds Nkr295, singles/doubles Nkr495/840*), south of the centre, is a large, functional building. **Radisson SAS Polar Hotel** (☎ 79 02 34 50; **e** sales@lyrzh.rdsas.com; *singles/doubles from Nkr1310/1580*) is Longyearbyen's most luxurious accommodation.

Huset (☎ 79 02 25 00; *mains Nkr195-255*), west of the centre, is a popular choice for both Arctic and French-style meals. In the central shopping mall, you'll find the **Svalbardbutikken** supermarket, and **Kafé Busen** (*mains under Nkr100*), which serves daily specials as well as typical cafeteria fare.

Getting Around Longyearbyen **Buss & Taxi** (☎ 79 02 13 75) charges Nkr80 to Nkr100 for a cab trip between town and airport. The airport bus (Nkr35) serves the various accommodation options.

Around Svalbard

Barentsburg, complete with Soviet-era relics, is Svalbard's only remaining Russian settlement and is a fascinating place that still mines and exports coal. There's a reasonable **museum** *(admission Nkr30)*, a **hotel** *(☎ 79 02 10 80; doubles Nkr500)* and a **workers' canteen**. Most people arrive by tour boat, but it's possible to hike from Longyearbyen in five days.

Ny Ålesund, at latitude 79°N, is a wild place with none-too-friendly scientists and downright hostile arctic terns (you may have to beat the latter off with a stick!). Relics of past glories include a **stranded locomotive**, previously used for transporting coal, and an **airship pylon**, used by Amundsen and Nobile on their successful crossing of the North Pole in 1926. There's a basic **camping ground** *(tent sites Nkr100)*.The **hotel** *(☎ 79 02 72 00; ⓔ booking@kingsbay.no; singles/doubles from Nkr975/2060)* is expensive, but prices include full board. The **King's Bay Cantina** *(☎ 79 02 72 00; full board Nkr460)* offers breakfast/lunch/dinner·for Nkr75/210/175.

Most visitors arrive in Ny Ålesund on tourist cruises, but **Kings Bay** *(☎ 79 02 72 00; ⓦ www.kingsbay.no)* offers air transport to/from Longyearbyen (Nkr2720 return, 25 minutes, two or three per week).

Climbers scaling Norway's Jostedalsbreen glacier

A bird's-eye view of a 19th-century stave church

A river of moss in Dovrefjell National Park

Tromsø's striking Arctic Cathedral

Arctic tropics: enjoy a warm swim on Langøya island, Vesterålen

The road to Geirangerfjorden

Take a walk in World Heritage Listed Bryggen

Amtmandens Datter, one of Tromsø's many pubs

Sweden

Every country has its stereotypes and cliches but, let's face it, who wouldn't want to live up to the image Sweden has in the outside world? A nation of tall, blonde, attractive types, famously open-minded and non-aggressive (well, at least in the recent past). A country full of athletic folk (think Bjorn Borg) at the cutting edge of technology (think Ericsson), well cared-for by the state and living very comfortable lives: flash cars parked in the garage (think Volvo and SAAB) and houses full of stylish, cleverly designed furniture (think IKEA), with the population spending their long summer days eating meatballs and listening to ABBA (OK, maybe that last bit is taking it too far...). To the casual observer it might well seem that the cliches are pretty spot on. But, as ever, there's a lot more to a country than its stereotypes. Dig even slightly below the glossy surface and you'll find even more to be impressed by.

Sweden has more than 25,000 protected Iron-Age graveyards and burial mounds, 1140 prehistoric fortresses, 2500 open-air rune stones, 3000 churches (almost one-third of them are medieval), thousands of nature reserves, 28 national parks and more than 10,000km of trekking and bicycle paths – not to mention 10 royal castles in the Stockholm area, hundreds of superb museums and 12 Unesco World Heritage Sites.

In the south, you'll find Danish castles and architectural influences in Helsingborg and Lund. The lovely capital city, Stockholm, has historic ties with France reflected in some of its stylish architecture. Stockholm's coastal *skärgård* (archipelago) consists of at least 24,000 islands and is served by one of the largest antique steamer fleets anywhere in Europe.

Sweden also takes in vast forested and lake-studded landscapes. The starkly beautiful wilderness areas of Norrland (northern Sweden) have the legendary midnight sun in summer, Kebnekaise (2111m; Arctic Scandinavia's highest mountain), and thousands of kilometres of hiking trails through immense protected areas.

There's one problem, however; Sweden can be quite expensive, but with the devaluing of the krona in recent years, costs for visitors are not as extortionately high as in the

At a Glance

Capital	Stockholm
Population	8.9 million
Area	449,964 sq km
Official Language	Swedish
GDP	US$210 billion
Time	GMT/UTC +0100
Country Phone Code	☎ 46

Highlights

- Finding out just how accurate Stockholm's slogan 'Beauty on Water' really is, with a boat cruise around the capital and a stroll through Gamla Stan (p429)
- Taking in the traditional culture and attractions of the pretty Lake Siljan area, with everything from artists' homes to music festivals, huge ski races and a bear park (p449)
- Following the example set by holidaying Swedes on Gotland: cycling and camping, and exploring delightful Visby (p477)
- Getting downright chilly and admiring the ingenuity at the breathtaking Ice Hotel in Jukkasjärvi, near Kiruna (p487)
- Enjoying the dramatic mountain landscapes and great trekking in the far north, particularly in and around Abisko National Park (p489)

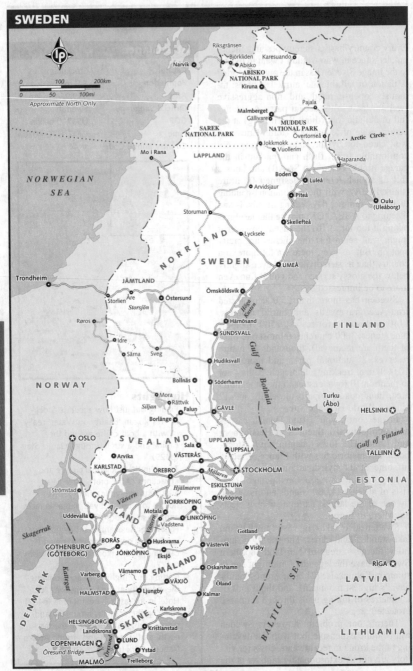

SWEDEN

Riksgränsen
Björkliden
Narvik
Karesuando
Abisko
ABISKO NATIONAL PARK
Kiruna
Pajala
Malmberget
Gällivare
MUDDUS NATIONAL PARK
Övertorneå
SAREK NATIONAL PARK
Jokkmokk
Arctic Circle
Mo i Rana
Vuollerim
Haparanda
LAPPLAND
Boden
Luleå
Arvidsjaur
Piteå
NORWEGIAN SEA
Storuman
Skellefteå
Lycksele
NORRLAND
SWEDEN
UMEÅ
Trondheim
JÄMTLAND
Örnsköldsvik
Storlien
Åre
Östersund
Storsjön
Härnösand
Höga Kusten
FINLAND
Røros
SUNDSVALL
Idre
Särna
Sveg
Hudiksvall
Gulf of Bothnia
Bollnäs
Söderhamn
NORWAY
Mora
Rättvik
Turku (Åbo)
Siljan
Falun
HELSINKI
Borlänge
GÄVLE
OSLO
SVEALAND
UPPLAND
Åland
Sala
Gulf of Finland
Arvika
VÄSTERÅS
UPPSALA
TALLINN
KARLSTAD
ÖREBRO
Mälaren
STOCKHOLM
Strömstad
Hjälmaren
ESKILSTUNA
ESTONIA
GÖTALAND
Vänern
NORRKÖPING
Nyköping
Uddevalla
Motala
LINKÖPING
Skagerrak
Vadstena
Vättern
Gotland
BORÅS
Huskvarna
Västervik
GOTHENBURG (GÖTEBORG)
JÖNKÖPING
Eksjö
Visby
SMÅLAND
Varberg
Värnamo
Oskarshamn
RĪGA
Kattegat
VÄXJÖ
Öland
LATVIA
HALMSTAD
Ljungby
Kalmar
DENMARK
Karlskrona
BALTIC SEA
HELSINGBORG
SKÅNE
Landskrona
Kristianstad
LITHUANIA
COPENHAGEN
LUND
Öresund
Ystad
Öresund Bridge
MALMÖ
Trelleborg

0   100   200km
0   50   100mi
Approximate North Only

SWEDEN

past. The quality of goods and services is generally high and many attractions are free, but when you must pay, you can pay dearly.

Facts about Sweden

HISTORY
The Pre-Christian Era
Written records survive only from late in the Middle Ages, but the number and variety of fortifications, assembly places, votive sites and graves is impressive. Of these, the highest concentrations are around the Mälaren valley, in Uppland (the ancient region centred on Uppsala) and on the Baltic islands of Gotland and Öland.

People and metallurgy made late appearances and only in the Bronze Age, after the arrival of Indo-Europeans, was there rich trade. However, the early cultural life is still eloquently expressed by the *hällristningar* (rock carvings) that survive in many parts of Sweden. They depict ritual or mythological events using the familiar symbols of warriors, boats, the sun and the beasts of the hunt. Stone settings in the shape of ships were in use in the Iron Age as graves or cenotaphs of this warrior society and its chieftains. In the Mälaren valley, the first known trading posts were established and monuments with runic inscriptions were raised.

In the 9th century the missionary St Ansgar visited Birka near modern Stockholm, just as the Viking Age was getting under way. The regions of Gotland and Svealand already had links throughout the Baltic area and Swedish adventurers had meddled in Russia. Roman, Byzantine and Arab coins have been found in huge numbers.

Rise of the Swedish State
The wealth and power of the Svea overwhelmed the southern Gauts (Götar) before the 11th century. This allowed a Christian, Olof Skötkonung, to be crowned king, paving the way for the emergence of a Swedish state. In 1164 an archbishopric was established in Uppsala.

King Magnus Ladulås instigated a national law code in 1350. Sweden avoided feudalism, but a privileged aristocracy owed allegiance to the king and the wealth of the church

grew. St Birgitta, the mystic, founded an order of nuns at Vadstena.

The south belonged to Denmark and was strongly influenced by it. The Hanseatic League established walled trading towns such as Visby and there was a strong German presence in early Stockholm. However, Denmark intervened and, together with Norway, joined Sweden in the Union of Kalmar in 1397. Danish monarchs held the Swedish throne for a while, tolerating an assembly of four estates which was the forerunner of the modern Riksdag (Parliament).

The Vasa Dynasty
The regent Sten Sture loosened the Danish hold in 1471. The execution of his son and namesake in Stockholm in 1520 by the Danish king, Christian II, caused further rebellion which began in Dalarna under the leadership of the young nobleman Gustaf Vasa. After being crowned Gustaf I in 1523, he introduced the Reformation and a powerful, centralised nation-state. In mainly Catholic Småland, Nils Dacke defied Gustaf, but Nils' death in 1543 left a strong throne firmly in control of a Lutheran Sweden.

A period of expansion began under Gustaf II Adolf, who championed the Protestant German princes in the Thirty Years' War and removed the imperial threat to his ambitions in the Baltic. Although he died in battle at Lützen in 1632, Sweden had gained territory on the Baltic coast and remained in control of Finland.

The Liberalisation of Sweden
The megalomania of the young Karl XII was crushed by Peter the Great at Poltava. Karl's adventures cost Sweden its Baltic territories and the crown much prestige. Greater parliamentary power marked the next 50 years.

Gustaf III led a coup that interrupted this development. He brought French culture to his court, and introduced a Swedish academy of culture. His foreign policy was less auspicious and in 1792, while at the opera in fancy dress, he was murdered by an aristocratic conspiracy. Unrestricted royal power was ended by aristocratic revolt in 1809 and Finland was lost to Russia.

That same year produced a constitution that divided legislative powers between king and Riksdag. The king's advisory council was also responsible to the Riksdag, which controlled

SWEDEN

taxation. An ombudsman was created as a check on the bureaucracy. Sweden also negotiated with Denmark to exchange Swedish Pomerania for Norway. Napoleon's marshal Bernadotte was chosen to fill a gap in the succession and, as Karl Johan, became regent. Thus began the rise of liberalism and Sweden's policy of neutrality. The enforcement of the 1814 union with Norway was Sweden's last military action.

Industrialisation
Industry arrived late and was based on timber, efficient steel making and the safety match (a Swedish invention). Iron-ore mining, then steel manufacture, began to expand and produce a middle class. However, the 1827 statute, which turned peasant farms into larger concerns, had more immediate and far-reaching effects – the old social fabric disappeared.

In 1866 a very limited franchise was introduced for a new and bicameral Riksdag. Many farmers preferred to migrate and endure hardship in the USA, but when US corn began to penetrate the Swedish market, tariffs became the great issue. This led to tensions with free-trading Norway and ultimately to the end of the union in 1905.

By 1900 almost one in four Swedes lived in cities, and industry (based on timber, precision machinery and hardware) was increasing. In this environment, the working class was radicalised.

Conscription was first introduced as a measure against Russia in 1901 and men aged over 24 years received the vote in 1907. Moves to cut wages caused 300,000 people to strike two years later. Temperance movements profoundly influenced the labour movement and alcohol restrictions became state policy.

The Welfare State
Sweden declared itself neutral at the outbreak of WWI, but a British economic blockade caused food shortages and civil unrest. Consensus was no longer possible and for the first time a Social Democrat and Liberal coalition government took control. Reforms followed quickly and suffrage for all adults aged over 23 years was introduced, as well as the eight-hour working day.

The Social Democrats dominated politics after 1932. After the hardships caused by the Depression, they took the liberal tendencies of the 1920s *statsminister*, Hjalmar Branting, and combined them with economic intervention policies and other measures to introduce a welfare state.

These trends were scarcely interrupted by Sweden's ambiguous approach to WWII. The Social Democrats sponsored models for industrial bargaining and full employment which allowed the economy to blossom in harmony under Tage Erlander.

The economic pressures of the 1970s began to cloud Sweden's social goals and it was under Olof Palme that support for social democracy first wavered. Palme's assassination in 1986 and subsequent government scandals led to a downturn in the fortunes of the Social Democrats.

Serious current account problems in the early 1990s provoked frenzied speculation against the Swedish krona, forcing a massive devaluation of the currency. With both their economy and national confidence severely shaken, Swedes voted in favour of joining the European Union (EU), effective 1 January 1995. Since then, Sweden's welfare state has undergone major reforms and the economy has improved considerably, with falling unemployment and inflation. The country has remained outside the single European currency, and a referendum is still to be held on the issue. It's expected that this referendum will occur sometime in 2003 and it's likely that the euro will be accepted.

GEOGRAPHY
Sweden covers an area of 449,964 sq km and its maximum north–south extent is 1574km. This size allows for a little diversity, but the dominant characteristics of the landscape go back to the time of the last glaciation. Flat and open, Skåne is similar to Denmark, but farther north the landscape is hillier and heavily forested.

The rocky west coast is most notable for its fjords and skerries, although they scarcely compare with the barrage of rocky islets that shield Stockholm. The islands of Öland and Gotland consist of flat limestone and sandstone.

There are approximately 100,000 lakes in Sweden. Lake Mälaren is the heart of the country, although Vänern is by far the biggest of the south and central lakes. In Norrland there is a nearly uniform expanse of forest cut by rivers and narrow lakes. The trees thin out in Jämtland and Lappland and the mountains assert themselves, providing a natural frontier with Norway in the northwest.

Geographical divisions in Sweden are complex. The two kingdoms which united in the 11th century form the southern half of the country: Götaland in the south and Svealand in lower central Sweden. Anything north of Svealand is called Norrland. The 25 historical regions (based on common dialect), or *landskap*, remain as denominators for people's identity and a basis for regional tourist promotion. Regional administration is based on 21 *län* (counties) which are responsible for things like *länstrafik* (regional public transport) and *länsmuseum* (regional museums).

CLIMATE

Most of Sweden has a cool temperate climate, with precipitation in all seasons, but the southern quarter of the country has a warm temperate climate. Sweden is shielded from rainy Atlantic weather systems and can be influenced by high pressure over Russia, giving fine weather instead. Stockholm has an average of about nine hours of sunshine daily from May to July, but Luleå leads the country in July with more than 10 hours. In January the average maximum temperature in the south of Sweden is -1°C and in the north -13°C (where minimum temperatures can be -50°C). Average maximum temperatures for July are 18°C in the south and around 14°C in the north, but long hot periods aren't unusual, with temperatures over 30°C.

ECOLOGY & ENVIRONMENT

Ecological consciousness is very high and reflected in concern for native animals, clean water and renewable resources. Swedes are fervent believers in sorting and recycling household waste (paper, glass, plastic etc), and the Swedish government strictly enforces its antipollution laws. Fishing in the clean waters surrounding central Stockholm isn't unusual, but, pollution and over-fishing of the seas around Sweden is becoming cause for concern, as is acid rain damaging the soils and lakes.

FLORA & FAUNA

The predominant tree species are Norway spruce, Scots pine, birch and, in central and southern Sweden, beech and oak. Large numbers of elk (moose) and deer live in the forests, while in Norrland there are sizable herds of reindeer (no longer truly wild, as each animal belongs to a local Sami community). Other animals peculiar to the north are the arctic fox and lemmings, small, hardy rodents famous for their reproductive capacity. European brown bears, Scandinavia's only surviving wild bear population, number about 1000 and live mainly in the remote northern areas.

National Parks

Sweden led Europe in setting up national parks in the early 20th century; there are now 28 scattered throughout the country (the biggest and best are in Lappland). Rules vary locally, but the constant is that responsible and careful people may have access to open areas (see Activities in the Facts for the Visitor section). In 1996, the 9400-sq-km Laponia area was placed on the World Heritage List – it includes the national parks Stora Sjöfallet, Sarek, Padjelanta and Muddus.

GOVERNMENT & POLITICS

Sweden has maintained its monarch as head of state under the constitution, but the statsminister is chosen by a majority of the *Riksdag* (Parliament). Since 1971 there has been only one chamber in the parliament. From it come the cabinet ministers, who then lose their parliamentary vote. After several constitutional reforms in the 1970s, cabinet was confirmed as the ultimate legislative body. The Riksdag, which has 349 members, is elected every four years in September (the latest in 2002), but representatives of union, business and cooperative movements also serve on its commissions.

Councils of the 21 *län* are convened by cabinet appointees, can levy taxes and are responsible for the administration of regional services such as public transport and health. At the municipal level, 289 *kommuner* (municipalities) provide housing, roads and water.

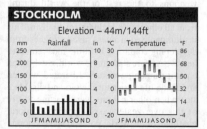

STOCKHOLM

Elevation – 44m/144ft

ECONOMY

Sweden is one of the strongest industrial nations in Europe (home to Volvo, Ericsson, SAAB and ABB) but, although it remains one of the wealthiest countries in the world, its tightly regulated and highly socialised 'economic model' is now viewed far more critically at home and abroad than before. Even the Social Democrats who built the system admit that the era of *folkhemmet* (the welfare state) is over. Yet, the idea of cradle-to-grave welfare is deeply entrenched in the Swedish psyche.

Sweden's service sector accounts for 74% of the domestic economy (amongst the highest in the world). Unemployment, which reached 14% in the early 1990s, has now fallen to about 4% and the krona has regained some of its strength. Taxes rank among the highest in the world.

Timber and mining are vital to industry. About half the country is forested and nearly half of this is in the hands of government or forestry companies. The iron-ore mines at Kiruna and Gällivare in the Arctic north are still of importance. Only 8% of Sweden is farmland and most of this is in the south.

POPULATION & PEOPLE

Currently, 8.9 million people live in Sweden, making it the most populous Scandinavian country. The density of the population is 21.5 people per sq km.

Low birth and mortality rates have made Swedes among the oldest population on earth, with 17% of the population over 65. Over 500,000 are foreign nationals, and an extraordinary 20% of the population is either foreign-born or has at least one non-Swedish parent.

There are two native minorities: the 15,000 Sami (formerly called Lapps) and about 30,000 Finns who live in the northeast. The Sami can be considered the indigenous inhabitants of the north. Today the Sami keep reindeer or are engaged in tourism and forestry.

Greater Stockholm has a population of over 1.8 million, the Gothenburg area is home to 800,000 people and Greater Malmö has 500,000 people. Apart from a sprinkling of towns along the Bothnian coast, settlement in Norrland is sparse – Umeå's municipality is the largest with just over 100,000 inhabitants.

ARTS & SCIENCES

The best known members of Sweden's artistic community have been writers, chiefly the influential dramatist and author August Strindberg and the widely translated children's writer Astrid Lindgren. Vilhelm Moberg, a representative of 20th-century proletarian literature, won acclaim with *The Immigrants* and *The Emigrants*. Ingmar Bergman remains one of the greatest cinema directors of all time.

To the Swedish soul the Gustavian balladry of Carl Michael Bellman is perhaps dearest. Sweden lacks a Grieg or Sibelius, but its modern music industry is one of the strongest in Europe. The popularity of music in Sweden is highlighted by the facts that Swedes buy more recorded music per capita than any other nationality, and the country is the third-largest exporter of music in the world (after the US and UK). Some 120 music festivals are staged annually, ranging from medieval and baroque to folk, jazz and rock. Some home-grown pop groups are internationally known; ABBA is the most famous Swedish pop group and were huge in the 1970s. In the late 1980s and into the 1990s, more mainstream pop acts such as Roxette, Ace of Base and the Cardigans held international attention. The latest Swedish bands to hit the big time are The Hives, Lambretta and Millencolin.

The most important figure from Swedish culture, however, has been the scientist Carl von Linné, the 18th-century botanist who pioneered plant taxonomy under Latin classifications which are still used. Even better known is Alfred Nobel, the inventor of dynamite and other explosives, whose will founded the Nobel Institute and the international prizes in 1901.

SOCIETY & CONDUCT

Sweden's reputation as a social reformer, albeit sometimes misunderstood, is justified. After having sold (as a neutral country) weapons to the rest of the world during WWII, Sweden decided to save the world from all other evils, including capitalism. This institutionalised niceness saved refugees from developing countries, built the most comprehensive welfare state in the world, established equality among workers, liberated women and made life easier for the old and disabled. Just when other nations were starting to tire of this over-zealous, self-appointed 'moral guardian' of the world, political and economic factors in the late 1980s forced Swedes to fundamentally reassess themselves.

Still, Sweden regulates, taxes and subsidises every step from cradle to grave. Even queuing is infallibly ordered: press a button for your own numbered ticket, then wait until it comes up on a digital display, even if you only want to buy a bottle of wine! All this is just *lagom* (satisfactorily acceptable) to Swedes who have created one of the cleanest, most comfortable and stylish societies anywhere – almost a perfect destination for travellers, if only you can afford it!

Although the strong rural traditions are not forgotten (the summer cottage is almost *de rigueur* – there are 600,000 second homes) modern Sweden is becoming increasingly urban. Late-model Volvos and SAABs are everywhere, and mobile phone ownership is sky-high. Its small population also has an impressive presence in world music charts and international sporting arenas.

RELIGION
Around 85% of Swedes belong to the (Lutheran) Church of Sweden, although fewer than 10% regularly attend church services. Women may be ordained. The state, however, guarantees religious freedom, and since 1994 citizens don't legally acquire a religion at birth but voluntarily become members of a faith. Church and state finally separated in 2000. Around 500,000 foreigners are non-Christians, including nearly 250,000 Muslims and around 20,000 Jews.

Facts for the Visitor

SUGGESTED ITINERARIES
Depending on the length of your stay you might like to see and do the following:

Two days
Visit Stockholm
One week
Visit Stockholm and Gothenburg, and a few nearby towns or regions, including the Stockholm archipelago and Uppsala
Two weeks
Visit Stockholm, Gothenburg and Uppsala, and tour the Dalarna and Skåne regions
One month
You can explore the country pretty thoroughly, including a few days in Abisko National Park
Two months
Visit almost all places mentioned in this chapter

PLANNING
When to Go
If you want sunshine, visit between late May and late July, bearing in mind that August can be wet. Light refraction increases the length of the day in the far north by 15 minutes both before dawn and after sunset. Malmö in the south gets 17½ hours of light around midsummer, Sundsvall has constant light during the second half of June, and Kiruna has 45 days of continuous light. Conversely, at 69° north, there's an average 'day' of only four twilight hours in December.

Quite a number of hostels, camping grounds and attractions open only in summer, from late June to mid-August. Summer can be hot, sunny and beautiful, but also busy with holidaying Swedes. Travel in winter is somewhat restricted and should be better planned, but there are opportunities for winter activities like skiing, or dog-sled and snowmobile safaris. The big cities are in full swing all year, but the smaller towns almost go into hibernation when the temperatures begin to drop.

Maps
Good maps (including town plans) are usually available free of charge from tourist offices and often from places to stay. The best tourist road maps are Kartförlaget's Vägkartan series (1:100,000) available from larger bookshops. Also useful, especially for hikers, are the Fjällkartan mountain series (1:100,000); these are usually priced from Skr80 to Skr110 and are available at larger bookshops, and also from outdoor equipment stores and Svenska Turistföreningen (STF) mountain stations.

The best road atlas is *Motormännens Sverige Atlas* for around Skr270.

What to Bring
A raincoat and jumper (sweater) are necessary at all times of the year. From at least November to April you'll need lots of warm clothes, including scarf, hat, gloves and anorak or overcoat. In the more temperate months, use layers of thinner clothing. Other useful items include a hostel sleeping sheet (saving Skr50 per day) or a tent and sleeping bag.

TOURIST OFFICES
Sweden has about 350 local tourist information offices. Most are open long hours in summer and short hours (or not at all) during winter and a few exhibit nomadic tendencies. The offices

SWEDEN

in big towns stock brochures from all around Sweden. The website ⓦ www.turism.se claims to list all of Sweden's tourist information offices and their contact details.

Tourist Offices Abroad

The official website for the Swedish Travel and Tourism Council is at ⓦ www.visit-sweden.com. The site contains loads of good information in many languages.

The following offices can assist with inquiries and provide tourist promotional material. In countries without a designated tourist office, a good starting point for information is the Swedish embassy.

France (☎ 01 53 43 26 27, ⓔ servinfo@suede-tourisme.fr) Office Suédois du Tourisme et des Voyages, 18 boulevarde Malesherbes, F-75008 Paris

Germany (☎ 040-32 55 13 55, ⓔ info@swetourism.de) Schweden-Werbung für Reisen und Touristik, Lilienstrasse 19, DE-20095 Hamburg

UK (☎ 020-7870 5600, 00800 3080 3080, ⓔ info@swetourism.org.uk) Swedish Travel & Tourism Council, 5 Upper Montagu St, London W1H 2AG

USA (☎ 212-885 9700, ⓔ info@gosweden.org) Swedish Travel & Tourism Council, PO Box 4649, Grand Central Station, New York NY 10163-4649

VISAS & DOCUMENTS

Citizens of the EU, Norway and Iceland can enter Sweden with a passport or a national identification card (passports are recommended). Nationals of Nordic countries can stay and work indefinitely but others require *uppehållstillstånd* (residence permits) for stays of between three months and five years.

Non-EU passport-holders from Australia, New Zealand, Canada and the US can enter and stay in Sweden without a visa for up to three months. Citizens of South Africa and other African, Asian and some Eastern European countries require tourist visas for entry; only available in advance from Swedish embassies (allow two months); the cost is Skr225/275 for permits allowing a maximum 30/90 days. It may be hard to extend your stay.

Migrationsverket (☎ 011-156000; ⓦ www.migrationsverket.se; SE-60170 Norrköping) is the Swedish 'migration board' and it handles all applications for visas and work or residency permits. A minimum of six weeks (allow eight) is needed to process an application, and you

may have to send your passport to have it stamped plus provide a number of personal details.

EMBASSIES
Swedish Embassies & Consulates

A complete list of Swedish diplomatic missions abroad is available on the Internet at ⓦ www.utrikes.regeringen.se.

Australia (☎ 02-6270 2700, ⓦ www.embassyofsweden.org.au) 5 Turrana St, Yarralumla ACT 2600

Canada (☎ 613-241 8553, ⓦ www.swedishembassy.ca) 377 Dalhousie St, Ottawa K1N 9N8

Denmark (☎ 33 36 03 70, ⓦ www.sverigesambassad.dk) Sankt Annæ Plads 15A, DK-1250 Copenhagen K

Finland (☎ 09-6877 660, ⓦ www.sverige.fi) Pohjoisesplanadi 7B, 00170 Helsinki

France (☎ 01 44 18 88 00, ⓦ www.amb-suede.fr) 17 rue Barbet-de-Jouy, F-75007 Paris

Germany (☎ 030-505 060, ⓦ www.schweden.org) Rauchstrasse 1, 107 87 Berlin

Ireland (☎ 01-671 5822, ⓦ www.swedishembassy.ie) 13–17 Dawson St, Dublin 2

Netherlands (☎ 070-412 0200, ⓦ www.swedenembnl.org) Burg Van Karnebeeklaan 6A, 2508 Den Haag

New Zealand (☎ 04-499 9895) 13th floor, Vogel Bldg, Aitken St, Wellington

Norway (☎ 24 11 42 00, ⓦ www.sverigesambassad.no) Nobelsgate 16, NO-0244 Oslo

UK (☎ 020-7917 6400, ⓦ www.swedish-embassy.org.uk) 11 Montagu Place, London W1H 2AL

USA (☎ 202-467 2600, ⓦ www.swedish-embassy.org) Suite 900, 1501 M St NW, Washington DC 20005-1702

Embassies & Consulates in Sweden

The diplomatic missions listed here are in Stockholm, although some neighbouring countries also have consulates in Gothenburg, Malmö and Helsingborg:

Australia (☎ 08-613 2900) 11th floor, Sergels Torg 12

Canada (☎ 08-453 3000) Tegelbacken 4

Denmark (☎ 08-406 7500) Jakobs Torg 1

Finland (☎ 08-676 6700) Gärdesgatan 9–11

France (☎ 08-459 5300) Kommendörsgatan 13

Germany (☎ 08-670 1500) Skarpögatan 9

Ireland (☎ 08-661 8005) Östermalmsgatan 97

Netherlands (☎ 08-556 93300) Götgatan 16A

New Zealand (☎ 08-660 0460) Nybrogatan 34

Norway (☎ 08-665 6340) Skarpögatan 4

UK (☎ 08-671 9000) Skarpögatan 6–8

USA (☎ 08-783 5300) Dag Hammarskjöldsväg 31

CUSTOMS

Going through customs rarely involves any hassles, but rules on illegal drugs are strictly enforced. Duty-free allowances for travellers from outside the EU are: 1L of spirits or 2L of fortified wine; 2L of wine; and 32L of strong beer. The limits on goods brought into Sweden from another EU country are more generous: 2L of spirits or 6L of fortified wine, 26L of wine and 32L of strong beer. People aged under 20 years are not allowed to bring in alcohol.

See the Customs section in the Facts for the Visitor chapter and W www.tullverket.se for further details.

MONEY

You should encounter few problems if you carry cash in any convertible currency or internationally recognised travellers cheques. Although not all machines are fully connected, the national Minuten and Bankomat ATM networks provided by Swedish banks accept international Visa, Plus, EC, Eurocard, MasterCard or Cirrus cards.

Forex, found in the biggest cities and most airports and ferry terminals, is one of the cheapest and easiest places to exchange money and charges Skr15 per cheque. Banks charge up to Skr60 per cheque.

You can buy foreign notes for no fee at Forex. The X-Change centres also offer good deals, but have fewer branches.

Currency

The Swedish *krona* (plural: *kronor*), usually called 'crown' by Swedes speaking English, is denoted Skr and divided into 100 *öre* (prices are rounded to the nearest 50 *öre*). Coins are 50 *öre* and one, five and 10 *kronor* and notes are 20, 50, 100, 500 and 1000 *kronor*.

Exchange Rates

The following exchange rates prevailed at the time of printing:

country	unit		kronor
Australia	A$1	=	Skr5.15
Canada	C$1	=	Skr5.99
Denmark	Dkr1	=	Skr1.25
euro	€1	=	Skr9.27
Japan	¥100	=	Skr7.56
New Zealand	NZ$1	=	Skr4.42
Norway	Nkr1	=	Skr1.24
UK	UK£1	=	Skr14.83
USA	US$1	=	Skr9.48

Costs

High prices mean that you may struggle to do and see it all in Sweden. The accrued costs of transport, food, accommodation and attractions, coupled with simple things like luggage storage (up to Skr70 at lockers in some cities), a cup of coffee (Skr20) or a beer (Skr40 to Skr50) mean that money disappears quickly. You may need to avoid alcohol to keep to a budget – boozing here is definitely for the wealthy.

However, Sweden *can* be cheap – with a tent you can sleep for free in forests. Bring sheets and an Hostelling International (HI) membership card, and you pay Skr80 to Skr200 per night in each of the 300-plus STF hostels, generally offering a very high standard of accommodation. Students with an ISIC card (and often seniors) are eligible for discounts in museums, theatres and cinemas. Big cities offer excellent hotel packages, which come with free entry to all attractions and public transport, and most hotels offer heavily discounted prices at weekends throughout the year and in summer (from mid-June to mid-August), sometimes with reductions on weekday room rates amounting to 50%.

Stuff yourself at the breakfast buffet for about Skr45 (included in the price in most hotels), or choose a *dagens rätt* (the lunch special) offered by numerous restaurants from around Skr50 instead of dining à la carte in the evening. Takeaway pizzas and kebabs are inexpensive options, and good kitchen facilities at hostels and camping grounds make self-catering easy.

Avoid overpriced tourist traps and instead visit any of the 30,000-odd historical or natural attractions that are free.

To save money on transport, don't just buy a one-way bus ticket – ask about daily or weekly passes. Get a rail pass and explore towns and regions by foot or on bike. If there's a few of you, sharing car rental for a weekend in order to see some out-of-the-way places is worth considering (some petrol stations offer small cars for as little as Skr200 per day).

That said, petrol prices are high (and more expensive in the far north). However, self-service pumps that take banknotes or credit cards are slightly cheaper (note that many of these self-service pumps won't accept foreign credit cards).

SWEDEN

Tipping & Bargaining

Service charges are usually included in restaurant bills and taxi fares, but there's no problem if you want to reward good service with a tip (or round up the taxi fare, particularly if there's luggage). Cloakrooms usually cost about Skr20.

Bargaining isn't customary: a price is generally a price, but you can get 'walk-in' prices at some hotels and *stugby* (chalet parks).

Taxes & Refunds

The main additional cost for the traveller is *mervärdeskatt* or *moms*, the value-added tax (VAT) on goods and services, which is included in the marked price. This varies but may be as much as 25%.

At shops that display the sign 'Tax Free Shopping', non-EU citizens making single purchases of goods exceeding Skr200 (including *moms*) are eligible for a VAT refund of 15% to 18% of the purchase price. Show your passport and ask the shop for a 'Global Refund Cheque', which should be presented along with your unopened purchases (within three months) at your departure point from the country (before you check in), to get export validation. You can then cash your cheque at any of the international refund points, which are found at international airports and harbour terminals. The *Tax Free Shopping Guide to Sweden* is available from tourist offices free of charge, or call ☎ 020 741741 for more information.

POST & COMMUNICATIONS
Postal Rates

Mailing letters or postcards up to 20g within Sweden costs Skr5, and Skr8 to elsewhere in Europe, or Skr10 beyond Europe. The *ekonomibrev* (economy post) option takes longer to reach its destination and costs marginally less (Skr4.50, Skr7 and Skr8 respectively). Airmail will take a week to reach most parts of North America, perhaps a little longer to Australia and New Zealand.

A package weighing 2kg costs Skr160/220 by airmail to Europe/outside Europe. The *ekonomibrev* option here is roughly Skr30 cheaper, but postage time may take up to a month.

Sending & Receiving Mail

At the time of writing, Posten (the Swedish postal service) was undergoing big changes, including moving to new premises all over the country. Service outlets of Posten are opening in some 3000 new venues, mostly in food stores and petrol stations, and will therefore be open long hours (many from 9am to 9pm daily). These outlets will offer all that most travellers will need, eg, *frimärken* (stamps), *brev* (letter) and *paket* (package) service. You can also buy stamps from many tourist offices, convenience stores, tobacconists and newsagents – look for the yellow post symbol on a pale blue background, which indicates that some postal facilities are offered.

Receiving poste-restante mail under the new postal system will be slightly more difficult for travellers. As many of the large, old-style post offices have closed or relocated, there is no central 'holding place' in most towns. The person sending you mail will need to specify which post outlet you will be collecting from, with a specific address and postal code.

Telephone

Almost all public telephones in Sweden take Telia phonecards. These cards cost Skr35, Skr60 or Skr100 (giving 30, 60 or 120 credits, respectively). Many Telia booths also accept credit cards, but there are virtually no coin phones in public areas (although some hostels, camping grounds and restaurants may have them).

For directory assistance dial ☎ 118118 (for numbers within Sweden) or ☎ 118119 (international), but note that these services aren't free.

For international calls dial ☎ 00 followed by the country code and the local area code. You can also dial your home operator for a collect call with these numbers:

Australia
Telstra (☎ 020 799061)
Optus (☎ 020 799161)

Canada
Canada Direct (☎ 020 799015)

New Zealand
Telecom (☎ 020 799064)

UK
British Telecom (☎ 020 795144)
Cable & Wireless (☎ 020 799044)

USA
AT&T (☎ 020 795611)
MCI (☎ 020 795922)
Sprint (☎ 020 799011)

International telephone calls can be made with the Telia Travel Card: a call to the UK/USA/Australia costs the equivalent of Skr3/4.50/7.50 per minute with a 50-unit card (Skr75, available from Telia shops). You can also buy a wide range of phone cards from tobacconists that give cheap rates for calls abroad. International collect calls cannot be made from payphones.

Calls to Sweden from abroad require the country code (☎ 46) followed by the area code and telephone number (omitting the first zero in the area code).

In addition to the typical yellow pages, Swedish phone books include green (for community services) and blue pages (for regional services). Numbers beginning ☎ 020 or ☎ 0200 are free but not from public phones (they can be called from abroad but are obviously not free then!).

Email & Internet Access

Internet cafés typically charge around Skr1 per online minute or Skr50 per hour. However, facilities to log on can be frustratingly rare outside big cities, largely due to the fact that most Swedes have Internet access at home. Many Internet cafés, where they do exist, are more amusement arcades than traveller hangouts, full of young guys playing advanced computer games.

Many tourist offices now offer a computer terminal for visitor use (sometimes for free). Nearly all public libraries offer free Internet access, but often the half-hour or hour slots are fully booked for days in advance by locals, and email facilities may occasionally be blocked.

DIGITAL RESOURCES

Most Swedish organisations have their own websites, and many of these have pages in English. Every town also has its own site – usually this is found by simply entering www., then the town's name, followed by .se, eg W www.vasteras.se.

The official website of the **Swedish Travel and Tourism Council** (W www.visit-sweden.com) contains loads of useful travel information in many languages. **Svenska Institutet** (W www.si.se), the Swedish Institute, is a public agency entrusted with disseminating knowledge abroad about Sweden, and its site is full of detailed information on countless topics. It maintains the **Virtual Sweden**

(W www.sweden.se) site, the 'official gateway to Sweden' with excellent links in various categories (including Culture, Nature & Environment and Sports & Leisure).

The **Swedish Tourism Trade Association** (W www.sverigeturism.se) maintains a huge site; its 'Smorgasbord' pages are rich in information. **CityGuide Sweden** (W www.cityguide.se) has detailed information pages for some 85 Swedish cities.

Other sites that may be useful for travellers include those of **Gula Sidorna** (W www.gulasidorna.se), the online version of Sweden's yellow pages directory; **Naturvårdsverket** (W www.environ.se), the Swedish environmental protection agency, which has good coverage of the country's national parks; and **Svenska Turistföreningen** (W www.meravsverige.se), or STF (the Swedish touring agency), which maintains an extensive network of over 300 excellent hostels throughout the country – details for all of them can be found on the website.

BOOKS

Lonely Planet's *Sweden* is the best guidebook for travellers, but bring your copy from abroad – books are expensive in Sweden. Lonely Planet also produces a city guide to Stockholm.

There's a good range of general books, with emphasis on the arts and literature, at the Sweden Bookshop in Stockholm (inside Sweden House, also home to the main tourist office). To get a handle on the country, try *A History of Sweden* by Lars O Lagerqvist or *A Journey Through Swedish History* by Herman Lindqvist. *Swedish Mentality* by Åke Daun will help you understand the Swedes themselves. Sam Erik's *Favorite Swedish Recipes* gives an insight into local cuisine. *True North: The Grand Landscapes of Sweden*, with text by Per Wästberg and Tommy Hammarström and pictures by some of Sweden's top nature photographers, contains some stunning images.

The arts are covered in *Great Royal Palaces of Sweden* by Göran Alm; *Creating the Look: Swedish Style* by Katrin Cargill; *Swedish Folk Art* by Barbro Klein; *The Decorative Arts of Sweden* by Iona Plath; and *The Frozen Image: Scandinavian Photography* by Martin Friedman. A good light fiction work is Selma Lagerlöf's *The Wonderful Adventures of Nils*.

NEWSPAPERS & MAGAZINES

Pressbyrån, usually at train stations in towns and cities, sells international news magazines and you can usually find copies of the *International Herald-Tribune*, the *Guardian in Europe* and the London dailies. A good, free option is to visit the local libraries in Sweden, which often have a reading area stocked with up-to-date newspapers from around the world.

RADIO & TV

National radio stations are on FM frequencies throughout the country, and stations play a wide range of international music, from pop to classical. **Radio Sweden International** (Ⓦ *www.radiosweden.org)*, the overseas network, broadcasts programmes nationally on 1179kHz (FM 89.6 in Stockholm), to Europe on 1179kHz, as well as to North America and Asia/Australia under various other frequencies (check the website for these).

Sweden has half a dozen TV channels (some on cable networks only) and satellites bring more English programmes within reach. Subtitled English films and series are common.

PHOTOGRAPHY & VIDEO

Film is expensive in Sweden. You can sort through bargain bins at photo stores for 24-exposure rolls for under Skr30, but generally you should expect to pay around Skr50/65 for a 24/36-exposure film. Fuji Velvia 36-exposure slide film costs Skr110. Prices for print processing vary widely, but it usually costs around Skr100/130 for 24/36-exposure film over three days, and is more expensive if you want one-hour processing. Slide processing costs around Skr40 for 36 exposures, excluding the mounts. You'll pay Skr50 for a 90-minute video film (Sony 8mm).

Don't risk photographing the military unless they are on public parade. Photography is forbidden in certain restricted (military) areas, particularly on the Baltic coast.

TIME

Sweden is one hour ahead of GMT/UTC, but summer time (from the end of March to the end of October) is another hour ahead. Otherwise, at noon in Sweden, it's also noon in Oslo, Copenhagen and Berlin but 6am in New York and Toronto, 11am in London, 3am in San Francisco, 1pm in Helsinki, 9pm in Sydney and 11pm in Auckland. The 24-hour clock is used.

WEIGHTS & MEASURES

Sweden uses the metric system. Some shops quote prices followed by '/hg', which means per 100g. Decimals are separated from whole numbers by a comma and thousands are indicated by points.

Don't be tricked by the Swedish word *mil*, which Swedes will often translate into English as 'mile'. The Swedish *mil* equals 10km.

LAUNDRY

The coin-operated laundrette is virtually nonexistent in Sweden. A *snabbtvätt* (quick wash), where you leave clothes for laundering, isn't available everywhere, may actually take several days and tends to be extremely expensive (up to Skr200). Most hotels offer a laundry service (also expensive). Thankfully, many hostels and camping grounds have laundry facilities costing around Skr50 for wash and dry. It's also a good idea to carry soap powder or a bar of clothes soap for doing your own laundry in basins.

TOILETS

Public toilets in parks, museums, shopping malls, libraries, and bus or train stations are rarely free in Sweden. Some churches and most tourist offices have free toilets. Except at larger train stations (where an attendant is on duty), pay toilets are coin operated, and usually cost Skr5.

HEALTH

No vaccinations are required for travellers. There's no general practitioner service in Sweden but *apotek* (pharmacies) sell nonprescription (and prescription) medicines as well as give advice on how to deal with everyday ailments and conditions. Nattapotek are open 24 hours and are found in major cities.

For emergencies and casualty services, go to a *vårdcentral* (local medical centre), or a *sjukhus* or *lasarett* (hospital). There are centres in all districts and main towns, listed by area under *kommun* (municipality) in the local telephone directory. EU citizens with an E111 form are charged around Skr120 to consult a doctor and up to Skr300 for a visit to casualty. Hospital stays cost Skr90 per day. Non-EU citizens should have adequate travel insurance or be prepared to face high costs, although some countries (eg, Australia) have reciprocal health-care agreements with Sweden.

Tandläkare (dentists) charge around Skr700 for an hour's treatment.

The general emergency number, including ambulance, is ☎ 112.

Visitors are attacked by mosquitoes until late July. These annoying creatures are worst in the northern lowlands near water, marshes and in some forests. Take a powerful repellent (eg, 100% DEET) with you since some preparations are banned from sale in Sweden, or ask a pharmacist for advice.

Winter travellers should note that there are long cold periods. If you're out of doors in the far north or during winter, exposure is a threat best avoided by common sense.

WOMEN TRAVELLERS

Sexual equality is very well emphasised in Sweden and there should be no question of discrimination. Solo female travellers are unlikely to face the sort of harassment received in parts of southern Europe. Some hostels have segregated dorms, and you can ask for a women-only compartment if you don't want male company in a 2nd-class rail sleeping section. Some Stockholm taxi firms offer discounts for women at night.

GAY & LESBIAN TRAVELLERS

Sweden is famous for its liberal attitudes and there are laws allowing same-sex 'registered partnerships', which grant most marriage rights. The organisation concerned with equality for lesbians and gays is **Riksförbundet för Sexuellt Likaberättigande** *(RFSL;* ☎ *08-736 0213;* W *www.rfsl.se; Sveavägen 59, Stockholm).* The website is mostly in Swedish.

One of the capital's biggest parties is the annual **Stockholm Pride** (W *www.stockholmp ride.org),* a five-day festival celebrating gay culture, held in late July-early August.

A good source of information is the free, monthly magazine *QX,* giving gay and lesbian information and listings (again, only in Swedish).

You can pick it up at many clubs, stores and restaurants, mainly in Stockholm, Göteborg, Malmö and Copenhagen. Its website (W www.qx.se) has some excellent information and recommendations in English.

DISABLED TRAVELLERS

Sweden is perhaps one of the easiest countries to travel around in a wheelchair. For information about facilities, contact the national

Emergency

In Sweden, dial ☎ 112 to be in contact with police, ambulance and fire services.

organisation for people with disabilities, **De Handikappades Riksförbund** *(*☎ *08-685 8000;* W *www.dhr.se; Katrinebergsvägen 6, Box 47305, SE-10074 Stockholm).*

People with disabilities will find special transport services and adapted facilities of a generally high standard, ranging from trains and taxis to hotels and grocery stores.

TRAVEL WITH CHILDREN

Swedes treat children very well, and domestic tourism is largely organised around children's interests: many museums have a children's section, and there are public parks for kids, plus theme parks, water parks and so on. Long-distance ferries and trains, hotels and even some restaurants may have play areas for children. Summer is very much a time for family vacations and in some areas cabins and camping grounds may be fully booked at this time.

DANGERS & ANNOYANCES

Sweden is a safe country, but crimes perpetrated against travellers (such as pickpocketing) do occur and are on the increase; take particular care in museums and transport terminals in Stockholm. Drug-related crime and a few trouble spots in big cities are also of some concern.

See also the Health section earlier and Car & Motorcycle under Getting Around later in this chapter.

BUSINESS HOURS

Businesses and government offices are open 8.30am or 9am to 5pm Monday to Friday, although they can close at 3pm in summer. Banks usually open at 9.30am and close at 3pm, but some city branches open 9am to 5pm or 6pm.

Most museums have short opening hours and many tourist offices are closed at weekends from mid-August to mid-June.

Normal shopping hours are 9am to 6pm Monday to Friday and 9am to between 1pm and 4pm on Saturday, but department stores are open longer and sometimes also on Sunday. Some supermarkets in large towns will open until 7pm or 9pm. In restaurants, lunch often begins at 11.30am and is over by 2pm. Stockholm has convenience stores like 7-Eleven that are open 24 hours.

Frustratingly, many hostels, especially those belonging to the STF network, are closed between 10am and 5pm. See Hostels under Accommodation later in this chapter for information.

PUBLIC HOLIDAYS & SPECIAL EVENTS

There's a concentration of public holidays in spring and early summer. The Midsummer public holiday brings life almost to a halt for three days.

Transport and other services are reduced, so read your timetables carefully and plan ahead: some food stores are open and many tourist offices (usually with reduced hours), but not all attractions. Some hotels are closed from Christmas to New Year and it's not uncommon for restaurants in larger cities to close during July and early August (when their owners join the holidaying throngs in beachside or lakeside areas). Note: some businesses will close early the day before a public holiday and all day the day after.

Public holidays are:

New Year's Day 1 January
Epiphany 6 January
Good Friday to Easter Monday March/April
Labour Day 1 May
Ascension Day May/June
Whit Monday late May or early June
Midsummer's Day first Saturday after 21 June
All Saints' Day Saturday, late October or early November
Christmas Day 25 December
Boxing Day 26 December

Christmas Eve, New Year's Eve and Midsummer's Eve are not official holidays, but are generally non-working days for most of the population.

Special events celebrated in Sweden include:

April
Walpurgis Night (30 April) Valborgsmässoafton is popular with students, who are easy to spot in Uppsala and Lund

May
May Day (1 May) This is observed by marches and other labour movement events which stop the traffic

June
Flag Day (6 June) The national day, but, surprisingly, it's not a public holiday
Midsummer's Day (first Saturday after 21 June) This is the festival of the year. Maypole dancing is a traditional activity on Midsummer's Eve and most people head for the countryside. For the folk touch, Dalarna is a good place to celebrate, but music, dancing and drinking are normal no matter where you are, so enjoy it – not much will be open.

December
Lucia Festival (13 December) Since 1927, the Lucia festival has become very popular. Oddly, it seems to merge the folk tradition of the longest night and the story of St Lucia of Syracuse. A choir in white, led by Lucia (who wears a crown of candles), leads the singing, and glögg (hot alcoholic punch) is drunk.
Christmas Eve (24 December) This is the main day of celebration during this season; it's the night of the smörgåsbord and the arrival of jultomten, the Christmas gnome carrying a sack of gifts
New Year's Eve (31 December) This is a fairly big event and it's a busy time for eating and entertainment; some places have midnight fireworks

ACTIVITIES

Outdoor pastimes are popular with Swedes, who are active on bicycles, forest jogging tracks, rivers and lakes, mountain trails and the snow and ice.

Right of Public Access

By law, you're allowed to walk, boat, ski or swim anywhere outside private property (ie, the immediate vicinity of a house and its garden and all fenced areas and cultivated land). You're can camp for more than one night in the same place, and you may pick berries and mushrooms. You may not leave any rubbish nor take living wood, bark, leaves, bushes or nuts. Fires may be set where safe (not on bare rocks) with fallen wood. Use a bucket of water to douse a campfire even if you think that it's out. Cars may not be driven across open land or on private roads. Close all gates. Do not disturb reindeer.

If you have a bicycle, look for free camp sites around unsealed forest tracks off the secondary country roads. Make sure your spot is at least 50m from the track and not visible from any house, building or a sealed road. Dry pine forests are your best bet. Bring drinking water and food, although running creek water can normally be used for washing (don't pollute the water with soap or waste food).

Skating

Wherever the ice is thick enough (usually between December and March), Stockholm's lake and canal system is exploited by skating enthusiasts seeking the longest possible 'run'. In Stockholm you can hire cheap skates, but if conditions aren't good, go and join a wild crowd of ice-hockey spectators instead.

Skiing

Cross-country (nordic) skiing opportunities vary depending on the snow and temperatures, but the northwest usually has plenty of snow from December to April (although not a lot of daylight in December and January). Practically all town areas (except the far south) have marked skiing tracks, often illuminated. There are large ski resorts catering mainly for downhill skiing in the mountainous areas of the west – Åre is the biggest. The websites W www .goski.com and W www.thealps.com have good pages reviewing the Swedish ski fields.

Hiking

Hiking is popular everywhere and the mountain challenge of the northern national parks is compelling. However, these parks are rarely snow-free and the jewel, Sarek, is only for experienced hikers. Good equipment is vital.

Easy walking trails are common. Many counties have a network of easy trails connecting sites of interest, and many *kommuner* have their own wilderness tracks (some off-the-beaten-track routes have free huts or shelters). The best hiking time is between late June and mid-September, but conditions are better after early August, when the mosquitoes have gone.

For information on organised group walks and the STF mountain huts, which are placed at intervals averaging about 20km along popular trails like Kungsleden, contact STF (see Accommodation later in this chapter). You may stay the night (or camp nearby) for a fee which is slightly higher than STF hostel rates. There are also nine STF lodges with shops, showers and restaurants. The free STF hostel guide *STF Vandrarhem och Fjäll* includes details of mountain huts and lodges. Conditions are self-service, similar to STF hostels, and you should bring sheets (sleeping bags in huts).

Canoeing & Kayaking

Sweden's superb wilderness lakes and white-water rivers are a real paradise for canoeists and kayakers. The national canoeing body is Svenska Kanotförbundet (☎ 08-605 6000; W www.kanot.com; Idrottens Hus, SE-12387 Farsta). It provides general advice and produces *Kanotvåg*, an annual brochure listing the 75 approved canoe centres that hire canoes (from Skr140/500 per day/week) throughout the country. According to the right of common access, canoeists may paddle or moor virtually anywhere provided they respect the basic privacy of dwellings and avoid sensitive nesting areas within nature reserves. More good information is available at W www.kanotguiden.com.

Fishing

There are national and local fishing restrictions relating to many of the inland waters, especially concerning salmon, trout and eel; check with tourist offices or local councils before dropping a line. You generally need a permit, but free fishing is allowed on parts of Vänern, Vättern, Hjälmaren and Storsjön Lakes and most of the coastline. Local permits (for *kommun* waters) can be bought from tourist offices and sports or camping shops and typically cost Skr50/280 per day/week. Good general fishing information is available at W www.top10fishing.se.

Boating & Sailing

Lake and canal routes offer pleasant sailing in spring and summer (canals are usually only open for limited seasons), but lock fees can be high. Some simpler harbours are free, but ones with good facilities average Skr100 per night. The *skärgård* (archipelago) areas, particularly around Stockholm, are a different and rather demanding setting for sailing or motor boats. A useful guide is the free *Gästhamnsguiden*, published by Svenska Kryssarklubben (Swedish Cruising Club), with details of some 500 guest harbours and facilities, prices, services etc. It's available from larger tourist offices and most of the guest harbours listed. Charts are available from **Kartcentrum** (☎ 08-411 1697; Vasagatan 16, SE-10126 Stockholm).

Other Activities

The opportunities for countless other activities exist, including cycling, mountaineering, rock-climbing, golf, horse-riding and rafting in summer, and skating, ice-fishing, ice-climbing, snowmobile safaris and dog sledding in winter. Tourist offices should be able to provide information.

WORK

Non-EU citizens need to apply for a work permit and residence permit (for stays over three months), enclosing confirmation of the job offer, a completed form (available from Swedish diplomatic posts), a passport photo and passport. Processing takes one to three months. EU citizens only need to apply for a residence permit within three months of arrival if they find work, then they can remain in Sweden for the duration of their employment (up to five years). Australians and New Zealanders aged 18 to 30 years can now qualify for a one-year working holiday visa. Full details of all permits and how you can apply are available online at W www.migrationsverket.se (the Swedish migration board's site).

Despite low unemployment (4%), work permits are only granted if there's a shortage of Swedes (or citizens from EU-countries) with certain skills, such as in technical manufacturing areas. Speaking Swedish may be essential for the job. Few organisations are looking for builders or people with social services or care skills, and service work opportunities are minimal. Students enrolled in Sweden can take summer jobs, but such work isn't offered to travelling students.

Helpful information is also available on the Internet at W www.ams.se (from the Swedish National Labour Market Administration website).

ACCOMMODATION
Camping

Sweden has hundreds of camping grounds and a free English-language guide with maps is available. Some camping grounds are open in winter, but the best time for camping is from May to August. Prices vary with facilities, from Skr70 for a basic site to Skr200 for the highest standards. Most camping grounds have kitchens and laundry facilities, but many camping grounds are extremely popular family holiday spots and have the works – swimming pool, minigolf, bike and canoe rental, restaurant, store etc. If you're a solo hiker or cyclist, you should be able to get a cheap site (around Skr80), otherwise you'll pay the full rate.

You must have the free Svenskt Campingkort to stay at Swedish camping grounds. Apply at least one month before your journey to **Sveriges Campingvärdars Riksförbund** (fax 0522-642430; e adm@scr.se; Box 255, SE-45117 Uddevalla). If this isn't possible, you'll be given a temporary card on arrival. The annual stamp on your card costs Skr90 and is obtainable at the first camping ground you visit. Visit W www.camping.se for lots of useful information. See also the Activities section for advice on free camping in Sweden.

Hostels

Sweden has well over 450 *vandrarhem* (hostels) and some 320 are 'official' hostels affiliated with **Svenska Turistföreningen** *(STF;* ☎ *08-463 2100;* e *info@stfturist.se; Box 25, SE-10120 Stockholm)*, part of Hostelling International (HI). STF produces a free detailed guide to its hostels, but the text is unfortunately in Swedish only (although the symbols are generally easy to understand). All hostel details are also found at W www.meravsverige.nu. Holders of HI cards stay at STF hostels for between Skr80 and Skr200. Nonmembers can pay Skr45 extra per night or join up at hostels (membership costs Skr275 for adults, Skr100 for those aged 16 to 25, free for children). In this chapter we have listed the prices at STF hostels for members.

Around 150 hostels belong to the 'rival' **Sveriges Vandrarhem i Förening** *(SVIF;* ☎ *0413 553 450;* e *info@svif.se; Box 9, SE-45043 Smögen)*. No membership is required; rates are similar to those of the STF. Pick up the free guide at tourist offices or SVIF hostels. Also look out for other hostels that are not affiliated with either STF or SVIF.

Hostels in Sweden have a unique problem; they're hard to get into outside reception opening times. Most of the day (and much of the winter) the doors are firmly locked. The secret is to phone and make a reservation during the (usually short) reception hours. These vary, but are generally from 5pm to 7pm. You may have to write down the four-digit entrance door code and ask where the room key will be. Theoretically, you could stay overnight without seeing another person until you pay in the morning. Written reservations are recommended, but cancellation is only accepted up to 6pm the previous day, otherwise you'll be charged for one overnight stay. Breakfast is often available (Skr40 to Skr55), but normally has to be arranged the night before. Always carry sheets and a towel to save some money. Many hostels have kitchens, but very occasionally you need your own utensils.

Outdoor sculpture at Millesgården, Stockholm

Ship ahoy at Stockholm's Vasamuseet

Ales Stenar, near Ystad, is a mysterious ship-shaped stone formation thought to date from 500 BC

You'll have a right royal time exploring the bridges of Stockholm

Skiing is a way of life in Sweden

Raukar limestone formations spice up Fårö sunsets

A little rain won't dampen Midsummer festivities

Solid as a rock: 13th-century walls surround the World Heritage Listed medieval trading town of Visby

Kayaking smooth waters in Dalarna

Country pumpkins in the rolling fields of Skåne

Be careful in December and check that the hostel is really open at Christmas and New Year. From June to August you can expect longer reception hours, but a reservation is recommended because many hostels are full. The principle is that you should clean up after yourself, although some hostels push optional 'cleaning fees' of up to Skr100!

Many mountain huts and lodges are run by STF and also charge overnight fees.

Cabins & Chalets

Daily rates for cabins and chalets at camping grounds offer good value for small groups and families and range in both facilities and price (Skr200 to Skr800). Some cabins are simple, with bunk beds and little else (you share the bathroom and kitchen facilities with campers), others are fully quipped with their own kitchen, bathroom and even living room. Local and regional tourist offices have listings of cabins and cottages that may be rented by the week and are very popular with Swedes in summer.

Hotels

There are few cheap hotels in Sweden. Budget travellers may find weekend and summer (mid-June to mid-August) rates reasonable, often below Skr700 for a luxurious en suite double. Some packages are good value if you plan ahead. Stockholm, Gothenburg and Malmö offer cut-price 'packages' that include a hotel room, free entry to the major attractions of the city and free local transport – plus an optional discounted return train ticket. Tourist offices and travel agents can usually give details.

Sometimes prices are expressed as 'per person in a two-bed room', so be careful. Discount vouchers are generally run by the big chains, eg, Radisson SAS, Scandic, First and Elite. Of particular interest to those on a budget are the two cheapest hotel chains, Formule 1 and Ibis, with flat rates for rooms. Formule 1 hotels are only found in four Swedish cities (Stockholm, Gothenburg, Malmö and Jönköping); small and bland but functional rooms with shared facilities cost under Skr300 and can sleep up to three people.

FOOD

Budget travellers should stuff themselves at breakfast buffets, look for lunch specials and visit supermarkets for self-catering dinners.

Stylish restaurants are numerous and offer a real splurge with dinner and drinks for around Skr200. *Fullständiga rättigheter* means a restaurant is fully licensed.

Husmanskost specials are solid, meat-based, cafeteria-style meals such as meatballs, fried meat and Swedish hash. They usually include potato and are high in cholesterol, but you'll pay as little as Skr45. The *sallad* is usually buffet coleslaw. For a reasonably priced lunch, look for *dagens rätt* (the day's special) which generally includes a main course, bread, salad, coffee and a drink. Lunch usually starts at 11.30am and is over by 2pm, and typically costs Skr50 to Skr65.

Chinese restaurants are less likely to be a cheap option in Sweden, but Middle Eastern fare including kebabs, felafel and pizzas are OK budget alternatives – many places offer this sort of fast food from Skr30. *Konditori* are old-fashioned bakery-cafés where you can get a pastry or a *smörgås* (sandwich) from Skr25, but there are also many modern, stylish cafés where you can do some good people-watching over pricier Italian coffees, gourmet salads and filled bagels and ciabattas. Pure vegetarian restaurants do exist but are not common; there will usually be at least one vegetarian main-course option on restaurant menus. Due to the strict licensing laws, most pubs and bars in Sweden serve a good range of meals too; chains like Harry's and O'Leary's are popular.

Self-Catering

Making your own meals is easy enough if you are hostelling or staying in camping grounds with good facilities. In supermarkets, both the item price and comparative price per kilogram have to be shown by law. Plastic carry-bags usually cost Skr1 or Skr2 at the checkout. The most prominent supermarket chains are Hemköp, Konsum, ICA and Rimi.

Bröd (bread) costs Skr15 to Skr18 for a loaf and *mjölk* (milk) costs around Skr6.50 per litre. The selection of fresh vegetables and fruit in small supermarkets might seem limited, but tends to be better at produce markets (these are commonly found on a town's main square).

DRINKS

Lättöl (light beers, less than 2.25% alcohol) and *folköl* (folk beers, 2.25% to 3.5% alcohol) account for about two-thirds of all beer sold in Sweden and can be bought in supermarkets.

SWEDEN

Mellanöl (medium-strength beer, 3.5% to 4.5% alcohol), *starköl* (strong beer, over 4.5% alcohol) and wines and spirits can only be bought at outlets of the state-owned alcohol store, **Systembolaget**, open to about 6pm weekdays and only for a few hours on Saturday.

You must be aged 20 or over to make a purchase. Alcohol prices are kept high as a matter of government policy, and the stronger a drink is, the more you'll pay for it. Pressure from the EU may force Sweden to relax its strict alcohol laws, but in the meantime Swedes go over the border to Denmark, the Åland islands or Finland to stock up (you can still buy tax-free products in the Åland islands).

Soft drinks are relatively expensive (Skr12 to Skr15 is the norm for 350mL). Carry a plastic bottle for tap water. Most plastic bottles and aluminium cans can be recycled – supermarket disposal machines give Skr0.50 to Skr1 per item.

ENTERTAINMENT

Discos and nightclubs usually admit no-one aged under 20, although the minimum age limit for men may be 23 and sometimes 25. Drinking at these places is an expensive option. Cover charges range from Skr60 to Skr150 and cloakrooms charge around Skr20. Pubs and restaurants charge around Skr40 to Skr50 for the standard 500mL *storstark* (strong beer), although the cheaper 300mL bottle is common.

Theatre tickets cost from Skr100 to Skr500. Cinema tickets usually cost around Skr60 to Skr70, but may be cheaper early in the week (and there are student and senior discounts). Foreign films are almost always screened in the original language (usually English) with Swedish subtitles.

SHOPPING

There's no shortage of examples of gorgeous Swedish design, especially in Stockholm and the larger cities, but souvenirs, handicrafts or quality Swedish products in glass, wood or pewter are relatively expensive, and some are not terribly easy to cart around or send home. Typically Swedish is the Dalarna painted wooden horse; if you want a good handmade one, go to the workshops in Dalarna (see the Mora section). See also the Glasriket section for glass factory shop details.

Sami handicrafts are usually expensive, look for the 'Duodji' label (a round coloured token of authenticity) on knives, textiles and trinkets, and beware of fakes. Handicrafts carrying the round token 'Svensk slöjd', or the hammer and shuttle emblem, are endorsed by the national handicrafts organisation, Svenska Hemslöjdsföreningarnas Riksförbund, whose symbol is displayed by affiliated handicraft shops.

If you want bargains look for the signs *lågpris, extrapris, rabatt* or *fynd*.

Getting There & Away

AIR

Although you may not find a cheap direct flight to Sweden from outside Europe, there are plenty of European companies that will sell an inexpensive flight to Stockholm via their hub. Note that Copenhagen airport is just 25-odd minutes by train from Malmö in Sweden. Check whether cheaper flights to Copenhagen are available.

Although **SAS** (⒲ *www.scandinavian.net*) is based in Copenhagen, it has plenty of direct international flights to Stockholm. The discount carrier **Ryanair** (⒲ *www.ryanair.com*) flies between London Stansted and Gothenburg, Malmö, and two airports about an hour from Stockholm (Skavsta in Nyköping, and Västerås) from only UK£45 return (plus taxes). **Good Jet** (⒲ *www.goodjet.com*) is a new Swedish budget airline offering cheap flights from Stockholm, Gothenburg and Malmö to Paris, Nice and Alicante.

Stockholm has an interesting flight market, with some inexpensive deals to/from the Asian cities of Delhi, Tokyo, Hong Kong and Bangkok. Sometimes you can be lucky enough to secure cheap last-minute charter flights to distant shores.

LAND

Direct access to Sweden by land is possible from Norway, Finland and Denmark. Train and bus journeys are also possible from the Continent – these vehicles go directly to ferries and if you sleep, you won't even notice the sea journey! Include ferry fares in your budget if you're driving.

The new Öresund toll bridge linking Copenhagen with Malmö was officially opened in July 2000, creating a major direct rail/road link with Denmark.

Eurolines (☎ 020-987377; Ⓦ www.eurol ines.se), the long-distance bus operator, is represented in Stockholm by Busstop in Cityterminalen. Tickets can also be purchased from the head office in Gothenburg (Kyrkogatan 40).

The Continent

Eurolines' bus services run between several European cities, including Stockholm and London (Skr1624/2524 or £95/152 one way/return, 30 hours, one to four a week) via Amsterdam and Hamburg. There are also services from Gothenburg to Berlin (Skr549 one way, 13 to 16 hours, daily) and Stockholm to Berlin (Skr818, 18 to 20 hours, three a week).

Direct overnight trains run between Berlin and Malmö (Skr800/1135 couchette/bed, nine hours, daily) via Trelleborg and Sassnitz. See Ⓦ www.berlin-night-express.com for details.

Denmark

Eurolines runs buses between Stockholm and Copenhagen (Skr433/482 low/high season, nine hours, five a week) and between Gothenburg and Copenhagen (Skr180/260, 4½ hours, daily). **Säfflebussen** (☎ 020 160 0600; Ⓦ www .safflebussen.se) buses also regularly connect the same cities, but are slightly cheaper on the daily Stockholm–Copenhagen route.

Trains run every 20 minutes between Copenhagen and Malmö (Skr70, 35 minutes) and connect with many towns in Skåne. Trains usually stop at Copenhagen airport. X2000 trains run between Copenhagen and Stockholm (10 a day) via Norrköping, Linköping, Lund and Malmö. A further five or six X2000 services operate between Copenhagen and Gothenburg via Halmstad, Helsingborg, Lund and Malmö. There are trains every hour or two connecting Copenhagen, Kristianstad and Karlskrona.

Finland

There are seven crossing points along the river border – see the Finland chapter for details. Bus services from Luleå to Haparanda, Övertorneå and Pajala on the Swedish side are operated by **Länstrafiken i Norrbotten** (☎ 020 470047). **Tapanis Buss** (☎ 0922-12955) runs express coaches from Stockholm to Tornio via Haparanda (Skr450, 15 hours, twice a week).

Train passengers can only reach Boden or Luleå in northern Sweden – from there it's necessary to continue by bus.

Norway

There are more than 20 border crossing points and formalities range from the non-existent to hardly noticeable.

Säfflebussen runs between Stockholm and Oslo (Skr250, 7½ hours, five a day) and between Gothenburg and Oslo (Skr150, four hours, six a day). **Swebus Express** (☎ 0200 218218; Ⓦ www.swebusexpress.se) runs three times daily on the Stockholm–Oslo route and six times daily between Gothenburg and Oslo, charging very similar prices.

Länstrafiken Västerbotten (☎ 020 910019) and **Länstrafiken i Norrbotten** (☎ 020 470047) run buses from Umeå to Mo i Rana (Skr210, 8½ hours, daily) and from Skellefteå to Bodø (Skr400, nine hours, daily). In a number of counties Länstrafiken run buses to within a few kilometres of the Norwegian border.

The main rail links run from Stockholm to Oslo, from Gothenburg to Oslo, from Stockholm to Östersund and Storlien (Norwegian trains continue to Trondheim), and from Luleå to Kiruna and Narvik.

SEA

See the Getting There & Away chapter for contact details of all the international ferry companies listed here.

Denmark

There are numerous ferries between Denmark and Sweden, although all boats between Malmö and Copenhagen ceased in 2002 (the opening of the new bridge saw ferry passenger numbers drop dramatically). The quickest and most frequent services are between Helsingør and Helsingborg (Skr18 to Skr22); passenger cars can do the journey with five passengers for Skr245.

There are also services between Jutland and Sweden. **Stena Line** sails between Gothenburg and Frederikshavn (Skr100 to Skr170, three hours, five to seven a day). Its fast ferry covers the same journey in only two hours (Skr140 to Skr195). Stena Line also sails numerous times daily between Grenå and Varberg (Skr100 to Skr140, four hours).

Bornholm Ferries sails daily from Ystad to Rønne. There are both conventional (2½ hours) and fast (80 minutes) services, two to nine times daily. Passenger fares are from Skr182 to Skr234.

Finland

Daily services throughout the year are available on Stockholm–Turku and Stockholm–Helsinki routes all via the Åland islands. There are inexpensive connections to Åland from Kapellskär and Grisslehamn, both accessible via Norrtälje, north of Stockholm. Further north, there's a connection from Umeå to Vaasa. See the various town sections and the Finland chapter for further details.

Norway

There are plenty of bus and train services between the two countries, but if you get stuck in Strömstad, there are frequent ferries to Sandefjord. See Strömstad for further details.

DFDS Seaways runs daily overnight ferries between Copenhagen and Oslo, via Helsingborg. Fares between Helsingborg and Oslo (14 hours) vary according to the season and day of the week, and range from Skr625 to Skr1025. DFDS Seaways also sails from Gothenburg to Kristiansand (Skr150 to Skr400, seven hours, three per week).

Germany

Trelleborg is the main gateway with more than a dozen ferries arriving daily. **TT-Line** sails between Trelleborg and both Travemünde and Rostock (prices for both from Skr270); **Scandlines** is cheaper and sails to/from Rostock and Sassnitz (Skr70 to Skr195).

Stena Line cruises between Gothenburg and Kiel daily (Skr310/370/610 low/mid/high season, 13½ hours).

Poland

There are daily summer services and less frequent services in winter between Świnoujście and Ystad (Skr450/520 low/high season, nine hours), provided by **Unity Line Polferries**; Gdynia and Karlskrona (Skr335/395 low/high season, 10½ to 12 hours), operated by **Stena Line**; and Gdańsk and Nynäshamn (Skr470/540 low/high season, 19 hours), run by **Polferries**.

Baltic Countries

Tallink sails daily between Sweden and Estonia on two routes: Stockholm-Tallinn (from Skr300, 16 hours) and Kapellskär–Paldiski

(from Skr175, 10 to 11 hours). **V-V Line** connects Paldiski and Västervik a few times a week (tickets are much more expensive than Tallink at Skr1000). V-V Line also connects Nynäshamn and Ventspils in Latvia daily except Monday (Skr800, 10 hours).

Lisco Line sails daily between Klaipėda in Lithuania and Karlshamn (Skr570, 18 hours). **Riga Sea Line** sails between Nynäshamn and Riga in Latvia every second day (Skr672, eight hours).

The UK

DFDS Seaways sails from Gothenburg to Newcastle (Skr550/1175 low/high season, 25 hours, twice a week) via Kristiansand (Norway).

Getting Around

Although Sweden takes time and money to travel through, public transport is well organised using 24 different *länstrafik* (regional networks); heavily subsidised, they offer good bargains. The general confusion of so many operators is partly solved by the Tågplus system, where one ticket is valid on trains and on *länstrafik* buses. Handy local timetables are available free or at nominal cost from tourist offices or the operators. National air and train networks have discount schemes available.

There's a helpful website at W www.tagplus .se, with timetables for all trains, boats and buses in Sweden.

AIR

Sweden's half-dozen domestic airlines mostly use Stockholm Arlanda as a hub. Flying is quite expensive, but substantial discounts are available, such as for Internet bookings, student and youth fares, off-peak travel, return tickets booked at least seven days in advance or low-price tickets for accompanying family members and seniors.

SAS (☎ 020 727000; W www.scandinavian .net) daily domestic flights serve the country from Malmö to Kiruna, but **Skyways** (☎ 020 959500; W www.skyways.se) runs a larger network. **Malmö Aviation** (☎ 020 550010; W www.malmoaviation.se) also flies between major cities.

Flying is quite expensive, but substantial discounts are available, such as return tickets booked at least seven days in advance or low-price tickets for accompanying family members and seniors.

If you're flying into Sweden from abroad with SAS, you can buy Visit Scandinavia Airpass flight coupons (up to a maximum of eight) for around US$65 per flight (see the Getting Around the Region chapter for more details).

BUS

You can travel by bus in Sweden either on national long-distance routes, or using any of the regional *länstrafik* networks.

Regional Traffic

Länstrafik is usually complemented by the regional train system, and one ticket is valid on any bus, local or regional. Rules vary but transfers are usually free within one to four hours. Most counties are divided into zones; travel within one zone will cost from Skr13 to Skr17. Every time you enter a new zone, the price increases, but there's usually a maximum fare.

Timetables explain the various discount schemes. There are good-value daily or weekly passes and many regions have 30-day passes for longer stays. The *värdekort* (value card), which you can 'top up' at any time, is also good: you pay, say, Skr200 for over Skr250 worth of travelling. Always ask how the regional discount pass works: you may have to run the ticket through a machine, press buttons, tell the driver where you want to go, get your ticket stamped or something else.

Express Buses

Swebus Express (☎ 0200 218218; W www .swebusexpress.se) has the largest 'national network' of express buses, but it only serves the southern half of the country (as far north as Mora). Fares for 'long' journeys (over 100km) are 30% cheaper if you travel between Monday and Thursday. **Svenska Buss** (☎ 0771-676767; W www.svenskabuss.se) and cheaper **Säfflebussen** (☎ 020 160 0600; W www.safflebussen.se) also connect many southern towns and cities with Stockholm. North of Gävle, good connections with Stockholm are provided by **Ybuss** (☎ 0200 334444; W www.ybuss.se) from Sundsvall, Östersund and Umeå.

If you're a student or senior, it's worth asking if the bus company will give you a discount – most will only give student prices to holders of Swedish student cards (the exception is Swebus Express, where you can use ISIC

cards). Only Swebus Express doesn't require advance seat reservations – it always guarantees a seat.

TRAIN

Sweden has an extensive railway network and trains are certainly the fastest way to get around, although travellers should be aware that many destinations in the northern half of the country cannot be reached by train alone. There are a few train operators in Sweden, although the national network of **Sveriges Järnväg** (SJ; ☎ 0771-757575; W www.sj.se) covers most main lines, especially in the southern part of the country. Its flag carriers are the X2000 fast trains running at speeds of up to 200km/h, with services from Stockholm to Gothenburg, Malmö, Karlstad, Växjö, Jönköping, Sundsvall and other destinations. **Tågkompaniet** (☎ 020 444111; W www .tagkompaniet.se) operates train services in the far north, and several counties run small regional train networks.

Full-price, 2nd-class tickets are expensive, but there are discounts, especially for booking a week or so in advance. Students (with a Swedish CSN or SFS student card if aged over 26) and people aged under 26 get a 30% discount on the standard adult fare. All SJ ticket prices are reduced in summer, from late June to mid-August. X2000 tickets include a seat reservation. Bicycles can be carried on many *länstrafik* trains without prior advice, unlike on SJ trains (which won't carry them).

In summer, almost 25 different tourist trains offer special rail experiences. The most notable is **Inlandsbanan** (☎ 063-194409; W www.inlandsbanan.se), a 1067km route from Mora to Gällivare and one of the great rail journeys in Scandinavia. Travel on this line is slow (the train travels at a speed of 50km/h) and it takes seven hours from Mora to Östersund (Skr240) and 15 hours from Östersund to Gällivare (Skr485). A special card allows two weeks' unlimited travel on the route for Skr950.

Station luggage lockers usually cost between Skr20 and Skr30 for 24 hours. Check that the station building will be open when you want to collect.

Train Passes

The Sweden Rail Pass, Eurodomino tickets and the international passes InterRail, Eurail and ScanRail are accepted on SJ services and most other operators, such as regional trains (they often cooperate closely with SJ). Exceptions are the local SL *pendeltåg* trains around Stockholm, and Inlandsbanan. The latter only gives ScanRail card-holders a 25% discount on the Skr950, 14-day ticket, but not on individual tickets. Inter Rail pass-holders under 26 can ride the Inlandsbanan for free.

X2000 trains require all rail pass-holders to pay a supplement of Skr50 (including the obligatory seat reservation). The reservation supplements for non-X2000 (ie, InterCity) trains (Skr50) aren't obligatory, and there are no supplements for regional *länstrafik* trains.

Due to restrictions, obtaining rail passes in Sweden isn't entirely convenient, but they can be arranged in advance through **Sweden Booking** (☎ 0498-203380; W *www.swedenbooking .com*) for a Skr115 fee.

For more information, see the Getting Around the Region chapter.

CAR & MOTORCYCLE

Sweden has good roads and the excellent E-class motorways don't usually have traffic jams. There are no public toll roads or bridges in the country. You usually only need a recognised full driving licence, even for car rental. If bringing your own car, you'll need your vehicle registration documents. If your vehicle breaks down, call the **Larmtjänst 24-hour towing service** (☎ 020 910040). Insurance Green Cards are recommended.

Billetautomat (automatic ticket machines) for street parking are common and usually cost from Skr5 to Skr10 per hour during the day, but may well be free in the evening and at the weekend. Cities have multistorey car parks (P-hus) that charge between Skr15 and Skr40 per hour.

In the north, privately owned reindeer and wild elk (moose) are serious road hazards, particularly around dawn and dusk. Report all incidents to police – failure to do so is an offence. Sandboxes on many roads may be helpful in mud or snow. Beware of trams in Gothenburg and Norrköping.

The Swedish national motoring association is **Motormännens Riksförbund** (☎ 020 211111, 08-690 3800; Sveavägen 159, SE-10435 Stockholm).

Road Rules

Basic road rules conform to EU standards. In Sweden, you drive on and give way to the right. Headlights should be dipped, but must be on at all times when driving. Seat belt use is obligatory. The blood-alcohol limit is a stringent 0.02%. The maximum permitted speed on motorways and remote highways is 110km/h. Other speed limits are 50km/h in built-up areas, 70km/h on narrow rural roads and 90km/h on highways. The speed limit for cars towing caravans is 80km/h. Police use hand-held radar equipment to detect speeding and impose on-the-spot fines.

On many highways broken lines define wide-paved edges, and the vehicle being overtaken is expected to move into this area to allow faster traffic to pass safely.

Rental

To rent a car you normally have to be at least 18 (sometimes 25) years of age, need to show a recognised licence (in some cases, an International Driving Permit), and may be required to pay by credit card.

International rental chains are expensive, starting at around Skr600 per day for smaller models. Fly-drive packages can bring some savings, and weekend or summer packages may also be offered at discount rates. All the major firms (eg, Avis, Hertz, Europcar) have desks at Stockholm's Arlanda airport and offices in most major cities. **Mabi Hyrbilar** (☎ 020 110 1000; W *www.mabirent.se*) is a good national company with branches in many major cities and competitive rates. Prices for a small car are Skr170 per day plus Skr1.70 per kilometre, or Skr495 including 300km. For weekly rentals, prices start at Skr2195, including 1500km.

Cars can be hired from petrol stations at better rates, but must be returned to the hiring point. **Statoil** (☎ 020 252525) charges from Skr150 per day plus Skr1.50 per kilometre. **OK-Q8** (☎ 020 850850) has small cars from Skr295 per day, including an allowance of 100km.

BICYCLE

Sweden is a flat country and it's ideal for cycling, with Skåne and Gotland particularly recommended. Cycling is an excellent way to look for points of interest and quiet spots for free camping. The cycling season is May to September in the south, and July and August in the north.

You can cycle on all roads except motorways (green sign, with two lanes and a bridge) and roads for motor vehicles only (green sign with a car symbol). The reasonably quiet and safe secondary roads are good for cycling.

You can take a bicycle on some *länstrafik* trains and most regional buses (free, or up to Skr50), and bikes are transported free on some ferries, including the Vägverket routes. Long-distance buses usually do not accept bicycles, and nor does SJ.

One-gear bike hire is free in some towns, but multi-gear bikes can cost up to Skr200/800 per day/week. If you want to buy one secondhand, try the bicycle workshops in university towns first.

Some country areas, towns and cities have special cycle routes – check with local tourist offices for information and maps. The well-signposted, 6300km-long Sverigeleden is the national route linking points of interest in suitable roads (mostly with an asphalt surface) and bicycle paths.

HITCHING

Hitching isn't popular in Sweden and it's likely that you'll have less luck getting lifts than in other European countries. However, the main highways (E4, E6, E10 and E22) aren't too bad and very long lifts are possible. Note, it's prohibited to hitch on motorways.

BOAT

The national road authority, Vägverket, operates dozens of car ferries, but many are being replaced with bridges. They're part of the road network and are free.

An extensive boat network opens up the attractive Stockholm archipelago and boat services on Lake Mälaren, west of Stockholm, are busy in summer. Gotland is served by regular ferries from Nynäshamn and Oskarshamn and there are summer services to many other small islands off the coast.

Boat passes are valid for 16 days (Skr385) and are available for the Stockholm archipelago. The quaint fishing villages off the west coast can normally be reached by boat with a regional transport pass – inquire in Gothenburg.

The canals provide cross-country routes linking the main lakes. The longest cruises, on the historic Göta Canal from Söderköping (south of Stockholm) to Gothenburg, run from mid-May to mid-September, take at least four days and include the lakes between.

Rederiaktiebolaget Göta Kanal (☎ *031-806315;* W *www.gotacanal.se)* operates three ships over the whole distance at fares of around Skr9500/13,600 a single/double, including full board and guided excursions. There are a number of companies that offer shorter trips on sections of the canal – tourist offices in the area can help.

LOCAL TRANSPORT

In Sweden, local transport is always linked with the regional *länstrafik* – rules and prices for city buses may differ slightly from long-distance transport, but a regional pass is valid both in the city and on the rural routes. There's usually a flat fare of around Skr15 in towns.

Stockholm has an extensive underground metro system, and Gothenburg and Norrköping run good tram networks. Gothenburg also has a city ferry service. Beware of getting ripped off by taxis – don't get in one without agreeing the fare first; in Stockholm, flag fall is around Skr32 then Skr7 per kilometre.

ORGANISED TOURS

There are many small tour companies around the country. The largest tour operator of interest is STF (see Hostels under Accommodation in the Facts for the Visitor section), which has scores of interesting events and tours around the country every season, mostly involving outdoor activities. Contact STF directly for information on these events – its detailed brochure and the website has this information in Swedish only.

Stockholm

☎ 08 • pop 755,000

Stockholm is without doubt one of the most beautiful national capitals in the world, and right now it's an extremely hip destination. Gamla Stan (the Old Town) is particularly lovely, although the city's fringe is industrialised and some suburbs seem to have been inspired by Kafkaesque and Stalinist baroque.

Stockholm is a royal capital that has always been ideally situated for trade and maritime connections. The 24,000 islands of the *skärgård* (archipelago) protect the urban islands from the open seas. Around 1.8 million people live in Greater Stockholm and over 15% of them are immigrants, making for a lively, international atmosphere.

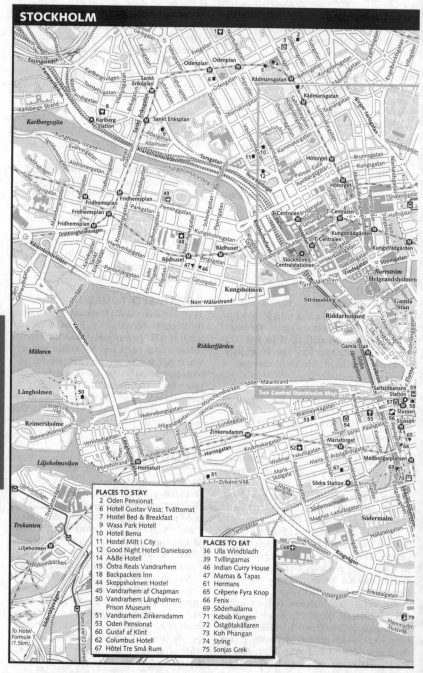

STOCKHOLM

PLACES TO STAY
2 Oden Pensionat
6 Hotell Gustav Vasa; Tvättomat
7 Hostel Bed & Breakfast
9 Wasa Park Hotell
10 Hotell Bema
11 Hostel Mitt i City
12 Good Night Hotell Danielsson
14 A&Be Hotell
15 Östra Reals Vandrarhem
18 Backpackers Inn
44 Skeppsholmen Hostel
50 Vandrarhem af Chapman
50 Vandrarhem Långholmen;
   Prison Museum
51 Vandrarhem Zinkensdamm
53 Oden Pensionat
60 Gustaf af Klint
62 Columbus Hotell
67 Hôtel Tre Små Rum

PLACES TO EAT
36 Ulla Windbladh
39 Tvillingarnas
46 Indian Curry House
47 Mamas & Tapas
61 Hermans
65 Crêperie Fyra Knop
66 Fenix
69 Söderhallarna
71 Kebab Kungen
72 Östgötakällaren
73 Koh Phangan
74 String
75 Sonjas Grek

SWEDEN

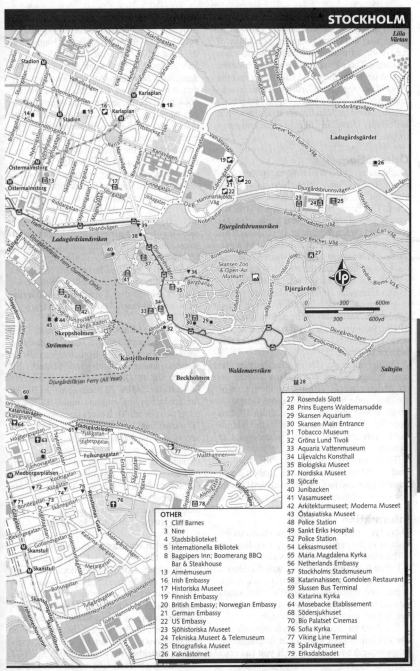

STOCKHOLM

27 Rosendals Slott
28 Prins Eugens Waldemarsudde
29 Skansen Aquarium
30 Skansen Main Entrance
31 Tobacco Museum
32 Gröna Lund Tivoli
33 Aquaria Vattenmuseum
34 Liljevalchs Konsthall
35 Biologiska Museet
37 Nordiska Museet
38 Sjöcafe
40 Junibacken
41 Vasamuseet
42 Arkitekturmuseet; Moderna Museet
43 Östasiatiska Museet
48 Police Station
49 Sankt Eriks Hospital
54 Leksasmuseet
55 Maria Magdalena Kyrka
56 Netherlands Embassy
57 Stockholms Stadsmuseum
58 Katarinahissen; Gondolen Restaurant
59 Slussen Bus Terminal
63 Katarina Kyrka
64 Mosebacke Etablissement
68 Södersjukhuset
70 Bio Palatset Cinemas
76 Sofia Kyrka
77 Viking Line Terminal
78 Spårvägsmuseet
79 Eriksdalsbadet

OTHER
1 Cliff Barnes
3 Nine
4 Stadsbiblioteket
5 Internationella Bibliotek
8 Bagpipers Inn; Boomerang BBQ Bar & Steakhouse
13 Armémuseum
16 Irish Embassy
17 Historiska Museet
19 Finnish Embassy
20 British Embassy; Norwegian Embassy
21 German Embassy
22 US Embassy
23 Sjöhistoriska Museet
24 Tekniska Museet & Telemuseum
25 Etnografiska Museet
26 Kaknästornet

SWEDEN

The city is best seen from the water but you'll also enjoy the parklands of Djurgården or the alleys of Gamla Stan on foot. Many of the 70 or so museums contain world-class treasures. The 10 royal residences include the largest palace in the world still in use, and the World Heritage Listed Drottningholm. Stockholm has the widest selection of budget accommodation in Scandinavia and, although it isn't really cheap, it's mostly clean and comfortable.

Orientation

Stockholm is built on islands, except for Norrmalm, the modern centre. Norrmalm is focused on the ugly square known as Sergels Torg. The large, busy tourist office is in the eastern part of Norrmalm; the popular garden Kungsträdgården is almost next door. This business and shopping hub is linked by a network of subways to Centralstationen (the central train station); and these subways also link with the metro (tunnelbana or T) stations.

The triangular island Stadsholmen and its neighbours accommodate Gamla Stan, separated from Norrmalm by the narrow channels of Norrström near the royal palace, but connected by several bridges. To the west of this is Lake Mälaren.

On the southern side of Stadsholmen the main bridge Centralbron and the Slussen interchange connect with the southern part of the city, Södermalm, and its spine Götgatan. From its top end the giant stadium Globen (looking like a golf ball) is the southern landmark, although you'll cross water again at Skanstull before reaching it.

To the east of Gamla Stan is the small island of Skeppsholmen, and farther down Strandvägen and past the pleasure-boat berths you cross to Djurgården, topped by Skansen.

Information

There are a number of useful publications for visitors to the capital – the best overall guide is the monthly *What's on Stockholm* (available free from tourist offices), which includes sections on shopping, restaurants, activities, events and sightseeing. There are two separate accommodation guides – one for camping, the other for hotels and hostels.

Excellent tourist information is available online in English (and many other languages) at **w** www.stockholmtown.com. If you can read Swedish, try **w** www.alltomstockholm.se.

Tourist Offices The capital's main tourist office is at **Sweden House** (*Sverigehuset;* ☎ 789 2490; **e** info@stoinfo.se; *Hamngatan 27; open 8am-7pm Mon-Fri, 9am-5pm Sat & Sun June-Aug; 9am-6pm Mon-Fri, 10am-3pm Sat & Sun Sept-May*), by Kungsträdgården. It has lots of good brochures and can help book hotel rooms, theatre and concert tickets, and packages such as boat trips to the archipelago. Also in Sweden House is a Forex currency exchange counter and a travel agency specialising in the Finnish province of Åland. Upstairs you'll find the Sweden Bookshop, with information in English about Swedish life and culture provided by the Swedish Institute.

Perhaps more convenient for arriving travellers is the busy **Hotellcentralen** (☎ 789 2490; *Centralstationen; open 9am-6pm daily mid-August–mid-June; 8am-8pm daily mid-June–mid-Aug*), inside the main train station. In addition to tourist information, they will reserve hotel rooms and hostel beds (for a fee), plus sell the Stockholm Package, Stockholm Card or SL Tourist Card, book sightseeing tours and sell maps, books and souvenirs.

Stockholm Card The Stockholm Card covers all transport and most sightseeing needs – it's available from tourist offices, some camping grounds and hostels, SL centers and the larger museums at Skr220/380/540 for 24/48/ 72 hours (Skr60/120/180 for accompanying children under 18, maximum two per adult). It gives free entry to over 70 attractions, free city parking, free sightseeing by boat and free travel on public transport (including the Katarinahissen lift, but excluding local ferries, some city buses and airport buses). To get maximum value, use two 24-hour cards over three days (with a rest day in between) but take care to note opening hours; Skansen remains open until late, whereas royal palaces are only open until 3pm or 4pm.

Stockholm Package This cut-price package, called Stockholm à la Carte, basically includes a hotel room and the Stockholm Card and is available weekends year-round and also throughout the summer (mid-June to mid-August). It costs from Skr450 per person, depending on the standard of accommodation (prices for central hotels start at around Skr600). For details, contact **Destination Stockholm** (☎ 663 0080, fax 664 1807; **w** www.destination-stockholm.com).

The website lists the 50-odd hotels involved in the scheme.

Money The exchange company **Forex** *(Arlanda airport • Centralstationen; open 7am-9pm daily • Vasagatan 14 • Sweden House; Hamngatan 27)* has about a dozen branches in the capital; at all of them the charge is Skr15 per travellers cheque.

There are ATMs all over town, including a few at Centralstationen, usually with long queues. There are banks around Sergels Torg and along Hamngatan.

Post & Communications The longest hours are offered by the busy **post office** *(open 7am-10pm Mon-Fri, 10am-7pm Sat & Sun)* in the Centralstationen. You can now send letters from a number of city locations, including newsagents and some supermarkets – keep an eye out for the Swedish postal symbol (yellow on a blue background) to indicate that postal services are offered at that location.

Email & Internet Access Café **Access IT** *(Sergels Torg; open Tues-Sun)*, downstairs in Kulturhuset, is a central Internet café where 30 minutes online costs Skr20. On the northern side of town, **Nine** *(Odengatan 44; open until midnight daily)* charges roughly Skr45 per hour – and there's a good café here too. **Ice** *(Vasagatan 42)*, close to Centralstationen and also open until midnight, charges Skr30/50 for 30/60 minutes online.

At the main city library, **Stadsbiblioteket** *(Sveavägen 73)*, free 'drop-in' computers are available 10am to 7pm daily (maximum 15 minutes online; email is accessible). The nearby **Internationella Bibliotek** *(Odengatan 59)* has drop-in spots available for 30 minutes (free) or you can book a one-hour slot (Skr15).

Travel Agencies STA *(☎ 545 26666; Kungsgatan 30)* and the nearby **Kilroy Travels** *(☎ 0771-545769; Kungsgatan 4)* both specialise in discount youth and student flights.

STF *(☎ 020 292929)* doesn't have a drop-in sales office, but you can make telephone bookings for tour packages.

Bookshops The **Sweden Bookshop** *(Sweden House; Hamngatan 27)* has the broadest selection of thematic books in English. For English-language newspapers and paperbacks go to **Pressbyrån** *(Centralstationen)*. For international and special interest magazines, try **Press Stop** at a few locations around town, including Drottninggatan 35. For guidebooks and maps, go to **Kartcentrum** *(Vasagatan 16)*, opposite Centralstationen. **Akademibokhandeln** *(Mäster Samuelsgatan 32)* is a good general bookshop.

Libraries **Kulturhuset** *(Sergels Torg)* has a reading room with international periodicals and newspapers as well as books in various languages. The main city library, **Stadsbiblioteket** *(Sveavägen 73)* is just north of the city centre. Opening hours vary.

Laundry Laundry options are limited and it's best to find a hotel or hostel with facilities or a fast washing service. A handy laundrette near the metro station T-Odenplan is **Tvättomat** *(Västmannagatan 61; open 8.30am-6.30pm Mon-Fri, 9am-3pm Sat)*. It costs Skr67 per machine load to wash and dry if you do it yourself. Last orders are accepted two hours before closing.

Left Luggage Three sizes of left luggage boxes at Centralstationen cost Skr20, Skr30 and Skr70 for 24 hours. Similar facilities exist at the neighbouring bus station and major ferry terminals.

Emergency & Medical Services The toll-free **emergency number** for the fire brigade, police and ambulance is ☎ 112. There's a 24-hour medical advice hotline you can reach on ☎ 644 9200. **CW Scheele** *(☎ 454 8130; Klarabergsgatan 64)* is a central 24-hour pharmacy.

In the suburbs, seek the nearest *vårdcentral* medical centre listed in the blue pages of the telephone directory.

The hospital **Södersjukhuset** *(☎ 616 1000)*, in Södermalm, handles casualties from the central city area.

Emergency dental treatment is available at **Sankt Eriks Hospital** *(Fleming-gatan 22)*. Call ☎ 654 1117 between 8am and 9pm, or contact the **duty dentist** *(☎ 463 9100)* for advice after 9pm.

The there are two 24-hour **police stations** *(☎ 401 0100; Torkel Knutssonsgatan 20, Södermalm • ☎ 401 0200; Kungsholmsgatan 37, Kungsholmen)*.

SWEDEN

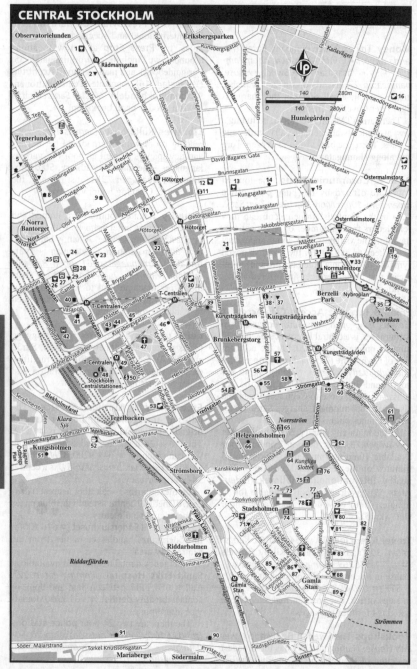

CENTRAL STOCKHOLM

CENTRAL STOCKHOLM

PLACES TO STAY
6 Pensionat Oden
8 City Backpackers
9 Queen's Hotel
40 Nordic Hotel Light
41 Nordic Hotel Sea;
   Ice Bar
90 Mälaren Den Röda Båten
91 M/S Rygerfjord

PLACES TO EAT
2 Souperb
4 Sabai Sabai
5 Carinas Pizzeria
7 Spice House
10 Kungshallen
15 Sturehof
18 Östermalms Saluhall;
   Örtagården
20 Sturekatten
22 Hötorgshallen;
   Filmstaden Sergel
23 Vetekatten
24 Kebab House
29 Waynes Coffee
31 Birger Jarlspassagen Cafes
33 Riche
37 Friday's American Bar & Café
44 Systembolaget
45 Hemköp
58 Operakällaren; Café Opera;
   Bakfickan
71 Hermitage
80 Pontus in the Greenhouse
81 Grill Ruby; Bistro Ruby
82 Gamla Stans Bryggeri

85 Källare Restaurang Movitz
86 Café Art
87 Michelangelo
88 Den Gyldene Freden
89 Zum Franziskaner

OTHER
1 Tip Top; RFSL
3 Strindbergsmuseet
11 STA Travel
12 Glenn Miller Café
13 The Loft
14 Kilroy Travels
16 French Embassy
17 New Zealand Embassy
19 Musikmuseet
21 Akademibokhandeln
25 Vasateatern
26 Jazzclub Fasching
27 Oscars Teatern
28 Ice Internet Cafe
30 Australian Embassy
32 Dubliner
34 Hallwyl Collection
35 Stockholm Sightseeing;
   Djurgården Boats
36 Strömma Kanalbolaget Boats
38 Sweden House;
   Sweden Bookshop; Forex
39 Kulturhuset;
   Access IT
42 Cityterminalen (Bus Station,
   Airport Buses)
43 CW Scheele Pharmacy
46 Press Stop
47 Klara Kyrka

48 Hotellcentralen; Forex;
   Post Office; Pressbyrån
49 Kartcentrum
50 Forex
51 Stadshuset
52 Lake Mälaren Boats
53 Canadian Embassy
54 Medelhavsmuseet
55 City Sightseeing
   (Tour Departures)
56 Danish Embassy
57 Sankt Jakobs Kyrka
59 Stockholm Sightseeing Office
60 Waxholmsbolaget Office &
   Ferry Terminal
61 National Museum
62 Svea Viking Boat
63 Gustav IIIs Antikmuseum
64 Museum Tre Kronor
65 Medeltidsmuseet
66 Riksdagen
67 Riddarhuset
68 Riddarholmskyrkan
69 Stargayte
70 Wirströms Irish Pub
72 State Apartments
73 Storkyrkan
74 Nobelmuseet
75 Skattkammaren &
   Royal Chapel
76 Livrustkammaren
77 Kungliga Myntkabinettet
78 Finska Kyrkan
79 Mandus
83 Ice Gallery
84 Tyska Kyrkan

Things to See

Almost all of the roughly 70 museums and other major attractions in and around Stockholm can be visited free with the Stockholm Card. Most are open daily in summer, but are closed Monday the rest of the year. Children under 16 are generally admitted for half-price and small children can enter free if accompanied by a paying adult.

A useful website for pre-trip research is w www.stockholmsmuseer.com; this site is in Swedish but has links to all museum homepages (and most of these have information in English).

Gamla Stan The oldest part of Stockholm is also its most attractive, containing old houses, vaulted cellar restaurants and the royal palace. Allow a day to explore Gamla Stan; include touristy Västerlånggatan, but don't miss the parallel alleys or quiet squares.

The city emerged here in the 13th century and adopted the trade and, partly, the accents of its German Hanseatic guests. It grew with Sweden's power until the 17th century, when the castle of Tre Kronor, symbol of that power, burned to the ground.

The 'new' royal palace **Kungliga Slottet** (☎ 402 6130; Slottsbacken; adult/child per attraction Skr70/35, combined ticket Skr110/65; most attractions open 10am-4pm daily mid-May–Aug, noon-3pm Tues-Sun Sept–mid-May) is built on the ruins of Tre Kronor and is a highlight. Its 608 rooms make it the largest royal palace in the world. Many visitors find the **State Apartments** the most interesting, with two floors of royal pomp and portraits of pale princes. Crowns are displayed at the **Skattkammaren** (Royal Treasury), near the **Slottskyrkan** (Royal Chapel). **Gustav III's Antikmuseum** (Gustav III's Museum of Antiquities) displays Mediterranean treasures acquired by the eccentric Gustav III. **Museum Tre Kronor** is in the palace basement and features the foundations and exhibits rescued from the medieval castle during the fire of 1697.

Livrustkammaren *(Royal Armoury; ☎ 5195 5544; Slottsbacken 3; adult/child Skr65/20; open 10am-5pm daily June-Aug, 11am-5pm Tues-Sun Sept-May)* has a large collection of royal memorabilia, including five colourful carriages. **Kungliga Myntkabinettet** *(Royal Coin Cabinet; ☎ 5195 5304; Slottsbacken 6; adult/child Skr45/12; open 10am-4pm Tues-Sun)* is opposite the palace.

Near the palace, **Storkyrkan** *(adult/child Skr20/free; open daily)* is the Royal Cathedral of Sweden. The most notable feature is the 1494 *St George & the Dragon* sculpture. On nearby Stortorget is the excellent new **Nobelmuseet** *(☎ 232506; Börsen Bldg; adult/child Skr50/20; open daily)*, presenting the history of the Nobel Prize and past laureates.

The island of Riddarholmen has some of the oldest buildings in Stockholm, including **Riddarholmskyrkan** *(☎ 402 6130; adult/child Skr20/10; open 10am-4pm daily mid-May–August, noon-3pm Sat & Sun Sept)* is no longer a church – it now houses the royal necropolis. **Riddarhuset** *(House of Nobility; ☎ 723 3990; Riddarhustorget 10; adult/child Skr40/10; open 11.30am-12.30pm Mon-Fri)* displays 2325 coats of arms.

The site of **Medeltidsmuseet** *(☎ 5083 1790; Strömparterren; adult/child Skr40/5; open daily July-Aug, Tues-Sun Sept-June)*, the museum of medieval Stockholm, had been allocated as parking space for members of the nearby **Riksdagshuset** *(Parliament House; ☎ 786 4000; Riksgatan 3A)*, but excavations revealed well-preserved foundations of the medieval town and it's now a museum. The Riksdagshuset has free guided tours in English at 12.30pm and 2pm Monday to Friday from late June to August.

The streets of the eastern half of Gamla Stan still wind along their 14th-century lines and are linked by a medieval fantasy of lanes, arches and stairways. Also worth a look is the lavishly decorated **Tyska kyrkan** (German church).

For something completely different, call in to the **Ice Gallery** *(☎ 790 5500; Österlånggatan 41; adult/child Skr50/25; open 11am-5pm daily)*. Here the gallery is kept at –7°C (warm clothing provided), and there's ice sculptures on show.

Central Stockholm Not many people like central **Sergels Torg** but it's the centre of activity much of the year. **Kulturhuset** has a café, library and an Internet café, and it hosts regular art exhibitions.

Stadshuset *(Town Hall; ☎ 5082 9058; Hantverkargatan; adult/child Skr50/free)* looks like a church, but features the mosaic-lined Gyllene salen, Prins Eugen's own fresco recreation of the lake view from the gallery, and the hall where the annual Nobel Prize banquet is held. Entry is by daily tour only (10am, 11am, noon, 2pm and 3pm from mid-June to mid-August), interrupted from time to time by preparations for special events. Climb the **tower** *(adult/child Skr15/free; open 10am-4pm daily May-Sept)* for a good view of Gamla Stan.

Klara kyrka, near Centralstationen, has information on Stockholm's other churches. Also worth a visit is **Sankt Jakobs kyrka** in Kungsträdgården.

The collections in **Medelhavsmuseet** *(Museum of Mediterranean Antiquities; ☎ 5195 5300; Fredsgatan 2; adult/child Skr50/free; open 11am-8pm Tues, 11am-4pm Wed-Fri, noon-5pm Sat & Sun)*, near Gustav Adolfs Torg, include Egyptian artefacts. The delightful **Hallwyl Collection** *(☎ 5195 5599; Hamngatan 4; adult/child Skr65/30)* is a private palace completed in 1898 and a tour is given in English at 1pm daily from late June to mid-August (1pm Sunday only for the rest of the year); more frequent tours are given in Swedish.

The **National Museum** *(Södra Blasieholmskajen; ☎ 5195 4300; adult/child Skr75/free; open 11am-5pm Tues-Sun)* has the main national collection of painting and sculpture but hosts other exhibitions, including design, so it's worth checking even if mainstream art isn't your thing.

Across the bridge, **Östasiatiska** *(Museet Museum of Far Eastern Antiquities; ☎ 5195 5750; Skeppsholmen; adult/child Skr50/free; open noon-8pm Tues, noon-5pm Wed-Sun)* displays ancient and contemporary ceramics, paintings and sculpture. You'll also find the **Moderna Museum** *(☎ 5195 5200)* and the adjoining **Arkitekturmuseet** *(☎ 5872 7000)*, the modern and architecture museums, although at the time of writing they were closed for repairs. Check with the tourist office for the latest details.

In Vasastaden, north of the centre, the **Vin & Sprithistoriska Museet** *(Wine and Spirits*

Museum; ☎ *744 7070; Dalagatan 100; adult/child Skr40/free; Tues-Sun)* sounds eccentric but might make sense of the weird story behind *brännvin* (snaps) and the birth of the conservative Swedish alcohol policy.

Strindbergsmuseet *(☎ 411 5354; Drottninggatan 85; adult/child Skr40/free; open noon-4pm Tues-Sun)* is in the preserved apartment where August Strindberg (1849–1912) spent his last years. **Musikmuseet** *(Music Museum;* ☎ *5195 5490; Sibyllegatan 2; adult/child Skr40/20; open 11am-4pm Tues-Sun)* is the best presented of the small collections, and you can handle and play some of the musical instruments and see genuine original ABBA paraphernalia from the 1970s.

The **Armémuseum** *(☎ 788 9560; Riddargatan 13; adult/child Skr60/30; open 11am-8pm Tues, 11am-4pm Wed-Sun)* has vivid displays of Swedish military history from the Vikings to the present, with some rather graphic depictions.

The main national historical collection at the **Historiska Museet** *(History Museum;* ☎ *5195 5600; Narvavägen 13; adult/child Skr60/free; open 11am-5pm daily June-Aug, 11am-5pm Tues-Sun Sept-May)* covers prehistoric, Viking and medieval archaeology and culture. Don't miss the incredible Gold Room with its rare treasures, including a seven-ringed gold collar.

Djurgården Djurgården is a 'must see' for visitors to Stockholm. **Skansen** *(☎ 442 8000; adult Skr30-60, child Skr20-30; park open 10am-8pm May, 10am-10pm June-Aug, 10am-5pm Sept, 10am-4pm Oct-Apr)* was the world's first open-air museum (it opened in 1891); over 150 traditional houses and other exhibits from all over Sweden occupy this attractive hill top. You could spend all day here, wandering between the zoo, the handicraft precinct, the open-air museum or the daily activities happening on Skansen's stages, including folk-dancing in summer. Trace the unhealthy history of smoking at the **Tobacco Museum** or visit the **aquarium** *(adult/child Skr60/30)* – en route to the fish you walk amongst the lemurs and see the smallest monkeys in the world.

Nordiska Museet *(☎ 5195 6000; Djurgårdordsvägen 6-16; adult/child Skr60/free; open 10am-5pm daily late June-Aug, 10am-5pm Tues-Sun Sept-May)* is housed in an enormous Renaissance-style castle, with notable temporary exhibitions and vast Swedish collections.

The award-winning **Vasamuseet** *(☎ 5195 4800; adult/child Skr70/10; open 9.30am-7pm daily June-Aug, 10am-5pm daily Sept-May)*, behind Nordiska Museet and on the western shore of Djurgården, allows you simultaneously to look into the lives of 17th-century sailors and appreciate a brilliant achievement in marine archaeology. The flagship *Wasa* sank within minutes of being launched in 1628 and tour guides will explain the extraordinary and controversial 300-year story of its death and resurrection. At the moorings behind the museum are the icebreaker *Sankt Erik* and the lightship *Finngrundet*.

Nearby, **Junibacken** *(☎ 5872 3000; adult/child Skr95/70; open 10am-5pm daily June-Aug, 10am-5pm Tues-Sun Sept-May)* re-creates the scenes of Astrid Lindgren's children's books, which might stir the imaginations of children and the memories of adults familiar with her characters. Minor museums around Djurgården include the **Biologiska Museet** (Museum of Biology), **Liljevalchs Konsthall** (an art gallery) and the **Aquaria Vattenmuseum** (yet another aquarium).

The crowded **Gröna Lund Tivoli** *(☎ 5875 0100; admission Skr50; open May–mid-Sept; noon-11pm most days mid-June–mid-Aug)* is a fun park with dozens of amusements – the Åkbandet day pass (Skr220) gives unlimited rides; individual rides range from Skr10 to Skr40.

Beyond Djurgården's large tourist traps are plenty of little gems. **Prins Eugens Waldemarsudde** *(☎ 5458 3700; Prins Eugens Väg 6; adult/child Skr70/free; open 11am-5pm Tues-Sun)* was the private palace of a painter-prince who preferred art to royal pleasures. The art galleries, buildings and the old windmill are surrounded by picturesque gardens. Farther north, **Rosendals Slott** *(☎ 402 6130; Rosendalsvägen adult/child Skr50/25)* was used by Karl XIV Johan in the 1820s, and guided tours run hourly between noon and 3pm Tuesday to Sunday from June to August. At the eastern end of Djurgården is **Thielska Galleriet** *(☎ 662 5884; Sjötullsbacken; adult/child Skr50/30; open noon-4pm Mon-Sat, 1pm-4pm Sun)* with a notable collection of Nordic art.

To get to Djurgården, take bus No 47 from Centralstationen or the Djurgården ferry services from Nybroplan or Slussen (frequent in

SWEDEN

summer). By the bridge you can rent bikes (see Getting Around later), and this is by far the best way to explore the area.

Ladugårdsgärdet North of Djurgården, in among the vast parkland, are more fine museums and attractions.

Sjöhistoriska Museet (☎ 5195 4900; Djurgårdsbrunnsvägen 24; adult/child Skr50/20; open 10am-5pm daily) exhibits maritime memorabilia. **Tekniska Museet** (☎ 450 5600; Museivägen 7; open 10am-5pm Mon-Fri, 11am-5pm Sat & Sun) contains exhaustive exhibits on Swedish inventions and their applications, and includes the **Telemuseum** (☎ 670 8100; Museivägen 7; combined entry adult/child Skr60/20; open 10am-5pm Mon-Fri, 11am-5pm Sat & Sun), which covers everything you ever wanted to know about telecommunications and LM Ericsson. **Etnografiska Museet** (☎ 5195 5000; Djurgårdsbrunnsvägen 34; adult/child Skr50/free; open 11am-5pm Tues-Sun) brings the entire world under one roof.

Nearby is the 155m TV tower, **Kaknästornet**, the tallest building in town. There's an **observation deck** (☎ 667 2180; adult/child Skr25/15; open 9am-10pm daily May-Aug, 10am-9pm daily Sept-Apr) for fine views.

To get to Ladugårdsgärdet, take bus No 69 from Centralstationen.

Northern Suburbs Among the popular attractions is the beautiful **Millesgården** (☎ 446 7594; Carl Milles väg 2, Lidingö; metro T-Ropsten then bus No 207; adult/child Skr75/20; open 10am-5pm daily May-Sept, Tues-Sun & Fri Oct-Apr), an outdoor sculpture collection by Carl Milles.

The extensive **Naturhistoriska Riksmuseet** (☎ 5195 4040; Frescativägen 40; metro T-Universitetet; adult/child Skr65/40; open 10am-7pm daily Apr–mid-Aug, 10am-7pm Tues-Sun mid-Aug–Mar) is the national museum of natural history, and includes the Imax theatre and planetarium **Cosmonova** (☎ 5195 5130; adult/child Skr75/50, combined museum & Cosmonova admission Skr120/80).

The large parks, extending from Djurgården in the south, form **Ekoparken**, a 27-sq-km national city park and the first such protected city area in the world. **Haga Park** is pleasant for walks and bicycle tours with attractions including the royal **Gustav III Pavilion** and the **Butterfly House**. Farther north is

the royal castle **Ulriksdal Slott** (☎ 402 6130; metro T-Bergshamra then bus No 503 or 540; adult/child Skr50/25; open daily mid-June–mid-Aug; guided tours run hourly noon-3pm Tues-Sun June-Aug), with Queen Kristina's coronation carriage and an Orangery housing Swedish sculpture.

Södermalm Mostly residential, Södermalm has more character than other parts of Stockholm. For evening walks, head to the northern cliffs for the old houses and good views. Especially fine neighbourhoods lie around **Katarina kyrka**, in the park near **Sofia kyrka**, around Hornsgatan, and on Lotsgatan and Fjällgatan, near the Viking Line terminal.

There are fine views from **Katarina-hissen** (☎ 743 1395; Slussen; open 7.30am-10pm Mon-Sat, 10am-10pm Sun) an old lift which takes you to the heights from Slussen (Skr5/free). At the top is one of the city's best restaurants, **Gondolen** (see Places to Eat).

Stockholms Stadsmuseum (☎ 5083 1600; Slussen; adult/child Skr50/10; open 11am-5pm Tues-Sun Sept-May; 11am-7pm Tues-Sun June-Aug) exhibits the streets and houses of Stockholm and is worthwhile once you've developed some romantic attachment to Stockholm. **Leksasmuseet** (☎ 641 6100; Mariatorget; adult/child Skr45/25; open 10am-4pm Tues-Fri, noon-4pm Sat & Sun; also Mon mid-June–mid-Aug), behind Maria Magdalena kyrka, is a toy museum and oversized fantasy nursery full of everything you probably ever wanted as a child. **Spårvägsmuseet** (☎ 462 5531; Tegelviksgatan 22; adult/child Skr20/10; open 10am-5pm Mon-Fri, 11am-4pm Sat & Sun), in the Söderhallen transport depot, is a transport museum with a large collection of vintage trams and buses.

Långholmen This small island once housed a prison and the **Prison Museum** remains in one of the cells – the remainder is now a hotel and STF hostel. There are some pleasant picnic and bathing spots.

Southern Suburbs One of Stockholm's more unusual 'attractions', **Skogskyrkogården** (Söckenvagen; metro T-Skogskyrkogården; admission free), a cemetery in a peaceful pine woodland setting. Surprisingly, the cemetery is on the Unesco World Heritage List, recognised by the organisation for its unique design and the harmony of function and landscape. The area is dominated by a large granite cross, and there's a number of chapels scattered throughout. It's a pleasant place to walk.

Fjäderholmarna These tiny, delightful islands (the 'Feather Islands') offer an easy escape from the city – they're just 25 minutes away by boat and are a favourite swimming spot for locals. The islands are off the east coast of Djurgården. Take one of the boats (Skr75 return) that leave from either Nybroplan (half-hourly) or from Slussen (hourly) from May to early September. There are a couple of restaurants here and the last boats leave the islands at around midnight, making them a perfect spot to enjoy the long daylight hours.

Activities

Stockholm offers a great variety of activities, and summer sees both the locals and visitors taking advantage of the good weather and long daylight hours. Many people head for the coast and the islands of the archipelago (with good swimming spots) or organise picnics in the parks.

Eriksdalsbadet (*☎ 508 40250; Hammarby slussväg 20)* has indoor and open-air swimming pools (Skr65) in the far south of Södermalm. From **Sjöcafe** (*☎ 660 5757)*, by the bridge leading to Djurgården, you can rent bikes, inline skates, kayaks, canoes and rowing boats (costs are from Skr60/200 per hour/day).

Organised Tours

Stockholm Sightseeing (*☎ 587 14020; W www.stockholmsightseeing.com)* runs frequent cruises from early April to mid-December around the central bridges and canals from Strömkajen (near the Grand Hotel), Nybroplan or Stadshusbron. There are one-hour tours from Skr90 to Skr110, but the two-hour 'Under the Bridges of Stockholm' (Skr150) covers more territory and passes under 15 bridges and through two locks. The land-based sister operation is **City Sightseeing** (*☎ 587 14030; W www.citysightseeing.com)*, which offers daily 1½- to 3-hour coach tours of the city from Skr170 to Skr280, and walking tours around Gamla Stan or Haga Park (Skr80, 1½ hours, daily). There are also combo trips offering sightseeing by coach and boat.

You can take a one-hour, English-language guided walk through Gamla Stan with an authorised guide (Skr50). In summer these tours start at 7.30pm Monday, Wednesday and Thursday, and from September to May they commence at 1.30pm Saturday and Sunday. Meet at the Obelisk at Slottsbacken, outside the royal palace; no reservation is needed. To go back even further in time, you can take a cruise in a great old wooden ship done up to resemble a Viking longboat. In summer the *Svea Viking (☎ 202223)* offers regular 1½ hour sightseeing cruises (Skr150) of the city's waterways and out into the archipelago. You can't miss the ship, moored outside the royal palace.

Special Events

There are many festivals, concerts and other events at Sergels Torg and Kungsträdgården throughout the summer, and major museums exhibit temporary exhibitions on a grand scale. *What's on Stockholm* lists events.

Places to Stay

Camping Open only in summer, **Östermalms Citycamping** (*☎ 102903; Östermalms Idrottsplats, Fiskartorpsvägen 2; metro T-Stadion, bus No 55; camping per person Skr60; open mid-June–mid-Aug)* is a cheap and central option.

Bredäng Camping (*☎ 977071; e bredangcamping@telia.com; Stora Sällskapets väg; metro T-Bredäng; camping per person/car Skr85/165, dorm beds Skr140; open mid-Apr–late Oct)* is 10km southwest of the city centre in a pleasant lakeside location. Bredäng is a well-equipped camping ground, with a hostel attached.

Hostels Stockholm has both HI-affiliated STF hostels (where a membership card yields a Skr45 discount) and independent hostels (no membership cards required). The choice includes four boat hostels, one in an old prison and some central options; two hostels are open in summer only and accommodation is in school classrooms! Most hostels fill up during the late afternoon in summer so arrive early or book in advance. May is also a very busy time for hostels, with large numbers of Swedish school groups visiting the capital. For a Skr20 fee, tourist offices in the city centre can assist you in getting a bed – or buy a phonecard and start dialling. All hostels listed here are open year-round unless otherwise specified; many have options for single, double or family rooms (obviously more expensive than rates for dorm beds), and a few have 24-hour reception (a rarity elsewhere in Sweden).

Most travellers head first to Skeppsholmen (take bus No 65 from Centralstationen). The popular STF boat hostel **Vandrarhem af Chapman** (☎ 463 2266; e *info@chapman.stfturist .se; dorm beds Skr120-150)* has done plenty of travelling of its own but it's now a big anchored hostel swaying gently in sight of the centre of the city. Bunks are below decks; breakfast is Skr55. On dry land beside the boat hostel, and with the same reception and prices, is the larger **Skeppsholmen Hostel**, with kitchen and laundry facilities. From August 2004, af Chapman will be closed for an estimated nine months while it undergoes a complete renovation. The land-based hostel will be open as usual during this time.

Also part of the STF network, **Backpackers Inn** (☎ 660 7515; e *backpackersinn@telia .com; Banérgatan 56; metro T-Karlaplan; dorm beds Skr110-150; open late June–mid-Aug)* has 300 beds in a school building. There are no kitchen facilities, but breakfast is available for Skr50. Nearby, the SVIF **Östra Reals Vandrarhem** (☎ 664 1114; Karlavägen 79; dorm beds Skr125-150; open mid-June–mid-Aug)* is also in an old school. There are kitchen facilities here – and no bunks!

Nearer to Centralstationen is **City Back-packers** (☎ 206920; e *info@citybackpackers .se; Upplandsgatan 2A; dorm beds Skr170-200)*, a clean, friendly and well-equipped hostel. There's a kitchen, sauna, laundry and Internet access. In the same area, a bit north, **Hostel Mitt i City** (☎ 217630; e *reservat ions@stockholm.mail.telia.com; Västmanna-gatan 13; dorm beds from Skr175)* occupies a few floors of an old apartment building. Rates here include breakfast.

Also north of the centre, **Hostel Bed & Breakfast** (☎ 152838; e *hostelbedandb reakfast@chello.se; Rehnsgatan 21; metro T-Rådmansgatan; dorm beds Skr150-175, annex beds Skr100)* is a pleasant, informal basement hostel with a kitchen and laundry, plus cheap breakfast (Skr25). There's a large summer annex here filled with beds, but it's not for those who like their privacy!

There are a fair number of hostels around Södermalm, a good 15-minute walk from the Viking Line boats and Centralstationen. The ship hostel **Gustaf af Klint** (☎ 640 4077; Stadsgårdskajen 153; dorm beds Skr120-150)* has beds in pretty down-at-heel rooms. West of the railway lines, the red-painted **Mälaren den Röda Båten** (☎ 644 4385; e *info@icts.se;*

Söder Malärstrand, Kajplats 6; dorm beds Skr185) is probably the cosiest of Stockholm's floating hostels and has a good summer restaurant. There are also pleasant hotel-standard cabin rooms here. A bit farther west is the unhelpful **MS Rygerfjord** (☎ 840830; e *hotell@rygerfjord.se; Kajplats 14; dorm beds from Skr180)*, with a hostel and hotel-style cabins, plus a restaurant.

In the west end of Södermalm near T-Zink-endamm, the well-equipped STF **Vandrarhem Zinkensdamm** (☎ 616 8100; e *mail@ zinkensdamm.com; Zinkens väg 20; dorm beds Skr155)* is a large, welcoming complex in a quiet location near a park. There is a reasonably priced hotel here too. Off the northwestern corner of Södermalm, the small island of Långholmen is home to STF **Vandrarhem Långholmen** (☎ 668 0510; e *vandrarhem@ langholmen.com; dorm beds from Skr175)*, formerly a prison. There are dorm beds in former cells (booking is essential) and slightly roomier hotel-standard rooms, with heavily reduced rates on weekends and in the summer season.

If things get desperate, there are more than 20 hostels around the county that can be reached by SL buses, trains or archipelago boats within an hour or so. Some options are mentioned in the Around Stockholm section.

Private Rooms A number of agencies, including **Bed & Breakfast Service** (☎ 660 6654; e *info@bedbreakfast.a.se; w www .bedbreakfast.a.se; rooms from Skr200)* and **Bed & Breakfast Agency** (☎ 643 8028; e *info@bba.nu; w www.bba.nu; rooms from Skr200)* can arrange good-value apartment or B&B accommodation.

Hotels At Centralstationen, **Hotellcentralen** (see Tourist Offices earlier) can usually find you suitable accommodation for a fee of Skr50. The handy booklet *Hotels and Youth Hostels in Stockholm* (free from tourist offices) lists most hotels and their room rates.

Most Stockholm hotels offer discount rates on weekends (Friday, Saturday and often Sunday night) and in the summer (mid or late June to mid-August). Discounts can be up to 50% off the normal price, making some hotels surprisingly affordable. Almost all hotel prices include breakfast.

Hotel Formule 1 (☎ 744 2044; Mikrofon-vägen 30; metro T-Telefonplan; rooms Skr290) offers perhaps the best value in Stockholm, with very cheap rooms that can accommodate up to three people for one flat rate (breakfast not included). Rooms are hardly inspiring, facilities are shared, and you're 4km southwest of town, but who can argue at that price?

In the middle of town is the pleasant **Queen's Hotel** (☎ 249460; e queenshotel@ queenshotel.se; Drottninggatan 71A; singles/ doubles from Skr650/750), offering comfortable rooms with either shared or private facilities. Just north of the centre is the clean and friendly **Hotell Bema** (☎ 232675; Upplandsgatan 13; singles Skr590-820, doubles Skr690-890), with modern, good-value rooms. Nearby, **Good Night Hotell Danielsson** (☎ 411 1065; Västmannagatan 5; singles/doubles Skr600/800, discounted to Skr550/750) is a simple, old-fashioned place with affordable rooms.

A bit farther north, **Hotell Gustav Vasa** (☎ 343801; e gustav.vasa@wineasy.se; Västmannagatan 61; singles/doubles from Skr725/ 1000) is a small family business.

Wasa Park Hotell (☎ 545 45300; Sankt Eriksplan 1; singles/doubles from Skr525/ 625, discounted to Skr495/595) is northwest of the central business district and is another affordable option. The small, pretty **A&Be Hotell** (☎ 660 2100; Grev Turegatan 50; singles/doubles from Skr490/690) in Östermalm is also good value.

The **Columbus Hotell** (☎ 503 11200; e columbus@columbus.se; Tjärhovsgatan 11; metro T-Medborgarplatsen; budget singles/ doubles/triples with shared facilities Skr595/ 795/995, hotel singles/doubles Skr1995/ 1495) is in a quiet part of Södermalm, set around a cobblestone courtyard and by a pretty park. As well as the budget rooms, there are excellent hotel-standard rooms.

Also in Söder, the cute **Hotel Tre Små Rum** (☎ 641 2371; e info@tresmarum.se; Högbergsgatan 81; metro T-Mariatorget; rooms Skr695) started off with three small rooms, as the name suggests, but has grown to seven. Bathroom facilities are shared.

The people behind welcoming **Oden Pensionat** (☎ 796 9600; e info@pensionat.nu; Kammakargatan 62 • Odengatan 38 • Horns-gatan 66, Södermalm; singles/doubles from Skr680/750, with bath Skr930/1025) must be doing well – the third 'branch' of this affordable pension has just been opened. Prices vary at different locations and according to

room size and facilities, and reasonable summer discounts apply.

There's no shortage of hotels in the area immediately surrounding Centralstationen; most are in the mid-to-upper price bracket but offer good weekend and summer prices. New and super-cool are the two Nordic 'design hotels'. **Nordic Hotel Light** (☎ 505 63000; Vasaplan; singles/doubles Skr2000/2200) and **Nordic Hotel Sea** (☎ 505 63000; Vasaplan; singles/doubles Skr2000/2200) feature sleek black-and-white and nautical blues and greens, respectively. Regular prices are very high, but summer prices are reasonable (up to 50% discount).

Places to Eat

Stockholm has thousands of restaurants, including inexpensive lunch cafeterias and some of the finest dining halls in Scandinavia. The cheapest snacks are found at the numerous **gatukök** outlets, which serve burgers, hot dogs and sausages. The main gatukök and hamburger restaurant chains are all over town, including Sibylla, Burger King and McDonald's, and there are countless places serving cheap pizzas and kebabs. There are also several 24-hour **7-Eleven** shops that serve coffee, sandwiches and snacks.

Self-caterers should ask at their hostel for the location of the nearest supermarket. The handiest central supermarket is **Hemköp** (Klarabergsgatan 50), and there's a **Systembolaget** (Klarabergsgatan 62) nearby for buying alcohol.

Market Halls The colourful market halls are excellent places to sample both local and exotic treats. **Hötorgshallen** (Hötorget) has many Mediterranean food stalls and good specialist shops. **Östermalms Saluhall** (Östermalmstorg) has some fine restaurants and upstairs you'll find **Örtagården**, which serves excellent vegetarian food. **Söderhallarna** (Medborgarplatsen) is a more modern food centre, and **Kungshallen** (Hötorget) has an enormous selection of food stalls where you can eat anything you fancy from Tex-Mex to Indian at budget prices.

Gamla Stan Tourists, not surprisingly, love Gamla Stan and many dine on Västerlånggatan in places like **Michelangelo** (dishes from Skr60) or drink their coffee in the stylish vaults of **Café Art**. Check out restaurants

SWEDEN

on nearby Stora Nygatan, including the vegetarian **Hermitage** *(Stora Nygatan 11; dinner Skr70)*, with good-value dagens rätt (daily special) for Skr60.

Locals often prefer traditional restaurants such as **Källare Restaurang Movitz** *(Tyska Brinken 34)*, in a brick-arched, 17th-century cellar. Along Österlånggatan you'll find the very classy **Den Gyldene Freden** and **Pontus in the Greenhouse** – restaurant mains at either are not cheap, but both offer bar menus that are more within a traveller's price range. Museum-like **Zum Franziskaner** *(Skeppsbron 44)* is the oldest restaurant in town and offers good-value hearty fare (German sausages and the like). On the same street but further north, **Gamla Stans Bryggeri** has reasonable food and its own brewery.

For something a little more modern, head to Österlånggatan, where the neighbouring Ruby restaurants play along a *Paris, Texas* theme. **Grill Ruby** *(Österlånggatan 14; bar meals from Skr80)* is a relaxed, American-style place with lots of meat and fish dishes from the grill on the menu, plus a good bar menu of light meals like burgers, burritos or salads. Next door's **Bistro Ruby** *(Österlånggatan 14)* is more low-lit and intimate, with a French-influenced menu.

City Head to the stalls along the eastern edge of Kungsträdgården for a range of fast food, including hot dogs, burgers and baked potatoes, and lots of ice-cream options in summer. **Friday's American Bar & Café** *(Kungsträdgården; meals from Skr130)* is in the middle of the bustling park and is a popular drinking spot. It has a long, American-style menu with salads, snacks, burgers, Tex-Mex and pasta.

A small store with a clever name, **Souperb** *(Sveavägen 92; soups Skr55)* serves up great soups (including seafood, chicken green curry or tomato and basil), with bread. Perfect for nightowls and close to Centralstationen, **Kebab House** *(cnr Vasagatan & Kungsgatan; open until 5am)* offers kebabs and burgers. **Carinas Pizzeria** *(Upplandsgatan 9B; lunch Skr29, dinner Skr35-55)* has very cheap pizzas especially at lunchtime.

Next to the Dubliner pub on Smålandsgatan you'll find the entrance to **Birger Jarlspassagen**, a great little arcade full of cool cafés. **Waynes Coffee** *(Vasagatan 7)* has great café fare and a Skr60 lunch buffet of appealing salads. **Vetekatten** *(Klara Norra Kyrkogatan 26)* is one of the city's most traditional cafés. Similar **Sturekatten** *(Riddargatan 4)* also has great atmosphere.

Upplandsgatan, near to a few of the hostels and budget hotels, has a couple of good eateries in the vicinity, including **Spice House** *(Upplandsgatan 6; mains from Skr75)* serving authentic Indian fare, and **Sabai Sabai** *(Kammakargatan 44; mains from Skr75)*, a Thai restaurant with good food and over-the-top decor.

Birger Jarlsgatan and Stureplan have many good, upmarket places, and **Riche** *(mains from Skr115)*, at No 4 on Birger Jarlsgatan, should be seen for its decor alone. Nearby **Sturehof** *(Stureplan 2; mains Skr105-175)* offers great people-watching from its outdoor tables. The menu includes simple, reasonably priced Swedish fare (herring, sausages), plus more upmarket dishes like grilled tuna and entrecote steak.

Trendy places at the back of the Opera House and facing Kungsträdgården are the late-19th-century, super-posh **Operakällaren**, the lively **Café Opera**, which is more a nightclub than a café, and the intimate, moderately priced **Bakfickan** *(dinner around Skr90)*, with Art Nouveau decor.

Södermalm For a quick, cheap fix, head to **Kebab Kungen** *(Götgatan 60; kebabs Skr25; open until 5am daily)*. This area is home to some great restaurants and cafés: there are many cool choices on Götgatan, including busy **Fenix**, at No 44, with a range of beers and a variety of meals. Another popular evening restaurant is **Sonjas Grek** *(Bondegatan 54)*, serving good Greek food.

Koh Phangan *(Skånegatan 57, dishes from Skr120)*, with its tacky tropical decor, is one of the area's coolest restaurants, as the queue for a table might suggest.

String *(Nytorgsgatan 38)* looks like a second-hand shop and almost everything is for sale (café fare from around Skr55). For budget vegetarian food try **Hermans** *(Fjällgatan 23A)*, with a great view of the city. **Crêperie Fyra Knop** *(Svartensgatan 4)* is an excellent choice of an evening. It's an intimate little place serving excellent crepes – savoury from Skr44, sweet from Skr28.

Östgöta Källaren *(Östgötagatan 41; light meals Skr45, mains Skr105-165)* is a popular, cosy restaurant-bar. **Gondolen** *(Stadsgården*

6; *mains Skr250)* is top of the heap – figuratively and literally. It's at the top of the Katarinahissen, with a spectacular view of the city and a menu to match. Gourmet main courses include lobster, duck breast and prime veal.

Elsewhere in Stockholm Over on Kungsholmen, the popular budget restaurants are around Scheelegatan, including the **Indian Curry House** *(Scheelegatan 6; dishes from Skr60)* and **Mamas & Tapas** *(Scheelegatan 3; mains Skr75)*, with a good selection of tapas plates.

With so many places on the touristy island of Djurgården, you won't go hungry. The old **Ulla Winbladh** villa along the northern loop road serves fine food in a garden setting. The restaurants on either side of the bridge to Djurgården, **Tvillingarnas** and **Sjöcafé** also do a roaring trade on fine summer days; come here for food or long leisurely drinks and good people-watching.

Entertainment

Pubs & Clubs Stockholm nightlife centres around neighbourhoods that offer pubs and bars within walking distance. In Södermalm, check the Götgatan, Östgötagatan and Skånegatan area. In Kungsholmen, go to Scheelegatan and Fridhemsplan, and in the northern centre (Vasastaden) try the Tegnérgatan and Rörstrandsgatan areas. For the fashionable late-night bars and nightclubs frequented by the city's hip, beautiful people, head to Stureplan and its surrounding areas.

In the city centre, the lively **Dubliner** *(Smålandsgatan 8)* has typical pub food and Guinness on tap. **The Loft** *(Regeringsgatan 66)* is another great Irish pub with restaurant-quality food. Around Rörstrandsgatan are a few pubs, including the **Bagpiper's Inn** (Scottish) and **Boomerang BBQ & Steakhouse** (Australian). The very popular **Cliff Barnes** *(Nortullsgatan 45)* is a great place, named after the loser from the *Dallas* TV soapie. On Gamla Stan, check out **Wirströms Irish Pub** *(Stora Nygatan 13)*. On a balmy summer evening, try the restaurant-bars on either side of the bridge leading across to Djurgården, **Tvillingarnas** and **Sjöcafé**.

When it comes to live music, jazz is extremely popular in the capital. The small and intimate **Glenn Miller Café** *(Brunnsgatan 21)* has live jazz a few nights a week, and the larger **Jazzclub Fasching** *(Kungsgatan 63)* is

one of Stockholm's main jazz venues. **Mosebacke Etablissement** *(Mosebacke torg 3)* in Södermalm is an excellent bar, nightclub and concert venue, featuring all sorts of music and performers. The outdoor bar here offers a great view of the city. Summer sees a lot of outdoor concerts at places like **Gröna Lund Tivoli**.

Head to the unique **Ice Bar** *(Vasaplan)* inside the Nordic Sea Hotel for a taste of life at the Ice Hotel (see under Kiruna later in this chapter). For an entry charge of Skr125 you get to play inside a bar filled with ice sculptures where the temperature is a constant -5°C (warm clothing and boots provided) and select a drink (alcoholic or otherwise) to imbibe from a glass made of ice.

The gay scene is well established, although Sweden's famous open-mindedness means that non-heteros are welcome in all bars and clubs. **Mandus** *(Österlånggatan 7)* is a very popular gay restaurant-bar in Gamla Stan; other hotspots include **Tip Top** *(Sveavägen 57)*, by the RFSL headquarters, and **Stargayte** *(Södra Riddarholmshamnen 19)*.

Cinema & Theatre The 10-screen **BioPalatset** *(Medborgarplatsen)* and **Filmstaden Sergel** *(Hötorget)* both show Hollywood films daily, and there are many more cinemas around town.

Stockholm is a theatre city, with outstanding dance, opera and music performances – for an overview, pick up the free *Teater Guide* from tourist offices. Tickets aren't cheap and are often sold out, especially for Saturday shows. **Operan** *(☎ 248240; Gustav Adolfs Torg)* is the place for opera and ballet. The classic **Oscars Teatern** *(☎ 205000; Kungsgatan 64)* runs 'Broadway' musicals, and the small **Vasateatern** *(☎ 102363; Vasagatan 19)*, around the corner, sometimes stages plays in English.

Getting There & Away

Air Stockholm's main airport, **Arlanda** *(☎ 797 6000)*, is 45km north of the city centre. **Skyways** *(☎ 797 7639)* and **SAS** *(☎ 020 727000)* have comprehensive networks of domestic flights.

International air services to Copenhagen, Oslo, Helsinki and Reykjavík are run by SAS. **Finnair** *(☎ 020 781100)* flies to Turku, Vaasa and Tampere and there are around 15 flights per day to Helsinki. **British Airways** *(☎ 0200 770098)*, **Air France** *(☎ 679 8855)*,

KLM (☎ 593 62430) and **Lufthansa** (☎ 020 228800) also have regular European services.

Bromma airport (☎ 797 6874) is 8km west of Stockholm and is used for some domestic flights. **Skavsta airport** (☎ 0155-280 400) is also used for domestic flights and also by some low-cost carriers, including Ryanair. It's 100km south of Stockholm, near Nyköping.

Bus Long-distance buses use Cityterminalen, next to Centralstationen. Here you'll find the **Busstop ticket office** (☎ 440 8570), which represents the big concerns such as Eurolines, Svenska Buss and Y-Bussen, along with many of the direct buses to the north. **Swebus Express** (☎ 0200 218218) has a ticket office on the second level.

Train Stockholm is the hub for SJ's national services. Direct trains to/from Copenhagen, Oslo, Storlien (for Trondheim) and Narvik arrive and depart from Centralstationen (Stockholm C), as do the SL *pendeltåg* – commuter services that run to/from Nynäshamn, Södertälje and Märsta.

In the basement at Centralstationen, small/medium/large lockers cost Skr20/30/70 for 24 hours and showers are Skr25.

Boat Silja Line (☎ 222140; W www.silja .com) ferries depart for Helsinki (from Skr333 with breakfast and cabin) and Turku (from Skr160) from Värtahamnen – walk from T-Gärdet or take bus No 76 from T-Ropsten.

Viking Line (☎ 452 4000; W www.vikin gline.fi) ferries sail daily to Turku (from Skr130) and Helsinki (from Skr270) from the terminal at Tegelvikshamn (bus from Cityterminalen, or walk 1.5km from T-Slussen).

Tallink ferries to Tallinn (Estonia) sail from Tallinnterminalen at Frihamnen – take a connecting bus from Cityterminalen (Skr20).

See the Around Stockholm section for other boat connections.

Getting Around

Storstockholms Lokaltrafik (SL; W www.sl .se) runs all *tunnelbana* (T or T-bana) metro trains, local trains and buses within the entire Stockholm county. At T-Centralen there are SL information offices in the basement of the station hall (open until 11.15pm daily) and at the Sergels Torg entrance. Both offices issue timetables plus sell SL Tourist Cards and the general Stockholm Card. You can also call

☎ 600 1000 for schedule and travel information from 7am to 9pm Monday to Friday and 8am to 9pm weekends.

The Stockholm Card (see the Information section) covers travel on all SL trains and buses in greater Stockholm. The 24-hour (Skr80) and 72-hour (Skr150) SL Tourist Cards differ from the Stockholm Card in that they only give free entry to a few attractions, but they're a much cheaper alternative if you just want transport. The 72-hour SL Tourist Card is especially good value if you use the third afternoon for transport to either end of the county – you can reach the ferry terminals in Grisslehamn, Kapellskär or Nynäshamn, as well as all the archipelago harbours. If you want to explore the county in more detail, bring a passport photo and get yourself a 30-day SL pass (Skr500).

On Stockholm's public transport system the minimum fare costs two coupons, and each additional zone costs another coupon (up to five coupons for four or five zones). Coupons are available individually for Skr10, or a better idea is to buy a 10/20-coupon discount ticket for Skr60/110. Coupons are valid for an hour and must be stamped at the start of the journey. International rail passes aren't valid on SL trains.

To/From the Airport The **Arlanda Express** train travels to Centralstationen (Skr160, 20 minutes, every 15 minutes from 5am to midnight). The cheaper option is the **Flygbuss** service between Arlanda airport and Cityterminalen (Skr80, 40 minutes, every 10 or 15 minutes). The same trip in a taxi costs from Skr350 to Skr450, but agree your fare first and don't use any taxi without a contact telephone number displayed.

There are bus services from Cityterminalen to Bromma airport (Skr60, 20 minutes) and Skavsta airport (Skr100, 80 minutes). Call ☎ 600 1000 for bus departure times to/from all airports.

Bus Bus timetables and route maps are complicated but worth studying. Inner-city buses can be replaced by the metro or by walking, but useful connections to suburban attractions radiate from Sergels Torg, Fridhemsplan (on Kungsholmen), Odenplan and Slussen; bus No 47 runs from Sergels Torg to Djurgården and bus No 69 runs to the Ladugårdsgärdet museums and Kaknästornet.

Check where the regional bus hub is for different outlying areas. Islands of the Ekerö municipality (including Drottningholm palace) are served by bus Nos 301 to 323 from T-Brommaplan. Buses to Vaxholm (No 670) and the Åland ferries (No 637 to Grisslehamn and Nos 640 and 631 to Kapellskär) depart from T-Tekniska Högskolan.

Train Local *pendeltåg* trains are useful for connections to Nynäshamn (for ferries to Gotland), to Märsta (for buses to Sigtuna and Arlanda airport) and Södertälje. There are also services to Nockeby (from T-Alvik), to Lidingö (from T-Ropsten), to Kårsta, Österskär and Näsbypark (from T-Tekniska Högskolan) and to Saltsjöbaden (from T-Slussen).

Tram The historical tram No 7 runs between Norrmalmstorg and Skansen, passing most attractions on Djurgården. Separate fees apply for Stockholm Card-holders, but the SL Tourist Card is valid.

Metro The most useful mode of transport in Stockholm is the *tunnelbana* (T), which converges on T-Centralen, and is connected by an underground walkway to Centralstationen. There are three main through lines with branches – check that the approaching train is actually going your way.

Car & Motorcycle Driving in central Stockholm is not recommended. Small one-way streets, congested bridges and limited parking all present problems – parking stations (P-hus) charge up to Skr50 per hour (the fixed evening rate is usually more reasonable). If you have a car, one of the best, hassle-free options is to stay on the outskirts of town and catch public transport into the centre.

Taxi There's usually no problem finding a taxi in Stockholm, but they're expensive (about Skr35 flag fall, then around Skr7 per kilometre) and always arrange the fare before getting in. At night, women should ask about *tjejtaxa*, a discount rate offered by some operators. Reputable firms are **Taxi Stockholm** (☎ *150000*), **Taxi 020** (☎ *020 939393*) and **Taxi Kurir** (☎ *300000*).

Bicycle Stockholm has an extensive network of bicycle paths, and in summer you won't regret hiring a bicycle. Tourist offices sell cycling maps but they are not usually necessary. Top day trips include: Djurgården; a loop going from Gamla Stan to Södermalm, Långholmen and Kungsholmen (on lakeside paths); Drottningholm (return by steamer); Haga Park; and the adjoining Ulriksdal Park. Some long-distance routes are marked all the way from central Stockholm.

Bicycles can be carried free on SL local trains, except from 6am to 9am and 3pm to 6pm Monday to Friday, and they're not allowed in Centralstationen or the metro, although you'll see some daring souls from time to time.

Sjöcafe (☎ *660 5757*), by the bridge across to Djurgården, rents bikes for Skr60/250 per hour/day and has options for longer rentals. It also rents inline skates at Skr60/200 per hour/day, which is a fun way of getting around.

Boat Djurgårdsfärjan city ferry services connect Gröna Lund Tivoli on Djurgården with Nybroplan and Slussen as frequently as every 10 minutes in summer (considerably less frequently in the low season); a single trip costs Skr20 (free with the SL Tourist Card).

Around Stockholm

You can explore the county of greater Stockholm with the SL Tourist Card or monthly passes that allow unlimited travel on all buses and local trains – pick up timetables from SL centers.

FERRY PORTS

Nynäshamn, about 50km south of Stockholm, is the main gateway to Gotland (see that section); there are also regular ferries to Gdańsk and Riga, and boats to the island of Utö in Stockholm's archipelago. Regular local trains run from Stockholm to Nynäshamn; you can use SL passes, but international rail passes are not valid.

Viking Line ferries sail up to three times daily from May to September between tiny **Kapellskär** (about 90km northeast of Stockholm) and Mariehamn on Åland (from Skr50). From mid-June to mid-August, boats also sail once daily to Turku (from Skr160) via Mariehamn. Viking Line has a direct bus from Stockholm Cityterminalen to meet the ferries (Skr55), but if you have an SL pass, take bus No 640 or 644 from T-Tekniska

SWEDEN

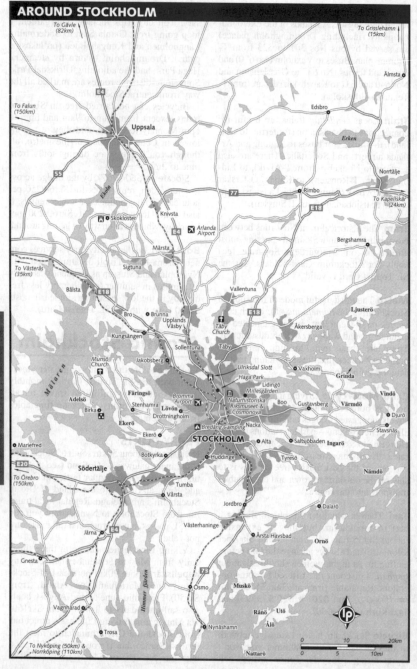

AROUND STOCKHOLM

To Gävle
(82km)

To Grisslehamn
(15km)

E4

Älmsta

To Falun
(150km)

Edsbro

Uppsala

Erken

55

Ekoln

Norrtälje

77

Skokloster

Knivsta

Rimbo

To Kapellskär
(24km)

E4

Arlanda
Airport

E18

Märsta

Bergshamra

To Västerås
(35km)

Sigtuna

Bålsta

E18

Vallentuna

Ljusterö

Bro

Brunna

E18

Upplands
Väsby

Åkersberga

Kungsängen

Jakobsberg

Täby
Church

Munsö
Church

Sollentuna

Täby

Mälaren

Ulriksdal Slott

Vaxholm

Grinda

Faringsö

Stenhamra

Haga Park

Bromma
Airport

Lidingö
Millesgården

Vindö

Adelsö

Lövön

Boo

Värmdö

Birka

Ekerö

Drottningholm

Naturhistoriska
Riksmuseet &
Cosmonova

Gustavsberg

Djurö

Ekerö

Bredäng Camping

Nacka

Stavsnäs

Mariefred

STOCKHOLM

Alta

Saltsjöbaden

Ingarö

E20

Botkyrka

Tyresö

To Örebro
(150km)

Södertälje

Huddinge

Nämdö

Tumba

Vårsta

Järna

E4

Jordbro

Dalarö

Ornö

Gnesta

Västerhaninge

Årsta Havsbad

73

Himmerfjärden

Muskö

Vagnhärad

Osmo

Rånö

Utö

Trosa

Nynäshamn

Ålö

To Nyköping (50km) &
Norrköping (110km)

Nattarö

0   10   20km
0   5   10mi

SWEDEN

Högskolan to Norrtälje and change there to No 631, which runs every two hours or so (infrequent at weekends).

The quickest and cheapest ferry to Finland departs from **Grisslehamn**, about 100km from Stockholm in the northern part of Stockholm's county; SL tickets apply on bus No 637 which runs four to nine times daily from Norrtälje. **Eckerö Linjen** (☎ *25800;* W *www.eckerolinjen .fi)* ferries sail from Grisslehamn to Eckerö (Åland; Skr50/80 low/high season, cars Skr50/ 70, bicycles free, two hours, five a day). Eckerö Linjen runs regular bus connections from Uppsala and from T-Tekniska Högskolan (Stockholm) to Grisslehamn two hours before most boat departures (Skr110/140 low/high season including boat ticket).

VAXHOLM
☎ 08 • pop 9500

Crowded Vaxholm, about 35km northeast of the city, is the gateway to Stockholm's archipelago and has a collection of quaint summerhouses that were fashionable in the 19th century. On an islet east of town, **Vaxholm slott** (☎ *5417 2156; admission Skr40; open daily mid-June–mid-Aug)* dates from 1544 but is now a museum. Admission includes the return ferry.

Take regular bus No 670 from T-Tekniska Högskolan, or frequent Waxholmsbolaget boats from Strömkajen (Skr55) or Slussen (Skr70).

STOCKHOLM ARCHIPELAGO
☎ 08

Depending on which source you read, the archipelago around Stockholm has anything between 14,000 and 100,000 islands, although the common consensus is 24,000. Whatever the number, a summer visit to one is highly recommended. Summer cottages on rocky islets are popular among wealthy Stockholmites, and regular boats offer options for outings.

The biggest operator is **Waxholmsbolaget** (☎ *679 5830;* W *www.waxholmsbolaget.se)* and timetables and information are available from offices outside the Grand Hotel on Strömkajen in Stockholm, and at the harbour in Vaxholm. Its Båtluffarkortet pass (Skr385), valid for 16 days, gives unlimited rides plus a handy island map. The ferries wind through the archipelago to Finnhamn, Stora Kalholmen, Möja, Sandön, Ornö, Utö, Öja and many more

islands. Bikes can be taken on the ferries for a fee, but it's a better idea to hire at your destination; bikes can be hired on many islands.

It's worth checking what **Cinderella Båtarna** (☎ *587 14050;* W *www.cinderellabata rna.com)* has to offer. Its boats *Cinderella I* and *Cinderella II* also go to many of the most interesting islands from Skeppsbron in Stockholm. If your time is short, a recommended tour is the Thousand Island Cruise offered by **Stromma Kanabolaget** (☎ *587 14000;* W *www .strommakanalbolaget.com)*, running daily between late June and mid-August. The full day's excursion departs from Stockholm's Nybrokajen at 9.30am and returns at 8.30pm; the cost of Skr625 includes lunch, dinner and guided tours ashore – the boat visits a number of interesting islands, and there are several opportunities for swimming.

Each island has its own character. **Sandhamn** is popular among wealthy sailors and is best visited on a day trip (90 minutes from Vaxholm). **Finnhamn** is quieter, but book in advance to stay at the **STF hostel** (☎ *542 46212;* e *info@finnhamn.nu; dorm beds Skr180)*. **Utö** is popular among cyclists; the **STF hostel** (☎ *504 20315; dorm beds Skr200; open Apr-Sept)* has its reception at the nearby Utö Värdshus, rated among the best restaurants in the archipelago.

EKERÖ DISTRICT
☎ 08 • pop 22,600

Surprisingly rural, Ekerö, 20km west of Stockholm, consists of several large islands on Lake Mälaren, the Unesco World Heritage Listed sites of Drottningholm, Hovgården and Birka, and a dozen medieval churches. Bus Nos 311 and 312 run from T-Brommaplan metro station in Stockholm.

Drottningholm

It certainly can be an expensive day out if you wish to see everything at the World Heritage Listed royal residence and parks of Drottningholm (☎ *402 6280; open daily May-Sept, Sat & Sun Oct-Apr)* on Lovön – it's a good idea to use the Stockholm Card here. The main Renaissance-inspired **palace** *(adult/child Skr60/ 30)*, with geometric baroque gardens, was built late in the 17th century, about the same time as Versailles. The highlights are the **Karl X Gustav Gallery**, in baroque style, and the painted ceilings of the **State Bedchamber**. The unique **Slottsteater** is the original 18th-century court theatre and is well worth a visit (hourly tours adult/child Skr60/30). Ask about musical performances here in summer.

At the far end of the gardens is the 18th-century **Kina slott** *(adult/child Skr50/25)*, a lavishly decorated 'Chinese pavilion' that was built as a gift to Queen Lovisa Ulrika. Admission includes a guided tour.

The most pleasant way to get to Drottningholm is by boat. **Strömma Kanalbolaget** *(☎ 587 14000; W www.strommakanalbolaget .com)* has boats departing from Stadshusbron in Stockholm daily from May to mid-September (Skr100 return).

Adelsö

Across the road from Adelsö's medieval church is **Hovgården**, a Unesco World Heritage Site of burial mounds that are associated with nearby Birka. SL bus No 312 runs to Adelsö kyrka from T-Brommaplan metro station via the medieval Ekerö kyrka and Munsö kyrka and the free Adelsö ferry.

The hostel **Adelsögården** *(☎ 383359; dorm beds from Skr165; open mid-June–Sept)* is just south of the ferry pier. There's a kitchen and a restaurant, and bikes and canoes can be hired. A walking trail from the hostel leads via some prehistoric sites to the church.

Birka

At the Viking trading centre of Birka *(☎ 5605 1445, open daily May-Sept)*, a Unesco World Heritage Site on Björkö in Lake Mälaren, archaeologists have excavated the town's cemetery, harbour and fortress. Cruises to Birka run from early May to late September. **Strömma Kanalbolaget** *(☎ 587 14000)* has day trips on its *Victoria* from Stadshusbron, Stockholm (Skr220 return). A visit to the small **museum** and a guided tour in English of the settlement's burial mounds and fortifications are included in the cruise price. From May to September there are also daily boats from Adelsö (Hovgården) to Birka (Skr70, including museum entry).

SIGTUNA
☎ 08 • pop 35,500

The most pleasant place in the vicinity of Stockholm is picturesque Sigtuna, about 40km to the northwest, and the oldest town in Sweden. The friendly **tourist office** *(☎ 592 50020; W www.sigtuna.se; Stora gatan 33)* can help with visitor inquiries.

There is a good deal of history here: **Stora gatan** is probably Sweden's oldest main street, and there are ruins of the 12th-century churches of **St Per**, **St Olof** and **St Lars** around town. **Mariakyrkan** has restored medieval paintings, and you can also visit the extensive **Sigtuna Museum** *(☎ 5978 3870; Stora gatan 55; open noon-4pm daily June-Aug, noon-4pm Tues-Sun Sept-May)*.

Unfortunately Sigtuna's summer hostel had closed at the time of writing; check with the tourist office. Otherwise, the only accommodation is quite pricey (although summer rates are more reasonable). **Sigtuna Stiftelsen Gästhem** *(☎ 592 58900; Manfred Björkquists allé 2-4; singles singles/doubles Skr800/1300, discounted to Skr500/600)* is a pretty place run by a Christian foundation. There are a number of good cafés and restaurants to choose from. **Tant Brunn Kaffestuga**, in a small alley off Stora gatan, is a delightful 17th-century café set around a pretty courtyard. **Båt Huset** is a classy wooden restaurant and bar, floating on the lake.

Travel connections are easy from Stockholm. Take a local train to Märsta, from where there are frequent buses to Sigtuna (No 570 or 575). In summer there are cruises from Stockholm and Uppsala (stopping at the baroque castle Skokloster).

Svealand

This is where Sweden was born. Viking rune stones and forts are reminders of the time when Lake Mälaren offered safe harbours and links to the Baltic Sea and Russia. The kingdom of the Svea became synonymous with the entire country, thus called Sverige or Svea Rike.

Farther northwest, amidst some picturesque lake and forest scenery, lies Dalarna (sometimes called Dalecarlia in English), a county of rich folk culture and beautiful landscapes centred around the smaller Lake Siljan and the twin branches of the Dalälven River. This region has become popular for travel and winter sports.

UPPSALA
☎ 018 • pop 191,100

Uppsala is the fourth-largest city in Sweden, and one of its oldest. Gamla (Old) Uppsala flourished as early as the 6th century. The cathedral was consecrated in 1435 after 175

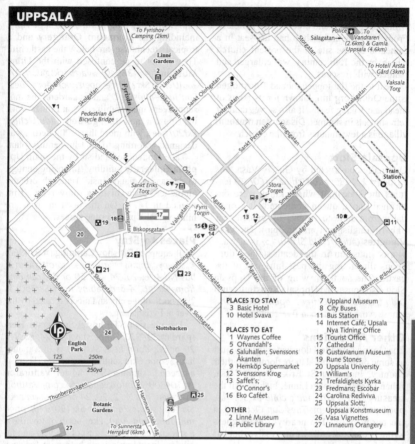

UPPSALA

PLACES TO STAY
3 Basic Hotel
10 Hotel Svava

PLACES TO EAT
1 Waynes Coffee
5 Ofvandahl's
6 Saluhallen; Svenssons Åkanten
9 Hemköp Supermarket
12 Svenssons Krog
13 Saffet's; O'Connor's
16 Eko Caféet

OTHER
2 Linné Museum
4 Public Library
7 Uppland Museum
8 City Buses
11 Bus Station
14 Internet Café; Upsala Nya Tidning Office
15 Tourist Office
17 Cathedral
18 Gustavianum Museum
19 Rune Stones
20 Uppsala University
21 William's
22 Trefaldighets Kyrka
23 Fredmans; Escobar
24 Carolina Rediviva
25 Uppsala Slott; Uppsala Konstmuseum
26 Vasa Vignettes
27 Linnaeum Orangery

SWEDEN

years of building and the castle was first built in the 1540s, although today's edifice belongs to the 18th century. The city's sprawling university is Scandinavia's oldest.

Information

The main **tourist office** (☎ 274800; ⓦ www .uppsalatourism.se; Fyristorg 8; open 10am-6pm Mon-Fri, 10am-3pm Sat year-round; noon-4pm Sun mid-June–mid-Aug) is central and helpful. Ask about the **Uppsala Card** (Skr75), valid for 24 hours and giving you free admission to many of the town's museums and sights.

The **public library** (cnr Sankt Olofsgatan & Svartbäcksgatan) offers free Internet access, but expect long waits. The **Internet café** (cnr Fyristorget & Drottninggatan) inside the

Upsala Nya Tidning newspaper office is right by the tourist office and charges Skr10 for 15 minutes online.

Gamla Uppsala

Uppsala began at the three great **grave mounds** at Gamla Uppsala (☎ 239300; open 11am-5pm daily May-Aug, noon-3pm Sun Sept-Apr), 4km north of the modern city (bus No 2 from Stora Torget; admission free; always open). The mounds are said to be the graves of legendary pre-Viking kings and lie in a cemetery including about 300 smaller mounds and a great heathen temple. A new, modern **historical centre** (adult/child Skr50/30; open daily) has museum-style exhibits of ancient artefacts excavated from Gamla Uppsala and the nearby archaeological sites.

Christianity arrived in the 11th century and with it the bishops and other church officials. From 1164 the archbishop had his seat in a cathedral on the site of the present **church** which, by the 15th century, was enlarged and painted with frescoes.

Next to the flat-topped mound **Tingshögen** is the **Odinsborg Inn**, known for its horns of mead and Viking feasts. It also serves daintier refreshments in summer. **Disagården museum village** is a few minutes from the church.

Uppsala Slott

Originally constructed by Gustav Vasa, this castle (☎ 272485; adult/child Skr60/15) features the state hall where kings were enthroned and a queen abdicated. It's open daily from June to August by guided tour only (in English at 1pm and 3pm). The **Vasa Vignettes** (adult/child Skr40/15) is a 'waxworks' museum in the death-stained dungeons illustrating the past intrigues of the castle. The southern wing of the Uppsala Slott also houses the **Uppsala Konstmuseum** (adult/child Skr30/free; open Wed-Sun), whose works of art span five centuries.

Other Attractions

The Gothic **cathedral** dominates the city, just as some of those buried there dominated their country, including St Erik, Gustav Vasa, Johan III and Carl von Linné. Inside, visit the **treasury** (☎ 187201; adult/child Skr30/free; open daily May-Sept, Tues-Sun Oct-Apr) in the north tower. The nearby **Trefaldighets kyrka** is not outwardly as impressive, but has beautiful painted ceilings.

Gustavianum Museum (☎ 471 7571; Akademigatan 3; adult/child Skr40/free; open 11am-4pm Tues-Sun) has an excellent antiquities collection and features an old 'anatomical theatre'. **Upplands Museum** (☎ 169100; Sankt Eriks Torg 10; adult/child Skr30/free; open noon-5pm Tues-Sun), in the old mill, houses county collections from the Middle Ages.

Carolina Rediviva (☎ 471 3900; Dag Hammar-skjöldsväg 1; adult/child Skr20/free; open daily mid-May–mid-Sept, Mon-Sat mid-Sept–mid-May) is the old university library and has a display hall with maps and historical and scientific literature, the pride of which is the surviving half of the 6th-century *Codex Argentus* (Silver Bible), written on purple vellum in the extinct Gothic language.

The excellent **Botanic Gardens** (open 7am-9pm May-Aug, 7am-7pm Sept-Apr), including the **Linnaeum Orangery** and a tropical greenhouse, are below the castle hill. They're not to be confused with the **Linné Museum** (☎ 136540; Svartbäcksgatan 27; adult/child Skr25/free; open noon-4pm Tues-Sun June–mid-Sept) and its garden. The museum keeps memorabilia of von Linnés work in Uppsala and the **garden** (adult/child Skr20/free), with more than 1000 herbs, was designed according to an 18th-century plan.

Take sandwiches and sit by the main **Uppsala University** building (imposing enough to demand a glance inside) and absorb the ambience of a historic university (first opened in 1477). On the lawn in front are nine typical Uppland rune stones.

Places to Stay

Well-equipped **Fyrishov Camping** (☎ 274960; e stugbycamping@fyrishov.se; Idrottsgatan 2; bus No 4, 6, 20, 24, 25, 50 or 54; camping from Skr115, 4-bed cabins from Skr350) is 2km north of the city and nicely located by the river at Fyrisfjädern.

The pleasant STF hostel **Sunnersta Herrgård** (☎ 324220; Sunnerstavägen 24; bus No 20 or 50; dorm beds Skr180) is in a manor house some 6km south of the centre. There is a second, summer STF hostel **Vandraren** (☎ 104300; e info@vandraren.com; Vattholmavägen; bus No 2, 20, 24 or 54; dorm beds Skr165, singles/doubles Skr190/370; open mid-June–mid-Aug), 2km north of town. It's a student residence the rest of the year and facilities, including private bathroom for each room, are excellent.

Uppsala Room Agency (☎ 109533; e uppsala.rumsformedling@swipnet.se; singles/doubles Skr250/350) will book private rooms in town. A 15-minute bus ride from Stora Torget is **Hotell Årsta Gård** (☎ 253500; Jordgubbsgatan 14; bus No 7 or 52; singles/doubles Skr525/675, discounted to Skr425/675), a small, family-run place.

Central **Basic Hotel** (☎ 480 5000; e reception@basichotel.com; Kungsgatan 27; singles/doubles from Skr690/790; both discounted to Skr600) has excellent rooms with their own self-catering facilities. This is a good place for families or small groups: four-bed rooms cost Skr760 year-round. **Hotel Svava** (☎ 130030; e info.svava@swedenhotels.se; Bangårdsgatan 24; singles/doubles Skr1295/1535, *discounted to Skr735/900)*, right opposite the train station, has all the facilties of an upper-range business-style hotel.

Places to Eat

There are several eateries on the pedestrian mall and Stora Torget. When it comes to fast food, **Saffet's** *(Stora Torget, meals Skr50)* has the works – burgers, enchiladas and tacos, baked potatoes, fish and chips, kebabs. **Of-vandahl's** *(Sysslomansgatan 3-5)* is a classy café full of old-world charm. Some of the best coffee in town and Italian-style food such as pasta and panini (Skr40-65) can be found at funky **Eko Caféet** *(Drottninggatan 5)*. Sleek **Waynes Coffee** *(Smedsgränd 4)* also has good coffee and café fare in stylish surrounds.

If you're self-catering, there's a central **Hemköp supermarket** *(Stora Torget)*. The indoor produce market, **Saluhallen** *(open Mon-Sat)*, is between the cathedral and the river at Sankt Eriks Torg (it's being rebuilt after a fire and should have reopened by the time you read this).

Svenssons Krog *(Sysslomansgatan 15)* is very popular, as is the sister venue **Svenssons Åkanten** – an outdoor, riverside restaurant and bar by Saluhallen. **William's** *(Övre Slottsgatan 7)*, in the university quarter, is an English pub with an adjacent Indian restaurant (lunch buffet Skr50). **O'Connor's** *(Stora Torget 1)*, upstairs from Saffet's, is a friendly Irish pub and restaurant (good pub meals from Skr50). There's also regular live music and a selection of over 85 beers. **Fredmans** *(Drottninggatran 12)* also has pub food and live music; next door is **Escobar**, a popular bar and nightclub.

Getting There & Away

The bus station is outside the train station. Bus No 801 departs at least twice an hour for nearby Arlanda airport (Skr80). Swebus Express runs regularly to Örebro, Stockholm, Gävle and Västerås. Frequent SJ trains run from Stockholm; all SJ services to/from Gävle, Östersund and Mora stop in Uppsala. SL coupons or passes take you only as far as Märsta from Stockholm.

Getting Around

A local bus ticket costs from Skr20 and gives unlimited travel for two hours – just enough for a visit to Gamla Uppsala. Catch a city bus from Stora Torget or outside Scandic Hotel Uplandia. **Upplands Lokaltrafik** *(☎ 020 114*

1414) runs regional traffic within the county; if you're staying long in the area, ask about rebate cards and the various passes available.

You can hire a bicycle at Fyrishov Camping or either of the STF hostels (or inquire at the tourist office). Regional buses of Upplands Lokaltrafik take bicycles for Skr20 but local trains don't.

VÄSTERÅS
☎ 021 • pop 127,800

Both an old and modern city, Västerås (the sixth-largest city in Sweden) is a centre for industrial technology. Ignore the sprawling suburbs and head for the old town centre and wooden buildings along the Svartån River, or relax on Lake Mälaren's shores.

The **tourist office** *(☎ 103830;* **w** *www .vastmanland.se; Stora Gatan 40; open daily mid-June–mid-Aug, Mon-Sat mid-Aug–mid-June)* can help with visitor information. The **public library** *(Biskopsgatan 2)* is opposite the fine late-14th-century **cathedral**.

Västmanlands Länsmuseum *(☎ 156100; Slottsgatan; admission free; open Tues-Sun)*, in Västerås Slottet (manor house), has a strong general historical collection; the nearby **Konstmuseum** *(☎ 161300; Fiskartorget; admission free; open Tues-Sun)* has temporary exhibitions by Swedish painters.

Vallby Friluftsmuseum *(☎ 161670; Vallby; bus No 12 or 92 from Vasagatan; admission free; open daily mid-June–mid-Aug)* is an open-air collection assembled by the regional museum. Among the 40-odd buildings, the highlight is **Anunds Hus** *(Skr20)*, a reconstructed Viking house. It's located off Vallbyleden, near the E18 interchange, 2km northwest of the city.

The city is surrounded by pre-Christian sites; the most interesting and extensive is **Anundshög** *(bus No 12 or 92)*, 6km northeast of the city. It has a full complement of prehistoric curiosities such as mounds, stone ship-settings and a large rune stone. From the Bjurhovda terminus walk 2km east.

Places to Stay & Eat

Västerås is no paradise for budget travellers, but you could visit the sights in half a day and catch a train somewhere else for the night. The closest camping ground is **Johannisbergs Camping** *(☎ 140279; bus No 25; camping Skr80, cabins from Skr250)*, 5km south of the city. Not far from the camping ground is the

SWEDEN

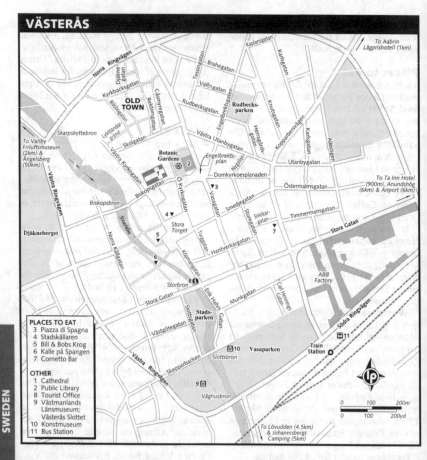

VÄSTERÅS

PLACES TO EAT
3 Piazza di Spagna
4 Stadskällaren
5 Bill & Bobs Krog
6 Kalle på Spangen
7 Cornetto Bar

OTHER
1 Cathedral
2 Public Library
8 Tourist Office
9 Västmanlands
  Länsmuseum;
  Västerås Slottet
10 Konstmuseum
11 Bus Station

STF hostel **Lövudden** (☎ 185230; **e** info@ lovudden.nu; dorm beds Skr150, hotel singles/ doubles Skr550/825, discounted to Skr390/ 625), off Johannisbergsvägen. It's a pleasant lakeside place with hostel and hotel accommodation. The only cheapish central possibility is **Aabrin Lågprishotell** (☎ 143980; Kopparbergsvägen 47; singles/doubles Skr545/605, discounted to Skr375/475), by the E18. Or try **Ta Inn Hotel** (☎ 139600; Ängsgärdgatan 19; singles/doubles Skr695/850, discounted to Skr395/550). Both have liveable rooms but are in totally uninspiring locations, each about 1km from the town centre.

Cornetto Bar (Kopparbergsvägen 23) has a good menu of salads, pastas, wraps and ciabattas. **Kalle på Spangen** (Kunsgatan 2) is by the river and serves café fare such as coffee,

sandwiches and cakes. Reasonably priced restaurants along Vasagatan include **Piazza di Spagna** at No 26, a popular Italian place with good pizzas from Skr63. **Bill & Bobs Krog** and **Stadskällaren**, on Stora Torget, are the pick of the restaurants for mid-priced and splurge dinners respectively.

Getting There & Away
The **airport** (☎ 805600) is 6km east of the centre and is connected by bus (No 41); budget carrier Ryanair flies here from the UK. The bus and train stations are just south of the centre. Swebus Express runs daily to Uppsala, Stockholm and Örebro. Västerås is accessible by hourly train from Stockholm and from towns around Lake Mälaren. Trains to Örebro and Uppsala are also frequent.

ÄNGELSBERG

Some 50km northwest of Västerås is the village of Ängelsberg, where the main object of interest is **Engelsbergs Bruk**, an ironworks dating from the 17th and 18th centuries and comprising a mansion and park, workers' homes and industrial buildings. The site features on Unesco's World Heritage List and is ranked as one of the most important examples from early industrial times. Guided tours run daily in summer (Skr30), and less frequently in May and late August; contact ☎ 13100 for details.

Regional trains run roughly hourly from Västerås to Ängelsberg (50 minutes); from the train station it's a 1.5km walk north to the site.

ÖREBRO

☎ 019 • pop 125,000

The most photogenic castle in Sweden stands by the river in the centre of Örebro, a very attractive city and a pleasant place to spend a day or two. The **tourist office** (☎ 212121; W www.orebro.se/turism; open 9am-7pm Mon-Fri, 10am-5pm Sat & Sun June-Aug; 9am-5pm Mon-Fri, 11am-3pm Sat & Sun Sept-May) is inside the castle. The **library** (Näbbtorgsgatan) is south of the town centre, and **Video Biljard**, the video store on Järntorget, also has Internet access.

Admission to the once powerful **Slottet** (☎ 212121; adult/child Skr45/free; open daily year-round), now restored, includes a castle tour (in English at noon and 2pm daily in summer). Outside the castle is **Länsmuseum & Konsthall** (☎ 168020; Engelbrektsgatan 3; adult/child Skr20/free; open 11am-5pm daily), the combined regional and art museums. A pleasant stroll east of the castle along the river will take you through Stadsparken. Here, the delightful **Stadsträdgården** greenhouse precinct has a café and, farther east, there's the excellent **Wadköping** museum village, which has craft workshops, a bakery and period buildings.

The commercial centre and some grand buildings are around Stortorget, including the 13th-century church **St Nikolai kyrka**. You can see Lake Hjälmaren from on top of **Svampen** (☎ 611 3735; Dallbygatan 4; admission free; open daily), the water tower, north of the city centre. Built in 1958, it was the first of Sweden's modern 'mushroom' water towers and now functions as a lookout; there's a café at the top.

Places to Stay & Eat

The very good **STF hostel** (☎ 310240; e vandrarhem@hepa.se; Fanjunkarevägen 5; bus No 16 or 31; dorm beds from Skr120) is quite well hidden, some 1.6km northeast of the train station. Hostel management also has a new complex of well-equipped apartments next door, **Livin' Lägenhetshotell**, which has the same contact details as for the hostel. Each apartment has a fully-equipped kitchen, bathroom and living area and costs Skr500.

Hotell Linden (☎ 611 8711; Köpmangatan 5; singles/doubles from Skr350/450, discounted to Skr250/320) is just off the main square and has comfortable rooms with shared facilties.

For cheap eats head to **Aladdin Café** (meals Skr40) on the slightly grungy Järntorget. It offers a wide range of pizza, pasta and baked spuds. **Hälls Konditori Stallbacken** (Engelbrektsgatan 12) is a classic old-style café with a courtyard. For something more upmarket head to **Slottskällaren** (Elite Hotel, lunch Skr69, dinner from Skr105), by the castle.

Getting There & Away

You're well placed to go almost anywhere in southern Sweden from Örebro. Swebus Express has connections in all directions: to Jönköping, Linköping and Norrköping; Karlstad and Oslo; Mariestad and Gothenburg; Västerås and Uppsala; and Eskilstuna and Stockholm.

Train connections are similarly good. Direct SJ trains run to/from Stockholm every hour, some via Västerås. To get to Gothenburg, take a train to Hallsberg and change there.

KARLSTAD

☎ 054 • pop 80,800

The port of Karlstad is on Vänern, Sweden's largest lake. It's also the gateway to outdoor experiences in the county of Värmland. **Karlstad Turistbyrå** (☎ 222140; W www.karlstad .se; Tage Erlandergatan 10E; open daily June-Aug, Mon-Fri Sept-May) has details on both town and county, including many activities in and on the region's forests, lakes and rivers.

The **STF hostel** (☎ 566840; e karlstad vandrarhem@swipnet.se; bus No 11 or 32; dorm beds Skr130) is off the E18 highway at Ulleberg, 3km southwest of Karlstad's centre. There are a number of central hotels opposite the train station, including **Hotell Freden** (☎ 216582; e info@fredenhotel.com;

SWEDEN

Fredsgatan 1; singles/doubles Skr480/580, discounted to Skr380/480), a pleasant place with comfortable rooms and shared facilities. Head to the main square, Stora Torget, and its surrounds for good eating and drinking options. On Vastra Torggatan you'll find **Kebab House**, serving good-value pizza, kebabs, pasta and salads, and its neighbour, **Gröna Trädgården**, offering mainly vegetarian selections.

Swebus Express has daily services along the Gothenburg–Karlstad–Falun–Gävle and Stockholm–Örebro–Karlstad–Oslo routes. Buses leave from the terminal on Drottninggatan. Trains between Stockholm and Oslo pass through Karlstad and several daily services also run from Gothenburg. Värmlandstrafik (☎ 020 225580) runs regional buses.

FALUN
☎ 023 • pop 54,600
Falun, traditionally the main centre of Dalarna, is synonymous with mining and with Stora, perhaps the world's oldest public company (first mentioned in 1288). The Falun Folkmusik festival, which has an international flavour as well as airing regional traditions, is held over four days in mid-July.

The **Falun tourist office** (☎ 83050; W www.visitfalun.se; Trotzgatan 10-12; open daily mid-June–mid-Aug, Mon-Sat mid-Aug–mid-June) can help with visitor information. **Billiard & IT Café** (Falugatan 4) is a central Internet café.

Things to See & Do
The **Falu koppargruva** copper mine (☎ 711475; W www.kopparberget.com; bus No 709; open 10am-5pm daily May-Sept, 11am-4pm Sat & Sun Oct-Apr) was the world's most important by the 17th century and drove many of Sweden's international aspirations during that period, but it closed in 1992 (it's now on Unesco's World Heritage List). The mine also provided, as a by-product, the red coatings that became the characteristic house paint of the age and is still in popular use today. The mine and museum are west of town at the top end of Gruvgatan. You can go on a one-hour tour of the bowels of the disused mine (adult/child Skr80/30 including museum entry) – bring warm clothing.

There's more folk culture at **Dalarnas Museum** (☎ 765500; Stigaregatan; admission Skr40/20; open 10am-5pm Mon-Fri, noon-5pm Sat & Sun). This fine museum features local culture and art, and Selma Lagerlöf's study is preserved here. The baroque interiors of **Kristine kyrka** (Stora Torget) show some of the riches that came into the town but don't miss **Stora Kopparbergs kyrka**, a bit north of the centre, the oldest building in town.

Falun is a winter-sports centre with plenty of ski runs, Nordic courses and toboggan runs, particularly in the Lugnet area.

Places to Stay & Eat
Lugnet Camping (☎ 83563; bus No 705 or 713; camping from Skr95, 2-bed cabins from Skr150) is in the ski area 2km northeast of the centre. The big, well-kept **STF hostel** (☎ 10560; e stf.vandrarhem.falun@telia .com; Vandrarvägen 3; bus No 701; dorm beds from Skr130) is 3km east of the town; take the bus to Kopparitorget, from where it's a 10-minute walk. The friendly SVIF **Falu Fängelse Vandrarhem** (☎ 795575; e info@ falufangelse.se; Villavägen 17; dorm beds Skr180) is a more central option, and accommodation is in the cells of an old prison, used up until the mid-1990s.

There are good hotel choices right by the tourist office, including **Hotel Falun** (☎ 29180; Trotzgatan 16; singles/doubles Skr540/740, discounted to Skr500/600), offering comfortable rooms with private toilet and shared shower (or you can pay extra for rooms with full private bathroom).

An excellent choice for lunch is **Café Kopparhattan** (Stigaregatan), attached to Dalarnas Museum. It serves sandwiches for around Skr40, soup for Skr52 and a vegetarian buffet for Skr65. **Lilla Pizzerian** (Slaggatan 10, pizzas to Skr55) does takeaway and eat-in pizzas and kebabs. There are a number of eateries on the main square and the adjoining pedestrian malls of Holmgatan and Åsgatan. **Banken Bar & Brasserie** (Åsgatan 41) is a classy place with a grand interior. The menu includes a 'gott & enkelt' (good and simple) category featuring the likes of burgers and pasta (Skr89 to Skr125), plus more upmarket options.

For self-caterers, there's a central **ICA supermarket** (Falugatan).

Getting There & Away
Falun isn't on the main railway lines – change at Borlänge when coming from Stockholm or Mora – but there are direct trains to/from Gävle (Skr95). Swebus Express has buses on the Gothenburg–Karlstad–Falun–Gävle route,

and also has connections to buses on the Stockholm-Borlänge-Mora route.

Regional traffic is run by **Dalatrafik** (☎ 020 232425) and covers all corners of the county of Dalarna. Tickets cost Skr15 for trips within a zone, and Skr15 extra for each new zone. A 31-day *länskort* costs Skr800 and allows you to travel throughout the county. Regional bus No 70 goes to Rättvik and Mora.

LAKE SILJAN REGION

This pretty, traditional area in the county of Dalarna is a popular summer tourist destination for boths Swedes and foreigners, with numerous festivals and reasonable-sized towns offering good facilities and attractions. **Siljansleden** extends for more than 300km around Lake Siljan and has excellent walking and cycling paths – maps are available from tourist offices. Another way to enjoy the lake is by boat: in summer, MS *Gustaf Wasa* has a complex schedule of lunch, dinner and sightseeing cruises from the main towns of Mora, Rättvik and Leksand. Inquire at any of the area's tourist office for a schedule.

Check out the Siljan area website at W www.siljan.se.

Rättvik
☎ 0248 • pop 10,900

Rättvik is a popular town on Lake Siljan, with sandy beaches in summer and ski slopes in winter. The **tourist office** (☎ 797210; W www .rattvik.se; open daily mid-June–mid-Aug, Mon-Fri mid-Aug–mid-June) is at the train station.

The 13th-century **church**, rebuilt in 1793, has 87 well-preserved **church stables**, the oldest dating from 1470. Farther north is **Gammelgården** (☎ 51445; admission free, guided tours Skr20; open noon-5pm daily mid-June–mid-Aug), an open-air museum with a good collection of furniture painted in local style. There are guided tours for Skr20 from mid-June to mid-August. **Kulturhuset** (☎ 70199; adult/child for both museums Skr20/free; open daily), in town near the Enån River, houses the library, art exhibitions and displays on local flora and fauna. Don't miss the longest wooden pier in Sweden, the 625m **Långbryggan** out over the lake. Views from surrounding hills and the ski slopes are excellent. Try the rodel run, a sort of summer bobsled chute that's lots of fun (Skr30/70 for one/three rides).

Dalhalla (☎ 797950; W www.dalhalla.se), an old quarry 7km north of Rättvik, is used as an open-air concert venue in summer – the acoustics are incredible and the setting is stunning. It's well worth going along to see a performance – tickets usually start at Skr150. See the tourist office for a programme of concerts.

Places to Stay & Eat On the lakeshore near the train station is **Siljansbadets Camping** (☎ 51691; camping low/high season Skr90/135, 4-bed cabins from Skr280/390). **Rättviksparken** (☎ 56110; camping low/high season Skr90/120, doubles Skr250, cabins from Skr275/400) is by the river off Centralgatan (1km from the train station).

STF hostel (☎ 10566; e rattviksparken@ rattviksparken.fh.se; Centralgatan; dorm beds Skr120), by Rättviksparken, is excellent. Also good value is the mission-run **Jöns-Andersgården** (☎ 10735; Bygatan 4; dorm beds Skr120), up on the hill (the view is superb), with beds in traditional wooden huts dating from the 15th century. The quiet, pretty **Stiftsgården** (☎ 51020; singles/doubles from Skr375/530) is by the lake and near the church.

The cheapest eateries are opposite the train station. **Fricks Bageri** (Torget) has sandwiches, cakes, pies and coffee, and **Erkut Pizzeria** offers pizzas (Skr40) and kebabs (Skr45). **Palmbergs** (Storgatan, lunch Skr65) has good coffee, fresh OJ and a range of sandwiches. Self-caterers will find three **supermarkets** on Storgatan.

Getting There & Away Buses depart from outside the train station. Dalatrafik's bus No 70 runs between Falun, Rättvik and Mora. Direct trains from Stockholm and Mora stop at Rättvik.

Mora
☎ 0250 • pop 20,000

The popular legend is that, in 1520, Gustaf Vasa fled on skis from Mora after hiding from the Danes. Two good yeomen of Mora, chose to brave the winter and follow. The huge ski race Vasaloppet, which ends in Mora, commemorates Gustaf's journey and involves 90km of gruelling nordic skiing. Around 15,000 take part on the first Sunday in March.

The **tourist office** (☎ 592020; W www .mora.se; open daily mid-June–mid-Aug, Mon-Fri mid-Aug–mid-June) is at the train station.

Vasaloppsmuseet (☎ 39225; Vasagatan; adult/child Skr30/10; open 10am-5pm Mon-Fri; 10am-5pm daily mid-June–mid-Sept) has interesting displays about the largest skiing event in the world, and the story behind it. **Zornmuseet** (☎ 16560; Vasagatan 36; adult/child Skr35/2; open daily) celebrates the works and private collections of the Mora painter Anders Zorn. The Zorn family house, **Zorngården** (☎ 10004; Vasagatan 36; open daily (short hours mid-Sept–mid-May), between the church and the museum, is an excellent example of a wealthy artist's house, reflecting his National Romantic aspirations. There are guided tours every 30 minutes for adult/child Skr45/10.

The most reputable of the painted Dalarna **wooden horses** (☎ 37200; open daily mid-June–mid-Aug, Mon-Sat mid-Aug–mid-June) or *dalahästar* are made by Nils Olsson Hemslöjd at Nusnäs, 10km southeast of Mora (bus No 108). You can inspect the workshops and buy up big at the souvenir outlet; both are open daily in summer.

Outside the town of Orsa (16km north of Mora) is **Grönklitt Björnpark** (☎ 46200; bus No 118; adult/child Skr75/40; open daily mid-May–mid-Sept, Sat & Sun only mid-Sept–mid-Oct), an excellent place where you can see bears, wolves and lynx in fairly natural surrounds. The bears are usually fed around noon, when you'll get a great view of them.

Places to Stay & Eat In a great spot by the river 400m northwest of the church, busy **Moraparken** (☎ 27600; camping from Skr75, 2/4-bed cabins from Skr250/350) has good facilities and is a popular spot for families.

The **STF hostel** (☎ 38196; e info@malkullann.se; Fredsgatan 6; dorm beds from Skr140) is owned by Ann of **Målkull Ann's Pensionat** (☎ 38190; Vasagatan 19; singles/doubles with shared facilties Skr450/ 600), who offers a good selection of accommodation in the centre of town. **Hotell Kung Gösta** (☎ 15070; Kristinebergsgatan 1; dorm beds from Skr120; singles/doubles Skr750/ 1090, discounted to Skr590/790), opposite the main station, has a hostel annexe in addition to its comfortable hotel rooms.

There are a few old-style cafés on Kyrkogatan, plus fast-food joints and supermarkets. By Zornmuseet is the excellent **Claras Restaurant** (Vasagatan; dagens rätt Skr75, light meals from Skr59). **Målkull Ann's**

(Vasagatan; meals Skr70-160) is a pretty restaurant and café opposite Vasaloppsmuseet.

Getting There & Away All Dalatrafik buses use the bus station at Moragatan 23. Bus No 70 runs to Rättvik and Falun. Bus No 170 goes to Särna, Idre and Grövelsjön, near the Norwegian border.

Mora is an SJ terminus and the southern terminus of Inlandsbanan, which runs north to Gällivare between mid-June and mid-August. The main train station is about 1km east of town, by the lake. The more central Mora Strand is a platform station in town but not all trains stop there, so check the timetable.

When travelling to Östersund, you can choose between Inlandsbanan (Skr240, 6½ hours) or bus No 45 (Skr255, 5¼ hours).

Skåne

The county of Skåne, sometimes anglicised as Scania, was Danish until the mid-17th century – the influence of the Danish is still easily detected in the dialect and architecture.

Bicycle trips are popular in Skåne; there are numerous attractions in the gently rolling landscape and more hostels than any other region of Sweden.

For information about the Skåne region, contact **Skåne Tourist Board** (☎ 046-350570; W www.skanetur.se), which publishes some very good brochures and maps.

MALMÖ
☎ 040 • pop 262,400
Malmö is a lively and friendly city, perhaps due to the influence of Copenhagen across Öresund. The new 16km Öresund bridge and tunnel link, which includes Europe's longest bridge (7.8km), has brought the two cities even closer.

Orientation & Information
Although the main square, Stortorget, is the focus of the city, there's also Lillatorg and Gustav Adolfs torg nearby. Centralstationen (the central train station) is just outside the city centre's encircling canals. Malmöhus slott guards the western end in its park setting.

The **tourist office** (☎ 341200; W www .malmo.se; open 9am-8pm Mon-Fri, 10am-5pm Sat & Sun June-Aug; 9am-6pm Mon-Fri, 10am-1pm Sat & Sun May & Sept; 9am-5pm

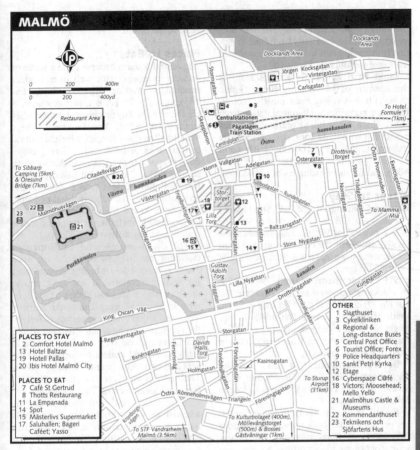

MALMÖ

0 | 200 | 400m
0 | 200 | 400yd

Restaurant Area

Docklands Area

Docklands Area

To Hotel Formule 1 (1km)

To Sibbarp Camping (5km) & Öresund Bridge (7km)

To Mamma Mia

To Sturup Airport (31km)

To Kulturbolaget (400m), Möllevångstorget (500m) & Bosses Gästvåningar (1km)

To STF Vandrarhem Malmö (3.5km)

PLACES TO STAY
2 Comfort Hotel Malmö
13 Hotel Baltzar
19 Hotell Pallas
20 Ibis Hotel Malmö City

PLACES TO EAT
7 Café St Gertrud
8 Thotts Restaurang
11 La Empanada
14 Spot
15 Mästerlivs Supermarket
17 Saluhallen; Bageri Caféet; Yasso

OTHER
1 Slagthuset
3 Cykelkliniken
4 Regional & Long-distance Buses
5 Central Post Office
6 Tourist Office; Forex
9 Police Headquarters
10 Sankt Petri Kyrka
12 Etage
16 Cyberspace C@fé
18 Victors; Moosehead; Mello Yello
21 Malmöhus Castle & Museums
22 Kommendanthuset
23 Teknikens och Sjöfartens Hus

SWEDEN

Mon-Fri, 10am-2pm Sat, Oct-Apr) is inside Centralstationen. The free official booklet *Malmö* is very useful, listing tourist information and a guide to events. The discount card Malmökortet allows free bus transport, free street parking, free entry to several museums and discounts at other attractions and on sightseeing tours. It's good value at Skr120/150/180 for one/two/three days.

Skånegården *(open daily)* is a tourist office on the E20, 800m from the Öresund bridge toll. It's designed purely to give information to motorists entering the country from Denmark, and can provide details on Malmö, Skåne and the whole of Sweden.

A **Forex** exchange counter can be found inside the tourist office within the train station. The **central post office** *(Skeppsbron 1)* is not far from here. **Cyberspace C@fé** *(Engelbrektsgatan 13)* offers Internet access at Skr22/44 for 30/60 minutes. Good information in English can be found at W www.malmo.com.

Things to See

The main museums of Malmö are based around **Malmöhus slott** *(☎ 344400; Malmöhusvägen)*; you can walk through the royal apartments with their interiors and portrait collections and see the **Stadsmuseum**, with its Malmö collection, and the galleries of **Konstmuseum**. Especially interesting are the **aquarium** and the **Naturmuseum**. The old **Kommendanthuset** arsenal is opposite the castle and **Teknikens och Sjöfartens Hus** is a short way to the west. The latter is a well-presented technology and maritime museum displaying aircraft, motor vehicles, steam engines and a walk-in submarine. The museums are open 10am to 4pm daily from June to August (otherwise noon to 4pm) and combined entry costs adult/child Skr40/10.

Sankt Petri kyrka *(Göran Olsgatan)* is characteristic of 14th-century Baltic Gothic style, although it has been mostly rebuilt. There's a magnificent altarpiece dating from 1611. There are restored parts of the late-medieval town at **Lilla Torg**, now occupied by restaurants, galleries and boutiques. It's worth wandering around Drottningtorget and down Adelgatan for more examples of old Malmö.

Places to Stay
Sibbarp Camping *(☎ 155165; Strandgatan 101; bus No 12B or 12G; camping Skr125-170, 2-bed cabins Skr260-390, 4-bed cabins Skr370-490)* is by the beach about 5km from the centre of town and has a great view of the Öresund bridge.

STF Vandrarhem Malmö *(☎ 82220; e info@malmohostel.se; Backavägen 18; bus No 21; dorm beds from Skr130)* is 3.5km south of the city centre. The hostel is big, bright and well equipped, offering breakfast for Skr50. Catch the bus from Centralplan in front of Centralstationen.

Bosses Gästvåningar *(☎ 326250, Södra Förstadsgatan 110B; singles/doubles from Skr275/325)* is a central SVIF hostel, close to Möllevangstorget.

Rooms or apartments from about Skr250 per person are available through **City Room** *(☎ 79594; e cityroom@telia.com)*. Otherwise, contact the tourist office.

Hotel Pallas *(☎ 611 5077; Norra Vallgatan 74; singles from Skr355, doubles Skr395-475)* is a recommended cheapish hotel near the train station; breakfast is an extra Skr30. **Hotel Formule 1** *(☎ 930580; Lundavägen 28; rooms Skr290)* is 1.5km east of Stortorget. Rooms can sleep up to three people. **Ibis Hotel Malmö City** *(☎ 664 6250; Citadellsvägen 4; rooms Skr540-680)* is a good, reasonably priced central option.

All of the better hotels offer discounts on weekends and in summer. Try **Comfort Hotel Malmö** *(☎ 611 2511; Carlsgatan 10C; singles/doubles Skr945/1095, discounted to Skr620/760)*, in the area north of the train station. **Hotel Baltzar** *(☎ 665 5700; e info@ baltzarhotel.se; Södergatan 20; singles/ doubles from Skr980/1300, discounted to* Skr700/850) is another good choice in the heart of the action.

Places to Eat
The central squares become quite a scene on summer evenings, with well over a dozen restaurants offering alfresco dining and drinking. Lilla Torget is a picturesque cobbled square lined by restaurant-bars and often teeming with people. Your best bet is to head to **Saluhallen** *(Lilla Torget)*, which has an excellent range of food stalls offering something to appeal to every taste, including pasta, sushi, kebabs, Chinese, and baked potatoes. Inside, **Bageri Caféet** *(meals from Skr20)* serves filled bagels, baguettes and ciabattas. Also here, **Yasso** *(lunch Skr58)* serves up Greek dishes, including a range of mezes (small appetiser dishes) from Skr30.

The cheap and cheerful **La Empanada** *(Själbodgatan 10; dishes Skr30-40; open 10am-7pm Mon-Sat)* is highly recommended for budget travellers. It has an extensive menu of mainly Mexican dishes served cafeteria-style; tacos, enchiladas and burritos. The area around Möllevångstorget reflects the city's interesting ethnic mix, and there's good, cheap food on offer from a mix of stalls, stores and student-frequented restaurants and bars. Also here is the popular **Krua Thai** *(Möllevångstorget 14; dishes Skr70)*, a large and long-standing Thai restaurant.

For excellent Italian sandwiches and salads, visit the stylish **Spot** *(Stora Nygatan 33)*; daily pasta and risotto dishes cost from Skr60. **Café St Gertrud** *(Östergatan 7)* is in the charming old St Gertrud courtyard. For a special treat and an atmospheric meal, try **Thotts Restaurang** *(Östergatan 10; mains Skr165, 2-course set menu Skr245)*, in a lovely half-timbered house. Enter via the SAS Radisson Hotel.

The central **Mästerlivs supermarket** *(Engelbrektsgatan)* is opposite the Temperance Hotel. The best produce market is on Möllevångstorget.

Entertainment
For evening diversions, head to Lilla Torget or Möllevångstorget and take your pick of bars. On Lilla Torget, **Victors**, **Moosehead** and **Mello Yello** stand side by side and compete for custom. On Möllevångstorget, **Nyhavn** is the drinking spot of choice, but there are numerous places in the vicinity.

Kulturbolaget *(Bergsgatan 18)* has regular live music or DJs. Other popular clubs are **Etage** *(Stortorget)*, with two dance floors and four bars, and the huge **Slagthuset** *(Jörgen Kocksgatan 7A)*.

Getting There & Away

Sturup airport *(☎ 613 1000)* is 31km southeast of the city and SAS has up to five direct flights to/from Stockholm daily. The low-cost carrier Ryanair also flies to Sturup from the UK. Trains run directly from Malmö to Copenhagen's main airport (Skr80), which has a much better flight selection.

An integrated Öresundregionen transport system is now operational, with trains from Helsingborg via Malmö and Copenhagen to Helsingør. Malmö to Copenhagen (Skr80) takes 35 minutes, trains leave every 20 minutes. For a round tour of the Öresund or a visit to Copenhagen, the Öresund Runt card (Skr199) gives two days' free travel on ferries and local trains. The cards can be bought at the Pågatågen train station in Malmo.

SJ runs regularly to/from Helsingborg and Gothenburg via Lund. Direct trains run between Stockholm and Malmö, including X2000 services.

Skånetrafiken *(☎ 020 567567;* W *www .skanetrafiken.skane.se)* operates the local buses and trains in the Skåne region. It sells a variety of value cards and passes, including a useful summer pass (Skr395), valid for 25 days of travel throughout the county from mid-June to mid-August. Pågatågen local trains run to Helsingborg, Lund, Ystad and other destinations in Skåne (bicycles are half-fare, but are not allowed during peak times, except in summer). The platform is at the end of Centralstationen; you buy tickets from a machine. International rail passes are accepted.

Regional and long-distance buses depart from Stormgatan, opposite the post office (behind the station). Swebus Express runs daily to Stockholm, Gothenburg and Oslo. Trains are best for trips across the Öresund bridge.

In 2002 all ferry services between Copenhagen and Malmo ceased. The bridge and excellent train connections between the two cities had made them obsolete.

Getting Around

The regular Flygbuss runs from Centralstationen to Sturup airport (Skr80); a taxi should cost no more than Sk350.

Malmö Lokaltrafik offices are at Gustav Adolfs torg and Värnhemstorget. Local tickets cost Skr14 for one hour's travel. The bus hubs are Centralplan (in front of Centralstationen), Gustav Adolfs torg, Värnhemstorget and Triangeln. The Malmökortet includes city bus travel.

Bicycles can be rented for Skr120/600 per day/week from **Cykelkliniken** *(☎ 611 6666)*, behind Centralstationen.

LUND

☎ 046 • pop 99,600

The second-oldest town in Sweden, Lund was founded by the Danes around 1000. Construction of the cathedral began about 1100 and Lund became the largest archbishopric in Europe. Much of the medieval town can still be seen. The university was founded in 1666, after Sweden took over Skåne. Today, Lund retains its quiet yet airy feel and has a youthful population.

The **tourist office** *(☎ 355040;* W *www .lund.se; Kyrkogatan 11; open daily June-Aug; Mon-Sat May & Sept; Mon-Fri Oct-Apr)* is opposite the cathedral. The **public library** *(Sankt Petri Kyrkogatan 6)* has free Internet access, but there's also the Internet café, **Studio 9** *(Lilla Gråbrödersgatan)*, nearby.

Things to See

The excellent **Kulturen** *(☎ 350400; Tegnerplatsen; adult/child Skr50/free; open 11am-5pm daily mid-Apr–mid-Sept, noon-4pm Tues- Sun Oct–mid-Apr)* claims to be the world's second-oldest open-air museum (it opened in 1892). Its impressive collection of about 40 buildings fills two blocks and includes period homes from the 17th century and countless displays. Nearby, **Hökeriet** *(☎ 255972; cnr St Annegatan & Tomegapsgatan; open daily June-Aug, Mon-Sat Sept-May)* is an old-fashioned general store worth a quick look.

The magnificence of Lund's Romanesque **cathedral** *(open daily)* is well known, but for a real surprise visit at noon or 3pm (1pm and 3pm on Sunday and holidays) when the astronomical clock strikes up *In Dulci Jubilo* and the figures of the three kings begin their journey to the child Jesus. Close by, you can find out about the cathedral at **Domkyrkomuseet**, and the attached **Historiska Museet** *(☎ 222 7944; open 11am-4pm Tues-Fri)* has pre-Viking Age finds. Both museums are

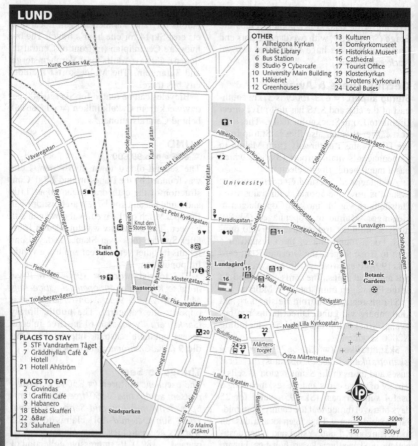

LUND

OTHER
1 Allhelgona Kyrkan
4 Public Library
6 Bus Station
8 Studio 9 Cybercafe
10 University Main Building
11 Hökeriet
12 Greenhouses
13 Kulturen
14 Domkyrkomuseet
15 Historiska Museet
16 Cathedral
17 Tourist Office
19 Klosterkyrkan
20 Drottens Kyrkoruin
24 Local Buses

PLACES TO STAY
5 STF Vandrarhem Tåget
7 Gräddhyllan Café & Hotell
21 Hotell Ahlström

PLACES TO EAT
2 Govindas
3 Graffiti Café
9 Habanero
18 Ebbas Skafferi
22 &Bar
23 Saluhallen

open Tuesday to Friday (combined entry adult/child Skr20/free).

Drottens kyrkoruin (*Kattesund 6*) are 11th-century church ruins; the **underground museum** (☎ 141328; adult/child Skr10/free; open 9am-4pm Tues-Fri, noon-4pm Sat & Sun) has models and exhibits of Lund's past.

The **main university building**, which faces Sandgatan, is worth a glance inside and Scanian rune stones are arranged in the park nearby. The **Botanic Gardens** with tropical greenhouses are east of the city centre.

Places to Stay & Eat

You could easily keep Lund as a base and take trains to nearby towns if you stay at the central **STF Vandrarhem Tåget** (☎ 142820; e trainhostel@ebrevet.nu; dorm beds Skr120),

behind the station (connected by overpass). You sleep in railway carriages set in parkland, with three bunks to a room – they're quiet yet tiny and perhaps too familiar to weary train travellers.

Private rooms can be booked at the tourist office from Skr200 per person plus a Skr50 fee. Book early for tiny **Gräddhyllan Café & Hotell** (☎ 157230; e graddhyllans@swipnet .se; Bytaregatan 14; singles/doubles Skr495/ 795, discounted to Skr400/600), which is a lovely place offering all of four rooms above a café.

Hotel Ahlström (☎ 211 0174; Skomakaregatan 3; singles/doubles from Skr575/725, Sat & Sun discounted to Skr525/625) is another central, mid-range option, but it's closed from Midsummer to mid-August.

Lund has plenty of eating possibilities ranging from fast-food eateries and library cafés to popular evening hang-outs. **Saluhallen** *(Mårtenstorget)* is a good place for reasonably priced food, from pasta to hamburgers and kebabs. For something a little more upmarket, **&Bar** *(lunch from Skr45)* on the same square, is a fashionable but relaxed place; it serves lunchtime meals of bagels, salads and various specials.

Habanero *(Kyrkogatan 21)* is good for an el cheapo Tex-Mex fill (lunch is Skr59). **Govindas** *(Bredgatan 28)* has a lunchtime vegetarian deal for Skr55. Nearby **Graffiti Café** *(cnr Paradisgatan & Bredgatan; meals from Skr30)* offers baked potatoes, salads and baguettes. **Ebbas Skafferi** *(Bytaregatan 5; lunch from Skr50)* is a delightful courtyard café well worth seeking out; there's a good lunchtime selection.

Getting There & Away

There are frequent SJ and Pågatågen departures from Lund to Malmö (Skr34, 15 minutes); some trains continue to Copenhagen. All long-distance trains between Stockholm and Malmö stop in Lund. Buses leave from outside the train station.

TRELLEBORG

☎ 0410 • pop 38,600

Trelleborg has Sweden's main ferry connections with Germany, but if you're arriving into here, there's no reason to linger in town long – better to move on to Malmö or Ystad. The town's few medieval remnants are complemented by a re-creation of a Viking fortress, **Trelleborgen** *(☎ 53049; admission free, guided tours summer free; open daily)*, off Bryggaregatan.

The **tourist office** *(☎ 53322; w www.trelleborg.se; Hamngatan 9)* is useful. If you need a place to stay, **Night Stop** *(☎ 41070; Östergatan 59; singles/doubles Skr199/299)* is diagonally opposite the town museum, about 500m from the tourist office.

Bus No 146 runs every half-hour or so between Malmö and Trelleborg's bus station, some 500m from the ferry terminals.

There are two ferry terminals, both behind the tourist office. **Scandlines** *(☎ 65000)* ferries connect Trelleborg to Sassnitz (five a day) and Rostock (three a day). **TT Line** *(☎ 56200)* ferries and catamarans shuttle between Trelleborg and Travemünde (three to five a day), and between Trelleborg and Rostock (three a day).

YSTAD

☎ 0411 • pop 26,200

Rambling cobbled streets and half-timbered houses remain in this agreeable medieval town that is visited by daily ferries from Bornholm and Poland. The friendly **tourist office** *(☎ 577681; w www.visitystad.com; open daily mid-June–mid-Aug, Mon-Fri mid-Aug–mid-June)* is opposite the train station. Next door is the large **Konstmuseum** *(☎ 577285; adult/child Skr20/free; open Tues-Sun)*. Don't miss the medieval **Sankta Maria kyrka** *(Stortorget)* or the historical **Ystads Stadsmuseum** *(☎ 577286; adult/child Skr20/free; open daily)* in the old monastery church of Gråbrödraklostret.

On the Baltic coast 19km east of Ystad is **Ales Stenar** *(bus No 322; admission free)* a mysterious pre-Viking stone formation forming an oval 67m along its long axis.

Places to Stay & Eat

Those with their own wheels can choose B&B or cabin options along the scenic coastal roads. The central **SVIF hostel** *(☎ 577995; e ystad .stationen@home.se; dorm beds Skr180)* is handily located in a renovated railway building at Ystad's train station. The **STF hostel** *(☎ 66566; bus No 572; dorm beds Skr135)* is 2km east of Ystad in a pleasant beachside recreation area. **Hotell Bäckagården** *(☎ 19848; Dammgatan 36; singles/doubles from Skr450/650)* is a cosy guesthouse in a 17th-century home behind the tourist office, and nearby **Hotell Tornväkteren** *(☎ 78480; Stora Östergatan 33)*, above a café on the main street, has similar prices.

There are some lovely cafés amongst the beautiful old buildings; **Bäckahästen** *(Lilla Östergatan 6)* is an inviting place with lots of garden seating. Most budget eating places are on Stora Östergatan, the main pedestrian street. If you feel like a treat, visit **Bryggeriet** *(Långgatan 20; lunch Skr65, dinner Skr95-195)*, an atmospheric restaurant and pub in an old brewery.

Getting There & Away

Buses depart from outside the train station. To get to Trelleborg by bus, first take bus No 303 to Skateholm then transfer to bus No 183. Pågatågen trains run roughly hourly to/from Malmö (Skr70).

Unity Line *(☎ 556900)* ferries sail daily between Ystad and Świnoujście in Poland. In

SWEDEN

Ystad, the ferry terminal is within walking distance of the train station. Frequent ferries also operate between Ystad and the Danish island of Bornholm (see the Denmark chapter).

HELSINGBORG
☎ 042 • pop 118,500

The busy port of Helsingborg is perched on the Öresund coastline. There's a summer boulevard atmosphere in Stortorget and the older buildings in the winding streets blend well with the newer shops. The seaside character is enhanced by an architectural pastiche of high beachfront houses. Denmark is only 25 minutes away by ferry.

The well-organised **tourist office** (☎ 104350; W www.visit.helsingborg.se; Stortorget; open 9am-8pm Mon-Fri, 9am-5pm Sat & Sun June-Aug; 9am-6pm Mon-Fri, 10am-2pm Sat Sept-May; 10am-2pm Sun May) can help with visitor inquiries. Most other travel-related needs are met inside the vast Knutpunkten complex at the seafront, including **Forex** for currency exchange. **First Stop Sweden** (☎ 104130; W www.firststopsweden.com; Bredgatan 2; open 9am-9pm daily June-Aug, 8am-5pm Mon-Fri Sept-

May), near the car-ferry ticket booths, dispenses tourist information on the whole country. The large **public library** (Stadsparken), near Knutpunkten, offers Internet access, and there's a small **Internet café** (Mariatorget 17).

Things to See

Too many travellers leave Helsingborg without seeing any more than the underground train station, but it's an appealing town with quality budget accommodation and it's worth taking some time to explore.

The eye-catching new **Dunkers Kulturhus** (☎ 107400, Kungsgatan 11; admission free; open 11am-6pm Wed & Fri-Mon, 11am-10pm Tues & Thurs), in the area just north of the transport terminals, opened in 2002 and houses the very good **town museum** and **art museum** (adult/child for both Skr60/free), plus a concert hall, restaurant and café. Take a stroll along the northern waterfront from here to admire the sleek and attractive apartment buildings and restaurants, all part of a very successful harbour redevelopment project.

You can access the square medieval tower **Kärnan** (☎ 105991; adult/child Skr15/5;

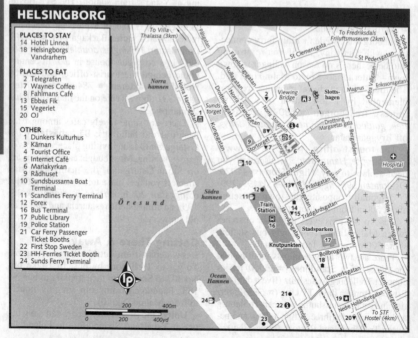

HELSINGBORG

PLACES TO STAY
14 Hotell Linnea
18 Helsingborgs Vandrarhem

PLACES TO EAT
2 Telegrafen
7 Waynes Coffee
8 Fahlmans Café
13 Ebbas Fik
15 Vegeriet
20 OJ

OTHER
1 Dunkers Kulturhus
3 Kärnan
4 Tourist Office
5 Internet Café
6 Mariakyrkan
9 Rådhuset
10 Sundsbussarna Boat Terminal
11 Scandlines Ferry Terminal
12 Forex
16 Bus Terminal
17 Public Library
19 Police Station
21 Car Ferry Passenger Ticket Booths
22 First Stop Sweden
23 HH-Ferries Ticket Booth
24 Sunds Ferry Terminal

open 11am-7pm daily June-Aug, Tues-Sun Sept-May) from steps near the tourist office. The tower is all that remains of a 14th-century castle; the view from the top (34m) overlooks Öresund to the Danish heartland and reminds visitors of struggles that finally delivered the fortress to Swedish hands. You can access the area from steps near the tourist office. Historic **Mariakyrkan** (Mariatorget) is worth a visit for its medieval features and choral and organ concerts.

Fredriksdals Friluftsmuseum (☎ 104500; adult/child Skr40/free; open daily) is off Hävertgatan, 2km northeast of the centre. It has a pretty manor, gardens and a museum village – it's a lovely place for a stroll. Highlights of the summer programme here include performances in the baroque open-air theatre.

Places to Stay

The SVIF hostel **Villa Thalassa** (☎ 380660; Dag Hammarskjöldsväg; bus No 219; dorm beds/singles/doubles from Skr160/275/400), 3km north of the city centre, is reached by walking 500m along a path from the bus stop at Pålsjöbaden. The villa and gardens are beautiful, but the hostel accommodation is in huts.

The **STF hostel** (☎ 131130; e boka@stfv andrarhem.helsingborg.nu; Planteringsvägen 69-71; bus No 1; dorm beds from Skr160), 4km south of town, offers high quality accommodation in a newly fitted and stylishly decorated hostel. The most central hostel is **Helsingborgs Vandrarhem** (☎ 145850; e info@ hbgturist.com; Järnvägsgatan 39; dorm beds from Skr165), an excellent place in a nondescript building about 200m from Knutpunkten.

A good mid-range hotel in the city is the charming **Hotell Linnea** (☎ 214660; e linne a@hotell-linea.se; Prästgatan 4; singles/ doubles from Skr795/895, discounted to Skr620/720). There are some expensive hotels on Stortorget and near the harbour that discount heavily at weekends and in summer.

Places to Eat

The quickest snacks and a good variety of restaurants are found upstairs in the **Knutpunkten complex**, but don't miss the city centre. **Fahlmans Café** (Stortorget) is the most traditional of the city's cafés, serving sandwiches and pastries; in contrast is trendy **Waynes Coffee** (Stortorget), opposite, serving the usual modern café fare (bagels, wraps, salads, muffins). Unique **Ebbas Fik**

(Bruksgatan 20) is styled in 1950s retro with superb results; there's an extensive café menu here too.

An inviting bar-restaurant is **Telegrafen** (Norra Storgatan; snacks Skr50), serving a good selection of pub snacks such as nachos, fish and chips, and chicken drumsticks. Vegetarians will rejoice at **Vegeriet** (Järnvägsgatan 25; lunch Skr48, dinner Skr65), an inviting veggie café and restaurant.

For self-caterers, the best central supermarket is **OJ** (Karl Krooks gata).

Getting There & Away

The main transport centre is Knutpunkten; the underground platforms serve both the SJ and pågatågen/Kustpilen trains departing for Stockholm, Gothenburg, Copenhagen, Oslo and nearby towns. At ground level and a bit south, but still inside the same complex, is the bus terminal where regional Skånetrafiken buses dominate, but daily long-distance services run to various destinations, including Gothenburg and Oslo.

Knutpunkten is the terminal for frequent **Scandlines** (☎ 186300) car ferries to Helsingør (Skr22). Across the inner harbour, **Sundsbussarna** (☎ 216060) has a terminal with passenger-only ferries to Helsingør every 15 to 20 minutes in summer (Skr20). The frequent **HH-Ferries** (☎ 198000) service to Helsingør is the cheapest, both for cars (from Skr245, including up to five passengers) and individual passengers (from Skr9, rail passes not valid).

DFDS Seaways (☎ 241000; w www.dfds seaways.com) runs ferries every evening to Oslo (from Skr675/975 low/high season) from the Sunds terminal.

Götaland

The medieval kingdom of Götaland joined Svealand and Norrland to become Sweden 1000 years ago, but remained strongly influenced by Denmark. Soon after Gothenburg was founded by Gustav II Adolf in 1621, Sweden conquered the rest of the region.

Pricey but unforgettable is the long journey along the Göta Canal – from the rolling country of Östergötland, north of Linköping, into the great Lake Vättern, before continuing into the county of Västergötland on the other side and farther to Gothenburg. See Getting Around earlier in this chapter.

GOTHENBURG

☎ 031 • pop 471,300

The sunny west coast is almost as island-studded as the east. Gothenburg (the Swedish name, Göteborg, sounds like 'yoo-te-bor'), Sweden's second largest city, is wedded to its port and has a more Continental outlook than Stockholm.

There's a lot more to Gothenburg than the showpiece Kungsportsavenyn boulevard and Konstmuseet, not least its heavy industries and heritage as a port. The Liseberg fun park, with its prominent 'space tower', is statistically Sweden's top attraction.

Orientation

The heart of the city is bordered by canals, which are now well suited to sightseeing. A branch of the canals snakes its way to Liseberg amusement park.

From the centre of the city, Kungsportsavenyn crosses the canal and leads up to Götaplatsen. 'Avenyn' is the heart of the city with boutiques, restaurants, theatres, galleries and street cafés.

The recently closed shipyards are on the island of Hisingen. They are reached by road via the monumental bridge Älvsborgs bron, southwest of the city by Götaälvbron near Centralstationen (the central train station), and the tunnel Tingstadstunneln.

Information

Tourist Offices The main **tourist office** (☎ 612500; ⓦ www.goteborg.com; Kungsportsplatsen 2; open 9am-6pm daily June-Aug; 9am-6pm Mon-Fri, 10am-2pm Sat Sept-May; 10am-2pm Sun May) is central and busy. There is also a **branch office** (open 9.30am-6pm Mon-Fri, 10am-4pm Sat, noon-3pm Sun) at Nordstan shopping complex.

Göteborg Pass Göteborg Pass is a discount card giving entry to Liseberg and a number of city attractions and city tours, as well as parking and public transport within the municipality. It costs adult/child Skr175/95 for 24 hours or Skr295/190 for 48 hours. The card is available at tourist offices, hotels and numerous Pressbyrån newsagents.

Money Forex offices are at Centralstationen, inside the Nordstan shopping complex, opposite the tourist office on Kungsportsplatsen, and at Kungsportsavenyn 22. Banks with ATMs can be found all over, including inside the Nordstan complex.

Post & Communications The **post office** (Nordstan complex; open 9am-7pm Mon-Fri, 10am-3pm Sat) has long hours. **Janemans IT Palats** (Viktoriagatan 14) is an Internet café charging Sk50 per hour.

Libraries Stadsbiblioteket (Götaplatsen), the city library, has plenty of imported newspapers and magazines, books in English, a modern computer section (with free Internet access, but the wait can be long and the time limit very short) and a good café.

Emergency & Medical Services Apoteket **Vasan** (☎ 804410; open 8am-10pm daily) is inside the Nordstan complex. The **hospital** (Östra Sjukhuset; ☎ 343 4000) is near tram terminus No 1. The **police station** (☎ 739 2000; Ernst Fontells Plats) is off Skånegatan.

Liseberg

Liseberg fun park (☎ 400100; tram No 4, 5, 6 or 8 from Brunnsparken; adult/child under 7 Skr50/free) is dominated by its futuristic spaceport-like tower. The ride to the top, some 83m above the ground, climaxes in a spinning dance and a breathtaking view of the city. The other amusements and rides seem tame by comparison but there's no lack of variety. You can buy a pass for Skr235 that allows you to ride the attractions all day, otherwise individual rides cost between Skr10 and Skr40 each. Opening hours are complex – it's best to check the website at ⓦ www.liseberg.se.

Museums

After Liseberg the museums are the strongest attractions and, if several take your fancy, use the Göteborg Card.

The **Stadsmuseum** (☎ 612770; Norra Hamngatan; adult/child Skr40/10; open 10am-5pm daily May-Aug, Tues-Sun Sept-Apr), in Östindiska huset, has archaeological, local and historical collections, including Sweden's only genuine Viking ship.

The main art collections are at **Konstmuseet** (☎ 611000; Götaplatsen; adult/child Skr40/10; open 11am-6pm Tues-Thurs, 11am-5pm Fri-Sun). This museum has impressive collections of Nordic and European masters and is notable for works by Rubens, Van

GOTHENBURG (GÖTEBORG)

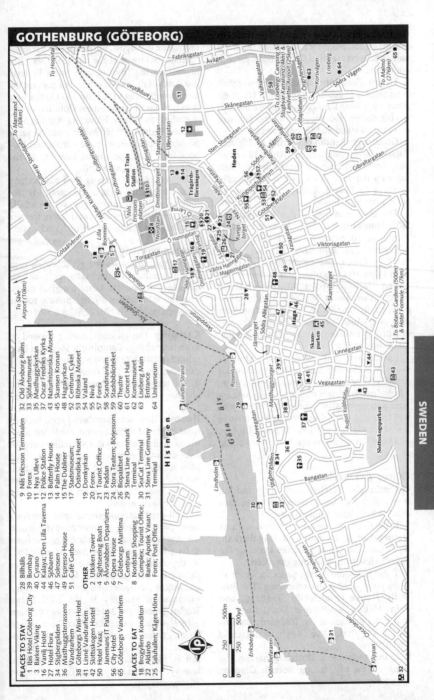

PLACES TO STAY
1 Ibis Hotel Göteborg City
3 Barken Viking
16 Vanil Hotel
27 Hotel Flora
34 Stigbergsliden
36 Masthuggsterrassens Vandrarhem
38 Göteborgs Mini-Hotel
41 Linne Vandrarhem
42 Slottsskogen Hostel
50 Hotel Vasa;
Janemans IT Palats
56 City Hotel
65 Göteborgs Vandrarhem

28 Billhälls
39 Bombay
40 Cyrano
44 Kalaya; Den Lilla Taverna
46 Sjöbaren
47 Solrosen
49 Espresso House
51 Café Garbo

PLACES TO EAT
18 Brogyllens Konditori
22 Aldardo
25 Saluhallen; Kåges Hörna

9 Nils Ericsson Terminalen
10 Forex
11 Nya Ullevi
12 Police Station
13 Butterfly House
14 Palm House
15 The Dubliner
17 Stadsmuseum;
Östindiska Huset
19 Domkyrkan
20 Forex
21 Tourist Office
23 Paddan
24 Stora Teatern; Börjessons
26 Biopalatset
29 Stena Line Denmark
Terminal
30 SeaCat Terminal
31 Stena Line Germany
Terminal

32 Old Älvsborg Ruins
33 Sjöfartsmuseet
35 Masthuggskyrkan
37 Oscar Fredriks Kyrka
43 Naturhistoriska Museet
45 Skansen Kronan
48 Hagakyrkan
52 Centrum Cykel
53 Röhsska Museet
54 Valand
55 Nivå
57 Forex
58 Scandinavium
59 Stadsbiblioteket
60 Theatre
61 Concert Hall
62 Konstmuseet
63 Liseberg Main
Entrance
64 Universeum

OTHER
2 Utkiken Tower
4 Sightseeing Boats
5 Älvsnabben Departures
6 Opera House
7 Göteborgs Maritima Centrum
8 Nordstan Shopping Complex; Tourist Office; Banks; Apotek Vasan; Forex; Post Office

SWEDEN

Gogh, Rembrandt and Picasso. The museum includes a sculpture section behind the main hall and the **Hasselblad Center** photographic collection.

The excellent **Röhsska Museet** (☎ 613850; Vasagatan 37; adult/ child Skr40/10; open noon-5pm Tues-Sun) covers modern Scandinavian design and decorative arts, but also contains classical and Oriental items.

Göteborgs Maritima Centrum (☎ 105950; Packhuskajen; adult/child Skr60/30; open daily Mar-Nov) claims to be the largest floating ship museum in the world and usually displays 13 historical ships, including the submarine Nordkaparen.

The main museum of maritime history, **Sjöfartsmuseet** (☎ 612900; Karl Johansgatan 1; museum & aquarium adult/child Skr50/10; open 10am-5pm daily May-Aug, Tues-Sun Sept-Apr), is near Stigbergstorget. There is an interesting aquarium attached.

The **Naturhistoriska Museet** (Natural History Museum; ☎ 775 2400; Slottsskogen park; adult/child Skr40/10; open 11am-5pm daily May-Aug, Tues-Sun Sept-Apr), the natural history museum, has a collection of some 10 million specimens.

By Liseberg is the striking new **Universeum** (☎ 335 6450; Södra Vägen; admission Skr80-110; open 10am-8pm June–mid-Aug, 11am-6pm Tues-Sun mid-Aug–mid-June), a huge and impressive 'science discovery centre' featuring everything from rainforests to a shark tank. It's got lots of good displays and hands-on experiments, but it's not cheap to visit.

Other Attractions
Gothenburg's churches aren't very old but they reflect Swedish architecture more than Stockholm's Italian imitations.

In addition to central churches, such as **Domkyrkan** (cathedral) and **Hagakyrkan**, don't miss the **Oscar Fredriks kyrka** or the superb view from **Masthuggskyrkan**.

There are some lovely parks in which to enjoy good weather in Gothenburg. The **Butterfly House** (adult/child Skr35/10) and **Palm House** (adult/child Skr20/free) are within the grounds of the **Trädgårdsföreningen** (City Park; Nya Allén; adult/child Skr15/free).

In the southwest is **Slottsskogsparken**, the 'lungs' of the city, and the **Botanic Gardens** are nearby.

Organised Tours
From June to August, **Börjessons** (☎ 609660) operates bus tours of the city (Skr75/50, 1½ hours), leaving from outside Stora Teatern, just south of the tourist office, but perhaps the most popular way to pass time in Gothenburg is to take a boat cruise on the Göta älv, or farther afield to the sea. From late April to September **Paddan** (☎ 609670) runs frequent 50-minute boat tours of the canals and harbour from Kungsportsbron, near the tourist office (adult/child Skr80/50).

Holders of the Göteborg Pass pay nothing to take one of the regular Älvsnabben ferries (otherwise Skr16) or to join cruises from Lilla Bommen to the ruins of Nya Älvsborg fortress near the river mouth (otherwise Skr85).

Places to Stay
Gothenburg offers several good hostels near the city centre and hotel prices are quite reasonable compared to other Swedish cities. The tourist office can arrange **private rooms** (singles/doubles Skr175/225) for a Skr60 fee.

Camping The closest camping ground to town is **Lisebergs Camping & Stugbyar Karralund** (☎ 840200; Olbergsgatan; tram No 5; camping Skr100-200), owned and operated by the fun park. It's geared for families and also has a range of cabins and rooms for rent.

Hostels There are a number of good hostels, most clustered in the central southwest area, in apartment buildings that sometimes inspire little confidence from the outside, but inside offer accommodation of a very high standard. All are open year-round, and usually offer double rooms for not much more than the cost of two dorm beds.

Well-run **Masthuggsterrassens Vandrarhem** (☎ 424820; e masthuggsterrassen .vandrarhem@telia.com; Masthuggsterrassen 8; tram No 3,4 or 9; dorm beds from Skr150) is very clean, quiet and close to the ferries to Denmark. Take the tram to Masthuggstorget and follow the signs (up the stairs behind the supermarket). Nearby is the STF hostel **Stigbergsliden** (☎ 241620; e vandrarhem .stigbergsliden@swipnet.se; tram No 3, 4 or 9; Stigbergsliden 10; dorm beds Skr115) in a renovated 18th-century seaman's house. Breakfast is Skr40 and there's a good kitchen, laundry, TV room and garden. Take the tram to Stigbergstorget.

STF's **Slottsskogen** (☎ 426520; e *mail@
slottsskogenvh.se; Vegagatan 21; tram No 1
or 2; dorm beds from Skr100)* is a friendly,
appealing place with excellent facilties. Take
the tram to Olivedalsgatan. Down the road is
another good option, the SVIF hostel **Linné
Vandrarhem** (☎ 121060; Vegagatan 22;
dorm beds from Skr160)*. Clean and inviting
Göteborgs Mini-Hotel (☎ 241023; e *info@
minihotel.se; Tredje Långgatan; dorm beds
from Skr130)* is located in the same area.

Göteborgs Vandrarhem (☎ 401050;
e *info@goteborgsvandrarhem.se; Mölndals-
vägen 23; tram No 4; dorm beds from
Skr150)* is just south of Liseberg in yet another well-equipped hostel. Take the tram to
Getebergsäng.

Hotels Probably the best accommodation
bargain in town, **Hotel Formule 1** (☎ 492400;
Axel Adlersgata 2; rooms Skr270)* is in Västra
Frölunda, about 7km south of the city centre.
Functional but bland rooms have shared facil-
ities and can accommodate up to three people.

Ibis Hotel Göteborg City (☎ 802560; Gullbergskajen 217; rooms Skr525-650)* is a large
floating hotel with comfortable, well-priced
rooms. The down side is that it is in quite an
isolated part of town. Better located is another
large boat-hotel **Barken Viking** (☎ 635800;
Gullbergskajen; singles Skr600-800, doubles
Skr800-1000)*, near Lilla Bommen. You can
pay extra for a little more luxury and private
facilties in an officer's cabin.

City Hotel (☎ 708 4000; e *receptionen@
cityhotelgbg.se; Lorensbergsgatan 6; singles/
doubles Skr395/495)* is in a fine location behind Kungsportsavenyn. For about Skr300
extra you can have a better standard of room
with private facilities. In a similar vein is
Hotel Flora (☎ 138616; Grönsakstorget 2;
singles/doubles Skr415/575)*, not far from
the tourist office. It also offers very comfortable rooms with private facilties in addition
to its budget rooms.

Vanilj Hotel (☎ 711 6220; e *info@
vaniljhotel.entersol.se; Kyrkogatan 38; singles
Skr545-795, doubles Skr795-995)* is a small,
cosy and personal place above a lovely café,
situated in the heart of town.

Hotel Vasa (☎ 173630; e *info@hotelvasa
.se; Viktoriagatan 6; singles/doubles Skr845/
995, discounted to Skr550/720)* is an attractive, family-run place handy to the cafés of
Vasagatan.

Places to Eat

Kungsportsavenyn, the Champs-Élysées of
Gothenburg, is lined with all kinds of restaurants and alfresco dining is popular when the
sun comes out. Vasagata and Linnégatan are
similar, with quite a few popular places. Unfortunately, many restaurants are closed on
Sunday.

If you need something quick, the enormous Nordstan shopping complex houses
many fast-food outlets. Right by the tourist
office, busy **Aldardo** (Kungstorget 12; meals
Skr25-35)* is a great spot to pick up authentic
Italian fast food – home-made pizza al taglio
(by the slice) and pasta. In the middle of
neighbouring Saluhällen, full of excellent
budget eateries and food stalls, **Kåges Hörna**
(meals Skr35)* serves some of the best cheap
food around – chicken salad, lasagne and
pasta specials.

Cafés are numerous and invariably of high
quality. **Café Garbo** (Vasagatan 40)* and the
very trendy **Espresso House** (Vasagatan 22)*
are two of several excellent places along the
leafy Vasagatan boulevard. **Brogyllens Konditori** (Västra Hamngatan 2)* is a lovely traditional place selling great breads and
pastries.

Near the hostels in the southwest, **Bombay**
(Andra Långgatan 8; dishes Skr70)* serves
good-value Indian dishes, including tandoori
and vegetarian selections. **Kalaya** (Olivedalsgatan 13; dishes Skr55)* has excellent Thai
dishes, and its neighbour, **Den lilla Taverna**
(Olivedalsgatan 17; mains Skr100)*, is a
charming place with authentic, reasonably
priced Greek dishes. **Cyrano** (Prinsgatan 7;
lunch Skr65, dinner from Skr135)* is a highly
regarded French restaurant. Cosy **Sjöbaren**
(Haga Nygata 25; dishes Skr95)* has excellent
Swedish seafood; classic dishes like *gravad
lax* (cured salmon) with potatoes, fish soup or
seafood pasta. Vegetarians should head for
nearby **Solrosen** (Karponjärgatan 4; dishes
from Skr60)*, a slightly grungy place with
great buffets.

The best supermarket is **Billhälls** (Hvit-
feldtsplatsen)*.

Entertainment

You'll find some good pubs and bars along
the main thoroughfares. **The Dubliner** (Östra
Hamngatan 50B)* is as authentic an Irish pub
as you'll ever find on the Continent and has
live music nightly in summer.

Kungsportavenyn, often referred to simply as Avenyn (the avenue) is the place to go for nightlife. Take a wander among the restaurant-bars and take your pick. **Nivå** at No 9 and **Valand**, on the corner with Vasagatan, are popular nightclubs.

Biopalatset *(Kungstorget)* cinema has 10 screens, and there are numerous other cinemas around town. Facing each other near Konstmuseet are the city **Theatre** and **Concert Hall**, often with interesting performances. The **Opera House** *(Christina Nilssons gata)* is also worth a visit.

Gothenburghers are avid sports fans, and the city has outdoor stadiums such as **Nya Ullevi** and the indoor **Scandinavium**, where pop and rock concerts are also held.

Getting There & Away
Air Landvetter airport (☎ *941000*) is 25km east of the city. There are frequent daily flights to and from Stockholm and daily services to many other European cities. **Säve** (☎ *926060*) is a minor airport some 20 minutes north of the city, used by Ryanair.

Bus The modern bus station, **Nils Ericsson Terminalen**, is next to the train station. There's a **Tidpunkten office** (☎ *0771-414300*) here giving information and selling tickets for all city and regional public transport within the Göteborg, Bohuslän and Västergötland region.

Eurolines (☎ *020 987377; Kyrkogatan 40; open 9am-5.30pm Mon-Fri*) has its main Swedish office in town. **Swebus Express** has an office at the bus terminal and operates frequent buses to most major towns (up to 10 daily to Stockholm, from Skr285). Cheaper **Säfflebussen** (☎ *020 160 0600*) runs to Copenhagen (Skr180, six a day), Oslo (Skr150, six a day) and Stockholm (Skr240, once or twice a day).

Train Centralstationen serves SJ and regional trains, with direct trains to Malmö, Copenhagen, Oslo and Stockholm. Tågkompaniet night trains run to the far north. Direct trains to Stockholm depart approximately hourly, with X2000 trains every one or two hours.

Boat Gothenburg is a major entry point for ferries, with several terminals.

Nearest the city centre, the **Stena Line** (☎ *704 0000*) Denmark terminal on Masthuggstorget (tram No 3, 4 or 9) has up to 11 daily departures for Frederikshavn in summer,

with 50% discount for rail pass-holders. Faster and dearer **SeaCat** (☎ *720 0800*) catamarans to Frederikshavn depart up to three times daily in summer from near Sjöfartsmuseet. Take tram No 3 or 9 to Stigbergstorget. Farther west is the Stena Line terminal for the daily car ferry to Kiel (in Germany). Take tram No 3 or 9 to Chapmans Torg.

DFDS Seaways (☎ *650650*) sails twice weekly to Newcastle from Skandiahamnen on Hisingen (buses leave 1½ hours earlier from Nils Ericsson Terminalen; Skr50).

Getting Around
You can catch the frequent Flygbuss to reach Landvetter airport from Nils Ericsson Terminalen (Skr50). There are also buses to Säve airport some 90 minutes before flight departures (Skr30).

Buses, trams and ferries run by **Västtrafik** (☎ *0771-414300*) make up the city public transport system; there are Tidpunkten information booths inside Nils Ericson Terminalen, on Drottningtorget and at Brunnsparken. An individual ticket on transport costs Skr16. Cheaper and easy-to-use 'value cards' cost Skr100 and reduce the cost considerably. A 24-hour *Dagkort* (day pass) for the whole city area costs Skr50. Holders of the Göteborg Card travel free.

The easiest way to cover lengthy distances in Gothenburg is by tram. There are 11 lines, all converging somewhere near Brunnsparken, one block from the train station. Also convenient and some fun are the Älvsnabben ferries, which run between Lilla Bommen and Klippan every 30 minutes or so. Västtrafik have regional passes for 24 hours (Skr190) or for 30 days (Skr1200) which give unlimited travel on all länstrafik buses, trains and boats within Gothenburg, Bohuslän and the Västergötland area.

Centrum Cykel *(Chalmersgatan 19)* offers bike rental for Skr100 per day.

MARSTRAND
☎ 0303 • pop 1300
Pretty Marstrand, with its wooden buildings and island setting, conveys the essence of Bohuslän fishing villages. Like many other places along the coast, it has become an upmarket weekend destination for wealthy sailors. The 17th-century **Carlstens Fästning** (☎ *60265; adult/child Skr60/20; open daily June-Aug*) fortress reflects a martial and penal history.

Båtellet (☎ 60010; dorm beds Skr185-235) is a private hostel 400m from the ferry dock; the attached **Restaurang Drott** serves lunch specials and à la carte selections, with a great view. There are numerous eating options along the harbour, including cheap **fast-food stalls** (one sells fresh fish and chips for Skr45), **cafés** and upmarket **restaurants**.

Marstrand is a good day-trip from Gothenburg (40 minutes). Take bus No 312 then cross to Marstrand by the frequent passenger ferry (Skr13) or, in summer, take a day trip by boat, which leaves from Lilla Bommen (Skr100/160 single/return, daily at 9.30am).

TANUMSHEDE
☎ 0525

Bronze Age rock carvings are well represented in Bohuslän, but the most famous are those on the World Heritage List at **Vitlycke** (admission free; always open), 2.5km south of Tanumshede. Nearby is an excellent **museum** (☎ 20950; adult/child Skr50/30; open daily Apr-Sept, Sat & Sun Oct-Dec) showing the carvings' origins and types, and with a reconstructed Bronze-Age farm.

Unfortunately transport connections are not great. If you catch a train to Tanum (on the Gothenburg-Strömstad line), you have to catch a connecting bus to the village of Tanumshede, then walk the 2.5km south to Vitlycke.

STRÖMSTAD
☎ 0526 • pop 11,200

Strömstad is an attractive fishing harbour and seaside resort near the Norwegian border, and is consequently very busy with Norwegian tourists taking advantage of Sweden's cheaper prices. The **tourist office** (☎ 62330; w www.stromstadtourist.se) is between the two harbours on the main square. There are good attractions, including **museums**, **beaches** and **boat trips** to nearby islands. The Koster islands are the most westerly in Sweden and are popular for cycling.

The central STF hostel **Crusellska Hemmet** (☎ 10193; Norra Kyrkogatan 12; dorm beds Skr140-160) is popular – book ahead. By the harbour, next door to the tourist office, is **Laholmens Fisk** (Norra Kyrkogatan) selling lots of fresh fish and good-value baguettes filled with seafood (Skr40 to Skr50). Not far away is **Göstases** (Strandpromenaden), with cosy nautical decor and a good menu of light meals.

Strömstad is the northern terminus of the Bohuståg train system, with regular trains to/from Gothenburg. Swebus Express buses between Gothenburg and Oslo also stop here.

Color Line (☎ 0526-62000; w www.colorline.com) ferries sail to Sandefjord (Skr130/160 low/high season, 2½ hours, two to six a day) in Norway.

HALMSTAD
☎ 035 • pop 85,700

Founded along the Nissen River, Halmstad was Danish until the 17th century. Medieval attractions include the 14th-century **church**, and the nearby **Tre Hjärtan** building, which also has a café (on Stora Torget). Along the river is a Danish **castle** (home to the tourist office) and an old boat, **Najaden** (admission free; open 5pm-7pm Tues & Thurs, 11am-3pm Sat mid-June–mid-Aug). North of the town centre is **Halmstad Museum** (☎ 162300; Tollsgatan; adult/child Skr20/5; open noon-4pm Tues-Sun). The beachside **Tylösand area** (bus No 10), 8km east of town, is an extremely popular summer spot for Swedes.

The **tourist office** (☎ 109345; w www.halmstad.se) can arrange **private rooms** (room per person Skr120), with self-catering and your own linen. The **SVIF hostel** (☎ 120500; e halmstad@hallonstenturist.se; Skeppargatan 23; dorm beds from Skr140; open late June–mid-Aug) is a central, summer-only choice. Near the beach at Tylösand, **Tylebäck** (☎ 32460; e info@tyleback.com; Kungsvägen 1; camping Skr150, dorm beds/singles/doubles Skr160/645/890) is in a rustic location and offers hostel, hotel and camping options.

Storgatan, particularly its northern end, has a great range of eating and drinking spots. For quick, cheap sustenance, **Nudelbar** (Storgatan; meals Skr50) is a small hole-in-the-wall serving takeaway noodle meals; the **Pasta Huset van** (Stora Torget; meals Skr29) does cheap pasta.

Swebus has regular bus connections with Malmö, Gothenburg and Jnköping. Regular trains between Gothenburg and Malmö stop in Halmstad.

VARBERG
☎ 0340 • pop 53,100

The main attraction in this pleasant coastal town is the **medieval fortress** (☎ 18520; adult/child Skr50/10; open daily), with its

SWEDEN

excellent museums. However, you might also want to brave the brisk Nordic weather and swim in **Kallhusbadet** (☎ 17396; adult/child Skr40/25; open daily mid-June–mid-Aug), a striking bathing house built in Moorish style on stilts above the sea. The town's **tourist office** (☎ 43224; W www.turist.varberg.se; Brunnparken) is in the centre of town.

The SVIF hostel **Vandrarhemmet Varbergs Fästning** (☎ 88788; e vandrarhem@turist .varberg.se; dorm beds Skr165-185), within the fortress, is one of the finest hostels in Sweden. It offers singles in old prison cells or larger rooms in other buildings. For dining, most cheap restaurants are along the pedestrianised Kungsgatan. **Harry's** (Kungsgatan 18, meals from Skr85) is a popular pub-restaurant serving a range of meals. However, the fortress **café** offers the best sea views in town.

Ferries from the Danish town of Grenå dock near the town centre. Trains between Gothenburg and Malmö (and on to Copenhagen) stop regularly at the train station. Buses depart from outside the train station.

NORRKÖPING
☎ 011 • pop 122,900

From the late 19th century, large textile mills and factories sprang up along Norrköping's swift-flowing Motala ström. Today this industrial-revolution architecture, complete with canals, locks and waterfalls, is a fine example of inner-city regeneration and well worth a look. Another key attraction is the animal park at Kolmården, 30km to the northeast.

The **tourist office** (☎ 155000; W www .destination.norrkoping.se; Dalsgatan 16; open daily late June-late July, Mon-Sat late July-late June) can help with visitor information. The city's **library** (Södra Promenaden 105) has free Internet access. There's also Internet available at **Norrköpings Biljard och IT Café** (Prästgatan 48).

Kolmården

Kolmården (☎ 249000; W www.kolmarden .com; bus No 432 or 433; open 10am-5pm daily May, 9am-6pm daily June-Aug; 9am-6pm Sat & Sun Sept) is billed as the largest zoo in Europe and has about 1000 animals from all continents and climates of the world. The complex is divided into two areas: the main **Djurparken** (zoo) with its excellent dolphin show **Delfinarium** (adult/child Skr195/ 95); and **Safariparken** (adult/child Skr80/

40), which you drive around (in a bus or your own transport). An excellent, separate **tropical house** (adult/child Skr70/45) opposite the entrance completes the attraction. A general 'maxi' ticket for the zoo and safari park costs Skr245/125. The cable car (Skr80/40) around the park gives a better view of the forest than of the animals.

You'll need all day to take the zoo in fully. Kolmården is 35km north of Norrköping, on the north shore of Bråviken – the bus trip costs Skr48.

Other Attractions

Pedestrian walkways and bridges lead around the ingenious system of locks and canals along the riverside. The industrial past is exhibited at the city museum, **Stadsmuseum** (☎ 152620; Holmbrogrämd; admission free; open 10am-5pm Tues-Fri, 11am-5pm Sat & Sun). Sweden's only museum of work, the excellent **Arbetets Museum** (☎ 189800; admission free; open 11am-5pm daily) is just across the bridge from the Stadsmuseum. A modern addition to the riverside scenery is the extraordinary **Louis de Geer Concert Hall** (☎ 155030; Gamla Torget).

The **Konstmuseum** (☎ 152600; Kristinaplatsen; adult/child Skr30/free; open Tues-Sun), the large art museum south of the centre at Kristinaplatsen, has some important early 20th-century works. For a view of the city and out to Bråviken, climb the 68m-high **Rådhuset tower** (Drottninggatan; admission Skr25; open mid-June–mid-Aug). **Sankt Olai kyrka**, in a small, central park, is one of the few noteworthy baroque churches in Sweden.

From early July to mid-August, the tiny vintage tram No 1 runs a short guided tour through the town centre. The tram leaves from outside the train station at 5pm Monday, Wednesday and Friday (Skr25).

Places to Stay

Himmelstalunds Camping (☎ 171190; camping per person Skr30) is near the city on the south bank of Motala Ström. There is also a huge, well-equipped camping ground 5km from Kolmården, **Kolmårdens Camping & Stugby** (☎ 398250; camping from Skr105, rooms/cabins from Skr395/495).

STF's **Turistgården** (☎ 101160; e info@ turistgarden.se; Ingelstagatan 31; dorm beds Skr145) is about 800m north of the train station and offers good accommodation. The

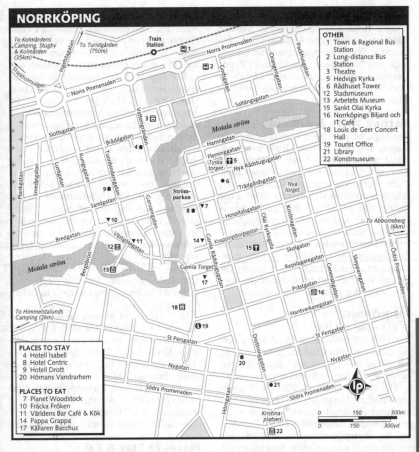

NORRKÖPING

OTHER
1 Town & Regional Bus Station
2 Long-distance Bus Station
3 Theatre
5 Hedvigs Kyrka
6 Rådhuset Tower
12 Stadsmuseum
13 Arbetets Museum
15 Sankt Olai Kyrka
16 Norrköpings Biljard och IT Café
18 Louis de Geer Concert Hall
19 Tourist Office
21 Library
22 Konstmuseum

PLACES TO STAY
4 Hotell Isabell
8 Hotel Centric
9 Hotell Drott
20 Hörnans Vandrarhem

PLACES TO EAT
7 Planet Woodstock
10 Fräcka Fröken
11 Världens Bar Café & Kök
14 Pappa Grappa
17 Källaren Bacchus

SWEDEN

second STF hostel, **Abborreberg** (☎ 319344; ⓔ info@abborreberg.nu; bus No 101 or 111; dorm beds Skr125; open May-Sept) is beautifully situated by the coast, 6km east of town. Accommodation is in cottages scattered through the surrounding park. Take the bus to Lindö. The third budget option is in the heart of town: **Hörnans Vandrarhem** (☎ 168271; ⓔ hornans.vandrarhem@telia.com; Hörngatan 1; dorm beds Skr160) is above a pub and has comfortable lodgings.

The best budget bet is the small **Hotell Isabell** (☎ 169082; Vattengränden 7; singles/doubles with shared facilities Skr450/550, discounted to Skr350/450). Pleasant **Hotel Centric** (☎ 129030; Gamla Rådstugugatan 18; singles/doubles Skr695/795, discounted to Skr390/490) and **Hotell Drott** (☎ 180060;

Tunnbindaregatan 19; singles/doubles Skr695/795, discounted to Skr390/490) both have similar rooms.

Places to Eat

There are plenty of cheap eateries in the shopping district along Drottninggatan, and also in the student quarter around Kungsgatan. There are some excellent options near the industrial area, including **Fräcka Fröken** (Kungsgatan 43), a cool café offering good coffee, sandwiches, salads and cakes, and the funky, colourful **Världens Bar Café & Kök** (Västgötegatan 15), with dishes – and music – from around the world. **Planet Woodstock** (Gamla Rådstugu gatan 11; dishes Skr60; open until 11pm Sun-Thur, until 5am Fri & Sat) has an extensive menu of bagels, baked potatoes and hot dishes like moussaka and lasagna. Heading upmarket, popular **Källaren Bacchus** *(Gamla Torget 4; lunch Skr63, dinner from Skr85)* has a great outdoor serving area, and lunch here is good value. **Pappa Grappa** *(Gamla Rådstugugatan 26; dishes from Skr95)* is a cosy, intimate place offering authentic Italian dishes.

Getting There & Around

The regional bus station is next to the train station, long-distance buses leave from a terminal across the road. Swebus and Svenska Bus have frequent services to Stockholm, Gothenburg, Jönköping and Kalmar, among others. Norrköping is on the main north-south railway line, and SJ trains run roughly hourly to Stockholm and Malmö. Frequent regional trains run south to Tranås (via Linköping).

Norrköping's urban transport is based on *länstrafiken* (see Linköping), and the minimum fare is Skr16. Trams cover the city and are quickest for short hops, especially along Drottninggatan from the train station.

LINKÖPING

☎ 013 • pop 134,000

Known for its medieval cathedral and modern aeroplane industries (SAAB is based here), Linköping is both a modern city and a preserver of traditions in its numerous museums.

The **tourist office** *(☎ 206835; www.linkoping.se; Klostergatan 68)* is inside Quality Hotel Ekoxen. It's open 24 hours, but is usually staffed during office hours. The striking city **library**, near the cathedral, has been rebuilt after a fire and offers Internet access. There's also a **Internet cafe** *(Bantorget 1)* not far from the long-distance bus stations.

Things to See & Do

The enormous **cathedral**, with its 107m spire, is the landmark of Linköping and is one of Sweden's oldest and largest churches. There are numerous gravestones and medieval treasures. The nearby castle houses the **Castle & Cathedral Museum** *(☎ 122380; adult/child Skr40/free; open 11am-4pm Tues-Fri, noon-4pm Sat & Sun Apr-Sept)*.

Just north of the cathedral, **Östergötlands Länsmuseum** *(☎ 230300; Vasavägen; adult/child Skr20/10; open 10am-5pm Tues-Fri, 11am-4pm Sat & Sun)* houses an extensive collection by a variety of European painters, including Cranach's view of Eden, *Original Sin*,

and Swedish art reaching back to the Middle Ages. The concrete floor of **Sankt Lars kyrka** *(Storgatan; open Mon-Sat)* was built above a medieval church crypt. Downstairs, you can see 11th-century gravestones and skeletons.

The best attractions are just outside the centre. Some 2km west of the city is **Gamla Linköping** *(☎ 121110; bus Nos 202 or 214; admission free; village & most museums open daily)*, one of the biggest living-museum villages in Sweden. Among the 90 quaint houses are about a dozen time museums, many shops and a small chocolate factory. You can wander among the 19th-century buildings at will. Just 300m through the forest behind the old village is the **Valla Fritidsområde**, a recreation area with domestic animals, a 'colony garden', a children's playground, minigolf, a few small museums and many old houses.

Some 7km west of the centre is **Flygvapenmuseum** *(☎ 283567; Malmslätt; bus No 213; adult/child Skr30/free; open 10am-5pm daily June-Aug, Tues-Sun Sept-May)*, with exhibits on air-force history, including 60 aircraft.

Most visitors to Sweden know about the engineering marvel of the Göta Canal, but Linköping boasts its own canal system, the 90km **Kinda Canal**. There are 15 locks, including the deepest in Sweden. A variety of cruises from early May to the end of September run along the canal. The trip on **MS Kind** *(☎ 0141-233370)* leaves the Tullbron dock on Wednesday and Thursday for Rimforsa and costs Skr235 (return by bus or train included).

Places to Stay & Eat

The excellent, central STF **Vandrarhem Linköping** *(☎ 149090; e lkpgvandrarhem@swipnet.se; Klostergatan 52A; dorm beds from Skr180, singles/doubles Skr595/680, Sat & Sun discounted to Skr455/550)* has dorm beds and a few hotel-style rooms, most with kitchenette. In the centre of Valla Fritidsområde is **Mjellerumsgårdens Vandrarhem** *(☎ 122730; dorm beds Skr160)*, which doesn't have a kitchen.

Not far from the train station is **Hotell Östergyllen** *(☎ 102075; Hamngatan 2B; singles/doubles with shared facilties from Skr350/500)* and its neighbour, **Stångå City** *(☎ 311275; singles/doubles Skr745/890, discounted to Skr445/595)*, both reasonable mid-range choices. The very central **Good Evening Hotel** *(☎ 129000; Hantverkaregatan*

LINKÖPING

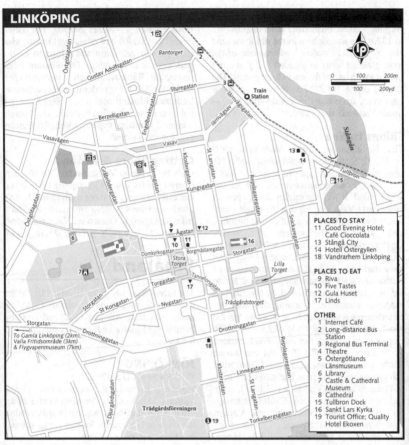

```
0        100        200m
0        100        200yd
```

PLACES TO STAY
11 Good Evening Hotel;
    Café Cioccolata
13 Stångå City
14 Hotell Östergyllen
18 Vandrarhem Linköping

PLACES TO EAT
9   Riva
10 Five Tastes
12 Gula Huset
17 Linds

OTHER
1   Internet Café
2   Long-distance Bus
    Station
3   Regional Bus Terminal
4   Theatre
5   Östergötlands
    Länsmuseum
6   Library
7   Castle & Cathedral
    Museum
8   Cathedral
15 Tullbron Dock
16 Sankt Lars Kyrka
19 Tourist Office; Quality
    Hotel Ekoxen

SWEDEN

1; singles/doubles Skr795/895, discounted to
Skr475/575) is another option.

Most places to eat (and drink) are on the
main square or nearby streets, especially
along buzzing Ågatan. **Five Tastes** *(Ågatan;
meals Skr50)*, opposite the cinema, offers a
decent selection of pizza and kebab meals.
New and trendy **Riva**, *(Ågatan 43; dishes
from Skr90)* has gourmet pizzas to fit the
decor, plus other pricey Italian dishes. **Gula
Huset** *(Ågatan; lunch Skr60, dinner Skr78)* is
more traditional. Around Stora Torget, **Linds**
(lunch Skr 59, dishes Skr45) serves both a
lunch buffet and à la carte meals including
nachos and pasta, and has a courtyard area.
Café Cioccolata *(Hantverkaregatan 1)* is a
stylish café offering a wide range of coffees
and filled panini or ciabatta (Skr35).

Getting There & Away
Regional and local buses have their terminal
adjacent to the train station. Long-distance
buses leave from 500m north of the train station. Linköping is on the main north-south railway line and SJ trains stop roughly every hour.

Regional (and local) traffic is run by **Öst-
götaTrafiken** *(☎ 0771-211010)*; there is an
information office at the station. Journeys
cost from Skr16; the 24-hour *dygnskort*
(Skr100) is valid on all buses and local trains
within the county.

VADSTENA
☎ 0143 • pop 7600
Beautiful Vadstena on Lake Vättern is a legacy
of both church and state power and now the
abbey and castle compete for the visitor's

interest. The dominant historical figure was St Birgitta, who established her order of nuns here in 1370. The atmosphere in the old town (and also by the lake) makes Vadstena one of the most pleasant spots in Sweden – if you don't meet up with one of the many local ghosts. The **tourist office** (☎ 31570; W www.vadstena .se/turism; open daily mid-June–mid-Aug) is inside Vadstena slott (castle).

Things to See
The Renaissance castle, **Vadstena slott** (☎ 31570; Slottsvägen; adult/child Skr50/10; open daily May-Sept, guided tours mid-May–mid-Sept), looks straight over the harbour and lake beyond. It was the mighty family project of the early Vasa kings and in the upper apartments there are some items of period furniture and paintings. The superb 15th-century **klosterkyrkan** (abbey church; ☎ 76807; Lasar-ettsgatan; admission free; open 11am-4pm daily mid-May–August) has a combination of Gothic and some Renaissance features. Inside are the accumulated relics of St Birgitta and medieval sculpture, including the saint depicted during revelation. Near the church is the **Klostermuseet** (adult/child Sk35/free; open daily mid-May-Aug), the old convent founded by St Birgitta in 1370. The old courthouse **Rådhus**, on the town square, and **Rödtornet** (Sånggatan) also date from late medieval times.

The area around Vadstena is full of history and deserves a closer look. Cycling is an option as the scenic flatlands around Vättern lend themselves to the pedal. A series of ancient legends is connected with **Rökstenen**, Sweden's most impressive and famous rune stone, by the church at Rök, just off the E4 on the road to Heda and Alvastra.

Places to Stay & Eat
The central **STF hostel** (☎ 10302; Skänninge-gatan 20; dorm beds Skr145) is open year-round, but from late August to early June it is essential to book in advance. A more appealing option is the lakeside **STF hostel** (☎ 20368, e info@borghamnsvandrarhem.nu; bus No 610; dorm beds Skr135), a friendly place in a lovely, quiet setting 15km southwest of Vadstena. It's about a 750m walk from the bus stop at Borghamn. The small, central **27:ans Natt-logi** (☎ 13447, Storgatan 27; singles/doubles from Skr500/600) has five rooms (some with private facilities, some shared) and breakfast is included in the price.

Pizzas are available at **Pizzeria Venezia** (Klostergatan 2, pizzas Skr50). For filled baguettes (Skr40) and other light meals, visit the open-air café **Hamnpaviljongen** in the park in front of the castle. The pleasant cellar restaurant **Rådhuskällaren** (Rådhustorget; mains Skr70-180) is under the old courthouse. **Vadstena Klosterhotel** (lunch Skr85), in the abbey area, serves a fine buffet lunch. There's a central **Konsum supermarket** (Rådhustor-get) for self-caterers.

Getting There & Around
Only buses run to Vadstena: bus No 661 regularly links the town with Mjölby (where you can catch trains to Linköping and Stockholm). Swebus Express bus No 840 runs once daily from Jönköping to Örebro via Vadstena. **Sport Hörnan** (☎ 10362; Storgatan 26) rents bikes.

Småland

The forested county of Småland is famous for glass production at its numerous factories, many of which you can visit, and was the homeland of many 19th-century emigrants to the USA.

JÖNKÖPING
☎ 036 • pop 117,900
Pleasantly located at the southern end of Lake Vättern, Jönköping is the main centre of an urban strip that stretches eastwards around the shore to Huskvarna, known for its sewing machines and motorcycles.

The **tourist office** (☎ 105050; W www .jonkoping.se; daily June-Aug, Mon-Sat Sept-May) is in the Juneporten complex, in the overpass connected to the train station (or accessed from Västra Storgatan). The large **public library** has Internet access and is adjacent to the Länsmuseum.

Things to See
The museum of the history of matches, **Tänd-sticksmuseet** (☎ 105543; Tändsticksgränd 27; adult/child Skr30/free; open daily June-Aug, Tues-Sat Sept-May) deals with this Swedish innovation that is much taken for granted, and is more interesting than it sounds! Nearby is the **Radio Museum** (☎ 713959; Tändsticksgränd 16; admission Skr20; open daily June–mid-Aug, Tues-Sat mid-Aug–May) with a collection of over

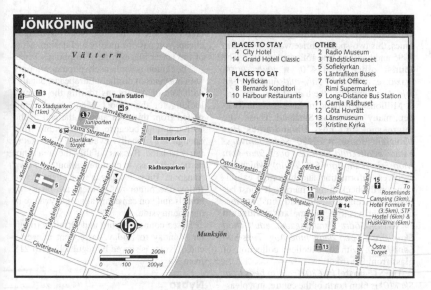

JÖNKÖPING

Vättern

Train Station

To Stadsparken (1km)
Juniporten
Järnvägsgatan
Västra Storgatan
Skolgatan
Djurläkartorget
Nygatan
Hamnparken
Rådhusparken
Östra Storgatan
Munksjön

Munksjön

0   100   200m
0   100   200yd

PLACES TO STAY
4 City Hotel
14 Grand Hotell Classic

PLACES TO EAT
1 Nyfickan
8 Bernards Konditori
10 Harbour Restaurants

OTHER
2 Radio Museum
3 Tändsticksmuseet
5 Sofiekyrkan
6 Läntrafiken Buses
7 Tourist Office;
   Rimi Supermarket
9 Long-Distance Bus Station
11 Gamla Rådhuset
12 Göta Hovrätt
13 Länsmuseum
15 Kristine Kyrka

To Rosenlunds Camping (3km), Hotel Formule 1 (3.5km), STF Hostel (6km) & Huskvarna (6km)

Östra Torget

1000 radio sets and related memorabilia – a playground for technical buffs.

In the old town square of Hovrättstorget are the 17th-century buildings of **Göta Hovrätt** and the red **Gamla Rådhuset**. The **Kristine kyrka** *(Östra Storgatan)* is in a restored part of the old town. Nearby are the collections of the **Länsmuseum** *(☎ 301800; Dag Hammarskjölds plats; adult/child Skr40/free; open 11am-5pm Tues-Sun)*, covering local history and contemporary culture; don't miss the childlike, yet strangely haunting fantasy works of John Bauer.

Places to Stay & Eat

Rosenlunds Camping *(☎ 122863; camping Skr160; cabins & rooms from Skr490)* is on the lakeshore off Huskvarnavägen 3km east of the town centre.

East of the town centre in Huskvarna, the **STF hostel** *(☎ 148870; ℮ 148870@telia.com; Odengatan 10; bus No 1; dorm beds Skr150)* is a good choice, with pleasant rooms and bikes for rent. **Hotel Formule 1** *(☎ 302565; Huskvarnavägen 76; bus No 1; 3-person rooms Skr270)* is another budget option, with basic rooms with shared facilities a few kilometres from the centre of town. **Grand Hotell Classic** *(☎ 719600; Hövrättstorget; singles/doubles from Skr690/840, discounted to Skr490/590)* is probably the cheapest central option; **City Hotel** *(☎ 719280; Västra Storgatan 25)* has similar discounted prices.

Most cheap eateries are on the pedestrian streets in the eastern part of the town centre. **Bernards Konditori** *(Kyrkogatan 12)* opened in the 1910s, and still serves tasty cakes and good coffee. In the area near the Tändsticksmuseet, **Nyfickan** *(lunch Skr50)* is an excellent café with a student atmosphere; sandwiches cost around Skr35. Head down to the harbour area's multitude of **restaurants** for good lunch specials (around Skr70) and crowds of a summer evening.

There's a **Rimi supermarket** in the Juniporten complex.

Getting There & Away

Long-distance buses depart from next to the train station; while most regional buses use the terminal on Västra Storgatan. Swebus Express bus services can get you to Gothenburg (Skr150), Stockholm (Skr265) and Malmö (Skr245).

Jönköping is not on the main train lines. From the central train station you can catch hourly regional trains, which connect with SJ services on the main lines in Nässjö and Falköping.

VÄXJÖ
☎ 0470 • pop 74,100

Växjö (quite unpronounceable – ask a local to demonstrate!) was a Catholic centre in medieval Sweden. By 1050, a wooden church was

SWEDEN

established where the imposing 15th-century **cathedral** now stands. Ravaged by fire many times, this two-spired edifice was renovated in 1995 and houses a fine 15th-century altar. The **tourist office** (☎ 41410; W www.turism .vaxjo.se; open daily July–mid-Aug, Mon-Fri mid-Aug–June) is at the train station.

Millions of Americans have roots in Sweden, many of them in Småland. Those who return shouldn't miss **Utvandrarnas Hus** (Emigrant House; ☎ 20120; Södra Järnvägsgatan; adult/child Skr40/5; open 9am-4pm Mon-Fri, 11am-4pm Sat & Sun), which has archives, information and historical exhibitions on the beckoning America. It's just behind the central train and bus station, conveniently close to **Smålands Museum** (☎ 45145; Södra Järnvägsgatan; adult/child Skr40/free; open daily June-Aug, Tues-Sun Sept-May), with an excellent collection of glass from Glasriket.

The **STF hostel** (☎ 63070; dorm beds from Skr110) is 6km north of the centre, in a pleasant lakeside recreational area (take bus No 1C). The cheapest central hotel is **Hotell Esplanad** (☎ 22580; Norra Esplanaden 21A; singles/doubles Skr650/750, discounted to Skr400/570). For sustenance, head to Storgatan for a decent array of eateries. **Orient Kebab** (Storgatan 28, meals Skr40) has the usual run of burgers and pizzas. Nearby **Wokie Dokie** (Storgatan; meals from Skr25) has great take-away Asian food. **Café Momento** at Smålands Museum is a great lunch spot, with an excellent selection of baguettes, salads and cakes, and a pretty courtyard.

Växjö lies between Alvesta and Kalmar and is served by SJ trains that run roughly hourly. Buses to other parts of the county also depart from the train station, with destinations including Oskarshamn, Kalmar and Västervik.

GLASRIKET

With dense forests and quaint red houses, Glasriket (W www.glasriket.net) is popular among tourists – it's the most visited area in Sweden outside Stockholm and Gothenburg. The 'Kingdom of Crystal' has at least 15 glass factories (look for signs saying 'glasbruk') scattered around the wilderness, and its roots go way back. Kosta was founded in 1742, and by the end of the 19th century there were 10 factories in full swing. Factory outlets offer substantial discounts on seconds – don't just come for glass and crystal since

there are ceramics, wood, leather and handicrafts for sale in the area. Not everything is cheap; you pay for quality and design. Most of the larger places offer a shipping service.

The region is immensely popular not only with busloads of northern Europeans, but also with lots of Americans touring the country looking for their roots. Many people emigrated from this area around the end of the 19th century because they couldn't find enough work locally. Even now, Glasriket is fairly isolated. Because of this, the area is not particularly easy to explore without your own transport. Bicycle tours are excellent if you follow the minor roads; there are plenty of hostels and you can camp almost anywhere in the countryside.

Buses connect Nybro and Orrefors (regular Monday to Friday, infrequent at weekends). Kosta is served by regular bus No 218 from Växjö.

Nybro
☎ 0481 • pop 19,800

Of the two glass factories in the eastern part of Glasriket, traditional **Pukeberg** is a worthwhile stop for its quaint setting and higher quality. The **tourist office** (☎ 45085; W www.nybro .se; Stadshusplan) is inside the town hall and can help with visitor inquiries. About 2.5km west of the town centre is the 200m-long **kyrkstallarna building**, which was the church stables but now house the excellent museum **Madesjö Hembygdsgård** (adult/child Skr25/5; open daily mid-June–mid-Aug).

Nybro Lågprishotell & Vandrarhem (☎ 10932; Vasagatan 22; dorm beds Skr130-170, singles/doubles Skr490/690), south of the centre near Pukeberg, is the local STF hostel. It's clean and comfortable and has a kitchen on each floor. You can also rent bikes here. The more upmarket **Stora Hotellet** (☎ 51935; Mellangatan 11; singles/doubles Skr790/895, discounted to Skr600/650) is on Stadhusplan, by the tourist office. There's a restaurant that's good for a meal (pizzas from Skr55).

SJ trains between Alvesta and Kalmar stop here every hour or two. Regional bus No 131 runs to/from Kalmar.

Kosta, Boda & Orrefors
These three small Småland villages are home to the three biggest names in Swedish glass production. Each namesake company is open daily and each factory complex has an outlet

store, museum or gallery and glass-blowing demonstrations.

The village of Kosta is where Glasriket started in 1742. At times it looks like the biggest tourist trap in southern Sweden, but it will be appreciated if you concentrate on the finesse and quality of the local craftsmanship and not on the tourist buses and discount stores. Boda is a quaint little village with a large factory outlet and several other shops. Founded in 1864, the glass factory is now part of the **Kosta Boda company** (☎ 0478-34500; W www.kostaboda.se). Much the same products are available at each factory.

Orrefors (☎ 0481-34195; W www.orrefors .se) was founded in 1898. The factory complex is impressive (check out the gallery) and there's a good hostel nearby, but the namesake village is pretty dull.

Places to Stay & Eat Across the road from the factory in Kosta, **Kosta Värdshus** (☎ 0478-50006; singles/doubles Skr400/650) serves inexpensive lunches and offers simple, comfortable accommodation. There's also a good café inside the factory's outlet store.

The **STF hostel** (☎ 0481-24230; e boda .vandrarhem@telia.com; dorm beds Skr120; open May–mid-Sept) in Boda is not far from the factory. The friendly, well-equipped **STF hostel** (☎ 0481-30020; dorm beds Skr110-150; open May-Aug) in Orrefors is conveniently located near the factory area. At the factory complex you can dine at **Orrefors Värdshus** (good but pricey lunches) but there's also a stall selling hot-dogs and ice cream. You can also get pizzas and kebabs from **Pizzeria Alexandra** in the village.

OSKARSHAMN
☎ 0491 • pop 26,200

Although important for boat connections to Gotland and useful for travel-related services, Oskarshamn isn't an immensely interesting town. Hantverksgatan is one of the main streets, where you'll find the **tourist office** (☎ 88188; W www.oskarshamn.se; Hantverksgatan 18), a good library that has free Internet access, and also two museums, **Sjöfartsmuséet** and **Döderhultarmuséet** (☎ 88040; combined admission adult/child Skr30/free; both open daily mid-June–mid-Aug), with wonderful woodcarvings by Döderhultaren (well worth a look) and maritime exhibits.

The well-run **STF hostel** (☎ 88198; e vandrarhemmet@oksarshamn.se; Åsavägen 8; dorm beds Skr80-130) is a few hundred metres from the train station and well positioned for the Gotland ferries. **Lilla Frej** (Lilla Torget; lunch Skr65, dinner from Skr70) serves lunch and evening meals including pizza, pasta and salads.

Länstrafik trains run from Nässjö, and there are regional buses running regularly on the Kalmar-Oskarshamn-Västervik route. Swebus Express has two daily buses between Stockholm and Kalmar that stop at Oskarshamn. Regular boats to Visby depart from near the train station (see Gotland).

KALMAR
☎ 0480 • pop 59,800

For a long time the port of Kalmar was the key to Baltic power and the short-lived Scandinavian union agreement of 1397 was signed at its grand castle. Kalmar was vital to Swedish interests until the 17th century and its streets and impressive edifices retain a strong historical flavour. Visit the **tourist office** (☎ 15350; W www.kalmar.se/turism; Larmgatan 6; open daily June-Aug; Mon-Sat May & Sept; Mon-Fri Oct-Apr) for information. The **public library** (Tullslätten 4) has free Internet access, but is outside the city grid.

Things to See
The once-powerful Renaissance castle **Kalmar Slott** (☎ 451490; adult/child Skr70/20; open daily Apr-Sept), by the sea south of the railway, was the key to Sweden before lands to the south were claimed from Denmark. The panelled King Erik chamber is the highlight of the interior, while another chamber exhibits punishment methods used on women in crueller times. The **Konstmuseum** (Art Museum; ☎ 426282; Slottsvägen 1D; adult/child Skr40/free; open 11am-5pm daily) is a few minutes' walk from the castle.

The highlight at **Kalmar Länsmuseum** (☎ 451300; Skeppsbrogatan; adult/child Skr50/free; open 10am-6pm daily mid-June–mid-Aug, Tues-Sun mid-Aug–mid-June), in the old steam mill by the harbour, is the exhibition of finds from the flagship Kronan, which sank controversially off Öland – a disaster to match the sinking of the Wasa, now on show in Stockholm. Aft and slightly to port is **Kalmar Sjöfartsmuseum** (☎ 15875; Södra Långgatan 81; admission Skr30; open

SWEDEN

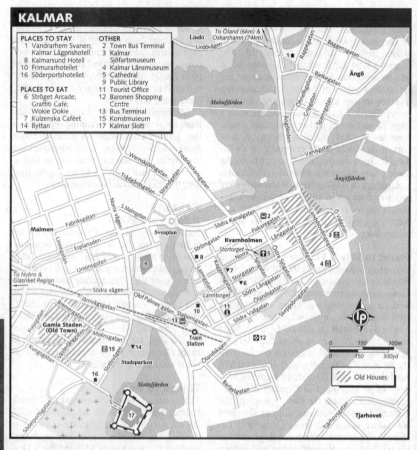

KALMAR

PLACES TO STAY
1 Vandrarhem Svanen;
  Kalmar Lågprishotell
8 Kalmarsund Hotell
10 Frimurarhotellet
16 Söderportshotellet

PLACES TO EAT
6 Ströget Arcade;
  Graffiti Café;
  Wokie Dokie
7 Kulzenska Caféet
14 Byttan

OTHER
2 Town Bus Terminal
3 Kalmar
  Sjöfartsmuseum
4 Kalmar Länsmuseum
5 Cathedral
9 Public Library
11 Tourist Office
12 Baronen Shopping
  Centre
13 Bus Terminal
15 Konstmuseum
17 Kalmar Slott

---

daily mid-June–mid-Aug, Sun mid-Aug–mid-June), a delightfully eccentric little maritime museum. A few blocks away is the baroque **cathedral** *(Stortorget)*, which was designed by Tessin, the leading 17th-century architect working for the Swedish crown.

Places to Stay & Eat
Vandrarhem Svanen *(☎ 12928; @ info@ hotellsvanen.se; Rappegatan 1; bus No 402; dorm beds Skr160)* is a well-equipped STF hostel attached to **Kalmar Lågprishotell** *(☎ 25560; singles/doubles Skr465/595)*, on the adjacent island of Ängö. **Söderports-hotellet** *(☎ 12501, Slottsvägen 1; singles/ doubles Skr350/530; open mid-June–mid-Aug)* is right by the castle and offers good summertime accommodation in student digs.

There are plenty of hotels in the city centre, but not much for those on a budget. Try **Frimurarhotellet** *(☎ 15230; Larmtorget 2; singles/doubles Skr875/1085, discounted to Skr625/795)*, in the heart of the action, or **Kalmarsund Hotell** *(☎ 18100; Fiskaregatan 5)*, with similar discounted rates. **Ströget arcade** *(Storgatan 24)* houses a small food hall, with a good selection of places – **Graffiti Café** *(meals Skr40-50)* serves salad, baguettes and baked potatoes, **Wokie Dokie** offers Asian noodles and stir-fry dishes. **Kulzenska Caféet** *(upstairs, Kaggensgatan 26)* is a gorgeous place with 19th-century atmosphere and a range of sandwiches and cakes. **Byttan** *(lunch Skr65, dinner from Skr155)* is a classy restaurant in the park by the castle, offering wonderful views of the town's major attraction.

Getting There & Away

All regional traffic is run by **Kalmar Län-strafik** (☎ 0491-761200), including the Rasken long-distance services and buses to Öland. A one-way ticket costs Skr16 to Skr117 within the county; a *Sommarkort* is valid from mid-June to mid-August on all buses and trains within the county and costs around Skr850. All regional and long-distance buses depart from the train station; local town buses have their own terminal on Östra Sjögatan.

SJ trains run every hour or two between Kalmar and Alvesta (with connections to the main north-south line) and to Gothenburg.

ÖLAND

☎ 0485 • pop 25,000

More windmills than Holland? There are 400 on Öland today, but there were once around 2000. Most are the characteristic wooden huts on a rotating base. Also prominent are the lighthouses at the northern and southern tips of the island. Öland is a popular summer destination for Swedes and there are plenty of budget accommodation options – some 25 camping grounds and at least a dozen hostels.

The island stretches 137km, and is reached from Kalmar via the 6km Ölandsbron (bridge), once the longest in Europe. Buses connect all main towns from Kalmar (bus Nos 101-106 all cross the bridge to Färjestaden; Nos 101 and 106 go to Borgholm).

Borgholm

The 'capital' of Öland is a pleasant small town with shops, cafés and an enormous ruined castle. The **tourist office** (☎ 89000; open daily mid-June–mid-Aug, Mon-Fri mid-Aug–mid-June) is at the bus station.

The town is dominated from the hill just to the south by **Borgholm Slottsruin** (☎ 12333; adult/child Skr50/20; open daily May-Sept). This castle was finally burned and abandoned early in the 18th century after being used as a dye works. There's an excellent museum inside; the ruins are often used as a venue for summer concerts.

Sweden's most famous 'summer house', **Solliden Palace** (☎ 15355; parks & pavilion exhibitions adult/child Skr50/free; open daily mid-May–Sept), 2.5km south of the town centre, is used by the royal family. It has beautiful parks and pavilion exhibitions.

Places to Stay & Eat

Coastal **Grönhags Camping** (☎ 72116; camping Skr100-150) is one of a half-dozen large, neighbouring camping grounds in Köping (about 4km north of Borgholm). Most are open from late April to mid-September, and prices are increased in the peak summer season (from Midsummer to mid-August).

Just outside the centre of town is the **STF hostel** (☎ 10756; Rosenfors Manor; dorm beds Skr110-160; open mid-May–Aug), set in a pretty garden. **Olssons rumsuthyrning** (☎ 77939; Tullgatan 12A; doubles Skr400-600) has some simple double rooms; prices exclude breakfast; but there is a kitchen guests can use. Stylish **Hotel Borgholm** (☎ 77060; Trädgårdsgatan 15; singles/doubles Skr890/990) has been transformed into a colourful boutique hotel. The owner is one of Sweden's most well-known chefs – the restaurant here is, naturally, very highly regarded. If you feel like a splurge, a two-course set menu starts from around Skr300.

The main square in town has the usual collection of fast-food stalls and ice-cream kiosks, and there are a few reasonable dining options nearby. **Pubben** (Storgatan 18; meals Skr40) is a classic English-style pub serving up snacks and light meals, washed down with a choice of many fine beers.

Northern Öland

Sandvik, on the west coast of Öland 30km north of Borgholm, has the more familiar Dutch-type **windmill** (☎ 26172; open daily May-Aug). In summer, you can climb the eight storeys for a great view back to the mainland (adult/child Skr15/7; open daily mid-June–mid-Aug) and a café and restaurant here.

The remains of the medieval fortified church **Källa ödekyrka**, at a little harbour 36km northeast of Borgholm off road 136, are fascinating, as it and other churches actually supplanted the mighty stone fortresses as defensive works. **Grankullavik**, in the far north, has sandy beaches and dense summer crowds, but the natural attractions in the nearby **Troll-skogen** nature reserve are worth a visit.

Northern Öland has plenty of camping grounds. The SVIF **Grankullavik Vandrarhem** (☎ 24040; bus No 106; dorm beds from Skr175; open May-Sept) has a kitchen, restaurant and a bakery. The **STF hostel** (☎ 22038; bus No 106; dorm beds Skr100-165; open May-Aug) is in Böda.

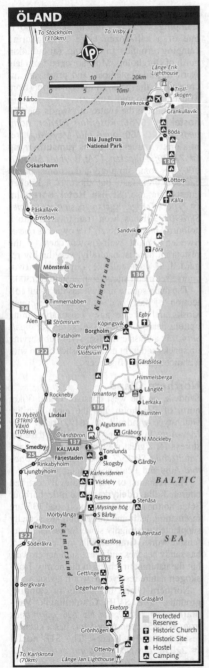

ÖLAND

To Stockholm (310km)
To Visby
Långe Erik Lighthouse
Fårbo
Byxelkrok
Trollskogen
Grankullavik
Blå Jungfrun National Park
Böda
Oskarshamn
136
Löttorp
Källa
Påskallavik
Emsfors
Sandvik
Föra
Mönsterås
Oknö
136
Timmernabben
Egby
Ålen
Strömsrum
Köpingsvik
Borgholm
Pataholm
Borgholm Slottsruin
Gärdslösa
Himmelsberga
Rockneby
Ismantorp
Långlöt
136
Lerkaka
Runsten
To Nybro (31km) & Växjö (109km)
Lindsal
Algutsrum
Gråborg
Ölandsbron
N Möckleby
137
Smedby
Torslunda
25
Färjestaden
Skogsby
Gårdby
Rinkabyholm
Karlevistenen
Ljungbyholm
Vickleby
BALTIC
Resmo
Stenåsa
Mysinge hög
Mörbylånga
S Bårby
Halltorp
Hulterstad
Söderåkra
Kastlösa
SEA
136
Stora Alvaret
Bergkvara
Gettlinge
Degerhamn
Gräsgård
Eketorp
Protected Reserves
Grönhögen
Historic Church
Historic Site
Hostel
Camping
To Karlskrona (70km)
Länge Jan Lighthouse
Ottenby

0   10   20km
0   5   10mi

SWEDEN

Färjestaden & Around

The long bridge from Kalmar lands you on the island just north of Färjestaden ('ferry town' – the pre-bridge name), where there's a large **tourist office** (☎ 560600; W www.olandsturist .se; open daily May-Aug, Mon-Sat Sept, Mon-Fri Oct-Apr) at the Träffpunkt Öland centre beside the road. The tourist office will book rooms (free of charge) or cabin accommodation (Skr50 fee) throughout the island.

Färjestaden itself has little of interest, but north of the bridge is the pricey **Ölands Djurpark** (☎ 30875; entry Skr160; open daily May-Aug), a zoo, amusement park and swimming pool popular with families.

The vast **Ismantorp fortress**, with house remains and nine mysterious gates, is 5km west of the Himmelsberga museum. It's an undisturbed fortress ruin, clearly showing how the village was encircled by an outer wall (Eketorp, described in the following Southern Öland section, is an imaginative reconstruction of similar remains). The area, just south of the Ekerum-Långlöt road, can be freely visited all year.

In the middle of the east coast at Långlöt, **Himmelsberga** (☎ 561022; open daily May-Aug) is a farm village from a bygone age. This isn't the only one on Öland, but here the quaint cottages have been repainted and fully furnished as a **museum** (adult/child Skr50/ free; open daily mid-June–mid-Aug).

The STF hostel **Ölands Skogsby** (☎ 38395; e info@vandrarhskogsby.se; bus No 103; dorm beds from Skr75; open mid-Apr–Sept) is 3km southeast of Färjestaden.

Southern Öland

The southern half of the island is chiefly a haven for nature and the relics of humankind's settlements and conflicts, attested to by the Iron Age fortresses and graveyards of all periods. It's now an area on Unesco's World Heritage List.

The unusual limestone plain, **Stora Alvaret**, is of interest to naturalists, especially those keen on bird life, insects and flora. The expanse takes up most of the inland southern half of Öland and can be crossed by road from Mörbylånga or Degerhamn. Late April, May and early June are usually good for venturing out by bicycle and for bird-watching.

The most southerly of the big ring forts, **Eketorp** (☎ 560607; open daily May-Aug), 6km northeast of Grönhögen, has been reconstructed to show what the fortified villages, which went in and out of use over the centuries, must have been like in early medieval times. The impressive fort can be viewed from the outside at any time, and inside there are reconstructed Iron-Age houses and a **museum** (☎ 560607; bus No 114; adult/child Skr50/20; open daily mid-June–mid-Aug). There are tours in English at 1pm daily from late June to late August. Take the bus from Mörbylånga.

In the small village of Mörbylånga, **Mörby Vandrarhem & Lågprishotell** (☎ 49393; Bruksgatan; singles/doubles Skr200/300; open May-Aug) has good accommodation. Öland's southernmost **STF hostel** (☎ 662062; camping Skr100, dorm beds Skr120) is near Ottenby, 7km south of Eketorp.

KARLSKRONA
☎ 0455 • pop 60,600
Karlskrona was reconstructed in grand baroque style after a fire in 1790 and became Sweden's greatest naval port. It's now on Unesco's World Heritage List. The **tourist office** (☎ 303490; W www.karlskrona.se/turism; Stortorget 2; open daily mid-June–mid-Aug, Mon-Sat mid-Aug–mid-June) can help visitors. The **public library** (Stortoget) offers free Internet access.

The finest attractions in Karlskrona are the extraordinary offshore **Kungsholms Fort** and the impregnable **Drottningskär kastell**; in summer, Skärgårdstrafiken sails from Fisktorget to the fort at 10am and 12.15pm (Skr70 return); book at the tourist office.

The striking **Marinmuseum** (☎ 53900; Stumholmen; adult/child Skr50/25; open 10am-6pm daily June-Aug, Tues-Sun Sept-May) has ship and historical displays. **Blekinge Museum** (☎ 304960; Fisktorget 2; adult/child Skr20/free; open 10am-6pm daily mid-June–mid-Aug, Tues-Sun mid-Aug–mid-June) features local cultural history and has a pleasant café.

A pleasant way to spend a sunny afternoon is touring Karlskrona's archipelago. A three-hour tour taking in the eastern islands costs Skr110; contact the Skärgårdstrafiken office at Fiskatorget for timetables and information.

Places to Stay & Eat
STF has two good hostels in the town centre: **Vandrarhem Trossö** (☎ 10020; e trossovandrarhem@telia.com; Drottninggatan 39; dorm beds Skr115), and **Vandrarhem Karlskrona**

(☎ 10020; Bredgatan 16; dorm beds from Skr130; open mid-June–mid-Aug). The newly renovated **Hotell Siesta** (☎ 80180; Borgmästaregatan 5; singles/doubles from Skr615/715, discounted to Skr495/615) is a decent mid-range option, right near Stortorget.

The northern side of the huge Stortorget and the street behind it, Ronnebygatan, are home to a good choice of eateries. **Red Light** (Ronnebygatan 21) has the usual fast-food selections (kebabs, pizzas etc). **Kings Crown** (Stortorget; meals Skr100), by the tourist office, is an English-style pub with good bar meals. Next door is **Glasslären** (open summer only), an extremely popular ice-cream café.

Getting There & Away
The bus and train stations are just north of the town centre. Svenska Buss runs once daily except Saturday to Kalmar and Stockholm. Train connections are better: direct trains run to Copenhagen via Malmö (10 a day). Regular trains also run to Emmaboda, and from there to Kalmar or Växjö and on to Gothenburg.

Stena Line ferries to Gdynia (Poland) leave from Verkö, 10km east of Karlskrona (take bus No 6).

Gotland

☎ 0498 • pop 57,400
Gotland, the largest of the Baltic islands, is also one of the most historical regions in Sweden – there are more than 100 medieval churches and an untold number of prehistoric sites. Other attractions include the odd *raukar* limestone formations (remains of 400 million-year-old coral reefs), and the walled, medieval trading town of Visby, which is on Unesco's World Heritage List. You could easily pass a week here seeing the highlights.

Gotland is probably the top budget travel destination in Sweden; bicycle travel is by far the best option, free camping in forests is easy and legal, most attractions are free and there are more than 30 hostels around the island. The island is jam-packed, however, with holidaying Swedes in July and August, and is *the* summer party spot for young Swedes, who come not for the history but for beaches and booze.

Prehistoric Sites
There are hundreds, perhaps thousands of sites around the island, many of them signposted,

SWEDEN

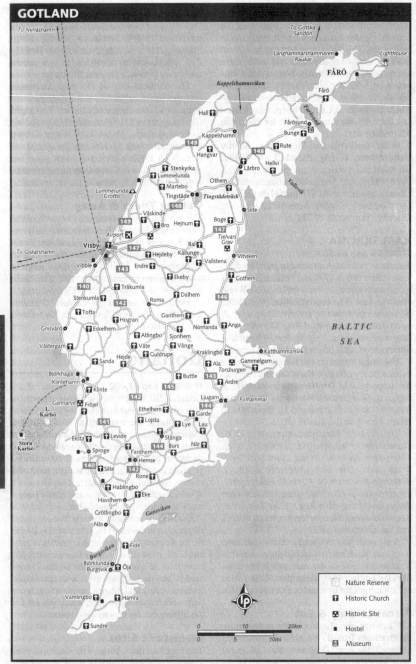

GOTLAND

To Nynäshamn

To Gotska Sandön

Langhammarshammaren Raukär

Lighthouse

FÅRÖ

Fårö

Kappelshamnsviken

Hall

Kappelshamn

149

Hangvar

148

Rute

Fårösund

Bunge

Lärbro

Hellvi

Stenkyrka

Lummelunda

Martebo

Othem

Lummelunda Grotto

Tingstäde

Tingstäderäsk

Slite

Väskinde

148

Bro

Hejnum

Boge

147

Airport

149

Visby

147

Hejdeby

Källunge

Bäl

Tjelvars Grav

Vallstena

Vitviken

To Oskarshamn

Vibble

143

Endre

Ekeby

Gothem

140

Träkumla

Roma

Dalhem

146

Stenkumla

142

Ganthem

Tofta

Hogran

Norrlanda

Anga

Gnisvärd

Eskelhem

Atlingbo

Sjonhem

BALTIC

Västergarn

Väte

Vänge

Katthammarsvik

SEA

Sanda

Hejde

Guldrupe

Kraklingbo

Ala

Gammelgarn

Björkhaga

Torsburgen

Klintehamn

Klinte

Buttle

143

Ardre

Gannarve

Fröjel

145

Ljugarn

Folhammar

L. Karlsö

141

Ethelhem

Garde

Lojsta

Lye

Lau

Stora Karlsö

Eksta

Levide

Stånga

När

Sproge

Fardhem

144

Burs

Hemse

140

Silte

142

Rone

Hablingbo

Eke

Havdhem

Grötlingbo

Gansviken

Nås

Burgsviken

Fide

Björklunda

Burgsvik

Öja

Vamlingbo

Hamra

Sundre

0   10   20km
0   5   10mi

	Nature Reserve
	Historic Church
	Historic Site
	Hostel
	Museum

including stone ship-settings, burial mounds and remains of hill-top fortresses to burial mounds. Keep your eyes open for the information boards along roadsides. You can visit these sites, as well as the numerous nature reserves, any time, free of charge.

Churches

Nowhere else in northern Europe are there so many medieval churches in such a small area. There are 92 of them outside Visby; over 70 have medieval frescoes and a few have very rare medieval stained glass. In addition, Visby has a dozen church ruins and a magnificent cathedral.

Each village had a church built between the early 12th and the mid-14th century, until wars ended the tradition. Each church is still in use, and all those medieval villages still exist as entities. Most churches are open 9am to 6pm daily, mid-May to late August. Some churches have the old key in the door even before 15 May, or sometimes the key is hidden above the door. *The Key to the Churches in the Diocese of Visby* is a useful English-language brochure available free from tourist offices.

Getting There & Away

Air Skyways flies between regularly between Visby and three mainland airports: Stockholm Arlanda, Stockholm Bromma and Norrköping. The cheaper local airline is **Gotlands Flyg** (☎ 222222; W www.gotlandsflyg.se), with regular flights between Visby and Stockholm Bromma (Skr495 one way, one to six a day). Book early for discounts, and inquire after standby fares (from Skr300).

The island's **airport** (☎ 263100) is 4km northeast of Visby and is served by buses.

Boat Destination Gotland (☎ 201020; W www.destinationgotland.se) operates car ferries year-round to/from Visby out of Nynäshamn and Oskarshamn. Departures from Nynäshamn are from one to five times daily (about five hours, or three by high-speed catamaran). From Oskarshamn, there are one or two daily departures (except Saturday, from early November until mid-March) in either direction (four to five hours).

Regular one-way adult tickets cost Skr174/276 for the ferry/catamaran, but from mid-June to mid-August there is a more complicated fare system, with prices ranging from Skr152 to Skr258 for the ferry trip, Skr236 to Skr474 for

the catamaran sailing (some overnight, evening and early-morning sailings in the middle of the week have the cheaper fares).

To transport a bicycle on the ferry/catamaran costs Skr35/62; a car usually costs Skr274/408, although again in the peak summer season a tiered system operates.

Getting Around

There are over 1200km of roads in Gotland, typically running from village to village through the pretty landscape. Bicycle tours are highly recommended, and bikes can be hired from a number of places in Visby. The forested belt south and east of Visby is useful if you have a tent and want to take advantage of the liberal camping laws.

Kollektiv Trafiken (☎ 214112) runs buses via most villages to all corners of the island. A one-way ticket will not cost more than Skr59 (taking a bike on board will cost an additional Skr40), but enthusiasts will find a monthly ticket good value at Skr590.

VISBY
☎ 0498 • pop 21,400

The narrow cobbled streets and impressive town walls of the medieval port of Visby, a living relic with more than 40 towers and the ruins of great churches, attest to the town's former Hanseatic glories. Today it's a World Heritage Listed town that leaves no tourist disappointed. From mid-May to mid-August cars are banned in the old town, and the highlight is the costumes and re-enactments of **Medieval Week** (W www.medeltidsveckan.com) during the first week of August. Book accommodation well in advance if you wish to visit at this time.

The **tourist office** (☎ 201700; W www .gotland.com; Hamngatan 4; open daily May-Sept, Mon-Fri Oct-Apr) can help with visitor information. The public **library** (Cramérgatan) is good for free Internet access.

Things to See

The town is a noble sight, with its 3.5km-long **wall** of 40 towers breached in only two places. Set aside enough time to stroll around the narrow roads and lanes. The ruins of 10 medieval churches, including **St Nicolai kyrka**, **Helge And kyrka** and **Sta Karins kyrka**, are all within the town walls and contrast with the old but sound **Cathedral of St Maria**. Ask at the tourist office about

SWEDEN

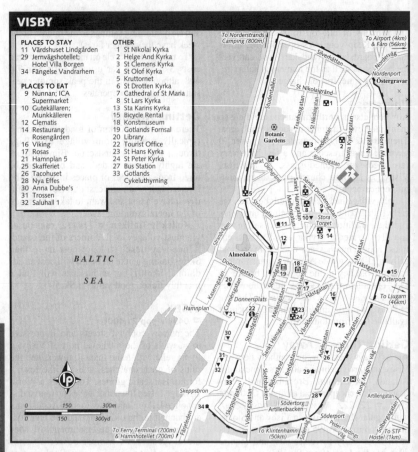

VISBY

PLACES TO STAY
11 Värdshuset Lindgården
29 Jernvägshotellet;
    Hotel Villa Borgen
34 Fängelse Vandrarhem

PLACES TO EAT
9   Nunnan; ICA
    Supermarket
10 Gutekällaren;
    Munkkälleren
12 Clematis
14 Restaurang
    Rosengården
16 Viking
17 Rosas
21 Hamnplan 5
25 Skafferiet
26 Tacohuset
28 Nya Effes
30 Anna Dubbe's
31 Trossen
32 Saluhall 1

OTHER
1   St Nikolai Kyrka
2   Helge And Kyrka
3   St Clemens Kyrka
4   St Olof Kyrka
5   Kruttornet
6   St Drotten Kyrka
7   Cathedral of St Maria
8   St Lars Kyrka
13 Sta Karins Kyrka
15 Bicycle Rental
18 Konstmuseum
19 Gotlands Fornsal
20 Library
22 Tourist Office
23 St Hans Kyrka
24 St Peter Kyrka
27 Bus Station
33 Gotlands
    Cykeluthyrning

walking tours of the town, conducted in English a few times a week in summer (Skr80, two hours).

Gotlands Fornsal (☎ 292700; Strandgatan 14; adult/child Skr50/free; open 10am-5pm daily May–mid-Sept, Tues-Sun mid-Sept–Apr) is one of the largest and best regional museums in Sweden – allow a couple of hours if you want to fully appreciate it. Extraordinary 8th-century, pre-Viking picture stones, human skeletons from chambered tombs, silver treasures and medieval wooden sculptures are highlights. The nearby **Konstmuseum** (☎ 292775; Sankt Hansgatan 21; adult/child Skr30/free; open 10am-5pm daily May–mid-Sept, Tues-Sun mid-Sept–Apr) has the same hours and displays varying art exhibitions.

Places to Stay

The closest camping ground is **Norderstrands Camping** (☎ 212157; camping Skr85-145; cabins Skr350-550; open late-Apr–mid-Sept), by the sea 800m north of Visby's ring wall (connected by a good walking or cycling path).

Gotlands Resor (☎ 201260; e info@ gotlandsresor.se; singles Skr240-285, doubles Skr380-425) is a travel agency that can book private rooms.

The **STF hostel** (☎ 269842; e carl.tholin@ tjelvar.org; dorm beds from Skr115; open mid-June–mid-Aug) is southeast of the town centre off Lännavägen in a school residence and therefore only open in peak season. The **Fängelse Vandrarhem** (☎ 206050; Skeppsbron 1; dorm beds from Skr150) offers beds in the converted cells of an old jail. You have to call ahead to book at **Jernvägshotellet** (☎ 271707; e staff@visbyjernvagshotell.com; Adelsgatan 9; dorm beds from Skr170), a small, central hostel.

Hamnhotellet (☎ 201250; Färjeleden 3; singles Skr560-640, doubles Skr600-760) is not far from the ferry terminal and offers uninspiring but cheap (for Visby) hotel rooms. **Värdshuset Lindgården** (☎ 218700; e lindgarden.vardshuset@telia.com; Strandgatan 26; singles Skr595-750, doubles Skr745-945) is a good, central option, with rooms set in a pretty garden beside a quality restaurant. **Hotel Villa Borgen** (☎ 279900; singles Skr860-910, doubles Skr970-1070) has pleasant rooms set around a pretty, quiet courtyard.

Places to Eat

Most restaurants and bars are around the Old Town squares, on Adelsgatan or at the harbour. There are a few cheap fast-food type places on Adelsgatan, including **Viking** (Adelsgatan 37; meals from Skr49) serving pizzas, kebabs etc. Nearby **Tacohuset** (Adelsgatan 22; meals from Skr42) has pizzas, pasta and salads, plus Mexican dishes such as tacos and burritos (Skr65). **Nya Effes**, just off Adelsgatan, is an eerie bar built into the town wall and is a good place for a meal or beer; there's regular live music here in summer.

Good places around buzzing Stora Torget include **Restaurang Rosengården**, (lunch Skr62) with weekday lunches, **Nunnan**, with a menu featuring Greek dishes, and the cellar restaurant-bars **Gutekällaren** and **Munkkälleren**, both home to nightclubs popular with the summer crowd.

Rosas (St Hansgatan 22), with a sunny courtyard, is an excellent lunch spot, serving baguettes, filled crepes, baked potatoes and the island specialty, saffron pancakes. **Skafferiet** (Adelsgatan 38) is similarly inviting.

In summer, visit atmospheric **Clematis** (Strandgatan 20; open mid-June–mid-Aug), a medieval restaurant serving food cooked according to medieval recipes, accompanied by music and entertainers, including the occasional fire-eater.

Hang-outs around the harbour are popular on warm summer days and evenings, including **Hamnplan 5**, **Anna Dubbe's**, **Trossen** and the cheap stalls selling ice cream, sandwiches and pizza at **Saluhall 1**.

There's an **ICA supermarket** (Stora Torget) for self-caterers.

Getting Around

Bicycles are highly recommended and can be hired from Skr60/300 per day/week from behind Saluhall on the harbour or at Österport. **Gotlands Cykeluthyrning** (☎ 214133), behind Saluhall, rents tents (Skr75/250 per day/week), or for Skr200/1000 you can hire its 'camping package' – two bikes, a tent, camping stove and two sleeping mats.

EASTERN GOTLAND

Ancient monuments include the Bronze Age ship-setting **Tjelvars grav**, 1.5km west of road 146, and its surrounding landscape of standing stones, almost all linked to Gutasaga legends. Mightier still is **Torsburgen**, a partly walled eminence that forms a fortification (the largest in Scandinavia) extending 5km around its irregular perimeter.

Although **Ljugarn** is more of a seaside resort, there are impressive raukar formations at **Folhammar nature reserve** 2km north. **Garde kyrka** has its original 12th-century roof, **Lye kyrka** has 14th-century stained glass and there's an impressive doorway to the nave in **Stånga kyrka**.

The **STF hostel** (☎ 493184; dorm beds from Skr115; open mid-May–Aug) has a fine spot at the eastern end of the Ljugarn village. In Garde is the **STF hostel** (☎ 491391; e gardavh@sverige.nu; dorm beds Skr115; open Feb-Dec).

NORTHERN GOTLAND & FÅRÖ

The picturesque northeastern tip of Gotland and the southern part of the adjacent island of Fårö remain a military zone, but access is now less restricted. Well worthwhile is a visit to the **Bunge open-air museum** (☎ 221018; admission Skr60; open daily mid-May–Aug), near the northeastern tip and not far from where the frequent, free ferries connect to Fårä. Recommended **churches** to visit include those in Lummelunda, Othem, Lärbro and Bunge, although there are a dozen more.

The **grotto** (☎ 273050; adult/child Skr60/35; open daily May–mid-Sept), south of Lummelunda is the largest in Gotland. Watch the sunset from the raukar formations at **Langhammarshammaren** on Fårö, the finest in Gotland.

There are good **STF hostels** in Fårö (☎ 223639; dorm beds from Skr85), 17km northeast of the ferry, and in Lärbro (☎ 225033; dorm beds Skr125). Both are open from mid-May to the end of August. There is an **SVIF hostel** (☎ 273043; dorm beds from Skr130) in Lummelunda.

SOUTHERN GOTLAND

Klintehamn, a reasonable sized town on the west coast, has a range of services. Boats to the island nature reserve **Stora Karlsö** sail from Klintehamn one to three times daily from May to August (Skr200 return, 30 minutes). You can visit the island as a day trip (with five or six hours ashore), or stay overnight at the hostel.

At **Gannarve**, 1km north of Fröjel, there's an 11th-century grave with an excellent reconstruction of a stone ship-setting. **Öja kyrka**, dating from 1232, has Gotland's highest church tower and excellent wall paintings. The **churches** in Hablingbo, Fardhem and Rone are also worth a look. **Lojsta** has the deepest lakes in Gotland, remains of an early medieval fortress and a very fine church.

Places to Stay & Eat

In Klintehamn **Pensionat Warfsholm** (☎ 240010; e warsholm@telia.com; camping Skr85, dorm beds Skr100, rooms per person Skr250) is in a pretty waterside spot and offers a range of accommodation, including an STF hostel, camping and rooms, as well as a restaurant.

You can stay on Stora Karlsö at the simple **STF hostel** (☎ 240500; e boka@storakarlso .com; dorm beds Skr150). There's a restaurant and café on the island.

The **STF hostel** (☎ 487070; e vandrarh em@gutevin.se; Hablingbo; dorm beds Skr150; open May-Sept) is next to **Gute Vin**, a good restaurant and commercial vineyard. In Björklunda, 2km north of Burgsvik, friendly **Värdshuset Björklunda** (☎ 497190; dorm beds/singles/doubles Skr165/590/790) is a delightful place reminiscent of a Greek villa. Meals at the restaurant here are good and reasonably priced.

Norrland

The northern half of Sweden, Norrland, has always been considered as separate from the rest of the country. It's closely associated with forest, lake and river, as well as the pioneers'

struggle to produce the timber and iron ore necessary for the construction of the railways that opened up the region. Sustainable logging continues, but most heavy mining has moved north to Kiruna and Malmberget. The Arctic wilderness attracts walkers, skiers and canoeists.

Inlandsbanan, the railway from Mora to Gällivare via Östersund, Storuman, Arvidsjaur and Jokkmokk, offers a great way to see the north. Otherwise, getting to the far north of the country by train is a night exercise only. Express buses follow most main highways but they may not be frequent.

GÄVLE
☎ 026 • pop 91,200

Gävle, the gateway to Norrland, is probably the most pleasant of the northern cities to walk in because of its architecture and parks; note the contrast between the wooden residences of Villastaden and Gamla Gefle. The helpful **tourist office** (☎ 147430; w www .gavle.se/turism; Drottninggatan 37; open daily June-Aug, Mon-Fri Sept-May) is not far from the train station. The **public library** (Slottstorget 1), near the castle, offers free Internet access.

Things to See & Do

The wooden old town of **Gamla Gefle**, south of the city centre, shows what Gävle was like before it was virtually destroyed by fire in 1869. The regional **Länsmuseum** (☎ 655600; Södra Strandgatan 20; adult/child Skr30/free; open Tues-Sun) has an excellent art collection and interesting historical exhibitions. The oldest of the churches in Gävle is **Heliga Trefaldighets kyrka** at the western end of Drottninggatan, which has an 11th-century rune stone inside. The buildings of the **castle** on the south bank of Gävleån are now in administrative use.

Railway buffs will enjoy the preserved steam locomotives of **Järnvägsmuseet** (☎ 144615; Rälsgatan; adult/child Skr40/free; open daily June-Aug, Tues-Sun Sept-May), the national rail museum, 2km south of the town centre, off Österbågen.

The leisure park and zoo **Furuvik** (☎ 177300; bus No 838; adult/child Skr95/75; open daily mid-May–Aug), 12km southeast of Gävle, aims to provide a little of everything; you can behave like a monkey on the amusement rides and then see the real thing. Tickets for rides cost from Skr10 to Skr40.

Places to Stay & Eat

The central **STF hostel** (☎ 621745; ℮ stf
.vandrarhem@telia.com; Södra Rådmans-
gatan 1; dorm beds from Skr120) is clean and
quiet and set around a pleasant courtyard.
Another STF hostel, **Engeltofta** (☎ 96160;
℮ engeltofta@swipnet.se; Bönavägen 118;
bus No 95; open June-Aug) is about 7km
northeast of the city.

Nya Järnvägshotellet (☎ 120990; singles/
doubles Skr395/525, discounted to Skr300/
450), opposite the train station, is the cheapest
hotel in town. **Hotell Boulogne** (☎ 126352;
Byggmästargatan 1; singles/doubles Skr445/
545, discounted to Skr350/450) is another
decent mid-range option.

A step up is **Hotel Winn** (☎ 177000; Norra
Slottsgatan 9; singles/ doubles Skr1150/1350,
discounted to Skr610/810), with well-priced
summer rooms.

Fashionable **Brända Bocken** (Stortorget)
is right in the heart of the action on the main
square, with meals from Skr64 and lots of
outdoor seating. Excellent, tiny **Söders Deli**
(Södra Kungsgatan 11; meals Skr40-75)
serves good coffee and authentic Italian ciabatta or pasta.

Nearby, **Wärdshuset Söderhjelmska Gården** (Södra Kungsgatan 2B; lunch Skr68, dinner Skr38-154) offers fine food in a great
setting; à la carte meals range from snacks to
traditional Swedish dishes.

Getting There & Away

There are numerous long-distance bus services: Y-buss runs daily to Umeå (Skr280) and
Östersund (Skr210). SGS Bussen (☎ 133030)
has services to Stockholm (Skr110, two to four
a day). Swebus Express runs to Uppsala
(Skr125) and Stockholm (Skr165) once or
twice daily.

SJ trains run to Stockholm via Uppsala,
and northwards to Sundsvall and beyond;
there are up to six X2000 services and several
slower trains daily. Other useful direct trains
include Gävle to Falun and Örebro.

HÖGA KUSTEN
☎ 0613

One of the most attractive parts of Sweden's
coastline, Höga Kusten (meaning the High
Coast) is a hilly area with many lakes, fjords
and offshore islands.

Although the scenery is not quite as dramatic as the name suggests, the region as a
whole was recently listed as a Unesco World
Heritage Site, recognised as a unique area
largely shaped by the combined processes of
glaciation, glacial retreat and the emergence
of new land from the sea (this retreat continues today at a rate of 0.9m per hundred
years).

Höga Kusten stretches from north of
Härnösand to Örnsöldsvik, both pleasant but
unremarkable towns with decent facilities.

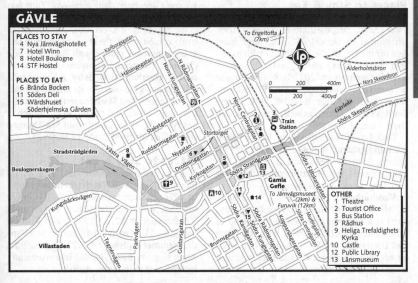

GÄVLE

PLACES TO STAY
4 Nya Järnvägshotellet
7 Hotel Winn
8 Hotell Boulogne
14 STF Hostel

PLACES TO EAT
6 Brända Bocken
11 Söders Deli
15 Wärdshuset
   Söderhjelmska Gården

OTHER
1 Theatre
2 Tourist Office
3 Bus Station
5 Rådhus
9 Heliga Trefaldighets
   Kyrka
10 Castle
12 Public Library
13 Länsmuseum

To Engeltofta (7km)

Alderholmsbron

Nora Skeppsbron

Södra Skeppsbron

0   200   400m
0   200   400yd

Gävlean

Train
Station

Stortorget

Stradsträdgården

Boulognerskogen

Gamla
Gefle

To Järnvägsmuseet
(2km) &
Furuvik (12km)

Villastaden

SWEDEN

There is a **tourist office** (☎ 50480; W www .hogakusten.com; open daily) in Hotell Höga Kusten, just north of the spectacular E4 suspension bridge over Storfjärden. There you can pick up information on attractions and accommodation options in the tiny villages along the coast.

There's also useful information on the Internet at W www.turistinfo.kramfors.se. Unfortunately, however, there's little by way of public transport (buses cruise along the E4 highway but don't make it into the region's villages).

Hence, this area is virtually impossible to explore without your own set of wheels – unless, of course, you wish to walk the **Höga Kustenleden**, a 127km hiking trail, stretching from Veda in the south, through Kramfors, and finishing near Örnsköldsvik, with shelters and cabins situated along its length

As well as the striking landscapes, the other major attractions of the region are the many well-preserved **fishing villages**, the pick of them being Barsta, Bönhamn and Norrfällsviken, and the lovely off-shore **islands**, especially Högbonden and Ulvön, both accessible by boat. Be sure also to visit **Mannaminne** (☎ 20290; admission Skr20; open daily), an eccentric collection of just about everything from farming to emigration and technology.

Places to Stay & Eat

You can stay at **Hotell Höga Kusten** (☎ 722270; singles/doubles Skr845/1095, discounted to Skr500/750), the large hotel just off the E4, by the bridge and with excellent views. There's also a good café here.

Mannaminne (☎ 20290; e info@mann aminne.se; singles/doubles Skr250/450, cottages Skr300), near tiny Häggvik, offers B&B accommodation as well as cottages, and there's a café here too.

Delightful Norrfällsviken has a good **camping ground** (☎ 21382; camping Skr110, cabins from Skr320), and a popular fish restaurant and pub, **Fiskarfänget**, with seating on a large deck over the water.

Vandrarhem Högbonden (☎ 23005, 42049; dorm beds from Skr195; open May-Oct) is a relaxing getaway on the island of Högbonden, reached by boat from Bönhamn and Barsta (Skr70). You'll need to book well in advance. There's a kitchen here, and also a café open in summer.

ÖSTERSUND
☎ 063 ● pop 58,400

This pleasant town by Lake Storsjön, in whose chill waters lurks a rarely sighted monster, has very good budget accommodation and is worth a visit for a couple of days. The area used to be Norwegian and many locals maintain an independent spirit.

The **tourist office** (☎ 144001; W www .ostersund.se/turist; Rådhusgatan 44; open daily mid-June-Aug, Mon-Fri Sept–mid-June) is opposite the town hall. The good-value Östersund Card (adult/child Skr120/ 55), valid for nine days between June and mid-August, gives discounts or free entry to many local attractions. The large **public library** opposite the bus station has free Internet access.

Things to See

Some attractions lie on the adjacent island of Frösön, reached by road or footbridge from the middle of Östersund (the footbridge is from the pleasant Badhusparken – nearby you can rent bikes, inline skates and canoes). The island features the animals at **Frösöns Djurpark** (☎ 514743; adult/child Skr100/50; open daily mid-June–mid-Aug) and the old **Frösöns kyrka** with its characteristic separate bell tower. For skiers there are slalom and Nordic runs on the island at Östberget, where there's a **viewing tower** (adult/child Skr10/5).

Don't miss **Jamtli** (☎ 150100; adult Skr60-90, child free; open daily June-Aug; Tues-Sun Sept-May), 1km north of the town centre. This is the highlight of Östersund, combining the lively exhibitions of the regional museum and a large museum village with staff in period clothing. The regional museum exhibits the curious **Överhogdal tapestry**, a Viking relic that's perhaps the oldest of its kind in Europe.

The refurbished **Stadsmuseum** is opposite the tourist office and the old town **church** is nearby. Lake cruises on the old S/S **Thomée** steamship cost from Skr65 to Skr95.

Places to Stay & Eat

You can live amongst Östersund's big attraction: the quaint STF **Vandrarhemmet Jamtli** (☎ 122060; dorm beds Skr140-160) is inside the Jamtli museum precinct. **Östersunds Vandrarhem** (☎ 101027; Postgränd 4; dorm beds Skr145) is in the town centre, and **Vandrarhemmet Rallaren** (☎ 132232; Bangårdsgatan 6; dorm beds Skr140) is conveniently located next to the train station.

Pensionat Svea (☎ 512901; e *pensionatsvea@spray.se; Storgatan 49; singles/doubles Skr440/540)* is a cosy place close to the heart of town; prices include breakfast. Atmospheric **First Hotel Gamla Teatern** (☎ 511600; e *bokning@gamlateatern.se; Thoméegränd 20; budget singles/doubles Skr902/1152, discounted to Skr502/652)* is in an old theatre. The budget rooms are OK and the summer prices are reasonable; a better standard of rooms cost Skr200 to Skr250 extra.

Kebab City (*Storgatan 31; meals around Skr50)* serves burger, kebab and falafel meals. Most restaurants are on Prästgatan, the main pedestrian street, including **Volos** (*Prastgatan 38; meals from Skr60)* with something for everyone's tastes – pizzas, pasta, nachos, salads, kebabs, Greek dishes and more.

Captain Cook (*Hamngatan 9; meals Skr50-150)* is an Australian-themed pub with a good menu of pub food, ranging from light snacks to more hearty fare and good local beer. Self-caterers should go to the **Domus supermarket** (*Kyrkgatan)*, near the bus station.

Getting There & Away

The train station is a short walk south from the town centre, but the main regional bus station is central on Gustav III Torg; local buses usually run to both. Local buses Nos 1, 3, 4, 5 and 9 go to Frösön.

Bus No 45 runs south to Mora twice a day; in summer the Inlandsbanan train runs once daily, to Gällivare (Skr485) or Mora (Skr240). Bus No 156 runs west to Åre; and bus No 63 runs twice daily northeast to Umea.

Direct trains run from Stockholm via Gävle, and some continue to Storlien (from where you can catch trains to Norway). You can also catch a train east to Sundsvall.

ÅRE & AROUND
☎ 0647 • pop 9600

Arguably Sweden's top mountain sports destination, the Åre area (W www.skistar.com/are) has 45 ski lifts that serve some 100 pistes and 1000 vertical metres of skiable slopes, including a superb 6.5km downhill run (day pass Skr270). The skiing season is from November to mid-May, but conditions are best from February, when daylight hours increase, and Easter is a hugely busy time. There are also excellent cross-country tracks in the area, and winter activities such as dog-sledding, snowmobile

safaris and sleigh rides (horse- or reindeer-drawn!) are available.

Åre also offers great summer outdoor recreation, including hiking, kayaking, rafting, fishing and mountain biking. The area west of Åre is popular among fell walkers: there's a network of STF wilderness huts and lodges here for enthusiasts. The main track is the Jämtland Triangle, just north of the Sylarna mountain range.

The Åre **tourist office** (☎ 17720; *open daily)* is in the train station. Most facilities are around the main square, which you reach by walking through the park opposite the station.

Places to Stay & Eat

In winter it's best to book accommodation and skiing packages via **Åre Resor** (☎ 17700; e *reservations@areresort.se).*

Åre Camping (☎ 50054; *camping Skr130)* is a good summer option. **Park Villan** (☎ 17733; Parkvägen 6; dorm beds Skr170), the yellow house in the park opposite the train station, offers good backpacker accommodation outside of the ski season. The **STF hostel** (☎ 30138; e *brattlandsgarden@user.bip.net; dorm beds Skr120)* is 8km east of Åre. Not all hotels stay open in summer, but those that do offer great bargains. **Åre Fjällby** (☎ 13600; e *reception@arefjallby.com; self-contained apartments from Skr520)*, for example, had an offer at the time of writing whereby you paid for two nights and received a third night free.

Like the hotels, the majority of restaurants are closed in summer, but there are still some very good choices, primarily centred on the main square. Typical Swedish fast food is available at **Åre Kiosk & Grill**, but nearby **Liten Krog** (*dishes from Skr70)* and **Werséns** (*dishes from Skr70)* have more style. **Villa Tottebo** (*dinner Skr145-220)*, opposite the train station, is a classy establishment, and there's an inviting bar upstairs. There's a **Konsum supermarket** on the square.

Getting There & Away

Regional bus No 156 runs from Östersund and connects Åre to the nearby winter-sports centre of Duved (much quieter and more family-oriented than Åre). Regular trains between Stockholm and Storlien, via Östersund, stop at Åre. Storlien is the terminus for SJ trains; change here for Norwegian trains to Hell and Trondheim.

SWEDEN

UMEÅ

☎ 090 • pop 105,000

Umeå has a large university and a port with ferry connections to Finland. It's among the fastest-growing towns in Sweden and has some 22,000 students, making it an agreeable place to just hang out for a spell. The **tourist office** (☎ 161616; Ⓦ www.umea.se/turism; Renmarkstorget 15; open daily mid-June–mid-Aug, Mon-Fri mid-Aug–mid-June) can help with visitor inquiries. **Spixel** (Skolgatan 44) is an Internet café not far from the hostel.

Gammlia, 1km east of the town centre, has several museums and shouldn't be missed. It includes the regional **Västerbottens Museum** (☎ 171800; adult/child Skr20/free), the modern art museum **Bildmuseet** and the **Maritime Museum**. The **Friluftsmuseet**, with old houses and staff wearing period clothes is also worth a visit. The museums are open daily in summer (closed Monday in winter; only the regional museum has an admission charge).

There are a number of **activities** in the surrounding area – including fishing, whitewater rafting, jet-boating and canoeing in or on the local rivers. The tourist office can help organise these. There are also a couple of islands to visit: **Norrbyskär**, with an interesting history, and sunny **Holmön**. In summer, buses connect with boats to both islands.

Places to Stay & Eat

The well-run **STF hostel** (☎ 771650; ⓔ info@vandrarhemmet.se; Västra Esplanaden 10; dorm beds from Skr115) is clean and central. **City Hotel** (☎ 702341; ⓔ mail@cityhotel.umea.com; Rådhusesplanaden 14; singles/doubles Skr395/595) is a good, central option, right beside Blå restaurant-bar. **Hotel Pilen** (☎ 141460; Pilgatan 5; singles/doubles Skr550/750, discounted to Skr450/550) is a family-run place, dated but comfortable, in a quiet area some 600m from the town centre.

Eldorado (Vasagatan 10; meals Skr50) serves pasta, felafel, kebabs and salads. **Waynes Coffee** (Storgatan 50) offers coffee, cake, salads and sandwiches in stylish surrounds. **Lottas Krog** (Nygatan; meals from Skr89) is a friendly pub-restaurant with an extensive menu that has something to appeal to everyone, while nearby **Blå** (buffet Skr99, dishes from Skr72) is trendier and has a nightly all-you-can-eat Thai buffet (not available in summer) or regular à la carte menu.

Getting There & Away

The bus station is near the train station. Umeå is the main centre for **Länstrafiken Västerbotten** (☎ 020 910019), the regional bus network that covers over 55,000 sq km. Direct buses run to Mo i Rana in Norway (daily); other daily destinations include Östersund, Skellefteå and Luleå. Tågkompaniet trains leave daily from Umeå to connect with the north-south trains between Stockholm and Luleå.

There are two companies operating ferries between Umeå and Vaasa in Finland. **RG Line** (☎ 090-185200; Ⓦ www.rgline.com) is more passenger-friendly. Boats depart at least five times a week (Skr360, four hours). A bus to the dock leaves from near the tourist office an hour before departure. **Botnia Link** (☎ 0611-550555; Ⓦ www.botnialink.se) is the second ferry company, used primarily for freight trucks. It is slightly cheaper, however (Skr310, four a week).

SKELLEFTEÅ

☎ 0910 • pop 72,000

Skellefteå is a likeable coastal town with a few noteworthy attractions. The **tourist office** (☎ 736020; Ⓦ turistinfo.skelleftea.se; Trädgårdsgatan 7; open daily mid-June–mid-Aug) is in the town centre. All attractions are in the parks along the river, west of the centre. A pleasant walk takes you to the Nordanå park that includes the **Skellefteå museum** (☎ 735510; adult/child Skr20/free; open daily) and several old houses, some of which contain handicraft shops.

West of Nordanå is **Bonnstan**, a unique housing precinct with 392 preserved 17th-century houses – many of them still inhabited in summer. Farther west is the 16th-century **church** and the small island of Kyrkholmen, with a lovely café. Cross the river on the **Lejonströmsbron**, Sweden's longest wooden bridge, built in 1737.

The idyllic, church-run **Stiftsgården** (☎ 725700; ⓔ stiftsgarden.skelleftea@svenskakyrkan.se; dorm beds Skr200, singles/doubles Skr650/1000, discounted to Skr460/625), behind the old church on Brännavägen, is home to both the STF hostel and a guesthouse offering bright, comfortable, hotel-standard rooms. You can get the usual fast food on the main square in town. **Monaco** (Nygatan 31; meals Skr65) offers good pizza and pasta, and the pretty nearby **Café Lilla Mari** serves to outside tables in a small courtyard (sandwiches from Skr25).

Bus No 100 runs every two hours on the Sundsvall–Umeå–Skellefteå–Luleå route (some buses continue as far north as Haparanda). Länstrafiken i Norrbotten has a bus from Skellefteå to Bodø (Skr400, nine hours, daily) in Norway, via Arvidsjaur. Skellefteå's nearest train station is Bastuträsk and bus No 27 connects there three times daily (Skr45).

LULEÅ
☎ 0920 • pop 72,000
One of Sweden's busiest airports lies just outside Luleå, the capital of Norrbotten. Norrbotten is Sweden's largest county, accounting for one-quarter of the country's total area. Storgatan is the main pedestrian mall; the **tourist office** (☎ 293500; W www.lulea.se; Storgatan 42) will help with inquiries; and the **library** (Kyrkogatan) has Internet access.

The **Norbottens Museum** (☎ 243500; Storgatan 2; admission free; open Tues–Sun) is worth a visit just for the Sami section. The neo-Gothic **cathedral** dates from 1893. Other attractions are outside the centre. **Teknikens Hus** (☎ 492201; bus No 17 or 35; adult/child Skr50/30; open daily mid-June–Aug, Tues–Sun Sept–mid-June), within the university campus 4km north, is a hands-on exhibition of technological phenomena (take bus No 17 or 35). In summer there are a number of boat trips to the surrounding archipelago.

The most famous sight in Luleå is the World Heritage Listed **Gammelstad** (bus No 32), or 'Old Town'. The stone church (from 1492), 424 wooden houses (the largest of the restored 'church villages', where the pioneers stayed overnight on their weekend pilgrimages) and six church stables remain. The open-air museum, **Hägnan**, and a nature reserve are nearby. There's a small tourist information office (☎ 254310) at Gammelstad, open daily in summer, and it organises guided tours (Skr30) of the church village.

Places to Stay & Eat
The SVIF **Luleå Vandrarhem** (☎ 222660; Sandviksgatan 26; dorm beds Skr150, twins per person Skr175) doesn't look like much from the outside, but inside is a clean and comfortable hostel. The large dorms are not so great (tri-level bunks) – better are the twin rooms. There are a number of mid-range options near the train station. **Park Hotell**

(☎ 211149; e hotellet@parkhotell.se; Kungsgatan 10; singles/doubles from Skr490/690, discounted to Skr390/550) offers pleasant rooms – some have a bathroom and cost a little extra. A step up, **Amber Hotel** (☎ 10200; e hotel.amber@telia.com; Stationsgatan 67; singles/doubles Skr790/950, discounted to Skr440/590) has rooms in a pretty, wooden guesthouse.

There are two very good cafés on either side of the tourist office, including the trendy **Roasters** (Storgatan 43). Bright, modern **Matstället** (cnr Nygatan & Storgatan; meals Skr40-60) is a good choice, with all sorts of fast food – pizzas, kebabs, burgers, pasta, Tex-Mex and Asian dishes. Friendly **Corsica** (Nygatan 14; meals Skr60-100), nearby, has an extensive menu of good-value meals, eg, salads, pasta, souvlaki and fish.

Getting There & Away
There are up to eight SAS flights daily to Stockholm. Take the airport bus from the bus station (Skr40).

Länstrafiken i Norrbotten (☎ 020 470047) buses cover the 100,000-sq-km county. The maximum fare is Skr270, a 30-day pass covering the entire county costs Skr1410 and bicycles are carried for Skr50.

Bus No 100 is one of the most useful for travellers – it runs between Haparanda, Luleå, Skellefteå, Umeå and Sundsvall at least four times daily. Bus No 21 goes to Arvidsjaur (via Boden and Älvsbyn), and bus No 44 to Jokkmokk and on to Gällivare (via Boden and Vuollerim).

Direct Tågkompaniet trains from Stockholm and Gothenburg run at night only. Most trains from Narvik and Kiruna terminate at Luleå.

HAPARANDA
☎ 0922 • pop 10,400
Haparanda was founded in 1821 as a trading town to replace Sweden's loss of Tornio (see the Finland chapter) to Russia. Now the two border towns almost function as one entity (both the krona and euro are accepted at most places in both towns; Tornio is one hour ahead of Haparanda). There are few sights in Haparanda and the ugly church looks exactly like a grain silo, but one noteworthy attraction is the unique golf course. The **Green Zone Golf Course** (☎ 10660) is right on the border of the two countries; during a full

SWEDEN

round of golf the border is crossed four times. The cost to play 18 holes is €22, club hire is an additional €10. You need to book in advance if you want to play under the midnight sun.

Haparanda's helpful tourist office (☎ 12010; W www.haparanda.se/turism; Torget 7) is in Stadshotellet. There is another, joint, Haparanda-Tornio tourist office on the 'green line'.

The excellent STF hostel (☎ 61171; e info@ haparandavandrarhem.com; Strandgatan 26; dorm beds from Skr110) is not far from the town centre. There's a kitchen and meals are available in the attached café. Further up the road, the Resandehem (☎ 12068; Storgatan 65B; singles/doubles Skr150/250) is a simple guesthouse. The large, once-grand Stadshotellet (☎ 61490; Torget 7; singles/doubles Skr1090/1390, discounted to Skr610/810; some budget beds Skr195 mid-June–mid-Aug) is the focus of the town, and its pub-restaurant, the Gulasch Baronen (meals Skr65-110) offers good, reasonably priced meals.

Regular buses connect Haparanda and Tornio (Skr10). There are regional buses from Luleå (Skr110) and towns farther south, and daily bus No 53 travels north along the border via the scenic Kukkolaforsen rapids, Övertorneå and Pajala, then continues west to Kiruna (Skr250).

ARVIDSJAUR
☎ 0960 • pop 7100

The small settlement of Arvidsjaur on Inlandsbanan was an early Sami market. Lappstaden (admission free), a well-preserved Sami church village, contains almost 100 buildings as well as forestry and reindeer-breeding concerns. Guided tours cost Skr25 (July only). From early July to early August an old steam train makes return evening trips to Slagnäs on Friday and Moskosel on Saturday (adult/child Skr140/free). Also in summer is the opportunity for white-water rafting on the nearby Piteälven for Skr330/165 (adult/child).

The tourist office (☎ 17500; W www .arvidsjaurturism.se; Garvaregatan 4) is behind the park by the main square and can provide useful information. Cosy Lappugglans Turistviste (☎ 12413; Västra Skolgatan 9; dorm beds Skr130) and stylish Rallaren (☎ 070-682 3284; Stationsgatan 4; open mid-June–mid-Aug; dorm beds Skr130), both near the train station, have excellent hostel accommodation. Kaffestugan (Storgatan 21; lunch Skr60) is a popular café by the main square, with good daily lunch specials, plus an assortment of cakes, sandwiches and light meals. Athena (Storgatan 10; dishes Skr100) offers pastas, salads and grill dishes. The town is bustling in winter, when test drivers from around Europe put their cars through their paces in the tough weather conditions.

The daily bus between Gällivare and Östersund (No 45) stops at the bus station on Storgatan. Bus No 200 runs daily between Skellefteå and Bodø (Norway) via Arvidsjaur. The Inlandsbanan train can take you north to Gällivare via Jokkmokk, or south to Mora via Östersund.

JOKKMOKK
☎ 0971 • pop 5900

The small town of Jokkmokk is just north of the Arctic Circle and started as a Sami market and mission. Since 1605 the Sami winter fair has taken place here. The three-day event attracts some 30,000 people and starts on the first Thursday in February, when you can shop seriously for handicrafts.

The tourist office (☎ 12140; W www .turism.jokkmokk.se; Stortorget 4; open daily mid-June–mid-Aug, Mon-Fri mid-Aug–mid-June) can help with information. The Ájtte museum (☎ 17070; Kyrkogatan 3; adult/ child Skr50/free; open daily mid-June–mid-Aug; Sun-Fri Oct-Apr) is the highlight of a visit to Jokkmokk; it gives the most thorough introduction to Sami culture anywhere in Sweden. It also offers exhaustive information on Lappland's mountain areas, with a full set of maps, slides, videos and a library. A research visit is recommended for planning wilderness trips (there are good opportunities for trekking in the areas surrounding Jokkmokk). Naturfoto (☎ 55765; open daily mid-June–mid-Aug), at the main Klockartorget intersection, exhibits and sells work by a local wilderness photographer.

About 7km south of Jokkmokk you'll cross the Arctic Circle; there's a café and campsite here.

Places to Stay & Eat
Gula Villan (☎ 55026; Stationsgatan; singles/ doubles Skr125/200) is the yellow guesthouse with the sign advertising 'rum' as you exit the train station; rooms are simple but

adequate. The STF hostel **Åsgård** (☎ 55977; e asgard@jokkmokkhostel.com; Åsgatan 20; dorm beds from Skr110) is a clean, comfortable place behind the tourist office. There's an unexpected surprise at the park by the tourist office; here you'll find a **caravan** (lunch Skr55) where you can buy authentic takeaway Laotian food. At the Ájtte museum **restaurant** (lunch Skr60) you can try local fish or a sandwich with reindeer meat. **Café Piano** (Porjusvägen 4; dishes Skr60) is another good choice – with a grand piano inside, a large garden outside and an extensive menu, including pasta and wok meals.

Getting There & Away

Bus Nos 44 and 45 run daily to/from Gällivare (Skr87), and bus No 45 to/from Arvidsjaur once daily (Skr133). Inlandsbanan trains stop in Jokkmokk. For main-line trains, take bus No 94 to Murjek via Vuollerim (up to six a day) or bus No 44 to Boden (Skr118) and Luleå (Skr139). Another alternative is bus No 36 to Älvsbyn to visit the spectacular 82m Storforsen, Europe's greatest cataract falls (best in May/June).

GÄLLIVARE
☎ 0970 • pop 19,700

The town of Gällivare and its northern twin Malmberget are surrounded by forest and dwarfed by the bald Dundret hill. The helpful **tourist office** (☎ 16660; W www.gellivare .se; Storgatan 16) is near the church in the town's centre. **Dundret** (821m) is a nature reserve with excellent views; you can see the midnight sun here from 2 June to 12 July. In winter there are four Nordic courses and 10 ski runs of varying difficulty, and the mountain-top resort organises numerous activities.

In Malmberget, 5km north of Gällivare, **Kåkstan** (admission free; open daily) is a historical 'shanty town' museum village dating from the 1888 iron-ore rush. Contact the Gällivare tourist office for details of the **LKAB iron-ore mine** tour (Skr150, July to August). Also of interest is the **Gruvmuseum**, covering 250 years of mining. Inquire about these attractions at the tourist office. Bus No 1 to Malmberget departs from opposite the Gällivare church.

Places to Stay & Eat

Gällivare Camping (☎ 10010; Hembygdsområdet; camping Skr100, 2-bed cabins Skr300;

open June-Sept) is in a lovely spot beside the river. The **STF hostel** (☎ 14380; Barnhemsvägen 2; dorm beds Skr120; closed May & Oct) is across the footbridges from the train station; bikes can be hired here.

Your best bet for anything other than fast food is the **Vassara Pub** at Quality Hotel Next (Lasarettsgatan 1; lunch Skr68, dishes from Skr70), offering lunch and à la carte dishes. The eastern part of Storgatan is home to two reasonable restaurants: **New Delhi** (Storgatan 17; lunch Skr65) serves a range of Indian meals; **Restaurang Peking** (Storgatan 21; lunch Skr65) has Chinese and Thai dishes on offer.

Getting There & Away

Regional buses depart from the train station. Bus No 45 runs daily to Östersund via Jokkmokk and Arvidsjaur, bus No 93 serves Ritsem and Kungsleden in Stora Sjöfallet National Park (mid-June to mid-September only), bus Nos 10 and 52 go to Kiruna and bus No 44 runs to Jokkmokk and Luleå.

Tågkompaniet trains come from Luleå and Stockholm (sometimes changing at Boden), and from Narvik in Norway. More exotic is Inlandsbanan, which terminates at Gällivare; the train journey from Östersund costs Skr485.

KIRUNA
☎ 0980 • pop 23,900

Kiruna is the northernmost town in Sweden and, at 19,446 sq km, it's the largest district in the country. The area includes Sweden's highest peak, Kebnekaise (2117m), and several fine national parks and trekking routes (see also the following Abisko section). It's worth making the effort to get up here! This far north, the midnight sun lasts from 31 May to 14 July and there's a bluish darkness throughout December and New Year. Many people speak Finnish, and the Sami are a small minority.

The helpful and efficient **tourist office** (☎ 18880; W www.kiruna.se; Lars Janssonsgatan 17; open daily mid-June–mid-Aug) is next to the Scandic Hotel and has loads of excellent brochures. Another excellent website for the town and surrounds is W www.lappland .se. The **library**, behind the bus station, offers Internet access.

Things to See & Do

The highlight is a visit to the fabulous **Ice Hotel** (☎ 66800; W www.icehotel.com; bus No 501; day visit adult/child Skr100/50),

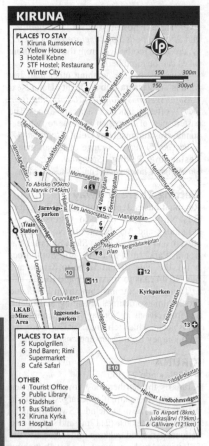

KIRUNA

PLACES TO STAY
1 Kiruna Rumsservice
2 Yellow House
3 Hotell Kebne
7 STF Hostel; Restaurang Winter City

PLACES TO EAT
5 Kupolgrillen
6 3nd Baren; Rimi Supermarket
8 Café Safari

OTHER
4 Tourist Office
9 Public Library
10 Stadshus
11 Bus Station
12 Kiruna Kyrka
13 Hospital

(it's expected that this will be an annual winter event). All this can be quite pricey for a budget traveller, but anyone can visit the hotel on a day visit.

In summer, after the Ice Hotel has melted away, visitors can still experience a little of the magic. Inside a giant freezer warehouse called the **Ice Hotel Art Center** (adult/child Skr100/50), at temperatures of –5°C, there are a few of the Ice Hotel features: a bar, ice sculptures, and even small igloos where guests can stay overnight. Day visitors are welcome (warm clothing supplied). See Places to Stay & Eat following for details of accommodation prices.

Also worthwhile in Kiruna is a visit to the depths of the **LKAB iron-ore mine**, 540m underground. English-language tours depart from the tourist office regularly from mid-June to mid-August (adult/child Skr140/50, 2½ hours); make bookings through the tourist office. **Kiruna kyrka**, the town church, looks like a gigantic Sami tent; it's particularly pretty against a snowy backdrop.

Places to Stay & Eat

The central **STF hostel** (☎ 17195; Bergmästaregatan 7; dorm beds Skr130-155) has good facilities and an adjacent Chinese restaurant. The SVIF **Yellow House** (☎ 13750; e yellowhouse@mbox301.swipnet.se; Hantverkaregatan 25; dorm beds/singles/doubles Skr120/300/400) also has excellent facilities, including a sauna, kitchen, laundry and TV in each room.

Kiruna Rumsservice (☎ 19560; e krs@kiruna.se; Hjalmar Lundbohmsvägen 53; doubles from Skr350) is a good option, especially for small groups. It offers rooms and apartments with a varying number of beds. Breakfast is additional (Skr45). Or try **Hotell Kebne** (☎ 68180; e info@hotelkebne; Konduktörsgatan 7; singles/doubles Skr945/1125, discounted to Skr595), with good summer rates.

Staying at the **Ice Hotel** (☎ 66800; w www.icehotel.com; Jukkasjärvi; rooms winter from Skr1960, igloos summer from Skr1000) is a unique experience. There are also stylish new hotel rooms (not made of ice), three-bed cabins with skylights enabling you to watch the northern lights in winter, and chalets that sleep up to four with kitchen. These are all available year-round – summer prices are quite reasonable.

truly a unique experience. Every winter at Jukkasjärvi, 18km east of Kiruna, an amazing structure is built from hundreds of tonnes of ice taken from the frozen local river. This 'igloo' has a chapel, bar and exhibitions of ice sculpture by international artists. It also has 50 'hotel rooms' where guests can stay, on beds covered with reindeer skins and inside sleeping bags guaranteed to keep you warm despite the –5°C temperatures (and in winter that's nothing – outside the hotel it can be as low as –30°C!). There are numerous activities for guests to pursue (snowmobile safaris, skiing, ice-fishing, dog sledding etc), and in the winter of 2002–3, there are plans to construct a replica of Shakespeare's Globe Theatre from ice, and Sami theatre groups will perform *Hamlet* in their local language

Kupolgrillen (*Vänortsgatan 2*) is a decent central spot for burgers and kebabs. Easily the nicest café in town is **Café Safari** (*Geologsgatan 4*), with good coffee, cakes and light meals. **Restaurang Winter City** (*lunch Skr65*) is at the STF hostel, offering Chinese and other Asian dishes, and **3nd Baren** (*Föreningsgatan 11*) is a popular, moderately priced restaurant and a lively drinking spot of an evening; the **Rimi supermarket** is next door.

Getting There & Away

The small **airport** (☎ 68000) 7km east of the town has nonstop flights to/from Stockholm with SAS (daily).

Regional buses to/from the bus station, on Hjalmar Lundbohmsvägen opposite the Stadshus (town hall), serve all major settlements around Norrbotten. To reach Karesuando (Skr46), Sweden's northernmost settlement, take bus No 50 (Sunday to Friday). Bus No 91 runs two or three times daily to Riksgränsen (Skr110) via Abisko (Skr87).

Regular trains connect Kiruna with Luleå, Stockholm and Narvik (Norway).

ABISKO

☎ 0980 • pop 180

The 75-sq-km **Abisko National Park**, on the southern shore of scenic Lake Torneträsk, is well served by trains, buses and the scenic mountain highway between Kiruna and Narvik. It's the soft option of the northern parks – distinctly less rugged and more accessible. There are some very good short hikes.

The popular **Kungsleden** trail follows the Abiskojåkka Valley and day trips of 10km or 20km are no problem from Abisko village. Kungsleden extends 450km south from Abisko and offers diversions to the summit of **Kebnekaise** or the magical national park of **Sarek** (no huts and few bridges). Waterproof (preferably rubber) boots are essential at any time of the year; the snow doesn't melt until June. July, August and September are recommended months for hiking although in July there's still some boggy ground where mosquitoes breed. It can still get cold very quickly, despite the midnight sun. Winter escapades are too risky for the uninitiated due to blizzards, extreme cold and avalanches.

The **Naturum** (☎ 40177; *open July–mid-Sept*), next to the STF lodge in Abisko, provides good information. The **Linbana** chair lift (from Skr70/95 one-way/return) takes

you to 900m on **Njulla** (1169m), where there's a **café** (*open 9.30am-3pm*). In Björkliden, 8km northwest of Abisko, **Hotell Fjället** (☎ 64100; ⓦ *www.bjorkliden.com*) offers various summer and winter activities, including a half-day cave tour for Skr195. Tours are also organised by STF at Abisko Turiststation; both places offer outdoor gear for hire.

Places to Stay & Eat

Abisko Fjällturer (☎ 40103; ⓦ *www.abisko .net; camping per person Skr60, dorm beds Skr125*), behind the town, is a backpackers' delight. The small hostel has comfortable accommodation and a wonderful wooden sauna, but the treat is in the reasonably priced activities on offer, especially in winter. Owner Tomas and his father keep a large team of sled dogs, and for Skr500 in winter you get a night's hostel accommodation plus the chance to drive your own sled, pulled by dogs, for about 10km. There are also very popular week-long sled trips for Skr7900, including all meals and accommodation – you'll need to book very early for this. In summer you can take mountain walks with the dogs.

Abisko Fjällstation (☎ 40200; ⓔ *info@ abisko.stfturist.se; dorm beds from Skr170*) is another option, kept to the usual high STF standards. Trekking gear can be hired here, and breakfast/lunch/dinner costs Skr70/70/155. There's an **ICA** supermarket in Abisko village for self-caterers, and a café nearby.

Self-service **STF huts** (*dorm beds members Skr160-220, nonmembers Skr210-270*) along Kungsleden are spread at 10km to 20km intervals between Abisko and Kvikkjokk; you'll need a sleeping bag. Day visitors/campers are charged Skr25/45. The excellent 100km trek from Abisko to Nikkaluokta runs via the STF lodge **Kebnekaise Fjällstation** (☎ 0980-55000; ⓔ *info@kebnekaise.stfturist.se; dorm beds from Skr260; open Mar-Apr & mid-June–mid-Sept*).

Getting There & Away

In addition to trains (stations at Abisko Östra and Abisko Turiststation) between Luleå and Narvik, bus No 91 runs from Kiruna to Abisko. Bus No 92 travels from Kiruna to Nikkaluokta (Skr64, four a day), at the Kebnekaise trail heads. Kvikkjokk is served by bus No 94 that runs twice daily from the Murjek main-line train station via Jokkmokk.

RIKSGRÄNSEN
☎ 0980 • pop 50

The best midnight (or daytime) skiing in June in Scandinavia awaits you at this rugged frontier area (Riksgränsen translates as 'National Border'). You can briefly visit Norway at full speed on downhill skis! Rental of downhill gear costs from Skr210 per day, and a day lift pass is Skr250. There's not much to the tiny settlement here, but you can visit Sven Hörnell's **wilderness photography exhibition** at his own gallery (☎ 43111; open daily Feb-Sept). The exhibition itself is free, but there's an excellent regular audiovisual show (Skr60; daily at 3pm in mid-June to mid-August; commentary is in Swedish only, but you don't have to understand to appreciate the stunning photography).

Katterjåkk Turiststation (☎ 43108; e katterjakk@kiruna.frilufts.se; dorm beds from Skr170; open Feb-Sept) is a well-run hostel 2km east of Riksgränsen. **Riksgränsen** (☎ 40080; e info@riksgransen.nu; rooms per person Skr405-715) is a large resort popular with skiers in winter and offering an 'alpine spa' retreat in summer, plus lots of organised wilderness activities in both seasons.

From Kiruna, bus No 91 goes to Riksgränsen (Skr110; two or three a day), via Abisko. Riksgränsen is the last train station in Sweden before the train rushes through tunnels and mountain scenery back to sea level at Narvik in Norway; three daily trains running on the Luleå–Kiruna–Narvik route here.

The historical 'Navvy Trail' walkway that follows the railway line takes you to Abisko (39km) or Rombaksbotn in Norway (15km).

Language

This language guide contains pronunciation guidelines and basic vocabulary to help you get around Scandinavian Europe. For a more detailed guide to the languages in this region, get a copy of Lonely Planet's *Scandinavian phrasebook*.

Danish

While the majority of Danes speak English, any effort to learn a few basic words and phrases will be greatly appreciated by the people you meet.

Danish has a polite form of address, using the personal pronouns *De* and *Dem*. The Danish translations in this book mostly use the informal pronouns *du* and *dig*, except where it's appropriate and/or wise to use the polite form. In general, you should use the polite form when speaking to senior citizens and officials, and the informal the rest of the time.

Nouns in Danish have two genders: masculine and neuter. In the singular, the definite article ('the' in English) is suffixed to the noun: *-en* (masculine) and *-et* (neuter). In the plural *-ne* is used for the indefinite ('some' in English) and *-ene* for the definite, regardless of gender.

Pronunciation

You may find Danish pronunciation difficult. Consonants are drawled, swallowed and even omitted completely, creating, in conjunction with vowels, the peculiarity of the glottal stop or *stød*. Its sound is rather as a Cockney would say the 'tt' in 'bottle'. Stress is usually placed on the first syllable or on the first letter of the word. In general though, the best advice is to listen and learn. Good luck!

Vowels

a	as in 'father'
a, æ	as in 'act'
å, o	
& u(n)	a long rounded 'a' as in 'walk
e(g)	as the sound of 'eye'
e, i	as the 'e' in 'bet'
i	as the 'e' in 'theme'
ø	as the 'er' in 'fern'
o, u	as the 'oo' in 'cool'
o	as in 'pot'
o(v)	as the 'ou' in 'out'
o(r)	as the 'or' in for' with less emphasis on the 'r'
u	as in 'pull'
y	say 'ee' while pursing your lips

Consonants

sj	as in 'ship'
ch	a sharper sound than the 'ch' in 'cheque'
c	as in 'cell'
(o)d	a flat 'dh' sound, like the 'th' in 'these'
ng	as in 'sing'
g	a hard 'g' as in 'get', if followed by a vowel
h	as in 'horse'
k	as the 'c' in 'cat'
r	a rolling 'r' abruptly cut short
w	similar to the 'wh' in 'what'
j	as the 'y' in 'yet'

Basics

Hello.	*Hallo.*
	Hej. (informal)
Goodbye.	*Farvel.*
Yes.	*Ja.*
No.	*Nej.*
Please.	*Må jeg bede/Værsgo.*
Thank you.	*Tak.*
That's fine/ You're welcome.	*Det er i orden/ Selv tak.*
Excuse me. (sorry)	*Undskyld.*
Do you speak English?	*Taler De engelsk?*
How much is it?	*Hvor meget koster det?*
What's your name?	*Hvad hedder du?*
My name is ...	*Mit navn er ...*

Signs – Danish

Indgang	Entrance
Udgang	Exit
Åben	Open
Lukket	Closed
Forbudt	Prohibited
Information	Information
Politistation	Police Station
Toiletter	Toilets
Herrer	Men
Damer	Women

491

Getting Around

What time does ... leave/arrive?	*Hvornår går/ ankommer ...?*
the boat	*båden*
the bus (city)	*bussen*
the bus (intercity)	*rutebilen*
the tram	*sporvognen*
the train	*toget*

Where can I hire a car/bicycle?	*Hvor kan jeg leje en bil/cykel?*

I'd like ...	*Jeg vil gerne have ...*
a one-way ticket	*en enkeltbillet*
a return ticket	*en tur-retur billet*

1st class	*første klasse*
2nd class	*anden klasse*
left luggage office	*reisegodsoppbevar ingen*
timetable	*køreplan*
bus stop	*bus holdeplads*
tram stop	*sporvogn holdeplads*
train station	*jernbanestation (banegård)*

Where is ...?	*Hvor er ...?*
Go straight ahead.	*Gå ligefrem.*
Turn left/right.	*Drej til venstre/højre.*
near/far	*nær/fjern*

Around Town

a bank	*en bank*
a chemist/pharmacy	*et apotek*
the ... embassy	*den ... ambassade*
my hotel	*mit hotel*
the market	*markedet*
a newsagent	*en aviskiosk*
the post office	*postkontoret*
the telephone centre	*telefoncentralen*
the tourist office	*turistinformationen*

What time does it open/close?	*Hvornår åbner/ lukker det?*

Accommodation

hotel	*hotel*
guesthouse	*gæstgiveri*
hostel	*vandrerhjem*
camping ground	*campingplads*

Do you have any rooms available?	*Har I ledige værelser?*
How much is it per night/ per person?	*Hvor meget koster det per nat/ per person?*

Does it include breakfast?	*Er morgenmad inkluderet?*

I'd like ...	*Jeg ønsker ...*
a single room	*et enkeltværelse*
a double room	*et dobbeltværelse*

one day/two days	*en nat/to nætter*

Time, Days & Numbers

What time is it?	*Hvad er klokken?*
today	*i dag*
tomorrow	*i morgen*
yesterday	*i går*
morning	*morgenen*
afternoon	*eftermiddagen*

Monday	*mandag*
Tuesday	*tirsdag*
Wednesday	*onsdag*
Thursday	*torsdag*
Friday	*fredag*
Saturday	*lørdag*
Sunday	*søndag*

0	*nul*
1	*en*
2	*to*
3	*tre*
4	*fire*
5	*fem*
6	*seks*
7	*syv*
8	*otte*
9	*ni*
10	*ti*
100	*hundrede*
1000	*tusind*

one million	*en million*

Faroese

Faroese is a Germanic language derived from old Norse, closely related to Icelandic and some Norwegian and Swedish dialects. In 1890, a standard written version of Faroese, Føroyskt, was made official and given equal status with Danish in public and government affairs.

All Faroese speak Danish, can handle Norwegian and Swedish, and some speak English. Nearly every Faroese learns Danish at school (and many also learn English and German), but foreign languages have had little impact on everyday life.

Pronunciation
In most cases, Faroese words are stressed on the first syllable. Grammar is very similar to that of Icelandic, but pronunciation is quite different due to a mix of Icelandic, Danish, and even Gaelic influences, eg, the name of Eiði village is inexplicably pronounced 'oy-yeh'; the nearby village of Gjógv is referred to as 'Jagv'; the capital, Tórshavn, gets the more or less Danish pronunciation, 'torsh-hown'.

Vowels & Diphthongs

a, æ	short, as the 'u' in 'cut'; long, as the 'ai' in 'hair'
á	short, as the 'o' in 'hot'; long, as the 'oi' in French *moi*
e	as in 'get'
i, y	short, as the 'i' in 'hit'; long, as the 'i' in 'marine'
í, ý	as the 'ui' in Spanish *muy*
o	as in 'hot'
ó	short, as the 'a' in 'ago'; long, as the 'o' in 'note'
ø	as the 'a' in 'ago'
u	as in 'pull'
ú	short, as a sharp 'u' – purse your lips and say 'ee'; long, as the 'ou' in 'you'
ei	as the 'i' in 'dive'
ey	short, as the 'e' in 'get'; long, as the 'ay' in 'day'
oy	as the 'oy' in 'boy'

Consonants

ð	silent in final position, otherwise taking on the value of surrounding vowels
ðr	as the 'gr' in 'grab'
dj	as the 'j' in 'jaw'
ft	as the 'tt' in 'bitter'

Emergencies – Faroese

Help!	*Hjálp!*
Call a doctor!	*Ringið eftir lækna!*
Call the police!	*Ringið eftir løgregluni!*
Go away!	*Far burtur!*
I'm lost.	*Eg eri vilst.* (m) *Eg eri vilstur.* (f)

g	silent in final position, otherwise taking on the value of surrounding vowels
ggj	as the 'j' in 'jaw'
hv	as 'kv'
hj	as the 'y' in 'yellow'
ll	as the 'dl' in 'saddle'

Basics

Hello.	*Hey/Halló/ Góðan dag.*
Goodbye.	*Farvæl.*
Yes.	*Ja.*
No.	*Nei.*
Please.	*Gerið so væl.*
Thank you.	*Takk fyri.*
Excuse me. (Sorry)	*Orsaka.*
Do you speak English?	*Tosar tú eingilskt?*
How much is it?	*Hvussu nógv kostar tað?*
What's your name?	*Hvussu eita tygum?*
My name is ...	*Eg eiti ...*

Getting Around

boat	*bátur*
bus	*bussur*
map	*kort*
road	*vegur*
street	*gøta*
village	*bygd*

I'd like a ...	*Kundi eg fingið ...*
one-way ticket	*einvegis ferðaseðil*
return ticket	*ferðaseðil aftur og fram*

1st class	*fyrsti klassi*
2nd class	*annar klassi*

Around Town

bank	*banka*
chemist	*apotekið*
the ... embassy	*... ambassaduni*
market	*handilsgøtuni*
the post office	*posthúsinum*
a public toilet	*almennum vesi*

| the telephone centre | telefonstøðini |
| the tourist office | ferðaskrivstovuni/ turistkontórinum |

Acommodation

hotel	hotell
guesthouse	gistingarhús
youth hostel	vallarheim
campground	tjáldplass

Do you have any rooms available?	Eru nøkur leys kømur?
How much is it per night/per person?	Hvussu nógv kostar tað fyri hvønn eina natt?
Does it include breakfast?	Er morgunmatur innifalinn?

I'd like (a) ...	Eg vil fegin hava ...
single room	eitt einkultkamar
double room	eitt dupultkamar

Time, Days & Numbers

What time is it?	Hvat er klokkan?
today	í dag
tomorrow	í morgin
yesterday	í gjár
morning	morgun
afternoon	seinnapartur
night	nátt

Monday	mánadagur
Tuesday	týsdagur
Wednesday	mikudagur
Thursday	hósdagur
Friday	fríggjadagur
Saturday	leygardagur
Sunday	sunnudagur

1	eitt
2	tvey
3	trý
4	fíra
5	fimm
6	seks
7	sjey
8	átta
9	níggju
10	tíggju
20	tjúgu
100	hundrað
1000	túsund

| one million | ein millón |

Finnish

Finnish is a Uralic language spoken by just six million people, the vast majority of whom live in Scandinavia and Russian Karelia. The most widely spoken of the Finno-Ugric family is Hungarian, but its similarities with Finnish are few. Suomi refers to both Finnish-speaking Finland and its language.

Staff at hotels, hostels and tourist offices generally speak fluent English. Bus drivers or restaurant and shop staff outside the cities may not, but they'll always fetch a colleague or bystander who does. You can certainly get by with English in Finland, but don't assume everyone speaks it.

Swedish is spoken on Åland, as well as on the west ('Swedish') coast and around Helsinki and Turku, and all Finns learn Swedish at school.

Pronunciation

Finnish pronunciation is more or less consistent – there is a one to one relationship between letters and sounds. There are nine vowels: a, e, i, o, u, y, ä, å and ö (the å has been adopted from the Norwegian and Swedish alphabets). The final letters of the alphabet are å, ä and ö (important to know when looking for something in a telephone directory).

Vowels

y	as the 'u' in 'pull' but with the lips stretched back (like the German 'ü')
å	as the 'oo' in 'poor'
ä	as the 'a' in 'act'
ö	as the 'e' in 'summer'

Consonants

Some consonant sounds differ from English:

z	pronounced (and sometimes written) as 'ts'
v/w	as the 'v' in 'vain'
h	a weak sound, except at the end of a syllable, when it is almost as strong as 'ch' in German ich
j	as the 'y' in 'yellow'
r	a rolled 'r'

Double consonants like kk in viikko or mm in summa are held longer.

Basics

| Hello. | Hei/Terve. |
| | Moi. (informal) |

Goodbye.	*Näkemiin.*
	Moi. (informal)
Yes.	*Kyllä/Joo.*
No.	*Ei.* (pronounced 'ay')
Please.	*Kiitos.*
Thank you.	*Kiitos.*
That's fine/You're welcome.	*Ole hyvä.* or *Eipä kestä.* (informal)
Excuse me. (sorry)	*Anteeksi.*
Do you speak English?	*Puhutko englantia?*
How much is it?	*Paljonko se makasaa?*
What's your name?	*Mikä Teidän nimenne on?*
My name is ...	*Minun nimeni on ...*

Getting Around

What time does ... leave/arrive?	*Mihin aikaan ... lähtee/saapuu?*
the boat	*laiva*
the bus (city)	*bussi*
the bus (intercity)	*bussi/linja-auto*
the tram	*raitiovaunu/raitikka*
the train	*juna*
I'd like a one way/ return ticket.	*Saanko menolipun/ menopaluulipun.*
Where can I hire a car?	*Mistä mina voisin vuokrata auton?*
Where can I hire a bicycle?	*Mistä mina voin vuokrata polkupyörän?*
1st class	*ensimmäinen luokka*
2nd class	*toinen luokka*
left luggage	*säilytys*
timetable	*aikataulu*
bus/tram stop	*pysäkki*
train station	*rautatieasema*
ferry terminal	*satamaterminaali*

Signs – Finnish

Sisään	Entrance
Ulos	Exit
Avoinna	Open
Suljettu	Closed
Kielletty	Prohibited
Huoneita	Rooms Available
Täynnä	No Vacancies
Opastus	Information
Poliisiasema	Police Station
WC	Toilets
Miehet	Men
Naiset	Women

Emergencies – Finnish

Help!	*Apua!*
Call a doctor!	*Kutsukaa lääkäri!*
Call the police!	*Soittakaa poliisi!*
Go away!	*Mene pois! (Häivy!)*
I'm lost.	*Minä olen eksynyt.*

Where is ...?	*Missä on ...?*
Go straight ahead.	*Kulje suoraan.*
Turn left.	*Käänny vasempaan.*
Turn right.	*Käänny oikeaan.*
near/far	*lähellä/kaukana*

Around Town

bank	*pankkia*
chemist/pharmacy	*apteekki*
... embassy	*... -n suurlähetystöä*
my hotel	*hotellini*
market	*toria*
newsagent	*lehtikioski*
post office	*postia*
stationer	*paperikauppa*
telephone centre	*puhelinta/puhelin*
tourist office	*matkailutoimistoa/ matkailutoimisto*
What time does it open/close?	*Milloin se aukeaan/ sul jetaan?*

Accommodation

hotel	*hotelli*
guesthouse	*matkustajakoti*
youth hostel	*retkeilymaja*
camping ground	*leirintäalue*
Do you have any rooms available?	*Onko teillä vapaata huonetta?*
How much is it per night/per person?	*Paljonko se on yöltä/hengeltä?*
Does it include breakfast?	*Kuuluko aamiainen hintaan?*
I'd like ...	*Haluaisin ...*
a single room	*yhden hengen huoneen*
a double room	*kahden hengen huoneen*
one day	*yhden päivän*
two days	*kaksi päivää*

Time, Days & Numbers

What time is it?	*Paljonko kello on?*
today	*tänään*
tomorrow	*huomenna*

yesterday	*eilen*
morning	*aamulla*
afternoon	*iltapäivällä*

Monday	*maanantai*
Tuesday	*tiistai*
Wednesday	*keskiviikko*
Thursday	*torstai*
Friday	*perjantai*
Saturday	*lauantai*
Sunday	*sunnuntai*

0	*nolla*
1	*yksi*
2	*kaksi*
3	*kolme*
4	*neljä*
5	*viisi*
6	*kuusi*
7	*seitsemän*
8	*kahdeksan*
9	*yhdeksän*
10	*kymmenen*
100	*sata*
1000	*tuhat*

one million	*miljoona*

Greenlandic

The official language of Greenland is Greenlandic, one of many Inuit dialects spoken in the Arctic. Regional variations do occur – West Greenlanders can understand variations of West Greenlandic, but their dialect is not mutually intelligible with East Greenlandic.

The second language of Greenland is Danish, which is spoken by nearly everyone. Only a small percentage of Greenlanders speak any language other than Greenlandic and Danish.

Pronunciation

Greenlandic pronunciation is difficult to demonstrate in a pronunciation guide. Consonants come from deep in the throat and some vowels are scarcely pronounced. Your best bet is to listen and learn.

Vowels

a	as the 'u' in 'hut'
aa	as the 'a' in 'father'
e	as the 'a' in 'ago'
i	as in 'marine'
o	as in 'hot'
u	as the 'oo' in 'cool'

Consonants

Consonants are pronounced as in English with the exception of the following:

g	as in 'goose'
j	as in 'jaw'
k	as in 'key'
l	as in 'leg'
ng	as in 'sing'
q	pronounced as a 'k' from deep in the back of the throat
v	as in 'van'

Basics

Hello.
Inuugujoq, kutaa/Haluu.
Goodbye, best wishes.
Inuulluarit (sg)/*Inuulluaritse* (pl)
Ajunnginniarna (sg)/*Ajunnginniarise* (pl)
(long-term parting)
Goodbye/See you soon.
Takuss'. (short-term parting)
Yes.
Aap.
No.
Naagga/Naamik.
Thank you (very much).
Qujanaq (qujanarsuaq).
That's fine/good.
Ajunngilaq.
Do you speak English?
Tuluttut oqalusinnaavit?
How much is it?
Qanoq akeqarpa?
What's your name?
Qanoq ateqarpit?
My name is ...
...-imik ateqarpunga.

Getting Around

What time does the ... leave/arrive?
Qaqugu ... aallartarpa/tikkiuttarpa?

boat	*ilaasortaat*
bus	*bussi*
plane	*timmisartoq*

I'd like a ... ticket. *... bilitsimik pisorusuppunga.*

one-way	*Siumuinnaq*
return	*Siumut-utimut*

Is it far from here?
Maanngaanit ungasippa?
Is it near here?
Maanngaanit qanippa?

Emergencies – Greenlandic

Help!	*Ikiunnga!*
Call a doctor!	*Nakorsamik kalerriigitsi!*
Call the police!	*Politiimik kalerriigitsi!*
I'm lost.	*Tammaqqavunga.*

Go straight ahead.
Siumuinnaq.
Turn left.
Saamimmut sangulluni.
Turn right.
Talerpimmut sangulluni.

Accommodation

hotel	*hoteli*
guesthouse	*unnuisarfik*
youth hostel	*angallatsinut unnuisarfik*
campground	*tupertarfik*

Do you have any rooms available?
Inimik attartungasaateqarpise?

How much is it ...?	... *qanoq akeqarpa?*
per night	*Unuinnarmut*
per person	*Inummut ataatsimut*

Does it include breakfast?
Ullaakkoorsioneq ilaareerpa?

I'd like ...	... *piumavunga.*
a single room	*Kisimiittariamik*
a double room	*Marluuttariamik*

Around Town

Where is a/the ...?	... *sumiippa?/Naak ...?*
bank	*banki*
... consulate/ embassy	*konsuleqarfik/ nunannut aallattitaqarfik*
my hotel	*hotelera*
market	*kalaalimineerniarfik*
police	*politeeqarfik*
post office	*allakkerivik*
public toilet	*anartarfik*
telephone centre	*oqarasuaat/ telefooni*
tourist office	*takornarissanut allaffik*

What time does it open/close?
Qaqugu ammassarpat/matusarpat?

Time & Dates

What time is it?	*Qassinngorpa?*
today	*ullumi*

tomorrow	*aqagu*
morning	*ullaaq*
afternoon	*ualeq*

Monday	*Ataasinngorneq*
Tuesday	*Marlunngorneq*
Wednesday	*Pingasunngorneq*
Thursday	*Sisamanngorneq*
Friday	*Tallimanngorneq*
Saturday	*Arfininngorneq*
Sunday	*Sapaat*

Numbers

Numbers in Greenlandic only go up to 12 – after 12 there is only *amerlasoorpassuit*, 'many'. From 12 onwards you have to use Danish numbers (see Danish section earlier in this chapter).

1	*ataaseq*
2	*marluk*
3	*pingasut*
4	*sisamat*
5	*tallimat*
6	*arfinillit*
7	*arfineq marluk*
8	*arfineq pingasut*
9	*qulingiluat*
10	*qulit*
11	*arqanillit*
12	*arqaneq marluk*

Icelandic

Icelandic belongs to the Germanic language family that includes German, Dutch and all the Nordic languages except Finnish. Its closest 'living relative' is Faroese. Both Icelandic and Faroese are derived from Old Norse and they've changed little since the time of the Vikings.

Icelandic grammar is very complicated; suffixes added to nouns and place names to indicate case may render a place name quite unrecognisable. This can lead to a great deal of confusion, especially when you're trying to read bus timetables and find names of towns spelt several different ways. For example, the sign that welcomes visitors to the town of Höfn reads 'Velkomin til Hafnar'. Hafnar is the dative of Höfn.

Fortunately, it's not essential for foreigners to speak Icelandic. The second language of most young people is English, followed by Danish (and therefore Swedish and Norwegian to some degree) and German. Some people also learn French, Italian or Spanish.

Other Icelanders will normally know enough English and German to do business and exchange pleasantries.

Pronunciation

Stress is generally on the first syllable. Double consonants are pronounced as such.

Vowels & Diphthongs

a	long, as in 'father' or short, as in 'at'
á	as the 'ou' in 'out'
au	as the word 'furry' without 'f' or 'rr'
e	long, as in 'fear' or short, as in 'bet'
é	as the 'y' in 'yet'
ei, ey	as the 'ay' in 'day'
i, y	as the 'i' in 'hit'
í, ý	as the 'i' in 'marine'
o	as in 'pot'
ó	as the word 'owe'
u	a bit like the 'u' in 'purr'
ú	as the 'o' in 'moon', or as the 'o' in 'woman'
ö	as the 'er' in 'fern', but without a trace of 'r'
æ	as the word 'eye'

Consonants

ð	as the 'th' in 'lather'
f	as in 'far'. When between vowels or at the end of a word it's pronounced as 'v'. When followed by l or n it's pronounced as 'b'.
g	as in 'go'. When between vowels or before r or ð it has a guttural sound as the 'ch' in Scottish *loch*.
h	as in 'he', except when followed by v, when it is pronounced as 'k'
j	as the 'y' in 'yellow'
l	as in 'let'; when doubled it's pronounced as 'dl'
n	as in 'no'; when doubled or word-final it's pronounced as 'dn' (unless nn forms part of the definite article *hinn*)
p	as in 'hip', except when followed by s or t, when it's pronounced as 'f'
r	always trilled
þ	as the 'th' in 'thin' or 'three'

Basics

Hello.	*Halló.*
Goodbye.	*Bless.*
Yes.	*Já.*
No.	*Nei.*
Please.	*Gjörðu svo vel.*
Thank you.	*Takk fyrir.*
That's fine/ You're welcome.	*Allt í lagi/ Ekkert að þakka.*

Excuse me. (Sorry)	*Afsakið.*
Do you speak English?	*Talar þú ensku?*
How much is it?	*Hvað kostar tað*
What's your name?	*Hvað heitir þú?*
My name is ...	*Ég heiti ...*

Getting Around

What time does ... leave/arrive?	*Hvenær fer/kemur ...?*
the boat	*báturinn*
the bus (city)	*vagninn*
the tram	*sporvagninn*

I'd like ...	*Gæti ég fengið ...*
a one-way ticket	*miða/aðra leiðina*
a return ticket	*miða/báðar leiðir*
1st class	*fyrsta farrými*
2nd class	*annað farrými*

bus stop	*biðstöð*
ferry terminal	*ferjuhöfn*
timetable	*tímaáætlun*

I'd like to hire a car/bicycle.	*Ég vil leigja bíl/reiðhjól.*
Where is ...?	*Hvar er ...?*
Go straight ahead.	*Farðu beint af áfram.*
Turn left.	*Beygðu til vinstri.*
Turn right.	*Beygðu til hægri.*
near/far	*nálægt/langt í burtu*

Around Town

bank	*banka*
chemist/pharmacy	*apótek*
... embassy	*... sendiráðinu*
my hotel	*hótelinu mínu*
market	*markaðnum*
newsagent/ stationer	*blaðasala/bókabúð*
post office	*pósthúsinu*

Signs – Icelandic

Inngangur/Inn	Entrance
Útgangur/Út	Exit
Opið	Open
Lokað	Closed
Bannað	Prohibited
Full Bókað	No Vacancies
Upplýsingar	Information
Lögreglustöð	Police Station
Snyrting	Toilets
Karlar	Men
Konur	Women

Emergencies – Icelandic

Help!	Hjálp!
Call a doctor!	Náið í lækni!
Call the police!	Náið í lögregluna!
Go away!	Farðu!
I'm lost	Ég er villtur. (m)
	Ég er villt. (f)

telephone centre	símstöðinni
tourist office	upplýsingaþjónustu fyrir ferðafólk

Accommodation

hotel	hótel
guesthouse	gistiheimili
youth hostel	farfuglaheimili
camping ground	tjaldsvæði

Do you have any rooms available?	Eru herbergi laus?
How much is it per night/per person?	Hvað kostar nóttin fyrir manninn?
Does it include breakfast?	Er morgunmatur innifalinn?

I'd like ...	Gæti ég fengið ...
a single room	einstaklingsherbergi
a double room	tveggjamanna-herbergi

one day	einn dag
two days	tvo daga

Time, Days & Numbers

What time is it?	Hvað er klukkan?
today	í dag
tomorrow	á morgun
yesterday	í gær
in the morning	að morgni
in the afternoon	eftir hádegi

Monday	mánudagur
Tuesday	þriðjudagur
Wednesday	miðvikudagur
Thursday	fimmtudagur
Friday	föstudagur
Saturday	laugardagur
Sunday	sunnudagur

0	núll
1	einn
2	tveir
3	þrír
4	fjórir
5	fimm

6	sex
7	sjö
8	átta
9	níu
10	tíu
20	tuttugu
100	eitt hundrað
1000	eitt þúsund

one million	ein milljón

Norwegian

Norway has two official languages – Bokmål and Nynorsk – but differences between the two are effectively very minor. In this language guide we have used Bokmål – it's by far the most common language travellers to Norway will encounter.

English is widely understood and spoken, especially in the urban areas and in most tourist destinations. In the rural areas (where Nynorsk predominates) you may come across people who speak very little English. If you show an effort to speak Norwegian, it will help a great deal in making contact.

Pronunciation
Vowels & Diphthongs

a	long, as in 'father'; short, as in 'cut'
å	as the 'aw' in 'paw'
æ	as the 'a' in 'act'
e	long as in 'where'; short, as in 'bet'; when unstressed, as the 'a' in 'ago'
i	long, as the 'ee' in 'seethe'; short, as in 'hit'
o	long, as the 'oo' in 'cool'; short, as in 'pot'
ø	long, as the 'er' in 'fern'; short, as the 'a' in 'ago'
u, y	say 'ee' while pursing your lips
ai	as the word 'eye'
ei	as the 'ay' in 'day'
au	as the 'o' in 'note'
øy	as the 'oy' in 'toy'

Consonants & Semivowels

d	at the end of a word, or between two vowels, it's often silent
g	as the 'g' in 'get'; as the 'y' in 'yard' before ei, i, j, øy, y
h	as in 'her'; silent before v and j
j	as the 'y' in 'yard'
k	as in 'kin'; as the 'ch' in 'chin' before ei, i, j, øy and y

ng	as in 'sing'
r	a trilled 'r'. The combination rs is pronounced as the 'sh' in 'fish'.
s	as in 'so' (never as in 'treasure'); as the 'sh' in 'ship' before **ei, i, j, øy** and **y**

Basics

Hello.	*Goddag.*
Goodbye.	*Ha det.*
Yes.	*Ja.*
No.	*Nei.*
Please.	*Vær så snill.*
Thank you.	*Takk.*
That's fine/You're welcome.	*Ingen årsak.*
Excuse me. (sorry)	*Unnskyld.*
Do you speak English?	*Snakker du engelsk?*
How much is it?	*Hvor mye koster det?*
What's your name?	*Hva heter du?*
My name is ...	*Jeg heter ...*

Getting Around

What time does ... leave/arrive?	*Når går/kommer ...?*
the boat	*båten*
the (city) bus	*(by)bussen*
the intercity bus	*linjebussen*
the train	*toget*
the tram	*trikken*

I'd like ...	*Jeg vil gjerne ha ...*
a one-way ticket	*enkeltbillett*
a return ticket	*tur-retur*

1st class	*første klasse*
2nd class	*annen klasse*
left luggage	*reisegods*
timetable	*ruteplan*
bus stop	*bussholdeplass*
tram stop	*trikkholdeplass*
train station	*jernbanestasjon*
ferry terminal	*ferjeleiet*

Emergencies – Norwegian

Help!	*Hjelp!*
Call a doctor!	*Ring en lege!*
Call the police!	*Ring politiet!*
Go away!	*Forsvinn!*
I'm lost.	*Jeg har gått meg vill.*

Where can I rent a car/bicycle?	*Hvor kan jeg leie en bil/sykkel?*
Where is ...?	*Hvor er ...?*
Go straight ahead.	*Det er rett fram.*
Turn left.	*Ta til venstre.*
Turn right.	*Ta til høyre.*
near/far	*nær/langt*

Around Town

bank	*banken*
chemist/pharmacy	*apotek*
... embassy	*... ambassade*
my hotel	*hotellet mitt*
market	*torget*
newsagent	*kiosk*
post office	*postkontoret*
telephone centre	*televerket*
tourist office	*turistinformasjon*

Accommodation

hotel	*hotell*
guesthouse	*gjestgiveri/pensjonat*
youth hostel	*vandrerhjem*
camping ground	*kamping/leirplass*

Do you have any rooms available?	*Har du ledige rom?*
How much is it per night/ per person?	*Hvor mye er det pr dag/ pr person?*
Does it include breakfast?	*Inklusive frokosten?*

I'd like ...	*Jeg vil gjerne ha ...*
a single room	*et enkeltrom*
a double room	*et dobbeltrom*

one day	*en dag*
two days	*to dager*

Time, Days & Numbers

What time is it?	*Hva er klokka?*
today	*i dag*
tomorrow	*i morgen*
yesterday	*i går*
in the morning	*om formiddagen*
in the afternoon	*om ettermiddagen*

Monday	*mandag*
Tuesday	*tirsdag*
Wednesday	*onsdag*
Thursday	*torsdag*
Friday	*fredag*
Saturday	*lørdag*
Sunday	*søndag*

0	*null*
1	*en*
2	*to*
3	*tre*
4	*fire*
5	*fem*
6	*seks*
7	*sju*
8	*åtte*
9	*ni*
10	*ti*
100	*hundre*
1000	*tusen*

one million   *en million*

Swedish

Swedish belongs to the Nordic branch of the Germanic language family and is spoken throughout Sweden and in parts of Finland. Swedes, Danes and Norwegians can make themselves mutually understood. Most Swedes speak English as a second language.

Definite articles in Swedish ('the' in English) are determined by the ending of a noun: *-en* and *-et* for singular nouns and *-na* and *-n* for plural.

If you learn a few common phrases, your attempts will be greatly appreciated by Swedes, who aren't used to foreigners speaking Swedish.

Sami dialects (there are three main groups) belong to the Uralic language family, and are ancestrally related to Finnish, not Swedish.

Pronunciation
Vowels
The vowels are pronounced as short sounds if there's a double consonant afterwards, otherwise they are long sounds. Sometimes the **o** in Swedish sounds like the **å**, and **e** as the **ä**. There are, however, not as many exceptions to the rules as there are in English.

a   long, as in 'father'; short, as the 'u' in 'cut'

o, u   long, as the 'oo' in 'cool'; short, as in 'pot'

i   long, as the 'ee' in 'seethe'; short, as in 'pit'

e   long, as the 'ea' in 'fear'; short, as in 'bet'

å   long, as the word 'awe'; short as the 'o' in 'pot'

ä   as the 'a' in 'act'

ö   as the 'er' in 'fern', but without the 'r' sound

y   try saying 'ee' while pursing your lips

Consonants
The consonants are pronounced almost the same as in English. The following letter combinations and sounds are specific to Swedish:

c   as the 's' in 'sit'

ck   as a double 'k'; shortens the preceding vowel

tj, rs   as the 'sh' in 'ship'

sj, ch   similar to the 'ch' in Scottish *loch*

g   as in 'get'; sometimes as the 'y' in 'yet'

lj   as the 'y' in 'yet'

Basics
Hello.	*Hej.*
Goodbye.	*Adjö/Hej då.*
Yes.	*Ja.*
No.	*Nej.*
Please.	*Snälla/Vänligen.*
Thank you.	*Tack.*
That's fine/ You're welcome.	*Det är bra/ Varsågod.*
Excuse me. (sorry)	*Ursäkta mig/Förlåt.*
Do you speak English?	*Talar du engelska?*
How much is it?	*Hur mycket kostar den?*
What's your name?	*Vad heter du?*
My name is ...	*Jag heter ...*

Getting Around
What time does ... leave/arrive?	*När avgår/kommer ...?*
the boat	*båten*
the city bus	*stadsbussen*
the intercity bus	*landsortsbussen*
the train	*tåget*
the tram	*spårvagnen*

I'd like ...	*Jag skulle vilja ha ...*
a one-way ticket	*en enkelbiljett*
a return ticket	*en returbiljett*
1st class	*första klass*
2nd class	*andra klass*

LANGUAGE

left luggage	*effektförvaring*
timetable	*tidtabell*
bus stop	*busshållplats*
train station	*tågstation*

Where can I hire a car/bicycle?	*Var kan jag hyra en bil/cykel?*
Where is ...?	*Var är ...?*
Go straight ahead.	*Gå rakt fram.*
Turn left.	*Sväng till vänster.*
Turn right.	*Sväng till höger.*
near/far	*nära/långt*

Around Town

bank	*bank*
chemist/pharmacy	*apotek*
... embassy	*... ambassaden*
my hotel	*mitt hotell*
market	*marknaden*
newsagent/ stationer	*nyhetsbyrå/ pappers handel*
post office	*postkontoret*
a public telephone	*en offentlig telefon*
tourist office	*turistinformation*

What time does it open/close?	*När öppnar/ stänger de?*

Accommodation

hotel	*hotell*
guesthouse	*gästhus*
youth hostel	*vandrarhem*
camping ground	*campingplats*

Do you have any rooms available?	*Finns det några lediga rum?*

Signs – Swedish

Ingång	**Entrance**
Utgång	**Exit**
Öppet	**Open**
Stängt	**Closed**
Förbjudet	**Prohibited**
Lediga Rum	**Rooms *Available***
Fullt	**No Vacancies**
Information	**Information**
Polisstation	**Police Station**
Toalett	**Toilets**
Herrar	**Men**
Damer	**Women**

Emergencies – Swedish

Help!	*Hjälp!*
Call a doctor!	*Ring efter en doktor!*
Call the police!	*Ring polisen!*
Go away!	*Försvinn!*
I'm lost.	*Jag har gått vilse.*

How much is it per night/ per person?	*Hur mycket kostar det per natt/ per person?*

Does it include breakfast?	*Inkluderas frukost?*

I'd like ...	*Jag skulle vilja ha ...*
a single room	*ett enkelrum*
a double room	*ett dubbelrum*

for one/two nights	*i en natt/två nätter*

Time, Days & Numbers

What time is it?	*Vad är klockan?*
today	*idag*
tomorrow	*imorgon*
yesterday	*igår*
morning	*morgonen*
afternoon	*efter middagen*

Monday	*måndag*
Tuesday	*tisdag*
Wednesday	*onsdag*
Thursday	*torsdag*
Friday	*fredag*
Saturday	*lördag*
Sunday	*söndag*

0	*noll*
1	*ett*
2	*två*
3	*tre*
4	*fyra*
5	*fem*
6	*sex*
7	*sju*
8	*åtta*
9	*nio*
10	*tio*
100	*ett hundra*
1000	*ett tusen*

one million	*en miljon*

Thanks

Many thanks to the travellers who used the last edition and wrote to us with helpful hints, useful advice and interesting anecdotes:

Alexandra Aebischer, Husain Akbar, Kasper Anderson, Elizabeth Andonovski, JM Aranaz, June Arber, Glenn Ashenden, Kris Ayre, Ali Baldwin, Kate Barker, Eleanor Barrett, Michele Beltrame, Koos Berkhout, Christian Bertell, Michael Bohames, Katarina Boijer, Peter Christian Bokelmann, Carmen Boudreau-Kiviaho, Kees Bouman, Ian Brazewell, Ingemar Brinkenberg, Julie Bromley, Thessa Brongers, Abe Brouwer, Chris Burin, Nikolajs Calenko, Ken & Diana Campbell, Michael Cassidy, Scott Caufield, Bradley Chait, Sutapa Choudhury, George Christensen, Meredith Cook, Karen Cooper, Ed Cornfield, Christine Crowther, Richard Daly, Jennifer Davidson, Sander de Vries, Chris Detmar, Nathan Dhillon, Birge Dohmann, Alexander Doric, Tom & Ann Dowd, Robert Edmunds, Hugh Elsol, Andrew Embick, Ket Ericson, Kelly Eskridge, Louisa Fagan, Eva Fairnell, Jimmy Fong, Graham Ford, Ludek Frybort, Martin Garvey, Claire Gibbons, Serge Gielkens, Martin Grandes, Phyllis Grant, Anthony Gray, Ed Graystone, Nicky Griffin, Patricia Grumberg, Martin Gstrein, David Gyger, Brian Aslak Gylte, Jean-Francois Hachey, Cedric Hannedouche, Armin Hass, Edgar Hee, Scott Hegerty, James Hemingway, Moritz Herrmann, Matt Hoover, Alex Hopkins, Marcel Huibers, Darcy Hurford, Steve Hutton, Ahmet Incesu, Trygve Jackson, Hilde Johnsen, Ludmila Johnsen, TC Jones, W Jules, Alexandra Kainz, Silke Kampowski, Teemu Kankaanpaa, Karles Karwin, Andrew Keeley, Erki Kurrikoff, Christine Laliberte, Naomi Lee, Lesley Leung, Bert Leunis, Marge Lilane, Andy Limacher, Jill Litwin, Hanne Lorimer, Jeff Lowe, Barbara Lund, PA MaCaitlem, Jonna Makkonen, Roberto Manfredi, Roy & Susan Masters, John McKenzie, Patrick McMorris, Gunnar Merbach, Gina Messenger, Susanne Meyer, Marius Moellersen, Pierre Moermans, Geraldine Moran, Hakon Mosseby, Jean Mounter, Wade Munsie, Sally Murphy, Tatu Myohanen, Ludwig Naf, Sofia Nilsson, Mick Nishikawa, Jen Noble, Mark Nutall, Anders Paalzow, Sandra Pagano, Luc Penninckc, Andrew Perry, Robertas Pogorelis, Graham Pointon, Barry Poole, Tony & Jill Porco, Kieth Porteous Wood, Ramu Pyreddy, Alexandra Rasch, Bard Reian, Vera Reifenberg, Benjamin Richter, Kim Riley, Nat Robbins, Nicola Romeo, Bjorn Ronnekliev, Jaroslaw Rudnik, David Rutter, Salvador Sanchez, Bernard Sayer, Wendy Scaife, Jacco Scheffer, Frede Scheye, Asya Schigol, Robert Schwandt, Larry Schwarz, GN Sellers, Alan Sirulnikoff, Mary-Louise Sloan, JM Haw Smalley, Mariella Smith, Anthony Snieckus, Robert Stroethoff, Ichiro Sugiyama, Jerker Svantesson, Kenneth Tangnes, Marianne Teglengaard, Aimi Theobald, Silje Figenschou Thoresen, Martin Torres, Nick Townsend, Danielle Treacy, Gordon Trousdale, Dana & Nick Tsamaidis, Riikka Tuomisto, Juliette Turner, Ronaldo Uliana de Oliveria, Jens Christian Ulrich, Marianne Undberg, Elzeline Van Der Neut, Aletta & Ruud van Uden, Stefan vanwildemeersch, Terese Wadden, Henrik Waldenstrom, Louise Walters, Dennis Waterman, Viktor Weisshaupl, Ian West, Froy Lode Wiig, Whui Mei Yeo

LONELY PLANET

Guides by Region

onely Planet is known worldwide for publishing practical, reliable and no-nonsense travel information in our guides and on our Web site. The Lonely Planet list covers just about every accessible part of the world. Currently there are 16 series: Travel guides, Shoestring guides, Condensed guides, Phrasebooks, Read This First, Healthy Travel, Walking guides, Cycling guides, Watching Wildlife guides, Pisces Diving & Snorkeling guides, City Maps, Road Atlases, Out to Eat, World Food, Journeys travel literature and Pictorials.

AFRICA Africa on a shoestring • Botswana • Cairo • Cairo City Map • Cape Town • Cape Town City Map • East Africa • Egypt • Egyptian Arabic phrasebook • Ethiopia, Eritrea & Djibouti • Ethiopian Amharic phrasebook • The Gambia & Senegal • Healthy Travel Africa • Kenya • Malawi • Morocco • Moroccan Arabic phrasebook • Mozambique • Namibia • Read This First: Africa • South Africa, Lesotho & Swaziland • Southern Africa • Southern Africa Road Atlas • Swahili phrasebook • Tanzania, Zanzibar & Pemba • Trekking in East Africa • Tunisia • Watching Wildlife East Africa • Watching Wildlife Southern Africa • West Africa • World Food Morocco • Zambia • Zimbabwe, Botswana & Namibia
Travel Literature: Mali Blues: Traveling to an African Beat • The Rainbird: A Central African Journey • Songs to an African Sunset: A Zimbabwean Story

AUSTRALIA & THE PACIFIC Aboriginal Australia & the Torres Strait Islands •Auckland • Australia • Australian phrasebook • Australia Road Atlas • Cycling Australia • Cycling New Zealand • Fiji • Fijian phrasebook • Healthy Travel Australia, NZ & the Pacific • Islands of Australia's Great Barrier Reef • Melbourne • Melbourne City Map • Micronesia • New Caledonia • New South Wales • New Zealand • Northern Territory • Outback Australia • Out to Eat – Melbourne • Out to Eat – Sydney • Papua New Guinea • Pidgin phrasebook • Queensland • Rarotonga & the Cook Islands • Samoa • Solomon Islands • South Australia • South Pacific • South Pacific phrasebook • Sydney • Sydney City Map • Sydney Condensed • Tahiti & French Polynesia • Tasmania • Tonga • Tramping in New Zealand • Vanuatu • Victoria • Walking in Australia • Watching Wildlife Australia • Western Australia
Travel Literature: Islands in the Clouds: Travels in the Highlands of New Guinea • Kiwi Tracks: A New Zealand Journey • Sean & David's Long Drive

CENTRAL AMERICA & THE CARIBBEAN Bahamas, Turks & Caicos • Baja California • Belize, Guatemala & Yucatán • Bermuda • Central America on a shoestring • Costa Rica • Costa Rica Spanish phrasebook • Cuba • Cycling Cuba • Dominican Republic & Haiti • Eastern Caribbean • Guatemala • Havana • Healthy Travel Central & South America • Jamaica • Mexico • Mexico City • Panama • Puerto Rico • Read This First: Central & South America • Virgin Islands • World Food Caribbean • World Food Mexico • Yucatán
Travel Literature: Green Dreams: Travels in Central America

EUROPE Amsterdam • Amsterdam City Map • Amsterdam Condensed • Andalucía • Athens • Austria • Baltic States phrasebook • Barcelona • Barcelona City Map • Belgium & Luxembourg • Berlin • Berlin City Map • Britain • British phrasebook • Brussels, Bruges & Antwerp • Brussels City Map • Budapest • Budapest City Map • Canary Islands • Catalunya & the Costa Brava • Central Europe • Central Europe phrasebook • Copenhagen • Corfu & the Ionians • Corsica • Crete • Crete Condensed • Croatia • Cycling Britain • Cycling France • Cyprus • Czech & Slovak Republics • Czech phrasebook • Denmark • Dublin • Dublin City Map • Dublin Condensed • Eastern Europe • Eastern Europe phrasebook • Edinburgh • Edinburgh City Map • England • Estonia, Latvia & Lithuania • Europe on a shoestring • Europe phrasebook • Finland • Florence • Florence City Map • France • Frankfurt City Map • Frankfurt Condensed • French phrasebook • Georgia, Armenia & Azerbaijan • Germany • German phrasebook • Greece • Greek Islands • Greek phrasebook • Hungary • Iceland, Greenland & the Faroe Islands • Ireland • Italian phrasebook • Italy • Kraków • Lisbon • The Loire • London • London City Map • London Condensed • Madrid • Madrid City Map • Malta • Mediterranean Europe • Milan, Turin & Genoa • Moscow • Munich • Netherlands • Normandy • Norway • Out to Eat – London • Out to Eat – Paris • Paris • Paris City Map • Paris Condensed • Poland • Polish phrasebook • Portugal • Portuguese phrasebook • Prague • Prague City Map • Provence & the Côte d'Azur • Read This First: Europe • Rhodes & the Dodecanese • Romania & Moldova • Rome • Rome City Map • Rome Condensed • Russia, Ukraine & Belarus • Russian phrasebook • Scandinavian & Baltic Europe • Scandinavian phrasebook • Scotland • Sicily • Slovenia • South-West France • Spain • Spanish phrasebook • Stockholm • St Petersburg • St Petersburg City Map • Sweden • Switzerland • Tuscany • Ukrainian phrasebook • Venice • Vienna • Wales • Walking in Britain • Walking in France • Walking in Ireland • Walking in Italy • Walking in Scotland • Walking in Spain • Walking in Switzerland • Western Europe • World Food France • World Food Greece • World Food Ireland • World Food Italy • World Food Spain **Travel Literature:** After Yugoslavia • Love and War in the Apennines • The Olive Grove: Travels in Greece • On the Shores of the Mediterranean • Round Ireland in Low Gear • A Small Place in Italy

LONELY PLANET

Mail Order

Lonely Planet products are distributed worldwide. They are also available by mail order from Lonely Planet, so if you have difficulty finding a title please write to us. North and South American residents should write to 150 Linden St, Oakland, CA 94607, USA; European and African residents should write to 10a Spring Place, London NW5 3BH, UK; and residents of other countries to Locked Bag 1, Footscray, Victoria 3011, Australia.

INDIAN SUBCONTINENT & THE INDIAN OCEAN Bangladesh • Bengali phrasebook • Bhutan • Delhi • Goa • Healthy Travel Asia & India • Hindi & Urdu phrasebook • India • India & Bangladesh City Map • Indian Himalaya • Karakoram Highway • Kathmandu City Map • Kerala • Madagascar • Maldives • Mauritius, Réunion & Seychelles • Mumbai (Bombay) • Nepal • Nepali phrasebook • North India • Pakistan • Rajasthan • Read This First: Asia & India • South India • Sri Lanka • Sri Lanka phrasebook • Tibet • Tibetan phrasebook • Trekking in the Indian Himalaya • Trekking in the Karakoram & Hindukush • Trekking in the Nepal Himalaya • World Food India **Travel Literature:** The Age of Kali: Indian Travels and Encounters • Hello Goodnight: A Life of Goa • In Rajasthan • Maverick in Madagascar • A Season in Heaven: True Tales from the Road to Kathmandu • Shopping for Buddhas • A Short Walk in the Hindu Kush • Slowly Down the Ganges

MIDDLE EAST & CENTRAL ASIA Bahrain, Kuwait & Qatar • Central Asia • Central Asia phrasebook • Dubai • Farsi (Persian) phrasebook • Hebrew phrasebook • Iran • Israel & the Palestinian Territories • Istanbul • Istanbul City Map • Istanbul to Cairo • Istanbul to Kathmandu • Jerusalem • Jerusalem City Map • Jordan • Lebanon • Middle East • Oman & the United Arab Emirates • Syria • Turkey • Turkish phrasebook • World Food Turkey • Yemen **Travel Literature:** Black on Black: Iran Revisited • Breaking Ranks: Turbulent Travels in the Promised Land • The Gates of Damascus • Kingdom of the Film Stars: Journey into Jordan

NORTH AMERICA Alaska • Boston • Boston City Map • Boston Condensed • British Columbia • California & Nevada • California Condensed • Canada • Chicago • Chicago City Map • Chicago Condensed • Florida • Georgia & the Carolinas • Great Lakes • Hawaii • Hiking in Alaska • Hiking in the USA • Honolulu & Oahu City Map • Las Vegas • Los Angeles • Los Angeles City Map • Louisiana & the Deep South • Miami • Miami City Map • Montreal • New England • New Orleans • New Orleans City Map • New York City • New York City City Map • New York City Condensed • New York, New Jersey & Pennsylvania • Oahu • Out to Eat – San Francisco • Pacific Northwest • Rocky Mountains • San Diego & Tijuana • San Francisco • San Francisco City Map • Seattle • Seattle City Map • Southwest • Texas • Toronto • USA • USA phrasebook • Vancouver • Vancouver City Map • Virginia & the Capital Region • Washington, DC • Washington, DC City Map • World Food New Orleans **Travel Literature:** Caught Inside: A Surfer's Year on the California Coast • Drive Thru America

NORTH-EAST ASIA Beijing • Beijing City Map • Cantonese phrasebook • China • Hiking in Japan • Hong Kong & Macau • Hong Kong City Map • Hong Kong Condensed • Japan • Japanese phrasebook • Korea • Korean phrasebook • Kyoto • Mandarin phrasebook • Mongolia • Mongolian phrasebook • Seoul • Shanghai • South-West China • Taiwan • Tokyo • Tokyo Condensed • World Food Hong Kong • World Food Japan **Travel Literature:** In Xanadu: A Quest • Lost Japan

SOUTH AMERICA Argentina, Uruguay & Paraguay • Bolivia • Brazil • Brazilian phrasebook • Buenos Aires • Buenos Aires City Map • Chile & Easter Island • Colombia • Ecuador & the Galapagos Islands • Healthy Travel Central & South America • Latin American Spanish phrasebook • Peru • Quechua phrasebook • Read This First: Central & South America • Rio de Janeiro • Rio de Janeiro City Map • Santiago de Chile • South America on a shoestring • Trekking in the Patagonian Andes • Venezuela **Travel Literature:** Full Circle: A South American Journey

SOUTH-EAST ASIA Bali & Lombok • Bangkok • Bangkok City Map • Burmese phrasebook • Cambodia • Cycling Vietnam, Laos & Cambodia • East Timor phrasebook • Hanoi • Healthy Travel Asia & India • Hill Tribes phrasebook • Ho Chi Minh City (Saigon) • Indonesia • Indonesian phrasebook • Indonesia's Eastern Islands • Java • Lao phrasebook • Laos • Malay phrasebook • Malaysia, Singapore & Brunei • Myanmar (Burma) • Philippines • Pilipino (Tagalog) phrasebook • Read This First: Asia & India • Singapore • Singapore City Map • South-East Asia on a shoestring • South-East Asia phrasebook • Thailand • Thailand's Islands & Beaches • Thailand, Vietnam, Laos & Cambodia Road Atlas • Thai phrasebook • Vietnam • Vietnamese phrasebook • World Food Indonesia • World Food Thailand • World Food Vietnam

ALSO AVAILABLE: Antarctica • The Arctic • The Blue Man: Tales of Travel, Love and Coffee • Brief Encounters: Stories of Love, Sex & Travel • Buddhist Stupas in Asia: The Shape of Perfection • Chasing Rickshaws • The Last Grain Race • Lonely Planet ... On the Edge: Adventurous Escapades from Around the World • Lonely Planet Unpacked • Lonely Planet Unpacked Again • Not the Only Planet: Science Fiction Travel Stories • Ports of Call: A Journey by Sea • Sacred India • Travel Photography: A Guide to Taking Better Pictures • Travel with Children • Tuvalu: Portrait of an Island Nation

LONELY PLANET

You already know that Lonely Planet produces more than this one guidebook, but you might not be aware of the other products we have on this region. Here is a selection of titles that you may want to check out as well:

Stockholm
ISBN 1 74059 011 2
US$14.99 • UK£8.99

Scandinavian phrasebook
ISBN 1 86450 225 8
US$7.99 • UK£4.50

Denmark
ISBN 1 74059 075 9
US$17.99 • UK£12.99

Copenhagen
ISBN 1 86450 203 7
US$14.99 • UK£8.99

Sweden
ISBN 1 74059 227 1
US$19.99 • UK£12.99

Iceland, Greenland & the Faroe Islands
ISBN 0 86442 686 0
US$19.99 • UK£12.99

Norway
ISBN 1 74059 200 X
US$19.99 • UK£11.99

Finland
ISBN 1 74059 076 7
US$21.99 • UK£13.99

Europe on a shoestring
ISBN 1 74059 314 6
US$24.99 • UK£14.99

Read This First: Europe
ISBN 1 86450 136 7
US$14.99 • UK£8.99

Available wherever books are sold

Index

Bold indicates maps.

Bold indicates maps.

MAP LEGEND

CITY ROUTES

Freeway	Freeway		Unsealed Road
Highway	Primary Road		One Way Street
Road	Secondary Road		Pedestrian Street
Street	Street		Stepped Street
Lane	Lane		Tunnel
	On/Off Ramp		Footbridge

REGIONAL ROUTES

	Tollway, Freeway
	Primary Road
	Secondary Road
	Minor Road

BOUNDARIES

	International
	State
	Disputed
	Fortified Wall

TRANSPORT ROUTES & STATIONS

	Train		Ferry
	Underground Train		Walking Trail
	Metro		Walking Tour
	Tramway		Path
	Cable Car, Chairlift		Pier or Jetty

HYDROGRAPHY

	River, Creek		Dry Lake; Salt Lake
	Canal		Spring; Rapids
	Lake		Waterfalls

AREA FEATURES

	Building		Market		Glacier		Campus
	Park, Gardens		Sports Ground		Cemetery		Plaza

POPULATION SYMBOLS

○ CAPITAL	National Capital	● CITY	City	Village	Village
◎ CAPITAL	State Capital	● Town	Town		Urban Area

MAP SYMBOLS

▪	Place to Stay	▼	Place to Eat	●	Point of Interest
✕	Airport	⌂	Cave, Cavern	♦	Monument	⊡	Shopping Centre
▣	Archaeological Site	⬡	Chalet, Hut	▲	Mountain	⊙	Spring
⊖	Bank	⊞	Church	⬚	Museum	⊠	Swimming Pool
↗	Beach	⊞	Cinema	)(	Pass	⚐	Ski Field
▢	Bus Terminal	▣	Embassy, Consulate	▣	Police Station	▣	Theatre
⬛	Camping	▥	Internet Cafe	▭	Post Office	❶	Tourist Information
▦	Castle, Chateau	⁎	Lookout	▨	Pub or Bar	▥	Zoo

Note: not all symbols displayed above appear in this book

LONELY PLANET OFFICES

Australia
Locked Bag 1, Footscray, Victoria 3011
☎ 03 8379 8000 fax 03 8379 8111
email: talk2us@lonelyplanet.com.au

USA
150 Linden St, Oakland, CA 94607
☎ 510 893 8555 TOLL FREE: 800 275 8555
fax 510 893 8572
email: info@lonelyplanet.com

UK
10a Spring Place, London NW5 3BH
☎ 020 7428 4800 fax 020 7428 4828
email: go@lonelyplanet.co.uk

France
1 rue du Dahomey, 75011 Paris
☎ 01 55 25 33 00 fax 01 55 25 33 01
email: bip@lonelyplanet.fr
www.lonelyplanet.fr

**World Wide Web: www.lonelyplanet.com *or* AOL keyword: lp
Lonely Planet Images: lpi@lonelyplanet.com.au**